from Sarah & Tony.
On their return from 5 weeks holiday
in Australia with James & Alice.
22. 8. 04

Foreword

The compilation of this my fifth major book on Wine and Food has been a true revelation and a wonderful and exciting journey of discovery and rediscovery. In my own life as in the lives of many others, the harmonious balance of the glorious natural beverages of Australia and New Zealand, principally wine and their clean green and caringly crafted foods, have become an increasingly meaningful and enjoyable experience

In the words of my dear friend and world wine legend, Robert Mondavi, "Wine is the temperate, civilized, sacred, romantic, mealtime beverage recommended in the bible, the liquid food praised 8,000 years ago since civilization began, by rulers, poets, philosophers and physicians for life happiness and longevity. Wine is the only natural beverage that feeds not only the body, but the soul and spirit of man, stimulates the mind and creates a more gracious and happy way of life". I cannot but agree with Robert's wise words and look back a number of years to the day I turned up in California's Napa Valley unannounced and through many strange coincidences (or do they really exist) I found myself that night preparing a meal for Robert and his friends amongst their majestic vineyards, it was his 82nd birthday, jokingly - I believe, he offered me the equivalent of several Michelin stars. I am sure the meal was not that good but great wines, good food and great company, in a beautiful part of nature's world certainly feeds more than just the body!

When once again I began my pilgrimage some 2 years ago to create a New Australian Pictorial Wine Atlas I had been amazed in a little more than a year my 98-99 Edition had sold out.

After several months of travel around Australia with my dear colleague and splendid photographer Frenchman, Stephane L'Hostis, in June 1999 we found ourselves in his homeland - at the worlds premier Wine Exhibition the Biannual Vin-Expo in Bordeaux. The showcase of the world's finest wines, the main exhibition hall is over a kilometer long and the "haut-couture" wine brands build entertaining facilities along the Lakeshore which would rival the Taj Mahal.

All wine countries have large integrated stands, to me some of the most exciting and innovative wines and vibrant stand belong to New Zealand, their industry had also doubled in size in only four years. Over the years many people have suggested I include New Zealand in my pictorial publication; after my Bordeaux experience I embraced their sentiments absolutely.

Stephane and I spent 17 action-packed days

of rally like experiences in New Zealand in November 1999. Starting in Christchurch we went south to Otago and Queenstown. After 7,000 kilometers, 12 wine regions, 150 wineries visited and photographed, we found ourselves in the Northland Region of Auckland. New Zealanders hospitality, their warm enthusiasm about their wines and the quality of their premises astounded me. The range of wines from such diverse climates and soils and the overall quality particularly their reds of the 1998 vintage blew me away.

In my own homeland the Australian Wine Industry has literally exploded in the last 3 years. The seemingly unattainable goal of a billion dollars in wine exports by the year 2000 (the industry revised downwards in early 1998 - not to be achieved until around 2003!!) In 1999 the billion dollars came and in 2000 it was over $1.38 billion, 34% up on the previous 12 months and in January 2001 the 12 months total was over $1.5 billion. Why this astronomic growth? When so many new and old world wine powers are pushing hard for markets without our success. Australia's climate, clean environment and great winemakers combine to make superb wines of all styles at all price points. We are rightfully the darling of the wine-drinking world.

The foresight of the industry in planting top premium grape varieties and clones in carefully chosen microclimates over the last 10 years is paying handsome dividends.

Planting continues at an annual rate of growth of around 10% whilst some concerns have arisen that too much red and not enough white varieties are being planted. The growth of the premium red market particularly in exports has proved that the balance is still good. Maybe now is the time to start again with a selective planting push for premium white varieties certainly sauvignon blanc, semillon, pinot gris, verdelho and viognier are in increasing demand and the riesling renaissance is now a reality.

The wine processing capacity is growing quickly with a number of specialist wine processing plants such as Boar's Rock in McLaren Vale, Kirribilly in Clare, Monarch in the Hunter, Fern Grove in Western Australia's Frankland River, Zilzie in Mildura, Belvidere and Langhorne Creek Wineries in Langhorne Creek plus a number of others often with no wine brand of their own are augmenting the traditional wineries both large and small which are also expanding their production facilities. None-the-less a real bumper harvest in a number of regions and with all the new plantings in full production will test our producers and marketers to the full.

Wine tourism, is booming and making the

wine adventure all that much more enjoyable.

Food has gained equal billing with wine in this book, I have included a growing food content in my previous editions but my move into the food arena in a full sense has amazed me. The variety and quality of Australian and New Zealand's natural foods is spectacular. I am thrilled to bring much of this variety to you.

The environmental impacts and sustainable growth of Wine, Food and other beverage industries has gratefully come more to the fore. In June 2000 the Australian Wine Industry Environment Program was inaugurated. My own mother, Dr Barbara Hardy, addressed their first annual conference in October 2000 conveying "A sustainable vision for the Wine Industry". Our clean, green image as versus the "old wine world" must be protected and promoted. We must use well and not abuse our fragile soils and scarce water. Wine is a natural product with virtually no additives. Our vineyards are increasingly organically run. We are in good shape, let's keep it that way.

For a number of years I have been compiling a "Who's Who of Wine in Australia and New Zealand". It has been a tough task and is by no means complete but I trust the details and in many case photographs of our industry's founders and key figures both past and present will be a useful and interesting addition to thumb through.

Although a new edition will not be published for 5 years my Internet Site (www.picwine.com.au) can keep you updated with changes both in the regions, wineries, food and hospitality houses.

So now to the new adventure and its many new facets!!

Cheers,

Tom Hardy

The only reason I drink wine, particularly red wine, is of course, for my health. The medical profession tell us this is good for us and I must say that I am eternally indebted to those medicos!!

I still have my "Learners plates" for wine knowledge but I take every opportunity to enhance it. It seems only a couple of years ago that we all loved a sweet moselle with a meal, thinking we were the "bees-knees". Then cam Riesling and in particular Yalumba's Pewsey Vale and Heggies, introduced to me by my mate and Manager, Austin Robertson as a "roady" or two before going out to a restaurant. Chardonnay became the "in" drink and I must say I imbibed freely in this new grape.

Red is the only drink; Rod Marsh kept telling me, and that I should broaden my wine horizon. So cab'savs became my nectar and the gutsier the better, in particular the Penfolds range. Shiraz then took my fancy but I kept going back to aged cab'savs and obtain non-cellar quantities of these gems from Vince at Beaucoll Cellars in Perth. Vince is also helping me broaden my drinking experiences by introducing me to other top wines. In fact he gave me an old Yalumba Dennis Lillee Collector's Port the other day and it is drinking beautifully twenty years on!

My favourite wines are aged and include such gems as the Leo Buring Leonay Eden Valley Riesling. Recently, I tried a 1994, which is drinking magnificently at the moment. This was accompanied by some great reds including a young Tower Shiraz - one for the future - a splendid drop.

Well, there it is in a nutshell, my wine history - which I hope to enlarge. What fun it will be trying!

I have known Tom for many years and it is with pleasure I have written a few words for his book. I have read his last two and soaked up the information on Aussie wines. I now look forward to the new section on the great New Zealand wines.

Tom, well done on a fabulous production again.

Cheers,
Dennis Lillee

The development and success of the Australian Wine Industry since the late 1960's has been spectacular, its performance over the last 15 years has been extraordinary.

Australian viticulturists and winemakers have a passion for success, they are prepared to innovate in the vineyard in developing techniques to grow the best grapes possible, so that the winemaker can use his experience and research to make outstanding and appropriate products, for our consumers at home and abroad.

Australian marketers have understood the essential need to deliver what our consumers want rather than what it is perceived that consumers should have. Export success is a fine example of that; an unbelievable performance.

In 1985 Australian exports totaled less than $25 million, fifteen years later in the year 2000 our exports had risen to $1.3 billion, an increase of some fifty times in fifteen years.

I firmly believe that we, as wine producers, are just at the lower rungs of the ladder that has many steps yet available if the wine industry of the future has the determination to take them. I believe we have the capacity, the will, the expertise and the vision today that the previous generation had when they put us on the road to International success.

Wine is very successfully grown across Australia today, not only does it bring financial stability to country areas but in many regions it encourages a significant Tourism industry. Tourism encourages all types of infrastructure, accommodation, food facilities, speciality gourmet food and cheese procedures, crafts and of course festivals.

However, all this needs to be communicated to the wine importer, wine distributor, retailer and of course, the wine consumer; whether new to wine or well informed. So this is why I have great pleasure in providing an introduction to Tom Hardy's new publication "The Australian and New Zealand Wine and Food Pictorial Atlas - Millennium Edition".

Not only does our wine industry need the viticulturist, the winemaker and retailer; it also needs the communicator who informs the consumer about wine; its history, its geography, its personalities and its excitement. I believe the industry is extremely fortunate to have Tom Hardy projecting it through this magnificent publication. Tom Hardy is a dedicated enthusiast of the finest order; a member of the famous Hardy family. He has used his well-respected journalistic skills to inform wine lovers about the joys of Australian wine and food for the last twenty years.

This Millennium Edition is his finest publication yet, I believe you will be enchanted by the photography and current information on the state of wine and food in Australia and New Zealand.

Please enjoy this magnificent work, Congratulations Tom!

Yours in Wine,
Brian McGuigan AM

Hermann Thumm on his 88th Birthday, 31st December 2000,
celebrating the opening of his grand new venture "Chateau Barrosa".
For over 80 years since he first worked on his father's vineyards in
Russian Geogia, he has faced incredible challenges, his vision and
pride remain undaunted.

History of Australian Wine

The history of Australian wine begins with the first settlers. Vine cuttings were brought into the country by Captain Arthur Phillip when he landed at Sydney Cove in 1788. Planted where Sydney's Botanic Gardens now stand, the cuttings, mainly because of unsuitable soil, did not thrive.

It wasn't long, however, before others, such as the great pastoralist and grazier, John Macarthur, moved on to more suitable areas around Parramatta. From there the vineyards extended to the rich, volcanic soils of the Hunter Valley, around the towns of Pokolbin and Cessnock. All southern mainland states had vineyards established within a few years of their founding.

Ethnic groups were a major influence in establishing the various vineyard areas. The Lutherans, having fled religious persecution in Germany, pioneered the Barossa Valley in South Australia. Their influence is still very obvious today. It can be seen in the picturesque churches and local townships, along with the classic Germanic-style rieslings and the unique German mettwursts, which are showcased in the Barossa's colourful and exuberant wine festival. This is a traditional German celebration, which was imported to the Barossa Valley to become the first of its kind in Australia, and is now held every two years.

Victoria's strong beginnings in the industry date back to the Swiss settlers who were encouraged to come to Australia by the first Governor, Charles LaTrobe and his wife, also Swiss. Victoria went on to become the premier Wine State, having three quarters of the country's total production until the 1890's.

Unfortunately, wine in Australia has always been subject to fashion, changes in taste and economic conditions. Only in the last couple of decades, when wine has become an integral part of the Australian way of life, has some sort of stability and steady growth taken place. Of course stability is also dependent on the forces of nature. The worldwide plague phylloxera swept through most of Australia's vineyards in the 1890's. This tiny vine louse eats into and eventually kills the root of the vine. South Australia was, fortunately, spared this threat and remains one of the very few areas in the world not devastated by this plague. Nevertheless, it still remains a threat.

In the early days winemaking, even at its very best, was a 'hit or miss' affair. With little knowledge worldwide as to the very nature of the process of fermentation from grape juice to wine, many wines were unsound. Some exceptional wines, however, which are now making a comeback, were made in cooler areas such as the Yarra Valley in Victoria.

Heavy fortified wines became increasingly popular as they were protected by blending with high quality grape spirit, thus ensuring their integrity. They could be produced in the warmer and often irrigated areas where crops were often of greater size per hectare than in the cooler, high quality table wine areas. The Great Depression of the 1930's reinforced the drinking of fortified wines. Not only was it the most affordable beverage, but it was also very palatable in its rich, sweet style.

The dominance of fortified wines lasted 70 to 80 years, only being reversed in the early 1970's when table wines eventually rose to above 50 percent of wine consumed. Many factors were at work. The heavy post-war immigration of Europeans brought to Australia their century-old tradition of drinking table wine with meals. This influence, along with the growing affluence of the average Australian, brought more leisure time, overseas travel and an interest in the finer things of life, and thus there was an upsurge in wine drinking. The industry accommodated this change with a reasonable price structure, and the introduction of bulk containers such as the flagon, which culminated in the ingenious Australian invention, the 'bag in the box' wine cask. People were now able to enjoy table wine whenever they so desired, without fear of the wine 'going off'.

Red wines certainly made a resurgence in the 1990s and the richness in colour, flavour, and the complexity and balance winemakers today are achieving with their reds is indeed marvelous. The best Australian reds are easily on the top rung of the world's great wines. Much credit for this and the overall outstanding quality of Australian wines comes right back to the vineyard. Soil selection, the aspect of the new plantings, micro-climates carefully chosen, the clonal selections of grape varieties now available, vine spacing, innovative trellising and pruning, are all contributing to better and better grapes and consequently wines.

Since the '60s, interest and investment have grown in the wine industry, particularly from the multi-national companies rationalisation has continued among the ownership of the bigger wine companies with many floating on the Australian Stock Exchange. Alongside this has been the enormous growth in 'boutique vineyards' and the expansion into new viticultural areas. We now have vineyards in all states of Australia and undoubtedly world-class wines. So many new areas for wine have opened up, in this edition you will find new chapters on Canberra, Young and Orange in Central New South Wales, Eastern Tasmania, Southern Fleurieu and Wrattonbully in South Australia. Almost all other Regions are greatly expanded; the number of Australian food and wine features has increased from 257 in 1998 to 420 in 2001.

Whilst much work has gone into the drawing up of definitive boundaries to each wine region in Australia, over the last 5 years through the Geographical Indications Committee of the Winemakers Federation of Australia, not all regions have yet been so defined. The maps in this book are thus more for the wine and food enthusiast and tourist not for strictly defining wine regions.

Australia is the best performed by far in any world wine competitions, during the last decade or so Australian wines have taken the wine world by storm. Wine exports have increased dramatically, wine is now one of Australia's main exports, and a very prestigious one at that.

To cope with this demand and future plans - among others, 4.5 billion dollars in wine exports by 2025, the

History of Australian Wine

huge plantings starting some 8 years ago continues at an even more frantic pace but we are still short of quality wine the world is demanding from us.

The heath benefits of wine are finally being properly acknowledged and red wine is a particular beneficiary of this although white wine is also healthy in moderation.

Exciting times and challenges are ahead for Australian wines. The Australian wine industry has really come of age. In this book, we look forward to guiding you to wineries, vineyards and food producers, large and small; a comprehensive tour which not only provides readily identifiable labels, up to the minute maps and sensitive photography, but

also experiences that you, the traveller, should seek out.

Wine Festivals and Gourmet Wine Food celebrations in all regions are booming bringing together food, art, music and people. Wine is the magic elixir enhancing our enjoyment of fine civilized living.

Australian Wine Producing Areas

WESTERN AUSTRALIA
19 Coastal Plains of WA
20 Margaret River
21 Great Southern
22 Swan Valley
23 Pemberton and Manjimup

TASMANIA
24 Northern Tasmania
25 Southern Tasmania
26 Eastern Tasmania

QUEENSLAND
27 Queensland

VICTORIA
12 Bendigo - Heathcote
12 Goulburn Valley
12 Mount Macedon
12 Sunbury
13 Gippsland
14 Geelong
15 Glenrowan
15 King and Alpine Valleys
15 Rutherglen
15 Victorian High Country
16 Mildura and Swan Hill
17 Grampians
17 Pyrenees
18 Mornington Peninsula
18 Yarra Valley

SOUTH AUSTRALIA
7 Adelaide Hills
7 Adelaide Plains
7 Barossa Valley
7 Clare Valley
7 Eden Valley
8 Currency Creek
8 Langhorne Creek
8 McLaren Vale
8 Southern Fleurieu
9 Coonawarra
9 Padthaway
9 Wrattonbully
10 Riverland
11 Coastal Regions of SA

NEW SOUTH WALES
1 Lower Hunter Valley
1 Upper Hunter Valley
2 Mudgee
3 Orange
4 Riverina
5 Canberra
5 Cowra
5 Young
6 Other Regions of NSW

Contents

Internet Guide

In 1998 the previous edition of this book , "The Australian Wine Pictorial Atlas" was published on the World Wide Web site **www.picwine.com.au**. Over the past four years, the site has enjoyed great success with hundreds of thousands of hits from all around the world. Picwine.com.au was also a finalist in the Jacobs Creek World Food Media Awards 1999, Best food and/or Beverage Cdrom or Internet Web Site section.

Picwine.com.au contains constantly updated editorial, fabulous pictures and information from wineries, fine food producers and hospitality venues throughout the Australian and New Zealand region.

It is our plan to increase the scope of the site to include the ability to purchase wine and foods, and also the booking of accommodation and restaurants for your wine touring needs.

The site can be accessed via the Internet using your favourite web browser. Picwine.com.au includes hyperlinks to the many wineries, food and hospitality web sites included on the web site.

We welcome any queries, feedback and suggestions on how we may improve picwine.com.au. This may be done on the web site or by simply sending an email to tom@picwine.com.au

Written By: Thomas K. Hardy
Photography: Stephane L'Hostis, Thomas K. Hardy
Publisher: Thomas K. Hardy
Project Assistant: Julie Idema
Photographic Assistance: Diana Dunstall
Page Makeup: Linda Hardy, Thomas W. Hardy
Maps: Linda Hardy, Thomas W. Hardy
Scanning: Image Digital, Adelaide, South Australia
Printed By: Graphic Print Group, Adelaide, South Australia

Published By: Vintage Image Productions
PO Box 42, Brighton, South Australia 5048
Tel/Fax 61 8 8377 5104
Email: tkh@picwine.com.au

Copyright © 2001

New South Wales was the first State to plant vines; in fact, the first vine cuttings arrived with Governor Phillip and the first fleet in 1788. The vines were planted at Farm Cove, which is now part of Sydney's Botanic Gardens. These vines unfortunately did not fare well due to poor soil conditions.

Vineyards soon sprang up in many areas around Sydney. The first commercial wine came from Gregory Blaxland, a member of the famous pioneering family, from his vineyard at Brush Farm on the Parramatta River, which is now part of metropolitan Sydney. Another included the Rooty Hill 'Minchinbury' Vineyard of Penfolds. None survive today.

Other vineyards sprang up around the State but it was not until vines were planted in the Hunter Valley in the late 1820's that the New South Wales wine industry became firmly established. The first vines in the Hunter were planted in the Branxton/Singleton area. This is some 20 kilometres north of the current main grape-growing area around Cessnock, referred to as the Lower Hunter Valley, although Wyndham Estate have a large and very successful vineyard at Branxton. The main pioneers were George Wyndham at Dalwood near Branxton, and James Busby at Kirkton. George Wyndham's classic old home 'Dalwood House', was built in 1828 and had fallen into disrepair. It was restored in a joint project by

Wyndham Estate and the National Trust of Australia for the Australian Bicentenary in 1988. George Wyndham also planted some 10 hectares of vines at Inverell in 1850. This vineyard produced until 1890. (No further vines were planted in the region until the mid 1960's when Gilgai Vineyard was established). James Busby established his vineyard at Kirkton between Branxton and Singleton in 1825.

Mudgee, situated in the northern part of the Great Dividing Range, some 300 kilometres north west of Sydney, was the next wine region to be opened up. It was pioneered in 1858 by Arthur Roth, a vineyard worker from Germany. He named his property Rothwein and his family was still involved in viticulture a century later. He was followed by other Germans, namely Andreas Kurtz and Frederick Buchultz. As in the Barossa Valley in South Australia, there was a notable German wine growing influence. Mudgee has seen huge new plantings in recent years, Rosemount now have nearly 2,000 acres of vines and Simon Gilbert a very large new Winery and Hospitality Centre.

Other areas of New South Wales planted in the latter part of the 19th century were Junee, Wellington, Molong, Bathurst and Young on the slopes of the Great Dividing Range. Today this area is enjoying a renaissance, with huge areas of vines being planted at Cowra, and other large vineyards such as McWilliam's

Barwang property near Young, a new chapter on this region and its wineries features in this Edition. Over the last decade or so the areas around Orange and Mount Canoblas have been rapidly growing. This cool, high country is producing excellent chardonnay and pinot noir with merlot and cabernet sauvignon really starting to show out very well, this region also features as a new chapter. Another new Region with substantial plantings but as yet only a few small wineries is the New England area around Tenterfield & Armidale.

Canberra has many small wineries and is now growing viticulturally with the location in the region of a winery and vineyards by BRL Hardy · Canberra also has a new chapter.

By far the largest wine region in New South Wales is the Riverina area, first planted to vines in 1912, and centered around the towns of Griffith and Leeton. This area produces almost 100,000 tonnes of grapes from nearly 5,000 hectares of vines, representing approximately one-sixth of Australia's total wine production. Some very high quality table wines come from this region with a number of companies crushing from 10,000 to 40,000 tonnes. Until the late 1950's the majority of wine produced in the region was fortified, but since the wine boom of the mid-60's table wine production has risen dramatically in both quantity and quality.

The Lower Hunter Valley was the first wine region to really cater for the wine-lover with properly turned out tasting areas, personal service by proprietors and a framework of restaurants, galleries, art and craft outlets and other venues of interest to attract visitors. Probably it was its proximity to Sydney and the fact that Australia's first boutique wineries sprang up here that the Hunter led the way.

The development of these small but very attractive wineries occurred in the early 1960's and their reputation for beauty and quality of produce has spread worldwide. The first such operation was Dr. Max Lake's 'Lake's Folly', established in 1963.

Today the Lower Hunter boasts around 70 wineries and many more vineyards. Nearly all are very keen to open their doors and offer hospitality to the visitor.

The larger companies such as McWilliam's, Lindemans, Hungerford Hill, Wyndham Estate, Tyrrells, McGuigan and others have responded by upgrading their facilities and staff, resulting in improved conditions for the visitor. Progress in this area over the last decade has been remarkable and has been augmented by the establishment of some great restaurants and accommodation houses which are fire-tuned to the wine traveller's needs. Peppers, the McGuigan Wine Village, Robert and Sally Molines at the Pepper Tree complex, Casuarina Restaurant and Tower Estate are just a few.

If there were an area in Australia that outwardly seemed totally unsuited to viticulture, it would be the Lower Hunter. The climate is hot. Many vineyards are on poor soil, and the sub-tropical climate can bring rain exactly when it isn't needed, at Vintage time. Why then does the Hunter produce some outstanding table wines? I believe part of the answer lies with the cool, afternoon sea breezes that seem to concentrate around the vineyard area and then die along the magnificent Brokenback Range, the backdrop to the whole region. This often prevents excessive temperatures, and when coupled with afternoon cloud in summer, results in protecting the grapes from direct heat, thereby conserving flavour components.

There is much feeling within Australia that only areas with cool climates can produce really top quality wines. The Lower Hunter is one of several regions that are certainly exceptions to this rule. After all it is the wine in the bottle that people enjoy (even the wine judges) that is the real proof of the pudding! I am sure it is the great beauty of the region that has attracted many of the winery proprietors to the Hunter despite its difficult climate and low yields from the vineyards. There are now approximately 4,000 hectares of vines planted. The wines that originally put the Hunter on the map were whites made from semillon (or Hunter River riesling as it was known in the area), and the dry reds from shiraz, often referred to as hermitage. Both are distinctive styles.

The semillon, particularly has come back into vogue after spending some years languishing in the shadows of the more 'trendy' varieties such as chardonnay and sauvignon blanc. Hunter semillons age exceptionally well, developing deep golden colour and rich toasty, nutty and honey-like flavours. There is too, a delightful

Lower Hunter Valley

crisp lemon-citrus finish, which stays with them all their life. The older wines of Lindeman, McWilliam, Tulloch, Tyrrell, Drayton and Rothbury often show these sought-after characteristics which make Hunter semillons such good food wines.

The late 1960's and early 1970's saw the start of the Australian wine boom and there was a veritable rush from Sydney to invest in the Hunter Valley. Many co-operative ventures started, including the Rothbury Estate,

brainchild of Len Evans, and Brokenwood where James Halliday and other notables were involved.

The Rothbury Estate has endured tough times but is now firmly established. The winery is magnificent with its banquet hall regularly used, and the light delicatessen-style luncheon you can enjoy on the lawns daily is excellent.

Many other regions have challenged the wine tourism strength of the Hunter. The Yarra Valley, Mornington Peninsula, the Barossa and McLaren

Vale along with Margaret River in Western Australia, but after a slight hiatus in growth in the mid-nineties. The expansion in multi-million dollar developments such as Cypress Lakes, Tower Estate, Audrey Wilkinson and small wineries with bed and breakfast such as Peacock Hill has once again revitalised the region. It is a must visit to experience the natural beauty, history, wonderful wines, beautiful wineries and to meet all the regions hospitable folk.

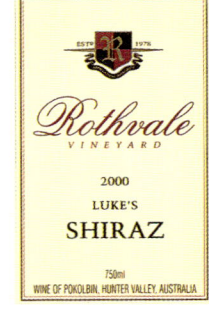

Lower Hunter Valley

Lower Hunter - NSW

1. Allandale Winery
2. Allanmere
3. Audrey Wilkinson
4. Beyond Broke Vineyard
5. Bimbadgen Estate
6. Blaxlands
7. Blueberry Hill
8. Brian McGuigan Wines
9. Briar Ridge
10. Broke Estate
11. Brokenwood
12. Brokes Promise Vineyard
13. Calais Estate
14. Catherine Vale
15. Cockfighter's Ghost Vineyard
16. Constable & Hershon
17. Drayton Family Wines
18. Gabriels Paddock
19. Gartelmann Estate
20. Golden Grape Estate
21. Honey Tree Estate
22. Hope Estate
23. Hungerford Hill
24. Hunter Ridge
25. Hunter Valley Cheeses
26. Ivanhoe Wines
27. Kevin Sobels
28. Lakes Folly
29. Lindemans Wines
30. Littles Wines
31. Margan Family Winery
32. Mount Pleasant
33. Mount View Estate
34. Nightingale Wines
35. Oakvale Wines
36. Peacock Hill
37. Pendarves Estate
38. Peppertree Wines
39. Petersons Champagne House
40. Petersons Wines
41. Piggs Peake
42. Pokolbin Estate
43. Pooles Rock Vineyard
44. Reg Drayton
45. Rothbury
46. Rothbury Ridge
47. Rothvale
48. Saddlers Creek
49. Sandlyn Wilderness Estate
50. Scarborough Wines
51. Serenella Estate
52. Tamburlaine
53. Terrace Vale
54. Tinonee
55. Tower Estate
56. Tulloch Wines
57. Tyrrells Vineyards
58. Van De Sheur Wines
59. Vinden Estate
60. Wilderness Estate
61. Wyndham Estate

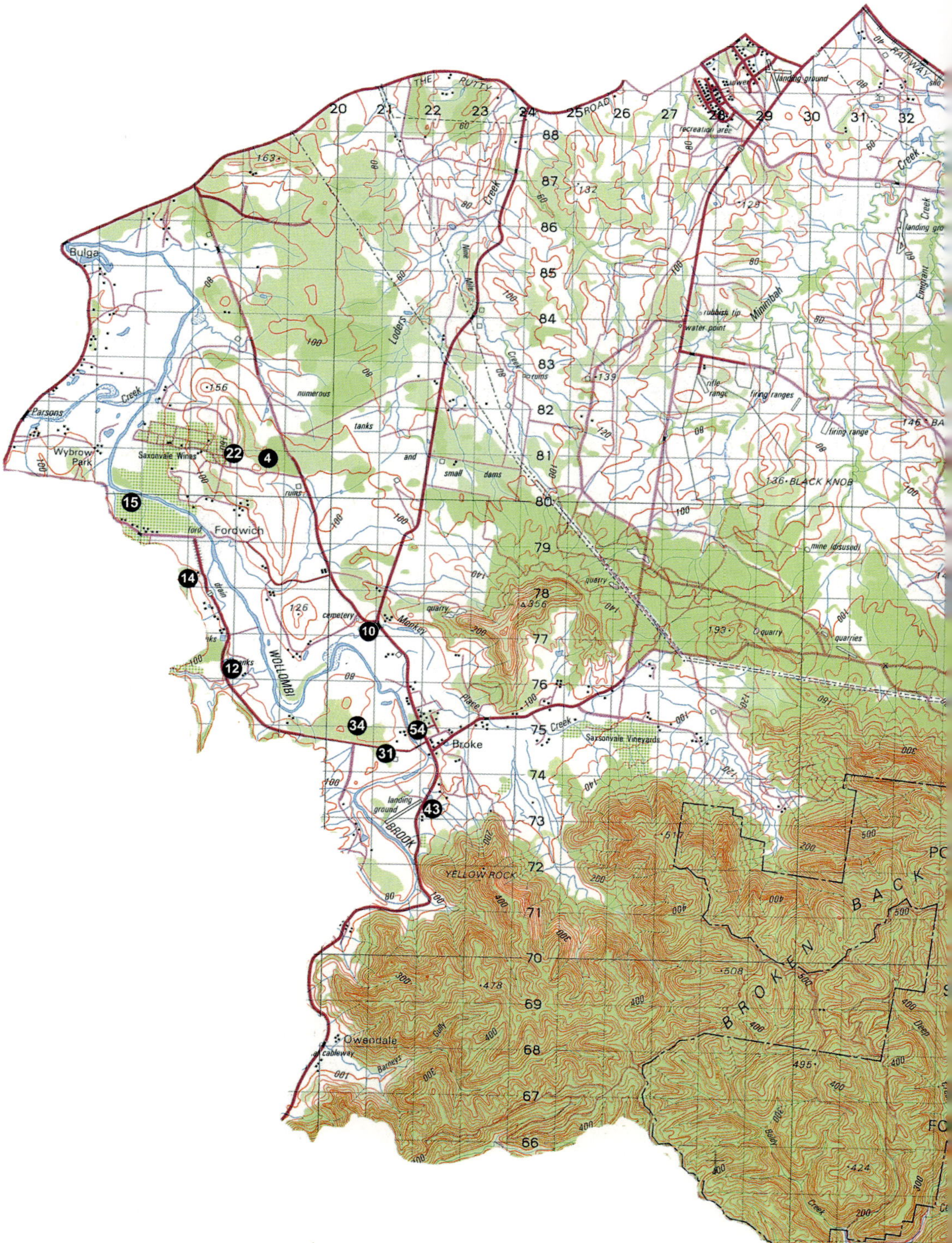

Lower Hunter Valley

Lower Hunter Valley

R&G DRAYTON WINES

POKOLBIN HILLS

CABERNET SHIRAZ

750mL

TOWER
ESTATE

Hunter Valley

SEMILLON

2000

PRODUCE OF AUSTRALIA   750ml

MOUNT
PLEASANT
ELIZABETH

MOUNT PLEASANT IS ONE OF THE MOST FAMOUS HUNTER VALLEY WINERIES, RENOWNED WORLD-WIDE FOR ITS AWARD-WINNING TABLE WINES. THIS CLASSIC BOTTLE-AGED SEMILLON CRAFTED USING HAND-PICKED GRAPES, IS A TRIBUTE TO THE GENIUS OF LEGENDARY WINEMAKER MAURICE O'SHEA, WHO FOUNDED MOUNT PLEASANT IN 1921.

HUNTER VALLEY SEMILLON
1997

11.0%vol   PRODUCE OF AUSTRALIA   750 ML

TYRRELL'S
MOON MOUNTAIN
CHARDONNAY
2000

TYRRELL'S
INDIVIDUAL
VINEYARDS
HUNTER
VALLEY

TYRRELL'S WINES

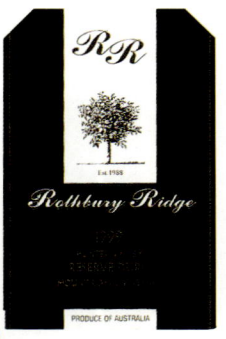

RR

Est 1988

Rothbury Ridge

PRODUCE OF AUSTRALIA

HOPE
ESTATE
HUNTER VALLEY

ESTATE GROWN

Shiraz
2000

1997

BOTRYTIS
SEMILLON

PRODUCT OF AUSTRALIA

375ML

WILDERNESS

ESTATE
1998
HUNTER VALLEY

RESERVE
Chardonnay

750ml PRODUCE OF AUSTRALIA

RR

Rothbury Ridge

1999
STEVEN
CHARDONNAY

HUNTER VALLEY
PRODUCE OF AUSTRALIA

TYRRELL'S
OLD WINERY
CHARDONNAY

HUNTER VALLEY · McLAREN VALE
1999

1999
Hunter Valley

NIGHTINGALE
WINES

Verdelho

PRODUCT OF AUSTRALIA
750mL

RESERVE

LITTLES
1998 Shiraz
HUNTER VALLEY

RR

Rothbury Ridge

1998
EDGAR
CHAMBOURCIN

HUNTER VALLEY

TOWER
ESTATE

Hunter Valley

SHIRAZ

1999

PRODUCE OF AUSTRALIA   750ml

MOUNT
PLEASANT
PHILIP

MOUNT PLEASANT IS ONE OF THE MOST FAMOUS HUNTER VALLEY WINERIES, RENOWNED WORLD-WIDE FOR ITS AWARD-WINNING TABLE WINES. THIS CLASSIC BOTTLE-AGED SHIRAZ IS A TRIBUTE TO THE GENIUS OF LEGENDARY WINEMAKER MAURICE O'SHEA, WHO FOUNDED MOUNT PLEASANT IN 1921.

HUNTER VALLEY SHIRAZ
1996

12.5%vol   PRODUCE OF AUSTRALIA   750 ML

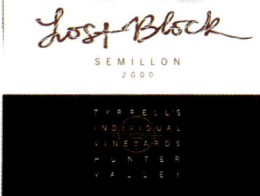

TYRRELL'S WINES
HUNTER VALLEY

Vat 47
Pinot Chardonnay

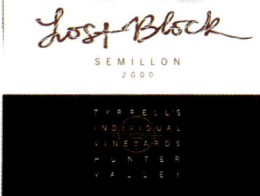

Lost Block
SEMILLON
2000

TYRRELLS
INDIVIDUAL
VINEYARDS
HUNTER
VALLEY

TYRRELL'S WINES
750ml

1999
Hunter Valley

NIGHTINGALE
WINES

Chardonnay

Unwooded

PRODUCT OF AUSTRALIA
750mL

MOUNT VIEW ESTATE

1998

Reserve Shiraz

Hunter Valley

750mL

Peacock Hill Vineyard
Hunter Valley
1999 Untamed Chardonnay

13.0% ALC./VOL.
750ML
PRODUCT OF AUSTRALIA

Vignron George Tinos
Peacock Hill Vineyard
Palmers Lane Pokolbin 2320
Ph/Fax (02) 4998 7661
Approx 2.7 Standard Drinks
Preservative (220)
Antioxidant (300) Added

ESTABLISHED 1828
WYNDHAM ESTATE
HUNTER VALLEY

POKOLBIN HUNTER VALLEY

Vinden Estate
2000 CHARDONNAY

750ML PRODUCE OF AUSTRALIA

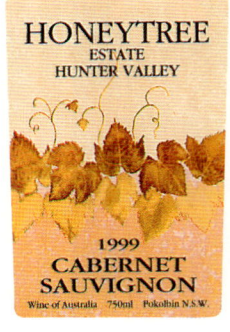

HONEYTREE
ESTATE
HUNTER VALLEY

1999
CABERNET
SAUVIGNON
Wine of Australia 750ml Pokolbin N.S.W.

ESTD 1978

Rothvale
VINEYARD

1999
RESERVE
CHARDONNAY
Barrel Fermented American Oak

750ml
WINE OF POKOLBIN, HUNTER VALLEY, AUSTRALIA

POKOLBIN HUNTER VALLEY

Vinden Estate
1998 SEMILLON

750ML PRODUCE OF AUSTRALIA

BIN
111

Verdelho

2000
VINTAGE

750ML

Allandale

winery', of which 'Allandale' was one of the first, established in 1978.

Allandale is situated on a hill with commanding views of its seven hectares of vines and the Brokenback Ranges.

The tasting area is in the winery itself and you are surrounded by French and American oak barrels quietly maturing the wines. The winery has been enlarged, upgraded and beautifully landscaped and is a must to visit during your next Hunter pilgrimage.

Enthusiastic and knowledgeable winemaker Bill Sneddon, a graduate of Charles Sturt University's wine course at Wagga Wagga, has been in charge for the last fifteen years and makes an excellent range of wines, including a semillon, chardonnay, pinot noir and shiraz which go under the Allandale label.

Allandale takes its name from the sub-region of the Hunter so named. This sub-region in turn, is part of the Lovedale area near the Cessnock Airport, which in fact was the wine capital of the Hunter Valley during the last century, boasting many vineyards and wineries, including the Hunter's largest, 'Daisy Hill'. This is the capital of the 'friendly boutique

Address: Lovedale Road ACTON 2601	Winemaker: Bill Sneddon & Steve Langham	Semillon	
Phone: (02) 4990 4526	Est: 1978 Vine Ha: 7	Principal Wines	Potential
Fax: (02) 4990 1714	Cases: 18,000	Chardonnay	2-5 yrs
Email: wines@allandalewinery.com.au	Public Hours: 9am-5pm, Mon-Sat;	Semillon	5-10 yrs
WWW: www.allandalewinery.com.au	10am-5pm Sun	Matthew Shiraz	5-10 yrs
Owner: Villa Villetri (Wines) Pty Ltd	Principal Varieties: Chardonnay, Pinot Noir,	Verdelho	2-3 yrs

Blueberry Hill

Charm and culture abound on Blueberry Hill. Former top level banker John Howarth and wife Wendy have created a true mecca. Their well tended vineyards surround the cellar door with panoramic views over the Brokenback Ranges to the south and the Barrington Range to the north. The cellar door is breezy and fresh with an outdoor patio. Although the Howarth's grow six varieties in their vineyard, only two are selected to carry the Blueberry Hills Reserve label. A full-bodied chardonnay and a traditional Hunter shiraz.

Secluded behind the cellar sales area, amongst splendid gardens, are two self contained queen suites also sharing the splendid views. You can also enjoy the pool and tennis court to really add to your thrill on Blueberry Hill.

Address: Corner McDonalds & Coulson Roads POKOLBIN 2320	Email: blueberryhill@hunterlink.net.au	Principal Varieties: Cabernet Sauvignon,
Phone: (02) 4998 7295 Fax: (02) 2998 7296	WWW: www.blueberryhill.com.au	Merlot, Sauvignon Blanc, Chardonnay,
	Est: 1973	Pinot Noir, Shiraz

Allanmere

Allanmere has gone through a real wine renaissance. The cellar door has been greatly expanded and is comfortable and classy providing an environment suitable for tasting the really excellent range of fruit driven wines.

Allanmere is a winemaking paradise. There is not one winemaker but four of the Hunter's most dynamic winemakers Greg Silkman, Gary Reed, Steve Allen and Craig Brown-Thomas. All have the zeal of youth but 60 years of winemaking experience between them and are all owners of the winery. Early in 1997 they bought the winery from founder

Dr Newton Potter, who with his wife Virginia began the enterprise in 1985 winning two gold medals with his first two wines in the Hunter Wine Show - a cabernet sauvignon and a hermitage (shiraz).

There is also a superb luxury cottage on the property with three suites, lounge and kitchen where up to six adults can spend a wonderful four days in this charming wine region. "Trinity Cottage" has an open fire for winter and is fully air-conditioned.

Allanmere, takes its name "Allan" from the Allandale region and "Mere" from the 10-acre lake in the Estate. The cellar door features cheese and

olive oil tastings accompanied by the wineries own home baked bread and of course great wines. Try the two Trinity wines, the red is a cabernet merlot shiraz blend and the white a chardonnay semillon sauvignon blanc blend or the classic 'Durham Chardonnay' of the lesser oaked Gold Label Chardonnay. For something different try the unoaked verdelho, it is a real fruit salad of flavour or the botrytis semillon-tokay with its luscious and lingering finish. Sip them under the shady verandah looking out over the pretty vineyard and the beautiful Brokenback Mountains.

Address: Lovedale Road POKOLBIN 2320	Winemaker: Greg Silkman	Durham Chardonnay	2-5 yrs
Phone: (02) 4930 7387 Fax: (02) 4930 7900	Est: 1985	Trinity White	Now
Email: winemasters@allanmere.com.au	Cases: 7,000	Trinity Red	Now
WWW: www.allanmere.com.au	Public Hours: 9am-5pm, weekdays; 9.30am-	Verdelho	2-5 yrs
Owner: Greg Silkman, Gary Reed, Craig	5pm, weekends	Shiraz	3-5 yrs
Brown-Thomas, Steve Allen	Principal Wines Potential	Cabernet Sauvignon	3-5 yrs

Audrey Wilkinson

From its majestic site perched some 250 metres above the valley floor the magnificent new Audrey Wilkinson Cellar Door Complex looks over seemingly endless slopes of vibrant vines growing in the rich red volcanic soils of the Brokenback Range foothills.

It is a far cry from 1899 when young Audrey Wilkinson and his brother Garth began building the family's new winery and cellars on the property their father Fredric had purchased in 1866, and shortly after planted vines. Fredric's own father Alfred, a career soldier, later to become an ordained Minister, had first come to Australia to establish missions for the Catholic Apostolic church in 1852. He also tried his hand at farming in Tasmania and Victoria without success and returned to England in 1859.

In 1861 the Crown Lands in New South Wales were opened up, it seemed an ideal opportunity to purchase land and plant vines to provide an opportunity for his sons, two of whom Fredric and John had studied viticulture and winemaking under Monsieur Lauser in the Fleury region of France and later in Germany, under Baron Justus Von

Liebig who had taught other Australian wine pioneers before them.

Tragically Fredric died of a chill at the tender age of 40 in 1883 leaving a young widow Florence with three children under 6, the eldest being son Audrey. On his deathbed he extracted a promise from his two sons they would never drink "any of the wine", a promise, according to Dr Max Lake, who interviewed Audrey two years before his death in 1960, he kept absolutely stating neither he or Garth "have ever swallowed a teaspoon".

The new Cellar Door Complex has been constructed on the site of the original winery and includes a museum with some of the original old tanks and equipment. The intention is to develop this museum as an ongoing project. The Cellar Door and Function Area was designed by the dynamic Chris Cameron, Chief Winemaker and

Managing Director for the James Fairfax owned Pepper Tree Group, the owners of "Audrey Wilkinson" and its surrounding 111 hectares of land as well as the splendid Peppertree Winery in Halls Road Pokolbin and extensive vineyards in Coonawarra.

The wines all come from the estate vineyard, originally named "Oakdale" by the Wilkinson Family. I found the wines all had great intensity of flavour, lots of fruit but elegant and fine. The semillon, from 30-year-old vines, will be one of the classic Hunter styles that improve for decades.

The chardonnay is French oak aged, again heaps of fruit in the stone fruit spectrum, fine and elegant. There is also a very aromatic traminer and a rich spicy shiraz that's already a trophy winner.

Audrey Wilkinson's rebirth, 100 years after the original cellars were built, is truly remarkable and the view is the best in the Hunter. It is a must visit.

Address: De Beyers Road POKOLBIN 2320	**Est:** 1866, re-created 1999	**Principal Wines**	**Potential**
Phone: (02) 4998 7411	**Cases:** 30,000	Semillon	5-7 yrs
Fax: (02) 4998 7303	**Public Hours:** 9am-5pm Mon-Fri, 9:30am-	Chardonnay	3-4 yrs
Winemaker: Chris Cameron	5pm Sat, Sun & public holidays; closed	Traminer	
Owner: James Fairfax	Christmas Day & Good Friday	Shiraz	5-8 yrs

Australian Wine Selectors

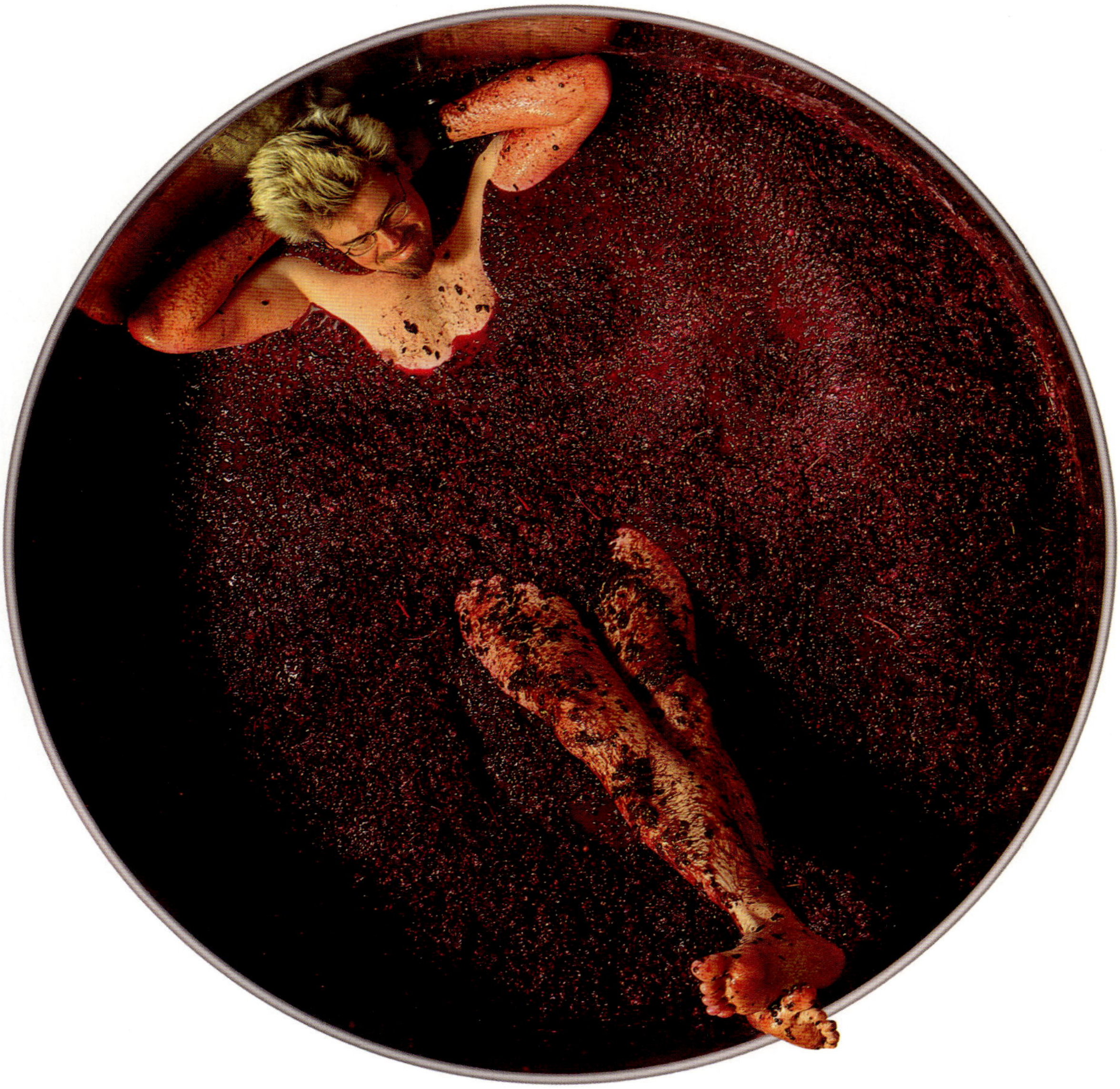

Enjoy wine with body.....and all the extras!

As a member of either the Hunter Valley Wine Society Pty Ltd or Société de Vignerons, you can get top quality wines, guaranteed by their stringent tasting and evaluation process, at significant savings off recommended prices.

The Hunter Valley Wine Society Pty Ltd started in the Hunter Valley almost 20 years ago, to help bring the region's often difficult to find boutique wines, to an Australia wide audience. The Société de Vignerons likewise to source great boutique wines from all Australian wine regions.

Today Australian Wine Selectors has brought these two great concepts together and added many other benefits for members. You can enjoy delivery to your door, comprehensive tasting notes, access to special events, plus member discounts on food, travel and accommodation.

Recently they launched a glossy, quarterly wine magazine "Wine Selector" which has quickly become the highest circulation wine publication in Australia.

The Australian Wine Selectors website, www.wineselector.com.au, has a wide range of information some available exclusively to members, like the matching of wine with food and fabulous member's specials.

If you enjoy wine with substance - Australian Wine Selectors certainly delivers.

Address: Wine Centre, Honeysuckle Newcastle NSW 2300

Phone: 1300 303 307
Fax: 1300 130 220

Email: contactus@wineselectors.com.au
WWW: www.wineselector.com.au

Briar Ridge

At the southern-most corner of the Hunter Valley is the Mount View sub-region unobtrusively nestled in the foothills of the Brokenback Range. It is the home of Briar Ridge Vineyard, current holder of the "Champion Australian Small Winery" title.

Briar Ridge Vineyard is the very essence of what a "Boutique Winery" should be. Started in 1971 by the enigmatic Murray Robson, it is now run by Neil McGuigan, the younger of the famed Australian winemaking McGuigan brothers. With fellow winemakers Adrian Lockhart and Karl Stockhausen, Neil's undying passion for winemaking (and the Hunter) is at once obvious and his desire to share this with visitors to the winery is apparent in every member of the Briar Ridge Vineyard team.

Don't expect a quiet, studious tasting session at Briar Ridge, this is wine in action. You will probably see the team sprinting around the winery, exchanging humorous but professional banter and springing up on top of tanks and wine casks, the contents of which are like children to them. Every vat receives lots of care and individual attention.

The winery's lively attitude shows up in the wines not to mention the various events staged on and around the stunning verandah and gardens. The "Mount View Autumn" and "Budburst" Festivals are so convivial they are now permanently etched in the calendars of hundreds of wine loving Briar Ridge loyalists.

The charming rustic winery is built from local timbers and retains a lovely country nature. The wines are excellent and largely snapped up by the "Briar Ridge Vintage Club" which is certainly worth joining. Briar Ridge Vineyard is the perfect place to start your tour of the Hunter and sets an ideal, if not appropriate, benchmark for the rest of your weekend tastings.

Recently Neil has taken an extra role in winemaking at the landmark Rothbury Estate for the Beringer Blass Company who have taken a half share in Briar Ridge. This association will assist Briar Ridge increase its international distribution while retaining its perfect "boutique" style and quality.

		Potential
Address: Mount View Road, Mount View, Via Cessnock CESSNOCK 2325	**Winemaker:** Neil McGuigan **Est:** 1972	**Principal Wines**
Phone: (02) 4990 3670	**Vine Ha:** 54	Signature Stockhausen Semillon 3-7 yrs
Fax: (02) 4990 7802	**Cases:** 18,000	Signature Stockhausen Hermatige 3-7 yrs
Email: indulge@briarridge.com.au	**Public Hours:** 9:30am-5pm, Monday-Saturday; 10am-5pm, Sunday	Briar Ridge Old Vines Shiraz 3-5 yrs
WWW: www.briarridge.com.au	**Principal Varieties:** Pinot Noir, Semillon, Shiraz, Verdelho, Cabernet, Chardonnay	Briar Ridge Hand Picked Chardonnay 3 yrs
Owner: John Davis and Beringer Blass		Signature McGuigan Chardonnay 3-5 yrs
		Signature McGuigan Cabernet Merlot 3-6 yrs

Bimbadgen Estate

Address: Lot 21 McDonalds Road
POKOLBIN 2320
Phone: (02) 4998 7585
Fax: (02) 4998 7732
Email: office@bimbadgen.com.au
WWW: www.bimbadgen.com.au

Winemaker: Kees van de Scheur
Est: 1996   **Cases:** 30,000
Vine Ha: 50
Public Hours: Restaurant - Lunch 7 days,
Dinner Wed-Sun
Principal Varieties: Chardonnay, Semillon,

Shiraz, Cabernet Sauvignon

Principal Wines	**Potential**
Signature Series	7-10 yrs
Bimbadgen Series	6-8 yrs
Grand Ridge Series	2-4 yrs
Bell Tower Series	2-4 yrs

Bimbadgen Estate

One of the most striking Wineries in Australia sits on top of a rise on McDonalds Road a kilometre or so north of the Centre of Pokolbin.

An impressive tower visible right around the valley caps off the whitewashed Spanish inspired mission style winery.

In 1999 the whole complex underwent a total rebuilding and now sports a sensational top class restaurant and café with majestic views and clever use of glass and wood to really put you almost amongst the vines and winery as you enjoy a top class meal.

The winery is constructed into the hillside, which provides for an efficient gravity aided operation plus cool and moist conditions in the underground section for barrel maturation of the wines.

Bimbadgen also has a large cellar door with splendid views over the vines and an impressive area set up as a restaurant. The rebuilding arrangement of this exciting venture has been under the careful eye of local identity and innovative winemaker Kees van de Scheur.

The Bimbadgen Estate has 50 hectares of local vineyards supplying estate-grown grapes for a classic range of wines - Chardonnay, Shiraz, Cabernet Sauvignon, Pinot Noir and Verdelho.

The wines I have seen are of such excellent quality that I am sure the future augurs well for Bimbadgen. It is great to see this fine Estate being put on track as one of the Hunters best.

Club Bimbadgen has recently been launched; one can become a member by the purchase twice a year of a six bottle tasting pack of the latest releases. Not only do members receive special bonus gifts such as insulated wine carry packs and classic corkscrews ideal for wines that need decanting, but a host of other benefits. Members can attend barrel tastings including lunch, private tastings and dinners by arrangement. Priority access to vintage wines, special events and priority accommodation at the Estate. Bimbadgen also runs Annual winemakers Dinners in Sydney and Melbourne.

Bimbadgen is a credit to the Hunter Valley - well done Kees!!

Brian McGuigan Wines

Brian McGuigan and his wife Fay are true legends of the Australian Wine Industry, two of the loveliest people you'll ever meet. Even with breakneck pace of their super busy lives, their achievements and the wealth they have created, they have time for everyone and for the simple pleasures and family values of life.

Since Brian formed his publicly listed company Brian McGuigan Wines Ltd in 1992 it has grown enormously. One of its great strengths has been Brian's concentration on securing vineyards in the best wine growing Regions of Australia. He started this move about 10 years ago and now has 23 different vineyard sites, many outside his beloved Hunter Valley. These many thousands of acres of different varieties of vines in different Regions sets up the ability for him to make wines of all styles from the best possible fruit. Large plantings have occurred in Cowra, ideal for chardonnay and red varieties, Mudgee mainly for reds, outside of

New South Wales he has planted extensively on the Terra Rossa Soils of the limestone coast in the South East of South Australia near Bordertown at his Howcroft Estate again mainly red. Brian also has

vineyards in the Barossa and Riverland regions of South Australia. When you're around the McGuigans magic things happen. I am sure they have a positive psychic power and it definitely transfers into their wines.

The McGuigan family has long been involved in the wine industry of the Hunter Valley. Brian's father Perc was the long time winemaker and manager for Penfolds at their Dalwood Winery in the northern part of the Lower Hunter Valley, a winery established in 1827 by George Wyndham. Brian and his father bought the run-down winery from Penfolds in 1971. By the mid '80's Brian, who had taken over from his father, owned 3 other Hunter wineries, Hunter Estate, Saxonvale and Richmond Grove. Shortly after, he bought Montrose and Craigmoor, the two biggest wineries in Mudgee.

In 1991, Brian who had formed a public company, sold his entire wine empire to the Orlando Wine Group, then owned by the giant French

Address: Cnr. McDonald & Broke Road POKOLBIN 2320
Phone: (02) 4998 7400
Fax: (02) 4998 7401
Email: mcguigan@onaustralia.com.au

Winemaker: Brian McGuigan, Peter Hall, Rodney Kemp and Brod Vallance
Est: 1992
Cases: 425,000
Public Hours: 10am-5pm, daily

Principal Varieties: Chardonnay, Merlot, Semillon, Cabernet Sauvignon, Shiraz, Verdelho, Traminer, Rhine Riesling, Chambourcin, Grenache, Petit Verdot, Sauvignon Blanc

Brian McGuigan Wines

Pernod Ricard Company. Being idle is not Brian McGuigan's favourite pastime and he quickly formed a vineyard investment company. He could see the coming need for more grape supply with export sales booming and the certainty that domestic sales would recover from their slight decline due to the recession of the late '80's and early '90's.

Brian was itching to get back into the mainstream of winemaking and marketing, which saw the formation in 1992 of McGuigan Brothers with his dynamic wife Fay. The company made a public float and Brian in his usual way took the show on the road. I ran into him one day in a leading Melbourne broker's office where he was delivering an address to their leading clients, followed naturally by a wine tasting.

Brian and Fay chose a most unusual symbol for their label, I am sure, inspired by their deep religious convictions. Many of their labels have the likeness of St. Francis Xavier, the patron saint of Australia, carrying his shepherd's crook. After forming the company, Brian and Fay took off to live and work in America for 6 months. They say St. Francis was working hard for them also, particularly in the very religious southern states.

At home since, the main McGuigan Wine Village and Winery have expanded. A fresh Bakery has been included, the "Gift Hunter Boutique" in the Village is thriving and the "Wine Country Souvenir Shop" in the main winery area - now with the hugely successful "Hunter Cheese Factory" both are going extremely well.

At a splendid inaugural Thanksgiving Dinner for over 600 guests in April 1997, Prime Minister John Howard sang praises of the wine industry. How suitable it was that Brian McGuigan was host, a last minute change of venue, which as usual the great man, his wife and team took in their stride.

Visiting Brian during the 2000 vintage in the Hunter I was again reminded of his incredible energy and devotion to making the best possible wines.

My photographer Stephane L'Hostis and I suggested we would like to capture the night harvesting and crushing of grapes, obviously spectacular, but also done to enhance the quality of the wine. The true enemy of quality table wine is heat particularly the searing direct sunlight of an Australian summer.

In the cool early hours of the morning, well before sunrise, the giant mechanical fingers of the

huge grape harvesters start their work quickly removing the grapes from the vines, each doing the work it would take several hundred human hands to do. The grapes are transferred to enormous trucks which head directly to the crushing pit at the winery where the cool grapes are converted into "must" (grape juice) which is immediately removed from the other · enemy · air which can oxidize the juice and resulting wines causing them to lose the intriguing delicate fruit flavours nature has built into them over the preceding four seasons.

As we pulled into the vineyard around 2am the car headlights hit the red soils, deep green leaves and plump golden chardonnay berries. Who should be there beside his loyal workers but the big man himself not only checking the crop but ready to take the first "Dog" (Brian's name for the massive truck and trailer used to bring some 20 tonnes of grapes at a time to the winery) that will eventually become 17,000 or so bottles of premium wine.

An hour or two later we are at the winery. Brian pulls up in the "Dog"

it's the first load of the vintage, the gate on the truck is stuck, so its Brian levering it open. Vintage has truly begun, the long journey which Brian McGuigan leads, not missing a step until he is once again promoting his great Australian liquid sunshine in the bottle in London, Dublin, Hong Kong and Atlanta inspiring the world

with his enthusiasm and deep belief in the goodness of wine.

The McGuigan wines are made for easy drinking by the widest range of people possible worldwide. For my mind, this is a noble goal and one which is making McGuigan liquid sunshine in the bottle, the flavour of Australia.

Calais Estate

As one enters the driveway of Calais Estate the impressive winery buildings come into view over the vines. The huge convict-hewn stones, the wide two storied verandahs with their intricate iron lacework trimmings all give a feeling of the Victorian colonial charm of yesteryear.

The winery started off in the 1970s under the name Woolundry Estate that was later changed when the Peterson wine clan became involved, they have since moved on but the same care and attention is certainly evident.

The cellar door also has much charm inside with huge wooden beams coming from early colonial buildings, giving it a warm solid atmosphere. Calais Estate also runs a corporate wine club and should you wish, would be delighted to send you the details. The restaurant, with its regional cuisine focus, caters only for functions.

The award-winning Calais range includes semillon, chardonnay, chambourcin, shiraz, cabernet sauvignon and botrytis semillon. Specially selected reserve wines are also available. The Calais wines are packaged in splendid tall imposing bottles, which do justice to their exciting quality.

Address: Palmers Lane POKOLBIN 2320	**Est:** 1975　**Vine Ha:** 9　**Cases:** 15,000	Calais Reserve Cabernet — 10+ yrs
Phone: (02) 4998 7654 **Fax:** (02) 4998 7813	**Public Hours:** 9am-5pm daily	Calais Reserve Chardonnay — 6+ yrs
Email: calaisestate@bigpond.com	**Principal Varieties:** Cabernet Sauvignon,	Chambourcin — 8+ yrs
Owner: Richard & Susanne Bradley	Chambourcin, Chardonnay, Semillon, Shiraz	Merlot — 6+ yrs
Winemaker: Adrian Sheridan	**Principal Wines**　　　　　　**Potential**	Calais Reserve Semillon — 10+ yrs

Drayton Family Wines

Drayton is a famous family wine name in the Hunter Valley with the winery being a real family affair. Max Drayton, a fourth generation member, owns and runs the business with his three sons. Eldest son, John, a giant of a man, returned to the fold in 1989 after tracking around NSW for some 14 years. Trevor, who graduated from Roseworthy Agricultural College as Dux of the course in 1977, is winemaker. Youngest son Greg is vineyard manager, helped along by his father Max. Greg has an Agricultural Diploma from Tocal Agricultural College where he passed all subjects with distinction.

The Drayton story commenced when Joseph Drayton, in his early twenties, set sail from England in 1852 with his wife Anna and two sons.

Tragically, during the voyage, he lost his wife, newborn daughter and one of his sons. Undaunted, he and his surviving son Frederick purchased a property in the Hunter in 1853. The dynasty retains this solid commitment which shows through in its large range of wines. The Drayton's are not flashy people - they go about their business producing great wines that they figure do the talking, and more power to them.

Address: Oakey Creek Road POKOLBIN 2320	**Est:** 1853 **Vine Ha:** 65	**Principal Wines**　　　　　**Potential**
Phone: (02) 4998 7513 **Fax:** (02) 4998 7743	**Cases:** 100,000	Chardonnay — 2-5 yrs
Email: drink@draytonswines.com.au	**Public Hours:** 8am-5pm, weekdays;	Verdelho — 2-5 yrs
WWW: www.draytonswines.com.au	10am-5pm weekends & public holidays	Semillon — 4-7 yrs
Owner: Members of the Drayton Family	**Principal Varieties:** Verdelho, Shiraz,	Bin 5555 Shiraz — 5-10 yrs
Winemaker: Trevor Drayton	Semillon, Merlot, Chardonnay,	Cabernet Merlot — 5-10 yrs
	Cabernet Sauvignon	Cabernet Sauvignon — 5-10 yrs

Constable & Hershon

At the very end of Gillards Road lies the intriguing Constable & Hershon Vineyards. Sharing the same rich red soils as Scarborough, the slopes face a splendid uninterrupted view of the Brokenback Ranges. A reasonably recent addition to the Hunter as a winemaker, the vineyards in fact have been planted considerably earlier.

Constable & Hershon are truly the gardens of the Hunter. The spectacular gardens at the rear of the cellar door feature beautiful box hedges interspersed with lavender and rosemary. Enclosed are four formal gardens "The Rose Garden" resplendent with 780 Japonica roses and 60 fragrant varieties also has a gazebo and pergola to relax under and enjoy the perfumes. You can also visit "The Knot & Herb Garden", "The Sculpture Garden" - featuring contemporary Australian art spreads

through to the top of the vineyard where Melinda Brown's sculpture of "The Skull" overlooks the property. "The Secret Garden" behind the full sized bronze lions has a mystique not to be missed.

Constable & Hershon have a range of very smart wines including chardonnay, semillon and a beautiful velvety cabernet merlot. They also have a Wine Club with many benefits - why not join up.

Address: 1 Gillards Road Pololbin 2320	Est: 1981 Vine Ha: 10	Chardonnay	3-6 yrs
Phone: (02) 4998 7887	Cases: 5,000	Unwooded Chardonnay	1-4 yrs
Fax: (02) 4998 7887	Public Hours: 10am-5pm daily	Cabernet Merlot	6 yrs
Email: mamerica@constablehershonwines.com.au	Principal Wines Potential	Shiraz	5-10 yrs
Winemaker: Neil McGuigan	Semillon 6-10 yrs		

Gartelmann Estate

In 1996, following a heart attack and by-pass surgery Jorg Gartelmann decided on a change of lifestyle. His wife, Jan going along with the whim to purchase a vineyard suddenly found herself a partner in this new venture. With the purchase of the George Hunter Estate, established by Sydney restaurateur Oliver Shaul in 1970, Jorg and Jan became the

proud owners of a new Hunter Valley label, Gartelmann Hunter Estate.

The first vintage 1997, Jorg made only Shiraz and Chardonnay before moving into full production in 1998, adding Semillon and Chenin Blanc. 1999 saw the addition of their wonderful Botrytis Chenin Blanc and finally the Merlot was released in 2001.

With over 30 medals to their credit they eventually broke though the GOLD barrier with the 1999 Chardonnay winning Gold at the Hunter Valley Wine Show in 2000 and Blue Gold at the 2001 Sydney International Wine Show. They are also very proud of their 1999 Methode Champenoise, a delightful Semillon/Chenin Blanc sparkling, which won the top medal, Silver, at the 2000 Hunter Valley Wine Show.

The award winning Cellar Door overlooks a small dam and the recently planted Muscat vines. The symbol of the Gartelmann Estate, the Magpie is proudly displayed on the side of the building. Why the Magpie? A bird that does not eat grapes, does eat the insects that would attack their grapes and chases away the grape-eating birds, certainly deserved their recognition.

Address: Lovedale Road LOVEDALE 2321	Est: 1970 Vine Ha: 16	Gartelmann Shiraz	5-9 yrs
Phone: (02) 4930 7113 Fax: (02) 4930 7114	Cases: 8,000	Gartelmann Chardonnay	3-5 yrs
Email: sales@gartelmann.com.au	Public Hours: 10am-5pm daily	Gartelmann Semillon	10 yrs
WWW: www.gartelmann.com.au	Principal Varieties: Chenin Blanc, Semillon,	Gartelmann Chenin Blanc	3 yrs
Owner: Jan & Jorg Gartelmann	Chardonnay, Merlot, Shiraz	Gartelmann Methode Champenoise	
Winemaker: Monarch Winemaking Services	Principal Wines Potential	Gartelmann Rose	

Gabriel's Paddock

It seems a guardian Angel has been watching over what was Sutherland's Wines. The vineyards and winery had gone through some tough times in recent years after a spectacular start in the 1980's when the wines won many awards and were right at the cutting edge of the Australian wine technology through bio-chemist and wine enthusiast Neil Sutherland.

In 2000 publishing and telecommunication executive Chris Anderson bought the property and has upgraded the well established vineyards along with the winery now incorporating a viewing area in the cellar door where one can observe the winemaking process.

The beautiful country residence that was the Sutherland's home has now been extended, renovated and will become an exclusive accommodation House. There is also "Boundary Cottage" with smaller accommodation facilities available for your Hunter stay. Both venues have exceptional sunset views of the Brokenback Ranges.

The wines are returning to their peak, try the chenin blanc, it's zesty and full of life almost angelic.

Address: Deaseys Road POKOLBIN 2321	Email: gabrielspaddocks@hunterlink.net.au	Principal Varieties: Cab Sauv, Chenin Blanc,
Phone: (02) 49987650 Fax: (02) 49987603	WWW: www.gabrielspaddocks.com.au	Semillon, Chardonnay, Pinot Noir, Shiraz

Ivanhoe Wines

Way back in the 1850's one of the early Hunter properties to grow wines and make wine was "Ivanhoe". It seems only appropriate that one of the fifth generation of the famous Hunter wine family, the Drayton's, has revived the name and built a beautiful winery replicating the original "Ivanhoe" amongst the terraced vines on the slopes of Mount Pleasant. Stephen Drayton and his wife Tracy are absolutely "hands-on" and run an extremely interactive winery where personal tours and seminars for groups large and small are a constant happening.

The majority of the vineyard at Ivanhoe is over 50 years old. Non-irrigated the low yielding vines produce very intense fruits, the whites, semillon, chardonnay, verdelho and gewurztraminer all exhibit great concentration of aromatic characters and the reds, a shiraz and cabernet sauvignon have deep colour with firm tamins. They will age extremely well. Ivanhoe also make a lovely chambourcin, a French hybrid, full flavoured but round and smooth.

The underground cellar and verandahs around the building keep it cool and pleasant and ideal for the aging of the wines and to make your visit not only enlightening but also extremely pleasant. "The Round Table Wine Club" started by Stephen and Tracy has been a huge success and easy to join.

Address: Marrowbone Road POKOLBIN 2320	Email: ivanhoewines@bigpond.com	Gewürztraminer, Shiraz, Chambourcin,
Phone: (02) 4998 7325	Est: 1996	Semillon, Verdelho
Fax: (02) 4998 7848	Principal Varieties: Cabernet Sauvignon,	

Golden Grape Estate

The history of Golden Grape Estate is like a mini history of Pokolbin. The site of the winery, on a prominent hill in the south end of the region, was the original site of the "Clayton" Winery. Taking its name from the property, first settled by George Wills in the mid 1800's, grapes were first planted on the property by James Connolly in 1866.

The Estate was purchased by Wesley 'Johnny' Drayton around the end of the First World War and passed on to Barry Drayton who operated it as "Happy Valley" Vineyard. Golden Grape purchased the property in 1985.

The complex, in addition to its cellar door outlet, has a Wine Museum, Gift Shop, Restaurant (winner of the Hunter Valley Tourism Award for Excellence, for the Best Tourism Restaurant) Picnic Areas, a Wine Trail and approximately 15 hectares of vines.

Golden Grape concentrates on sales of wine through tastings on the Estate or at client's own homes or business premises, Australia wide. Golden Grape also offers customised labels for selected premium white, red, sparkling and fortified wines. Why not visit Golden Grape and enjoy a meal at its award-winning Restaurant or if you cannot make it to the Hunter give the winery a call and arrange for a tasting to come to you.

Address: Oakey Creek Road POKOLBIN 2320	Semillon, Merlot, Chardonnay, Cabernet Sauvignon	Verdelho 3-5 yrs
Phone: (02) 4998 7588		Merlot 5-7 yrs
Fax: (02) 4998 7730	**Principal Wines** **Potential**	Mount Leonard Cabernet Sauvignon 8-10 yrs
Est: 1853 **Vine Ha:** 16	Semillon 4-6 yrs	Cabernet Hermitage 5-7 yrs
Principal Varieties: Verdelho, Shiraz,	Chardonnay Reserve 4-6 yrs	

Honeytree Estate

His is one of the few vineyards still growing the unusual white variety "Clairette" and makes a very fragrant white that is well worth the visit to their homely cellar door to try, along with their semillon, shiraz and cabernet sauvignon.

Right in the heart of Pokolbin they also have the gorgeous 2 bedroom Honeytree Cottage, ideal for your vineyard stay set in 1fi acres of beautiful landscaped gardens. It's air-conditioned for summer and there is a potbelly stove to make it nice and cosy in winter. You also have a swimming pool and barbecue at your disposal. Quite a number of restaurants are within walking distance and it's close to everything.

Henk & Robyn Strengers are very much at home on their Honeytree Estate. Their care and attention to detail is evident in all they do. Henk is passionate about his vineyard and keeps it an absolute picture. He seems to know almost every vine and is most aware of the different soils and microclimates of each area of the 30-year-old vines and each variety.

The 22 acres of vines under Henk's careful eye produce all the wines. His care and control are evident in the finished product.

Address: 16 Gillards Road POKOLBIN 2320	Est: 1970 Vine Ha: 10	Principal Wines	Potential
Phone: (02) 4998 7693 Fax: (02) 4998 7693	Cases: 5,000	Clairette	Great drinking young
Email: honeytree@bigpond.com	Public Hours: 11am-4pm Wed & Thurs;	Semillion	5-10 yrs
WWW: www.honeytreewines.com	10am-5pm Fri, Sat & Sun	Shiraz	5-10 yrs
Owner: Robyn & Henk Strengers	Principal Varieties: Shiraz, Semillon,	Cabernet Sauvignon	5-12 yrs
Winemaker: Contract	Clairette, Cabernet Sauvignon	Vintage Port	10-25 yrs

Hunter Valley Cheeses

In early 1995 a joint venture was agreed to between dynamic wine producer and gourmet cheese lover, Brian McGuigan, and pioneer specialty cheesemaker, David Brown, from the Milawa Cheese Company, just down the road from Brown Brothers Wines in Victoria.

A cheese factory was built into a section of the McGuigan Brothers Winery at Pokolbin. It has viewing windows along the long verandah where one can watch the cheeses being made.

A range of fine cheeses is produced, taking their names from the region: Branxton Brie, Busby Blue, an assertive gorgonzola style; Pokolbin White, with a soft texture a Cessnock Cheddar and a multi-faceted Pokolbin Club Blue. Hunter Valley Gold is a washed rind cheese and the Fromage Blanc a farmhouse cheese. There are three goat's milk cheeses, Hunter Valley Chevre, Hunter Valley Aged Ashed Chevre and the Hunter Valley Table Chevre in a pyramid.

Master Cheesemaker is Peter Curtis who operates the business with his partner in life Rosalia Lambert. A visit to the Hunter Valley Cheese Company is a great learning experience. It will help you get to know one of wine's great accompaniments. Why not purchase a plate of their cheeses and other produce and enjoy them on the verandah with a glass or two of McGuigan wines.

Address: McGuigan Cellars Complex, McDonalds Road POKOLBIN 2320	Email: cheesehuntervalley@bigpond.com	Rosalia Lambert
	WWW: www.huntervalleycheese.com.au	Est: 1995
Phone: (02) 4998 7744 Fax: (02) 4998 7269	Owner: David and Anne Brown, Peter Curtis,	Public Hours: 9am-5:30pm, daily

Hunter Ridge

The Hunter Ridge Winery began its life in 1985 as The Richmond Grove Hunter Winery built by Brian McGuigan under the Wyndham Estate Group banner. Brian unfortunately lost the winery with the Orlando buyout in 1990 but retained the vineyards with a syndicate group. In late 1993 Brian bought back the winery relaunching it under the Hunter Ridge name.

The cellars and equipment are state of the art and set in a magnificent vineyard scene. The cool maturation cellars are in the lower half of the expansive buildings.

In 1997 a joint venture between Brian McGuigan and BRL Hardy has seen Hardy's take on the management and marketing of the wine, whilst Brian McGuigans' team with input from Hardy winemakers, producing the Hunter Valley wines.

The wines of Hunter Ridge are only available from the Cellar Door. This marvellous facility now has had a second story added with panoramic views of the vineyards and Brokenback Range.

Hungerford Hill

A product of the wine boom of the 1960's, Hungerford Hill's first vines were planted in 1967. Over a period of five years, the original area expanded to well over 200 hectares, much of which was shiraz grapes. By the time the first Hungerford Hill reds came onto the market, red wine popularity was in a dramatic decline. A drastic rationalisation program followed, which saw the Hungerford Hill wines back on the rails to success.

Hungerford Hill is becoming a specialist in making wines from the newer grape growing regions of N.S.W. such as Cowra, Young and Tumbarumba. These include a cellar door range with wines of strictly limited quantities only available at the winery such as the Tumbarumba Pinot Gris. The winemaking and marketing skills of Hungerford Hill can be relied upon to give you a consistent and enjoyable experience.

In 1996 Hungerford Hill found a new home just down the road from Lindemans, a charming old weatherboard church is now resounding in the praises for their fine wines and the French petanque pitch outside resounds to the clatter of this ancient bowls game and happy contented Hungerford Hill fans.

Lake's Folly

Lake's Folly - Australia's first true boutique winery, created by the visionary Dr Max Lake in 1963 has just changed hands but that's about all that will change. Perth identity, Peter Fogarty, bought the winery from the Lake Family in May 2000. Stephen Lake who has been running the winery and making the wines for the last 20 years will be staying on as consulting winemaker, his assistant for the last 17 years, Peter Payard, is also staying on.

Rodney Kempe, a local winemaker with 13 years Hunter Valley experience, is the new General Manager/Winemaker. Along with his wife and family Rodney will be living in the Lake's Folly residence above the winery where he can keep a constant eye on the vineyard and winery that have consistently produced a cabernet sauvignon and chardonnay that rank in the absolute top echelon of Australian wines with great consistency.

The plan at Lake's Folly is not to change anything and continue on the tradition. On a recent flight over the Lower Hunter in a light aircraft the best looking vineyard by far was Lake's Folly. Its deep green canopy and diligently tilled soils are a real joy to look at. The deep red volcanic soils with limestone under for drainage are perfect. The 35-year-old vines are heavily pruned for low yields of quality grapes. Care, attention to detail, long experience and top class French oak does the rest. The only problem is there is never enough of these classic wines to go around.

Address Broke Road POKOLBIN 2320	**Winemaker:** Rodney Kempe	**Principal Varieties:** Chardonnay, Cabernet
Phone: (02) 4998 7507 **Fax:** (02) 4998 7322	**Est:** 1963	Sauvignon, Merlot, Shiraz, Petit Verdot
Email: folly@ozemail.com.au	**Vine Ha:** 12	**Principal Wines** **Potential**
WWW: www.lakesfolly.com.au	**Cases:** 4,000	Chardonnay up to 12 yrs
Owner: Peter Fogarty	**Public Hours:** 10am-4pm, Mon-Sat	Cabernet up to 20 yrs

Reg Drayton Wines

In 1994 an airline tragedy robbed the Hunter Valley of two of its true stalwarts, Reg Drayton and his wife Pam, on their way to a well-earned holiday.

Happily daughter Robyn, a fifth generation Drayton, has continued the family tradition and is now firmly ensconced as a female vingeron in the Hunter.

Reg Drayton Wines is a true family winery with the cellar door at the rear of Robyn and Craig's home on a prominent corner travelling between Lindeman's and McWilliam's under the shelter of the spectacular Brokenback Range. Robyn is involved in a more than full-time basis of managing, promotions and winemaking whilst Craig runs the vineyard and also involved in the Mining Industry.

When you visit and take in the warm family hospitality and enjoy the characterful wines, the Lambkin Semillon is a favourite of mine. You are greeted to walk through the Cellar Door and admire the magnificent leadlight windows and rustic Australian timbers. Choose from unique Australian products from the Gift Gallery, browse through the Drayton Family Museum dating back to 1853. Wine tasting on hand crafted timber furniture, barbecue and picnic including giant checkers and dominoes set amongst the tranquility of the vines.

Address: Cnr McDonalds and Pokolbin Mountain Roads POKOLBIN 2320	**Winemaker:** Tish Cecchini & Robyn Drayton	Lambkin Semillon	8-10 yrs
	Est: 1989 **Vine Ha:** 18 **Cases:** 4,000	Pokolbin Hills Chardonnay Semillon	4-5 yrs
Phone: (02) 4998 7523 **Fax:** (02) 4998 7523	**Public Hours:** 10am-5pm daily	Pokolbin Hills Chardonnay	6-7 yrs
Email: mail@regdraytonwines.com.au	**Principal Varieties:** Semillon, Chardonnay,	Pokolbin Hills Shiraz	10+ yrs
WWW: www.regdraytonwines.com.au	Verdelho, Shiraz	Lambkin Verdelho	4-5 yrs
Owner: Robyn Drayton	**Principal Wines** **Potential**	Pokolbin Hills Cabernet Shiraz	7-8 yrs

This famous winery, formerly known as the Ben Ean Winery, was purchased by Lindemans from John MacDonald in 1912. The company Lindemans was founded at a much earlier date, however, by the famous Dr Lindeman, a Royal Navy surgeon who settled in the Hunter Valley in 1842. With his three sons, Dr Lindeman bought and established vineyards at Cawarra, Coolalta, Catawba, Warrawee and Kirkton.

The Lindemans also purchased the name of 'Porphyry' along with all remaining stock of the wine (the vineyard had ceased to exist) from the Carmichael family. Porphyry had an enviable reputation and had been served to Queen Victoria in 1851. Lindemans still produce Porphyry Sauternes, of which the Carmichael family would have been proud, improving as it does with every year in the bottle.

Lindemans Hunter River Wines are probably Australia's best-known wine 'family', with their simple but bold label and distinctive four-figure bin classification. The Hunter Valley whites are made mainly from semillon and chardonnay grapes. The major wines marketed under this label are the Lindemans Hunter River Semillon and the Hunter River Chardonnay. These wines are produced each year and the four figure bin numbers change each vintage. They age exceptionally well and develop into classic and unique wines of world class, which dominate

Australian wine shows.

When young, Lindemans Hunter Valley semillons are pleasant, but often simple. They usually have a grassy, herbaceous character both in the aroma and on the palate, with a distinct lemon-citrus flavour in the aftertaste. As they approach ten years of age however, marvellous things begin to happen. Flavours develop which include toast, honey and nuts and the finish is enhanced by the beautiful lemon-citrus character. The colour too, develops into a bright yellow gold, but does not tarnish. The Hunter River Chardonnay has also shown this good aging potential.

Until 1978, Lindemans chardonnays were not aged in new imported oak casks, as is the trend today, and so the wines exhibited pure, although complex fruit flavours. Since then, however, some wood aging has

become part of the style. This procedure, combined with temperature control and modern white wine making techniques, has produced wines with more fruit enhanced by vanilla oak characters. Grape selection has also changed with the times; fruit now comes to Lindemans from various parts of the Hunter Valley, including vineyards in the Broke Region. These changes were brought about by Karl Stockhausen who made the wines from 1960 until the late 1980's.

The red wines from the Hunter Valley winery have nothing to fear from the reputation of the whites. They are Steven Vineyard Shiraz and various Hunter River Shiraz with different bin numbers every year. These wines develop a silky feel in the mouth as they do not necessarily have deep colour or heavy body, but always have long and interesting flavours combining Hunter River 'leather' and an earthy character, they are well balanced with a soft silky finish and are usually reasonable buying when young. Although good drinking while young, these wines improve further with aging.

In 1986 after Karl Stockhausen took up a senior marketing position with Lindemans his winemaking position was filled by Gerry Sissingh, who had assisted Len Evans in establishing Rothbury Estate. The current winemaker is Pat Auld, from a famous South Australian winemaking family, who in 2000 completed his twenty-seventh Hunter vintage. In 1999 the winery was completely upgraded and now includes a Function & Hospitality Complex including the Laragby Loft, the Steven Room and a Wine Museum.

Littles Wines

fermenting wine in his large cool room.

The wines are all made from their two vineyards in Palmers Lane. The "Winery" and "Homestead" blocks are now greatly expanded in fact, from the initial 40 acres of vines Little's purchased, they now either own or control some 125 acres which includes the "Daisy Hill" vineyard of 52 acres purchased in 1997.

Little's now have 3 distinct ranges of wines. At the top is their Reserve Series, a semillon made in a traditional Hunter style. No wood, cold fermentation, a little skin contact and extended cold storage on yeast lees, a wine that has won a large number of gold medals, but needs around 10 years to bring it to its complex best. There is also a Reserve Shiraz, fermented in open topped French Barriques with hand plunging and a top class barrel fermented chardonnay. Little's also have a Premium Hunter Range from their own vineyards and a New South Wales Range, complimented with grapes from premium regions such as Cowra, Canberra and Orange. These carry the distinctive original label but you always look to Little's Labels for unique styles and lots of flavour. You can also join "The Little Wine Club".

The Little family purchased the vineyard established by the late Dr. Quentin Taperell on Palmers Lane. That was back in 1983. Ian Little studied biochemistry in England and worked at Tooth's Brewery in Sydney on arriving in Australia.

Ian took the wine course at what is now the Charles Sturt University at Wagga Wagga and worked with Geoff Merrill at Chateau Reynella during the 1981 and 1982 vintages. Ian

also had some experience at Penfolds, working in their champagne cellars. After buying the vineyard, the Little's quickly established a winery on the property.

I well remember visiting the winery during its early days. I was, and still am, very impressed by their wines and the quiet no-nonsense way they go about producing and promoting them. Ian is meticulous with his picking, and chills all the grapes and

Address: Lot 3, Palmers Lane POKOLBIN 2320	Est: 1983 Vine Ha: 50	Chardonnay	4 yrs
Phone: (02) 4998 7626 Fax: (02) 4998 7867	Cases: 18,000	Semillon	6 yrs
Email: littleswinery@bigpond.com	Public Hours: 10am-4:30pm, daily	Gewurztraminer	2 yrs
WWW: www.littleswinery.com	Principal Varieties: Cabernet Sauvignon,	Shiraz	8 yrs
Owner: Little & Kindred Families & partners	Chardonnay, Pinot Noir, Semillon, Shiraz	Cabernet Sauvignon	8 yrs
Winemaker: Ian Little	Principal Wines Potential		

McWilliams Mount Pleasant

There are probably very few family-owned companies as proud or as conscious of their heritage as McWilliam's Wines, who are well into their second century of winemaking. In addition to being one of Australia's largest wine producers, the company is entirely family-owned and controlled.

The McWilliam's are a close-knit family, and members of the last three generations can be found throughout the company. While most of those involved are working in the managerial area, or the running of one of their huge wineries in the Riverina, Yarra Valley, Coonawarra, Hilltops or at Robinvale, the McWilliam's are not above a hard day's work in whatever field demands their attention.

Both the winery itself and the wines from Mount Pleasant are close to the heart of the McWilliam family, not surprising given the outstanding show record of Mount Pleasant's wines over many decades. In what must be an expensive exercise, Mount Pleasant is one of the few remaining wine producers to cellar-age commercial quantities of bottled table wines until they are at their peak. This enlightened policy allows wine lovers to enjoy fully mature, five year old whites and reds at very reasonable prices. There is also a regular release of even older wines. This conscious policy by McWilliams is to be applauded.

The birth of the winery and vineyards at Mount Pleasant began in 1880 when Charles King planted vines on some of the best red volcanic soil in the region. Exciting things started to happen when the property was purchased by the O'Shea family. The young Maurice O'Shea was sent to study winemaking at Montpelier in France and upon his return in 1921,

quickly established a reputation for himself as perhaps the greatest and most celebrated winemaker of his time. During the most dismal period of the Great Depression in 1932, O'Shea was forced to sell half of the property at Mount Pleasant to the McWilliams, who later completed the purchase by buying the remaining half, while allowing Maurice O'Shea to stay on as winemaker and winery manager until his death in 1956.

The wines made by Maurice O'Shea are legendary and their longevity is astonishing, with some wines of more than 40 years of age still drinking magnificently. It was O'Shea who started a tradition, now adopted by McWilliams, of naming his wines after friends of the family. Some well-known examples are their 'Elizabeth', made from semillon (often referred to in days gone by as Hunter River Riesling), and 'Philip',

(formerly 'Philip Hermitage') made from shiraz. In recent years McWilliams have released a 'Maurice O'Shea Chardonnay' and a 'Maurice O'Shea Shiraz'.

Other great wines in Mount Pleasant's Individual Vineyard range are a shiraz from the Rosehill Vineyard and another from the Old Paddock and Old Hill Vineyards. Keep an eye out too for regular re-releases of some of the older vintages of Mount Pleasant Elizabeth under the 'Museum Release Label'.

The current long-serving winemaker at Mount Pleasant is Phil Ryan, a quiet, astute man who is also a terrific host - if you can track him down. Phil was one of the first graduates from the new winemaking course at Charles Sturt University, and has been with McWilliams for many years - like the winery name, he is a very pleasant chap. The cellar door facility has been rebuilt and extended and is delightful including a café and facilities for group catering and large functions.

I well remember a tasting at the winery some 15 years ago, I'm not sure my late friend Milan remembered it so well as he kept asking me how I could spit out the exquisite wines. After 23 wines, all more than 15 years old, finishing with a 1946 Maurice O'Shea Sauterne of which McWilliams at that stage still had over 1,000 dozen, Milan found out why I do spit them out. As we exited the tasting room, the moon was rising. That was our first day working together and I had to help him put the camera on the tripod. He took one of his greatest photos ever.

Address: Marrowbone Road
POKOLBIN 2320
Phone: (02) 4998 7505 **Fax:** (02) 4998 4408

Email: mcwines@mcwilliams.com.au
WWW: www.mcwilliams.com.au
Winemaker: Phil Ryan   **Est:** 1921

Principal Varieties: Cabernet Sauvignon, Merlot, Riesling, Shiraz, Cabernet Franc, Chardonnay, Pinot Noir, Semillon, Verdelho

Mount View Estate

Mountview Estate is located high on a ridge in the classic Mountview Region at the southern end of the Hunter Valley.

The vineyards and winery were established in 1971 by Harry Tulloch, a fourth generation member of the famous Tulloch Family of winemakers. He and his wife Ann recently retired and the property has been taken over by John and Polly Burgess. The soil and in fact the total terroir at Mountview is ideal for premium grape growing. John and Polly are totally committed to nurturing the vineyard further and to making wines in the fine tradition the Tullochs established.

The 16 acre vineyard has the traditional Hunter varieties, shiraz, cabernet sauvignon, semillon and chardonnay but also grows verdelho - one of the first vineyards in the Hunter to plant this increasingly popular variety. Mountview also grow pinot noir and merlot. The terraced vineyards are a picture and the view over them to the Brokenbacks is magic.

The mature vines, grown on the volcanic soils over limestone, produce superb fruit and the upgraded cellar door is a great place to try these hidden gems - wines that have not been easy to find in the past but are truly great, and with the commitment of the team at Mountview will scale even greater heights.

| **Address:** Mount View Road via Cessnock 2325 | **Phone:** (02) 4990 3307 **Fax:** (02) 4991 1289 **Winemaker:** Keith Tulloch **Est:** 1971 | **Principal Varieties:** Cab Sauv, Merlot, Semillon, Verdelho, Chard, Pinot Noir, Shiraz |

Peacock Hill Vineyard

The history of the "Hill" dates back to the beginnings of European settlement with John Jenkins Peacock, who is listed on the 1828 census as "owner-farmer, born in the colony", being granted 100 acres of land c.1841.

A peach and apricot orchard was established in the 1900's. A large well for holding water used to wash fruit remains and has been incorporated into the property's gardens.

Becoming part of the Rothbury Estate in 1968-69, Peacock Hill was recognised as ideal for planting to Shiraz and Cabernet vines. Chardonnay soon followed in 1984. After a number of owners, in October 1995 charming couple George Tsiros and Sylvia Laumets took over the property and put it on a firm commercial footing.

Implementation of a careful, environmentally friendly vineyard management programme has resulted in improved vine health and increased yield. Bill Sneddon has recently taken over the job of Consultant Winemaker from David Lowe who has an increasing involvement in Mudgee. The wines have a history of Gold, Silver and Bronze medals and are made using premium oak barrels.

George and Sylvia have just completed a splendid new building with a very cool cellar for maturation and storage of wines.

The Cellar Door is open amongst the gardens and Lodge guests can enjoy tennis, petanque, a private wine tasting and sunset vineyard tour as part of their Peacock Hill experience.

George and Sylvia are great hosts. Avail yourself of their hospitality soon.

| **Address:** Palmers Lane POKOLBIN 2320 **Phone:** (02) 4998 7661 **Fax:** (02) 4998 7661 **Email:** peacockhillwines@hunterlink.net.au **Owner:** George Tsiros and Sylvia Laumets **Winemaker:** Bill Sneddon & Steve Langham **Est:** 1968 **Vine Ha:** 5 **Cases:** 1,800 | **Public Hours:** Fri, Sat-Mon 9am-5pm; public & school holidays 10am-5pm; other times by appointment **Principal Varieties:** Cabernet Franc, Cabernet Sauvignon, Chardonnay, Shiraz **Principal Wines   Potential** | Faith Cabernet Sauvignon   7+ yrs Jaan Shiraz   7-10+ yrs Top Block Chardonnay   3-5 yrs Untamed Chard (wild yeast ferment)   3-5 yrs Cabernet Sauvignon/Shiraz   5-7 yrs Absent Friends Unoaked Chardonnay 1-3 yrs |

Van de Scheur

Kees Van de Scheur and his partner in life Helen Palmer have created a piece of paradise in Pokolbin. A delightful cluster of historic old buildings on O'Conners lane (formerly the Ingleside Winery founded in 1872) has become a captivating winery complex. Kees is an old hand at the winemaking game whilst his youthful enthusiasm and lively imagination has come up with a great hands on concept. "City Vignerons", he and Helen were faced with the aged old dilemma of the wine industry, the large investment it takes to set up a vineyard and winery and finance the aging and packaging of the wine. They floated the idea of an involvement of friends and city dwellers looking for an earthy outlet and to expand their horizons and change their lifestyle.

They have been inundated by keen amateur vignerons buzzing with excitement as teams of "city" winemakers who compete in a winemaking challenge (they all made 2 barrels of the same variety from the same vineyard).

Often they may be making wine from the vineyard they have helped plant. Why not become a City Vigneron contact Van de Scheur, you won't regret it.

Address: Lot 2 O'Connor Lane POKOLBIN 2320 Phone: (02) 4998 7789 Fax: (02) 4998 7847 Email: vandescheurwine@ozemail.com.au Owner: Kees Van de Scheur & Helen Palmer	Winemaker: Kees van de Scheur Est: 1994 Vine Ha: 10 acres Cases: 2,000 Public Hours: 10am-5pm, daily Principal Varieties: Shiraz, Semillon, Cabernet Sauvignon, Chardonnay	Principal Wines	Potential
		Shiraz	8-12 yrs
		Semillon	6-10 yrs
		Chardonnay	4-6 yrs
		Cabernet Sauvignon	4-6 yrs

Catherine Vale Vineyard

Classic Hunter white grape varieties semillon and chardonnay were planted at Catherine Vale by Bill and Wendy Lawson in 1993. Verdelho and Italian red varieties dolcetto and barbera were planted in 1998 and produced their first crop in 2001. All four vintages since the premier release in 1997 have produced excellent wines and with the vines maturing the future looks bright. Bill and Wendy were runners up in the viticulture section of the 1998 Hunter Farmer of the Year.

The 1914 Singleton Uniting Church Manse re-located to Catherine Vale is nestled below the rugged Hunter Range. Wide verandahs look over the vineyard and provide a spectacular view of the Broke Fordwich area.

The region has grown quickly over the last 15 years and has a long history dating back to the early 1920's. Take a trip out along Milbrodale Road and see the vineyards. Make sure you drop in to taste the wines at Catherine Vale.

Address: 656 Milbrodale Road BULGA 2330 Phone: (02) 6579 1334 Fax: (02) 6579 1334 Email: catherinevale@hotmail.com WWW: www.catherinevale.com.au Owner: Bill & Wendy Lawson	Winemaker: John Hordern Est: 1993 Vine Ha: 4.5 Cases: 750 Public Hours: 10am-5pm weekends (closed Christmas Day, New Years Day, Easter Sunday, check for Australia Day)	Principal Varieties: Barbera, Chardonnay, Dolcetto, Semillon, Verdelho

Principal Wines	Potential
Chardonnay 1998, 1999, 2000	7 yrs
Semillon Chardonnay 1999, 2000	4 yrs
Semillon 1997, 1998, 1999, 2000	10 yrs

Hope Estate

In 1997 Pharmacist Michael Hope bought the almost derelict Saxonvale winery Complex aptly naming it Hill of Hope. The winery has since been renamed Hope Estate. Michael had in fact purchased his first vineyard, some 40 acres, near Broke in 1994. He followed this by purchasing 200 acres of red basalt land at Fordwich which is now planted with 100 acres of shiraz, cabernet sauvignon and merlot.

The winery had been used for storage only, by Orlando Wyndham and needed extensive refitting, all was operational for the 1997 vintage. A real highlight of the vintage was the verdelho which went on to be chosen by Qantas to feature on its First Class wine list. Verdelho, originally from the Island of Madeira and used to make their famous fortified wines, has been a real success in the Broke-Fordwich region. Its tropical fruit aromas and flavours are balanced by a full palate and a clean citrus like finish. The 1997 Reserve Shiraz has also gone on to be a gold medal winner.

In 1998 Michael Hope appointed up and coming young winemaker Peter Howland, a Roseworthy Honours Graduate who has made wine in a wide range of locations and climates, Mount Pleasant in the Hunter, Cassegrain at Port Macquarie,

Southern Italy and in Margaret River with the legendary David Hohnen. Peter uses some quite "avant garde" techniques including use of the grapes own wild yeasts rather than cultured yeasts for the chardonnay along with barrel fermentation with some of the grapes solids.

The investment in and variety of French oak at Hope Estate is quite amazing, eight different French coopers supply the barrels, each sourcing wood from around six different forests. Peter uses the various combinations along with a little American oak to subtly enhance

the characters of each variety, not overpower them.

Peter is also using whole berry fermentation with about a third of his shiraz to give a bigger, smoother mouthfeel to the resultant wine when it is blended back with the traditionally fermented wine. In Peter's own words "our aim is to produce a balance of the sweet New World and savoury Old World flavours". The 1999 Chardonnay has just won a gold medal at the 2000 Royal Sydney Show against many better known and more expensive wines.

The Winery Restaurant, available for private functions, on the upper level of the Hope Estate Winery has panoramic views over the Broke-Fordwich Valley and surrounding Wollemi Ranges and includes the Mezzanine Restaurant with its full glass windows and French doors, opening to the balcony where one can eat. There is also The Barrel Hall where functions of up to 600 can be catered for.

Late in 2000 Michael Hope took over the assets of Vincorp which also included the icon vineyard and winery Virgin Hills which I will cover in a later chapter. Well done Michael your hope and determination have breathed new life into two great wine producers.

Address: Cobcroft Road BROKE 2330	**Winemaker:** Peter Howland	Hope Estate Shiraz	10 yrs
Phone: (02) 6579 1161	**Est:** 1996 **Vine Ha:** 87.9	Hope Estate Chardonnay	10 yrs
Fax: (02) 6579 1373	**Public Hours:** Cellar door: 10am-4pm, daily	Hope Estate Merlot	10 yrs
Email: info@hopeestate.com.au	**Principal Varieties:** Merlot, Shiraz,	Hope Estate Verdelho	5 yrs
WWW: www.hopeestate.com.au	Chardonnay, Semillon, Verdelho	Hope Estate Semillon	10-15 yrs
Owner: Michael Hope	**Principal Wines** **Potential**	Hope Estate Blanc De Noir	5 yrs

A real plus for the Broke-Fordwich renaissance is Nightingale.

In fact, this marvellous vineyard and winery came about from a wager between ex-schoolteacher Paul Nightingale and his wife Gail, back in 1991. At a dinner with 20 or so friends, a new wine label appeared · McGuigan Brothers Chardonnay · the first wine from Brian McGuigan's new company. A dispute about the label erupted and Paul said to Gail "I'll give you $10,000 if your right". The very next morning, Paul saw a newspaper article, but so did Gail!! The result... Gail became the proud owner of $10,000 of shares in Brian McGuigan Wines Ltd.

The shares rocketed ahead and the Nightingales became regular attendees at the McGuigan shareholder events. Gail joked with Brian McGuigan at one event that they should plant a vineyard and McGuigan's should buy the grapes. With a definitive "yes" from McGuigan, the search began.

Gail informed Paul she had enrolled him in Steve Gell's Viticultural Course at the Kurri Kurri TAFE.

After several existing vineyard deals fell through, Paul decided to start afresh with some virgin land near the start of Milbrodale Road. The land became a pilot project for the Kurri Kurri class with soil testing, evaluation and planning of the

vineyard. Paul and Gail decided having ventured that far, they should become true vignerons so a winery and cellar door were built.

Gail is the power behind the wine, a real pocket dynamo. Her father a former Australian Featherweight Boxing Champion became a coal miner in the Hunter Region. Gail came along as the 9th child of 11 so she really had to be a fighter.

In 1984, Paul and Gail lent their hand to writing some children's educational books. This lead to the establishment of Nightingale Press Pty Ltd in 1989, now Australia's second largest primary school textbook publisher. Their extension of education, Nightingale Software, producing children's educational CD-Roms, has become a world leader and significant exporter.

Gail and Paul are right behind the Broke Fordwich revival. I am sure that John Younie Tulloch, who pioneered grape growing in the region over 100 years ago, would be proud of their efforts.

The first vintage was made from purchased grapes by Andrew Margan in the small winery, their own vines produced the 2000 vintage with the wine fermenting in their growing winery. In 2001, the grapes are being crushed in their own winery · a vintage of around 70 tonnes is envisaged. The 2001 reds have just been racked and have come up exceptionally well. The first export to England of 1056 dozen has just been dispatched as I write.

With their enthusiasm and energy their wines are full of life, character and quality, the future of Nightingale is bright indeed.

Address: 1239 Milbrodale Road BROKE 2330	Owner: Paul & Gail Nightingale	Nightingale Oaked Chardonnay	5 yrs
	Winemaker: Andrew Morgan	Nightingale Verdelho	3 yrs
Phone: (02) 6579 1499 Fax: (02) 6579 1477	Est: 1997 Vine Ha: 30 acres Cases: 7,000	Nightingale Shiraz	5 yrs
Email: gail@nightingalewines.com.au	Principal Wines Potential	Nightingale Cambourcin	
WWW: www.nightingalewines.com.au	Nightingale Semillon 5 yrs	Gail Force Port	Enjoyment

Oakvale Wines

In 1893, one of the Hunters first pioneers, J.D. Elliot, was granted over 100 acres of land at the base of the Brokenback Ranges. Soon after, he and his wife planted and cultivated one of the Hunter Valleys first vineyards, adjacent to their colonial homestead (now a museum). Constructed of hand-hewn slabs of spotted gum with roof timbers of mountain pine. A high-pitched iron roof protects the pine rafters, which remain in their original strong condition.

An old peach tree leans comfortably into the homestead lending its name to the acclaimed Oakvale Reserve Semillon and Chardonnay ranges. Wild pink roses abundantly grow over a covered well where icy water flows far below, the cold storage for some of the first vintages, chilled to perfection and retrieved by strings attached to their necks. Who knows how many Hunter treasures are still cooling their heels, waiting for recovery!

Oakvale has since prospered from the generations of hard work and sweat, along with wonderfully rich soils on which it lies. The winery's renowned old growth vines still flourish with their talisman - the gnarled Peppertree imparting special terroir characters into the much acclaimed Oakvale Reserve Peppercorn Shiraz.

Richard Owens is the proprietor of Oakvale Wines and Milbrovale Vineyard at Broke, established in 1995. This 85 acre property is considered by many to be the viticultural showpiece of the Hunter Valley. Milbrovale uses state of the art technology, including computerized irrigation and fertilization systems, soil structure, water, and integrated pest management, which are pivotal to the operation of the vineyard.

Milbrovale's location and microclimate produces some of the best fruit the Valley has to offer. This premium fruit is blended with that produced at Oakvale to produce the exceptional wines. Both vineyards are managed to restrict fruit yields, thus concentrating the resulting flavours.

Richard's purchase of Oakvale and Milbrovale fulfills his passion of 40 years to make wines which are the very best in the region. He believes by concentrating on growing the finest grapes, the result will be elegant, premium wines of the highest quality. He believes the grape absorbs and reflects its heritage, environment, elements and skill of those nurturing it. It can't lie. This has become the Oakvale and Milbrovale motto - In the grape there is truth.

Recent vintages continue to win

medals at major wine shows in Australia and London, including a trophy and gold medal in Sydney for the 1999 Oakvale Verdelho. The varieties grown and produced are those that the Hunter does best, namely Semillon, Chardonnay, Verdelho and Shiraz. However, a Merlot Cabernet has also been released.

Oakvale strives to produce fruit driven wines of elegance and structure, which are unique and exciting styles, yet, loyal to their Hunter terroir.

The refurbished cellar door houses the winery, a wine shop of premium boutique Australian and International wines, and one of the largest food and wine bookshop in New South Wales. A gourmet deli and coffee shop are more recent additions, with locals now proclaiming it the best espresso and cake in Pokolbin.

Or if you prefer pristine air and serene skies - spend some time in the vineyard. The Café will pack you a picnic, leaving you to meander through the grounds or set up on one of the many picnic tables. Let the children enjoy the kiddie's playground and take them back in time to enjoy the historic Homestead, now housing an 1800's shop and museum. Whichever way you would like to spend your visit, you must drop into Oakvale.

Address: Broke Road POKOLBIN 2320
Phone: (02) 4998 7088 **Fax:** (02) 4998 7077
Email: info@oakvalewines.com.au
Owner: Richard Owens
Est: 1893 **Vine Ha:** 45 **Cases:** 14,000

Public Hours: 9am-6pm, daily
Principal Varieties: Semillon, Verdelho, Chardonnay, Shiraz
Principal Wines Potential
Oakvale Classic Semillon 2-10 yrs

Oakvale Classic Verdelho	2-5 yrs
Oakvale Classic Merlot Cabernet	2-6 yrs
Oakvale Reserve Peach Tree Chard	4-12 yrs
Oakvale Reserve Peppercorn Shiraz	5-20 yrs
Milbrovale Owens Family Semillon	2-10 yrs

Pepper Tree Wines

Vying for the title of Australia's prettiest winery is Pepper Tree Wines. Pepper Tree is situated amongst ancient pepper trees at the end of Halls road, almost opposite Rothbury, off the main Broke road.

The verdant gardens and vines enclose the New England style wooden barns that house a truly great winery.

Media mogul James Fairfax has spared no expense to ensure the wines and winery are world class. A number of New South Wales Tourism Awards have been awarded to Pepper Tree.

With the luxury of owning and managing its own vineyards under the watchful eye of Carl Davies, Pepper Tree Wines has 50 hectares of land locally at Pokolbin, much of it on the site of the original Oakdale Vineyards high on the slopes of the Brokenback Range overlooking the Hunter Valley. Grapes are also grown in a 10 hectare block in Coonawarra and marketed with reference to that area after being processed in their Hunter Winery.

Winemaker and Managing Director Chris Cameron is passionate and focussed on producing truly great wines. In 1999 his quest to produce the worlds best merlot was rewarded when he won the "R & de R Fredricksberg" trophy for the Best Merlot Worldwide at the 1999 International Wine and Spirit Competition in Bordeaux with the 1996 Reserve Coonawarra Merlot. Pepper Tree has a wide range of wine styles and labels. A tasting visit to the cellar door is a real adventure with cellar door staff showing classic red and white varieties. The winemaking team also work wonders with merlot, malbec, cabernet sauvignon and cabernet franc and their Bordeaux style blends are sensational. Gewürztraminer and black muscat are used to produce some wines different to the normal Hunter theme.

All this adds up to a great wine experience when you make your obligatory pilgrimage to Pepper Tree, you should also drop into Roberts for lunch or dinner and finish your trek at the Convent.

Address: Halls Road POKOLBIN 2320	
Phone: (02) 4998 7539 **Fax:** (02) 4998 7746	
Email: ptwinery@peppertreewines.com.au	
WWW: www.peppertreewines.com.au	
Owner: Bridgstar Pty Ltd	
Winemaker: Chris Cameron	
Est: 1993	

Vine Ha: 60
Cases: 85,000
Public Hours: 9am-5pm daily, except Christmas Day & Good Friday
Principal Varieties: Cabernet Sauvignon, Chardonnay, Gewürztraminer, Malbec, Merlot, Semillon, Shiraz

Principal Wines	Potential
Semillon	5-8 yrs
Shiraz	5-8 yrs
Chardonnay	6 yrs
Traminer	up to 10 yrs
Verdelho	2-3 yrs
Malbec	5 yrs

Pendarves Estate

Dr Philip Norrie is a general practitioner in a northern beaches suburb of Sydney. He is also President and Founder of the 'Austral an Medical Friends of Wine Society'. With his wife Belinda he established Pendarves Estate in 1986. Philip's family actually first settled in the Hunter Valley in 1839. Pendarves vineyards are planted on the "Belford Dome of Limestone" with red clay topsoil over limestone as distinct from the usual Hunter volcanic soils. This region was first planted in 1825 when James Busby

planted his Kirkton Vineyard and has long proved its suitability for premium wine production. Philip is one of a long line of doctors, going right back to Dr Henry Lindeman, who have been prime movers in the Hunter Valley wine industry. The roll call of doctors who have started wineries in Australia is now up to at least 200, proving beyond doubt that medical practitioners at large, believe in the medicinal value of wine.

Dr Norrie has published a booklet entitled "Wine and Health" with the

help of McWilliams Wines. This most informative booklet quotes the world's leading Epidemiologist and Oxford Professor, Sir Richard Doll, who states, "The positive affect of wine consumption in moderation has been conclusively proved". Dr Norrie has also published several significant Historical books, two on the most famous of Australia's Wine Doctors. Firstly Dr Henry Lindeman. This book was published in 1993. Secondly Dr Christopher Rawson Penfold, published in 1994. A most enlightening book followed these two on Leo Buring "Australia's First Wine Authority". He also rewrote the early history of Australia's wine industry with his book "Vineyards of Sydney" (1990) and his latest book is "Wine and Health - A New Look At An Old Medicine" (2000). Dr Norrie is a credit to our great industry to whom I toast "good health".

Address: 110 Old North Road BELFORD 2335 Phone: (02) 9913 1088 Fax: (02) 9970 6152 Email: w nedoc@sreaker.net.au WWW: www.winedoctor.md Owner: Dr P.A. and Mrs B.J. Norrie	Winemaker: Greg Silkman Est: 1986 Vine Ha: 20 Cases: 11,000 Public Hours: Sat & Sun 11am - 5pm Principal Varieties: Chambourcin, Chardonnay, Malbec, Merlot, Pinot Noir, Sauvignon Blanc, Shiraz, Verdelho	Principal Wines	Potential
		Merlot-Malbec-Cabernet	10 yrs
		Chardonnay	5 yrs
		Shiraz	10 yrs
		Pinot Noir	2-5 yrs
		Verdelho	5-10 yrs
		Chambourcin	2-5 yrs

Pokolbin Estate

Pokolbin Estate is housed in a magnificent sandstone cottage on McDonalds Road in the heart of Pokolbin. The cottage was built over 100 years ago; some 15kms away in lower Belford, near where James Busby planted the Hunters first vines in the 1820's.

In 1980 the cottage was moved stone by stone to its present location with its high ceilings and verandahs, it's full of character with a log fire in winter and cooling in summer. It is very pleasant to sit around the wine barrel tables and taste the great wines. I was most surprised to find a number of back release wines some 7 - 8 years old. Some of the shiraz and semillons I tried had really developed superbly. You can join the wine club and get the opportunity to buy some of these special releases and some of the excellent fortified wines.

The old building really has a special feeling to it and makes a great starting point to take a Pokolbin Horse Coach ride around the valley, its wineries and other attractions. The characterful coaches and

colourful coach drivers know their beautiful Clydesdales and the wineries well. It is a special way to take in the splendid scenery and history of the Hunter.

Address: McDonalds Road POKOLBIN 2321 Phone: (02) 4968 7524 Fax: (02) 4968 7765 Email: pokolbinestate@netaus.net.au Owner: Richard Friend & John Hindman	Winemaker: Andrew Thomas Est: Early 1920's Vine Ha: 15 Cases: 2,500 Public Hours: 10am-6pm, daily Principal Wines Potential	Pokolbin Estate Shiraz now-10 yrs Small Barrel Tawny Port (Avg aged 40 yrs) Pokolbin Estate Semillon now-10 yrs Pokolbin Estate Vintage Port 6-8 yrs Pokolbin Estate Riesling (The only Hunter grown) 5 yrs

Petersons Wines

style tasting room in front of the winery opens out to a delightful garden, which has elevated views in all directions over the orderly vines and the rich fertile valleys surrounding them. As a backdrop the steep slopes of the impressive mountains not only add a grandeur to the whole scene, but give a sheltered yet surprisingly cool micro-climate.

Petersons was founded in 1971 and quickly began to collect awards at the Hunter Valley Wine Show, particularly with its chardonnay, and forging an enviable reputation for all the wines in a very short time.

The family is very involved in the operation and are modest, open and friendly people.

Son Colin, with the assistance of his father and the rest of the family, also put together the exciting 'Petersons Champagne House', a publicly-

floated venture, producing outstanding methode champenoise in the French tradition, from a superb 'maison', prominently located on the corner of Branxton and Broke Roads. They have every reason to toast its success. The Petersons are a credit to the Hunter Valley.

The name Mount View is most applicable as a location for one of the Hunter Valley's most revered wineries, Petersons. The cottage-

Address: Mount View Road MOUNT VIEW 2325 Phone: (02) 4990 1704 Fax: (02) 4991 1344 Email: petersonswines@hotkey.net.au Owner: Ian, Shirley & Colin Peterson Winemaker: Colin Peterson Gary Reed	Est: 1971 Vine Ha: 20 Cases: 10,000 Public Hours: 9am-5pm Mon-Sat; 10am-5pm Sun Principal Varieties: Merlot, Cabernet Sauvignon, Shiraz, Chardonnay, Semillon, Pinot Noir, Malbec	Principal Wines	Potential
		Back Block Shiraz	8-10 yrs
		Back Block Cabernet Sauvignon	8-10 yrs
		Semillon (Show Reserve)	5 yrs
		Chardonnay	3-5 yrs
		Botrytis Semillon	3 yrs

Petersons Champagne House

It seems absolutely right that the gateway to the Hunter should be resplendent with a world class "Champagne House". This, the only Hunter sparkling wine production house began in 1995. It provides the ideal tipple to celebrate the beginning or the end of your Hunter adventure.

Colin Peterson is a courageous entrepreneur with a great capacity for coolness under pressure also runs the family winery at Mount View.

One thing is for sure, true Methode Champenoise -Sparkling Wine made in the true French tradition should have life and vitality, if a wine is a reflection of its maker as I truly believe, then the Petersons Sparkling Wine has an abundance of these vital qualities.

Your essential visit here is

accompanied by personal table service and a tutored tasting

together with cheese and bread. Don't miss it!!

Address: Corner Broke and Branxton Roads CESSNOCK 2325 Phone: (02) 4998 7881 Fax: (02) 4998 7882 Email: bubbles@petersonhouse.com.au WWW: www.petersonhouse.com.au	Winemaker: Colin Peterson Est: 1994 Vine Ha: 4 Cases: 5,000 Public Hours: 9am-5pm, daily Principal Varieties: Chardonnay Principal Wines Potential		
		Semillon - Pinot Noir	3 yrs
		Chardonnay - Pinot Noir	3 yrs
		Merlot	3 yrs
		Shiraz	2-3 yrs
		Pinot - Chardonnay - Meunier	3 yrs
		Chambourcin	3 yrs

Piggs Peake

A welcome new winery on Hermitage Road is Piggs Peake. The brainchild of dynamic winemaker Steve Dodd who with two partners has virtually built the whole winery from laying the cement slab to welding the stainless steel tanks himself. Steve is still a young man but has a wealth of experience starting in the Hunter in the mid-eighties at Saxonvale. After the Orlando Wyndham takeover he worked for them in the Hunter.

The philosophy at Piggs Peake is to source the very best grapes from New South Wales regions to basically make regional wines separately at one location and market them direct through their pleasant informative cellar door. When I asked Steve why the name? He just said "why not".

The wines I saw were a real knockout. The unoaked chardonnay was crisp and zingy with loads of melon and lemon citrus flavours, a chardonnay from the Rylestone region about half way from the Hunter to Mudgee had lovely grapefruit like highlights with a smooth vanilla like palate. The Hunter Shiraz from 50 year old dry grown vines near Broke had lovely intense raspberry like fruit and pepper ·· excellent. The 1999 vintage of 110 tonnes was handled by Steve with just one assistant · that's a big job. Piggs Peake are all about innovation, watch out for them.

Address: 697 Hermitage Road POKOLBIN 2335 **Phone:** (02) 6574 7000 **Fax:** (02) 6574 7070	**Email:** piggspeake@cn-newc.com.au **Winemaker:** Steve Dodd **Est:** 1998	**Public Hours:** 10am-5pm, daily; closed Public Holidays **Principal Varieties:** Shiraz

Rothbury Estate

The brainchild of Wine Guru, Len Evans. Rothbury began its life in the seventies as an opportunity for people to become involved in a true winery operation. "The Rothbury Society" was founded to give hands on involvement in premium wine.

An impressive winery was built on an imposing hill on the main Broke road at Pokolbin. A cathedral like large hall was incorporated in the construction "The Great Hall" and became the venue for legendary Dinners and Celebrations that continue today.

Rothbury also pioneered the Cowra Region, making a chardonnay that quickly captured the wine drinkers imagination.

Today the enterprise is in the hands of the progressive and innovative Mildara Blass Group. Local identity, the innovative and enthusiastic winemaker Neil McGuigan has just taken on the winemaking job. I am sure this will only add a further zest to the wines.

Rothbury Ridge Wines

Rothbury Ridge Wines specialise in producing unique Hunter wine styles from both traditional Hunter varieties and new varieties recently introduced into the Hunter Valley.

A top class addition to the Hunter Valley is Rothbury Ridge Wines with its recently refurbished accommodation venue Rothbury Ridge Winemakers Cottage.

Rothbury Ridge is located on a ridge south of Talga Road and enjoys splendid views of the Brokenback Ranges and surrounding Valley.

The Cellar Door has been constructed using Australian timbers, antiques and oak barrels overhead creating a great atmosphere for visitors to taste beautifully crafted wines. The Semillon and Chardonnay are packed with fruit flavour and I was very impressed by two unusual red varieties in which Rothbury Ridge Wines specialise. The first being Durif, a variety mainly grown in Northern Victoria, its deep colour, full-bodied, rich blueberry flavours are truly exciting. The other variety being Chambourcin, a French hybrid that is well suited to the Hunter climate, with its smooth cherry like character and complexity, equally impressive.

Address: Talga Road ROTHBURY 2320	**Est:** 1988	**Vine Ha:** 13.3	**Cases:** 8,400	Reserve Durif	10+ yrs
Phone: (02) 4930 7122 **Fax:** (02) 4930 7198	**Public Hours:** 8am-5pm weekdays; 10am-			Reserve Chambourcin	7+ yrs
Email: rothburyridge@telstra.easymail.com.au	5pm weekends			Reserve Semillon	10-15 yrs
WWW: www.rothburyridgewines.com.au	**Principal Varieties:** Cabernet Sauvignon,			Premium Shiraz/Cab Sauvignon	7-10 yrs
Owner: Rothbury Ridge Wines	Chard, Semillon, Chambourcin, Durif, Shiraz			Premium Shiraz/Chambourcin	7-10 yrs
Winemaker: Peter Jorgensen	**Principal Wines**		**Potential**	Rosé Trad. Methode Champenoise	7 +yrs

Rothvale Vineyard & Winery

The Rothvale vineyard and winery property also boasts "The Hunter Habit" Four romantic cottages set amongst the vines where one can truly experience life on a working vineyard.

Former Veterinarian Max Patton bought the property from Tyrrells in 1997 and the 25 acres of 30 year old vines have really performed well for him. The vineyard has been doubled in size. Max's family are all very active in the business with partner Ann Wilson very active in the sales and promotional area. Son Luke, who has a commerce degree in Land economics, is General Manager and assists his father in the vineyard and winery. Daughter Tilda has a Bachelor of Arts in Information Technology and assist in this area of business. Max's other son Angus is also involved with Food and Beverage Management and has worked at Casuarina, a leading Hunter restaurant, as well as for the Disney Cruise Line.

The four vineyard cottages that make up "The Hunter Habit" are beautifully secluded amongst the vines. There is a choice of one, two or three bedroom cottages and each has a fully equipped kitchen and an open fireplace. When you take a stroll along the creek you could even come across a wombat or platypus.

The wines at Rothvale are all domain sourced from their own vineyards. I was most impressed by the Reserve Chardonnay a voluptuous wine with marmalade and vanilla and a very silky mouthfeel. The "Tilda" Shiraz is a substantial wine, which will certainly age well. Rothvale have a Vintage Club with regular functions being held.

Address: Deasys Road POKOLBIN 2321	**Email:** rothvalehunterhabit@bigpond.com	**Principal Varieties:** Chardonnay, Shiraz,
Phone: (02) 4998 7290 **Fax:** (02) 4998 7290	**WWW:** www.users.bigpond.com/rothvalehunterhabit	Cabernet Sauvignon, Semillon **Est:** 1998

Saddlers Creek

A lively and interesting winery, attracting much interest over recent years, is Saddler's Creek. Located at the beginning of Marrowbone Road, in fact an ideal spot to commence your journey through the Hunter Wineries, as it is not far from the town of Cessnock and gives you a very pleasant start to the day.

A number of enthusiastic partners have put together a great Enterprise. They have recently introduced "Club Equus", a wine club which they conduct on a very personal basis with the simple aim of giving their best customers the best service and priority at all times. You can join Club Equus, its free!! It will give you three times a year a special selection

dozen at a great price. You will also be updated on new releases and receive first choice of purchase. You also obtain free invitations to pre-release barrel tastings and wine previews. The Bluegrass Room offers tutored, personal tastings by appointment as well as the normal cellar door tastings.

The winery produces wines on site under the distinctive label names of Bluegrass, Equus and Marrowbone. The wines are increasingly being seen in top restaurants around Australia.

Along with their innovative approach Saddler's Creek's packaging is exquisite. Magnums are offered along with some extraordinary dessert wines in a sensational wax sealed presentation, which is totally in keeping with the wines quality. The Bluegrass Cabernet Sauvignon & Marrowbone Chardonnay have both

won trophies and gold medals at recent Hunter Valley Boutique Winemakers Shows. These wines, along with a traditionally fermented sparkling blend and their superb Classic Hunter Semillon, the 2000 scoring 5 stars for quality and value in the 2000 Penguin Wine Guide & Sydney Morning Herald & Melbourne Age Uncorked feature, contribute to what is an extraordinary range for a Boutique winery.

Saddler's has a reputation for putting on some of the best luncheons in the Hunter and their Annual Barrel Tasting is both unique and incredibly popular.

A taste of their wines and their hospitality is well worth the effort.

Address: Corner Marrowbone & Oakey Creek Roads POKOLBIN 2320	Winemaker: John Johnstone		
	Est: 1989 Vine Ha: 15		
Phone: (02) 4991 1770	Cases: 15,000	Bluegrass Cabernet Sauvignon	6-10 yrs
	Principal Varieties: Cabernet Sauvignon,	Marrowbone Chardonnay	3-5 yrs
Fax: (02) 4991 2482	Chardonnay, Merlot, Semillon, Shiraz	Equus Hunter Shiraz	5-8 yrs
Email: info@saddlerscreekwines.com.au		Equus McLaren Shiraz	8-10 yrs
		Reserve Selection Merlot	5-8 yrs
WWW: www.saddlerscreekwines.com.au	Principal Wines Potential	Classic Hunter Semillon	10-12 yrs

Scarborough Wines

Ian and Merralea Scarborough are perfectionists. Their idyllic setting perched on top of a substantial hill looking over Pokolbin with the Brokenback Ranges as a backdrop has been carefully chosen. The vineyard, perfectly tended all year round, is on rich red terra rossa soil, a rarity in the Hunter, but one of the worlds most sought after viticultural soil types. It is ideal for the two wines they produce a rich opulent chardonnay and a regal pinot noir both with definite burgundian styles.

Scarborough's are virtually the only Boutique Winery who give their wines bottle aging. Both are aged for 3 years before their release.

The hilltop winery is meticulously kept and adjoins a charmingly appointed tasting room, delightfully decorated in a provincial style with splendid views in all directions. Every visitor gets to sit down and have a properly tutored tasting of all the current release wines, here you are really in the hands of a caring professional wine family.

The Scarborough's are a close family. Son Jerome and daughter Sally all pull their weight in the enterprise. This vineyard and winery demands a visit - do not leave the Hunter without visiting it!!

Address: Gillards Road POKOLBIN 2320	**Winemaker:** Ian Scarborough	Semillon
Phone: (02) 4998 7563	**Est:** 1987	**Principal Wines** **Potential**
Fax: (02) 4998 7786	**Vine Ha:** 10 **Cases:** 10,000	Scarborough Traditional Yellow Label 5-6 yrs
Email: sales@scarboroughwine.com.au	**Public Hours:** 9am-5pm, daily; except	Scarborough Export Blue Label 3-4 yrs
WWW: www.scarboroughwine.com.au	Christmas Day	Scarborough Pinot Noir 3-5 yrs
Owner: Ian & Merralea Scarborough	**Principal Varieties:** Chardonnay, Pinot Noir,	Scarborough Semillon Should cellar well

Kevin Sobels Wines

Kevin Sobels comes from a family steeped in wine history going back to the early 1800's when his ancestor was trained in the art of winemaking in France & Germany. Coming to Australia and opening his own winery in 1850 in the Barossa Valley before moving onto Clare in 1869 to what became Buring & Sobels Quelltaler Estate. Kevin's wife Margaret comes from a well-known Riverland Wine Family and son Jason is involved in the vineyard and winery operations.

In 1991 the Sobels bought their Broke road Pokolbin property and its 23-acre vineyard planted by Greg Ross in 1980. In 1995 the Sobels built a unique circular winery and cellar door on the main Broke road to give the visitor a real family greeting often accompanied by their faithful St Bernard "Plonk", the only thing missing, being the mini barrel of brandy around his neck!!

The Sobels wines are carefully made using minimal amounts of preservatives and include some sweeter table wine styles, sparkling and fortified wines as well as dry reds and whites. You can be sure to find something to suit your palate.

Larger groups are welcome and picnic tables and barbecue facilities are freely available.

The Sobels boast on their brochure "open every day whilst the doors are open or the lights are on:" so there is no excuse not to drop in.

Address: Corner Halls and Broke Road POKOLBIN 2320	**Est:** 1992 **Vine Ha:** 8 **Cases:** 6,000	Chardonnay 3-5 yrs
	Public Hours: 7 days whilst the doors are	Semillon 3-5 yrs
Phone: (02) 4998 7766 **Fax:** (02) 4998 7475	open and or the lights are on	Shiraz 5 yrs
Email: kevin@sobelswines.com.au	**Principal Varieties:** Chardonnay, Pinot Noir,	Cabernet / Merlot 3-5 yrs
WWW: www.sobelswines.com.au	Semillon, Shiraz, Traminer	Hunter Sparkling Red 3-5 yrs
Winemaker: Kevin Sobels	**Principal Wines** **Potential**	Gewürztraminer 1-2 yrs

Tower Estate

How do you set up the ideal winery and finest hospitality venue in Australia?

Wine Industry icon and Hunter Valley stalwart Len Evans had time to think about this after the Mildara Blass Wine Group had bought out his love and brainchild Rothbury Estate, he had the vision and founded Rothbury and its accompanying Wine Society with a few friends in 1969. Len acted as its guiding light for 27 years.

Len was not ready to take to the backwaters although he has his own wine enterprise, Evans Family Wines, and a splendid Villa on Palmers Lane. The thought of another large wine enterprise gave Len no joy at all, but his thoughts crystalised around a Boutique Wine and Hospitality concept absolutely devoted to quality.

Tower Estate is the pinnacle encompassing Len's philosophies of Wine and Life. 1000 dozen only will ever be produced of each Tower Wine, that's all, this requires about 15 tonnes of the best fruit available. Len's concept was to get the best 15 tonnes of each variety available in Australia from the region and vineyard that produced the best. Len's coterie of wine legend friends became his answer. But first where to put the winery, it had to be in the Hunter in a prominent location. Happily close friend Fay McGuigan, wife of human dynamo wine legend Brian, had a large block on the corner of Halls Road and the main Hunter artery Broke Road right in the heart of Pokolbin. I well remember Brian and Fay chatting to me about the happy times they had enjoyed living under the gums in the makeshift cottage in the early nineties when the Wyndham takeover had left them homeless.

Len's mates came to the fore, Brian Croser a friend and associate of Len for 25 years sourced 15 tonnes of the best riesling grapes from the Clare, Watervale and Eden Valleys. Michael Hill-Smith, a sixth generation

Address: Corner Halls & Broke Road POKOLBIN 2320	Owner: Tower Estate Pty Ltd	Hunter Valley Chardonnay	up to 10 yrs
	Winemaker: Don Dineen	Hunter Valley Shiraz	10-12 yrs
Phone: (02) 4998 7989	Est: 1999	Coonawarra Cabernet	12-15 yrs
Fax: (02) 4998 7919	Cases: 10,000	Hunter Valley Semillon	10+ yrs
Email: sales@tower-lodge.com.au	Public Hours: 10am-5pm, daily	Clare Valley Riesling	up to 10 yrs
WWW: www.towerestatewines.com.au	Principal Wines Potential	Barossa Shiraz	12-15 yrs

Tower Estate

wineman who Len had know since childhood, found 15 tonnes of prime Adelaide Hills sauvignon blanc, the 15 tonnes of shiraz came from the master of the Barossa Peter Lehmann, 44 years Len's mate and only a few days his elder. Robert Hill-Smith found 15 tonnes of prime Coonawarra cabernet sauvignon from his Menzies Vineyard. A Hunter semillon, verhelho, chardonnay and a shiraz completed the 1999 first vintage of eight wines.

The Tuscan style Tower Winery and tasting area is a real picture imposing yet intriguing with its huge 1895 French coachhouse doors. The splendidly equipped winery became the workshop for talented young winemaker Dan Dineen. Another of Len's great mates Iain Riggs, Chief of Brokenwood where Dan was Chief Winemaker, released him for the new project. I met Dan about 4 years ago when he was understudy for Phil Ryan at Mt Pleasant and fresh from an overseas study tour, he's certainly fired up.

Tower has developed dramatically into a fabulous complex, supported by 14 shareholders handpicked by Len with names like Basil Sellars, John David and Ken Cowley, the power and influence is obvious, Brian McGuigan and Tower builder Keith Stronach form the Executive Committee.

Tower Lodge opened in August 2000. A real win has been the acquisition of Roberts Restaurant and the involvement of Robert & Sally Molines, it's right next door to Tower and Len's favourite restaurant. Certainly as far as I am concerned it is in the top 10 restaurants in Australia.

Blaxlands Restaurant on the other Broke Road side of Tower has also been purchased and under Len's daughter Jodie's control will become a classic all-hours true Brasserie. The new Tower Lodge includes 12 suites all with a special individual feature plus separate lounge area and courtyard. The Chairmans suite is even larger with a separate meeting room.

The Conference facilities are truly complete, the large Boardroom seats up to 30 people and has a large French oak refectory table, leather chairs and every conceivable communication and audio-visual facility.

There are also two syndicate rooms, a dining room and lounge with a huge open fireplace and a library and courtyard. Roberts and Blaxlands make up a complete package. Guest services are five star quality, the corporate market has already embraced Tower strongly.

Tower Estate have created the "Tower 200" an exclusive club, the 200 Members places are all now taken but you can join the waiting list. One case of each wine is available to members along with magnum sized bottles exclusively. There are many other benefits including guided tastings by Len Evans and Dan Dineen.

The seven wines entered in wine shows from the initial 1999 vintage have already gained 2 trophies, 3 gold and one silver medal. Some Tower wines are already being exported to leading restaurants worldwide. Although buying direct at the vineyard is the main way to secure these exclusive wines Vintage Cellars fine wine outlets have a small stock, you may even run into them on Qantas who took the 99 Sauvignon Blanc for 1st class internationally and the 99 Riesling domestically.

Len has created a towering concept, more power to him, his friends and their beloved Hunter Valley.

Terrace Vale Wines

It was a syndicate of 20 Sydney businessmen and their families who started Terrace Vale. Most remain and other than winemaker Alain Le Prince and some administrative staff, the rest of the 'workers' are the syndicate members and families. Work, including cellar door sales, is handled on a roster basis and the result of this extraordinary co-operation is a congenial 'family' atmosphere.

The Terrace Vale vineyard was planted in 1971 and the first vintage was produced in 1974 at Tyrrell's Winery. The first vintage to be made in the new winery at Terrace Vale was in 1976. As his name suggests, winemaker Alain Le Prince is French and from the Touraine region of the Loire Valley. Alain is a gentle but extremely passionate person who cares deeply for his wines.

The Bin 2 Chardonnay was an early success story for the winery when the 1979 vintage won many medals and trophies. Alain's semillons are made in a quite French style firm with restrained citrus characters. When young they are rather restrained but really develop superbly with bottle-age and some of the older vintages in my cellar are magnificent drinking now when well over 10 years old.

Terrace Vale reds are often big, fruity wines particularly the shiraz which will improve with several years cellaring. The pinot noir is usually a lighter style wine with pronounced fruit, while the cabernet sauvignon is a more elegant wine that develops well in the bottle. There is a stunning view of the Brokenback Ranges from Terrace Vale and this, combined with lovely wines and warm hospitality, makes it a charming place to visit.

Address: Deasy Road POKOLBIN 2320
Phone: (02) 4998 7517 **Fax:** (02) 4998 7814
Winemaker: Alain Leprince

Est: 1971 **Vine Ha:** 36.69
Cases: 10,000-12,000
Public Hours: 10am-5pm, daily

Principal Varieties: Semillon, Chardonnay, Shiraz, Cabernet, Pinot Noir, Gewürztraminer, Sauvignon Blanc

Tamburlaine

Found in the heart of Hunter Wine Country, in the shadows of the Brokenback Mountain Range, Tamburlaine has been evolving since the mid 60's with a huge base of active members, who take almost the entire production of excellent wines, including some great botrytised wines, an old fortified muscat and a framboise (raspberry liqueur). Tamburlaine has achieved significance amongst Hunter Winemakers, both in terms of innovation and production growth, for many years winemaking has been under the guidance of Chief Winemaker and Managing Director, Mark Davidson.

Grape growing on the Winery site in Pokolbin began before the current day boom and the cellar maintains some traditional Australian charm.

Tastings at the winery are unhurried and personal, particularly during the week. Informative and enthusiastic staff introduce the wines you would like to know more about, as well as those with which you may be familiar.

The wines are not widely available; however the limited releases each vintage are well worth tasting and buying at the cellar door.

Address: McDonalds Road POKOLBIN 2320	**Est:** 1966 **Vine Ha:** 40 **Cases:** 40,000	**Principal Wines**
Phone: (02) 4998 7570 **Fax:** (02) 4998 7763	**Public Hours:** 9am-5pm, daily	Tamburlaine Hunter Reserve Range
WWW: www.mywinery.com	**Principal Varieties:** Syrah, Cab Sav,	Tamburlaine Orange Reserve Range
Winemaker: Mark Davidson &	Semillon, Merlot, Chambourcin, Malbec,	Tamburlaine "Blue" Label Range
Michael McManus	Sauvignon Blanc, Chardonnay, Verdelho	Marlowe (To be released)

Tulloch Wines

In 1883 John Younie Tulloch became the slightly reluctant owner of a vineyard. In settlement of a debt to his store at Branxton, he accepted a 17-hectare property around the corner from Lindemans. Although a devout Methodist, John obviously saw no sin in developing nature's gift of the grape.

After rejuvenating the small shiraz vineyard, Tulloch made his first wine in 1895. By the 1920s, he had bought much surrounding property and had more land under vine than any other local winemaker. Tullochs, like many other winemakers, sold their wine in bulk to large wine merchants in the capital cities, including Rhinecastle and Leo Buring.

John Younie's son Hector succeeded him in 1940 and established the first Tulloch label in the early 1950s. The company is now managed by Pat Auld whose family are steeped in Wine Tradition, Jay Tulloch having recently retired. The renovated cellar door, with its beautiful pergola and façade in the shadow of The Brokenbacks, is worth a visit. Tulloch wines are consistently excellent. They are individual in style and the verdelho is particularly good each year. Tullochs have a reputation for their white wines, which have managed to remain consistently good throughout the company's tumultuous history.

Tullochs also make an excellent Vintage Sparkling wine from chardonnay and semillon under the label "Hunter Cuvee" which has regularly won major wine awards.

Their Glen Elgin Estate is a pretty place with vineyards planted over the undulating countryside. It has a very settled happy feeling about it, which is reflected in the characterful wines of recent years.

Tyrrells Wines

Tyrrell's has expanded into a very significant Australian Wine Company and is now ably run by fourth generation Bruce Tyrrell. His father Murray sadly passed on late in 2000, he was undoubtedly one of the great characters of the Hunter Valley. He was awarded the Order of Australia for his services to the wine industry and was very outspoken in support of Australian wine, in particular that of the Hunter Valley.

When Murray took over Tyrrell's in 1959, the company sold only bulk wine to other wine companies, such as McWilliam's, where Maurice O'Shea blended them with his own. O'Shea also bottled some of Tyrrell's wines and sold them under the 'Richard' label. As soon as he had taken charge, Murray Tyrrell instigated some major changes. He developed a label and began exhibiting wines successfully in many shows. Visitors soon flocked to the winery's cellar door and sales boomed. From only several hundred tonnes in the 1960's, Tyrrell's now crush many thousands of tonnes and have invested in vineyards in other regions such as McLaren Vale and Coonawarra in South Australia.

Tyrrell's have a number of traditional labels such as their top selling 'Long Flat' wines and the 'Old Winery' label. The Tyrrell's Vat 47 Chardonnay was really the first commercial

chardonnay in Australia and has celebrated many successful vintages, regularly winning gold medals and trophies in wine shows. This 'Vat' series, which includes a number of white and red wines, really put Tyrrell's on the map, when they were launched by Murray in the mid-1960's, at the start of the wine boom.

Tyrrell's also made some of the first pinot noirs in Australia. Their pinot noir vineyard is planted in rich, red volcanic soil over shale and limestone, on the Brokenback Range to the rear of the winery. This is an ideal location for this grape variety and Tyrrell's have produced some incredible wines. In 1979 Tyrrell's Pinot Noir won the Gault Milleau World Olympics of Wine in France, this led to worldwide publicity and acclaim for Tyrrell's, which was

further enhanced by Murray's own distinctive way of passing on good news.

The history of Tyrrell's Hunter Valley Winery is the longest and most continuous progression of any of the winemakers in the district. In 1998, they celebrated 140 years of operation. The business was begun by Edward Tyrrell, who was granted 330 acres of land at Pokolbin in 1858. This property was ideally suited to the vine, with its rich volcanic soils on well-drained slopes. A slab hut (which is still preserved by the family) was built and vines planted, with the first vintage occurring in 1864. Edward's son Dan took over winemaking in 1885 at the age of 15, and proceeded to make 75 vintages, surely a world record. It was not until a fall from a ladder in 1958 that Dan was forced into retirement.

Murray took the helm in 1959 and his son Bruce is now Managing Director. Bruce astutely handles the marketing and business side of the company, after serving his apprenticeship well in the winery under his late father. Tyrrell's also produce some wonderful methode champenoise wines from semillon, pinot and chardonnay grapes. Tyrrell's have expanded quite significantly into the McLaren Vale Region of South Australia, where their own vineyards provide their "Rufus Stone" range of wines and also into the Heathcote Region of Victoria.

Address: Broke Road POKOLBIN 2320	Mark Richardson	Principal Wines	Potential
Phone: (02) 4993 7000	Est: 1858	VAT 47 Chardonnay	5-10 yrs
Fax: (02) 4998 7723	Vine Ha: 610	Moon Mountain Chardonnay	3-6 yrs
Email: tyrrells@tyrrells.com.au	Cases: 850,000	VAT 1 Hunter Semillon	10 + yrs
WWW: www.tyrrells.com.au	Public Hours: 8am-5pm Mon-Sat	VAT 9 Hunter Shiraz	10 + yrs
Owner: Bruce Tyrrell	Principal Varieties: Semillon, Chardonnay,	VAT 6 Hunter Pinot Noir	5-10 yrs
Winemaker: Andrew Spinaze &	Pinot Noir, Shiraz	VAT 8 Shiraz Cabernet	5-10 yrs

Vinden Estate

Sydney Solicitor Guy Vinden and his wife Sandra, have created a first class Vineyard Estate in the heart of Pokolbin on Gillards Road.

Their combined home and cellar door is certainly one of the most beautiful buildings in the Hunter. The cellar door is in the spacious western wing of the house. The décor and ambience are truly superb and the sandstone and glass furniture is of their own design, under the "Vindoni" Label. Some pieces are available for purchase, along with the classy Vindoni garments.

Guy has probably the Hunters smallest winery where he proudly showed me his first red wine still not released, seven barriques only, of a silky 1998 shiraz. Made in tandem with his good friend, the talented winemaker John Baruzzi, with Guy's care and John's passion and

knowledge they have created a great wine. The 2001 vintage has seen the first merlot from the Vinden Vineyards, a wine to look out for.

The semillon and chardonnay both of the 1998 vintage, the wineries first release, were packed with flavour and extremely well balanced - expect great things from this winery.

Vinden Estate also boasts "The Stables Cottage" accommodation. This restored rural cottage, in a beautiful garden setting, shows all the skills of design and décor, that Sandra and Guy have used in the cellar door. With its lounge and separate bedroom, it can happily house a family of four with a fully equipped kitchen, air-conditioning and an outside entertaining area, it is a great place to stay a day or two. The location is also great, being within walking distance of a number of great restaurants, golf courses

and other attractions.

You can join the Vinden Estate Wine Club or mailing list, to ensure you have access to their limited releases and activities.

		Semillon, Shiraz	
Address: 17 Gillards Road POKOLBIN 2320	**Cases:** 1,000		
Phone: (02) 4998 7410 **Fax:** (02) 4998 7421	**Public Hours:** Fri, Sat, Sun, Mon & Public	**Principal Wines**	**Potential**
Owner: Sandra & Guy Vinden	Holidays 10am-5pm otherwise by	Semillon	5 yrs
Winemaker: John Baruzzi & Guy Vinden	appointment	Shiraz	4 yrs
Est: 1998 **Vine Ha:** 4	**Principal Varieties:** Chardonnay, Merlot,	Chardonnay	4 yrs

Sandalyn Wilderness Estate

On Wilderness Road to the northern part of the Lovedale Region of the Hunter Valley is the magnificent and unique building of Sandalyn Wilderness Estate with its vaulted ceilings in a conservatory style. Light, airy and resplendent not only with the excellent wines of the Estate but many gourmet products and the crafts of local artisans.

Owners Sandra and Lindsay Whaling with their daughter Sally established the Estate in 1988. The vineyard is a beautifully maintained 30 acres and the wines continue to win critical acclaim each year. The range includes a Semillon Verdelho which proves how well these complimentary varieties can blend with the tropical and passionfruit of the Verdelho with the grassy Semillon with its honey and citrus in the background.

Another wine with a distinct difference is the Semillon-Late Harvest with a touch of luscious apricot aromas and flavours crisp and clean, whilst the Methode Champenoise sparkling Chardonnay/Verdelho has proved to be a unique trophy winning combination.

The Sandalyn Conservatory Shiraz is fine structured with loads of spicy fruit. A number of other wines are produced. If you wish you can take your glass out under the Rose Arbour or beside the six metre high bronze sculpture of Henry Moore set in the lovely gardens, probably the Maitre d' Bacchus, a loping golden retriever will be delighted to share your experience and your company.

Address: Wilderness Road Lovedale 2320	**Winemaker:** Adrian Sheridan	Semillon Verdelho	5-6 yrs
Phone: (02) 4930 7611	**Est:** 1988	Chardonnay	4-6 yrs
Fax: (02) 4930 7611	**Vine Ha:** 30 acres	Pinot Noir	3-5 yrs
Email: sandalyn@hunterlink.net.au	**Cases:** 4,500	Verdelho	3-4 yrs
WWW: www.huntervalleyboutiques.com.au	**Public Hours:** 10am-5pm daily	Semillon Late Harvest	up to 5 yrs
Owner: Sandra & Lindsay Whaling	**Principal Wines** **Potential**	Shiraz	5-10 yrs

Located on the banks of the Hunter River, Wyndham Estate was founded by one of the earliest pioneers in the region, George Wyndham, who planted his first vines in 1828 on a property called "Dalwood". The classic old homestead, Dalwood House was restored as an official Australian Bicentenary Project as an important part of Australia's Heritage and is now open for tours at 11.30am Wednesday through Sunday.

Vines and winemaking were a large part of George Wyndham's rural interests, however he is also credited with introducing the first Hereford cattle to mainland Australia.

George Wyndham purchased property throughout New South Wales and planted vines as far north as Inverell near the Queensland border. Under careful handling by his son, the wine business grew until it was the second largest Wine Company in the State. Unfortunately with the death of both Wyndhams by

1870 and a subsequent depression, the Wyndham Company was reduced to bankruptcy, to be bought by H. Wilkinson in 1901. The vineyards, winery and related interests were bought by Penfolds, who kept the Dalwood name and gave it great circulation, with their "Dalwood" series of table wines. The winery was sold to their winemaker Perc McGuigan, whose son Brian began Wyndham Estate Pty. Ltd., which was then purchased by current owners Orlando Wyndham. Wyndham Estate is now one of the largest and perhaps most widely-known winery in the Hunter Valley, with its wines also well known on the international market, through the marketing prowess of parent company, Orlando Wyndham.

Wyndham Estate wines reflect the vibrant team that produces them and always seem to have a liveliness and zest to them along with rich fruit flavours. The Bin TR2 and Bin 222 Chardonnay are amongst Australia's market leaders in their price range

and are superb fruit driven wines. The Oak Cask Chardonnay is extremely good, and benefits from a few years' bottle aging. The Wyndham range also includes a verdelho, the grape of the Island of Madeira, which always exhibits beautiful tropical fruit flavours with a crisp dry finish. The Bin 555 Selected Hermitage made from shiraz grapes, is a wine of drinkability, ideal as a lunchtime red. Bin 444 Cabernet Sauvignon is a rich, round wine, full-bodied, but with typical Wyndham approachability.

This historic winery has been brought back to its former glory, with extensive refurbishment and now houses a wonderful cellar door, restaurant, function facilities, wine education centre and caters for daily tours. The gardens at Wyndham are also superb, with riverside barbecue and picnic grounds, in fact the whole estate is wonderfully turned out and a must for a visit on your Hunter pilgrimage.

Address: Dalwood Road DALWOOD 2335	**Est:** 1828	**Principal Varieties:** Shiraz, Semillon, Chardonnay, Cabernet Sauvignon, Traminer, Riesling, Merlot
Phone: (02) 4998 3444 **Fax:** (02) 4998 3422	**Public Hours:** 9am-5pm, Mon-Sat; 10am-5pm, Sun	
Owner: Orlando Wyndham Group Pty Ltd		

THE WINE GUARDIAN
AUSTRALIAN WINE SYSTEMS
HEAD OFFICE: 61 BRUCE STREET, COOKS HILL
NEW SOUTH WALES, AUSTRALIA 2300
PHONE: (02) 4929 4269 FAX: (02) 4926 4360

The ebullient Brett Fairclough has come up with a real winner, in The "Wine Guardian" Wine Dispensing System, which not only beautifully preserves the wine but also protects and dispenses it, with the unique Argon gas, to keep the wine in absolutely first class condition for up to 2-4 weeks. The taps that fit into the bottles have clip on gas lines, each wine can therefore be removed from the wooden unit and stored under its gas shield in the cupboard or refrigerator and put back on the system at any time, thus 20 - 30 or more wines, can be protected at any one time. When you look at the price of premium wine, you can protect a couple of thousand dollars worth and have each ready to serve, to enjoy all its nuances of aroma and subtleties of flavour at a moments notice. For those in the hospitality business it is indispensable!!

Brett is a real wine enthusiast and long time wine lover. He has also arranged a leasing system for the unit and as I have experienced first hand the Wine Guardian System Service is a real winner. A number of Australia's leading restaurants and wine enthusiasts swear by the system.

Address: 41 Annie Street WICKHAM 2293   **Phone:** (02) 4927 6566   **Fax:** (02) 4927 6789

Wilderness Estate

"Out of the Wilderness - into the limelight" would well describe the progress of Wilderness Estate founded in 1985 by Austrian born Hunter grapegrower and winemaker Joe Lesnik.

The Wilderness winery is right at the crossroads of the Hunter on the corner of Broke and Branxton roads. Joe has green fingers and has extensive vineyards on the rich terra rossa style soils on his Wilderness Road Vineyards and on the fertile loams around the winery. The winemaking facility was built in 1985 and is well equipped with the most up-to-date technology.

The Wilderness Wines are full of rich fruit flavours and extremely drinkable. They represent extremely good value for money and are taking the Export markets by storm, along with the main range are Black Creek and Lesnik labels. Plans are afoot for major renovations to the cellar door so keep an eye on this major intersection of the wine roads of the Hunter for exciting developments.

Address: Branxton Road POKOLBIN 2320	Public Hours: 9am-5pm daily	Wilderness Estate Merlot	4 yrs
Phone: (02) 4998 7755 Fax: (02) 4998 7750	Principal Varieties: Merlot, Chard., Verdelho,	Wilderness Estate Cabernet Merlot	6 yrs
Owner: Josef Lesnik	Semillon, Pinot Noir, Shiraz, Cabernet	Wilderness Est Individual Block Sem.	5 yrs
Winemaker: John Baruzzi	Principal Wines Potential	Black Creek Verdelho	3 yrs
Est: 1985 Vine Ha: 40 Cases: 20,000	Wilderness Estate Chardonnay 6 yrs	Black Creek Chardonnay	4 yrs

Upper Hunter Valley

The area loosely called the Upper Hunter Valley surrounds the Hunter and Goulburn Rivers and their tributaries, and the towns of Denman, Muswellbrook, Sandy Hollow and Scone. The landscape is striking and diverse with both rich alluvial plains and steep mountain ranges. It is rich country with deep red and black soils over many coal deposits, this being one of the region's major industries.

Vines have been grown in the Upper Hunter since early in the 19th century. One of the first winegrowers was George Bowman who established Arrowfield and other properties and made wine at his property, Archerfield. Other wines in the area were made mostly as a hobby. In 1960, Penfolds bought a large property at Wybong (just north of Sandy Hollow), where they planted several hundreds of hectares of vines of a great variety. A winery and dam were constructed on the property, but there were only limited supplies of water available at times, causing some problems. This property was sold to Rosemount in 1977 and is now Barrington Estate.

The period of real growth for the Upper Hunter started in 1969 when Arrowfield began a huge development at Jerry's Plains. This became the largest single vineyard in Australia consisting of more than 800,000 vines by 1977. Also in 1969, Bob Oatley bought a large tract of land at the junction of Wybong Creek and Goulburn River, which became Rosemount Estate. The period saw other beginnings for the Upper Hunter with David Hordern planting a vineyard at Wybong.

The old Oak Factory at Muswellbrook has been converted to a winery by Simon Gilbert, with the help of John Hordern. John has now taken over the cellars with partner Rex d'Aquinio from Orange and further renovations have been undertaken.

Although the Upper Hunter receives less rain than the Lower Hunter, there is an abundant water supply in the local rivers and nearly all new vineyards rely on drip irrigation to become established. The mature vines in the area seem to be producing better fruit each vintage. The area historically has produced white grape varieties more successfully than red and it was the Rosemount's rieslings and traminers, produced in the '70's by John Ellis, that first brought the area wide acclaim.

Since then, the Upper Hunter has become best known for its chardonnays, with Philip Shaw of Rosemount winning accolades worldwide. Other whites such as wood-aged semillons and sauvignon blancs have also brought credit to Rosemount and others. As the vines mature the red wines are really turning out to be top class, as evidenced by red specialist grower Cruickshank Callatoota with their cabernet sauvignon.

Newcomers to the wine scene Inglewood Vineyards have large holdings of mature vineyards.

The Upper Hunter has seen some large increases in vineyard areas during the last 5 years some under the McGuigan banner, and as the existing vineyards mature the wines are improving each vintage. It is a region with a great depth of winemaking talent and they all seem to work well together, spurring each other on.

Upper Hunter Valley

Upper Hunter - NSW

1. Arrowfield Wines
2. Barrington Estate
3. Cruickshank Callatoota Estate
4. Hordens Horseshoe
5. Inglewood Vineyards
6. James Estate
7. Kenmarie Vineyard
8. Oak Wine Services

Arrowfield Wines

Arrowfield's history dates back from 1824 when George Bowman, one of the first settlers in the Upper Hunter region, received several large land grants from Governor Macquarie. A vineyard was planted and a horse stud and grazing property developed.

In 1969, new owners established a large vineyard and winery and by 1977 it was the largest single vineyard in Australia with 1,200 acres of vines. The collapse of the red wine market in the late 1970's saw a rationalisation of the vineyard keeping only the best plantings on the best soil types and aspects.

The nucleus of Arrowfield Wines now consists of the best 150 acres of this most picturesque valley. The remainder of its grapes are sourced from other premium regions around Australia · shiraz from McLaren Vale, cabernet sauvignon from King Valley and chardonnay from the Cowra region. The Arrowfield Cowra Chardonnay is generally acknowledged as the best of the region and a leader in the premium chardonnay market.

A growing proportion of Arrowfield's sales are from premium wine exports to markets in USA, UK, Hong Kong, Malaysia, Ireland, Germany,

Singapore, Japan and New Zealand. The growth in these markets is driven by the "New World" wine styles made in the high tech winery. The artistry of the winemaking team is led by Chief Winemaker Blair Duncan a Biochemistry graduate of the Adelaide University. Blair was involved with scientific research before turning his hand to winemaking helping his parents in their vineyard and winery in the Clare Valley.

In 1981 Blair attended Roseworthy College and following these further studies went to New Zealand, making wines in the Gisborne region for

Matawhero Wines. Returning to Australia he joined the Lindemans team, with the Southcorp takeover, he moved to Wynns Coonawarra, where he took charge of winemaking for a year. Blair spent the next 10 years as Southcorp's research oenologist, troubleshooting throughout their Australia wide winery operations.

He joined Arrowfield in late 1999. I am sure the Arrowfield wines will go from strength to strength under his guidance.

In the search for quality and innovation Arrowfield believe there is no finishing line.

Address: Denman Road JERRYS PLAINS 2330	Est: 1969	Vine Ha: 59	Cases: 100,000	Show Reserve Chardonnay	5 yrs
Phone: (02) 6576 4041 Fax: (02) 6576 4144	Public Hours: Cellar door 10am-5pm, daily			Show Reserve Shiraz	6 yrs
Email: sales@arrowfieldwines.com.au	Principal Varieties: Chardonnay, Semillon,			Hunter Valley Chardonnay	2 yrs
WWW: www.arrowfieldwines.com.au	Shiraz, Cabernet Sauvignon, Merlot, Pinot			Hunter Valley Shiraz	4 yrs
Owner: Hokuriku CCBC	Noir, Ruby Cabernet, Sauvignon Blanc			Arrowfield Chardonnay	1 yr
Winemaker: Blair Duncan	Principal Wines		Potential	Arrowfield Semillon Chardonnay	1 yr

Barrington Estate

During the mid 1960's Penfold's "Dalwood Estate" was the Hunter Valley's largest single vineyard. Jeffery Penfold Hyland, Max Schubert, Percy McGuigan and others had selected the site on Yarraman Road in 1958.

The property comprises 1,100 acres and at one stage held some 400 acres of vines. This Wybong site was chosen for its ideal soil types, climate and water supply from the Wybong Creek. The property was acquired by Rosemount in 1974 before passing to the current dynamic owners.

The vineyards are surrounded by mountainous hills riddled with caves and covered with native Australian Black Cypress Pencil Pines. The huge lake in front of the vineyard supports over 100 bird species including Black Swans and Pelicans.

Today the vineyards have been expanded with an extra 50 acres of vines since the late 1990's and a further 150 acres planted prior to 1998 including some merlot. The vineyard area is now up to 200 acres.

In 1998 work began on upgrading the winery and expanding it greatly. This has been completed and I can assure you it is a most impressive sight looking out over the whole operation from the platform near the crusher.

Barrington Estate is becoming a major player in the Australian Wine Industry producing several excellent ranges of wine. This includes the flagship brand "Barrington Estate Yarraman Road" (Yarraman is aboriginal for horse). The next range is under the name "Barrington Estate Pencil Pine" named after the Black Cypress Pencil Pines, which look over the property. A third range "Barrington Estate Banjo" pays homage to the Bushmans poet A.B. "Banjo" Paterson. The wines reflect that character, hearty and full flavoured and the labels feature illustrations inspired by several of his more graphic animal ballads. White Cockatoos Chardonnay, Frogs in Chorus, Premium White Brumbys Run Shiraz and Black Swans Premium Red.

Winemaker Stephen Hagan has had 8 years experience as an International flying winemaker and is producing excellent fruit driven wines.

Barrington Estate has already captured the upper echelon of Sydney wine lovers with their exceptional wines and are also exporting wines to a number of countries.

Address: Yarraman Road WYBONG 2333	Winemaker: Stephen Hagan	Chardonnay, Gewürztraminer, Merlot, Shiraz	
Phone: (02) 6547 8118	Est: 1960 Wybong Park, 1994 Barrington	**Principal Wines**	**Potential**
Fax: (02) 6547 8039	Estate	Yarraman Road Chardonnay	2-5 yrs
Email: info@barringtonestate.com.au	Cases: 10,000	Yarraman Road Shiraz	2-3 yrs
WWW: www.barringtonestate.com.au	Public Hours: 10am-5pm, Mon to Sun	Pencil Pine Gewürztraminer	2-5 yrs
Owner: Private Unlisted Company	Principal Varieties: Cabernet, Chambourcin,	Pencil Pine Chambourcin	2-5 yrs

Cruickshank Callatoota Estate

A true individualist, John Cruickshank has had a long love affair with wine. He founded the Canberra Wine & Food Society in 1953. He planted his vineyard with only two grape varieties, cabernet sauvignon and cabernet franc in 1973. From this unique vineyard only four wines were produced. Two cabernet sauvignons, one a lighter style than the other, the third a blend of cabernet sauvignon and franc. The fourth wine is a very good cabernet rose. In 1996, five acres of shiraz were added to extend the length of vintage as it is an earlier ripener than cabernet and provides some new characters for the Callatoota wines.

The vineyard has deep red alluvial soil and good water access. The vines chosen were specially selected clones that have grown beautifully.

The first four hectares were planted in 1974 and the winery was built in 1981. John uses American Oak and the resulting wines are of a high quality that will age very well in the bottle. The cabernet franc is released as a straight varietal wine and also blended with cabernet sauvignon.

John Cruickshank, who has been involved in engineering and management consulting, approached the establishment of the vineyard as a factory producing the best possible material (grapes) for the finished product (wine).

The unique industrially designed trellises presenting the strong vines in the form of a giant glass with four arms holding the bowl. This gives great exposure to the leaves and fruit as helps prevent disease. Two eagles protect the vineyard from small grape-eating birds.

The winery visitor's centre won the 1995 Hunter Tourism Award For Excellence as "The Most Significant Local Tourism Attraction" for the entire region, a fine achievement. You can also join the Callatoota Club and receive regular mailings. A light lunch is now available at the winery everyday.

		Principal Wines	Potential
Address: 2656 Wybong Road WYBONG 2333	**Winemaker:** John Cruickshank	Cabernet Rosé	2-3 yrs
Phone: (02) 6547 8149 **Fax:** (02) 6547 8144	**Est:** 1973 **Vine Ha:** 10	Cabernet Sauvignon Pressings	10+ yrs
Email: john@nobbys.net.au	**Cases:** 7,000	Cabernet Sauvignon	10+ yrs
WWW: www.cruickshank.com.au	**Public Hours:** 9am-5pm, daily	Cab Sav / Cabernet Franc	10+ yrs
Owner: JHF Cruickshank	**Principal Varieties:** Cabernet Sauvignon, Shiraz, Cabernet Franc	Cabernet Franc	10+ yrs

Hordern's Horseshoe

This small vineyard, owned and operated by the Hordern family, was established in the late 1960's. However, it was not until 1987 that the first commercial Horseshoe wines were released on the market.

John Hordern is one of the few winemakers in the Upper Hunter who was raised in the region, developing his interest in wine from his father, who first planted the classic Hunter stalwarts semillon and shiraz on the family property.

John's philosophy that 'specialisation is one of the most important elements for success in the wine industry' has certainly proven very successful for Horseshoe. They have won a swag of gold medals for their semillon and chardonnay.

John is a very much hands on winemaker and works extremely long hours particularly at vintage. He has helped establish a winery in the magnificent old oak Dairy at Muswellbrook with Simon Gilbert and now runs it along with partner Rex d'Aquino from the Orange region.

Small amounts of Horseshoe wines have been exported to the United Kingdom, USA and Japan. In 1993 the Horseshoe Vineyards 1991 Chardonnay Semillon was awarded the UK Critics Choice for the best imported dry white wine. The Horseshoe wines are full flavoured with both elegance and complexity and will age gracefully with cellaring.

		Principal Wines	Potential
Address: Horseshoe Road, Horseshoe Valley DENMAN 2328	**Est:** 1969 **Vine Ha:** 10	Classic Hunter Semillon	10 yrs
	Cases: 3,000	Classic Hunter Chardonnay	5 yrs
Phone: (02) 6547 3528 **Fax:** (02) 6547 3542	**Principal Varieties:** Shiraz, Semillon, Chardonnay	Unwooded Semillon	10 yrs
Owner: Anthony Hordern and Sons Pty Ltd		Classic Hunter Shiraz	10 yrs
Winemaker: John Hordern		Cabernet Sauvignon	10 yrs

Inglewood Vineyards

One of the most impressive vineyards in Australia, covers the hillsides overlooking the confluence of the Hunter and Goulburn Rivers. The vineyard was started in 1988 and most plantings are now quite mature, producing outstanding fruit. Whilst a winery is yet to be built, Inglewood have been successfully making their wines under contract for many years. Their wines have been very successful; the main brand is under the "Two Rivers" label, the name chosen because of the location, at the junction of the two main rivers of the region.

A cellar door has been approved and will be constructed near the top of the vineyard, with breathtaking views over the vines, valley and rivers.

The property has been under the able management of husband and wife team, Brett and Linda Keeping. With well over 400 acres under wine, Inglewood have the opportunity of selecting the best parcels of each variety, for their own wines, whilst selling the rest to large winemaking groups.

The vineyard includes one of the largest mature plantings in Australia, of the exciting variety verdelho.

They also grow semillon and chardonnay in the whites, plus pinot noir, shiraz, cabernet sauvignon, merlot and the unusual ruby cabernet in the reds.

Inglewood are well set to produce significant quantities of top premium wines and have already established some good export markets.

Soon you will be able to visit this splendid property and taste their wines, whilst you marvel over the beautiful tended vines, almost as far as the eye can see.

Address: 2 Yarrawa Road DENMAN 2328
Phone: (02) 6547 2556
Fax: (02) 6547 2546

Email: inglewood@hunterlink.net.au
Est: 1988

Principal Varieties: Cabernet Sauvignon, Merlot, Ruby Cabernet, Shiraz, Chardonnay, Pinot Noir, Semillon, Verdelho

James Estate

James Estate has truly majestic views over the Goulbourn River. Its vineyards planted on the sweeping slopes of the large rural property go back to 1968 when Giancarlo Cecchini began planting. He retired from his engineering business in 1990 and with his daughter Tish (Letitia) built a winery naming it Serenella Estate. Unfortunately Giancarlo died at the winery during vintage in 1993. Tish carried on and made many excellent wines.

In 1998 David James bought the Estate. The cellar door and winery have been upgraded to make the most of their location. The vineyards also have had an enormous amount of work done on them and extensive new plantings are underway, soon you will look out over a sea of vines, as you taste the wines.

A rare variety planted at James Estate is white sylvaner, which makes a very aromatic delicate wine with a distinct floral bouquet, refreshing,

crisp and elegant. I was most impressed by this wine on my visit.

The new packaging at James Estate has a vibrant international feel about it reflecting the lifted character of the wines which are gaining a real foothold on the export markets mainly in Japan, Singapore and the USA.

Estate grown grapes only are used in

the winemaking. The range also includes chardonnay, verdelho, pinot noir, merlot, shiraz and cabernet sauvignon. I found them all packed with flavour.

It's certainly an awesomely beautiful spot with the hills and Wollemi National Park behind and the river in front. I see a very bright future for James Estate and their wines.

Address: 951 Rylstone Road BAERAMI 2333 **Phone:** (02) 6547 5168 **Fax:** (02) 6547 5164	**Winemaker:** Peter Orr **Public Hours:** 10am-4pm, daily **Principal Varieties:** Cabernet Franc, Merlot,	Riesling, Semillon, Sylvaner, Cabernet Sauvignon, Pinot Noir, Sauvignon Blanc, Shiraz

Oak Wine Services

The imposing classic art deco building, situated on Hunter Street at Muswellbrook in the heart of the Upper Hunter, has had a new lease of life. Built in 1954 as the "Oak Milk Factory" its conversion to a wine making facility has been helped enormously by the fact milk products, like wine, require sterile and cool conditions during the production and maturation process.

The large premises have at one end, large open areas stretching up several stories high, ideal for fermentation and housing large tanks in a cool environment. The other areas consist of dual level underground cellars ideal for wine maturation.

The transformation from milk to wine began in 1995; John Hordern was heavily involved.

In July 2000 a new enterprise began when John was jointed by Rex D'Aquino to form "Oak Wine Services". The business has taken off in a big way and the winery is crushing 3000 tonnes of premium grapes, from 40 different vineyard properties throughout South Eastern

Australia. The wine boom and more particularly the boom in vineyard planting, means the need for top professional winemaking services. Many of these new winegrowers want to produce and market their own wines and to set up their own winemaking facilities, with a huge

capital outlay and to be used for only a month or so each year, makes no sense at all.

Oak Wine Services not only makes wine but consults on grapegrowing, vineyard management and has fully equipped laboratories for analysis

and quality control.

Partners John Hordern and Rex D'Aquino both have strong grapegrowing and winemaking backgrounds. John's family started in the wine business in the 1850's, he is a fifth generation winemaker with his own vineyards. Rex's family have large vineyard holdings and a wine and hospitality centre at Orange where they pioneered the wine industry in 1946, making Orange's first wine in 1952.

Rex & John are also both graduates of Roseworthy's famous Oenology Course between them they have 80 years of winemaking experience having both started with their families in their youth.

Oak Wine Services also bottle most of the wine produced in the winery and have contract bottling facilities.

A cellar door has just been opened where all wines produced on the premises will be sold; it's quite a range!! With 23 acres of land around them "Oak" is solidly set for the future. I toast their bold and brilliant venture - Wine the milk of the Gods!!

Address: Hunter Street MUSWELLBROOK 2333 Phone: (02) 6541 3512 Fax: (02) 6541 3514	Email: oakwine@hunterlink.net.au Owner: Oak Wine Services (Australia) Pty Ltd Winemaker: John Horden Est: 2000	Cases: 250,000 Public Hours: 9am-5pm, daily Principal Wines Contract Services (over 60 brands)

Rosemount Estate

Rosemount Estate stands out as one of the great success stories of the modern Australian wine industry. During a visit to their head office in Sydney, I posed the question, "What does the Latin expression under your crest mean?" Founder Bob Oatley's son Ian replied, "We always land on our feet."

Certainly the family was blessed by a great premonition when they chose these words. The Oatley's selected the best areas of the Upper Hunter for planting and have consistently produced grapes of exceptional quality.

A young John Ellis was appointed as Rosemount's first winemaker in 1973, he proved himself more than capable and produced some white wines of extraordinary quality which excited the wine-drinking public and got Rosemount off to a flying start.

The vineyard began as a small and successful operation planted by Carl Brecht in the 1860's. It was bought by Bob Oatley in 1969 and a winery was built in 1973. The first wines were successful on the show circuit, which generated great publicity for Rosemount and brought the wines to the attention of both Australian and International wine drinkers.

Spurred on by this success, Rosemount expanded their home vineyard, planted vines at Roseglen on the banks of the Goulburn and planted fifteen hectares at the Edinglaissie homestead. With a greater amount of fruit each vintage and demand for its wines exceeding

Address: Rosemount Road DENMAN 2328
Phone: (02) 6549 6400 **Fax:** (02) 6549 6499
Email: rosemount@winery.com
WWW: www.winery.com
Owner: Mr Robert Oatley

Winemaker: Philip Shaw
Est: 1969 **Vine Ha:** 700
Cases: 700,000
Public Hours: 10am-4pm, Mon-Sat; 10am-4pm, Sun (Summer); 12pm-4pm, Sun (Winter)

(Closed Christmas Day & Easter Friday)
Principal Varieties: Chardonnay, Semillon, Shiraz, Cabernet Sauvignon, Gewürztraminer, Pinot Noir, Merlot, Petit Verdot, Grenache, Mourvedre

Rosemount Estate

supply, the Rosemount winery was soon bursting its seams. In 1983, Rosemount purchased a further 400 hectares at Mt. Danger, where now more than 100 hectares are under vine.

The prize purchase by Rosemount has proved to be their Roxburgh vineyard. Bought from Denman Estate the plantings of chardonnay have produced the true Australian classic. It is an extraordinary wine.

Rosemount also produces other chardonnays. The Show Reserve has achieved worldwide acclaim as the best wine of its variety, both in price and quality. The Yellow Label Chardonnay is also of a similar rich style and as such is incredibly popular with wine drinkers.

Rosemount Wines really came of age under current winemaker Philip Shaw, who has made the wines at Rosemount for the last 20 vintages. Philip is definitely one of the three or four most gifted winemakers in Australia. After graduating from Roseworthy College, he spent two years working for Lindemans where he was in charge of developing their range of premium wines. He is a laconic character but takes his position very seriously.

Philip also makes the wine from Rosemount's various vineyard interests in Victoria and Coonawarra as well as other NSW regions, a challenging job that he takes in his stride. He also has overall responsibility for the Ryecroft winery in McLaren Vale producing a good deal of red wine for the Rosemount label as well as it's own full range of

Ryecroft wines. The Rosemount Black Label Shiraz has been a huge success; several times being awarded the World's Best Shiraz accolade by the American Wine Spectator Magazine, beating wines at many times its modest price.

Rosemount have invested heavily in premium vineyards in both traditional and new cool climate Australian wine regions. At Mudgee they have now planted huge areas at their Mountain Blue and Hill of Gold vineyards mainly to shiraz and cabernet sauvignon, whilst at Orange in the Central Highlands of NSW chardonnay, cabernet sauvignon, merlot and pinot noir have been planted. In South Australia a massive vineyard of over 300 hectares has been planted at Langhorne Creek to shiraz and cabernet sauvignon with a little chardonnay grenache, merlot and

petit verdot. Another vineyard has also been planted in the new exciting area of Kuitpo in the Southern Adelaide Hills and they have a long established vineyard Kirri Billi at Coonawarra.

Rosemount has created a truly great international feel to its whole operation. The great success of Rosemount on the export market, particularly in the USA, has been hard won. Rosemount has taken tough and expensive individual initiatives that other wine exporters would do well to note, but in the long run, it is the consistently high quality of its whole wine range that has gained it fame and outstanding sales results. I remember Rosemount produced 100,000 cases of wine back in 1986 on my first visit, today they produce over 4fi million cases. At Rosemount, they always land on their feet and keep running!

Mudgee

Like the Barossa Valley in South Australia, the viticultural roots of the Mudgee area were planted by German immigrants. In the case of Mudgee, the Germans were invited to Australia by William Macarthur to tend his vineyard at Camden, now part of outer Sydney.

Vines were first planted at Mudgee by one of these 'vine dressers', Adam Roth, who was given a grant of 37 hectares in 1858. Although gold was discovered in the area in 1872, Roth was not tempted to change his interests. By 1880, six out of the thirteen wineries in the area were operated by Roth and his sons.

Andreas Kurtz, another of the German immigrants, planted the second vineyard in the area. The largest vineyard of 80 hectares was planted by Fredrich Bucholz, and later bought by the Roth family. The Australian Surgeon General of the time, Thomas Fiaschi, purchased the Augusine Vineyard from the Roth Family in 1917. By 1930, Jack Roth had bought out his brother at Fothview, the original winery, and was the only surviving winemaker in the area, although several growers remained. He consolidated winemaking at the Craigmoor winery and there made a dry white wine containing a nameless grape variety. The

wine fared very well. The same nameless variety was planted by a descendant of Andreas Kurtz. Eventually, it was identified by a French viticulturist as a chardonnay, one of the best disease-free clones he had seen. In this way, Mudgee became the first wine-growing area in Australia to grow chardonnay, and other areas used this stock to start their own chardonnay vineyards.

Two more wineries were established in Mudgee in 1969, the Botobolar Winery by Gil Wahlquist and Huntington Estate by Bob Roberts. The 1970's saw a number of new wineries open, including Mirimar and Pieter Van Gent. There are now over 20 wineries in the region; outside of the large Montrose and Craigmoor operations, the impressive new Winery Estate of Andrew Harris and Simon Gilbert's impressive winery complex in the southern part of the

region. All the other wineries are small individual boutiques.

Many locals are pioneering organic grape-growing and winemaking, learning every day the wonderful balance in nature. I am sure this work will reap its rewards as our world becomes ever more conscious of our fragile, precious environment, our own health and the health of future generations.

Mudgee grapes are much sought-after due to their rich flavours. Although on the same latitude as the Hunter Valley, vintage in Mudgee is almost a month later. The district is 500-1,000 metres above sea level and thus cooler. The grapes have a long ripening period. As a result, local table wines have 13, 14 and even 15 percent alcohol.

The well-made wines of the area, particularly the whites, exhibit well-defined varietal flavours. It was the first region in Australia to introduce a wine appellation scheme. This occurred in 1979, and all wines are guaranteed free of defects and of 100 percent Mudgee fruit.

Mudgee is undergoing a large vineyard expansion. Rosemount have planted several hundred hectares and Asian interests many hundreds of hectares more.

Blue Wren Wines

It's no wonder the family of blue wrens that watch over the vineyards of James and Diana Anderson feel content to stay around; everything is a picture of order and natural beauty.

Blue Wren have two vineyards. The original Stoney Creek Road Vineyard, is some 20km north of Mudgee at an altitude of 580 meters in the Cooyal Valley. The vines are 20 years old, on the edge of the Great Dividing

Range and the Wollemi National Park, New South Wales' largest wilderness area.

The second vineyard just 3km north of Mudgee is part of the old Augustine Vineyard, the location of a new tasting room, café and restaurant complex, opened early 2001. New plantings of shiraz, verdelho and merlot will produce their first harvest in 2002. The new architect designed blue colourbond

building is fast becoming a highlight of every Mudgee wine tour. James' experience as a civil engineer and Diana's horticultural background are evident in the style of the development.

The wines of Blue Wren are very fresh and aromatic due to the long slow ripening period of the grapes with hot summer days and cool autumn nights, ripening late, hand picked and carefully crafted into semillon, chardonnay, cabernet, merlot and shiraz wines. I liked their other white port, made from chardonnay. Their 1999 Merlot was highly awarded with two gold medals and two trophies in 2000 winning the Best Boutique Wine of the NSW Small Winemakers Show.

Blue Wren produce a very informative newsletter with information about Mudgee events.

Address: Cassilis Road Mudgee 2850	**Winemaker:** Simon Gilbert	Blue Wren Semillon	15 yrs
Phone: (02) 6372 6205 **Fax:** (02) 6372 6206	**Est:** 1998 **Vine Ha:** 15 **Cases:** 2,500	Blue Wren Chardonnay	6 yrs
Email: sales@bluewrenwines.com.au	**Public Hours:** 10:30am-4:30pm Thurs-Mon,	Blue Wren Shiraz	10 yrs
WWW: www.bluewrenwines.com.au	dinner from 6pm	Blue Wren Merlot	15 yrs
Owner: James & Diana Anderson	**Principal Wines** **Potential**	Blue Wren Cabernet Sauvignon	20 yrs

Mudgee

Mudgee - NSW

1. Andrew Harris Wines
2. Blue Wren Wines
3. Botobolar Vineyard
4. Craigmoor Winery
5. Miramar Wines
6. Montrose Wines
7. Pieter Van Gent Winery
8. Rosemount
9. Rosemount Cumbandry
10. Simon Gilbert
11. Steins Wines

Andrew Harris Wines

Andrew Harris has performed in an impressive way, rising with great vision from small beginnings in 1991, to a multi-million dollar winery, that saw its first vintage in 1997.

Andrew's family had been in cotton and soyabeans in a substantial way. During the late 1980's two important things happened for Andrew. He met his bride to be at the Lightning Ridge Races and he embarked on a vinous path, purchasing a 730 acre sheep station east of Mudgee, on rich clays over limestone and with plentiful water from the Cudgegong River. It seemed ideal.

I well remember visiting the property in 1995, its splendid vineyards and majestic views were inspiring and a complete surprise as we arrived in Mudgee at sunset. Today the vineyards cover 111 hectares. Andrew is fastidious about his vineyard, with careful canopy management to control the foliage, allowing the grapes to be exposed to abundant sunlight and gentle air currents, which enhance wine colours and flavours. 1994 was the first vintage under Simon Gilbert, who then continued through until 1996 producing the wines at his own winery facility and then the 1997 at the new Andrew Harris winery. As a trial 14 entries were exhibited in wine shows from the 1994 vintage, 11 medals and a trophy the result. This outstanding result was even eclipsed by the 1995 vintage.

The 1995 Andrew Harris The Vision

Shiraz-Cabernet Sauvignon, took all before it at the 1997 Royal Sydney Easter Show. The Rudy Komon Memorial Trophy for the best medium bodied red wine of the show and the Leslie Kemeny Memorial Trophy, for the best 1995 red table wine of the show.

The Andrew Harris label, a painting of Andrew surveying his Estate and new plantings from high on the hill where his winery now stands surrounded by vines, captures well his vision.

Andrew had another part of his vision still not realised - a great resident winemaker to complete the picture - particularly to make the best red wine. In his own words "if you want to make the best red wine then there is only one thing to do - hire the man who makes the best red wine - 'Grange' no less". In January 1999 Frank Newman joined as Chief

Winemaker, trained by the legendary Max Schubert, he became Penfolds Red winemaker and made Grange for some years. After 16 years at Penfolds he spent 11 years as Angoves Chief Winemaker, assisting in their renaissance. A further 3 years at BRL Hardy added to his illustrious career.

So far Andrew Harris's medal tally stands at 195, with 12 major trophies incredible for a new winery of moderate size.

The Andrew Harris wines are in 3 ranges - "The Andrew Harris", "The Reserve" for long term aging and finally aptly named "The Vision" the limited release range, a fulfillment of Andrew Harris's dream, to produce wines with all the complexities that would captivate and intrigue the unacquainted palate and charm the connoisseur. Touché Andrew, well done!!

Address: Sydney Road MUDGEE 2850	Cases: 20,000	Andrew Harris 2000 Semillon	4-5 yrs
Phone: (02) 6373 1213 Fax: (02) 6373 1296	Principal Varieties: Cabernet Sauvignon,	Andrew Harris 2000 Merlot	3-4 yrs
Email: ahv@andrewharris.com.au	Merlot, Riesling, Semillon, Verdelho,	Andrew Harris 1999 Shiraz	5-7 yrs
WWW: www.andrewharris.com.au	Chardonnay, Petit Verdot, Sauvignon Blanc,	Andrew Harris 2000 Verdelho	2-3 yrs
Winemaker: Frank Newman	Shiraz, Zinfandel	Andrew Harris 2000 Chardonnay	3-4 yrs
Est: 1991 Vine Ha: 111	Principal Wines Potential	Andrew Harris 1999 Cab Sav	5-8 yrs

Botobolar Vineyard

some natural substances, to keep the vines healthy but no chemicals.

As the vineyard is basically dry grown, the mid nineties saw drought reduce the crop dramatically during several vintages, 1995 in particular. Kevin has now built a large dam, to help avoid the vines stressing too much when drought strikes.

One of Australia's truly great vineyards, Botobolar, was the pioneer of the organic vineyard management concept. It is now about six years since Chicago born Kevin Karstrom and his wife Trina bought the vineyard and winery, from founder Gil Walquist, who planted the vineyard in 1971, after a career in journalism. All is well at Botobolar - a native word coined by the local Kouri tribe, for the black native pines that grow on the property.

Kevin and Trina are totally committed to the organic vineyard system, which includes planting a mixture of specially chosen cover crops, to attract vineyard friendly insects, that ward off vine predators and diseases. The Karstrom's also use

The reds at Botobolar are awesome, powerful yet with great complexity and even a touch of elegance. A very good marsanne is produced with its typical honeysuckle character and a lovely rich chardonnay. Several other varieties such as riesling, traminer and pinot noir, means Botobolar can offer a number of wines rarely seen in the region.

The outdoor area under a pergola has been sensitively constructed from old barrels and natural materials. It is a great place to try the wines and marvel at the natural way it's all happened.

Address: 89 Botobolar Road MUDGEE 2850
Phone: (02) 6373 3840
Fax: (02) 6373 3789
Email: botobolar@winsoft.net.au

WWW: www.botobolar.com
Winemaker: Kevin Karstrom
Est: 1971
Public Hours: 10am-5pm, Mon-Sat; 10am-

3pm Sun & public holidays
Principal Varieties: Chardonnay, Marsanne, Pinot Noir, Shiraz, Cabernet Sauvignon, Gewürztraminer, Mataro, Riesling

Rosemount

Rosemount have always been the innovative individual company, self-motivated and self-assured on the cutting edge of Australian Wine. They have put a tremendous effort into marketing and promoting premium Australian wines overseas, the fact that they have been extremely successful in the 30 years of their existence, being self-evident.

The Rosemount policy over the last few years, has been to expand their vineyard holdings, in the leading Australian Wine regions. This they have accomplished with gusto. Firstly, Coonawarra followed by vineyards and a winery in McLaren Vale, Langhorne Creek and Kuitpo in the Adelaide Hills. Now Mudgee has joined the push and hundreds of hectares have been planted to shiraz, cabernet sauvignon, chardonnay and merlot.

Three properties have been planted; the first "Mountain Blue" is on rich red soils on a westerly sloping site, almost opposite Craigmoor. The 1998 vintage saw a small crop with

the vineyard coming on stream in 1999. The second vineyard, much larger and some 10 kilometres further north is called "Hill Of Gold" named during the 1870's gold rush. The third is "Cumbrandry" - 28

kilometres north of Mudgee near Gulgong. As ever the family crests motto, the Latin version of "we always land on our feet" seems sure to echo loudly, through these well thought out ventures.

Stein's Wines

Robert Stein is a very strong character, somewhat reclusive, he lives amongst his two loves, his vines and his fine collection of vintage motor bikes, displayed in a large shed amongst the vines.

Being in the less habitated part of the region, at dawn and dusk most days you can see plenty of large kangaroos gently moving amongst the vines, doing them no harm at all.

Robert is a descendent of the family that brought riesling cuttings to Australia, almost 200 years ago from Germany. The families 30 acre property at Mudgee proved quite a temptation for Robert, to rediscover his wine heritage, he planted shiraz in 1976 and followed this with six other varieties, chardonnay, semillon, cabernet sauvignon, traminer the rare black muscat and naturally riesling. The colonial style tasting room surrounded by large healthy vines, is a great place to try the great wines.

The winery has been put together by Robert who has quite a mechanical flair. This is a real hands on family winery and a must visit in Mudgee, if you get there. Late afternoon you may even catch a glimpse of a statuesque Kangaroo or two.

| **Address:** Pipeclay Lane MUDGEE 2850
Phone: (02) 6373 3991
Fax: (02) 6373 3709 | **Winemaker:** Robert Stein
Est: 1976
Public Hours: 10am-4:30pm, daily | **Principal Varieties:** Cabernet Sauvignon, Riesling, Shiraz, Black Muscat, Gewürztraminer, Semillon |

Miramar

Ian Macrae is a talented and resourceful individual, in control of all the operations of his Estate, in the rolling hills, north of the township of Mudgee. On our visit just prior to the 2000 Vintage, he was busy welding a trailer to take the grape bins, before leaping on his brand new tractor to trim the very vigorous vines. Being at an altitude of 570 metres, he enjoys a unique microclimate, with vintage often several weeks behind some of the region. The deep red soils at Miramar also adds character to the wines, which can be very full-bodied, but with elegance and balance.

Ian, an honors graduate from Roseworthy, worked for giants of the industry Penfolds and Hardys, before branching out into a winery design consultancy, designing a number of well-known wineries.

In 1975 Ian arrived in Mudgee as winemaker for Montrose. He began establishing Miramar, making his first vintage there in 1977. He has won numerous National and International awards over the years and has a large range of wines, providing a great cellar door tasting area, in his rustically charming cellars adjoining his home.

Address: Henry Lawson Drive MUDGEE 2850 **Phone:** (02) 6373 3874 **Fax:** (02) 6373 3854 **Winemaker:** Ian Macrae **Est:** 1977 **Vine Ha:** 25 **Cases:** 8,000 **Public Hours:** 9am-5pm, daily	**Principal Varieties:** Chardonnay, Semillon, Sauvignon Blanc, Riesling, Shiraz, Pinot Noir, Cabernet Sauvignon **Principal Wines** **Potential** Chardonnay 10 yrs	Semillon 10 yrs Fumé Blanc 5 yrs Sauvignon Blanc 5 yrs Riesling 15 yrs Cabernet Sauvignon 10 yrs

Pieter van Gent

Pieter van Gent is one of the strong characters of the Mudgee region. He arrived in the area in 1970 to work for Craigmoor Wines, after previously spending eleven years at Penfolds working with champagne and fortified wines.

Fortified wines are a favourite of Pieter's and he is the only winemaker in Mudgee to make them consistently. His Pipeclay Port is a rich, unique style with intense flavours and a smooth quality. It is a hit with visitors to the winery.

The winery is charming with wide verandahs, wooden vats and casks and a warm friendly atmosphere. There is an earthen floor and the furnishings include pews from an old church. Pieter was one of the first chardonnay makers in Australia, producing award winners for Craigmoor, he now makes his own, and also a White Port along with a range of unusual wine varieties. Pieter has expanded his production and cellar door sales areas in the same characterful style.

Pieter van Gent and his family are delightful hosts. Their approach to winemaking and visitors is a sincere, honest and no-fuss one, which makes you feel right at home. Pieter has many fans in his own Dutch homeland and some of his wines find its way there too.

Address: 141 Black Springs Road MUDGEE 2850 **Phone:** (02) 6373 3807 **Fax:** (02) 6373 3910 **Winemaker:** Pieter van Gent & Philip van Gent **Est:** 1979 **Vine Ha:** 15	**Cases:** 7,500 **Public Hours:** 9am-5pm Mon-Sat; 11am-4pm Sun **Principal Varieties:** Cabernet Sauvignon, Chardonnay, Müller Thurgau, Semillon, Shiraz, Verdelho	**Principal Wines** **Potential** Mudgee White Port 2 yrs Pipeclay Port 5 yrs Cornelius Port Vintage Shiraz Chardonnay

Poets Corner

Australia's greatest "poet of the bush", Henry Lawson, spent much of his life in Mudgee. Local mythology tells how the tranquil beauty of the landscape inspired some of his greatest works. The popular Poet's Corner wines were named in his honour.

Poet's Corner was born from the premium Mudgee brand Montrose, which along with Criagmoor, the region's oldest established winery were purchased by Orlando Wyndham Group in 1989.

Craigmoor is also known as the birthplace of chardonnay in Australia as it was Jack Roth, the original owner of Craigmoor, who planted cuttings of a particularly fine clone of chardonnay given to him indirectly from either William Busby or William Macarthur. This small planting was to become the source block of much of Australia's chardonnay. Craigmoor released a chardonnay from the 1971 vintage making it a pioneer of the variety in Australia. This great wine is still the flagship of the Craigmoor range.

Since Orlando Wyndham Group purchased Craigmoor and Montrose much capital has been invested to improve the vineyards and expand the Montrose Winery. The capital investment has seen the Montrose Winery become one of the region's most highly technological wineries and the vineyards producing the quality of grapes required by the viticulturists and winemakers alike.

In 1999 the Craigmoor Winery was closed and re-opened at Poet's Corner Wines Cellar Door. The Montrose Winery was also closed to the public and renamed Poet's Corner Winery. At Poet's Corner Cellar Door, guests can sample the complete range of Poet's Corner Wines as well as Montrose and Craigmoor Wines, which are produced at the Poet's Corner Winery.

The facilities for visitors to Poet's Corner Wines are first class with a rustic ambience including the Craigmoor Restaurant, tasting area, museum, containing old winemaking and viticultural equipment, a picnic area, cricket oval and even a petanque pitch.

Poet's Corner Wines has a delightful unspoilt feel about it, with sweeping lawns and the picnic area going down to the creek with the beautiful Mudgee ranges in the background. This beautiful setting inspired Aboriginals to name it Mudgee, translating to "nest in the hills".

At Poet's Corner Winery, under the guidance of the extremely talented young winemaker, James Manners, the philosophy is to produce wines with well-defined regional and varietal characters and freshness of fruit. Every Poet's Corner, Montrose and Craigmoor wine has a style all of its own from the innovative Montrose Stony Creek Chardonnay to the traditional Craigmoor Chardonnay, from the boutique Montrose Italian varieties of Sangiovese and Barbera to the traditional Mudgee Henry Lawson Cabernet Sauvignon.

Just as Mudgee inspired Henry Lawson to write his masterpieces, this same scenery has been the inspiration behind Poet's Corner, Montrose and Craigmoor, wines which reflect the premium nature of the region.

Address: PO Box 67 MUDGEE 2850
Phone: (02) 6372 2208 **Fax:** (02) 6372 4464
Email: gameaun@orlando.com.au
WWW: www.poetscornerwines.com
Winemaker: James Manners **Est:** 1858

Public Hours: 10am to 4.30pm Mon-Sat;
10am-4pm Sundays & Public Holidays
(closed Christmas Day)
Principal Wines
Poets Corner Unwooded Chardonnay

Poets Corner Shiraz Cab Sav Cabernet Franc
Poets Corner Semillon Sav Blanc Chard
Henry Lawson Cabernet Sauvignon
Henry Lawson Shiraz
Henry Lawson Chardonnay

Simon Gilbert

Simon Gilbert, a fifth generation winemaker, was christened in the Chapel at the Pewsey Vale Vineyard in the Barossa Ranges. His great-great-grandfather Joseph Gilbert, a well-respected Adelaide identity, first planted this vineyard on his 1,100 acres overlooking the Barossa Valley, from cuttings he had bought with him on his voyage from Pewsey in Wiltshire, England.

Simon well remembers his first taste of wine at age 11, in the Yalumba boardroom, the wine a pre-release of the first Pewsey Vale Riesling; Simon made up his mind to become a winemaker.

Joseph Gilbert also established other vineyards, the grapes of which were sold to Leo Buring until 1950. Ironically, it was there that Simon began his first hands-on winemaking experience during his studies in winemaking at Roseworthy Agricultural College, from which he graduated in 1977.

Subsequently he worked for the Lindemans Group at Karadoc, the Barossa, the Hunter and Coonawarra. In 1985 he became Chief Winemaker at Arrowfield in the Hunter. In January 1994, Simon established his own company, Simon Gilbert Wine Services.

Since then, he has grown significantly, firstly located in the former Hunter Valley Dairy Coop

building on the outskirts of Muswellbrook. In early 2000 just in time for vintage Simon moved into the Mudgee region in a big way to be near many of his existing clients and to provide winemaking services for the fast growing wine regions of central New South Wales.

The new Simon Gilbert Winery at Appletree Flat south of Mudgee is nothing short of spectacular not only providing a large state of the art winemaking base for Simon but a superb Cellar Door, Café and Restaurant looking out over the home vineyard and the ranges surrounding them.

Simon is a custom winemaker and consultant to the wine industry and has become recognised as a personalised producer of the highest quality premium wines, after six years of operation. Simon and his winemaking team employ current best practice technologies.

On behalf of their clients, they produce tailor-made wines. Simon has received more than 40 trophies and over 1200 medals at National and International Wine Shows in his 28 year winemaking career. His client-base regions include: The Hunter Valley, Southern Queensland, Cowra, Orange and Mudgee.

The 2000 vintage has also seen Simon launch several wine ranges. The "Card Series" wines all carry an

intriguing playing card, the Mudgee Shiraz with its proud red "Rooster" is sure to steal a big market share worldwide, it is a rich voluptuous style, aromatic with some rose petal in the bouquet, the red currant and cherry flavours are highlighted with a little white pepper on the finish, its silky mouth feel beckons another glass, it's also a great value for money buy. The card series also features a Hunter chardonnay, Hunter Verdelho and a blended Semillon Sauvignon Blanc. The Simon Gilbert Regional wines are slightly dearer. There is also a Family Selection Range, a Pinot Noir from Orange, a Central Ranges Cabernet Merlot, a Mudgee Shiraz and a McLaren Vale Grenache/Shiraz, Simon's South Australian connections have helped him source some extraordinary fruit from, McLaren Vale, over many years. The ultimate statement of this is his "Wongalere" Shiraz and Abbaston Cabernet Sauvignon both opulent wines with deep colour, richness and complexity aged in a mixture of Allier, Troncais and Vosges French oak and new fine grained American oak, more French is used for the cabernet.

Simon is a consummate winemaker reveling in his splendid new home, expect greater things from him in the future and certainly visit his magic place soon.

Address: 1220 Castlereagh Highway APPLETREE FLAT 2850
Phone: (02) 6541 2399 **Fax:** (02) 6541 2401

Email: sgwsmudg@sinsoft.net.au
Winemaker: Drew Tuckwell
Est: 1994

Principal Varieties: Cabernet Sauvignon, Merlot, Sangiavese, Zinfandel, Barbera, Chardonnay, Petit Verdot, Shiraz

Riverina

Centred on the thriving towns of Griffith and Leeton in the Murrumbidgee Irrigation Area, the Riverina grows more than half the total grape crop in New South Wales. With more than 150,000 tonnes of grapes produced by over 500 growers in a normal year, the region has the highest proportion of premium varietal fruit of any of the major inland grapegrowing region.

Semillon and shiraz are widely planted as well as large plantings of chardonnay, cabernet sauvignon, sauvignon blanc, while newer varieties such as merlot, marsanne and verdelho represent an increasing proportion of the Riverina's varietal portfolio.

Being an efficient, low cost producer, the Riverina's grapes are now keenly sought for Australia's burgeoning export market, and in recent years there has been considerable investment in new broad acre viticulture on the adjacent rice farms.

There are a dozen wineries in the region ranging from the large scale of De Bortoli and McWilliam's to the boutique wineries such as Lillypilly in Leeton and West End Wines in Griffith. While in the past the area was dominated by McWilliam's and Penfolds, the Riverina is now the home of many of Australia's larger remaining family wine companies including McWilliam's, De Bortoli, Miranda, Rossetto and Toorak, with the growing enterprises of Riverina Wines, Cranswick Estate and the new enterprise of Casella.

While in the past much of the wine produced was bulk white and red destined for the cask market, increased interest in Australian wine overseas over the past dozen years now sees much of the region's wine exported. Improved viticultural and winemaking techniques have seen the overall quality of bottled varietal wine improve dramatically, with the region's semillon · chardonnay blends prominent.

By far the region's star performer is the botrytised semillons that have swept the world by storm taking award after award in International contests. Pioneered by the De Bortoli Family with the 1982 vintage, there are now more than a dozen different botrytised wines produced locally.

The region was founded in 1912 when John James McWilliam planted his first vines in Hanwood (some of these have been retained at Hanwood and still bear fruit!), the area now produces almost every style of wine from the more than forty grape varieties. Following the First World War, the area became the new home for returned soldiers, followed in the 1920's by many Italian immigrants who contributed greatly to the wine industry's development. The Riverina's cultural heritage is still prominent today.

The area is probably the most efficient wine producer in Australia, with its large yields approaching an average of twenty tonnes of grapes per hectare. The area pioneered the use of mechanical harvesting which enables picking of fruit at optimum ripeness and in the cool of the night, thus enhancing wine quality. The Riverina was also in the forefront of the development of mechanical pruning. A sense of purpose and a desire to meet the challenges of modern viticulture and winemaking pervades the Riverina · it's an exciting, positive feeling.

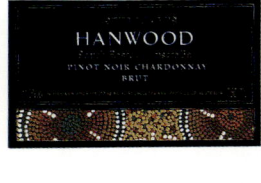

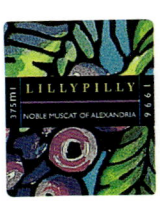

Riverina

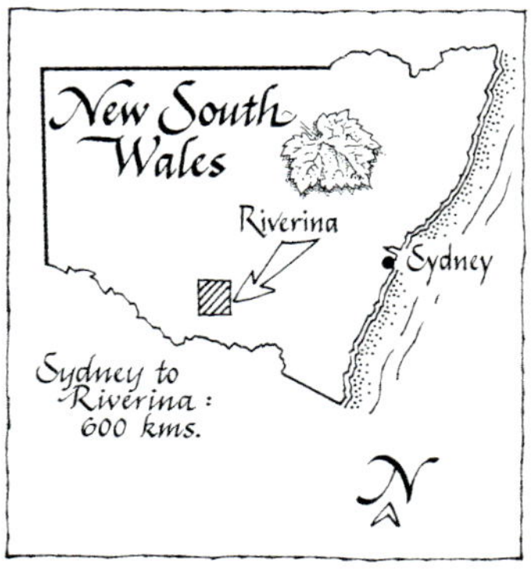

Riverina - NSW

1. Casella Wines
2. Cranwsick Estate
3. De Bortoli Wines
4. Lillypilly Estate
5. McManus Wines
6. McWilliams Hanwood Winery
7. McWilliams Yenda Winery
8. Miranda Wines
9. Riverina Wines
10. Rossetto Wines
11. Toorak Wines
12. West End Wines
13. Wilton Estate
14. Zappacosta Estate Wines

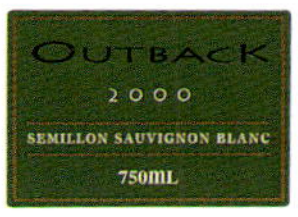

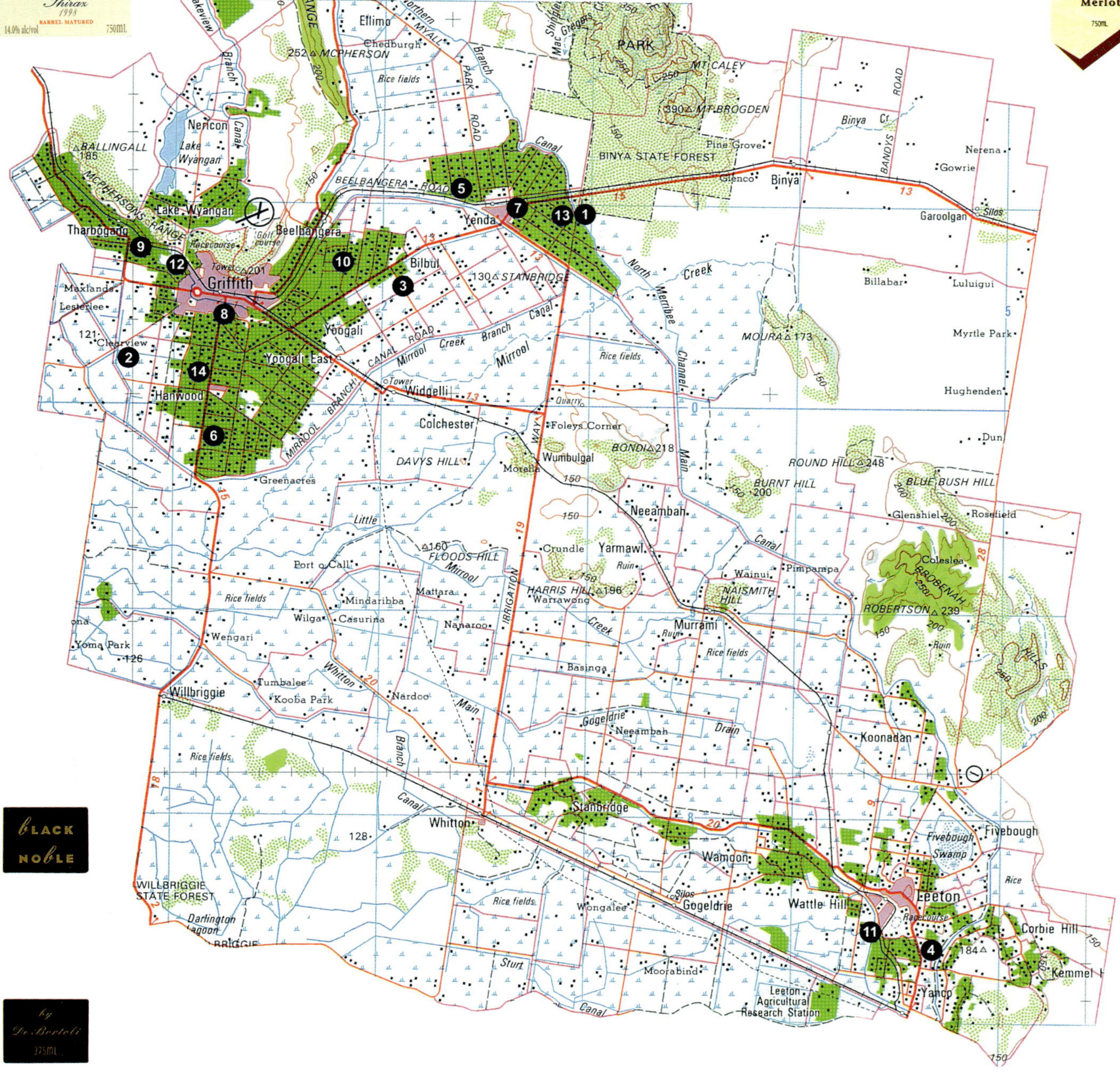

New South Wales

Riverina

Sydney

Sydney to Riverina : 600 kms.

N

73

Casella Wines

John Casella's parents Filippo and Maria arrived as Italian immigrants in the early 1950's, settling on a small fruit block near Yenda in the Riverina. The Casella's had generations of grape growing in rural Italy behind them and didn't take long to set up a small winery on their vineyard to make the traditional family wine each year.

Gradually many of the family friends started to come by to replenish their wine cellars. The family grape and fruit growing business remained the main focus. By 1965 Filippo was convinced wine was the future and purchased a large block near Yenda and began planting more vines.

Then son John became a trained winemaker and for many years was in charge of the winemaking at the giant Riverina Wine Company, the other side of Griffith. Things began to change rapidly in 1994, when John commissioned a huge modern building to house a large winemaking operation. As the 1995 vintage started, work on the building and the winemaking centre was still in frantic progress. The massive stainless steel tanks holding hundreds of thousands of litres of wine were

soon full and John breathed a sigh of relief knowing his dream and vision were fast becoming a reality. The subsequent vintages have been a great success and the winery has grown even further in size during this time. Tucked away in the corner of the old family shed is the first fermenting tank of his fathers, proudly shown to me by John.

The Casella wine label has now been released and the wines shape up

superbly. Wine exports of Casella have become a mainstay of the business. Enthusiastic and talented winemaker Alan Kennett works in tandem with John to handle an extremely big crush with very few hands around the cellars.

John Casella well represents the new entrepreneurial wave of young winemakers Australia really needs to satisfy the worldwide thirst for new world wines.

Address: Farm 1471, Wakely Road YENDA 2681
Phone: (02) 6968 1346 **Fax:** (02) 6968 1196
Email: info@casellawine.com.au

WWW: www.casellawine.com.au
Owner: Filippo & Maria Casella
Winemaker: Alan Kennett
Est: 1969 **Vine Ha:** 280 **Cases:** 500,000

Principal Varieties: Cabernet Sauvignon, Chardonnay, Durif, Merlot, Petit Verdot, Sangiovese, Semillon, Shiraz, Viognier, Tempranello

Cranswick Estate

One of Australia's most progressive and successful wine companies is the Cranswick Estate. They are in the top ten in size, being Australia's seventh largest wine exporter.

The Cranswick Estate is a totally professional operation - its history dates back to 1931 when the Cinzano Family of Italian Vermouth fame began winemaking in Australia. In 1974, they built one of Australia's most modern and best-equipped wineries and began making table wines under contract, as well as their own Vermouths. In 1991 the management team, led by dynamic Managing Director Graham Cranswick Smith, bought out the business. Their immediate focus was on fine-tuning the winemaking and establishing exciting brands to attack the premium bottled wine export market.

Their success speaks volumes for their courage and foresight. One might also say "well done Ken Done" - his uniquely Australian Barramundi design wine labels have flooded the export market and sales overseas have rocketed from nothing to a substantial volume.

Barramundi has a distinct Australian feel with its design, and carries graphically the message 'Australian

wine - sunshine in the bottle'.

Cranswick also has a more traditional range of varietal wines under the Cranswick Estate label. The 1996 Botrytis Semillon 'Autumn Gold' has carried all before it on the wine show scene.

Cranswick growers work hand in hand with the winemaking team to get the botrytised (noble rot) grapes to perfect condition, a risky business in which they can lose everything, but this sense of trust and teamwork typifies the Cranswick operation. In 1993, Cranswick spent $2 million on a 400-hectare property on the slopes (a rarity in the Riverina) near Scenic Hill. The property has been named Cocoparra, Aboriginal for Kookaburra. This massive investment on this vineyard of perfect soils and good well-drained slopes and drip irrigation, also a rarity in the Riverina, has already shown great results. Expansion at the winery has seen the ability to give the reds long fermentation, adding to body, flavour and quality.

Cranswick Estate's Managing Director, Graham Smith is also a keen private pilot, a suitable pastime for his high-flying style of taking Cranswick Estate to the top.

In June 1996 at 'Wine Australia', after their export success, Cranswick Estate launched their Australian range of wines. Already the wines have enjoyed incredible success on the show circuit.

The 1996 Semillon won the top gold in that year's Melbourne Wine Show. The 1996 Chardonnay also scored a highly commended award in the same show. The Autumn Gold continued its success with 2 trophies and 4 gold medals during 1996. Cranswick wines have continued their success. Qantas have served a number of vintages in their first class cabin.

Cranswick Premium Wines Limited have now floated on the Australian stock exchange and expanded into other regions with their purchase in the late nineties of the Alambie Wine Company including a major production facility near Mildura and Haselgrove Wines who have just built a large, entirely new state of the art winery in McLaren Vale which is not only processing local fruit but increasing quantities of grapes from the Haselgrove vineyards in the new region of Wrattonbully in the south east of South Australia. Their Wrattonbully wines including their "Bentwing" label are just great.

Address: Walla Avenue GRIFFITH 2680	**Est:** 1931 **Vine Ha:** 150	Cranswick Estate Unoaked Chardonnay 5 yrs	
Phone: (02) 6966 9600 **Fax:** (02) 6962 2888	**Cases:** 800,000	Barrel Fermented Semillon	8-10 yrs
Email: info@cranswick.com.au	**PublicHours:** 10am-4pm, daily	Cranswick Estate Semillon	5 yrs
WWW: www.cranswick.com.au	**Principal Varieties:** Chardonnay, Shiraz,	Pinot Chardonnay upto	10 yrs
Owner: Cranswick Premium Wines Limited	Merlot, Cabernet Sauvignon, Marsanne	Young Vine Chardonnay	6 yrs
Winemaker: Andrew Schulz / Tim Pearce	**Principal Wines** **Potential**	Conlon Block Marsanne	6 yrs

DeBortoli Wines

Vittorio De Bortoli arrived in Australia from Northern Italy in 1924. By working hard he was able to save and purchase land in Bilbul in 1927, the site of his winery today. His son Deen joined him in the family business in the 1950's. Deen expanded the winery and developed a bulk sparkling system. Deen's son Darren, a graduate of Roseworthy College in South Australia, joined the company ranks in 1982.

Darren made his mark on the industry, experimenting with semillon grapes, which had been left on the vines until two months after vintage and were heavily infected with mould. Unsure as to whether the grapes contained 'noble rot' (botrytis cinerea), he had to make the wine before he could be sure. The result has passed into Australian wine history. The 1982 De Bortoli Semillon Sauternes won more gold medals within a relatively short period of time than any other Australian wine. Now called Noble One, De Bortoli Botrytis Semillon is sold worldwide.

Today the winery at Bilbul has a storage capacity of over 50 million litres and produces the equivalent of over three million cases of wine annually. More than 150 people are employed in production, marketing and distribution through branches in Sydney, Melbourne and Brisbane, United Kingdom, United States and Europe. Darren De Bortoli is Managing Director and oversees a team of six winemakers. Because of the large varietal mix, vintage lasts from early February through to late April/May with the picking of the botrytised grapes for Noble One.

In 1987 De Bortoli purchased a winery in the Yarra Valley Victoria. This move has been totally successful and the Yarra operation (which is covered in the relevant chapter of this book) makes a range of premium wines and has an award winning restaurant on site. The family's faith in the Yarra Valley was rewarded in 1997 when their 1996 GS Reserve Shiraz won the prestigious Jimmy Watson Memorial Trophy making it the second for the vineyard and only the third Victorian

wine in thirty years.

The Deen Vat Series premium range, the fortified wines including Black Noble (another Darren De Bortoli creation), Emeri sparkling and Sacred Hill value range from the Bilbul winery are of outstanding quality. Like everything else the De Bortoli family does these wines reflect great credit on the company and the Australian Wine Industry.

Address: De Bortoli Road BILBUL 2680	Est: 1928 Vine Ha: 250	Principal Wines	Potential
Phone: (02) 6964 9444	PublicHours: 9am-5.30pm, Mon-Sat; 9am-4pm Sun	Noble One	10+ yrs
Fax: (02) 6964 9400		Rare Dry	5-10 yrs
Email: dbw@debortoli.co.au	Principal Varieties: Cabernet Sauvignon, Chardonnay, Colombard, Durif, Pinot Noir, Riesling, Sauvignon Blanc, Semillon, Shiraz, Traminer, Trebbiano, Verdelho	Deen Vat Series	2-5 yrs
WWW: www.debortoli.com.au		Willowglen Range	2-3 yrs
Owner: De Bortoli Family		Montage Range	2-3 yrs
Winemaker: Darren De Bortoli		Premium Fortified Range	

McWilliams Hanwood

In 1912, shortly after completion of the Murrumbidgee Irrigation Scheme, J.J. McWilliam arrived with his bullock wagon loaded down with 40,000 cuttings from the family's vineyard at "Markview", near Junee and planted the area's first vines. The Hanwood winery was built in 1917 and is the centre of McWilliam's operations in the Riverina. They also have a large winery at Yenda.

The Hanwood winery is enormous and its entrance is modelled to appear like a huge barrel. This is the tasting and visitors' entertainment area. Alongside the barrel is a giant bottle on its side, of about 25 metres in length. This houses a museum, which details the history of McWilliam's. The winery itself produces mainly white and red varietal table wines but is also the wood maturation centre for McWilliam's range of sherries and ports.

Perhaps the best known of these is 10 year old Hanwood Port, one of Australia's most popular and finest tawny ports · a wine that still contains a drop of the original blend of 1926. McWilliam's also make an excellent vintage port at Hanwood. Total storage capacity at Hanwood is a massive 25 million litres, about six per cent of Australia's annual wine consumption.

The genius behind this modern set up was the late Glenn McWilliam who foresaw the swing in popularity away from fortified to table wines, and changed the emphasis in production at McWilliam's accordingly. He was also responsible for building the Robinvale Winery on the Murray River in Victoria in 1961. Glenn McWilliam refurbished and expanded the local McWilliam's wineries with equipment of his own design in the 1950's and my family had many dealings with him. After graduating from an engineering course at Adelaide University in 1948, my father went to work for Glenn at Hanwood, where he picked up valuable information and

experience. This was later utilised when he designed all of Hardy's new winery equipment and additions, over the next few decades.

Glenn's contribution to McWilliam's Wines and the Australian wine industry cannot be underestimated, he was a typical member of an extraordinary family, who are not surprisingly well into their second century of winemaking. McWilliam's was one of the first wine companies in the Riverina and Australia, for that matter, to market varietal table wines some 35 years ago. The focus today is on vibrant wines with young fresh obvious varietal character. The Hanwood Range · a chardonnay, semillon/chardonnay, shiraz and

cabernet sauvignon, have been re-dressed in a distinctively Australian style with labels featuring Aboriginal dot art from the artists living on the Napperey Station, 200 kms north-west of Alice Springs. These wines at great value prices have already gained a good slice of the export market. Production Director in charge of all of McWilliam's wineries is Doug McWilliam, a graduate from the famous Davis University's oenology course in California. Day to day management of the Hanwood Winery itself is in the very capable hands of his cousin, the genial, Brian McWilliam. Long may the great family stay independent and continue their great work.

Address: Jack McWilliams Road HANWOOD 2680	Est: 1916	Principal Wines	Potential
Phone: (02) 6963 0001	Vine Ha: 376	Hanwood Verdelho	2 yrs
Fax: (02) 6963 0002	PublicHours: 9am-5pm Mon-Sat	Hanwood Sauvignon Blanc	2 yrs
Email: mcwines@mcwilliams.com.au	Principal Varieties: Cab. Sav, Chardonnay,	Hanwood Semillon Chardonnay	2-3 yrs
WWW: www.mcwilliams.com.au	Malbec, Merlot, Pinot Noir, Riesling, Ruby	Hanwood Chardonnay	2-3 yrs
Winemaker: Jim Brayne	Cabernet, Sauvignon Blanc, Semillon, Shiraz,	Hanwood Merlot	4 yrs
	Touriga, Traminer, White Frontignac	Hanwood Shiraz	3 yrs

Miranda Wines

Frank Miranda came to Australia with his new bride Caterina in 1938 to start a new life. A professor of languages in his homeland, he and Caterina bought a half share in a general store in Kooyoo Street, Griffith. Frank was interned during World War II at the Loveday Camp, Barmera, but not before making his first vintage, three tonnes of grapes crushed with his bare feet in the old Italian tradition.

Frank's winemaking career took an unusual turn at the prison camp in Katherine, an unlikely a place to make wine, as you could imagine, but not for the innovative Frank. From dried sultanas, re-hydrated and many winemaking books in his hand he became a very popular individual indeed.

Two years after his release in 1944, he began building a winery and in the early 50's employed his first winemaker, the equally innovative Ron Potter.

Frank was totally devoted to his family and friends and in his life

expanded Miranda with the help of his three sons and their families, to be one of the largest privately owned wine companies in Australia.

The hospitality flows freely at Miranda and the generously flavoured wines follow this theme.

This impressive Riverina winery is the head office for Miranda Wines. It is at this winery where Sam, Jim and Lou Miranda as the sons of the founder Frank Miranda gather as the Board of Directors.

The winery boasts over 200 stainless tanks and 4,000 French and American oak barrels with the total storage capacity being over 28 million litres.

The modern state-of-the-art administration area houses the sales operations as well as a large cellar door sales complex.

The cellar door has been expanded into a hospitality centre. This transformation has encompassed the beautification of the existing building and grounds. Miranda Wines

premium image has been intensified as all visitors to the hospitality centre are welcomed into the elegantly designed tourist information bureau, a show case for all Miranda world class wines.

The brothers, with their comprehensive knowledge of the wine industry, have had the foresight to expand their premium areas to include the Barossa Valley of South Australia and the King Valley of Victoria, where they have wineries.

Miranda Wines has not only forged a reputation for being a progressive family owned company but also as a producer of nationally and internationally recognised wines. This was never more true when Miranda Wines received the Mission Hill Trophy for the Best Chardonnay Worldwide at the 1996 London Wine and Spirit competition.

So with such accolades and no doubt more to follow Frank Miranda would be justly proud of his family's achievements.

Address: 57 Jondaryan Avenue GRIFFITH 2680	Owner: Sam, Jim & Lou Miranda	Principal Wines	Potential
Phone: (02) 6962 4033	Winemaker: Luis Simian	Mirrool Creek Range	Up to 5 yrs
Fax: (02) 6962 6944	Group Winemaker: Gary Wall	Somerton Range	Up to 3 yrs
	Est: 1939	Golden Gate Sparkling	
Email: info@mirandawines.com.au	Cases: 1,500,000	Fireside Port Up to	5 yrs
WWW: www.mirandawines.com.au	PublicHours: 10am-5pm daily	Miranda Kilkenny Creams	

Lillypilly Estate

Post war immigrant to Australia Pasquale Fiumara brought to his new homeland the expertise of thousands of years of viticultural and winemaking heritage. Vines were planted on Pasquale's property in 1972. With seven sons to keep busy, a winery was the logical choice. Son Robert, a giant of a man, went to Charles Sturt University as one of the first students under wine guru Brian Croser's instruction. The first vintage was made at Lillypilly in the new winery in 1982. Robert coined a name for a wine he made from traminer and semillon, 'Tramillon'®. It was an instant hit, not only with the wine-drinking public but also with the wine judges, winning a trophy at the 1983 Royal Sydney Easter Show. It has also proven to age well.

Lillypilly have won many awards since this first success. Robert has definite skill in making the late harvest and botrytised dessert wines. His Noble Semillon, Noble Riesling, Noble Traminer and Noble Muscat of Alexandria all have similar luscious characters. Often, the grapes are not picked until May or June - a risky business, but the rewards to the drinker are high. Lillypilly won a National trophy in their first vintage in 1982 and they have won hundreds of awards since. A very interesting wine is their "Red Velvet"® a blend of 12 varieties and the perfect summer red. I am certain if you visit Lillypilly and enjoy its charming atmosphere, you will also fall in love with at least one of the Fiumara's fine wines.

Address: Lillypilly Road LEETON 2705
Phone: (02) 6953 4069 **Fax:** (02) 6953 4980
Email: info@lillypilly.com
WWW: www.lillypilly.com
Owner: P & A Fiumara & Sons Pty Ltd
Winemaker: Robert Fiumara

Est: 1982 **Vine Ha:** 30 **Cases:** 10,000
PublicHours: 10am-5pm Mon-Sat
Principal Varieties: Chardonnay, Cabernet Sauvginon, Traminer, Semillon, Muscat of Alexandria, Riesling, Shiraz, Sauvignon Blanc

Principal Wines	Potential
Tramillon	4-5 yrs
Red Velvet	4-5 yrs
Sauvignon Blanc	4-5 yrs
Noble Harvest	10 yrs
Noble Muscat of Alexandria	6-10 yrs
Cabernet Sauvignon	5-10 yrs

Toorak Wines

Francesco Bruno Snr migrated from Sicily in 1950. Three years later he purchased a small 18 hectare property that was then planted with fruit trees. In 1963, together with his two sons, Frank Jnr and Vincent, he decided to expand into winegrape growing. In 1965 they established a small winery and produced regional wines. The winery has expanded during the last 30 years to now produce over 3 million litres of mainly table wines. Each vintage some 100,000 cases of varietal wines, such as chardonnay, semillon, cabernet, shiraz and traminer are sold under the Willandra Estate and Amesbury Estate Label. These wines have been accepted world wide and represent Australian produce well. Frank Jnr looks after the production and Vincent the administration, while Frank's son Robert is the winemaker.

Over the years they have won many awards at major Australian Shows and they continue to produce local wines of exceptional character and flavour.

The Willandra Estate Chardonnay, Cabernet Sauvignon and Traminer all display excellent varietal character and are made from 100% Riverina fruit. Frank Senior Port and Liqueur Muscat are well regarded by consumers and the trade.

Address: Toorak Road LEETON 2705
Phone: (02) 6953 2333
Fax: (02) 6953 4454
Winemaker: Robert Bruno
Est: 1966 **Vine Ha:** 30
Cases: 150,000

PublicHours: 9am-5pm, Mon-Sat.
Tours daily at 10.30am
Principal Varieties: Semillon, Chardonnay, Shiraz, Cabernet Sauvignon, Colombard, Sauvignon Blanc, Ruby Cabernet, Fortified and Dessert wines

Principal Wines	Potential
Cabernet Sauvignon	3-5 yrs
Ruby Cabernet	3 yrs
Semillon Chardonnay	3 yrs
Headmaster Port	
Liqueur Muscat	

Riverina Wines

roots. He is happiest when working with his men out in his enormous rural and vineyard holdings, he's much happier at the wheel of his four-wheel drive than behind his seldom used desk.

Joe's father who was born in 1912, migrated from his native Italy to the Riverina, he had 9 children, 8 daughters and 1 son.

From small beginnings, Riverina now rates as the eighth biggest winery in Australia. At present, the Sergi's have a massive 1,100 hectares of vines which ensures they have the varieties and quantities needed for their ambitious expansion programme.

The spread of varieties planted includes a substantial quantity of chardonnay, but also 40 hectares of verdelho, the famous variety of the Island of Madeira which also makes an exciting, fruity, full bodied white wine and is ideally suited to a warm climate like the Riverina, there are also substantial plantings of sauvignon blanc. Tony Sergi also runs a number of vineyards for other members of his family. Riverina are one of the most self sufficient wineries in the region which also gives them good quality control over the grapes they process.

The winemaker is the young genius Sam Trimboli who makes an impressive range of wines.

At a masked tasting I conducted all the Judges agreed that his wines shone out, often out-pointing much more expensive wines. The sparkling burgundy made mainly from shiraz impressed all the judges.

The winery has just gone through a total upgrade and expansion with the accent on winemaking equipment to enhance quality, a further expansion and bottling hall is being completed as I write. The Riverina Winery has a large and attractively appointed tasting area and a pleasant leafy covered outdoor alfresco area, a pleasant place indeed to wile away a few moments whilst tasting the impressive range of wines.

Tony Sergi is a hardworking, down to earth man. Reflecting his solid Italian

Address: 700 Kidman Way GRIFFITH 2680	PublicHours: 9am-5.30pm, daily		
Phone: (02) 6962 4122 Fax: (02) 6962 4628	Principal Varieties: Chardonnay, Semillon,	Warburn Estate Durif	4 yrs
Email: rivwines@webfront.net.au	Sauvignon Blanc, Merlot, Verdelho, Shiraz,	Warburn Estate Shiraz	4 yrs
Owner: Antonio and Angela Sergi	Cabernet Sauvignon, Pinot Noir, Chenin	Warburn Estate Cabernet Merlot	4 yrs
Winemaker: Sam Trimboli	Blanc, Barbera, Ruby Cabernet	Warburn Estate Verdelho	4 yrs
Est: 1969 Vine Ha: 1,100 Cases: 250,000	Principal Wines Potential	Warburn Estate Chardonnay	4 yrs
		Warburn Estate Merlot	4 yrs

Rossetto Wines

The Rossetto winery was founded in 1930 by Angelo Rossetto who had arrived in Australia in 1923 as part of the wave of post World War One Italian immigration. His first experience in his new homeland was working at Broken Hill, so the Riverina to him must have seemed like a real oasis. Coming from the Northern Italian town of Treviso, he purchased a farm and planted vines in 1928 making his first wine two years later. In 1962 son John took over the running of the Company, with his unfortunate passing in 1998 it was left to his widow Bianca and the third generation of the family run the vastly expanded business, crushing an average of 12,000 tonnes of grapes each vintage. The Family has its own vineyards, known as Beelgara Estate, which adjoins the winery in the Beelbangera district of the Riverina.

The three Rossetto brothers, Garry, Brian and Kevin are true gentlemen and a great, positive, pleasant and energetic team. They run the enterprise and control everything, from the viticulture, through their modern well-equipped winery, to their own bottling line, making the most of the richly flavoured ripe grapes, produced from the fertile soils of their region. The Rossetto's, like many long-established wineries, make a large range of wines - table, fortified, sparkling and even cocktail styles - all representing excellent value for money.

Rossetto were the real pioneer of commercial chardonnay winning a silver medal with their 1969 pinot chardonnay at the Adelaide Show 2 years before the emergence of the first Hunter chardonnays.

Rossetto have invested heavily in new equipment and expansion of the winery and in 1997 introduced a top premium range "Promenade Family Reserve" including a chardonnay, cabernet merlot and a riesling from Watervale fruit. A botrytis semillon has joined the range. The reviews of the first few vintages of Promenade have been outstanding. Two new premium table wine ranges under the Promenade were released in 1998. "Silky Oak" and a fighting varietal range "Wattleglen". An ultra premium label "Mitchell Brook" sourcing the best parcels of various varieties from leading regions has also just been released and I am sure will show their skills as winemakers, plus help them on the International Market. The cost of all this development has put a little strain on the company financially, but with the Rossetto motto 'from the heart of the grape" I am sure they will get through because the family's heart is certainly in the right place.

Address: Farm 576 BEELBANGERA 2680	**Cases:** 100,000	Shiraz	5 yrs
Phone: (02) 6966 0288 **Fax:** (02) 6966 0298	**PublicHours:** 9am-5pm, Mon-Sat	Cabernet Merlot	5 yrs
Email: rossetto@ozemail.com.au	**Principal Varieties:** Semillon, Shiraz,	Cabernet Sauvignon	5 yrs
Owner: Garry Brian & Kevin Rossetto	Colombard, Chardonnay, Gordo, Trebbiano,	Chardonnay	3 yrs
Winemaker: Belinda Morandin	Merlot, Cabernet Sauvignon	Unwooded Chardonnay	3 yrs
Est: 1930 **Vine Ha:** 50	**Principal Wines** **Potential**	Rhine Riesling Eden Valley	5 yrs

were born.

Bill is one of the nicest and positive people in our great industry. I heartily applaud his achievement but it's been a long tough journey.

In 1945 Francesco and Elizabeth Calabria harvested and vintaged their first wine in the Riverina region of Australia. These wines were made in the tradition of their Italian heritage and with the excellent grape growing conditions the Riverina provided; a new boutique winery had emerged.

Westend Wines, now under the guiding hand of their son, Bill, has sought to increase both the quality and range of, wines offered. Testimony to his success is the collection of medals won at major Australian and International Wines Shows.

Bill, has never been able to consume any amounts of wine due to an allergy.

So to produce these wines, he has a unique palate to create such great wines from just tasting.

Westend's premium wine under the '3 Bridges' label to date have been awarded 6 trophies, 15 Gold and 42 Silver medals guaranteeing the quality and high standard of these great wines. Westend also have two other excellent wine ranges 'Richland' and 'The Outback Series'.

Situated right in Griffith, Westend Estate Wines is in the heart of New South Wales' largest grape producing area. Bill, is a true master of creating exceptional wines.

Bill Calabria got the New Millennium off with a real bang. As the clock struck midnight on 31st December 1999 and fireworks were firing everywhere Bill and his team began harvesting the first 2000 grapes. All these grapes were picked by 2am and 10 buckets were crushed straight away. By 5.30am all the grapes had been crushed, their juice on the pathway to being wine. Bill had a few competitors including a vineyard at Bourke but their grapes had to be trucked to Mudgee and were way behind Bill. Dennis Hornsby at Alice Springs was on the job too but half an hour behind Bill, his dream and plans had become a reality, 1,100 numbered bottles of "Eternity No. 1 Chardonnay"

Address: Brayne Road GRIFFITH 2680	Est: 1945 Vine Ha: 21	Principal Wines	Potential
Phone: (02) 6964 1506 Fax: (02) 6962 7512	Cases: 84,000	Richland Chardonnay	3 yrs
Email: westend@webfront.net.au	PublicHours: 8:30am-5pm Mon-Fri,	Richland Sauvignon Blanc	2 yrs
WWW: www.westendestate.com	10am-4pm Sat	Outback Traminer Riesling	2 yrs
Owner: William Calabria	Principal Varieties: Sauvignon Blanc,	Outback Semillon Sauvignon Blanc	2 yrs
Winemaker: William Calabria &	Semillon, Shiraz, Cabernet Sauvignon,	3 Bridges Cabernet Sauvignon	10 yrs
James Ceccato	Chardonnay, Durif, Merlot	3 Bridges Chardonnay	6 yrs

Cowra

during the rather dry summers.

Situated in the heart of New South Wales, not far from Orange and the National Capital, Canberra, Cowra is probably best known for the infamous 'Cowra Breakout' of Japanese prisoners from the Cowra Prison Camp during the Second World War. Cowra is a pretty town and features a Japanese War Cemetery Garden and Cultural Centre. The town is built around a huge granite rock; a nesting place for wedgetail eagles. From this lofty viewpoint, the vine rows seem to stretch into eternity.

The vineyard expansion in recent years has been astounding. Richmond Grove's vineyard alone now covers over 400 hectares, the largest vineyard venture ever undertaken in Australia in one year. More than 1,700 hectares are now covered with vines on the fertile soils. These are made up of broken down granite and basalt, with alluvial loam brought down by the Lachlan River, which also provides supplementary irrigation

Five main vineyards dominate the region - Cowra Estate the first established vineyard in 1973, followed by Rothbury and Richmond Grove. The O'Dea Family's Windowrie Estate 15 kms north of town with a large vineyard next door planted by a consortium lead by Brian McGuigan. Arrowfield have had a long association with the region and long-term contracts with some of the few independent growers. Several small wine producers have also sprung up over recent years such as Danbury Estate, Kalari,

Chiverton, Mulyan and Hamiltons Bluff near Canowindra.

Cowra is fast becoming the chardonnay capital of Australia. Rothbury have made a strong statement with this variety in recent years, as have Arrowfield, Cowra Estate and now, Richmond Grove. The chardonnays are ripe, rich and fleshy with strong stone fruit peach-nectarine characters often with some nuttiness in the background, finishing with easy-drinking acids. (Brian Croser helped launch chardonnay from Cowra in his days as lecturer at what is now Charles Sturt University). Other varieties, both red and white, seem to thrive in this climate with its good soils and water. The region is now a major player in the Australian wine scene.

The long established Quarry Restaurant and Cellars and the newly established Cowra Mill Winery and Restaurant in an historic bluestone former flour mill add a delightful wine tourism feel to the town.

Cowra Chardonnay 1998

Cowra - NSW

1. Chiverton Wines
2. Cowra Mill
3. Cowra Vineyards
4. Danbury Estate
5. Hamiltons Bluff
6. Kalari
7. Mulyan
8. Richmond Grove Vineyard
9. Rothbury Vineyard
10. The Quarry
11. Windowrie Estate

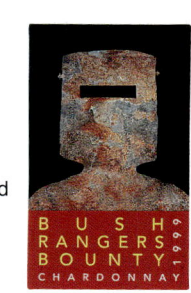

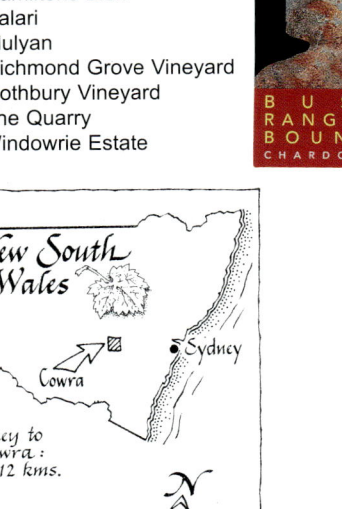

New South Wales

Sydney

Cowra

Sydney to Cowra : 312 kms.

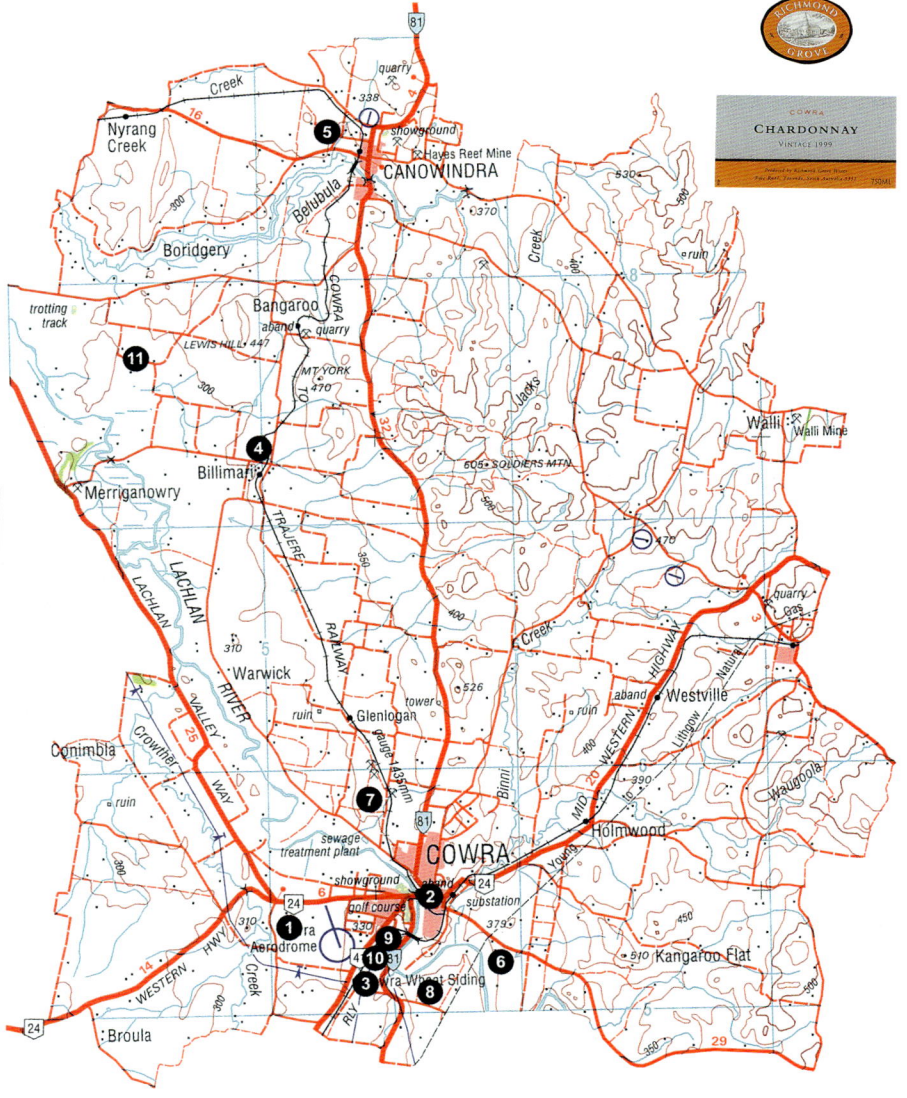

Chiverton Wines

Greg Thompson has had a very active business in the Cowra region

business. In 1993 he bought Chiverton, a property with a long and fascinating history, in fact in the 1800's it was a small village, all that remains of it on the property today is an old stone building that was the school house.

The Chiverton homestead is a lovely large old wooden colonial bungalow with spacious verandahs and in 1998 a cellar door facility was incorporated into the building.

The hardworking team under Greg and his wife Linda have created a picture book vineyard, they hand select the best parcels of each variety for their own wines, as they supply grapes to other winemakers.

The friendly, family hospitality and handcrafted premium wines make a visit to this picturesque vineyard and homestead a joy. I am sure their wines will find their way to many top wine outlets around the world as time goes by.

supplying irrigation equipment, largely to the booming grape growing

Address: 605 Mid Western Highway COWRA 2794 **Phone:** (02) 6342 9308 **Fax:** (02) 6342 9314 **Owner:** Greg Thompson	**Winemaker:** Simon Gilbert **Est:** 1994 **Vine Ha:** 136 **Public Hours:** 10am-4pm Weekends **Principal Wines**	Shiraz Cabernet Sauvignon Chardonnay Semillon

Danbury Estate

I first met the delightful young couple Jonathan and Margaret Middleton, the proprietors of Danbury, in Canberra at a Cowra Wine promotion. They represent the forward thinking, progressive boutique vignerons, that are making Cowra a real force in the Australian

Wine industry.

They escaped the city life in Sydney and Jonathan obtained his viticultural experience working at Windowrie Estate, before they purchased a carefully chosen property and planted 20 acres of

vines. They named the property Danbury Estate after Jonathan's Mothers Family Estate originally in Sydney.

Danbury is situated close to Billimari, midway between Cowra and Canowindra. The vineyard planting only started in September 1996, but their wines have already won a number of medals in wine shows.

The striking label features the Middleton family crest originating in England in the year 1250. They are particularly proud of their Middleton Chardonnay, which carries the crest. They aim for the aromatic style, peachy with a lifted citrus blossom bouquet. I noticed they are using top class French oak which gives the wine a nice creamy character and texture. Their cabernet merlot is a fine lifted and slightly spicy style, well rounded for easy drinking.

Address: PO Box 605 COWRA 2794 **Phone:** (02) 6341 2204 **Fax:** (02) 6341 4690 **Email:** middo@westserv.net.au **WWW:** www.cowraregionwines.com **Owner:** Jonathan Middleton	**Winemaker:** Peter Howland **Est:** 1996 **Vine Ha:** 8.2 **Cases:** 5,000 **Public Hours:** The Quarry Restaurant / Cellar Door 10am-4pm, Tues-Sat **Principal Wines** **Potential**	Middleton Chardonnay Reserve Chardonnay Cabernet Merlot Sparkling Chardonnay Fortified Semillon	3-4 yrs 5-10 yrs 2-3 yrs 2 yrs 5 yrs

Kalari

1995 seems to have been a watershed years in the Cowra Region, this was the year also when Valto and Pamela Heikkinen and Bob and Carmel Clark started planting their vineyard on the banks of the Lachlan River, about 5kms east of the Cowra township. The vineyard is a real picture of health and the views over the Lachlan are spectacular. They have built a charming rustic cellar door secluded away in the heart of the vineyard. This is a true boutique, where you meet and enjoy not only the wines but the Company knowledge and experience of the owners.

I found their verdelho particularly impressive, full of tropical fruit and soft round flavours on the palate. They also make a late picked verdelho fruity and luscious but crisp and clean. If you looking for a great after dinner drink, you can also try the fortified verdelho liqueur it's a knock out.

Kalari also produce a great unwooded chardonnay and a chardonnay with some oak handling, both show lovely nectarine and peach stonefruit characters. The range is completed by a vibrant shiraz full of berry flavours, with a nice peppery finish. Look out for the Kalari Wines and make sure you visit the vineyard if you're in Cowra.

Address: 120 Carro Park Road COWRA 2794	Andrew Margan	Principal Wines	Potential
Phone: (02) 6342 1465 Fax: (02) 6342 1465	Est: 1995 Vine Ha: 13	Dry Verdelho	3-5 yrs
Email: kalari@westserv.net.au	PublicHours: 10am-4pm, Fri-Mon & Public	Late Picked Verdelho	
Owner: Valto & Pamela Heikkinen,	Holidays, other times by appointment	Chardonnay	3-5 yrs
Bob & Carmel Clark	Principal Varieties: Chardonnay, Semillon,	Unwooded Chardonnay	upto 5 yrs
Winemaker: Jill Lindsay, Jon Reynolds &	Cabernet Sauvignon, Merlot, Shiraz, Verdelho	Shiraz	upto 5 yrs

The Quarry

The Cowra Region has virtually only one winery but a number of vineyards are wine producers, making their wines at facilities outside the region but strictly from the best grapes of their own vineyards. The Quarry has been and still is a godsend to them and a wonderful way for visitors to the region to try and buy the great Cowra wines. Many small wine producers such as Danbury Estate and Mulyan don't have a cellar door, neither does the larger established winemaker "Cowra Estate" whose vineyards surround the Quarry.

Large producers, Richmond Grove and Hungerford Hill also have their wines available at the Quarry, which is situated a few kilometres south of Cowra on the Boorowa Road. Wines from all these vineyards plus many more are available online at www.cowraregionwines.com.

Secluded in its tree-covered gardens there is a delightful cellar door wine room on one side and a cosy intimate restaurant on the other. You can enjoy over twenty great and different Cowra wines in either. Anne Loveridge looks after the wine and is a great hostess, husband Paul is the chef, his food is renowned in the region with good reason it's innovative, fresh and delicious.

The cellar door opens from Tuesday to Sunday from 10am - 4pm. The restaurant opens each of these days at Noon for lunch and Friday and Saturday for Dinner from 7.00pm. It's a must visit on your Cowra trip.

Address: Boorowa Road COWRA 2794	Fax: (02) 6341 4191	
Phone: (02) 6342 3650	Owner: Anne & Paul Loveridge	Public Hours: 10am-4pm, Tues-Sun

Hamiltons Bluff

In 1995 world renowned Architect John Andrews, designer of The C & N Tower in Toronto and The Intelsat Headquarters in Washington D.C., turned his hand to viticulture and established a vineyard on the outskirts of Canowindra in the Cowra region.

John and his son James were impressed by the well drained soils and chose splendid slopes that rise above the pretty cellar door, surrounded by lawns and gardens with its outdoor patio James and his wife, production manager, Julia, lived upstairs for a time until they built their new residence.

The vineyard is now quite large covering 110 acres of premium chardonnay, semillon, cabernet sauvignon, shiraz and sangiovese.

The first wines were made in 1998 by top Hunter winemaker Andrew Margan. The chardonnays he produced, have won medals at every show they have been exhibited in so far. Hamiltons Bluff is the top label, but a second label Canowindra Grossi has been a huge success named after a unique 360 million year old fish fossil, discovered in 1956, identified by German Scientist

Walter Gross and named Canowindra Grossi.

The 1998 Canowindra Grossi Chardonnay was used by Qantas Internationally and the 2000 vintage in Business Class. Hamiltons Bluff also make a Methode Champenoise, a Blanc de Blanc from Chardonnay, with 20 months yeast lees aging. I tried it at the vineyard, it's superb.

The Andrews have another string to their bow. Some 30 kilometres from the vineyard at Eugowra they breed

and raise some of the best red Deer in the country and produce "Mandagery Creek Australian Farmed Venison".

Once a year during the award winning Marti Balloon Fiesta, Hamiltons Bluff host "Breakfast Under The Balloons, it's around Easter time each year and the towns population swells to 25,000 from its normal 1,700. It's a great time to visit Hamiltons Bluff and enjoy the best that the country has to offer.

Address: Longs Corner Road
CANONWINDRA 2804
Phone: (02) 6344 2079
Fax: (02) 6344 2165
Email: hambluff@netconnect.com.au
WWW: www.hamiltonsbluff.com.au

Owner: Andrew Family
Winemaker: Andrew Morgan
Est: 1995 **Vine Ha:** 43
Cases: 3,000
Public Hours: 10am-4pm weekends & public holidays or by appointment

Principal Wines   **Potential**
Canowindra Grossi Chardonnay   Now - 5 yrs
Canowindra Grossi Cab Sav   Now - 3 yrs
Hamiltons Bluff Chairmans Reserve
Chardonnay
Sangiovese

Mulyan

Mercurial could well describe the exploits of the Fagan Family over five generations. Back in 1862 John Fagan was driving the stagecoach past Escort Rock near Eugowra, when legendary outlaws · Ben Hall and Frank Gardiner pulled off

Australia's biggest ever gold hold-up, half the bullion was never recovered.

Certainly the liquid gold that now comes from the family property Mulyan was far from his thoughts, when he purchased the large land holding in 1886. Mulyan is the aboriginal name for Eagle Hawk, the native bird and symbol of the region, today there a 100 acres of vines with another 50 acres going into the ground in 2001. The plantings are largely chardonnay and shiraz mostly contracted to Orlando Wyndham. The new plantings will include viognier and merlot. The final area under vine will be a massive 250 acres. ·

In the gardens of the Family homestead is a statue of Mercury sitting high amongst the statuesque palms. It was placed there in 1912 by Peter Fagan's grandmother. Mercury was the stepfather of the god of wine, Bacchus as well as messenger for all the other gods, he

is well placed on the label of the Mulyan Wines. Peter and his wife Jenni have three children, 26 year old James completed a Farm Management degree at the Orange Campus of the University of Sydney, where he topped viticulture in his last year. Second son Edward 25 has completed an Ag-commerce degree at Orange and the youngest daughter Sarah is in her second year of a Wine Science degree at Charles Sturt University at Wagga Wagga.

Peter's father was a car-racing driver in the 1930's and the cellar door is full of historic memorabilia. Mulyan is well set for a mercurial future.

Address: North Logan Road COWRA 2794 **Phone:** (02) 6342 1336 **Fax:** (02) 6341 1015	**Email:** mulyan@westserv.net.au **WWW:** www.mulyan.com.au **Winemaker:** Simon Gilbert	**Public Hours:** 10am-5pm, weekends & public holidays (weekdays by appointment) **Principal Varieties:** Chardonnay, Shiraz

Richmond Grove

One of the most impressive looking vineyards in Australia is the massive 780 acre Richmond Grove Estate Vineyards, that spread over the rolling hills surrounding the city of Cowra, its an awesome sight to survey the beautifully manicured vines as they sweep over the hills to the horizon.

The rich red volcanic soils and splendid aspects of the slopes, along with the excellent climate of Cowra, ensure that the considerable quantity of wine, that appears under the Richmond Grove Cowra label around the world, is all first class.

Richmond Grove had its beginnings in the late 1970's at the height of the wine boom; marketing wizard Mark Cashmore really put them on the map. The brand then came under the wing of wine dynamo Brian McGuigan, who ensured the wines really came of age.

Wyndham Estate with its Richmond

Grove wines was then taken over by Orlando and the giant Pernod-Ricard Company. Their search for a large premium vineyard opportunity ended up at Cowra.

They have been delighted with the results, winning an award in France

recently as the Worlds Best Chardonnay with their 1998 Cowra wine. When you pull the cork on any of the "Richmond Grove" great value Cowra wine, you can take part in the celebration of this vast vineyard venture.

Address: Para Road TANUNDA 5352 **Phone:** (08) 8563 2204 **Fax:** (08) 8563 2804 **Winemaker:** John Vickery **Est:** 1897	**Public Hours:** 10am-5pm, weekdays; 10.30pm-4.30pm, weekends and public holidays	**Principal Varieties:** Riesling, Cabernet Sauvignon, Shiraz, Semillon, Chardonnay, Verdelho

Windowrie Estate

The splendid new Windowrie Estate Winery was finished just in time for the 2000 vintage. Situated on a hilltop it has majestic views over the region from atop the considerable tank farm. The winery is a natural development for the growing enterprise of the O'Dea Family.

David O'Dea was early to recognise the potential of Cowra as a viticultural region when he planted his first vines in 1988. Today he has 45 hectares of his own vines and manages almost 200 more hectares of vines adjoining his property for clients such as a consortium of growers supplying Brian McGuigan Wines. David's vineyards are located in sweeping valleys between Cowra and Canowindra. His first client was Arrowfield Wines who have been very successful with chardonnay from the O'Dea vineyards.

The O'Dea's are a large family and youngest son Jason is involved in viticulture having worked in vineyards in South America and California's Napa Valley. Daughter Dimity is studying Wine Marketing at Roseworthy in South Australia.

Eldest son Steph has had a different mission, a builder, he has renovated and restored the classic old bluestone flourmill in Cowra, built in 1861, which had lain dormant for almost 90 years. With the clever use of recycled timbers and natural materials he has transformed it into a splendid Restaurant and Wine Tasting Centre featuring the Windowrie Estate Wines from the family's vineyards and a specially launched label "The Mill Wines". The Mill is now landscaped with fruit bearing vines; it has a fantastic ambience. The food is innovative and the three story building has a great cellar door featuring local produce on the ground floor, the restaurant is on the second floor and under the verandahs on the first floor. The third floor is a function area.

All the Windowrie and Mill wines are from their estate and made at the new Windowrie Estate Winery from specially selected parcels of each variety. The Windowrie Wines, a chardonnay and a cabernet sauvignon, are both matured for a time in French oak and have some bottle age. The Mill range includes chardonnay, sauvignon blanc, traminer riesling, cabernet merlot and shiraz.

The Windowrie wines have already achieved Wine Show success, a gold at the highly competitive Chilean Wine Show in South America and a gold medal for their chardonnay in Adelaide. At Windowrie they make sure they're winners.

Address: Windowrie Road
CANOWINDRA 2804
Phone: (02) 6344 3264 **Fax:** (02) 6344 3227

Email: windowrie@windowrie.com.au
WWW: www.windowrie.com
Winemaker: Rodney Hooper

Est: 1988 **Vine Ha:** 44
Principal Varieties: Chardonnay, Cabernet Sauvignon, Sauvignon Blanc

Orange

The Orange Region is situated around 280kms west of Sydney and is known as "The food basket of Australia" as it produces an astonishing array of fresh produce.

Planting of vines commenced in 1983 and the climate of a true continental nature and cooled by being over 600 metres above sea level, has proved a winner for many grape varieties. Orange also has a reliable rainfall of 800mm p.a. with a dry autumn, ideal for the vintage period.

Today over 2,500 acres have been planted, large companies are sourcing fruit from the region. Rosemount's renowned chief winemaker, Philip Shaw, has his own vineyard in the region and in 1999 at the world's largest wine fair Vin Expo in Bordeaux carried off the trophy for the world's best chardonnay from these vines.

Nearly all styles seem to do well, currently more than 15 wine producers are marketing and selling wine from Orange.

There are also a number of delightful Winery Boutiques to visit, some with food and hospitality facilities. Nearly all the vineyards and wineries have the majestic Mt Canobolas towering above them, it gives the region a regal feeling. A number of vineyards, some extremely large, such as the Cabonne Limited's huge vineyard holdings and massive Quondong Winery at Cudal stretch up to 30 · 40 kms from Orange. A champion of the region for over ten years has been Jon Reynolds, who has his own vineyard and has now merged his Reynolds Wine Company with Cabonne, he is now making all the wine at the Quondong Winery.

Orange is fast becoming an icon Australian Wine Region.

Orange

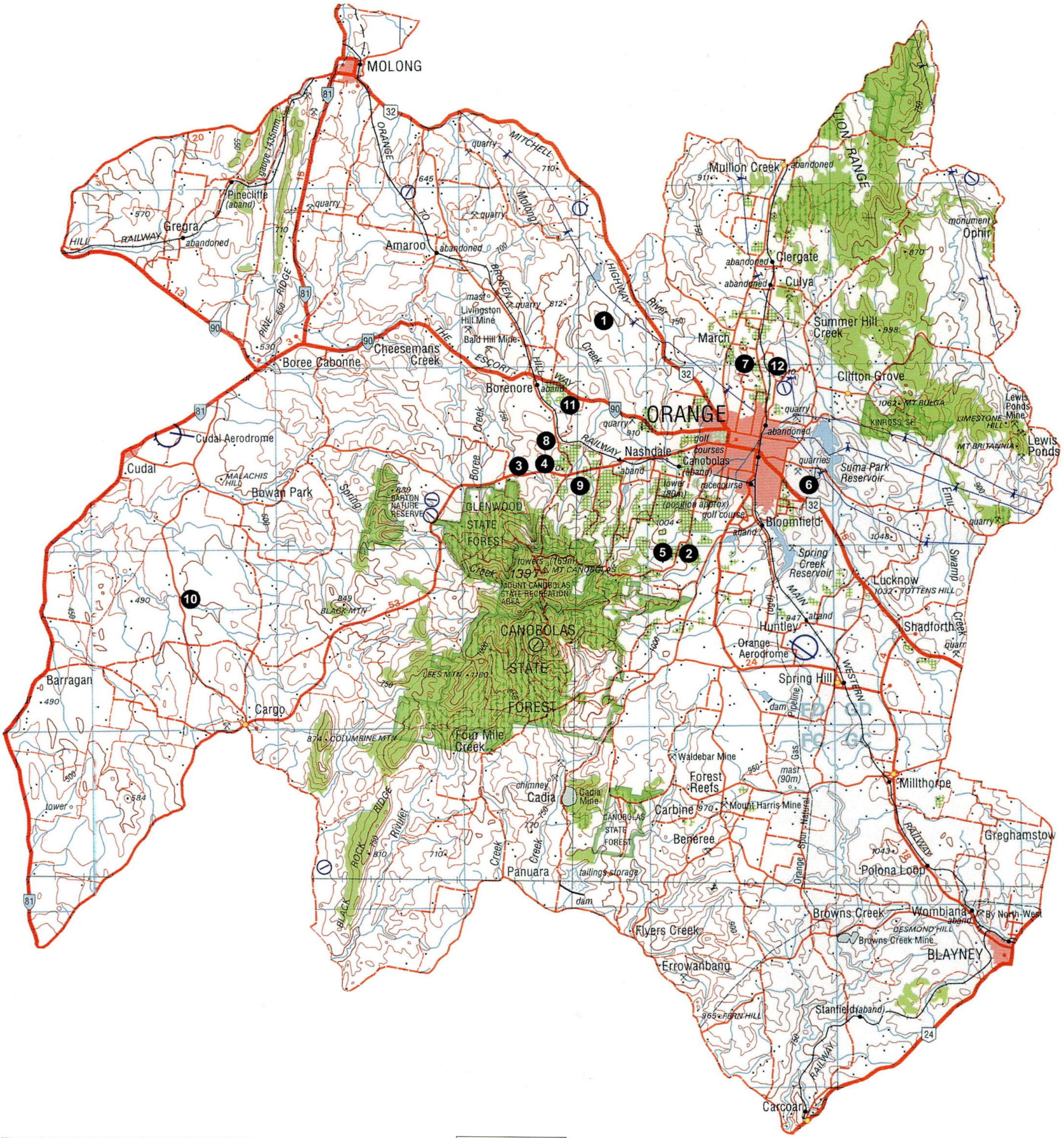

MOLONG

New South Wales

Sydney

Orange

ROSEMOUNT

Orange - NSW

1. Bloodwood Estate
2. Brangayne of Orange
3. Canobolas Smith
4. Cargo Road
5. Donnington Wines
6. Highland Heritage
7. Ibis Wines
8. Nashdale Vineyard
9. Osmond Wines
10. Quondong Wines
11. Rosemount
12. Templers Mill

Cabonne

Cabonne Limited is quickly becoming one of Australia's largest premium wine producers and by Vintage 2002, it should be well cemented in the top 20 wineries, ranked by the volume of wine produced.

Cabonne Ltd. was registered on the Australian Stock exchange in May 1999, as a vineyard owner, developer and manager, since then it has quickly become a fully integrated Wine Company.

Cabonne is the name of the district, close to Orange, in the cool western slopes of New South Wales Great Dividing Range, where the Cabonne vineyards are planted.

Cabonne is already the 9th largest vineyard operator in Australia, with over 2250 acres of premium grape varieties planted, the vineyards are predominately red varieties and include Shiraz, Cabernet Sauvignon and Merlot, with some white varieties including Chardonnay, Riesling, Vendelho, Sauvignon Blanc, Semillon and Marsanne.

The winery is already profitable and also processes grapes from a number of vineyards in the central NSW regions. By vintage 2003 Cabonne will produce around one million cases of wine from their own vineyards.

The first stage of the massive winery was opened by NSW premier, the Hon. Bob Carr in March 2000. Stage two was completed in time for the 2001 vintage.

Cabonne have been extremely fortunate to secure the services of top winemaker Jon Reynolds, who has some excellent large company winemaking experience, as former Chief Winemaker for Houghton Wines in WA and at Wyndham Estate wines in the Hunter Valley. Cabonne purchased The Reynolds Wine Company in September 2000 including the very successful Reynolds wine brand, which was increasingly focused on Jon's Orange vineyards and contract growers in the Orange region,

where Jon has been a pioneer winemaker.

How to find markets for such massive quantities of premium wines? In December 2000 this challenge came a lot closer to achievement, when a global alliance was struck with the Trinchero Family Estates, a huge American Wine group which owns American's largest wine brand, Sutter Home. With this alliance Cabonne has become their exclusive Australian Wine Supplier. It is anticipated the first year 175,000 cases of premium Reynolds Wines will be sold in the USA and throughout the world.

Cabonne have just launched their "Little Boomey" brand in the United Kingdom, 50,000 cases have been selected from the 2000 vintage, so things are certainly on the move at Cabonne. This is one of Australia's truly grand international wine ventures, showing clearly already, that our countries wines are well worthy on the world's wine stage.

Address: Cargo Road CUDAL 2864
Phone: (02) 6364 2330 **Fax:** (02) 6364 2388
Email: quondong@cabonneltd.com.au
WWW: www.cabonne.com
Winemaker: Jon Reynolds

Est: 1994 **Vine Ha:** 900
Principal Varieties: Cab Sav, Marsanne, Riesling, Sem, Verdelho, Chard, Merlot, Sauv Blanc, Shiraz
Principal Wines
Moon Shadow Chardonnay

Jezebel Cab Sav
Landscape Sav Blanc
Landscape Cab Merlot
Little Boomey Sauv Blanc
Little Boomey Chardonnay

Cargo Road

Firstly James is an expert viticulturist and along with Neil and Ian Fletcher from the Cowra region runs a successful vineyard management business, Rural Development and Management, which looks after over 10 vineyards in the central New South Wales grape growing regions.

The Cargo Road range of wines includes zinfandel, a deep coloured and spicy red famous in California and gewürztraminer, the spicy white variety from Alsace. They also produce a merlot, cabernet merlot, riesling and a sauvignon blanc.

The charming winery also has an active gallery and a restaurant café "Pippin" with a balcony sporting stunning views over the vineyard and region. Quick and light meals from the local "food bowl of Australia" produce are served or you can settle down to a T-bone with ratatouie and while away a few hours enjoying the Cargo Road reds - either way I am sure you will be charmed.

Cargo Road Winery is a hive of activity. Owner James Sweetapple is a dedicated enthusiast, who brings together an exciting wine and food enterprise, that is a must visit if you are in the Orange district.

Address: Cargo Road FERNLIDSTER 2800 **Phone:** (02) 6365 6100 **Fax:** (02) 6365 6001	**Email:** cargo@ix.net.au **Public Hours:** 11am-5pm, weekends (or by appointment)	**Principal Varieties:** Cabernet Sauvignon, Merlot, Sauvignon Blanc, Gewürztraminer, Riesling, Zinfandel

Donnington Wines

Located at the pretty Campbells corner on Pinnacle road 960 metres above sea level, on the upper slopes of Mt Canobolas, Donnington Vineyard is very picturesque. The vineyards are surrounded by orchards and stands of European trees, which wear spectacular colours in autumn.

The recently constructed cellar door is a delight and has an uninterrupted view of the vineyards, sweeping up towards the summit.

The extremely cool viticultural conditions give the grapes a very long growing season and help retain the essential acid levels for crisp flavoursome wines. The first vines were planted in 1991; the vineyard has expanded greatly through further plantings and is now 15 acres, with quite a number of varieties, including cabernet sauvignon, which often does not ripen until May.

Jamie Gordon and his wife Sharyn decided to become vignerons after picking grapes for and assisting Orange pioneer winemaker Murray Smith. Jamie is a Neurologist and Sharyn a Nuclear Physician. Jamie studied the wine degree course at Charles Sturt for 2 years before health problems prevented him continuing, he intends making the wines himself when their enterprise has grown a little more. Sharyn is in the last year of seven years of the viticultural degree course at Charles Sturt. They hope to expand the vineyard to around 40 acres.

The Donnington name comes from the Donnington Castle near Oxford in England home of Sir John Packer an ancestor of Jamie's mother.

I found both their pinot noir and chardonnay particularly complex and impressive.

Address: Campbells Corner ORANGE 2800 **Phone:** (02) 6365 3509 **Fax:** (02) 6361 8139 **Email:** donnvine@ix.net.au **Owner:** James Gordon & Sharyn Russell **Winemaker:** John Hordern	**Est:** 1992 **Vine Ha:** 6 **Public Hours:** 9am-5pm, Mon-Fri; 11am-4pm Sat, Sun & Public Holidays **Principal Varieties:** Chardonnay, Merlot, Riesling, Semillon, Cabernet Sauvignon,	Malbec, Pinot Noir, Sauvignon Blanc **Principal Wines** Chardonnay Pinot Noir Cabernet Sauvignon Sauvignon Blanc

Highland Heritage

Highland Heritage is a name well chosen. The D'Aquino family became the pioneers of the now blossoming wine industry around Orange, when founder Carmelo D'Aquino moved there in 1946 and set up a small winery in a tin shed.

Carmelo was born in Sicily in 1902; in January 2001 he celebrated his 99th birthday and can look back on a life of incredible achievement. In 1932 he arrived in Australia in the middle of the great depression, he went back to Sicily to marry his childhood sweetheart in 1934 and brought her back to Australia with him the same year. Carmelo put is farming background to good use when he established a group of fruit shops in Sydney. At the urging of a friend he moved to Orange in 1946. In 1952 he built a new winery on the site where the companies head office is today. His first commercial vintage that year consisted of six barrels; it was the first commercial wine ever made in the Orange Region. In 1949 a distant relative Illuminato Leo D'Aquino came to Australia "the land of opportunity". He arrived in Darwin speaking no English and was promptly robbed of all his possessions. He came to Sydney and worked in Carmelo's fruit shops, in 1955 he married Carmelo's daughter and in 1958 they moved to

Orange to assist Carmelo in his growing enterprise.

In 1970 Leo and Zina bought the business from her father who is still enjoying his long retirement. Their son Rex is General Manager of the D'Aquino Group of Companies that includes a large liquor wholesaling, retailing and distribution locally and in Brisbane and Sydney. Rex gained his winemaking degree from Roseworthy in 1981 he controls a vintage of around 3,000 tonnes mainly made at the Oak Wine Services Winery in Muswellbrook, in which D'Aquino's have a share in the ownership with John Hordern a fellow

Roseworthy graduate. Whilst D'Aquino's make wines from many regions their 40 acres of vines on their 250-acre Highland Heritage property, 3kms east of Orange, provides the grapes for their Highland Heritage Estate Wines.

The flagship wines are the Mt Canobolas range, individual vineyard selections and limited releases. The second range "Wellwood" is named after the original settlers grant by Governor Macquarie, of which the Highland heritage Estate is part of. The "Wellwood" wines are all from the Orange region.

The third range is the Gosling Creek Wines, named after the historic waterway that runs through the property. These wines are blended from premium wine regions around southeastern Australia. There are also a number of export brands to keep the D'Aquino's bottling business busy.

The tasting room at Highland Heritage is a rail car complete with signals and their multi award winning restaurant and function centre seats up to 250 people, it is a popular wedding venue.

Why not celebrate your visit to Highland Heritage, with a glass of the Mt Canobolas Ice Crystal Sparkling Pinot Noir, a Methode Champenoise that spends 54 months on yeast lees - it's full of character just like the D'Aquino Family.

Address: Mitchell Highway ORANGE 2800	Winemaker: Rex Daquino	Principal Wines	Potential
Phone: (02) 6362 7381 Fax: (02) 6362 6183	Est: 1946 Vine Ha: 16.5	Mt Canobolis Range	10-20 yrs
WWW: www.highlandheritageestate.com	Cases: 13,000	Wellwood Range	5-15 yrs
Owner: Fernbrew Pty Ltd	Public Hours: 9am-5pm, daily	Gosling Range	3-5 yrs

Rosemount

Philip Shaw found his Orange Vineyard site in a most unusual way some dozen years or so ago. He was looking for a new challenge, to find a region where he could plant a vineyard to produce grapes that would give him styles and opportunities entirely different than he currently had. For a year or two he looked at the Yarra Valley but the opportunities didn't come and something just didn't feel right to him.

Flying on a trip down to the Yarra

from Denman, the plane flew close to Mt Canobolas near Orange. Philip was struck by the orchards and the look of the region, on returning home to the Upper Hunter he jumped in his car and almost immediately he found the land and the climate he was looking for. Today he has a 100-acre vineyard with some colleagues and Rosemount have a 100-acre vineyard alongside. Planting commenced in 1989.

Philip firmly believes the high

altitude has a lot to do with the quality of the grapes. The high ultra violet level sunrays help mature the fruit, with loads of flavour and great colour, after around 28°C the vine shuts down to a degree thus in warm regions the vine is just not working to ripen the fruit a lot of the time. Central New South Wales can be super hot, in the 2001 summer temperatures have risen to 46°C but at his Orange Vineyard 36°C has been the hottest day. Philip's careful analysis of the total terroir has been spot on. The wines produced are the final proof of the pudding. At Vin Expo in Bordeaux in 1999 the 1997 Rosemount Orange Chardonnay was chosen as the best in the world. It also triumphed at the International Wine & Spirits competition in England. Recently the 1999 Shiraz won gold in Sydney. Pinot Noir is in fact the biggest planting but a number of other varieties make up the vineyard including cabernet sauvignon. I am sure we will hear a lot more of the Rosemount "Orange" Wines as the century unfolds.

Templer's Mill

Templer's Mill is the official wine label of the University of Sydney using grapes grown at their Orange Campus.

The name and label were inspired by one of Australia's first flour mills,

which provided flour for the early goldfields at Ophir near Orange. The ruins rest on the adjacent property "Narrambla" which is also famous as the birthplace of writer A.B. (Banjo) Paterson, creator of "The Man from

Snowy River". The label features a nostalgic watercolour and ink painting by local artist Ron Noble.

The 20ha vineyard is a key enterprise at the University of Sydney - Faculty of Rural Management, that is also used for viticultural management education and research. Templer's Mill wine is made by Jon Reynolds who has recently taken over as winemaker at the large Quondong Winery near Cudal in the west of the region.

The Chardonnay wines have received critical acclaim and a number of medals. A spicy Shiraz is becoming a signature wine alongside complex Cabernet Sauvignons that show intense berry flavours. Sauvignon Blanc and Merlot are also grown to provide a stimulating range of cool climate wine.

Address: The University of Sydney, Leeds Parade ORANGE 2800	Owner: The University of Sydney	Principal Wines	Potential
Phone: (02) 6360 5509	Winemaker: Jon Reynolds	Chardonnay	5-8 yrs
	Est: 1997 Vine Ha: 20	Sauvignon Blanc	3-4 yrs
Fax: (02) 6330 5698	Cases: 1,500	Shiraz	10+ yrs
Email: temp ersmill@orange.usyd.edu.au	Public Hours: 10am-4:30pm, Weekdays or	Cabernet Sauvignon	10+ yrs
WWW: www.orange.usyd.edu.au	by appointment	Merlot	5 yrs

Young

The history of vines and wine in the Hilltops region, encompassing the shires of Young, Harden and Boorowa, goes back to the 1860's when in the aftermath of the turbulent gold rush days, vines were planted chiefly by the Dalmatian Settlers for their own use. The grape industry grew to around 300 acres of vineyards but gradually these diminished until all but disappearing in the 1950's. Some of the few remaining vines planted in 1886 are on the renaissance vineyard of Grove Estate on the outskirts of Young.

After a department of agriculture report in the mid 60's recommending the area for premium grape growing a few tentative small vineyards were planted. By the mid 80's some 15 vineyards and half a dozen boutique

wineries were operating. The first major vineyard began in 1969 when Peter Robinson planted at Barwang off the Boorowa road. This vineyard was purchased by McWilliams in 1989 and now covers over 240 acres.

The winemaking renaissance in the Hilltops region began when Jill and Phil Lindsay made their first commercial wine in 1986 from vines they planted in 1978.

The Hilltops name originates from the unique soils partly made up of wind blown up soil from the Riverina plain combining on the broad elevated ridge tops with the red granite volcanic soils, together forming deep fertile volcanic loams. The Hilltops were planted for this reason and to ensure air drainage to avert late spring frosts damaging the budding cherrytrees and later grape vines. A yearly festival - Hilltops Flavours of the Harvest Food and Wine, is held each February and in late November the National Cherry Festival which has been held each year for over 50 years.

Today the Hilltops has a number of active boutique wineries and some large commercial vineyards being planted.

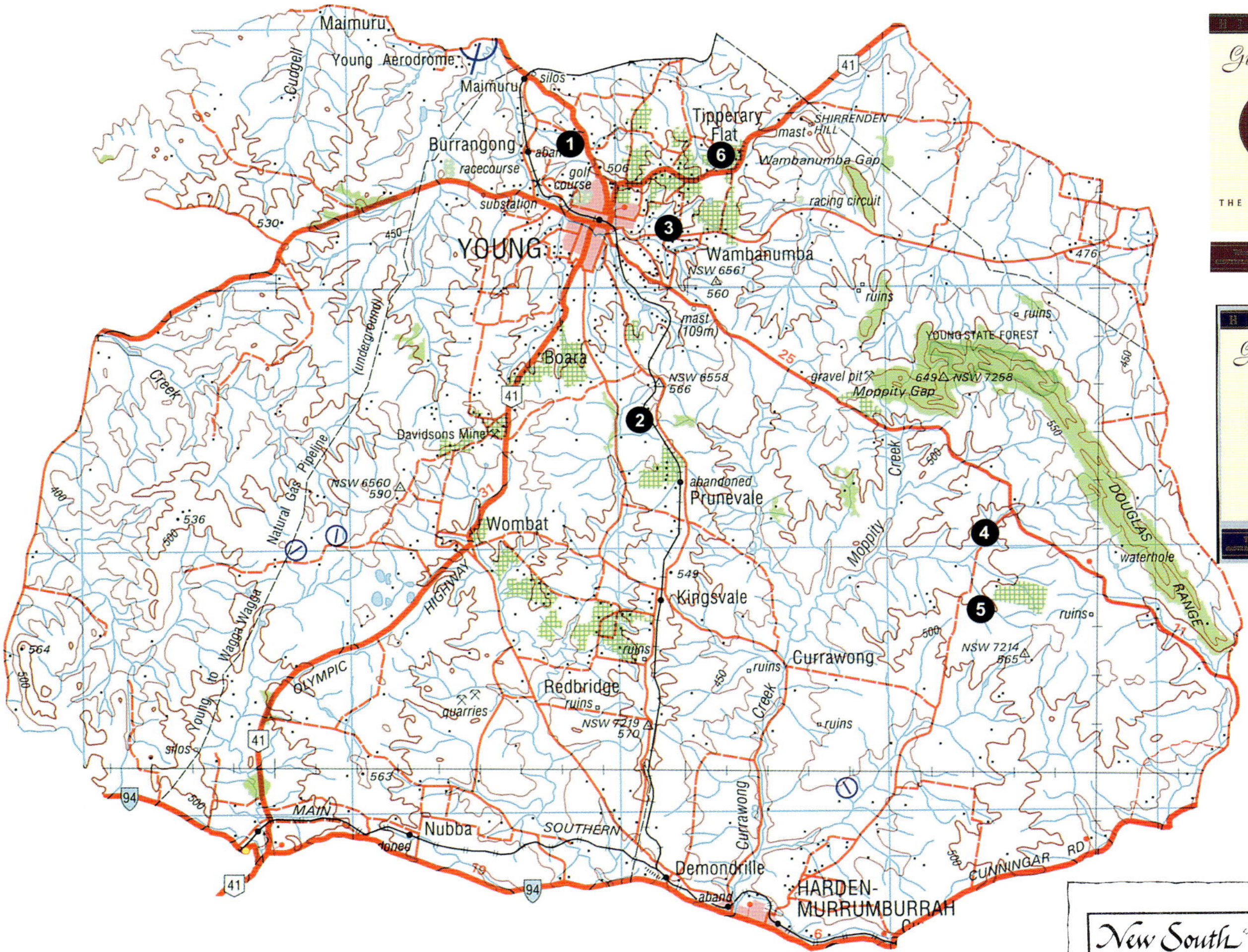

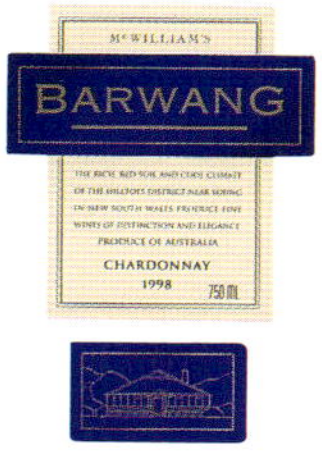

Young - NSW

1. Chalkers Crossing
2. Demondrille Vineyards
3. Grove Estate
4. Hansen
5. McWilliams Barwang
6. Woodonga Hill

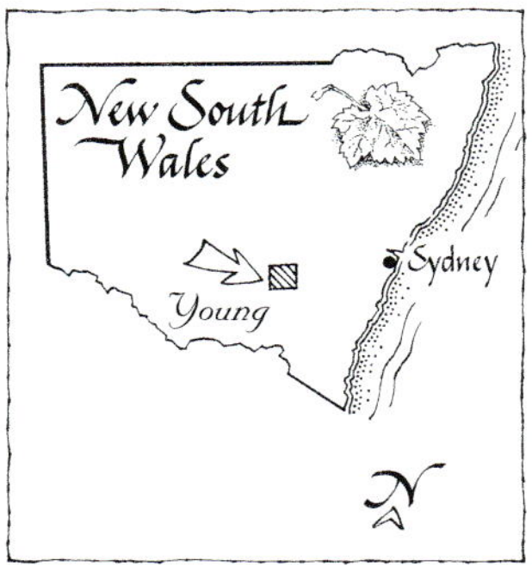

On the south-western slopes of the Great Dividing Range some 25 kilometres east of Young, at an average height above sea level of 600 metres, is the impressive McWilliam's Barwang Vineyard. The vineyards covers over 100 hectares of rolling hills of the 400 hectare property and the view over the patchwork quilt of vines from the furthest hill is quite something. The soils are deep red decomposed granite impregnated with basalt, and I'm sure this comes through in the strength and complexity of the red wines.

This remote cool climate location was first planted back in 1969, 13 hectares along the high ridges to avoid the worst of the frosts that are common in the area.

McWilliam's bought the vineyard in 1989 from the founders, the Robinson family, whom McWilliam's had been supplying with vine cuttings since the vineyard's founding. McWilliam's immediately planted a further 87 hectares, and today it is all bearing. The grapes are crushed on site and then make the three-hour journey as chilled 'must' (grape juice).

The vineyard is chiefly planted to cabernet sauvignon, shiraz and chardonnay with smaller quantities of merlot, pinot noir, semillon, sauvignon blanc and riesling.

The wines from Barwang have been spectacularly successful in wine shows and are often confused with those from Coonawarra. The first vintage shiraz, a 1989, won five gold medals and the 1991 Cabernet Sauvignon has won two trophies and two gold medals. In all, the McWilliam's Barwang wines have won more than 100 medals in only seven short years. Qantas and a number of prestigious 5-star hotels have included Barwang on their wine lists, along with other Australian classics, proving McWilliam's aim of developing fruit-driven wines from the excellent viticultural conditions to be absolutely correct.

Address: Barwang Vineyards YOUNG 2594	**Owner:** McWilliams Wines Pty Ltd	Barwang Semillon	5 yrs
Phone: (02) 6382 3594	**Winemaker:** Jim Brayne	Barwang Chardonnay	2-5 yrs
Fax: (02) 6382 3594	**Est:** 1969 **Vine Ha:** 103	Barwang Cabernet Sauvignon	10 yrs
WWW: www.mcwilliams.com.au	**Principal Wines**	**Potential** Barwang Shiraz	8 yrs

Grove Estate

On the eastern outskirts of Young on the Murringo Road is the impressive

Grove Estate Vineyard of the Mullany, Kirkwood and Flanders families. Planting started in 1989 with the aim of producing premium cool-climate grapes on the red volcanic soils. Today 100 ha of superb looking vines fan out from the cellar door on the peak of their ridge just off Murringo Road.

Grove Estate have a piece of Australia's wine heritage, some ancient vines planted in 1886. DNA research is currently being carried out to determine the variety.

In 1997 the partners at Grove Estate

decided to keep small parcels of various varieties and produce a range of premium wines. The first release was a 1997 Cabernet Sauvignon and a 1998 Chardonnay. A Shiraz, Semillon, Zinfandel, Riesling and Pinot Noir have now been released, with the 1999 Cabernet Sauvignon winning a gold medal in the 2001 Sydney International Wine Show.

The cellar door is an original building that has been lovingly transformed and opens onto an outdoor area ideal for a picnic with spectacular views.

Address: Murringo Road YOUNG 2594 **Phone:** (02) 6382 6999 **Fax:** (02) 6382 4527 **Email:** grove_estate@yol.net.au **Owner:** Brian Mullany, Mark Flanders, John Kirkwood **Winemaker:** Greg Silkman	**Est:** 1989 **Vine Ha:** 110 **Cases:** 4,000 **Public Hours:** 10am-5pm, Sat & Sun **Principal Varieties:** Barbera, Cabernet Sauvignon, Petit Verdot, Semillon, Zinfandel, Chardonnay, Sangiovese, Shiraz, Merlot	**Principal Wines** **Potential** The Partners Cabernet Sauvignon 10 yrs Cellar Block Shiraz 10 yrs Hilltops Semillon 6 yrs Murringo Way Chardonnay 8 yrs

Chalkers Crossing

Ted and Wendy Ambler began planting their Chalkers Crossing vineyard and olive grove just south of Young in 1997. The vineyard is situated on the highly prized red aeolian soils for which the Hilltops Region is renowned and is producing shiraz, cabernet, merlot, semillon and riesling. A small number of olive trees have been planted around the vineyard, with more substantial plantings being planned for the future.

With a clear focus on producing premium quality cool climate wines, the company receives grapes from the Hilltops, Southern Highlands and Tumbarumba

Regions of NSW. The Chalkers Crossing Winery, located just north of the town, was completed in early 2000 in time for the 2000 vintage making riesling, semillon, shiraz and cabernet from Hilltops grapes, and chardonnay, sauvignon blanc and pinot from Tumbarumba grapes.

In early 2001 Chalkers Crossing installed a modern, continuous process, olive press adjacent to its winery and is producing premium quality Extra Virgin Olive Oil.

The Chalkers Crossing 2000 Cabernet Sauvignon has just been awarded a trophy for the best Cabernet/Merlot at

the 2001 Canberra Regional Wine Show. With a trophy, two silver and nine bronze medals from seven wines in its first vintage Chalkers Crossing is worth watching and is certainly worth a visit if you are in the Hilltops area.

Address: 387 Henry Lawson Way YOUNG 2594 **Phone:** (02) 6382 6900 **Fax:** (02) 6382 5068 **Email:** ted@chalkerscrossing.com.au **WWW:** www.chalkerscrossing.com.au	**Winemaker:** Celine Rousseau **Est:** 2000 **Vine Ha:** 10 **Cases:** 7,000 **Public Hours:** 10am-4pm, daily **Principal Wines** **Potential**	Riesling Hilltops 5 yrs Semillon Hilltops 5 yrs Merlot Hilltops 5 yrs Cabernet Sauvignon Hilltops 5 yrs Shiraz Hilltops 5 yrs

Woodonga Hill

Jill and Phil Lindsay began planting at Woodonga Hill in 1978. Their plan was to start a commercial boutique winery; it was a brave move as there were no producing

wineries left in the region since its demise in the 1950's.

They chose a ridge of the Hilltops soil, rich red volcanic loam about 10kms north east of Young on the Olympic Highway, The site also had excellent air drainage to help avert the frost hazard always present around Young.

Jill began her wine studies at Wagga's Charles Stuart University, today she has her Oenology Degree and is consulting winemaker for a number of boutique wineries in Central New South Wales.

The first vintage of the new winery was in 1986. Both her first two wines, a 1986 Dry Riesling and 1986 Cabernet Sauvignon, won medals in wine shows.

I recently drank a bottle of 10 year old Dry Riesling, it was in prime condition and absolutely superb.

The wineries cellar door has a fantastic family feel about it. Phil and Jill's enthusiasm and passion for their wines really rubs off on you.

You can taste their extended range of award winning wines and a Cherry Liqueur.

Address: Cowra Road YOUNG 2594 **Phone:** (02) 6382 2972 **Fax:** (02) 6382 2972 **Email:** lindsays@yol.net.au **Owner:** Phil & Jill Lindsay	**Winemaker:** Jill Lindsay **Est:** 1978 **Vine Ha:** 12 **Cases:** 5,000 **Public Hours:** 9am-5pm, daily **Principal Wines** **Potential** Hilltops Riesling 14 yrs	Sauvignon Blanc 5 yrs Pinot Meunier 5 yrs Chardonnay 5 yrs Hilltops Shiraz 15+ yrs Hilltops Cabernet Sauvignon 15+ yrs

Canberra

The Canberra wine regional history goes right back to the 1820's to a famous vineyard planted by explorer Hamilton Hume at Cooma Cottage. There were vineyards and wineries around Yass in the 1850's. The establishment of the new Canberra Wine region started in the 1970's.

Today the region has more than 20 wine producers and a number of boutique wineries with cellar doors. Currently nearly 1,000 acres are under vine but this is increasing quickly, with the current production of around 2 million bottles of wine set to double in the next five years.

A major development has been a

recently opened Wine Centre at the Canberra horse racing track constructed by Wine giant BRL Hardy, who are contracting large quantities of grapes from the region.

In all there are three distinct areas with clusters of vineyards and

wineries. Hall slightly to the north-west, further north Murrumbateman and to the east and north-east Lake George. The general climate and microclimates of each area is quite distinct and different, allowing a full range of premium wines to be made in the general region. Many medals and trophies in wine shows over the last 25 years attest to their quality.

The very personal cellar doors are charming usually with spectacular views and often with walking trails, it's a charming region. The "Days of Wine-Roses" Festival each October is a good time to visit.

Canberra - ACT

1. Brindabella Hills
2. Clonakilla
3. Doonkuna Estate
4. Helms Wines
5. Kamberra
6. Lake George
7. Lark Hill
8. Madew
9. Murrumbateman
10. Pankhurst

Brindabella Hills

In 1986 they carved out an 8-acre vineyard in rugged, hilly country, with spectacular views over the Murrumbidgee River Valley near Hall. The red and yellow duplex soils are similar to those of Great Western in Victoria, Mt Barker in Western Australia and Clare/Watervale in South Australia. They are well drained and the wines they craft from riesling, semillon, sauvignon blanc, chardonnay, merlot, shiraz, cabernet franc and cabernet sauvignon have received critical acclaim. The cellar door, tucked away amongst the trees and gardens has much charm.

Dr Roger Harris has a PhD in Chemistry from the Adelaide University and a Wine Science degree from Charles Sturt University. He and his wife Faye had had a life long interest in wine and were inspired to search for a vineyard site by several visits to the classic winemaking regions of Europe and America.

Address: 156 Woodgrove Close HALL 2618	**Est:** 1986 **Vine Ha:** 4.5 **Cases:** 3,000	Cabernet (Blend Cabernet Sauvignon, Cabernet
Phone: (02) 6230 2583 **Fax:** (02) 6230 2033	**Public Hours:** 10am-5pm w/e & public holidays	Franc, Merlot) 5+ yrs
Email: brindabellahills@bigpond.com	**Principal Varieties:** Cab Franc, Chardy, Riesling,	Chardonnay(Barrel Fermented) 5+ yrs
Owner: Roger & Faye Harris	Semillon, Cab Sav, Merlot, Sav Blanc, Shiraz	Sauvignon Blanc/Semillon
Winemaker: Dr Roger Harris	**Principal Wines** **Potential**	Riesling 5+ yrs Shiraz 5+ yrs

Helms Wines

By anyone's stretch of their imagination Ken Helm is a genuine character. Ken and wife Judith were early pioneers of the Canberra region of Murrumbateman, they planted in 1973 with a winery following in 1977. Ken is a 4th generation descendant of a German vine dressing family who established vineyards in the 1850' and 1880's in Albury and Rutherglen. The family tradition continues with their daughter Stephanie, at 15 she has already made 5 vintages, won a trophy, gold, silver and bronze medals with her wines.

The 1880 Schoolhouse - now the tasting room is papered with awards, clippings and memorabilia including photographs of Helm wine enthusiasts with bottles of their wines from Moscow to the Antarctic.

Ken's 22 years as an insect ecologist in vineyards and orchards with the CSIRO, until becoming full time at the property in 1988 has assisted him in becoming a

Nationally recognised premium winemaker. His selfless service to the industry and community are also legendary.

Pankhurst

granitic ridge above the Murrumbidgee River valley. It has good cold air drainage, preventing frost damage at critical times. The land was formerly used for grazing and has good organic and water retaining properties. Expert regional winemaker Sue Carpenter makes the wines. I was most impressed with the 1997 Pinot Noir, the champion red and dual trophy winner at the 1999 Canberra Wine Show. They also produce Chardonnay, a Sauvignon Blanc/Semillon and a Cabernet Merlot. Visitors to Pankhurst Wines are rewarded with stunning views of the Brindabellas.

Christine and Allan Pankhurst are perfectionists; she a Pharmacist and he an Agricultural Scientist. Their 12 acre vineyard is planted on the north facing slopes of "Old Woodgrove", part of the historic "Woodgrove" property being on a

Address: Old Woodgrove WOODGROVE 2618	**Winemaker:** Sue Carpenter	Pinot Noir 10+ yrs
Phone: (02) 6230 2592 **Fax:** (02) 6230 2592	**Est:** 1986 **Vine Ha:** 5 **Cases:** 2,000	Chardonnay 5 yrs
Email: pankhurst@ozemail.com.au	**Public Hours:** 10am-5pm w/e, p/h & by appointment	Sauvignon Blanc-Semillon 3 yrs
Owner: Allan & Christine Pankhurst	**Principal Wines** **Potential**	Cabernet 10 yrs

Lake George

On the shores of Lake George lies the historic Lake George Vineyard & Winery, the pioneer vineyard and winery, started by Scientist and wine legend Dr Edgar Riek in 1971.

Although Edgar has sold the property to the Karelas Family, proprietors of Manuels-Potatoes, a Canberra institution, he remains as winemaker. On my visit during vintage he was busy with Sam and Bill Karelas, who were absorbing every word and deed, as they made the wines together with the master. I tried an exquisite Muscat and a 98 Pinot Noir which had no additives or acid or sulphur and no fining or filtering, a completely natural wine and of gold medal standard. Look for Lake George wines, this is an icon producer.

Address: Fedral Highway COLLECTOR 2581	Est: 1971 Vine Ha: 3.5 Cases: 750	Lake George Semillon	3 yrs
Phone: (02) 4848 0039 Fax: (02) 4848 0039	Principal Varieties: Chardonnay, Pinot Noir,	Lake George Cabernet Sauvignon	7-10 yrs
Email: sam@lakegeorgewinery.com.au	Cabernet Sauvignon, Merlot, Semillon	Lake George Merlot	7-10 yrs
WWW: www.lakegeorgewinery.com.au	**Principal Wines** **Potential**	Lake George Pinot Noir	3-5 yrs
Winemaker: Angus Campbell	Lake George Chardonnay 5 yrs	Lake George Botrytis Semillon	10+ yrs

Lark Hill

Definitely the highest profile winery in the Canberra District is the Lark Hill winery established by Dr David and Sue Carpenter in 1978. They process over 100 tonnes of grapes, one of the largest crushes in the district. Winemakers Dave and Sue also make wine for a number of other produces.

Lark Hill is on the top of the escarpment overlooking Lake George, at an altitude of 860m. The site is particularly suited to Riesling, Chardonnay and Pinot Noir, for which Lark Hill has forged an enviable reputation. Lark Hill also produce an excellent Méthode

Champenoise. The 1998 Pinot Noir I tasted was magnificent, loads of cherry fruit, gamey and spicy with a long, long palate. The 1996 Cabernet Merlot was just superb; the other wines in their range are all very good.

Address: RMB 281 Bungendore Road	Owners/ Winemakers: Dave & Sue Carpenter	Pinot Noir	5-10 yrs
BUNGENDORE 2621	Est: 1978 Vine Ha: 10	Shiraz	3-5 yrs
Phone: (02) 6238 1393 Fax: (02) 6238 1393	Public Hours: 10am-5pm, daily	Cabernet Merlot	5-10 yrs
Email: larkhill@dynamite.com.au	**Principal Wines** **Potential**	Riesling up to	10 yrs
WWW: www.larkhill.com.au	Chardonnay 5-10 yrs	Sauvignon Blanc	2-3 yrs

Murrumbateman

Duncan Leslie has created a little piece of vinous paradise. Apart from his boutique winery and the 9-acre vineyard he tends himself, he also has a licensed Restaurant, Function Centre and the Vine View Gallery that showcases regional Canberra art.

On my visit the autumnal scene was an absolute picture, with the colourful leaves and filtered light through the trees adding to the already pretty place.

Duncan has won tourism awards in 1995, 1996 and 1997 and I am sure will win many more. His wines including, chardonnay, sauvignon blanc, riesling, cabernet sauvignon and shiraz have also won many medals, he also makes a mead. There are so many reasons to come and enjoy his warm hospitality.

Address: Barton Highway MURRUMBATEMAN 2582	Est: 1972 Vine Ha: 5 Cases: 1,500	Sauvignon Blanc	6 yrs
Phone: (02) 6227 5584 Fax: (02) 6227 5987	Public Hours: 10am-5pm (Except Tues-Wed)	Cabernet Sauvignon	8 yrs
Email: cabsavleslie@ozemail.com.au	**Principal Wines** **Potential**	Cabernet Merlot	8 yrs
Winemaker: Duncan Leslie	Chardonnay 5 yrs	Shiraz 8 yrs	Rose 5 yrs

Hardy's Kamberra

The first land granted in the region now known as Canberra, was to Joshua John Moore in 1824, he named his property Canberry after hearing the local Aboriginals using the term Kamberra.

In 1901 following Federation the search for the site for a National Capital began. In 1908 Canberra was chosen and American Walter Burley Griffin won the competition to design the Capital in 1911.

The establishment of the Canberra wine region is attributed to John Richard Hardy, who in 1853 planted a vineyard at Hardwicke near Yass. Ironically in that same year, one of the founders of the Australian wine industry and J R Hardy's namesake Thomas Hardy, planted his first vines on his property Bankside, on the banks of the River Torrens in Adelaide, South Australia.

The Canberra/Yass wine region unfortunately ground to a halt in the latter half of the nineteenth century, due to reduced trade restrictions between the states following Federation, the Depression of 1893 and the predominant demand for fortified wines produced in the warmer areas.

The winegrowing renaissance in Canberra began in the 1970's and today there are 24 wineries and many more vineyards in the region.

BRL Hardy has long taken an interest in the region. In fact I saw a photograph of my father Thomas Walter Hardy on the wall of Helm's winery. It was taken in the 1970's,

my father was standing alongside Ken Helm offering support to the fledgling Canberra wine industry. My grandfather Tom Mayfield Hardy lost his life in the Kyeema air disaster in 1938, on his way to a National Wine Industry meeting in Canberra. There is even a winery named Kyeema at Murrumbateman.

For many years Hardys have sourced fruit from the Canberra region, some of which has found its way into its flagship Eileen Hardy wines.

The Kamberra Wine Company was established in 2000, as a result of this long held belief and commitment to the region and its potential. The complex, including a cellar door, winery, art gallery and restaurant, is located just five minutes from the centre of the city, on the edge of the Canberra racecourse, amongst 6 acres of

landscaped gardens, waterways and an outdoor ampitheatre.

The Kamberra Wine Company is the gateway to the Canberra wine district, featuring information and displays on all 24 regional wineries. Kamberra and Meeting Place wines are available for tasting at the cellar door and winery tours are available by appointment. The Kamberra range is made solely from fruit sourced in the Canberra region, while the Meeting Place wines also include fruit from districts further afield.

Fine regional food from areas such as Batemans bay, the Southern Highlands, Cowra and Bethungra is served in the "Meeting Place Bistro", while the complex also caters for functions, seminars and concerts.

The Kamberra Wine Company is the national capital's meeting place.

Other NSW Areas

near Shoalhaven Heads and Nowra.

Other emerging regions, with wine quality reputation growing fast and large plantings such as the New England area around Tenterfield demonstrate the potential of NSW wines from regions with higher altitudes.

Vineyards stretch to the north through Port Macquarie, where one of the state's most heralded wine producers, Cassegrain, has a large winery and restaurant complex, right up to the Queensland border. One can only admire the intrepid souls who have so diligently sought out the regional conditions and micro-climates and who prove that, with attention to site and variety, and in caring hands, the vine is a marvellous plant, always able to produce fine wines with the right love and attention applied.

Being the first Australian State, and the first wine-producing State, established in Australia with the arrival of vines with the first fleet, New South Wales has vineyards in all areas, including the far west. As well as the main wine-producing regions, excellent wines are found in the cool south near Bega, with Grevillea Estate, and on the mid-south coast

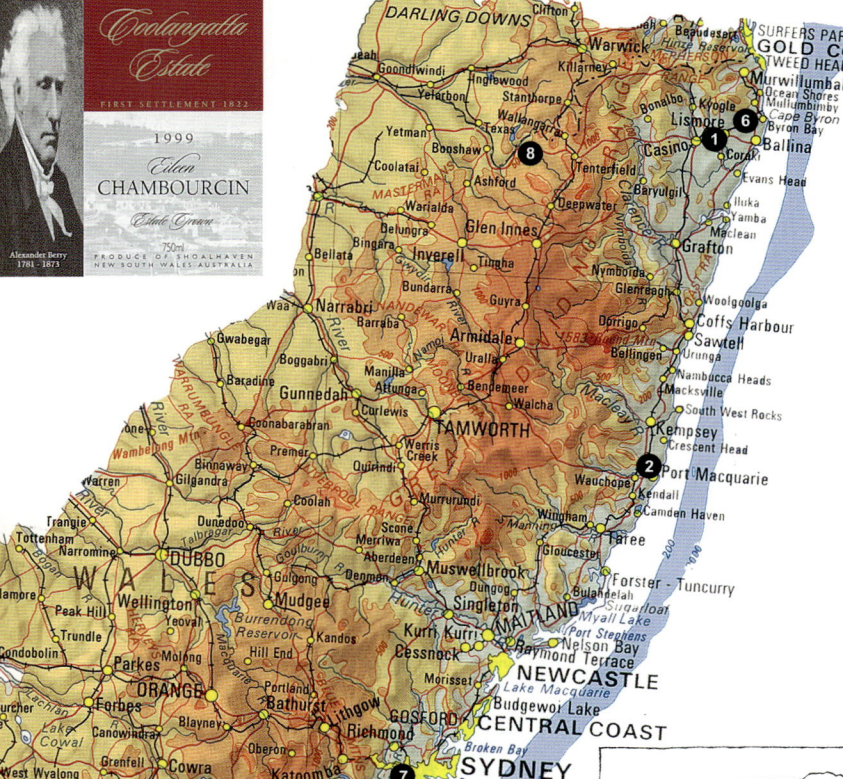

Other NSW Areas

1. Australian Macadamia
2. Cassegrain Wines
3. Charles Sturt University
4. Cobbitty Wines
5. Coolangatta Estate
6. Pacific Plantations
7. Primo Smallgoods
8. Reedy Creek Wines

Coolangatta Estate

On the temperate coast a couple of hours south of Sydney the new wine region of Shoalhaven has emerged. The convict built Coolangatta Estate dates back to the regions founding in 1822 by Alexander Berry.

Energetic wine enthusiast Greg Bishop has a 10 hectare vineyard and is making some fine wines, he also has a superb award winning function and conference centre with accommodation, Alexander's Restaurant and the Great Hall for banquets, there is a 9 hole golf course. The vineyard is planted to chardonnay, semillon, sauvignon blanc, verdelho, shiraz, cabernet sauvignon, merlot and sangiovese chambourcin and already boasts many medal-winning wines. The wines are made at Tyrrells.

This historic pretty estate nestles between the coast and the "Coolangatta" mountain. If in Sydney the drive to this idyllic escape is truly breathtaking and worthy of the effort.

			Principal Wines	Potential
Address: 1335 Bolong Road SHOALHAVEN HEADS 2535	Mark Richardson		Coolangatta Estate Semillon	10 yrs
Phone: (02) 4448 7131	**Est:** 1988 **Vine Ha:** 10		Elizabeth Berry Cabernet Sauvignon	8 yrs
Fax: (02) 4448 7997	**Cases:** 5,000		Coolangatta Estate Vintage Port	15 yrs
Email: coolangatta@shoalhaven.net.au	**Public Hours:** 10am-5pm, daily		Alexander Berry Chardonnay	6 yrs
Owner: Greg Bishop	**Principal Varieties:** Chardonnay, Sauvignon Blanc, Verdelho, Semillon, Cabernet		Coolangatta Estate Chambourcin	4 yrs
Winemaker: Andrew Spinaze &	Sauvignon, Shiraz, Merlot, Chambourcin		Coolangatta Estate Verdelho	5 yrs

Reedy Creek

Norina De Stefani is a strong and determined woman; her late husband was a hardworking and courageous man, and a former alpine soldier. With Norina they carved out a rural enterprise from rugged country in an isolated area, west of Tenterfield in northern New South Wales. The main crop was tobacco for 25 years, until the federal government bought back tobacco quotas in 1994. Vineyard plantings commenced in 1969 and a total of 16-acres has been planted to date, including some interesting varieties such as durif, malbec, mataro and white italia.

Norina and her son Nick, who is studying viticulture at Charles Sturt University, look after the very healthy vineyard.

The wines have already received critical acclaim the 1998 Chardonnay was awarded top ranking from Winestate Magazine with 5 stars, I found it had lots of exotic tropical flavours with a lovely fresh French baguette toastiness and a hazelnut/cashew finish. Their 1998 Shiraz/Mouvedre was equally impressive with dark cherries and chocolate and ironically with a hint of herbaceous tobacco, a complex wine; I noted it of gold medal standard.

Luckily although isolated Reedy Creek is near the Glenlyon Dam tourist-fishing park that receives 40,000 visitors each year so hopefully their cellar door will benefit; the wines so far are certainly stunning.

		Principal Wines	Potential
Address: Reedy Creek via Tenterfield TENTERFIELD 2372	**Winemaker:** Bruce Humphrey Smith	Reedy Creek Bianco Alpino	2-4 yrs
	Est: Vineyard 1969, Cellar door 1997	Reedy Creek Rosso Alpino	2-4 yrs
Phone: (02) 6737 5221 **Fax:** (02) 6737 5200	**Vine Ha:** 8	Reedy Creek Unwooded Chardonnay	2-5 yrs
Email: reedycreekwines@halenet.com.au	**Cases:** 2,500	Reedy Creek Chardonnay	2-8 yrs
WWW: www.reedycreekwines.com.au	**Public Hours:** 9am-5pm, daily	Reedy Creek Old Vine Shiraz	5-10 yrs
Owner: De Stefani Family	**Principal Wines** Potential	Reedy Creek Shiraz Mourvedre	5-10 yrs

Primo Smallgoods

The journey that has taken Primo to its place as the number one smallgoods producer in Australia has been long and hard.

In a small village just outside the small town of Miskolc in Hungary some 180 years ago an entrepreneurial resident by the name of Lederer began trading with cattle, grain and some meat with his neighbours. His children were influenced and their children, generation after generation. In 1957 Andrew Lederer and his family migrated to Australia following the Soviet invasion of Hungary. He brought with him the families secret recipes for continental smallgoods, cured hams and bacon.

He began a small deli business in the chic Sydney suburb of Annandale. It wasn't long before news of his great produce spread far and wide, particularly amongst Europeans who made up the large wave of post war migration to Australia.

Andrew then founded a large smallgoods business before selling to Japanese interests and putting all his efforts and knowledge into creating Primo with partners John Hunt, Paul Lederer, Steven Lederer and David Beverley. Their aim evident by the name Primo was to be number one in size and quality. In 1985 they started operating in Homebush with a staff of 37. In 1998 it became time to move and build a huge, state of the art plant at Chullora in part to make way for the Olympic site. The

staff had grown to 400 and they were the biggest smallgoods producer and exporter in Australia.

The new plant is astounding, when I visited in late 2000 I was amazed. $60 million has been spent to create the world's finest, safest and most efficient meat processing facility. Quality control and work practices are leading the world.

What have been Primo's secrets for this successful giant step forward? I'd say it is the Lederer's insistence on care and quality at every step of the process and the long serving loyal workforce they have inspired and educated over many years. A high percentage of staff have been with the family for over 20 years.

The equipping of the plant has been

a huge undertaking, but even here it has been many of Primo's long serving suppliers with special relations with the company, who have helped make it all happen. For instance Andrew Lederers relationship with the Globas group goes back 40 years. Co founder, the late Paul Stern, started making the first man made sausage casings in 1949. Andrew asked Paul to supply an uneconomic small run of 500 casings, this was done without question and the Lederer's have never forgotten it. Paul's children now deal with Andrew's nephew and Managing Director Paul Lederer and his staff.

Primo has now grown to a yearly turnover of $250 million plus. The plant processes over 1500 pig carcasses per day plus beef and veal processing 250 tonnes a day and a further 60 tonnes at their Brisbane plant. 280 different products are produced both cooked and cured such as Prosciutto and Pancetta. The factory is basically divided into two different areas totally sealed off. All services such as maintenance; drains, staff and staff amenities are separate. Nearly all maintenance is located in the rooftops to make it

easy for the staff and save invading the hermetically sealed production areas. All positive air pressure to stop any airborne bacteria entering.

So what does this mean for us the consumer? a fabulous range of tasty, healthy and safe smallgoods. Traditional leg ham products both boned and boneless, plain cooked, smoked or with honey and mustard Flavours. There is a full range of rolled leg hams including a 97% fat free 'Lite Ham'. There are also 0.5kg and 0.4kg portions and pre pack units of only 100 gramms sliced which also includes roast pork, beef, silverside and other processed products and naturally champagne ham.

Bacon of all sorts, pork loin, smoked spec, neck and so many other products such as cured and air dried Prosciutto and Pancetta.

Primo produces a huge range of salami's, bratwursts and other wursts of all sorts. Naturally Frankfurts and the 'little boy' cocktail variety. The Lederer's haven't forgotten their Hungarian origin either with a range of Csabai sausages highly seasoned with paprika, which can be eaten like salami or even barbequed. I love their Spanish style Chorizos · red hot and loaded with paprika.

Primo opeates two abattoirs, one in Port Wakefield and the other in Scone, and is looking to buy more in the future.

Primo are making great strides on the export market with growth in Asian markets particularly strong.

I noticed in some of the 1950's and 60's photographs from the Lederer archives that wine was often present in the tasting promotions they held in the delis. Just as the post war European influx helped change and enrich our wine drinking habits so has it enriched our eating habits.

As I write this feature my mouth waters with the thoughts of the huge range of red, white and sparkling wines I could enjoy with Primo's extraordinary range and the meals I could create around them both, so "Bon·Appetit".

Cassegrain

Cassegrain Wines was established in 1980 when Gerard and Francoise Cassegrain planted a vineyard near Port Macquarie, on the New South Wales Mid-North Coast, heralding a rebirth of viticulture in the Hastings River district. They believed that the district's temperate maritime climate would be ideally suited to the production of premium table wines, a belief justified by the awards and accolades that Cassegrain's wines have received since production of the first vintage in 1984.

Their son John, an oenology graduate from South Australia's renowned Roseworthy College and rapidly emerging as one of Australia's most highly regarded winemakers, was ideally suited to taking the helm, in a winery which blended the best of Old World tradition with New World technology. He had worked 10 vintages with Tyrrells winery in the Hunter Valley, experienced vintages in burgundy and the Loire Valley, and had presented a thesis on natural fermentation at California's Davis University.

John's winemaking philosophy is based very firmly on the belief that great wines are made in the vineyard and he put enormous emphasis on

ensuring that he has access to only the highest quality fruit. In the winery his principal aim is to ensure that the characteristic flavours of that premium fruit are maintained and enhanced during the winemaking process and delivered in the bottle to the consumer.

In early 2001 John and his wife, Eva, in conjunction with three partners, purchased the winery from the family and embarked on a new era for Cassegrain Wines. While they retain a solid commitment to utilising the best available fruit from Hastings River, they are also expanding their

horizons by sourcing grapes from other areas. Some of these areas, such as the Hunter Valley and Coonawarra, are well established as among the world's best. Others, especially the New England region just across the Great Dividing Range from Port Macquarie, are really only just emerging but offer exciting new vistas for winelovers.

Principal wine styles include semillon, chardonnay, verdelho, cabernet merlot and chambourcin. Chambourcin is a French hybrid red variety ideally suited to the Hastings' humid climate and produces soft, rich supple wines with a distinctive spicy flavour. Cassegrain's highly regarded Reserve Chambourcin is made from bio-dynamically grown fruit.

Cassae, a version of Cognac's famous Pineau-des-Charantes, is literally made from grape juice fortified with brandy. Chilled it makes an excellent aperitif and it can also be served with light desserts.

Cassegrain's winery features a splendid restaurant overlooking vineyards and gardens which boast 2,500 roses. If any winery has a claim to paradise in Australia, it's Cassegrain.

Address: 764 Fernbank Creek Road
PORT MACQUARIE 2444
Phone: (02) 6583 7777 **Fax:** (02) 6584 0354
Email: info@cassegrainwines.com.au
Owner: Private Company
Winemaker: John Cassegrain & Ben Wurst
Est: 2001 **Vine Ha:** 12

Cases: 45,000
Public Hours: 9am-5pm, daily (except Christmas Day & Good Friday)
Principal Varieties: Chardonnay, Semillon, Verdelho, Sauvignon Blanc, Pinot Noir, Chambourcin, Merlot, Shiraz, Cabernet Sauvignon, Cabernet Franc

Principal Wines	Potential
Chambourcin	5+ yrs
Semillon	5+ yrs
Chardonnay	2-5 yrs
Five Mile Hollow	2+ yrs
Merlot / Cabernet Franc	3+ yrs
Cassae	

Cobbitty Wines

vineyard at Cobbitty in 1964, this has now grown to 25 acres. Their Cobbitty vineyard is planted with barbera, shiraz, trebbiano, grenache and muscat with the remainder of grapes purchased from South Australia. John's son Joseph Cogno who runs the Middlebrook Winery at McLaren Vale, takes care of the premium end of the market producing wines under the new Cogno Brothers label.

The company has now diversified into the manufacturing of Wine Base Liqueurs that are produced on premise as substitutes for imported Liqueurs. The majority of all wines produced are for exclusive sale through cellar door, local bottle shops and restaurants.

Cogno Brothers · Cobbitty Wines is open every day for tastings and there are barbecue and picnic facilities, with a wide range of wines, as the family motto states "The best wine is the one you like".

The Cogno's arrived in Australia in 1950 and planted their 14-acre

Address: 40 Cobbitty Road COBBITTY 2570	**Winemaker:** John Cogno		5.30pm Sun
Phone: (02) 4651 2281 **Fax:** (02) 4651 2671	**Est:** 1964 **Vine Ha:** 5 **Cases:** 10,000		**Principal Varieties:** Trebbiano, Grenache,
Owner: Cogno Bros.	**Public Hours:** 9am-5.30pm, Mon-Sat; 12pm-		Muscat, Barbera, Shiraz

Charles Sturt University

Australia's first degree course in winemaking, Bachelor of Applied Science (Wine), was introduced by the Riverina College of Advanced Education, (now the Charles Sturt University) at Wagga Wagga in 1975. The course can be studied full-time or by external studies and there are currently 600 students enrolled. The winery has since been expanded and now processes around 500 tonnes each vintage, producing 20,000 cases under their own C.S.U. Label. Some of the multiple award winning wines are their Sparkling from Tumbarumba fruit, a Chardonnay from Cowra grapes and a Cabernet dominant red from the University vineyard at Wagga Wagga which now cover over 50 acres.

Brian Croser was the first winery director and the first crush was in 1977. Today winemaking is in the capable control of Greg Gallager formerly at Taltarni in Victoria. The winery and vineyard enterprise demonstrates an accountable commercial operation and provides stimulating training for those students fortunate enough to be employed (winery scholarship). In association with the formal teaching, the practical experience the students obtain will prepare them for challenging careers in the wine industry.

Address: Boorooma Street	**Public Hours:** Monday to Sunday 11am-4pm	Cabernet/Shiraz/Merlot	5-8 yrs
WAGGA WAGGA 2650	**Principal Varieties:** Cabernet Sauvignon,	Limited release Cabernet Sauvignon	10+ yrs
Phone: (02) 6933 2435 **Fax:** (02) 6933 4072	Chardonnay, Merlot, Pinot Noir, Semillon,	Limited release Shiraz	10 yrs
Est: 1977 **Vine Ha:** 25	Shiraz, Tinta Coa, Touriga, Traminer	Pinot Noir - Chardonnay Sparking	5 yrs
Cases: 15,000	**Principal Wines** **Potential**	Chardonnay	3 yrs

Australia's Macadamia

From the seeds of an Australian rainforest tree the world has discovered a health nut with an irresistible taste for today's modern lifestyle.

Australia's indigenous people feasted on this seed, known as Kindal Kindal, for thousands of years. Now known as the macadamia, it is the only native Australian bush food

to be developed commercially. Chefs and food lovers alike are finding a place for macadamias in recipes, from stir fry to parfait, or as a simple, delicious snack.

Macadamias are mainly grown in the lush subtropical rainforests of northern New South Wales and south east Queensland where the original native trees flourished.

The unique taste of the macadamia and its soft 'crunch' are making the nut a winner with the public and recent scientific research suggests it can make a great contribution to

a healthy diet. The oil in macadamias is not only cholesterol free, but actually helps to lower total blood cholesterol.

In fact, a handful a day can significantly reduce the risk of heart disease. On top of this macadamias are high in fibre and contain the important anti oxidant vitamin E.

Australian macadamia nuts are widely available in supermarkets, health food shops and on the nut stand at most good liquor outlets. There is nothing better than a handful of macadamias with a glass of your favourite wine!

Australian Macadamia Society
Address: Level 1,113 Dawson Street, LISMORE NSW 2480
Phone: (02) 6622 4933 **Fax:** (02) 6622 4932
Email: admin@macadamias.org
WWW: www.macadamias.org

DID YOU KNOW?
Macadamias are native to Australia. The nut is grown between Nambucca Heads in NSW and Atherton in Queensland. Australia's production area is 14,000ha planted with 4 million trees. Australia produces more than 40% of the world's production and exports more than 70% of its crop.
Major destinations for the Aussie nut are USA, Japan and Germany.

Pacific Plantations

Pacific Plantations has been involved in the Macadamia Nut industry since the mid 1970's. It's Macadamia Nut Plantation, processing plant and confectionery factory are located in Northern New South Wales. The rich volcanic soils and temperate climate are ideal for growing this Australian native nut. Begun by the MacRae family, famous for their Speedo swimwear, Pacific Plantations is Australia largest privately owned Macadamia Plantation and Processing Plant.

The Macadamia Nut is wholly indigenous to Australia, discovered in the early 1800's near Brisbane it was named after Dr John Macadam, the first secretary of the Philosophical Institute in Melbourne. Ludwig Leichhardt, in his first romp around Queensland brought the nut back to Victoria and presented it to the Herbarium, who promptly grew a tree or two. Another free settler, Walter Hill, gathered the nuts from a rainforest and gave them to a young chap who worked for him with instructions to crack the nut so that it could be grown. The young lad cracked the nut and ate it, informing his boss that it had a delicious taste indeed. His boss, who had been told by the Aborigines that the nut was poisonous, feared for the boys life but after a day or two, the lad showing no ill effect, the boss

gobbled a couple down himself. The Australian Bush Nut was on its way to becoming one of the most popular eating nuts in the world.

Unfortunately, Australia wasn't in the vanguard of promoting the nut to the world. Plantations in Hawaii, grown from Australian seed, took the honours and it is only now that Australia is proving to the world that its own nut, grown in Australia, is of better quality than those grown outside its natural habitat. The Macadamia Nut is principally marketed in the USA but also in Asia and Europe.

The Macadamia tree comes in many different varieties and each variety yields different quantities of kernel at different times of the season. Plantations consist of many varieties. A Macadamia tree can effectively produce Macadamias on a commercial basis until the age of around 50 years. The mature tree is approximately 35 feet high and 32 feet in diameter. The Macadamia Tree produces its crop on a seasonal basis, picking from March until September.

The Nut is only ready for harvest once it has dropped to the ground, it consists of the kernel which is surrounded by a very hard shell, this is also covered by a green husk. This nut in husk is picked off the ground by highly efficient mechanical

harvesters, these machines can run up to 16 hours a day 7 days a week, ensuring that the freshest produce reaches the consumer.

The nuts are then put through highly efficient dehusking plant. The nuts are then stored in large silos at a certain kernel moisture content. Pacific Plantations prides itself on its unique drying system, which dehumidifies the nuts and reduces the moisture content using low temperature. Once dried, the

Macadamia still in its shell is sent into the processing plant. Once the various styles are sorted, they are dusted and then either packed in bulk packs, or sent to Pacific Plantations value added facility.

Macadamia Nuts contain polyunsaturates, protein, carbohydrates, fibre, water, calcium, phosphorus, iron, thiamine, niacin and riboflavin, but no cholesterol plus its oil is of the good gang · mono-unsaturated.

Macadamias go extremely well with Methode Champenoise Wines as their creamy taste and texture finds an ideal balance with the crisp fruit flavours. They are also excellent companions for the richer styles of Chardonnay. In cooking both savoury and sweet dishes, can be enhanced by their imaginative use.

Name: Pacific Plantation
Address: Friday Hut Road BROOKLETt (via

Bangalow) 2479
Phone: (02) 6687 1472

Fax: (02) 6687 1075
Email: pacplant@bigpond.com

Although one of the last settled states in Australia, by 1887 South Australia was leading Australian wine production.

In 1837, only one year after the state's founding, J.B. Hach and George Stevenson planted vine cuttings from Tasmania in North Adelaide. Later that same year Richard Hamilton planted his Ewell vineyards in what is now the suburb of Marion. Shortly afterwards, John Reynell planted his first vines at Reynella.

In 1844 Dr Christopher Rawson Penfold established his Grange vineyard at Magill. The 1840's were the period when the German Lutheran immigrants began arriving in the Barossa Valley and Johann Gramp planted his Jacob's Creek Vineyard. English immigrant and brewer Samuel Smith established Yalumba in 1849.

During the 1850's, the wake of the gold rush saw a flurry of new vineyards, Thomas Hardy, Jesse Norman and the Holbrook family all commenced winemaking and established vineyards in what are now inner suburbs of Adelaide:

Woodley's vineyard was established at Glen Osmond in 1858.

Back to the Barossa, where Joseph Seppelt commenced planting in 1851 and Samuel Hoffmann even earlier in 1847. The names of the early pioneers of wine in South Australia have lived on and continue to dominate the wine scene in the state. One of these early pioneers, like many others, was a medical practitioner, Dr Alexander Kelly, who planted his Trinity Vineyard at Morphett Vale in 1843. An entrepreneur at heart, he later formed the Tintara Vineyard Company and planted extensive vineyards at McLaren Vale, later to be bought out of bankruptcy by Thomas Hardy.

We must not to forget Clare, where John Horrocks put his first vines in the ground in 1840; he was only 22 years of age, but managed to convince many others to plant vines in this beautiful valley. By the 1860's more than 6,000 acres of vines covered many areas of the state. In fact, the first wine surplus was at hand and the vignerons of the state made their first assault on the English market. The logistics and

time involved meant this push had a very limited affect, thus many growers and suppliers to the larger wineries were forced to make their own wine or see their grapes go to waste. Unfortunately there was a flood of cheap, poorly-made wine which affected the industry's reputation badly for a period; however, the earlier established companies and well known names today such as Hardy, Seppelt, Penfold, Orlando and Yalumba continued to focus on quality and grew stronger through the period, although overall production decreased dramatically.

South Australian wine began to secure markets in the other states; this progress was halted somewhat late in the century with tariffs being imposed by NSW and Victoria on South Australian wine, by then the nation's leading producer. At this time the dreaded vine louse phylloxera struck the vineyards in Victoria and to a degree, New South Wales. South Australia being more remote and on lighter soils, escaped this blight which destroyed other states' vineyards. In fact, South Australia remains one of the few

producing regions of the world where phylloxera has never struck; vine quarantine regulations are understandably strict.

It was with great interest that I read a collection of contemporary "letters to the editor" contained in a scrapbook kept by my great-great-grandfather at Bankside in Adelaide. Dated 1869-1870 that chronicled the differences of opinion in certain matters pertaining to wine and vines between Messrs. Hardy and Seppelt of South Australia and Messrs. Morris and Chambers of Victoria. By the outbreak of the World War I, South Australia was producing 18 million litres of wine, more than half the nation's output. Fortified wines had started to make in-roads in the market; they were easier to keep pure and in good condition and during the next 50 years dominated the wine scene in South Australia.

It was the influx of European immigrants after World War II that started to tip the scales back in favour of table wines and changed our drinking habits; it was only in 1970 when table wine production actually exceeded that of fortified wines and the culture of nearly

universal enjoyment of table wines with meals began. Development over the last two decades in the South East of the state started with Coonawarra in the early 1950's with Samuel Wynn and also Ron Haselgrove from Mildara reviving Coonawarra as a wine region, almost 100 years after John Riddoch had founded the regions' wine industry as part of his 'Penola Fruit Colony'. Padthaway, Cape Jaffa, more recently Wrattonbully north east of Coonawarra, the Wirrega/Bordertown area and other parts of this region, from Bordertown down to Mt. Gambier and across to Robe, promise this Limestone coast is set to be a huge world-renowned quality wine region.

Langhorne Creek near the mouth of the mighty Murray River has a cool but mild climate and has had vineyards since the last century. Stonyfell with their Metala and Wolf Blass have shown in the last few decades the capabilities of the region. Huge vineyard plantings here are continuing.

The resurgence of wine growing in the Adelaide Hills has been quite remarkable with modern day

pioneers such as Brian Croser, Stephen Henschke and Tim Knappstein forging the way. South Australia richly deserves its title of "The Wine State", producing more than 50% of Australia's wines. With suitable land and climate, water is really the only problem in the driest state on the world's driest continent.

South Australians are determined, inventive and proud of the impact their wines are having on the world market. In 2001 the S.A. Wine Exports totalled $1,007 million up 24% on the previous year. The state's wine industry enjoys over 65% of the nation's wine exports.

The South Australian Government is understandably very supportive of its wine industry and the burgeoning wine tourism industry. Naturally food and particularly seafood has been fast growing, in 2000 seafood exports from South Australia's ocean catch and aquaculture amounted to $438 million up 21%, meat $209 million up 32%, horticultural and other food products are also growing enormously. The state is fast developing, cheers to South Australia's wine and food success story.

Adelaide Plains

Although this area saw the birth of South Australia's wine industry, Adelaide's urban sprawl has all but wiped out viticulture within the greater metropolitan area, however vineyards and wineries still remain.

The Magill Cellars and Vineyards, the spiritual home of Grange Hermitage, along with the original home of founder Dr. Christopher Rawson Penfold, remain an active part of Australian wine and are protected by National Trust classification.

Richard Hamilton's original Ewell Vineyards, planted in 1837, a year after the state's settlement, have fallen to housing and a transport depot but the century old Marion Vineyard has recently been revived by Dr Richard Hamilton a sixth generation direct descendant, Patritti's in Dover Gardens are still going strong along with Crestview, Hardy's Chateau Reynella and Mt. Hurtle in the Happy Valley regional area.

Many changes have occurred in the consolidation of the wine industry of South Australia. Hamilton's moved to the Eden Valley, Woodleys went to the Barossa and were taken over by Seppelts and Normans have expanded by moving to Angle Vale as well as buying the Coolawin Winery at Clarendon in the Adelaide Hills. Hardys moved from their Bankside Winery after it was destroyed by fire in 1904. They established Mile End Cellars close to the city and Champagne Cellars in Currie Street in the city.

In 1983, Hardys moved lock, stock and barrel to Reynella and the former

property of early settler, Walter Reynell. The wonderful old homestead and Chateau were restored and a new winery, bottling and storage facilities were constructed.

Angoves had extensive vineyards and a winery at Tea Tree Gully, a north-eastern Adelaide suburb. Their Tregrehan vineyard was famed for its red wine but unfortunately, and much to the disgust of the Angove family, it was compulsorily acquired by the State Housing Commission. Douglas A. Tolley of Pedare fame had an operating winery and vineyard until 1995.

The significant vineyards of the Adelaide Plains area are now found around Angle Vale near Gawler and around the entrance to the Barossa Valley. There have been grapes grown in this area since the first days of the industry.

The new Valley Growers Co-op Ltd took over a foundering winery in 1984 at Angle Vale, employing Colin Glaetzer who produced some great wines, stylishly packaged. This operation is now named

Barossa Estates and is in the process of moving to the Barossa Valley to a huge new facility near Seppeltsfield.

Norman's also have a large vineyard at Angle Vale called Evanston Estate, where many grape varieties are planted, and in 1973, in the same area, the Grilli family established Primo Estate. The region is very warm, but with the moderating effects of sea breezes from St. Vincents Gulf the climate is not too harsh.

The soil is the result of a rich alluvial flood plain and fruit picked at the right time, and handled well, produces award-winning wines. However, with the heat and low rainfall, irrigation is essential. Adelaide Plains is renowned for producing high quality wines. At the northern end of the region lies the famous Roseworthy Agricultural College where so many of Australia's great winemakers have trained. The Adelaide Plains is also a huge fruit and vegetable growing area and many successful food producers have fast expanding operations in the region with booming export business.

Adelaide Plains

1. Australian Cider
2. Chilli Cap
3. Coopers Brewery
3. Leabrook Farms
4. Haighs Chocolates
5. Joes Poultry
6. Macro Meats
7. Mitani Spices
8. Vilis Cakes & Pies

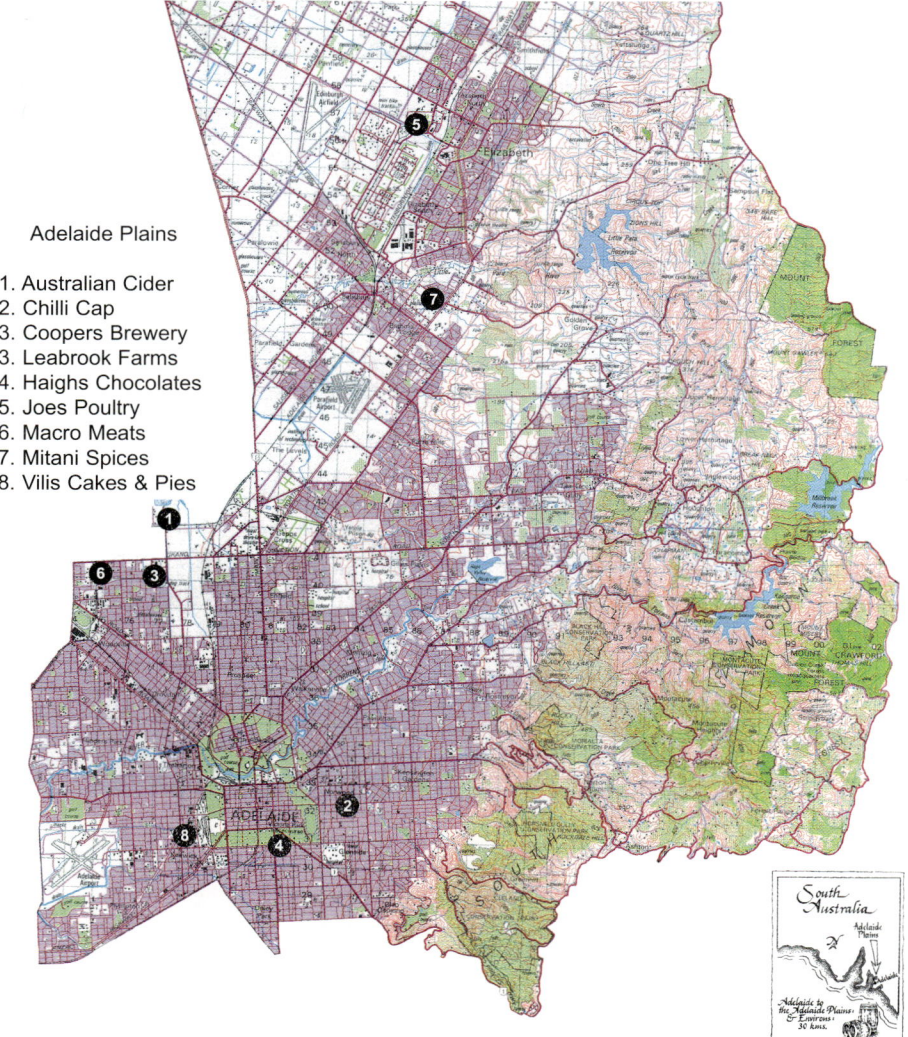

Chilli Cap

A Gourmet Delight to take your cap off to. Chilli Cap is a great South Australian culinary success. Meghan Johns entertained guests many a time and commenced the evening with serving what she described as her Chilli Cap.

A mouth-watering blend of Fresh Capsicum, Fresh Chilli, Fresh Lemon Juice, Sugar, Vinegar, Garlic and Almonds to add texture and taste.

Meghan's guests enjoyed the taste and the versatility of the Gourmet Dip, which made Meghan decide to extend the enjoyment to consumers all over Australia - providing The Perfect Entertainer on a commercial basis.

Whilst creating the original Chilli Cap, Meghan had a few strong culinary principles she wanted to adapt to the product and these were that the product would be manufactured in South Australia, fresh ingredients would be used, it would be preservative free, cholesterol free, suitable for vegetarians and 99.5% fat free. The product would be versatile and could be served hot or cold.

The heat really did rise in the kitchen when Meghan initially supplied Retail Gourmet Outlets Nationally with the product. The demand from consumers for more heat, gave Meghan the vision to create Hot Stuff her second product on the market, with distribution of both products throughout Gourmet Centres around Australia.

You will find this attractively packaged product on shelves, as the products only needs refrigerating after opening. The long use by date giving consumers the product guarantee they deserve.

The serving suggestions for Chilli Cap are only inhibited by your imagination. Serve as a glaze for meat, chicken and seafood, delightful on oysters. A hot sauce for vegetables and pasta. Liven up your salads. Add to your special stir-fry or as designed originally as a cap over cream cheese.

Try Chilli Cap, it's The Perfect Entertainer.

Address: 64 Kensington Road
ROSE PARK 5067
Phone: (08) 8332 8018 **Fax:** (08) 8333 1211

Email: chillicap@dwjohns.com.au
Owner: Chilli Cap Pty Ltd
Est: May 1997

Public Hours: Normal Week Days
Principal Varieties: Chilli Cap Mild, Chilli Cap Hot Stuff

Coopers Brewery

The secret of brewing is much like winemaking. The brewers palate must be like the palate of a winemaker. History plays an instrumental part in the uniqueness of the beer. Cooper's is brewed with a yeast strain that was harnessed over 90 years ago and has been kept alive to this day. This yeast provides a secondary fermentation in the style of champagne, which leaves the characteristic cloudy sediment, and it's this that some folk consider to be the most nutritious part (although claiming nutritional value sounds suspiciously like a good excuse to drink more beer).

The Coopers still craft beer the traditional way and still have least one family member in charge of the brewery.

Dear Brother,
   We are now in the Brewing Business.

Those were the words written by Thomas Cooper to his Brother in England after establishing his Brewing business in South Australia in 1862.

His talent as a Brewer was discovered when his wife asked him to brew up a batch of ale from an old family recipe to help cure an illness. The ale was well accepted, he found himself brewing and delivering by horse and cart the now world famous Coopers Sparkling Ale and Extra Stout. The loyalty of customers grew and grew.
A family of tradition has ensured and

there is now a real family of beers. Thomas Cooper died in 1897 and the brewing continued with the expertise of his sons John, Christopher, Samuel and Stanley.

Coopers today is Australia's sole remaining family owned brewery which has survived the great depression of the 1930's and the turmoil and trouble of two world wars. The strength of the Coopers Family shows in the family of beers they have created over the years.

Coopers Sparkling Ale is Australia's world class ale with a solid head. Its distinctive, full-bodied flavour is enhanced by a soft fruity character and sediment, which give it its famous cloudy appearance.

Coopers Best Extra Stout - a fine example of a robust, full flavoured stout. Its unique, rich and dark texture comes from our specially roasted black malt.

Coopers Original Pale Ale has a full fruity ale flavour. Naturally fermented in the "Burton-on-Trent" style, its secondary fermentation creates a cloudy, fine residue in the finished products.

Coopers Dark Ale is another of our naturally brewed ales. A judicious blend of roasted and chocolate malts are used to give Dark Ale its unique flavour.

Coopers Light - Never light on flavour, Coopers Light is our popular

low alcohol beers with tons of character. Its strong, malty style belies its low alcohol content.

Coopers Genuine Draught is a full and flavoursome beer displaying a dry and clean palate with a good "bitter" after taste. If offers traditional "off the tap" flavour that's crisp, dry and very refreshing.

Coopers DB has a refreshingly crisp, dry taste that's been created by eliminating the residual sugars during a double pitching of the yeast.

Coopers Extra Strong Vintage Ale is designed to improve with age (its flavour will improve for up to 18 months). Because each vintage is available only as a limited release, it's an eagerly awaited beer each year.

Coopers Premium is a chill filtered ale, brewed using malted and unmalted grains to give a rounded and full-bodied palate, a golden colour and a good creamy head.

Thomas Cooper's Finest Export is a handcrafted brew of blended malts and hops. Maturation in Coopers cold cellars results in a beer with a smooth finish and brilliant clarity.

The Coopers family are a world-renowned brewing family and fine South Australians. I am proud to count as friends and have shared more than the odd glass of Black Velvet with - Champagne blended with Stout, what a drink to toast to!!

Leabrook Farms

In the cool cellars of Coopers not only are the many tastes of Beer being brewed but too this hive of activity has become the home of Leabrook Farms pure Australian Honey.

The production of the sweet golden textures of Leabrook Farms honey is now around 2,500 tonnes a year. Just as wines are blended, the master Honey Blender, gently hovers over his honey like a doting parent with pride and passion, carefully filtering and blending to produce six of the best honeys in Australia.

The taste difference is enhanced by the secret ingredients the Bee itself adds. The Bees drawn from a range of secluded locations, which only the Bee Keepers and Blender know.

The Extended Honey Family - fine specific Flora Honeys are produced.

Leabrook Farms Blue Gum - The Blue Gum tree (Eucalyptus, Leucoxylan) grows in the forests and flat hilly areas in South Australia and Victoria. The honey itself displays a bright clear pale straw colour with a distinct flavour and his highly prized for its extraordinary density. Available in 325g and 500g jars.

Leabrook Farms River Red Gum - The River Red Gum tree (Eucalyptus Gamaldulensis) is the most common of all Eucalypt species. It grows along the banks of rivers, waterways and tributaries or any other areas where there is a high moisture content. The honey is light amber in appearance with a distinctive mild

wood flavour. Available in 325g and 500g jars.

Leabrook Farms Strawberry Clover - Strawberry Clover (Trifolium Repens) is a ground cover that grows chiefly in the South East region of Australia, where there is high rainfall and good moisture. The honey itself is a very light colour and has a sweet mild flavour and aroma. Available in 325g and 500g jars.

Leabrook Farms Yellow Box - The Yellow Box tree (Eucalyptus Melliodora) grows mainly in the slopes and tablelands of New South Wales, Victoria and Queensland. It is a dense aromatic honey. It has a clear golden colour and stores without crystallisation for long periods of time. Available in 325g and 500g jars.

Leabrook Farms Leatherwood - The Leatherwood tree (Eucryphia Lucidia and E Milligani) is unique to Tasmania. It grows in the forests along the West Coast of Tasmania, an area renown for its rugged landscape and high rainfall. The honey is light amber in colour and is renowned for its unique strong flavour and scented aroma. Available in 325g jar.

Leabrook Farms also produce a range of Blended Honeys.

Leabrook Farms Pure - At Leabrook Farms they believe in producing only the finest honeys. Our pure honey is a blend of specially selected honeys from around Australia, brought together to meet the flavour, colour

and aroma characteristics preferred by the majority of honey customers. Available in 325g, 500g and 1kg jars.

Leabrook Farms Squeeze Pack - At last, a squeeze pack, which really works. Now Leabrook Farms honey can be dispensed quickly, cleanly and efficiently, without the need for spoons or knives. The trick is a non-drip valve that stops the mess and dribbles normally associated with honey in jars. Never before has honey been so easy and fun to use! The durable plastic bottle can easily be stored upside down on its cap, ready for immediate use. Available in 500g plastic bottle.

Leabrook Farms Mixed Blossom - Like wines, each honey is different. This can depend on the types of blossoms and flowers the bee gathers the nectar from, climatic conditions and geographical regions. Mixed Blossom is our very special honey, carefully selected from a range of blossoms and flowers and then blended by our master blender in much the same way a winemaker blends grapes. The results is a honey of unrivalled quality. Available in 1.5kg can.

Haighs Chocolates

As the grape is to the vine so to is the Cocoa Bean to Chocolate. Like wine grapes, cocoa beans have regional characteristics. Haigh's select cocoa beans from exotic locations around the world.

Haigh's is the only retail chocolate company in Australia and one of only a handful in the world still making chocolates directly from the beans.

The characteristics of the Cocoa Bean depend on the variety, area of origin and the processing. From the selection of the beans Simon Haigh controls the blending and the processing as meticulously as any fine winemaker. Simon's highly developed sense of taste and smell is projected throughout each process providing for you the quality and uniqueness of Haigh's.

Founded in 1915 by Alfred Haigh, Haigh's Chocolates is now Australia's oldest family owned chocolate manufacturer.

In 1933, Alfred's son Claude took over as Managing Director. The Haigh's business grew as shops were opened in Hindley Street, Rundle Street, Glenelg Beach, Broken Hill, Gawler and Murray Bridge.

The war years saw rationing of supplies. Fortunately for Haigh's, Australia grew its own sugar and the production of boiled sweets continued. Haigh's delighted the Armed Forces by making wrapped toffees. John Haigh today's Chairman remembers packing them at night.

John Haigh was considering a university degree in veterinary science when he decided to join the Haigh's family business. He realised that the chocolate industry would be an interesting and challenging career; continuing the family tradition.

At 19 years of age he spent some time in Switzerland working with famous makers Lindt and Sprungli.

Today both John's sons Alister and Simon have taken the reins with him, running the company.

Simon is Chief Chocolatier he controls production at the Parkside factory in Adelaide.

The beans are roasted to extract the moisture and enhance the flavour, then fed into the winnower, which removes the outer husks and breaks the beans into small nibs. These are ground to a liquid in the nib mill, the mass is transferred to the melangeur, where icing sugar and pure cocoa butter for consistency are added. Milk powder is also included for milk chocolate.

The process continues in the roller-refiner, where the chocolate paste is

converted into a fine flake. This is placed in the conche for the final refinements, where paddles beat in the cocoa butter and lecithin for up to 72 hours. This is critical for the final smoothness of the chocolate.

Although the factory was enlarged in 1995, manufacturing is still done in small batches to ensure premium quality and freshness.

More than 50% of Haigh's chocolates are made by hand and many are individually dipped, a process now recognised in the industry as an artisan skill.

Simon and Alister spend time with each staff member to ensure they remain part of the vital Haigh's team.

Traditional recipes are still being used including the Original Chocolate

Fruits that company founder Alfred Haigh made back in the 1920s, above his Beehive Corner store.

Many new products have been introduced to meet ever changing tastes and trends. Sitting alongside old favourites such as Apricot Fruits or Ginger are new creations such as Cointreau truffles, Cappuccino Bars, Praline Centres, Liquorice Chocs (bullet sized pieces of dark liquorice coated in smooth milk chocolate), and Hot Cross Bun Chocolates, flavoured with fruit bun spice.

The Parkside factory is set up for small batches, enabling the production of more than 150 different products and the flexibility to quickly introduce new ones.

Wherever possible, Haigh's sources its ingredients in Australia · the world's finest ginger from Buderim in Queensland, stonefruit from South Australia's Riverland and nuts from Queensland. New centres introduced recently include blackberry jelly, plum liqueur, hazelnuts, brazil nuts and raisins.

It wouldn't be South Australia without wine, so in recent years Haigh's has introduced Champagne Truffles and Sparkling Shiraz Truffles.

In 1992, the Royal Melbourne Show introduced awards for chocolate-making. In the seven years since, Haigh's chocolates has won the Championship Award five times. In 1999, Haigh's won a record 13 gold medals for different products proving the consistency of quality across its range.

Haigh's was one of the first manufacturers to produce a chocolate Bilby. Haigh's has become the home of the Easter Bilby, with part proceeds of all Bilby sales going to the Rabbit Free Australia Foundation. Funds are also raised for endangered Frogs. The Haigh's Frog is their best selling item with more than a million being sold each year.

In Adelaide's city centre the warming phrase "meet me at Haigh's" is often heard, a phrase referring to the Beehive Corner, the landmark building that has been home to Haigh's since founded in 1915.

Haigh's also welcome you to their Visitor's Centre at Greenhill Road, Parkside which incorporates their factory viewing and interpretative area.

Macro Meats

Macro Meats Gourmet Game are true pioneers in the processing, wholesaling and exporting of Kangaroo Meats and Skins.

1987 marked the beginnings of what is now Australia's largest supply chain of Kangaroo Meat.

From nil consumption to a worldwide acceptance with a view to have Kangaroo placed on Menu's throughout the world. Ray and Rita Borda today's Managing Directors have lead this journey not only for their company Macro Meats Gourmet Game, but for the entire industry.

They began this journey by developing regulations, through committees and associations to set and to strengthen the establishment of the industry itself. Today we can see the results in the growth of the industry.

The culling, processing, distribution and consumption of Kangaroo needed to be addressed, Ray and Rita's passion and determination for Kangaroo has now assisted many in the true understanding of the industry. It was in 1990 when Kangaroo was recognised as a meat, this was the beginning of the first SA hygiene regulations for Kangaroo Meat.

Kangaroos are a natural and important resource of Australian wildlife and culture. Although a threat to some agricultural practices, there are approved Government management plans, which aim at a balanced approach toward sustaining an acceptable population. Of the forty-eight Kangaroo species only four are harvested commercially within strict management plans and predetermined quotas. Similarly the commercial harvesting of two

Wallaby species is permitted.

It's natural! 100% Natural. Kangaroo being a wild animal, the meat is completely free of antibiotics, chemicals, growth hormones or any artificial invention.

The lean meat makes cooking time for skilled chefs or the home chef very minimal. Macro Meats Gourmet Game has implemented a "Paddock To Plate" program, which gives all consumers a guarantee of quality control right from the paddock to the plate.

Raising the awareness of Kangaroo is the next step Ray and Rita are continually working towards, ensuring that Kangaroo is understood and enjoyed.

The question If Kangaroo Meat becomes popular, will kangaroos be in danger of becoming extinct? Is often asked.

Absolutely not! The culling of kangaroos is a strictly controlled program overseen by the Department of Environment and Heritage. The

program operates only in South Australia, Western Australia, New South Wales and Queensland and not all of each state is open to commercial harvesting.

Nevertheless, permits are occasionally issued to landholders for the taking of kangaroos where they are shown to be causing significant damage to crops or pastures etc.

A Kangaroo field processor is only allowed to harvest the number of kangaroos that the Department of Environment and Heritage has allocated to each property that has applied for a permit. Every kangaroo has to be tagged with a number, which can be traced, from beginning to end. Macro Meats will not accept any kangaroos, which are not tagged. All part of the Quality Assurance Program designed and implemented by Macro Meats Gourmet Game.

Driven by Ray and Rita Borda the entire team at Macro Meats Gourmet Game maintains an active commitment to the responsible development of the Kangaroo industry in Australia. Everyone is working together with government organisations to constantly ensure that the regulations and controls of kangaroo harvesting and processing deliver the highest standard and the "world's best practise", principles in animal welfare, conservation management, environmental issues and meat hygiene.

Marco Meats Gourmet Game entice you to discover Kangaroo as a healthy delicacy.

Vilis Cakes & Pies

How did a Hungarian immigrant who started with nothing come to be an icon in an industry which produces the Australian Icon, the humble, but celebrated, Aussie pie?

When I came back to live in Adelaide some 8 years ago, after an absence of 22 years, I was fascinated by the sandwich boards outside many delis and cafes, with the big blue "V" promoting Vili's cakes and pies. After several months, curiosity got the better of me and I tried a Vili's pie. I was an instant convert - pure beef in a succulent gravy encased in Vili's hallmark light and flaky pastry, it blew me away. I particularly love the Hungarian Goulash pie, which was first produced some 12 years ago, and the Bushmans pie is another firm favourite of mine.

Vili now produces an extensive range of gourmet products, using only the finest ingredients, for only the best is good enough.

For Vili it all started when, as a nine year old, he arrived with his family in Adelaide on the 6th January, 1958. It is a date he remembers well, for it was also the 6th January that he registered his new business back in 1967.

His father chose to settle in Australia because, Australia has no borders. In Adelaide, the Milisits family shared a half-fronted cottage in Carrington Street in the city. 16 people shared the cramped quarters.

Later, when Vili's father became ill, Vili was obliged to leave school at age 14 to commence work as an apprentice pastry chef in a small Kent Town bakery so that he could help support his family.

It was during those hard years, getting up at 4am every day that, in his own words, "I had a dream, and my dreams have come true". He dreamt of having a family of his own, a house, car and a good fishing boat.

Married at a young age to a vivacious lass, Rosemary, he purchased an aging bungalow at 14 Manchester Street in the tough, unfashionable suburb of Mile End South, and it was here that he brought his new wife, and started to pursue his dream with only $50 capital. At that time, little did he realise that one day he would acquire much of the property around him, and that by the turn of the century, his baking business would stretch to South Road or that he would have satellite bakeries in Sydney and Melbourne.

Interestingly, it was not always pies, when Vili began his business and for the first ten years, he primarily produced exquisite European-style cakes, tortes and pastries. His philosophy was then, as it is today - Quality, Service and Commitment.

To satisfy customer demand for pies and pasties from patrons of his

sister's snack bar, Vili began his odyssey of repositioning the traditional Australian pie as a "value for money taste sensation".

Vili has always been innovative, thinking outside the square, and a great advocate of common sense. If no ones done it before that is a good reason for him to give it a go. I asked Vili what he thinks has been the most help to him in creating his baking empire. His first reaction was 'being underestimated' followed by 'be willing to do what no one else dares to do'. He is like a good chess player, five moves ahead of his opposition, and with a phenomenal ability to anticipate today's cosmopolitan society's taste preferences. To some extent, he not only satisfied demand he plays a significant role in creating it.

From that first Beef pie the product range has grown to include Steak & Mushroom, Hungarian Goulash, Gourmet Chicken, Beef Rendang, Satay Chicken, Kangaroo Rendang, Kangaroo and Bush Tomato, Lamb and Mint and now a Roasted Vegetable Pie. In addition, Vili also produces the Vili Dog, a kransky sausage wrapped in Vili's unique

Vilis Cakes & Pies

flaky pastry, initially designed for the USA market but now being readily accepted by Asian consumers. A spin off from the bakery is another business venture which could one day outstrip in size his baking enterprise - Café de Vili's.

To satisfy the lunchtime needs of local workers and the after hours needs of shift workers, Café de Vili's, a 24 hour licensed café, was established. The menu is quite extensive, with reasonable prices and caters to most tastes. From fresh cut sandwiches, to pie, chips and gravy or to a satisfying meal from the menu board. Additionally patrons are given the opportunity to purchase quality wines by the glass or partake in a range of quenching ales. Even Vili is surprised by its success. It has become a trendy late nightspot for the young, a great family restaurant, and an informal meeting place as well as catering to workers' needs.

The concept is now being tested overseas in Japan and there has been intense interest from UK developers. Vili's son, Simon, is now spending considerable time overseas promoting, not only Vili's products but also the Café de Vili's concept.

Vili is an extremely proud family man. It was a joy seeing him around the table in the Café de Vili's with wife, Rosemary, a sheer delight, and

his children Simon and Alison, just chatting about old times and good memories of the business growth.

Vili can always have a good laugh. In fact, another of his well found philosophies is "it helps to have a helluva sense of humour in business" - not much can phase him!!

The Milisits family have happily shared their good fortune with the community. The list of their support to the less fortunate, the community generally and sport is outstanding. Recently Vili launched the new Grange surf lifesaving surfboat "The

Pie Floater" - ask any South Australian, they'll understand.

Vili's acknowledged passion is 'wine & food'. He has a substantial cellar in his home, Northgate House, in which for eleven years, until he got too busy, he and Rosemary ran one of Adelaide's finest Reception Centres in one wing. Vili likes nothing better than to share a bottle or two of good red wine with a few mates as they have a game of snooker at home.

What of the future? His first grandson, Josh, arrived on Vili's day, the 6th January 1992 - a tradition is growing. Vili is respectful of tradition but in his words "tradition is good to remember, nice to think about, should never be forgotten, but it may not be the market of the day. Evolution in food is forever - remember, wine was once for plonkies, when I arrived in Australia. I was born Hungarian, I am Aussie by choice, my home is Adelaide, blue skies and starry nights. It's my 5 million star hotel, the food is fantastic all year".

Vili's is a successful business partnership between Vili & Rosemary. They are very humble and conscious of their good fortune. It is they who have created it, their fine concepts and products are a credit to them and their family.

Address: 2-14 Manchester Street MILE END SOUTH 5031 **Phone:** (08) 8234 5711	**Fax:** (08) 8351 9856 **Email:** vilisbak@camtech.net.au **WWW:** www.vilis.com	**Owner:** Vilmos & Rosemary Clarke Milisits **Est:** 1967 **Public Hours:** 24 hours a day, 7 days a week

Joes Poultry

From our family to yours, a truer statement could never be written.

This is exactly how Joe Fazzari viewed his family business, Joe's Poultry, in relation to his customers who became his friends.

Born in the Taurinova, province of Italy in 1942, Joe had the privilege of growing up with strong Italian values and family beliefs.

Joe arrived in Australia as a penniless migrant in 1953 and made his living as a skilled market gardener. In 1980 a work injury caused him to look for a new challenge and he found that challenge in a retail chicken outlet in Adelaide. The business grew and within 3 years the demand for fresh chicken gave Joe the vision to create a production outlet of his own. With a strong belief that families and business grew by sticking together,

his first employee was his son Nat, today's General Manager. With determination and sheer hard work Joe built a large enough establishment to employ all his children as they completed their school years. He had achieved a heart felt goal and that was the foundation of a strong family business.

Joe's constant striving to achieve the best quality, the most efficient work practises and the best equipped plant have characterised the company from its earliest days.

A quote from one of Joe's first customers Ben (Red Rooster) - "My first recollection of Joe was when he knocked on our business back door, looking like he had just walked out of the factory, having worked 24 hours straight without a shave, scruffy and tired looking. He came in and asked if he could be given a break as he had just started out in business and had 5 little mouths to feed. His mannerisms and genuine approach made my decision to deal with him. From that instant I knew Joe was a special person who I could trust and respect. I respected Joe for his honesty and he never let us down since".

From that day Joe has built not just a business but an empire, a South Australian empire with strong family values and a business that now employs over 150 South Australians with a multi-million dollar turnover.

From fresh chicken the produce range has grown to a fully cooked range of products and value added meal solutions. All of Joe's dreams,

with his strength, determination and vitality became a reality.

Six weeks before his death, Joe was told he had cancer. Throughout that time he showed the same strength of character, determination and courage that he always had. He has left a family keeping his vision and strong principles in mind. The family, together with the team of loyal staff, with their dynamic energy coupled with their admiration and respect for Joe, will continue to build business and grow from strength to strength, providing South Australians with employment and consumers both nationally and internationally with quality, service and family values that were always given by Joe himself.

The Australian Cider Company

Cobbley's Cider made its debut in 1971. Made in the Adelaide Hills by a prominent wine maker, it gathered a huge following in hotels known as Scrumpy and attracted many day-trippers to its cellar door. As the years went by the following remained loyal and steady, even when Cobbley's stopped producing kegs to focus on bottling a range of ciders, to tempt a wide range of cider lovers.

A new era in cider began in 1995 when Mel. Scrivens, along with his wife, Christine and three children, Luke, Keryn and Nicholas became involved in the cidery. Mel, who spent most of his child hood in England around places like Dorset and Devon was an avid cider drinker. Much of his time was spent scrumping apples from the orchards surrounding his home to brew their own home made cider. Mel jumped at the opportunity to relive his childhood and has now committed himself to producing the finest quality cider available.

The family's fresh, innovative approach has seen the company once again focus on kegs. In a strategical move they changed the name from Cobbley's Cider to The Australian Cider Co. The cider is still made to the same recipe as was originally used in the 70's, and the family is committed to using only Australian ingredients in their cider.

Premium Aussie Cider is 100% Australian and totally natural. Made in the traditional way it uses only the freshest Australian apple juice, which gives it a crisp, refreshing flavour. The Cider is now produced in the Barossa Valley, internationally recognised for its fine wines and food produce.

Today with a new generation, Premium Aussie Cider has made a huge comeback in the bars of many hotels. Fresh, clean, sparkling and refreshing it still attracts many of its original 70's tipplers, as well as an enormous number of people who have never heard of Cobbley's. It is fast becoming a favourite choice in bars everywhere.

While the family is focusing on its Premium Aussie Cider in kegs and bottles it hasn't forgotten Cobbley's origins in the 70's and continues to make some of the old favourites. Still available are the Cobbley's Traditional Cider, available in casks and the age-old potent scrumpy, guaranteed to warm you in Antarctica.

As the company continues to grow it still keeps its main objective in sight: to make fresh, high, quality, entirely Australian cider.

Look out for limited release, numbered bottles of "Vintage Scrumpy"

Premium Aussie Cider, Scrumpy and Cobbley's Tradition Cider are available from the Australian Cider Company. Door to door delivery Australia wide is available.

Phone: (08) 8349 9977   **Fax:** (08) 8349 9977   **Email:** ozicider@senet.com.au

Adelaide Hills

Adelaide Hills region stretches from Mount Pleasant in the north to Mount Compass in the south. Together with Eden Valley it forms Australia's largest cool climate viticultural region, outside of Coonawarra/Padthaway in the south east of South Australia, with vineyards at a height of more than 400 metres above sea level.

The region is quickly forging a strong reputation worldwide with high profile winemakers such as Brian Croser at Piccadilly, Tim Knappstein, Stephen and Prue Henschke, Geoff Weaver and Nepenthe at Lenswood.

Pinot Noir is becoming a shining star for the Hills with Henschke and Knappstein being pressed for supremacy by some great pinots from the small wineries of Ashton Hills, Pibbin and Hillstowe. In the southern Adelaide Hills, Geoff Hardy's large Kuitpo Vineyard is the showpiece vineyard of Australian viticulture, supplying the likes of exclusive wine producer Shaw and Smith along with the large companies. Geoff keeps his favourite little patches of the vineyard to make his stunning Geoff Hardy Kuitpo varietal wines and won the first great Australian Shiraz Challenge in 1995 with his 1993 Kuitpo Shiraz. Rosemount also have a large vineyard near Kuitpo.

This diverse hills region is certainly at the forefront of the quality wine development of Australia. The sky is the limit so to speak. Perhaps one day we will see the hundreds of vineyards in the Hills that the last century boasted.

The food produce of the Adelaide Hills region particularly around Hahndorf is a fast growing industry. Hahndorf Venison, Bird in Hand Olive Oil, Beerenberg Jams and various smallgoods are some of the main movers. Wine tourism in the hills is also really taking off.

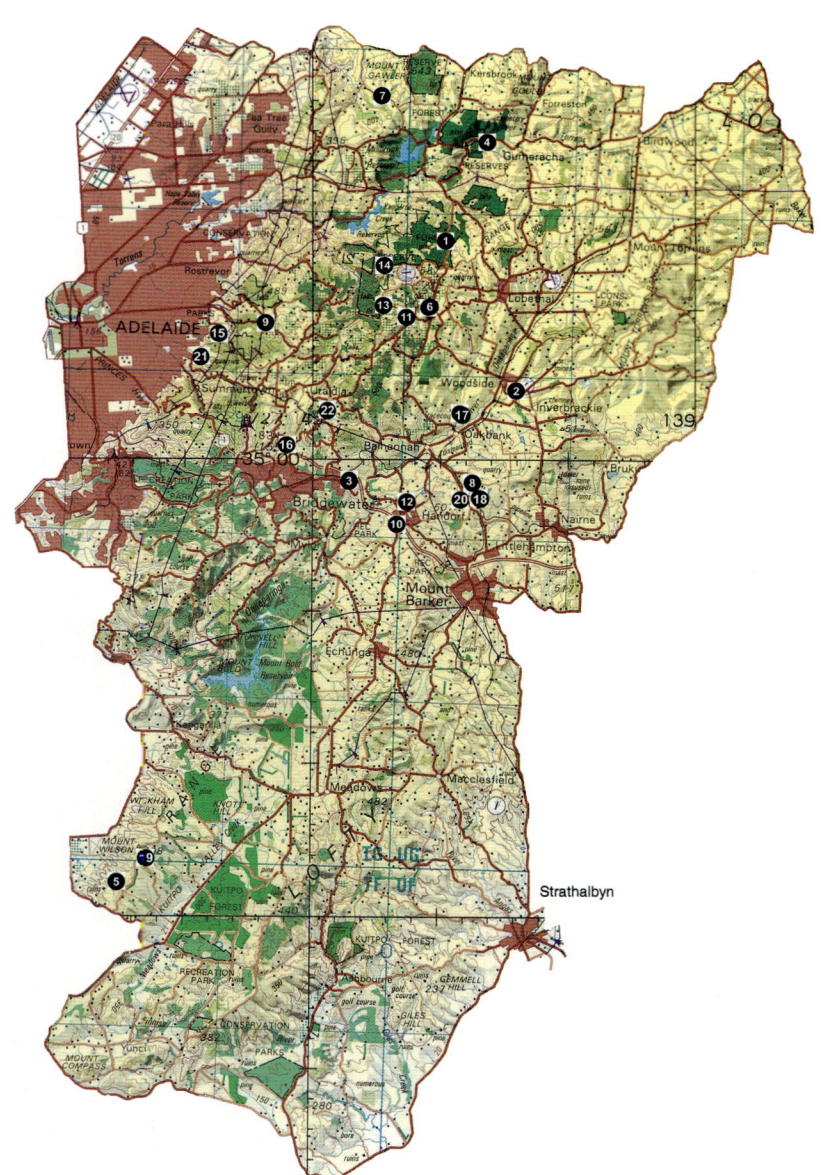

Adelaide Plains - SA

1. Ashbourne
2. Bird in Hand
3. Bridgewater Mill
4. Chain of Ponds
5. Geoff Hardy Kuitpo
6. Geoff Weaver
7. Glenara
8. Glenhurst
9. Grove Hill
10. Hahndorf Venison
11. Henschke
12. Hillstowe
13. Lenswood
14. Nepenthe
15. Penfolds Magill
16. Petaluma
17. Pibbin
18. Ravenswood Lane
19. Rosemount
20. Shaw and Smith
21. Stonyfell Winery
22. Whisson Lake

Adelaide Hills

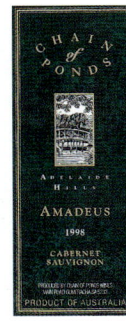

Bridgewater Mill

In between Aldgate and Mount Barker in the pretty Adelaide Hills lies one of the gems of the wine industry and a monument to good taste and cultured living. The Bridgewater Mill is fully restored even to it's giant wheel quietly ticking over as the tranquil stream flows by.

Brian Croser was searching the hills to find a suitable location for a cellar for his methode champenoise; solid, cool and somewhat humid were the basic demands. In the Bridgewater Mill, he found all those things plus a handsome historic building. The cellars hold some of his beloved Croser Sparkling, whilst the internal structure now holds a multi level gallery and restaurant. When Brian and long time friend Len Evans were giving the Mill the once over, Len remarked it would make a marvellous theatre. The cleverly designed internal roof of the tasting area and bar is actually on a hydraulic system and lowers to form a genuine stage.

Like the ambience of the Mill, the wines are a real treat. The

Bridgewater Mill Sauvignon Blanc is fresh and fruity with a keen exotic oriental edge to its flavour and the finish is a winner. The Riesling Methode Champenoise is superb and the reds very fruity and balanced. Put a lunch at the Bridgewater Mill on your must-do list now.

Chain of Ponds

Caj and Genny Amadio are legends in their own time. Following many years of entrepreneurial ventures attacked with remarkable success, and being from generations of Italian winemaking tradition, it was only a matter of time before they ventured into the wine producing business themselves. Several photographs on the walls of the tasting room, which also features an alfresco restaurant, show both Genny and Caj's family's vineyards in hilly northern Italy in terrain very similar to that they have at Gumeracha.

After having pioneered the now much sought after Adelaide Hills subregion of Gumeracha in 1985, this is what they have to say:

"We grow our vines on an enhanced trellising system and hand pick all our fruit to ensure fruit quality and flavour is maintained; combine all the personal care and attention with the ideally cool microclimate of Gumeracha in the Adelaide Hills and you have very special wines".

Wine judges have agreed by honouring them with many achievements: Best Performer · Adelaide Hills Wine Show '96, '97

&'98, Best Performer · Australian Boutique Wine Awards '96, '97, '98 & '99, A commendation, "Best New

Winery '96" by Vogue Entertaining National Magazine and Nominated for "The 21 Hottest Wineries of the

Chain of Ponds

World" by Decanter International Wine Magazine. Chain of Ponds is now the most highly awarded Boutique Winery in Australia.

In 1995 the enormously successful Italian style light red, "Novello Rosso", was launched. It has rapidly increased its market share every vintage since. It is a vibrant, young, full flavoured Grenache/Sangiovese blend, which is ideal for the Australian/Alfresco environment.

In fact, why not visit the gorgeous Chain of Ponds Winery, it's only a stone's throw from Adelaide. Grab a bottle of the Novello Rosso and enjoy a picnic in this beautiful part of the hills. The steep north facing slopes of their vineyards ripen even the cabernet fully but with elegant cool climate characteristics.

The Chain of Ponds Sauvignon Blanc shows why the Adelaide Hills is the premier Australian region for this variety. The semillon and the chardonnay have also been

successful in wine shows.

Caj's son Danniel Amadio is now also heavily involved.

And by the way, they are also helping

to develop a world of wine on Kangaroo Island. You can taste the excellent results of that venture at the Cellar Door too - you'll be very pleasantly surprised.

Address: Main Road GUMERACHA 5233	Vine Ha: 21		Shiraz	5-10 yrs
Phone: (08) 8389 1415	Cases: 5,000		Chardonnay	5-7 yrs
Fax: (08) 8389 1877	Public Hours: 10.30am-4.30, daily		Semillon	5-7 yrs
Winemaker: Caj Amadio	Principal Wines	Potential	Sauvignon Blanc-Semillon	3-5 yrs
Est: 1985, 1993 (First Vintage)	Cabernet Sauvignon "Amadeus"	5-10 yrs	Riesling	10+ yrs

Bird in Hand Wine & Olive Oil

One of the most exciting food and wine ventures I have seen in Australia is the Bird in Hand olive, oil and wine enterprise of the Nugent Family, at Woodside in the Adelaide Hills. The Hahndorf-Balhannah-Woodside region of the hills is only a 20-minute drive out of Adelaide. It's a region rapidly becoming a gourmet food bowl for local and export markets, as well as a fast growing super premium wine region.

The property is a former dairy and features two massive grain silos. Having climbed to the top with a camera in hand, I can vouch for their height. From here one can see the magnificent vineyard and olive grove is bordered by a commercially designed olive hedge and has spectacular gum trees amongst the vines. The substantial buildings include an old yogurt factory that has become an olive production centre (it will soon house the winery, cellar door and café) and historic stables built in the 1850's.

Dr Michael Nugent, formerly an owner and director of Tatachilla Winery bought the property in 1997 with son Andrew, daughter Susan and son-in-law Steven Marshall and planted 90 acres of vineyard and olive groves.

Andrew and Susie Nugent live in the magnificent old farmhouse on the property, they were married in the gardens there in 1999. After graduating from Roseworthy, Andrew has owned and managed substantial

vineyards throughout South Australia and has developed a reputation as a viticulturist who is scrupulous with his vines with an unsurpassed attention to detail. His work with

olives is just as impressive, he manages one of the largest mature olive groves in Australia, turning the neglected 35yr old grove into a productive and valuable one. The family has since bought this old grove and the production from the 125 acres of trees supplements their Woodside olives.

Justin, who has an extremely successful legal and corporate

background, recently took over the marketing of Bird in Hand. He has a boundless energy, enthusiasm and love for the Adelaide Hills, which takes him all over Australia and the world promoting the area as a food and wine mecca.

Michael, the eldest, is a GP in Clare and lives on a property boasting 100-year-old feral olive trees and world class Riesling and Shiraz viticultural country. The Clare produce also supplements the Bird in Hand range.

Bird in Hand wines benefit from Andrew's experience as both a viticulturalist and winemaker. The Nugent family vineyards produce a variety of premium cool climate wines including: Sauvignon Blanc, Pinot Noir, Merlot and Cabernet. The wines I have tasted are stunning.

The range of premium olive oils began as a small business by Andrew's wife Susie in 1997. Through her passion and insistence on quality the Bird in Hand range of oils now rival anything produced anywhere. The range includes a "First Reserve" or early season pressing, a "Gourmet" pressing and a "Late Harvest" blend. All are extra virgin quality and cold pressed on site. There are now also 3 types of premium Bird in Hand table olives; Verdale (green), Manzanillo & Kalamata (black). The Bird in Hand olives and oils adorn the shelves of every genuine gourmet retail outlet throughout Australia, and are increasingly being appreciated on an international scale.

You'll be seeing plenty of magic from the Bird in Hand wine and olive products, they're certainly worth much more than two in the bush.

Address: Bird in Hand Road WOODSIDE	Est: 1997	Adelaide Hills Sauvignon Blanc	1-5 yrs
Phone: (08) 8232 9033	Vine Ha: 24	Bird in Hand Adelaide Hills Pinot Noir	3-5 yrs
Fax: (08) 82329066	Principal Varieties: Cabernet Sauvignon,	Cabernet Sauvignon/Merlot	5-10 yrs
Owner: The Nugent Family	Merlot, Sauvignon Blanc, Pinot Noir	Adelaide Hills Sparkling Pinot Noir	1-5 yrs
Winemaker: Andrew Nugent	Principal Wines Potential	Bird in Hand Fleurieu Shiraz	8-10 yrs

Glenhurst

Nothing has been left to chance by the Crowhurst Family in their quest to create one of the greatest Australian Vineyard and Wine Estates.

The company has been named after the property settled near Gumeracha in the Adelaide Hills, by Bruce Crowhurst's great great grandparents in 1848, which they named Glenhurst when they arrived from the Village of Crowhurst in England.

In 1992, Bruce decided to sell the family's successful national paint business started in 1923. Both Bruce and his son Greg were thinking about farming. Bruce bought 3,000 acres in Wrattonbully (adjacent to Coonawarra). About this time major plantings of vines were beginning in the region and Bruce soon began planting on the best terra rossa soils on his property.

In 1997 planting began at the Glenhurst property at Hahndorf in the Adelaide Hills, situated right across the road from the celebrated

Shaw and Smith Winery. Today there are 100 acres of vines at Wrattonbully and 55 acres at Hahndorf. The Crowhurst's are perfectionists and nothing is left to

chance. Both vineyards have sophisticated weather stations and this combined with careful vine monitoring minimises disease and subsequent controls. Greg has trained at Roseworthy College; the vineyards are a picture, as are the rose gardens surrounding the cellar door at the Hahndorf property.

Glenhurst grow shiraz, cabernet sauvignon and the Italian variety dolcetto at Wrattonbully and chardonnay, sauvignon blanc and pinot noir complete the picture at Hahndorf. They therefore have a presence in two of Australia's most prestigious wine growing areas.

The first wines are being released as I write and you can find out more about them by joining The Glenhurst Wine Buffs Club. I predict they will be a leading Australian super premium producer in quick time.

Address: PO Box 44 HAHNDORF 5245	**Public Hours:** 11am-4pm Wed-Sun (except Christmas Day, Boxing Day & Good Friday)	Cab Sav "The Nobelman" 8-10 yrs
Phone: (08) 8388 4439 Fax: (08) 8388 4439		Glenhurst Shiraz "The Zealia" 8-10 yrs
Email: glenhurst@chariot.net.au	**Principal Varieties:** Chardonnay, Pinot Noir, Shiraz, Cabernet Sauvignon, Dolcetto, Sauvignon Blanc	Glenhurst Dolcetto 2-5 yrs
Owner: Bruce, Deidre & Greg Crowhurst		Glenhurst Pinot Noir "The Dark Lady" 5-8 yrs
Winemaker: Bruce Crowhurst		Chardonnay "The Doretta" Up to 5 yrs
Est: 1992 **Vine Ha:** 60 **Cases:** 2,500	**Principal Wines** **Potential**	Sauvignon Blanc "The Eleaner" 0-3 yrs

Shaw & Smith

Cousins Michael Hill Smith and Martin Shaw have taken the high ground in Australian Wine and are well credentialed to do so. Michael is a sixth generation member of the prominent wine family that began Yalumba Wines in 1849. Michael became Australia's first Master of Wine when he passed their extremely rigorous examination in London in 1988, in 1992 he set up the highly successful Universal Wine Bar in Adelaide.

Martin has an impeccable winemaking background, he graduated from Roseworthy in 1981, after which he worked with Brian Croser at Petaluma in the Adelaide Hills for 8 years, before setting up the "Flying Winemakers Network" in France, Spain, Chile, Australia and New Zealand he still consults to a number of leading wineries worldwide.

Over a long lunch in 1989 Martin and Michael decided to realize a long held dream to make wine together - Shaw and Smith was born, for the first 10 years they focused on white, firstly sauvignon blanc followed by

chardonnay, my brother Geoff supplying them with Adelaide Hills grapes amongst others. In 1994 they began planting their own

vineyards at Woodside. A contemporary state of the art winery was built in 2000, on a 46 acre property they bought at Balhannah in 1999, further vineyards have been planted around the winery.

In 1998, under pressure from their mothers, who prefer red, they produced their first red a merlot. Pinot noir and riesling will join the range. There are two chardonnays, one un-oaked the other a single vineyard called M3 in limited quantities which is barrel fermented in top French oak and designed for the long haul.

The winery has a spacious private dining room and separate reception area and is ideal for top level functions and events, the views over the vineyard are breathtaking, the food exquisite.

Address: Lot 4 Jones Road BALHANNAH 5242	Matthew Hill Smith	Sauvignon Blanc
	Winemaker: Martin Shaw & Willy Lunn	**Principal Wines** **Potential**
Phone: (08) 8398 0500	**Est:** 1989 **Vine Ha:** 38 **Cases:** 20,000	Shaw & Smith Sauvignon Blanc 1 1/2 yrs
Fax: (08) 8398 0600	**Public Hours:** 9am-4pm Monday to Friday (closed weekends)	M3 Vineyard Chardonnay 5-7 yrs
Email: shawandsmith@shawandsmith.com		Shaw & Smith Unoaked Chardonnay 3-5 yrs
Owner: Martin Shaw, Michael Hill Smith &	**Principal Varieties:** Chardonnay, Merlot,	Shaw & Smith Merlot 10 yrs

Geoff Weaver

Geoff Weaver was a pioneer in the Lenswood area of the Adelaide Hills, when he began plating his vineyard on the sheltered eastern slopes of Stafford Ridge in 1982. Long renowned for its orchards, the Lenswood area is now home to the neighbouring vineyard of icon winemaker Stephen Henschke and a number of other high profile producers.

Geoff has had a most distinguished career in wine, following gaining his degree in Agricultural Science from Adelaide University he taught Science at the tertiary and secondary levels. Geoff joined Orlando in 1972 after 6 months he decided to see the world of wine and spent 7 months travelling wine regions and teaching institutions in the USA and Europe. After a couple of years making wine under Mark Tummel at Orlando, Geoff joined Hardys in 1975 rising from white winemaker to become group Chief Winemaker in 1988 and Chief Winemaker at BRL Hardy until he left in 1992 to concentrate fully on his Stafford Ridge Vineyard and making his own wines.

Geoff is a real artist not only in his winemaking where his blending of intensity of fruit with subtle complexities of flavour is world class, but also with a paint brush and artists palate, he has painted some extraordinary canvases capturing the exquisite light of early morning over his vineyard with inspired skill.

Geoff is undoubtedly in the top few chardonay makers in Australia and he has won many top awards including the best South Australian Wine of the Year, in the 1998 Hyatt Advertiser Wine Awards and many appearances in James Halliday's Annual Top 100 Australian Wines. Geoff also produces a riesling, sauvignon blanc and a velvety cabernet merlot, all are wines of true distinction, beautifully balanced that will improve with bottle ageing.

Geoff Weaver shares his skill with many, through his wine industry appointments and top industry consulting jobs. He is a consummate master of the vine and its glorious progeny · wine.

Henschke - Lenswood

During the 1980s Henschke's conducted a search to find vineyard land to produce the highest quality table wines. Their search led them to the heart of the Adelaide Hills, where they purchased an existing 40-acre apple orchard and began establishing a picture book vineyard at Lenswood, which is 50 kms south of their Keyneton vineyards.

Prue and Stephen Henschke met during their studies at Adelaide University in the 1970s, where Prue was then majoring in Botany and Zoology. After marrying, they travelled to Germany, where they both studied at the famous Geisenheim Wine Institute. Prue worked closely with the world-renowned viticulturist and vine breeder Dr Helmut Becker for two years, learning the German's meticulous and rigorous approach to viticulture in particular.

The quality of the grapes Prue is producing is truly world class and the wines have been truly wonderful and one wonders just how good the Henschke wines of the future will be. I for one await them with keen anticipation.

Grove Hill

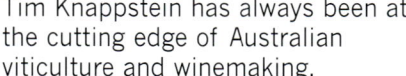

Nestled among rolling hills and lush valleys is the delightful Grove Hill Estate. Planting began here in 1978 and continued in the 1980's. A few original shiraz vines still ramble from last century. Marguerite Giles a fifth generation member of the founding family runs the vineyard which is one of the oldest in the cool climate Adelaide Hills region. It is very close planted, with only 1.2 metres between rows.

The soil is a clay loam with underlying slate. Large slate flagstones taken from the ground are evident in the historic buildings and stone walls on the property; a testament to the very hard work of yesteryear.

The grapes are hand pruned and hand picked and they are usually dry grown. Viticultural practice produces low yields, which are compensated by the intense flavours of the berries.

The wines produced are all white, bunch pressed and fermented on natural yeast from this single source vineyard.

Currently 3 styles are produced, a soft, fruity and elegant riesling with mineral undertones, it is reminiscent of the alsace style. The chardonnay is both fermented and matured in Burgundian barriques. It is kept on lees for approximately 10 months until bottling; this wine has great structure, length and depth of flavours. The 1996 vintage was recently awarded 91 points by the U.S. Magazine, Wine Spectator.

The Sparkling Marguerite is 100% barrel fermented. This Pinot Noir/Chardonnay, Methode Champenoise is a complex wine with great flavours and it is produced in limited quantities.

Only 20 minutes from Adelaide this rural retreat is producing some outstanding boutique wines. The historic building housing the cellar door has some extraordinary souvenirs from the families pioneering days. It is a delight, not to be missed.

			Principal Wines	Potential
Address: 120 Old Norton Summit Road NORTON SUMMIT 5136	David Powell		Grove Hill Chardonnay	5-10 yrs
Phone: (08) 8390 1437 **Fax:** (08) 8390 1437	**Est:** 1978 **Vine Ha:** 3 **Cases:** 500		Grove Hill Riesling	5-10 yrs
Owner: Marguerite Giles	**Public Hours:** Cellar door on Sun 11am-5pm		Grove Hill Marguerite Sparkling	10+ yrs
Winemaker: Roman Bratasiuk &	**Principal Varieties:** Chardonnay, Pinot Noir, Riesling		Grove Hill Pinot Noir	5-10 yrs

Lenswood Vineyard

Tim Knappstein has always been at the cutting edge of Australian viticulture and winemaking.

During the late 1960's and early 1970's he revolutionised the wines at his family's Stanley Wine Company in Clare. The Leasingham Bin5 and Bin 7 Rhine Rieslings took all before them on the show circuits and his Bin Reds, the 56 Cabernet Malbec and Bin 49 Cabernet Sauvignon wine, were benchmarks of the industry.

Tim was looking for a way to add another dimension to his wines so in 1981 he and his wife Annie purchased a steep sloped property at Lenswood between the Mawson Bike Trail and the Heysen Walking Trail in the cool Adelaide Hills. Theirs was the first vineyard in the region. Chardonnay was planted in October 1981.

The Ash Wednesday bushfires in 1983 destroyed the remains of the apple orchards on the property and about 50% of the vines.

Tim and Annie persevered. The original 18-hectare property was expanded to 45 hectares in 1990 and now there are some 27 hectares under vine.

The Knappstein Lenswood Vineyard wines are sensational. The pinot noir is a knockout, the chardonnay and sauvignon blanc and cabernet sauvignon/merlot/malbec blend are also superb.

Annie and Tim have a private tasting and entertaining area with exquisite views over the vineyards in part of what is now their home. They have a true paradise and know what to do with it.

Geoff Hardy Kuitpo

inland from McLaren Vale, in the Adelaide Hills wine region.

Today he has some 85 acres of Australia's most revered vineyards. His grapes are eagerly sought after by the cream of the best winemakers. Geoff selects his favourite rows of the vineyard, to make his own few hundred dozen super premium wines.

In 1995 his 1993 Kuitpo Shiraz outpointed 400 of Australia's best shiraz wines from any vintage, to win the inaugural Australia Shiraz Challenge, sponsored by Qantas and held in the Goulburn Valley, Victoria. All three judges, James Halliday in Melbourne, Brian Croser at Bridgewater and Geoff Merrill at Reynella chose this wine as Australia's Best Shiraz, totally independently.

Geoff also runs a vine nursery at the vineyard during springtime, supplying millions of cuttings to the burgeoning viticultural boom around Australia. Geoff Hardy, who happens to be my brother, is a credit to our great industry.

In 1980 a youthful 24 year old, Geoff Hardy, purchased the Old Ryecroft vineyards in the foothills behind McLaren Vale with the then vineyard manager Ian Leask.

They quickly made a reputation as top-flight grapegrowers and

viticulturists, winning the first South Australian Vineyard of the Year award in 1990.

Geoff was keen to develop a truly cool climate vineyard and chose a site near the Kuitpo pine forests, high in the ranges, 9 or so kilometres

Rosemount Kuitpo

Rosemount's movement into establishing their own vineyards in the premium cool climate areas of Australia, took a big step forward some years ago, when managing director Bob Oatley saw Geoff Hardy's Kuitpo vineyards and tasted the wines.

During a dinner between the two friends he made Geoff a very generous offer to buy the vineyard. Geoff gave the offer much thought. That night he awoke to the realisation he could not part with his gem in this hills, but he did know of a great site on Range Road, so he

and Bob worked out a deal and Geoff designed and laid out a picture book vineyard, which has proved to be a viticultural jewel in the glittering Rosemount Crown, particularly producing sauvignon blanc and chardonnay of exciting quality.

Hahndorf Venison

Hahndorf Venison is a family owned and operated South Australian business. The DeLaine family introduced farmed Venison to the hospitality industry of South Australia during the 1970's, clearly leading the way and successfully achieving many initiatives.

Today, Hahndorf Venison operate a fully government approved and accredited quality assured "Category 6 · Meat Wholesaling/Boning Room". Having undergone the introduction and implementation of a HACCP based Quality Assurance program they now meet and exceed the requirements of the Primary Industries Meat Hygiene Unit of South Australia.

Hahndorf Venison successfully maintain a rigorous process approach, with the implementation of an 'on farm' industry based Deer Farming Best Practise Program, a first in Australia. Hahndorf Venison's overall concept of 'paddock to plate' is indeed a reality.

Hahndorf Venison purchase their livestock within the Wistow Farm environment for improved dietary intake for prime selection. They are depastured and then presented to the preferred government approved

processing facility located just 15 minutes from the lush pastures of Wistow.

Hahndorf Venison practice 'On Farm' processing procedures, enabling the origin of all products processed to be identified with 'trace back' to its origin, maintaining the integrity of all products.

Hahndorf Venison has the experience and resources to meet the commitments and demands of country and interstate trade successfully. The company has unrestricted trade throughout Australia and access into some

international markets. In addition to the restaurants of Adelaide and regional South Australia, Hahndorf Venison regularly features on the fine dining menus of Australia's best.

The DeLaine's welcome you to personally view their farm at Hahndorf and extends an invitation into the Boning Room to discuss the 'Paddock To Plate' concept and the unique processing features of Hahndorf Venison.

Whilst visiting you should get Des DeLaine to surprise you with his eye opening collection in his museum with a twist.

Haven Lamb

Haven Lamb is on the cutting edge of the meat Industry. Founder, the energetic and dynamic Robbie Robertson, began his career in the meat Industry as a clerk at City Meat in Adelaide in 1976, by 1984 he had become State manager of Thomas Borthwick, a large traditional meat business.

In 1986 he set out on his own with the strong belief there needed to be a meat processor and wholesaler, that presented consistent top quality branded meat, with a quality assurance for the consumer.

The Fleurieu Peninsula includes the Adelaide Hills Region and the Southern Vales down to Cape Jervis and across to Goolwa. This region is not only majestically beautiful but one of the cleanest and greenest environments for grazing, one could find anywhere in the world. The Fleurieu pastures are rich but its not too wet and the hilly nature of the country side provides the sheep with plenty of exercise to build firm muscle structure.

As far back as 1851 my own great grandfather Thomas Hardy worked on a grazing property at Normanville and drove 500 head of cattle across to Ballarat to the gold diggings twice, to raise the capital to start his wine enterprise. Normanville is also the home for the Abattoirs ably run by Bruce Wedd that handle the Lambs and the young cattle for the milk fed veal which Haven also produce,

under their gold seal brand.

The lambs for Haven's processing are carefully selected under strictly laid out criteria. Fred Leishman along with Robbie Robertson personally carry out the selection, most of the lambs selected then spend about six weeks on Havens own feed lot.

The main criteria for selection are, breed, weight, age, fat content and confirmation - a meat industry term for the form of each animal, normally the lambs have a weight of 18-20 kgs. Processing is done at Normanville under surgically clean conditions. Before the dressed carcasses are ready to receive the "Haven Gold" branding. Haven are

working on some value-added products such as seasoned roasts, tunnel boned legs and other gourmet products.

For a short season, October-January, Haven also market Kangaroo Island Lamb under the "K.I. Gold" label.

The Haven Lamb is always pink in colour, even, but not excessive fat cover and very importantly, moist. Havens commitment is to have recognisable 'gold branded' meat products that the consumer can have full confidence, in their superior quality and consistency, with a money back guarantee.

Haven have a second very successul business "Fleurieu Fresh". They pack meat in special colour coded packs which are sealed with clear plastic, enclosing a modified atmosphere consisting of 20% pure carbon dioxide with 80% surgical grade oxygen, this prolongs shelf life dramatically from 4 days to 11 days and from 2 days to 6 days for mince meat. Haven pack lamb in green containers, beef in cream and pork and veal in blue, these can be found in the chillers of convenience supermarkets.

Robbie and his hard working, French born wife Jacqui , are doing a superb job. I hope their Haven lamb and other meat products find a happy Haven in your home with a great South Australian Shiraz to wash them down.

Hillstowe Wines

The Hillstowe story began with Buxton Forbes Laurie, a pioneer of viticulture in South Australia an ancestor of Dr Chris Laurie and his son Hamish.

In 1853, in the lush foothills near Port Elliot, Buxton laid the foundation of his family home "Southcote" on land chosen for its suitability as a vineyard. The first vines were planted in the winter of 1853 and in 1857 the first vintage was harvested. By 1866 his vineyard produced top quality Shiraz, Cabernet, Grenache and Riesling wines. The legacy of Buxton Forbes Laurie imbued in his descendent the desire to continue the tradition of producing premium quality wines for Australia and export.

Udy's Mill was a 19th century timber mill located in the heart of the Adelaide Hills in bushland at Carey Gully near Lenswood, where the ancient Stringy Bark gums were felled by timber cutters until the late 1900's. More than a century later, the clearings left in the forest have been planted to Chardonnay and Pinot grapes by the Laurie family.

The Hillstowe philosophy of 'better vines better wines'; its concentration on high quality grapes and focus on winemaking techniques has led to a string of international and national awards.

Hillstowe Wines cellar door is in Hahndorf, the heart of the Adelaide Hills wine-growing region. Hillstowe's complex of stone cottages nestles amongst trees and gardens in this historic township. On the main street is Thiele's Cottage (circa 1845), believed to be the oldest building still standing in Hahndorf: A collection of cottages, in the style of German villages of Thiele's era, huddle behind...and here Hillstowe have created a café following through to the Cellar Door, tastings are offered of Hillstowe's award winning single vineyard and wines from both

the Adelaide Hills and McLaren Vale. All wines are available for purchase by the glass or to enjoy with a meal in the café.

A large picnic area beckons from across the creek dividing the grounds. A stroll over a bridge to a large grassy meadow, dappled with stunning Willows and Australian Native Trees, takes you to the perfect spot for throwing a rug, relaxing with a bottle of wine and some local cheeses.

Address: 104 Main Road HAHNDORF 5245	Est: Vineyards 1980; Hillstowe Wines 1991	Adelaide Hills Ucy's Mill Chard	8-10 yrs
Phone: (08) 8388 1400 Fax: (08) 8388 1411	Public Hours: 10am-5pm, daily	Adelaide Hills Ucy's Mill Pinot Noir	6-8 yrs
Email: wines@hillstowe.com.au	Principal Varieties: Chardonnay, Pinot Noir,	Adelaide Buxton Sauvignon Blanc	
WWW: www.hillstowe.com.au	Sauvignon Blanc, Merlot, Shiraz, Cabernet	McLaren Vale Buxton Merlot Cab	8-10 yrs
Owner: The Laurie Family	Sauvignon, Pinot Gris	McLaren Vale Buxton Chardonnay	6-8 yrs
Winemaker: Chris Laurie Vine Ha: 14	Principal Wines Potential	McLaren Vale Buxton Shiraz	12-15 yrs

Nepenthe

"Nepenthe" in "The Odyssey" of Homer was an Egyptian herbal drink so powerful that it eased grief and banished sorrow from the mind.

High profile business Executive Ed Tweddell and his wife Sue had the vision for Nepenthe · in Ed's own words;

"I guess my wife and I had always thought about the possibility of owning a vineyard and a winery and having our own label. We used to think about the curious satisfaction of pulling a cork on your own brand and enjoying a slow reflection on a number of past vintages while entertaining family and friends.

We actually had a brief excursion into vineyards in the late '60s when we owned a cattle and sheep property in central Victoria. We established a small vineyard in an area which a hundred years previously had grown prime grapes. Our vineyard was one of the early ones established in the Avoca area · now a thriving wine region. We had some good Shiraz made for us. We still have a few bottles in the cellar from those early days and enjoy them on the odd ceremonial occasion.

We sold the property when we moved to the US and we spent the next fifteen years as expatriate Australians living a wonderful life in New York,

Montreal, Nairobi, Hong Kong and Tokyo. I was working as a physician in the pharmaceutical industry so there was no chance of growing grapes or making wine, but I must say our international sojourn taught us to appreciate a wide variety of wines from around the world.

On returning to Australia we settled in Adelaide, South Australia which is rightfully known as the Wine State. With our interest in wine I guess it is not strange that we started thinking very seriously in the early '90s about establishing a vineyard and possibly a winery in South Australia.

We were attracted to high altitude viticulture as we had a great admiration for Adelaide Hills winemakers · figures such as Brian Croser, Tim Knappstein and the Henschkes · and we had particularly fallen in love with the Burgundies and the Loire Valley Sauvignon blancs while we had been living out of the country.

Our first plantings were Chardonnay, Sauvignon Blanc, Pinot noir and Zinfandel. We also established some Merlot, Semillon, Riesling and Pinot gris.

High altitude viticulture is not without its challenges, but because we are firmly committed to quality we will continue to produce distinctive wines from relatively low

yielding premium vines. We are proud of the reputation the Nepenthe brand has already developed both in Australia and in the UK, and will not compromise our commitment to high standards.

The management of Nepenthe is in the hands of our son James, who has developed a tremendous team to support and develop the business.

As a family we appreciate art and music and beautiful things. It was important for us to develop vineyards that reflected these aesthetic interests, and especially important that our beautiful vineyards should produce even more exquisite wines. When we sit back and contemplate an inviting glass of Nepenthe, our fascination with the beautiful is completed: a total absence of sorrow indeed".

The Nepenthe Lenswood vineyards, where the winery is located and the Charleston vineyards provide ample visual testimony to the exceptional beauty of the Adelaide Hills.

Of the two, Lenswood is more undulating, at a higher altitude, and has a tremendous variety of natural vegetation. With under half of the property cleared, Lenswood constitutes a number of small vineyards separated by tracts of natural scrub.

Situated in broad sweeping hills dotted with huge eucalypts, the larger Charleston vineyard is marked by the old homestead that dates back to the earliest days of white settlement.

Together, the two vineyard areas' extensive variety of soils and diverse topography add to the wonderful complexity and richness of the Nepenthe wines.

At high altitude, our premium vines produce frighteningly low yields · but what they lack in quantity they more than make up for in quality and concentrated flavour.

Nepenthe concentrate on doing everything in a consistent and thorough way, and stunning wines are the result.

Address: Vickers Road LENSWOOD 5240	**Winemaker:** Peter Leske	Sauvignon Blanc 1-2 yrs
Phone: (08) 8431 7588	**Est:** 1994 **Vine Ha:** 100 **Cases:** 40,000	Pinot Gris 1-5 yrs
Fax: (08) 8431 7688	**Principal Varieties:** Chard, Sauv Blanc,	Unwooded Chardonnay 1-5 yrs
Email: plimpus@nepenthe.com.au	Merlot, Pinot Noir, Cab Sav, Semillon,	Riesling 1-15 yrs
WWW: www.nepenthe.com.au	Zinfandel, Pinot Gris	Chardonnay 1-10 yrs
Owner: Ed Tweddell Family	**Principal Wines** **Potential**	Semillon 1-15 yrs

Penfolds Magill

Dr. Christopher Rawson Penfold and his wife Mary arrived in Adelaide in 1844. Being a great believer in the healing powers of red wine Dr Penfold planted vine cuttings he had brought from the south of France. He built a solid stone cottage which he called 'The Grange', and which is today classified under the National Trust.

The soil at the Magill Estate is rich and red and Dr Penfold's vines thrived. After his death in 1870, his wife, daughter Georgina and son-in-law Thomas Francis Hyland took over the company, opening offices in Melbourne and Sydney.

Penfolds wines were increasingly successful and by 1913, the company had purchased Wyndham's Dalwood vineyards in the Hunter Valley, Pridmore's Southern Vales winery south of Adelaide, the Minchinbury winery and cellars on the outskirts of Sydney, and they had established the Nuriootpa Cellars in the Barossa Valley. Penfold also established a winery at Griffith in New South Wales in 1921.

Over the next 40 years the company purchased further properties in the Hunter Valley, Coonawarra and next door to their own winery at Magill, the latter being the old Auldana Cellars.

By 1950, 95 per cent of Penfolds production was based on fortified wines. The management decided to change the company's direction and develop a range of table wines. The man chosen to head this project was

Max Schubert, who had been with Penfolds since his youth.

As a youngster, Max had worked each night after school, mucking out stables and priming gas lanterns, for the princely sum of 2 shillings and sixpence (25 cents) a week.

Max was sent to Europe to study winemaking and while in France met one of the Bordeaux region's most famous winemakers, Christian Cruse. After observing his winemaking techniques and tasting some very old Bordeaux wines, Max was determined to create a new style of Australian red wine, one that would age well for decades. The wine he produced in 1951 was the first vintage of Australia's most famous wine, "Grange".

Very few people recognised the quality or potential of the wine and it received some aggressive criticism. Today, however, Grange's of the early 50s sell for many thousands of dollars a bottle at auction.

Penfolds revoked their support of the wine, but secretly Max persisted until they were forced to capitulate as it grew in popularity and acclaim during the 1960's.

Like "Grange", Penfolds St. Henri, made at the Auldana Cellars, was not instantly accepted by the public. As with Grange, St. Henri was considerably ahead of its time. So were Penfolds Bin 389, a cabernet shiraz blend aged in the previous Grange hogsheads, Bin 28, a soft, full, Kalimna Shiraz and Bin 128, an elegant, Coonawarra Shiraz.

Koonunga Hill is a similar style of wine, although more commercial and excellent value for money.

In 1985, Penfolds released their 1983 Magill Estate. This special wine was made entirely from the remaining 5 ha shiraz vines at the famous Grange Vineyards. Originally covering 77 ha, the vineyard has been reduced to 5 ha by Adelaide's suburban sprawl.

Even in his retirement, Max spent much of his time in his laboratory office which was always open to anyone who wanted to bring in their old Penfolds wines for "Dr" Max to check over and if necessary restore to good health with a top-up or a new cork.

John Duval, the chief winemaker for Penfolds, is a protege of Max Schubert and is doing an excellent job with all the Penfolds wines, which cover the whole gambit of styles · reds, whites, the fortifieds · up to the great 'Grandfather Port' and many excellent sparkling wines.

Magill Estate, with Dr Rawson Penfold's old cottage and its vineyards remains the spiritual home of Penfolds and has undergone a major restoration, to make it a splendid showpiece of the wine industry.

The complex includes the truly first class "Magill Estate Restaurant" which has panoramic views over the city of Adelaide, a visit is a must as it is less than 15 minutes from the city centre.

Petaluma

The pursuit of excellence is becoming a well-worn phrase, but when used in reference to Petaluma, it is most appropriate.

Petaluma is the brainchild of the brilliant Brian Croser. Brian Croser graduated with honours from Adelaide University in 1972, and joined the winemaking team at Thomas Hardy and Sons, where he assessed the entire winemaking, bottling and vineyard production areas. In 1973, he went to Davis University in California for further study and returned in 1974 in time to take over the year's white wine production.

Brian did his best to introduce his philosophy and technique of oxygen exclusion from the time grapes arrive in the winery to the time of bottling. Whilst working with Brian, I well remember dragging cylinders of carbon dioxide around the winery at Waikerie at 4.00am, attempting to cover and protect wine being loaded for transport to Adelaide for bottling, the winery workers thinking I had screws loose!!

In 1975, Croser convinced Hardys to invest in new equipment, refrigeration and improved storage facilities. He helped introduce oxygen exclusion, cold settling of wines, filtering before fermentation, careful yeast choice and long slow fermentation, the rest is history. The 1975 white wines took the industry and market by storm. They dominated the white wine classes in every wine show in Australia, and overnight Brian Croser became a legend.

Despite an offer of Chief winemaker's position, Brian left Hardys in 1976 and joined the staff at the Riverina College of Advanced Education at Wagga Wagga in New South Wales, where he did much to introduce modern winemaking skills, which have helped our entire industry so much. The first Petaluma wine, a spaetlese rhine, was made at the College winery in 1976 from Mitchelton fruit.

By 1978, Brian had left the College and begun a wine consultancy business, where he instantly amassed a huge group of clients. In the same year, he constructed a winery and planted a vineyard for champagne, at Piccadilly. Brian brings in his grapes from selected regions, which he believes have the potential to best produce the varietal characteristics he is looking for.

Petaluma has large vineyards in the Clare Region, specialising in riesling, in the high cool Polish Hill River region. The reds largely come from Petaluma's Coonawarra and Sharefarmers vineyards in the cool southeast of South Australia, rich in the famed terra rossa soils. The chardonnay and sparkling wines under the Petaluma and Croser labels, largely come from the Adelaide Hills, as does the Bridgewater Mill Sauvignon Blanc.

Petaluma has become a very successful public company and also owns Knappstein Wines of Clare, the Mitchelton Winery in Victoria and now Smithbrook in Western Australia. Brian has put much effort in the maximisation of wine quality and production efficiency, of these additions to Petaluma's wine stable.

The Bridgewater Mill, a beautiful historic mill nearby to Petaluma in the hills, was a derelict shell when Brian took it over in the early 1980's; today it is a splendid Restaurant and Gallery, that also holds concerts. It is a successful cellar door for Petaluma as well as marketing a Bridgewater Mill Label, encompassing some exciting and different fresh fruit driven wine styles.

Brian Croser has been a true crusader for the wine industry in its fight against potentially huge increases in wine taxes. Over two years, at least half his working life was devoted to fighting for the industry, creating a plan and blueprint for the Australian wine and grape industry for the 21st Century. Due to his efforts the industry now has the government support and understanding it so richly deserves, considering its employment, export success and tourism multiplier effects. Petaluma and Brian Croser are a credit to wine in Australia.

Brian has also been awarded the Annual Maurice O'Shea Award for services to the industry, a richly deserved honour.

Whisson Lake

Mark Whisson has one of the steepest and most spectacular vineyards I have seen anywhere in the world. The awesome north east facing slopes at Uraidla are commonly refered to as "Heart Attack Hill". Mark tells the story of how he and his former boss Brian Croser, were running up the slopes back in 1985, when out of breath three quarters of the way up, they stopped and looked around both dumb struck by the spectacular view. Mark built his swiss style chalet home on this spot and is now surrounded by 14 acres of magnificent mature Pinot Noir Vines, Australia's only specialist Pinot Noir Domaine.

Mark developed the property with a partnership interest from Bruce Lake, hence the name.

In 1977 Mark graduated with an Honors degree in Botany from Adelaide University, he went on to do further studies in Plant Bio Chemistry in the University of Alberta in Edmonton Canada gaining his Masters degree in 1981.

In 1983 Mark found himself pulling

out blackberries and arranging Brian Croser's gardens at Petaluma. Brians vineyard manager at the time, Alan Dean, left to teach viticulture at Wagga Wagga, suddenly Mark was also vineyard Manager for Petaluma.

In 1985 Mark bought the Whisson Lake property and began planting his Pinot Noir carefully colonal selection has ensured great balanced wines. Mark is a fastidious viticulturalist

and constantly pushing the parameters of vinegrowing for premium wines, he utilises a number of trellising systems, pruning techniques and the expensive policy of bunch thining limiting each vine to an exact number of bunches.

All is in the search of the ultimate wine. The vineyard has been dry grown, i.e. no irrigation since 1995. The intensity of his Pinot Noir is extraordinary as its complexity in his 1996, the first dry grown vintage, I could detect a real strawberry conserve character overlain by meaty roast lamb, with some herbaceous tobacco mint and anise highlights.

Mark also runs a big viticultural consulting and vineyard management company which runs over 30 vineyards in the Adelaide Hills. He has also been heavily involved in the establishment of the 720 acre "Kayinga" Vineyard at Langhorne Creek.

Mark Whisson has a passion for Pinot Noir and like his passion for sports cars he likes them powerful, sleek and definitely racey !!

Ravenswood Lane

Ravenswood Lane is about style.

Conceived in France and created in the Adelaide Hills, Ravenswood Lane wines are neither European or Australian in style, rather the best of both worlds.

These wines have the structure and finesse of Europe's best, complimented by intense fine fruit flavours and spice, a produce of Australian sunlight and the terroir of Ravenswood Lane. Ravenswood Lane sits high in the Adelaide Hills nearby the tiny village of Hahndorf.

It is also the home of the Starvedog Lane wines which emerged from a very similar premise that developed the Ravenswood Lane wines. That is a focus on quality, structure, character and mouthfeel.

Ravenswood Lane & Starvedog Lane wines are world wines from the Adelaide Hills.

Address: HAHNDORF 5245	**Winemaker:** Stephen Pannel, Glenn James, Ed Carr & Rob Mann	Beginning Chardonnay	5 yrs
Phone: 0419 862 811 **Fax:** (08) 8388 7233		Reunion Shiraz	10+ yrs
Email: thelane@olis.net.au	**Est:** 1992 **Cases:** 5,000	Starvedog Lane Sauvignon Blanc	2 yrs
WWW: www.ravenswoodlane.com.au	**Principal Wines** **Potential**	Starvedog Lane Shiraz	5-7 yrs
Owner: J & H Edwards	Gathering Sauvignon Blanc 3 yrs	Starvedog Lane Cabernet Sauvignon	5-7 yrs

Two Dogs International

Two Dogs has a true pedigree, in 1993, Duncan MacGillivray created a world first. After his Adelaide Hills orchardist neighbour asked what he could do with hundreds of under-sized and over-sized lemons, that he could not sell. Duncan joked, I'll try brewing them". Duncan brewed up the excess lemons and made a delicious all-natural and totally refreshing Lemon Brew and just for fun, he called it "Two Dogs". Almost overnight Two Dogs became a success throughout Australia. Sales soared and within months a whole new category of alcoholic drinks was created.

This traditionally, fermented natural beverage is made only from fresh Australian Lemons, it's light to medium in body, has a pleasant aroma with a clean citrus palate and a fresh and slightly dry finish with low alcohol level (4.2%), make it perfect for health conscious consumers, Two Dogs is finding an enthusiastic market. Fresh lemons are selected at their peak, the latest

technology is employed involving an innovative Australian designed process to enhance the volatile aromatic compounds found in fresh lemons, which are usually lost during processing, giving an ideal acid/sugar balance with moderate levels of carbonation and alcohol that produces a good mouth feel.

'Lemon Brew' is the company's flagship product, the worldwide sales are approaching 3 million cases per year. 'Orange Brew' was first produced in response to an oversupply of oranges in the Riverland, Australia's largest citrus producing area.

The thirst for Two Dogs grew so much the race was on to distribute this appealing product outside Australia. The UK was the first market to be entered, in time for the summer of 1995. Around 1,000,000 cases sold in six months, an exceptional achievement, given initial estimates of 300,000 cases in the first 12 months. Not to be stopped, Two Dogs then forged on into Europe, with countries including Denmark, Finland, France, Germany, Italy, Netherlands, Norway, Sweden and Switzerland. In 1995, the USA market was established.

Two dogs is a genuine revolution in the world's Beverage Industry and a delightful drink, you should try, for your health's sake.

Eden Valley

The Eden Valley Region has been in recent years tied in with the Adelaide Hills climatically as both regions are in the Mt Lofty Ranges. However, from a wine tourism point of view, traditionally the region has always been aligned with the Barossa Valley and often known as the Barossa Ranges. The climate is cool with most vineyards located 400 metres or more above sea level.

Many vineyards such as Pewsey Vale planted firstly by Joseph Gilbert date back to the 1840's. The development in the region over the last two decades has been astonishing. The Hill-Smith's of Yalumba fame have planted large vineyards at Pewsey Vale, Hill-Smith Estate and Heggies. Southcorp have large vineyards at Tollana-Woodbury and Seppelts Partalunga, on the border with the Adelaide Hills. Mountadam is most impressive and others such as Jim Irvine and Karl Seppelt join with traditional long-term vineyards and wineries such as Henschke at Keyneton. The region stretches from Mt Pleasant in the south to Moculta in the north and borders on the Barossa Valley on the west. The main towns with long wine traditions are Springton and Keyneton. Riesling thrives and makes exceptional wines but all classic varieties do well in this cool climate region with many varying soils and slopes.

Eden Valley

Eden Valley - SA

1. Craneford Wine Co.
2. Henschke
3. Irvine
4. Karl Seppelt Grand Cru
5. Mount Adam

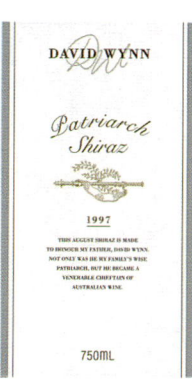

Henschke

The Henschke family have a long and rich winemaking history in Australia. They are dignified and private people, who are purposeful and enthusiastic in their desire to produce individual and exceptional wines.

Johann Christian Henschke arrived in South Australia in 1841, initially settled in the Barossa Valley at Bethany, and moved to Keyneton in the Barossa Ranges in 1862. Henschke's is now the only winery in the immediate area but it was once one of many established by German and English settlers in the last century.

The first wine was made at Henschke in 1868 and Johann's grandson Paul Alfred helped his father build substantial cellars at the turn of the century. The wines were mainly fortified until 1951 when Cyril Henschke took over the business, and began bottling and labelling Henschke table wines. In 1970 he received a Churchill Fellowship and travelled the world studying wine making.

Henschke wines are now made and managed by Stephen Henschke who was educated at Adelaide University and at the Geisenheim Wine Institute in Germany. He has updated and

restored much of the winery, and the cellar door area is superb. The winery exudes an air of history and the wonderful 130-year-old Henschke home next door is set in a beautiful garden.

Stephen Henschke's white wines are exciting. The improvements to the winery and his study have paid off, producing a range of excellent white varietal wines including a chardonnay, semillon, riesling, sauvignon blanc, gewurztraminer and a magnificent noble riesling. The Henschke reds are still living up to their big reputation with Mount Edelstone and Hill of Grace (from a nearby vineyard near the Gnadenberg Church meaning 'Hill of Grace') being outstanding.

The Henschke's are a real team with Stephen's wife and chief viticulturist Prue Henschke providing him with fantastic grapes for his great wines, which easily ranks the winery in the top few of Australia's best.

Address: Henschke Road KEYNETON 5353	**Est:** 1868 **Vine Ha:** 75 **Cases:** 35,000	Mount Edelstone	7-10 yrs
Phone: (08) 8564 8223 **Fax:** (08) 8564 8294	**Public Hours:** 9am-4.30pm, weekdays; 9am-12pm, Sat; 10am-3pm, public holidays	Keyneton Estate	7-10 yrs
Email: info@henschke.com.au		Johann's Garden Grenache	3-5 yrs
WWW: www.henschke.com.au	**Principal Wines** **Potential**	Julius Eden Valley Riesling	5-7 yrs
Winemaker: Stephen Henschke	Cyril Henschke Cabernet Sauvignon 7-10 yrs	Hill of Grace	10+ yrs

Karl Seppelt Grand Cru

After a long search Karl and Lotte Seppelt found an ideal property to plant vines and start their own wine enterprise. They purchased 120 hectares in 1981, located a couple of kilometres south of Springton, which originally belonged to George Fife Angas.

The stone buildings are quite special and the Estate has developed remarkably since then. Karl is a meticulous person with a grand plan and the Tower he has built at the entrance to the winery is distinctly reminiscent of Chateau La Tour, the famous French Grand Cru.

Four hectares were planted to chardonnay and cabernet sauvignon

in 1981. This was to be a retirement project for Karl and Lotte after his long working life with Seppelts. However things did not stop there, in 1985 a further four hectares were planted and the first vintage from the Estate was made. Expansion continues to this day.

Karl has made wines that are of truly exceptional quality. His Brut Sauvage Methode Champenoise is bone dry and an ideal aperitif style. He also makes a Chardonnay Brut Sparkling and a Shiraz Sparkling also by the Methode Champenoise process.

The table wine range includes a chablis style chardonnay dry and

crisp. A rhine riesling and a long living bordeaux style cabernet sauvignon. Added to this is a shiraz from Langhorne Creek grapes. Long a devotee of fortified wines, Karl makes an exquisite dry flor fino sherry which often graces my dinner table - "try it with or in the soup" a vintage and a tawny port. Over 100 medals have been won in major shows.

The Estate has a wonderful cellar door and a function cellar ideal for a dinner or lunch. Karl's son Peter is now involved at Grand Cru. It is an Estate not to be missed on your wine journey.

Address: PO BOX 153 MOUNT PLEASANT 5235	**Public Hours:** 10am-5pm daily	Sparking Shiraz
Phone: (08) 8568 2378 **Fax:** (08) 8568 2799	**Principal Varieties:** Pinot Noir, Riesling,	Cabernet Sauvignon
Email: grandcru@adelaide.on.net	Cabernet, Chardonnay, Merlot, Meunier	Chardonnay Riesling
Owner: K. J. Seppelt	**Principal Wines**	Merlot Shiraz
Est: 1981 **Vine Ha:** 12 **Cases:** 5,000	Sparkling Brut Sauvage & Chardonnay Brut	Fino Sherry Vintage Port - Tawny Port - Muscat

Irvine

High up in the Eden Valley is the Springhill Manor of Jim and Marjorie Irvine, built in 1860. Jim is a real gentleman and without doubt one of Australia's busiest and most sought-after winemaking consultants.

Over the years Jim has made wine on a consulting basis for some 45 different wineries, all of whom speak highly of his professionalism and ability.

In 1993, he achieved the ultimate accolade when a wine made by him for the Elderton Winery won the Jimmy Watson Trophy. For his own label, Jim has chosen the high ground; he makes and absolute stunner of a merlot. Many years ago when consulting for Normans, at a lunch, he tasted the Chateau Petrus, the world's most expensive red wine - a 100% merlot from the Pomerol district near Bordeaux.

Jim has successfully made his own version of the taste he fell in love with that day. The merlot spends almost four years in wood and yet is still fresh, but so silky smooth and complex. It earns every bit of its

regal name 'Grand Merlot' dressed in its regal robes - probably Australia's best-packaged wine. The 1988 Merlot won the World Merlot Competition from hundreds of entrants and he has since repeated the same feat in Switzerland in 1997.

Jim also make several superb methode champenoise wines including a straight meslier, an unusual variety used in the Champagne region of France to help the acidity in the base wines during warm years: its zesty fruit makes it the ideal aperitif.

The Irvine Blanc de Blanc Chardonnay normally spends 4 - 5 years on yeast lees but often longer, his merlot red methode champenoise is exquisite.

For over 50 years since his first job in the laboratory at Glenloth as a sixteen year old, Jim Irvine has weaved his creative magic with wine, never losing his enthusiasm and zest for life, shared wholeheartedly by his wife Marjorie and their two daughters. The elder, Joanne, traded in her nursing theatre sisters degree to study winemaking. The Irvine wines of the future look assured.

Craneford

One of the freshest brightest and innovative wineries and hospitality houses is Craneford, right in the middle of the little town of Truro, which is situated on the top of the Barossa Ranges at the Northern end of the Eden Valley.

The gorgeous Café Restaurant fronts onto the main road and is run by John Zilm, his wife Bev and son Steven. The Zilms also have a hairdressing salon next door and a delightful residence opposite. The family certainly have a lot of artistic flair as one sits in the café enjoying the fresh vibrant food, you can look in on a full working winery. The wines are pressed and fermented before your eyes and the reds quietly mature in oak barrels all around you. The building has been rebuilt with beautiful 90 year old black butt timber from the old Jetty at Port Pirie. The Zilms still have plenty left for future expansion.

John has a wine science degree and has had heaps of experience

winemaking since the early 1980's. He not only makes his own wines but is in high demand as a consultant winemaker and makes wine for other small producers in his boutique facility.

Craneford was founded in 1978 by Colin Forbes and forged a top reputation. When the Zilms bought the Company in 1998, they decided to move the operation from the sleepy town of Springton to Truro where the main road from Adelaide to Sydney carries some 2,500 cars a week. The move has been an unqualified success.

John's Craneford wines have been most successful, his 1998 Riesling being chosen as the Penguin Wine Guide, white wine of the year, it was also dual winner of the Prestigious Advertiser Hyatt Wine Awards.

Craneford grow and make an excellent Tempranillo - a vibrant Spanish red variety.

On your travels make sure you drop in and enjoy the wine, food and hospitality of the Zilm family.

Address: Moorundie Street TRURO 5356
Phone: (08) 8564 0003 **Fax:** (08) 8564 0008
Email: johnzilm@dove.net.au

WWW: www.cranefordwines.com
Winemaker: John Zilm   **Est:** 1978
Public Hours: 10am-5pm daily

Principal Varieties: Cabernet Franc, Chardonnay, Merlot, Semillon, Cabernet Sauvignon, Grenache, Riesling, Shiraz

Mount Adam

Adam Wynn is a real winner, focused, positive and urbane, his technical skills rank with the world's best, but his creative flair and love of music and art give extra dimensions to his wines that are truly exciting.

His family's achievements in Australian wine have been extraordinary; he is one of the most likeable and natural people you would be likely to meet.

The Wynn wine saga commenced in Poland just after the turn of the century. Samuel Wynn made a yearly pilgrimage to the Black Sea and returned to Poland with dried raisins which he reconstituted and turned into wine. At 21 years of age, he arrived in Australia keen to pursue a career in wine; this began with a wine bar in Bourke Street Melbourne, where he came up with the classic barrel-design Wynns 2 litre flagon. Samuel lived until 90 years of age, a testament to a life tempered by good wine.

Adam's late father David truly put the Wynn family on the wine map. In 1950 he purchased the run down old Coonawarra Estate, featuring its famous three-gabled roof on his Wynn's Coonawarra label. The world recognition of this region bear testament to David's greatness, but he did much more. A very talented artist, he was chairman of the

Adelaide Festival Trust for many years and created the concept of the highly successful Barossa Music Festival, which he served until his death as its founding chairman.

David and Adam had enormous vision; their search for the top viticultural region in Australia ended 600 metres above the Barossa and Eden Valleys. A visit to Mountadam is a rare treat, set high on Eden Ridge in rugged rocky country, habitat for the majestic wedgetail eagle, the symbol of the winery, prominently displayed in the huge granite sculptures on the impressive stone pillared entrance to the

vineyard. The setting just on the lee side of the ridge gives protection to the vines from harsh winds, and provides an ideal frost-free microclimate; the resultant outstanding fruit is the cornerstone of Adam's wines. Adam followed a degree in agricultural science with a postgraduate degree in oenology from Bordeaux in France, where he was dux of the course in 1981.

Rarely have I seen so many expensive French oak barrels in any winery, let alone the modestly sized Mountadam. Adam follows a no expense spared philosophy, using French Troncais oak, tight-grained and with subtle but distinct flavour characteristics. Barrel fermentation, careful selection and individual treatment of the many hundreds of barrels for the chardonnay and the reds, produces complex wines that shine at the top of Australia's wine tree.

Adam produces a 50/50 merlot cabernet wine simply called 'The Red', which is simply superb. The cornerstone of the product range is the Mountadam Chardonnay. The David Wynn range of quality Eden Valley varietals and the Eden Ridge organically grown range complement the domain-grown Mountadam wines. Adam Wynn has literally taken the high ground of Australian wine.

Address: High Eden Road	Winemaker: Adam Wynn & Andrew Ewart	Principal Wines	Potential
EDEN VALLEY 5235	Est: 1972 Vine Ha: 51	Mountadam Chardonnay	2-5 yrs
Phone: (08) 8564 1101 Fax: (08) 8564 1064	Cases: 40,000	Mountadam Pinot Noir	5-10 yrs
Email: office@mtadam.com	Public Hours: 11am-4pm, daily	Mountadam The Red	5-15 yrs
WWW: www.mountadam.com	Principal Varieties: Chardonnay, Pinot Noir,	Mountadam Cabernet Sauvignon	5-15 yrs
Owner: Adam Wynn / Lumn	Cabernet Sauvignon, Merlot	Mountadam Merlot	5-15 yrs

Barossa Valley

Without doubt the most famous of Australia's wine regions is the Barossa Valley. Something of an institution with Australian wine lovers, the area has a personality all its own. The turn of the Century in 2000 has seen a real renaissance in the region.

Its unique character is mainly due to the Barossa's large German population who began to arrive in 1842. Having sought a new start in a new land, many hundreds of German Lutherans were settled on the huge properties of George Fife Angas. Many of these immigrants had already been involved in viticulture in Germany and soon planted vine cuttings they had brought with them to Australia.

Significant amongst these first commercial plantings were those made by Johann Gramp at Rowland Flat, which saw the beginning of the Orlando Company and that of Samuel Smith at Angaston, which became Yalumba. The Seppelt family company was established with Joseph Seppelt's planting in 1851.

The first wines produced in the Barossa were table wines, but as fortifieds gained in popularity by the turn of the century, winemakers were forced to alter the emphasis of the production. This transition was easy due to the valley's temperate climate, rich soils and sheltered environment, which enabled new grape varieties, such as grenache and pedro to reach production relatively quickly. Popular tastes have reverted to premium table wines, as a result, the area under vine in the Barossa is currently less than its peak, as many vignerons are still replanting their vineyards with grapes more suitable for table wine and water to establish the vines is scarce.

Companies such as Peter Lehmann, Basedow, St. Hallett, Rockford and others are producing excellent premium table wines and have recently been joined by newcomers on the boutique arena such as Burge Family, Bethany, Charles Melton, Charles Cimicky, Grant Burge, more latterly Ross Estate, Schild Estate, H. Thumm's magnificent Chateau Barossa and others. The Barossa Valley is home to many large companies such as Penfold's and Kaiser Stuhl, Orlando, Seppelts, Yalumba, Wolf Blass, Tollana, Krondorf, Leo Buring and Saltram.

All these wineries are totally committed to Barossa fruit and have a full recognition of the Barossa's solid viticultural base. Many vineyards have been in the same families and worked by them for five - six generations.

Many vineyards of shiraz, grenache and semillon have 50 year old vines and some over 100 years old, whilst other regions have changed dramatically viticulturally, the Barossa has not, but there has been a renaissance of quality in bottled table wines. The growing emphasis on wine tourism has led to the establishment of the likes of Kaesler Wines with its restaurant, conference and seminar facilities and cottage accommodation. The list goes on, with many fine restaurants and Bed and Breakfast Inns being established during the last decade. The sensational Novotel Barossa All Seasons Resort alongside the Tanunda Golf Course has been a welcome addition.

Every two years the Barossa Valley is the setting for a wonderful Vintage Festival. Commencing on Easter Monday, the festival runs for a week and is centred around the Tanunda oval. There is a giant fair and all the local wine companies set up marquees for public tastings. A colourful parade passes through the streets and a Vintage Festival Queen is crowned.

The highlights of this celebration are the huge banquets, held in Tanunda's enormous hall, consisting of a sit down Barossa feast for roughly 2,000 people at a time. The entertainment provided at these functions is excellent, particularly the comedian · who is the local undertaker. In addition, the Ledertahl Choir and Tanunda Brass Band usually perform to delighted crowds who, by the end of the evening are usually standing on their tables clapping to the music.

The Festival wine auction is also worth attending and must be the best of its kind held in Australia.

The Spring Barossa Music Festival features two weeks of outstanding concerts at wineries, the valley's beautiful churches and other venues. This event is not only of National but International significance and is already a major South Australian Tourism attraction. The Valley also boasts some of the best bakeries and small goods makers in Australia. Put a trip to the Barossa on your travel agenda. Until then, why not enjoy some of her fine wines.

Barossa Valley

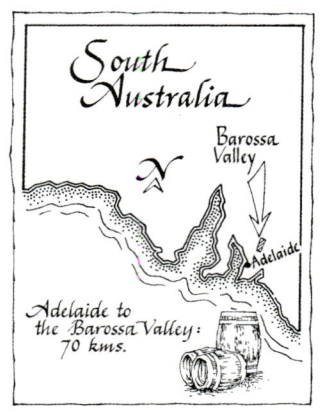

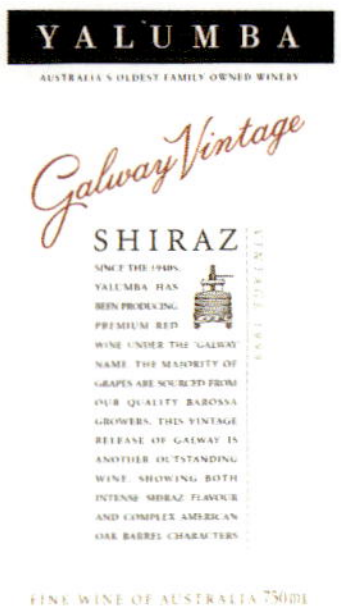

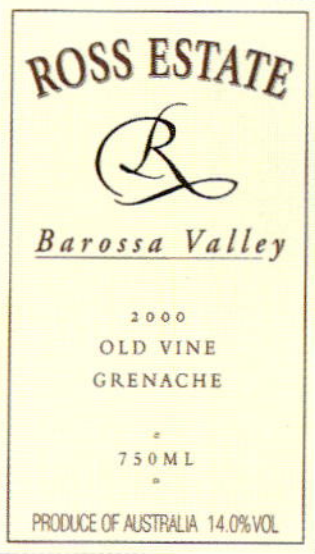

South Australia

Barossa Valley

Adelaide

Adelaide to the Barossa Valley: 70 kms.

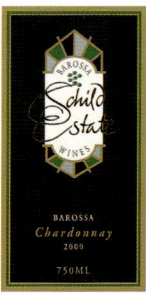

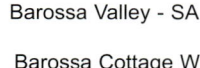

Barossa Valley - SA

1. Barossa Cottage Wines
2. Barossa Helicopters
3. Barossa Settlers
4. Barossa Valley Estate
5. Basedow Wines
6. Bethany Wines
7. Burge Family Wines
8. Charles Cimicky
9. Charles Melton
10. Chateau Barrosa
11. Chateau Dorrien
12. Chateau Yaldara & Motor Inn
13. Dorrien Estate
14. Elderton Wines
15. Gnadenfrei Estate
16. Grant Burge Wines
17. Hamiltons Ewell
18. Heritage Wines
19. High Wycombe Wines
20. Jenke Vineyards

21. Kaesler Wines
22. Kellermeister Wines
23. Kies Estate
24. Krondorf Wines
25. Langmeil Wines
26. Liebichwein
27. Miranda Wines
28. Novotel Resort
29. Orlando Wines
30. Penfold's Wines
31. Peter Lehmann Wines
32. Richmond Grove
33. Rockford Wines
34. Ross Estate
35. Saltram Wine Estate
36. Schild Estate
37. Seppeltsfield
38. St Hallett Wines
39. Stanley Brothers
40. Stockwell Wines
41. Tarac Technologies
42. Twin Valley Estate
43. Whistler Wines
44. Wolf Blass Winery
45. Yalumba

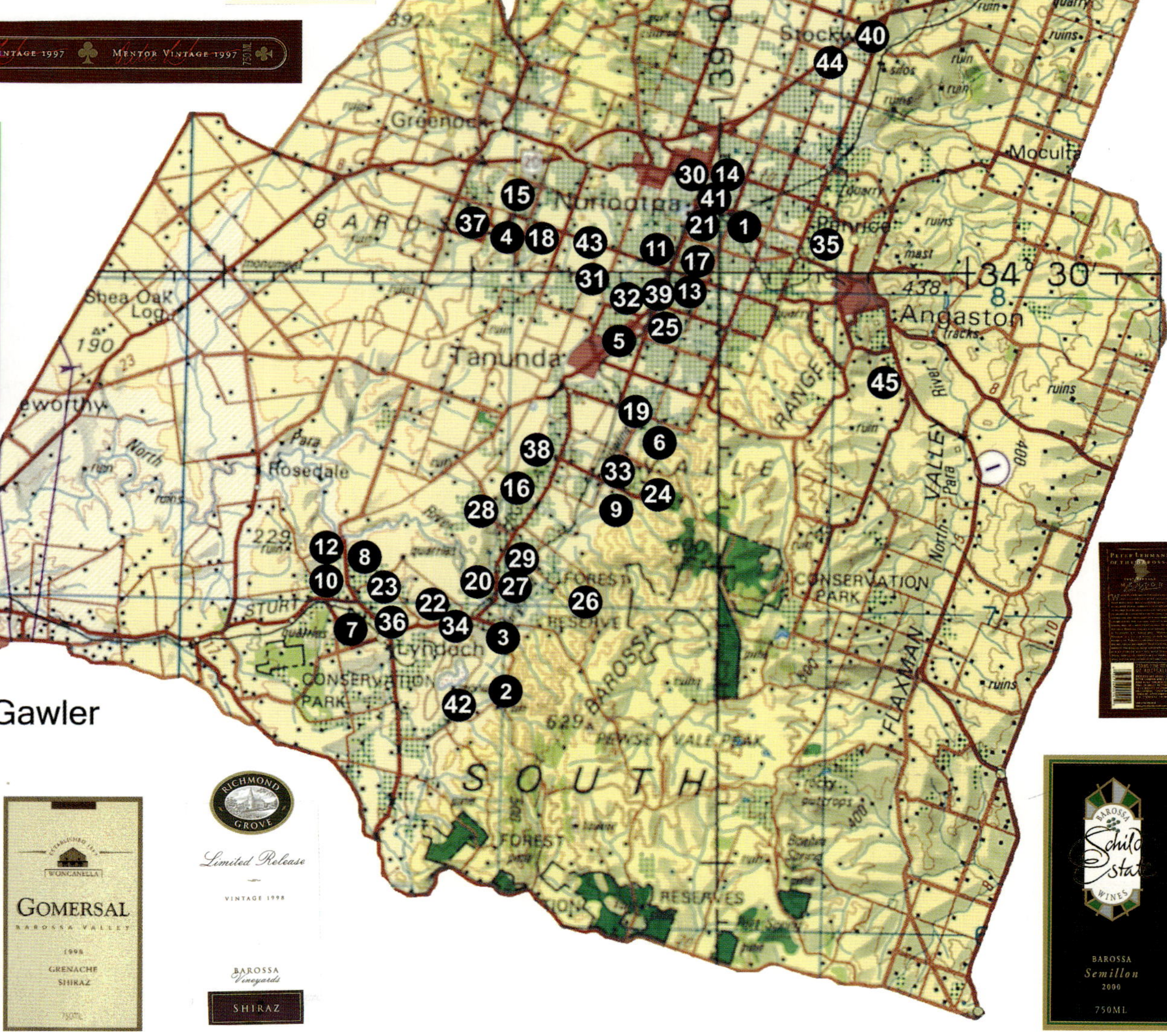

Gawler

Barossa Valley

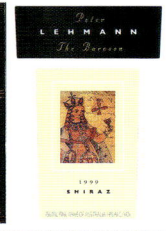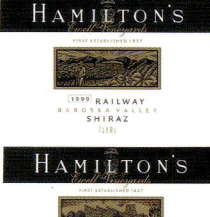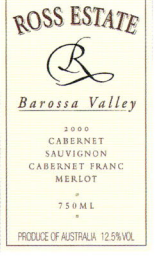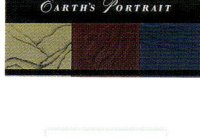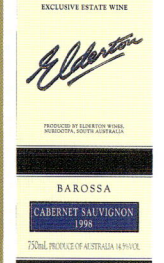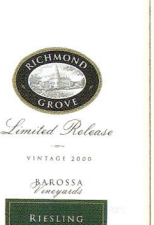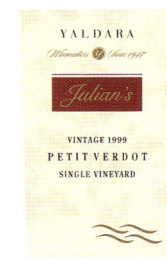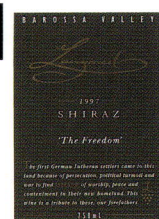

Barossa Helicopters

Tucked away in the Historic Hoffnungsthal Valley (a German name meaning Valley of Hope) is the dynamic Helicopter enterprise of Peter and Sandra Kies, Peter's ancestors came to the Valley in the mid 1800's his father Ken was heavily involved in grape growing and winemaking. The Kies have a beautiful property accessible from the Lyndoch Williamstown road. Statuesque Palms line the driveway to the Helicopter Hangars, they are surrounded by the Kies 150 acre vineyard which includes about 12 acres of Shiraz planted in the 1890's, some of the crop may have even found itself in "Grange" over the years.

Barossa Helicopters offer a number of tours over the Barossa and Eden Valley, ranging from 6 minutes to an hour, for as little as $25 per seat, it is a great way to see this unique area and its many inaccessible hills and valleys.

Barossa Helicopters also offer sunrise and sunset flights, Airport transfers and are available for charter. I can vouch for their suitability for aerial photography having chartered and flown in them several times, it is a fantastic feeling.

People of all ages are welcome and prepaid vouchers for all scenic flights are available making an unusual and exciting gift. Why not shout yourself or your friends a fantastic experience.

"Dr." Max and his baby
"Grange-Schubert's Unfinished Symphony"

Barossa Valley Estate

Barossa Valley Estate Winery was initially established at Angle Vale just south of the Barossa in 1985 as a co-operative with the objective of making and marketing premium bottled wine. The grape growers and the winemakers have a very close relationship due to this structure and the synergy that has developed is evident in the richness and depth of flavours in the wine. The winery has recently been relocated to Marananga near Seppeltsfield, to provide winemaking facilities in the Barossa Valley close to its grape growers to further enhance quality wine production.

The labels include the E & E Black Pepper Shiraz which has won world acclaim, being awarded trophies in the International Wine Competition in London and rated in the USA's Wine Spectator's Top 10. The E & E Sparkling Shiraz as well as the

Ebenezer range have been bestowed with awards both nationally and internationally. This gives great testament to the quality of wines made from this premium grape growing area. The Moculta range of premium selection reds and whites as well as the Spires Chardonnay Semillon and Shiraz Cabernet make

up the remainder of the portfolio.

The recently established winery at Marananga near Seppeltsfield crushes approximately 3,000 tonnes of fruit and is situated in a picturesque setting providing modern tasting facilities as well as landscaped picnic areas.

Address: Seppeltsfield Road MARANANGA 5117	**Public Hours:** 9am-5pm weekdays, 10am-4pm Saturday	E&E Black Pepper Shiraz	10-15 yrs
Phone: (08) 8563 1311		E&E Sparkling Shiraz	5-10 yrs
Email: bve@chariot.net.au **Est:** 1985	**Principal Varieties:** Cabernet Sauvignon,	Ebenezer Range	5-10 yrs
WWW: www.bve.com.au **Cases:** 90,000	Shiraz, Chardonnay, Merlot, Semillon	Moculta Range	2-4 yrs
Winemaker: Natasha Mooney	**Principal Wines** **Potential**	Spires Range	1 yr

Bethany Wines

The Schrapel family, with Robert as winemaker and Geoff as marketing/sales/ viticulturist, represent one of the oldest grape-growing families in the region, going back to the German pioneers of the last century.

In 1977 they set up a beautiful winery, with a stunning panoramic view over the entire valley, by building into an old disused quarry. The natural cellar and insulation this has provided at minimal expense shows their good sense.

Like many Barossa wineries, they first made a mark with their riesling and today make a fine range of premium table and fortified wines including the aptly-named 'The Old Quarry Port'.

In 1994, at the Canberra National Wine Show, Bethany Wines won the trophy for the best dry red table wine, shiraz predominant, with its 1992 Bethany Shiraz.

If you are ever in the valley for any Barossa event weekend, don't miss Bethany. The folk there always put on a great show with food, wine and dancing and the location is a knock out.

Address: Bethany Road TANUNDA 5352	**Est:** Vineyard 1850, Winery 1981	**Principal Varieties:** Riesling, Chardonnay,
Phone: (08) 8563 2086 **Fax:** (08) 8563 0046	**Vine Ha:** 25 **Cases:** 18,000	Shiraz, Semillon, Cabernet Sauvignon,
Owner/Winemaker: Rob & Geoffrey Schrapel	**Public Hours:** 10am-5pm, Mo-Sa; 1pm-5pm, Sun	Grenache

Novotel Barossa Valley Resort

Late in 1999 Tourism in the Barossa Valley rose to another level with the opening of the Barossa Valley Resort. The Barossa has always prided itself on being Australia's premier wine tourism region and was the first wine region to have a vintage festival, which is held in April every second year. The Barossa's international reputation has also increased dramatically over the last decade or so, since the Australian wine export boom has been in full swing.

All these things were particularly positive but something had always been missing, accommodation and conference facilities of an international standard, this has now changed with the Novotel Barossa Valley Resort.

The site chosen for the Resort is spectacular running along the sheltered side of a Ridge, high above Jacobs Creek and Rowland Flat, the panoramic views over the vines, the statuesque white gums lining the bed of Jacobs Creek and the Barossa Ranges as a backdrop, its perfect.

On the other side of the Ridge a short walk from the resort is the Tanunda Golf Course which is in the process of being upgraded with help from the Resort.

Novotel is part of the French Accor Group, the world and Australia's largest Hotel and Resort operators. Accor really understand wine tourism, they have resorts in French wine regions such as the Loire Valley, Burgundy, Bordeaux, Champagne, Alsace and also in the Swan Valley in Western Australia. The Barossa Novotel is their 20th Resort in Australia, it also joins in with the Novotel in Adelaide's Hindley Street and the superb Grand Mercure Mt Lofty House also both operated by Accor.

The 140 studio and two bedroom apartments are spread along the top of the resorts natural amphitheater, all have panoramic views over the valley.

The resort has a splendid lounge come dining room with 270 degree view over the valley it also has 8 function rooms and can host conferences with up to 340 delegates, already its hosting many product launches, executive seminars, incentive groups, exhibitions and special events.

Apart from the Golf course and naturally visits to the Barossa's many wineries, both large and small, there

Novotel Barossa Valley Resort

are many other leisure activities to participate in. The Resort has a large swimming pool surrounded by gardens, again overlooking the valley, a health club-gymnasium, tennis courts and a kids club.

In 2000 the resort was rightly awarded "The Most Outstanding Contribution to tourism in South Australia".

Novotel have a great advantage, their worldwide network is already bringing many overseas visitors to the Barossa. The increasingly sophisticated wine, cuisine and culture offered in regions like the Barossa, with all its history and natural beauty, is sure to bring them back again.

The Barossa wineries food and tourism businesses have embraced

the resort, it's a great partnership that's already developing.

When you visit the Novotel Barossa Valley Resort, maybe on one of the great value packages they offer, you will get the "Complete Experience" of the Barossa Wine, Food, Culture, Sightseeing, Recreation and Relaxation, literally in the Lap of Luxury. At the Novotel they really know how to look after you.

Chateau Barrosa

An extraordinary event happened on New Years Eve 2000, Hermann Thumm A.M, the human dynamo who founded Chateau Yaldara in 1947 opened his new Grand Venture "Chateau Barrosa" on his 88th Birthday. Hermann has always been affectionately known as HT, he was born on 31 December 1912 in Georgia, the last of 10 children, his father a German Cooper who had started his own winery. HT grew up working in the family's extensive vineyards and went on to become manager of the business when only 19 years old. He survived the Russian Revolution and escaped swimming across the Arax River into Persia, after his two companions were both captured in front of him by a Russian border guard. He spent 10 turbulent years in Persia where he invented a new way of making hard soap from linseed and sunflower oils, he then helped build the Trans-Persian railway and worked for a German wine shipper establishing vineyards and a winery near Tehran.

In 1941 HT arrived in Australia as a prisoner of war at a camp in the Murray Valley, it wasn't long before he was putting his winemaking skills to good use with the local grapes

and his home fashioned champagne in beer bottles was a huge hit.

When the war finished HT was able to stay on and set about realising his dream of becoming a well-to-do wine and champagne manufacturer, little did he imagine his dreams and much more would come to reality. With an introduction to a Pastor in the

Barossa Valley from his own Lutheran Religion, he arrived at the Tanunda Railway Station, a job was arranged for him at a family winery near Lyndoch, he did much to help his employers to improve their business but his burning desire to begin his own business, saw him search for a suitable place to start.

In October 1947 he bought a huge stone building which had started its life as a flour mill in 1862. At one point of its life it had been converted to a winery, now it had no roof but was in reasonably good condition. Five months later after an incredible amount of hard work, with a young builder HT had befriended, by some miracle on the 1 March 1948 Yaldara - an aboriginal word meaning "Sparkling" crushed its first grape.

In 1950 he married Ingeburg the daughter of the local priest Th. Hebart their strong partnership has helped them prosper over the last 50 years. With their two sons Robert and Dieter they built Chateau Yaldara into a huge pre-eminent Australian winery. HT's foresight in seeing the immense benefits of wine tourism was way before his time. He was a real pioneer of cellar door trade and direct marketing in the 1950's and 1960's partly to overcome the restrictive distribution of wine through hotels, where small wineries and newcomers were at an almost

impossible disadvantage to the large established wineries.

In 1958 HT decided to create a centrepiece for his enterprise to integrate his wine with the arts and to use as a means of expanding wine tourism and its benefits. The European inspired Chateau he built is magnificent and gave him a home for his growing porcelain and art collection, many music concerts and recitals followed its first use, by the world renowned Australian musical group "The Seekers".

Shortly after the Chateau was finished he began building the Barossa's first modern accomodation and Hospitality centre, the Circular Barossa Motel, on its elevated site as one enters the Valley from Adelaide, this was the real beginning of true National and International tourism for the Barossa Region.

In his wine enterprise he was as usual restless for a challenge which had its outlet in a remarkable development. HT was looking for a way to make grape spirit for his fortified wines but also protect his beautiful environment and create some new products from the vine, for healthy enjoyment. He wanted to tackle the general supermarket food

trade plus the untapped markets of Asia and the middle East where alcohol is practically banned. His creation of a vacuum distillation method (under a vacuum alcohol boils off at about 60oC) does not destroy the delicate flavours of the wine, there is no oxidation because no oxygen is present under a vacuum. By distilling wine with half the grape sugar still in it he was also able to create non-alcoholic wines

and a unique grape spread no waste, no pollution, and still get his grape spirit.

HT also built a splendid imposing Reception Centre overlooking a lake and a indoor outdoor restaurant and bistro overlooking the stream and stately gums at the rear of the property.

As the millennium closed HT sadly sold Yaldara but another dream was emerging for him, he immediately began landscaping the gardens around his now Barrosa Park Motor Inn planting 18,000 roses (possibly the largest Rose garden in the Southern Hemisphere) and building his "Chateau Barrosa".

This true cultural centre for the Barossa Valley is a building of truly impressive dimensions, where his huge collection of porcelain, glass and a wine museum could have a proper home. The building will also be a major visitor centre and host concerts and cultural events of all kinds.

"Chateau Barrosa" is set to grow even bigger in the next few years and, I am sure will fulfill the dreams of its extraordinary creator. It was my very humble privilege to share a glass or two of HT's new Chateau Barrosa sparkling, with the master and photograph him on his 88th birthday as he christened his new baby.

Address: Gomersal Road LYNDOCH 5351	**Winemaker:** James Irvine	9am-5pm, weekends
Phone: (08) 8524 4200 **Fax:** (08) 8524 4678	**Est:** 1947 **Vine Ha:** 65 **Cases:** 550,000	**Principal Varieties:** Cab Sav, Merlot, Shiraz,
Owner: Thumm Family	**Public Hours:** 8.30am-5.00pm, weekdays;	Chard., Semillon, Sav Blanc, Pinot Noir, Grenache

Basedow Wines

of his fast-growing production, took over the winery, upgrading it even further. The 1995 Basedow Chardonnay won the white wine of the year trophy at London's prestigious International Wine Challenge.

In 1996 progressive wine merchant Terry Hill, whose Hill International Wines in Sydney is a highly successful premium wine distributor, took over Basedow. Terry is a long time friend of Grant Burge and was also born in the Barossa Valley. In another amazing coincidence Terry's great grandmother travelled to Australia from Germany on the same ship as Johannes and settled in the Barossa in the 1840s, Terry released a stunning "Johannes" Barossa Shiraz 1996 vintage to celebrate Basedows centenary. The tradition will continue with Basedows best Shiraz appearing under this label each year. Grant remains in charge of the winemaking activities also making wine for Terry's two great McLaren Vale wineries, Marienberg and Fern Hill.

The Basedow wines and label today represent a quality boutique style wine at bargain prices. The underground tasting cellar is one of the best in the valley. Drop in while you are in Tanunda - it's easy to find.

In 1996, Basedow celebrated their centenary. The winery, built beside a creek in the centre of Tanunda by brothers Martin and Johannes Basedow, was taken over by Martin's son Oscar and renamed O. Basedow and Sons.

Basedow's history and reputation had been forged with fortified wines, although John Basedow won the coveted Jimmy Watson Trophy in 1970 with his dry red. The real transformation for Basedow came during the mid 70's when Peter Lehmann's son Doug took over the reins, restoring the lovely old sandstone buildings, upgrading the facilities and expanding the winery's capacity considerably.

Doug began contract crushing for the likes of Wolf Blass as well as upgrading the Basedow wines. The Basedow White Burgundy was the real pioneer for wood-aged semillons. In 1993, Grant Burge, who had been using the Basedow winery for most

Address: 161-165 Murray Street TANUNDA 5352	Winemaker: Craig Stansborough Est: 1896	Chardonnay	5-7 yrs
Phone: (08) 8563 0333 Fax: (08) 8563 3597	Public Hours: 10am-5pm daily, not Xmas+GF	Riesling	10 yrs
Email: info@hillwine.com.au	Principal Wines Potential	Shiraz	7-10 yrs
Owner: Terry Hill & Family	Grenache 5 yrs	Semillon	7-10 yrs

Burge Family

Back in 1928 the Burge family founded Wilsford Wines. Today carrying on that fine tradition is Rick Burge, a big genial fellow with both winemaking and hospitality skills at his fingertips.

I first ran into Rick in Rutherglen some 15 years ago when Milan Roden and I were researching our first book. He was running the Poachers Paradise, an excellent restaurant and tavern in the main street. Rick did a stint as winemaker at St. Leonards but decided home in the Barossa Valley and the family wine business was for him.

Rick has built a beautiful winery on the family's property at Lyndoch, just as you enter the town. Functionally and aesthetically, it is very well done. Rick has also phased in the new name Burge Family Winemakers and runs the Wilsford label for his fortified wines.

The Burge family run a number of wine, food and music events, always innovative, informative, interesting and lots of fun. Rick's great interest in music has translated into the production of a number of CD's which play at the cellar door as you enjoy the wines.

The Burge Family's wines certainly have nothing to fear from competition.

Address: Barossa Highway LYNDOCH 5351	Public Hours: 10am-5pm,daily except Christmas and Good Friday	Draycott Shiraz	5-10 yrs
Phone: (08) 8524 4644		Draycott Homestead Blend	5-10 yrs
Fax: (08) 8524 4444	Principal Varieties: Shiraz, Cabernet	Draycott Merlot	2-5 yrs
Owner: Rick and Bronwyn Burge	Sauvignon, Merlot, Grenache, Touriga,	"Old Vines" Grenache	2-5 yrs
Winemaker: Rick Burge	Cabernet Franc, Riesling, Muscat Blanc	Olive Hill Riesling	2-5 yrs
Est: 1928 Vine Ha: 12 Cases: 3,300	Principal Wines Potential	Muscat Blanc Late Harvest	2-5 yrs

Liebichwein

Liebichwein was founded in 1992 by Ron Liebich, but his family history in grapegrowing and winemaking goes back considerably further. His family began winemaking in 1919 at Rowland Flat where they started Rovalley wines. Liebichwein not only includes the family name but literally means "I love wine" in "Barossa Deutsch".

The premium bottle wines coming from the elevated Eastern slopes of the Valley are certainly extremely good and very well priced. I am sure those that invest in Ron's latest reds will not be disappointed. The vineyard property was settled in 1848 by South Australia's first Potter, Samuel Hoffmann. The rich red and black soils he chose for his craft, also proved ideal for vines, giving wines of rich character.

Liebichwein is one of the few wineries selling bulk fortifieds · they also bottle great aged fortifieds.

A visit to the Liebich's charming cellar door is a real pleasure and takes one back a little in time, to a more relaxed and personal era of the wine industry.

Address: Steingarten Road ROWLAND FLAT 5342	Owner: Ron & Janet Liebich	The Darkie Shiraz	10-20 yrs
	Winemaker: Ron Liebich	The Potters Merlot	5-10 yrs
Phone: (08) 8524 4543 Fax: (08) 8524 4047	Est: 1992 Vine Ha: 32 Cases: 2,000	Riesling of the Valley	10-20 yrs
Email: liebichwein@primus.com.au	Public Hours: 11am-5pm, daily	The Lofty Cabernet Sauvignon	10-20 yrs
WWW: www.liebichwein.com.au	Principal Wines Potential	Ron's Blend Bulk Tawny	

Grant Burge

Grant Burge comes from a family long involved in grape-growing in the Barossa Valley. I first met Grant some 25 years ago when, as young lads, we used to travel to wine shows together. Grant was working as a winemaker for the Southern Vales Co-operative in McLaren Vale just across the road from Hardy's where for a couple of years I prepared the show wines for the company.

Grant then, as now, was a quiet but happy sort of fellow, very committed to his quality winemaking. Some years later, he formed a partnership with colleague Ian Wilson - Burge and Wilson. They created a label and made wine together using their good contacts in both McLaren Vale and the Barossa to source very high quality grapes.

This partnership purchased the Krondorf Winery in the Barossa from the Seagram Wine Estates Group. Ironically it was right next door to the old Burge Winery, Wilsford. Grant and Ian were highly successful and had been using the winery since 1976, a few years before purchasing it. In 1983, Krondorf went public to help with capital expenditure and expansion and two years later, Mildara purchased it, retaining Burge and Wilson as consultant winemakers.

In 1988 Grant decided to go out on his own and bought the original Jacob brothers' winery, the beautiful Moorooroo Cellars at Jacobs Creek, which were restored in the 1970's by Colin Gramp and run as a restaurant called Gramps Winekeller, then renovated again by Helen, Grant's wife in 1988. This base gave Grant the chance to develop a high profile for his excellent wines. His many talents and the help of his wife in the marketing area, has seen Grant Burge wines through a period of explosive growth. Grant won the Telecom South Australian Small Business of the Year in 1993.

Grant Burge has quietly amassed large vineyard holdings around the Barossa Valley and Barossa Ranges.

At present, 850 acres are planted in strategic locations and planting is still underway. Grant's total land holdings are around 2,000 acres, so he has further potential to expand his vineyards. He is already in fact, one of the largest grape-growers in the valley.

This control of the vineyards is what gives Grant the opportunity to make the styles of wine he wants. For many years Grant has used the Basedow Winery for his making which has been expanded and brought up to the absolute state of the art technically speaking. Grant's flagship is the "Meshach" one of Australia's top ten reds, a regal shiraz from 70 year old vines on Grant's Filsell Vineyard and named after his great-grandfather who started the family wine enterprise in the 1860.

Recently in another bold move Grant and wife Helen have bought back the Krondorf Cellars, next to their home, looking out over their beloved Barossa Valley, they have renamed it Barossa Vines Winery. This purchase will add more capacity to make and mature the wines of the expanding Grant Burge stable which are of truly fine quality.

Grant pays great credit to all his staff who have pulled together in this remarkable success story. Grant's wines have won many awards and are all very approachable in their rich fruit-driven style.

Address: Barossa Valley Way, Jacobs Creek TANUNDA 5352	Est: 1988 Vine Ha: 400	Principal Wines	Potential
	Cases: 100,000	Meshach	25 yrs
Phone: (08) 8563 3700	Public Hours: 10am-5pm, daily except	Shadrach	15 yrs
Fax: (08) 8563 2807	Christmas Day and Good Friday	Sauvignon Blanc	4 yrs
Email: gbwines@dove.com.au	Principal Varieties: Riesling, Sauvignon	Merlot	8 yrs
Owner: Grant and Helen Burge	Blanc, Chardonnay, Semillon, Shiraz,	Shiraz	10 yrs
Winemaker: Grant Burge	Cabernet Sauvignon, Merlot	Cabernet Sauvignon	10 yrs

Elderton Wines

I well remember the emergence of Elderton onto the wine market in the early 1980's. Two shiraz wines then labelled as Hermitage, a 1982 and a 1983, captured the wine drinkers imaginations with their rich flavours and velvety textures.

In 1982 the Ashmead family bought the 40-hectare Tolley vineyard and classic old homestead, on the rich alluvial river flats of the North Para River, on the southern edge of Nuriootpa. The robust old vines, the oldest of which are around 70 years, produce rich complex wines.

In 1993 the 1992 Elderton Cabernet Sauvignon won the coveted Jimmy Watson Memorial Trophy at the Royal Melbourne Show. A just reward for 10 years of exceptional red wines. Consummate, consultant winemaker Jim Irvine uses all his skill and many years of experience, to handcraft all the wines. Elderton's cellar door is delightfully appointed and has recently been enlarged and incorporates a beautiful garden courtyard. A new temperature controlled red wine maturation cellar has just been completed, on the outskirts of Nuriootpa and will give the red wines a chance to become even better if that is possible. Elderton also now make a merlot and a cabernet-shiraz-merlot blend both are silky and top class, like the shiraz and the cabernet sauvignon. The top Elderton drop is "The Command Shiraz" rich and complex with a seductive velvety texture, its right up there with the best super premium wines produced in Australia.

Elderton's whites are by no means overshadowed by their reds. The semillon, riesling, chardonnay and the botrytis semillon are in the top echelon of Barossa whites. If your celebrating try the pinot chardonnay methode champenoise sparkling and toast to Elderton's great wines.

Address: 3 Tanunda Road NURIOOTPA 5355	**Est:** 1982 **Vine Ha:** 35	**Principal Wines**	**Potential**
Phone: (08) 8562 1058 **Fax:** (08) 8562 2844	**Public Hours:** 8.30am-5pm, weekdays; 11am-	Elderton Tantalus White	
Email: elderton@chariot.net.au	4pm, weekends and public holidays	Elderton Eden Valley Riesling	10 yrs
WWW: www.eldertonwines.com.au	**Principal Varieties:** Shiraz, Cab Sauvignon,	Elderton Barossa Chardonnay	7 yrs
Owner: Lorraine Ashmead	Chardonnay, Merlot, Riesling, Semillon	Elderton Golden Semillon	6-8 yrs

Kaesler Wines

Reid Bosward is a young man who's dream has really come true, a year or two ago he talked three other investors into buying the Kaesler Wine Complex, complete with its marvellous vineyard and gnarly old shiraz vines, 108 years old, from which he produces an exquisite "Old Vine Shiraz". From the same vines he has also just released the "Old Bastard" Shiraz - the best two barrels of the old vine wine - about 50 doz. only of one of the best wines you'd ever find. Its not cheap but still a bargain in the super premium arena.

Reid first became aware of Kaesler in 1996 when he was working at Cellarmasters down the road, they were purchasing grapes from Kaesler and Reid noted they were consistently amongst the best fruit in the valley. Reid has had some great experience in winemaking, taking him from the Hunter Valley to Moldova in Eastern Europe to South Africa and even to Bordeaux in France.

Reid also makes a classic Old Vine Semillon, picked young and full of crisp citrus and apple flavours its unwooded and will age exceptionally well. The other reds are the "Stone Horse" shiraz from 40 year old vines and a vibrant grenache.

Reid is currently expanding and improving the winery and cellars. The tasting room in the old stables building is full of character and the welcome truly warm. You must come and see what great wines Reid is creating.

The charming and multi-faceted Kaesler Estate is located on the main road, just south of the township of

Nuriootpa.

The whole complex has a real feel of old Australiana, with its corrugated iron roofs and verandahs; indeed some of the buildings were German pioneers' cottages. The property was restored in 1986. In 1990 came the tasting area and the delightful vine and pergola-covered courtyard, then the lake with its mini bridges and landings. The initial development was followed by an alfresco style restaurant and then a conference and seminar area expanded further in 1997. In 1994 it was decided to convert some of the older buildings into high-class bed and breakfast accommodation with a superb central lounge area where one can gaze out over the vineyards to the Barossa Ranges beyond.

Kaesler also make some excellent old fortifieds, well worth seeking out.

Kaesler's laid-back style, its cosy, warm atmosphere, great wines and friendly hospitality make a visit here one to look forward to.

Address: Barossa Valley Way NURIOOTPA 5355	Winemaker: Reid Bosward	Principal Wines	Potential
Phone: (08) 8562 4488 Fax: (08) 8562 4499	Public Hours: 10am-5pm, daily	Old Bastard	10 yrs
Email: lisa@kaesler.com.au Est: 1893	Principal Varieties: Cabernet Sauvignon,	Old Vine Shiraz	5 yrs
WWW: www.kaesler.com.au Vine Ha: 25	Grenache, Mourvedre, Pinot Noir, Riesling,	Old Vine Semillon	10 yrs
Owner: Dural Wines Pty Ltd Cases: 15,000	Semillon, Viognier, Shiraz	Stonehorse Shiraz	10 yrs

Kaesler Restaurant

Michael McMahon has been the chef at the Kaesler restaurant and conference centre since its inception in 1994. These days he is ably assisted by his wife Heather, they are now the proprietors of the hospitality side of Kaesler, which also includes three charming self, contained bed and breakfast cottages. The "Shiraz", "Burgundy" and "Cabernet" rooms, traditional in style are cosy and romantic, decorated in rich textures with baltic pine furnishings and brass fittings. There is also a sunroom with spectacular views over the vineyard where you can relax and even sit by the fireside in winter. You won't be bored as you can play a game of petanque or croquet or if your feeling like an energetic outing you can whip out on one of the bicycles that are available for guests.

Michael, still a young man, has been a chef or a good deal of his life. When he was 16 he cooked with his mother in their open house restaurant in England. They then moved on to a Country House Hotel in Sussex where he really honed is skills. At 18 he entered the British duck Cuisine Awards with a duck dish he had created which had a slightly royal air about it, designed around Prince Charles and Princess Di, against stiff competition he won first prize. He still sometimes features the dish at Kaesler. Michael went on to work in some famous English restaurants such as The Café Royale in London and The University Arms in Cambridge.

Michael's modern Australian cuisine is innovative and features much of the local produce and Barossa specialities. At Kaesler there are many choices of where to eat, you can have a cosy dinner for two by the fireside in the intimate A la Carte Restaurant on the ground floor or upstairs in the lounge area with exceptional views over the vineyards, this room is decorated with historic memorabilia, work tools from days gone by and colonial furniture; it's a delightful walk back in time. If you feel like something alfresco, you can eat out around the lake under an umbrella or the winery verandah. "The Fernery" overlooking the cottage gardens seats up to 100 people it's a great wedding venue or ideal for conferences and seminars.

Kaesler also run some great theatre nights featuring local identity Laurie Evans and his "Barely Together Theatre Troupe" it's a real rollicking night out. If your thinking of spoiling yourself or your friends, you can take a ride to Kaesler in one of Chris Carpenter's "Mirror Image Chauffeured Chevrolets", they're 1955 classics and a really fine way to do it in style on your day out.

Kaesler naturally feature their own wines but also many great Barossa and other regional wines, they are also one of the few places you can enjoy the award winning "Nurihannam" wines made by students at the Nuriootpa High School.

Michael and Heather have three young sons now at school, so Heather is being a real support in their growing business each day.

The Kaeslers cuisine, cottages and hospitality complex are full of character and the ambience is superb. Take time out to go to this special place.

Glaetzer Wines

In 1995 one of Australia's most respected winemakers Colin Glaetzer left his long term position as Chief Winemaker and Manager for Barossa Valley Estates to start his own family winery in the heart of the Barossa. His winery was built by the late Cyril Henschke and had lain idle for many years. Colin has now been joined by his son Ben, who is fast developing a top reputation as an innovative winemaker.

Along with handcrafting their own range of just eight wines, which are of truly exciting quality, they also make a large vintage in a new 'state-of-the-art' production facility adjacent, owned by an elite group of winemakers including Glaetzer Wines.

Colin and Ben have amassed a huge array of medals and trophies in wine shows around the world. I loved the 'Semillon Ratafia', a great aperitif cold or with dessert. Their Sparkling Pinot Noir and Sparkling Shiraz are outstanding examples of great Australian sparkling wines.

The Rhone style Grenache/Mourverdre is scrumptious. They also make a Bushvine Semillon, soft and full of flavour along with two Classic Barossa Shiraz Wines · Glaetzer Shiraz and Glaetzer Bishop Shiraz, another stunning wine is Glaetzer Malbec/Cabernet Sauvignon. The tasting room on the top floor of the winery with windows both into the winery and onto the balcony is a great stop-off on your Barossa tour.

Address: 34 Barossa Valley Way TANUNDA 5352 **Phone:** (08) 8563 0288 **Fax:** (08) 8563 0218 **Email:** glaetzer@glaetzer.com **WWW:** www.glaetzer.com	**Owner:** Glaetzer Family **Winemaker:** Colin + Ben Glaetzer **Est:** 1996 **Vine Ha:** Fruit purchased from Barossa Valley Grape Growers **Cases:** 3,500 **Public Hours:** 10.30am-4.30pm, Mon-Sat;	1.30am-4.30pm, Sunday and public holidays **Principal Varieties:** Shiraz, Malbec, Cabernet Sauvignon, Semillon, Grenache, Mourvedre, Pinot Noir, Pinot Meunier, Chardonnay **Principal Wines** **Potential** Glaetzer Barossa Valley 8+ yrs

Hamiltons Ewell

Mark Hamilton is a man with a mission. A sixth generation member of South Australia's oldest wine producing family, founded by Richard Hamilton in 1837.

In 1979 Mark was the youngest director of the family wine company, then the nations sixth largest wine produce. His hopes of leading the 142 year old family business into the new millenium were dashed, when Hamilton's Ewell was bought by Mildara, the first of their major acquisitions. By 1988 the Hamilton's Ewell brand had disappeared from the marketplace. However by this time Mark, a lawyer by profession, and his wife Deborah gained the Hamilton's Ewell name back in 1991.

Now they are the largest private vineyard proprietors in the Barossa Valley floor, they have a vineyard and winery in the Eden Valley and a large vineyard on the Terra Rossa Soils at Wrattonbully near Coonawarra.

In November 1999 they opened a cellar door in an old cottage on the main highway between Tanunda and Nuriootpa, decorated with many classic old sepia prints of the Hamilton's Ewell vineyards and wineries, a classic part of Australia's wine heritage.

The first vintage of the revived Hamilton's Ewell was in 1998 supervised by Mark and his father Robert. The wines are impressive, the Fullers Barn Vineyard Shiraz and the Railway Shiraz are both lovely rich opulent wines typically Barossa. The stonegarden Grenache is a vibrant fruity red, an ideal lunchtime wine.Hamilton's Ewell were always famous for their whites the modern versions are top wines. The Railway Chardonnay is rich and complex, the unwooded Chardonnay a fresh crisp style. The Railway Shiraz was recently awarded 5 stars in winestate, putting it in the top 5 Barossa wines from 250 entries.

Mark has set up a unique online cellar door with a live web camera and a real time video conferencing facility on his site www.hamiltonewell.com.au, already export business is streaming in, why not check it out before you go to the Barossa.

Address: Siegersdorf Vineyard, Barossa Valley Road NURIOOTPA 5355 **Phone:** (08) 8562 4600 **Fax:** (08) 8562 4611 **Email:** cellardoor@hamiltonewell.com.au	**WWW:** www.hamiltonewell.com.au **Est:** 1991 **Vine Ha:** 149 **Public Hours:** 10am-5pm Mon-Fri, 11am-5pm weekends	**Principal Varieties:** Cabernet Franc, Chardonnay, Malbec, Riesling, Semillon, Cabernet Sauvignon, Grenache, Merlot, Sauvignon Blanc, Shiraz

Langmeil

Langmeil was the second village settled in the valley after Bethany and is on the western fringe of the town of Tanunda.

The beautiful complex of buildings which form the Langmeil Winery date back to the middle of the 19th century and rumour has it that the old vineyard behind the winery was planted in 1843. Some of the gnarled old vines certainly are truly ancient but still bearing a good crop of characterful grapes.

The first winery on the site was established in 1932 by the Hanisch family and operated under the name of 'Paradale Wines' until the late 1960's when it was transferred to Bernkastel Wines.

In February 1996 three friends, Richard Lindner, Chris Bitter and Carl Lindner got together and undertook their first vintage at the

winery. This is truly a family operation. Richard's son Paul is in charge of cellar operation while you will find Chris's son Tyson either in the cellar or out in the vineyard.

They have sensitively restored the stone buildings and upgraded the winery. Their wines have certainly

been of the highest quality. Carl Lindner has large vineyard holdings in the valley and through the group's other contacts Langmeil is assured of top class grapes to work with. Great things are afoot at this classic old winery and I applaud this group of Barossa stalwarts.

Address: PO Box 551 TANUNDA 5352	**Cases:** 10,000	Cabernet Sauvignon	10 yrs
Phone: (08) 8563 2595 **Fax:** (08) 8563 3622	**Public Hours:** 11am-4.30pm, daily	Shiraz	10 yrs
Email: langmeilwinery@dove.net.au	(Closed Christmas Day and Good Friday)	Selwins Lot (Cab Grenache Shiraz)	5 yrs
WWW: www.langmeilwinery.com.au	**Principal Varieties:** Grenache, Shiraz,	Bella Rouge Cabernet Sauvignon	3 yrs
Winemaker: Paul Lindner	Cabernet Sauvignon	Semillon	10 yrs
Est: 1932, Langmeil since 1996 **Vine Ha:** 17	**Principal Wines** **Potential**	Liquor Shiraz Tawny	

Tarac

Tarac had its beginnings in 1929 when Founder Alfred J Allen began experimenting in his backyard garage with a pilot plant he had designed to recover residual alcohol from the residual grape marc and yeast lees from winery operations. He also

discovered a way to do this and recover tartrates for commercial use. He built his first recovery plant in the Barossa Valley the following year.

Today the Company is also Australia's largest distiller and marketer of spirits and has a plant

which can recover red wine from fermented grape skins. Tarac now own the famous Beenleigh Rum Distillery in Queensland, Australia's first licensed distillery, and also have a commercial wine and spirit bottling and packaging contract division.

Recently the Tarac has set up a unique cellar door. The full scale "still" inside shows you exactly how spirits are made, you can sample a complete range of spirits and liqueurs plus gourmet foods made using Tarac spirits and liqueurs. Gourmet food platters, tea and coffee can also be purchased. Tarac have a very interesting and informative video presentation. The area is also available for corporate and functions and parties. The Centre is right opposite the giant Penfolds winery and is a great place for a different experience on your Barossa Pilgrimage.

Address: 43-51 Barossa Valley Way NURIOOTPA 5355	**Email:** tarac@dove.mtx.net.au	**Public Hours:** 10am-4.30pm Mon-Fri,
	WWW: tarac.com.au	10.30am-4.30pm Sat, 12-4.30 Sun & public
Phone: (08) 8562 1522 **Fax:** (08) 8562 2031	**Winemaker:** Lyn Tasker **Est:** 1934	holidays

Peter Lehmann Wines

Peter Lehmann is a legend. His long and rich winemaking career has spanned over five decades and encompasses all the ups and downs of the Australian Wine Industry over the last 50 years.

The successful listing of Peter Lehmann Wines Ltd, on the Australian Stock Exchange on the 5th of August 1993, was the high point in an extraordinary career in the wine industry. The Company now secure, could move forward with confidence under the leadership of his eldest son, Douglas Lehmann as Managing Director. The outstanding growth and financial stability makes it one of the "winery stars" of public wine company listings.

The winemaking team is headed by Andrew Wigan who joined Peter in 1976. Andrew's contribution to the Company's reputation for making wines of outstanding quality was recognised by the Barons of Barossa who named hin Barossa Winemaker of the Year, 2001. Andrew and his team, Ian Hongell and Leonie Lange have built upon the solid foundations and philosophy of Peter Lehmann to create a string of National and International award winning wines.

It is the only wine company to win three years in a row, trophies for "The World's Best Wine" in the prestigious UK International Wine & Spirit Competition. 1995 saw the Peter Lehmann 1993 Cabernet Sauvignon

scoop the pool; in 1996, the 1989 Mentor Blend was given the nod, followed by the 1993 Eden Valley Reserve Riesling in 1997. By 2000, Peter Lehmann Wines had won 3 trophies in that competition for Riesling.

Andrew Wigan and his team were equally delighted with places in Wine Specator's Top 100, for 1999 and 2000 as well as Red Wine of the Year in the International Wine Challenge, London for the 1998 Shiraz. A stunning string of wine success, to say the least.

The flagship wine is Stonewell Shiraz. The Barossa is the heartland of the noble Shiraz grape and Stonewell, made from old vine, dry

grown, low yielding Shiraz is the distilled essence of that great variety. Only ever released as a five year old wine, Andrew Wigan describes the grapes selected for Stonewell as "little black jewels".

Stonewell quickly gained national recognition. In 1994, I enjoyed one of the best wine releases ever held, when the 1989 Stonewell Shiraz, winner of the 1990 Jimmy Watson Memorial Trophy, was released. More than 70 guests arrived at the winery to be greeted by the growers, then, after a casual stroll up the hill to the Lehmann home where a long table for 70 had been set, we enjoyed a superb meal prepared by Maggie Beer.

Peter Lehmann Wines

The icing on the Lehmann cake was that several weeks previously the Stonewells had absolutely blitzed the other red wines at the Royal Adelaide Show when the 1990 Stonewell won the Adelaide Trophy for the Best Red of that Show and the 1989 was again a trophy winning wine for the Best Medium Bodied Dry Red.

Now Stonewell has been joined by a another super premium, Eight Songs Shiraz, 100% French oak fermented and matured, the 1996 vintage of which was first released to great acclaim in 1999. Eight Songs Shiraz celebrates a wonderful collaboration beween all the arts; music, poetry, painting and wine.

Peter Lehmann is staunchly Barossa. He eats, drinks and breathes the Barossa. His winemaking career began at Yalumba where he remained for 13 years before joining Saltram where he spent 20 vintages creating wine history through wonderful wines; most notably the Mamre Brook dry red, the 1996 winning the Jimmy Watson in 1967. These classics occasionally surface today and are eagerly sought by collectors.

In 1978, during a period of red wine surplus, Peter was appalled by the orders of the then owners of Saltram not to buy any red grapes from its Barossa growers; growers to whom he had given his word that if they

looked after Saltram, then the Company would look after them. So he found partners and founded a wine compnay. This he named Masterson Barossa Vignerons after the famous Damon Runyon character, gambler Sky Masterson. At that time he said of the company which was the saviour of the independent Barossa grape growers, "If anything is a gamble, this is it."

He adopted The Queen of Clubs, the gambler's card, as his logo. However, in his mind he never felt it was such a gamble, for he always had utter faith in the quality of Barossa grapes - a faith which has been well and truly vindicated. The packaging has since been given a lift. Artists were commissioned to create and Queen of Clubs expressive of each wine style. The wines and their

labels are true works of art.

Peter Lehmann Wines still draws most of its fruit from over 700 individual great Barossa vineyards lovingly cared for by those loyal growers he helped more than two decades ago. It has the pick of the best Barossa vineyards meticulously tended by 5th and 6th generation Barossans. Since 1993, the Company has also bought three vineyards, including the famous Stonewell Vineyard.

Peter Lehmann Wines has achieved great export success, with over 50% of its bottled wine sold overseas; the most important markets being the UK, USA, Germany, Switzerland, Scandinavia and New Zealand. It has become a well known and highly respected brand world wide, with overseas drinkers eagerly seeking the rich Barossa reds and discovering the joys of Barossa Semillon, the top selling Lehmann white wine.

Throughout these great developments, Peter Lehmann has never changed. His favourite spot is still the cosy weighbridge building during vintage, where he greets all the growers with a warm welcome, a cold drink or a glass of wine and always a stick of Barossa Mettwurst whilst weighing their grapes and directing them to the appropriate crusher. Correction, one thing has changed. He now operates the weighbridge computer with aplomb!

Here's a toast to a great winemaking team with their stalwart Barossa growers, and a very special family!

Address: Para Road TANUNDA 5352	Public Hours: 9.30am-5pm, daily; 10.30am-4.30pm weekends and public holidays	Peter Lehmann Stonewell Shiraz	20+ yrs
Phone: (08) 8563 2500 Fax: (08) 8563 3402		Peter Lehmann Mentor	20+ yrs
Winemaker: Peter Lehmann, Andrew Wigan,	Principal Varieties: Shiraz, Cabernet	Peter Lehmann Barossa Shiraz	8+ yrs
Peter Scholz, Leonie Lange. Managing	Sauvignon, Grenache, Merlot, Semillon,	Peter Lehmann Barossa Semillon	5+ yrs
Director: Doug Lehmann	Chardonnay, Riesling, Chenin Blanc	Clancy's Gold Preference	5+ yrs
Est: 1979	Principal Wines Potential	Clancy's White	2+ yrs

Orlando Wines

Johann Gramp, one of the early German Settlers in the Barossa Valley, planted the first grapes back in 1847 at Jacob's Creek. In 1877 Johann's son, Gustav, transferred the winemaking from Jacob's Creek to the more expansive site at Rowland Flat. The name "Orlando" (the German name for Roland) later became the Company's Brand name.

During the early 1950's, Colin Gramp went to Germany and brought back with him some German pressure controlled stainless steel fermenting tanks, which started the most significant technological breakthrough yet, in the history of the Australian wine industry. The control of the rate, temperature and length of the fermentation, produced white wines with much more aromatic, floral and fruit driven flavours and naturally, being sealed, prevented oxidisation of the wines. These radically different and improved white wines quickly gained popularity and set the stage for the white wine boom of the early 1970's.

Colin Gramp also brought to Australia, German winemaking genius Guenter Prass, Guenter spent more than 30 years with Orlando, finishing as Managing Director and overseeing the remarkable development of Orlando, into one of the largest and most respected wine companies in Australia. Capital demands and the need to build an international distribution network, led to a buyout by world wine and spirit giant, the Groupe Pernod Ricard.

Orlando have been at the forefront of many winemaking developments. Barossa Pearl in its unique pear-shaped bottle, was introduced as Australia's first bulk fermented sparkling wine and at a never before seen affordable price, it became "de rigeur" when courting a young lady, to crack a bottle or two of this exciting new wine. Orlando produced Australia's first commercial chardonnay in the late 1970's.

In the mid 70's Orlando released four premium wines in the popular price bracket, Lyndale Riesling, Moorooroo White Burgundy, Fromm's Spaetlese and Jacob's Creek Claret. Although most of the advertising and promotion was directed at Lyndale, it was the Jacob's Creek Claret, named after the site of Johann Gramp's original vineyard, which stole the show.

Jacob's Creek is an incredible success story; today the red wine, a blend of shiraz and cabernet, the biggest selling bottled wine in England. The trickle of the creek has turned into a river, which is flowing around the world. Jacob's Creek Chardonnay has also had great success, winning a number of trophies and awards, including a top French honour, quite a feat for a wine which sells at under $10 Australian.

Old stalwarts such as the Steingarten Riesling from the "Garden of Stones" vineyard, high on Trial Hill behind the valley, produces incredibly small crops of exceptional wines which capture the wine lovers imagination.

The Orlando Saints - St. Helga Eden Valley Riesling, St. Hugo Coonawarra Cabernet Sauvignon and the more recently released St. Hillary Chardonnay, from Padthaway are all rich in flavour and truly great bargains in their price bracket.

In the super premium area, Orlando has three individual vineyard red wines, Lawson's Shiraz from Padthaway, Jacaranda Ridge Coonawarra Cabernet Sauvignon and Centenary Hill Shiraz from the Barossa. These are consistently in the top few great Australian red wines.

The Russet Ridge Cabernet blend from Coonawarra, first released in 1993, is a great success in the medium-priced area. Orlando have a very well balanced and well-rounded range of wines. Their winery and its state of the art packaging centre is world class. One would be remiss not to mention their great sparkling wines - Jacob's Creek Chardonnay Pinot Noir, Trilogy, a pinot noir, chardonnay and pinot meunier cuvee and Carrington. Why not toast their success with these fine sparklers?

Address: Barossa Valley Way ROWLAND FLAT 5352 **Phone:** (08) 8521 3111 **Fax:** (08) 8521 3100 **WWW:** www.jacobscreek.com.au **Owner:** Orlando Wyndham Group Pty Ltd	**Winemaker:** Philip Laffer Est: 1847 **Public Hours**: 10am-5pm, weekdays; 10am-4pm, weekends and public holidays **Principal Varieties:** Cab Sav, Merlot, Chard, Riesling, Sem, Cab Franc, Pinot Noir, Sauv Blanc, Shiraz	**Principal Wines** Jacob's Creek Saint Range Trilogy Gramp's Range Lawson's Padthaway Shiraz Jacaranda Ridge Coonawarra Cabernet Sauvignon

Richmond Grove

At long last a 50-year-old dream has been realised at Richmond Grove. Leo Buring dreamt of erecting tunnels, towers and spires, on the winery he renamed, Chateau Leonay, when he bought the Hoffman's Orange Grove Winery, in 1945. Unfortunately his death in 1961 interrupted these plans. Leo's famous "apprentice" and now Wine Industry Legend John Vickery, finally convinced current owners Richmond Grove to finish the job and the two copper spires they have added recently, are befitting of this fine building and its great wines. The winery is right across the lawns from the Peter Lehmann Winery.

This leading Australian wine label which had its beginnings in the Upper Hunter in New South Wales was taken over some years ago by the Orlando Wyndham Group, who started looking for a home in the Barossa for Richmond Grove.

The beautiful old Chateau Leonay Winery, built around the turn of the century, lay idle. Today the winery is a buzzing beehive of activity. John Vickery, the living legend of Australian white winemaking, who put Buring's on the map in the 1960's and 70's, is back at his beloved Chateau Leonay after a long absence.

The cellar door has been enlarged and beautifully styled. John's first 'back home' vintage in 1994 produced some great wines, including two exquisite riesling's, one from the Barossa and another from Watervale. The tradition has recommenced, the 2000 vintage has seen the real renaissance of riesling and John Vickery has bottled his gems under the Stelvin Cap, which will ensure they improve for decades into the new millennium.

Richmond Grove has played host to some great cultural events and has been a major sponsor of the Barossa Music Festival and a popular venue for many events. Richmond Grove's success and expansion has breathed life into a great winery. Why not check it out for yourself?

Address: Para Road TANUNDA 5352
Phone: (08) 8563 2204 **Fax:** (08) 8563 2804
Winemaker: John Vickery **Est:** 1897

Public Hours: 10am-5pm, weekdays; 10.30pm-4.30pm, weekends and public holidays

Principal Varieties: Riesling, Cabernet Sauvignon, Shiraz, Semillon, Chardonnay, Verdelho

Miranda Wines

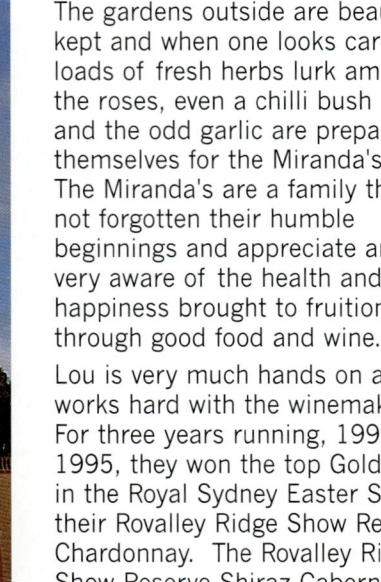

The gardens outside are beautifully kept and when one looks carefully, loads of fresh herbs lurk amongst the roses, even a chilli bush or two and the odd garlic are preparing themselves for the Miranda's table. The Miranda's are a family that have not forgotten their humble beginnings and appreciate and are very aware of the health and happiness brought to fruition, through good food and wine.

Lou is very much hands on and works hard with the winemaker's. For three years running, 1993 - 1995, they won the top Gold Medal in the Royal Sydney Easter Show for their Rovalley Ridge Show Reserve Chardonnay. The Rovalley Ridge Show Reserve Shiraz Cabernet won

The Miranda's are very close and hardworking family. Their patron, the late Frank Miranda, affectionately called "Poo", who came to Australia in 1939, loved his adopted land.

He didn't waste time, honing his winemaking skills in of all places; Katherine in the Northern Territory, making wine from dried sultanas and raisins, during the second World War.

On returning to Griffith he began making wine commercially. Today, Miranda is Australia's seventh largest winery and becoming a bigger and

bigger player in the premium wine market every year.

In 1991, the Miranda's took over the Rovalley Winery from the Leibich family, who had founded it in 1919. Likeable Lou Miranda and his wife Val moved over from Griffith to run the winery. Lou has overseen a rejuvenation of the winery in terms of equipment, new oak barrels and a whole new attitude. This has been followed by the building of a truly grand cellar door and hospitality area one of the best in the valley.

the trophy at the Royal Perth Show for the best red wine. The "Old Vine Shiraz" has had considerable success winning a trophy in London.

Miranda is fast forging a reputation for top quality wines at very affordable prices. Why not drop in on your way through the Barossa it's on the main road and one of the first wineries you pass on your pilgrimage. I am sure you will enjoy the Miranda's warm hospitality and their exceptional wines.

Address: 57 Jondaryan Avenue GRIFFITH 2680	Winemaker: Luis Simian, Jane Gilham & Jeff Martin	Mirrool Creek Range	Up to 5 yrs
Phone: (02) 6962 4033 Fax: (02) 6962 6944		Somerton Range	Up to 3 yrs
Email: info@mirandawines.com.au	Est: 1939 Cases: 1,500,000	Golden Gate Sparkling	
WWW: www.mirandawines.com.au	Public Hours: 10am-5pm daily	Fireside Port	Up to 5 yrs
Owner: Sam, Jim & Lou Miranda	Principal Wines Potential	Miranda Kilkenny Creams	

Rockford

Robert O'Callaghan has built a winery that captures the spirit of the traditional Barossa. The original 1850's stone buildings have been restored and extended in the same style. Rockford retains the feel of a Barossan farmyard and winery; the thick stone walls provide insulation that makes them ideal for maturing wine in wood.

In 1965 Robert left school to become an apprentice winemaker with Seppelt's at Rutherglen. His time with Seppelt's took him through their wineries at Rutherglen, Chateau Tanunda, Dorrien and Seppeltsfield. He was part of the modernisation of the Australian wine industry.

Robert uses grapes from low yielding vineyards, hand pruned and picked, open fermenters, wooden crushers and basket presses, combined with handed down knowledge to produce the rich earthy complex red and white wines, for which Rockford are renowned. Basket Press Shiraz, was

one of the first wines to re-establish this traditional style. The 'coup de grace' of the Rockford range is their Black Shiraz, a sparkling red that is

well-named, inky black in colour, with a kaleidoscope of flavours. It is swallowed up literally straight away, when the small batches are released.

Address: Krondorf Road TANUNDA 5352	**Winemaker:** Robert O'Callaghan	**Public Hours:** 11am-5pm, Mon-Sat
Phone: (08) 8563 2720	**Est:** 1984	**Principal Varieties:** Grenache, Riesling,
Fax: (08) 8563 3787	**Cases:** 15,000	Shiraz, Cabernet Sauvignon, Semillon

Whistler Wines

Whistler is English for the German word Pfeiffer, and legend has it that Martin Pfeiffer whistles wherever he goes. With 27 years of experience

with Penfolds, Martin, and his wife Sally, along with brother Chris, wife Jayne and Iain and Rae Grierson, have opened this dynamic new wine

company on their 80 acre Heysen Estate, in the heart of the Barossa Valley. Plantings currently consist of Shiraz, Semillon, Merlot and Cabernet. Wines from these varieties are now available although volumes are low and demand high. The limited release "Black Piper" Sparkling Shiraz, is made with the help of Graham Stallard who has joined the team to assist with making and marketing.

The drive to the cellar door is lined with red and white roses, and the building itself nestles under ancient gum trees in an area of peaceful virgin landscape. Built of modern materials in the tradition of the old German cottages, the cellar door reflects the contemporary approach to viticulture and wine styles, and is an exciting new addition to the Barossa wine scene.

Address: Seppeltsfield Road MARANANGA 5355	**Est:** 1999 **Vine Ha:** 22 **Cases:** 1,500	Cabernet Merlot	5 yrs
Phone: (08) 8562 4942 **Fax:** (08) 8562 4943	**Public Hours:** 10:30am-5:30pm weekends	Merlot	5 yrs
Email: whistler@chariot.net.au	& public holidays	Cabernet	5 yrs
WWW: www.whistlerwines.8k.com	**Principal Varieties:** Cab, Merlot, Sem, Shiraz	Shiraz	7 yrs
Owner: M & S Pfeiffer, C & J Pfeiffer, I & R Grierson	**Principal Wines** **Potential**	Semillon	3 yrs

Seppeltsfield

Joseph Seppelt arrived in Australia in 1849. Purchasing a large area of land near Tanunda in 1852, he built a homestead, which is known as Seppeltsfield.

In addition to planting vines, Joseph originally attempted to establish corn, wheat, tobacco as well as grazing cattle. Initially wine facilities were not a priority as in fact the first vintage was made in the dairy.

With the exception of tobacco, all Joseph's endeavours were successful but wine emerged as his main interest. In 1867, Joseph commenced work on the magnificent stone buildings, which make up Seppeltsfield and by the turn of the century; the company was the largest wine producer in Australia with 2 million litres of wine being produced annually.

Seppelt purchased another large winery in 1916, Chateau Tanunda, built in 1890, this impressive stone construction was equal to Seppeltsfield in its grandeur. He not only acquired an historic landmark, but also inherited large stocks of brandy. The early years of this century saw Seppelt purchase wineries and vineyards at Great Western in Victoria and Dorrien near Tanunda, both of which were later furnished with the characteristic Seppelt turrets.

Throughout the difficult 1930's Seppelt's were most considerate to their staff. Although on reduced wages, the employees not only kept their jobs but also were provided with food and shelter, if necessary. In return, employees were requested to

plant date seeds to a set pattern at each of their wineries. This elegant feature has become another distinguishing characteristic of Seppelt wineries. The impressive family mausoleum stands on a hill overlooking a valley of palm-lined avenues, magnificent stone buildings and turreted tanks. This picture is completed by the rolling greens and golds of Australia's first contoured vineyard.

James Godfrey is in charge of the Seppelt range of fortified wines. Having judged fortified wines with James a few times, I can attest to the fact he is as skilled and knowledgeable about fortified wines as any person could be. Seppeltsfield has always stored huge quantities of ageing top class fortified wines, which in the case of the old Seppelt Para Liqueurs go back to the 1878 vintage.

Occasionally, these old Para's are bottled for special occasions · they are almost liquid gold, the essence of wine and history in a glass. The Seppelt fortified wines are all superb, right down to the commercial sherries, ports and muscats. The Mt. Rufus and Old Trafford Ports are particularly good value. The DP 90, a drier style tawny is superb, as is the richer Para Liqueur.

The Seppelt old fortified sherries in the DP series; the fino, amontillado and oloroso are a must in the aperitif cabinet or to add that classy zest to a soup or casserole. It's a real myth to use old opened or oxidised wine in cooking. Wine is a food and an ingredient when you cook · you wouldn't use limp vegetables or meat that's on the turn so why handicap your cooking with spoiled wine? The secret with good fortified wines is to have old stocks in a solero system (ironically the name of the Seppelts range of Sherries) where new wine is added to old in a gradual process each year. With more than 15 million litres of old fortifieds in their Seppeltsfield stronghold, Seppelt has a unique asset. Seppelts also make many excellent premium table wines.

The Seppeltsfield buildings are some of the finest and best-kept Australian colonial architecture and a must for a visit whilst in the Barossa. The palm-lined avenues, the mausoleum, the peaceful grandeur of the place have a special spiritual feel to it. Seppeltsfield is a winery with soul · I'm certain yours will be enriched by visiting there.

Ross Estate

In 1993 Darius Ross and his wife Pauline decided it was time for a change. Darius who was born in Poland had spent more than 30 years running his own engineering and lighting business in Adelaide. They often visited the Barossa Valley with friends and slowly fell in love with the region.

The moment they set eyes on the 110 acre property near Lyndoch, that has become their home, they had to have it, signing the purchase contact the very next day. The existing vineyard of 50 acres was somewhat rundown, but included some gems, 80 year old Grenache, 35 year old Semillon and 20 year old Merlot vines. 15 acres of unsuitable varieties were replaced and a further 60 acres planted, the current vineyard covers 110 acres. Shiraz, Cabernet Sauvignon, Cabernet Franc, Sauvignon Blanc and Chardonnay have been added.

Darius had not thought of a winery until he bought the property but it became a mission for him immediately he moved there, he just hoped Pauline would share this

mission with him. Together they have created a splendid estate. Darius designed the Colonial German and Polish inspired winery and cellar door, surrounded by lawns and Rose gardens - it's a real picture.

Darius is a real perfectionist and was lucky enough to snare top experienced winemaker Rod Chapman, who was anxious to get back home to Lyndoch after many years working for giants of the Industry Orlando, Saltram and Penfolds. Together they have set up a superb state of the art 400 tonne

capacity winery, totally enclosed and airconditioned it is the envy of many in the valley and Rod is also producing for a number of smaller vineyards under contract.

The early wines under the Ross Estate label have been stunning. Their first show outing was in the Sydney show 2000, when they won four medals including a gold medal for their 1998 Cabernet Sauvignon, Cabernet Franc, Merlot blend.

I found their Semillon Riesling and Chardonnay to be really polished complex wines. They also produce a blended white wine under the "Beekeepers Blend", it has got a certain slightly sweeter style and is so named because beehives were kept in the property at the turn of the century.

Ross Estate is easy to find, it is less than a kilometre up the road from Lyndoch heading towards Rowland Flat on the Barossa Highway, its beautiful buildings and gardens are under the shade of some monstrous Pines. Do not miss this Barossa newcomer, of which the wine world will hear much of in the future.

Address: Barossa Valley Way LYNDOCH 5351	**Public Hours:** 10am-5pm, Mon-Sat; 1pm-5pm, Sun	Semillon	4 yrs
Phone: (08) 8524 4033 **Fax:** (08) 8524 4533	**Principal Varieties:** Riesling, Sem,	Beekeepers Blend	Now
Owner: Darius & Pauline Ross	Grenache, Chard	Chardonnay	5 yrs
Winemaker: Rod Chapman	**Principal Wines**	**Potential**	Sauvignon Blanc/Semillon (blend)	2 yrs
Est: 1999 **Vine Ha:** 44 **Cases:** 15,000	Riesling	4 yrs	Grenache	4 yrs

Schild Estate

Managing Director and owner, Ed Schild has been a vigneron since 1952, starting with a small parcel of land at Rowland Flat in the heart of the Barossa Valley.

Progressively over the next forty odd years, Ed continued to purchase parcels of land around the Lyndoch, Rowland Flat area. These vineyard holdings now total over 300 acres!

The Moorooroo Block (Jacob's Creek) has some of the oldest Shiraz vines in Australia - 150 years old! Ed bought this beautiful parcel of land during the "vinepull" in the 80's. Everyone thought he was mad as the government was paying to pull out your vines and Ed was buying up vines! His incredible foresight has certainly paid off now.

Ed decided that he wanted to make wine under his own label some 10 years ago. It was a dream that he chose to pursue relentlessly until it became a reality. During a visit to California, Ed saw some of the delightful architecture that graces the Napa Valley's Cellar Doors and wanted to use some of these concepts in the base design on his Cellar Door - wherever that was going to be!

In 1998, the local ANZ Bank was listed for sale. It was your typical 1980's cream brick "ugly duckling". The location was fantastic-the main street in Lyndoch on the corner-everyone entering the Southern part of the Barossa would have to drive past! Everything was going for it

except the building. It was sad and tired and certainly lacked street appeal.

Ed hired the services of well respected Architect, Fred Phillis to transform the building. Fred came up with plans based on what Ed saw in the Napa Valley, along with some innovative blending of raw timbers, stone and slate. It was a mix of the old and the new, traditional and modern. It was fantastic! After over six months of tenders, dust, dirt and

hammering and banging, it was transformed. The "ugly duckling" had become a "beautiful swan" in the township of Lyndoch. The vista of sails, sandstone and slate says everything that Ed wanted.

On July 21 2000 the Cellar Door was quietly opened to the public to test the waters and iron out any problems. The first day's trading saw a mixture of "locals, family, friends and the odd tourist or two", all checking out this transformation.

After its official opening, the Cellar Door and Café has settled down to a thriving business.

As Ed now takes the reins of the Cellar Door, Michael, Ed's son is running the vineyards. Michael has worked with Ed in the Vineyards for over fifteen years, learning everything possible about vines, soil, climate, and anything else that comes with growing vines. With his apprenticeship well and truly done, Michael has the great responsibility of running the vast vineyard holdings.

Ed's focus is now clearly on the Cellar Door and domestic and export markets, using his experience and insight into the Australian Wine industry. Having tasted Ed's impressive range of wines with him, I am confident that the Schild Estate Wine label will grow and prosper into a Barossa icon.

Address: 1 Lyndoch Valley Road LYNDOCH 5351 Phone: (08) 8524 5560 Fax: (08) 8524 4333 Email: schildest@chariot.net WWW: www.schildestate.com.au Owner: Ed, Lorraine & Michael Schild	Winemaker: Rod Chapman Est: 1998 Vine Ha: 110 Cases: 5,000 Public Hours: 11am-5pm, daily Principal Varieties: Cabernet Sauvignon, Chardonnay, Riesling, Shiraz, Pinot Noir, Semillon	Principal Wines	Potential
		Barossa Shiraz	8-10 yrs
		Barossa Cabernet Sauvignon	8 yrs
		Barossa Riesling	10 yrs
		Barossa Chardonnay	5-7 yrs
		Barossa Semillon	5-7 yrs

Saltram

Although now owned by Beringer Blass a strong family tradition continues at Saltram. The winemaker Nigel Dolan, is the son of famed Saltram-Stonyfell winemaker the late Bryan Dolan, an industry legend and a former winner of the Jimmy Watson Trophy.

Saltram was founded in 1859 by William Salter, who purchased a property on the banks of a creek naming it Mamre Brook. Longtime winemaker for 20 years was Peter Lehmann, making famous the Mamre Brook and Metala labels as amongst Australia's best reds.

Saltram is a classic old winery with its open fermenting tanks for the reds but much money has been spent upgrading the white winemaking facilities and barrel ageing cellars.

The characterful cellar door now leads into a classy café style restaurant, both of which look out over the splendid stone villa "Mamre Brook House" a fine example of Victorian inspired colonial architecture and classified by the National Trust of Australia.

The Saltram wines and winery are a credit to our great industry.

Stanley Brothers

Lindsay Stanley is undoubtedly one of the true characters of a region that seems to breed such personalities. One should not however be fooled by his laid back laconic nature. He is a really first class winemaker and a deep thinker who has learned well from his 28 years of winemaking experience including working early in his career with the legendary Max Schubert.

Through their many friends and contacts in the valley, the Stanley Brothers have access to some of the best dry grown Barossa grapes, from very old vines grown in many of the valley's unique sub-regions.

Lindsay's interest in horse racing translates into some of his best selling wines. The Thoroughbred Cabernet with its rich, ripe, upfront flavours and the Full Sister Semillon, which is full bodied a real red wine drinkers white.

Stanley Brothers also do great things with the Germanic white variety. Sylvaner, fruity and spicy, it is great with Asian dishes.

If you do happen to corner Lindsay, a reluctant raconteur, get him to tell you of his duck shooting day with Doug Lehmann, I am sure it will be a highlight of your day in the Barossa!!

Address: Barossa Valley Way TANUNDA 5352
Phone: (08) 8563 3375 **Fax:** (08) 8563 3758
Email: stanleybros@mtx.net.au **Est:** 1990
WWW: www.stanleybros.mtx.net **Vine Ha:** 23
Owner: Klomer Estate Pty Ltd **Cases:** 8-10k
Winemaker: Lindsay Stanley

Public Hours: 10am-5pm, weekdays; 11am-5pm, weekends
Principal Varieties: Cabernet Sauvignon, Chardonnay, Grenache, Semillon, Shiraz, Sylvaner
Principal Wines   **Potential**

Thoroughbred Cabernet	7-10 yrs
John Hancock Shiraz	up to 15 yrs
Blacksheep Malbec/Merlot	2-3 yrs
Grenache	Now
Full Sister	up to 5 yrs
Pristine Chardonnay	Now

St Hallet Wines

In 1988, a small band of Barossa stalwarts joined Carl Lindner at the St Hallett winery, to create a bolder image and style for St Hallett.

Carl commenced the "revival" through vineyard acquisitions and development, with winemaker Stuart Blackwell assigned to upgrade the winery and equipment.

The third in the partnership, Bob McLean his niche as "marketer". Applying a very simplistic approach to St Hallett marketing, he feels others in the industry often say "too much, many people lose sight of the fact they are in the business of producing 750 mls of happiness". How basic it all is.

St Hallett believes the Barossa is one of the most unique wine producing regions of Australia. The valley extends over many boundaries, from the cool heights of the Barossa Ranges, to the warm flat plains of

the valley floor. Soils differ from dark clay to river loam, to sandy types and varying microclimates enable enormous diversity in the

wine styles produced.

St Hallett is in a unique position sourcing fruit from its own vineyards and purchasing fruit from growers with very old vines, this enables greater flexibility and access to some of the best fruit of the Barossa region.

The Old Block Shiraz, was the forerunner of a number of premium Australian reds, made from the grapes of very old vines. A number of traditional Barossa growers produce grapes for The Old Block; the vines vary from around 70 years old to over a century. The wine has been a huge success. Medium-priced wines of exceptional quality include The Poachers Blend, named after the old story involving poachers and the creek at the end of the winery's land; these wines have been most successful additions to the St Hallett stable.

Address: St. Halletts Road, Hallett Valley TANUNDA 5352	**Cases:** 40,000	Old Block Shiraz 5-10 yrs
	Public Hours: 10am-5pm, Mon-Sat; 10am-5pm, Sun (Summer); 11am-5pm, Sun (Winter)	Cabernet Sauvignon 5-10 yrs
Phone: (08) 8563 2319		Cabernet Franc Merlot 2-5 yrs
Fax: (08) 8563 2901	**Principal Varieties:** Shiraz, Cabernet	Gamekeeper's Reserve 2-5 yrs
Winemaker: Stuart Blackwell	Sauvignon, Semillon, Chardonnay	Chardonnay 2-5 yrs
Est: 1944 **Vine Ha:** 50	**Principal Wines** **Potential**	Semillon-Sauvignon Blanc 2-5 yrs

Wolf Blass Wines

In a very short space of time, Wolf Blass built one of Australia's most successful wine companies. The company was founded in 1973 and went public in 1984.

Wolf was born in East Germany and worked as an apprentice on his grandfather's vineyard. He graduated from university as the youngest ever holder of the Kellermeister Diploma (Master degree) in Oenology. He came to Australia at the invitation of Kaiser Stuhl in 1960 and it was not long before the industry was sitting up and taking notice of this outspoken new winemaker.

He left to become Australia's first freelance winemaker since Leo Buring made a similar move in 1919. Earning $2.50 per hour, Wolf drove from winery to winery, seven days a week, in his old Volkswagen. Many small wineries were eased into table wine production with his assistance

In the course of his time spent later at Tollana, Wolf purchased a couple of hectares on the Sturt Highway north of Nuriootpa. There, he built a large shed, which became his winemaking headquarters. Today, it is a magnificent complex, set among gardens and fountains; it has recently significantly expanded. The

first Wolf Blass wine was a red; a shiraz made in 1966.

In 1975, Wolf Blass became the first ever to win the Jimmy Watson Trophy at the Melbourne Show for three consecutive years. The company also won the Montgomery Trophy, for the best commercially available red wine at the Adelaide Show, six years running and the best red wine in the Sydney Show for the years 1981 to 1983.

Throughout this period, Wolf only produced red wines. Today the

company produce a wide range of red, white and sparkling wines. The Black Label Cabernet is one of Australia's most sought after wines and the 100% Langhorne Creek Grey Label red is one of my personal favourites.

Wolf Blass wines continue to please the palates of an ever-growing wine drinking public around the world. The Beringer Blass team of winemakers have continued the good work and Wolf Blass Wines are a real cornerstone in this success story. Ein Prosit Wolfie!!

Yaldara Wines

Yaldara Wines and its magnificent Chateau have long been recognized as one of the most picturesque and attractive wine tourist destinations in Australia. Located just outside the township of Lyndoch in South Australia's Barossa Valley, the 340-acre property centres on the imposing European-style Chateau, built in the 1950's, of yellow hand hewn sand stone as a focal point. This Chateau, along with the Winery, a Reception Centre and a Distillery are surrounded by landscaped gardens, natural lakes with fauna and flora leading to the Cellar Door tasting facility and a Garden Bistro, it's picturesque setting overlooking the North Para River.

Yaldara receives 75,000 visitors each year. Guided tours of the Chateau, including the cellars are conducted at regular intervals most days of the year. The cellar door is open daily 9:00am-5:00pm for tastings and sales. Tours of the winery are conducted daily, at 10:15-10:45am, 1:15-2:15pm, 3:15-4.15pm. The Garden Bistro is open daily for coffee, cakes, snacks or meals

9.00am-4:00pm, it adjoins the Cellar Door and provides a wonderful opportunity to enjoy regional cuisine in a most hospitable environment.

Conducted tours for special groups are also catered for, not only by providing a tasting experience but also lunch accompanied by some of Yaldara's great wines, its a combined wine and tourism experience never to be forgotten.

In December 1999, Simeon Wines Ltd, Australia's second largest wine making company, bought Yaldara Wines from the family who had established the winery in 1947. At the time of acquisition, Yaldara Wines was selling approximately half a million cases of wine a year, making it the 25th largest winery in

Yaldara Wines

Australia. Using Simeon's resources, Yaldara has significantly improved the quality of the products in the portfolio and also embarked upon a major modernisation program, incorporating the best features of the existing winery, along with new state of the art technology.

With the current growth anticipated in winemaking at Yaldara, the site is undergoing major changes to cater for this increase. So far three Million dollars has been spent on upgrading the winemaking facilities and the number of stainless steel wine storage tanks will be significantly increased in the near future.

New technology being introduced in 2002 will enable pre-selection of grapes in the vineyard, which will mean an earlier identification of when the premium grapes are in absolutely perfect balance.

Yaldara now sources grapes from many of Australia's most premium grape growing areas, such as the Hunter Valley, Cowra, Yarra Valley, Mornington Peninsula, Limestone Coast , Adelaide Hills and Langhorne Creek.

Yaldara produces an excellent range of table wines, sparkling wines, ports, brandy and a selection of de-alcoholised grape products.

The premium wines, are under the "Farms" label and there is a limited release range under the "Julian's" label, including one of only three varietal Petit Verdot wines available in Australia.

In today's market place presentation and wine quality are paramount. Since the change of ownership, many of the company's wines have featured in Wine State magazine, Australia's premier wine magazine and several wines under the "River Run" and "Lakewood" labels have appeared in their Top 40 Best Buys.

Yaldara retains its classic charm and beauty but is a winery on the move in terms of innovation and quality. If you can't visit this beautiful place, seek out their wines which are more often than not also great value for money.

Address: PO Box 62 LYNDOCH 5351
Phone: (08) 8524 4200
Fax: (08) 8524 4678
Email: yaldara@yaldara.com.au

WWW: simeon.com.au
Winemaker: Matt Tydeman
Est: 1947   **Cases:** 500,000
Vine Ha: Estate: 80, Vineyards: 54

Public Hours: 9am-5pm, daily
Principal Varieties: Cabernet Sauvignon, Chardonnay, Grenache, Merlot, Pinot Noir, Riesling, Sauvignon Blanc, Semillon, Shiraz

Yalumba Wines

Yalumba is at the forefront of premium wine production in Australia. It is Australia's oldest family owned winery, established in 1849. The Hill Smith family manage their business in an innovative way, encouraging open communication and a team spirit. The relationship between staff and management is also excellent and this harmony has contributed markedly to their success.

Unlike the majority of Barossa Valley Wine companies, which were established by German immigrants, Yalumba was founded by an Englishman, Samuel Smith, a Dorset brewer whose first work in Australia was for George Fife Angas at Angaston. Whilst employed for Angas, Smith bought 14 acres of land near Angaston, which he planted with vines. He called his property "Yalumba" which is Aboriginal for "all the land around". This was ultimately an auspicious choice as the Yalumba empire grew to cover just that.

In 1852, like many others, Smith headed to the Victorian goldfields and with singular luck, struck gold. He returned to the Barossa, purchased a further 30 acres and established a winery. Although he did not live long enough to see it, by the turn of the century Yalumba was one of the most successful wine companies in Australia.

Robert Hill-Smith and his brother

Sam are the proprietors of Yalumba, having guided an amicable family buy-out in 1989, assisted by their late father, Wyndham. Robert and Sam are the fifth generation of Smith's at Yalumba.

The Yalumba family have ongoing projects aimed at producing the best possible grapes for their winemaking team to work with. Under the eye of their chief viticulturist Robin Nettelbeck, Yalumba have established a substantial vine grafting operation and vine nursery. Their good work is obvious when you visit any of their vineyards in the Eden Valley or The Menzies Vineyard at Coonawarra; these vines are a joy to behold. Needless to say, the

Yalumba wine stable since the late 1980's is flawless, each year the wines just keep getting better. Clonal selection, fruit evaluation trials and grafting techniques might all sound a bit obscure and highbrow, but their relevance comes through loud and clear in the finished wines.

Yalumba choose the best possible and most suitable microclimates for each grape variety they wish to plant. A great example of this has been the successful planting of viognier in the Eden Valley. They have developed three individual vineyards in the Eden Valley region being Pewsey Vale, Heggies Vineyard and Hill-Smith Estate. All three vineyards are separate, self-sufficient concerns, with wines appearing under their respective names. Common resources are shared at Yalumba where all the fruit is individually processed.

Yalumba owns additional vineyards at Oxford Landing near Waikerie, the 'Menzies' vineyard in the Coonawarra and vineyards in the emerging winegrowing region of Wrattonbully.

Yalumba Wines

Yalumba have a unique way of honouring those family members, friends or business associates who have in some way assisted or been very dear to the company. The idea occurred to Wyndham Hill Smith when Sir Robert Menzies described a 1961 Yalumba Special Reserve Stock Galway Claret as 'the finest Australian wine, I have ever tasted!'

Yalumba began holding back the best red each year and releasing them only when they felt the wine had achieved sufficient maturation both in wood and bottle. The flagship wine series became known as 'The Signature', a cabernet sauvignon and shiraz blend and only released at 4 years of age.

I once had the pleasure of tasting every 'The Signature' release from the inaugural 1962 through to the 1991; what a wonderful way to imbibe in Australia's wine history. From 1988 onwards, the wines have become richer and more full-bodied, they would be great to put down in the cellar. My pick of 'The Signatures' were the wines commemorating the winemakers of their era's, Rudi Kronberger (1967) and Peter Wall (1990).

In 1990, Yalumba began a new red wine tradition when it released 'The Octavius' made from very old vine Barossa Shiraz. These substantial vines are aged in 80 litre casks called Octaves, the smallest casks used commercially for wine maturation, made at Yalumba in their own Cooperage The combination of Missouri oak, seasoned for a minimum of eight years, rich powerful Shiraz fruit and extended maturation in the Octaves, produce wines that are simply awesome.

Yalumba and the Hill-Smith family celebrated their 150 years of wine making in 1999 publishing a superb book "Earth Vine Grape Wine" written by Rob Linn for the occasion.

The pioneering spirit that drove the founder Samuel back in 1849 is as evident today at Yalumba at it was then. Five generations later, this family owned company remains innovative and exciting across the broad disciplines of winemaking whilst maintaining a laid back but professional demeanour.

Address: Eden Valley Road ANGASTON 5353	Est: 1849 Vine Ha: 600 Cases: 600,000	Principal Wines	Potential
Phone: (08) 8561 3200 **Fax:** (08) 8561 3393	**Public Hours:** 9am-5pm, weekdays; 10am-5pm, Saturdays; 12pm-5pm, Sundays and public holidays	Yalumba "The Virgilius"	
Email: info@yalumba.com		Yalumba "The Signature"	15 yrs
		Yalumba "The Octavius"	20+ yrs
WWW: www.yalumba.com	**Principal Varieties:** Cabernet, Grenache, Merlot, Riesling, Sauvignon Blanc, Shiraz, Viognier	Yalumba "The Menzies" Coonawarra	10 yrs
Owner: Robert and Sam Hill Smith		Yalumba "D" Méthode Champenoise	5 yrs
Winemaker: Brian Walsh & Alan Hoey		Yalumba Riesling	5 yrs

Clare Valley

The region known as the Clare Valley incorporates four main river systems and stretches for 30 - 35 kilometres in length. There are five sub-divisions within the valley, proceeding south from the northern end; they are the sub-regions of Clare, Sevenhill, Watervale, Polish Hill River and Auburn. Each area has its own geographic and climatic characteristics. Some of the vineyards are quite elevated, and although the general climate could be descr bed as continental, each small area is subject to its own microclimate. Many Clare wines exhibit distinct cool climate characteristics and intense varietal fruit flavours.

Compared to the Barossa Valley, the

Clare Valley has a later growing period and vintage, with fruit ripening after the intense heat of summer.

John Horrocks first settled in the area very early in the state's history in 1840. He named his property Hope Farm and planted some vines there. While on a trip to England, Horrocks ordered some South African vine cuttings to be sent back to his property and planted them. Unfortunately Horrocks died in a shooting accident at the age of 28, having set the area on its viticultural course.

Another early settler, Irishman Edward Gleeson, named the Valley after his home, County Clare. Gleeson brought many new vine

cuttings into the area, and the industry progressed slowly until the 1890's when planting greatly increased. The Clare Valley was planted largely with red grape varieties such as shiraz, cabernet sauvignon and malbec. These were gradually replaced with higher yielding varieties as the demand for fortified wines grew.

In 1894, the Stanley Wine Company was established and it quickly became one of the largest vignerons in the state.

The four companies still operating in Clare after the depression were Stanley, Buring & Sobels, Sevenhill and Birks Wendouree. During the 1950's, a number of companies re-established themselves for table wine production by planting high quality grape varieties, particularly riesling. Today, riesling has almost become synonymous with the Clare Valley and recently major wine companies such as BRL Hardy, Penfold and Petaluma have planted riesling vineyards in the area. Taylors have extensive new vineyards near Auburn.

The Clare Valley has continued to attract winemakers as an exciting area for premium wine production. Some of the fruit grown in the region however is moved to wineries in other areas for processing. Clare Valley grapes, particularly riesling, are very much in demand all over Australia. Larger developments, like the massive Kirribilly Vineyards and Winery north east of Clare at Farrell's Flat, have heralded a changing face for the region.

Nonetheless Clare is the spiritual home of the small boutique winery and many great ones have opened in recent years. Today, there are more than 25 wineries in the region and its reputation and new plantings are both rapidly increasing.

In 1984, Clare became the first region to introduce the concept of a gourmet weekend of wine, food, music and art, a celebration of the culture of wine, and each May this most successful event reconfirms the Clare Valley's elevated position in the Australian wine industry.

Winery Name: Reilly's Wines
Address: Corner Burra & Hill Streets MINTARO 5415
Phone: (08) 8843 9013 **Fax:** (08) 8843 9013
Email: reillys@ozemail.com.au

WWW: www.winetitles.com.au/reillys.html
Winemaker: Justin Ardill   **Est:** 1994
Public Hours: 10am-5pm, Sun-Fri & public holidays; 10am-5:30pm, Sat

Principal Varieties: Cabernet Sauvignon, Grenache, Semillon, Chardonnay, Riesling, Shiraz

Clare Valley

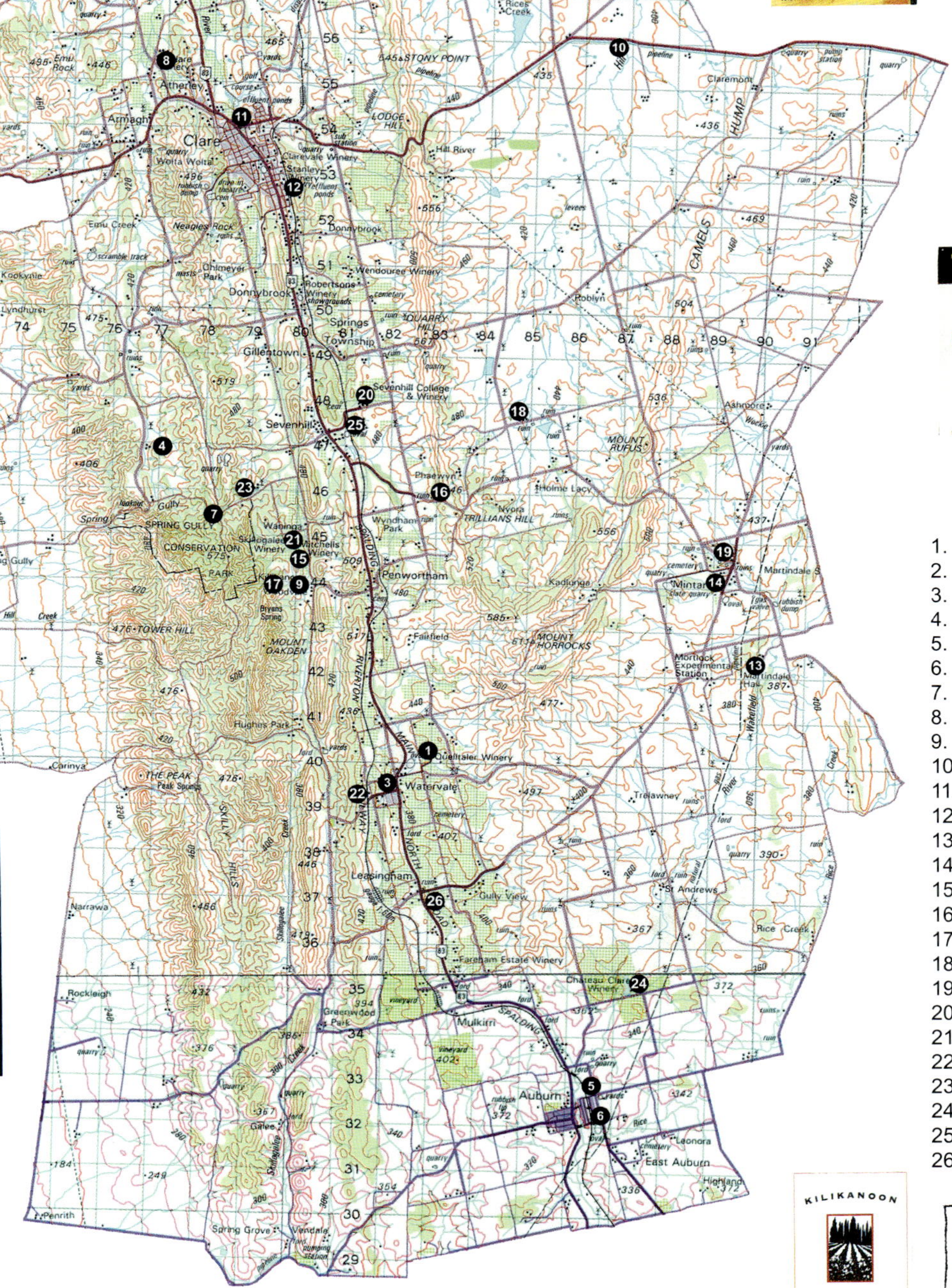

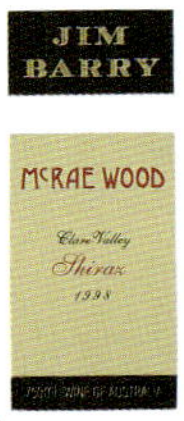

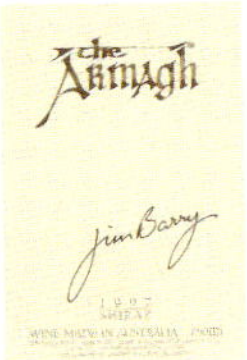

Clare Valley - SA

1. Annies Lane
2. Brian Barry Wines
3. Crabtree of Watervale
4. Eldredge Vineyards
5. Grosset Wines
6. Horrocks Wines
7. Jeanneret Wines
8. Jim Barry Wines
9. Kilikanoon Wines
10. Kirribilly Wines
11. Knappstein
12. Leasingham Wines
13. Martin Dale
14. Mintaro Wines
15. Mitchell Cellars
16. Paulett Wines
17. Penna Lane Wines
18. Pikes Wines
19. Reillys Wines
20. Sevenhill College & Winery
21. Skillogalee
22. Stephen John
23. Stringybrae Wines
24. Taylors Wines
25. Thorn Park Country House
26. Tim Gramp Wines

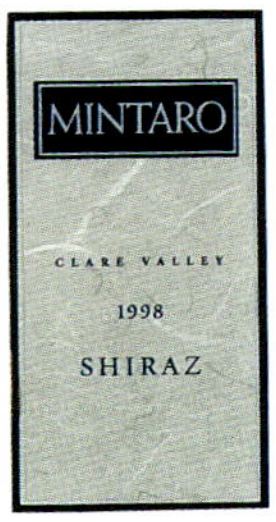

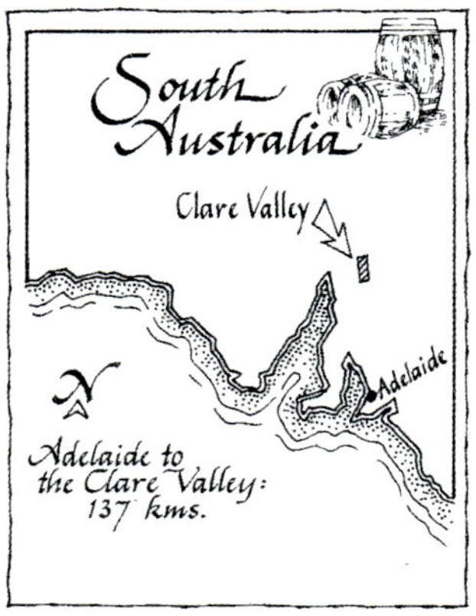

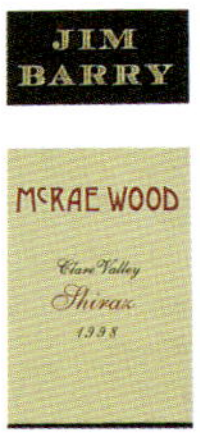

Jim Barry Wines

Jim Barry is a legendary Clare identity. After graduating from the first post-war Roseworthy course in 1946 he became the first Roseworthy graduate to work in the valley in 1947 and brought with him the first pH (acid meter) used in Clare winemaking, when he began 22 years with the Clarevale Co-operative Winery, many of these as its general manager.

In 1959 Jim began to plant his own vineyards with a view to beginning a family wine business involving his children. Gradually, Jim and his hardworking wife Nancy, bought land around the Valley and with his children's assistance planted vines. Their cellar door operations began in 1974 and today four of Jim's six children are directly involved in the business. Peter is general manager, Mark is winemaker, with Julie and John both toiling hard in various areas of the wine business. Jim Barry and his family now have over 500 acres of their own vines planted throughout the valley - from the northern flats on the edge of town to the high, cool ranges in the east, and the famous 'Florita' vineyard at Watervale where the Jim Barry Watervale Riesling is produced.

With their 1985 vintage the Barry's started a great tradition with 'The Armagh', a shiraz of mammoth proportions from their extremely low-yielding Armagh Vineyard on the western side of the valley, planted by Jim back in 1968. The name Armagh, which was given circa 1859, to a settlement 4 kms west of Clare, dates back to the County Armagh and was bestowed by the Irish settlers of the region.

Jim Barry has also released a second shiraz from the 1992 vintage called 'McRae Wood', named after a vineyard planted on land bought by Jim from an old friend, Duncan McRae Wood. It is like a junior version of the opulent Armagh; both are huge wines, yet balanced, flavoursome and approachable even when young.

The Barry family have also restored to original, a classic FJ Holden. Bought new back at Clare in 1956 by Jim's father, Frederick James Barry, it has travelled only 63,000 miles and is in mint condition. Jim and Nancy Barry have enjoyed a prosperous career making wine in Clare, a tradition which is being continued by their children.

Address: PO Box 321, Craigs Hill Rd CLARE 5453	9am-4pm, weekends and public holidays	"The Armagh" 10+ yrs
Phone: (08) 8842 2261 **Fax:** (08) 8842 3752	**Principal Varieties:** Riesling, Shiraz,	Watervale Riesling 2-10 yrs
Email: jbwines@jimbarry.com.au	Sauvignon Blanc, Chardonnay, Cabernet	Personal Selection Cab Sav 5-10 yrs
Owner: Jim Barry **Winemaker:** Mark Barry	Sauvignon, Semillon, Pinot Noir, Cabernet	Personal Selection Chardonnay 2-5 yrs
Est: 1959 **Vine Ha:** 200 **Cases:** 60,000	Franc, Merlot, Malbec	McCrae Wood Shiraz 5-8 yrs
Public Hours: 9am-5pm, weekdays;	**Principal Wines** **Potential**	McCrae Wood Cabernet Malbec 3-5 yrs

Brian Barry

Brian Barry has had a long and illustrious career in the wine industry. As one of the first post war graduates from Roseworthy he was the dux of the course in 1948. Brians first job was at Hamiltons Ewell vineyards and winery at Glenelg one of the last metropolitan wineries in Adelaide, he not only made wine but Whisky and Gin as well, his first gold medal was for in fact for a whisky, although he's gone on to win

thousands more for wine since and even the revered Jimmy Watson memorial trophy for Australia's best one year old red wine with the Berri Estate 1972 Cabernet Shiraz the only time a wine from the irrigated Murray regions has won. Brian was winemaker at Berri/Renmano from 1952 - 1976.

In 1976 whilst wine making for Stanley ·Leasingham he bought a 63 acre property next to the Leasingham

vineyards and began planting in 1977. He named it Jud's Hill after his son Jud.

The vineyard is planted to Riesling, Cabernet Sauvignon and Merlot.

Brian won a trophy in the Adelaide show with his 1983 Riesling which continued to drink magnificently over the next 15 years. Brians wines are made for the long haul. The vineyard is strictly non irrigated, an expensive rarity these days. Brian estimates his 2000 Riesling cost him some $600/tonne just to handpick with the bunches so small and scarce, but the intensity of flavours makes up for it.

Brian also has a second label Gleesons Ridge named after a Clare Pioneer. Brian is a renowned wine judge being the inaugural chairman of the National Wine show in Canberra in 1976 and the Barossa Valley in 1977.

Brian Barry and Gleesons Ridge wines are now available in the Valley through the Leasingham Village Restaurant which is on the main road through the Valley and acts as his Cellar door.

Eldredge

Leigh Eldredge is a fifth generation member of a Clare Valley farming family, who arrived in the region in 1865.

He grew up working on the farm, but in 1978 in his late teens began working vintages at the Stanley Wine Company. Wine Legend Mick Knappstein offered him a full time position when he was 18, Leigh decided against it feeling his weakness in Chemistry may be a handicap. Nonetheless he worked 12 straight vintages at Stanley followed by another four at Quelltaler with Stephen John. He and his wife Karen also purchased his parents 400-acre farm, interest rates leapt up to 21%, in 1991. They decided to sell and bought 113 acres just west of the Skillogalee Valley, to plant vines making their first wine in 1991, a Cabernet Sauvignon. Leigh added about 10% Shiraz. Tim Adams offered them his Cottage behind his

Winery, their short stay ended by up being four years as they first concentrated on turning the cottage on their property into a Cellar Door. In 1995 Leigh started selling his first vintage in Adelaide to restaurants from the back of his car. I met him at this time and was most impressed by his wine, buying some for Chesser Cellars in Adelaide.

The Eldredges now live on their property and have a great Cellar door and Restaurant open Thursday to Sunday for lunches and wine dinners of 12 or more, they serve modern contemporary food using fresh local produce.

The Eldredge Wines now includes a Cabernet Sauvignon, a Shiraz called "Blue Chip", a Mourvedre-Shiraz-Grenache blend, Riesling, and a recently released Sangiovese with a touch of Cabernet added. Leigh has completed the wine marketing course at Roseworthy and has taught

winemaking at the Clare TAFE for many years.

Eldredge have been most successful in Wine shows. Their 1995 Cabernet won Top gold and a trophy, in Adelaide in 1997, their 1999 Riesling won a gold in the same show.

Address: Spring Gully Road CLARE 5453
Phone: (08) 8842 3086 **Fax:** (08) 8842 3086
Email: bluechip@capri.net.au

Winemaker: Leigh Eldredge
Est: 1992
Public Hours: 11am-5pm, daily

Principal Varieties: Cabernet Sauvignon, Merlot, Sangiovese, Shiraz, Malbec, Riesling, Sauvignon Blanc

Stephen John

Stephen John is a world class winemaker. For 25 years he worked for large winemakers, rising from Laboratory Technician at Seppelts, to the Chief Red Winemakers position, before joining Wolf Blass Wines as Chief White Winemaker and then finally General Manager of Operations which took him often to the Quelltaler Winery. This is only a stones throw from where Stephen and his wife Rita have set up their own winery and cellar door, in an 80 year old stable, on the 6 hectare vineyard of old dry grown vines, which in Stephen's experienced hands, are producing great wines.

Stephen still holds the record of 9 gold medals in one show for his Wolf Blass whites in Brisbane. This skill is obvious in his Watervale Riesling and a very interesting Watervale Pedro Ximenez, a white made in a soft, lightly oaked style, from this Spanish variety, I enjoyed this wine a lot and it is very affordably priced.

Stephen also makes a shiraz and cabernet sauvignon, as well as a family favourite, a shiraz based methode champenoise sparkling called "Traugott Cuvee" a rich, soft and velvety wine ideal with roasts and game dishes. This is one of the great new boutique wineries of recent years.

Address: PO Box 345, Government Road WATERVALE 5452
Phone: (08) 8843 0105 **Fax:** (08) 8843 0105
Owner: Stephen and Rita John
Winemaker: Stephen John

Est: 1994 **Vine Ha:** 5.5 **Cases:** 3,500
Public Hours: 10am-5pm, weekdays; 11am-5pm, weekends and public holidays
Principal Varieties: Riesling, Shiraz, Cab Sav, Chard, Pedro Ximenez

Principal Wines	Potential
Watervale Riesling	10 yrs
Watervale Pedro Ximenez	4 yrs
Clare Valley Cabernet Sauvignon	10 yrs
Clare Valley Shiraz	5-10 yrs
Traugott Cuvee Sparkling Red	5 yrs

Annies Lane

Through many changes of name and many great winemakers, this beautiful old winery in the centre of the Clare Valley at Watervale remains as a reminder of the grandeur of days gone by.

Over recent years, the winery has been thoughtfully and thoroughly restored. Quelltaler's history goes back to 1860 when Walter Hughes purchased the property. Vines had already been planted and as these came to bear fruit, Hughes hired Carl Sobels to supervise winemaking and the construction of a winery. After his employer's death, Sobels formed a partnership with Herman Buring and they bought the property in 1890. To formalise the establishment of this new business the property was re-named 'Quelltaler', which is derived from the German translation of 'Spring Vale'. The stone houses built at Quelltaler to accommodate Carl Sobels' growing family, are still lived in and beautifully maintained. The Sobels family remained with Quelltaler until the 1960s.

The winery is now owned by the progressive Beringer Blass Company who have invested heavily in the vineyards. The Annies Lane brand named after the road leading to the property, has become extremely successful over recent years and synonymous with extremely high quality wines at affordable prices. The reds have been particularly impressive.

Leasingham

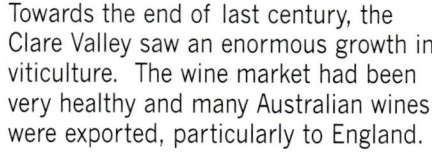

Towards the end of last century, the Clare Valley saw an enormous growth in viticulture. The wine market had been very healthy and many Australian wines were exported, particularly to England.

A grape surplus looked imminent. A syndicate was formed, including J H Knappstein, the area's largest grower, they purchased the Clare jam factory for conversion into a winery. Stanley's first vintage was in 1895, their first winemaker being Alfred Basedow, of the famous winemaking family.

By 1911 Knappstein had bought out his partners. During the 1940's, Stanley were selling bulk wine to most major companies and they began developing their vineyards at Leasingham, near Watervale. Rhine riesling and cabernet sauvignon were the major grape varieties planted.

Stanley began marketing bottled wine under their own label during the 1960's. In 1970 the first vintage of the multi-award winning Leasingham Bin 56 Cabernet Malbec was released.

Current owners BRL Hardy have spent considerable capital on up-grading the winery and vineyards.

Recently a premium range of wines under the label 'Classic Clare' were introduced featuring a shiraz and a cabernet sauvignon and more recently a rhine riesling.

They have been awarded many accolades, including the 1995 Jimmy Watson Trophy.

Mintaro Wines

Peter Houldsworth is a genuine character with more than an air of a sporting legend about him. He travelled through Mintaro as a visitor from New South Wales and fell in love with this historic little village. Mintaro is one of the most unspoiled and characterful towns you'll ever see. It's stepping back into the 19th century, Mintaro slate is much sought after and almost every

building in the town is a classic example of its use. There is also the Mintaro Maze and abolsutely fascinating one acre live, hedged maze. The town has a number of charming bed and breakfast cottages, where you should spend

the night. Mintaro is an absolute must to visit on your trip to the Clare Valley, it is on the eastern fringes of the region and one travels some 10 kms or so through the Polish River region from the main Clare road to get there.

Peter makes a traditional range of wines that have won numerous medals at wine shows. His "Dry Riesling" is a great food wine with all the floral fragrance and lime characters that come through in the Clare region but exceptionally dry and crisp.

The Mintaro Shiraz and the Mintaro Cabernet Sauvignon are rich opulent wines with the strong character of their maker coming through. Peter has recently launched the 'Monarch' range of wines, which is really proving enormously successful. The range includes a "dry" Riesling, Semillon Chardonnay (uwooded), Cabernet Sauvignon and Shiraz. Both the reds are full-bodied styles; already the Monarch wines are achieving export success, but are also available on the Australian market.

Mintaro is a true boutique winery where you can talk and taste with the winemaker and his team and discover some great unique wines.

Address: Leasingham Road MINTARO 5415	Cases: 5,000	Shiraz	5+ yrs
Phone: (08) 8843 9046 Fax: (08) 8843 9050	Public Hours: 9am-5pm, daily	Riesling	2+ yrs
Email: mintaro@hotmail.com	Principal Varieties: Cabernet Franc,	Sem-Chard Unwooded	2+ yrs
Owner: Peter Houldsworth	Cabernet Sauvignon, Chardonnay, Riesling,	Cabernet Sauvignon	5+ yrs
Winemaker: Peter Houldsworth	Semillon, Shiraz	Late Picked Riesling	2+ yrs
Est: 1984 Vine Ha: 20	Principal Wines Potential	Sparkling Cabernet Shiraz	5+ yrs

Neagles Rock

A new face on the Clare scene is Neagles Rock. Between them Jane Willson and Steve Wiblin have 30 years experience as top level wine marketers with wine industry giants.

They decided on Clare as the place to settle with their young family and join the boutique wine brigade, but with their eyes wide open.

They chose a 20 acre block mainly of older vines on the west side of the main road as you approach Clare from Adelaide. The block was very run down and they affectionately named it "Misery", two years later it is anything but. They have renovated the rundown cottage which is now a substantial airy cellar door and have a spacious and beautifully appointed Café Restaurant adjoining called "[Georges] of Clare" all set amongst the vines.

A name for their well thought out venture perplexed them, they thought about the name of the look-out above their first vineyard on the south west corner of the Clare township, but the name "Neagles Rock" sounded somewhat harsh, but they looked into it further and a rather romantic story evolved.

George Neagle was an early pastoralist in the region, after his death, they named the lookout after him and turned the area into a Flora and Fauna Park. It became a popular spot for courting couples, a real "Lovers Retreat".

Thus their new wine venture and Café had their names. The Neagles Rock labels are strong and earthy each featuring a name and artists impression. The Grenache Shiraz is "Lovers Retreat". The Riesling is named "Roof tops" the view from Neagles Rock. The Semillon "Serenity". The Cabernet "Break of Day" paying homage to the many friends and family who worked dawn 'til dusk to help establish their enterprise. The Shiraz is named "Misery" showing their vineyard and cellar door before renovations.

A liqueur Tawny Port "Richard Lincoln" and Botrytis Riesling "Sweet Dorothy" acknowledge the incredible help and support from Jane's parents, completes the range. There's also a N.V. Sparkling Chardonnay Pinot Noir only available at the Cellar door and [Georges] Café shop. Drop in and try it and help celebrate this welcome addition to Clare.

		Principal Wines	Potential
Address: Main North Road CLARE 5453	**Cases:** 4,000	Neagles Rock Vineyard Cab Sauv	5-8 yrs
Phone: (08) 8843 4020 **Fax:** (08) 8843 4021	**Public Hours:** 10am-5pm 6 days - Closed	Neagles Rock Vineyard Riesling	5-6 yrs
Email: neaglesrock@bigpond.com	Wednesday; Restaurant open 10am-5pm 6	Neagles Rock Vineyard Shiraz	6-8 yrs
Owner: Stephen Wiblin & Jane Willson	days & open Fri & Sat nights	Neagles Rock Vineyard Grenache	3-5 yrs
Winemaker: Neil Pike & Steve Wiblin	**Principal Varieties:** Cabernet, Riesling,	Neagles Rock Vineyard Semillon	3-4 yrs
Est: 1997 **Vine Ha:** 15	Semillon, Grenache, Sangiovese, Shiraz		

Knappstein

The Knappstein name has been involved in the wine business in Clare since 1895 when the local brewer, the local doctor, a solicitor and J H Knappstein began the Stanley Wine Company in the premises of the Clare Jam Factory.

The Stanley Wine Company achieved wine show success second to none, in this early era of the modern premium Australian wine business in Clare. After the sale of the Stanley Wine Company, Tim Knappstein began Enterprise Wines in the old Enterprise brewery building, in the township of Clare.

The Knappstein Vineyards adjoins Petaluma's Hanlin Hill Vineyard and the more recently planted 45 hectare Yertabulti Vineyard, all are on rich red soils over limestone, they are all planted with premium varieties to supply Knappstein Wines. The Knappstein riesling, fume blanc and cabernet merlot owe much of their commercial success to the qualities of these concentrated grapes.

Petaluma purchased the Knappstein Winery in 1992 and the vineyards in 1995. Petaluma's chief Winemaker of seven years, Andrew Hardy took over the reins as manager and winemaker a number of years ago. Although owned by Petaluma, Knappstein Wines operates as an independent premium quality winery. Andrew Hardy is doing a great job at Knappstein Wines producing wines that are the "essence of Clare" and most especially the world renowned dry riesling and full bodied ripe fruit reds.

		Principal Wines	Potential
Address: 2 Pioneer Avenue CLARE 5453	10am-5pm Sat; 11am-4pm, Sun	Hand Picked Riesling	5-10 yrs
Phone: (08) 8842 2600 **Fax:** (08) 8842 3831	**Principal Varieties:** Chardonnay, Merlot, Cab	Gewurztraminer	3-6 yrs
Winemaker: Andrew Hardy	Sav, Shiraz, Sauvignon Blanc, Semillon, Cab	Cabernet Merlot	8-10 yrs
Est: 1976 **Vine Ha:** 80	Franc, Gewürztraminer, Riesling, Malbec	Enterprise Cabernet Sauvignon	10-15 yrs
Public Hours: 9am-5pm, weekdays;		Enterprise Shiraz	10-15 yrs

Jeanneret Wines

Denis Jeanneret, a Swiss Chemist, and his wife Pat fell in love with the natural beauty of a property on the edge of the Spring Gully Conservation Park not far from the group of wineries in the Skillogalee Valley.

They planted vines and for a number of years as they grew Denis worked for Robert Crabtree at Watervale honing his winemaking skills.

The first Jeanneret Wines were made in 1992. The winery is on top of a hill in quite dense bushland but the cellar is neatly tucked under the families lovely stone home. In spring the natural bush gardens are resplendent with thousands of daffodils. Denis unfortunately passed on prematurely but son Ben has been involved for a number of years and making excellent wines. The family are generous and open

with lots of character, like their wines.

I particularly like their shiraz, resplendent with wild berry flavours

and lots of pepper and spice.

Jeanneret is a little off the beaten track, but well worth the effort to visit.

Address: Jeaneret Road SEVENHILL 5453	**Cases:** 4,000	Semillon	5-10 yrs
Phone: (08) 8843 4308 **Fax:** (08) 8843 4251	**PublicHours:** 11am-5pm, weekdays; 10am-5pm, weekends & public holidays	Denis Shiraz	10+ yrs
Email: jwines@bigpond.com		Sparkling Grenache	2-3 yrs
WWW: www.ascl.com/j-wines	**Principal Varieties:** Cabernet Sauvignon, Grenache, Riesling, Semillon, Shiraz	Riesling	5-10 yrs
Winemaker: Ben Jeanneret		Shiraz	5-10 yrs
Est: 1992 **Vine Ha:** 4	**Principal Wines**　　　　　**Potential**	Grenache Shiraz	4-6 yrs

Stringybrae

Owned by Donald and Sally Willson, the family's picturesque Stringy Brae property is located near the Spring Gully Conservation Park, two kilometres West of Sevenhill.

The cellar door has just moved into a magnificent new home, "Waldie's Shed", a contemporary Australian building with slate based verandahs and a vast lawned area designed for a marquee for special functions.

Stringy Brae now boasts a 'total experience' incorporating wine, food and accommodation. Waldie's Shed caters for lunch during normal cellar door hours as well as special events and private functions.

The first Stringy Brae wine was produced in 1988 with the first vineyards being planted in 1991 through to 2001. The Stringy Brae label produces Riesling, Shiraz and

Cabernet Sauvignon, whilst the Mote Hill label provides Special Reserve wine currently consisting of 1994 1.5 litre Cabernet Sauvignon and a blend of five vintages of Shiraz under the Black Knight label.

The two self-contained cottages situated on the Northern side of "Mote Hill" overlooking the dam, vineyards and sweeping valleys towards Clare. This combined with the wines and the unforgettable charming hospitality of Donald and Sally makes Stringy Brae an ideal country getaway retreat.

Address: Sawmill Road, Sevenhill CLARE 5453	**Est:** 1988	**Vine Ha:** 10 　**Cases:** 1,500	Riesling	8 yrs
Phone: (08) 8843 4313 **Fax:** (08) 8843 4319	**PublicHours:** 10am-5pm Fri, Sat, Sun, Public Holidays, School Holidays; Weekdays refer to road sign		Shiraz	8-10 yrs
Email: admin@stringbrae.com.au			Cabernet Sauvignon	8-10 yrs
WWW: www.stringybrae.com.au			Mote Hill 1994 1.5L Cabernet Sav	15-20 yrs
Owner: DB and SM Willson	**Principal Varieties:** Riesling, Shiraz, Cab Sav		Mote Hill "Sir Lancelot" Shiraz	10 yrs
Winemaker: Contract	**Principal Wines**　　　　**Potential**		Mote Hill "Black Knight" Shiraz	10 yrs

Kilikanoon

Kevin Mitchell has a good deal of wine history, training and experience behind him, his father has vineyards, in Clare Valley, supplying grapes to Kevin's uncles winery, Mitchells of Clare, who are ironically located just up the road from Kilikanoon, in the

pretty Skillogalee Valley.

Kevin established Kilikanoon in 1998, before this he had worked in a number of wineries in Australia and the USA, since graduating with a degree in Oenology from Adelaide University in 1992.

The Kilikanoon Cellar door is in a beautifully restored 1880's cottage in Penna Lane and surrounded by pretty English gardens. Kevin has been making his wine off site so far but his 2002 vintage will be made on site, in a winery he is constructing.

Kevin manages his vineyard and makes his wine using very traditional methods, all wines are fermented in small batches to maintain individual varietal and district characters, the reds are all fermented in open tanks and basket pressed.

Kilikanoon are set to expand considerably over the next 5 years, whilst remaining a hands on boutique operation. Kevin is already selling 70% of his wine overseas. Kilikanoon have got all their bases well covered and you should make the effort to visit them, in their very pretty location in their special part of the Clare Valley.

Address: Penna Lane PENWORTHAM	**Public** Hours: Weekends, public holidays	Kilikanoon Cabernet Sauvignon	6-10 yrs
Phone: (08) 843 4377 **Fax:** (08) 843 4377	**Principal Varieties:** Cabernet Sauvignon,	Kilikanoon Prodigal Grenache	3-8 yrs
Email: kilikan@capri.net.au	Grenache, Riesling, Semillon, Shiraz	Kilikanoon Morte Block Riesling	5-10 yrs
Owner/Winemaker: Kevin Mitchell	**Principal Wines** **Potential**	Kilikanoon Semillon	2-5 yrs
Est: 1998 **Vine Ha:** 6 **Cases:** 5,000	Kilikanoon Oracle Shiraz 8-15 yrs	Kilikanoon Sauvignon Blanc	2-5 yrs

Penna Lane Wines

Ray and Lynette Klavins have spent 7 years of enormously hard work turning a neglected farm in the Skilly Hills, adjacent to Penwortham, into a Picture Book Vineyard and a delightful Cellar door. Nowadays their newly constructed home looks out over a splendid vista, but it was not always so.

In 1991 Ray was looking for a change of direction and went back to study Viticulture and Oenology at Roseworthy. Here he met Stephen Stafford-Brookes who was on a similar mission. Today they are partners in Penna Lane Wines, a name they chose in 1999.

When Ray and Lynette bought the 35 acre property in 1993 it was covered in the noxious weed Salvation Jane with a derelict dairy and a tumble down piggery. After 20 truckloads of

rubbish were removed, with friends and family they set to work. Today 11 acres are under vine and the old dairy that also served as a shearing shed and for a time the Klavins home, is now a great Cellar door with an outdoor alfresco eating area and a log fire for winter. Lynette produces a range of oils and condiments from her own garden and serves food

platters at the Cellar door. There are also Barbeque facilities for a picnic under the trees.

The Penna Lane Wines I found a real surprise for such a young enterprise. The Semillon from 30 year old unirrigated vines grown nearby was intense and enriched by partial barrel fermentation and a little time in older French Oak.

The Cabernet Sauvignon was elegant, full of plum and red berry flavours with a very long finish.

The Shiraz had very deep mauve colour, lots of spice with very lifted fruit. Riesling has been added to the range in 2001. It is an intensely aromatic wine with a fresh, lingering finish.

Penna Lane is a fine addition to the Clare Valley and will undoubtedly gain much kudos as time goes by.

Address: Lot 51 Penna Lane PENWORTHAM via CLARE 5453	**Owner:** Ray & Lynette Klavins & Stephen Staffors - Brookes	Cabernet Sauvignon, Semillon	
		Principal Wines	**Potential**
Phone: (08) 8843 3464	**Est:** 1998 **Vine Ha:** 4.5 **Cases:** 1,500	Penna Lane Riesling	5+ yrs
Fax: (03) 8843 4349	**Public Hours:** 11am-5pm, Thurs - Sun	Penna Lane Shiraz	5-10 yrs
Email: klavins@rbe.net.au	or by appointment	Penna Lane Cabernet	5-10 yrs
WWW: www.pennalanewines.com.au	**Principal Varieties:** Riesling, Shiraz,	Penna Lane Semillon	4-5 yrs

Paulett Wines

Neil and Alison Paulett quickly made their mark with their riesling after commencing their well-integrated vineyards and winery in 1983. Several years ago they made the bold move of building a new stone winery at the apex of their property. The view from this hilltop winery with its return verandahs looking out over the entire Polish Hill River Valley is awesome.

The winery has been cleverly designed to take advantage of gravity to make the wines with a minimum of human and mechanical intervention.

The visitor to the winery also has a birds eye view, not only of the vineyards in the valley, but the working winery as well from the elevated tasting area.

The Paulett wines include riesling both dry and late-picked styles, chardonnay, sauvignon blanc, shiraz and cabernet merlot. They have carved out a solid reputation both in Australia and on several overseas markets.

If in the Clare Valley make sure you drop in and catch the view along with tasting the excellent wines. Local artists works grace the tasting room walls and are worth seeing.

Address: PO Box 50, Sevenhill via CLARE 5453	Public Hours: 10am-5pm, daily except Christmas Day and Good Friday		
Phone: (08) 8843 4328 Fax: (08) 8843 4202		Andreas (Reserve Shiraz)	10-15 yrs
Owner: Neil and Alison Paulett	Principal Varieties: Cab Sav, Chardonnay,	Riesling	8-10 yrs
Winemaker: Neil Paulett	Merlot, Riesling, Sauvignon Blanc, Shiraz	Shiraz	6-8 yrs
		Cabernet Merlot	6-8 yrs
Est: 1983 Vine Ha: 12.5 Cases: 12,500	Principal Wines Potential	Sauvignon Blanc	2-4 yrs

Tim Gramp

Tim Gramp has been directly associated with the wine industry since the mid 70's.

Tim is a fifth generation member of the family that made Orlando famous. His grandfather, Hugo Gramp, was a former Managing Director of Orlando. His father, "Snowy" Gramp was a former Director and Viticultural Manger.

The Gramp family sold the company in the early 70's, but Tim continued the tradition with his own his personal label. In 1991, after graduating from Roseworthy College in the Wine Production and Marketing course he worked in the McLaren Vale region for a number of years.

His 1991 Shiraz quickly found success on the wine show circuit, winning 1 Trophy, 6 Gold and 2 Silver medals and a Gold at the renowned

Intervin International Wine show in New York City. Following vintages have continued to win awards, the Shiraz is his flagship wine.

A 1993 Grenache was the next addition to the TG range, specifically aimed as a versatile food wine.

Tim was searching for a base. It was by chance when he was trying to coerce quality Riesling fruit from a Watervale grower, in early 1996, that a winery site came up for sale.

It was the ideal location to establish a base for production and cellar door sales. Tim and Kathy purchased the property in February 1996.

The winery complex is nested in the hamlet of Leasingham (2 kilometres south of Watervale) the 1860's cottage which houses cellar door sales was originally used as a "halfway house" by the Burra copper miners en route to the Port Wakefield wharves.

Although based in the Clare Valley, Tim continues to produce top quality McLaren Vale Shiraz and Grenache complemented with the two local wines of Riesling and Cabernet Sauvignon.

Tim recently planted a new Cabernet Sauvignon vineyard designed using a unique Italian "Sylvoz" trellising system · the first of its kind in the Clare Valley.

Address: Mintaro Road LEASINGHAM 5452	Est: 1990 Vine Ha: 2 Cases: 5,000	Principal Wines	Potential
Phone: (08) 8843 0199	Public Hours: 10:30am-4:30pm weekends &	Tim Gramp Watervale Cabernet Sav	4-6 yrs
Fax: (08) 8843 0299	public holidays	Tim Gramp McLaren Vale Shiraz	5-7 yrs
Email: timgramp@timgrampwines.com.au	Principal Varieties: Grenache, Cabernet	Tim Gramp Watervale Riesling	5-10 yrs
Owner/Winemaker: Tim Gramp	Sauvignon, Riesling, Shiraz	Tim Gramp McLaren Vale Grenache	2-3 yrs

Sevenhill Cellars

Brother John May celebrated his 30th vintage as winemaker at Sevenh ll Cellars in 2001 as the 8th winemaker in the 150 years of Clare's oldest winemaking establishment. Sevenhill, which was founded by the Jesuit Society who fled Austria in 1848, to escape religious persecution.

Only Brother John Schreiner the first winemaker who presided over 35 vintages from 1851-1884 has made more vintages.

The society began winemaking to provide sacremental wine for religious use, this still forms 25% of the vintage at Sevenhill and all demon nations are supplied throughout Australia and even as far away as P.N.G., Indonesia and India.

The Jesuits grow all their own grapes in their 115 acres of vineyards where 18 varieties are planted. The vintage usually comprises around 500 tonnes and all the wines are made bottled and labelled by them on the premises. A full range of table wines both red and white are produced. The reds can be of fairly heroic proportions and age particularly well. Sevenhill also produce a range of fortified wines which includes sherries, liqueurs, frontignac and three parts a vintage, a tawny and one made from the Portugese variety Touriga.

The buildings at Sevenhill are quite breath taking, the Church was commenced in 1864 but construction halted in 1866 as no funds were available, it resumed in 1870. Construction was never fully completed and the North Transept was added in 1910 and the South Transept added in 1997. The Construction from Stone quarried on the property local red gum timbers and Mintaro slate is set to last many lifetimes. The church is one of few in Australia with a Crypt. The first burial there being Brother Sadler who was killed blasting building stone in the quarry in 1865.

In amongst the vines is a gorgeous grotto with a pure white statue of the Virgin Mary. There is also a peaceful picnic areas on the lawns with tables seats and plenty of shade from the trees You can not only taste in the Cellar door and visit the winery but also the grotto, the Church and even the Crypt.

Thorn Park Country House

David Hay and Michael Speers have created a truly magnificent Country House from the Classic old Homestead and outbuildings they found in decay in 1986. Thorn Park is a 60 acre rural retreat almost directly opposite Clare's oldest winery, the historic Sevenhills Cellars of the Jesuit Brothers.

Thorn Park's undulating hills are studded with towering gums and the dam near the Homestead is resplendent with native ducks and other bird life. The gardens around the homestead and guest rooms are truly enchanting, particularly at sunrise and sunset.

The Homestead was built in the 1850's from stone quarried on the

property and Mintaro slate. The décor and furnishings in the living rooms and library are superb and available to guests to relax in and enjoy at any time. The bedrooms in the homestead and outbuildings are beautifully appointed with their own private facilities. The kitchen is truly spacious and includes an eating area where one can chat with David, a trained chef who also runs cooking classes for guests, or Michael who has a wealth of knowledge on the Clare Valley and all the things you can do.

The Dining room is available for

functions as is a larger function area and the gardens all make a great places for a special celebration. Thorn Park is very central and within easy reach of the regions attractions, such as Spring Gully Conservation park, the unspoilt colonial charm of Mintaro and Martindale Hall, you can even discover Geralka Rural Farm or visit the Historic copper mining town of Burra.

For me I'd be just as happy to lay back and absorb the beautiful ambience created by David and Michael in their very special place and their relaxed country hospitality.

Pikes Wines

Neil and Andrew Pike have a very positive attitude to life. Their family has long been heavily involved in the beverage industry. Over the last two years they have greatly expanded their winery also adding a splendid new cellar door and a beautiful vaulted function area on the first floor. The design and construction from regional stone blends in superbly with the classic old buildings. The whole complex is a credit to them and their heritage.

Henry Pike, their great grandfather arrived in South Australia in 1878. He settled in the pretty town of Oakbank in the Adelaide Hills and established a brewing and soft drink business, the symbol of which was the distinctive English pike fish.

In 1972, the business was sold; however by this time Edgar Pike, Neil's father, was vineyard manager for a large wine company and dabbling in his own private winemaking. Neil and his brother Andrew both studied viticulture and winemaking at Roseworthy Agricultural College. Andrew is involved in viticulture and

management, whilst Neil handles the winemaking and marketing, they are a great team.

Their vineyard was established in 1984 and they made wine from the region the following year. The cool Polish Hill River is a genuine sub-region of the Clare Valley, ripening several weeks after most of the valley, giving the wines that extra depth of flavour and keen cool climate edge.

All the Pikes wines will age well; the only problem is they just haven't been able to keep up with demand, particularly from the restaurant trade. The riesling led the way and runs out each year, as does their succulent shiraz with its

approachable Rhone Valley character.

Pikes also have a reserve shiraz, a rigorously selected wine from the best few barrels of the year. The first wine was a 1992 vintage; the wine is only released in excellent years, the 1993 didn't rate a reserve selection, but the wines since have been sensational. Neil and Andrew dedicated the first reserve to their hardworking inspirational parents, Edgar and Merle.

Look for the pike fish and make sure he's not the one that got away and was served on someone else's table! After the shiraz and riesling, try the sauvignon blanc and the cabernet with a touch of merlot and cabernet franc.

Address: Polish Hill River Road, Sevenhill SEVENHILL 5453 **Phone:** (08) 8843 4370 **Fax:** (08) 8843 4353 **Email:** info@pikeswines.com.au **WWW:** www.pikeswines.com.au **Owner:** Neil & Andrew Pike **Winemaker:** Neil Pike	**Est:** 1984 **Vine Ha:** 34 **Cases:** 35,000 **Public Hours:** 10am-4pm, daily (except Good Friday & Christmas day) **Principal Varieties:** Cabernet Sauvignon, Chardonnay, Merlot, Pinot Grigio, Riesling, Sangiovese, Sauvignon Blanc, Shiraz	**Principal Wines** Riesling Sauvignon Blanc Chardonnay Shiraz Cabernet Sangiovese	**Potential** 6-10 yrs 3-4 yrs 6-10 yrs 8-12 yrs 5-8 yrs

Skillogalee

Skillogalee is located in the beautiful Skillogalee Valley that runs in a north south direction on the western side of the region on the edge of the Spring Gully Conservation Park. This sub region in the Penwortham Section of the Clare Region is now home to some 9 wineries, the most of any of the sub regional districts.

This secluded Valley is absolutely spectacular at any time of the year with its long contoured vineyards, waterways and areas of native bushland, interspersed with stands of European trees that are cloaked in vibrant colours in Autumn.

The beautiful property, with its 55 acres of mature vines, was bought by Management Consultant David Palmer and his wife Diana in 1989. They not only make stunning wines but set up a truly first class restaurant some 10 years ago in the 146 year old cottage, built by the first settler on the property John Trestrail, a Cornish miner who developed the property significantly from virgin bushland, with the help of his 13 children. The history of the property however goes back to the early 1840's.

Father of the region, Explorer John Horrocks was returning from an expedition to the Flinders Ranges, running short of food his party of explorers had existed on a makeshift version of a celtic dish called Skillogalee, a thin porridge of grass seeds and water. On returning home to the Clare Valley and better nutrition, they were enjoying a meal on the banks of the stream, which runs through the base of the Palmers property, they named it Skillogalee Creek. The first vines on the property were planted in 1969 by Spencer and Margaret George.

The elevated site some 475 metres above sea level is one of the coolest and latest picked vineyards in the Clare region. The wines are all made from the Palmers own grapes. The Riesling has an enviable reputation and Skillogalee also produce an excellent aromatic Gewurztraminer. The Reds are exceptionally full flavoured and spicy, along with traditional Shiraz and Cabernet Sauvignon, they also grow Cabernet Franc and Malbec and even a little Muscat from which they make an excellent fortified Liqueur. I like their Vintage Port a rare variety now a days. You can also enjoy a flute of their Sparkling, Methode Champenoise Riesling as an apéritif before you eat in the Restaurant.

The Skillogalee Restaurant has developed a great deal of respect in the Hospitality Industry. Diana Palmer a former school teacher also studied as a chef and she is extremely talented. The setting of the restaurant, its views, the rustic charm of the old stone cottage and gardens is enchanting. They are open for lunch 7 days a week and also serve morning and afternoon teas. There is no excuse not to visit Skillogalee and all its charms.

Address: PO Box 87 Sevenhill via Clare 5453
Phone: (08) 8843 4311 **Fax:** (08) 8843 4343
Email: skilly@capri.net.au

Owner: Efira Services Pty Ltd **Est:** 1970
Winemaker: Dave Palmer **Vine Ha:** 27
Principal Varieties: Cabernet Sauvignon,

Frontignac, Grenache, Merlot, Riesling, Cabernet Franc, Chardonnay, Gewürztraminer, Malbec, Muscat, Shiraz

Taylors

In 1969, Bill Taylor Snr., along with his sons John and Bill, purchased a holding of 178 hectares by the Wakefield River in Auburn. The site was carefully chosen for the red brown loam over limestone soils (known as terra rossa) and the cool climate of the Clare Valley. The initial planting consisted of 178 hectares, of which 149 hectares were Cabernet Sauvignon. Later, a further 145 hectares were purchased and planting of Chardonnay, Shiraz and Riesling were added. With thoughts firmly fixed on the successful future of Taylors Wines, the family aptly named the new addition the "Promised Land".

The excellent Bordeaux wines such as Mouton-Rothschild had long held a fascination for the Taylor brothers and this led them to strive towards producing wines of comparable quality in Australia. In 1973 the first Taylors estate grown and bottled Cabernet Sauvignon received gold medals at every national wine show. Since then every vintage produced has won awards at national and international wine shows. The Taylors went on to produce Shiraz, Chardonnay, Riesling, Pinot Noir and White Burgundy (a Chardonnay/Crouchen blend). Recent new releases include an Unwooded Chardonnay, Shiraz/Cabernet, Semillon, Merlot and Gewurztraminer. In true Taylors tradition, these wines all regularly receive awards both nationally and internationally, earning them the reputation of being Australia's most consistently awarded winemaker.

In 1995 expansion continued with the purchase of two adjoining properties, totalling 405 hectares, alongside the original Taylors estate. The additions make the Taylors property one of the largest contiguous estates in Australia. One of the purchases included a disused, historic winery called St. Andrews and in 1999 the family recreated history with the first release of Taylors' premium St. Andrews range of wines.

Still proudly family owned, Bill Taylor is chief executive officer of the company, his eldest son Mitchell is managing director in addition to continuing the tradition of family winemaking, while younger brothers Justin and Clinton have key roles in national sales and marketing.

The philosophy at Taylors Wines is to make soft, easy drinking wines and to hold them back from the market until they are ready to drink. This fact, together with an obsession for quality, sparing no expense, make Taylors one of the best value wines in the country.

Address: Taylors Road AUBURN 5451	**Public Hours:** 9am-5pm, weekdays; 10am-5pm, Sat and public holidays; 10am-4pm, Sun	Taylors Estate Cabernet Sauvignon	5-10 yrs
Phone: (08) 8849 2008 **Fax:** (08) 8849 2240		Taylors Estate Chardonnay	2-5 yrs
Email: info@taylorswines.com.au	**Principal Varieties:** Chardonnay, Merlot, Cabernet Sauvignon, Shiraz, Pinot Noir, Riesling, Semillon, Crouchen	Taylors Estate Shiraz	5-10 yrs
WWW: www.taylorswines.com.au		Taylors Estate Merlot	5-10 yrs
Owner: Taylor Family **Est:** 1969		Taylors Estate Semillon	2-5 yrs
Winemaker: Adam Eggins **Vine Ha:** 550	**Principal Wines** **Potential**	Taylors Estate Pinot Noir	2-5 yrs

Coonawarra

After making a fortune selling supplies to gold prospectors and running stores in Ballarat and Geelong, John Riddoch and his family moved to Coonawarra in 1861. Riddoch purchased 200 acres (80 ha), but within 20 years he owned the extensive property Yallum Park, which covered tens of thousands of hectares.

On the advice of a local gardener, Riddoch subdivided much land into 25-75 ha blocks, forming the Penola Fruit Colony. This land was bought by 'blockers' as they came to be known, who planted and later sold grapes to Riddoch. Until the bank crash in 1893, the Fruit Colony prospered, due to the magic 'terra rossa' soil of the area. This soil covers about 4,800 ha of land in a strip about 1.6 km wide and 14.5 km long.

With 140 ha under vine at Yallum Park, Riddoch built substantial cellars in which to store the wines made from the blockers' fruit. These were largely shiraz, cabernet sauvignon, malbec and some pinot noir. The cellars were built with three distinct gables and have come to be very well known as the building on the Wynns Coonawarra Estate woodcut labels. The cellars were designed to store 340,000 litres of wine, but with the depressed market and large vintages, they soon became inadequate. The Yallum shearing sheds at Katnook provided further storage space for Riddoch's wine.

John Riddoch died in 1901 at a time when fortified wines were becoming increasingly popular. The property was taken over by trustees, who gradually disposed of the land, vineyards and wine. Bill Redman arrived in Coonawarra the year of Riddoch's death and started work at Yallum Park. By 1907, at 20 years of age, he had reached the position of head cellarman and was able to purchase a 16 ha block from Riddoch's estate. Redman's first wine was made using an old cheese press and was fermented in

hogsheads purchased from Douglas A. Tolley who had agreed to buy the wine for one shilling per gallon (4.5 litres).

After Yallum Park was purchased by Chateau Tanunda in 1919, Redman became the only winemaker in the area, as the wine remaining from Riddoch's estate was distilled into fortifying spirit and brandy · a shocking waste of excellent reds.

In 1945 Woodleys bought the Yallum Estate, winery, distillery and vineyards and renamed the property Chateau Comaum. Bill Redman and family were commissioned to run the winery. Wynns purchased the property in 1951, renaming it Wynns Coonawarra Estate. There are now more than 20 wineries in the region and many more wine companies around Australia either own vines or purchase grapes or wine from the region.

The climate in Coonawarra is cool and occasionally frosts and ripening are problems. There is a constant underground water supply, but the layer of limestone between it and the terra rossa, makes establishing vines both difficult and expensive, as the limestone must be ripped through under each row of vines to enable their roots to reach the water source. Once established, vines are protected from the vagaries of annual rainfall by a constant water supply.

Internationally, Coonawarra is the first region in Australia to gain a reputation for its wines and their style, as distinct from just being an Australian wine. The south east of South Australia now has wines growing far and wide, new multi-million dollar wine planting schemes seem a dime a dozen, but the name Coonawarra still has the magic which has been hard-earned and deserved.

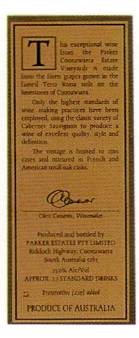

Coonawarra

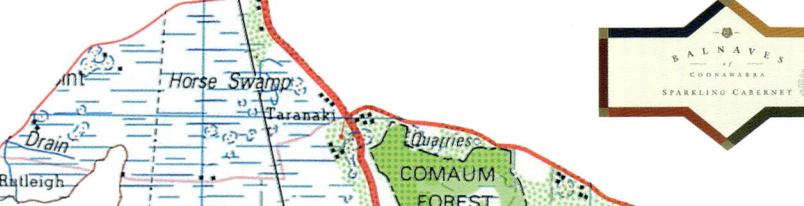

Coonawarra - SA

1. Balnaves of Coonawarra
2. Blok Estate
3. Brands Laira
4. Chardonnay Lodge
5. Gartner Wines
6. Hollick Wines
7. Katnook Estate
8. Leconfield Wines
9. Majella Wines
10. Mildara Jamieson's Run Wines
11. Parker Estate
12. Penley Estate
13. Punters Corner
14. Redman Wines
15. Rosemount - Coonawarra
16. Rouge Homme
17. Rymill Wines
18. S. Kidman Wines
19. Weatherall Wines
20. Wynns Coonawarra Estate
21. Zema Estate

Adelaide to Coonawarra: 375kms.

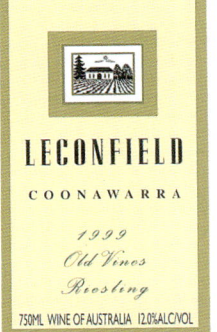

Brands Laira Wines

Eric Brand married into the wine industry in 1950 when he wed Nancy Redman, Owen's sister. He bought a small property from Redman, which was mostly orchards, but also included several hectares of vines, some of which were amongst the first planted in Coonawarra in 1896.

There are still walnut trees along the drive and visitors can buy pickled walnuts from the cellar door. The original vineyard, with its one hundred-year-old vines, continues to produce outstanding red wines, but the early fruit orchards have long since given way to Brand's expanding vineyards.

Eric Brand sold his grapes for to local winemakers for many years but began making his own wine in 1966. Hardy's winemaker Dick Heath supplied Brand's with a crusher and other necessary equipment. The resulting wine was sold to Hardy's directly after vintage. Redman's also made wine at Brand's winery before completion of their own.

During the late 60's, Brand's began bottling and selling some wine under the 'Laira' label, from their cellar door. 'Laira' was the ship owned by Captain Stentiford, the first owner of Brand's property. The red wines released under this label have developed a legendary reputation, and under Eric's sons, Bill and Jim some interesting new wines and styles have evolved. Brand's made steady progress in the market place and were, in fact, innovators in some areas - they produced Coonawarra's first pinot noir in 1982, and were one of Australia's first wineries to produce straight merlot.

The demand for cash to fund expansion and the challenge of marketing and distributing their wines meant more capital was needed. This led to an arrangement with McWilliam's, the strong family wine company from New South Wales. The balance was perfect; McWilliam's were looking to expand into a number of premium table wine regions, Brand's fitted the bill, so in 1990 they took a half share in the company.

Brand's Wines leapt ahead and in 1994 McWilliam's purchased the remaining half of the company. At the same time McWilliam's purchased an additional 200 hectares immediately adjacent to Brand's existing vineyards making it one of the largest landholders in the Coonawarra area. Sensibly McWilliam's have let Jim and Bill Brand stay on and manage things in their very thorough, diligent style. The Brand's wines are consistently among the best in Coonawarra and remain great value for money.

<table>
<tr><td>Address: Riddoch Highway
COONAWARRA 5263
Phone: (08) 8736 3260 Fax: (08) 8736 3208
Winemaker: Jim Brand and Bruce Gregory
Est: 1965 Vine Ha: 180</td><td>Public Hours: 9am-4.30pm, weekdays;
10am-4pm, weekends and public holidays
Principal Varieties: Chardonnay, Merlot,
Cabernet Sauvignon, Shiraz, Pinot Noir,
Cabernet Franc, Malbec, Riesling</td><td>Principal Wines
Cabernet Merlot
Cabernet Sauvignon
Shiraz
Chardonnay</td><td>Potential
0-4 yrs
7-8 yrs
5+ yrs
2-4 yrs</td></tr>
</table>

Balnaves

Doug Balnaves commenced his career in the Wine Industry when he developed and managed the Hungerford Hill Vineyards in Coonawarra in the early 1970's. In 1975, the family began planting their own vineyards and today they have a magnificent 120 acre vineyard at the southern end of the cigar shaped terra rossa strip, in the heart of Coonawarra.

The predominant variety at Balnaves is cabernet sauvignon, but other varieties include shiraz, merlot, cabernet franc and chardonnay. In 1991 the Balnaves launched their own wine label and opened a state of the art tasting and cellar door sales area overlooking a small lake, always resplendent with native bird life.

Doug's wife, Annette, is a great photographer and the cellar door sales area often features some of her excellent work.

Balnaves of Coonawarra uses only about 20% of the grapes for their own wines. The wines include the flagship cabernet sauvignon, a wine called 'The Blend', a superb cabernet sauvignon, merlot and cabernet franc blend, shiraz, chardonnay and a sparkling methode champenoise made from cabernet sauvignon.

Kirsty Balnaves is responsible for the office administration, cellar door and sales and Peter Balnaves manages the vineyards. In 1996 a modern winery was built and Peter Bissell joined the company. The winery tower is well visible from the main road and the distinctive Australiana flavour and colours of the buildings are aesthetically most pleasing. Balnaves is a high quality family wine business and a great asset to Coonawarra.

Address: Main Road COONAWARRA 5263	**Winemaker:** Peter Bissell	Petit Verdot, Shiraz
Phone: (08) 8737 2946 **Fax:** (08) 8737 2945	**Est:** 1975 **Vine Ha:** 49 **Cases:** 10,000	**Principal Wines** **Potential**
Email: kirsty.balnaves@balnaves.com.au	**Public Hours:** 9am-5pm weekdays,	The Blend 2-5 yrs
WWW: www.balnaves.com.au	10am-5pm, weekends & public holidays	Cabernet Merlot 6-8 yrs
Owner: Doug, Annette,	**Principal Varieties:** Cabernet Franc,	Cabernet Sauvignon 8-10 yrs
Kirsty & Peter Balnaves	Cabernet Sauvignon, Chardonnay, Merlot,	Chardonnay

Blok Estate

The most welcoming boutique wine producer in Coonawarra is the Blok Estate of Di and John Blok. Originally Di ran Haselgrove wines from a delightful home on the main road in the middle of the region.

In 1998 along with her husband John they bought the business.

Their hospitality and their bright fresh approach to wine is both warm and enlightening. Their tasting centre has been revamped, the rustic redgum tasting bench and mantle pieces and the polished floor boards give a perfect atmosphere to taste and enjoy their wines. An open fire adds to the ambience in winter. The new Blok labels are also bold and fresh. The N.V. Sparkling Pinot Chardonnay with its creamy yeastiness and subtle floral character is a great starter. They also produce a Riesling, Chardonnay, Shiraz and a Cabernet Sauvignon from their own, and selected other Coonawarra vineyards. Their wines are all exceptionally good value.

If you can't get to Coonawarra to enjoy the pleasure of a visit to the Bloks, you can join their mailing list. They despatch orders of as little as 6 bottles at a time, and even with the inclusion of freight and insurance you'll be pleasantly surprised by the value for money prices.

Address: Riddoch Highway	**Est:** 1998	Shiraz 5-7 yrs
COONAWARRA 5063	**Public Hours:** 10am-4pm, daily	Chardonnay
Phone: (08) 8737 2734 **Fax:** (08) 8737 2994	**Principal Wines** **Potential**	Riesling
Owner: Dianne Blok	Cabernet Sauvignon 5-7 yrs	Pinot Noir Sparkling Chardonnay

Gartner Wines

Michael Gartner is a quiet achiever, at present he is constructing a huge state of the art winery, in a quarry site about a kilometre from the Riddoch Highway on the Sydney Road, as it heads towards Edenhope. In charge of the winery project and winemaking is high profile winemaker Peter Douglas, who has just returned home to Coonawarra, after stints making wine in USA and Sicily. Before this Peter had spent 18 years at Wynns Coonawarra, the last 15 years as winemaker and manager where he planned and supervised their enormous extensions of recent years.

Peter is well known to many, from the very competent job he did as compere of the Australia wide live video event, Wynnsday, held each year to release their wines, Peter also reintroduced the legendary Michael Hermitage.

Michael and Peter are building the 6,000 tonne capacity winery with unique barrel maturation cellars which will be underground in the old quarry site, using the natural cool and humid conditions, which will be enhanced by natural earth inlaid into the floor. These conditions are ideal for the barrel maturation of premium reds.

Michael Gartner came to Coonawarra some 40 years ago, when he bought 1,000 acres of grazing land. He could see the potential for horticulture and began developing a huge mechanised market garden, producing mainly potatoes and onions, today this business is thriving under his sons Greg and David, his other son Philip manages the vineyards. Currently the Gartners have 7,000 acres of land which includes 1,050 acres of vines. Daughter Dianne, Greg and David also have their own vineyards. The Gartners began planting in 1988.

They also developed a large vineyard of 260 acres in the Pemberton region in South West Western Australia for B.R.L. Hardy this has since been purchased by B.R.L Hardy.

Garner also have a highly respected viticulturist who works hand in hand with Philip Gartner, Lee Haselgrove is a cousin of the famous Haselgrove clan, that were such an important part of the Coonawarra renaissance in the 1950's. Lee has a masters degree in viticulture gained at Adelaide University, the last awarded under the guidance of legendary viticulturist Peter Dry.

Gartners first commercial vintage was 1998 prior to this all their grapes were sold to leading wineries. Gartner have the luxury of being able to "pick the eyes" out of their vast vineyards. The wines so far have been exceptional.

| **Address:** PO Box 1 COONAWARRA 5263
Phone: (08) 8736 5011 **Fax:** (08) 8736 5006
Email: gartwine@coonawarra.mtx.net.au | **Winemaker:** Peter Douglas
Est: 1999
Public Hours: 10am-4pm, Mon-Fri | **Principal Varieties:** Cabernet Sauvignon, Merlot, Semillon, Chardonnay, Riesling, Shiraz |

Chardonnay Lodge

Set among the vines, bordering the main road in the heart of Coonawarra, is the impressive Chardonnay Lodge. It was built in 1984 by the Yates, Coop and Giles families. In 1999 major additions were made including a whole new wing of luxury rooms equipped with spas.

Approaching the main arched doorway, visitors are impressed by the magnificent leadlight glass panelled entrance produced by Barry Mulligan of the district's St. Mary's Vineyard.

The classic Victorian Australian inspired complex spreads out comfortably, surrounded by the poplar trees traditionally used in

Coonawarra as wind breaks. The rooms are spacious with high timber ceilings; a family can happily spread out here.

Partners, James and Anne Yates have managed the establishment for more than ten years and managed it most efficiently. The food in the restaurant is creative and uses many local ingredients and the seminar and function facilities are large and

beautifully appointed. Chardonnay Lodge was a pioneer in terms of offering the wine traveller a truly wine integrated experience. The expanded function and seminar facilities are a welcome development for the region. Open every day of the year, Chardonnay Lodge provides an ideal stopover on your visit to Coonawarra.

Hollick Wines

Ian and Wendy Hollick purchased 55 acres of land at the southern end of Coonawarra in 1974. At the time, Ian was employed by one of the larger Coonawarra wine companies, and in their spare time the couple began developing a vineyard.

Cabernet sauvignon, riesling, merlot, chardonnay and pinot noir were planted during the following six years, until in 1983 the decision was made to build a winery. The winning of the Jimmy Watson Trophy in 1985, with only their second vintage, gave the Hollick's further incentive to expand and in 1987 they purchased the nearby 'Wilgha' property. With total land holdings of over 250 acres, about half under vine, the Hollick's have plenty of scope for expansion. The lane leading to Wilgha also provided them with a name used for their super premium cabernet sauvignon.

The Hollick's have a most beautiful home and tasting area for their wines, right in front of the winery in the form of a cottage that was the home of the poet, John Shaw Nielson, and built in the 1870's. The cottage has been lovingly restored and the Hollick's take delight in dispensing their warm hospitality along with their wines. Hollick also

produce a silky smooth sparkling merlot and a luscious botrytis "The Nectar" made in extremely small quantities from riesling, sauvignon blanc and semillon affected by the noble rot.

All the Hollick wines are top class and their charming cellar door is not to be missed on your Coonawarra pilgrimage.

Address: PO Box 9B COONAWARRA 5263	Public Hours: 9am-5pm, daily except	Shiraz Cabernet Sauvignon	4-7 yrs
Phone: (08) 8737 2318 Fax: (08) 8737 2952	Christmas day & Good Friday	Reserve Chardonnay	3-5 yrs
Email: admin@hollick.com Est: 1982	Principal Varieties: Cabernet Sauvignon,	Sauvignon Blanc Semillon	up to 3 yrs
WWW: www.hollick.com Vine Ha: 83	Chardonnay, Merlot, Pinot Noir, Riesling,	Cabernet Sauvignon Merlot	7-10 yrs
Owner: Ian & Wendy Hollick Cases: 30,000	Sauvignon Blanc, Semillon, Shiraz	Ravenswood Cabernet Sauvignon	10+ yrs
Winemaker: Ian Hollick/David Norman	Principal Wines Potential	Hollick Wilgha Shiraz	10+ yrs

Katnook

Katnook is a winery with a history that goes back to the early settlement of Coonawarra. John Riddoch arrived in Coonawarra in 1861. He named his first Coonawarra property 'Yallum Park', Yallum being derived from an aboriginal word meaning grassy.

Riddoch constructed a magnificent sandstone mansion surrounded by splendid gardens. His land holdings quickly grew to 250 square kilometres. Riddoch became known as the 'Squire of Penola' and his restored home, 'Yallum Park' can be visited when you are in Coonawarra.

Riddoch's first enterprises in Coonawarra were grazing and wool, to this end; he built a woolshed calling it 'Katnook'. Today, it is an historic monument and the winery for Katnook wines.

In 1890 Riddoch decided Katnook

could support closer settlement and horticulture, and he formed the Coonawarra Fruit Colony at Katnook and sold off 10-acre blocks at 10 pounds per acre, a considerable sum in those days.

Twenty-six colonists began planting fruit and vines on their blocks. The second vintage in 1896 was made at Katnook in the woolshed. During the 1960's, Melbourne businessman, Peter Yunghaans purchased the property, replanting vines and building a high-tech winery, within the historic old woolshed.

Katnook today is vastly expanded and a further 250 acres of vines were planted in 1996. Wayne Stebbens is the capable, affable winemaker. Katnook also produce the Riddoch label; these wines are great examples of the best of Coonawarra. Katnook produces a great sauvignon blanc, which has won many gold medals and trophies. John Riddoch would indeed be proud to see the way his old woolshed winery has been restored and the great wines it is producing.

Address: Riddoch Highway COONAWARRA 5263	**Est:** 1978 **Vine Ha:** 330 **Cases:** 50,000	"Odyssey" Cabernet Sauvignon	10-20 yrs
Phone: (08) 8737 2394 **Fax:** (08) 8737 2397	**Public Hours:** 9am-4.30pm, daily; 10am-	Katnook Estate Sauvignon Blanc	8-15 yrs
Email: katnook@wingara.com.au	4.30pm, Saturday; Noon-4.30pm, Sunday	Cabernet Sauvignon	10-18 yrs
WWW: www.katnookestate.com.au	**Principal Varieties:** Cab Sav, Shiraz, Merlot,	Katnook Estate Merlot	8-15 yrs
Owner: Wingara Wine Group	Chardonnay, Sauvignon Blanc, Riesling	Katnook Estate Chardonnay	10-18 yrs
Winemaker: Wayne Stehbens	**Principal Wines** **Potential**	Katnook Estate Chardonnay Brut	8-12 yrs

Majella

Brian and Anthony Lynn began planting vines back in 1969 when modern day Coonawarra was in its infancy. The two brothers are third generation farmers whose main specialisation was wool; their father named the property Majella after Saint Gerard Majella, a Spanish saint

and the patron paint of motherhood. All the produce of the large property goes out under the brand of Majella.

Up until 1991 all the crop from their 85 acres of vines was sold to winemakers in the region. In 1991, they decided to produce a Majella red wine at Brand's Wines made by Bruce Gregory. The

vineyard has been expanded to over 100 acres, all red grape varieties, about one half cabernet sauvignon and one half shiraz.

The Lynn's are a gregarious family and you can now share their hospitality at their new cellar door in the state of the art winery finished for the 1997 vintage. Winemaker Bruce Gregory has been quietly doing a great job. Many of the "Prof" Brian Lynn's mates have dubbed him as the "Trophyless Prof" until a year or two ago he hadn't landed even a gold medal - since however Majella has won more medals and trophies than any other winery of its size in Australia.

If you cannot get to Coonawarra go out and get yourself a succulent steak and wash it down with a Majella red with its striking label and great flavour.

Address: Lynn Road COONAWARRA 5263	**Est:** 1967 **Vine Ha:** 60 **Cases:** 10,000	**Principal Wines**	**Potential**
Phone: (08) 8736 3055 **Fax:** (08) 8736 3057	**Public Hours:** 10am-4.30pm, daily except	Riesling (Steluni cap)	10+ yrs
Email: prof@penola.mtx.net.au	Christmas Day and Good Friday	Shiraz	7-10 yrs
Owner: The Lynn Family	**Principal Varieties:** Shiraz, Cabernet	Cabernet	10-15 yrs
Winemaker: Bruce Gregory	Sauvignon, Riesling	Sparkling Shiraz	10-12 yrs

Mildara Jamiesons Run

Jamieson's Run has taken the wine world by storm. Mildara launched the name along with an exciting new red wine in 1987, a blend of cabernet sauvignon, shiraz, merlot and cabernet franc and in some years a little malbec is added for balance. Their aim is to produce a rich, smooth style that is consistent and recognisable year after year.

The choice of the name Jamieson's Run is particularly apt as it was the name of the property at Mildura where the Chaffey Brothers built their original winery, 'Chateau Mildura', back in 1888. This became the forerunner of Mildara Wines. The connection is even more appropriate because of Mildara's Coonawarra investment in the early 1950's through long time technical and managing director, Ron Haselgrove who, along with David Wynn, rediscovered Coonawarra and really put it on the wine map.

The proof of the pudding came in 1989 when the 1988 Jamieson's won the Jimmy Watson memorial Trophy, the grand prix of Australian wines.

After this victory, Jamieson's Run became a truly recognised Australian wine.

Jamieson's Run chardonnay is no slouch either, a very drinkable wine

showing good barrel fermented complexity. In fact, any wine bearing the Mildara Coonawarra label is a guarantee of real enjoyment.

Redman

One hundred years a go in 1901 fourteen year old Bill Redman arrived in Coonawarra and began working for Riddoch's winery, thus beginning a long and distinguished career in the wine industry. In 1908, Bill gained his independence by forming a partnership with his family in the acquisition of established vineyards, later known as Rouge Homme. After 1920, when winemaking all but ceased in Coonawarra, he remained the area's only producing winemaker for many decades.

In 1937 Bill was joined in the business by his son Owen, and this alliance lasted until the sale of Rouge Homme to Lindemans in 1965. Owen then purchased a 40-acre vineyard as well as extra land to build his own winery. Today, Redman's winery is very well set up with the tasting area having

picturesque views of the vineyard and the winery.

Bill Redman died in 1979 at 92 years of age, having presided over 65 vintages, his contribution to the wine industry was enormous and he can

be truly called one of the fathers of Coonawarra. His grandsons Bruce and Malcolm Redman are continuing this heritage, having not only taken over the management of their father's winery, but also expanding its size and reputation.

Redman's wines had traditionally produced only two wines, a shiraz and a cabernet sauvignon (they're real red men); recently they have introduced a third wine, a cabernet merlot.

In recent years, they have beefed up the colour and body in their wines and used more small oak. The Redman's vineyards, some of which date back to before the turn of the century, produce superb fruit. The wines I have seen in recent years are certainly doing these fine vineyards justice.

Address: Riddoch Highway COONAWARRA 5263 Phone: (08) 8736 3331 Fax: (08) 8736 3013 Owner: EM, BM, DM & MM Redman	Winemaker: Bruce and Malcolm Redman Est: 1966 Vine Ha: 34 Public Hours: 9am-5pm weekdays; 10am-4pm, weekends & holidays Principal Varieties: Merlot, Cabernet	Sauvignon, Shiraz	
		Principal Wines	Potential
		Redman Shiraz	4-6 yrs
		Redman Cabernet Sauvignon	6-8 yrs
		Redman Cabernet Sauvignon Merlot	5-7 yrs

Leconfield

The Leconfield vineyard was planted in 1974 and the winery built in 1975 by Sydney Hamilton at the age of 76. Sydney was a 4th generation descendant of Mr Richard Hamilton, South Australia's first vigneron ca.1837.

After retiring from Hamilton Ewell in the mid 50s, Syd searched the Australian continent for the site to make the classic Australian Red table wine. He decided that Coonawarra had the potential to achieve this life long ambition.

In 1974 Syd planted the vineyard of 30 acres mainly to Cabernet Sauvignon and the following year used his considerable engineering skills to build the Leconfield winery. Syd created a legend with his early vintages, the 1978 and 1980 Leconfield Cabernets.

In 1981 Leconfield was acquired by Syd's nephew, Dr Richard Hamilton, a noted Adelaide Plastic Surgeon. Richard Hamilton is the proprietor and founder of Hamilton Wines (aka Richard Hamilton Wines) with historic vineyards and winery at McLaren Vale, established in 1972.

The Leconfield Cabernets have all been superb wines. The inclusion of Cabernet Sauvignon, with small proportions of Merlot, Petit Verdot and Cabernet Franc into the Cabernet blend by passionate winemaker Philippa Treadwell, has made Leconfield Cabernet arguably one of Australia's great red wines, thus perpetuating the legend of Sydney Hamilton and the pioneering Hamilton winemaking family.

Leconfield, an imposing Romanesque style building constructed of limestone, is situated right on the main road. It strikes me as some other Coonawarra vineyards do, with its similarity to a Bordeaux chateau. Certainly its Cabernets are in the mould of the very best Bordeaux.

The Leconfield Cabernet, with power and elegance, is Classic Coonawarra.

Address: Riddoch Highway COONAWARRA 5263	Winemaker: Philippa Treadwell	Principal Wines	Potential
	Est: 1974 Vine Ha: 25 Cases: 15,000	Chardonnay	5+ yrs
Phone: (08) 8737 2326 Fax: (08) 8737 2285	Public Hours: 10am-5pm, weekdays;	Cabernet Franc	5+ yrs
Email: leconfield@coonawarra.mtx.net.au	11am-5pm, weekends and public holidays	Merlot	10+ yrs
WWW: www.leconfield.com.au	Principal Varieties: Cabernet Sauvignon,	Shiraz	5-10 yrs
Owner: Dr Richard Hamilton,	Shiraz, Merlot, Cabernet Franc, Petit Verdot,	Cabernet	10+ yrs
The Hamilton Wine Group	Chardonnay, Riesling	Petit Verdot	5+ yrs

Parker Coonawarra

John Parker was the founding chairman of Hungerford Hill Wines in the late 1960's as well as its Chief Executive. Until its corporate take over and loss it was in this role that he first had dealings in Coonawarra, establishing vineyards that were capably run by Doug Balnaves.

John always had a strong desire to produce a truly great red wine, without normal commercial restraints. He decided to act on this desire and purchased in 1985 a 50-acre property on the main road in the heart of the famous Terra Rossa Strip.

Parker Coonawarra Estate First Growth was a wine before its time and like a great Bordeaux it is made for the long term. The grapes are all grown in Parker's own vineyard with great attention paid to limiting the crop and berry size, getting real intensity of flavour into the wines.

The varieties grown are Cabernet Sauvignon, Merlot and Cabernet Franc. The blend of varieties used in First Growth each vintage depends on the vintage conditions.

The result is always a substantial wine which receives first class French oak maturation in specially selected Barriques. It's in the absolute top league of Australia's super premium Reds. Parker also has a Cabernet Sauvignon made from the domaine, it is also a great wine.

John chose to make only red wine and only two reds, to ensure in the true Bordeaux tradition, that they were as perfect as man could make. They now produce a 500 case run of straight varietal Merlot each year as well.

In 2001 Parker have finished their fine Mount Gambier Limestone headquarters on the vineyard which will add an extra dimension to their wines and the noble Coonawarra region.

Address: Riddoch Highway (PO Box 305) COONAWARRA 5263	Owner: John Parker	Cabernet Franc, Merlot	
	Est: 1985 Vine Ha: 21 approx.	Principal Wines	Potential
Phone: (08) 8737 3525 Fax: (08) 8737 3527	Cases: 5000	Terra Rossa "First Growth"	20 yrs
Email: pk@parkercoonawraestate.com.au	Public Hours: 10am - 4pm	Terra Rossa "Merlot"	15 yrs
WWW: www.parkercoonawraestate.com.au	Principal Varieties: Cabernet Sauvignon,	Terra Rossa "Cabernet Sauvignon"	10 yrs

Penley Estate

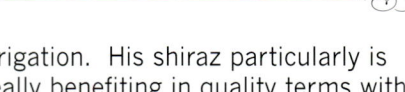

irrigation. His shiraz particularly is really benefiting in quality terms with half!! the crop levels it's an expensive business.

Kym has released a "Hyland-Shiraz" a super premium to commemorate his Penfold-Hyland family connection. Penley also produce a finely tuned Pinot Noir and an opulent Merlot, a Shiraz Cabernet as well as a traditional Cabernet Sauvignon with two styles "Pheonix" and "Flagship", a stylish chardonnay. Assistant winemaker Matthew Copping is reveling in the challenge also.

Over 12 vintages Penley Estate have won 20 trophies, 80 gold, 108 silver and 258 bronze medals in Australian and International wine shows. Extraordinary!!

Penley's have 225 acres of vines comprising cabernet sauvignon, pinot noir, shiraz, chardonnay, merlot, cabernet franc and pinot meunier.

Penley Estate utilise the very best of the crop, the rest is sold to other premium winemakers.

Kym's winemaking philosophy is "Every wine must be the best I can produce". Creating a perfect balance between fruit, tannin and acid to give balance and length of flavour, great fruit, good wood, time, attention to detail and a dose of luck are Kym's well-managed ingredients. Kym's wines must reflect what he feels, in his own words - "My objective has always been to produce the best wines I can, and I will continue to do in years to come. If something is worth doing, it's worth ding well".

Penley's packaging is a revolution; Kym has spared no effort of expense to package the wines he is so proud of in the most beautiful way. Kym also produces a 100% Coonawarra Methode Champenoise, 90% pinot noir and 7% chardonnay and 3% pinot meunier.

Kym oversees every part of the Penley operation and has added even more lustre to the reputation of Coonawarra as a world class wine region. In 2001, at last a cellar door is opening at the new winery an event to be celebrated by all who visit Coonawarra.

Kym Tolley is steeped in wine history. His father is Reg Tolley, former chairman of the Tolley Wine Company, his mother was a Penfold Hyland, niece of Jeffrey Penfold Hyland, and in fact his great great great grandfather was Penfold's founder, Dr Christopher Rawson Penfold.

Kym, a Roseworthy graduate winemaker, worked for 17 years at Penfolds before striking out alone and forming Penley Wines in 1988.

Early in 1999 Kym completed the new winery on his Coonawarra property. Purpose built from his long experience it is on one hand a dream for him but on the other a nightmare - the winery is superb but Kym's fastidious approach, gives some pretty tough logistical headaches - like 32 separate batches of 2000 Cabernet Sauvignon from 9 different vineyard lots. Individual barrel fermentation with the wine going in and out of barrels 4 0 5 times during the winemaking process creates a huge workload but that what true winemaking is all about. Kym has also reduced the yields on his maturing vineyard through pruning techniques and minimal

Address: McLeans Road COONAWARRA 5263
Phone: (08) 231 2400 **Fax:** (08) 231 0589

Owner/Winemaker: Kym Tolley
Est: 1988 **Vine Ha:** 68 **Cases:** 15,000

Principal Varieties: Cab Sav, Pinot Noir, Shiraz, Chardonnay, Merlot, Cab Franc, Pinot Meunier

Punters Corner

In August 2000 Punters Corner realised their venture was no gamble! They won the coveted Jimmy Watson Memorial Trophy at the Royal Melbourne Wine Show, their 1999 vintage repeating the feat their neighbours Hollick Wines achieved in 1985.

Winning the 2000 Jimmy Watson Trophy has brought well deserved recognition to this consistently high quality Coonawarra producer with its cellar door located off the main road and the lane to the local racetrack.

Grapes are accessed from their four central Coonawarra vineyards which now total 150 hectares. The finest 150 tonnes are selected each vintage for their own wines with the balance sold to other leading local producers.

David Muir, co-owner of the business, is managing director. The cellar door is extremely well managed by Sue Hood as is the exciting modern accommodation centre located on a picturesque corner of the V & A Lane vineyard. For those wine lovers seeking accommodation in Coonawarra, a stay at the Punters Corner Retreat is a must. The modern contemporary design of the retreat features timber floors with floor to ceiling glass giving panoramic views over the vineyard from the four bedrooms and a mezzanine dining area. The entire area is air-conditioned and has a slow combustion wood heater for winter. The kitchen is fully equipped with a microwave and dishwasher, there is also a laundry. A television, video and sound system ensures entertainment is at your fingertips. The retreat has four mountain bikes to get about on. Full breakfast is provided. A selection of Punters Corner wines is available and makes the retreat a perfect getaway.

As well as winning the 2000 Jimmy Watson Trophy with the 1999 Spartacus Reserve Shiraz, the 1999 Cabernet also featured well with a gold medal at the Melbourne Wine Show. Their cabernets have also twice been selected as representing Coonawarra's finest cabernets in the 1997 and 1998 Coonawarra Cabernet Celebrations. Their chardonnay and cabernet merlot are also fine quality award winning wines.

Punters Corner now exports some third of their wines. The decision taken by this family owned business to significantly expand their vineyards in the area is now paying dividends. Their access to fruit from four separate vineyards all located within central Coonawarra should ensure a bright future for its range of fine quality wines.

Address: PO Box 28 COONAWARRA 5263	**Public Hours:** 10am-5pm, daily except	Coonawarra Cabernet Sauvignon 5-8 yrs
Phone: (08) 8737 2007 **Fax:** (08) 8737 3138	Christmas Day and Good Friday	Coonawarra Shiraz 3-5 yrs
Email: punters@coonawarra.mtx.net.au	**Principal Varieties:** Cabernet Sauvignon,	Coonawarra Cabernet / Merlot 2-5 yrs
Owner: Muir & Hance families	Merlot, Shiraz, Chardonnay	Coonawarra Chardonnay 2-3 yrs
Vine Ha: 150 **Cases:** 10,000	**Principal Wines** **Potential**	"Spartacus" Reserve Shiraz 3-10 yrs

Rosemount

In line with the Oatley family philosophy of growing their own grapes in each region, Rosemount established their Kirri Billi vineyard at Coonawarra in 1980. Rosemount specialise in what they believe Coonawarra does best - Cabernet Sauvignon. After crushing, the wine is made at the main winery in the Upper Hunter Valley. Hand pruning and hand picking of Rosemount's premium fruit, a rarity in Coonawarra, shows Rosemount's determination to make a no expense spared classic Coonawarra Cabernet.

The concern that the Oatley family takes in the selection, planting and management of this vineyard is at the heart of this remarkable company's rapid success.

Rosemount, have for their size been the most successful exporter and ambassador for Australian wines overseas, particularly in North America. With Coonawarra's growing reputation far from our shores, Rosemount have put their Coonawarra Show Reserve Cabernet Sauvignon, well and truly on the world wine map.

Rymill

Peter Riddoch Rymill has much to be proud of, Peters great grandfather was the legendary John Riddoch, who set up the Penola Fruit Colony on the Terra Rossa soils of Coonawarra.

John Riddoch a wine and general merchant in Geelong arrived at Penola in 1861, the home and gardens he developed at "Yallum" is now a national treasure. He also started the timber industry in the South East. His properties covered over 50,000 acres. He also planted vines and built the regions first winery in 1897, this property is now the famous Wynn's Coonawarra Cellars.

Riddoch's daughter Mary married Robert Rymill, widowed with two infant sons she ran the family's 28,000 acre property. Mary's son John (Peter's father) became a famous explorer. His 1934-1937 expedition to the Antarctic, in the ship "Penola", proved that the Antarctic was in fact a continent not an archipelago.

Peter Rymill is an extremely successful equestrian, winning the Australian show jumping championship. He studied science at Adelaide university and developed a distinctive composite breed of cattle through genetic technology. He also

planted an experimental vineyard in 1968 and in 1977 the large Riddoch Run vineyards, Peter's wife Judy looked after the farm, whilst Peter completed a degree in wine science and a diploma in wine marketing. In 1990 they built a winery, this is a show piece of the region. The design influenced by the gabled structure of his great grandfathers winery, its use of glass makes it absolutely spectacular, the equine statues at the entrance pay homage to his family's passion.

The Rymill wines are equally spectacular, Peters approach is a no compromise mission to make the best possible wine. He also produces a marvellous methode champenoise. Winemaker John Innes capably carries through Peters philosophies. You must visit Rymill when in Coonawarra.

Address: The Riddoch Run Vineyards, Riddoch Highway COONAWARRA 5263
Phone: (08) 8736 5001 **Fax:** (08) 8736 5040
Email: winery@rymill.com.au
WWW: www.rymill.com.au
Owner: Peter & Judy Rymill

Winemaker: John Innes
Est: 1990 **Vine Ha:** 165 **Cases:** 50,000
Public Hours: 10am-5pm daily, closed Christmas Day
Principal Varieties: Cabernet Sauvignon, Chardonnay, Merlot, Sauvignon Blanc, Shiraz

Principal Wines	Potential
Rymill Cabernet Sauvignon	8-10 yrs
Rymill Shiraz	5-8 yrs
Rymill Mc2	2-5 yrs
Rymill Sauvignon Blanc	
Rymill June Traminer	

Wynns Coonawarra

The Wynns Coonawarra Estate story began in 1890 when John Riddoch, who had vast landholdings in the area, developed the Coonawarra Fruit Colony, selling off 10-acre blocks of this land to hopeful farmers.

Riddoch himself planted vines and built a large stone winery, which was completed in 1895. The façade of this building has adorned Wynns Coonawarra Estate wine labels since the 1950's.

Riddoch's venture failed to prosper and Coonawarra languished for the first half of the 1900's. Were it not for David Wynn, who purchased the estate in 1951, the winery would almost certainly have become a woolshed and the vineyards a sheep run.

One of the two flagship reds of today's Wynns Coonawarra Estate is John Riddoch Cabernet Sauvignon, a majestic wine that wins trophies and gold medals in Australian and International Wine shows with monotonous regularity.

The first John Riddoch was the 1982, a wine of such incredible richness, mouthfeel and velvet-like texture that

it almost defied description.

I first encountered it in a lineup of the celebrated 1982 Bordeaux first and second growth wines. All were masked and to my mind it was at the top of the class. If anything, the John Riddochs of the 1990's are even better.

If John Riddoch Cabernet commemorates the founder of Coonawarra, the second Wynns Coonawarra Estate flagship red links us with the family that re-established Coonawarra.

Michael Hermitage, a best-of-vintage Shiraz, takes its name from the legendary wine of 1955, created by David Wynn as a memorial to his young son who had died suddenly the previous year.

This wine was reintroduced with the 1990 vintage and has quickly become one of Australia's most talked-about wines.

Wynns most widely-available reds are the black label Coonawarra Estate Cabernet Sauvignon, the white label Coonawarra Estate Shiraz and the Coonawarra Estate Cabernet-Shiraz-Merlot blend.

All are fine-textured, full-flavoured wines often displaying a minty, herbaceous character over the fruit flavours.

The estate also produces whites of great quality.

Wynns Coonawarra Estate Riesling is exceptional value and always exhibits very good floral and fruity aromas and flavours. The Wynns Coonawarra Estate Chardonnay shows excellent peach/apricot flavours, beautifully integrated with subtle oak.

Each year on a Wednesday a special tasting release is held at the winery and beamed by satellite to functions in major cities where tastings and dinners are held. Wynnsday is a world famous wine event.

Both the underground cellars at Wynns, and the newer, air-conditioned, ground level facilities, are brimming with great wines in a forest of the world's finest oak; it's one of the great liquid assets of Australia.

John Riddoch's vision has finally been fulfilled.

Rouge Homme

Right in the heart of Coonawarra are the Rouge Homme vineyards. Their history dates back to 1908 when the Redman family purchased part of John Riddoch's Penola Fruit Colony. For half a century, Rouge Homme supplied wine to other companies and merchants, but it was not until the release of the 1954 Cabernet Sauvignon, wearing the first Rouge Homme label, that the brand itself began to attract some fame. The translation of the name 'Rouge Homme' · French for 'red man'. The 'Richardson's' label was introduced with the 1992 vintage and named in honour of Henry Richardson. In 1892 Richardson purchased land offered for sale by Riddoch's Coonawarra Fruit Colony and established a vineyard and winery on the property.

In 1965 the Redman family sold the vineyards and winery which became rouge Homme. Occupying about 150 acres, the vineyards are planted the classic varieties including shiraz, cabernet sauvignon, cabernet franc, merlot and pinot noir, with a small amount of chardonnay.

Because of the cold winters and springs, the vines at Rouge Homme are trained over especially high trellises, with overhead mist sprinklers to protect them from frosts during spring. Five Rouge Homme wines are produced today in contemporary labels reflecting the earthy colours of the Coonawarra.

The original claret which forged Rouge Homme's early reputation is still made but is today varietally labelled as a shiraz cabernet. This was followed by the straight cabernet sauvignon, a wine of power and presence. Rouge Homme produces a pinot noir, which consistently exhibits good colour and varietal character. 'Richardsons Red Block' is a blend of the classic Bordeaux varieties of cabernet sauvignon, malbec, merlot and cabernet franc. The chardonnay also shines in the white arena.

With a considerable reputation as classic Coonawarra, Rouge Homme wines are frequent gold medal winners · particularly the reds. In 1994, Rouge Homme received what is regarded by many to be the wine industry's greatest accolade · the Jimmy Watson Memorial Trophy.

S Kidman

Sid and Susie Kidman have one of the most charming cellar doors in Coonawarra, on the northern fringes of the region. It is in former stables on their property, built in the 1860's.

Their lovely sprawling old colonial Australian home behind the winery dates back even further, to the 1840's. The 'paradise lost' garden behind the homestead would do 'Home and Garden' proud and is lovingly tended by Susie.

The Kidman's have been landowners and farmers in the region since pioneering days. Even during his school years, Sid used to love jumping on the tractor to do some work on the property and, in fact, he still occasionally drives the old 1960 tractor he learnt on. Sid helped his father establish a large vineyard across the road from 'The Ridge' in partnership with Melbourne wine merchant, Dan Murphy, in the 1970's.

In 1984 Susie and Sid changed their vineyard from grape production to wine production. Their riesling is excellent, often showing fruit flavours in the mandarin fruit spectrum and quite full-bodied. Sid has planted more shiraz and has been very successful with the variety, with complex and characterful wines that live on for many years. Why not drop into S. Kidman Wines and share the history and warm hospitality of the Kidman's.

Address: PO BOX 25 COONAWARRA 5263	Winemaker: John Innes	Vine Ha: 15	Principal Wines	Potential
Phone: (08) 8736 5071 Fax: (08) 8736 5070	Public Hours: 9am-5pm, daily Cases: 8,000		S. Kidman Cabernet Sauvignon	7 yrs
Email: kidman@coonawarra.mtx.net.au	Principal Varieties: Cabernet Sauvignon,		S. Kidman Shiraz 5 yrs S. Kidman Riesling 4 yrs	
Owner: Suzie and Sid Kidman Est: 1984	Shiraz, Sauvignon Blanc, Riesling		S. Kidman Sauvignon Blanc	4 yrs

Wetherall Wines

Wetherall Wines became a part of the Coonawarra story over 30 years ago when the family began planting their vineyard.

Michael Wetherall graduated from the respected Roseworthy agricultural College and has had a wealth of experience since. He has not only run his families vineyards, making their no expense spared wines but also assisted top level Winemaker Kym Tolley at Penley Estate .

Wetherall did not enter the wine making arena until their wines were very mature. The first Wetherall wine was a Cabernet Sauvignon of the 1990 vintage, they struck instant success with a gold medal in the following years Melbourne wine show.

Wetherall have built a top class cellar door and production facility overlooking a steep sided lake overhung by statuesque gums. The soil profile of rich red Terra Rossa over limestone is very evident, as you

look out from the terrace of "The Hermitage" Restaurant which forms part of the complex.

Wetherall use top class small imported oak barrels to ferment and age their wines, which come from the choicest parts of their own

vineyards, they produce a Cabernet Sauvignon, Shiraz, Merlot and Chardonnay. The Wetherall wines are not that easy to find outside the region. I suggest you join their mailing list.

Address: PO Box 20 COONAWARRA 5263 Phone: (08) 8737 2104 Fax: (08) 8737 2105 Email: wetherall@coonawarra.mtx.net.au	Owner: Wetherall Family Est: 1970 Ha: 115 Winemaker: Michael Wetherall Cases: 2000 Principal Varieties: Cab Sav, Shiraz	Principal Wines	Potential
		Wetherall Cabernet Sauvignon	5-10 yrs
		Wetherall Shiraz	4-8 yrs

Zema Estate

Zema Estate has come a long way since the family made their first wine in an open hayshed on their property, in the heart of Coonawarra's Terra Rossa Strip in 1982. The winemaking equipment included a milk tanker and a couple of cheese vats. From such humble beginnings the Zemas have flourished into a highly respected top class producer. Their red wines are typically robust, rich and flavoursome.

In 1959 Demetrio Zema arrived in Coonwarra to marry his fiancée Francesca, he established himself in Penola as the local painter but he

had always harboured a dream to have his own vineyards and produce his own wines, he had certainly come to the right spot!!

Like many of his countrymen he made his own wine at home, it fired his dream even further. In 1982 the dream got closer to reality when Demetrio now with this two sons Matt and Nick, bought a parcel of Terra Rossa right in the heart of Coonawarra.

The family are vigorously traditional in their approach to winemaking. Their vines are not irrigated and are hand pruned, giving them the intense

fruit they want. The original 20 acre block has now expanded to 120 acres of vines.

Matt and Nick have set up a state of the art modern winery, they oversee all the traditional processes and part ferment and age their reds - they only make red - in top class, small oak barrels.

The Zema's Shiraz has become a true icon wine for the region, they also produce a regal Cabernet Sauvignon and a Bordeaux Blend called "Cluny" from Cabernet Sauvignon, Merlot, Malbec and Cabernet Franc. The top Zema wine is aptly named "Family Selection" Cabernet Sauvignon, full rich and perfectly balanced, this is a wine with the firm structure to put down in the cellar and salute the Zema's skill and commitment in many years to come.

Address: Riddoch Highway COONAWARRA 5263 Phone: (09) 8736 3219 Fax: (08) 8736 3280 Email: zemaestate@zema.com.au WWW: www.zema.com.au Est: 1982 Owner: The Zema Family Vine Ha: 48.5	Winemaker: Tom Simons Cases: 12,000 Public Hours: 9am-5pm daily, closed Good Friday & Christmas Day Principal Varieties: Merlot, Cab Sav, Shiraz Principal Wines Potential	Zema Estate "Family Selection" Cabernet Sauvignon	20 yrs
		Zema Estate Cabernet Sauvignon	10-15 yrs
		Zema Estate Shiraz	10-15 yrs
		Zema Estate Cluny (blend)	5 yrs

Padthaway

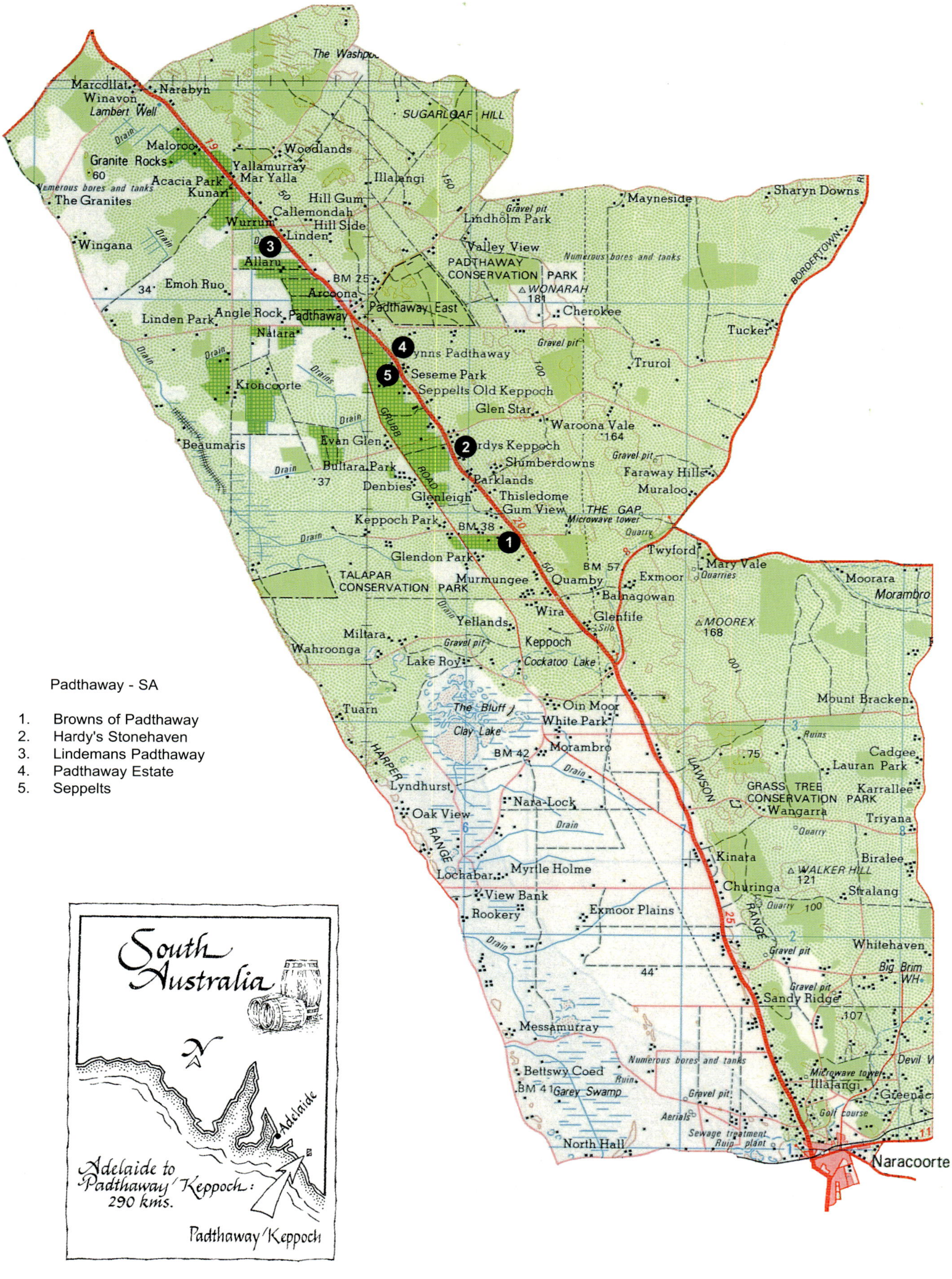

Padthaway - SA

1. Browns of Padthaway
2. Hardy's Stonehaven
3. Lindemans Padthaway
4. Padthaway Estate
5. Seppelts

South Australia

Adelaide

Adelaide to
Padthaway/Keppoch:
290 kms.

Padthaway/Keppoch

Padthaway

When land in Coonawarra became increasingly scarce and expensive, many of Australia's major wine companies were forced to search for an alternative area to develop for the production of premium wine.

The Padthaway region, 80 kilometres north of Coonawarra, proved to be the most suitable. Made up of a similar terra rossa soil over limestone, the strip of rich, red soil is 16 kms long and 1 to 1.5 kms wide. The area has a slightly warmer climate, providing a stability that produces less variation in vintages.

Rainfall is lower, but like Coonawarra, there is a good supply of underground water, and, once established, the vines grow very well. Before Seppelts established the first vineyards in 1963, the region was divided into seven large grazing-oriented properties, the most famous being Padthaway House, home of the Lawson family, descendants of Henry Lawson.

Padthaway House was refurbished in the late 1920's; it is one of the most beautiful old colonial homes where

you can stay in Australia.

Padthaway has been developed largely by the bigger companies namely Seppelts, Hardy's, Lindemans, Wynns and Orlando, but with others such as the Brown family, who began winemaking in 1994, after many years as a major grape grower in the region.

Although originally envisaged as a red wine area, this region has proved to be extremely versatile, producing white wines of many styles. Rhine riesling, chardonnay and sauvignon

blanc along with pinot noir have been successful grape varieties, producing excellent results. Padthaway now has a comparable area under vine to Coonawarra.

The intense varietal character found in the high-grade fruit of the area; Padthaway is becoming of increasing importance to the industry. The Padthaway Estate Winery was the only actual producer and cellar door in the region but has recently been joined by the superb state of the art Hardys Stonehaven Winery and Hospitality Complex.

Padthaway Estate

Padthaway was settled in 1847 by Robert and Eliza Lawson, when they took up pastoral leases of 53,760 acres. Their main income coming from wood and breeding Arab horses, they built an eight room stone cottage in which they raised their 6 children. This is now home to the resident chef.

Robert died in 1876, by this time his holdings had risen to 81,760 acres.

Eliza managed the property and supervised the building of the magnificent 22 room homestead which is today one of Australia's finest bed and breakfast retreats. She also built a massive 13 stand shearing shed in which 1,100 sheep a day could be shorn. Today this has been converted to a winery and includes Australia finest true champagne press imported from

France.

In 1980 the property was purchased by Dale Baker and Ian Gray. They established a large vineyard, planting Pinot Noir Chardonnay, Pinot Meunier particularly to make a top class Australian Methode Champenoise Sparkling they went on to name "Eliza", after the founders wife. It has been extremely successful, they also planted Shiraz and Cabernet Sauvignon.

The grapes from the "Eliza" sparkling take a team of 20 pickers 10 days to gather, the vines are also hand pruned.

Plans are afoot to transform the "Doctors House" into a showcase for the homestead and property. This along with a new location for the Cellar door will also help truly reflect Padthaway Estate as the premium, boutique wine producer of the region.

Address: Riddoch Highway PADTHAWAY 5271	Winemaker: Ulrich Grey-Smith Cases: 5,000	Eliza Sparkling Cuvee	5 yrs
Phone: (08) 8765 5235 Fax: (08) 8765 5294	Public Hours: 10am-4pm daily	Padthaway Estate Unwooded Chard	1yr
Email: pad_estate@bigpond.com Est: 1980	Principal Varieties: Cabernet, Chard, Pinot Noir	Padthaway Estate Chardonnay	3 yrs
Owner: Dale Baker & Ian Gray Vine Ha: 50	Principal Wines Potential	Padthaway Estate Cabernet Sav	10 yrs

Browns of Padthaway

In 1959, fourth generation Yorke Peninsula farmer, Don Brown purchased a 720 acre property at Padthaway.

The Browns' were looking for land, which could be irrigated for their Border Leicester and Southdown stud sheep. Padthaway is actually derived from an Aboriginal word for 'Good Water'. Don and his wife Glenda named the property 'Glendon

Park' and gradually they have expanded it to more than 6,120 acres. The original 10 acres of irrigation has been expanded drastically.

During the 1960's Don developed his 'small seed production' business before planting vines in 1970. Today the vineyard has expanded to 500 acres. Don also began a contracting company specialising in grape

harvesting and transportation.

For many years his eagerly sought after grapes were purchased by large companies such as Orlando, then in 1993, the Browns' launched their own label beginning with a riesling and an unwooded chardonnay. They have more than enough vines to supply their needs.

Their three children all live and work on the property. Andrew and David both have degrees in farm management from Roseworthy, whilst daughter Sue has the Roseworthy wine marketing diploma. Daughter-in-law Lisa, has a business degree and son-in-law Michael, an agricultural degree. All in all it's a pretty formidable team at Browns' and the wines so far have reflected this. The wines are all great value for money. Expect great things from Browns' of Padthaway, I'm sure they won't let you down.

Address: PMB 196 NARACOORTE 5271	Shiraz, Malbec, Cabernet Sauvignon,	"T-trellis" Shiraz	3+ yrs
Phone: (08) 8765 6063 **Fax**: (08) 8765 6083	Sauvignon Blanc, Verdelho	"Redwood" Shiraz/Malbec	2+ yrs
Est: 1970 **Vine Ha**: 150 **Cases**: 30,000	**Principal Wines** **Potential**	"Redwood" Verdelho Sauvignon Blanc	
Principal Varieties: Chardonnay, Riesling,	"Myra" Family Reserve Cab Sav 5+ yrs	Sparkling Shiraz	2+ yrs

Hardys Stonehaven

Stonehaven is situated just 6 kilometres south of the township of Padthaway, ideally positioned to capitalise on the quality fruit being sourced from the SA's Limestone Coast vineyards in Padthaway, Wrattonbully & Coonawarra.

Stonehaven gets its name from one of its vineyards, which originally

formed part of the pioneering Hynam Station, established by one of the region's first settlers Adam Smith in 1846.

Dedicated to the release of fine contemporary Australian wines that reflect the unique 'terroir' in which they are propagated, Stonehaven sources the finest fruit from the

Limestone Coast regions and processes it with the latest oenological expertise and equipment.

Opened in March 1998, Stonehaven is a 12,000 tonne winery that features the latest in high technology developments for producing premium cool climate wines. It has been designed to provide the winemaker with maximum control and flexibility over the winemaking process. While being at the forefront of winemaking technology, Stonehaven also acknowledges its reliance on the local 'terroir' and on traditional winemaking practices, combining all three to produce award winning wines.

Since opening, the winery and its wines have won numerous awards, including a number of gold medals at major national and international wine shows and an engineering excellence award. In 2000 Stonehaven was honoured to be named 'International Winery of the Year' at the prestigious San Francisco International Wine Competition.

Wrattonbully

Aptly the name Wrattonbully is an interpretation of an Aboriginal expression meaning "a place of rising smoke signals" this is exactly what this, the most recent wine region in South Australia is doing in the world of wine. There are huge investments by the big players BRL Hardy with their Stonehaven Venture vineyard, Beringer Blass, Yalumba and Cranswick's Haselgrove Wines. There are also some private ventures such as Heathfield Ridge, which has the only winery in the region so far, Glenhurst wines, Picarus and others.

Wrattonbully is located to the north and east of Coonawarra and some further distance South and east of Padthaway it is the most central wine region of the Viticultural zone "The Limestone Coast". In fact, the famous soil structure of Terra Rossa over limestone so revered in Coonawarra is prevelant in Wrattonbully caused by the breakdown of the limestone base of a series of ancient coastlines, then overlain with clay and organic matter, iron rich, this has oxidised into a deep russet red colour.

The vineyards are planted on the undulating hills between 75-105 metres altitude in what is in fact the low Naracoorte Ranges. The cool climate and gentle ripening period is ideal particularly for red wine, large areas of Shiraz and Cabernet Sauvignon have been planted, however at least 17 classic varieties are planted, including some of the more exotic Italian, French and Austrian varieties. The latest world leading Viticultural practices are being used, over 6,000 acres of vines have so far been planted in the region.

The world famous Naracoorte caves can be visited, these are recognised as one of the five richest fossil deposits in the world, a top class indoor/outdoor restaurant serves local food and wines and "The Sheeps Back" an award winning museum is worth visiting. Nearby Bool Lagoon is an internationally recognised wetlands its 7090 acres providing home to more than 150 bird species.

Wrattonbully's wines so far have been extremely impressive it will soon become a large powerful world recognised premium wines region.

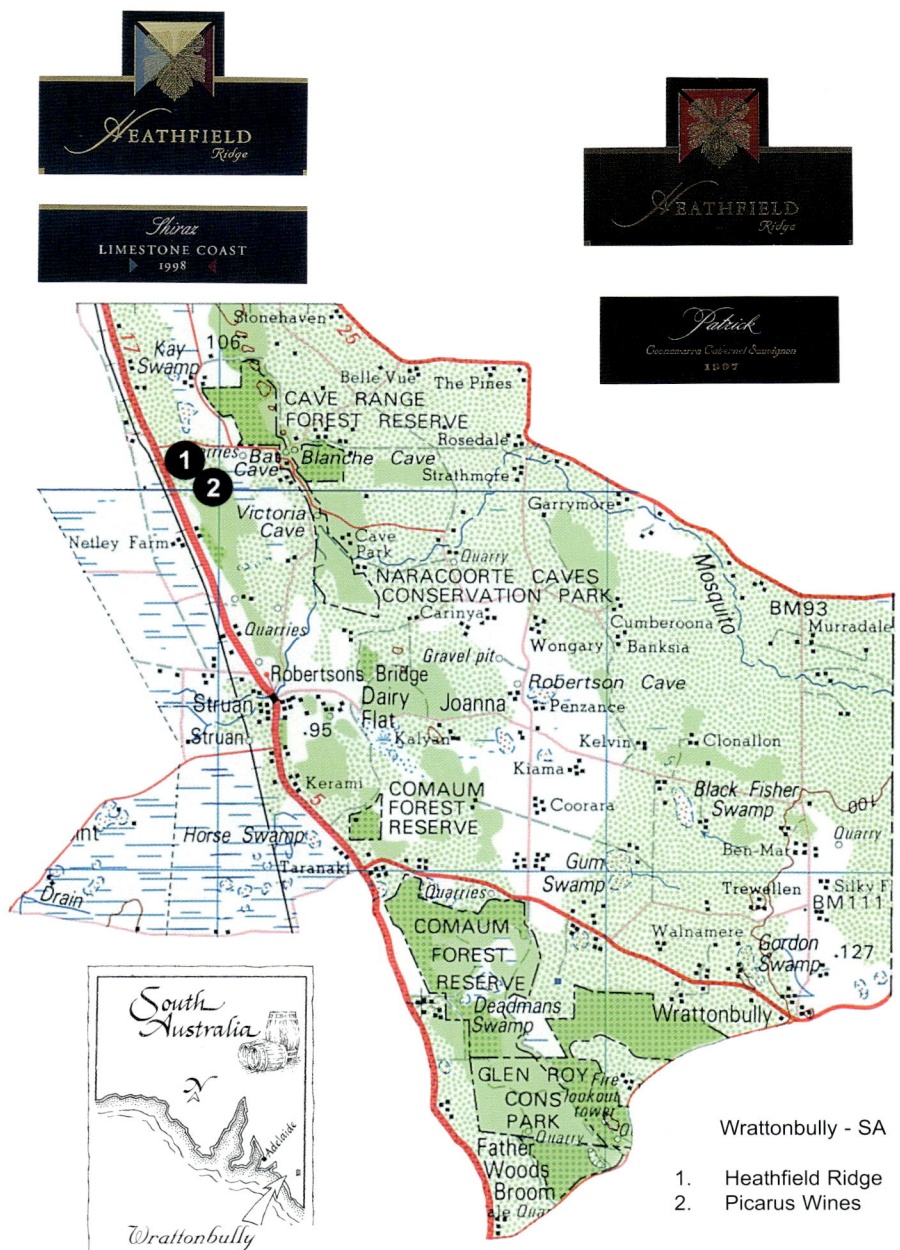

Wrattonbully - SA

1. Heathfield Ridge
2. Picarus Wines

Heathfield Ridge

Heathfield Ridge Wines is located on the corner of Caves Road and Riddoch Highway, 10 kms south of Naracoorte in the heart of the Limestone Coast Region of South Australia, officially it is in the Wrattonbully district. The state of the art processing facility was built in 1997/98 to meet the demand created by the massive vineyard growth within the Limestone coast. The winery has a licence to crush up to 10,000 tonnes and currently boasts some of the larger wine companies in Australia as its primary clients.

Heathfield's vineyard at Bool Lagoon is located in the heart of the National Park Heathlands towards Lucindale. The 260 acre vineyard was planted in 1995/96 supplying excellent fruit for their Sauvignon Blanc, Chardonnay, Shiraz, Cabernet Sauvignon, Merlot and includes a new planting of Petit Verdot. The winery site is surrounded by vineyard totalling 80 acres including varieties such as Semillon, Pinot Noir, Shiraz and Cabernet Sauvignon.

The Cellar Door sales area was opened in February 2000 coinciding with the release of the premium

Heathfield Ridge range of wines, which includes a Sauvignon Blanc, Reserve Chardonnay, Shiraz and a Cabernet Sauvignon. They also released their Wonambi Range

emphasising a push for tourism in the region by supporting the ongoing research and development of the Wonambi Fossil Centre, which is part

of the World Heritage listed Naracoorte Caves not more than 4 kms east of the winery.

Their two flagship wines - a 1997 Patrick Reserve Cabernet Sauvignon and a 1998 Jennifer Reserve Shiraz have just been released. "Jennifer Shiraz" commemorates the Proprietors, the Tidswell family's daughter Jennifer, who tragically lost her life in an automobile accident at a young age.

The winemaker and an important figure behind the Heathfield Ridge project is Pat Tocacui, with a rich career of winemaking at Tollana and Hollicks behind him he is the "Patrick" in the flagship Cabernet Sauvignon's name. Another wine legend who made wine with Pat and played league football with him at North Adelaide many years ago. John Baruzzi is helping guide the quick progress of the Heathfield Wines in the market place.

The striking Heathfield Ridge winery is easy to spot in the top of the Ridge as you travel on the Riddoch Highway. The tasting area is world class with an exceptional view don't drive past it drop in instead!!

Address: Cnr Caves Rd & Riddoch Highway NARACOORTE 5271
Phone: (08) 8762 4133 **Fax:** (08) 8762 0141
Email: winery@hthfieldwine.mtx.net
WWW: www.hthfieldwine.com.au
Owner: Tidswell Family

Winemaker: Pat Tocaciu, Neil Dodridge & Paul Gobel
Est: 1997 **Vine Ha:** 350
PublicHours: 10am-5pm, Mon-Sat; 11am-4:30pm Sun & Public Holidays
Principal Wines

Reserve Chardonnay
Shiraz
Sparkling Chardonnay Pinot Noir
Sauvignon Blanc
Merlot
Cabernet Sauvignon

Picarus Wines

A powerful partnership of dynamic, experienced winemaker and marketer John Baruzzi with entrepreneur and wine lover Mark Arnold has created an exceptional new wine producer, Picarus, this is the name of their main vineyard in the new Wrattonbully district of the Limestone Coast region of south eastern South Australia. The grapes from their estate are supplemented by strictly controlled, contracted vineyards in the Limestone Coast region. Cutting edge Viticultural techniques including minimal pruning, regulated deficit irrigation and specialised canopy management ensure the crop levels are very modest, the berry sizes are small and the flavour in the grapes is truly intense.

To sum up all these factors and their total philosophy about their wine, Mark and John coined the word PICARUS, P-Pedical, the stalk of an individual flower which becomes the short stem in the bunch bearing a single grape, I · Iron, an essential mineral for vine growth an in abundance in their vineyard, C · cepage, French for grape variety, A · Adega, Portugese for wine cellar or winery, R · Reserve the finest wines of the vintage, U · United the fision of the importise of the Picarus team, S · a celebration of the science of winemaking.

The Picarus range included three Limestone coast wines. Cabernet Sauvignon, Shiraz and Chardonnay, Reserve 1 · Coonawarra Cabernet Sauvignon and Reserve A · Padthaway Shiraz.

I found the wines to be concentrated complex and individual in style. I am sure they will be very successful in overseas markets as well as locally.

Nothing has been spared in terms of investment in producing simply great wines which the team at Picarus are committed to.

Fleurieu Peninsula

Wine has become more a part of the Fleurieu Peninsula over the last two decades. In the 1960's and 70's McLaren Vale and the so called Southern Vales contained nearly all the vineyards and wineries on the Fleurieu Peninsula. As the 80's and 90's unfolded the Adelaide Hills portion of the Fleurieu exploded with vines and wineries, this has worked south through Hahndorf, Macclesfield, Echunga, Meadows, Kuitpo and Kangarilla across to Yankallila and Normanville down through Mt Compass to Middleton, Compass Creek and across to a much enlarged Langhorne Creek region.

Fleurieu is a French name given to the large Peninsula stretching from the mouth of the Murray River, past Port Elliot and Victor Harbour around Cape Jervis and up to the Southern metropolitan areas of Adelaide, it stretches across to Murray Bridge in the east. French explorer Baudin on his journey east met Flinders on his journery west, many of the names west of Encounter Bay (as they named their meeting place near Victor Harbour) carry French names. Baudin and his botanist were taken by the trees and wildflowers on the Peninsula they had just rounded naming it Fleurieu, literally the Flowering Peninsula, it has certainly blossomed over recent years not only with vineyards and wineries but many new gourmet food producers. Strawberries, venison, jams and preserves, olive oil, bakery produce, asparagus and many other products fall under the "Fleurieu Gold" food banner.

Hospitality and wine and food tourism has boomed with specialist resorts such as Paradise Cove at Wirrina, with top class accomodation, championship golf course and all possible ammenities. Whalers Haven and others have transformed the region. Many wineries now have Restaurants, function facilities and accomodation.

The topography of the Peninsula is striking and varied from the incredible ghost gums, made famous by Hans Heysens paintings, to the rugged coast south of Normanville, beautiful bays and spectacular hills, valleys, and a climate suited perfectly to the vine, its a paradise future generations will appreciate more than we ever realise today.

Bruce Gordon is the ideal person to be running the finest regional wine and food tourism centre in Australia, he truly understands its mission. Bruce explained it to me, "it's the sorting area, it's about demystifying wine and helping visitors to the region to have a truly enjoyable and personally rewarding visit". Bruce knows the 56 cellar doors in the McLaren Vale region and the couple of dozen others in the Southern Fleurieu Peninsula, Currency Creek, Middleton, and Langhorne Creek regions like the back of his hand. He's a gregarious fellow who makes it his business to chat with all the visitors who come to the centre to find out as he says "the romance" they are seeking in wine and food.

The centre also features an excellent indoor/outdoor café "Stump Hill" which looks over the lawns and the Shiraz vineyard which was established by the winemakers of the region, to produce the "Stump Hill Shiraz" made by Mike Farmilo at Boars Rock Winery, usually around 5,000 cases are produced. The proceeds of the sale of this great wine help fund the centre. The Stump Hill café serves light innovative food, created entirely from local produce. It is open from mid morning for lunch seven days a week. The large area including The Thomas Hardy Tower is often used for art exhibitions, weddings and other functions, full conference and seminar facilities are also available.

The Centre has a large range of wines for tasting and purchase, including wines from half a dozen or so producers who don't have their own cellar door. Bruce will consolidate wine orders for visitors and arrange delivery virtually anywhere in the world.

The centre has regular wine appreciation courses which usually run over 4 weeks, one night per week for around $100, this includes a guest winemaker each week and a range of wines to taste accompanied by suitable food.

Theme nights are often held at the centre such as "Merlot in May" where a range of Merlots will be tasted and discussed with the winemakers accompanied by a meal. All these services are featured through the "McLaren Vale Wine Club" which has periodic mail outs and is free to join.

Next summer Bruce will be running an outdoor cinema, he's just bursting out with good ideas. Bruce left his home near Toronto, Canada, as a youth, spending much of his life travelling and working in the wine and hospitality industries through Europe, North Africa, Asia and America. It's certainly sharpened his palate, focussed his thinking and fed his passion for wine, food and good company. I first met him some years ago at Wirilda Creek Winery in McLaren Vale where he spent 2 $\frac{1}{2}$ years. I am pleased to see him at this great cultural centre and urge you to drop in and see him too, he'll help you discover the great gourmet regions of McLaren Vale and the Fleurieu Peninsula.

McLaren Vale

The McLaren Vale wine region stretches from the southern suburbs of Adelaide including Reynella in the north to Aldinga and Willunga in the south. The region is bordered by the Adelaide Hills to the east and the Gulf of St Vincent to the west.

John Reynell planted the first vines of the region at Reynella in 1838. He was followed by Dr Alexander Kelly, who founded the Tintara Vineyard Company and developed a considerable property covering 712 acres.

The first vines planted by Dr Kelly are still bearing fruit, which has traditionally been used in a fortified dessert wine. In 1850 George Manning established the Hope Farm Vineyard, which is now Seaview. By late 1880 wine industry development was booming throughout Australia.

In McLaren Vale, new businesses were founded by J.G. Kelly with the Tatachilla Vineyard, the Kay family with their Amery winery, the Johnstons' Pirramimma Wines and Robert Wigley with Wirra Wirra. Much of the wine produced in McLaren Vale/Reynella was exported to England. The area was subject to export market vagaries and grew slowly until the table wine boom of the 1950's.

Larger companies such as Lindemans and Penfolds started purchasing McLaren Vale red wines for blending and many existing local companies began to bottle and market their own wine. Towards the end of the decade and through the

early 70's new companies blossomed throughout McLaren Vale. There are now more than 50 wineries in the area and the 1980's and 1990's have seen the area under vines expand dramatically. More importantly, the awareness of McLaren Vale Wines and their reputation for quality has grown even more dramatically.

I can well imagine how the beauty of the region would have captured the heart of my own great-grandfather, Thomas Hardy, as he drove his horse and buggy over the final rise of the southern Adelaide Hills and saw the peaceful Valley spread out before him, the time-worn fingers of the hills holding its final exit into St. Vincents Gulf (by coincidence, St. Vincent is the patron saint of winemakers). The gentle undulating hills have traditionally supported vines, olives and almonds. The almonds in blossom around the first week or so in August gives the Valley a special glow.

During the 1870's, the area had fallen on hard times, the over-cropping of cereals and over-grazing leading to diminishing rural returns. Thomas Hardy set about promoting the vine and olive, educating farmers in their cultivation. He also bought the grand, but bankrupt, Tintara Vineyard Company and the disused Flour Mill in the centre of town converting it to a winery, soon having the region well on its feet, with his own flourishing enterprise.

McLaren Vale is one of the world's best-placed wine regions, being only

45 minutes drive south of the Adelaide city centre. This, combined with its physical beauty, has led to a boom in tourism through which; fortunately, the region has lost none of its charm or the individual character of its winemakers.

Forerunner among this development was David Hardy, great-grandson of pioneer Thomas, along with renowned artist, David Dridan. They set up the wine-inspired restaurant, The Barn, in 1970 with its vine-covered courtyard and 'choose your own' wine cellar. It was an innovative and welcome addition to Australia, let alone McLaren Vale.

David also founded the Wine Bushing Festival in 1974, based on the old Elizabethan tradition of hanging a bush outside the inn when the new wine was ready. In October each year, this tradition continues. The makers of the best commercially available McLaren Vale wine are crowned "Bushing King and Queen" at the annual Winemakers' Luncheon. The month kicks off with the McLaren Vale Continuous Picnic on the October long weekend, a Sunday and Monday celebration of wine and food. Some 30 wineries all have a guest restaurants cooking, and all manner of entertainment.

Bushing Week usually starts with the McLaren Vale Wine Show, a varietal workshop and the Winemakers' Luncheon, which showcases the show's award winning wines, complemented by regional produce from the Fleurieu Peninsula. All

McLaren Vale

awards from the wine show are presented during the luncheon, the highlight being the crowning of the "Bushing King and Queen".

The festival culminates with the Bushing Festival Street Procession and Fair Day when the whole town stops and stalls and entertainment reign supreme. In between, wineries have dinners, concerts, theatre pieces and all manner of other music, art and cultural experiences.

McLaren Vale has long been known for its full-bodied red wines, aided by the complex soils and mild temperate climate. These rich round generous wines can really warm the soul. The region also produces great whites and although its chardonnays led the way, they have latterly been joined by sauvignon blancs, which are becoming a regional speciality and highly regarded by the wine cognoscenti.

Much of the industry's success originally was based on fortified ports and sherries and while sherry making has ceased, the ports of the region are outstanding; both the

vintage and tawny styles excel. The number of winery restaurants, bed and breakfasts and regional eating houses is growing daily and they are superb. The Barn has been joined by The Salopian Inn at the other end of town and the McLarens on the Lake restaurant, function and accommodation centre is splendid, indeed. Woodstock has a superb large restaurant and function centre, The Coterie, a Sunday lunch here is compulsory. Middlebrook has a restaurant, Wirilda Creek features a casual restaurant and great bed and breakfast, at the McLaren Vale Olive Groves you can taste a great range of olive and other produce - they also serve light meals, Geoff Merrill's historic Mt. Hurtle Winery also has a function area. The new cellar door at d'Arenberg and d'Arry's Verandah Restaurant with its spectacular views over the vines, hills and the waters of St Vincents Gulf is one of the very best wine hospitality centres in Australia.

"Magnums" at the Hotel McLaren and the Almond Train are at the entrance

to Hardy's Tintara Winery in McLaren Vale's main street which has many other new cafes and restaurants.

The new Fleurieu Regional Visitor Centre (opened in late 1996) is located near the McLaren Vale township's western entrance. The centre offers visitors a glimpse of what they can discover in the McLaren Vale region and beyond on the Fleurieu Peninsula. In 1998 Australia's richest landscape art competition was inaugurated the "Fluerieu Biennale". The $50,000 prize and the prestige of becoming Australia's best Landscape Artist, has drawn many of Australia's finest landscape painters, many producing works on the beautiful Fleurieu Peninsula. Many wine and food events surround this very successful venture.

Any visitors to Adelaide with an interest in wine should spend a day or two exploring the magnificent scenery, beaches, wines and food of the McLaren Vale Wine Region - Adelaide's playground.

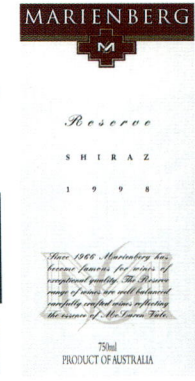
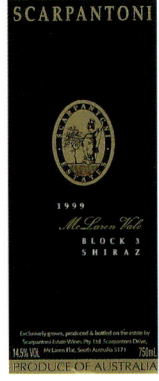

McLaren Vale

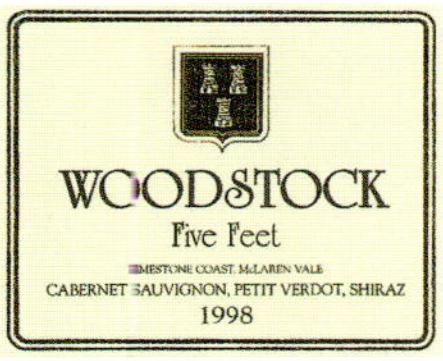

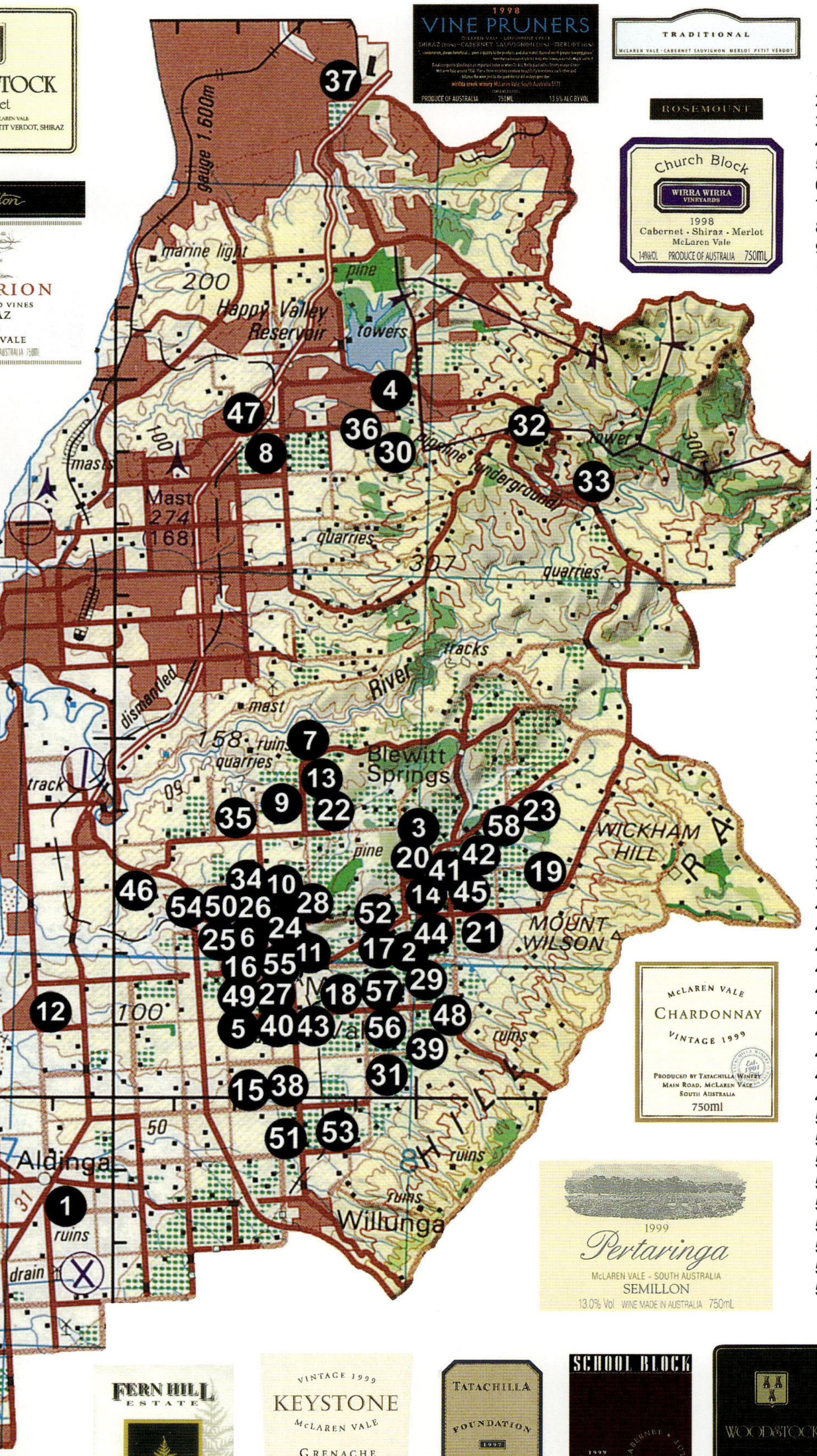

McLaren Vale - SA

1. Aldinga Bay Wines
2. Aldinga Turkeys
3. Andrew Garrett Wines
4. Beresford Wines
5. Boars Rock
6. Brewery Hill
7. Chapel Hill Winery
8. Chateau Reynella Winery
9. Coriole Wines
10. D'Arenberg Wines
11. Dennis of McLaren Vale
12. Dyson Wines
13. Edwards & Chaffey Wines
14. Fernhill Estate
15. Fox Creek Wines
16. Hardy's Tintara Winery
17. Haselgrove Wines
18. Hugh Hamilton
19. Hugo Winery
20. Ingoldby
21. Kangarilla Road
22. Kay Bros
23. Maglieri Wines
24. Manning Park Winery
25. Marienberg Winery
26. Maxwells Wines
27. McLaren's on the Lake
28. Merrivale Winery
29. Middlebrook Wines
30. Mount Hurtle Vineyards
31. Noon's Winery
32. Normans Wines
33. Old Clarendon Winery
34. Olive Groves
35. Oliverhill Wines
36. Patritti Reynella
37. Patritti Wines
38. Pennys Hill
39. Pertaringa Vineyards
40. Pirramimma Winery
41. Rosemount Ryecroft
42. Ryecroft Vineyards
43. Salopian Inn
44. Scarpantoni Estate Wines
45. Shottesbrooke
46. Simon Hackett Wines
47. St Francis Winery
48. Tanami Red Wines
49. Tatachilla Winery
50. The Barn
51. The Hamilton Wine Group
52. Tinlins
53. Tyrrells Rufus Stone
54. Visitors Centre
55. Wayne Thomas
56. Wirilda Creek Winery
57. Wirra Wirra Vineyards
58. Woodstock Winery

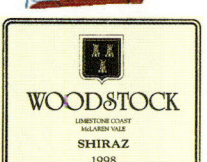

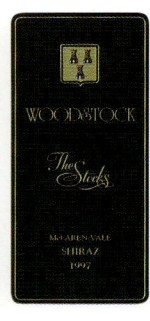

McLaren Vale

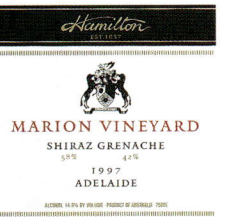

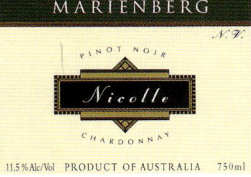

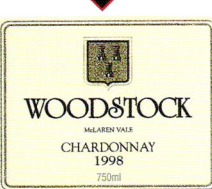
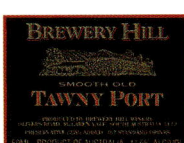

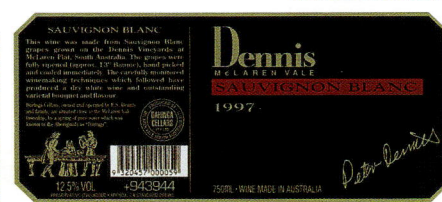
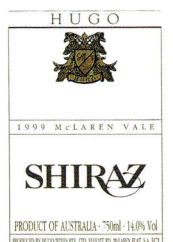

Mt Hurtle

One of the most beautiful old gravity flow wineries of the last century is Mount Hurtle, which was built in 1897 by Mostyn Owen.

The winery was disused and storing hay when Geoff Merrill, then the high profile winemaker at Chateau Reynella, bought it back in the early 80's.

The Mount Hurtle winery is a picture. A small lake reflects the winery as one enters the tree-lined drive. The front section of the winery has been turned into a splendid function area with polished wooden floors and a balcony where one can view the working winery and barrel cellar below. Many weddings and other events now take place in this stunning setting.

Geoff is certainly not the shy and retiring type, with his huge handlebar moustache enhancing his happy smiling face. He is a serious, fastidious winemaker and all his wines reflect this care in their great balance and sophisticated styles. The Mount Hurtle and the super premium Geoff Merrill reds are often in the more herbaceous spectrum, with fine tannins and clean varietal characteristics. The whites are rich and ripe in style, showing classy wood treatments.

Geoff is a passionate cricket fan and a close friend of cricket legends Ian Botham and Bob Willis. Every year they hold a charity cricket event in England, sponsored by Geoff and Mount Hurtle, which raises hundreds of thousands of dollars for charity. Well done Geoff Merrill!!

Address: 291 Pimpala Roa WOODCROFT 5162
Phone: (08) 8381 6877 **Fax:** (08) 8222 2244
Owner: Geoff Merrill **Est:** 1987 **Cases:** 100k
Winemaker: Geoff Merrill and Goe DiFabio

Public Hours: 10am-4pm M-F; 12pm-5pm Sun
Principal Wines

Principal Wines	Potential
Geoff Merrill Reserve Cabernet Sauv	10-15yrs
Geoff Merrill Reserve Chardonnay	5-15 yrs

	Potential
Mount Hurtle Sauvignon Blanc Semillon	1-4yrs
Mount Hurtle Grenache Rose	1-2 yrs
Geoff Merrill Shiraz	1-4 yrs
Geoff Merrill Cabernet Merlot	5-8 yrs

Aldinga Bay Wines

Situated on the southern end of the Willunga plain, just as you begin to climb nto the ranges of the Southern Fleurieu Peninsula, is the Aldinga Bay Vineyards and winery of the Girolamo family.

A mere two and a half kilometres away are the beautiful sandy beaches of Aldinga Bay, which is around 45 kilometres south of the centre of Adelaide.

The moderating affect of the sea all year around and the afternoon sea breezes in summer, provides a temperate environment ideal for enhancing and preserving all the intriguing flavours and varietal characters in the grapes.

Don Girolamo's love of vineyards, wine and winemaking began in his native taly. In 1973 along with his wife Olga, he selected 35 acres in the gentle slopes below the Sellicks Hills. The fertile Bay of Biscay soils which had washed down from the Hills have

proved ideal for vines, since these early days the Girolamo's land holdings have expanded considerably and their vineyards now cover 175 acres.

The original varieties planted

included Cabernet Sauvignon, Merlot, Cabernet Franc, Shiraz, Sauvignon Blanc, Chardonnay and Rhine Riesling. Although Don set up his vineyard to supply grapes to wineries in the McLaren Vale region,

Aldinga Bay Wines

the temptation to make his own wine proved too much for him. By 1979 he had outgrown his small winemaking facility and a modern winery was constructed and a range of table and fortified wines were launched. Shortly after this time Don's son Nick had completed his degree in Oenology from Roseworthy and returned home after winemaking experience overseas.

Today Nick runs the family enterprise and the wines are marketed under the fresh bright "Aldinga Bay" labels. The more recent plantings at Aldinga Bay have included some Italian red varieties, Nebbiolo, Sangiovese and Barbera along with Semillon, Verdelho, Malbec, Petit Verdot and Ruby Cabernet. The new varietal and

blended wines using these varieties are just coming on stream as I write.

The Cellar door run by Sophie Scipioni is open from 10.00 a.m. 5.00 p.m. every day except Christmas Day and Good Friday. The location on the main road through to Myponga and Yankalilla, is ideal for a visit if you are on a trip around the beautiful and varied Fleurieu Peninsula. You can drop in on your way south or on your way back northward towards Adelaide from the southern coast and Victor Harbor. It can also make a great pit stop if you are driving down to take the Ferry to Kangaroo Island from Cape Jervis.

Aldinga Bay also have a very good Wine Club which is free to join, it includes a Premier Membership

card. The Aldinga Bay Wine Club, not only gives you special prices and bonus wines with your order, but keeps you informed about the considerable number of interesting new release wines coming from this genuine family winery.

Aldinga Bay Wines have been a huge hit in Sydney's finest and most exclusive Restaurants, who now account for a high percentage of their sales.

I have found the Aldinga Bay Wines have exceptionally full varietal flavours. This is a special family winery where Don and Nick can be seen proudly working together in their vineyards and winery to produce fine premium wines.

		Principal Wines	Potential
Address: Main South Road ALDINGA 5173	**Cases**: 8,000	Aldinga Bay Shiraz	3-7 yrs
Phone: (08) 8556 3179 **Fax:** (08) 8556 3350	**Public Hours**: 10am-5pm, daily	Aldinga Bay Cabernet Sauvignon	3-7 yrs
Email: aldingabay@ozemail.com.au	**Principal Varieties**: Barbera, Cabernet Franc,	Aldinga Bay Merlot	2-5 yrs
WWW: www.aldingabaywine.com.au	Cabernet Sauvignon, Chardonnay, Malbec,	Aldinga Bay Sangiovese	2-5 yrs
Owner: Girolamo Family	Merlot, Nebbiolo, Petit Verdot, Sangiovese,	Aldinga Bay Chardonnay	2-5 yrs
Winemaker: Nick Girolamo	Semillon, Verdelho, Riesling, Sauvignon	Aldinga Bay Verdelho	2-5 yrs
Est: 1979 **Vine Ha**: 54	Blanc, Shiraz		

Aldinga Turkeys

by their two sons Simon who controls production and Anthony who is running the Turkey Kitchen.

The theme is a "Country Kitchen" with visitors being able to taste the famous Aldinga naturally smoked turkey breast and other products. There is an opportunity to learn many things about turkey and its nutritional value. Recipes and menus are available, along with a complete range of fresh and frozen Turkey products - Aldinga Turkeys has the largest range in Australia including Turkey Bacon, Turkey "Virginia" ham, marinated Turkey steaks, Turkey and sage sausages. Italian Turkey thigh Schnitzels, smoked turkey wings as well as the naturally smoked breast and many other treats.

The processing facility is almost next door so the produce is absolutely fresh. Turkey is one of the highest protein leanest fat and lowest calorie meats available and many of the Aldinga range products proudly display the "Heart tick" showing they have been approved by the National Heart Foundation, you can literally "eat Turkey to your hearts delight"

The Aldinga Turkey Kitchen is interactive and a great way to experience and learn more about Turkey, whilst on your wine journey around McLaren Vale.

Set amongst the vines in Foggo Road McLaren Vale is the Aldinga Turkey Kitchen and "Chiller" door sales outlet for this innovative turkey products processor. This total retail, information and tasting facility, features an exciting range of fresh frozen and fully cooked turkey, in what was the Haselgrove Wineries Cellar door and restaurant just off the main McLaren Vale to McLaren Flat roads.

Aldinga Turkeys was founded by Terry and Carol Crabb in 1973. In the early eighties they were looking for a way to expand their business

further and produce turkey products with a distinctly Australian flavour. Terry had seen some smoking ovens on the west coast of America and wondered how Australian Red Gum sawdust would work in them, he sent over the sawdust and the results were great. Aldinga Turkeys imported an oven and began smoking their own, they now have four ovens and their smoked turkey products are a huge success.

In 1973 Aldinga sold 54 fresh Turkeys at Christmas, during December 2000 they sold 20,000. Terry and Carol have now been joined

Address: Foggo Road MCLAREN VALE 5171	Email: turkman@aldingaturkeys.com.au	Principal Product
Phone: (08) 8323 8077 Fax: (08) 8323 8954	PublicHours: 10am-4pm daily Est: 1979	Aldinga Naturally Smoked Turkey Breast

Andrew Garrett

Andrew Garrett arrived on the wine scene like a whirlwind. Not since the early days of Wolf Blass's arrival a decade earlier had Australia's wine drinkers imagination been captured so fully.

His wines were exciting. A chardonnay packed full of fruit flavour, with good oak treatment, and methode champenoise of exceptional quality, lifting people's sights well above the ordinary. The Garrett reds were also lively and fruit driven. Andrew's flamboyant marketing style also had a Blass-like ring about it.

Andrew Garrett became part of the Beringer Blass stable some years ago and Andrew moved on to other projects. The wines are of absolutely the highest quality and the growth of the brand I am sure will accelerate even further, both domestically and overseas. The Andrew Garrett N.V. Pinot, a Non-Vintage Methode Champenoise Cuvee with its very faint blushing colour and delectable pinot noir nuances, is a rightful market leader.

The Garrett Red Sparkling is a truly regal rich red at the pinnacle of its class. In the table wine area the quality and styles are equally well conceived and created. The chardonnay and the "bold" shiraz stand out, but all the wines are outstanding.

The Andrew Garrett range of wines are available for tasting at the recently renovated and re-opened Ingolby cellar door.

Address: Kangarilla Road MCLAREN VALE 5171	**Public Hours:** 10am-4pm, daily	Andrew Garrett Sauvignon Blanc	2-4 yrs
Phone: (08) 8323 8853 **Fax:** (08) 8323 8271	**Principal Varieties:** Chardonnay, Cabernet	Andrew Garrett Bold Shiraz	3-5 yrs
Owner: Mildara Blass Limited	Sauvignon, Grenache, Sauvignon Blanc, Pinot Noir	Andrew Garrett Botrytis Riesling	3-5 yrs
Winemaker: Phil Reschke	**Principal Wines** **Potential**	Andrew Garrett Brut	2-3 yrs
Est: 1983 **Vine Ha:** 120 **Cases:** 120,000	Garrett Shiraz Cabernet Franc 2-5 yrs	Andrew Garrett Sparkling Burgundy	2-3 yrs

Ingoldby Wines

In May 1995, Beringer Blass purchased Ingoldby Wines, they quickly realised that Ingoldby as a brand presented a great opportunity. Much of this is to the credit of the previous owner and winemaker, Walter Clappis.

Walter is one of those characters who is truly larger than life - his infectious enthusiasm, love of life and the buzz he got from producing great wine was a joy to behold.

Walter began working with Jim Ingoldby at Ingoldby Wines in 1981. Jim established the winery in 1971 and the Ingoldby name has been associated with the McLaren Vale region since the turn of the century.

In 1982, Jim was looking at a change in lifestyle and to go and live at his beloved Walkers Flat on the River Murray.

Ingoldby is the only winery in the region to win the Dan Murphy Trophy three times for the best Cabernet Sauvignon, awarded each year at the McLaren Bushing Festival. The whites also tend to be rich and round, appealing to the red wine lover.

Recently the cellar door has been renovated and re-opened, you can now taste the Ingoldby along with the

Andrew Garrett wines.

Ingoldby Wines continue to reflect the individuality and distinctiveness that were their signature under Jim Ingoldby and Walter Clappis.

Address: Kangarilla Road MCLAREN VALE 5171	**Est:** 1973 **Vine Ha:** 7+ **Cases:** 20,000	Ingoldby Sauvignon Blanc	2-4 yrs
Phone: (08) 8323 8853 **Fax:** (08) 8323 8271	**Public Hours:** 10am-5pm, daily	Ingoldby Grenache	3-4 yrs
Owner: Mildara Blass Limited	**Principal Wines** **Potential**	Ingoldby Shiraz	3-5 yrs
Winemaker: Phil Reschke	Ingoldby Chardonnay 2-4 yrs	Ingoldby Cabernet Sauvignon	3-5 yrs

Maglieri

Maglieri Wines was founded by Steve Maglieri who was among the post-war influx of Italian grape growers, who did such good work in developing McLaren Vale in the 1950's and 60's.

Maglieri's expanded the plantings of premium grape varieties largely supplying their grapes to the bigger wineries. Being Italian of course, they had to make their own vino for the casa. They could not resist selling some of the wines, which were of excellent quality and value, thus was born Gully Wines in 1972, changing its name to Maglieri Wines in 1979.

A huge success story for Maglieri has been their excellent market-leading Australian Lambrusco, made in the style of this soft, fruity, slightly sweet Italian red wine. Maglieri's, however, make many seriously great table wines and have won hoards of trophies and gold medals. The winery is in the beautiful Blewitt Springs area of the Valley, rising up into the foothills of the Adelaide Hills and reminiscent of the rolling countryside of Tuscany.

The winery is now ultramodern, crushes over 3,000 tonnes of grapes and is blessed with top class oak and stainless steel storage.

The four ranges of Maglieri wines start with two lambruscos, followed by the 'Ingleburne Estate' range of affordable premium table wines and finally the flagship Maglieri Label.

Address: Douglas Gully Road MCLAREN FLAT 5171	11am-4.30pm, Sun	Cabernet Sauvignon	5-10 yrs
Phone: (08) 8383 0177 **Fax:** (08) 8383 0136	**Principal Varieties:** Shiraz, Cab Sav, Sem, Merlot,	Ingleburne Unwooded Semillon	2-5 yrs
Winemaker: John Loxton	Riesling, Chard., Traminer, Sav Blanc, Grenache	Ingleburne Cabernet	5-10 yrs
Est: 1972 **Vine Ha:** 150 **Cases:** 250,000	**Principal Wines** **Potential**	Chardonnay	2-5 yrs
Public Hours: 9.30am-4pm, Mon-Sat;	Shiraz 5-10 yrs	Semillon	2-5 yrs

Beresford Wines

The Beresford Wines story began in 1989 when the historic Old Horndale Winery built in 1896, was purchased and refurbished with the most up to date, state of the art equipment. The result is a unique blend of tradition, history and modern technology to ensure production of premium quality wines.

Success in export markets in particular were so spectacular that in 1996 Beresford purchased "Belleville Estate", 110ha of vineyard in the famous Langhorne Creek region. The vineyard comprises of Cabernet Sauvignon, Shiraz, Merlot, Chardonnay, Pinot Noir, Petit Verdot and Sangiovese.

Winemaker Scott McIntosh joined Beresford Wines in 1999. Having worked in the industry since 1985 and nurturing a vineyard of his own, Scott has an intimate knowledge and passion for grape production.

Today Beresford Wines is one of Australia's largest producers making over 300,000 cases of premium wine under various labels.

All wines are not only top quality but are exceptional value for money.

Address: 49 Fraser Avenue HAPPY VALLEY 5159	**Est:** 1985	**Vine Ha:** 96	**Cases:** 300,000	Beresford Cabernet Merlot — 5-8 yrs
	Public Hours: 11am-5pm, daily			Beresford Chardonnay — 3-5 yrs
Phone: (08) 8322 3611 **Fax:** (08) 8322 3610	**Principal Varieties:** Cabernet Sauvignon,			Beresford Semillon Sauvignon — 1-2 yrs
Email: info@beresfordwines.com.au	Petit Verdot, Shiraz, Merlot, Sangiovese,			Highwood Chardonnay — 2-4 yrs
WWW: www.beresfordwines.com.au	Chardonnay, Pinot Noir			Highwood Sauvignon Blanc — 1-2 yrs
Winemaker: Rob Dundon & Scott McIntosh	**Principal Wines**		**Potential**	Highwood Shiraz — 3-5 yrs

Coriole Wines

Dr Hugh Lloyd purchased Chateau Bonne Sante (ironically French for good health) and surrounding vineyards in 1968.

The property had a long history, with vines planted in 1920 and the ironstone buildings built in 1860.

Now known as Coriole, the property is set on the hill west of the Seaview vineyards.

The small viticulture region around Coriole is prized for its distinctive red brown loams over ironstone or limestone.

The Coriole shiraz is a consistent and impressive wine and the company's flagship. The top of the range wine is the Lloyd Reserve Shiraz. First produced in 1989, it is made from 80 year old vines grown at Coriole, it is very rich with great complexity and has long cellaring potential.

Sangiovese has become a speciality

of the winery. Coriole has led the way with this Italian variety in Australia. Sangiovese is a late variety with good acidity that is well suited to McLaren Vale. The lighter

bodied style with its savoury characters and gentle grip gives a wine that contrasts with their other reds.

Coriole is one of the few Australian wine companies to produce chenin blanc, which was rediscovered in the McLaren Vale region by a French ampelographer. Coriole Chenin has great depth of flavour · tropical, apple and quince characteristics abound.

The other wines include a shiraz cabernet call 'Redstone', a semillon sauvignon blanc and a top of range cabernet blend named 'Mary Kathleen', after Mark Lloyd's late mother.

The wines are predominantly estate grown. The old cottage and gardens now also include a café restaurant area with its long views of the surrounding countryside.

Address: Chaffeys Road MCLAREN VALE 5171 **Phone:** (08) 8323 8305 **Fax:** (08) 8323 9136 **Winemaker:** Stephen Hall **Est:** 1968 **Vine Ha:** 20 **Cases:** 25,000 **Public Hours:** 10am-5pm, weekdays; 11am-	5pm, weekends and public holidays **Principal Varieties:** Shiraz, Cabernet Sauvignon, Chenin Blanc, Sangiovese, Semillon **Principal Wines** **Potential** Shiraz 5-10 yrs	Redstone Shiraz/Cabernet Sauvignon 5-10yrs Sangiovese 2-5 yrs Cabernet Sauvignon 5-10 yrs "Mary Kathleen" Cabernet/Merlot/Cabernet Franc 5-10 yrs Lloyd Reserve Shiraz 10+ yrs

Boars Rock

Established in 1997 to service the growing processing needs of the Australian wine industry, Boar's Rock Winery is an independent, specialist contract processing facility located in the heart of the McLaren Vale wine region. It has a crushing capacity of 10,000 tonnes and offers a complete range of winemaking services, short and long term tank storage and barrel maturation.

The winery processes fruit to must, juice and ex-fermenter/gross lees stage for a number of Australia's major wine companies while smaller wineries utilize Boar's Rock full services to process fruit through to finished, bottle ready wine. Several major independent grape growers value-add their fruit by processing it and selling it as bulk juice or finished wine.

General Manager/Chief Winemaker and a partner in the venture is Mike Farmilo (former Group Red Winemaker at Southcorp).

Mike has had extensive experience in making and developing wines for significant Australian wine brands

such as Penfolds, Seaview, Wynns and Lindemans.

Address: Tatachilla Road MCLAREN VALE 5171	**Phone:** (08) 8323 9955 **Fax:** (08) 8323 9966 **Email:** winery@boarsrock.com.au	**Winemaker:** Mike Farmilo **Est:** 1997

d'Arenberg Wines

d'Arenberg is one of the most significant wine companies in McLaren Vale. In 1912 Joseph Osborn, purchased the well established Milton Vineyards in the hills just north of the township of McLaren Vale.

Joseph's son Frank left medical school, choosing to forsake the scalpel for pruning shears, selling the grapes from his 195 acres of vineyards to local wineries until the construction of his own cellars were completed in 1928.

In 1943 Frank's son d'Arry returned from school, aged 16, to help his ill father run the business, eventually assuming management of d'Arenberg in 1956, bottling the first of the famous diagonal red stripe labelled wines the following year. d'Arry's wines of the 1960's gained immediate cult status amongst imbibers and judges. One cabernet sauvignon won a Jimmy Watson Trophy and another Grenache based wine was awarded 7 trophies and 29 gold medals from Australian Capital City wine shows. By the 1970's d'Arenberg Wines had become very fashionable indeed.

After graduating from Roseworthy College and visiting other Australian and European wine regions, d'Arry's son Chester took over the reigns as chief winemaker in 1984, immediately rejuvenating the then 70 year old cellars and 19th Century vineyards.

Investing in new oak, lots of small stainless steel tanks and refrigeration resulting in immediate white dividends with his Dry Dam Riesling, Broken Fishplate Sauvignon Blanc, Olive Grove Chardonnay and botrytis affected Noble Riesling all winning gold medals and trophies.

In 1990 Chester was crowned McLaren Vale Bushing King. In 1995 d'Arry was invested as a patron of the Wine Industry of Australia, two years after completing his 50th consecutive vintage.

It is not surprising that with a "Red Stripe" in their blood, d'Arry and Chester's wines, have continued to win numerous national and international medals, trophies and critical acclaim.

In 1999 Chester was named the inaugural Winestate Australian Winemaker of the year, the same year d'Arenberg was named as in US

Wine and Spirits Top 70 Wineries in the World. d'Arenberg won in two consecutive years (1999 and 2000) The Wine Society Perpetual Trophy for the Most Successful Winery of the Competition at the Sydney International Top 100 Competition. June 2000 saw Chester Osborn voted Person of the Year at the 8th Annual Hospice du Rhone celebration (Pasa Robles, USA), in recognition of outstanding contribution to Rhone Wines. d'Arenberg was awarded the inaugural wine.com Hall of Fame in August 2000". d'Arenberg is continuing to produce wines under many unique labels like The Custodian Grenache, The Twentyeight Road Mourvedre, The Coppermine Road Cabernet Sauvignon and The Dead Arm Shiraz underlining Chester and d'Arry's commitment to the region. They have superbly renovated these 19th Century homestead incorporating one of Australia's finest cellar door tasting areas and a restaurant, aptly named "d'Arry's Verandah" both with imperious views overlooking McLaren Vale and Willunga escarpment to the Gulf of St Vincent. d'Arenberg is indeed a McLaren Vale tradition to be proud of.

Address: Osborn Road MCLAREN VALE 5171	
Phone: (08) 8323 8206 **Fax:** (08) 8323 8423	
Email: winery@darenberg.com.au	
WWW: www.darenberg.com.au	
Owner: Osborn Family **Winemaker:** Chester Osborn	
Est: 1912 **Vine Ha:** 150 **Cases:** 100,000	

Public Hours: 10am-5pm, daily
Principal Varieties: Riesling, Sauv Blanc, Chard, Marsanne, Rousanne, Viognier, Chambourcin, Grenache, Shiraz, Mourvedre, Cab Sav, Petit Verdot
Principal Wines   **Potential**

Wine	Potential
Stump Jump Red & White	1-4 yrs
The Dry Dam Riesling	10+ yrs
The Broken Fishplate Sauv Blanc	1-4 yrs
The Olive Grove Chardonnay	5-10 yrs
The Noble Riesling (375mL)	5-10 yrs
Peppermint Paddock Sparkling Chamb.	1-4 yrs

d'Arenberg Restaurant

d'Arry's Verandah Restaurant has the dress circle view of McLaren Vale and the hills beyond out to the waters of St Vincents gulf · its awesome.

In early 2000, it came under the wing of two top restauraters Pip Forrester and her brother Michael Ewers. Pip and Michael have both had lives enriched by food and wine, since they were tiny tots. A couple of years after Pip was born her parents took off to Paris, her father worked at the world headquarters of UNESCO. Michael was born in Paris and for these formative five years of their lives, the two young children were exposed to truly great food, their mother who now lives in McLaren Vale, had a great interest in cooking and as Michael put it "we absorbed knowledge about food by osmosis". After Paris they took off to Tehran spending a good deal of time with their French born tutor and often in the kitchen with the household staff. From there they went to New York a couple of years and then back to Paris. Pip studied in England, whilst Michael went to a bilingual school in Paris. It wasn't until they got back to Sydney in 1968 they really realised the cultural differences in their homeland, the charred roast with three veggies (cooked to death). A few years later they found themselves running a trendy restaurant on the northshore serving Pizza, Pasta and other Italian style food. Pip was in the front of the house, with Michael cooking. About this time Michael made a career choice, he became a film cinematographer working around the world, whilst Pip got her B.A. in Teaching.

Pip married and moved to South Australia, it was during the Dunstan Era a cultural, food and wine renaissance. Whilst working in her chosen profession at Flinders University successfully, Pip was drawn to hospitality food and wine. She spent some time in charge of the front of the house at "The Barn" restaurant and gallery in McLaren Vale.

In 1988 the historic Salopian Inn came up for sale, a few years after it had started out as a restaurant. Pip bought it and made it a huge success, turning it into one of Australia's best and most awarded restaurants, over the last 13 years. She has also catered for many of McLaren Vale's most important events. For the last 4 years she has also handed the catering at the large BRL Hardy function areas at Reynella.

In 1997 Pip called brother Michael in Sydney she had just got the Hardy's contract and the McLaren Vale Bushing Festival was coming up, she was "flat-out" so Michael came over and helped out, their natural teamwork and intuitive working relationship impressed them both, so Michael stayed moving his own family over some months later.

d'Arry's Verandah started its life several years ago focussing on fine dining. Pip and Michael are in the process of changing the direction a little, with innovative seasonal dishes, vineyard platters and the like, cutting edge cuisine and very regional foods, at Café prices and with a casual atmosphere. One will be able to follow their tasting, at the beautiful d'Arenberg tasting room next door, with a relaxed affordable meal inside or outside under the giant sails, wherever you are you will have a fantastic view, fine food and a memorable experience, not to mention the great d'Arenberg wines to complete the picture.

Dennis of McLaren Vale

Peter Dennis makes some of the great wines of the region, from his own vineyards located a little way from his cellars, on the eastern side of the valley.

All the Dennis wines have heaps of honest McLaren Vale character and intensity, they represent some of the best value in terms of quality and value for money prices, you will find anywhere in Australia.

Peter's father passed away a few years ago, Egerton Dennis was one of the real gentlemen of the wine industry.

During the 1960's he and Jim Ingoldby created McLaren Vale Wines Pty. Ltd. Based at Ryecroft, to market the wines of the district. Their vision in fact predated the wine boom. In 1969 Dennis's Daringa Cellars was borne.

Egerton's vineyard had been established in the early 1900's on the eastern side of the valley and still is the only source of grapes used, to make wines under the Dennis label.

The winery is located right on the edge of the town just opposite McLarens on the Lake.

The wines are all made by Peter who is ably assisted by his wife Margaret.

Dennis was one of the pioneers of chardonnay in the region and their full-flavoured reds are excellent value, the traditional shiraz and cabernet sauvignon have now been joined by an excellent merlot and a spicy grenache made from old bush vines. Dennis is the quiet achiever of the region and worth seeking out.

Address: Kangarilla Road	Est: 1970 Vine Ha: 22 Cases: 5,000-10,000	Shiraz	5-10 yrs
MCLAREN VALE 5171	Public Hours: 10am-5pm, daily	Cabernet Sauvignon	5-10 yrs
Phone: (08) 8323 8665 Fax: (08) 8323 9121	Principal Varieties: Shiraz, Cabernet	Merlot	5-10 yrs
Owner: Dennis Family	Sauvignon, Merlot, Chardonnay, Sauv Blanc	Chardonnay	2-10 yrs
Winemaker: Peter Dennis	Principal Wines Potential	Sauvignon Blanc	2-5 yrs

Fox Creek Wines

One of McLaren Vales more recently established wineries has already forged an enviable reputation, particularly with its red wines, notably its Reserve Shiraz.

Fox Creek is owned by Jim & Helen Watts, their son viticulturist Paul Watts and John & Lyn Roberts. Paul Watts began planting in 1985 with chardonnay followed by many other varieties, modern trellising, hand pruning and expert viticultural management, has ensured Fox Creek have truly great grapes for their winemaking. Jim's daughter Sarah, a Roseworthy wine graduate, married the 1988 Roseworthy Dux "Sparky" Marquis. They made the first vintage at Fox Creek in 1994. The first vintage Shiraz won the Annual McLaren Vale Bushing Trophy in 1994. The wine has since gone on to win a number of other gold medals. Their 1995 Reserve Shiraz was also very successful, being the highest pointed one year old shiraz in the prestigious Qantas Great Australian Shiraz Challenge, a National event open to all winemakers and all vintages. The 1996 Reserve Shiraz continued the success, it won two Trophies and was named the Penguin Wine Guide Shiraz of the Year for 1997. The J.S.M. Shiraz Cabernet Franc (named after the original settler on the property James Stanley Malpas) recently won the trophy for best red blend at the 2000 Adelaide Show. Fox Creek released

their first merlot a 1997 vintage which was awarded a trophy as best merlot in the 1998 Adelaide Show.

Fox Creek also has an excellent Reserve Cabernet Sauvignon and other interesting wines including "Vixen", a Sparkling Cabernets/Shiraz. The new winemakers at Fox Creek Daniel Hills and Tony Walker are already making their mark and commissioned the new 1,000 tonne winery for the 2000 vintage. A huge barrel maturation cellar has also just been commissioned.

The attractive 100-year-old stone cottage which houses the cellar door has an open fire for winter and glorious views of the vineyards. Come and picnic beside the lake and enjoy the large variety of bird life on the property.

The vineyard with its Scott Henry trellising seems to be making better wines each vintage. Why not become a Fox Creek preferred customer cardholder and receive their regular newsletter and great wine offers?

		Principal Wines	Potential
Address: Malpas Road WILLUNGA 5172	**Est:** 1995 **Vine Ha:** 60	Reserve Shiraz	10+ yrs
Phone: (08) 8556 2403 **Fax:** (08) 8556 2104	**Cases:** 35,000	Reserve Cabernet Sauvignon	10+ yrs
Email: sales@foxcreekwines.com	**Public Hours:** 11am-5pm, daily (except Good	JSM Shiraz-Cabernet Franc	5+ yrs
WWW: www.foxcreekwines.com	Friday & Christmas)	Merlot	5+ yrs
Owners: Jim, Helen & Paul Watts,	**Principal Varieties:** Cabernet Franc,	Vixen Sparkling Shiraz-Cabernet	5+ yrs
John & Lyn Roberts	Cabernet Sauvignon, Chardonnay, Merlot,	Verdelho	3 yrs
Winemakers: Daniel Hills & Tony Walker	Sauvignon Blanc, Semillon, Shiraz, Verdelho		

Brewery Hill

The classic old ironstone building that houses the Brewery Hill winery was constructed more than 150 years ago by George Manning. In its early days it was used as a grain mill and stables. On the Hill behind the winery was one of South Australia first breweries, which operated from 1853-1867.

The Brewery Hill Cellars are unique, the building is actually built with the walls following the slope down the hill, rather than the normal stepped construction, it is striking indeed.

Owners Peter Huffam and Bill Bell are very experienced winemen, having successfully run the St Francis Winery for many years. They concentrate on producing small parcels of premium varietal wines from leading South Australian Regions.

In the Cellar Door they have large Oak Barrels and vats filled with a variety of Fortified wines, you are welcome to bring your own containers, to fill and pay for by the litre at very good value prices.

Brewery Hill also specialise in customised client labels for wines and minatures of Port, they can also arrange delivery Australia wide.

At Brewery Hill you'll be looked after with great personal service, if you can't make it to this characterful winery, you can join their free mailing list.

Address: Clivers Road MCLAREN VALE 5171 **Phone:** (08) 8323 7344 **Fax:** (08) 8323 7355 **Owners:** Peter Huffam & Bill Bell	**Est:** 1990 **Cases:** 15,000 **Public Hours:** 9am-5pm weekdays, 10am-5pm weekends	**Principal Wines** Peter William Brewery Hill

Dyson Wines

It would be hard to find someone more happy with his lot in life than Allan Dyson. Allan started winemaking back in 1965 at Seaview, when Ben Chaffey was still at the helm, after which he travelled over to the Hunter Valley in 1970 and made wine for Hollydene for six years.

By 1977 Allan was back in McLaren Vale making wine at Middlebrook. The same year, he started planting vines on his estate near the coast, not far from Australia's first "naturist" beach. He planted all the vines by hand himself and knows everyone of them intimately. In fact, in his own words "I've got 10,220 reasons to be happy".

Looking extremely young for his years, Allan tends his vines, makes the characterful wines, including a methode champenoise which he ferments in the cellars, and even does his own disgorging, all by himself.

One would think he was too busy to say 'G'day'; not Allan - he loves people, and it shows in his wines which are bursting out with flavour and character. His lovely garden and tasting cottage also make this a memorable visit.

Address: Sherriff Road MASLIN BEACH 5170 **Phone:** (08) 8386 1092 **Fax:** (08) 8327 0066 **Email:** dyson@dove.net.au **Owner/Winemaker:** Allan Dyson	**Est:** 1977 **Vine Ha:** 6.5 **Cases:** 1,500 **Public Hours:** 10am-5pm, daily **Principal Varieties:** Cabernet Sauvignon, Chardonnay, Sauvignon Blanc, Pinot Noir, Pinot Primeur	**Principal Wines** Cabernet Chardonnay Handmade Methode Champenoise Fortified Liqueur Chardonnay	**Potential** 10 yrs 3-6 yrs 2-5 yrs 2-4 yrs

Edwards & Chaffey

Recently renamed Edwards & Chaffey, the Seaview Cellars have a long history. In 1850, George Manning planted vines on his newly purchased Hope Farm in McLaren Vale. A winery and cellars were built 40 years later.

The name Seaview was coined by the owners Ben Chaffey and his partner friend Henry Edwards, who found they could see St Vincents Gulf from various hillcrests on the property.

The winery itself sits attractively, surrounded by vines in the centre of a bowl-shaped valley, splendidly landscaped with vines. Seaview is one of Australia's best known and best selling wine brands. The Seaview Cabernet Sauvignon has developed a reputation as the 'value for money' cabernet of Australia, and is also often awarded gold medals in Australian and International wine competitions.

The humble shiraz is also an extraordinarily good wine for its price - look out for it. The Seaview whites have an added a lustre in recent times, with the chardonnay winning a prestige International award in 1994. Its rich melon and stone fruit flavours and great balance are consistent from year to year.

The hidden gem of the Seaview whites has been their semillon sauvignon blanc. Again a wine to look out for. A milestone in 1994 was the release of three super premium wines under the Edwards and Chaffey banner, a shiraz, a cabernet sauvignon and a chardonnay all made from the best grapes available in McLaren Vale in an "absolutely no expense spared" style. They are sensational wines and have been joined by an exquisite pinot chardonnay methode champenoise 'Edwards & Chaffey'.

Visiting the Edwards & Chaffey cellars is a great way of catching up with McLaren Vale's history and some of its best wines.

Fernhill Estate

In the heady days of the wine boom back in 1975, the gregarious Wayne Thomas and his late wife Pat, began a winery opposite Ryecroft and just down the road from Ingoldby. Fern Hill became a much-respected label.

Early in 1994 the Thomas's sold the winery to dynamic Sydney Wine entrepreneur and former Barossa boy Terry Hill, proprietor of the Hill Wine Group.

Small scale production; low quantities of super premium wines are being handcrafted.

At present these include a chardonnay fermented in French oak and a semillon fermented and aged very briefly in American oak. The reds comprise a cabernet sauvignon plus a shiraz both made in a no-compromise fashion from selected vineyards in the McLaren Vale Region.

The accent in the cellar door is also very much on the wine quality with a very personal and educational approach. The cellar door is relaxed, set under shady trees amongst flowers and ferns and ideal setting for tasting the fine wines with their elegant fern inspired labels.

		Principal Wines	Potential
Address: Ingoldby Road MCLAREN FLAT 5171	**Est:** 1975 **Vine Ha:** 20 **Cases:** 7,500	Chardonnay	5-7 yrs
Phone: (08) 8383 0167 **Fax:** (08) 8383 0107	**Public Hours:** 10am-5pm, daily except	Semillon	5-7 yrs
Email: info@fernhill.com.au	Christmas Day and Good Friday	Shiraz	7-10 yrs
Owner: Terry Hill & Family	**Principal Varieties:** Chardonnay, Semillon,	Cabernet Sauvignon	7-10 yrs
Winemakers: Grant Burge & Brian Light	Cabernet Sauvignon, Shiraz		

Hugh Hamilton

Hugh Hamilton is a 5th generation member of the family that first planted vines in South Australia. Wine has always been an integral part of his life.

Describing how he feels about wine Hugh quotes Theophile Malvezin -

"Wine is made to be drunk as women are to be loved. Profit by the freshness of youth or the splendour of maturity. Do not await decrepitude".

Hugh feels wine is not a mysterious substance only understood by the chosen few, but rather is an integral part of our daily lives to be enjoyed along with fine food and good company, wine must be affordable and drinkable. These are the values that help him shape the character of his wines.

Hugh has three main vineyards, the original McLaren Vale "Church Block",

the "Black Sheep Block" and "Barry's Block". All are located south of the township of McLaren Vale, within 500 metres of each other. They are part old vines and part replanted. Red varieties grown are Cabernet Sauvignon, Shiraz, Merlot and Sangiovese, planted in 1999. White varieties are Chardonnay and Verdelho. "Barry's Block is a recent acquisition where three other varieties have been planted in 2000, these are the French · Viognier and Petit Verdot, and the Spanish · Tempranillo.

Hugh is now in a position where he can satisfy all his requirements for grapes, other than a small parcel of Chardonnay which he purchases from the Adelaide Hills each year.

Hugh's recently constructed cellar door is set amongst the vines, on the highest point of the property. It's circular structure with glass panels has panoramic views over the valley and coastline.

Address: McMurtrie Road MCLAREN VALE 5171 **Phone:** (08) 8323 8689 **Fax:** (08) 8323 9488 **Email:** hugh@hamiltonwines.com.au	**WWW:** www.hamiltonwines.com.au **Est:** 1991 **Winemaker:** Hugh Hamilton **Vine Ha:** 18.5 **Public Hours:** 10am-5pm Mon-Fri, 11am-5pm	weekends & public holidays **Principal Varieties:** Cab Sav, Merlot, Shiraz, Chardonnay, Sangiovese, Verdelho

Haselgrove Wines

Haselgrove moved into their brand new winery on the eve of vintage 2000. The impressive new cellars feature much equipment designed by Nick Haselgrove who is the well credentialled winemaker. His grandfather, Ron Haselgrove put Mildara on the map many decades ago and his great uncle Colin was a winemaking legend at Hardy's and then Reynella.

Nick won the 'Bushing King' title in 1993 with his 1992 Futures Shiraz. This is Haselgrove's premium wine sourced from their own vineyard in McLaren Vale. Since 1984 this wine has been pre-sold to the winery's mail-order customers.

The Haselgrove wines are certainly among the best in the region. The cellar door, is situated at the new winery which is worth seeing,

cleverly built into the hillside with large insulated storage cellars chocked full of maturing red wines, in top quality imported oak casks.

Haselgrove also have extensive vineyards in the new Wrattonbully

district of the limestone coast in the south east of South Australia. They are producing some great reds from this region as well as their traditional excellent McLaren Vale range.

Address: Sand Road MCLAREN VALE 5171 **Phone:** (08) 8323 8706 **Fax:** (08) 8323 8049 **Email:** winery@haselgrove.com.au **WWW:** www.haselgrove.com.au **Winemaker:** Nick Haselgrove **Est:** 1981 **Cases:** 50,000	**Vine Ha:** 13, 300 Ha contracted vineyards **Public Hours:** 9am-5pm, weekdays; 10am-4pm, weekends **Principal Varieties:** Chard, Merlot, Shiraz, Viognier, Cab Sav, Grenache, Sauv Blanc, Tempranillo **Principal Wines** **Potential**	H Shiraz Cabernet Merlot Shiraz Chardonnay Sauvignon Blanc Bentwing Reds Cab & Shiraz Viognier	10+ yrs 2-5 yrs 2-5 yrs 12 mths 5-8+ yrs 1-2 yrs

Hardy's Chateau Reynella

One of South Australia's first settlers, John Reynell obtained vines in South Africa en-route to Australia and planted them in the rich soil of Reynella in 1838.

By 1845, he had completed the country's first underground cellar, now known as the 'Old Cave', which, due to its historical importance, has been classified by the National Trust.

After the death of John Reynell, the business became a family company but unfortunately, two world wars exacted a toll on the male line that resulted in the appointment, in 1953, of Colin Haselgrove as managing director of the winery. Under Colin's guidance, Reynella released some excellent red and fortified wines. The Reynella Alicante Flor Sherry, in particular, was one of Australia's best. Similarly, the Vintage Reserve clarets and burgundies released during the 1950's were remarkable wines and generally drastically underpriced. Colin Haselgrove remained at Reynella after the take-over by Hungerford Hill in 1970. The following year he produced what he considered to be his best vintage and indeed the 1971 Vintage Port and Cabernet Sauvignon are today, considered to be amongst Australia's greatest.

Thomas Hardy & Sons purchased the company in 1982 and spent millions of dollars restoring the Chateau, winery and other buildings to their former glory. Having moved their head office and bottling cellars to Reynella. In 1992 Berri Renmano Limited and Hardys merged to form BRL Hardy Limited and the old Reynell homestead houses the company's executive offices and boardroom.

In addition to the careful restoration of the buildings, the century-old botanical gardens planted by John Reynell, have also been rejuvenated and this has resulted in Chateau Reynella becoming one of the most beautiful wineries in Australia.

Chateau Reynella has long been known for its exquisite, long-living vintage ports and its mellow tawny port styles (Old Cave Port). These wines continue to be leaders in their styles and successfully promote the name of Reynella throughout the world.

The winery now produces wines made exclusively from McLaren Vale fruit. The "Basket Pressed" range of reds feature · Shiraz, Cabernet Merlot and Cabernet Sauvignon. The winemakers have worked closely with the viticulturists monitoring cropping, irrigation and trellising methods to obtain the highest quality fruit. Small open fermenters and the ability to maintain small batches of individual vineyard wine until the blending stage gives maximum flexibility in the quest for quality. The basket press is used to press the skins following fermentation; this process results in fine tannin structure without the bitterness sometimes associated with mechanical pressing. Chateau Reynella reds are big, rich, generous wines typical of McLaren Vale style.

There is also an award winning McLaren Vale Chardonnay in the range that is barrel fermented, stored on lees and a portion undergoes malolactic fermentation resulting in a rich, vanillin, buttery chardonnay style.

The Chateau Reynella renaissance has seen not only the restoration of a great winery, but also the development of a new elegant label along with the launching of an excellent range of table wines. The return to good management and proficient winemaking has seen the restitution of this winery to its well-deserved position as one of the country's leading premium wine producers. The beautiful Reynella complex is only 20 minutes drive south from the Adelaide GPO.

The winery has catering facilities for large functions, seminars and conventions, the Thomas Hardy room forming part of the complex. A visit whilst you are in Adelaide is virtually obligatory.

Hardy's Tintara McLaren Vale

At 20 years of age, Thomas Hardy arrived in the new colony of South Australia in 1850 with thirty pounds in his pocket. Within 40 years he had built Australia's largest wine company. Along the way, he somehow found time to travel overseas several times, write a book on fruit and wine growing in California, keep extensive diaries and scrapbooks, and educate those people with whom he worked.

Within weeks of his arrival in South Australia, Thomas Hardy obtained a year's work with Walter Reynell at Reynella Farm. Later, while employed on a grazing property at Normanville he became gripped with gold fever and left for the Victorian gold fields, where he was promptly arrested for mining without a licence. Deciding there were easier ways of making money, Hardy persuaded his former employer to let him drive 400 head of cattle to the gold fields, where they were butchered and sold to the miners. This venture was so successful that Hardy repeated the exercise and was then able to return to Adelaide and purchase a property on the banks of the Torrens, which he called 'Bankside'. Vines, fruit and olive trees were planted, cellars were constructed and as soon as the vines began to bear fruit, winemaking commenced.

Hardy's wine quickly found ready markets both locally and in England, giving him the necessary assets to purchase the Tintara Vineyard Company in 1876. The cellars of this new property were full of barrels of rich burgundy, which Hardy sold in England, recouping his purchase price in one year. The company steadily expanded with additional purchases of a bottling plant at Mile End, champagne cellars at Currie Street in Adelaide and a disused flour mill in McLaren Vale.

By 1893, Thomas Hardy controlled the largest wine company in Australia. Thomas Hardy died in 1912, leaving his son Robert in charge of the company. Currently, fourth generation member, Sir James Hardy OBE is on the board of directors of the parent company, the successfully merged BRL Hardy. In 1903, fire destroyed the cellars at Bankside. This fire occurred on a Sunday and as no fire brigade was

available to attend, the fire was extinguished by pumping wine onto the flames. Some of the charred casks remain and are used in the maturation of fortified wines at McLaren Vale.

In 1968, Hardy's established extensive vineyards in the Padthaway area. The purchase of the Emu Wine Company in 1976 included the Western Australian Houghton Winery and a large winery at Morphett Vale. The next acquisition was Chateau Reynella in 1982 - ironically, a return of the name Hardy to the winery where Thomas Hardy began his working life in Australia more than 130 years before. In 1992 Thomas Hardy & Sons merged with Berri Renmano Limited to form Australia's second largest wine group, BRL Hardy Limited.

Currently, the flagship wine in Hardy's extensive portfolio is Eileen Hardy. Named after the widow of

Tom Mayfield Hardy, the first of this line, a 1970 McLaren Vale Shiraz, was released in 1973 to honour her 80th birthday. Eileen Hardy Chardonnay was launched in 1986 to partner the Shiraz.

In 1994 'Eileen' was joined at the Hardy's red wine pinnacle by the Thomas Hardy Coonawarra Cabernet Sauvignon. Other Hardy products that are household names in Australia are - Sir James Cuvee Brut and Brut de Brut, Siegersdorf Rhine Riesling and Chardonnay, the Nottage Hill range and Black Bottle Brandy.

During 1994/95 large sums of capital were spent expanding the Company's premium vineyard holdings. Hoddles Creek vineyard in the Yarra Valley of Victoria was acquired to supply sparkling wine fruit for the Sir James range including the new Sir James Vintage, a premium Australian sparkling wine. New vineyards in Padthaway, Wrattonbully, Furner (near Robe), Coonawarra and Langhorne Creek will supply fruit for existing and planned new labels under the Hardy banner.

New premium wines recently introduced are the Bankside range - Shiraz, Grenache and Chardonnay and the Padthaway range of unwooded Chardonnay and Cabernet Sauvignon. The Banrock Station range supporting the environment has been a huge success.

Hardy's are continuing to produce and market wines of which the company founder would be proud.

The beautiful ironstone Tintara winery in the heart of McLaren Vale, incorporating the town's original mill, has been lovingly restored during the last decade and features the fabulous Driden Art Gallery and Fleurieu Showcase. A pilgrimage to this shrine of wine is a must for any visitor to McLaren Vale.

The Hamilton Wine Group

faith in the potential of McLaren Vale. Burt spent the last 18 years of his long life lending Richard a hand, working right up until his death in his 90th year in 1994 after a record 71 vintages. From this extraordinarily long commitment to the wine industry by the Hamiltons, Richard Hamilton has re-established the proud tradition founded by his ancestors.

All Hamilton Wines are home grown on Richard's 4 historic vineyards in the McLaren Vale and Willunga. The range consists of 3 red table wines including Gumprs Block Shiraz from old vines planted on limestone and ironstone, Hut Block Cabernet from old dry grown vines planted in 1947, and Lot 148 Merlot from the first planted Merlot in McLaren Vale. All are stylish wines showing the richness and flavour of McLaren Vale to perfection.

Among the whites the characterful Signature Chardonnay leads the way with the Slate Quarry Riesling and a tangy Semillon Sauvignon Blanc. A Viognier is soon to be released.

Richard Hamilton has been instrumental in the revival of the Rhone varieties Grenache and Shiraz in McLaren Vale. To this end Hamilton produce a family of limited release and highly sought after Single Vineyard Reserve Wines (aka SVR) when the quality is right.

These include The Burton's Vineyard Grenache-Shiraz, a truly great drop made from very old bush vines planted by Burton; The Centurion Shiraz vintaged from historic vines planted in 1892 - and now well over 100 years old; and the unique Marion Vineyard Grenache Shiraz from the last remaining suburban vineyard planted by Richard's grandfather Frank Hamilton in 1907.

Currently the Hamilton wines are vintaged at Leconfield. However a new McLaren winery and cellar door facility with tourist access to the wine making and maturation processes is soon to be built.

Richard Hamilton's wine interests have expanded greatly over recent years including "Hamilton" at McLaren Vale and "Leconfield" at Coonawarra.

A noted Plastic Surgeon, Richard Hamilton is both great great grandson and namesake to one of the founders of South Australia's wine industry. His great great grandfather was Mr Richard Hamilton 1st who established the Hamilton Ewell Vineyard in 1837 at Marion now a suburb of Adelaide, just one year after the settlement of the colony of South Australia. After several generations of innovative Hamiltons including Henry, Frank,

Sydney and Burton a marvelous wine business and dynasty was seemingly entrenched, only to see the old Hamilton firm decline.

Richard Hamilton relaunched the Hamilton name in 1972 by building his McLaren Vale winery and releasing a sensational 1972 Willunga - McLaren Vale Shiraz from 80 year old vines and a unique barrel fermented Riesling, both from historic Hamilton family McLaren Vale Vineyards planted in 1892. Richard planted the districts' first Chardonnay vineyard in 1975.

Richard's late father, Burton, affectionately known as 'Burt', was a dedicated vigneron with enormous

Address: Main Road WILLUNGA 5172	Est: 1837, relaunched 1972 Vine Ha: 60	Principal Wines	Potential
Phone: (08) 8556 4705 Fax: (08) 8556 2868	Cases: 30,000	Centurion Shiraz	10+ yrs
Email: hwg@hamiltonwines.com	Public Hours: 10am-5pm, Mon-Sat; 11am-	Marion Vineyard Grenache Shiraz	10+ yrs
WWW: www.hamiltonwinegroup.com.au	5pm, Sun & Public Holidays	Hut Block Cabernet	5-8 yrs
Owner: Dr Richard Hamilton,	Principal Varieties: Cabernet Sauvignon,	Burton's Vineyard Grenache Shiraz	10+ yrs
The Hamilton Wine Group	Chardonnay, Grenache, Merlot, Riesling,	Gumprs Block Shiraz	5-8 yrs
Winemaker: Philippa Treadwell & Tim Bailey	Sauvignon Blanc, Semillon, Shiraz, Viognier	Lot 148 Merlot	5-8 yrs

Hugo Wines

I might start this expose on Hugo Wines with a few words of philosophy from winemaker John Hugo – "the McLaren Vale region is a region of small winemakers, people who know their craft – ply it well – I firmly believe that we have to be specialists, people who pick a path in wine production and then follow that course".

John Hugo's philosophy is basically to use his own grapes from his 50-acre vineyard, established by his father, Colin in 1950.

John is a fastidious viticulturist and the quality of his grapes are renowned in the region. He first began work in the family enterprise in 1970 and established the winery in 1982. He planted another 18 acres of vines, which came into

bearing in 1997. His reds, a cabernet sauvignon, grenache and a shiraz, are rich and full-bodied in the tradition of the region and there is also a chardonnay, and more recently, a sauvignon blanc. The tawny port from the 'Solero' started by John in the 1970's is worth the trip to the cellar door to find.

The winery is the highest in the McLaren Vale and has a wonderful panoramic view. This has been well capitalised on by the Hugo's who have built a splendid cellar door and hospitality complex displaying local artist paintings, which opened in 1999. The cellar door construction with the earthy red ochre colour of the McLaren Vale ironstone soil and the lovely gardens surround it make it one of the best in the region.

Address: Elliott Road MCLAREN FLAT 5171	5pm, Sat	Hugo Chardonnay	3-4 yrs
Phone: (08) 8383 0098 **Fax:** (08) 8383 0446	**Principal Varieties:** Cab Franc, Cab Sav,	Hugo Unwooded Chardonnay	2 yrs
Owner: John & Liz Hugo **Est:** 1982 **Ha:** 31	Chardonnay, Grenache, Sav Blanc, Shiraz	Hugo Cabernet Sauvignon	5-6 yrs
Winemaker: John Hugo **Cases:** 10,000	**Principal Wines** **Potential**	Hugo Sauvignon Blanc	2 yrs
Public Hours: 10.30am-5pm, Sun-Fri; Noon-	Hugo Shiraz 5-6 yrs	Hugo Tawny Port	

Kangarilla Road

In 1997 Kevin O'Brien took over the Cambrai Winery which had begun its life in 1975, founder Graham Stevens was very successful with his red wines and won three titles as McLaren Vales bushing king for producing the best wine of the vintage.

Kevin has had a mercurial career in wine, he completed his studies in Oenology in 1984 and joined the dynamic duo of Mark Swann and Robert Hesketh. He assisted them in planning their very successful vineyard Cuppa-Cup, in the Limestone Coast Region near Bordertown, he also made wine for Mark's very successful export brands and for the burgeoning interwinery speculative wine market. He traveled the world assisting Swan and Hesketh in their international wine interests.

Kevin succesfully handled various other consulting wine making commissions, before becoming the

General manager of the Australian Wine Export council in 1997, he played a pivotal role, in the enormous growth of Australian wine sales on overseas markets.

Kevin has carried his innovative methods into the operations of his own winery, he renamed "Kangarilla Road vineyard and winery". The vineyard has been partially replanted and now boasts two new exciting varieties Zinfandel and Viognier. The initial few vintages of Zinfandel, a variety enormously successful in California, have been stunning, rich

strong and spicy wines it is a variety ideally suited to McLaren's climate. Kevin is making very supple reds, which are well balanced and although full bodied, havegood aging potential drink very well in their youth.The first vintage Viognier from the 2001 vintage is being released as a white it's a vibrant wine.

The Kangarilla Road winery has been rebuilt and includes a large area which hosts many events and corporate functions, lookout for this dynamic well credentialed winery, a great addition to the region.

Address: Kangarilla Road MCLAREN VALE 5171 **Phone:** (08) 8383 0533 **Fax:** (08) 8383 0044	**Winemaker:** Kevin O'Brien **Est:** 1997 **Public Hours:** 9am-5pm, Weekdays; 11am-5pm, Weekends & Public Holidays	**Principal Varieties:** Cabernet Franc, Chardonnay, Viognier, Zinfandel, Cabernet Sauvignon, Shiraz

Maxwells Wines

Mark and Ken Maxwell established Maxwell Wines in 1979. Maxwell's new home is truly remarkable built into the chalk hill on the southern fringes of the McLaren Vale township.

Mark Maxwell planned this bold move for many years even planting a hedge maze some ten years ago which should be ready as a visitors amazing entrance in a year or so. The pathway from the maze leads to an ancient

mushroom cave, which Mark is connecting, into the lower level barrel ageing cellars. The winery complex has an impressive function area, terrace and fully equipped kitchen.

During the nine months of the year between vintages, winery equipment usually remains idle. Maxwell's however, utilise their winery throughout these months for the production of mead (honey wine). Meads are released, including a standard mead, which makes a delightful cool mixed drink; a spiced mead, which can be served hot; and a liqueur mead, which contains a higher degree of alcohol and is a delicious after-dinner drink.

Mark Maxwell's dynamic drive and innovative style will make Maxwell Wines' future exciting indeed, in their amazing cellars that just seem to have mushroomed from nowhere!!

Address: Olivers Road MCLAREN VALE 5171	**Cases:** 6,000 wine, 6,000 mead	Unwooded Semillon	1-10 yrs
Phone: (08) 8323 8200 **Fax:** (08) 8323 8900	**Public Hours:** 10am-5pm, daily	Chardonnay	1-6 yrs
Owner: Maxwell Family	**Principal Varieties:** Shiraz, Cabernet	Cabernet Merlot	1-3 yrs
Winemaker: Mark Maxwell	Sauvignon, Merlot, Sauvignon Blanc	Lime Cave Cabernet Sauvignon	7-10 yrs
Est: 1979 **Vine Ha:** 8	**Principal Wines** **Potential**	Ellen Street Shiraz	8-15 yrs

Middlebrook Wines

Middlebrook has recently been beautifully restored and enhanced to make it one of the most beautiful winery complexes you will find in Australia.

Joseph Cogno from the well known Cogno wine family, is the new owner. The Cognos also have "Cobbitty Wines" in New South Wales, Joseph has done a superb job in redeveloping this fine property, he has been in the McLaren Vale region for a number of years and was Manager of the large Maglieri Winery. Joseph certainly has a feel for the vineyards and wines of the district and an obvious flair in the aesthetics of winery design.

The new Middlebrook complex includes a spacious tasting area with floor to ceiling windows overlooking a landscaped, tuscan style terrace garden, lawns and the classic rotunda. Later this year Middlebrook will open a superb Art Gallery at the rear of the Cellar Door area.

The Middlebrook winebar and restaurant is in the centre of the building with a long vine covered verandah where one can also eat. On the Sand Road entrance is the Medlow Confectionery factory producing unique fruit gels and chocolates.

Middlebrook is surrounded by its own 15 acre vineyard which Joseph has put considerable work into, reviving the old vines which are now producing wonderful fruit full of character.

Middlebrook also have an 80 acre vineyard called Highcrest a little further into the Hills near Kangarilla.

The Middlebrook Estate wines are great examples of the rich full flavours produced by the rich ironstone soils in the Willunga scarp area. Apart from his range of premium table wines Joseph is now producing the famous Cogno Lambrusco at Middlebrook. This is one of the largest selling Lambruco's in Australia.

Joseph is also reviving a unique liqueur created some 25 years ago by David Hardy the then proprietor. This is a combination of fortified wine blended with cumquat at a strength of around 23% alcohol, it certainly is a delicious after dinner drink and great base for cocktails and long drinks. Joseph found a couple of barrels of the original blend beautifully mature and has used this as his base for the new blend. I tasted it recently and if anything he has improved on my uncle's old blend.

Middlebrooks history goes back to 1880 when wine pioneer Thomas Hardy bought and planted a fertile block of land between two streams east of McLaren Vale, calling it "Glen Hardy". Ironically after a number of changes of ownership it was purchased in 1978 by Thomas's great grandson David and his two sons Christopher and John, they renamed the property Middlebrook.

When you are in the McLaren Vale region, it's a absolute must to search out Middlebrook, although it's not far from either McLaren Flat or McLaren Vale - it is a little tucked away, but make sure you find it, it's well worth the trouble.

Address: 43 Sand Road McLaren Vale 5171	Est: 1947 Vine Ha: 16 Cases: 30,000	Middlebrook Semillon	2-5 yrs
Phone: (08) 8383 0600 Fax: (08) 8383 0557	Public Hours: 10:30am-4:30pm daily	Middlebrook Sauvignon Blanc	2-5 yrs
Email: mail@middlebrookestate.com.au	Principal Varieties: Barbera, Chardonnay,	Middlebrook Cabernet Sauvignon	5-10 yrs
WWW: www.middlebrookestate.com.au	Riesling, Sauvignon Blanc, Shiraz, Cabernet	Middlebrook Chardonnay	5+ yrs
Owner: Cogno Brothers	Sauvignon, Grenache	Middlebrook Shiraz	5-10 yrs
Winemaker: Joseph Cogno	Principal Wines Potential	Highcrest Grenache Shiraz	5+ yrs

Middlebrook Restaurant

Middlebrook's Restaurant and wine bar is a truly special complex, its airy Tuscan style and classic furnishing gives one a sense of grandeur, whilst still maintaining a relaxed atmosphere. With seating capacity of around 250 people including the vine covered verandah, it is also an ideal setting for a wedding or other large function. The landscaped lawns can happily house a large marquee and the Rotunda amongst the vines has a very special atmosphere.

The Wine Bar is also complemented by a cigar bar and there is a large boardroom ideal for a special formal dinner for up to 30 people or as a business conference facility.

Middlebrook have just secured the services of one of South Australia's great chefs Andrew Davies, who was the founding chef at d'Arry's verandah restaurant in the region, gaining for it an enviable reputation. Andrew was also highly successful as chef at the Flying Fish restaurant at Port Elliot, he trained and worked overseas in leading hotels and

restaurants. Andrew makes his own Pate with port liqueur its sensational, his steamed mussels with fresh tomato puree, shallots, white wine and cream is a delicious dish, some

of the offerings have a definite east meets west flavour it's a great cultural as well as culinary treat to eat at Middlebrook.

Medlow Confectionery

To complete a great complex at the Sand Road entrance is the Medlow Confectionery business of David Smith, great great grandson of pioneer Samuel Medlow who arrived in the Colony of South Australia in 1845. David certainly has his ancestors pioneering spirit and has put together a unique place to create his confectionery, where you can view the confectioners as they go about their craft. Medlow fine Gels are a new and delicately textured confectionery, which David has created from the finest pectin (a pure derivative of fresh fruits). The Gels deliver a clean fresh and delightful palate experience full of natural fruit flavours. The Gels are produced in two varieties, sugar dusted and choc coated. They have already found themselves in famous places, such as the premier Hyatt Hotel chain.

Medlow is a fascinating place to visit, after viewing the gels being made you can taste them and make your selection from the mouthwatering display. A great way to finish your tour of Middlebrook truly contented.

McLarens on the Lake

In the early 1980's, entrepreneur Jack Weinart built a splendid complex on the outskirts of McLaren Vale, on the road to McLaren Flat, which he called 'Hazelmere Estate'.

The complex included a modern winery, a la carte restaurant, function and souvenir facility along with 30 large attractive accommodation suites. The Victorian/Australian architecture reminds me somewhat of the grand old wineries at Rutherglen, reminiscent of a bygone era.

The whole property is sensitively and beautifully landscaped around a man-made lake, all the huge old redgums have been retained and the cry of the corellas at dawn and dusk is a pleasant reminder that one is amongst nature in a beautiful country region.

The bird life on the lake is multitudinous, ducks, swans, cygnets, even seagulls happily share this large expanse of water as it blends more naturally into the environment each year. The name 'Hazelmere' was changed some years ago to 'McLarens on the Lake'.

All this aside, the McLarens on the Lake complex is idyllic and runs like a well-oiled machine.

The Courtyard Conservatory Restaurant is superb, the more formal McLarens Room Restaurant and in the seminar function area where weddings abound are magnificent.

The McLarens Complex has recently been purchased by local identity, winemaker Steve Maglieri, all the accommodation suites have been redecorated and refurnished.

Steve is also in the process of entirely redesigning and re-equipping the winery and to launch his new wine brand - Serafino (in fact his true Italian christian name). Steve still owns and runs his own extensive vineyards in some of the regions best locations. So I am sure some stunning wines are not long off.

Marienberg Wines

Ursula Pridham became Australia's first woman winemaker back in the late 1960's when she started her own winery at Happy Valley.

After 25 years of excellent winemaking and hard work she decided to step back a little. Sydney wine dynamo, Terry Hill, who was born in the Barossa, saw an ideal opportunity and late in 1990 he bought the Marienberg brand.

Coinciding with this move, he also bought the old 'Limeburners Cottage', opposite The Barn Restaurant in McLaren Vale. The Marienberg range has expanded, with six table wines led by a very elegant chardonnay and a rich round cabernet sauvignon. These are complemented by a non-vintage pinot noir/chardonnay methode champenoise under the name 'Nicolle' after one of Terry Hill's daughters, plus a 12 year old Tawny Port. The wines are from selected vineyards in the McLaren Vale area and made under the watchful eye of Grant Burge, an old school days chum of Terry's.

The Marienberg labels really stand out with their art deco inspired look.

I have been singularly impressed by all the wines, particularly their very approachable style, delivering clean crisp flavours, mouthfilling but extremely well balanced. The restrained use of top quality oak in some of the wines is particularly well handled.

Marienberg have done a fine job with the 'Limeburners Cottage' which is now a fine café, restaurant and wine bar. The glassed in Conservatory style, with French doors is perfect for alfresco dining and the outdoor patio areas are resplendent with trees and flowers.

Next door is the Marienberg cellar door where one can try all their excellent wines. Marienberg is a true haven for the wine traveller to drop into as you enter or leave McLaren Vale.

Address: 2 Chalk Hill Road MCLAREN VALE 5171	Est: 1966 Vine Ha: 35 Cases: 32,000	Principal Wines	Potential
Phone: (08) 8323 9666 Fax: (08) 8323 9600	Public Hours: 10am-5pm daily except	Reserve Chardonnay	5-7 yrs
Email: info@hillwine.com.au	Christmas Day and Good Friday	Reserve Shiraz	5-7 yrs
Owner: Terry Hill & Family	Principal Varieties: Cabernet Sauvignon,	Reserve Grenache	5 yrs
Winemakers: Grant Burge & Brian Light	Chardonnay, Grenache, Shiraz	Reserve Cabernet Sauvignon	5-7 yrs

Merrivale Wines

Merrivale with its pretty name and picturesque location was always a Cinderella winery searching for the fairy godmother.

Jack Starr started up the winery in the renaissance days of the nearly 1970's and got off to a flying start. The winery travelled through some troubled waters until its saviour came along in the form of the innovative winemaker Brian Light and his effervescent wife Kay.

Between them, they really rejuvinated Merrivale. Much of the 26 acre vineyard was either revived or replanted. In August 1997 Gerard Industries purchased Merrrivale.

The new team of Merrivale includes General Manager, Fred Howard a dynamic young man who has worked

in the wine industry overseas, and at local wineries such as Woodstock.

The new Winemaker is John Ketley, an innovative young winemaker. With the input from the powerful Gerard Industries the winery complex at Merrivale, is undergoing an upgrade and expansion program in the vineyard and the winery. The varieties planted include Pinot Noir and the exotic Muscat of Alexandria along with regional Stalwarts Chardonnay, Shiraz and Cabernet Sauvignon.

Merrivales range of wines includes the highly respected Tapestry label, which boasts a Riesling Bin 228 from McLaren Vale's high country, Chardonnay Bin 288, a Shiraz Bin 338 and a Cabernet Sauvignon Bin 388. The Tapestry concept is to emphasise the various elements of

the viticulture and oenology process, which when interwoven produce a work of art. The wines are 100% McLaren Vale from the very best available grapes, grown in Merrivale's own vineyards, which include significant holdings in the renowned Bakers Gully area, towards Kangarilla and by selected growers. The wines all have great structure flavour and the ability to improve with bottle maturation. They are rich and complex and typically McLaren Vale.

Merrivale also have a splendid barbecue and picnic area as well as a playground for children. Elevated high above the vineyard and McLaren Vale and the Gulf of St Vincent. To be in the Merrivale Cellar door, with a glass of wine in hand, it's an exhilarating feeling.

Address: Olivers Road MCLAREN VALE 5171	**Winemaker:** Pam Dunsford **Cases:** 15,000	Tapestry Chardonnay 2-5 yrs
Phone: (08) 8323 9196 **Fax:** (08) 8323 9746	**Public Hours:** 11am-5pm, daily	Tapestry Spaetlese Muscat of Alexandria 1-3yrs
Email: wineclub@merrivale.com.au **Est:** 1971	**Principal Varieties:** Shiraz, Cab Sav, Chard	Tapestry Cabernet Sauvignon 5-10 yrs
WWW: www.merrivale.com.au **Vine Ha:** 10	**Principal Wines** **Potential**	Tapestry Shiraz 5-10 yrs

Normans Wines

Jesse Norman arrived in Australia from England in 1851 and very soon purchased 18 acres of land near the town of Thebarton, on which he planted vines.

A winery was later established at Underdale and another vineyard planted at Sturt. Both vineyards prospered. Unfortunately with the spread of Adelaide's urban areas the company's land was purchased by the South Australian Housing Trust. As a result 130 acres were purchased at Gawler River, and planted to vines. This vineyard still exists today, and is now known as Evanston Estate. Normans continued to develop slowly until 1982 when the company was bought by the Horlin-Smith family. Having had a century-long association with the hospitality industry, the Horlin-Smith's were already well acquainted with many aspects of winemaking and marketing. Jim Irvine, long-time family friend and creator of Hardys famous Siegersdorf Rhine Riesling, was asked to join the management team.

Following the modernisation of the Underdale winery a new high quality range of wines was developed which quickly won wide acclaim.

The facilities at Underdale were inadequate when coping with greater volumes. So, Normans purchased the Coolawin winery and adjacent 10 acre vineyard at Clarendon, high in the Adelaide Hills.

Renamed Normans Clarendon Winery, the new property was soon fitted with the most modern winemaking equipment and ranks with the most efficient wineries in the state. All of Normans wines are now made at Clarendon. Located near the crest of Chandlers Hill, Normans winery commands magnificent views of the nearby coastline and the rolling hills of Clarendon. High altitude and onshore winds combine to bring the cool climate ideal for the production of premium table wines. Consequently, the vineyard next to the winery is planted with classic grape varieties · cabernet sauvignon, shiraz and chardonnay.

Normans have purchased a large parcel of land called "Eringa Park" near Kangarilla, this has some wonderful old bush vine grenache vineyards and hundreds of acres of new vines have been planted, mainly red varieties, these are just coming into bearing.

The Normans Chandlers Hill range represents great value for money and the exclusive Chais Clarendon range of three wines, a shiraz, a cabernet sauvignon and a chardonnay, rank on the very highest rung of Australia's wines.

Normans is now a public company. The influx of much needed capital has catapulted the company to even greater heights.

Address: Grants Gully Road CLARENDON 5157	Public Hours: 9am-5pm Mon-Sat, 10am-5pm	Old Vine Shiraz & Grenache	3-5 yrs
Phone: (08) 8383 6138 **Fax:** (08) 8383 6457	Sat, 11am-5pm Sun & Public Holidays	Lone Gum	2-4 yrs
Email: info@normanswines.com.au	**Principal Varieties:** Chardonnay, Verdelho,	Jesse's Blend	2 yrs
WWW: www.normanswines.com.au	Chenin Blanc, Cabernet Sauvignon, Merlot,	Chais Clarendon	4-7 yrs
Winemaker: Rebecca Kennedy	Shiraz, Pinot Noir	Encounter Bay	3-5 yrs
Est: 1853 **Vine Ha:** 230 **Cases:** 500,000	**Principal Wines** **Potential**	Chandlers Hill	2 yrs

⤜The Olive Grove McLaren Vale⤛

Nestled high above the pretty township of McLaren Vale, just 40 minutes drive from Adelaide, lies The Olive Groves.

The history of olives in McLaren Vale goes back to my own great great grandfather, Thomas Hardy, who planted olive trees on all the roads and spare land on his property and advised his neighbors to do likewise. The beautiful olives, olive oil and other products were not only a great adjunct to the table but added a welcome extra source of income. Some of the century - old trees can be seen on this property.

The Olive Groves is a family run business managed by Steve and Pam Seymour.

The Kalamata table-olives are hand-picked and pickled over 12 months using the traditional Greek method, whereby fresh water is used to remove the acid; followed by a relatively low-salt brine and vinegar mixture. Olive Grove olives have been described as *"the best in Australia"*. The cold pressed, award-winning, extra virgin oil is processed in the traditional way using woven mats as well as a more modern in-line method.

In the summer months visitors can come and sample the fruits of the harvest in the Gourmet Specialty Cottage, along with locally made jams and preserves, arts and crafts. Tours of the factory are available by

previous appointment. In front of the cottage is a gorgeous gazebo, which is obtainable for hire for functions.

In recent years The Olive Groves has diversified and is now producing premium wine to complement the olives and take advantage of the McLaren Vale soils and mild temperate climate, which lend themselves to the production of full-bodied red wine. Seymour Estates Shiraz will be a wine to look out for in the not-to-distant future!

Why not complete your visit to McLaren Vale with this unique experience and make the magic connection between the olive and the vine.

Address: Warners Road MCLAREN VALE 5171
Phone: (08) 8323 8792 **Fax:** (08) 8323 8833
WWW: www.olivegroves.com.au
Owner: Waren Seymour
Principal Wines
Seymour Estates Shiraz

Patritti Wines

Giovanni Patritti arrived in Australia in the early 1920's from the Italian region of Piedmont. In 1926 he founded his wine business at Dover Gardens, now a superb of Adelaide, crushing his first grapes in the late 1920's. The family tradition has continued and the much expanded winery is still in operation today under the ownership of his widow, three sons and daughter.

During the 1950's urban expansion claimed part of the vineyard, when the State Housing Trust, compulsorily acquired the land. The remaining vineyards were acquired in 1962 for a high school.

The Patritti family began establishing vineyards in the McLaren Vale region, during the 1960's, including Aldinga and Blewitt Springs. As an added business since 1977 the winery has produced non alcoholic sparkling fruit juices, including dark grape juices, golden muscat, medium white and a sparkling apple juice. These are proving extremely popular in Asia and Middle East markets.

Geoff Patritti who runs the production recounted how legendary wine transport guru Frank Sheppard's first job was transporting a Gollin & Schmidt press from Penfolds to Patritti. Geoff is an engineer by profession and worked at the Loxton Winery from 1966-1969 before starting at the family winery.

The winery has undergone much updating over recent years with the installation of a new Bucher press, new fermentation facilities, new tanks and a sophisticated refrigeration system for the white wine production. Patrittis produced mainly fortified and bulk wine up until a decade ago but today most of the production is premium bottled table wines.

The third generation of the family is now involved. Daughter Ines's son James Mungall is working in the winery as well as studying Oenology at the Waite Campus of the University of Adelaide.

Patritti also employ a winemaker with a real international background Lado Uzunashvili from the Russian Georgian wine region, studied winemaking for 6 years in Moscow. He worked in the Georgian Wine Institute before immigrating to Australia and has worked for Angoves and Miranda Wines as well as at the Australian Wine research institute before coming to Patritti.

Geoff Patritti remembers back to 1968/69 when Shiraz prices went from $55 to $110 per tonne and his father thought the wine industry would collapse, today with Shiraz prices around $2000 per tonne, local and export sales are booming, Patritti's are pleased they planted more vineyards back in the 1970's.

Patritti's are innovative, they also have a range of de-alcholised white, red, rose and a sparkling brut, made by a multi step process to remove the alcohol from the wine and preserve the aromas and flavours, they are very good indeed and a bonus for health and those on a low calorie diet, this brand "Billabong" has been very successful in the Muslim markets of Asia and the Middle East.

Whilst the focus at Patritti is on premium table and sparkling wines, they still make a fortified range including vermouth and marsala. At their two cellar doors, the Dover Gardens winery and Reynella, you can also purchase Brandy and a range of spirits.

Patritti are proud of their heritage and progressing positively into the future.

Address: 13-23 Clacton Road DOVER GARDENS 5048 Phone: (08) 8296 8261	Fax: (08) 8296 5088 Winemaker: Geoffrey Patritti Est: 1926 Vine Ha: 80	Public Hours: 9am-6pm, Mon-Sat Principal Varieties: Cabernet Sauvignon, Shiraz, Pedro, Grenache, Riesling

Pertaringa Wines

Geoff Hardy and Ian Leask purchased their first vineyard in 1981. It was planted mainly with shiraz grapes and later other varieties were grafted to old rootstocks These included chardonnay, sauvignon blanc, white frontignac, semillon, cabernet sauvignon, cabernet franc and pinot noir. The vineyard now has quite extensive plantings and the Pertaringa grapes are sought after by a number of major wine companies

A cabernet sauvignon from the 1990 vintage was their first commercial effort and an outstanding wine. Each year a cabernet sauvignon, shiraz, sauvignon blanc and an enticing barrel fermented semillon are produced. A liqueur frontignac completes the range and is blended from the base wine that dates back to 1980.

Pertaringa won the inaugural South Australian Vineyard of the year in 1990 and their wines have proven to be as successful as the vineyard. The Pertaringa wines are now exported to more than eight countries and have received outstanding reviews from the likes of James Halliday in Australia, Decanter Magazine in the UK and The Wine Spectator in the US. The Pertaringa shiraz has been flying high in Qantas Business Class.

A visit to the pretty vineyard setting and the cosy cellar door on the corner of Hunt and Rifle Range Roads offers the opportunity to taste and purchase the exceptional range of wines. The wines are made in small quantities and can be hard to find.

Ian Leask and Geoff Hardy have become significant players in McLaren Vale winemaking and grape growing. Their vines will continue to improve as they age and are expected to last at least 100 years while the wines will continue to offer the intense and luring varietal flavours of McLaren Vale.

Address: Corner Hunt & Rifle Range Roads MCLAREN VALE 5171 **Phone:** (08) 8323 8125 **Fax:** (08) 8323 7766	**Email:** wine@pertaringa.com.au **WWW:** www.pertaringa.com.au **Est:** 1980 **Vine Ha:** 33 **Cases:** 6,000	**Public Hours:** 9am-5pm, weekdays; 11am-5pm, holiday weekends **Principal Varieties:** Cab Sav, Semillon, Shiraz

Penny's Hill

Tony Parkinson is a successful Adelaide businessman who leaves nothing to chance. He and his wife Susie have set up a picture book vineyard at Penny's Hill on the eastern side of the McLaren Vale Region.

The climate is slightly cooler than the valley floor and the vines have been planted east west rather than north south by renowned viticulturist David Paxton. The summation of all these elements and Tony's meticulous care, gives grapes which not only have rich varietal fruit flavours but also lots of spice and pepper.

The Penny's Hill Shiraz is already becoming somewhat of an icon, both the 1997 and 1998 have received huge critical acclaim, from as lofty a source as Robert Parker from the Wine Advocate in the USA, some of his comments on the 1997

"A big succulent peppery black fruit scented and flavoured Shiraz, which promises to drink well for 6-8 years - "90 points".

Penny's Hill also produce a great Red called "Specialized" a Shiraz Cabernet/Merlot, a vintage Shiraz (port style) fortified in 500 ml bottles and a Chardonnay of some force. Ben Riggs the well respected Wirra Wirra winemaker makes them all superbly.

The Parkinsons have also bought the historic old Ingleburne homestead on the Main McLaren Vale Willunga Road. It was constructed from hard hewn stone in 1954 by Thomas Goss, who bought the property after returning from the Victorian

Goldfields with 1,500 pounds, a real fortune in those days. The Parkinsons purchased the property in 1998 from Keith Rowland, Thomas Goss's great great Grandson, whose family had farmed the property for almost 150 years.

Ingleburne is being completely redeveloped as a cellar door, function area and gallery. A stone wall is being built around the property. Ingleburne will host conferences, weddings and other functions plus regional food, wine, art and music events. Renowned local artist David Dridan is helping establish the gallery. The Salopian Inn just up the road will provide the food. Ingleburne will also have accomodation to allow wine industry visitors and invited artists to stay and work in the region. Penny's Hill is nobly enriching the region, with its fine wines and cultural philanthropy.

Address: Willunga Road MCLAREN VALE 5171 **Phone:** (08) 8556 4460 **Fax:** (08) 8556 4462 **Email:** bdarley@pennyshill.com.au	**WWW:** www.pennyshill.com.au **Winemaker:** Ben Riggs **Est:** 1988 **Vine Ha:** 42.5 **Cases:** 6,000 **Public Hours:** 10am-5pm, daily	**Principal Wines** "Specialized" (Shz/Cab/Mer) Penny's Hill Shiraz Penny's Hill Chardonnay	**Potential** 8-10 yrs 8-10 yrs 4-6 yrs

Frederick Wilkinson came to South Australia in 1879 from Manchester in England to work for the Bank of South Australia. He decided banking was not for him and in 1884 he purchased 160 acres at McLaren Flat.

Planting began in 1886, with the Cellars in readiness for the 1895 vintage, including a large underground cellar where 800 gallon vats kept the temperature of the fermenting wines in check, long before the days of refrigeration. Much of the original winery remains intact today.

Wilkinson's only son, Lewis, lost his life in the First World War and the winery was sold in 1919 to James Ingoldby, a 23 year old survivor of the war, and his father-in-law T.C. Walker, chairman of the Lion Brewery and the General navigation Co. They expanded the vineyard area to 165 acres, with the help of the stalwart Aubrey "Aub" Chapman who had remained on from Wilkinson's days.

The wines, mainly full-bodied reds from the rich ironstone-riddled clay soils, went from strength to strength.

Ingoldby's eldest son tragically died in the Second World War, but his younger son, Jim, a budding artist, survived several years in the Air Force and came back to finish his arts degree, but the pull of Ryecroft was too strong. By 1970 with "Ege" Dennis's help he had built Ryecroft into a specialised premium red producer, they then sold the business, the new owners didn't really understand the quality wine business, it was not until Rosemount wines purchased Ryecroft in the early 1990's that the winery's direction was redefined and a program of expansion initiated.

Today, under winemaker, Charles Whish and viticulturist, Paul Buttery, Ryecroft is growing quickly in the making and marketing of the highest possible quality table wines. During vintage it's a wonderful heady experience seeing and smelling all that fermenting red in the traditional open fermenters. It is the most comforting and uplifting experience any human being could wish for.

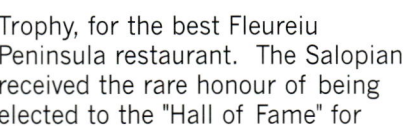

Salopian Inn

The historic old building on the corner of the main South Road and McMurtrie Road as you travel south from McLaren Vale was commissioned as an inn way back in 1856.

During the 1970's The Salopian (the name for someone born in the English County of Shropshire) was purchased by David Hardy with a view to resuscitating it as an historic inn.

The licensing laws changed however and David sold the property, which was finally restored and turned into a restaurant and wine cellar.

The Salopian has forged a name as a high quality, friendly restaurant and deserves every bit of praise heaped upon it. Proprietor since 1988 Pip Forrester has turned it into a top rung Australian Restaurant, in 1999, after three years winning the American Express Restaurant Awards

Trophy, for the best Fleureiu Peninsula restaurant. The Salopian received the rare honour of being elected to the "Hall of Fame" for 2000, 2001 and 2002.

The classic old colonial windows look out on vineyards in all directions. The décor is rustic but classy, brother Michael is also extremely personable and is the other half of the management team. They run a tight ship with great support from the local wineries. The view from the restaurant over the valley of vines is spectacular.

Treat yourself to a meal at the Salopian, I'm sure it will be a memorable one.

The Barn

The Barn was Australia's first hospitality house in a wine region when it was created back in 1970 by David Dridan, one of Australia' foremost artists, and David Hardy, great-grandson of Thomas Hardy, the wine pioneer who had in fact owned what was the old stage stop for changing horses between Adelaide and Victor Harbor.

The gorgeous whitewashed thatched-roof cottage sits serenely on the Chalk Hill road corner as one enters

the main street of McLaren Vale coming from Adelaide.

The entrance is a quaint and

characterful gallery, warmed in winter by a lovely log fire. The exhibitions are always changing and full of interest. The main restaurant opens up into a vine-covered courtyard, protected from inclement weather. Leading off the restaurant is the marvellous cellar, where one can wander and choose from a superb array of the region's wines.

As you enter, a warm welcome greets you from proprietors Daryl Moyle, who made the Three Brothers Arms at Macclesfield a culinary success, and his partner Phillip Taylor. Downstairs is the cellar function room, which has hosted many a fine wine and food function over the years. It's even complete with its resident spirit, a kindly soul from the last century, who has made her appearance from time to time over the years; the most vivid, to comfort a child crying on the steps, she materialised in a beautiful Victorian Regency dress. I always look forward to my next pilgrimage to this special place.

Simon Hackett

Simon Hackett is steeped in wine history. In 1860 his great great uncle attended Roseworthy Agriculture college, his father was a graduate of the inaugural Roseworthy Oenology course in 1938.

Simon grew up in the Barossa Valley, his father was for many years a director and general manager of the Tarac Wine distillery, the family lived alongside the Saltram winery at Angaston. At 18 years of age he decided to become a winemaker and joined the team at the Saltram Winery, serving his apprenticeship under the watchfull eye of master winemaker Peter Lehmann.

In 1970 Simon worked a vintage in the Hunter Valley in NSW, before returning to Saltram for another couple of years.

In 1973 Simon moved to McLaren Vale working with famous winemaking team of Grant Burge and Ian Wilson at Southern Vales Winery (now Tatachilla). After 8 years at Southern Vales Simon became the Chief Winemaker.

In 1984 Simon decided to launch his own wines, I remember conducting a wine tasting of his first release wines with him in Melbourne that year and being most impressed with them.

Simon sources his grapes from his own vineyards and long term contract growers, mainly with very old vines, in the McLaren Vale, Barossa Valley and the Adelaide

Hills. These include a small Shiraz vineyard near Angaston planted in the 1890's. His legendary Foggo Road vineyard in McLaren Vale is planted with Grenache, Cabernet Sauvignon, Shiraz in 1924. The remainder of Simon's McLaren Vale grapes come from vineyards, near Willunga, some in the foothills area. Simon has also established a 10 acre vineyard in the Adelaide Hills where he has planted Cabernet Sauvignon and Shiraz, these are just coming into bearing in 2001.

Simon has made his last few vintages in his new winery, beautifully situated on the last rise

as you enter the McLaren Vale region from Adelaide, situated just off the Main South Road, he has spectacular views over the valley and St Vincent's Gulf. The cellar door is magnificently appointed and has a long arched verandah looking out over the vines.

Simon's two whites a Semillon and a complex Chardonnay come from the Brightview vineyard in the heart of the Barossa Valley.

His McLaren Vale Shiraz and McLaren Vale Cabernet Sauvignon, both have generous fruit flavours and are particularly good value.

Simon produces two Reserve limited release wines, the "Anthony's Reserve" Shiraz and the "Foggo Road" Cabernet Sauvignon. They are all from old vines and extremely concentrated and complex, he uses top class imported oak barriques to mature them in, these are wines to seek out for the long haul, for super premium wines, they are extremely well priced. Simon has recently added an "old vine" Grenache to his range.

Simon Hackett wines have been extremely well received in England the USA where much of his wine is sold, he is certainly a quiet achiever, who doesn't say too much but lets his wines talk for him, they say plenty and you should seek them out.

Address: Budgens Road MCLAREN VALE 5171
Phone: (08) 8323 7712 **Fax:** (08) 8323 7713

Email: simon@simonhackettwines.com.au
Winemaker: Simon Hackett **Est:** 1981

Principal Varieties: Cab Sav, Grenache, Petit Verdot, Shiraz, Chardonnay, Merlot, Semillon

Pirramimma

Situated on the Willunga Plains, the Pirramimma property was purchased by Mr A.C. Johnston in 1892. Pirramimma is still wholly owned and run by the Johnston family, Alex being the General Manager and Charles Sturt University graduate Geoff, the winemaker. Pirramimma's first wine was made in 1900; the original cellars being constructed two or three years prior to that date.

The early success of Pirramimma was due to the company's excellent fortified wines and full-bodied reds. Geoff has also built up a commercial vineyard of petit verdot from a small number of original cuttings.

The recent bottlings of this distinctive red wine have been successful with gold and silver medals being awarded at recent Australian wine shows.

Most of the Johnston wines until the early 1970's were sold in bulk, a great proportion being exported to England.

Pirramimma released their first rhine riesling in 1979 and their first chardonnay two years later. Both of these wines are full flavoured and well balanced.

A semillon produced from Geoff's Kuitpo vineyard has been added to the range showing the delicate fruit intensity from this cool region in the Adelaide Hills.

Pirramimma and Johnston Family have large vineyard holdings in the region and pick the best grapes for their own label before selling the rest of the crop to other premium makers.

Just prior to the 1995 vintage, they completed a large and innovative barrel ageing cellar, but into the hillside above the winery was constructed with rammed earth. The very thick walls offer ideal insulation for the cellaring of the wine, its light ochre colour also blends happily into the hillside. The cellars have since been greatly expanded.

In a very sensible move, the family converted a number of 1,000 gallon French oak vats, built by Babidge Coopers in 1904, into 65 gallon hogsheads (the Babidges did this job too). The Shiraz, bottled to celebrate Pirramimma's centenary, went into these hogsheads. The wine was one of the best reds ever made in McLaren Vale. Pirramimma are undoubtedly on the move and we the wine drinkers are the beneficiaries.

Address: Johnston Road MCLAREN VALE 5171	5pm, Sat; 11.30am-4pm, Sunday and holidays	Pirramimma Cabernet Sauvignon	5-10 yrs
Phone: (08) 8323 8205 **Fax:** (08) 8323 9224	**Principal Varieties:** Shiraz, Semillon, Cab Sav,	Pirramimma Cabernet Merlot	5-10 yrs
Winemaker Geoff Johnston	Chard, Merlot, Petit Verdot, Grenache, Sav Blanc	Pirramimma Chardonnay	2-5 yrs
Est: 1935 **Vine Ha:** 170 **Cases:** 20,000	**Principal Wines** **Potential**	Pirramimma Stock's Hill Semillon/Chardonnay	2-5yrs
Public Hours: 9am-5pm, weekdays; 11am-	Pirramimma Shiraz 5-10 yrs	Pirramimma Stock's Hill Classic Riesling	2-5 yrs

Shottesbrooke

Nick and Chris Holmes have created a splendid home for their Shottesbrooke wines near McLaren Flat. Their sensitively and cleverly conceived modern winery blends beautifully into its vineyard setting nestled under the nearby hills. With its brick-paved courtyard adorned with flowers and native shrubs, this is one of the most impressive new wineries I've seen. There's a delightful picnic area by a tree-lined creek with shelter provided by a restored pickers' hut.

Nick graduated from Roseworthy in 1971 and spent the next decade winemaking in Australia and overseas. In 1981 he bought a property at Myponga on the Fleurieu Peninsula south of Adelaide. He named it Shottesbrooke after the parish in England, where his grandfather was vicar. Nick planted 20 acres of cabernet sauvignon, sauvignon blanc, merlot and malbec and released his first wines in 1984. He and Chris since have expanded to include 50 acres around their McLaren Flat winery planted to shiraz, merlot and chardonnay. Today the family-run Shottesbrooke is a true boutique winery producing elegant white and red wines of great quality and value. It's a must on the McLaren Vale wine circuit. While there don't forget to stock up on the merlot - it's a knockout!

Address: Bagshaws Road MCLAREN FLAT 5171	**Est:** 1981 **Vine Ha:** 32	**Principal Wines**	**Potential**
Phone: (08) 8383 0002	**Public Hours:** 10am-4.30pm, weekdays;	Cabernet/Merlot	5-8 yrs
Fax: (08) 8383 0222	11am-5pm, weekends & public holidays	Merlot	2-3 yrs
Email: shottesbrooke@senet.com.au	**Principal Varieties:** Sauvignon Blanc,	Shiraz	3-6 yrs
WWW: www.shottesbrooke.com.au	Cabernet Sauvignon, Merlot, Chardonnay,	Sauvignon Blanc	1-2 yrs
Owner/Winemaker: Nick Holmes	Shiraz	Chardonnay	2-4 yrs

Scarpantoni Wines

Dom Scarpantoni arrived in Australia as part of the post second world war immigration movement into this country. He secured a job at the vineyards of David Hardy and shelter in a shed in the backyard of Bob Hagley, manager of the Hardy's Tintara Winery in the middle of the township of McLaren Vale. Dom shared his meager quarters with his best friend, who had come out from Italy with him. Dom decided it was time to get married, his friend offered to help, showing him a photograph of one of his sisters, Paula, so it happened that one of the happiest and fruitful partnerships in the wine industry began.

Dom is an incredibly hard worker and blessed with a most helpful and pleasant nature. Gradually, as he established himself in his new land, he also began planting his own vineyards at McLaren Flat. During the 1960's and 70's he supplied grapes to Hardy's and others but as the wheel of fortune of wine accelerated he decided to extend his own family winemaking enterprise and build his own winery which he opened in 1979.

Today Scarpantoni is an expanding premium wine business and Dom has taken a little step back, leaving the day-to-day business to his two sons Michael and Filippo and daughter Mirella. All fortunately have inherited the charm and hardworking nature of their parents.

Many times I have enjoyed their special brand of sincere hospitality, an impromptu country style meal prepared by Dom's wife Paula, always a culinary treat, accompanied by the most delicious, truly opulent reds you could taste.

Often we have reminisced over the renaissance of McLaren Vale over the last few decades, it's a very special feeling and a sense we have all enjoyed something very strong in the welding of the cultures of Europe and Australia and the richness this has brought to not only our wine and food, but to our whole nation.

Long live the Scarpantoni's and all these European families who have enriched Australia so much.

Address: Scarpantoni Drive MCLAREN FLAT 5171 Phone: (08) 8383 0186 Fax: (08) 8383 0490 Email: scarpantoni.wines@bigpond.com.au WWW: www.scarpantoni-wines.com.au Owner: Domenico, Paula, Michael & Pilippo Scarpantoni	Winemaker: Michael & Filippo Scarpantoni Est: 1979 Vine Ha: 32 Cases: 15,000 Public Hours: 10am-5pm, weekdays; 11am-5pm, weekends Principal Varieties: Cab Sav, Shiraz, Chard, Sauv Blanc, Gamay, Merlot, Riesling	Principal Wines	Potential
		Cabernet Sauvignon	10-15 yrs
		Shiraz	10-15 yrs
		Sauvignon Blanc	1-2 yrs
		School Block	10 yrs
		Gamay	2-3 yrs
		Black Tempest Sparkling Burgundy	3-6 yrs

Tatachilla Winery

Tatachilla has made enormous progress during the last 6 years since its relaunching in 1995 and recently became part of the Banksia Wine Group listed on the Australian Stock Exchange. Tatachilla are definitely sailing on the right course.

The events that were to create Tatachilla began late in the last century, when Horace Pridmore bought land at McLaren Vale and using wattle slabs built a small cellar in 1901. His brother Cyril joined him from England; they bought a property in the main street of the town and constructed stone cellars, calling the winery 'The Wattles'. The original foundation stone was unearthed during recent renovations and has been restored to its rightful place.

Since the launch of the modern day Tatachilla in March 1995 the team headed by CEO, Keith Smith have gathered accolades from around the globe. Gold Medals in Australia and London represent the commitment to excellence in both viticulture and winemaking.

Tatachilla Winery has quickly claimed its place in the Australian wine industry earning recognition in many forms. In December 1996 prestigious food and wine magazine Vogue Entertaining nominated Tatachilla as

'Winery of the Year'. Next was a scoop in the pool of medals at the London International Wine Challenge, of the six wines entered all were awarded medals including a Gold Medal for Partners. In September 1997 Tatachilla Winery was named National Winner of the Federal New Exporters awards by the Australian British Chamber of Commerce, a month later Senior Winemaker Michael Fragos was crowned Bushing King for his Tatachilla 1996 McLaren Vale Chardonnay. In 1999 both Justin McNamee and Michael Fragos were crowned Bushing King for the 1997 McLaren Vale Cabernet Sauvignon and in 2001 Tatachilla Winery picked up the Tucker Seabrook award for the Best Wine exhibited on the National

Wine Show circuit for the previous 12 months.

Michael Fragos was brought up in McLaren Vale and literally grew up amongst the vines in his father's vineyard. Surrounded by grape growers and winemakers it wasn't a difficult decision to become a winemaker. A Bachelor of Science degree and a Graduate Diploma in Winemaking, provided Michael with the technical ability to oversee the entire wine production at Tatachilla. However his passion is for the backbone red varieties of McLaren Vale; Grenache and Shiraz. Careful vineyard selection, small batch ferments and fastidious blending enable him to craft wines that capture the essence of McLaren Vale. Michael is quick to point out the support from winemaker Justin McNamee, success has not come in isolation.

Michael's experience over the last eight vintages has shown him where the best fruit is. He spends much time in the vineyards, works with the growers and keeps all parcels of grapes separate at harvest during vintage. He also spends time setting up trials of small batch ferments. "Our aim at Tatachilla is to make a wine that has great complexity and flavour rather than pure varietal character. We want to create a wine that the consumers will find challenging". Michael has certainly more than achieved his objectives; Tatachilla's stunning success bears this out!!

Address: 151 Main Road MCLAREN VALE 5171	Est: 1901 Vine Ha: 20 Cases: 250,000	McLaren Vale Chardonnay	3-5 yrs
Phone: (08) 8323 8656 Fax: (08) 8323 9096	Public Hours: 10am-5pm, Mon-Sat; 11am-	"Growers"	1-3 yrs
Email: enquiries@tatachillawinery.com.au	5pm, Sunday and public holidays	"Partners"	2-4yrs
WWW: www.tatachillawinery.com.au	Principal Varieties: Chardonnay, Cabernet	McLaren Vale Merlot	3-6 yrs
Owner: Banksia Wines Ltd	Sauvignon, Shiraz, Merlot	McLaren Vale Shiraz	5-10 yrs
Winemaker: Michael Fragos, Justin McNamee	Principal Wines Potential	McLaren Vale Cabernet Sauvignon	8-10 yrs

Tyrrell's Rufus Stone

Tyrrells involvement in the wine industry goes back to 1858 in the Hunter Valley of New South Wales. Wine Legend Murray Tyrrell, who ably ran the Company from 1959 until recent years, unfortunately passed on late in the year 2000. Son Bruce has been at the helm now for a number of years and has presided over a considerable expansion in the Company's operations.

Tyrrells have long had close associations with the McLaren Vale wine region and have over the years purchased wine to assist in their blended brands such as the old winery range. This association has eventually led them to purchasing their own vineyards.

In 1997 the Tyrrell family launched "Rufus Stone" to market wines from their vineyards in McLaren Vale and Coonawarra in S.A. and Heathcote in Victoria. The wines from these vineyards were already going into their "Old Winery" range, but the family realised that the exceptional varietal wines should have their own banner.

Tyrrells searched their family history which goes right back to William the Conqueror in 1066 and all that!! King William the 2nd (Rufus) son of William the Conqueror was believed to have been killed by an errant arrow fired by Sir Walter Tyrrell whilst on a stag hunt in the new forest in the year 1100. King William was not a popular King but Sir Walter was nonetheless obliged to flee England to France in fear of his life. The Rufus Stone marks the site of the incident and is now the foundation stone for the Tyrrells' new venture.

The Rufus Stone vineyard in McLaren Vale was purchased in 1994. It is situated on the rising Eastern slopes of the valley, just north of Willunga in the cooler part of the region, 97 acres are now under vine. A new 1000 tonne crushing facility was constructed in time for the 1997 vintage. The juice is transported to the Tyrrells Ashmans Winery in the Hunter Valley for fermentation, maturation and bottling.

The vineyards were first planted with Chardonnay and Sauvignon Blanc but are now 70 per cent Red with Cabernet Sauvignon, Shiraz, Merlot and pinot Noir plantings. There is also a small quantity of Riesling planted.

The Rufus Stone range receives the super premium fruit with the old winery and Twin Wells wines receiving the rest.

Paul Matthews who has been with Tyrrell's for some years now runs the vineyard and crushing facility with great skill and efficiency.

Rufus Stone wines have struck their target true, just like the arrow from Sir Walters Bow.

Wirilda Creek

Kerry Flanagan and Karen Shertock opened the Wirilda Creek Winery in 1993 and it is really an extension of their lives.

Kerry has a rich and varied background in the wine and hospitality areas. He graduated from Roseworthy in 1980, having spent some time in the Penfolds red wine cellars during his course. He worked at Wirra Wirra during the time Brian Croser and Petaluma were involved in the winemaking. This experience was followed by a stint in the Hunter, then he returned to McLaren Vale and assisted at Hazelmere, Coriole, Woodstock and the old Southern Vales (now Tatachilla).

Kerry has a definite flair in the hospitality side of wine, and saw the Old Salopian Inn as an ideal opportunity to combine the two. Having secured the Salopian, he proceeded to dig out the cellars and launched the McLaren Vale Wine Centre. Kerry and gifted chef Russell Jeavons created a fine reputation for the lovely venue.

Kerry sold the Salopian and took off overseas, travelling the wine regions of Europe and the USA. On returning, he and Karen set about building Wirilda Creek. The building of rammed earth fits discreetly into the vineyards and the casual alfresco dining area is a delight. They also have several excellent rustic style accommodation suites, all tastefully appointed with full facilities including a country kitchen.

The wines are equally as impressive. Wirilda Creek is a place not to drive past.

Address: RSD 90 McMurtrie Road MCLAREN VALE 5171 **Phone:** (08) 8323 9688 **Fax:** (08) 8323 9260 **Owners:** Kerry Flanagan & Karen Sherlock **Winemaker:** Kerry Flanagan **Est:** 1992/93　　　**Cases:** 2,000-3,000	**Vine Ha:** McLaren Vale, 3; Kangaroo Island, 3 **Public Hours:** 11am-5pm, daily **Principal Varieties:** Shiraz, Cabernet Sauvignon, Malbec, Merlot, Chardonnay, Verdelho **Principal Wines**　　　**Potential**	Shiraz　10+ yrs Shiraz 'Rare'　10+ yrs Cabernet Merlot　5-10 yrs Vine Pruners - the blend Cabernet, Merlot, Shiraz　5-10 yrs Grape Pickers white blend Verdelho

Wayne Thomas Wines

The compilation of this book is tinged with sadness, McLaren Vale and the whole wine industry has lost one of its "true troupers" Wayne Thomas's marvellous wife Pat succumbed to a short tragic illness in early 2001. Theirs was a very special partnership in life. They truly enjoyed their vocation and the company of the people it brought them in contact with. Their friendly open and gregarious natures definitely shone through in their wines - complete with a star on the label, which must surely now be Pat's own special sign.

Wayne's winemaking career began at Stonyfell in 1961 and led onto studies at Roseworthy in 1964. Stints at Ryecroft and Saltram led to a consultancy business in the mid 1970's.

In 1975 Wayne and Pat set up "Fern Hill" Winery winning 5 trophies and 140 medals over 20 vintages. After selling Fern Hill in 1994 they set up the Wayne Thomas label and found a home, the old Maxwell Winery on Kangarilla Road as it leaves McLaren Vale township. They did a great job in refurbishing and re-enlivening the cellar and the cellar door is most tastefully appointed.

The wines, a cabernet sauvignon, shiraz, chardonnay and a riesling are all excellent and has been joined by a methode champenoise chardonnay - named 'Patricia'. Think of Pat when you have your "elevenses" and all the joy she brought to the world.

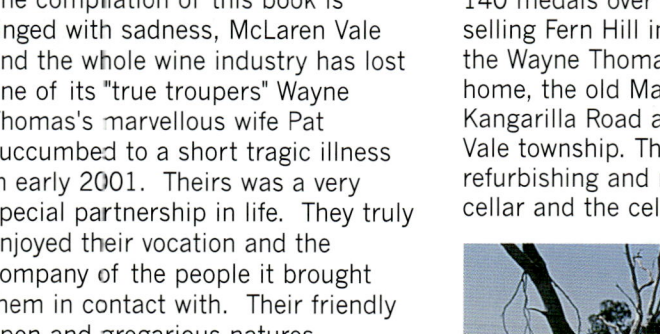

Address: 26 Kangarilla Road MCLAREN VALE 5171 **Phone:** (08) 8323 9737 **Fax:** (08) 8323 9737	**Owner/Winemaker:** Wayne Thomas **Est:** 1994　　**Cases:** 5,000 **Public Hours:** Noon-5pm, daily **Principal Varieties:** Cabernet Sauvignon,	Chardonnay, Riesling, Shiraz **Principal Wines**　　　**Potential** McLaren Vale Shiraz　6-8 yrs McLaren Vale Cabernet Sauvignon　6-8 yrs

Wirra Wirra

I first remember strolling into the ironstone relics, now the heart of the substantial high profile 'Wirra Wirra Winery', way back in 1972. I was searching for red grapes for my family's Tintara Winery and grower Greg Trott was on my hit list.

As I recounted this little bit of trivia to Greg some little time ago; he filled in the details. The man has an incredible memory for detail of the distant past, but ask him what he did yesterday; he'll probably have a few problems filling you in!

Greg Trott is also an acute observer of life and one of the most visionary people I have encountered in the world of wine. Wirra Wirra is in fact a partnership between Greg and his cousin Roger; they have released a methode champenoise called 'Cousins' to celebrate this connection. This exceptional Pinot Chardonnay Cuvee spends almost four years aging on the yeast lees in the bottle, and is one of the best sparkling wines you could find in Australia. Greg has a connection also to the Johnston family, large landholders and owners of 'Pirramimma' wines - Greg's mother was a Johnston.

Working life for Greg in McLaren Vale began, in his own words, 'as a mixed-up farmer', growing almonds, grapes, prunes and apricots and producing dried fruits. In 1969, Greg and cousin Roger bought the old ironstone cellars of Wirra Wirra, built in 1893 by Robert Strangways Wigley and disused since his death in 1924.

A big job lay ahead of them. The first grapes were crushed in 1970 - along with the 'Church Block' (cabernet, shiraz, merlot). By 1979 the rhine riesling had become a mainstay of their business when Greg coined the name 'hand picked' capturing the care and quality concerns always to the fore at Wirra Wirra.

The last 14 vintages have been made by Ben Riggs, a gentle giant of a man whose enthusiasm and creativity match his physical proportions. Ben deals with the estate grapes from Roger Trott's 'Moray Park' and Greg's 'Bethany' and 'Scrubby Rise' vineyards, along with other premium growers in the region. The winery has just been considerably extended.

An outstanding success for Wirra has been their 'Church Block' a cabernet sauvignon, shiraz and merlot blend, named after the vineyard opposite the winery which surrounds an old Methodist Church. Greg has built a large bell-tower outside the winery from which hangs the 'The Angelus'. The tower has recently been enclosed. This enormous bell is rung each year by the winemaker to herald the first crushing of grapes from the region. Wirra Wirra have two super premium wines bottled in exceptional years, 'The Angelus', a cabernet sauvignon and 'RSW Shiraz'. Look out for them. Wirra Wirra have many dinners, concerts and exhibitions at the winery, reflecting Greg Trott's loves, along of course with his beloved Wirra Wirra wines.

Address: McMurtrie Road MCLAREN VALE 5171	Est: 1969 Vine Ha: 31 Cases: 70,000	Church Block	5-10 yrs
Phone: (08) 8323 8414 Fax: (08) 8323 8596	Public Hours: 10am-5pm, Mon-Sat;	Hand Picked Riesling	5-10 yrs
Email: info@wirra.com.au	11am-5pm, Sunday and public holidays	The Angelus Cabernet Sauvignon	10-15 yrs
WWW: www.wirra.com.au	Principal Varieties: Shiraz, Sem, Cab, Merlot,	R.S.W. Shiraz	10-15 yrs
Owner: Greg & Roger Trott	Riesling, Sauv Blanc, Chard, Grenache	Chardonnay	2-5 yrs
Winemaker: Ben Riggs, Samantha Connew	Principal Wines Potential	Sauvignon Blanc	2-5 yrs

Woodstock Wines

Modern McLaren Vale is full of success stories, none more befitting than that of Scott and Anne Collett.

Scott, his brothers Ian and Stephen and their father, wine consultant Doug, established the winery in 1974. Doug bought the property, then named Woodstock, in 1973 and quickly rejuvenated the old vineyard.

Before settling down at Woodstock, Scott had some diverse training in the wine industry. He left Roseworthy with a degree, before making wine at a big Griffith winery for three years, six months of travelling California with a mobile wine bottling line and other visits to winemaking areas of Italy, Germany and France broadened Scott's experience.

Returning to Woodstock in 1982, a young Scott attacked the winemaking with real enthusiasm and a great deal of vision. Scott released high quality McLaren Vale reds and whites under the Woodstock label. In 1986, he won the Wine Bushing Crown for the best Wine of the Region, and was named South Australian Winemaker of the Year. His wines have gone on to achieve National distribution as well as International sales to several overseas countries.

On the home front, Scott, his wife Anne and their three children, Max, Peter and Sophia, live in a big home overlooking the Woodstock vineyards. Anne and Scott believe wine should be enjoyed with food, so they built a magnificent restaurant and entertaining venue next to the winery, naming it 'The Coterie'. The Coterie blends superbly into the environment; constructed of ochre-coloured rammed earth by Scott's brother Ian, its clever design is like a giant slice of cake with the full length windows and French doors opening out to a native garden under the stately gums. Across the road, one can see kangaroos and wallabies peacefully grazing in the Douglas Scrub Sanctuary.

Woodstock Wines

Chef Kay Cazzolato, husband Reg and her young enthusiastic staff run a really top class restaurant, generally open only for lunch on Sundays and holiday Mondays, but splendid vineyard platters are available everyday if you're a bit peckish. Each Easter Woodstock Coterie hosts a "Food, Wine, Music and Art Affair". Featuring an art exhibition, sculpture, glassware, music, fine crafts, furniture and a display of exotic roses, along with the food and wine · a real cultural extravaganza superbly staged. Woodstock Coterie also joins the regional food and wine events "From The Sea and The Vines" in early June and "The Continuous Picnic" in early October.

The Coterie often invite guest Restaurants to Woodstock. These restaurateurs enjoy a refreshing new kitchen and a visit to McLaren Vale, and the coterie guests enjoy a varied menu from some of Adelaide's better restaurants.

For Scott and Anne Collett, the vision became a reality. They grow and make a range of premium McLaren Vale wines; the "Stocks Shiraz" from Scott's century old vines is a sensation. Scott's entire wine range are not only wonderful rich fruit driven styles but exceptional value for money. The 2000 Semillon is one of

the best white wines I've ever enjoyed, but the Woodstock wines all shine. Scott has two other brands, the interesting "Five Feet" named after the "wooden stocks" at the entrance where there are footholes for five feet. Scott blends some of these wines with fruit from vineyards he has a share in, from Wirrega in the limestone coast and the Angas Vineyards at Langhorne Creek. The other brand Douglas Gully is a real value for money drop. At the coterie they offer them with superb food in

delightful surroundings. Scott is a real regional stalwart and put in several solid years as the McLaren Vale Winemakers Association Chairman.

The fabulous McLaren Vale & Fleurieu Visitor Centre at the gateway to the region would be nowhere near as brilliant without his tenacity and capacity for hard work.

Set aside a lazy Sunday to enjoy Woodstock's side of the wonderful McLaren Vale Wine Region.

Address: Douglas Gully Road MCLAREN FLAT 5171	**Est:** 1974 **Vine Ha:** 24 **Cases:** 15,000	Cabernet	5-10 yrs
Phone: (08) 8383 0156 **Fax:** (08) 8383 0437	**Public Hours:** 9am-5pm, weekdays; 12pm-5pm, weekends and public holidays	Shiraz	5-10 yrs
Email: woodstock@woodstockwine.com.au	**Principal Varieties:** Cab Sav, Shiraz,	Chardonnay	2-5 yrs
WWW: www.woodstockwine.com.au	Grenache, Chardonnay, Riesling, Semillon	Botrytis Sweet White	2-5 yrs
Winemaker: Scott Collett	**Principal Wines** **Potential**	Sauvignon Blanc	2-5 yrs
		Semillon	2-5 yrs

Southern Fleurieu

The Southern Fleurieu will undoubtedly be a substantial wine region of the 21st century, It's history goes right back to the pioneering days of the Colony of South Australia. The first oral surgeon Dr. Norman p'anted vines on his property at what is now Normanville in the 1840's and made wine. My own great great grandfather Thomas Hardy worked in the region in 1851/52.

Over the years small vineyards have come and and gone but during the last two decades of the 20th century vineyards became firmly established. The climate is cool but with the hills and valleys, there are many ideal micro climates and soils, rainfall is generally higher than further north at Mclaren Vale.

Nick Holmes planted 20 acres of vines

near Myponga in 1981. There are now quite extensive vineyards in the Mt Compass area and small vineyards near Yankalilla, Normanville and Victor Harbour. Several have cellar doors two have wineries, Twin Bays Estate and Allusion Wines. I am sure all this will change very shortly with many new plantings and wineries being built.

Wine tourism is very much alive and well

on the Southern Fleurieu Peninsula. The Paradise Resort at Wirrina Cove is spectacular with an 18 hole championship gold course, tennis, swimming, bush walking, a yacht harbour and marina and horse riding. Their Heysen Restaurant, Café and great conference facilities, are world class, the suites are superb with incredible views, peace and tranquility.

The Whalers Inn at Victor Harbour sheltering behind the bluff also has great suites, leisure activities and a first class restaurant bar and conference facilities.

There are many food producers on the Peninsula and lots of quaint Inns and Cafes in pretty little towns it's a real discovery tour, the Hills and Coastline are truly majestic.

Southern Fleurieu - SA

1. Allusion Wines
2. Middleton Estate
3. Paradise Wirrina Cove
4. Twin Bays
5. Whalers Inn

Allusion Wines

Steve and Wendy Taylor bought their property near Yankalilla in 1980. Since then they have planted 35,000 trees and 10 acres of vines. In 1998 they launched Allusion Wines and opened its cellar door to the public.

In 1996 Steve nearly met his fate, in a fishing accident where he had to swim for his life through a storm in pitch blackness. The name Allusion was derived from the name of another vessel, sunk as a snapper reef off Kangaroo Island, not far from where Steve's boating accident occurred.

Steve spent 20 years as a chef · at one time at my Uncle David's Middlebrook Winery Restaurant · he held a dream to create authentic, regional, single-vineyard wines.

Allusion Wines reflect Steve's love of European wines, developed during extensive overseas travels. The vines are

hand picked and pruned. Allusion uses only the finest French barriques.

Allusion make a Shiraz Viognier, a rare and innovative blend in Australia. The Shiraz is co-fermented in barrel with the Viognier (5%), to create a very interesting middle palate. Steve recommends it "with simple foods" such as rare beef, lamb, or grilled chicken, which won't overpower the lovely soft apricot character of the "Viognier". A Viognier white is also produced along with a Semillon/Sauvignon Blanc and a an award winning Cabernet Sauvignon.

Allusion is a true boutique vineyard and winery to seek out.

Address: Smith Hill Rd YANKALILLA 5203	Winemaker: Beck Kennedy & Steve Taylor	Shiraz/Voignier	5-6 yrs
Phone: (08) 8558 3333 Fax: (08) 8558 3333	Est: 1990　Vine Ha: 4　Cases: 1,500	Voignier	3-4 yrs
Email: allusion@dove.net.au	Public Hours: 11am-5pm, Thurs-Sun	Semillon/Sauvignon Blanc/Viognier	3-4 yrs
Owner: Steve & Wendy Taylor	Principal Wines　　　　　Potential	Cabernet Sauvignon	5-6 yrs

Twin Bays

The truly captivating view from this well thought out Boutique Vineyard and Winery is spectacular. Set on the slopes above Normanville, the rugged Rapid Bay and the tranquil Lady Bay spread out before you with Kangaroo Island often visible across the gulf waters of St Vincent · the patron Saint of winemakers.

Respected Adelaide Obstretician/Gynaecologist and Endoscopic Surgeon Bruno Giorgio gave birth to the venture with plantings in 1989. Twin Bays was the first commercial vineyard and winery in the area. The cool maritime climate, good rainfall and deep soils have proved perfect for the vine giving a long even growing season.

From his 5 acres of vines Bruno produces a range of excellent wines with the help of experienced winemaker Alan Dyson. The Twin Bays Riesling I found exquisite with beautiful floral aromas and flavours. The shiraz, cabernet sauvignon and grenache all have well defined varietal fruit flavours. The 2000 Home Block Shiraz is an absolute knockout.

An hour of picturesque coastal driving from Adelaide brings you to Twin Bays. Twin Bays won a special award for regional excellence in Wine Tourism at the Fleurieu Tourism 2000 Tourism Awards.

Address: Martin Road YANKALILLA 5203	**Est:** 1989 **Vine Ha:** 2	Twin Bays Fleurieu Cabernet Sauvignon 8-10 yrs
Phone: (08) 8267 2844	**Public Hours:** 10am-5pm weekends, school	Twin Bays Fleurieu Shiraz 8-10 yrs
Fax: (08) 8239 0877	and public holidays	Twin Bays Fleurieu Riesling 3-5 yrs
Email: twinbays@merlin.net.au	**Principal Varieties:** Cab Sav, Shiraz, Riesling	Twin Bays Fleurieu Wild Grenache 5-7 yrs
Winemaker: Bruno Giorgio and Alan Dyson	**Principal Wines** **Potential**	Twin Bays Fleurieu Light Red Current

The Whalers Inn

Nestled at the base of The Bluff overlooking Encounter Bay towards Victor Harbor, is the outstanding Whalers Inn Resort with undoubtedly the best sea view in South Australia. The Complex has been built in two stages by Adelaide Entrepreneur, Roger Thompson. The building of a further 18 apartments has recently been completed and together with the original apartments, the 4.5 star Resort is a very popular venue for conferences, seminars, weddings and other functions. There are four multipurpose function areas all with full seminar facilities and breathtaking views over the Bay. They take their names from the meeting that took place at Encounter Bay in 1802 between English Captain Matthew Flinders in his ship the Investigator and French Captain Nicholas Baudin. The Investigator room can cater for up to 130 people theatre style or 100 for a banquet, with the Encounter, Flinders and Baudin rooms catering for smaller groups.

The apartments have either two or three double bedrooms with two bathrooms and a mirrored double spa bath. They are fully self-contained and their "glass walls" and balconies have magnificent views over Encounter Bay, Victor Harbor and the Southern Ocean. The restaurant which is open seven days a week for lunch and dinner, enjoys the same wonderful views. Its Mediterranean influence and its extensive use of fresh produce from the Fleurieu Peninsula have earned it many awards and an excellent reputation.

The Resort features two swimming pools. The magnificent "horizon" pool is the first of its type in South Australia and overlooks the Bay, private lawned BBQ area and tennis court. There are many leisure activities available close to the Resort with two championship golf courses less than five minutes drive away. Fishing, River Murray cruises and winery visits are just a few of the other activities that are close at hand.

The Whalers Inn began its life as tea rooms before being redeveloped by Roger Thompson. South Australia should be very grateful for the great resort he has built.

Address: The Bluff, Franklin Parade VICTOR HARBOR	**Phone:** (08) 8552 4400 **Fax:** (08) 8552 4240 **Email:** whalers.inn@granite.net.au	**WWW:** www.whalers.com.au **Owner:** Rodger Thompson **Est:** 1989

Paradise Wirrina Cove

On the majestic coastline of the Fleurieu Peninsula, some 90 kilometres south of Adelaide, high on the cliffs overlooking the Gulf of St Vincent, with Kangaroo Island in the background, is Paradise Wirrina Cove Resort.

Paradise is a name well chosen. The Resort site has a certain grandeur about it and this carries through in the splendid hospitality, function and conference facilities and the 87 suites and rooms. There are also a number of self contained one, two and three bedroom appartments ideal for family breaks.

Heysens Restaurant, named after celebrated artist Hans Heysen, whose famous Landscape paintings of the scenes of the Fleurieu Peninsula and Hills are reminiscent of what you see looking out from the Restaurant and friendly coffee shop.

The Paradise Resort has a fabulous championship golf course sweeping over the slopes with breathtaking views of the Gulf. You may even share a fairway or two with a kangaroo. If you are more moved by marine life, the Cove features a fully serviced Marina with 210 berths for yachts and pleasure craft. The Resort also offers scuba diving in the Gulf waters of the Cove. Secluded amongst the fairways of the Golf Course is a large lake, where one can test their kayak skills. If you feel like a real challenge you can shoot an arrow or two on the archery range which is fully equipped with tuition from a champion archer.

To really explore the full beauty of Wirrina, horse back trail rides and mountain bikes are available. For those of a more tranquil nature, bushwalking trails, with various levels of challenge, take you through all the natural beauty the Fleurieu Peninsula has in full abundance.

Wirrina is also in the middle of a vinous paradise, you are only a half an hour's beautiful drive from one of the world's leading wine regions · McLaren Vale · featuring more than 50 wineries many with restaurants and cafés. Even closer at Twin Bays winery near Normanville, 10 minutes away, you can taste some great wines.

If a trip to the unspoilt Kangaroo Island and the Flinders Chase Reserve is of interest the car ferry is only 20 minutes away at Cape Jervis.

Paradise Wirrina Cove

Victor Harbor, Adelaide's holiday resort, the seaport of Goolwa and the Murray mouth are only another half an hour's journey away. You can even take a trip across the controversial new Hindmarsh Island bridge.

If you really feel like doing the body a favour, there is a mini-gym with spa, sauna and a heated pool. For the more adventurous you can take a scenic ride in the Fleurieu on a Harley Davidson or experience the fun of a Quad Bike trail ride. You can climb into combat gear and try the light hearted war games of "Paintball" or "Skirmish". By now, if you are totally tired out, you can retire to your room, with the in-house movies, full mini bar, tea, coffee and snack facilities, or just call for the prompt room service. Sitting out on Café Piazza terrace you can take in the beautiful natural surroundings, in peace, with a glass of fine wine in hand.

A special treat awaits you at night, after dinner you can indulge in the milky way through the powerful telescope and marvel at the stars in the crystal clear skies and the pristine environment, that is an abundance at Wirrina. There's even an experienced astronomer to guide your star gazing journey.

It's paradise at Wirrina Cove-that's for sure!!

Address: Cape Jervis Road
SECOND VALLEY 5204

Phone: (08) 8598 4001
Fax: (08) 8598 4037

Email: reservations@wirrina.com.au
WWW: www.wirrina.com.au

Currency Creek

Some 30 kilometres southwest of Langhorne Creek, close to the resort towns and fishing port of Goolwa and Victor Harbour, lies a distinctive wine region. At present it supports three wineries, but is already supplying grapes to many of South Australia's top winemakers. Late in the year 2000 it became a fully fledged wine region under the Australian Geographical Indications Scheme.

The Great Southern Ocean influences the truly maritime climate. In fact, it is one of South Australia's coolest climates overall, but in winter one of its mildest, both ideal for the vine, giving an exceptionally long growing

season, building and retaining loads of elegant flavours in the wines.

Wally and Phillip Tonkin's Currency Creek Wines, established in 1969, produces a large range of elegant wines and has a delightful country-style restaurant and six superb vineyard villa's.

Likewise, Middleton Winery, under the experienced and innovative Nigel Catt, makes outstanding wines and has a most pleasant alfresco style holiday and weekend restaurant tucked into the winery itself. A new winery has just been completed, the Ballast Stone Estate Winery of the Shaw family which already has a capacity of 3,500 tonnes to make wine from their 750 acre Currency Creek vineyards and their 150 acres of vines in McLaren Vale.

The sandy loams of the area with good drainage also help produce the unique styles this exciting new region will surely become famous for.

Currency Creek - SA

1. Ballast Stone
2. Currency Creek Winery
3. Middleton Winery

Ballast Stone

Ballast Stone is a bold venture in the newly proclaimed region of Currency Creek. The Shaw family have planted an 800 acre vineyard in the region to add to the 150 acres of vines they already own in McLaren Vale.

Richard Shaw started out at Beaudesert in Queensland as a mixed farmer. After coming to South Australia with his wife Marie he owned a concrete truck. In 1972 they purchased 15 acres of land at McLaren Vale and planted Shiraz, Cabernet Sauvignon, Riesling and Chardonnay. Richard's oldest son Philip joined him, and gradually they expanded the family's vineyard holdings driving concrete trucks at the same time to supplement the family's finances.

In 2001 a further 200 acres will be planted at Currency Creek and in 2002 a further 150 acres, primarily of Chardonnay and Pinot Noir. Late in 2000 the extremely capable and experienced winemaker John Loxton, joined Ballast Stone, after 19 years at Maglieri in McLaren Vale where he won numerous Australian and International trophies for his wines, particularly Shiraz.

The winery was constructed in 2000. The 2001 vintage saw a crush of 2000 tonnes. They envisage the crush expanding quite considerably over the next few years as new plantings start producing. Ballast

Stone Estate Wines are releasing their range of wines in August 2001 including Riesling, Sauvignon Blanc, Chardonnay, Grenache, Cabernet Sauvignon and Shiraz.

The Ballast Stone name has been derived due to many of the buildings on the property being built from stones carried out from England by the huge grain clippers as ballast. The ballast was discarded in Goolwa when they picked up their load of grain to sail back to England. Some of the stones making up the building, which will eventually

become part of the Cellar door, are etched with markings showing their origin.

Richard's two younger sons are involved, Mark is Winery Operations Manager and Nathan the company Viticulturist and Vineyard Manager. The Shaws liked Currency Creek's availability of excellent land, with sandy loam over clay, friable to make it easy for the water and the vine roots to penetrate. They also liked the drier disease free environment and the cool summers and mild winters, their choice of site has been spot on.

Curiously Currency Creek was once surveyed as the Capital of South Australia before Adelaide was built and it has the same square mile road grid with the same street names. Goolwa was to be its Port, it obviously never happened but it gave me an eerie feeling when John showed me the survey map and I saw all the familiar Adelaide street names.

Ballast Stone is certainly set to be a capital of wine though and I for one cannot wait to taste their first wines. I'm sure they will show the perfumed lift and defined varietal characters, the long growing season the mild maritime climate gives to the wines.

Address: Myrtle Grove Road CURRENCY CREEK 5214	**Winemaker:** F. John Loxton	Sauvignon Blanc	1-3 yrs
	Est: 2000 **Vine Ha:** 440 **Cases:** 10,000	Chardonnay	4-5 yrs
Phone: (08) 8666 4215 **Fax:** (08) 8555 4216	**Public Hours:** 10am-4:30pm, Weekdays;	Merlot	7-10 yrs
Email: enquiry@ballaststone.com.au	12pm-5pm Weekends & Public Holidays	Riesling	1-3 yrs
WWW: www.ballaststone.com.au	**Principal Wines** **Potential**	Grenache	1-3 yrs
		Cabernet Sauvignon	7-10 yrs

Currency Creek Winery

Wally Tonkin was born and raised in the region, but his bubbling energy and constant search for a new challenge to tackle, led him to Adelaide where he very successfully operated a property development business and a travel business at the same time.

His main challenges met, his love for the country of his youth, and animals, ed him to purchase a large rural holding on the Finnis and Currency Creeks near Goolwa. Always with a desire to be different, he "ran" a number of unusual animals and birds, from deer to ostriches and peacocks, along with his main love, horses.

He also planted a large vineyard, with most of the grapes being sold to eager winemakers further north, but he set up his own innovative little winery. Today, the winery is complete with a restaurant and function centre and six superb vineyard villas.

The peacocks proudly parade, past the windows, on the expansive lawns as you sip some superb Currency Creek wines with the succulent meals in the casual and charming restaurant. The Currency Creek region is blessed with ideal viticultural conditions, one of the coolest summers and mildest winters in South Australia, providing long growing seasons giving clean and complex fruit flavours in the wines.

The sauvignon blanc has been particularly successful, as has their sparkling cabernet and one of Australia's finest botrytised wines, their Noble Riesling, several times

Currency Creek Winery

the Australian Champion in the small wineries sweet white category.

Whilst Wally is busy winning many races with his self-trained stable of horses, Phillip is busy planting new vineyards for Currency Creeks expanding markets around the world. The vineyard villas are truly magnificently appointed, queen sized beds, spas, a kitchen, dining areas and outdoor courtyards. Set in amongst the dappled white gums, overlooking the Tookayerta Creek within an hour of Adelaide in the heart of the fabulous Fleurieu Peninsula. Why not put this, one of Australia's most colourful and characterful wineries, on your next wine adventure itinerary and stay the night after a sumptuous dinner.

Address: Winery Road CURRENCY CREEK 5214	**Winemaker:** Phillip Tonkin & Warren Randall	"Princess Alexandrina" Noble Semillon 0-5 yrs
Phone: (08) 8555 4069	**Est:** 1969 **Vine Ha:** 48 **Cases:** 8,000	Currency Creek Sauvignon Blanc 3-6 yrs
Fax: (08) 8555 4100	**Public Hours:** 10am-5pm, daily	Currency Creek Chardonnay 4-7 yrs
Email: ccw@granite.net.au	**Principal Varieties:** Chard, Semillon, Sauv	Currency Creek CabSav 5-10 yrs
WWW: www.currencycreekwines.com.au	Blanc, Rhine Riesling, Pinot Noir, Shiraz, Cab Sav	Currency Creek Shiraz 6-10 yrs
Owner: Wally & Rosemary Tonkin	**Principal Wines** **Potential**	Currency Creek Methode Traditionale 0-6 yrs

Langhorne Creek

Situated some 80 kms south-east of Adelaide, along the banks of the River Bremer, lies the grape-growing region of Langhorne Creek.

The rich alluvial plain is periodically flooded by the Bremer River, an event that the local growers look forward to as it brings much needed water and fertile silt to the vineyards.

Planting of vines at Langhorne Creek began in the middle of the last century. The oldest and largest winery in the region is Bleasdale, established by Frank Potts back in 1850. Today the Potts family still manage this historic winery.

Many of the great winemakers from around Australia have used Langhorne Creek grapes in their winemaking. The first wine to acknowledge this on the label was the famous Stonyfell Metala with its distinctive label explaining its origins.

During the late 60's and early 70's, Wolf Blass relied heavily on Langhorne Creek fruit, a significant ingredient of his trio of Jimmy Watson trophies. Today, seven excellent wineries including three new large production facilities Belvidere Winery and Langhorne Creek Winery at the Strathalbyn end of the region and the Belleville Winery of Beresford Wines. These share the region with many grape-growers, including a recent influx of larger companies and vineyard ventures, the area under vine has increased at least seven fold in the last 6 years and there are now well over 10,000 acres of vines planted in the region. Orlando Wyndham have established a huge $25 million vineyard development and Rosemount have planted 950 acres of vines in one single vineyard. It is a spectacular sight and had its first crop in 1998.

The wine industry and the State Government have just implemented a massive irrigation scheme, bringing water in a large pipeline from Lake Alexandrina; this sense of co-operation in South Australia's future is welcome.

Why not visit the region and see the historic Bleasdale and the fast developing family wineries, Lake Breeze, Temple Bruer and the delightful Bremerton with its excellent restaurant. The region is also home to the historic Newmans Horseradish business of the Meakins family who make a number of other condiments of exciting quality.

Langhorne Creek

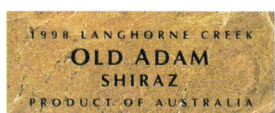

Langhorne Creek - SA

1. Bleasdale Wines
2. Bremerton Wines
3. Lake Breeze Wines
4. Langhorne Creek Winery
5. Metala
6. Newmans Horseradish

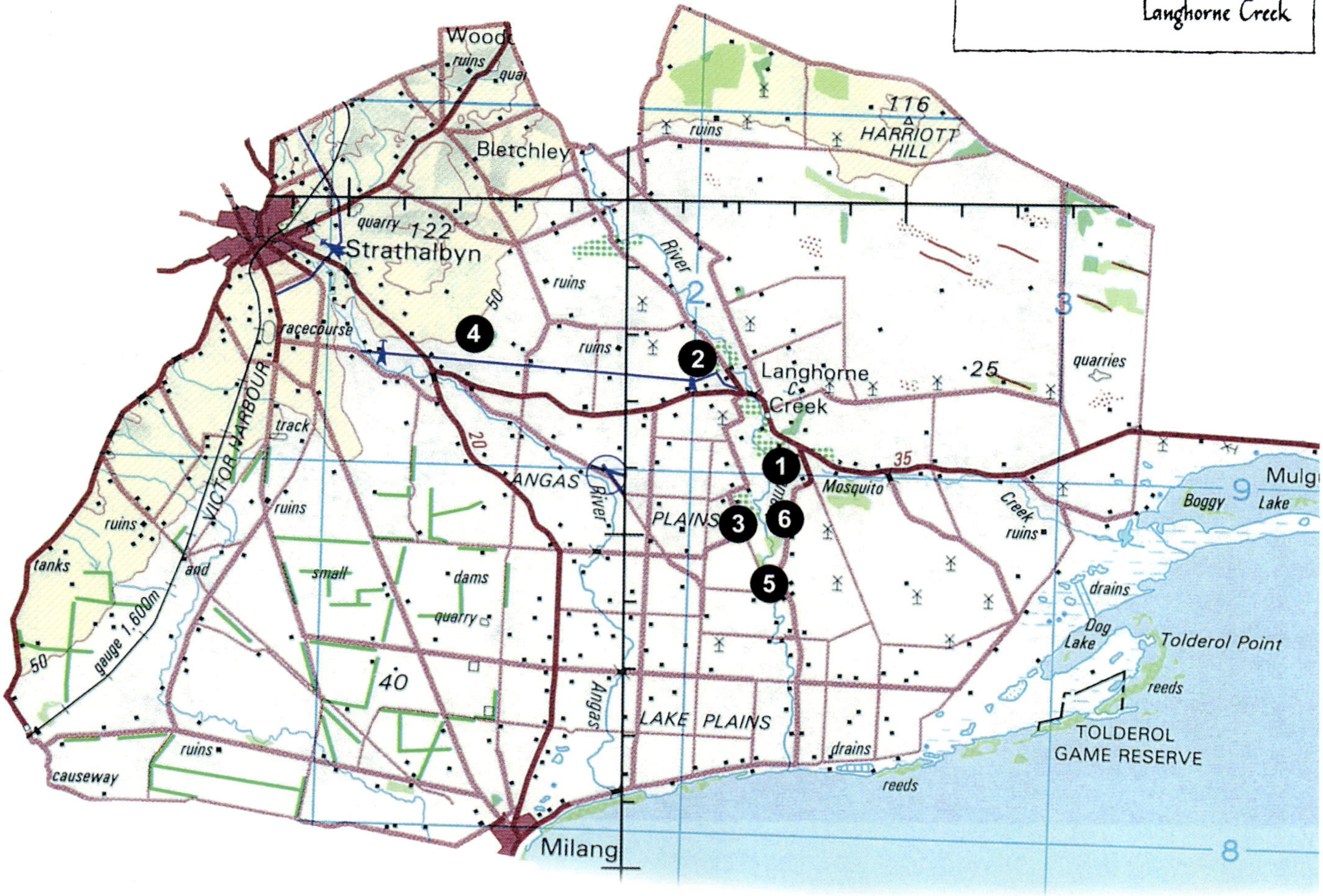

Bleasdale Wines

modern winemaking equipment and increased oak barrel storage. The reds, the chardonnay and the verdelho (table wine) have really shown the benefit of this investment and Michael's skill, combined with the superb fruit from the Langhorne Creek vineyards, has seen some sensational wines. The flagship "Frank Potts" a cabernet sauvignon, malbec, merlot and cabernet franc blend is a long living wine of real distinction. The Bleasdale Malbec a straight varietal wine is also worth searching out. The verdelho white table wine is a real mouthfull of flavour. The Langhorne Crossing Red and White are great value. I particularly like the Bleasdale Sparkling Shiraz, they also make a White Sparkling Chardonnay/Pinot Noir blend which is excellent.

The winery's tasting room is full of old photographs by family member, Diddy Potts, and paintings by his brother, A.B. Potts. Drop in to Bleasdale and immerse yourself in our wine history. Plans are afoot for a new cellar door and hospitality area, which will sensitively combine the historic past with the needs of the wine tourist.

Bleasdale is one of Australia's oldest family owned and operated wineries. On the 2rd May, 2000 the Potts Family celebrated the 150th anniversary of the founding of the company by Frank Potts in 1850 and the invited guests gathered around the classic old lever press which was once again swung into action by a crew of family and friends. It was a celebration not to be missed and befitting of this historic winery and the Potts family's commitment to quality wine. Little has changed in parts of the winery. Potts was one of the State's original settlers, landing in Adelaide on the first ship the H.M.S. Buffalo in 1836. An energetic and entrepreneurial chap, he also built 3 large paddle steamers which plied the Murray River for many years. The old part of the winery is on the National Trust and National Heritage register and makes a fascinating visit; the huge old red gum lever press is truly incredible.

Until the late 1950's, Bleasdale produced only fortified wines, including a number of ports, sherries and a madeira, made from the rare grape variety, verdelho. Bleasdale

still makes great fortifieds but today their table wines form the greater part of their business.

Winemaker is Roseworthy graduate and family member, Michael Potts. Michael has continued installing

Address: Wellington Road LANGHORNE CREEK 5255	Cases: 100,000	Cabernet/Malbec/Merlot	5-10 yrs
	Public Hours: 9am-5pm, weekdays; 11am-5pm, Sun	Cabernet Sauvignon	5-10 yrs
Phone: (03) 8537 3001 Fax: (08) 8537 3224		Special Vintage Shiraz	5-10 yrs
WWW: http://www.wineaustralia.com.au	Principal Varieties: Cabernet Sauvignon, Shiraz, Malbec, Verdelho	Verdelho	2-5 yrs
Winemaker: Michael Potts		Pioneer Port (Tawny Port)	10+ yrs
Est: 1850 Vine Ha: 50	Principal Wines Potential	Madeira (Verdelho)	10+ yrs

Bremerton Wines

Craig Willson and his delightful wife, Mignonne, have restored a group of beautiful century-old stone buildings comprising Bremerton Lodge they bought in 1985. Craig was a publisher of country newspapers based at Whyalla so it was quite a change of lifestyle. In 1992 floods devastated the property and buildings, since then they have constructed an earth barrier, it also forced them to refocus their property on vineyards and wine. Today they have over 100 acres of vines and a 40% share in another 175 acres.

The tasting area of Bremerton is housed in stables built in 1866 it features many historic items from the region and opens out to an outdoor patio which is delightful on a summer's day. It has recently been revamped and expanded.

The sweeping circular driveway adds to the beautifully balanced overall impression. In the winery with its high roof, the eating area is on a mezzanine above the cellars where the wine quietly ages and Mignonne serves her "mood food" on weekends, it's a great place to book for lunch. In 1998 the Willson's built a full-scale production winery which was extended in 2000 to include a temperature controlled barrel store. Daughter Rebecca who is a trained

winemaker has taken on all the winemaking duties and the Willson's second daughter Lucy is marketing and administration manager, Mark Roberts is winery manager.

The care and aesthetic understanding of the Willson's shows through in their wines which are beautifully balanced and good examples of the top quality that Langhorne Creek is famous for. Rebecca won the winery's first trophy, her 1997 Cabernet Sauvignon being awarded the Best Boutique

Cabernet Sauvignon in Sydney. Their "Old Adam" Shiraz and "Young Vines" Shiraz have also been successful. Bremerton have a blended red "Tamblyn" which is very well balanced and has averaged 6 show medals each vintage, try their verdelho too it's great.

Why not wend your way around Langhorne Creek one weekend and then breeze into Bremerton. I'm sure Mignonne's food or their great value cheese platters will suit your mood.

Address: Strathalbyn Road LANGHORNE CREEK 5255	Est: 1988 Vine Ha: 110	Bremerton Old Adam Shiraz	10 yrs
	Cases: 23,000	Bremerton Cabernet	10 yrs
Phone: (08) 8537 3093 Fax: (08) 8537 3109	Public Hours: 10am-5pm daily	Bremerton Young Vine Shiraz	6-8 yrs
Email: info@bremerton.com.au	Principal Varieties: Cabernet Sauvignon,	Bremerton Tamblyn	
WWW: www.bremerton.com.au	Chardonnay, Malbec, Merlot, Petit Verdot,	(Cabernet/Shiraz/Merlot/Malbec)	4-6 yrs
Owner: Craig and Mignonne Willson	Sauvignon Blanc, Shiraz, Verdelho	Bremerton Verdelho	1-2 yrs
Winemaker: Rebecca Willson	Principal Wines Potential	Bremerton Sauvignon Blanc	1-2 yrs

Lake Breeze

Greg Follett is one of the best young winemakers in Australia and has a cabinet full of trophies and medals to prove it. The Follett family are youthful, exuberant and dynamic. Father Ken still hasn't hung up his Aussie Rules footy boots and is one of the fittest men of his age you're ever likely to meet. Quietly spoken Ken is a fastidious hard-toiling farmer, whose superb vineyard and the wonderful fruit it produces is respected by winemakers from near and far.

After many years supplying grapes to Australia's leading winemakers, Ken decided to start a small winery to put his growing family to work. His three sons are the driving force of the winery · Roger is a viticulturist and assists his father in the vineyard, Tim helps in the vineyard and Greg the highly successful winemaker. Lake Breeze uses only the top ten percent of their crop for their own wines and sell the rest.

Greg's lightning rise to fame began when he graduated from Roseworthy in 1991. He followed this with a vintage at Hardy's, and then a vintage at Geyser Peak winery in California. Then he worked in France at Domaine du Vaissiere for the world famous winemaking Lurton family in the Minervois region south of Bordeaux.

Ken Follett's sons are doing him proud.

Address: Step Road LANGHORNE CREEK 5255	**Principal Varieties:** Cabernet Sauvignon, Shiraz, Chardonnay, White Frontignac, Grenache	"Bernoota" Shiraz/Cabernet	5-10 yrs
Phone: (08) 8537 3017 **Fax:** (08) 8537 3267		Winemaker's Selection Shiraz	10+ yrs
Winemaker: Greg Follett		Winemaker's Selection Cabernet	10+ yrs
Est: 1991 **Vine Ha:** 70 **Cases:** 6,000-8,000	**Principal Wines** **Potential**	Grenache	3-5 yrs
Public Hours: 10am-5pm, daily	Cabernet Sauvignon 5-10 yrs	Chardonnay	3-5 yrs

Langhorne Creek Winery

The newly established Langhorne Creek Winery is an independent contract processing winery modeled on, and managed by, the successful Boar's Rock Winery, McLaren Vale.

Langhorne Creek Winery, which began operations for the 2001 vintage has a current production output of 5,000 tonnes with plans to grow to a total capacity of 15,000 tonnes. The facility was established to service the rapidly growing processing and storage needs of the Australian wine industry.

The winery processes fruit to juice, must or ex fermenter/gross lees stage for several of Australia's major wine companies and also processes fruit for independent grape growers to sell in bulk as juice or finished wine. Smaller wineries utilize the full range of winemaking services on offer to process fruit through to finished, bottle ready wine. The Chief Winemaker is Mike Farmilo (former Group Red Winemaker at

Southcorp). Mike has had extensive experience in making and developing wines for significant Australian wine

brands such as Penfolds, Seaview, Wynns and Lindemans.

Address: PO Box 64 Langhorne Creek 5255	**Fax:** (08) 8537 0623	**Winemaker:** Mike Farmilo
Phone: (08) 8537 0600	**Email:** winery@langhorne.com	**Est:** 2000

Metala

Metala was the creation of renowned winemaker the late Bryan Dolan, whose son Nigel is current custodian of the famous brand.

Metala has a unique place in the history of the Australian wine industry. The fruit is sourced from a single vineyard in Langhorne Creek, from vines first planted in 1891.

The vineyard is planted to Cabernet Sauvignon and Shiraz in almost equal proportions. Since its inception the wine has always been a blend of these two great varieties.

The 1961 vintage of Metala was the first wine to win the Jimmy Watson Trophy at the Melbourne Wine Show. The first in a long, proud line.

This much loved wine has a dense, dark colour with intense plum, cherry and blackcurrant fruit character, supported by the hints of eucalyptus and licorice that are typical of the Langhorne creek Region.

In exceptional years such as 1995, 1996 and 1998, there is a special limited release "Metala Original Plantings Shiraz", which is made solely from the 1891 Shiraz vines, look out for this classic.

Rosemount

Over the last 5 years Rosemount have planted a massive 900 acres of vines on a huge panoramic site on the western banks of the Bremer River, mainly shiraz and cabernet sauvignon. The first vintage was in 1997 and now a truly massive quantity of absolutely top quality grapes is flowing into the Rosemount Ryecroft winery at McLaren Vale. The whole Rosemount range of reds are benefiting from the Super Premium Balmoral, GSM, Traditional, the Diamond label Shiraz and the Diamond label Cabernet Sauvignon.

In the hands of chief winemaker, Philip Shaw and the McLaren Vale winemaker Charles Whish, who are both amongst the top rung of the industry's winemakers the exceptional Langhorne Creek fruit is making superb wines.

From the Earth to your Taste Buds.

So it grows, in rich river flooded alluvial soils.

As the soils are rich and strong so is the brand name F.C. Newman. Fred (F.C.) Newman began producing prepared horseradish to supplement his nursery business in the Depression. He sold the red labelled jars from the back of a dray in the East End Market. The same red label is now seen throughout supermarkets nationally.

In 1946 the Meakins family bought Fred's business and have kept the same branding and similar principles in their production outlet today, as Brian and Anne Meakins realise the strength and brand loyalty Fred created.

The horseradish is now grown on this beautiful property at Langhorne Creek, part of South Australia's Fleurieu Peninsula. The rich soil found here is a result of flooding from the river and the cool nights experienced, making the soil develop perfect conditions for growing horseradish.

This Langhorne Creek property hosts the horseradish farm, the production outlet and a farm shop which visitors from all over the world come to enjoy. What they enjoy is the basic concept of good farming principles, the simple intelligence of concepts behind production and the taste, the unique taste of Newman's Horseradish.

So how does the horseradish move from the earth to your taste buds? Simple, the product is made weekly ensuring that the product is as fresh as can be when purchased. The use by dates are important to the Meakins as the horseradish is at its best and the taste, aroma and flavours at their height when the product is freshly made. The heat you experience when enjoying the horseradish is purely horseradish alone, which means there is nothing

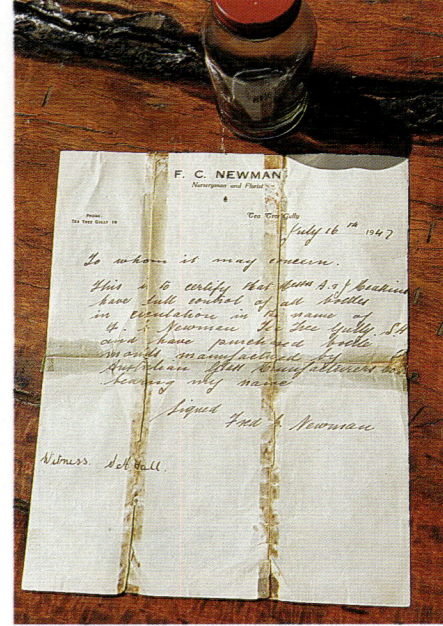

added to enhance the heat and flavours of the product.

Brian and Anne Meakins were one of the first to value-add to the horseradish and through research, determination and old fashion hard work have created a range of horseradish products for your enjoyment. You will find our jars in the refrigerated cabinets of supermarkets, gourmet delis and health food shops. Newman's also caters to the needs of chefs and restaurateurs with the foodservice range of 1 kg and 2.25 kg - a prefect accompaniment to so many dishes.

The Coastal Regions of South Australia are generally suitable for viticulture except for the West Coast and Upper Spencers Gulf, which are too hot and dry. Others such as Yorke Peninsula would need significant supplementary irrigation, as South Australia is the driest State on the driest continent of the World. This of course has its advantages as vine diseases prove less of a problem with the low humidity. The lighter soils that the State has is probably a factor that phylloxera, the dreaded vine louse that destroyed the vineyard of Europe and the Eastern States of Australia late last Century, has never attacked South Australia, with the advantage the State has many vineyards on their original roots that go back to the mid 1800's.

Vineyards have sprung up around the coast over the State's history but it is only since the mid 1980's that wine regions have really emerged, with the exceptions of the McLaren Vale and Langhorne Creek regions, which are quite maritime and Currency Creek founded in 1969 and Middleton Estate in 1978.

The Port Lincoln area now has Boston Bay Wines and Delacolline, both planted in 1984. Kangaroo Island has a number of vineyards, most small, but with a 20-acre vineyard at Emu Bay, Robin Moody from Penfolds being one of the partners in this venture. A lovely bordeaux blend red comes from the Florance family's vines at Cygnet Cove.

The Mount Benson region near Cape Jaffa is truly exciting with some 800 acres already planted and some exciting wines from Cape Jaffa, Mt Benson, the Black Wattle brand of Cellarmaster, Chapoutier from the Rhone Valley in France and the new Kreglinger Winery.

Near Robe BRL Hardy have large plantings in the Woak Coastal Ranges and Southcorp are developing large vineyards. The coastal climate with its long temperate growing season is ideal and abundant terra rossa soils completes the quality viticultural picture.

A little further south near Mt Gambier the Winter family and the characterful Sandy Haig have vineyards and wines on the market.

The future for the State's Coastal regions viticulturally seems assured with the state's sensational seafoods and the good tourism infrastructure things look rosy indeed, adding another dimension of enjoyment for the intrepid wine traveller to seek out!

Coastal Regions

Costal Regions - SA

1. Boston Bay Wines
2. Cape Jaffa - Rock Lobster
3. Chapoutier
4. International Oyster & Seafoods
5. Kreglinger
6. Mitani Spices
7. Oysa Oysters
8. Robe Haven Motel

Boston Bay
Cabernet Sauvignon
1998
750mL

Boston Bay
Shiraz
1998
750mL

Boston Bay Wines & Prawns

Established on the coastline of Port Lincoln with majestic views over the waters of Spencer Gulf, which provide much of the catch of the world renowned South Australian prawns, is the vineyard of the Ford Family's Boston Bay Wines.

Graham Ford, a deep-sea diver and salvage expert and his wife Mary came to live at Port Lincoln in the early 1970's. Loving their new environment, they began to think of the future with their young family. The answer came in planting a vineyard, the first in the region.

The climate was ideal with even temperatures due to the surrounding waters of Spencer's Gulf and the Great Australian Bite. The French explorer Baudin recommended viticulture here, undoubtedly seeing the similarity to Bordeaux. He named what is now Boston Bay "Port d' Champagny" referring to the soil type, with underlying limestone often the sign of good viticultural country. The Boston Bay vines have flourished and the wines won much acclaim far from their shores.

At vintage the grapes are handpicked and transported to the Clare Valley, where they are under the expert care of winemakers David O'Leary and

Nick Walker. Varieties include riesling, chardonnay, merlot, cabernet sauvignon and shiraz.

The cellar door is open for visiting on weekends, school and public holidays. The spacious function room and pretty garden setting are perfect for entertaining and are available to hire for that special occasion.

South Australia's Western King prawns are some of the most sought after in the world. 39 of the 52 licensed fishes operate in Spencer Gulf the other fisheries being St Vincent's Gulf and the West Coast. There are no official seasons. The fisheries are constantly monitored and trawling is permitted when stocks are adequate and only in restricted areas.

The total catch in the 1999/2000 season was 2416 tonnes with a value of some 27 million dollars. The industry employs around 650 people either directly or indirectly.

The South Australian Prawn Industry has received scientific support and recognition for the sustainability of their fishing practices. Every 2 years a "Prawn Fest" Festival is held in Wallaroo and the industry does much to promote South Australian Prawns worldwide. The industry is also very active in the Quality Assurance area.

Anyone who has ever enjoyed succulent South Australian Prawns, fresh and prepared in the myriad of ways with a cold crisp Boston Bay Riesling or Chardonnay will vouch for their delicious flavours and textures - try them soon, what a marriage!!

Address: Lincoln Highway PORT LINCOLN 5606	**Winemaker:** David O'Leary & Nick Walker	Boston Bay Riesling	5 yrs
Phone: (08) 8684 3600 **Fax:** (08) 8684 3637	**Est:** 1984 **Cases:** 3,500 **Vine Ha:** 7.5	Boston Bay Chardonnay	5 yrs
Email: bbw@bostonbaywines.com.au	**Public Hours:** 11.30-4.30, weekends,	Boston Bay Merlot	5-8 yrs
WWW: www.bostonbaywines.com.au	school and public holidays	Boston Bay Cabernet Sauvignon	10 yrs
Owner: Graham and Mary Ford	**Principal Wines** **Potential**	Boston Bay Shiraz	10 yrs

Cape Jaffa - Rock Lobster

South Australia not only has some of the worlds finest wines, but some of the worlds most succulent Rock Lobster. South Australia has a long coastline bordering on the Great Southern Ocean being the driest state on the driest continent in the world, apart from the outlet of the River Murray, South Australia has no other river system running into its waters, there are few industrial installations on the coastline and in summary the state has some of the cleanest waters in the world.

The state is divided into two fisheries the Southern Zone, covering all the state waters south of the Murray Mouth to the Victorian border and the Northern Zone, covering all the waters north of the Murray mouth over to the Western Australian border.

The two fisheries are extremely tightly managed paying respect to the necessity for the Lobsters to breed and in no way upsetting the delicate marine environment. The season operates from 1st November and operates until 31st May. 1990-2000 yielded a total of 2718 tonnes of which 63% comes from the Southern Zone. The catch was up some 10% on the previous year and its ever-increasing value totaled over 80 million dollars. Much of the harvest is exported with Asia being an ever-growing market. There are 253 licenses and 2,100 are employed people directly or indirectly.

Lobster and great white wines obviously go hand in hand. Over the last decade the areas around Cape Jaffa, Mt Benson and Robe, the hinterland of the Southern Rock Lobster Fishery have developed strongly as wine regions.

Cape Jaffa Wines was founded by Kym and Sue Hooper who have had a long-term love of wine. As a stock buyer for the family abattoir Kym noticed that the sheep coming from around the Cape Jaffa/Mount Benson area had a red tinge in their wool, just like those from Coonawarra. The Hooper's, along with partners, highly respected winemaker Ralph Fowler and his wife, bought their vineyard site, in the rolling hills, in the northern reaches of the new Mount Benson wine region.

The winery was carved into a limestone hillside with the cellar door built from limestone rocks, picked off the property. They are now producing an increasing vintage each year. Son, Derek Hooper, is the innovative and energetic winemaker and vineyard manager. Derek has worked closely with Ralph Fowler, and has also worked vintages in various districts of France. The winery is well designed with its natural rock insulation and gravity flow.

The climate is cool like Coonawarra but with some four degrees less seasonal temperature variation. The warmer winters and cooler summers, due to the maritime influence, give a longer, more even growing season. I noticed the red wines have very fine velvety tannins.

The first Cabernet Sauvignon a 1995 won a gold medal in the Royal Melbourne Show. I found all the wines have very floral overtones and although big wines very supple, which seems to be a desirable regional characteristic.

The Cape Jaffa tasting room on top of the hill has panoramic views of the region and the southern ocean in the distance. It is one of the loveliest in Australia.

Cape Jaffa is a truly exciting new winery and vineyard in a great new region.

Address: PO Box 437 ROBE 5276	Est: 1993 Vine Ha: 18	Principal Wines	Potential
Phone: (08) 8768 5053 Fax: (08) 8768 5040	Public Hours: 10am-5pm, daily	Chardonnay	5 yrs
Email: capejaffawines@picknowl.com.au	Principal Varieties: Chardonnay, Merlot,	Cabernet Sauvignon	10+ yrs
www.picknowl.com.au/homepages/capejaffawines	Cabernet Sauvignon, Shiraz, Sauvignon Blanc,	Merlot	10+ yrs
Winemaker: Derek Hooper	Pinot Noir, Semillon, Cabernet Franc, Petit Verdot	Sauvignon Blanc/Semillon	3-4 yrs

S.A. Marine Scalefish

South Australia's coastal waters support some of the nation's prized scalefish species. The marine scalefish fishery makes a significant contribution to South Australia's economy and is an important part of the fabric of many regional communities.

The marine scalefish fishery is defined as all species of fish, crustaceans, molluscs and other animals in the marine waters of the State, with the exception of prawns, rock lobster, abalone and blue crabs, which are managed independently.

The commercial sector of the marine scalefish fishery is the oldest commercial fishing industry in South Australia. For more than 160 years, many small business, often family run, have relied on fishing to supply a good quality fish for the domestic market. Today, there are 442 commercial licence holders catching around 9,500 tonnes of scalefish annually. The estimated gross market value of these fish is about $20.8 million.

It is a multi method and multi species fishery, taking in excess of 60 species of fish and using up to 27 different devices and methods.

The pilchard fishery is the largest marine scalefish fishery by weight with almost 4,000 tonnes being caught in 1999/2000. King George whiting is the most valued fishery worth almost $5 million each year. Other important marine scalefish species include snapper, squid, and garfish.

The most common methods of fishing are handline and nets. Handlines include the use of squid jigs and troll lines and account for more than 60% of the commercial

fishing effort (measured in boat days). Of the 442 commercial fishers, 105 have an endorsement to use a fish net and target mainly on the schooling fish including Australian herring (tommy ruffs), garfish, Australian salmon, sea mullet, snook and yellowfin whiting. The pilchard fishery was established in 1993 by permitting 14 fishers to use a special purse seine net.

Fishing for marine scalefish species is also a sport and recreation activity for many South Australians and attracts numerous visitors to the State. A survey in 1997 estimated that approximately 450,000 people over the age of five enjoyed the experience of recreational fishing in the waters of South Australia each year. For many recreational fishers, the social aspect of fishing is the most important factor in making a fishing trip satisfying, but the majority of fishers still consider that catching fish combined with eating the catch as the major motivation for going fishing.

The estimated proportion of fish taken by recreational fishers compared to commercial fishing varies between species, from 5% of Australian salmon, 15% of snapper and 35% of King George whiting.

The fisheries management deals with the swings from one target species to another in response to market opportunities and fluctuations in species abundance.

Much of the knowledge of the life cycle and habitat of fish species is based on scientific research, the results of which provide a sound basis for the future conservation of harvested species.

Current research activities are focused on monitoring the impacts of fishing activity on key biological performance indicators of King George whiting, snapper, squid, garfish and sand crabs. About $1.4 million is spent on the research and monitoring program for the marine scalefish fishery each year of which approximately 60% is contributed by the commercial fishery through licence fees.

South Australian Snapper, King George Whiting and Garfish in my opinion have no peer in the seaworld. When there you wash them down with an Adelaide Hills Sauvignon Blanc an Eden Valley or Clare Riesling or a top Chardonnay, from any one of South Australia's great wine regions, you will be in for a heavenly experience.

Kreglinger

What a real breath of fresh air it is to find a new winery that has so much potential and innovative thinking packed into it, as I found at the new Kreglinger winery in Mount Benson.

Kreglinger (Australia), perhaps better known to most Australia's as a bit of giant in the sphere of global agribusiness and other diverse industries, it a refreshing example of the extent to which old world companies are putting their new world ideas into practice and doing it well.

Coaxed initially by the burgeoning success of new world wines in the global market, but, perhaps not surprising y by Australian wines in particular, Kreglinger conducted and exhaustive search for the right site and location and has now set up and established a truly enterprising and promising new winery and vineyard in the Mount Benson region of The Limestone Coast.

Nestled between the attractive coastal towns of Kingston and Robe, Mount Benson, a region initially planted in the late-80's, has begun to deliver on its early signs of promise. That 'early promise' mind you had a lot to do with the fact that the region sits just a short distance west of Coonawarra. However on the basis of the wines that are now beginning to come through, the indications are strong that local climatic factors promise to push the quality boundaries out even further for some of the wines.

The combination of its mild maritime climate, long growing season, low frost risk, ample supply of high quality water and the fortuitous outcropping of abundant terra rossa over limestone, makes the vision and ambitions of a company like Kreglinger something to watch over the next few years.

Kreglinger emphasises that it has taken up the challenge of making this clean, green and highly attractive vineyard and winery operation the lynchpin of a foray into the world of global wine exports because Mount Benson is simply such a good place to start. If the same quality of thinking and execution that has evidently gone into what they have done so far, goes into the branding and distribution, it looks like they will deliver 'with bells on'.

They have engineered and built a genuinely state of the art elegant winery, which fits snugly into the gently rolling landscape of its own 250 acres of newly planted vines. Kreglinger have thoroughly examined the soil types and micro climates of their beautiful rolling hills and planted a number of classic varieties to suite each location. They are well set to create a fascinating mix of new world interpretations of old style wines and new wine styles that are only just beginning to take off here and around the world. Kreglinger will be well worth keeping your eyes on.

Chapoutier

One of the Rhone Valley in France's most prominent producers, M Chapoutier has begun three joint ventures with successful Australian producers, in cool climate regions. A strong accent is being placed on Shiraz a traditional Rhone Valley variety, that has been enormously successful in Australia.

The main and first Chapoutier venture is in the Limestone Coast Region of South Australia at Mount Benson, at their own domain, "Tournon". This was begun in 1998 and is also the first overseas venture by Chapoutier. Cape Jaffa wines are a minor joint venture partner. The first wine a Syrah 1998 (Shiraz) was released mid 1999. The mild summers with their cool nights, gives the Chapoutier wines a certain elegance and suppleness.

The vineyards which now cover 88 acres have an ideal "terroir". The deep red sandy loam's are based on free draining sandstone, the coastal ranges protect them well from the prevailing winds. The vineyards are organically managed and will soon be fully bio-dynamically managed.

The wines are made in open fermentors and undergo long maceration in the skins after fermentation for 3 to 4 weeks, a combination of new and older French oak barrels are used for maturation, so as not to overpower the fruit structure of the wines. The vineyard also has the Rhone white varieties of Viognier and Marsanne planted, as well as Cabernet Sauvignon. At present the wines are being marketed in Europe, Asia, USA, New Zealand and in Australia.

Chapoutier are also developing two other joint ventures with prominent wine makers in Victoria their H Cambrian venture with Ron Laughton from Jasper Hill and a venture at Malakoff in the Grampians with Trevor Mast and their U.S. distributor Paterno Imports.

Chapoutier are quietly and professionally doing great things in Australia, which will soon have worldwide significance.

Robe Haven Motel

Looking out over the picturesque Robe Boat Haven, surrounded by lawns and gardens is the impressive Robe Haven Motel, its whitewashed walls contrasting with the deep blue sea just across the lawns. Butlers Restaurant on the southern side, is warm and friendly, serving local produce and the succulent fresh lobster which has virtually crawled across the road.

The suites are large and airy, all with large colonial windows and exceptional views, recently redecorated, they have a completely furnished lounge area, desk, fridge and large wardrobes, they certainly make you feel like staying for a week

or so. It's a pleasant stroll of a few minutes into the historic coastal township or past the boat harbor to the lighthouse, perched high above the southern ocean on the cliff tops. It's hard to think of a more beautifully located place to have a real holiday or a reviving stop over.

There are plenty of activities nearby such as golf, tennis, squash, bowls or you can even try a spot of fishing, swimming or other water sports.

Robe is well situated for a drive over to Coonawarra wineries or to Mount Gambier's Blue Lake or the world heritage listed Naracoorte caves.

Mine Host is the extremely affable Mellie Welsh, she and her staff are most helpful and certainly make you feel right at home.

Oysa Oysters

The pristine clean clear waters of the oceanic bays of the west coast of South Australia have proved an absolute haven for the growing of Pacific Oysters. In a short time the South Australian Oyster Industry has grown into a highly regarded producer of world class oysters.

Oysters are farmed from the far west at Ceduna through Smoky Bay, Streaky Bay, Coffin Bay, around the base of Eyre Peninsula to Cowell, also at the bottom of Yorke Peninsula and around Kangaroo Island.

In 1994 38 oyster grower members formed OYSA, to guide and control the growing and marketing of oysters in South Australia. Today there are 68 growers involved by the year 2000, sales reached 30 million oysters a year and by 2002 production should reach 50 million, with a retail value of around $30M. Exports are growing rapidly to Asia including Hong Kong, Singapore and Japan, the U.K. and South Africa.

South Australia's central and western half is ideal for oysters. There is no industrial run-off, with no rivers emptying waste into the sea and no rural run off, in the driest state on the driest continent. The tidal waters also mean the oysters spend some 30% of their life above sea level which helps them develop strong muscles to assist in prolonging their shelf life. The pure nutrients in the ocean waters and the natural action of the waves also helps keep the shells clean of parasites and creates an even-shaped shell which adds a visual dimension to their eating enjoyment.

OYSA insists all oysters under their banner are guaranteed by the South Australian Sanitation Quality Assurance Program (SASQAP).

The waters of all farming leases, are checked regularly and tested to all current world standards. Samples are also taken and tested.

OYSA also works with the oyster hatcheries where the oyster "spat" is raised and sold to growers when between 4mm and 10mm in size.

OYSA oysters are graded 6-8 times before they are marketed in three categories, "Bistro" 50-60mm across the top shelf, "Plates" 60-70 mm and "Standards" 70-85 mm.

Oysters provide some of the best nutrients available - glycogen, taurine, amino acids - the building blocks of life, and zinc.

OYSA has also set up a chain of chiller rooms in all producing bays so growers can place their oysters in an ideal temperature before refridgerated trucks take them to Adelaide and onto the world. AQUIS accreditation at the Adelaide packing station further ensures quality.

Curiously South Australia had a thriving oyster industry in the early years of the states history, a round native oyster was collected by dredging, in 1870 at Coffin Bay alone, thirty sailing cutters manned by 80 men, collected over six and a half million oysters during the year. Unfortunately these practices meant the oysters were eventually fished out by the 1940's. Todays industry under OYSA, growing Pacific Oysters, is very well managed making sure the oyster business is a totally renewable resource and grown in an environmentally friendly way.

Oysters and South Australian wines are a perfect match. The Sauvignon Blancs from the Adelaide hills, McLaren Vale and other coastal regions are a perfect companion for natural oysters. Of course oysters can be served in so many ways, cold with many condiments and dips, cooked traditionally Kilpatrick style or mornay, but in so many other ways. A fresh creamy oyster soup made with South Australian snapper head stock and white wine is my favourite, or how about Carpet bag Steak, Lamb, Kangaroo, or Venison fillets stuffed with oysters served very rare - Yum!!

Why not celebrate anytime with a glass of Coopers Stout and Champagne (Black Velvet) and half a dozen natural oysters.

So the choice of wines for oysters is endless. I like OYSA's slogan "Our worlds the Oyster" and the world should celebrate.

International Oyster & Seafoods

I have never seen fresher or better seafood than the produce the Del Medico family at International Oyster & Seafoods process. The Del Medico family really know their seafood!

Their premises are situated in the heart of Adelaide at 241 Franklin Street.

The presentation of their display and sales area is absolutely mouth watering and behind the scenes, the processing area is as clean as a whistle and smells as sweet as a rose.

The large premises was purpose built in 1980, but the family's bond with the sea and it's bounty goes back a lot further.

The founder of the business, Diego Del Medico (known as Dick), arrived as a six year old in 1936. His father, Giuseppe came to Australia in the early 1920s from Molfetta on the Adriatic coast of Italy where his family had been fishermen for centuries. Giuseppe landed his first job as a fisherman at Port Pirie. In 1929 he went back to Molfetta and married his wife Giulietta. In October 1930, Diego was born and Giuseppe came back to Port Pirie alone, to long hours as a fisherman to establish a home for his family who joined him in 1936. Additions to the family of two boys and a girl followed.

When Diego was 17, he came to Adelaide boarding in Waymouth Street and working for seafood merchants Cappo Brothers in Grote Street. In 1952 Diego married Angela (known as Lina) and together they bought the Bluebird Fish Café at South Road, Black Forest. After two years, they moved to Carrington Street where Diego's father and mother now had their own fish shop. Later they moved to Hutt Street

where Lina ran the shop with her father.

In 1958 Diego started the International Oyster Bar and Restaurant in Hindley Street, an "avant garde" move for Adelaide at the time. By 1960 his oysters had such a reputation he started wholesaling to famous restaurants and nightclubs at the time such as The Lido Barbecue, Paprika and the Whisky-au-go-au-go, ensuring his oyster supply business grew quickly.

In 1960 Diego bought the wholesale business back to his Carrington Street property. In 1978 the business had well and truly outgrown its home and the Franklin Street property was bought and building commenced. By 1980, 15 people were working in the business and today 25 people work at International Oyster & Seafoods. The building was extended in 1999 and they now process and supply large volumes of oysters and seafood to the hospitality industry.

Diego's eldest son Giuseppe (known

as Joe), joined the business in 1975 (who has now left the business to pursue his own interests), Vito (who is married to Julie - Diego and Lina's daughter) joined the business in 1972, Mario the next son, joined the business in 1978 (Marios's wife Dorina pictured - also worked in the business up until a short time ago) and Angie the youngest son joined the business in 1981. Another brother, Trevor (twin of Angie) lives in America with his family). The business is very much a family affair as Julie (wife of Vito) Lina (wife of Angie) and Deborah (daughter of Vito and Julie) all working in the business.

The Del Medico family are all happy, hard working and extremely proud of their work. They pride themselves on the quality and freshness of all their products. Their delivery vans are all refrigerated and in pristine condition.

When in Adelaide, you must drop in to their place, as it is in an easy parking precinct of the city and you never know who you will bump into. The day I was photographing the family, a South Australian legend Kym Bonython breezed in, a regular customer who really knows his food and wine.

An Adelaide Hills Sauvignon Blanc or a Clare Valley Riesling, some oysters and seafood from the best fish suppliers I know - it's a heavenly thought.

Address: 241-249 Franklin Street ADELAIDE 5000
Phone: (08) 8231 6441 **Fax:** (08) 8231 7349
Owner: Delmedico Family   **Est:** 1958

Public Hours: 8:30am-5pm, Weekdays; 8:30am - 12 noon, Saturdays
Principal Brands: Fresh oysters from South Australian waters and other fresh Australian

oysters in season. Comprehensive range of fresh fish and seafoods of all varieties are available wholesale and retail sales at the premesis.

Mitani Spices

The Mitani family (Elia and wife Trianka and three month old Tas) arrived in Australia in 1954, as a part of the post World War II influx of European immigrants.

The family first settled in the Riverland town of Barmera, to work at a vine nursery.

They then moved on to Adelaide and finally settled on a farm formally the homestead for the area now known as Pooraka and Ingle Farm.

Tas Mitan now the managing director remembers his father Elia manually pulling down the stables at night making way for the glass houses, so that he could plant his tomato crop.

The family business began to evolve, as the business grew so did the family with four sons Tas, Con, Jim and Les, the family began to wholesale food out of the old former picture theatre in Gawler, the gateway to the famous Barossa Valley.

Here they started blending herbs and spices to produce the now famous Mitani Chicken Salt. The business continued to grow and in 1981 they constructed a purpose built processing facility at Salisbury, a little closer to Adelaide. By the mid 1980's the Mitani family were producing seasoned stuffing for the poultry industry and really now look at their business as value adding to the meat and particularly the poultry industry.

The main Mitani product, their chicken salt infact like wine improves with age, provided it is stored in the right conditions.

Spices are like wine; they must be kept at a constant cool temperature protected from the air to avoid oxidation and hence preserving their aromatic properties.

The family keeps some of each batch and has noticed the improvements as they age. The individual herbs and spices interact together to produce a very mellow blend of all natural ingredients. This product is now replacing table salt as it provides the benefit of sea salt together with a highly refined blend of herbs and spices.

Quality control at Mitani is extremely rigorous before and after the batches are made all ingredients are weighed to double check the exact quantities of each ingredient that have gone into the blend. Salt is a staple of life like wine, its not to be abused but ads zest to many foods. Chicken salt can uplift many dishes either as a condiment, for instance on potato wedges or used in cooking of dishes, such as the Coq au vin (chicken and red wine casserole).

A century or two ago salt was literally as valuable as gold as before refrigeration it was the only way to preserve meat as those who travelled from Europe to Australia in the 18th and 19th century by ship would have vouched.

Their products are currently available at all major supermarkets through out Australia and New Zealand including venues such as the Melbourne Cricket Ground . Exporting to the rest or the world is in their sights with stocks now available in South Africa and Singapore .

The whole of the Mitani family is committed to today's quality standards and continue to work close together which has been the main attribute to their success story.

Address: 77 Saints Road
SALISBURY PLAINS 5109
Phone: (08) 8258 4477 **Fax:** (08) 8281 4310

Owner: Mitani Family　　**Est:** 1958
Principle Brands: Chicken salt and other naturally flavoured salts and spices. Also a full

gourmet food range, freshly packed and frozen. Full catering supplies are available at the premesis.

Riverland

The Chaffey brothers, who had pioneered many successful irrigation schemes around Victoria, were asked by the South Australian Government to examine the possibility of implementing such schemes along the course of the Murray River as it wound its way through the state.

During the late 1880's the brothers set up the scheme with canals and channels, bringing life giving water to the rich orange-red alluvial soils. With the addition of this magic ingredient, the region began producing excellent quality crops of citrus and stone fruits. Grape growing and winemaking spread quickly and by the beginning of the new century it was already a substantial contributor to the Australian vintage. Today it is Australia's largest wine growing region. The massive Berri Winery, now under the banner of BRL Hardy, and agruably Australia's largest wine producer, is complemented by its sister winery, Renmano. Angove's fast expanding winery and distillery, producing its famous St. Agnes brandies, was the first established in the region in 1910, followed by large Australian companies such as Yalumba, Orlando Hardy's, Tollana, Normans, Seppelt and Penfold's all have vineyards in the region. The Riverland, however, is dominated by individual grape-growers, many of whose families took advantage of the soldier settlement program after the First World War to begin a new life planting their blocks with government assistance, a brilliantly conceived and managed scheme. The second major development in the region came with the post - Second World War European immigration flood. The newcomers with their strong link to wine and hard work developed the region quickly, inspiring others by their success.

Such immigrants were the Moularadellis family whose Kingston Estate is a premium wine success story expanding from a 60 tonne crush in 1986 to over 20,000 tonnes in 2001, and winning many trophies and gold medals around the world along the way. A huge success story has been the Hardy's Banrock Station project near Kingston. The vineyards are interspersed by wetlands which have been preserved and enhanced by owners BRL Hardy, every one of the tens of millions of the excellent Banrock Station table and sparkling wines sold helps land care in Australia. In March 2001 a new wetlands educational walkway was opened by the Honorable Joan Hall, S.A. Minister of Tourism.

Viticultural developments with techniques such as minimal pruning, leading to smaller bunches of berries and increased wine quality, have been most successful. Moisture control and minimum irrigation is also contributing to increased wine quality.

Winemaking methods and technology combine with top quality grapes to produce some exciting wines, in this important Australian wine region, whose future looks bright.

The region offers much to the visitor as it enjoys a very mild-pleasant climate all year round. The attractions of the river with its water sports, houseboat cruises and the many golf courses on its banks, beckons one to come and have a break anytime.

Bonneyview Wines

Bonneyview Wines was a concept well ahead of its time. In 1975 Robert Minns established his winery with a restaurant café incorporated. His pioneering and innovative nature can also be seen in the fact he was the first in the Modern Era of the Australian Wine Industry to plant Petit Verdot, rescuing a bundle of cuttings from the nearby Loxton Research Station in 1979, just before they were to be discarded. He planted these in his vineyard. Petit Verdot now features in various blends and may be released as a straight varietal by Bonneyview's new owners shortly.

In 2000, 25 years after its founding Robert sold Bonneyview to a group of Riverland growers Chris and Mick Zahos, George Simos and winemakers Rob Patonowski, now making wine in California and Chris Polymidas who has made wine for Australian vintages at Loxton.

The winemaking will be expanded, as the 3 growers produce 600 tonnes of premium grapes between them. The award winning restaurant at Bonneyview has a warm and friendly atmosphere and is renowned for its hearty servings of home cooked food. The steaks are particularly succulent and an open fire welcomes you in winter. The open Yiros grill has also proved a real winner.

Bonneyview is a must visit when you travel through the Riverland.

R i v e r l a n d

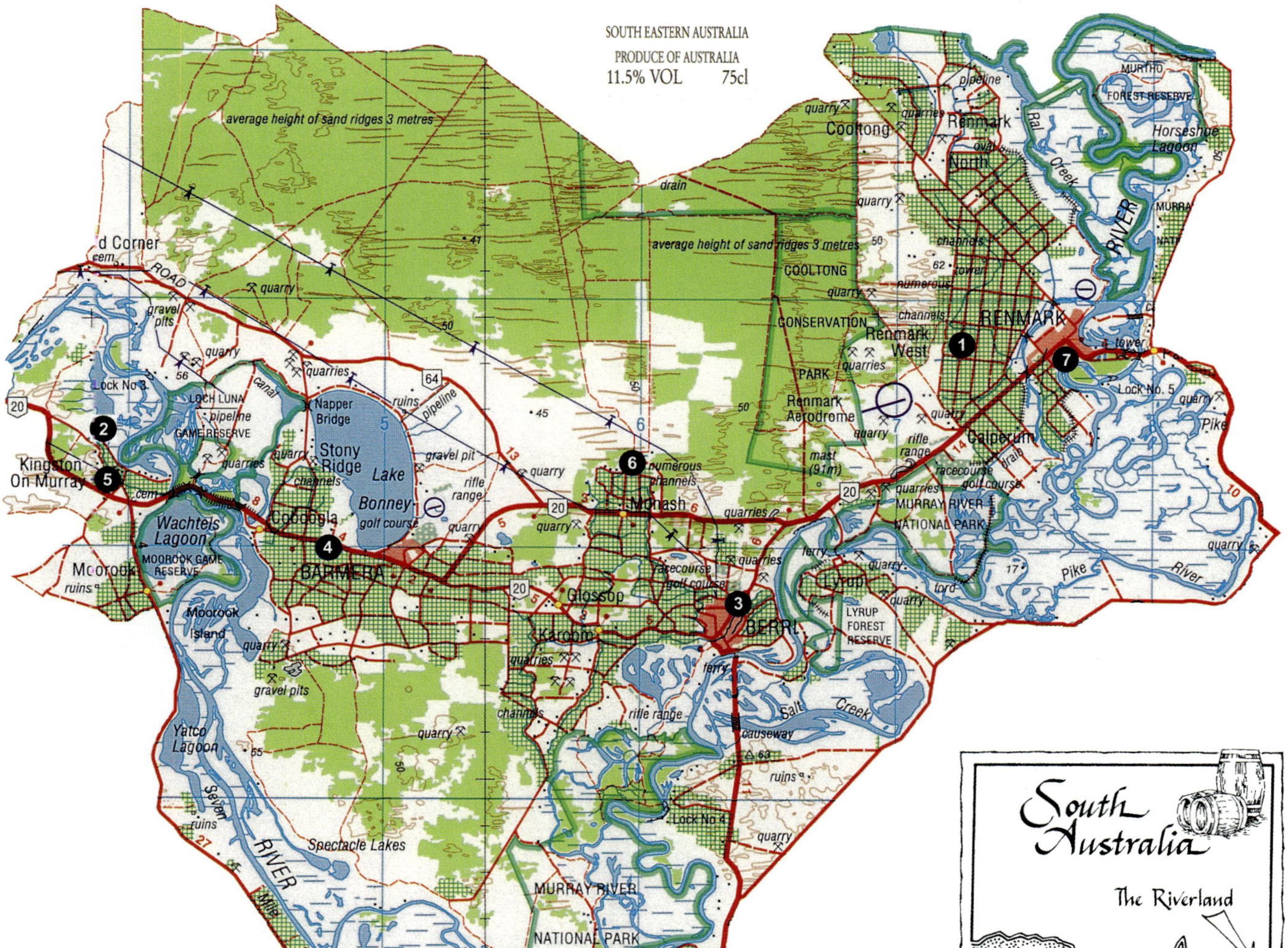

Riverland - SA

1. Angoves
2. Barrock Station
3. Berri Estates
4. Bonneyview Wines
5. Kingston Estate
6. Normans Lonegum
7. Renmano

Angoves St Agnes Brandy

No book on Australian Wine would be complete without a feature on brandy, an essential beverage of the wine and grape industry. What is brandy? Brandy is the distilled spirit of wine made from fresh grapes. Australia has some of the world's strictest controls on the production and maturation of this age-old essence of wine.

The first step in the production of brandy is the fermentation of grape juice to produce wine, often referred to as brandy wash. Brandy wash is then distilled, a process that extracts the alcohol and a wide range of volatile flavour components, called congeners, from the wine. It is the mystical distillation process that gives rise to the production of brandy from wine, but before it can be called brandy it must be matured in wood for a period of not less than 2 years. This time of quiet maturation allows the spirit to mellow and soften, and gain extra interest and complexity of flavour by interaction with the oak. Longer maturation is not uncommon in order to produce even better quality brandy.

There are two distinct alternative methods of distillation. The first and most important is the classic "pot still" method (the only method used for all Angove's St Agnes brandies). This technique has been utilised by the best French cognac houses for centuries. The pot still is "charged" with brandy wash or wine, which is gently heated. As boiling occurs the most volatile components vaporise first. These are called "heads" and are undesirable in the brandy and

after condensation are kept separate from the "heart" of the distillation that follows as the boiling point temperature continues to rise. Towards the end of the distillation the heavier least volatile components are vaporised and condensed and are called "tails", these are oily, and are also undesirable in the brandy. The heart of the distillation is often called "Brandy Low Wine" it contains about 50% alcohol by volume. The brandy low wine is returned to the pot still and distilled a second time with the heart of this second distillation being of sufficient purity to be matured in oak barrels for brandy.

A second distillation method utilises a continuous still and as the name implies is a continuous process where wine is constantly fed into the still, the alcohol stripped from the wine by steam generated heat and in a second column the steam alcohol mixture is successively distilled and condensed over a series of specially designed 'plates'. Spirit can be extracted from the column at up to 95% alcohol by volume. This is an excellent method for the production of fortifying spirit for addition to ports, sherries, vermouths etc., but is not the most ideal for production of quality brandy.

St. Agnes Brandy is double distilled pot still brandy, produced by the Angove Family in Renmark, South Australia, it's been a flagship of the company for many years and has earned many trophies and medals in Australia and Overseas. St. Agnes Very Old XO Brandy has been awarded many international honours

including the Championship Trophy in France against brandies from around the world.

In the early 1970's the Federal Government severely wounded this important segment of the wine and grape industry with callous ill-conceived tax increases. At this time brandy was on a strong growth curve and Angove's were increasing the size of their distillery to accommodate a new pot still to add to the three existing stills; this space still remains vacant some 30 years later. Recent growth in St. Agnes sales may herald new opportunities for expansion and the fourth pot still may yet find its way into the system.

The age of a brandy is the age in wood of the youngest component of any blend. By this rule, St. Agnes 3 Star Brandy is usually between two and a half and three years of age. It is a great value, superb brandy. St. Agnes Old Liqueur 5 Star Brandy has a minimum age of 10 years in wood and St. Agnes Very Old XO Brandy has a minimum age of 20 years in wood. These are superb spirits that the gods would be proud of. Older brandies are very expensive to produce with money tied up in stock for 20 years or more. Additionally, 2 - 3% of the volume of brandy in each barrel is lost to evaporation each year. This is called the "angel's share".

The Angove family is led by wine industry stalwart Tom Angove, with more than 65 vintages under his belt and his son John as Managing Director. This fine family company's commitment to quality wine and brandy production, always seeking to improve and give their customers extra value, is admirable. St. Agnes, the patron saint of purity, would be proud of them.

Angoves Wines

On July 12, 2001, Angove's celebrated 115 years of involvement in the Wine & Brandy industry. Dr William Angove planted the company's first vines in 1886 at Tea Tree Gully, near Adelaide.

Dr Angove as well as being a medical practitioner was a highly successful winemaker and marketer and his business thrived. By the turn of the century his wines were well known throughout the country with many show awards to their credit. The company expanded, establishing the first winery and distillery in the Murray Valley, at Renmark, in 1910. Further developments followed, with the construction of another winery at Lyrup, southwest of Renmark in 1913, and the export of large volumes of wine to England during the 1920's.

Angove's continued to expand and consolidate their business and in

Angoves Wines

1968 plantings commenced at Nanya Vineyard, a few kilometres east of Renmark. Now one of Australia's largest single vineyards, planted with at least 22 different varieties, the Nanya Vineyard produces a large range of varietal table wines including riesling, sauvignon blanc, chardonnay, chenin blanc, colombard and cabernet sauvignon.

The quality of the wines in the different Angove's ranges is exceptionally high and their value extraordinary. Their Classic Reserve wines are the best selections of their premium varieties, which receive special treatment in the winery in small batches, and in the case of the reds and chardonnay, small barrel fermentation and ageing. The Sarnia Farm label is now the top of the range and named after the original Tea Tree Gully properties. The wines are all regionally selected, with the Padthaway region in SA's southeast featuring prominently.

Angove's have a tremendous depth of products of the vine, producing one of Australia's finest brandies under the St Agnes label, along with Australia's best commercial fino sherry, a range of vermouths under the Marko label and the Stone's Green Ginger wine.

Angove's wines are currently produced at Renmark in the Riverland of South Australia. Tea Tree Gully, though originally constructed as a winery, now houses a Cellar Door sales facility as well as the State Branch Office. Vineyards that surrounded the Tea Tree Gully winery no longer exist, as they were compulsorily purchased by the South Australian Government to provide land for housing in the mid 70's.

Having played a major role in establishing the Murray Valley as a wine producing area the Angoves have not only contributed to the economic welfare of the state but have also furthered the reputation of Australian wine worldwide. Tom Angove although officially retired, still assists and helps keep everything on an even keel. He has contributed enormously to Australian wine and brandy in so many ways and is a true treasure of our great industry.

Address: Bookmark Avenue RENMARK 5341	Est: 1886 Vine Ha: 480 Cases: 1,000,000	Sarnia Farm Cabernet	5-10 yrs
Phone: (08) 8580 3100 Fax: (08) 8580 3155	Public Hours: 9am-5pm, weekdays	Sarnia Farm Chardonnay	2-5 yrs
Email: angoves@angoves.com.au	Principal Varieties: Chardonnay, Chenin	Classic Reserve Chardonnay	1-3 yrs
WWW: www.angoves.com.au	Blanc, Sauvignon Blanc, Cabernet Sauvignon,	Classic Reserve Cabernet Sauvignon	2-5 yrs
Owner: Angove Family	Rhine Riesling, Shiraz, Colombard, Pinot Noir	Classic Reserve Sauvignon Blanc	1-3 yrs
Winemaker: Hane Gilham	Principal Wines Potential	Butterfly Ridge Colombard/Chard	1-3 yrs

Banrock Station

Just north of Kingston-On-Murray is the historic Banrock Station, some 4,500 acres within a loop of the majestic River Murray and its magnificent red cliffs encircling three sides with 12 kilometres of river frontage.

The first settlement was made during the last century by a Sydney based drover called Wigley, who fell in love with the property and grazed cattle there. The ruins of his original homestead remain, but often being flooded, he relocated to a site which became Kingston-On-Murray. The historic Cobb and Co. Staging Station was just opposite the property, which passed through a number of owners gradually turning towards horticulture.

Thirteen acres of vines were planted by the Jackson Family to which legendary identity Jack Warne added a further 20 acres in 1975. Today BRL Hardy have developed 1,000 acres of premium vineyards. The first wines, a semilllon/chardonnay and a cabernet/shiraz, proved most successful in both bottles and 2 litre wine casks. A premium unwooded chardonnay and a premium shiraz were added in 1996.

The property includes a declared conservation protected wetlands which BRL Hardy are helping restore. A royalty on all Banrock Station Wines is going towards this worthwhile project. In April 2001 a new wetlands trail was opened by the S.A. Minister of Tourism, Joan Hall. You should check out Banrock Station, visit the hospitality centre and let your enjoyment help nature!!

Berri Estate

The largest wine producer in Australia has rather humble origins, as a grower co-operative. The co-operative's first wine and brandy spirit was produced in a small distillery with makeshift equipment, from a surplus of raisins and sultanas left over after the Riverland harvest of 1918. Within four years, local fruit production had greatly increased with the influx of repatriated soldier settlers to the area and the Berri Growers Co-operative was formed to manage the business.

Berri's first commercial vintage was made in 1922. In 1958 a new winery was constructed to cater for the swing in public tastes towards table wines. Wines were marketed in both bottles and flagons with impressive results. Sales figures skyrocketed during the early 1970's with the introduction into the market of the 'bag in the box' wine cask.

Berri quickly developed their five-litre cask, the wine inside the cask is of high quality and is great value for money.

Berri also developed a range of premium table wines during the 1970's. winemakers Brian Barry and Ian McKenzie won more than 1,000 show medals over an eight-year period including the illustrious Jimmy Watson Trophy and the 1977 Most Successful Exhibitors Trophy from the National Wine Show in Canberra.

The stars of the Berri range have been their cabernet sauvignons and cabernet blends. Today Berri Estate is part of the BRL Hardy Wine Company and quality is on a constant improvement curve.

Normans Lonegum

Situated at Monash, in the upper reaches of South Australia's Riverland, is a large winery formerly known as Wein Valley Estates.

In 1994 Wein Valley merged their operations, including a bottling line in Northgate Victoria, with Normans and floated what has become another successful public wine company, Normans Ltd.

The winery has been totally upgraded in a quality sense and expanded with an anticipated crush in 2001 of 20,000 tonnes, putting it in the top league of Australian Wineries.

The Lone Gum and Jesse's Blend (named after the legendary Jesse Norman) labels are focussing on the export and value for money Australian markets. The wine quality is well above average and the prices exceptionally good value. The sunshine good soils and careful winemaking have once again triumphed, in this, Australia's biggest wine region.

Address: Nixon Road MONASH 5342
Phone: (08) 8583 5255 **Fax:** (08) 8583 5444
Email: info@normans-wines.com.au

WWW: www.normans-wines.com.au
Owner: Normans Wines Limited
Winemaker: Stuart Auld

Public Hours: 9am-5pm, weekdays
Principal Varieties: Chardonnay, Semillon, Chenin Blanc, Cabernet Sauvignon, Shiraz

Renmano

In 1915, 130 Riverland grape growers banded together to form the country's first co-operative winery.

They purchased the Chateau Tanunda distillery situated just south of Renmark and produced spirit for

twenty years until fortified wines became popular, and production was altered accordingly. A range of table wines was developed during the late 1950's with Renmano's first varietal release being a cabernet sauvignon

in 1962. Other varieties followed in subsequent years, although most wines were sold in bulk to other companies until the 1970's. In addition to Renmano's cask and flagon wines, a premium range of table wines is also produced and marketed under the Chairman's Selection label. This range, cabernet sauvignon, shiraz and chardonnay represent excellent value for money and have been highly successful on the export market. The Chairman's Selection range really came into prominence when the 1998 Chardonnay won 4 trophies including the Tucker Seabrook Caon Trophy for the best show wine over the 1990 Wine Show season.

Renmano also produce a range of premium varietal 2 litre wine casks, these remain among the best and most popular wines in this field.

There is an excellent cellar door at the winery in the heart of Renmark and it makes a good visit if you are passing through the region.

Kingston Estate

In 1994 Kingston Estate were awarded the South Australian business of the Year award, an accolade that could not have been more deserved.

The winery and its young winemaker, Bill Moularadellis is one of the success stories of the Australian wine industry. Kingston has carved out a niche in the export market and have repeated this success within Australia. Although Bill's parents both came from Greece, they actually met in the Riverland. For many years they ran their fruit and vine block, selling grapes to large wine producers As their grapes were always among the best in the region and in demand, they decided to build a small winery in 1979. By 1986, the winery was still only crushing 60 tonnes. Today it is one of Australia's largest, crushing over 20,000 tonnes.

Bill attended Roseworthy and graduated with his winemaking credentials in 1985, followed by a vintage in the Hunter Valley. He then returned to Kingston and concentrated on creating a modern winemaking facility with state-of-the art equipment and expanded capacity.

At the outset the Moularadellis family set quality and value-for-money as the main criteria for their wines to meet and as rapid as the growth of the winery has been, Bill has always had a clear objective to continually improve the quality of the wines being produced, plus refining his style of winemaking.

Bill liaises strongly with his growers, assisting and encouraging in the pursuit of excellence at every level. To translate this fruit quality into wine Bill has introduced a system based on small tanks and open fermenters enabling he and his team to isolate and personally handle those batches of grapes showing outstanding potential.

Kingston Estate make two main ranges of wine - the elegantly packaged 'Kingston Estate' and the prestige 'Kingston Reserve' range featuring rich, truly powerful wines. In 1994, the 1991 Reserve Chardonnay won the double gold at the San Francisco International Wine Show and the Hyatt Advertiser Award for South Australia's best Chardonnay. Other whites produced are a wood-matured semillon and a semillon/sauvignon blanc blend - both classy wines, full of character. Recently released is the Kingston Reserve Petit Verdot a rich red

Bordeaux variety which has proved well suited to the Riverland. The 'Kingston Estate Cabernet Sauvignon, Merlot and Shiraz' are all award winners. Kingston Estate has pioneered many export markets such as China.

Kingston wines are proud of the Riverland and Bill pays tribute to the rich sandy loams of the region and the untiring efforts of his grapegrowers. Kingston have expanded their operations and now also crush grapes from other regions and are releasing special regional selections often of unusual varieties, such as the recent releases of zinfandel from the Alpine Valleys in Victoria and Durif from Northern Victoria.

The ultimate wine produced by Kingston is "Tessara" a limited edition, classy, complex Bordeaux blend, the first vintage a 1998 is a blend of 65% cabernet sauvignon from the Riverland with 15% cabernet franc and 10% merlot both from Victoria's Alpine Valleys, plus 10% petit verdot from the Riverland.

Bill Moularadellis is a 'new breed' of winemaker, unconstrained by outmoded concepts of winemaking and marketing. Bill's view is global and he has built a team of young professionals around him, who share his passion for excellence in every area of his business. Always in the background and caring for everything, down to keeping the fermentation area clean, are his devoted and proud parents.

Address: Sturt Highway KINGSTON-ON-MURRAY 5331	Est: 1979 Vine Ha: 200	Kingston Tessera (Cab/Cab Franc/Merlot/Petit Verdot) 3-5 yrs
Phone: (08) 8583 0510 Fax: (08) 8583 0505	Principal Varieties: Cabernet, Chardonnay, Merlot, Petit Verdot, Shiraz	Kingston Reserve Wines 5-7 yrs
Email: kewines@riverland.net.au	Principal Wines Potential	Kingston Estate Range Drink now
Owner/Winemaker: Bill Moularadellis	Sarantos Soft Press Chardonnay Drink now	Kingston Special Releases 2-7 yrs

Victoria has been through a wine revolution in the last two decades. The number of wineries has exploded - at last count, there were more than 350 wineries in the state, the most of any state in the Australia. However, Victoria accounts for less than 20 per cent of the nation's production.

One important factor is that Victoria is truly a premium wine producer. Well over 90% of the wineries are small, boutique, premium bottled wine producers. No state has such a wide spread of vineyards and virtually no region of the state is without a vineyard, showing how suitable the climate and soil are for vines.

In 1838 William Ryrie planted Victoria's first vines in the Yarra Valley at Yering Station. Within five years many vineyards had been established in Geelong, the Yarra Valley, and in and around metropolitan Melbourne. Suburban vineyards, some as large as 30 acres, were located at South Yarra, Toorak and Brighton. This development was due largely to the arrival of groups of Swiss immigrants who brought both vine cuttings and viticultural knowledge to the new colony. In particular, Paul and Hubert de Castella and the Baron Guillaume de Pury were influential in establishing a new viticultural industry, throughout the Yarra Valley. Swiss settlers also spread winemaking knowledge to Geelong where vines were first planted in 1842.

The gold rush of the late 1800's encouraged many thousands of people to travel inland in the search for easy wealth. New areas were settled and towns were consequently established. Winemakers travelled, developing vineyards in Great Western, Avoca, Ballarat, Bendigo, the Goulburn Valley and as far north as Rutherglen.

By the end of the century Victoria was producing more wine than any other colony. Unfortunately this booming industry went into decline owing to a change in public tastes and an attack from a tiny aphid called Phylloxera Vastatrix which kills vines by eating through their roots. The louse first attacked vines in Geelong in 1875 and gradually spread north through the state. In an attempt to protect Rutherglen, Victoria's principal wine-producing area, affected winemakers were ordered to destroy all vines and chemically sterilize their soil, making replanting financially impractical. By some quirk of fate, the Yarra Valley was spared this parasite, but both here and in other unaffected areas, production soon ceased due to the growth in popularity of fortified wines and the competitive prices of interstate producers.

The only regions still producing wine by 1921, were the Goulburn Valley and Glenrowan, Great Western, Rutherglen and the North-Western Murray River. With Victoria's wine production thus affected, redevelopment did not begin until the 1960's when table wine again became popular.

A few new districts were planted to vines however, such as Drumborg in the south-western corner of the state, the high elevated cool regions in the Central Highlands, King and Ovens Valleys and the Mornington Peninsula. Each of the 11 wine-producing areas of Victoria (with many subdivisions), produces distinctly characteristic wines.

When purchasing a Victorian wine the wine-lover is now confronted with an incredible array of wine styles and varieties. Despite almost total eradication, the wine industry of Victoria has re-asserted itself across the state.

Wines currently produced cater for all tastes and compare favourably with those of other states. Generally of a very high quality, Victorian wines are finding a ready market both Australia wide and internationally.

Bendigo Heathcote

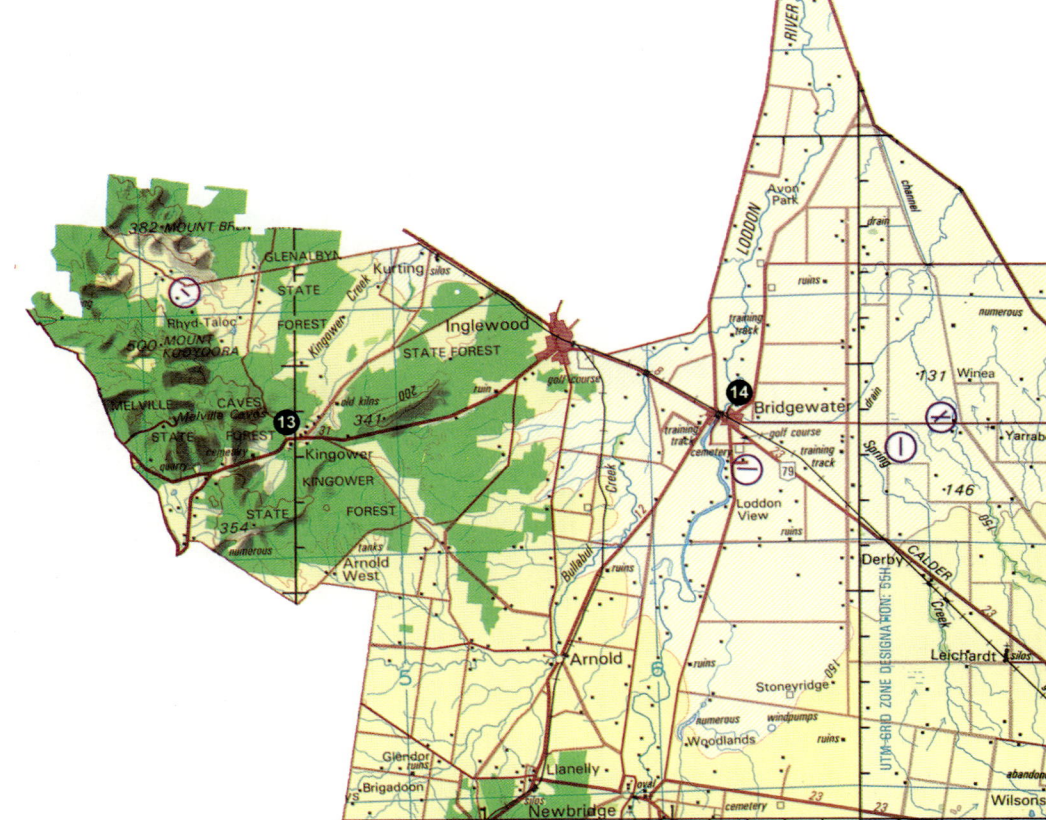

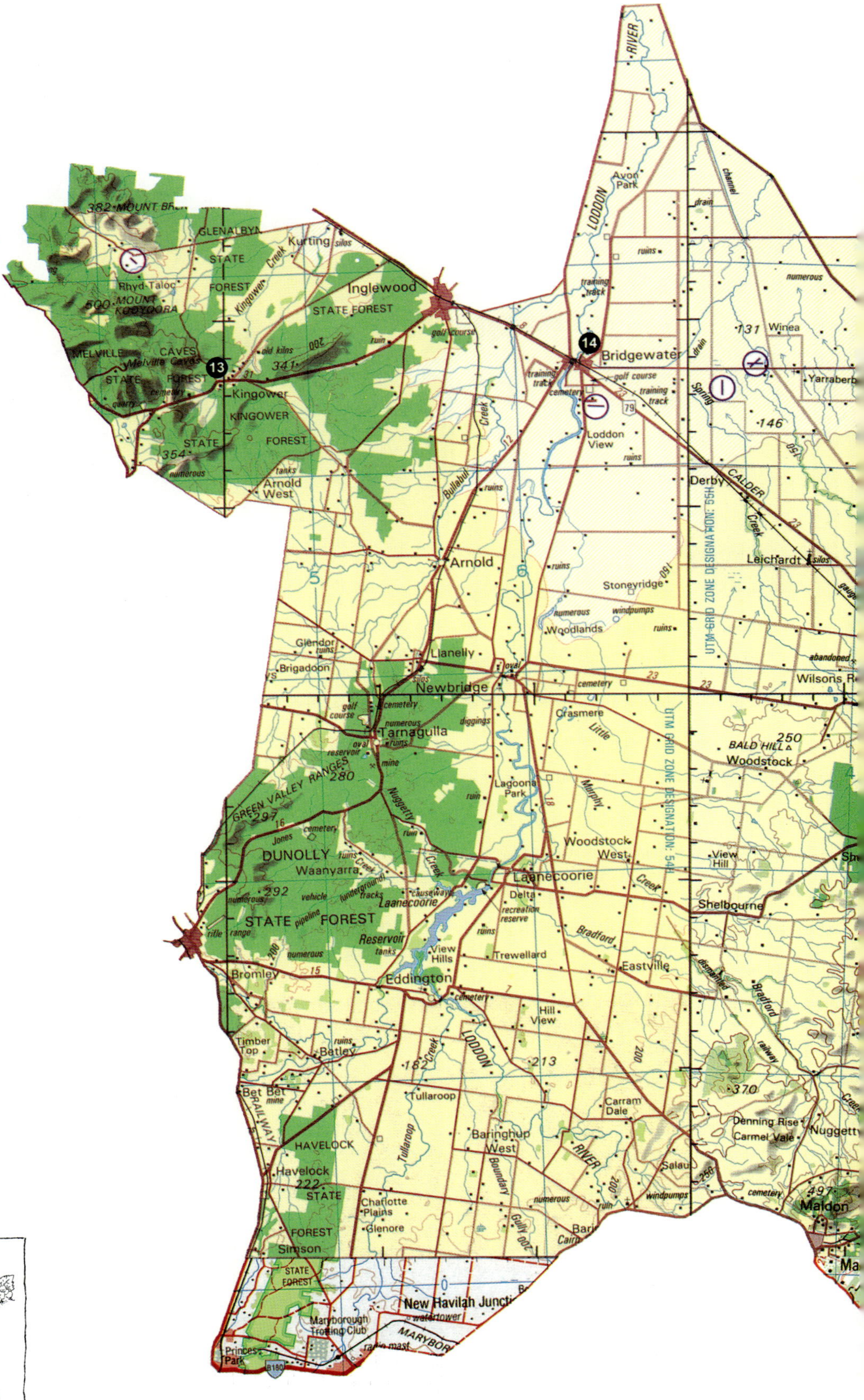

Bendigo - VIC

1. Ealgownie Estate
2. Eig Hill Vineyard
3. Elackjack Vineyards
4. Castlemaine Small Goods
5. Chateau Dore
6. Chateau Leamon
7. Eppalock Ridge
8. Harcourt Valley Vineyards
9. Heathcote Winery
10. Huntleigh Vineyards
11. Jasper Hill Vineyard
12. Mount Ida
13. Passing Clouds
14. Waterwheel Vineyards
15. Wild Duck Creek Estate
16. Zuber Estate

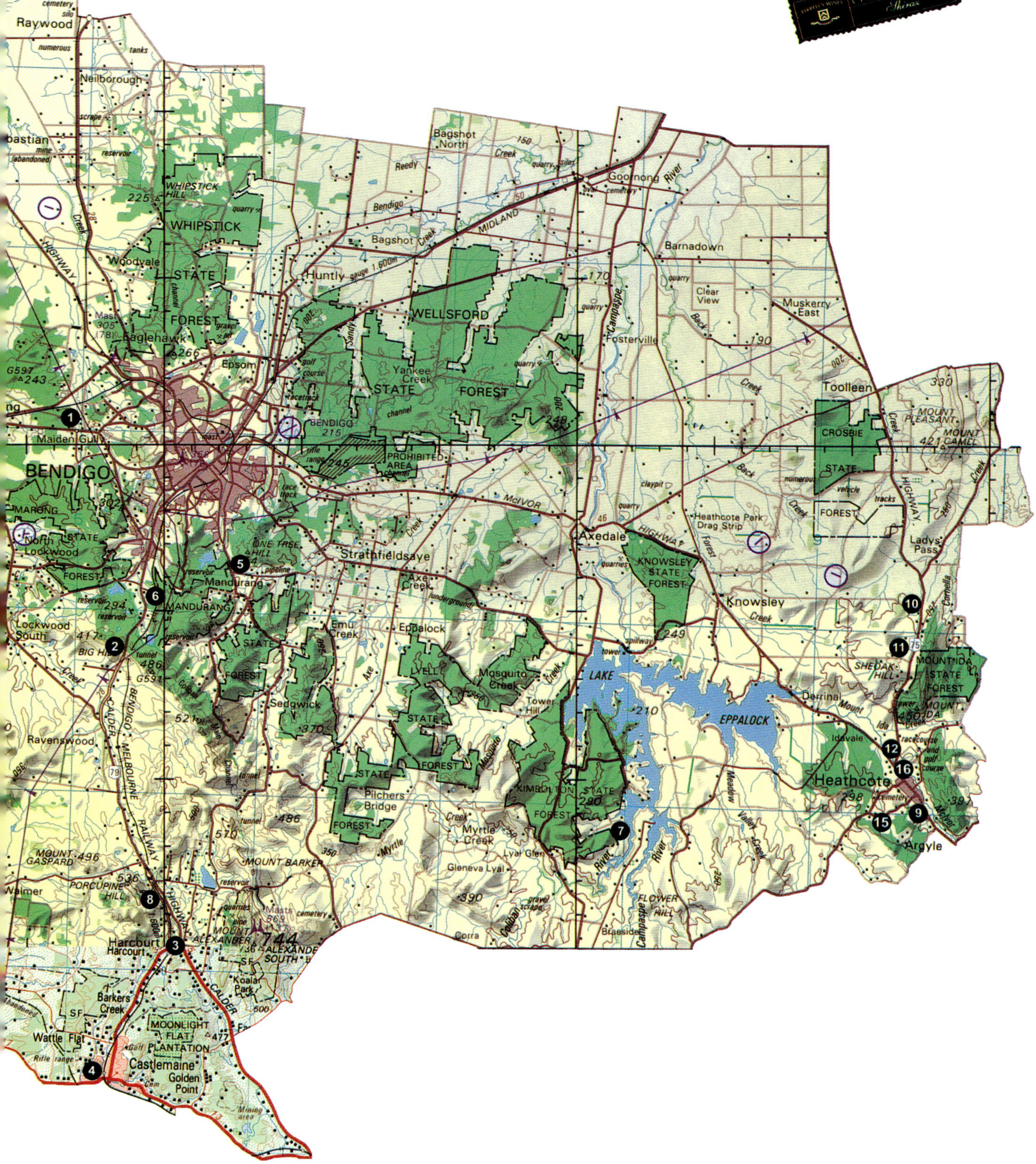

Bendigo Heathcote

Although a few vineyards existed around Bendigo during the late 1840's, the area did not fully develop until gold was discovered in 1851. Within 30 years, there were more than 100 wine producers in the region, making very high quality wines.

Phylloxera, the scourge of Victoria's vignerons, was discovered in Bendigo in 1893, thus bringing a thriving industry to a grinding halt. As in the Geelong district, local winemakers were forced to destroy their vines and the area was not replanted until 1969.

In that year, Stuart Anderson established the Balgownie vineyard northeast of Bendigo. Since then, the area has once again attracted winemakers, although only a small proportion of the original number. Heathcote is now a fast growing region. During the 1970's some exciting wines came on to the market. Artist Len French's Mt Ida

vineyard became very famous for its Shiraz and Cabernet. Ron Laughton's Jasper Hill Vineyards made quite a reputation for itself, which continues today. The Heathcote winery started in 1978 and produces innovate wines which are great value for money.

Many large vineyards are going in at present, over 100 acres is being planted by village road show chief Rob Kirby, near Mt Jasper, Southcorp, Tyrrells and others are planting huge vineyards on the Terra Rossa Slopes of Mt Camel to the north of Heathcote.

Shiraz seems to do particularly well giving wines of lifted cherry and raspberry flavours with some eucalypt and strong, peppery character. The areas potential is at last being realized.

While the Bendigo region produces some premium wines, physical conditions of the area are far from ideal. The average annual rainfall for

Bendigo is a low 500-550mm which is compensated for in various ways. Some winemakers irrigate their vineyards, others rely on an underground water supply, while still others depend on clay subsoils to retain what rain does fall. Furthermore, the impervious nature of widespread clay soils can prove to be a problem by restricting growth of vine roots.

Once these difficulties have been overcome, however, winemakers have followed Stuart Anderson's excellent lead to produce outstanding wines from this colourful region. Innovative winemakers such as Peter Cumming from Waterwheel and Ken Pollock and Ian McKenzie's Blackjack Vineyards have done much to conquer the elements and enhance this region's reputation.

In total there are now 18 wineries on the Granite Slopes and in the Loddon Valley regions.

Castlemaine Bacon Co.

Whilst Castlemaine began its life in this picturesque country Victorian town in 1905 producing mainly bacon, today the company produces more than 500 individual smallgoods of every shape, style and size.

Cured and fermented meat products have long accompanied the wines in European countries. Most wine-growing families in countries such as France, Italy, Spain and Germany make their own cured hams, salamis, terrines and pates. I well remember helping my neighbours each year in the Cognac region of France to turn a complete pigs carcass into an astonishing array of delicacies.

My favourite was the cured prosciutto style ham, I even pressed a couple of legs myself and cured them in the smoke filled tower of my Chateau Hotel · a slight accident as the grand fireplace was not working too well. The next year my neighbours wanted to hang their's there also · French oak smoked ham · it was a winner · a little secret was massaging them with "Eau de Vie" 70% alcohol cognac first, but back to Castlemaine.

In 1882 John Weetman arrived in Melbourne from his native England. He set up 3 or 4 small pork shops in the cosmopolitan St Kilda area, producing his own bacon and smallgoods.

In 1905, with his daughter and prospective son-in-law Wright Harris, he set up business in Castlemaine curing and processing 5 pigs a week in the old Castlemaine Butter Factory. In 1913, with business expanding, he moved to the current site in Richards Road.

After Weetman's death in 1922 Wright Harris carried on the business. By 1930, 500 pigs a year were being processed.

In 1946 Harris formed the Castlemaine Bacon Company with his seven sons, by the 1950's Castlemaine became the first company in Australia to install a vacuum packaging machine. Production had expanded to 15,000 pigs a year by 1967 and the workforce was up to 80 people and much new machinery had been installed. 1979 saw a large world class abattoir installed with a capacity of 1700 pigs a day.

A little like wine, to ensure supply of quality meat, Castlemaine set up their own pig raising facilities at Girgarree and Bears Lagoon. 45,000 animals are now housed at these facilities.

Castlemaine purchased Otto Wurth in 1991 to assist in the production and marketing of European delicacies.

In 1999 Castlemaine purchased two Victorian smallgoods manufacturers · Stuarts & Farmhouse. This was followed by the purchase in February 2000 of Meapro; a major NSW smallgoods manufacturer.

Castlemaine has remained a family business, operated by five successive generations of the Harris family. Their dedication and quality focus has seen the company grow to employ 900 people.

Like the specialist little German sausage and smallgoods makers in the Barossa Valley, Castlemaine are proud of their product and I am sure you can find one of their 500 or more superb products to suit the wine you like!!

Balgownie

While on a visit to the Bordeaux district of France in 1950, Stuart Anderson fell in love with the region and it's wines. He began a continuing association with the area, and gained much of his considerable winemaking knowledge there.

In 1969, Stuart planted approximately 30 acres of vines a short distance north-east of Bendigo. The property was named 'Balgownie' and although only 5,000-6,000 cases of wine were produced annually, these wines were of such high quality that they sold out quickly each year. The Balgownie Cabernet Sauvignon

was the star of the range which also included a Shiraz. The Cabernet has great depth with berry/cassis flavours and a beautiful hint of sweet oak and is consistently one of the best wines of this variety in Australia. The Balgownie Shiraz is of a similar style with a peppery character. Beringer Blass Wines saw the potential of Balgownie and purchased the vineyard and winery in 1985.

In 1999 the Estate returned to private ownership being bought by the Forrester Family, since their purchase the vineyards have been

expanded and now cover 75 acres. The winery has also been expanded and many improvements made. New winemaker Tobias Ansted has had plenty of cool climate experiences in the Canberra region after studying and working at Charles Sturt University winery he went overseas and has made wine in Romania, France and Argentina. He is reveling in his new task making the wines and managing Balgownie.

It is good to see Balgownie returning to the heights of its heyday, I'm sure the future at Balgownie is bright.

Address: Hermitage Road MAIDEN GULLY 3551	**Est:** 1969 **Vine Ha:** 100 **Cases:** 9,000	Balgownie Premier Chardonnay	2-4 yrs
Phone: (03) 5449 6222 **Fax:** (03) 5449 6506	**Public Hours:** 10.30am-5pm, Mon-Sat	Balgownie Premier Shiraz Cabernet	3-5 yrs
Owner: Mildara Blass Limited	**Principal Varieties:** Cabernet, Merlot, Shiraz	Balgownie Estate Cab Sav	5-8 yrs
Winemaker: Lindsay Ross	**Principal Wines** **Potential**	Balgownie Estate Shiraz	5-8 yrs

Heathcote Winery

Located in the heart of the historic and pretty town of Heathcote is the innovative Heathcote Winery, a blend of the past with a state of the art winery.

Thomas Craven arrived in the fledging wayside stop of Heathcote, during the gold rush days of the 19th Century. In 1884 he built a miners produce store, which included a wine and spirits license. Today this store is the characterful cellar door of Heathcote with the modern winery located at the rear.

In 1979 the Tudhope family established the winery in its main street location, plus 30 acres of vines on Newlans Lane, some 5 kms out of town. The Cellar Door has been totally restored and visitors may now experience the history of the building with its display of memorabilia and art gallery in the refurbished Grain Store room. The

new owners have rehabilitated the vineyards considerably and the winery has been expanded and updated.

The main focus at Heathcote is Shiraz and the new exciting white variety Viognier. Passionate and enthusiastic wine maker Mark Kelly is doing great things with the wines. Heathcote Winery, owned by Stephen

Wilkins and a band of wine lovers, run a great wine club, you can enjoy the benefits by joining up and also get a supply of the great wine each year.

The Heathcote region is fast becoming a top mainstream Australian wine region. There are many charming bed and breakfasts in the area, it's a great place to visit.

Address: 185 High Street HEATHCOTE 3523	**Winemaker:** Mark Kelly **Cases:** 5,000	Curagee Viognier 3 yrs
Phone: (03) 5433 2595 **Fax:** (03) 5433 3081	**Public Hours:** 11am-5pm, Thurs-Sun &	Heathcote Winery Chardonnay 3 yrs
Email: winemaker@heathcotewinery.com.au	Public Holidays, or by arrangement	Mail Coach Shiraz 10-12 yrs
WWW: www.auscellardoor.com.au **Est:** 1979	**Principal Wines** **Potential**	Heathcote Winery "Violet" 3 yrs
Owner: Stephen Wilkins **Vine Ha:** 30	Curagee Shiraz 10-12 yrs	Thomas Craven Chardonnay 3 yrs

Water Wheel

Water Wheel was a pioneering vineyard in the renaissance of the Bendigo Wine region, when vines were planted on the property at Bridgewater-on-Loddon, about 40kms north west of Bendigo, in 1970.

The initial vineyards have been greatly expanded, since local horticulturist Peter Cumming purchased the property in 1989. The 20-acre vineyard has now been increased to more than 200 acres of

vines, located on three different sites. The reds are planted on the heavier clay soils and the whites on lighter freer draining soils.

The vines are a picture, beautifully maintained on tall trellises giving plenty of exposure to the sun for the leaves and fruit, building full flavours and ripeness in the cool climate.

Water Wheel have been very successful not only on the local market but also overseas selling in Canada, USA, New Zealand, UK, Belgium, Austria and Switzerland.

The Water Wheel wines include Sauvignon Blanc, Chardonnay, Shiraz and Cabernet Sauvignon. I like their full round flavours and they are certainly well priced for top premium wines, it's not a wonder they often sell out before the new vintage is ready. Water Wheel have a friendly tasting area so drop in if your driving through the region.

Address: Raywood Rd BRIDGEWATER-ON-LODDON 3516	**Winemaker:** Bill Trevaskis **Est:** 1972	
Phone: (03) 5437 3060 **Fax:** (03) 5437 3082	**Public Hours:** 11am-5pm, daily (Oct-Apr); 11am-5pm, Mon-Fri & 1pm-4pm weekends & public holidays (May-Sep)	**Principal Varieties:** Chardonnay, Shiraz, Cabernet Sauvignon, Sauvignon Blanc
Email: waterwheel@bigpond.com		

Macedon Ranges

The Macedon viticultural region, closer to Melbourne than some parts of the Yarra Valley, stretches from North of the Sunbury Region to Boynton and from Mt William, west to Malmsbury. It is really divided into two separate regions, the wineries grouped around the central Lancefield-Woodend-Macedon area, then further north around Kyneton.

Initial development in the region started with the gold rush in the 1850's. Within 60 years however, due to the phylloxera plague and changes in wine drinking tastes, the industry had faded from existence.

The 1970's saw a renaissance of the area when the Knight family at Granite Hill and Tom Lazar at Virgin Hills established vineyards in the area. Other winemakers who followed were Flynn and Williams at Kyneton, Gordon and Judy Cope-Williams at Romsey, John and Ann Ellis at Hanging Rock, Keith and Lyn Brien at Cleveland Estate and many others. There are now more than 40 grape-growers in the region, supplying more than a dozen wineries.

To play such a major role in the production of high quality fruit in such a short period of time is an attribute to the endeavours of all who have been involved in the re-establishment of the area as a viticultural region. The French-based champagne house, Moet and Chandon with their Australian offshoot, Domaine Chandon, have shown great interest in the potential of this district for sparkling wine.

Subsequently, most grape growers have planted and are planting chardonnay and pinot noir vines for the production of fruit suitable for methode champenoise wines which are an obvious strength of the region. The Northern District is also renowned for its red wines, with Virgin Hills, Knight's, Hanging Rock and many others making extremely long-living wines. Shiraz particularly, does extremely well in the cool climate and granite soils.

Some great rieslings, sauvignon blancs and chardonnays are also made, particularly in warmer years.

Vying for the title of Australia's coolest viticultural region with its volcanic and granite soils, the tough conditions challenge the vignerons' and viticulturists' skills to the limit, but great wines are the result. Wine tourism is fast becoming a way of life for many of the region's producers.

Cope-Williams at Romsey has an extraordinary spread-eagled, but superbly planned hospitality complex, complete with a cricket ground, pavilion and large 'Clubroom' restaurant - and a full "Royal" Tennis Court housed in its own high building, you can feel like a lord for the day. The beautifully restored Cleveland Mansion of Keith and Lyn Brien is an absolute gem and they also have bed and breakfast accommodation, while Hanging Rock has a casual eatery, Mt Macedon Winery has a charming Tea Room tasting area. The list continues, it's so close to Melbourne and yet has a majestic isolated feel that touches the soul.

Macedon Ranges

Macedon Ranges - VIC

1. Cleveland Vineyard
2. Cobaw Ridge Winery
3. Cope Williams
4. Glen Erin Grange
5. Knight's Wines
6. Mount Macedon Wines
7. Mt William Winery
8. Porttree Vineyard
9. Rochford Wines
10. The Hanging Rock Winery
11. Virgin Hills

Victoria

Macedon

Melbourne

Melbourne to
Macedon:
55 kms.

Cope Williams

Architect Gordon Cope-Williams, a most successful designer of country houses, moved to the lush rolling Romsey countryside with his wife Judy in the early 70's to breed Welsh mountain ponies and grow a few grapes, indulgent hobbies if you like.

The initial Rocky Hill Vineyard was planted on an exposed slope, causing considerable problems with ripening fruit. Gusty winds and a high altitude maintained lower temperatures which resulted in very low grape yields.

Consequently, in 1982, a second vineyard was established in a more protected location close to the winery. Named the Coniston Vineyard, it was planted with pinot noir, chardonnay and small plots of cabernets and merlot.

Construction at Romsey is on a grand scale. The towered manor was the first construction large enough to accommodate guests. The building did not stop there. Gordon, an avid cricket fan has created an English village cricket ground, complete with a charming pavilion and a large clubroom, furnished with old leather

chairs, that can cater for up to 120 guests.

The coup de grace of the maison is their Romsey Brut a fine elegant Methode Champenoise. The stalwarts of their table wine range

are a pinot noir and chardonnay.

The Cope-Williams Estate is surrounded by stately conifers providing a necessary windbreak for the vines and the intrepid cricketers.

In 1998 a conference facility with 21 self contained suites and two sizable syndicate rooms with full audiovisual facilities, was constructed.

The "Coupe de grace" has been the incredible Royal Tennis Court, there are only 39 of these courts in the world, its an exact replica of the Cloisters of a medieval monastery where the game was first played. The game is played with a ball made of wound tape that hardly bounces and a bent racquet, its something like a blend of squash and chess. The court is surrounded by the dining rooms Banquet hall, lounges, change rooms, a gymnasium plus The Hare and Spaniel Wine bar. Whilst Cope-Williams "Coniston" is essentially a country club but the award winning wines are still the core business. All in all, Cope-Williams have performed a real hat trick of wine, hospitality and cricket, not necessarily in that order!!

Address: Glenfern Road ROMSEY 3434	**Public Hours:** 9am-5.30pm, daily	Cope-Williams Romsey Rosé	5+ yrs
Phone: (03) 5429 5428 Fax: (03) 5429 5655	Principal Varieties: Chardonnay, Pinot Noir,	Pinot Noir	5-10 yrs
Owner: Judy, Gordon & Michael Cope-Williams	Cabernet Sauvignon, Merlot	Chardonnay	5-10 yrs
Winemaker: Michael Cope-Williams	**Principal Wines** **Potential**	Cabernet/Merlot	10+ yrs
Est: 1977 **Vine Ha:** 14	Cope-Williams Romsey Brut 5+ yrs	Romsey Willow	5-10 yrs

Knights Granite Hills

Pioneers of cool climate viticulture in Australia, Gordon and Heather Knight planted their first vines at Granite Hills in 1970. Although this is one of Australia's highest vineyards at 550 metres above sea level and prone to strong winds, the grapes ripened well and further plantings followed. The vineyard now totals 30 acres and includes Cabernet Sauvignon, Shiraz, Pinot Noir, Riesling and Chardonnay, with some smaller plantings of Cabernet France and Merlot. Whilst earlier wines were made by contract, since 1979 the wines have been made by son Llew Knight at Granite Hills winery.

The first release was from the 1976 vintage, but it was the 1979 and '80 Granite Hills Shiraz which took the wine world by storm and continues to be a benchmark for the peppery, cool climate version of this Australian classic red. The Cabernet

Sauvignon also with early recognition is a more generous style with the inclusion of up to 15% Cabernet Franc and Merlot in the later vintages. The classic white varieties also perform well in this climate. The Riesling now with over 25 vintages, expresses its cool climate origins through a floral-citrus character and a long seamless natural acid finish.

Similarly, the Chardonnay is quite a big, fruit driven and touch minerally style, with soft integrated oak and clean natural acid backbone. Recent developments include a very serious Vintage Sparkling, made from Pinot Noir and Chardonnay, 1995 the first release, and also small quantities of red Pinot Noir.

				Principal Wines	Potential
Address: 1481 Burke & Wills Track BAYNTON 3444	**Est:** 1970	**Vine Ha:** 12	**Cases:** 7,000	Shiraz	14 yrs
	Public Hours: 10am-6pm, Mon-Sat; 1pm-6pm, Sunday			Cabernet Sauvignon	9 yrs
Phone: (03) 5423 7264 **Fax:** (03) 5423 7288	**Principal Varieties:** Cabernet Franc, Cabernet Sauvignon, Chardonnay, Merlot, Riesling, Shiraz			Riesling	14 yrs
Email: ghknight@iaa.com.au				Chardonnay	4 yrs
Owner: Knight Family				Vintage Sparkling	5 yrs
Winemaker: Llew Knight					

Virgin Hills Vineyard

Well known Hunter Valley vigneron Michael Hope has proved a real saviour for Virgin Hills vineyard and winery, producer of a true Icon amongst great Australian Red wines. He has brought hope back to a "grand vision".

In 1968 Tom Lazar, a truly eccentric Hungarian Born Restaurateur and sculptor, bought 300 acres of rugged bushland in the Macedon Ranges near Kyneton. Tom came to Melbourne in the 1950's from Paris. He established the acclaimed "Little Reata" restaurant followed by "Lazars".

Tom had great vision and quite a sense of humour. I remember him coming to a party at my home in Melbourne in the mid seventies, he gave me a bottle of red wine wrapped in the Kyneton Gazette. I gave it a cursory glace, seeing the label "1975 Virgin Hills" and put it in my cellar. Tom said to me "Look at it properly you stupid b_ _ _ _ _d". I did · to find the classic old hand blown bottle had a label on the other

side "1874 Chateau Lafite firsts", when I eventually opened it some

years later it was like a "grand old dame" still holding together well.

Lazar's vision was well represented in this extremely generous gesture. He aimed with Virgin Hills to create a complex rich red wine in the classic Bordeaux style, the first wine was a 1974 vintage. He certainly succeeded, there is only one wine made at Virgin Hills from the Cabernet Sauvignon, Cabernet Franc, Merlot, Malbec, Shiraz and Pinot Noir Lazar planted.

From 1979 to 1998 Melbourne Hotel identity Marcel Gilbert, bought the property from Lazar, assisted by winemaker Mark Sheppard, they kept Virgin Hills on course. It all looked a bit shaky in 1998 but in 2000 Michael Hope bought the vineyard and winery from a publicly listed company that couldn't make up their mind what to do with it.

On a recent visit I was pleased to see much investment being made in the vineyards and winery. The future glory of the vision of Virgin Hills looks well assured.

Hanging Rock

Hanging Rock was made famous by the novel 'Picnic at Hanging Rock', adapted into a superb world-renowned film by Australian director Peter Weir. Like the heroines in this mysterious story, I'm sure you'd like to lose yourself in this truly beautiful part of Australia.

Each year, the racetrack tucked under the awesome granite boulders that form this striking landmark comes to life with that particular Australian phenomenon, the picnic race meeting. Four kilometres away, on a slope of the opposing range, spreads the vineyards of a first class winery, 'Hanging Rock'. The winery is also the home to an extremely hospitable and well credentialled wine family.

John Ellis was the first winemaker for Rosemount Estate in the 1970's, and he really put them on the map. One of the most gifted winemakers in Australia and highly regarded by his peers, he was sought out by Dr. Peter Tisdall when he launched his wine enterprise at Echuca. John was most taken by The Tisdall Mount Helen Vineyard in the cool Strathbogie Ranges. The wines he made from this vineyard were sensational.

John married Ann Tyrrell, daughter of legendary Hunter Valley Winemaker, the late Murray Tyrrell. They were searching to put down their roots and establish their own vineyard and winery and chose their stunning site in the extremely cool Hanging Rock Valley in the centre of the Macedon Ranges Region, fast becoming one of Australia's foremost cool climate wine regions. John is convinced and certainly with some reason that the best Methode Champenoise sparkling wines come from the Macedon region, probably the coolest region in Australia and the most like the French Champagne Region in terms of climate. John also makes a good deal of wine under contract for other wineries.

The innovative winery, which incorporates the family home, with windows looking down into the fermentation and press room, it's truly amazing. The front of the winery has an incredible view of the weathered extinct volcano, Hanging Rock and sports a classy tasting room. Nearby is "The Picnic Café where local produce is turned into some innovative dishes to rival anything world wide. The view of Hanging Rock is sensational.

Why not head for Hanging Rock, picnic at the winery before going on your own exploration tour of this magic granite outcrop, John and Ann's wide range of still and sparkling wines will be the perfect accompaniment. If your thinking one day at Hanging Rock is not enough, you can spend the night at the Ellis's Winery Retreat - Dryden's Run, where the four spacious suites all have ensuites. There is a totally equipped kitchen, dining and lounge area and it's set on the private hill side above the winery with majestic views over the Valley and Mount Macedon and Camel's Hump.

Address: Jim Road NEWHAM 3442	**Est:** 1982 **Vine Ha:** 6 **Cases:** 25,000	Hanging Rock Macedon (Sparkling)	
Phone: (03) 5427 0542 **Fax:** (03) 5427 0310	**Public Hours:** 10am-5pm, daily (except	Hanging Rock Jim Jim Sauv Blanc 2-5 yrs
Email: hrw@hangingrock.com.au	Christmas Day and Good Friday)	Hanging Rock Picnic Red & White
WWW: www.hangingrock.com.au	**Principal Varieties:** Chardonnay,	Hanging Rock Victoria Cab Merlot 2-5 yrs
Owner: John and Ann Ellis	Gewürztraminer, Pinot Noir, Sauvignon Blanc	Hanging Rock Victoria Chardonnay 2-5 yrs
Winemaker: John Ellis	**Principal Wines** **Potential**	Hanging Rock Heathcote Shiraz 5-10 yrs

Mt Macedon Winery

As one winds around the road on the slopes of Mt Macedon with the lush forest of the conservation park both sides one wonders if there really is a winery somewhere around the corner.

Then all of a sudden above you on the slopes of the mountain in a neatly cut out clearing is a beautifully ordered vineyard with a gorgeous cottage winery and cellar door beneath it.

The view from the tasting room over a sea of gums as far as the eye can see makes one feel much further away than less than an hour out of Melbourne. The Vineyard and winery was established in 1989 by high profile newspaper executive Don Ludbey as a very much hands-on operation.

The Climate is extremely cool at an elevation of 680 metres one of the highest vineyard locations in Australia. In 1999 Brian and June Neylon who already had a vineyard in the region at Pipers Creek bought the vineyards and winery.

The Mount Macedon Range includes Macedon Ranges Brut Cuvee Sparkling, an Unwooded Chardonnay, a barrel fermented Chardonnay, Pinot Noir, a Pinot Noir Rose called "Saignee", a Cabernet-Merlot and a Shiraz. Winemaker Ian Deacon has been responsible for the wines since

1998, but he has moved on and Mount Macedon Winery now has a new winemaker, Andrew Byers, a Microbiologist who also has a Masters Degree (Hons) in Applied Science (Viticulture and Oenology), hails from New Zealand. His wines have won awards in New Zealand and his experience ranges from wineries in Canterbury and Marlborough in New Zealand, the Loire Valley and Languedoc in France to Loxton in South Australia. With fruit being contracted from other growers in the region and a new winemaker, the Neylons are looking forward to a "new

beginning" in the winery.

Mt Macedon is extremely pretty all year around but it is truly glorious in autumn, with the vines vibrant leaves catching the golden rays as the sun sets.

The cellar door is reminiscent of a Victorian tea room, furnished and decorated in great style where you can taste their excellent range of wines.

Mount Macedon Winery has two vineyards, 20 acres at the winery site and 10 acres on the Neylons' original property at Pipers Creek.

Address: Bawden Road WOODEND 3442	Winemaker: Andrew Byers	Pinot Chardonnay Brut Cuvee	5-10 yrs
Phone: (03) 5423 5252	Est: 1989 Vine Ha: 30 acres	Macedon Ranges Chardonnay	3-5 yrs
Fax: (03) 5423 5272	Public Hours: 10am-5pm, daily (except Good	Macedon Ranges Pinot Noir	5-10 yrs
Email: snowdon@netcon.net.au	Friday & Christmas Day)	Unwooded Chardonnay	3-5 yrs
WWW: www.mountmacedonwinery.com.au	Principal Varieties: Chardonnay, Pinot Noir	Shiraz	5-10 yrs
Owner: June & Brian Neylon	Principal Wines Potential	Cabernet Merlot	5-10 yrs

Sunbury / Myrniong

The Viticultural Region at Sunbury is Melbourne's closest. Ironically it is also one of the oldest, having been first planted in the 1850's.

The renaissance of the area began in 1976 when the Carmody Family replanted the Craiglee Vineyard, first planted with vines in 1864 by James Johnston, a politician, who gained international fame for the region, when he won an International Award for his 1872 "Hermitage" at an exposition in Vienna. The Carmody's have restored the old bluestone winery and cellars, which are well worth visiting.

Across the road is the impressive Goona Warra Vineyard Estate of John and Elizabeth Barnier, with its beautiful bluestone buildings, now magnificently restored as vineyard, winery, function complex and restaurant. James Goodall Francis, an early Victorian Premier, first planted vines on the property in 1858.

These famous historic wineries have since been joined by another winery even closer to Melbourne. Under the flight path of the jets as they fly into Tullamarine Airport is the Wildwood Vineyard of surgeon, Dr Wayne Stott. The even newer Sunbury wineries of Longview Creek and Diggers Rest Vineyard now also have wines on the market.

For a day tripper or a serious wine enthusiast, Sunbury, birth place of the famous cricket ashes, is a great wine region to visit just a cricket balls throw or so from Melbourne's famous Melbourne Cricket Ground.

In recent years a number of wineries have been established eastward from Sunbury towards Gisborne where Mt Gisborne Winery and Mawarra Vineyard both have Cellar Doors near Melton. The Witchmount Estate Vineyard and Winery also has a large Hospitality · function centre and restaurant, as has the St. Annes Winery on the Main Western Highway at Myrniong going towards Ballarat from Melton.

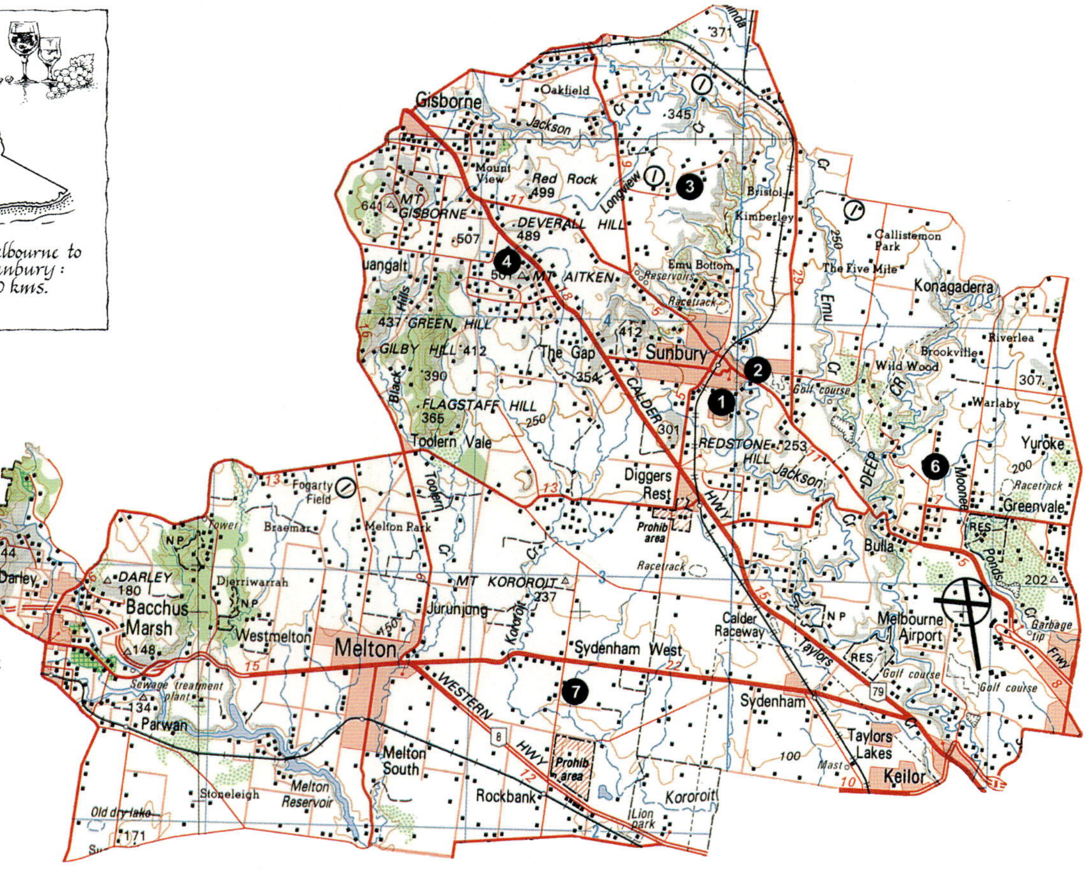

Sunbury / Myrniong - VIC

1. Craiglee
2. Goonawarra
3. Longview
4. Mt Aitken
5. St Annes
6. Wildwood
7. Witchmount Estate

Craiglee

The unspoilt historical bluestone buildings and magnificent 140 year old trees around the Craiglee Winery, give one a strong sense of the commitment and hard work of our forebears.

James Johnston founded Craiglee in 1864, his 1872 Hermitage (Shiraz) won an award at the Vienna Exhibition. The Johnston family continued to make wine until the late 1920's.

When the Carmody family purchased Craiglee in 1961 it was a grain and grazing property. In 1976 they decided to re-establish the vineyard, planting 10 acres of Shiraz. The vineyard now covers 22 acres and also includes Cabernet Sauvignon and Chardonnay.

The Craiglee Shiraz of the modern era has many awards, the 1997 being another trophy winner. The Cabernet Sauvignon is always a ripe full flavoured and full bodied wine,

but like the Shiraz, has great elegance. Craiglee also makes one of Australia's best Chardonnays.

Patrick Carmody makes the wines, he has an Agricultural science degree and is a graduate of the wine course at Charles Sturt University.

Craiglee's unique living history is just fascinating, its only 35 minutes from the heart of Melbourne or 10 minutes from Tullamarine airport, so there is no excuse not to visit, just give the Carmodys a call first.

Address: Sunbury Road SUNBURY 3429	Winemaker: Patrick Carmody	Principal Wines	Potential
Phone: (03) 9744 4489 Fax: (03) 9744 4489	Est: 1976 Vine Ha: 10	Shiraz	7-10 yrs
WWW: www.craiglee.com.au	Cases: 2,000	Chardonnay	5-10 yrs
Owner: Patrick Carmody	Public Hours: 11am-5pm, Sunday	Cabernet	7-10 yrs

Goona Warra

Former State Premier James Goodall Francis planted vines on his property "Goona Warra" in 1858. Sadly, the economics of the day saw the vineyard ceasing production before the end of the century. This historic vineyard has since been re-established by John and Elizabeth Barnier in 1983, and the first "new" vintage was made at Goona Warra in 1986.

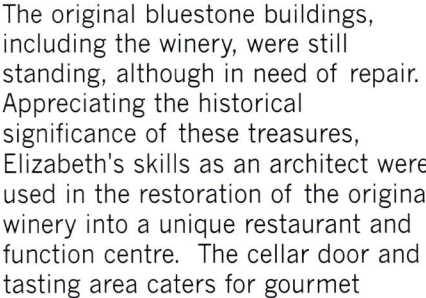

The original bluestone buildings, including the winery, were still standing, although in need of repair. Appreciating the historical significance of these treasures, Elizabeth's skills as an architect were used in the restoration of the original winery into a unique restaurant and function centre. The cellar door and tasting area caters for gourmet

lunches and afternoon teas on Sundays whilst the tastefully appointed Great Hall has become a popular venue for weddings and corporate dinners.

But let's not forget the wines. In a sound varietal line-up expressing the local terroir, the rarely grown Cabernet Franc stands out and early indications from a new Shiraz planting look very promising too.

Sunbury is the closest wine region to Melbourne, and by far the easiest to get to. One drives north out of the city on the Tullamarine Freeway, past Melbourne Airport and it takes less than half an hour to get there.

When in Melbourne why not drop in on the delightful cultured couple, John and Elizabeth Barnier. It will be a visit to remember.

Address: Sunbury Road SUNBURY 3429	Public Hours: 10am-5pm, daily	Chardonnay	2-5 yrs
Phone: (03) 9740 7766 Fax: (03) 9744 7648	Principal Varieties: Cabernet Franc,	Semillon / Sauvignon Blanc	2-5 yrs
Winemaker: John Barnier & Nick Bickford	Cabernet Sauvignon, Chardonnay, Merlot,	Pinot Noir	2-5 yrs
Est: Founded 1863/Re-established 1983	Pinot Noir, Semillon, Shiraz	Cabernet Franc / Merlot	2-8 yrs
Vine Ha: 5 Cases: 2,500	Principal Wines Potential	Shiraz	3-10 yrs

S t   A n n e s   V i n e y a r d

St Anne's Vineyards is a family owned wine company, established some 3 years ago in the Pentland Hills at Myrniong, South Victoria. Since humble beginnings the company has expanded with substantial vineyard development at Perricoota, Moama Southern NSW.

St Anne's Myrniong is located only 1 hour's west of Melbourne on the Western Freeway. Upon arriving you will find extensive parklands and an abundance of landscaped gardens. The cellar door is constructed from solid bluestone, common to the area, with open truss ceilings, providing a distinct colonial theme. The property has enjoyed significant growth in its 30 years. New additions include a double story barrelhouse, cooperage and recently the construction of a 300-seat restaurant. All buildings feature similar design, utilizing solid bluestone and open truss ceilings.

The Myrniong viticultural site is high and cool with Riesling the flagship. Other plantings consist of Cabernet, chardonnay and Sauvignon Blanc. A typical Myrniong growing season is long with harvest in mid-late April. This challenging environment provides low yielding high quality fruit, perfect for the production of medal winning wines.

At Anne's is one of the few Australian Wine companies still to utilize the services of a full time cooper. The St Anne's cooperage produces hand made barrels for port enthusiasts and non-commercial winemakers. Barrels are produced from both French and American oak and made under a strict regime of quality i.e. no glue, no nails and no wax.

St Anne's Perricoota is out latest development, located on the banks of the Murray less than 1-hour North of Bendigo at the popular tourist haven of Echuca-Moama. The St Anne's Perricoota cellar door is in true St Anne's tradition, one of a kind. Constructed from rammed earth and corrugates iron, the cellar door has an outback theme with contemporary design.

Perricoota (meaning Red Kangaroo) is one of Australia's most recent and fastest growing wine regions in Australia. The area features deep red loam soils, consistent growing seasons with very high sunshine hours, crucial for ripening late varieties. Vineyard plantings consist of Chardonnay, Semillon, Petit Verdot, Durif, Merlot, Cabernet Sauvignon, Cabernet Franc, Shiraz, Mataro and Grenache. The St Anne's vineyards are still relatively young at just 10 years of age, however early signs indicate that the majority of our varieties are well suited to this climate, with medals won for all at premium level. Particularly successful has been the Cabernet, Shiraz and Chardonnay.

At Echuca-Moama you'll find a number of wineries to peruse. Not to be missed is the historic Ironhouse Cooperage located in the Echuca Wharf tourist precinct. At this commercial cooperage, you can witness the traditional trade of the cooper laboriously producing premium oak barrels for the Australian Wine Industry. Along with the historic port area you'll find the famous Rich River Golf Club in Moama, an abundance of fine restaurants and of course the majestic Murray River.

Both St Anne's two facilities are great to visit so make sure you drop in and enjoy their hospitality, great wines, food and other attractions when you are travelling in their vicinity.

St. Annes Myrniong		Principal Wines	Potential
Address: Western FWY MYRNIONG 3341	**Email:** stannes@hyperlink.net.au	Perricoota Shiraz	8 yrs
Phone: (03) 5368 7209 **Fax:** (03) 5368 7595	**WWW:** www.st.annes.com.au	Perricoota Cabernet	8 yrs
St. Annes Perricoota	**Winemaker:** Richard McLean	Perricoota Chardonnay	2 yrs
Address: 24 Lane MOAMA 2731	**Est:** 1972 **Vine Ha:** 200	Myrniong Riesling	6 yrs
Phone: (03) 5480 0099 **Fax:** (03) 5480 0077	**Cases:** 5,000	Myrniong Cabernet	5 yrs
	Public Hours: 9am-5pm, daily		

Witchmount Estate

The Witchmount vineyards are planted on some of the best looking rich red granite soils I have seen. In 1991 the Ramunno family decided, contrary to local opinion, to plant vines in the volcanic plains between Melton and Taylors Lakes, on the outskirts of Melbourne's Metropolitan area, which was once the Wheat and Barley "bread basket" of Melbourne. Although officially in the Sunbury wine region it is about equidistant and very accessible from both the Calder Highway near Diggers Rest or Melton on the Western Highway.

Gaye and Matt Ramunno have a number of their children involved in the winery and a fine hospitality centre they have created the beautiful bluestone buildings have been constructed in a striking Gothic style and are surrounded by magnificent gardens, a lake and vineyards. They operate a 60 seat restaurant which serves excellent classic Italian food and opens Wednesday to Sunday for lunch and dinner. The Ramunnos also cater splendidly for weddings, seminars and other events, on Sundays they often have live Jazz, so it pays to get their program of events.

Experienced winemaker in the Region Peter Dredge makes the wines from the Estates vineyards, they have a number of varieties planted including Sauvignon Blanc, Semillon, Chardonnay, Merlot, Malbec, Cabernet Sauvignon, Cabernet Franc, Shiraz and the traditional Italian red grape variety Nebbiolo.

Apart from some excellent dry table wines, they also make two sweet style blended whites.

Their vineyard of 38 acres, is large for the region and they are very happy with the quality of the wines its producing. Being one of the very closest wineries to Melbourne its very convenient to visit for a tasting and to stay on for a meal, in the delightful setting, I'm sure both the wine and the food will please your palate.

| **Address:** 557 Leakes Road ROCKBANK 3335 **Phone:** (03) 9747 1155 **Fax:** (03) 9747 1744 | **Winemaker:** Peter Dredge **Est:** 1991 **Public Hours:** 12pm-10pm, Wed-Sun. Restaurant open Wed-Sun for lunch & dinner | **Principal Varieties:** Cabernet Sauvignon, Malbec, Nebbiolo, Semillon, Cabernet Franc, Chardonnay, Merlot, Sauvignon Blanc, Shiraz |

Gippsland

Victoria's most isolated wine-producing area is Gippsland in the south-eastern corner of the state. Most vineyards are small, of less than 20 acres and are spread over a large area which extends from Lakes Entrance in the far south-east to Phillip Island in Western Port Bay. The southernmost groups of wineries in mainland Australia are the cluster in South Gippsland, between Wilsons Promontory and Phillip Island - Lyre Bird Hill, Bass Phillip, Paradise Enough, Tarwin Ridge and Windy Ridge.

There are a growing number of grape growers in the area, many aiming to make their own wine and open cellar door sales. The first vignerons to plant vines since the nineteenth century were Pauline and Dacre Stubbs at Lulgra Wines of Lakes Entrance, now part of the Wyanga Park Estate.

Gippsland is grouped into the three subregions of South Gippsland, Central Gippsland and the Lakes District. The region covers quite a range of territory, topography and climate. Wines generally exhibit the spiciness inherent in cool climate fruit and consist of classic varieties such as pinot noir, cabernet sauvignon, shiraz, chardonnay, riesling and sauvignon blanc. Some of the best pinot noirs in the country have appeared from these tiny vineyards, notably from Lyre Bird, Bass Phillip and Windy Ridge.

Although still largely a cottage industry, winemaking in Gippsland is continuing to develop and the fine wines so far produced are a credit to the far-flung pioneers who created them.

Gippsland

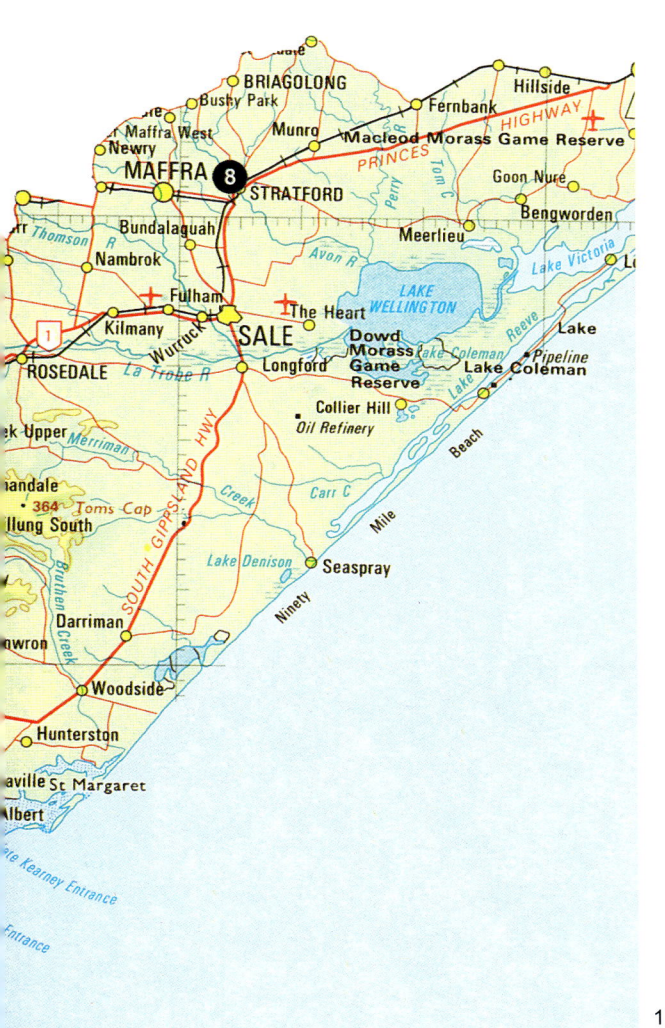

Gippsland - VIC

1. Bass Phillip
2. Coalville Vineyard
3. Lyre Bird Hill Winery
4. Paradise Enough Winery
5. Phillip Island Vineyard & Winery
6. Tarago River Cheeses
7. Tarwin Ridge
8. Wa-de-lock Vineyard
9. Westernport Estate Winery
10. Windy Ridge Winery

Lyre Bird Hill

Owen and Robyn Schmidt have a deep love and a passion for their vines, the Lyre Bird Hill Winery and the Country House they have shaped with hard work by their own hands. The property, one of the most southerly vineyards on mainland Australia, is set in the serene bucolic beauty that is South Gippsland near Wilsons Promontory. Among the stately gums and ferns they found their little piece of paradise.

Owen had been an accountant at BHP. Although born in Queensland, he travelled Australia, spending a few years in South Australia. Robyn's career was in catering, mainly in the school area, spending a number of years victualling the hungry young students at Melbourne's Wesley College. They decided that they would both give up their careers and set up a winery and provide a hospitality house on their weekend property near Koonwarra in South Gippsland, where they had already planted a vineyard.

Guests are welcomed into their home - the guest rooms are tastefully and practically appointed with spacious, yet cosy comfort. All rooms open onto a verandah surrounded by vines and bushland. Dinner is a table d'hote affair with Owen and Robyn showcasing their cuisine, wines and delightful company.

Lyre Bird Hill is a wonderfully restorative place to recharge the batteries and get back to nature.

Address: Inverloch Road KOONWARRA 3954	**Public Hours:** 10am-6pm, weekends, phone first for weekdays	Riesling	5-10 yrs
Phone: (03) 5664 3204 **Fax:** (03) 5664 3206		Pinot Noir	3-7 yrs
Email: rowen@lyrebirdhill.com.au	**Principal Varieties**: Cabernet Sauvignon,	Shiraz	5-10 yrs
WWW: www.lyrebirdhill.com.au	Chardonnay, Pinot Noir, Riesling, Shiraz,	Cabernet Sauvignon	5-10 yrs
Owner: Owen and Robyn Schmidt	Traminer	Chardonnay	2-5 yrs
Winemaker: Owen Schmidt **Est:** 1993	**Principal Wines** **Potential**	Traminer	2-5 yrs

 # Tarago River Cheeses

Tarago River Cheese factory is on the main road between Neerim and Neerim South, just an hour or so from Melbourne, it's idyllic green grazing country overlooks the Tarago River Lake.

In 1982, two families, the Jensens (cheesemakers) and the Johnstons (farmers) agreed that Australian specialist cheeses needed a shake up. The 250 acre farm and its 300 cows (mainly friesians) became suppliers to a small cheese factory built by the two families. Today a second farm of 850 acres has been secured and about 800 cows are milked a day from both properties. Some 45 people work in the total operation. The Jensen and Johnston families are still the proprietors and running the business.

The first cheese to find fame was Gippsland Blue, the first name of the enterprise. This Gorgonzola style developed a loyal following, and Tarago River decided to expand the range of blue cheeses to include Royal Victorian Blue, a "Stilton" style, Shadows of Blue, similar to "Blue Castello" and Blue Orchid, a "Roquefort" style. Tarago also make a traditional Brie and a Gippsland Brie, also a hard matured cheddar-style Tarago Mature and Tarago Lavender, infused with the herb of well being.

Cheeses from goats milk, and a new mild washed rind - "Jensens Red" (similar to 'Port Saulte') are the latest additions.

Tarago River is equidistant from the Yarra Valley and Mornington Peninsula. Why not pay them a visit?

Mornington Peninsula

The Mornington Peninsula Vineyards begins 50 kilometres south of the Melbourne C.B.D., near the Dromana area, a one hour drive south of the city. A few vineyards existed during the 19th century, but due to factors similar to those in the Yarra Valley, viticulture did not continue into the 20th century.

In the late 1940's leading wine judge and Melbourne wine merchant, the late Doug Seabrook, established a vineyard on the slopes of Arthur's Seat, near Dromana. Although this venture petered out within 10 years it was followed by a re-introduction of vines to the area by several intrepid souls during the 1970's.

The first of these was Baillieu Myer in 1972 at his 'Elgee Park' situated at Merricks North. A new, technically superb winery was completed in time for production of the 1984 vintage. Nat White was another vigneron to contribute to the early re-development of the Mornington Peninsula's wine industry, with the establishment of Main Ridge Estate in 1975. George and Jacquelyn Kefford followed, founding Merricks

Estate in 1977 and Stoniers Merricks vineyard one year later. There are now more than 150 vineyards in the area, covering over 2,000 acres, supporting more than 35 wineries. There have been a number of large plantings over the last 3 years including the Yabbie Lake Vineyards of the Kirby family of Village Roadshow fame.

By both Australian and European standards, the climate of the Peninsula is very cool, somewhat like the Bordeaux region in France. As the area is virtually surrounded by ocean, vines receive adequate rainfall throughout the growing season, and the high level of humidity in summer prevents vines from suffering stress.

Vineyards of the Mornington Peninsula produce table wines of clean, well-defined varietal characters, and crisp acidity. These features result in refreshing wines with considerable ageing potential. The predominant varieties are chardonnay and pinot noir, used in both table and sparkling wine-making. Other varieties include cabernet sauvignon, merlot, shiraz,

riesling, sauvignon blanc, semillon and pinot gris.

The Mornington Peninsula has produced some excellent wines since the re-establishment of viticulture in the area. Given the expertise and skill of the winemakers, this should continue and currently available wines are of a very high standard.

The physical beauty of the peninsula and its tourist pull has been well catered for by such excellent winery restaurants as Dromana Estate, where Margaret Crittenden and her family run a really fine establishment overlooking their lake and vineyards. Sir Peter and Lady Averil Derham have awesome views of Westernport Bay from their indoor/outdoor restaurant in front of the winery. Hann's Creek have a lovely French-style Sunday lunch with the strains of Piaf pumping through the winery. Fine Bed and Breakfasts abound, whilst restored mansions such as Glynt are world class. Mornington's rebirth as a wine region is a joy to behold.

Mornington Peninsula

Victoria

Mornington Peninsula

Melbourne

Melbourne to Mornington Peninsula: 55 kms.

N

Mornington Peninsula - VIC

1. Dromana Estate
2. Eldridge Estate
3. Elgee Park
4. Glynt Manor
5. Hanns Creek Estate
6. Hickinbotham Wines
7. Kings Creek Vineyard
8. Lindenderry
9. Main Ridge Estate
10. Mantons Creek
11. Paringa Estate
12. Redhill Estate
13. Stonier's Winery
14. T'Gallant
15. Tuck's Ridge
16. Willow Creek Vineyard

Dromana Estate

Garry Crittenden is one of the Australian wine industry's most dynamic and visionary people. Garry sold a chain of plant nurseries to concentrate on his vineyard at Dromana on the Mornington Peninsula. For a number of years he also operated a viticultural consulting business.

Garry and his wife Margaret are both heavily involved in the Dromana Estate operation and have built a colonial-inspired home on the property which enjoys superb views over their lake and vineyard.

Garry searched for a climate where delicate, yet intense flavours could be produced. He found this at Dromana Estate.

I have noticed on a number of visits to the Peninsula that Dromana enjoys its own special microclimate.

Whereas it can be cloudy, cold and windy on the Red Hill Ridge, Dromana can be bathed in sunshine. This combination of very cool climate, coupled with loads of sunshine, really makes his wines smile.

The pretty gardens surrounding the winery and lake reflect his love of plants. Garry is most innovative; always experimenting, learning and seeking perfection in his wines. Garry has introduced a second label, 'Schinus' under which he makes wines from grapes sourced in other regions. A certain fascination with Northern Italian wines and his penchant for a challenge has seen him produce a range of Italian varietals. Garry's hardworking and talented wife Margaret, has a real culinary flair and serves a seasonal

menu or simple tasty snack platters, depending on your mood. If you wish to bring your own tucker, there is a free barbeque area in front of the winery. Hospitality is the key note of the Crittenden's business.

In 2000 Dromana Estate listed as a public company to assist the Crittenden's to fund their expanding business. They have also taken over the vineyards of Mornington Estate Wines and are marketing their wines, along with the Dromana Estate, Schinus and Italian Varietals. Garry is the chief winemaker, ably assisted by Judy Gifford Watson and Garry's son Rollo.

They see a bright, bright future for the region and it's wines and wineries, with very good reason. Their family is an integral part of this future.

Address: Harrisons Road DROMANA 3936	**Winemaker:** Garry Crittenden	**Public Hours:** 11am-4pm, daily (except
Phone: (03) 5987 3800 **Fax:** (03) 5981 0714	**Est:** 1982 **Vine Ha:** 4	Christmas Day, Boxing Day and Good Friday)
Email: devyd@onaustralia.com.au	**Cases:** 3,500 from own vines for Dromana Estate label,	**Principal Varieties:** Chardonnay, Pinot Noir,
Owner: Garry and Margaret Crittenden	10,500 for Schinus label, 3,000 for Garry Crittenden	Cabernet Sauvignon, Merlot

Eldridge Estate

David Lloyd eventually had to buy a winery. I remember him growing up as the youngest son of our local parish priest in Brighton, a suburb of Adelaide. He was always an enthusiast and passionate about what he did.

David has an honors degree in Science. During the late 1970's he started making wine as a hobby, firstly in 1978 with Rutherglen grapes, then with Coonawarra Cabernet blends from 1979-85, winning the equal top gold for his 1982 vintage in the Lilydale show against commercial wineries, quite an achievement!!

In 1981 David won the trophy for the most successful exhibitor at the National Amateur wine show, after more amateur winemaking, he began making wine for wineries in the Yarra Valley and Mornington Peninsula from 1981 through to 1995. In

1995 he and his wife Wendy purchased an empty shell of a winery, 7 acres of vines mainly Cabernet · certainly unsuitable for the micro climate on the top of the main Red Hill Ridge. David and Wendy have painstakingly grafted over all the vines, they now produce Pinot Noir, Chardonnay and an exciting Semillon/Sauvignon Blanc.

The 98 Chardonnay was Winewise Small Vigneron Chardonnay of Year. The 99 was runner up and received Top Score at the Bathurst Wine Show and 5 stars from Winestate. They also produce a Merlot and a stunning Gamay, a vibrant fruity red which wine guru James Halliday rates as Australia's best by far. David also makes an excellent Methode Champenoise "P.F" from 100% Pinot Noir.

The name Eldridge comes from the breed of Cavalier King Charles Spaniels which David and Wendy have bred for over 20 years, two of their puppies were tragically killed on the main road above the winery. At Eldridge they do everything by hand with the help of their many friends and have lots of fun doing it, you can join in the fun, just contact them and don't miss them on your visit to the Red Hill area.

Address: 120 Arthurs Seat Road RED HILL	Winemaker: David Lloyd	Principal Wines	Potential
Phone: (03) 5989 2644 Fax: (03) 5989 2089	Est: 1986 Vine Ha: 3	Semillon Sauvignon Blanc	Drink Now
Email: fizz@eldridge-estate.com.au	Cases: 1,200	Chardonnay	5-10 yrs
WWW: www.eldridge-estate.com.au	Public Hours: 11am-5pm, Weekends, Public	Gamay	Drink Now
Owner: David & Wendy Lloyd	Holidays & School Holidays	Pinot Noir	5-10 yrs

Elgee Park

Baillieu Myer's property, 'Elgee Park' is primarily a horse and cattle stud. Vines were planted on the northern face of a naturally sheltered amphitheater in 1972, the first vineyard on the Mornington Peninsula. The vines are closely planted and include Cabernet Sauvignon, Merlot, Chardonnay, Riesling and Viognier.

The vineyard is very picturesque and was further enhanced in 1983 by the construction of a striking gazebo in the midst of the vines. Red gum was employed to build both the 'Vineyard Folly' and the magnificent post and rail fences which surround the property.

The wines were either made at other wineries or under makeshift conditions at the property until 1984, when Dr. Tony Jordan of Oenotec was called on to design a winery for Baillieu Myer. Today, Elgee

Park has a very close relationship with Stonier's Winery and coincidentally, winemaker Tod Dexter has a vineyard of his own near Elgee Park.

The Elgee Park vines benefit from an excellent micro-climate, sheltered from the prevailing winds by a heavily timbered ridge behind the vineyard. On a clear day, one can see

the distant skyline of Melbourne from the winery. An artist's impression of this view features on the Elgee Park labels. The mature vines and first class winemaking by Tod Dexter provide complex, elegant wines with which Baillieu makes an eloquent statement for the Mornington Peninsula.

Address: Junction Road MERRICKS NTH 3926	WWW: www.elgeeparkwines.com.au	Birthday Winter Wine weekend only
Phone: (03) 5989 7338	Winemaker: Tod Dexter, T'Gallant	Principal Varieties: Viognier, Cabernet
Fax: (09) 5989 7738	Est: 1972 Vine Ha: 5 Cases: 1,500-1,800	Sauvignon, Chardonnay, Curvee Brut, Merlot,
Email: elgee@pac.com.au	Public Hours: 11am-5pm, Sunday Queen's	Pinot Gris, Pinot Noir, Riesling

Glynt Manor

Glynt has new proprietors as of January 2001. Mike Puttock and his partner in life Diane have taken the reins, of this magic country manor. Mike spent some years travelling the wine regions of Australia, supplying essential products for winemaking. Diane has a delightful and charming personality and will put her experience in top level corporate management and her computer skills to great use in their new business.

Inspired by a Scottish castle, Glynt was built in the early years of this century as a summer residence for a prominent Melbourne family. Entertaining was a priority and the grand manor hosted many a gracious soiree. Over the years the family's needs waned and Glynt fell into disrepair, although the superb granite and stucco building was as solid as a rock.

The rebirth of the grandeur of Glynt began when the estate and it's surrounding land was bought by Sir Peter Derham for building development project. Ironically, Sir Peter is now a full-time Mornington Peninsula vigneron at Red Hill Estate. Glynt, situated some 100 metres from Port Philip Bay at Mount Martha, was left with two and a half acres of its grounds still intact in the middle of the development.

Sir Peter, then Chairman of the Australian Tourism Commission, mentioned Glynt to fellow commissioner, legendary outback tourism pioneer Bill King. Perhaps it was the glint in his eye that made Bill mention it to his wife Val. Sir Peter suggested they have a look at it.

Bill describes their first visit, climbing through a fence, battling the brambles and head-high grass. Val was about to turn back, but once they saw the mansion cloaked in its

Virginia Creeper, they fell in love with it instantly. Fortunately, among their children they had the experts in all the building trades and during

several years they painstakingly restored the building and grounds. To say they are a showpiece would be an understatement. In 1997 The Estate was taken over by renowned International Television Producer and Director Mark Callan and International Hairdresser William Gilchrist. They both have great taste and added two new suites, a stunning development of the turreted tower complete with a glass pyramid ceiling, one can star gaze through or reach behind the huge bed push a button and a horizontal blind draws across, it also has an outdoor courtyard and spa with views over the bay to Melbourne 50 kilometers away. A second new suite at the rear looks out over a splendid Hillside garden its awesome. There are now six exquisite suites · most with their own drawing rooms and all furnished with antiques as well as every modern convenience that would do a 5 star hotel proud. There are three other Garden and the large Bay View Suite which will take your breath away.

A full English breakfast is served in the vast garden room, with arched windows overlooking Port Phillip Bay. The licensed dining room is beautifully appointed. It creates an ideal ambience to enjoy a memorable dining experience.

Personally guided tours of the Peninsula wineries and world class golf courses are offered. Situated in the centre of the wine growing region, Glynt provides the ideal base from which to explore.

Name: Glynt by the Sea   **Address:** 16 Bay Road, Mount Martha 3934   **Phone:** (03) 5974 1216

Hanns Creek

Tony Aubery-Slocock has a strong background in horticulture, his family in England had a famous Rhododendron Nursery at Woking near London. On his mothers side was a famous Irish family headed by the Earl of Iveagh who formed a brewery in Dublin in 1649, that preceded Guiness. He certainly took the long road around getting into the wine business. During the 1950's he became a professional actor on the stage and radio, travelling Australia and New Zealand. After 5 years he went to England and studied dentistry at the Famous Guy's Hospital in London, where he

became a top class rugby player with the Harlequins.

Although Tony was born in Perth, he only came back to Australia in 1961, as his father was in Brisbane with a terminal illness. In 1962 he set up a dentistry practice in Melbourne, which he ran until 1989, by this time he had met his wife to be, Denise and they began planting a vineyard, in 1987 on the farm Tony had bought at Red Hill in 1985.

Tony had seen some great Mornington Peninsula wines at the Peninsula Golf Club and a fellow member wine journalist Tony Hitchin

encouraged him to plant vines. Denise has a zest for life and astounding energy - it's impossible to be around her and not feel the joy of life flowing over you. Denise's strong and most disarming French accent is from her native Brittany. She met Tony while running her own little restaurant in Melbourne, earning a living to bring up her children alone, hard work is no hardship for Denise.

On my first visit, Denise was busy summer grafting some shiraz, between running the cellar door and packing wine orders, always with a huge smile and a mischievous sense of humour. Tony makes the wines, which have already won a number of awards.

The vineyard is in a clearing on the lee side of the prevailing winds with a northerly aspect providing a sunny sheltered environment. It produces an excellent cabernet sauvignon. The French influence is obvious, with the winery also providing a crisp rose and burgundian-style pinot noir and a chardonnay.

Each Sunday, Hanns Creek really comes to life with a French-style lunch amongst the barrels, complete with gingham table cloths and the strains of Piaf in the air. It's a three hour affair starting at 1.00 pm.

If you are in need of a little exercise between courses, Tony will instruct you in the art of petanque, the French provincial game of bowls. When on the Peninsula, head for Hanns Creek for a most uplifting experience.

Address: Kentucky Road MERRICKS NTH 3926	Est: 1987 Vine Ha: 4 Cases: 1,500	Chardonnay	5 yrs
Phone: (03) 5989 7266 Fax: (03) 5989 7500	Public Hours: 11am-5pm , daily	Pinot Noir	10 yrs
Email: hannscreek@nex.net.au	Principal Varieties: Cabernet Sauvignon,	Rosé	5 yrs
Owner: Tony and Denise Aubrey-Slocock	Pinot Noir, Shiraz, Chardonnay	Cabernet Sauvignon	10 yrs
Winemaker: Tony Aubrey-Slocock	Principal Wines Potential	Cabernet Shiraz	10 yrs

Hickinbotham

As my photographer Stephane and I arrived at Hickinbotham's Dromana Estate just before sunset on the 23rd of March 1999, we could sense something special was in the air. We were absolutely right, it just happened to be the 70th birthday of a true legend of Australian wine · Ian Hickinbotham. When I first met Ian in the early 1970's he was proprietor of a top class restaurant "Ginis" in Toorak, an exclusive Melbourne suburb and doing some wine consulting work. Ian's winemaking background goes back a long way to the early 1950's, he was part of the Coonawarra renaissance as winemaker at Wynns Coonawarra Estate. He went on to become winemaker at Kaiser Stuhl in the late 1950's and early 1960's and had much to do with the white and sparkling wine revolution, with his incisive technical skills.

Ian's sons Stephen, who was tragically killed in a plane accident a number of years ago and Andrew, who now runs their Dromana Winery and hospitality centre, have followed in their father's footsteps.

Always innovative the Hickinbothams pioneered a wine style, with their "Cab Mac" a carbonic maceration · soft easy drinking red which they first made at their winery near Anakie, in the Geelong region, which they took over in the late 1970's.

As befits their pioneering nature they were one of very early full time vignerons on the Mornington Peninsula.

The Hickinbotham vineyards and Winery are easy to find its on the left side of the main Mornington Flinders Road one of the first wineries you come to before Dromana.

A huge clock formerly from Melbourne's Flinders St Railway Station is near the entrance. This will be about the only time you'll think of time, once you enter this special winery, you can learn so much about wine in a very relaxed atmosphere, there are some very innovative wines such as "Taminga" a unique grape variety, developed by the C.S.I.R.O. to suit Australian conditions, one of its parents is the exotic Gewurztraminer of Alsace in France. Taminga produces an aromatic crisp and delightful wine in the cool climate of the Mornington Peninsula, in the hands of master winemakers such as the Hickinbothams. "Taminga" is aboriginal for "Place of White Gums" a name the Kaurna tribe used for the site of Adelaide before its settlement.

You can also lunch at Hickinbothams where they specialise in superb vineyard platters of the best fresh foods of the Peninsula. The Hickinbothams range of wines changes a little with each vintage but the wines are always first class and interesting you should check out this innovative winery and indulge yourself in a little of Australia's wine history.

Address: 194 Nepean Highway DROMANA 3936	**Winemaker:** Andrew Hickinbotham		Pinot Noir (from 15 clones)	3 yrs
Phone: (03) 5981 0355	**Est:** 1988 **Vine Ha:** 15 **Cases:** 5,000		Taminga	2 yrs
Email: info@hickinbothamwinemakers.com.au	**Public Hours:** 11am-5pm, daily		Shiraz	8 yrs
WWW: www.hickinbothamwinemakers.com.au	**Principal Wines**	**Potential**	Chardonnay	5 yrs

Lindenderry

Vying for the title of Australia's finest wine regional Country House Hotel is Lindenderry, in the heart of the Mornington Peninsula at Red Hill.

One enters this world of Leisure and Luxury through a winding tree lined drive, surrounded by Lindenderry's own beautifully manicured vineyards.

Time at Lindenderry takes on another dimension, everything is designed to please the senses in every way. The building is imposing yet not intimidating, a blend of formal French and casual Mediterranean.

The décor inside is subtle yet striking, large picture windows gaze out at many angles on the magnificent gardens, landscaped into the rolling country side. The colours are light, yet soft and warm adding to the classic furnishing, antique English walnut and eighteenth century fruitfood pieces, contrast perfectly. The sofas are garbed in classic fabrics. The various lounge areas invite you to sit back for a while and enjoy the good things of life, and contemplate a little, away from the hustle and bustle of the city, which seems so far away, large open fires burn in winter.

The rooms are sumptuous and very private. The garden rooms open out onto their own verandah, with views over the landscaped gardens, lawns and lakes. Their spa baths and king-sized beds really help you relax. Some of the garden rooms even have their own fireplaces.

The Lake View Rooms have king-sized beds, an in-room bar and open out to a verandah looking over the landscaped garden and lakes.

The Courtyard Rooms with queen sized beds look out in the courtyard, lawns and ornamental pond, featuring the very appropriate sculpture "Journey".

The first time I visited Lindenderry was the launch of the Peninsula's "Pinot Week" in March 1999. The Canapés with classic peninsula Methode Champenoise were sensational, the setting of the main dining room with ice sculpture and all was exquisite, the banquet just superb.

Peter and Jan Clark are the creators and proprietors, ably assisted by their daughter Kate Ridell-Clark. They also have another country house hotel "Lancemore" near Lancefield in the Macedon Ranges, wine region and are developing a third property in a similar fashion in Northern Victoria.

The Linden Tree restaurant at Lindenderry has panoramic views over the vineyard and features

modern Australian cuisine from fresh local produce. At lunch there is a set price menu with choices and at dinner it's a full a la carte menu.

The extensive wine list features the best of the Mornington Peninsula vineyards.

There are plenty of things to do whilst your staying at Lindenderry. You are in the heart of some of Australia finest golf courses. "The National" - with its three classic courses, "Peninsula" - with two courses, "The Dunes" and "Flinders" are all in the top 60 courses in the Country. You can also try your hand at Clear Water Fly fishing with tuition or a fishing trip on the bay or the ocean. Naturally you can take one of the many walking trails or tour the numerous wineries, even in the Rolls Royce Silver shadow, gliding in style from destination to destination with a gourmet picnic hamper on board.

The Peninsula is a cultural and gourmet paradise. The famous Red Hill market day is not to be missed. There are also stacks of art galleries and antique shops. In summer you can even swim with the dolphins and you can watch the seals all year round.

Lindenderry also make their own wines from their Estate vineyards under the guidance of master winemaker Lindsay McCall of Paringa Estate.

So I,m sure we will be seeing you at Lindenderry, leisurely indulging in luxury - as you deserve!!

Address: Andrews Lane RED HILL 3937
Phone: (03) 5989 2933
Fax: (03) 5989 2936

Email: lrh@lindenderry.com.au
WWW: www.lindenderry.com.au
Owner: Lancemore Group

Winemaker: Lindsay McCall
Est: 1995 **Vine Ha:** 10
Principal Varieties: Chardonnay, Pinot Noir

Main Ridge Estate

Nat White, a graduate in oenology from Charles Sturt University, and his wife Rosalie, were the modern-day pioneers who began the rebirth of the Mornington Peninsula as a wine region. In the centre of the Peninsula on the cool, elevated Main Ridge, Nat and Rosalie cleared a sheltered hillside and planted vines in 1975. The vines today are strong, well established and producing complex wines which are full of character.

Nat believes that marginal, cool climates produce Chardonnay and Pinot Noir of great elegance, finesse and intensity but achievement of full potential requires far more attention to detail in the vineyard that in warmer areas. Low cropping levels, bunch and shoot thinning and pre-vintage removal of green or diseased fruit are all processes demanding meticulous manual labour.

The winery, sculptured into the hillside at the top of the property, has a cool underground cellar with a beautiful tasting room gallery above. The gardens around the winery and vineyard are superb, with more than 100 species of roses planted. Nat's former occupation as a civil engineer shows through in the pleasing layout of the estate. The Whites' deep love of nature and their estate is well captured in the verse I noticed on the verandah:

"The kiss of the sun for pardon
The song of the bird for mirth
One is nearer God's heart in the garden
Than anywhere else on earth".

Address: 80 William Road RED HILL 3937	Winemaker: Nat White	Principal Varieties: Chardonnay, Pinot Noir	
Phone: (03) 5989 2686 Fax: (03) 5931 0000	Est: 1975 Vine Ha: 3 Cases: 1,000	Principal Wines	Potential
Email: mrestate@mre.com.au	Public Hours: 12pm-4pm, Weekdays; 12pm-	Chardonnay	3-10 yrs
WWW: www.mre.com.au	5pm, Weekends and Public Holidays, lunch	Half Acre Pinot Noir	4-10 yrs
Owner: Nat and Rosalie White	served on Sundays	Pinot Noir	3-8 yrs

Kings Creek

In 1981 Kings Creek Winery began planting vines on the sheltered slopes on the Westernport side of the Mornington Peninsula near Bittern.

Their Pinot Noir, Chardonnay and Cabernet Sauvignon wines soon began winning medals in wine shows.

Kings Creek have some of the most mature vines on the Peninsula, this combined with the warmest climate and leanest soils, gives wines of more generous flavours and fuller body than other parts of the Peninsula.

The initial vineyards covered 10 acres, it has been increased to 50 acres in 1998/99, planting of a further 115 acres of vineyard is underway.

The more recent planting have enabled Kings Creek to extend their range which now includes an intense Pinot Gris, a Sauvignon Blanc, a Shiraz and a Savgiovese.

The Reserve label Pinot Noir is full in colour with loads of berry flavours, there is nothing insipid about this Pinot. The Reserve label Chardonnay is also a rich opulent style.

Kings Creek Cellar Door is full of character, lots of timber and a huge open fire for winter. There is a casual restaurant serving delicious light "Tapas" dishes from local produce, or you can bring your own picnic to enjoy in the outdoor area amongst the vines. Kings Creek is one of the closest Peninsula vineyards to Melbourne and an excellent place to start your Peninsula Pilgrimage.

Address: 237 Myers Road BITTERN 3918	Email: kcwinery@pac.com.au	Est: 1981
Phone: (03) 5983 2102 Fax: (03) 5983 5153	Winemaker: Brien Cole & Daneil Greene	Public Hours: 11am-5pm, daily

Paringa Estate

The spectacular Winery Restaurant and Hospitality Centre that was opened in 1998 at Paringa Estate represented another bold move in the success story, former school teacher, the tenacious Lindsay McCall has pulled together.

In 1999 at the Sydney International Wine Competition, the wine world was stunned when Paringa carried off the most prestigious trophy of the show. The Chairman of Judges trophy for "The Best Wine" was awarded to the 1997 Paringa Shiraz, extraordinary because the Mornington Peninsula hardly has any Shiraz planted and the pundits opinion is, it's too cold to make a decent Shiraz, Lindsay is not one to be swayed by others. His determination to succeed is evident in all his wines, which are in the absolute top echelon of Australia's finest, whilst his Shiraz wines have won a hoard of trophies and medals, his Pinot Noirs (the regions specialty) have won even more. Lindsay uses expensive tight grained French Troncais oak barriques from France for all his wines which also includes a Chardonnay, its restrained elegant character, shows off the finely structured Mornington Peninsula fruit perfectly.

A glass in hand of fine wine on the expansive wooden decking which opens out from the Restaurant, high above the vineyard with spectacular views over Westernport Bay, one could well be in a Paradise at Paringa.

Address: 44 Paringa Road RED HILL SOUTH 3937 Phone: (03) 5989 2669 Fax: (03) 5931 0135	Email: paringa@cdi.com.au Winemaker: Lindsay McCall Est: 1985	Public Hours: 11am-5pm, daily Principal Varieties: Pinot Gris, Shiraz, Chardonnay, Pinot Noir

Stoniers

Leading publisher Brian Stonier bought 112 acres of grazing country in 1977. The property has a sensational view over Western Port at Merricks. At the urging of his wife Noel they planted half an acre of Chardonnay vines adjacent to their home, replacing an old lemon grove that had outlived its useful life. They very basically prepared the land, dug the holes and planted the vines themselves using as their only guide a textbook entitled "General Viticulture" by Winkler. This has led 24 years later, to one of the largest wine producers on the Peninsula with vineyards covering 125 acres.

Stonier's can lay claim to being Australia's most successful 'new' winemaker. In 1994, at the prestigious Royal Adelaide Show, they were awarded two trophies for their 1993 Reserve Pinot Noir. One for the best pinot noir at the show and the other for the best varietal red table wine, against the best big reds of cabernet sauvignon, shiraz, merlot and other varieties, on South Australia's home ground. This extraordinary event marked the coming of age of the Mornington Peninsula as a wine region.

Stonier's winemaker for 14 vintages, Tod Dexter, began his career far off in the Napa Valley. At Cakebread

Cellars across the road from the legendary Robert Mondavi Winery, Tod learnt much in seven vintages before returning to Australia in 1985.

Tod credits the vineyards at Stoniers with producing fruit that makes his job rewarding. Tod also has a 15 acre vineyard at Merricks North which supplies the Stonier Winery with an important 'warmer' climate part of the vintage. Stonier's have a "Unique Barrique Club" started in 1991, where a barrique holding 25 dozen wine can be purchased in advance. The wine carries a Stonier Reserve label with the purchasers name or names added. Stoniers also produce a Sauvignon Blanc and a bordeaux-style cabernet sauvignon for sale at the cellar door only. Their new trade distributor Distinguished Vineyards, concentrate on chardonnay and pinot noir.

Address: 362 Frankston-Flinders Road MERRICKS 3916 Phone: (03) 5989 8300 Fax: (03) 5989 8709 Email: stoniers@stoniers.com.au WWW: www.stoniers.com.au Owner: Stonier Wines Pty Ltd	Winemaker: Tod Dexter Est: 1978 Vine Ha: 20 Cases: 16,000 Public Hours: 12pm-5pm daily; summer hours 11am-5pm (closed Christmas Day) Principal Varieties: Chardonnay, Pinot Noir, Cabernet Sauvignon, Cabernet Franc, Merlot	Principal	Wines Potential
		Stonier Pinot Noir	2-5 yrs
		Stonier Chardonnay	2-5 yrs
		Stonier Cabernet	3-5 yrs
		Stonier Reserve Pinot Noir	2-6 yrs
		Stonier Reserve Chardonnay	3-8 yrs

Red Hill Estate

historic property "The Briars", on the warmer north western part of the peninsula where the grapes ripen several weeks before the cooler Red Hill vineyards. Virtually all of the Red Hill Estate Cabernet Sauvignon comes from The Briars vineyard and the Chardonnay and Pinot Noir go into Red Hill Estate's superb Methode Traditionelle wines, the Pinot Noir · Pinot Meunier based "Blance de Noirs" and the Chardonnay based "Blanc de Blanc".

Red Hill produce a Pinot Grigio which is doing very well on the Peninsula, it comes from one of the vineyards which Red Hill contract, an important move as the micro climates and soils of each Mornington Peninsula site vary so much.

Winemaker Michael Kyberd arrived just before the 1998 vintage and has shown his innovative talents with the last few vintages, working in tandem with meticulous vineyard manger Tyson Lewis.

The beautifully manicured gardens at Red Hill Estate give visitors a taste of what is to follow · great wine and food in a relaxing and unique environment which truly gives it a commanding view of the Mornington Peninsula.

Red Hill Estate's views over Western Port Bay and Philip Island has to be seen to be believed and is even more enjoyable with a glass of Sparkling, followed by Max's fine food!!

A successful businessman and a person of incredible vision and energy, Sir Peter Derham has turned his retirement project into a more than full-time occupation. No job on his beloved Red Hill Estate is too trivial for Sir Peter's hands to tackle.

The vineyard was established in 1989, on the vibrant red soil which often supports some of the world's best pinot noirs. The hard work put in by Sir Peter and Lady Derham was well repaid in 1994, when they won the coveted Department of Agriculture "Victorian Vineyard of the Year Award". The vineyard has panoramic views over Western Port Bay and Phillip Island. To take advantage of this view, a restaurant was added to the front of the winery in 1994 and it proved instantly successful, with a focus on fresh local produce. One can also sit outdoors, although the ever changing vista can be viewed from any point in the restaurant.

In 1996 Executive Chef Max Paganoni joined Red Hill Estate to run the Restaurant and his dishes have received much critical acclaim.

Recently the Restaurant was renamed 'Max's at Red Hill'.

Red Hill Estate have grafted over all the Cabernet Sauvignon and Cabernet Franc to various clones of Pinot Noir, the vineyards of 24 acres are now planted to Pinot Noir, Chardonnay, Sauvignon Blanc, Pinot Meunier and Merlot. Red Hill Estate also manage a 5 acre vineyard at the

Address: 53 Shoreham Road
Red Hill South 3937
Phone: (03) 5989 2838

Fax: (03) 5989 2855
Email: info@redhillestate.com.au
WWW: www.redhillestate.com.au

Owner: Sir Peter & Lady Derham
Winemaker: Michael Kyberd   **Est:** 1989
Public Hours: 11am-5pm, daily

Mantons Creek Vineyard

Christmas 2000 will be quite a memorable one for Michael and Judy Ablett, they were on a weekend trip to the Mornington Peninsula to buy a Christmas Tree, casually looking at properties, when they saw a For Sale sign at Mantons Creek Vineyard. Within three months of first tasting the wines they were the proud owners.

Michael had been a Senior Lecturer in Medicine and a Consultant Cardiologist at the Otago Medical School in Dunedin, NZ, and his career brought him to Melbourne 10 years ago. His interest in the property probably stems from his upbringing at his parents' country hotel in rural Wales. His hospitality background should prove of great benefit to him as Mantons Creek not only produces fine wines, but also has a splendid 40-seat restaurant with delightful outdoor eating areas overlooking the vineyard as well as four bed and breakfast suites. There are two deluxe and two superior rooms, each with a verandah looking over the vines, and a guest lounge with an open fireplace.

The Mantons Creek wines include the up-and-coming Pinot Gris, already an award winner, and the little-grown red varieties Tempranillo and Pinot Meunier. Amongst the other Mantons Creek wines to impress me was the 1999 vintage Chardonnay, which scored 95.5/100 from me, with loads of melon, cashew and grapefruit, a very good, complex wine. They also have a Pinot Noir, a superb Traminer, nice and spicy, and a delightful desert wine blended from the Traminer, Muscat and Sauvignon Blanc. Consummate winemaker Alex White, formerly of Lillydale Vineyards, is doing a great job with the still wines whilst the Methode Traditionelle Sparkling is crafted at the Cope-Williams Winery. The Mantons Creek fruit is produced by skilled viticulturalist Carl Tiesdell-Smith who has been managing the vineyard for the ten years since its planting.

In its sunny clearing amongst groves of trees, including large, ancient pines, Mantons Creek is literally a hidden jewel of the Peninsula and it is well worth taking the trouble to find it to taste the wines. I am sure that you will want buy some wine and sit and have lunch in the gorgeous Tuscan-style restaurant which serves fresh, innovative dishes prepared from local ingredients - why not eat and stay the night.

Michael and Judy will celebrate each Christmas in honour of their special gift.

Address: 240 Tucks Road MAIN RIDGE 3928
Phone: (03) 5989 6264 **Fax:** (03) 5989 6286
Email: mantonscreek@hotmail.com
WWW: www.mantonscreekvineyard.com.au
Winemaker: Alex White
Est: 1989 **Vine Ha:** 10 **Cases:** 4,500 - 5,000

Public Hours: Dec-April: Cellar Door, 11am-5pm, daily. Restaurant, daily. May-Nov: Cellar Door, 11am-5pm, Thurs-Sun. Restaurant, Lunch, Fri-Sun, Dinner, Sat
Principal Varieties: Chard, Sauv Blanc, Traminer, Brown Muscat, Pinot Noir, Tempranillo
Principal Wines   **Potential**

Principal Wines	Potential
Chardonnay	3-6 yrs
Pinot Gris	3-4 yrs
Pinot Noir	3-4 yrs
Tempranillo	5-8 yrs
Sparkling Chardonnay/Pinot Noir	3-6 yrs
Pinot Meunier	4-6 yrs

Willow Creek is one of the show piece wineries of Australia, situated on top of a ridge, with views over the vineyards sweeping down the valley both sides to a large expanse of water, resplendent with bird life and stocked with trout, its spectacular.

The glorious red brick, slate roofed homestead at the entrance to the property and home to proprietors Peter and Sue Harris, was built in the 1870's and is one of the few original homes of "the grand era" left on the Peninsula.

The State of the Art Winery has been constructed in red brick, toning in beautifully with the historic homestead.

On the south west corner of the Winery, with floor to ceiling windows overlooking the valley of vines and dam, is a top class café restaurant, which opened in 1998 and has since been expanded and can now cater for functions, its a popular place to tie the wedding knot. The cellar door is equally spectacular and has a seperate menu with a choice of light fresh food, if you're on a tight schedule to see other Peninsula wineries.

The vineyard planting began in 1989

and now covers 32 acres. Willow Creek produced one of the few Sauvignon Blancs on the peninsula, a variety well suited to the maratime climate. Their unoaked Chardonnay is very aromatic and their "Tulum" Chardonnay barrel fermented in a blend of top class French Troncais, Allier and Nevers oak barriques, its complex and full bodied. Willow Creek is in the warmer part of the Peninsula sheltered by The Red Hill Ridge and their Cabernet Sauvignon with a touch of Merlot and Cabernet Franc, has been a consistent trophy winner. Naturally Willow Creek make a Pinot Noir, one of the best in the region, and also a good Shiraz, a

rarity in the area.

Young Winemaker Simon Black has already a number of vintages under his belt at Willow Creek and also supervises the vineyards. The well equipped winery and plenty of top quality French oak gives him every opportunity to make great wines and he revels in the challenge, winning many wine show awards.

Willow Creek run lots of special functions and events in their hospitality centre, and its worth contacting them for a calendar of events. You may be able to lock one of them into your Peninsula Pilgrimage.

Address: RMB 6535, 166 Balnarring Road MERRICKS NORTH 3926 **Phone:** (03) 5989 7448 **Fax:** (03) 5989 7584	**Email:** admin@willow-creek.com.au **WWW:** www.willow-creek.com **Winemaker:** Simon Black **Est:** 1988	**Public Hours:** 10am-5pm, daily **Principal Varieties:** Cabernet Franc, Chardonnay, Pinot Noir, Shiraz, Cabernet Sauvignon, Merlot, Sauvignon Blanc

Goulburn Valley

The area known as the Goulburn Valley was first explored and deemed suitable for development by Major Thomas Mitchell in 1836. Many graziers settled the area and despite the emphasis on farming, vines were first planted as early as the 1850's.

In 1860 a successful group of landowners and merchants formed the consortium 'Tahbilk Vineyard Proprietary'. Purchasing 260 hectares of land for the purpose of establishing a vineyard and winery, the group, and in particular, Mr John Pinney Bear, energetically set about creating favourable conditions for making good wines. Mr John Pinney Bear prompted rapid growth of the vineyard by advertising Australia-wide for vine cuttings.

Chateau Tahbilk prospered, not only because of the dedication of all those involved, but also because of innovative marketing, a kind climate and ideal topography. Today it is a most significant winery in the area and is the only winery to have remained continuously in production. Although hit by the phylloxera scourge at the turn of the century, some of the company's vineyards survived unharmed, allowing the manufacture of wines to continue. Chateau Tahbilk is now run by the Purbrick family who have utilized the original winery buildings and facilities and thus preserved the heritage of the property.

The architectural elegance of the winery coupled with the graceful layout of the surrounding grounds make Tahbilk one of the most beautiful wineries in Australia. Within the last 20 years many other winemakers have planted vines in the Goulburn Valley. In addition to Chateau Tahbilk the largest concern is the Mitchelton Winery and Vineyards.

Mitchelton's 500 acre property is bordered on one side by the Goulburn River and is widely recognised by its distinctive tower which became a part of the landscape in the early 1970's. In comparison to Chateau Tahbilk, Mitchelton has a more contemporary appearance, bit it too is one of the country's most striking wineries.

The Somerset Crossing Winery in the town of Seymour has not only great wines but an excellent winery restaurant. Two new large wineries have been built in the region since my last edition. The Dalfarras Winery of Chateau Tahbilk's Alister Purbrick and the McPherson Winery of Andrew McPherson, a long time exporter of premium Australian wines. In total, there are some 20 or so wineries in the region, as well as many small growers who supply high quality fruit, both throughout this area and elsewhere. As the region includes diverse microclimates, soils and altitudes, wine styles of the Goulburn Valley are many and varied. Both red and white wines are produced and although there are some discrepancies in quality, most are highly regarded.

The Goulburn Valley Winemakers have also taken a wonderful initiative in creating the "Great Australian Shiraz Challenge", an annual judging to find the best Shiraz of any vintage in Australia, graciously sponsored by Qantas. I had the great honour of accepting the inaugural trophy in 1995 on behalf of my brother Geoffrey and his 1993 Kuitpo Shiraz.

Goulburn Valley

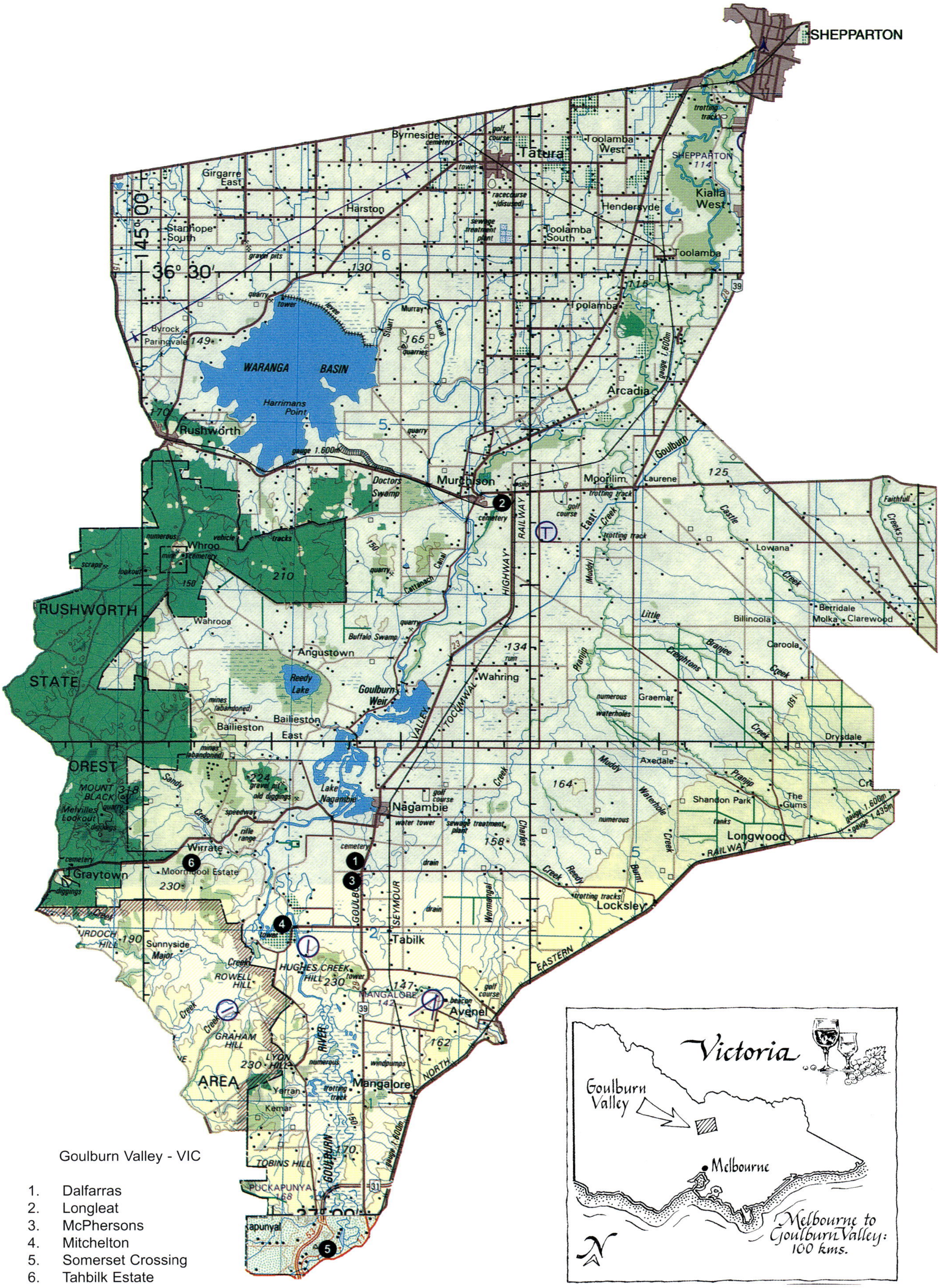

SHEPPARTON

Girgarre
East

Stanhope
South

Harston

Byrock
Paringvale 149

Rushworth

WARANGA BASIN

Harrimans
Point

gauge 1.600m

Doctors
Swamp

Whroo
cemetery

RUSHWORTH

STATE

Wahrooa

Angustown

Reedy
Lake

Baileston
East

Baileston

Goulburn
Weir

OREST

MOUNT
BLACK

Melvilles
Lookout

Wirrate

Graytown

Moorneool Estate
230

Nagambie

Lake
Nagambie

Tabilk

URDOCH
Sunnyside
Major

HUGHES CREEK
HILL 230

ROWELL
HILL

MANGALORE
142

Avenel

39

GRAHAM
HILL

AREA

Yarran

Kemar

Mangalore

NORTH

TOBINS HILL

PUCKAPUNYA

apunyal

Byrneside
cemetery

Tatura

golf
course

Toolamba
West

SHEPPARTON
114

Kialla
West

racecourse
(disused)

sewage
treatment
plant

Toolamba
South

Hendersyde

Toolamba

Murray
Canal

olamba

165
quarries

Arcadia

5

Murchison

cemetery

Moorilim

Laurene

Goulburn

125

golf
course

trotting track

Lowana

Billinoola

Carool a

Berridale
Molka Clarewood

Wahring

Graemar

numerous
waterholes

Branjee

Drysdale

Axedale

164

Shandon Park

The
Gums

Longwood

RAILWAY

Locksley

gauge 1.600m
gauge 435m

trotting tracks

golf
course

EASTERN

Goulburn Valley - VIC

1. Dalfarras
2. Longleat
3. McPhersons
4. Mitchelton
5. Somerset Crossing
6. Tahbilk Estate

Victoria

Goulburn
Valley

Melbourne

Melbourne to
Goulburn Valley:
100 kms.

325

Tahbilk Estate

Established in 1860, Tahbilk Estate is one of Victoria's most beautiful and historic properties. Situated 122 kilometres north of Melbourne, on the east bank of the Goulburn River, at a site the Aboriginals call "tabilk-tabilk".

The property comprises some 1,214 hectares of the richest river flats in the Goulburn Valley, with a frontage of 11 kilometres to the river and approximately 8 kilometres of permanent running back waters and creeks.

One of the most interesting and picturesque features of the Estate is the cellars, the main part of which is underground and eminently suitable for the maturation of high-quality table wines. The original cellar and storage, built in 1860, (and surmounted by a tower) which is classified by the National Trust, is 92 metres in length, whereas the "New Cellar", constructed in 1875 and running at right angles, is 60.5 metres long. An idea of the size of the cellars may be obtained from the fact that the roof area alone covers 1 hectare.

Throughout its career, Tahbilk has obtained over 1000 awards for wines produced on the Estate at all the world's principal exhibitions. These awards include the Diploma of Honour, the highest award obtainable at the Greater London Exhibition of 1899. Also First Order of Merit and Medals in London, Philadelphia, Paris, Bordeaux, Calcutta, Brussels, Amsterdam, Melbourne, Adelaide and Dunedin. More than 60 firsts have been obtained at the Royals Shows of Melbourne, Adelaide, Sydney and Brisbane, and since the introduction of the medals awards in 1965, 11 Trophies, 65 Gold, 188 Silver and 619 Bronze medals have been awarded.

The Estate was purchased by Reginald Purbrick in 1925 and by 1931 his son Eric had taken over management and winemaking responsibilities at Tahbilk. Eric was joined by his son, John, in 1955 and John's son Alister, a graduate of the Winemaking course at Roseworthy College, took over the role as winemaker and manager in 1978.

The vineyard comprises 182 hectares of vines with classical varieties such as cabernet sauvignon, cabernet franc, shiraz, merlot, malbec, riesling, marsanne, roussanne, viognier, chenin blanc, sauvignon blanc, chardonnay and semillon grown.

The process of vinification at Tahbilk unites traditional winemaking methods with modern, up to date technology. The exquisitely made whites exhibit intense, varietal fruit flavours when young and with bottle age, develop marvellous complexity and character.

The reds are produced with a commitment to the traditional winemaking values held at Tahbilk for over 140 years. As young wines they show a remarkable balance of complex fruit flavours and natural grape tannins which evolve with considerable bottle age into wines of great power and distinction.

The Tahbilk Museum was officially opened in October 1995 and is lodged in the "Old Church" built in 1875. This unique building now contains a vast array of fascinating historical pieces and also provides a wonderful setting for exclusive Tahbilk Wine Club dinners and functions.

Phone: (03) 5794 2555	**Est:** 1860 **Vine Ha:** 182 **Cases:** 125,000		Tahbilk Marsanne	5-10 yrs
Fax: (03) 5794 2360	**Public Hours:** 9am-5pm, Mon-Sat; 10am-		Tahbilk Shiraz	10-20 yrs
Email: admin@tahbilk.com.au	5pm, Sun & Public Holidays except Xmas Day		Tahbilk Cabernet Sauvignon	15-25 yrs
WWW: www.tahbilk.com.au	**Principal Varieties:** Cabernet Sauvignon,		Tahbilk 1860 Vines Shiraz	20-35 yrs
Owner: Purbrick Family	Shiraz, Chardonnay, Marsanne, Riesling		Tahbilk Reserve Cabernet Sav	30-50 yrs
Winemaker: Alister Purbrick	**Principal Wines**	**Potential**	Tahbilk Chardonnay	3-5 yrs

McPhersons

McPherson Wines had its beginnings in 1969 when the brand was launched by Andrew McPherson. Between 1971 and 1973, he was responsible for planting and developing over 1,000 acres in the Hunter Valley for a new group of investors. In 1974, McPherson established his own winery facility and took over as winemaker. The winery continued to grow for five more years until it was sold enabling McPherson to pursue other roles in the booming Australian wine industry.

Following the sale of McPherson Wines in 1979, Andrew McPherson acted as consultant winemaker to numerous wineries throughout Australia and New Zealand. During this time, he refined his skills, in the technological area of winemaking and was instrumental in applying this technology to Australia's burgeoning wine business and to other facilities around the world. Cold fermentation systems, high-speed centrifugation, and rotary drum vacuum filtration were some of the processes McPherson used to help his clients succeed.

In 1989, McPherson helped develop the export business along with that of his old friend, Geoff Merrill, one of Australia's most highly regarded winemakers. McPherson Wines was reformed in 1993 with principal vineyard holdings in the Murray-Darling region near Mildura, one of Australia's most exciting new regions for grape-growing. The recent acquisition of 350 acres in the Goulburn Valley of "red brick dust" soil with deep gravel offers even greater promise for cooler climate red wines in the McPherson portfolio. New trellising systems and a better

understanding of canopy management are some of the recent changes occurring at McPherson to further improve wine quality.

Since the inception of the McPherson brand, the goal has been to produce accessible, fruit-forward wines with varietal integrity at a fair price. McPherson describes the style of his wines as "sunshine in a bottle."

McPherson's Semillon-Chardonnay, Chardonnay, and Shiraz and Shiraz-Cabernet are offered in the U.S. through an exclusive U.S. distribution relationship with Brown-Forman Corporation in Louisville, Kentucky.

McPhersons's have also set up a unique association with Suzi McKay and her historic Restaurant and Country Hotel, Harvest Home, built in the 1870's at Avenel. Suzi also pioneered the Avenel Farmers market and began producing her own breads

growing her own vegetables and herbs, plus smoking fresh local fish. Suzi is also doing wonderful things with the famous Goulburn Valley fruits and naturally with the McPherson range of wines, with food matching recommendations and recipes, not only at her own restaurant but also on the Internet · why not check them out and find out more about the McPerhson Innovative wines at the same time.

Mitchelton

The late Ross Shelmerdine, an imaginative and ingenious man, made his mark on the Australian wine industry by creating one of the country's most exciting and unusual winery complexes. Ross commissioned Colin Preece to select a site anywhere in South Eastern Australia suitable for his ambitious project, Freece selected the Blackwood Park grazing property on the banks of the Goulburn River near Mitchellstown. In 1969 he purchased the 200 hectare property. Preece was also retained as a consultant for the first few vintages, giving the winery a solid foundation on which to develop.

In late 1972 work began on the winery complex which now includes extensive underground cellars. The complex was named after Mitchellstown, the site where Major

Thomas Mitchell set up camp during his exploration of the area in 1836.

The first small vintage was processed at Brown Brothers Winery in 1972. The vines originally planted by Colin Preece continued to bear excellent fruit for the production of high quality wines, by winemaker, Don Lewis, who has now made 29 vintages at the winery. Mitchelton Winery is now part of the Petaluma Wine Group and the support and impact of Brian Croser and his team has only enhanced the quality of the already excellent wines.

Mitchelton relies on its own vineyards for about half of its grapes and has contracts with cool climate growers in central Victoria for the rest. Don Lewis's first vintage was only 73 tonnes back in 1973. In 2001 this was well over 3,000 tonnes.

A unique wine in the Mitchelton range is the Wood Matured Marsanne with its distinctive honeysuckle character. It also ages remarkably well. Mitchelton and the Goulburn Valley has a well earned reputation for rhone varieties like marsanne and shiraz.

Mitchelton has an award winning restaurant which focuses on regional produce, an art gallery and accredited nature reserve. In fact, the level of quality afforded to the visitor by Mitchelton gained recognition in 1994 and again in 1995 with the Victorian Tourism Award in the Wineries section. This is a showpiece winery which also holds occasional concerts and hosts cultural events of various kinds. Things are well in balance at Mitchelton so why not drop in and absorb its great ambience.

Address: Mitchellstown NAGAMBIE 3608	**Est:** 1974 **Vine Ha:** 150 **Cases:** 220,000	Print Shiraz 20+ yrs
Phone: (03) 5794 2710	**Public Hours:** 9am-5pm, daily	Michelton Cabernet Sauvignon 15+ yrs
Fax: (03) 5794 2615	**Principal Varieties:** Cabernet Sauvignon,	Michelton Chardonnay 15+ yrs
Email: mitchelton@mitchelton.com.au	Shiraz, Riesling, Marsanne, Merlot,	Goulburn Valley Marsanne 10+ yrs
WWW: www.michelton.com.au	Chardonnay	Goulburn Valley Shiraz 10+ yrs
Winemaker: Don Lewis	**Principal Wines** **Potential**	Blackwood Park Shiraz 15-20 yrs

Dalfarras

Established in 1991 The Dalfarras Collection of fine wines and art combines the unique talents of husband and wife team Alister Purbrick - Graduate Oeonologist from Roseworthy Agricultural College and winemaker at Victoria's oldest family owned winery, Tahbilk and Rosa Purbrick (nee Dalfarra) - one of Australia's most talented artists whose highly acclaimed paintings have featured in exhibitions and galleries in Australia, Paris and New York.

Each Dalfarras release encapsulates the close link between fine wine and fine art and exhibits stunning images of a visual and sensory nature.

The fruit for the Dalfarras Collection is the finest available from preferred vineyard sites throughout Australia. Dalfarras have already won some top awards including The Douglas Seabrook Memorial Trophy for the Best Red Wine in the 1998 Melbourne Show with their 1991 Cabernet.

Stage one of the $4.5 million Dalfarras Winery was completed in early 1999.

March 15, 1999 marked the first day of harvest.

Unlike Tahbilk, which produces traditional wines from estate-grown vines in a history-rich environment, Dalfarras produces more modern, cutting-edge styles.

Within the next three years, 630 acres are expected to be under vines at four sites, as well as a Coonawarra-blended Cabernet

Sauvignon and both a Shiraz and Sauvignon Blanc blended with McLaren Vale, Margaret River and Nagambie Lakes fruit.

Expansion will see the 2003 vintage process about 7,000 tonnes. A cellar door complex, complete with ornamental lake and spire, will join the site, maintaining the theme of towers and lakes that predominates in Nagambie's wine-growing district.

Longleat

Longleat is a picturesque vineyard on the outskirts of the pretty town of Murchison, which features some of the most charming Victorian Colonial architecture in the State.

The vineyard is a picture of health and vigour on the rich river loams on the west bank of the Goulburn River. The property was planted to vines by the Schulz family, Peter Schulz's great great grandfather arrived in Australia in 1838.

The vineyards are now under new ownership and the vineyard has been revitalized and is currently being expanded to 31 acres. The vines are all hand pruned and the grapes are all hand picked to ensure maximum quality and to protect the root structure of the vines.

The wines also have been revamped and now sport classy labels boldly featuring the original Longleat Lion-crest. The Longleat Riesling has always been a favorite of mine, it now bears the "River Edge" label. The "First Crossing" Semillon Sauvignon is named after the nearby bridge, the first built over the Goulburn in the 1850's to link the areas various Goldfields. There is also a "Founders Reserve" Semillon and a "Campbells Blend" Cabernet Sauvignon, a rich opulent wine that pays homage to many of the early settlers, who did much to develop Murchison.

Longleat have won many awards for their wines, they are a little hard to find so its worth coming to their delightful wine cellars, surrounded by vine covered pergolas and picnic facilities, to stock up your own cellar, they also cater for functions.

Address: MURCHISON Victoria 3610
Phone: (03) 5826 2994 **Fax:** (03) 5826 2510
Email: longleat@longleatwines.com
WWW: www.longleatwines.com

Owner: Longleat Pty Ltd
Winemaker: David Traeger
Est: 1975 **Vine Ha:** 10 **Cases:** 3,000
Public Hours: Thursday - Monday

Principal Varieties: Cabernet Sauvignon, Semillon, Riesling, Shiraz
Principal Wines
Old Weir Road Shiraz

Victorian High Country

Some of the most awesomely beautiful country in Australia lies between the towns of Yea Alexandra and Mansfield. The two most striking features being Lake Eildon and Mount Buller whose snow capped peak dominates the vineyards of Delatite Winery, the first winery in the modern day history of this region.

There are only six or so wineries in this region but only four are of any size. Delatite whose vineyard planting began in 1968, the Murrindindi Vineyards of the Cuthbertson Family, Hugh Cuthbertson is a young legend of the industry and now works for a major wine company, Antcliff's Chase at Caveat and Plunkett Wines with their large vineyards in the Strathbogie Ranges of the region and their winery with its café near Avenel on the Hume Highway.

There are a number of large vineyards in the region also, including the Mount Helen vineyards of Tisdall and Mitchelton's Strathbogie vineyard.

The region is an outdoor persons paradise with skiing, bushwalking, canoeing, ballooning, trout fishing and horseback riding and camel trekking being amongst them. Why not exercise your sense of adventure in this glorious country soon - the wines are worth seeking out.

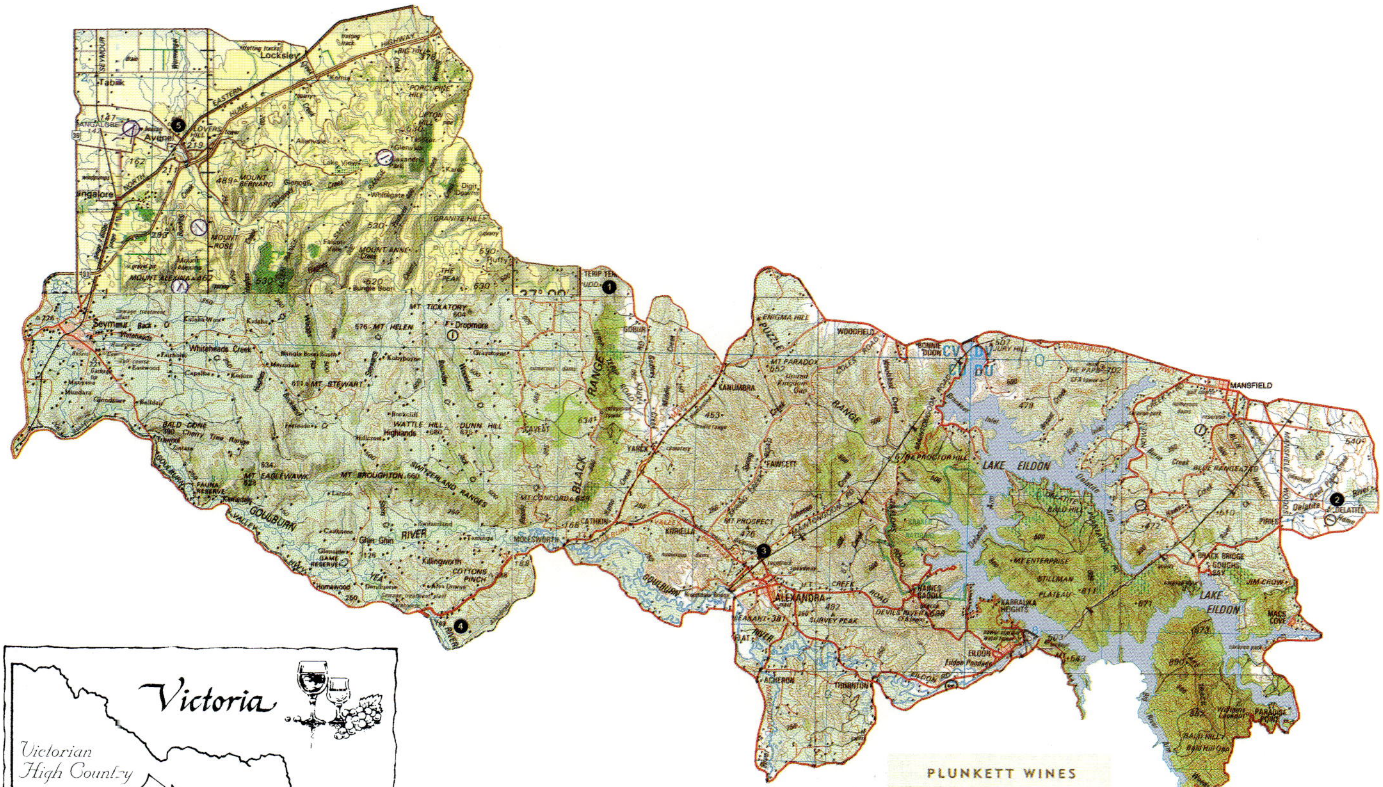

Victorian High Country - VIC

1. Antcliff's Chase Wines
2. Delatite
3. Goulburn River Trout
4. Murrindindi Vineyards
5. Plunkett Wines

PLUNKETT WINES

RESERVE   RESERVE

STRATHBOGIE RANGES
1998 SHIRAZ

750 mL | 12.5% ALC/VOL
PRODUCE OF AUSTRALIA

Goulburn River Trout

Hugh Meggitt and his family arrived from South Africa in 1979. Hugh, however, proudly describes this as a "homecoming" as his forbears settled in Paramatta in 1827 and his great grandfather Henry William Meggitt pioneered Australia's oilseed industry through his public company Meggitt Limited.

After spending 7 years living in Melbourne, Hugh felt he needed a change from city life and decided to swap his career in merchant banking for the challenge of trout farming in country Victoria. In 1986 the Meggitt family bought Walnut Island, an ideal trout farming site (plus 6000 black walnut trees), situated on a seasonal island in the Goulburn River near Alexandra. A huge learning curve followed for Hugh and his wife Gay. Once their two sons Edward and Derrick had graduated from university they joined the business and visits were undertaken to America, Britain, Scandinavia and Italy to learn more about trout farming, which is predominantly a Northern hemisphere activity. Prior to the Walnut Island trout farm being established, the Leake family, who were the first truly commercial trout farmers in Australia, agreed to sell Goulburn River Trout to the Meggitt family. The Leake's trout farm and processing factory were also situated in Alexandra, 5 kilometres upstream from the Walnut Island trout farm. This acquisition brought with it considerable experience and an established market presence.

Goulburn River Trout, which now includes the Walnut Island trout farm, currently produces an

expanding 900 tonnes of rainbow trout a year, accounting for about 40% of Australia's freshwater trout production. Its two grow-out farms and hatchery are situated on the Goulburn River about 15 kilometres below Lake Eildon. Due to irrigation releases from the depths of Lake

Eildon in summer the trout grow in ideal cold, clear, unpolluted water throughout the year, thereby avoiding the severe problems of trying to grow cold-water fish in warm low-flow rivers in summer.

The Meggitts do their own

processing, smoking and freezing in premises approved by the Australian Quarantine Inspection Service. Once processed the chilled, smoked and frozen trout products are distributed to the leading wholesalers, supermarkets, caterers and frozen food handlers in the major centres throughout Australia and also to a number of Asian countries. In addition to plate size trout, Goulburn River Trout supplies the markets with large King Trout, ranging in sizes from 1.5 to 2.5 kgs. The Meggitts pride themselves on the consistency, quality and freshness of their trout which is high in protein and rich in Omega 3. Their smoked trout, smoked in Europe's best Afos and Maurer smokers has been described as the "food they eat in heaven". Indeed a smoke trout fillet, brown bread and butter, black pepper and a squeeze of lemon with a good chardonnay is something out of this world.

Goulburn River Trout is very much a family business with Hugh and Gay handling much of the administration and sons Edward and Derrick looking after most of the production, processing and domestic sales. Other family members, including daughter Diana and daughters-in-law Sally and Donna, are also involved in the business which has 36 experienced and highly qualified members of staff. The success of the business has been based on hard work, customer service, stringent quality control and learning to live with the stress of intensive fish farming where all staff members are trained to be prepared and expect the unexpected.

Delatite

Robert and Vivienne Ritchie were pioneers of the modern Victorian Wine industry when they planted vines on their cattle property, Delatite, in 1968. They sold the grapes to Brown Brothers from 1972 - 1981 and completed the winery at Delatite in time for the 1982 vintage. Their daughter Rosalind returned to be the family's winemaker in 1982, having completed a degree in oenology at Roseworthy in South Australia. Her brother David manages the vineyards with father Robert looking after the farming enterprise. Vivienne is the dynamic and vivacious promoter and marketer of Delatite and makes sure the world knows about these exciting, clean and complex wines which keep winning trophies and awards every vintage.

As well as the famous Delatite Riesling and Gewürztraminer there is a sensational Sauvignon Blanc and an Unwooded Chardonnay.

The Devil's River, a Bordeaux style, Cabernet Sauvignon blended with Merlot, Malbec and Cabernet franc, is a top class wine with minty and conserve-like fruit intensity plus lovely cassis fruit characters.

Delatite also has a small range of intensely flavoured red varietals - Shiraz, Malbec, Merlot and Cabernet Sauvignon. The Ultimate Wines are their "R.J." Premium Red Blend and their "V.S." Premium Riesling, both only released in exceptional years.

The Pinot Noir and Chardonnay - 100% varietal wines - are aged in new Alliers, Vosges and Troncais (French) oak and the Demelza is a lovely 100% Pinot noir sparkling wine, only available at the cellar door.

The winery has a tasting room with sensational views over Mount Buller and Mount Stirling, underlining its cool mountain location.

Address: Corner Stoneys & Pollards Roads MANSFIELD 3722
Phone: (03) 5775 2922 **Fax:** (03) 5775 2911
Owner: The Ritchie

Winemaker: Rosalind Ritchie
Est: 1982 **Vine Ha:** 26 **Cases:** 12,000
Public Hours: 10am-5pm, daily (Closed Christmas Eve, Christmas Day, Good Friday

& Anzac Day)
Principal Varieties: Riesling, Pinot Noir, Gewürztraminer, Cabernet Sauvignon, Merlot, Chardonnay

Plunketts

One of the best unwooded chardonnay's I have tasted, comes from this little known winery with extensive vineyards in the very cool Strathbogie Ranges. Every time I drink this wine under their other label - Blackwood Ridge, its vibrant, fresh fruit flavours and lovely almond like nuttiness just blows me away

and I notice all my friends glasses are easily drained, it is moreish in the extreme.

Alan Plunkett began farming at "Whitegate" in the Strathbogie Ranges in 1966. The cool climate enhanced by being 500 metres above sea level, seemed ideal for growing premium table wine grapes.

In 1968 Alan pioneered grape growing in the Strathbogie's when he planted 3 acres to 25 varieties. Drought and the demands of a 3,200 acre grazing property during the rural depression shelved this experiment but Alan found which varieties thrived in his lofty environment.

In 1980 25 acres were planted, this is now up to 250 acres. Plunketts also have 9 acres around their winery on the Hume Highway at Avenel which includes a "Winery Cafe".

I have been most impressed by the Plunkett Merlot a supple style with lovely cherry and plum overtones. They have also just released an extremely fine Reserve Shiraz.

Alan's son Sam is quietly spoken, but his wines are saying plenty for him!!

Address: Lambing Gully Road AVENEL 3664
Phone: (03) 5796 2150 **Fax:** (03) 5796 2147
Email: winery@eck.net.au
WWW: www.plunkett.com.au
Owner: Alan Plunkett **Winemaker:** Sam Plunkett
Est: 1991 **Vine Ha:** 110 **Cases:** 10,000

Public Hours: cellar door: 10am-5pm, daily; restaurant, 10am-5pm, Thurs-Mon
Principal Varieties: Chardonnay, Sauvignon Blanc, Semillon, Gewürztraminer, Riesling, Shiraz, Pinot Noir, Merlot, Cabernet Franc, Cab Sav
Principal Wines **Potential**

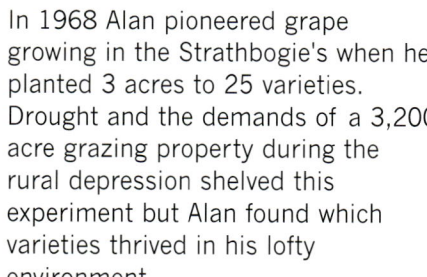

Principal Wines	Potential
Reserve Shiraz	7-10 yrs
Strathbogie Ranges Merlot	3-5 yrs
Strathbogie Ranges Cabernet Merlot	4-6 yrs
Blackwood Ridge Shiraz	3-5 yrs
Blackwood Ridge Unwooded Chard	1-3 yrs
Blackwood Ridge Sauv Blanc / Sem	1-3 yrs

Geelong

Geelong is one of the most southerly wine regions in Australia, the others being Tasmania, Mornington Peninsula and South Gippsland.

Situated 70 kilometres south-west of Melbourne on Corio Bay, Geelong has a cool, maritime climate. The growing season for fruit extends from September to May and grapes achieve great depth and complexity of flavours.

Developed by Swiss immigrants with vine cuttings from Tasmania, Switzerland and France, during the 1850's to 1870's Geelong was the largest and most significant wine region in Victoria. In 1878 Phylloxera Vastatrix was discovered in the region and a severe Government eradication programme brought this era to a close.

Vines were again replanted in 1966 when Daryl and Nini Sefton established Idyll Vineyard in the Moorabool Valley on the site of one of the region's early vineyards.

Other vignerons followed the Sefton's lead, including Maltby's, Mt Anakie - later purchased by the Hickinbotham family, Staughton Vale, Asher, Lovely Banks, Hoopers, Bannockburn, Griffiths, Batesford, Prince Albert,

Waybourne and Austins, Campbells at Mt Duneed, The Minya at Connewarre, Scotchman's Hill at Drysdale and their superb historic Spray Farm hospitality centre, Kilgour and Bellarine, with several other vineyards producing grapes late in 2000, a spectacular development on the southern side of Geelong in the Colac Road "The Geelong Epicentre" opened its doors, surrounded by its own vineyards, it's a showcase for the regions wines and gourmet food, with several restaurant, a café and function facilities, housed in a giant adobe building it's a must visit.

The quality of Geelong wines remains high and Geelong is once again returning to pre-eminence in the Victorian wine scene.

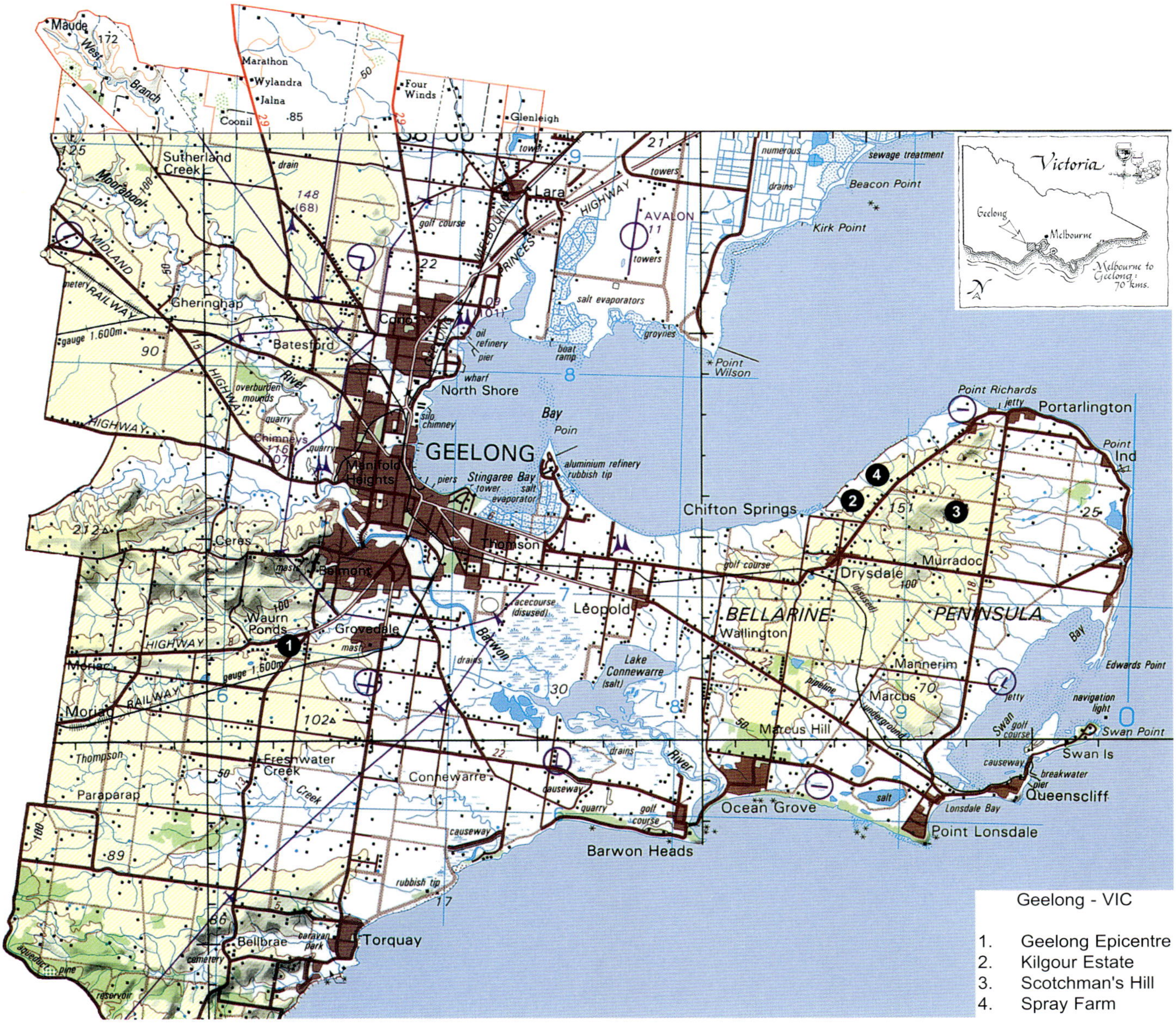

Geelong - VIC

1. Geelong Epicentre
2. Kilgour Estate
3. Scotchman's Hill
4. Spray Farm

Geelong Epicentre

Probably the most spectacular wine and food venture, in any wine region for many years is "The Geelong Epicentre". This incredible initiative by "Local Boy come home" Rodney Wade is also probably the worlds largest "Adobe" building, constructed out of 6000 bales of hay on a steel frame, concrete rendered and finished with messmate timber from the nearby Otway Ranges.

Rodney Wade left Geelong in his early 20's, his background in hospitality and restaurants is impeccable, his father created the famous large, "Long John's" Restaurant and his mother "Fishermans Peir" Restaurant, both in Geelong. Rodney went from work as a Ski instructor in America, to driving Safari trucks from Nairobi to Kenya, after other intinerate work, he turned

his hand to cooking, culminating in running two of his own restaurants, and a nightclub in Aspen Colorado. There he hosted many of Hollywood's rich and famous. In his travels Rodney fell in love the "Adobe" Villas in Santa Fe, New Mexico, he built an adobe home for himself, in Aspen. This began a dream for him of moving back to Geelong to plant a vineyard and build a hospitality centre on the prominent corner of the Anglesea Road and Princess Highway, where his family owned 60 acre property.

In 1999 Rodney planted Pinot Noir Vines on the property with a view to making his own Methode Champenoise.

In 2000 he commissioned his huge Adobe complex to his own design. through a Castlemaine Company, Strawbale Australia. A farm north east of Bendigo provided the hay, which is the stubble of wheat and rice crops after they are harvested, rather than burning it (creating harmful greenhouse gases) it is put to good use.

This method of construction creates

Geelong Epicentre

walls over 40 centimetres thick which are wonderful energy saving insulation, perfect for a wine and food operation.

The Centre includes a marvelous four sided tasting bar in a huge atrium area, where one can taste the best of Geelong and surrounding areas wine and food. There is a 160 seat restaurant and Californian inspired delicatessen, where one can purchase foods including meats and seafood's of all kinds and cook your own barbecue on the many cooking facilities in the huge rear courtyard. There are also expansive lawns and gardens, which include a large Tee Pee, in an area set aside for children, its got a wild west look but is filled with Australian Heritage items. There

is also a large stage which is used for concerts and cultural events

featuring local musicians and actors.

The expansion Adobe walls are covered in local artists works, it's truly a cultural Mecca, you certainly have no opportunity to be bored it's a fascinating fun and inspiring place. Rodney plans to build a Micro Brewery and a winemaking facility which he will operate in conjunction with the Geelong TAFE, who are building a Hospitality studies facility across the road.

The Building is impressive with its rounded shape, ochre colours and rustic textures blending into its environment amongst the vines perfectly, already it has the feel of a much older historic place. This Epicurean paradise is a wonderful bold move in Australia's wine and food world and truly worth whatever effort it takes to get yourself there.

Glenrowan

The region is located west of the Hume Highway, south of the rural city of Wangaratta and in view of the Victorian Alps.

The long established producers of the area, Bailey's and Booth's, have had a long history, both being established before 1900 and more recently Michael and Nancy Reid's Auldstone Cellars.

The climate is continental with extremely cool nights and winters. Being on the slopes of the Warby Ranges the soil is

alluvial and rich, eroded Granites from ancient volcanic activity it also has good air drainage protecting the vines from Spring frosts.

Traditionally the Glenrowan area has been renowned for deep complex red

wines of great longevity, the rich blackcurrant flavours further enhanced when the wines are cellared for at least 5 years. Chardonnay also does well producing rich mouthfilling wines.

These styles, combined with rich fortified muscat and tokays from all three producers at Glenrowan, creates great appeal and diversity.

Signposted from the Hume Highway near Glenrowan, makes it easy to find. The region has a grandeur not to be missed.

Glenrowan - VIC

1. Auldstone Cellars
2. Bailey's Of Glenrowan
3. Booths Taminick Cellars

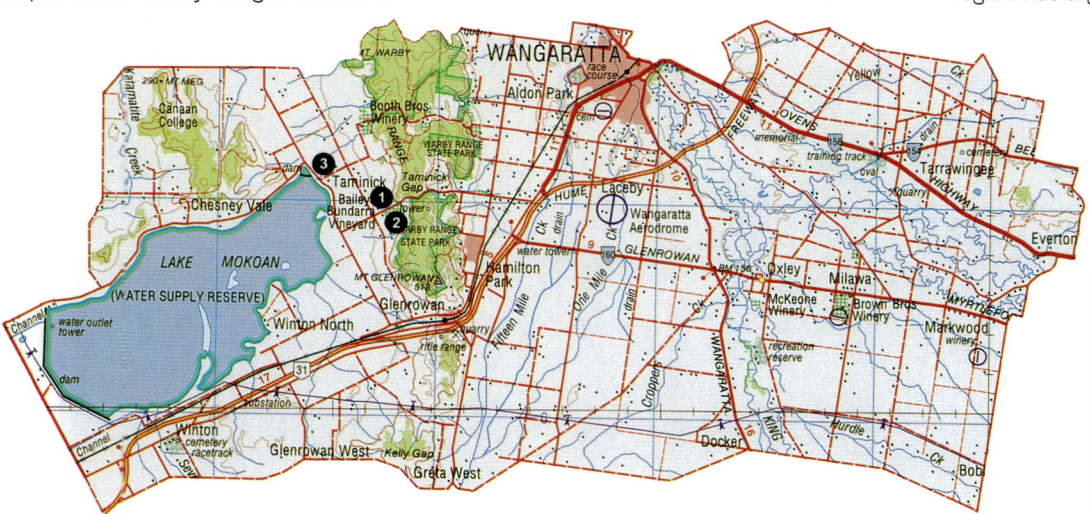

Booths Taminick Cellars

The magic ingredient of many of Australia's greatest red wines over many years, has been the wine they

have purchased from the Booths familys vineyards near Taminick in the Glenrowan Region.

Their penetrating berry flavours and earthy full bodied style makes them truly wines of great character, that mature magnificently.

One of the true characters of the wine industry is the sprightly octogenarian Cliff Booth, with his luxuriant silver grey hair and cheeky grin, he's a philosopher one could listen to for hours, it's a true honour to spend some time with Cliffy, tasting his wonderful rich reds, ports and muscats in the Booth family's historic cellars, gazing out over their legendary vineyard and the breathtaking grandeur of the Glenrowan Region.

Booths winemaking and management is now under the control of Cliffs son Peter, who also makes some full bodied whites from Chardonnay and Trebbiano (sometimes known as White Hermitage).

Booths Taminick Cellars is a treasured part of Australia's wine hirstory, one hopes it will always remain so.

Auldstone

In 1988, Viticulture and farming trade instructor Michael Reid and his economics trained wife Nancy, rescued the old Herceynia Vineyard and Cellars, when they bought them from Baileys 100 years after they had been established by Robert Cox. He originally planted in the 1880's and built the Cellars in 1891, mainly to produce wine for the "Jug" trade and Brandy spirit for fortifying Port and Sherry. In 1909 Robert tragically died of Peritonitis, due to the remoteness from medical facilities. His widow Barbara who had already lost two infant sons decided to sell and move to town with her two daughters. Baileys bought the vineyards but about this time Phylloxera devastated the 60 acres of vines. Bailey replanted 70 acres but the cellars no longer needed, fell into despair.

During the 1970's Baileys planted a further 50 acres but some not on resistant stock saw Phylloxera again

take its toll, with no irrigation the remainder of the vineyard could not produce commercial qualities of grapes.

The Reids heard Herceynia was on the market and bought the property in 1988. They have done a superb job restoring the historic old buildings and the Cellar door is full of character, they feature local art

and on weekends Nancy serves tempting gourmet lunches. The vineyards have also been brought back to their former glory. In 1990 an irrigation pipeline to Lake Mokoan was constructed, ensuring consistent vintages and continued vineyard health. The Reids won a gold medal for the best current vintage Muscat with their first vintage in 1988. The wine show successes have continued. They also produce Riesling, Chardonnay and two slightly sweeter whites, a Traminer Riesling and a late picked Riesling. In the reds they produce a Shiraz, a Cabernet Sauvignon and a Cabernet/Merlot blend. All big and full bodied but with velvety soft tannins. Their sparkling Shiraz is a taste sensation. They also have a Tawny Port and naturally a Muscat that is young but truly luscious. In winter the tasting room has a roaring log fire and the delightful gardens are a great place to relax on a hot summers day.

Address: Booths Road TAMINICK 3675	**WWW:** www.auldstone.com.au	Holidays; 10am-5pm, Sun
Phone: (03) 5766 2237	**Winemaker:** Michael Reid	**Principal Varieties:** Chard, Merlot, Riesling,
Email: winery@auldstone.com.au	**Public Hours:** 9am-5pm, Thu-Sat & Public	Cab Sav, Gewürztraminer, Muscat, Shiraz

Baileys

Richard Bailey arrived in Melbourne in the 1830's. He spent a decade as a cartage contractor before moving to Glenrowan and opening the towns first general store. Following the gold rush he bought land which his family farmed and planted some vines.

In 1855 his son Varley found a strip of deep red granite soil on the slopes below the Warby Ranges giving his red and fortified wines immense colour and strength, the muscat was particularly successful.

During the 1970's Harry Tinson became winemaker working hand in hand with Alan Bailey, great grandson of the founder. The Baileys 1920 Block Shiraz (long known as Hermitage) has always been sought after for its big robust colour and flavour. The muscats and tokays under various labels and prices are absolutely top wines in the unique rich Australian style that is taking many of the old world wine markets by storm.

The late 1990s saw the reintro-duction of Baileys Cabernet

Sauvignon and the limited release of Baileys 1904 Block Shiraz - both

wines made by the new winemaker Daniel Bettio.

King & Alpine Valleys

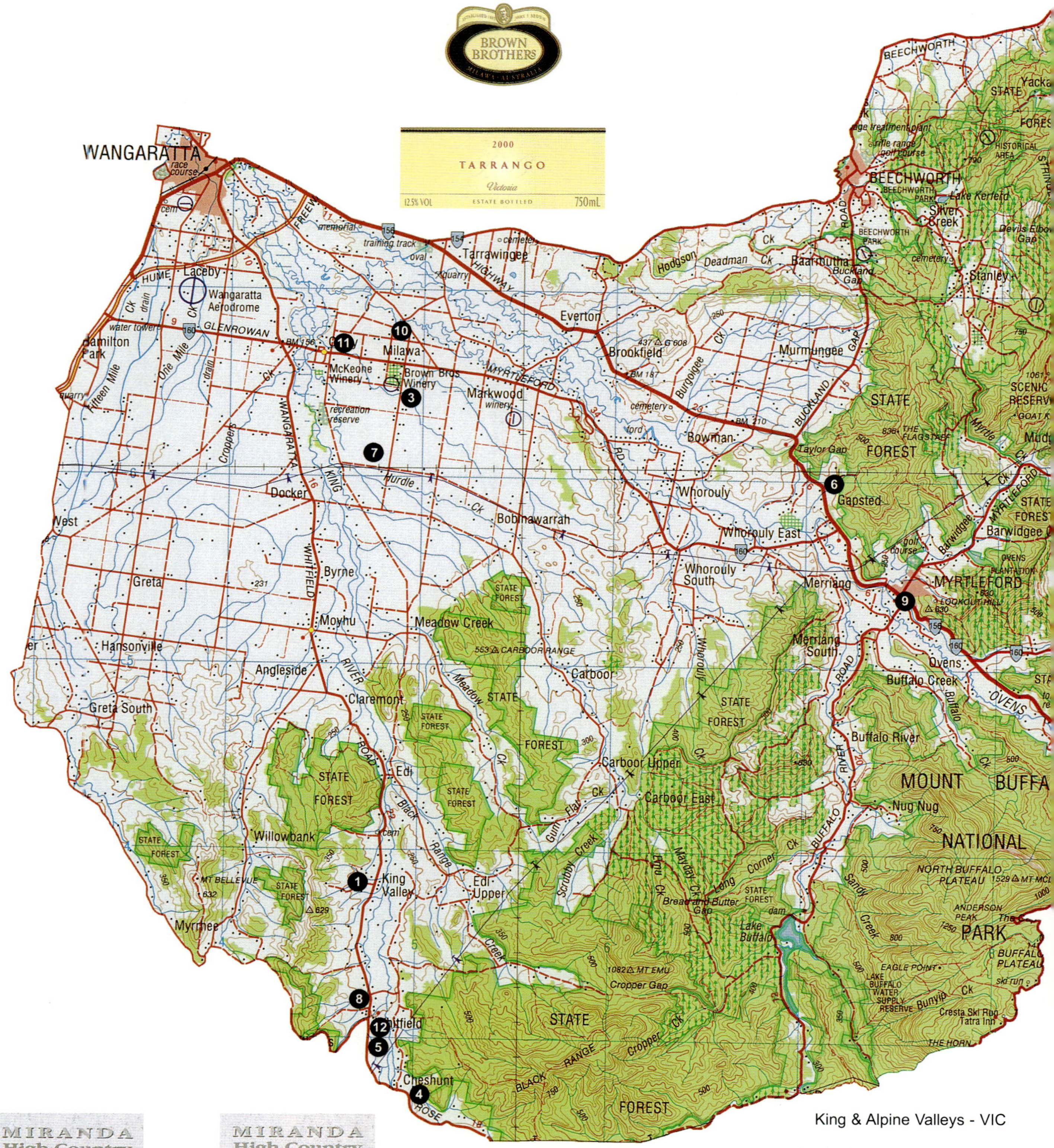

BROWN BROTHERS
MILAWA AUSTRALIA

2000
TARRANGO
Victoria
12.5% VOL   ESTATE BOTTLED   750mL

King & Alpine Valleys - VIC

1. Avalon
2. Boynton's of Bright
3. Brown Brothers
4. Chrismont Wines
5. Darling Estate
6. Gapsted Wines
7. John Gehrig Wines
8. King Valley Wines
9. Michelini Wines
10. Milawa Cheeses
11. Miranda Wines
12. Pizzini-Lana Trento

MIRANDA
High Country
1997
SHIRAZ
KING VALLEY · KIEWA VALLEY
PRODUCT OF AUSTRALIA · 750mL

MIRANDA
High Country
1999
CHARDONNAY
KING VALLEY · OVENS VALLEY
13.5% VOL · PRODUCT OF AUSTRALIA · 750mL

BROWN BROTHERS
MILAWA AUSTRALIA

EVERTON
1999
SHIRAZ,
CABERNET SAUVIGNON, MALBEC
Victoria
13.5% VOL   ESTATE BOTTLED   750mL

King & Alpine Valleys

It is little known that the King Valley has the largest area of vines (over 3,500 acres) of any cool climate grape growing region of Victoria. Situated high in the foothills of the Victorian Alps it supplies many of the top class, large Australian wineries with premium grapes. Brown Brothers still source almost half the crop from the region which is approaching over 20,000 tonnes of grapes per annum, planting is continuing at a rapid pace.

The region is very isolated and has few wineries in the high country. These include Avalon, the Darling Estate Winery, the Pizzini Lana Trento Winery and Chrismont. The 2,000 vintage saw the large new winery, King Valley wines crushing its first grapes. The region is very much in two entirely different climates. The plains, close to Milawa and Oxley, where Brown Brothers, the New Victorian Alps Winery, Miranda, Michelini and others are situated. The valley proper is at some 200 - 800 metres above sea level and some 30 - 40 kilometres south of Milawa around the towns of Whitfield and Cheshunt on deep volcanic soils.

Some problems have been experienced with isolated outbreaks

of phylloxera aided somewhat by the heavy soils, high rainfall and humidity. These have been contained and most vines are being planted on resistant root stock. The wines from The King Valley have very clean and strong varietal characters and good acid balance.

Most vineyards use high vertical trellising and double cordon training of the vines to get maximum leaf exposure to the sun for flavour building photosynthesis and some bunch exposure to the sun, to help also with disease control and to add full ripe characters to the wines. Recently The Pizzini Brothers and Guy Darling have set up a winery and crushing facility, "King Valley Wines", which crushes and supplies juice to about 20 wineries who buy grapes from the region.

The Ovens Valley has long been respected as a grapegrowing area as witnessed by the long term success of Wynns Ovens Valley Shiraz. Several small wineries around the towns of Ovens and Bright are doing good things and further north in a separate valley near Beechworth Stephen Morris has his Pennyweight Winery and Rick Kinzbrunner makes very good wine at Giaconda Vineyard.

Brown Brothers

The first member of the Brown Family to plant grapes for winemaking at Milawa was John Francis Brown in 1885. In 1889 he produced his first vintage.

The original property is still in use. The Canadian style barn built in 1860 and used as the first winery, is today used to age fortified wines in wood.

The enterprise flourished. By 1900, a larger winery was needed to accommodate the increase in production. And then, in 1915, disaster struck. The phylloxera infection that swept through the district all but wiped out John Francis Brown, but he hung on and replanted on phylloxera resistant American rootstock. By 1920, the vineyard was again flourishing.

The area had always been renowned for its fortified wines. Yet, John Francis Brown decided the future of the Milawa vineyard lay in the production of table wines. His foresight and willingness to experiment with new grape varieties was inherited by his only son, John Charles Brown, who joined his father in 1934. John Brown Senior, as he is known today, was one of the first winemakers in the area to recognise the potential of the areas quite remarkable climatic diversity for the cultivation of more varieties of grapes than had previously been

thought possible.

From sun drenched river plains through the rich, rolling hills of the King Valley, to Whitlands, one of the highest and coolest vineyards in Australia, these areas produce climatic and soil conditions so diverse, that Brown Brothers now produce the largest selection of grape varieties grown in any Australian vineyards.

John Brown Senior and his wife Pat raised four sons. John Graham, Peter, Ross and Roger until his early tragic death in 1990, all have been a part of the family's enterprise and shared the dedication to the development of varietal winemaking.

Their questioning and testing of the boundaries of winemaking has resulted in the creation, alongside the main winery, of a mini winery call the Kindergarten. Within this state of the art environment, small batches of wines can be assessed under different wine making techniques.

John Brown Senior's eldest son John Graham joined him in 1958 and did a marvellous job as winemaker for many years. John Graham held the position of winemaker to the company until 1988 when his father handed over the company's management to him. Until earlier this year, he held the position of Chairman and Chief Executive Officer of Brown Brothers and led the company into the modern era of Australian wine as a powerful and progressive force. John Graham remembers his first vintage in 1958, five people were employed and 100 tonnes of grapes were crushed.

Today Brown Brothers crushes over 12,000 tonnes of premium wine grape varieties with the vineyards being as varied as the wines and wine styles. Within a 50-kilometre radius of Milawa, there is a range of climatic conditions: from cool alpine areas to lush temperate valleys to sun-drenched plains. It is because of these sites that Brown Brothers can produce its impressive range of

premium wines. Acquired in 1982, Whitlands Vineyard at 800 metres above sea level, is one of Australia's highest and coolest vineyards. It is here that Brown Brothers grows its grapes for the company's award winning sparkling wines. Other varieties that prosper here are Sauvignon Blanc, Riesling and Pinot Grigio. A short distance away is the Banksdale Vineyard, which at 480 metres is the home of such varieties as Chardonnay, Shiraz, Merlot and Cabernet Sauvignon as well as Barbera and Pinot Grigio · the more unusual Italian varieties in Australia.

In addition to producing premium wines, matching wine and food is also a passion for the Brown family. So much so, that in 1994 they opened their Epicurean Centre, a restaurant where they match the various dishes to their wines. Each dish on the menu is creatively paired with a glass of Brown Brothers wine to perfectly complement its flavours and textures.

1994 was also the year that the fourth John Brown joined the family enterprise to continue the traditions built up over 100 vintages.

In April 2001 John Graham relinquished the role of CEO but has retained the Chairman's position, albeit in a non-executive capacity. The relinquishment of the CEO role has seen his brother Ross assume the role of CEO thus ensuring the continuance of active family involvement in the day to day management of the company.

Address: MILAWA 3678	Wendy Cameron, Matt Fawcett	Non Vintage Pinot Noir & Chard. Drink now
Phone: (03) 5720 5500	**Est:** 1885	Sauvignon Blanc 2-3 yrs
Fax: (03) 5720 5511	**Cases:** 770,000	Moscato 2 yrs
Email: bbmv@brown-brothers.com.au	**Public Hours:** 9 am-5pm, daily (closed	Tarrango 2 yrs
WWW: www.brown-brothers.com.au	Christmas Day & Good Friday)	Dolcetto & Syrah 2 yrs
Winemakers: Terry Barnett,	**Principal Wines** **Potential**	Everton 2-4 yrs

Milawa Cheeses

David and Anne Brown are pioneers of the modern gourmet Australian cheese industry. Inspired by cheese they had experienced in France and Northern Italy they sought out the abandoned butter factory at Milawa. It's location close to the famous Brown Brothers Winery, the Snow Road and the tourist attractions of North East Victoria was perfect. Cow's milk was available from the Ovens and Kiewa Valleys and a new industry of milking sheep and goats was about to begin.

The first cheeses made were based on European models; Milawa Blue derived from Dolcelatte from Northern Italy and the pungent Milawa Gold from the washed rind cheeses of France.

Using these foundation stones David Brown has developed a range of uniquely Australian styles, ranging from delicate fresh curd cheeses of sheep and goat's milk to the authoritative blue styles Milawa Roc (sheep's milk) and Mt Buffalo Blue (goats milk). The washed rind range has grown to include the delicate King River Gold as well as washed rind goat and sheep cheeses.

The complete range is available for tasting at the factory shop and espresso coffee and ploughman's luncheons are available all day. The Brown's have also expanded their premises greatly over recent years and it now includes a greatly expanded restaurant, function areas and a newly installed bakery producing fresh country style breads and pastries of all sorts. It's a gourmet's paradise and not to be missed when you visit the other famous Browns of wine fame on the other side of the Snow Road through Milawa.

Boynton's of Bright

Boyntons family winery has gone through quite a metamorphosis in 2001. In early recent times Bruce and Jenni Chalmers, principals of Chalmers nurseries joined the Boyntons as equity partners. They bought with them two vineyards. The "Two Rivers" vineyard at Piangil near Swan Hill and the "Pine Hills" vineyard near Euston on the NSW side of the Murray. The impressive assortment of Italian and French varieties will go into a new second label "Paiko" named after a creek that runs through the Euston property, which may have once been the original course of the Murimbidgee River. The wines will be largely aimed at the export market.

The winery has also gone through great changes, during the 2001 vintage 240 tonnes, by far the largest crush ever, took place amongst the builders frantically finishing a new

stone winery. Kel Boynton a stone mason, in his former life, has just completed a beautiful new stone cellar door and café from sandstone sourced from his "Hill" vineyard.

Winemaker Eleana Anderson recently graduated as Dux of the Charles Sturt University oenology degree course, she makes a large range of wines which includes Pinot Gris, Sauvignon Blanc, Chardonnay, Riesling and an excellent botrytised wine "Gold". The reds include "Pinots" a blend of Pinot Noir and Pinot Meunier, Shiraz, Merlot and "Alluvium" a Reserve Bordeaux blend. She also makes Boyntons Black a 10 year old sparkling red and a tawny port. The Boyntons wines have a cult following, for good reason, why not drop in and enjoy a meal in their café and taste their wines, you will receive a warm welcome.

Address: Great Alpine Road BRIGHT 3741	Public Hours: 10am-5pm, daily except Christmas Day	Cabernet Sauvignon	7-10 yrs
Phone: (03) 5756 2356 Fax: (03) 5756 2610	Principal Varieties: Shiraz, Cab Sav, Merlot,	Merlot	7-10 yrs
Owner: Kel and Carolien Boynton	Chardonnay, Semillon, Sauvignon Blanc	Chardonnay	1-3 yrs
Winemaker: Kel Boynton	Principal Wines Potential	Semillon	2-7 yrs
Est: 1987 Vine Ha: 16	Shiraz 7-10 yrs	Sauvignon Blanc	1-2 yrs

Chrismont

Arnie Pizzini is the son of migrants from Northern Italy who grew up amongst the tobacco fields in the King Valley. In the early 1980's Arnie sought a diversion to delay taking up a horticultural science course.

An invitation from Brown Brothers to supply grapes saw Arnie say goodbye to tobacco and in 1980 he planted his first vines, 7 acres of Riesling. In 1981 extra varieties were planted and in 1984 the first Italian planting in the King Valley, Barbera.

The current sizeable vineyard is 200 acres including Riesling, Chardonnay, Sauvignon Blanc, Merlot, Cabernet Sauvignon, Shiraz and Italian varieties Barbera, Marzemino, Pinot Grigio, Sangiovese and Arneis.

Originally all fruit produced was sold to Brown Brothers. Today the company supplies fruit to large

wineries including Brown Brothers and retains 150 tonnes for the production of Chrismont and La Zona labels.

Arnie and his wife Jo commenced producing wines under the Chrismont label in 1996 with Riesling, Chardonnay and Barbera approximately 1,000 cases in all. In 1997 both Shiraz and Cabernet/Merlot were added, followed by Pinot Grigio and Marzemino. A further two new Italian labels will extend the La Zona range. The King Valley has proven most suited to many wine grape

varieties. Detailed studies comparing the climates of Australian and Italian wine regions provides evidence that the King Valley has the edge. Temperatures and rainfall are similar to those in the famous regions of Piedmont and Tuscany.

The Pizzini's have two labels, Chrismont for classic French varieties and German Riesling and La Zona for the Italian varieties. The La Zona brand label translates to "The Area".

The Melbourne restaurant trade has welcomed these Italian varieties with open arms. The Italian varieties are a little different in flavour and colour and gives the consumer something different to try.

Chrismont have just opened a new cellar door at their Cheshunt property, it presents a great chance to try their innovative wines.

Address: Upper King Valley Rd CHESHUNT 3678	Winemaker: Warren Proft & Arnie Pizzini	La Zona Pinot Grigio	3 yrs
Phone: (03) 5729 8220 Fax: (03) 5729 8253	Est: 1980	La Zona Barbera	3+ yrs
Email: cmtwines@cnl.com.au	Public Hours: 11am-5pm, daily	Chrismont Riesling	3+ yrs
WWW: www.chrismontwines.com.au	Principal Varieties: Pinot Grigio, Sangiovese, Shiraz,	Chrismont Shiraz	5+ yrs
Owner: Arnie & Jo Pizzini	Ries, Sauv Blanc, Barbera, Cab Sav, Chard, Merlot	La Zona Marzemino	5+ yrs
Vine Ha: 80 Cases: 10,000	Principal Wines Potential	Chrismont Cabernet/Merlot	7+ yrs

Michelini Wines

In the middle of the pretty town of Myrtleford, in Victoria's Alpine foothills, is the new exciting Michelini wines with its splendid winery and hospitality complex on the main Ovens Valley Highway.

The Michelini story began when Emo and Olga Michelini arrived in Australia from Roverto in Italy in 1949. After living in Sydney and making smallgoods for a local butcher in Redfern, they moved to the Ovens Valley where Emo successfully grew tobacco.

Emo longed to make his own wines, as his family had done for over a century in the Trentino Alps in Northern Italy. Emo and his two sons, Ilario and Dino chose a site for their vineyards in the Buckland Valley cradled between the snow capped peak of Mt Buffalo and the pristine waters of Devils Creek. In 1982 they planted cuttings of various grape varieties, they had sourced from Orlando in South Australia. The

grapes from their vineyard in the cool elevated slopes, forming the main part of the base wine for Orlando's celebrated Trilogy Sparkling. The main varieties planted being Chardonnay and Pinot Noir, however they also planted Riesling, Shiraz, Cabernet Sauvignon and Merlot and the very traditional Northern Italian variety Marzemino renowned for its wines of steely, flinty structure with intense plummy fruit and a cedarwood like finish.

The cool summer nights and long growing season of Michelini's Alpine vineyards builds wines of crisp intense flavours. Recently experienced Tasmanian Pioneer winemaker Greg O'Keefe has become winemaker, I'm sure he will find the Michelini fruit superb to work with.

After deciding they would make their own wine, the Michelini's laid the foundations for their winery in October 1996, five months later they were crushing their first grapes.

The winery is well located for visitors on the main road in the middle of Myrtleford, the Cellar door is spacious and has been beautifully appointed.

In 1997 two whites and four reds were released including a very interesting wine "Marzemo" a blend of equal quantities of Marzemino and Merlot.

On my visit I tasted the 1998 Marzemino, I found it a lively vibrant red, spicy but not too heavy. The 1998 Michelini Cabernet Sauvignon really impressed me, its floral rose like bouquet and deep cassis like fruit led to a silky supple feel in the mouth, with a long sweet finish, easily a gold medal standard to my palate.

Michelini are a serious wine producer and well set to make a big impression on the premium wine market.

Address: Great Alpine Road MYRTLEFORD	**Winemaker:** Greg O'Keefe	Unwooded Chardonnay	1-2 yrs
Phone: (03) 5751 1990 **Fax:** (03) 5751 1410	**Est:** 1996 **Vine Ha:** 36 **Cases:** 4,000	Pinot Noir	2 yrs
Email: micheliniwines@bigpond.com	**Public Hours:** 10am-5pm, daily	Chardonnay	2-4 yrs
WWW: www.micheliniwines.com.au	**Principal Wines** **Potential**	Marzemino	2-5 yrs
Owner: Michelini Family	Riesling 2-6 yrs	Shiraz	2-3 yrs

Miranda

In 1997 Miranda Wines expanded their operations with the purchase of a 140 acre property located on the corner of the Whitfield and Snow Roads at Oxley, Victoria. Only a few hours from Melbourne, its quickly becoming a favourite of many lovers of fine wine and food.

The Miranda King Valley Winery, celebrated its first vintage in 1998 and in 2001 had the first vintage from its own vineyard, producing Merlot, Cabernet Sauvignon, Shiraz, Petit Verdot and Chardonnay.

The Cellar Door is set amidst a rustic décor of old timber, hessian, bales of pea straw, wine barrels, a corral, pictures of local high country huts and an old campfire setting, complete with camp oven and billy. A little piece of shearing shed atmosphere was created with the use of an old wooden wool sorting table, complete with some very old fleeces.

Reflecting the high country hut

atmosphere, this is complemented by a display of authentic items of interest, which include a 100 year old wagon, spring cart, horse collars, cross cut saws, and lanterns.

The King Valley Winery, home to Miranda's High Country range, is a great new place to visit on your pilgrimage to the Milawa Gourmet Region, Bright and the Snowfields.

Address: Corner Whitfield & Snow Roads OXLEY 3678	WWW: www.mirandawines.com.au	Principal Varieties: Cabernet Sauvignon, Merlot, Chardonnay, Shiraz
Phone: (02) 6960 3000 Fax: (02) 6962 6944	Owner: Sam, Jim & Lou Miranda	
	Winemaker: Jeff Martin	Principal Wines Potential
Email: info@mirandawines.com.au	Est: 1997 Vine Ha: 62 Cases: 1,500,000	Miranda High Country Up to 5 yrs

Gapsted Wines

The settlement of Gapsted, in northeast Victoria, began with gold mining, when reefs were discovered around Myrtleford in the 1850's. Today the population is less than 50, with the exciting new winery being the biggest feature.

Gapsted Winery was formed in 1997 after award-winning, former Californian winemaker Shayne Cunningham followed his dream, to establish a winery of his own and fell in love with the Alpine and King Valley. The winery was established

with the help of some experienced regional viticulturists and a close winemaker friend, a unique combination of winemakers, grapegrowers and marketers. Located on the main road to the major ski fields of Mount Hotham and Falls Creek, the winery enjoys picturesque views of Mount Hotham, Mount Buffalo and the Ovens Valley.

In 1997 storage and fermentation tanks were constructed onsite and a small crushing facility. In 1998 vintage 1200 tonnes of fruit were processed. Today Gapsted Winery crushes close to 6000 tonnes of grapes sourced from the King, Buckland, Ovens and Buffalo Valleys, as well as fruit from Tumbarumba, Strathbogie Ranges and Beechworth.

Michael Cope-Williams is Shayne's assistant he is responsible for Ballerina Canopy range of wines and brings a wealth of experience,

vintages in the Napa and Oregon in the USA, Champagne and Burgundy in France as well as the Hunter Valley, Clare Valley, Macedon and the Pyrenees.

Gapsted have been very successful in wine shows, already winning 5 trophies and 25 gold medals.

The cellar door opened in late 2001. The grounds and lake area are available for picnics and barbecues. A Cellar Club has been launched providing special offers and services to members.

Address: Great Alpine Road GAPSTED 3737	WWW: www.gapstedwines.com	Public Hours: 10am-4:30pm, daily
Phone: (03) 5751 1992	Winemaker: Shayne Cunningham & Michael Cope-Williams	Principal Varieties: Cabernet Franc, Chardonnay, Merlot, Shiraz, Cabernet Sauvignon, Durif, Sauvignon Blanc
Fax: (03) 5751 1368		
Email: gapstedwines@netc.net.au	Est: 1999	

Mildura / Swan Hill

Most of the wine grapes processed in Victoria are grown in the north-western corner of the state, along the Murray River. The region stretches from Mildura to the east, along the state border to Echuca. Irrigation is necessary as rainfall is very low.

The area was originally developed by the men who initiated the local channel irrigation, the Chaffey brothers. George Chaffey purchased Mildura Station after his arrival from California in 1886. The name 'Mildura' is appropriate to the rich burnt-coloured landscape along the Murray, being aboriginal for 'red rock'. However, even though the soil was fertile, lack of water made the area barren.

The South Australian Government, realising the potential of their Murray River region, and the Chaffey Brothers' irrigation successes in California, hired George and his newly arrived brother William to open up the Renmark area. The ensuing

success of this project, saw the Victorian Government hire the pair for a repeat operation in the dry north-western corner of the state. The region quickly became a major fruit-growing area. Although many grape-growers sold their fruit to wine companies, the greater proportion of grapes were used in dried fruit production.

Wine companies were naturally drawn to the Murray Valley. The huge scale of production underway, particularly after the Soldier Settlement Scheme, produced a glut of grapes on the market for attractive development potential. The Murray Valley, concentrating mainly on the production of spirits, prospered during the fortified wine boom.

While much fortified wine is still manufactured in the area, the Mildura Region now provides some 25 percent of Australia's wine, involving production in three states · Victoria and several enormous

wineries just across the river in New South Wales at Buronga and grapes which are trucked into South Australia.

Viticultural techniques such as minimal pruning, which sees huge bushy vines producing many small bunches with small tasty berries, has seen wine quality soar. The percentage of excellent bottled premium table wines from the region has grown enormously. Trentham Estate, Milburn Park, the giant new Zilzie Winery, Lindeman's Matthew Lang and the Deakin Estate typify this revolution. Further down river, Best's at Lake Boga, Bullers at Beverford and Tisdall at Echuca make excellent premium wines.

Australia's competitive position on the world wine market is benefiting greatly from this innovative region. A trip along the river by riverboat to the lovely Trentham Winery Restaurant is a must when you visit.

Mildura / Swan Hill

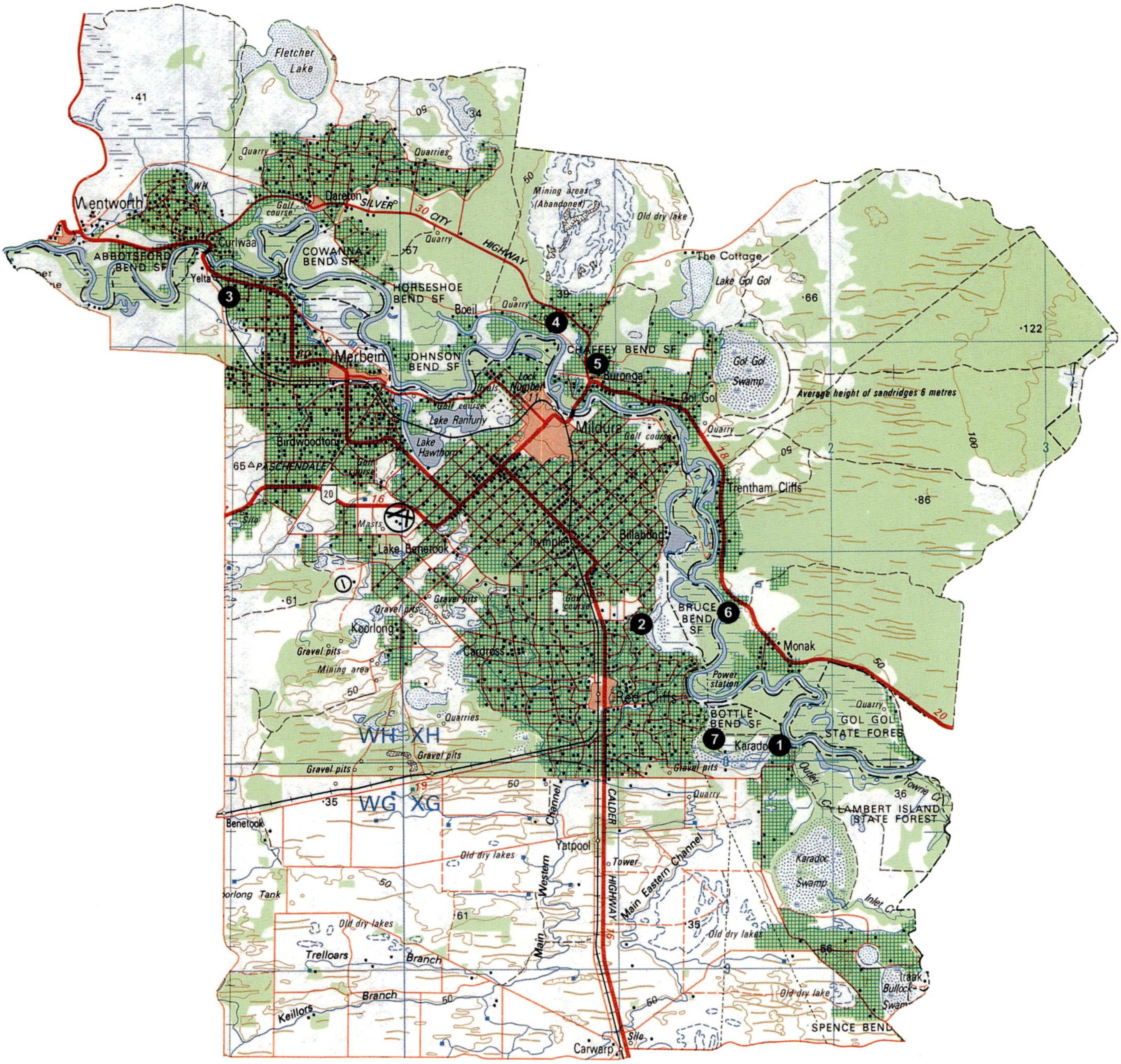

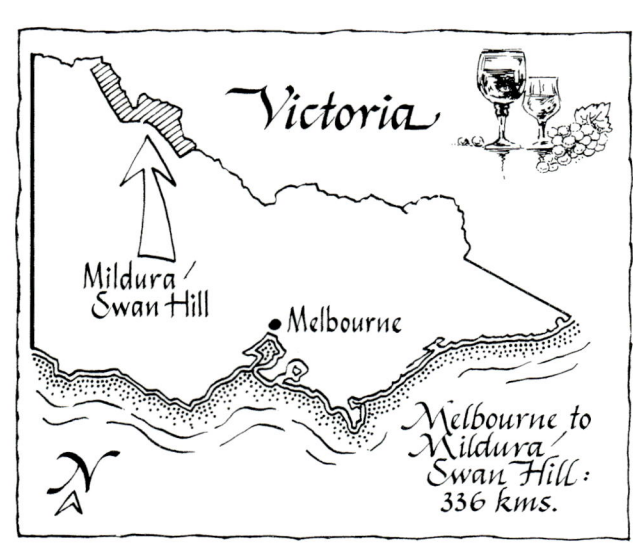

Mildura / Swan Hill - VIC

1. Lindeman's Karadoc Winery
2. Milburn Park
3. Mildara Merbein
4. Simeon Wines
5. Stanley Wines/Buronga
6. Trentham Estate
7. Zilzie Wines

Milburn Park

Rising rapidly through Australian wine industry ranks, the dynamic Cranswick Estate company now stands among the nation's top ten wine producers. It's recently acquired Milburn Park Winery was established 25 years ago by agricultural scientist, Peter McLaren.

Milburn Park now boasts extensive vineyards. From origins as a small concern processing grapes to add to its rural value, Milburn Park today produces premium wines at its Irymple winery for national and export markets. Company controlled vineyards mean that quality of

production is supervised by its winemaking team from vineyard to bottle.

Chief winemaker and manager is Krister Jonnson who worked previously with Capel Vale in W.A, he praises the viticultural techniques that have created strong, disease and drought-resistant vines, that produce grapes in small berried bunches yielding concentrated flavours. Technological developments have continued each year since the company's inception, assisting in producing critically acclaimed wines. Milburn Park also has large vineyard holdings in the exciting new vineyard area of Wrattonbully in the south east of South Australia.

In value-for-money wine and quality terms, all the Milburn Park wines including the Milburn Park, Salisbury and Wild Ant Brands are outstanding.

Address: Campbell Avenue IRYMPLE	**Winemaker:** Krister Jonsson & Gary Magilton	Milburn Park Chardonnay	4-5 yrs
Phone: (03) 5024 6800	**Est:** 1980 **Vine Ha:** 200	Milburn Park Cabernet Merlot	4-5 yrs
Fax: (03) 5024 6605	**Cases:** 400,000	Milburn Park Shiraz	4-5 yrs
Email: mpark@cranswick.com.au	**Public Hours:** 10am-4:30pm, Mon-Sat	Salisbury Chardonnay	3-4 yrs
WWW: www.milburnpark.com.au	**Principal Wines** **Potential**	Salisbury Sauvignon Blanc	3-4 yrs

Mildara Merbein

The wine dynasty, that has now become one of the worlds largest and most powerful premium wine groups, Beringer Blass, with its Historic American wineries and a string of Australia's leading wine producers, had its humble beginnings on the banks of the Murray River at Merbein just west of Mildura.

During the 1880's the renowned American duo, the Chaffey Brothers, revolutionized the Murray Region with their irrigation schemes. In 1888 they established a winery, Chateau Mildura at Irymple it failed financially as did the Mildura Wine Company at Merbein, begun by Willman Chaffey in 1911.

In 1924 William established Mildara Wines at Merbein, using the plant and equipment of the previous Mildura Wine Company, it prospered, mainly making fortified wines and selling them in the U.K.

In 1935 Ron Haselgrove was appointed Technical Director it began a long association of his family with

Mildara. He revolutionized their sherries with some great Flor yeast techniques and the Mildara "George" Fino "Supreme" dry and "Chestnut teal" medium, remain market leaders today, as does the Mildara Brandy produced in Merbein, in Victoria's few active distilleries. In the early 1950's Ron was one of the modern

day pioneers of Coonawarra, leading Mildara into this premium table wine region.

A visit to Mildara Merbein gives one a great insight into fortified wines and brandy, as well as a chance to taste and buy from the prestigeous Beringer Blass stable of wines.

Trentham Estate

One of the best located and prettiest wineries in Australia sits on the elevated banks on a perfect bend of the Murray River. Trentham Estate winery has a large glassed-in café-style restaurant affording panoramic views of the river in both directions over the sweeping lawns.

In front of the winery is a landing where each Thursday the historic paddle steamer Rothbury, built in 1881, pulls in after leaving Mildura at 10.30am. After a leisurely lunch at the winery, you disembark at Mildura at 3.30 pm.

The trip includes a guided tour of the winery by winemaker Anthony Murphy whose family owns the property. They first planted vines back in 1909 at Merbein. After graduating with a Bachelors degree in Oenology from Roseworthy, Anthony worked at Mildara for some 11 years, while he makes the wine his brother Pat manages the 117 acres of premium grape varieties, with 17 varieties including Viognier and Petit Verdot. Trentham are forward thinking and their wines win many awards, they are of a truly

international class. Aside from table wines, they produce both sparkling and fortified wines. I was particularly impressed by the chardonnay, the Shiraz and the vintage port.

The Restaurant area at Trentham has been upgraded over recent years, the food is extremely innovative, modern Australian in style with Mediterranean and Asian influences. The menu features the fresh horticultural produce of the region and game dishes such as "Pan seared Kangaroo Sirloin" served

around roasted beetroot risotto with redcurrant and rosemary glaze, its mouth watering stuff and the décor and view are superb.

You can also cook your own barbecue outdoors on the terrace and lawns, which have shelter from the sun and full facilities, you can purchase anything you need for your picnic from the restaurant.

The Murphy's have put together a wine and food mecca well ahead of its time.

Address: Sturt Highway TRENTHAM CLIFFS 2738	Public Hours: 8.30am-5pm weekdays,		Riesling	4 yrs
Phone: (03) 5024 8888	9.30am-5pm, weekends		Chardonnay	5 yrs
Fax: (03) 5024 8800	Principal Varieties: Cabernet Sauvignon,		Sauvignon Blanc	2 yrs
Owner: Nola, Anthony & Patrick Murphy	Chardonnay, Merlot, Pinot Noir, Ruby		Merlot	5 yrs
Winemaker: Anthony Murphy	Cabernet, Sauvignon Blanc, Shiraz		Cabernet Sauvignon Merlot	5 yrs
Est: 1988 Vine Ha: 40 Cases: 40,000	Principal Wines	Potential	Shiraz	6 yrs

Zilzie Wines

Zilzie Wines is wholly owned by the Forbes family of Karadoc, in North West Victoria. The family, fourth generation farmers have resided on the Karadoc property, Zilzie Estate, since 1911. Ian and Ros Forbes currently run Zilzie Estate with their two sons Steven and Andrew. Ian's father Gordon, although retired is still actively involved in the family business. The Estate has seen a diversity of farming activities through the generations, from general stock, cereal growing, vegetable production and now grape growing. The family are from hardy Scottish stock, who settled in the Karadoc area before irrigation was common and have progressed the property to where now, through perseverance, hard work and innovation, it constitutes one of the most successful family grape growing businesses in the Mildura region.

The origin of the name "Zilzie" can be traced back through the Forbes' Scottish heritage, it was the name given to the property in 1911 and translates to "First Home".

The first vines were planted in 1971, the property currently has over 1000 acres under vine producing high quality premium varieties. The Forbes family are the largest suppliers of premium fruit in the district to Southcorp Wines. The vineyards are state of the art, with computer controlled drip irrigation, integrated pest and disease management practices and a management

commitment to quality grape production. The soils are sandy loam over limestone, the topography is undulating with sweeping views of vineyards and scrubland. There is a significant remnant of Buloke, an uncommon native tree on the property, which is the northernmost stand of Buloke in Victoria. To ensure that this area will be protected in perpetuity, the Forbes family have made a voluntary contribution of the area, the "Buloke Reserve" which is now administered by community groups and DNRE. The first wines bottled for release in Australia- the Buloke Reserve range, feature this achievement.

Zilzie appointed talented winemaker Bob Shields, formerly at Alambie Wines to oversee the construction of their State of the Art Winery, which was commissioned for the 2000 vintage it is one of the largest and most modern in Australia. In 2001 over 16,000 tonnes of grapes were processed.

Zilzie basically have three distinct ranges of wines. They start with the "Buloke Reserve" range which offer true varietal characters wines, that are great value for money and ready to drink now. They have already picked up a number of medals in wine shows in 2000. This range includes a Chardonnay with a hint of oak, full of fresh melon and peach flavours, a Merlot with black cherry flavours and a silky soft palate, an honest direct Cabernet Sauvignon

with blackberry flavours and some vanilla and chocolate overtones, there is also a Shiraz rich in black fruit flavours with some pepper and spice.

The second range "Forbes Family Wines" are targeted at export markets.

The ultimate range is under the Zilzie Estate Banner. These vintage varietal wines are produced from the best fruit sourced from the Zilzie vineyards and selected growers, new imported oak is used to maximise complexity and give the wines extra aging potential the range includes a Chardonnay which although powerful through barrel fermentation has loads of stonefruit and melon fruit characters with elegance and complexity. The Merlot has deep colour and concentration with silky oak, underlying the plum and cherry flavours. The Shiraz is deep purple in colour with red berry and cassis flavours. The final Zilzie Estate wine, is a regal Cabernet Sauvignon from a selection of North West Victorian vineyards, maximising the influences of various "terroir" fine tannins compliment the rich blackberry and cassis flavours, with sweet vanilla overtones from the new oak maturation.

Zilzie is a well thought out and executed venture, producing excellent wines, which are great value by anyone's standards.

Rutherglen

Like other Victorian wine-producing areas, Rutherglen's fortunes have fluctuated over the years. Rutherglen has seen so many natural and economic changes throughout its history, that one must admire both the courage of the families who continued to persevere with the industry and the strength and quality of the wines that has enabled them to carry through.

The Rutherglen region was first settled by Lindsay Brown, who purchased the large Gooramadda property in 1839. Several of his farm-workers were from Germany and had brought vine cuttings with them, which were fully planted. Under pressure from these workers, Brown was encouraged to plant his own vines, which were also highly successful.

The discovery of gold in Rutherglen in 1860 was an event, which greatly increased the local population. Within 10 years, however, the ore had become scarce and people turned to

vines to make their fortune. By 1870 a number of large winemaking enterprises were in operation throughout the district. Some of these properties were built on a grand scale and included such magnificent homesteads as Camille Reau's, 'Tuilleries' and Alexander Caughey's 'Mt Prior'. Many family companies were established at this time, some of which are still in existence. Development of the wine industry continued to expand towards the turn of the century, with the further construction of imposing mansions and wineries. A grand castle was erected by the Sutherland Smith family, they called All Saints, and the Morris family also built a

magnificent mansion at Fairfield, with enormous cellars capable of storing three million litres of wine. The burgeoning popularity of fortified wines was crucial to these developments, particularly as Rutherglen had ideal conditions for the production of Australia's best fortified wines.

Unfortunately the threat of phylloxera became a reality in 1899, when it was identified in the area, temporarily halting the growth of Rutherglen's wine industry. Many vineyards were destroyed but others were replanted with vines on resistant rootstocks. This was encouraged by the government who subsidised the price of the new vines. Some vignerons were unable to meet the costs of replanting, however, and by the outbreak of the First World War, these companies had faded from existence. Export of fortified wines to the United Kingdom sustained many companies throughout this time until the market

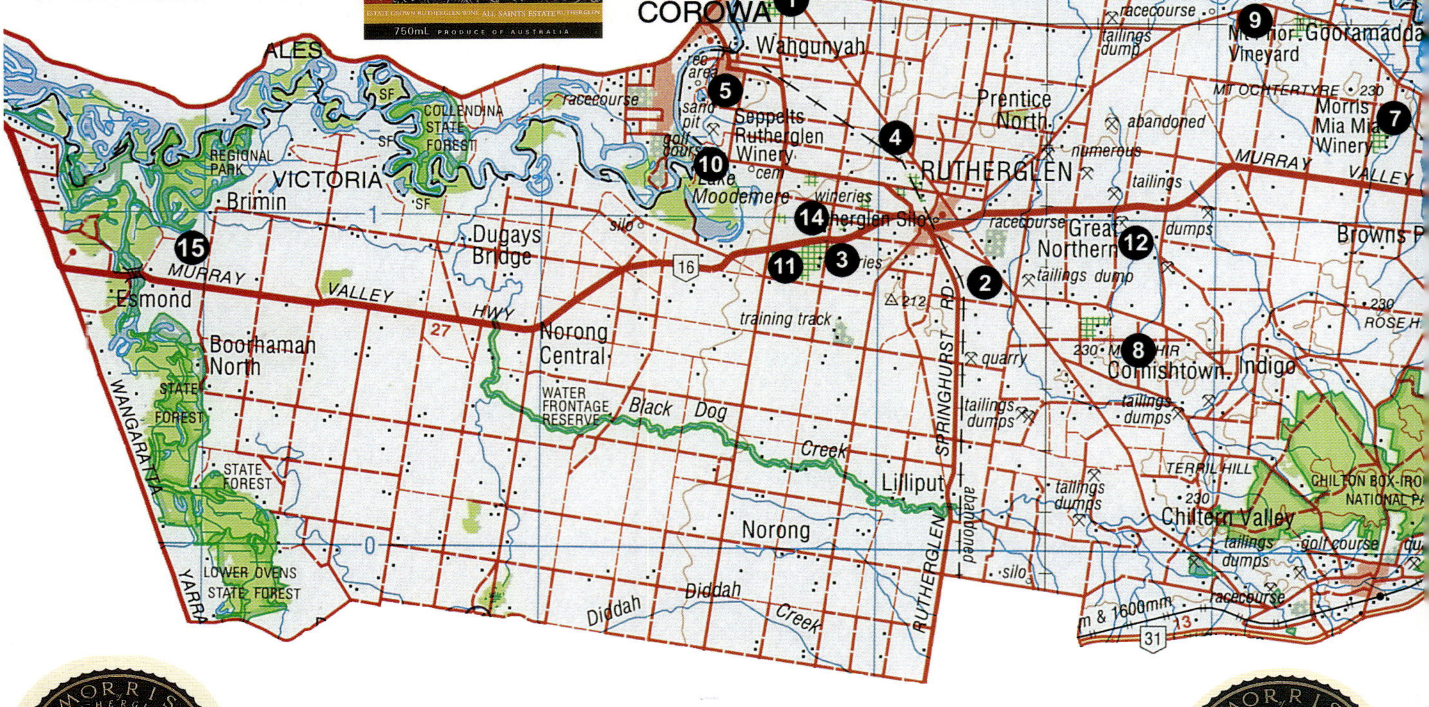

Rutherglen

collapsed during the Depression. Wine prices slumped and the government was forced to ration beer supplies to assist the ailing wine industry. Fortified wines again became locally popular and Rutherglen experienced a period of relative growth and prosperity. Public tastes were also veering toward table wines and several companies, including Campbell's, Bullers, All Saints and the Morris family developed new ranges of wines. For the most part red wines were produced but recent years have seen the production of high quality white wines in the area. Both semillon and chardonnay grapes are proving to be very successful and Mount Prior, St Leonards and Campbell's have excellent examples showing the potential of these varieties.

The liqueur muscats, tokays and frontignacs of the Rutherglen area are, without doubt, the best in Australia and are quite probably the best in the world. These wines are truly unique to Australia and are

saluted by critics the world over.

Following the success of Rutherglen's table wines and a resurgence of interest in its fortified's, many local winemakers have renovated, new wineries have been built and old ones re-opened. The restoration of the beautiful old All Saints 'Castle' Winery by Peter Brown of the Brown's of Milawa family, the gardens and the restaurant function area are really world-class.

Chris Pfeiffer, formerly with Lindemans has done an excellent job restoring and setting up with his wife Robyn, an excellent winery in the old Seppelts distillery at Wahgunyah. Campbell's Winery, which has a fine reputation for the wines of four generations, is beautifully presented and provides visitors with the opportunity of walking through their 128-year-old cellars.

The Sutherland Smith family continue to be a force in the region. Andrew Sutherland Smith fifth generation member of the family

that founded All Saints is making great wines at his Warrabilla Winery west of Rutherglen. A new large processing facility for the growing vineyards of Northern Victoria Rutherglen Estates was opened in time for the 2000 vintage, they will shortly launch their own brand.

Rutherglen was the first region in Victoria to run a wine festival. These became legendary events during the 1970's. The region now has a number of successful wine events. In March, the Labour Day weekend hosts the Tastes of Rutherglen when the finest restaurants in the region bring their gourmet treasures to the wineries.

The Gourmet Getaway follows on the next week (which is a long weekend in Canberra). The Queen's Birthday weekend in June sees the famous Winery Walkabout, food and entertainment featuring at all the wineries. Winner of many tourism awards, something for all the family, Rutherglen is back with a vengeance.

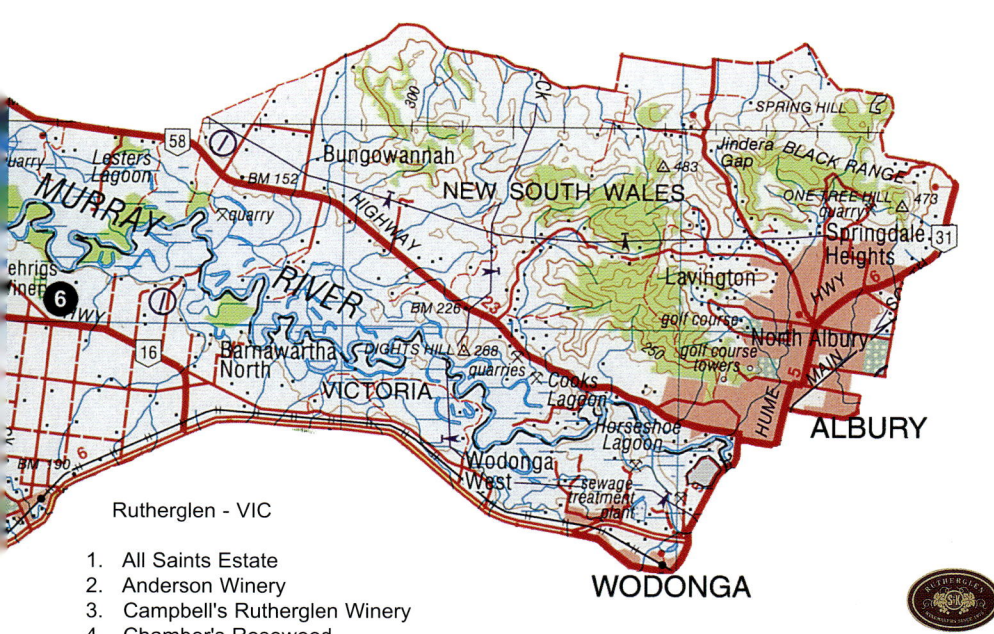

Rutherglen - VIC

1. All Saints Estate
2. Anderson Winery
3. Campbell's Rutherglen Winery
4. Chamber's Rosewood
5. Cofield Wines
6. Gehrig's Winery
7. Morris Wines
8. Mount Ophir
9. Mount Prior
10. Pfeiffer Wines
11. R.I. Buller (Calliope Vineyard)
12. Rutherglen Estates
13. St Leonards
14. Stanton & Killeen
15. Warrabilla Wines

All Saints

All Saints Estate must vie for the title of one of Australia's most imposing and impressive wineries. It has been restored and enhanced to a breathtaking degree by proprietor Peter Brown of the Brown Family of Milawa. He has created a hospitality centre, beautifully and sensitively blended it into this classic, Scottish castle inspired winery.

The history of All Saints Estate goes back to 1864 when George Sutherland Smith and his brother-in-law John Banks purchased a 1,300 acre property at Wahgunyah on the banks of the Murray River. Both Sutherland Smith and Banks had been tradesmen at the Castle of Mey in Caithness in northern Scotland and the winery was built to resemble this building. The winery's name is after the Castle of Mey's location in the parish of All Saints.

All Saints Estate is one of the premier producers of old fortified dessert wines. Its Museum releases contain predominantly 70 year old wines aged in old oak casks that line the winery's huge barrel hall. The table wines are also amongst the region's best, with recent awards including "Best Boutique Shiraz" at the Boutique Wines of Australia competition, and "Best Young

Rutherglen Red" trophy at the Rutherglen Wine Show.

In a separate cellar building which overlooks the splendid formal gardens, there is a special North East Victoria Winemakers hall of fame which certainly has more living history and past glory than any other Australian wine region. The indoor/outdoor Terrace Restaurant has an innovative menu featuring local produce and the Great Hall is a wonderful venue for special functions.

All Saints Estate has what is probably Australia's best-conceived winery club which has been running since the mid 1980's. All Saints Estate and St Leonards (their sister winery in the region) wines are featured. Four times a year members receive a 4 bottle home tasting pack, from a choice of 4 options. They are usually priced at less than $80 per pack, and there are no membership fees.

Club members have their own Pioneer Wine Club privilege card, providing a range of benefits including access to limited release wines, member functions and savings on all wine purchases. Special prices are offered at the Terrace Restaurant and The Lazy Grape Café at St Leonards, which has jazz every first and third Sunday of the month.

All Saints Estate also has a cooper making barrels at "The Keg Factory" on site and a blacksmith making wrought iron creations at his "Forge and Anvil" workshop.

The winning trifecta of quality wines, outstanding food at the Terrace Restaurant and one of Australia's most picturesque wineries makes All Saints Estate a "must visit" destination.

Address: All Saints Road WAHGUNYAH 3687	Public Hours: 9am-5.30pm, Mon-Sat; Sun from 10am, closed Christmas Day	Carlyle Durif	10 yrs
Phone: (02) 6033 1922 Fax: (02) 6033 3515		Carlyle Ruby Cabernet	10 yrs
Email: wine@allsaintswine.com.au	Principal Varieties: Cabernet Sauvignon, Chardonnay, Durif, Marsanne, Merlot, Muscat, Riesling, Ruby Cabernet, Shiraz, Tokay	Carlyle Chardonnay	6-8 yrs
WWW: www.allsaintswine.com.au		Carlyle Shiraz	10 yrs
Owner: Peter Brown		Cabernet Sauvignon	5-7 yrs
Est: 1864 Vine Ha: 58 Cases: 35,000	Principal Wines Potential	Shiraz	5-7 yrs

Anderson Winery

Howard Anderson literally does nearly everything with his own hands, in his true boutique winery on the Chiltern Road. His daughter Christobelle is studying Oenology at Adelaide University and helps him, particularly with the disgorging, when she is home on holidays. Howard has had a long career in wine, over 35 years, including 14 years of premium and Methode Champenoise winemaking at Seppelts Great Western Cellars. His aim when he started his own winery in March 1993, was to maintain the best of the traditional Rutherglen styles but with more finesse and complexity. Howard specialises in Methode Champenoise, which he makes totally in his small winery, using authentic equipment, imported from France.

Howard uses some fruit from the King Valley, for instance the Pinot Noir portion of his Methode

Champenoise Pinot Noir Chardonnay, which certainly has some elegance. He also makes a Chenin Blanc Champenoise, very crisp and fruity, great with Thai food. The third sparkling is Doux Blanc, soft and with just a hint of sweetness, a good dessert Champenoise. The last Sparkler is the Shiraz, which is big rich and ripe, soft and full of fruit, ideal with roast lamb, kangaroo, venison, or burgundy beef.

Anderson also has a range of premium still wines. Chenin Blanc,

oaked and unoaked Chardonnays, and Doux Blanc in the whites. Pinot Noir, Merlot, Soft Cabernet (ideal with pasta), Shiraz, a big rich Cabernet Sauvignon, and (starting from the 2001 Vintage) Durif in the reds. Howard also makes a great Botrytis Tokay in half bottles.

Anderson Winery has an active Cellar Club and it's a great way to secure their unique wines (not available in bottle shops), if you can't visit Rutherglen.

Address: Chiltern Road RUTHERGLEN 3685	**Winemaker:** Howard Anderson	Merlot	3-5 yrs
Phone: (02) 6032 8111 **Fax:** (02) 6032 7151	**Est:** 1993 **Vine Ha:** 6 **Cases:** 1,500	Soft Cabernet	2-4 yrs
Email: andersonwinery@telstra.easymail.com.au	**Public Hours:** 10am-5pm, daily	Methode Champenoise Pinot Noir Chardonnay	3-12 mths
WWW: www.andersonwinery.bigstep.com	**Principal Wines** **Potential**	Methode Champenoise Shiraz	3-12 mths
Owner: Howard & Margaret Anderson	Methode Champenoise Chenin Blanc 3-12 mths	Cabernet Merlot	2-4 yrs

Bullers Calliope

Lieutenant Commander Reginald Langdon Buller purchased his vineyard, 5 kms west of Rutherglen, in 1921 after returning from active service in the 1914-18 war. He named the vineyard 'Calliope' after the sturdy British warship in A.B. (Banjo) Patterson's stirring 'Ballad of the Calliope'.

In 1951 Reginald Buller left 'Calliope' in the hands of his son Richard (Dick), and moved to Beverford, north of Swan Hill, to establish a second vineyard and winery. Reginald Buller retired in 1966 and lived out his days in Melbourne. Dick Buller, who had developed a reputation as a talented winemaker, also had a distinguished career as a wine show judge and in 1996 was honoured by his peers with the title of a 'Rutherglen Legend'. He died in 1997.

Today R.L. Buller & Son is in the

hands of Dick's sons, Richard (Rick) and Andrew. Rick heads up the family company and oversees Beverford while Andrew is winemaker/manager at Rutherglen.

Rutherglen, from its non-irrigated vineyard, produces a range of full-bodied reds of which the flagship wine is the Calliope Shiraz. It is also

here that the famous Buller fortified wines are made - Muscats, Tokays and Ports. The Muscats and Tokays in particular have won medals and trophies in Australia and overseas. Andrew Buller also has a vineyard in the cool Indigo Valley and produces an excellent Bordeaux style blend from merlot, cabernet sauvignon and cabernet franc grown there.

Bullers have always released innovative wines and have put out some vibrant rhone style wines recently using Grenache with Cinsaut and Mataro (Mourvedre) and Shiraz.

The Beverford range includes a first class wood aged Semillon, a Shiraz, which is consistently good, and several varietals offering excellent value for money. An added attraction at Bullers of Rutherglen is Val Buller's Bird Park, which is open to the public, and was a finalist in the 1997 Victorian Tourism Awards.

Address: Three Chain Road RUTHERGLEN 3685	**Winemaker:** Andrew Buller	**Principal Varieties:** Cabernet Sauvignon,
Phone: (02) 6032 9660 **Fax:** (02) 6032 8005	**Est:** 1921	Durif, Marsanne, Muscat, Cabernet Franc,
Email: bullers@albury.net.au	**Public Hours:** 9am-5pm, Mon-Sat; 10am-	Chardonnay, Grenache, Merlot, Pinot Noir,
WWW: www.rlbullerandson.com.au	5pm, Sun	Sauvignon Blanc, Shiraz, Viognier

Campbells

In 2000, the Campbell clan celebrated their 130th vintage, a significant achievement as the winery, one of the oldest in Australia, has been owned by the Campbell family from the planting of its first vine.

Scotsman John Campbell arrived in Australia in 1858 and immediately set out for the Beechworth goldfields, a short time later he married and moved to the 'Bobbie Burns' diggings at Rutherglen. Campbell stayed on in Rutherglen and established a farm. He chose a 75-acre parcel of land adjacent to the gold diggings which he aptly called 'Bobbie Burns', the following year, he was granted a further 120 acres by the government.

Campbell planted 2 acres of vines, by 1885, this had increased to 38 acres. A winery was built in 1898, the vineyard was devastated by

phylloxera, Campbell's son David, restored the cellars and replanted vines on resistant rootstocks. In turn, his son Allen carried the business through the difficult years of the Depression.

Allen's sons, Malcolm and Colin, currently run the business. Malcolm handles the vineyards while Colin, a Roseworthy graduate, manages the winemaking and winery. His Bobbie Burns Shiraz has developed a cult following and the super premium, Barkly Durif looks set to go the same way. Campbell's fortifieds including tokays and muscats are marvellous, they also make very good whites.

The winery is a picture of beautifully maintained history as can be seen on the self-guided tour. The Campbell's are proud of their past and dedicated to the future

Address: Murray Valley Highway RUTHERGLEN 3685 Phone: (02) 6032 9458 Fax: (02) 6032 9870 Email: wine@campbellswines.com.au WWW: www.campbellswines.com.au Owner: Campbell Family	Winemaker: Colin Campbell Est: 1870 Vine Ha: 55 Cases: 35,000 Public Hours: 9am-5pm, Mon-Sat; 10am-5pm, Sun Principal Varieties: Shiraz, Muscat, Durif, Cab Sav, Riesling, Chard, Semillon, Tokay Principal Wines Potential	Bobbie Burns Shiraz	10+ yrs
		The Barkly Durif	10+ yrs
		Chardonnay	5 yrs
		Chardonnay Semillon	2-5 yrs
		Liqueur Muscat	
		Liqueur Tokay	

Chambers

In a region that boasts many of the true legends of the Australian Wine Industry - Bill Chambers is their Doyen. Bill is not one to stand on ceremony, his bright blue eyes shine with an intelligence that saw him well through Roseworthy many years ago. Bill is happiest on his farm, which just happens to have some of the greatest vineyards and wines this great wine nation can boast.

Bill's one that firmly believes a good wine sells itself. A select coterie of knowledgeable wine lovers have beaten a path to his cellar door for many years, but try as he may, he's found fame and fortune hard to avoid.

The Chambers Rosewood Rare Tokay and Muscat in half bottles sell in the United States for at least US$130 each. The Rare Tokay was awarded

98 points out of 100 in a September 1997 Wine Spectator tasting. The Penfolds Grange Hermitage is the only other Australian wine ever to achieve this incredible feat. The Special Tokay and Special Muscat were not far behind both with 95 points.

Late at night I love sipping the Special Tokay Bill gave me a few years ago. Its velvety texture and complex nutty character - its exquisite liquid gold!!

Chambers make some splendid red and white table wines. This is a cellar door where bulk wine and some real bargains can still be found. If your lucky enough to catch Bill in the tasting area - as he just loves to be in the winery or out on the farm - a conversation with him is a most enlightening experience indeed. Bill's son Stephen is now carrying on the family tradition with Bill, he is the sixth generation at Rosewood to do so.

Seek out this hidden jewel the Chambers have been keeping a secret since 1858 - your life will be richer for its discovery.

Address: Barkly Street RUTHERGLEN 3685 Phone: (02) 6032 8641 Fax: (02) 6032 8101 Email: wchambers@netc.net.au Owner: Bill Chambers Winemaker: Bill Chambers Est: 1858 Vine Ha: 53 Cases: 10,000	Public Hours: 9am-5pm, Mon-Sat; 11am-5pm, Sun (except Christmas Day & Good Friday) Principal Varieties: Shiraz, Cabernet Sav, Blue Imperial, Touriga, Rutherglen Muscat, Muscadelle, Chard, Palomino, Riesling Principal Wines Potential	Cabernet Sauvignon	10+ yrs
		Shiraz	10+ yrs
		Riesling	5+ yrs
		Chardonnay	5+ yrs
		Muscat (Special and Rare)	
		Tokay (Special and Rare)	

Gehrig Wines

Victoria's oldest winery, established in 1858, is situated alongside a magnificent early Victorian building "Barnawartha House" home to the Gehrig family for five generations.

The mansion was completed in 1879 from clay bricks formed and fired on the property. The three story Belltower overlooks the Gourmet Courtyards Restaurant and the adjoining citrus and walnut grove, with its display of historical farming implements.

The sense of history and the real heritage of the early days of wine in Victoria, come across strongly in this unspoilt Vinous paradise, which to a large degree has seen time stand still. Coming from Albury/Wodonga it's the first winery of the region you see.

Bernard Gehrig a fourth generation family member, has worked through many years of the wine industry's post Second World War boom, many

under his father Barney, a great industry character. Bernard has taken a step back these days and his son Brian, a graduate from Charles Sturt, is making the wines. The wines are typical Rutherglen, full bodied and full flavoured made using traditional and modern methods to bring out the best from the mature vineyards. The Chenin Blanc is the favourite white to have with lunch at the Courtyard Restaurant, as well as the Chardonnay Late Harvest Muscadelle. The main reds are the taditional style Shiraz, Cabernet and Durif. If you're a sherry lover try the Ye Olde dry amontillado or the rich Oloroso. They also make old sweet white Fortified 'Classic Muscadelle' plus an old Classic Tawny Port, a Vintage Port to put down for years and naturally, a Classic Muscat.

Gehrig Estate will give you the opportunity to imbide in Australia's rich wine history.

Address: Murray Valley Highway BARNAWARTHA 3688 Phone: (02) 6026 7296 Fax: (02) 6026 7424	Email: gehrig@hotkey.net.au Winemaker: Brian Gehrig Est: 1858 Public Hours: 9am-5pm, Mon-Sat; 10am-5pm, Sun	Principal Varieties: Cabernet Sauvignon, Chardonnay, Chenin Blanc, Durif, Muscadelle, Muscat, Pinot Noir, Riesling, Shiraz, Trebbiano

Pfeiffers

Chris Pfeiffer was fortified winemaker for Lindemans Wines, his last position being just across the Murray River from Rutherglen, in Corowa. In 1984 he and his wife Robyn purchased the grand old Seppelt's Distillery in Wahgunyah, and renovated the 19th Century Winery.

The tasting area is full of character, and the scenic picnic area on the banks of the river provides an idyllic location for enjoying Pfeiffer's gourmet lunch hampers.

The original 25-acre vineyard was planted in 1963, and since 1984 this has been expanded to 75 acres. Chris has a small planting of the elusive grape variety Gamay, which he crafts into an early drinking style of spicy wild berry flavours. The old low yielding Pinot Noir vines produce a red of great character. Since 1984 Chris has had some Cabernet Sauvignon, Riesling and Shiraz vines grown in the cooler alpine regions of

north east Victoria. The lifted aromatics of these grapes enhance the elegance of style and balance for which Pfeiffer Wines are renowned. The delicate dry Riesling in particular benefits from this influence and wins many medals.

The Auslese Tokay is a beautiful dessert wine, and an impressive

selection of fortified wines · Muscat, Tokay, Vintage Port and a Tawny Port containing 26 varieties · complete the range. Pfeiffers also have a second range of wines under the Carlyle label with true varietal and regional characteristics at great value prices. These have been very successful in overseas and domestic markets.

Address: Distillery Road WAHGUNYAH 3687 Phone: (02) 6033 2805 Fax: (02) 6033 3158 Email: pfeifferwines@iprimus.com.au	Winemaker: Chris Pfeiffer Est: 1880 Public Hours: 9am-5pm, Mon-Sat; 11am-4pm, Sun	Principal Varieties: Cabernet Franc, Cabernet Sauvignon, Chardonnay, Gamay, Malbec, Merlot, Muscat, Pinot Noir, Shiraz

Morris

In 1859, George Morris purchased a property at Browns Plains, which he called 'Fairfield'. Morris expanded his vineyard so that by 1872 he had 617 acres under vine.

During the 1880's Morris built the imposing Fairfield mansion, which became one of the showpieces of the area. More than half of Fairfield's output was exported to the United Kingdom. In fact George Morris had such a reputation that in 1886 he was appointed Wine Commissioner at the Indian Colonial Exhibition in London.

In fact by the 1890's George Morris was in charge of Australia's largest winery. George's son Charles Morris, purchased his own property three kilometres east of Fairfield at Mia Mia in 1887 and also planted vines. The resultant fruit was sold to and processed at Fairfield.

The Fairfield vineyards were attacked

suddenly by phylloxera at the turn of the century. Wine production rapidly declined and following the founder's death, the company ceased

production altogether. However, at Mia Mia, after the devastation wrought by the vine louse, Charles Morris replanted and continued to make fortified wines.

Today, the winery is run by its founder's great-grandson, David. David carries on the family tradition producing a range of red table wines including Durif, which is a wine of great body and character. Likewise his chardonnay is great with both excellent fruit and strong varietal character.

The Morris fortifieds are made skillfully and compare favourably with the best in the world. Morris Wines was sold to Orlando in 1970 but fortunately Mick Morris (wine industry legend and David's father) was retained. Since Mick's retirement David Morris is carrying on the fine family tradition of more than a century.

Address: Mia Mia Vineyard RUTHERGLEN 3685	**Principal Varieties:** Chardonnay, Semillon,	Morris Old Premium Liqueur Tokay
Phone: (02) 6026 7303 **Fax:** (02) 6026 7445	Shiraz, Cabernet Sauvignon, Durif, Muscat,	Morris Canister Range
Owner: Orlando Wyndham Group Pty Ltd	Tokay, Muscadelle, Blue Imperial	Morris Black Label Range
Winemaker: David Morris **Est:** 1858	**Principal Wines**	Morris Rutherglen Durif
Public Hours: 9am-5pm, Mon-Sat, 10am-5pm, Sun	Morris Old Premium Liqueur Muscat	Morris Rutherglen Shiraz

Stanton & Killeen

Timothy Stanton and his son John Lewis Stanton came to Victoria in 1855 from Suffolk in England, in search of gold. They finally settled in Rutherglen where they planted vines on their farm, making their first wine in 1875.

The vineyard, known as 'Park View', was destroyed by phylloxera around the turn of the century. The vineyard was replanted but succumbed again to the depression of the 1930s. Timothy's grandson, John Richard, became a successful vigneron in his own right and in 1921 presented his son, John Charles (Jack) Stanton with 30 hectares of land which became known as 'Gracerray'. While still working for his father Jack planted his own winery and his first vintage was in 1925.

Norm Killeen arrived in Rutherglen in 1940 as a young graduate in

agricultural science to work at the Research Institute. In 1948, he married Jack Stanton's daughter, Joan, and joined Jack at the winery in 1953, becoming winemaker in 1967. The business became known

as Stanton & Killeen. Jack died in 1990 at 95 years of age. I well remember photographing him in the new tasting area in 1986.

Norm's son Chris Killeen took over the winemaking in 1981 after farm management and tertiary winemaking studies. A new vineyard specialising in red was planted of Moodemere in 1968 and another 6 hectares in 1978 called 'Quandong', the property's name before Gracerray. Some of the original vineyards planted by Jack Stanton in 1921 are still bearing, producing some of the finest wines in the district most notably "Jack's Block Shiraz" a super premium red work seeking out. The Stanton & Killeen fortifieds which include tokay, muscat and vintage port are also outstanding. Chris also makes some very respectable whites.

Address: PO Box 15 RUTHERGLEN 3685	**Principal Varieties:** Cabernet Franc, Chard,	Durif	5-10 yrs
Phone: (02) 6032 9457 **Fax:** (02) 6032 8018	Merlot, Muscat, Tinta Coa, Cabernet	Vintage Port	15-25 yrs
Owner: CJ, NC & J Killeen	Sauvignon, Durif, Muscadelle, Shiraz, Touriga	Classic Rutherglen Muscat	
Winemaker: Chris Killeen	**Principal Wines** **Potential**	Classic Rutherglen Tokay	
Est: 1875 **Vine Ha:** 30 **Cases:** 15,000	"Jacks Block" Shiraz 5-10 yrs	Grand Rutherglen Muscat	

Mt Ophir

On the 4th February 1904, the following article appeared in the Rutherglen regional newspaper; entitled,

"An Advance in the Wine Industry" - "A new Departure - opening of the Winery at Mount Ophir Vineyard - a splendid gathering".

The story went on "It is now close on 35 years since the firm of P.B. Burgoyne of London first had dealings with Mr. T Hardy of South Australia in connection with Colonial Wine". In about 1884 Mr.G.F.Morris from Rutherglen began dealing with Burgoynes, a large English Wine merchant. Burgoynes were at the time buying large quantities of rich "Burgundy" wines made from Shiraz, Malbec and "Carbinet" (Cabernet Sauvignon) for the English market. They decided to have their own vineyards and in 1894 bought 150 acres with 100 acres of vineyards known as "Gleesons" on a prominent Hill some 4 kilometres from

Rutherglen. They constructed a magnificent winery. At the opening "The Splendid Gathering" included many prominent Victorians, the then Minister for Agriculture Mr. Tavener was conspicuous by his absence, (phylloxera was at the time having a devastating affect on Rutherglen and other Victorian regions).

Ironically my photographer Stehpane L'hostis and I were looking for accomodation early in February 2000 on a rush trip through the region, we

somehow found our way to "Mt Ophir". I was completely oblivious to the fact 96 years ago almost to the day, my great great grandfather had been there as a special guest of honour at the Grand opening.

The Cellars and homestead at Mt. Ophir have a grandeur and majesty that even many decades of decay were unable to destroy. Ruth Hennesey is a courageous and strong woman who has done a wonderful job restoring the Cellars and homestead which also operates as a marvelous bed and breakfast. The experience of staying there and immersing yourself in this fascinating piece of Australia's history is truly enlightening.

Ruth is also a superb cook and makes many jams, pickles and preserves, some from the original orchards planted some 120 years ago.

Australia owes Ruth Hennesy a true debt of gratitude!!

Address: Stillards Lane RUTHERGLEN 3685 **Phone:** (02) 6032 8920 **Fax:** (02) 6032 9911 **Email:** info@mount-ophir.com	**WWW:** www.mount-ophir.com **Owner:** Ruth Hennessy **Est:** 1891, restoration commenced 1988	**Vine Ha:** 5 **Public Hours:** Only by booking as guests or tour group

Warrabilla

Andrew Sutherland Smith is a young powerhouse of the Australian wine scene, he is also a fifth generation member, of a famous wine family that founded Rutherglens All Saints Winery in 1864.

Andrew is a graduate of Charles Sturt University's Wine degree course having won a Ron Potter Scholarship. His extensive experience has included working for Seppelts, Yellowglen, Mildara, Stanley, McWilliams, Chambers and Fairfield and All Saints all since 1981.

Andrew relishes having his own vineyards of 40 acres, as well as his own winery and being able to make his own styles, he is a real red enthusiast and his reds are powerful and positive, he uses traditional methods from the last century, open fermentors and a classic 1950's model Gradon Whitehill airbag press, he looks after his wines like his children. The Warrabilla reds have

intense purple hued colour lots of fresh fruit flavours, firm but balanced tannins and plenty of alcohol, he uses top class imported oak barrels for maturation.

Apart from his own vineyards around the winery, which is on the Murray Highway west of Rutherglen about half way to Yarrawonga, he also sources grapes from Glenrowan, Walla Walla and the King Valley, which gives him the various styles of

wine he is looking for to make his wines complete in flavour. Apart from his beloved reds he makes a very good Chardonnay which is a real mouthfilling style.

Andrew also has a Victorian Regional Range including his 01 Riesling, a real gem, and in 2001 their first Marsanne is being released.

Today Andrew gave me a real tip - try his 2001 Warrabilla Durif he assures me its going to be a world beater.

Address: Murray Valley Highway RUTHERGLEN 3687 **Phone:** (02) 6035 7242 **Fax:** (02) 6035 7242	**Email:** warrawin@rutherglen.albury.net.au **Winemaker:** Andrew Sutherland Smith **Est:** 1989	**Public Hours:** 10am-5pm, daily **Principal Varieties:** Cabernet Sauvignon, Chardonnay, Durif, Merlot, Shiraz

Rutherglen Estates

Rutherglen's history is a reflection of the whole Australian wine industry. Like other regions, Rutherglen lived it up through the boom times of the 1800s, suffered through during the depression years and then the nadir of the 1950s, before the boom in table wine consumption started in about 1970. During the hard times, Rutherglen hung on through the strength of its outstanding fortified wine but, for most of its history, it was red wine that brought if fame and success.

Before the depression, the Burgoyne family's estates of Mount Ophir and Mount Athos totalled nearly 700 acres of vines, with Shiraz, Cabernet Sauvignon, Malbec and Portuguese varieties. Now a group of Rutherglen families and their colleagues have re-establishing vineyards on the original Mount Athos. The vineyards were established by Michael Murtagh, Rutherglen born, who has managed properties in the Yarra Valley and elsewhere. Another partner is Nick Butler, a flying winemaker, who has made wine in France, Italy, Spain,

Greece, Chile, Argentina, and many Balkan states, as well as Australia. Steve Wallis, another son of the Rutherglen region, is the cellar foreman who supervises the "Cellar rats". His 29 years of industry experience are proving invaluable and his wicked larrikin humour is making sure that any tendency toward pomposity receives the ridicule it deserves.

The vineyards contain a mixture of the varieties that have been the backbone of Rutherglen Estates over centuries with a smattering of the new. Thus, Shiraz, Grenache and Durif now rubbed shoulders with the Spanish varieties Mataro (or Mourvèdre) and Tempranillo, and the exotic Sangiovese and Nebbiolo from Italy. Whites are not neglected, as the reds are joined by the Marsanne and Viognier varieties from the Rhône Valley of France, two warm region specialists which should prove ideally suited to Rutherglen's generous summers. The plantings of these varieties now total over 1000 acres.

David Valentine is the winemaker and has a brand new state-of-the-art winery to work in. The new stainless steel and galvanised building provides a striking contrast to the tradition timber wineries of the Rutherglen region. David's overriding goal is to produce "nothing but the best at an affordable price". He also makes wine on contract for other new Rutherglen vineyards, which have not yet built wineries, and for companies outside the area, both large and small, which have brought local grapes.

Architects are currently designing a new Cellar Door facility, which will open in 2002 to entertain visitors to the Rutherglen estates. Here, they will be able to buy small parcels of premium wines that are not available elsewhere.

The combined talents of this new team, building on the traditional strengths of the Rutherglen region, will ensure a great future for Rutherglen estates.

Grampians

In previous Edition's the dispersed nature of viticulture throughout Victoria and the enormous distances encountered from region to region, it had not been possible to devote an entire chapter to the Grampians so I am pleased to be able to do so in this edition.

The Grampians includes the areas close to Ararat and Great Western plus the Grampians proper around Halls Gap. I have also included Ballarat and the coastal areas around Drumborg although strictly speaking they are outside the Grampians Region.

The best-known area is Great Western, 218 kilometres west of Melbourne. Centred around a small town of the same name, the district is hilly, of poor soils and is at the mercy of extreme climates, including frosts. Fruit yields are therefore low but, due to the slow ripening period which creates high sugar levels, and great flavours, these are of excellent quality.

Since its inception out of the gold rush, the Great Western district has produced long living, high quality wines. Vines were planted in the 1860's by two Frenchmen, Jean Trouette and Emile Blampied and the Best family. In time, the former property faded from existence, leaving the Best family's Great Western vineyards to prosper and expand. Following the death of Joseph Best, the Great Western concern was sold to Hans Irvine who emphasised champagne production. B. Seppelt and Sons bought Great Western in 1918.

Of the 44 district vine growers of 1893, only two, Seppelt Great Western along with the Thomson family, at what was formerly Best's Concongella Vineyard, survive today. A number of wine ventures have started around Ararat led by McRae's Montara and Mt Langi Ghiran both founded in 1970.

During the 1960's Seppelt decided to expand their operations in Victoria and began a search for suitable land. Owing to quarantine regulations it was not possible to take cuttings from South Australia. As the company wished to continue producing fruit from cool climate areas, an alternative site in Victoria was required. Karl Seppelt purchased property at Drumborg outside Portland, which he first planted to vines in 1964. The coastal climate is milder than at Great Western and, since Seppelt's successful establishment at Drumborg, others have been encouraged to plant in this area.

The Halls Gap Region is awsomely beautiful overhung by the mountainous Grampian Ranges. On the northern slopes of the foothills, The Gap Vineyard is a top place to visit originally the Boroka Vineyard, in 1999 it was taken over by the talented Mast family from Mt Langi Ghiran, already great wines are emerging. It's also an easy visit if your staying at Halls Gap.

The Grampians are one of Australia's natural treasures as are the wines the region produces.

Grampians

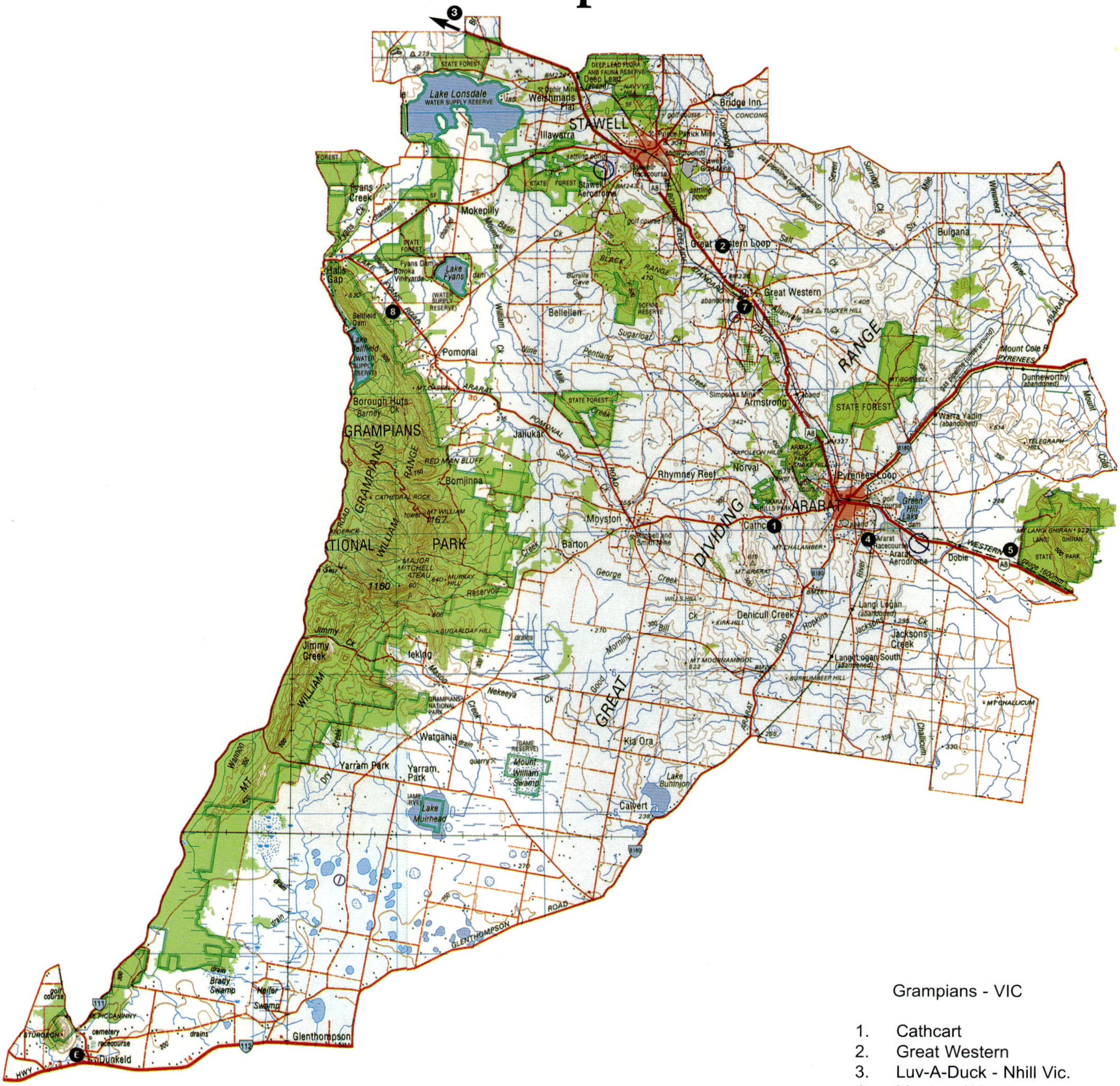

Grampians - VIC

1. Cathcart
2. Great Western
3. Luv-A-Duck - Nhill Vic.
4. Montara Winery
5. Mt Langi Ghiran
6. Royal Mail Hotel
7. Seppelts Great Western
8. The Gap Vineyard

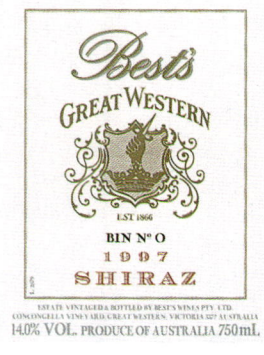

Bests Great Western

At St Andrews they produce superb concentrated fortified wines in the classic North-Eastern Victorian style. The winery also has a Best's Victoria label in the value for money section of the market. These wines are mainly from St Andrews, but often contain some Great Western material. The Victoria Chenin Blanc and Riesling both have lovely lifted fruit character and the Victoria Shiraz and Cabernet are mouthfilling, great value wines.

The 'piece de resistance' is the Great Western 'Bin O Shiraz', an incredibly long living wine. Viv Thomson and I sat down and drank the 1962 alongside the 1992 released to celebrate the family's centenary in 1993. We agreed the older wine was one of the finest and freshest old reds we had ever tried - its lifted pepper and wild berry flavours with a touch of mint were so seductive and full of the vibrancy of youth.

The Great Western Chardonnay, Riesling, Cabernet Sauvignon, Pinot Noir, Pinot Meunier and the Dolcetto Red, the latter 2 being from 130 year old wines, and their Concongella Cuvee Sparkling are world-beaters. Make sure you beat a path to their door to see the original winery and the historic vineyard, with more than 50 vine varieties, all 100-plus years old.

Although the Thomson family did not establish Best's Wines, the family have been growing grapes and making wine for more than 100 years in the Great Western region. On 13th November 1893 at 11.30am William Thomson became the proud owner of 'St Andrews', a vineyard and winery established by pioneer John Lorimer at Rhymney Reef. Thomson was a born entrepreneur - in 1888 he was appointed a caterer to the Great Colonial Exhibition in Melbourne.

His energy and 'hands' on approach have flowed down five generations of the family. Best's Wines is certainly ranked in the top ten Australian Wineries, with wines of extraordinary quality, ageing potential and, above all, individuality! Much credit must go to their unique vineyard at Great Western, taking its name from the Concongella Creek, which flows through the bottom of the property. Most of the original vines are still there, planted from 1866 to 1870. This is no museum piece of recreated history, but a working vineyard, which came into the Thomson family's hands in 1920. It must be close to being one of the oldest working vineyards in the world.

Best's also have a vineyard, winery and distillery at Lake Boga, called St. Andrews after William Thomson's original vineyard at Rhymney Reef, which they established in 1930 in the heart of the depression - a word that does not exist in the family's vocabulary.

Viv Thomson and his charming wife Chris have ably run the whole operation for many years, today they are assisted by their three sons Ben, Hamish and Marcus and daughter Yvette.

Address: Best's Road GREAT WESTERN 3377	Est: 1866		Bests Victoria Range	3-5 yrs
Phone: (03) 5356 2250	Vine Ha: 70	Cases: 30,000	Bin No 0 Shiraz	
Fax: (03) 5356 2430	Public Hours: 10am-5pm, daily		Great Western Pinot Noir	
Email: bests@netconnect.com.au	Principal Wines	Potential	Great Western Cabernet Sauvignon	
Winemaker: Viv Thomson & Hamish Seabrook	Bests Great Western	5-20 yrs	Great Western Riesling	

LUV·A·DUCK

Duck and Wine: the perfect recipe – Duck and wine have long been among the most favoured ingredients of chefs and those who love good food. Together they are "meat and drink" with the ability to transform a meal into a celebration.

Australia is blessed with an abundance of fine wines but it was not always so with ducks. In earlier days, duck in any form was a rare menu item indeed.

Today, the young ducklings grow up in huge, airy, covered enclosures on the company's modern 500-acre Wimmera property. Clean and green is the order of the day. Hormones and chemicals are unknown. Here the ducks are the centre of attention, growing up under the watchful eyes of specialists in husbandry, nutrition and veterinary care. Luv-a-Duck does everything in its power to help ensure a comfortable and stress-free environment for its fast-growing ducklings.

wheat, oats, barley, oil seeds, lucerne and clovers. This is the highly nutritious raw material helps to make Luv-a-Duck Australia's favourite duck.

Setting a fine table – Ducks and wine get along famously and forge a highly complementary dining partnership. Combine a good red or white wine with your favourite duckling dish and there is little else that even a seasoned gourmet could desire. No wonder the popularity of duck, in much the same way as wine, has increased rapidly over the past decade. Once the preserve of exclusive five-star restaurants, duck is now rarely off the menu in bistros, cafes, hotels, function centres and even on airlines. Wine is the prefect ingredient to add to duck sauce and any fruit or liqueur served with duck is guaranteed to highlight the flavour of the meat.

From the heart of the Wimmera Wheatlands comes the future in duck.

In the late 1960s similar thoughts went through the mind of 30 year old Arthur Shoppee in the small rural centre of Nhill in Victoria's Wimmera. Realising there was a year-round and virtually untapped market for these feathered delicacies, he started in a small way with some twenty white Pekin ducklings in his backyard. He incorporated the new concept of a balanced diet of nutritious grains as opposed to kitchen scraps.

An idea that grew – Experience was Arthur's only teacher and soon he took the risk of renting a small disused turkey farm on the outskirts of the town. In those early days, the raising of ducks on open runs almost led to the demise of the idea before it found its feet. Many ducks perished from exposure to the elements – heat, cold and rain. The young ducks were attacked by crows, mauled by foxes and threatened by disease from numerous avian pests. But Arthur was blessed with the pioneering spirit and a will to succeed – he was determined never to quit.

In less than thirty years, the man from Nhill and his fledgling enterprise, now known far and wide as Luv-a-Duck, have grown to become not just Australia's most successful producer of duck meat but also the largest in the Southern Hemisphere.

Arthur Shoppee's table duck is a unique white Pekin breed developed from local and imported strains to produce a fully flavoured lean meat, with the lowest fat content of any table duck available. In fact, lean duck meat is lower in fat than lean chicken meat. As Arthur explained, "It's the breeding of the ducks themselves that our business is built on. It's how they plate and taste that we're all about. We look for high breast meat thickness that's both tender and tasty."

Technically speaking – Adjacent to the farm is Luv-a-Duck's all-new state of the art, automated plant where the six week old ducklings are processed. This is the only Halal certified and export licensed duck plant in Australia.

Production and distribution of Luv-a-Duck is now big business with over two hundred staff closely involved. They include many professionals from disciplines as diverse as nutrition, poultry veterinary science, engineering, building, food technology, microbiology, cooking, marketing, sales and management.

The mild climate of the Wimmera region is perfect for the comfort of the table duck. At harvest time, the town of Nhill is an island in a sea of golden grains as the surrounding grainfields produce their bountiful harvest of

Ready for the bigger future – What does the future hold for this 21st century duck? Currently Luv-a-Duck is available whole, portioned, filleted, marinated, confit, roasted, sliced, and in medallions, smallgoods and finger foods. Luv-a-Duck is working with the booming hospitality industry, improving quality, crafting new dishes, and researching more convenient ways to present duckling in a world which has less and less time for "slow" food.

The company's own chef is closely involved in the development of new duck products as well as being available to assist customers with any questions they may have about the cooking and presentation of duck dishes.

So there are quite a few ways which duck and wine share a common future, and it's possible that some of our leading wines owe a lot more to the duck industry than you may have imagined. For example, composted duck litter is prized as a fertiliser by vignerons for a number of the more select wine labels.

In a way, it's pleasing to know that Luv-a-Duck is playing an important part in the dynamic growth of Australia's wine industry while achieving its own goal of making duck easy to use and available everywhere.

LUV·A·DUCK

Luv-a-Duck have a range of portion control,
ready to heat duck products available.
Confit of Duck Leg (main picture)
Duck Medallions (top insert)
Smoked & Sliced Duck Breast (middle insert)
Roasted & Sliced Peking Duck Breast (bottom insert)
It's so easy to serve duck.

LUV-A-DUCK PTY LTD
National Sales Office 151 Boundary Street (PO Box 185) Port Melbourne Victoria 3207 Australia
Telephone +61 3 9646 9000
Facsimile +61 3 9646 9020
Website www.luvaduck.com
Email sales@luvaduck.com

DAIRY FARMERS

Both MilLel Superior –
the mark of extraordinary cheese –
and MilLel Cheesemakers Selection – consistently
superb Australian cheese – present a range of award winning
flavours to show that Dairy Farmers cheeses are in a class of their own.

MilLel Superior Grana Cheeses

Cheese and wine – it just sounds right together doesn't it? And there are very good reasons for this as they both enhance the flavours and tastes of each other.

Ask any wine expert what is the best accompaniment for the not so arduous task of wine tasting and inevitably the answer will be cheese.

But you don't have to be a professional wine taster to enjoy the benefits of the cheese and wine combination and you must not be phased by people telling you what wine is best with so and so cheese and that this wine should not be drunk with that cheese.

One of the greatest joys of eating cheese and drinking wine together is in the experimentation and the courage to say 'I like this cheese with this wine'. Certainly experts are always on hand to suggest cheese and wine combinations and to tell you how to get the best out of your respective choices, but only the individual with his or her own preferences and unique pallet will tell you what is right for you! Yes, certainly some things don't work, but you will quickly learn that for yourself!

MilLel Cheesemakers Selection Double Brie and Double Camembert

Over the years, Dairy Farmers has built a solid reputation for producing the best locally produced Grana cheeses in the country. The multi-awarded Mil Lel Superior Parmesan, Pepato, Romano and Pecorino have repeatedly been recognised both nationally and internationally as some of the finest cheeses of their kinds. Proven to be a winner with wine drinkers as well, these hard (or grana – the Italian word for grainy) cheeses are ideal either as cheeseboard cheeses or as cooking cheeses. Their strong flavours are ideally matched with the more robust wines in the cellars – but also not only traditional reds and ports. These cheeses go equally well with strong wooded chardonnay or crisp Chablis.

MilLel Cheesemakers Selection Vintage Cheddar

In the past 12 months, Dairy Farmers has launched a new range of cheeses also ideally suited to the cheese/wine combination. Both the new style Mil Lel Cheesemakers Selection Double Brie and Double Camembert have struck a chord with the cheese going public. Both of these cheeses are unique in their style and production – easily distinguished from similar cheeses by their characteristic hole in the middle of the wheel.

The Mil Lel Double Camembert displays an earthy aroma with a creamy lightly salted taste while the Mil Lel Double Brie displays a lighter smell with a slightly less creamy texture and both are made with a thin non-traditional more appealing tasting rind. Both of these cheeses go very well with either red or white varietal or generic wines but go particularly well with a good Chardonnay.

Generally speaking the more acidic the cheese – the greater the need to match it with an equally acidic wine – which is why Feta cheeses go so well with Sauvignon Blanc or Sancerre and why the Cheesemakers Selection Vintage Cheddar is ideally matched with a mature Cabernet

MilLel Swiss

or Merlot or Shiraz. Its Blue Vein is best matched with traditionally sweet wines such as Tokay's, Muscats or Ports and its Swiss Cheese best served with light whites so as not to overpower the delicate taste of the cheese.

Mil Lel Superior Grana Cheeses and the Mil Lel Cheesemakers Selection are available from most good delicatessens throughout the country and Dairy Farmers has a number of recipe flyers just brimming with ideas on how to use them. Call 1800 777 556 for your set.

Caboolture Blue Vein

The recipe cards are clearly seasonal indicating just how versatile the range of cheeses is for both cooking and eating throughout the year.

Mt Langi Ghiran

Langi is aboriginal for 'home of' and Ghiran is the yellow-tailed black cockatoo. Langi is also the home of two of the best red wines in Australia. The Langi Shiraz, with its pepper, mulberry and cedar cigar box character, and the cassis and cedar wood like Cabernet Sauvignon Merlot, are as awesome as the spectacular vineyard location spread across the valley between Mount Langi Ghiran and Mount Cole. This cool isolated location was originally apple country, back in the gold rush days of the 1850's. Vines were first planted in 1880, but saw their demise around 1920, like much of Victoria's other vineyards.

In 1968 the vineyards were replanted by the Fratin brothers from Ararat they also began their own winemaking enterprise after some years and in 1979 they appointed Trevor Mast as consultant winemaker. Trevor s a graduate of the highly respected Geisenheim Wine Institute in Germany and has made wine at various wineries in Germany, France, Hungary, Portugal and South Africa going right back to the 1970's, long before the trendy flying winemakers took off. Trevor was so impressed with the Fratin's vineyards and wines that he purchased the property in 1987 with partner Ian Menzies

Recently Trevor has found a great

new partner, in European Wine identity Riquet Hess, former C.E.O. of German wine giant H. Sichel & Co, who purchased Menzies shares. The development of the vineyards has been astounding. Trevor has always had trouble with wind, birds, kangaroos and other animals in his best shiraz vineyard bringing the yields down to as low as / tonne per acre, absolutely uneconomic. Late in 1996 an enormous 27-acre permanent net was erected over the vineyard, it now crops at around 3.5 tonnes per acre from the protected vines and is of superb quality, each year it's improving.

A huge new winery is now operating and a large vineyard development some 10 kilometres north of the existing vineyard has been established under Trevor's masterly control. I am sure more exciting times and wines lie ahead.

Mt Langi maintain a strong philosophy of the organic vineyard concept and minimal intervention during winemaking, using only natural chemicals in extremely low concentrations.

The Blue Label Mt Langi Ghiran labels are reserved for wines selected from the mature Mt Langi vineyards. The shiraz and cabernet merlot have long been ranked in the absolute top rung of Australia's reds and

recognised worldwide. The Yellow Black Cockatoo range of whites, includes a much acclaimed aromatic riesling, chardonnay and a recently introduced pinot gris. The Billi Billi Creek range is made from fruit from the younger Mt Langi vineyards blended with fruit from other premium regions. The name comes from a creek which runs through the property named after Aboriginal elder King Billi Billi who died in 1869.

Mt Langi Ghiran have contracted a small vineyard in the Wrattonbully region of the limestone coast in South Australia, which Trevor has shown makes magnificent softer earlier natural cabernet sauvignons. This wine comes out each year under the name "Joanna" from "The Hundred of Joanna" where the vineyard is located.

Mt Langi have also taken over the Boroka vineyard and winery near Halls Gap renaming it "The Gap", exciting things are now underway there.

They have just released a new label "Cliff Edge Shiraz" from 17 year old vines under the netting at the Mt Langi Ghiran site.

Trevor Mast is a true master winemaker and a visionary person, he easily ranks in the top ten of Australia's best winemakers.

Address: Warrak-Buangor Rd BUANGOR 3375
Phone: (03) 5354 3207 **Fax:** (03) 5354 3277
Email: langi@netconnect.com.au

Winemaker: Trevor Mast   **Est:** 1970
Public Hours: 10am-5pm, Weekdays;
12pm-5pm, Weekends

Principal Varieties: Cabernet Franc, Cabernet Sauvignon, Chardonnay, Merlot, Pinot Grigio, Riesling, Sangiavese, Shiraz

The Gap Vineyard

Recently Mt Langi Ghiran the high profile winery and vineyard, bought Boroka Wines and Vineyards, about 5 kms East of the Tourist Mecca of Halls Gap in the Grampian Ranges.

They sit on the North Eastern Slopes of the Grampian foothills, it's one of the most spectacular vineyard sites in Australia. The imposing northern ridge of the Mt William Range rises directly behind the vineyard and extends each side of the property as far as the eye can see.

The Vineyard of some 23 acres was somewhat rundown when Mt Langi Ghiran took over but has been quickly put back into shape. Some extra planting and grafting has also been done.

The Cellar Door has been extended and a Terrace put in place, to make the most of the view. There is even a small playground for children.

Trevor Mast's wife Sandra and their daughter Daliah run the business. The spacious bright and airy Cellar Door also doubles as a gallery for prints produced by Daliah. They feature vines, wine and epicurean scenes. The works of guest artists are also sometimes displayed.

There are plans to serve light foods, in a café style environment in the next couple of years, which will feature the growing gourmet produce of the region.

The main varieties in the Gap Vineyards are Shiraz, Cabernet Sauvignon and Riesling. The Gap also use grapes from other Grampians Vineyards. The wines are all made under control of Consummate winemaker Trevor Mast at Mt Langi Ghiran.

At The Gap you can also taste a selection of Mt Langi and Four Sisters wines. Sandra Mast makes a point of always having an interesting wine on offer, often at a bargain price. These include Bin Ends and Cleanskin Wines from Mt Langi Ghiran. As an added incentive, not that its really necessary, to visit this beautiful vineyard.

Address: Vine Road BUANGOR 3375	**Est:** 1969 **Vine Ha:** 90 **Cases:** 30,000	Cabernet Sauvignon Merlot	15 yrs
Phone: (03) 5354 3207 **Fax:** (03) 5354 3277	**Public Hours:** 9am-5pm, Weekdays;	Joanna Cabernet Sauvignon	8 yrs
Email: langi@netconnect.com.au	12pm-5pm, Weekends & Public Holidays	Cliff Edge Shiraz	8 yrs
Owner: Riquet Hess & Trevor Mast	**Principal Wines Potential**	Billi Billi Creek Shiraz Cab Grenache	8 yrs
Winemaker: Trevor Mast	Langi Shiraz 15 yrs	Pinot Gris	2-3 yrs

Seppelts Great Western

One of the most fascinating legacies of Australia's wine industry is Seppelt Great Western. Built by Joseph Best during the mid 1860's, the winery features more than two and a half kilometres of underground cellars which have come to be known as the 'Drives'. They were excavated by local gold miners originally under the direction from Joseph Best, and serve to house maturing sparkling wines.

Throughout the history of the winery many drives have been opened or visited by contemporary celebrities and as such bear their names. 'Dame Nellie Melba Drive' for example, is named after the famous opera singer who is reputed to have bathed in champagne during her visit. The Drives, classified with an 'A' rating by the National Trust, are still in use, their constant temperature of 15 degrees being well suited to the storage of sparkling wines.

Over recent years, Seppelt has concentrated their efforts on improving their very popular bottle fermented wines, Great Western Imperial Reserve and Great Western Brut. A number of premium methode champenoise wines have also been introduced, starting with Fleur de Lys, released in the early 1980's, followed by the exquisite Salinger.

As part of this program, extensive plantings of new vines have been carried out behind the winery at Great Western, as well as Drumborg near Portland, plus Padthaway and the Coonawarra region in South Australia. The grape varieties planted are those best suited to sparkling wine production and include chardonnay, pinot noir and pinot meunier. Production of these wines has been radically improved. The base wines are produced and blended in the winery and transferred to the tirage preparation area where sugar and yeast are added prior to tirage bottling. Secondary fermentation and maturation in bottle then occur at the required temperature.

By now the yeast is dormant, its distinctive flavour permeating the wine. This process lasts a minimum of six months, but can take up to three years or more in the case of Salinger and some of the other special limited releases, including the marvellous Show Sparkling Burgundies. The wine is then disgorged (that is the dead yeast or lees removed). The new complex at Great Western can process a total of 20 million plus bottles per year.

The Seppelt Victorian Portfolio wines with their distinctive classy labels have been a big success - the 1991

Harpers Range Red, in fact, won the Jimmy Watson Memorial Trophy.

The background of many of the early settlers in the region, including Hans Irvine, was French, which I am sure had much to do with the sparkling wine focus. The cool climate is both ideal, both for the special kind of viticulture needed for sparkling wine grapes and the making and ageing of the wines.

Over the years, Seppelt Great Western has been blessed with some extraordinary winemakers. Skilled and talented, these men of vision have greatly contributed to the Australian wine scene. Firstly Joseph Best in early days of the 1860's, through to Hans Irvine and Seppelt's first manager, Reginald Mowatt, paved the way for the great Colin Preece who took over form Mowatt in 1932, giving Australia such classic wines as Moyston Claret, Chalambar Burgundy, Rhymney Chablis and Arawatta Riesling.

Colin's enormous talents contributed largely to Great Western's establishment as a major winemaking force and this tradition of excellence is today being continued by a professional team of winemakers who are developing exciting wines that bring credit to the Australian wine industry.

Montara Winery

Planting began at Montara in 1970. The vineyards and winery are a very much hands on enterprise of the McRae family.

Only a few minutes south of Ararat, the winery and cellar door are perched on a hilltop surrounded by gardens and with breathtaking views over the vineyards and ranges beyond. The rich red loam soils have proven ideal for vines and the wines all exhibit intense spicy characters.

Each year during the April harvest celebrations of the Grampian's region wineries, the McRaes run a unique 'Scarecrows in the Vineyard' competition to find the best scarecrow. Some of the entries are astounding and a fantastic picnic day at the winery is held to announce the winning scarecrow.

Montara's wines are all handcrafted from the estate's 20 hectare vineyard. Montara is one of the region's few producers of Riesling which is always very aromatic. The Montara barrel fermented Chardonnay is rich, stylish and complex. The Shiraz is loaded with wild berry fruit and quite peppery and the Cabernet Sauvignon is very good. However, Montara is most renowned for the intense spicy Pinot Noir, one of the best Australian examples of the variety.

The mud brick cellar door has loads of charm, views are superb and the McRaes' warm welcome and personal attention make Montara Winery a great place to visit.

Address: Chalambar Road RMB 2105 ARARAT 3377	Owner: The McRae Family	Est: 1970	Montara Chardonnay	3 yrs
	Winemaker: Mike McRae	Vine Ha: 20	Montara Shiraz	4-6 yrs
Phone: (03) 5352 3868 Fax: (03) 5352 4968	Public Hours: 10am-5pm, Mon-Sat; 12-4pm Sun		"M" Pinot Noir Shiraz	2 yrs
Email: montara@netconnect.com.au	Principal Wines	Potential	Montara Pinot Noir	2-3 yrs
WWW: www.montara.com.au	Montara Riesling	4 yrs	Montara Cabernet Sauvignon	4-6 yrs

Yellowglen

What has become one of Australia's most successful wine ventures was originally established in 1971 as a hobby vineyard by Ballarat businessman and gastronome, Ian Home. The Yellowglen Vineyard at Smythesdale is situated 18 kilometres south-west of Ballarat.

A number of red and white wines were released under the Yellowglen label. In 1978 the first sparkling wine was made at Yellowglen.

In 1982 Ian Home went into partnership with Dominique Landragin, previous sparkling winemaker for Seppelt. Born in the Champagne district of France, Dominique trained at Beaune in Burgundy, working for several major champagne houses before leaving for Australia. The two men decided to concentrate their efforts on the creation of a superior range of methode champenoise wines.

Two years later the classic yellow-labelled Yellowglen Brut Non Vintage was released, followed by Australia's first rosé methode champenoise, and a brut cremant a year later, containing half the gas of other sparkling wines and spends a longer time on yeast lees, creating a classic 'creamy' style. Such was the success of this range that Yellowglen was able to develop from a small concern to one of Australia's leading premium sparkling wine suppliers in little more than a decade.

Beringer Blass purchased the company in 1984. Home and Landragin stayed on for a time, but today this hugely successful business is run by the extremely competent Beringer Blass team.

Royal Mail Hotel

Situated at the Southern end of the spectacular Grampians at Dunkeld, is the Historic Royal Mail Hotel. The property has been extensively renovated and enhanced making it one of the finest Gastronomic Winery regional stop overs in Australia. The Hotel has a number of beautifully appointed accomodation units with sweeping views over Mt. Sturgeon and the Southern Grampians.

The fine dining facilities in the Café Bar and Restaurant are superb, opening out onto a landscaped courtyard and lawns beautifully sheltered, with panoramic views of the Grampians.

The wine list is one of the best I have ever seen, it showcases the Grampians and Western Victorian wines from the smallest boutique to the industry's giant, it also offers an extensive selection of aged Australian and French wines, which would do a three star Michelin Restaurant proud.

The Hotels proprietors also own the Riddoch Estate vineyards in Coonawarra and the Royal Mail is their Cellar Door, so don't miss out on tasting these excellent wines when you call in.

For those who live in Melbourne, Dunkeld is about half way to or from Coonawarra and makes a great stop over either overnight or for a meal or both.

For the wine and food aficionado the annex lounge is equipped with a custom designed demonstration kitchen utilised by guest Chefs, for cooking schools and for private functions or small conferences. Larger conferences are catered for up to 120 people and full seminar/conference electronic equipment is available.

Just 5 minutes away the Royal Mail have eight Historic Bluestone Cottages totally restored and decorated in a country colonial theme. They all have en suite bathrooms, cooking facilities and lounges with open fireplaces.

The cottages look out on the breathtaking beautiful Southern Grampians and the imposing Mt Sturgeon, bushwalking and rock climbing is right on your doorstep.

The Royal Mail Hotel can not only provide you with breakfast but also a picnic basket or a hikers hamper.

These Mount Sturgeon cottages are located on an operating farm. The Woolshed built in the 1870's used to house 35 shearers who handled 35,000 sheep each year. Its bluestone and timber construction has lasted magnificently well and it is now a fabulous conference centre, ideal for corporate events or private functions for up to 150 people, naturally the Royal Mail cater for you in style.

The Royal Mail Hotel has a splendid swimming pool facilities. Golf, tennis and bowls are close at hand and Dunkeld has a fine historical museum and beautiful gardens.

Apart from walking in the Grampians and seeing the MacKenzie and Silverband falls, you can arrange a days fishing on the lakes nearby.

The Royal Mail has certainly brought good news to the Southern Grampians, one of Australia's most awe inspiring districts.

Pyrenees

The Pyrenees winemaking district, includes Avoca, Moonambel and Redbank. Located north-west of Ballarat in the Pyrenees range, the undulating landscape provides ideal conditions for the making of a wide range of wines. Vines were first planted in the 1840's by Adams at Mountain Creek, closely followed by a Mr Mackereth in 1848. The Mackereth concern was sold and dismantled in 1929 and Mountain Creek closed operations in 1947.

In 1963, John Robb arrived at Avoca and planted extensive vineyards for a consortium of the Remy Martin Company from France and an Australian wine merchant, Nathan and Wyeth. Although initially established for brandy production, Chateau Remy, now known as Blue Pyrenees Estate, has since changed direction, specialising in fine sparkling wines. During the early 1970's, other vineyards were established in the Pyrenees, including Taltarni, Warrenmang and Dalwhinnie. In 1973 Neill and Sally Robb established the Redbank Winery, which have since acquired an outstanding reputation for their red wines as has Summerfield founded in 1980.

Winemakers of the Pyrenees region are highly successful at producing a large selection of wine styles, ranging from the excellent sparkling wines of Taltarni and Blue Pyrenees Estate to the minty reds produced by Redbank and others. Local conditions have contributed to their prosperity. Although fruit yields tend to be low and the climate is cold and rainfall moderate, the grapes are first rate.

The Pyrenees region seems able to produce any variety of wine desired, diverse in style and direction. All the winemakers share a commitment to the winemaking industry of Victoria and, as a result, produce wines of distinction. Many wineries, such as Warrenmang with its full resort facilities, have hospitality facilities adding to the pleasure of visiting this region.

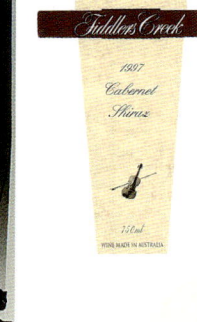

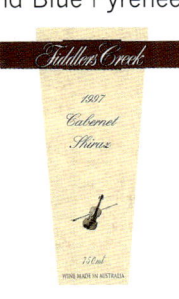

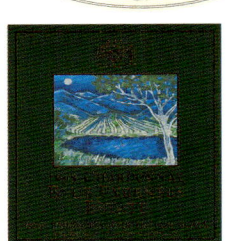

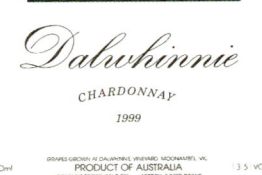

Pyrenees

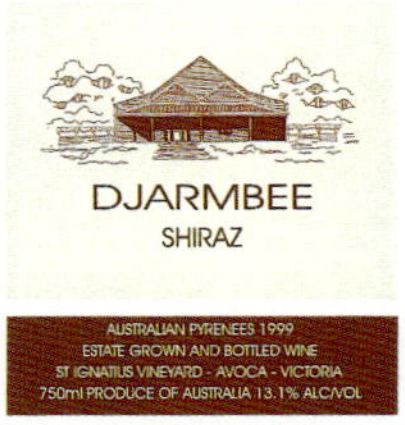

Pyrenees - VIC

1. Avoca Wines
2. Blue Pyrenees
3. Dalwhinnie
4. Karakara
5. Redbank
6. St Ignatius
7. Summerfield Wines
8. Taltarni
9. Warrenmang

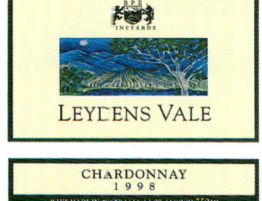

Dalwhinnie

Dalwhinnie vineyard is now recognised as one of Australia's elite small wine producers, a tribute to the vision and hard work of its founder Ewan Jones, which has been followed in full force by his eldest son David, who has since purchased the vineyards from his family.

When Classic Australian wines such as "Grange" and "Hill of Grace" and Wynns "Michael" are tasted, often Dalwhinnie is in their midst and more than holding its own.

Dalwhinnie is one of the most awesome vineyard sites in Australia at nearly 600 metres above sea level, it nestles in a sheltered rocky amphitheater under the Pyrenees highest peaks. This giant bowl at the extremity of the region beyond Tarni is cool but collects noticeable warmth and fierce thunderstorms which provide much needed water, a scarce commodity in the Pyrenees. The Ridges are the home of the King of the Skies. The powerful Wedgetail Eagle which features as an absolutely suitable symbol on the "Eagle"

Dalwhinnie label, which is their ultimate and most powerful wine. 45 acres are now under vine planting began in 1976 after 3 years of careful planning, much of the 320 acre property is too rugged to plant. Legendary Viticulturist Keith Farnsworth also instrumental in the planting of Taltarni's vineyards, assisted the Jones Family in their

vineyards formative years.

David and his wife Jenny have recently purchased another property nearer to Moonambel and are developing a new vineyard, which could grow to 100 acres.

In 1985 Ewan, an architect, designed and built, with David, a beautiful cellar door with spectacular views of the vineyards and mountains.

The Shiraz, Cabernet Sauvignon, Pinot Noir and Chardonnay are all great wines and David's "Eagle" series a very limited specially packaged wines, usually Shiraz, is in the absolute top echelon of Australia's unique wines.

The name Dalwhinnie came from the Scottish Highlands where Davids late mother's family hailed, as well as one of Scotland finest malt whiskies, ironically her family · famous country grocers and wine merchants, the Ritchie family marketed wine under the Dalwhinnie label many years ago.

Make your way to Dalwhinnie, it's a soul enriching experience.

Address: RMB 4378 MOONAMBEL 3478	**Est:** 1976	**Vine Ha:** 26	**Cases:** 4,500	Dalwhinnie Chardonnay	8 yrs
Phone: (03) 5467 2388 **Fax:** (03) 5467 2237	**Public Hours:** 10am-5pm, daily			Dalwhinnie Pinot Noir	8 yrs
Email: dalwines@origin.net.au	**Principal Varieties:** Cabernet Sauvignon,			Moonambel Shiraz	10 yrs
Owner: D.K. and J.E. Jones	Chardonnay, Pinot Noir, Shiraz			Moonambel Cabernet	10-15 yrs
Winemaker: David Jones	**Principal Wines**		**Potential**	Eagle Series Shiraz	10-15 yrs

Blue Pyrenees

A renaissance in viticultural activity in the Pyrenees region occurred in 1961 when the French Cognac giant, Remy Martin, teamed with the Australian wine and spirit merchants, Nathan & Wyeth, to form Chateau Remy.

They chose a site on the open alluvial soils which had attracted thousands of gold seekers a century before and with access to a permanent unlimited water supply the company had chosen one of the most versatile cool climate locations within Australia to begin its winemaking activities.

Although the focus of operation in the early years was on brandy production, the company quickly realised the potential this vineyard site had for the production of premium table and sparkling wines and quickly the Chateau Remy label established itself as a leading Australian brand of Methode Traditionelle.

During the 1980's the company consolidated its holdings at this prime Avoca site. Change came quickly with massive vineyard expansion, the erection of a totally new winery and the construction of vast underground cellars. In 1996

the estate name changed to Blue Pyrenees with the concept being to reflect the characteristics of this unique Pyrenees location in the wines produced there.

To meet this Estate appellation, only sections of the vineyard were used where fruit consistently met strict flavour criteria. This fruit was used as the basis for the original 'Blue Pyrenees Reserve' - a Bordeaux style red, the Reserve Chardonnay and the exquisite Midnight Cuvee and Vintage Brut Methode Traditionelle sparkling wines, which now also appears under this distinctive label.

The Blue Pyrenees Estate Reserve range of wines undoubtedly represents the pinnacle of winemaking achievement so far in the evolution of this Estate. Their high quality is a reflection of both the nature of the Estate grown cool climate fruit, and the care and expertise with which it has been handled.

The beautifully fresh and delicate, "Midnight Cuvee" sparkling wine is a Blanc de Blanc style i.e. pre-dominantly estate grown, chardonnay with a touch of pinot noir, it has established a strong niche for itself in the quality end of the market.

In 2000 the company released a range of pure Pyrenees varietal wines carrying the Blue Pyrenees label. These wines represent that special combination of cool climate Pyrenees district vineyard characteristics and the winemaking skill to create wines where the true varietal character is regionally expressed. The range consists of a Chardonnay, Cabernet Sauvignon, Shiraz, Sauvignon Blanc and Merlot.

Blue Pyrenees Estate has more than 430 acres under vine and is one of the most exciting viticultural developments in Australia. Moreover, with its picturesque location, nearby waterfalls and lookout, and surrounded by extensive gardens. Its award winning visitors centre is also becoming an increasingly popular visitor and tourist destination.

There is now also a restaurant on site or you can use the barbeque facilities, there are some wonderful bush walks at your doorstep or you could try your hand at the ancient French bowls game of Petanque.

Blue Pyrenees Estate is a mecca of culture in a breathtakingly beautiful natural setting.

Address: Vinoca Road AVOCA 3467	Est: 1963 Vine Ha: 185 Cases: 100,000	Blue Pyrenees Reserve Red	8-10 yrs
Phone: (03) 5465 3202 Fax: (03) 5465 3529	Public Hours: 10am-5pm, daily	Blue Pyrenees Reserve Chardonnay	3-5 yrs
Email: ken.field@bluepyrenees.com.au	Principal Varieties: Cabernet Sauvignon,	Blue Pyrenees Cabernet Sauvignon	4-7 yrs
WWW: www.bluepyrenees.com.au	Chardonnay, Merlot, Pinot Meunier, Pinot	Blue Pyrenees Shiraz	4-7 yrs
Owner: Remy Cointreau	Noir, Sauvignon Blanc, Shiraz, Viognier	Blue Pyrenees Chardonnay	2-4 yrs
Winemaker: Greg Dedman & Stuart Bourne	Principal Wines Potential	Fiddlers Creek Wines	2-4 yrs

Fiddlers Creek

The Pyrenees region is rich in gold mining history and was a hive of industry in the middle of the 19th century. In fact, from 1852 to 1864, records show that 624,115 ounces of gold were mined, valued at 2,496,000 pounds.

Fiddler's Creek winds its way down across the plains just to the north of the Blue Pyrenees Estate and was named after two musically inclined miners who discovered a significant gold reef. They tried to disguise their find, but were heard in the still of the night playing their fiddles for joy at their new found riches.

Fiddler's Creek has been appropriately chosen to label a second source of wines produced by Blue Pyrenees. Fruit sourced from premium Australian Wine regions to supplement that grown on the estate to produce a range of quality varietal wines that are marketed at good value prices. The selection includes a Chardonnay, Shiraz/Cabernet and a Cabernet Merlot.

Blue Pyrenees Varietals

Great wines start in the vineyard with the pursuit of a unique and premium Pyrenees character. This philosophy does not stop at the production of Reserve wines but also forms the cornerstone in the production of their range of "Pure Pyrenees" Varietal wines, and relates to the insistence on using only the most select Pyrenees district and Estate grown fruit for these wines.

The Blue Pyrenees Varietals wines represent that special combination of widely acclaimed cool climate Pyrenees district vineyard characteristics and the winemaking skill to create wines where the true varietal character is best expressed. The range consists of Chardonnay, Cabernet Sauvignon, Shiraz, Merlot and Sauvignon Blanc.

Kara Kara

Hungarian Steve Zsignond and his Mauritian wife Marlene have a definite flair for hospitality, they host many banquets and other functions at their gorgeous Estate, located on a ridge of the Pyrenees Mountain range alongside native bushland not far south of the town of St Arnaud.

Continuing the French connection in the Pyrenees region, the mining town that grew up during the gold rush in 1855 was later named St. Arnaud, honouring the victorious allied leader of the Crimea, Marshall Jacques Lee Roy De St Arnaud.

Kara Kara, aboriginal name, meaning "Gold Quartz" was the name of the surrounding farmland and local shire. Kara Kara was in the heart of the Gold mining rush of the mid 1800's and the "Poppet Head" used in mining features on their label.

Steve is a hard working fastidious Vigneron, he and Marlene began planting vines on the property in 1977. After selling their grapes to other wineries for a number of years they decided to produce their own wines from their Estate vineyards, their first wines were vintaged in 1991.

Marlene carves on the French tradition so strong in the Pyrenees, she was born and bought up in the island of Mauritius a former French

colony. She is passionate about her food and wine and puts on regular banquets, featuring her French inspired Cuisine for guests.

Each event has a theme they have ranged from a traditional "Mauritian" banquet to celebrate the release of their 1998 wines to a real touch of the Follies Bergere and the Moulin Rouge for the Parisian Café style banquet for the 1999 release.

During my visit to the winery they were busy finishing off the Cellar, which has been, dug into the Hillside below the Cellar door looking out over the vines and the rolling Hills

of the Pyrenees Ranges.

The 1999 Sauvignon Blanc impressed me with its lifted tropical style, melon like flavours and a real honey like finish. The 1998 Chardonnay, a Gold Medal winner had loads of stonefruit with honey and some hazelnut/cashew nuttiness. The 1998 Shiraz Cabernet I also found exceptionally complex and interesting.

Steve and Marlene's two sons, Andrew and Steven have both joined the company and the future of Kara Kara looks as if it will be in good hands.

Address: Sunraysia Highway REDBANK 3478
Phone: 5496 3294 **Fax:** 5496 3294
Email: kara@ruralnet.net.au
WWW: www.pyrenees.org.au/karakara
Owner: Marlene & Steve Zsigmond

Winemaker: Steve Zsigmond & John Ellis
Est: 1977 **Vine Ha:** 8 **Cases:** 2,500
Public Hours: 10am-6pm, daily
Principal Varieties: Chardonnay, Semillon, Cab Sauvignon, Sauvignon Blanc, Shiraz

Principal Wines	Potential
Kara Kara Vineyard Estate Chard	4-6 yrs
Kara Kara Sauvignon Blanc	Drink Now
Kara Kara Vineyard Estate Semillon	8 yrs
Kara Kara Vineyard Shiraz Cabernet	5-8 yrs

Mount Avoca Vineyard

Melbourne Stockbroker John Barry and his wife Arda established a vineyard near Avoca in the Pyrenees in 1970 after a long search for a suitable spot to begin a premium boutique wine business. The first crops were sold to other wineries with the 1976 vintage being the first released under the Mount Avoca label although made off site, a winery was built in time for the 1978 vintage it has since been expanded and improved the winemaker is now Matthew Barry Johns son, who has a degree Microbiology from Monash University, he is both extremely talented and extremely energetic and passionate in his work.

The Mount Avoca vineyards supply all the grapes for their domain bottled wines (as they also have their own sophisticated bottling wine). The vineyard area has now grown to 60 acres and the 3,000 case production in 1978 has now grown to 18,000 cases which is the level the Barrys feel is perfect for top premium wines.

In 1998 Mount Avoca released a white under the Trioss label a blend of estate grown Sauvignon Blanc, Chardonnay and Semillon, its crisp, refreshing with leads of flavour and at a great value price its proved very popular with the critics and Cellar door visitors alike. This café range also includes a Trioss Red.

Mount Avoca's main range includes Sauvignon Blanc, Chardonnay, Shiraz and Cabernet Sauvignon.

In recent years a Reserve Range has been added. These are wines of exceptional quality, are released in outstanding years only and are limited in number to between 100 and 500 dozen. Each bottle is numbered.

The Reserve Range includes Merlot, Shiraz, Cabernet Sauvignon and a bottle aged Semillon. (A special limited release of a 1994 for the Millennium celebrations is a great wine to search out).

The pinnacle of Mount Avoca's wines is "Arda's Choice" which is a truly exceptional wine limited to 200 dozen packed in wooden boxes. To date it has only been released in 1992 and 1996. A number of Reserve wines are also available in magnums.

Mount Avocas best red is released under Arda's choice label which is packed in wooden boxes and released only in exceptional years.

Arda Barry is an architect by profession and she has designed the splendid buildings at Mount Avoca which included an impressive Rotunda with views over the vineyard there are also picnic tables and an electric barbecue visitors are welcome to cook their own BBQ whilst looking out over the vines you an even purchase a cheese platter at a modest price and wine by the glass. There is also a French Pétanque pitch which makes for a great after lunch game.

In 1973 a 4 acre olive grove was planted, and Mount Avoca now produce a superb cold pressed extra virgin olive oil and herbed olives which are available at the Cellar Door.

Mount Avoca is a superb estate producing great wines with exceptional care and enjoying deserved success.

Matthew Barry has also created an excellent web site (address below) that is often updated, it's worth checking out.

Address: Moates Lane AVOCA 3467
Phone: (03) 5465 3282 **Fax:** (03) 5465 3544
Email: info@mountavoca.com
WWW: www.mountavoca.com **Est:** 1970
Owner: The Barry Family **Vine Ha:** 24

Winemaker: Matthew Barry **Cases:** 16,000
Public Hours: 9am-5pm, weekdays; 10am-5pm, weekends & public holidays
Principal Wines
Mount Avoca Reserve Cabernet Franc

Mount Avoca Reserve Merlot
Mount Avoca Sauvignon Blanc
Mount Avoca Reserve Cabernet
Mount Avoca Reserve Shiraz
Mount Avoca Reserve Semillon

Redbank

Neill Robb worked at various wineries in South Australia before taking a position as Champagne-maker at Chateau Remy in 1970. In 1973 Neill left Chateau Remy to develop his own vineyard and winery at Redbank, in the Pyrenees region of Western Victoria, at the same time consulting on the development of Yellowglen and Bannockburn.

Neill and his wife, Sally, planted 45 acres of vines and, using local century-old red bricks, built their steep-gabled winery and colonial-style home. Redbank named after the small town three kilometres to the north, is a credit to the Robb's, being both elegant and distinctly Australian.

As well as their own grapes Redbank processes other high quality fruit, brought in from growers around Central and Western Victoria. It is Neill's policy to process each load of fruit separately. The best known Redbank wine from their own grapes is the blend of cabernet sauvignon, shiraz, malbec, merlot and cabernet franc named 'Sally's Paddock'. This is an extremely well-structured red wine, with intense colour, flavour and adequate but soft tannins, it ages extremely well. Several years ago, Neill and Sally introduced a range of wines under the Redbank 'Long Paddock' label, sourced from cool regions of south-eastern Australia.

These wines represent excellent value for money and solve the shortage of wine, often a difficulty for the Robb's and provides a valuable export wine alternative.

Address: REDBANK 3478	Est: 1973 Vine Ha: 20 Cases: 55,000	Principal Wines	Potential
Phone: (03) 5467 7255 Fax: (03) 5467 7248	Public Hours: 9am-5pm, Mon-Sat;	Sally's Paddock	10-20 yrs
Email: neillrobb@bigpond.com	10am-5pm, Sun	Long Paddock	2-5 yrs
WWW: www.redbankwines.com	Principal Varieties: Cabernet Sauvignon,	Goldmine Series	5-10 yrs
Winemaker: Neill & Sally Robb	Shiraz, Cabernet Franc, Pinot Noir	Mountain Forge Hundred Tree Hill	5-10 yrs

St Ignatius

Enrique and Silvia Diaz have put together with their own hands a beautiful boutique winery and planted their own vineyards, on the Sunraysia Highway 4 1/2 kilometres South of Avoca.

Enrique's winemaking heritage has followed him over 3 continents, his great grandfather Fernando was a winemaker in the Reggio Emilia - Parma Region in Italy, he migrated to Argentina where he also made wine. Enrique and Silvia migrated to Australia, they chose a site to plant vines near where a group of Frenchmen discovered gold in 1859, creating the famous "Clare Castle" gold rush. They started planting in 1992, today the vineyard has grown to 20 acres and is planted to Shiraz, Cabernet Sauvignon, Sauvignon Blanc, Chardonnay, Merlot and Sangiovese.

On the 6th March 1999, their new Winery - Cellar door and hospitality centre opened its doors, designed by Silvia who is an architect by profession, its high roof and wide verandahs providing a cool environment in summer and an ideal place to enjoy the meals Silvia

prepares by appointment, with an Argentinean flair.

Enrique is an electronics engineer by profession and has designed and built much of the winemaking equipment, he is meticulous in his winemaking and on my visit I noticed his winery was spotlessly clean and well organised.

The wines at St Ignatius carry names connected with events in the region. Djarmbee is the name for their Shiraz - its aboriginal for friend - some of their other names are Hangmans Gully, Graveyard Hill, Clare Castle, Black Widow and Tango - a little South American touch.

The St. Ignatius wines certainly do justice to the Diaz's motto; "Vinum Amore Effectum" - we care about our wines with love and dedication - a visit to St Igantius is one that warms the soul.

Address: Sunraysia Highway AVOCA 3467	Est: 1992		Vine Ha: 8	Hangmans Gully (Cabernet Sav)	4-15 yrs
Phone: (03) 5465 3542 Fax: (03) 6465 3542	Cases: 700			Black Widow (Sangiovese)	4-15 yrs
Email: greatwines@telstra.easymail.com.au	Public Hours: 10am-5pm, daily			Clare Castle (Merlot)	4-15 yrs
Owner: Enrique & Silvia Diaz	Principal Wines		Potential	Tango (Premium Red Reserve)	4-15 yrs
Winemaker: Enrique Diaz	Djarmbee (Shiraz)		4-15 yrs	Graveyard Hil (Chardonnay)	1-4 yrs

Summerfield Wines

Ian Summerfield is a quiet achiever, he doesn't talk too much about what he's going to do, he just gets in and does it, his dogged persistence and goods sense of humour have got him past some pretty tough challenges. It's now over the thirty years since he first planted vines on the lower slopes of the majestic Blue Pyrenees Ranges. Every few years without fail he loses most of his crop to frost, but often in those years when his crops are so cruelly and drastically reduced, he creates some incredible red wines, that take all before them on the show circuit. Such a year was 1988 when he made a Shiraz that took 2 trophies. Since then countless medals and no less than 16 trophies have been awarded to Summerfield Wines.

Ian's son Mark has been part of a great team at Summerfield now for quite a number of years.

Although the first vines were planted in 1970, it was not until 1979 when a winery was built and Summerfield had its first vintage. It didn't take long for the accolades to come, the 1980 Shiraz was selected as the top wine in its price category in the Australian Newspaper's revered annual wine review.

The Summerfields have since built a characterful Cellar door from Bluestone and old bricks, it has a splendid solid Blackwood tasting bar and beautiful leadlight windows featuring bunches of grapes, the slate floor is from stone quarried from the nearby Donkey Hill.

On my visit there just before the 2000 vintage, Ian and Mark proudly showed me through their newly expanded and upgraded winery,

its hard to imagine the Summerfield wines getting any better, but it certainly looks like a distinct possibility.

If your looking for a great day out Summerfield is only two hours from Melbourne and they have excellent barbecue facilities with tables and benches under the trees, with the Pyrenees in the background.

If you feel like staying the night or even the weekend, they have a number of friendly and spacious homestead style units, beside the winery. With full kitchen facilities, beautifully decorated and furnished, they are in the centre of the region at Moonambel and ideally located for you to come and go on your discovery tours.

If you enjoy great wine and hospitality without the fuss, Summerfield is your place and your wine.

Address: RMB 4355 Main Road MOONAMBEL 3478	Winemaker: Ian & Mark Summerfield	Sauvignon Blanc, Merlot, Shiraz	
	Est: 1979	Principal Wines	Potential
Phone: (03) 5467 2264 Fax: (03) 5467 2380	Cases: 3,500	Reserve Shiraz	10 yrs
Email: sumerfld@origin.net	Public Hours: 9am-5:30pm, daily	Reserve Cabernet	10 yrs
Owner: Ian Summerfield	Principal Varieties: Cabernet Sauvignon,	Shiraz	8 yrs

Taltarni

Taltarni was purchased by Mr John Goelet in 1972 after a 3-year search of the worlds finest wine regions, looking for a site where wines similar to those of Bordeaux in France could be made. The property encompasses 1,750 acres. Between 1972 and 1975, the original 90 acre vineyard was expanded to 275 acres. Currently there are 340 acres with plans for even more plantings.

The site chosen is nestled in a natural sheltered amphitheatre at the western end of the Pyrenees region. The climate is cool, somewhat continental Mediterranean. The soils are well-drained sandy loam, interspersed with broken down quartz. The mature cabernet sauvignon, merlot, cabernet franc and shiraz vines are producing wines of finesse, complex character and distinctive regional characteristics. The flagship Cabernet Sauvignon, first vintaged in 1977, is always firm and full and one of the best premium Australian reds to put down for the long haul. The merlot/cabernet is more supple and approachable younger, Taltarni also now produce a silky smooth straight merlot and a traditional peppery shiraz. The whites at Taltarni have always been wonderful. They virtually pioneered sauvignon blanc and certainly produce the most consistently good version of this racy variety in Australia, it's also certainly more affordable than many versions of the variety.

Taltarni have just released two great blended wines which are refined versions of their former Blanc and

Reserve de Pyrenees wines. The Fiddleback is a native gum surrounding the Taltarni vineyards its special grain makes it sought after by artisans who work in wood. Under the distinctive label are a white - a blend of chardonnay, chenin blanc, sauvignon blanc and riesling, the inaugural 2000 vintage shows an intense tropical bouquet with zesty lemon, apple and pear on the palate, it's soft creamy texture certainly makes it a moorish drop.

The 1999 Fiddleback red is made from classic estate grown red varieties with subtle oak maturation, it's vibrant ripe berry aromas and flavours are underpinned by notes of cedar and vanilla with soft tannins, its mellow style makes it very approachable for drinking now or

over the next year or two.

Taltarni have long produced superb sparkling, fully bottle fermented. Their Classic Taltarni Brut has a blended base of chardonnay, pinot noir and pinot meunier from their Pyrenees vineyards and their Clover Hill vineyards in Northern Tasmania, they established in 1986. They also produce a Brut Taché with a touch of salmon pink colour.

Taltarni also make one of Australia's best dry Rosés from shiraz and malbec. Its bright neon pink colour and vibrant refreshing fruit make it the ideal summertime meal accompaniment. The Moonambel weather is usually very dry in Autumn but in 1999 an unusual rainstorm and the humid conditions that followed brought the "Noble Rot" botrytis to the grapes on their mature riesling vines. The have created their first botrytised wine a 1999 Late Harvest riesling, it's a real concentrated cracker!!

Taltarni host and sponsor a number of events each year at the winery and in the region. Their Easter Harvest Picnic is a winner, as is their Taltarni Cup race day in October at the Avoca racecourse on the Saturday, followed by a traditional Recovery Day celebration including music at the winery on Sunday. Taltarni also sponsor events of that ancient French bowls game "Petanque" on the Avoca "Piste".

Taltarni have reason to celebrate, in the words of World Wine Authority Robert Joseph it's "one of the most beautiful vineyards on the planet".

Warrenmang

The Warrenmang vineyard planting began in 1974 but it was not until the mid-1980's under the dynamic drive of restaurateurs, Luigi and Athalie Bazzani, that things really began to happen. Warrenmang's Restaurant is now one of Victoria's most celebrated vineyard resorts, set high on a hill, overlooking the vineyards and valleys of the Pyrenees. Its restaurant, recipient of numerous awards has achieved Hall of Fame status plus star rating in the Age Good Food Guide for the past 10 years.

Recently Luigi was awarded "The Age newspaper's Special Award for Professional Excellence". This prestigious annual award recognises an individual's outstanding contribution to the restaurant scene in Victoria. The Age went on to describe Luigi's achievements "The Doyen of Victoria's Country Restaurateurs, Luigi Bazzani has exemplified the highest standards of hospitality for nearly 3 decades. He founded the Copper Pot in Bendigo and La Scala in Ballarat, both the best provincial restaurants at their time. Now he runs the outstanding Warrenmang "unquestionably Victoria's finest Vineyard Resort". He has been honored by the "Wine & Food Society of Australia" for his "Distinguished personal contribution and consistent emphasis on excellence in the elevation of standards of Food and Wine".

The menu at Warrenmang varies with the seasons and is always innovative with such dishes as Roasted Redbank Pheasant on truffle scented potato puree with fresh figs and grapes followed by Roasted Pear Tatin with Bluecheese Icecream!!

Guests can enjoy outdoor dining in the summer on the spacious sundeck overlooking the vines - and in winter there is always a roaring log fire.

When Luigi created the restaurant in 1989 he knew that guests would find it hard to leave the warm inviting atmosphere and the wonderful surroundings so he built a charming little wine village of cottages and chalets where guests could retire after savouring the pleasures of his table.

Today the Resort has four different styles of accommodation, from cosy attic style cottages to luxury penthouse suites, all with sensational views of vineyards, valleys and typical Australian bushland.

Warrenmang also has a separate, fully equipped conference centre for 100 delegates with two tennis courts, swimming pool, an indoor/outdoor heated hot tub in a unique location overlooking the vines and a large barbecue pavilion.

The Warrenmang wines are led by the Grand Pyrenees, a huge opulent red blend - mainly merlot and cabernets, plus the multi award winning Shiraz which has gained much acclaim Australia wide and overseas. Robert Parker assessed the wine at 96/100 resulting in a flood of orders from around the world. Warrenmang recently released "Luigi Riserva" in the Italian tradition of refermenting an old wine (a cabernet/merlot blend 1991) with a young wine (1997 shiraz) with the resultant 1991 - 1997 blend giving the best of both worlds. James Halliday says it is one of the most unusual wines ever released in Australia and rated it at 97/100.

Recent acquisition of the Mountain Creek Vineyard has seen the addition of Sauvignon Blanc and a 100% Cabernet to the Warrenmang wine list. But it is the Black Puma from his experimental vineyard in Avoca in which Luigi Bazzani takes most pride - it is big, black rich, but soft and inviting Shiraz which was released in 2000 to much acclaim and which sold out within a matter of weeks. The late harvest traminer and the 'Bazzani' label wines including a vintage port are all popular styles produced at the vineyard. Visitors can enjoy complimentary wine tours and tastings daily, with the added bonus for houseguests of 20% discount off wine purchases.

The Resort was named winner of the Goldfields Tourism Award (wineries category) in 2000 and 2001.

Address: Mountain Creek Road MOONAMBEL 3478	Winemaker: Simon Clayfield	Principal Wines	Potential
	Est: 1974 Cases: 7,000	Warrenmang Grand Pyrenees	10+ yrs
Phone: (03) 5467 2233 Fax: (03) 5467 2309	Public Hours: 10am-5pm, daily	Warrenmang Estate Shiraz	10-15 yrs
Email: mail@pyreneeswines.com.au	Principal Varieties: Barbera, Cab Franc, Cab	Black Puma 100% Avoca Shiraz	10-15 yrs
WWW: www.bazzani.com.au	Sav, Chard Traminer, Dolcetto, Merlot, Pinot	Warrenmang Estate Chardonnay	5+ yrs
Owner: Luigi and Athalie Bazzani	Grigio, Sauv Blanc, Nebbiolo, Sangiavese, Shiraz	Warrenmang Estate Cabernet	5+ yrs

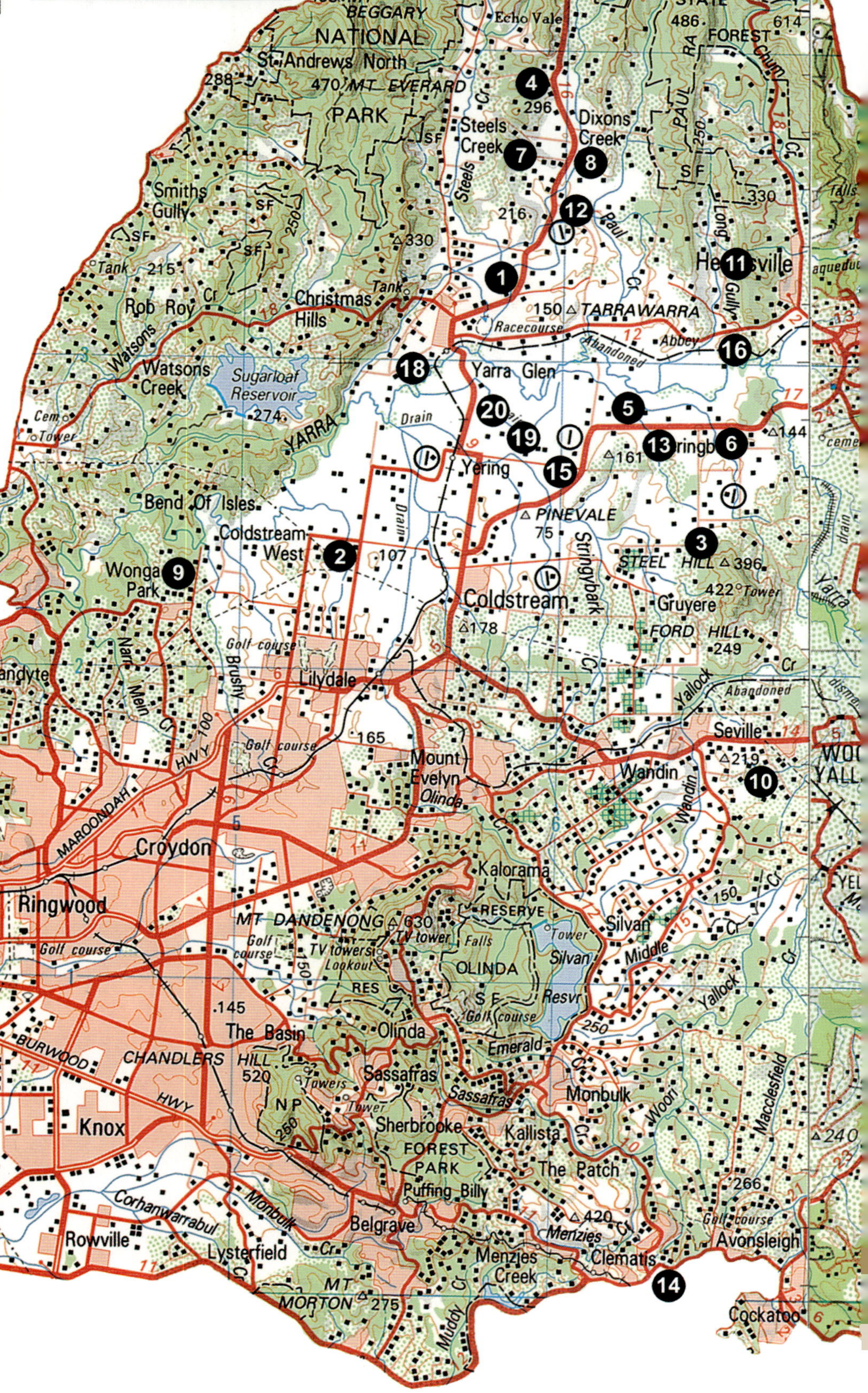

Yarra Valley - VIC

1. Andrew Garrett
2. Bianchet Winery
3. Coldstream Hills
4. Debortoli Winery
5. Domaine Chandon
6. Eyton on Yarra
7. Fergusson Winery
8. Henkell Vineyards
9. Kellybrook Winery
10. Lillydale Vineyards
11. Long Gully Estate
12. Lovey's Estate
13. Oakridge Estate
14. Paternoster
15. St Huberts Vineyard
16. Tarrawarra Estate
17. Yarra Burn Hoddles Creek
18. Yarra Ridge Vineyard
19. Yarra Valley Dairy
20. Yering Station

Yarra Valley

The history of wine in Australia has an amazing way of repeating itself. Fashions n taste change, economic conditions and the scourges of nature take their toll, but the truly great wines and vineyards that bear them will always re-emerge. Such is the history of the Yarra Valley in Victoria. The district is situated around the towns of Lillydale, Yarra Glen and Healesville with some vineyards in the outer suburbs of Melbourne.

Vines were first planted in the Yarra Valley around 1840 by William Ryrie, a farmer who came south from New South Wales in search of good land. This district, however, blossomed with the Swiss settlers who were encouraged to emigrate to Victoria by Sophie, wife of the first Governor of Victoria, Charles La Trobe. Sophie was the daughter of the Swiss Counsellor of State and was well-connected, mixing in circles which included the brothers Hubert and Paul de Castella, ancestors of our famous marathon runner, Robert de Castella. Hubert founded St. Hubert's Winery in 1854 and another of his countrymen, Baron de Pury, founded Yerinberg in 1862.

These Swiss pioneers were well versed in winemaking and viticulture and had a great influence on the growth and success of the area as a wine-producing district. St. Hubert's Winery won the German Emperor's Grand Prize for the Best Australian Wine Exhibitor in the Great Melbourne Exhibition in 1880, for which the grand Exhibition Buildings in Melbourne were built. The prize reflected the ideal wine-growing conditions of the area.

Vineyard areas in the Yarra Valley expanded rapidly and by the late 1860's they covered around 150 hectares. By 1890, Victoria produced almost 60 percent of Australia's wine - more than all the other states combined.

Unfortunately, around this time, tastes changed and fortified wines became the fashion. The lack of knowledge about bacterial spoilage meant, too, that bad wines abounded, as fortification became the norm. Cool climate, low-yielding areas that produced fine table wines, such as the Yarra Valley, died out and by the early part of the 20th century, most vineyards in the Yarra had ceased operating. The last vintage was at Yeringberg in 1921.

It is often thought that the vine louse, phylloxera, was responsible for the demise of the Yarra Valley, but surprisingly it was one of the few areas in Victoria not attacked and decimated by this disease. The re-birth of the Yarra Valley came more than 40 years after that last vintage in 1921.

There is a certain rivalry between the new pioneers as to who was actually the first in the renaissance. However, I feel the honour should be shared. In 1963, Reg Egan, a Melbourne solicitor, set up residence and started a small vineyard of several hectares in the outer Melbourne suburb of Wantirna South. Now he crushes about 15 tonnes each vintage. Although a little south of the Yarra region proper, I feel this is rightly classified as a Yarra Valley vineyard. A little north of Wantirna Estate is Kellybrook in the suburb of Wonga Park. Darren Kelly founded his enterprise in 1962 and made both still and sparkling wines from apples grown in his orchard; today the vines vastly outnumber the apple trees. In the 1960's renowned winemaker Dr John Middleton also began growing vines and making wines as a hobby.

The true renaissance started in the Yarra Valley in 1968/69 when St. Hubert's Yarra Yering, Fergussons and Yeringberg all got underway with planting. They were followed closely by Chateau Yarrinya (now de Bortoli's) and Seville Estate in 1971 and more lately by Yarra Burn and Warramate in 1976. Many other ventures have been successfully launched since. Chief among them is Domaine Chandon, the offshoot of the French Möet and Chandon Champagne company. This venture started a wine tourism bonanza with many wineries building restaurant, galleries and other hospitality adjuncts. These include the fabulous Yering Station complex, the state of the art Eyton on Yarra, the restaurant at Lillydale Vineyards, Fergussons were certainly in the forefront of this move, today the visitor to the Yarra Valley is extremely well catered for.

Wine tourism has gripped the Yarra, the annual Grape Grazing in March sees this at its zenith with wine, food and music pumping out. Many excellent restaurants and cellar door hospitality areas each week attract thousands of keen wine drinkers, from all corners of the world. The Yarra Valley is once again a wine mecca.

Coldstream Hills

Coldstream Hills began its life with lofty ideals in a lofty location high on the slopes of Steel Hill with sweeping panoramic views over the Yarra Valley.

Highly respected wine writer and winemaker James Halliday planted vines in 1985 in this spectacular north-facing amphitheatre.

In 1996 James merged with a large wine company. James is as ever deeply involved and active on a day to day basis with all aspects of his beloved Coldstream Hills.

The vineyard came into production and a winery was constructed for the 1988 vintage. The 1986 and 1987 vintages were made off-site, these vintages amassed 5 trophies, 12 gold, 6 silver and 8 bronze medals from only 39 entries attesting to James Halliday's skill as a winemaker.

The wines at Coldstream Hills have continued to win a huge number of trophies and medals as the vines mature.

The vineyards all closely planted on carefully chosen hilly microclimates surrounding the winery, also at Briarston, Gladysdale near Hoddles Creek and the Fernhill Vineyard.

With over 230 acres of vines most of the wines are made from estate grown grapes, a huge quality advantage.

The Coldstream Hills winery, perched above the vineyards has been expanded and includes a classy cellar door that is now open 7 days a week.

Coldstream Hills produce award winning Chardonnay, Sauvignon Blanc, Pinot Noir, Cabernet Sauvignon, Cabernet Merlot, a red Bordeaux blend "Briarston" and three Reserve Wines, Reserve Chardonnay, Reserve Pinot Noir and Reserve Cabernet Sauvignon. Rigorous selection produces some of Australia's finest wines of which James Halliday can be justly proud.

Eyton on Yarra

The Eyton on Yarra Winery and Restaurant is situated on Maroondah Highway at Coldstream.

The winery, cellar door, restaurant and surrounding acres of vines are the realisation of the vision of Yarra Valley grazier, the late Newell Cowan and is one of the premier winery and restaurant complexes in the country.

The winery took its name from the Cowan's "Eyton on Yarra" property, which was originally established by the Syme Family - of publishing fame - in the mid 1880's.

In the late 1980's he saw an opportunity to plant vines on the land, and, not a man to do things by halves, subsequently acquired the nearby Coldstream Winery. At this point, shortly after his 80th birthday, he decided to take the grape growing process one step further and

produce the wine as well.

Grapes from 120 acres of vines grown on the two Eyton on Yarra properties go to make the stylish wines. With the unique and distinctive regional fruit character of

the Yarra Valley. They comprise a pinot chardonnay methode champenoise, a chardonnay, a cabernet merlot, a reserve shiraz, a sauvignon blanc and a pinot noir. The Eyton on Yarra Winery and Restaurant is a visitor-oriented winery offering fine food and premium wines in a relaxed and inviting environment. A spiral staircase rises from the centre of the open plan restaurant to a platform giving viewing access over the working winery and Eyton tower which provides magnificent views across the vineyards and the Yarra Valley.

It is an absolute must to visit this Rolls Royce winery. Newell's daughter Deidre has assembled a great team under her and runs a very professional operation.

Address: Corner Maroondah Highway & Hill Rd COLDSTREAM 3770	**Est:** 1995 **Vine Ha:** 50	Eyton Chardonnay	5 yrs
	Cases: 10,000	Eyton Pinot Noir	5 yrs
Phone: (03) 5962 2119	**Public Hours:** 10am-5pm, daily	Eyton Cabernets	6-8 yrs
Fax: (03) 5962 5319	**Principal Varieties:** Chardonnay, Pinot Noir,	NDC Shiraz	6-8 yrs
Email: eytonwines@doncaster.starway.net.au	Cabernet Sauvignon, Merlot, Sauvignon Blanc	Dalry Road Chardonnay	Now
Winemaker: Matt Aldridge	**Principal Wines** **Potential**	Dalry Road Pinot Noir	Now

De Bortoli Yarra Valley

One of the largest and most successful family wine businesses in Australia is De Bortoli. It has risen from virtual obscurity to a prominent respected position in the premium wine industry in less than a decade.

The company's foundation goes back to 1928, four years after Vittorio De Bortoli arrived in the Riverina area of New South Wales from his homeland in northern Italy. Vittorio and his hard working wife, Giuseppina, established a 22 hectare vineyard at Bilbul and eight years later, were making 550,000 litres of wine per year. The original vats and winery are now housed inside the giant complex at Bilbul. De Bortoli really arrived on the wine map when winemaking dynamo Darren, Vittorio's grandson, made a botrytised semillon sauterne-style dessert wine in 1982. It took the wine world by storm, becoming one of the most awarded wines in Australia's history. The Noble One is a sensational wine each year. After a long search for a contrasting cool climate vineyard and winery, the family purchased Miller's Chateau Yarrinya vineyard and winery in 1987.

The vineyards have been dramatically expanded by De Bortoli, as has the winery which is partially underground. A separate winery building was constructed in 1995 and the vineyard expansion continues. The winemaking is in the capable hands of Steve Webber, who worked for a time at Lindeman's (Rouge Homme) in Coonawarra. Steve is married to Chief Executive Deen De Bortoli's daughter Leanne, who runs the showpiece restaurant and hospitality centre on the hill above the winery. The restaurant is large and extremely professionally run, with the feel of a Tuscan bistro and very warm and friendly service. The restaurant also enjoys sweeping panoramic views over the vineyards and the mountain ranges in the distance.

The first crush in 1987 was only 30 tonnes; in 2000 this was elevated to 3,500 tonnes and future growth is planned. There are four labels produced at De Bortoli Yarra Valley. Melba takes pride of place among the red wines. Blended from the best parcels of red wine from each vintage, the wine is matured in the finest French oak, selection from these barrels ensures that Melba is an outstanding wine. De Bortoli Yarra Valley is a classic, elegant label with the range featuring Chardonnay, Pinot Noir, Shiraz and Cabernet Sauvignon. There is a new Yarra Valley label Gulf Station which has been produced as a result of the family's involvement with the National Trust. The De Bortoli vineyard was in early times the 'Summer Paddock' of historic Gulf Station and the very original label depicts the old homestead. Windy Peak is the very popular label which is a selection of wines made from grapes grown in premium Victorian regions. In 1997 De Bortoli was awarded the prestigious Jimmy Watson Memorial Trophy, the second for this vineyard.

De Bortoli is a well-founded, professional family business which does credit to the Yarra Valley and demands a visit.

Address: Finnacle Lane DIXONS CREEK 3775	**Winemaker:** Stephen Webber, David Slingsby-Smith & David Bicknell	Yarra Valley Cabernet Sauvignon 5-10 yrs
Phone: (03) 5965 2271 **Fax:** (03) 5965 2464		Yarra Valley Shiraz 5-10 yrs
Email: dbw@debortoli.com.au	**Public Hours:** 10am-5pm, daily	Yarra Valley Pinot Noir 5-10 yrs
WWW: www.debortoli.com.au **Est:** 1987	**Principal Wines** Potential	Gulf Station Cabernet Sauvignon 4-6 yrs
Owner: De Bortoli Family **Vine Ha:** 130	Melba Reserve 5-10 yrs	Gulf Station Riesling 4-6 yrs

Domaine Chandon

The world's largest champagne house, Moët & Chandon, is no stranger to the New World of Wine. It set up a superb Methode Traditionelle cellar and restaurant complex in the Napa Valley back in 1973 having already established cellars in Argentina, Brazil and Spain.

John Wright, President of the Californian operation, was very impressed with the potential of Australia for still and sparkling wine during visits he made in the mid 1980's. He convinced Moët & Chandon that they should invest in sparkling production in Southern Victoria.

Careful perfectionists in all they do, Moët chose top-flight oenologist Dr. Tony Jordan to head up its Australian venture. As soon as the sites in the Yarra Valley were chosen, vines were planted, but Tony had already made sparkling wine base material in 1986. The resulting sparkling wines were already lying on tirage as the contract for the Yarra Valley property was being signed - forethought and planning are a big part of Methode Traditionelle making.

Tony was assisted with blending in the early years by firstly, Edmond Maudiere (he has an uncanny resemblance to the monk Dom Perignon) and then Richard Geoffroy, both oenologists from Moët & Chandon.

The beautiful buildings housing the winery, sparkling wine tirage cellars, and the stunning tasting and hospitality area were completed in December 1990. The first wine, a 1986, was released to celebrate the occasion and to start the necessary cash flow. Moët at first saw only the local market as of interest and planned a total production of 50,000 cases. Local sales now exceed this.

Exports (under the Green Point by Chandon label) to Europe and Asia now account for 25 per cent of the production and over 100,000 cases are now produced. I am sure the future will see even bigger production.

Even in the days of modern

machinery and technology, methode traditionelle production is an art form, a mosaic, bringing together an enormous number of pieces like a giant jigsaw, which takes time and a great deal of human skill and effort. Apart from its own extensive Yarra Valley and Strathbogie Ranges vineyards, Domaine Chandon has a network of growers under contract, mainly in the cool regions of Victoria and also from Southern Tasmania and Coonawarra.

The base wines are all made separately, then comes the assemblage by the Chandon winemaking team, pulling the base wines together to form the cuvees for the secondary fermentation. For this exacting task, an absolutely tranquil environment is needed. The architects (Allen Jack & Cottier of Sydney) designed this assemblage room in a tower above the winery, absolutely isolated, where the winemaking team can concentrate 100 per cent on their work to find the perfect matches for the master cuvee for each of the various

Domaine Chandon blends.

Needless to say, the finished product celebrates the skill and experience of centuries of champagne making, combined with the innovation and skill of the Australian winemakers, not forgetting the great grapes that form the base of it all.

Domaine Chandon has quietly been producing limited quantities of still wines since 1990.

Now, because of export demand, still production has now become a significant part of the business. The still wines are released under the 'Green Point' (the historic name of the Yarra Valley property) label and the current range includes Chardonnay, Pinot Noir and Shiraz.

When you visit Domaine Chandon, you can sit in the vaulted tasting area with its spectacular view of the vineyards and mountains, and for a small fee, enjoy a crystal flute of any of the Domaine Chandon range with a delicious gourmet platter. What better way to celebrate a visit to the Yarra Valley?

Address: Green Point Maroondah Highway COLDSTREAM 3770
Phone: (03) 9739 1110 **Fax:** (03) 9739 1095
WWW: www.domainechandon.com.au

Owner: Moet Hennessy Group
Winemaker: Wayne Donaldson
Est: 1985
Vine Ha: 40

Cases: 100,000
Public Hours: 10.30am-4.30pm, daily
Principal Varieties: Chardonnay, Pinot Noir, Pinot Meunier

Fergusson Winery

Peter Fergusson planted vines on his property near Yarra Glen in 1968. The business has since become one of the most popular wineries in the Yarra Valley, with much to offer the visitor

Fergusson is owned and managed by Peter Fergusson and his wife Louise. Their excellent restaurant is housed in an attractive colonial-style building and features innovative country cuisine devised and prepared by Louise, a gold medallist at the Culinary Olympics and a graduate of La Varenne in Paris. In fact, she has released a superb cook book "The Beginning & End of Cooking" featuring Yarra Valley cuisine and wines of the region which is available

in the winery's Australiana shop and selected local wineries and book shops. Fergusson's menu includes fresh home-grown herbs and vegetables, local yabbies, mountain trout and farm cheeses which are made by Louise. The Fergusson's had a disastrous fire some years ago, and the entire restaurant area was destroyed only to be immediately rebuilt bigger and better. The hard work involved in establishing this award-winning tourist attraction has been carried over into the vineyard and winery.

The vineyard was initially planted to a majority of red grape varieties but expanded to include chardonnay and sauvignon blanc. Fergusson's have

both a black label Estate range and the more affordable Tartan range of Victorian wines plus a unique product called 'Winter Warmer'. Peter's training as an industrial chemist has helped him to be an innovative and successful winemaker.

The Fergusson Restaurant is constructed with solid native timbers. The antique spit in the huge fireplace does not remain idle and Peter Fergusson is a deft hand with the carving knife. The cathedral ceilings and refectory furniture add atmosphere to the many functions held at the winery and entertainment is often at hand. Hot air balloon rides leave the winery each day.

Address: Wills Road YARRA GLEN 3775	**Winemaker:** Chris Keys	**Principal Varieties:** Chardonnay, Shiraz,
Phone: (03) 5965 2237 **Fax:** (03) 5965 2405	**Est:** 1968 **Vine Ha:** 10 **Cases:** 5,000	Cabernet Sauvignon, Cabernet Franc, Merlot,
Owner: Fergusson Family	**Public Hours:** 11am-5pm, daily	Pinot Noir

Henkell Vineyards

Whilst Hans Henkell is reasonably new to the Yarra Valley his family's vinous roots go back to the 1830's just before the Yarra Valley's first vineyards were planted.

Hans is the great-great-grandson of Adam Henkell who began the Henkell sparkling wine empire in the heart of the Rhine Valley in Germany

ironically, not far from Switzerland where the wine pioneers of the Yarra Valley left for Australia.

Hans and his father Otto visited the Yarra Valley in 1980. Plans began which led to the development of Henkell vineyards. The cellar door is resplendent with memorabilia of the Henkell's wine tradition behind the

signature gates on the Melba Highway some seven kilometres past Yarra Glen. Henkell produce a range of wines, naturally including a sparkling wine and these can be tasted along with light meals.

Hans Henkell's bold venture certainly adds another cultural dimension to the Yarra Valley.

Address: Melba Highway DIXON'S CREEK 3775	**Est:** 1989	**Principal Varieties:** Cab Sav, Chardonnay,
Phone: (03) 5965 2016 **Fax:** (03) 5965 2016	**Public Hours:** 12pm-5pm, Wed-Sun	Pinot Noir, Sauvignon Blanc, Shiraz

Oakridge Estate

In 1978 Jim Zitzlaff began planting vines on a ridge above Windin in the South Eastern wing of the Yarra Valley. Several huge English Oak trees marked the entrance to the vineyard hence the name. Jim's son Michael joined the business and together the Zitzlaff's built their winery.

Oakridge were looking to expand but didn't have the suitable land and their grand vision required a considerable financial input. In 1997 Oakridge Estate formed a public company and moved to the Maroondah Highway at Coldstream, just up the road from Domaine Chandon, where they have planted further vineyards and built a splendid state of the art winery and hospitality complex. Here they host functions and exhibitions, also serving light lunches. It's a great

place to sit back and enjoy the creative cuisine, with a glass or two of fine Oakridge wine while enjoying the panoramic views of the valley.

Oakridge make two ranges of wine, their premium range inlcudes Sauvignon Blanc, Chardonnay, Cabernet Merlot, Pinot Noir, Shiraz and Merlot. Michael Zitzlaff also

makes an ultra premium Reserve Range, which regularly wins some of the worlds most prestigious wine awards.

Oakridge have certainly put together a beautifully integrated, professional operation and are quickly developing a fine reputation, world wide.

Address: 864 Maroondah Highway COLDSTREAM 3770	**Winemaker:** Michael Zitzliaff	Merlot	5-7 yrs
	Est: 1981 **Vine Ha:** 10 **Cases:** 25,000	Shiraz	5-7 yrs
Phone: (03) 9739 1920 **Fax:** (03) 9739 1923	**Public Hours:** 10am-5pm, daily	Sauvignon Blanc	1-2 yrs
Email: info@oakridgeestate.com.au	**Principal Wines** **Potential**	Pinot Noir	3-5 yrs
WWW: www.oakridgeestate.com.au	Chardonnay 3-5 yrs	Cabernet/Merlot	5-7 yrs

Lillydale Vineyards

Lillydale Vineyards began its life as part of the second wave of the vinous re-establishment of the Yarra Valley in 1976 when vineyards were planted in the southern part of the Yarra Valley, just off the Warburton Highway at Seville. The soil in this part of the valley is a rich red colour, formed by ancient volcanic action. Pinot noir and chardonnay seem to thrive in a cool climate and this soil type

The first white wines really made an impact in the early 1980's. An aromatic spicy gewurztraminer and a floral intense riesling became eagerly sought after. This was followed by a classic chardonnay of the finer-boned structure-melons and tropical fruit with a subtle almond nuttiness and a vanilla bean character, enhanced by judicious ageing in French oak. The pinot noir and the cabernet sauvignon with a touch of merlot were equally as impressive.

The quality and style of Lillydale's wines and it's beautiful outlook on the Warburton Ranges did not escape the notice of the McWilliam family wine company, anxious to expand into premium cool regions.

In 1994 McWilliam's Wines bought Lillydale Vineyards. Max McWilliam moved to live on site and take charge of the operation, which has since been expanded, both for production and a new cellar door, visitors centre and restaurant added.

Lillydale have pioneered a great concept in the Yarra Valley, taking a leaf out of the book of "Nibs" restaurant in Coonawarra, around the corner from their Brand's of Coonawarra Winery and co-founded by Jim Brand. The old schoolhouse was converted to a restaurant, where you cook your own food on the excellent grills and hotplates provided, with loads of great condiments at your finger tips. Lillydale vineyards have incorporated this concept into their restaurant and also feature a fabulous range of regional cheeses and great desserts.

The Lillydale wines are, if it is possible, getting even better with the maturing vineyards and the capital input of McWilliam's. The sauvignon blanc is a stunner and both the chardonnay and the cabernet merlot were named Best Victorian Wines in their respective categories.

When on your travels through the Yarra, you must drop in and try these exciting wines, and cook up a storm to go with them.

Address: Davross Court SEVILLE 3139
Phone: (03) 5964 2016 **Fax:** (03) 5964 3009
Email: mcwines@mcwilliams.com.au
Owner: McWilliam

Winemaker: Max McWilliam
Est: 1976 **Vine Ha:** 13
Public Hours: 11am-5pm, daily
Principal Varieties: Chardonnay, Merlot,

Cabernet Sauvignon, Sauvignon Blanc, Pinot Noir, Gewürztraminer
Principal Wines
"Lillydale Vineyards"

Long Gully

Reiner Klapp had an extremely successful electronics business. When colour television first came to the Australian market in the early 1970's, Reiner was at the forefront with the top selling German Brands, then the market leaders.

At the same time he bought a beautiful property in the Yarra Valley near Healesville at the apex of 'Long Gully', which runs between the Warburton Ranges and a smaller range of hills which divides it off from the main part of the Yarra Valley. Reiner and his delightful wife Irma, built a lovely weekend home in amongst a grove of trees. They ran a few horses and hereford cattle, but Reiner is not an idle person and he had heard of the vineyard revolution that was sweeping the valley, so it wasn't long before he planted vines.

The first vintage was in 1982 with a riesling. Today, Long Gully Estate is like a well-oiled German motor car. The vineyards are lush with substantial vines, but neatly trimmed. The winery is spotless, even during vintage, and a pretty Alsatian inspired Cottage forms and

ideal tasting and entertaining area.

Long Gully has been extremely successful in international wine shows. In 1993, they pulled off an incredible 'Coup' at Intervin, the New York/Toronto massive wine show held annually. The Long Gully wines entered, were their 1991 Merlot and 1991 Cabernet Sauvignon. 12,000 entries were fined down to 800 odd finalists. After rewarding several hundred gold, silver and bronze medals, 5 only trophies were issued. From this world's best selection, Long Gully won two of the 5, an incredible achievement!

Long Gully Estate make extremely good whites, including a chardonnay, semillon and a sauvignon blanc. Some years a sauvignon blanc/semillon blend is also made. The reds include award-winning pinot noir, shiraz, merlot and cabernet sauvignon. All the wines have very refined, almost European characters to them. The tannins in the reds are very fine.

In 1998 Long Gully in their usual innovative fashion made Australia's first "Icewine" a Reserve "Ice Riesling".

This traditional wine is made in Germany and in Canada - grapes are left on the vines until the heart of winter then picked and pressed frozen yielding a very concentrated wine, as the water frozen into ice crystals stays in the press with the grape skins. Although the Yarra Valley can get below freezing temperatures Long Gully have to also put the grapes into a fruit freezing cool store before pressing them, the results have been spectacular with the 1998, 1999 and 2000 vintages selling out quickly.

Long Gully have recently launched a second range of wines "The Victoria Collection" from premium Victorian regions. The labels feature four parts of a collage created by renowned artist Naomi Benheim, "The Twelve Apostles", "Yarra Valley Vineyards", "Melbourne City" and the "Mount Dandenong Ranges" with Puffing Billy.

Long Gully Estate is a class winery that is well worth seeking out. Look out for the Irma's Cabernet, which has received many gold medals - its great.

Address: Long Gully Road HEALESVILLE 3777	**Winemaker:** Peter Florance	Sav, Shiraz, Sauvignon Blanc, Pinot Noir,
Phone: (03) 9510 5798 **Fax:** (03) 9510 9859	**Est:** 1982 **Vine Ha:** 35 **Cases:** 25,000	Riesling, Semillon, Cabernet Franc, Malbec
Email: longgully@netspace.net.au	**Public Hours:** 11am-5pm, daily	**Principal Wines** **Potential**
WWW: www.longgullyestate.com	(except Christmas Day)	Long Gully Estate 5-15 yrs
Owner: R & I Klapp	**Principal Varieties:** Chardonnay, Merlot, Cab	Victoria Collection 2-5 yrs

Otto Wurth

Smallgoods are like wine; you simply cannot rush quality. There are very few things in this world that improve with aging. Wine is of course one, vintage cheeses another and quality smallgoods of various types another. All share in common, also the need for the best natural ingredients. This takes time and care to put in place.

Otto Wurth's motto is "good is not good enough". Otto arrived in Australia escaping the European depression in 1928 only to be thrown into our own depression. He managed to find two days a week as an assistant butcher with the firm of

Grobbeckers, later to become Austral Smallgoods.

In 1934 he started his own business, Otto Wurth, in Church Street, Richmond producing continental sausages by night and selling them from the basket off his bicycle by day. The "A" Model Ford followed a short time later and his first employee in the same year. His rapid expansion led to larger premises in Johnston Street, Fitzroy. In 1958 Otto Wurth moved to the Watson & Paterson site in Preston where the first smallgoods had been made in the 1860's.

Otto Wurth's range is wide, encompassing the wursts he first became famous for, continental sausages, salamis, mettwursts, cooked and cured meats of all types.

The most delicate wursts can happily be enjoyed with aromatic whites such as rieslings and sauvignon blancs, whilst the pastrami type meats go hand in hand with the biggest of reds and the multitude of delicacies in between can be matched by the myriad of fine wines Australia produces.

TarraWarra Estate

TarraWarra Vineyard is one of Australia's most picturesque wine Estate's. One enters via a tree line circular driveway mounting the steep knoll on which a winery of distinctive modern lines is located, above lawns and vines running down to a lake.

Owner Marc Besen established TarraWarra Vineyard in 1983 with the vision of creating world class pinot noir and chardonnays. The Vineyard's reputation for wines of classic magnitude was established beyond doubt when the 1991 TarraWarra Pinot Noir won Best Dry

Red in the Open Classes at the 1993 Royal Melbourne Wine Show - an unprecedented success for a pinot noir. The chardonnay is also in the rich, complex mould, with state-of-the-art equipment in the winery and top class oak being used innovatively and to perfection.

The fact that TarraWarra concentrates on these two classic Burgundian varieties contributes to their success in producing benchmark examples of Yarra Valley pinot noir and chardonnay - rated amongst the finest wines in Australia.

TarraWarra use only their own estate grown grapes. They also grow shiraz and merlot. Their vineyard holdings include 63 acres around the winery and their "Tin Cows" vineyard at Coldstream of 112 acres.

TarraWarra also have a second wine brand of excellent quality wines under the "Tin Cows" label. Two wines that have recently appeared under this label are the first shiraz and first merlot produced at TarraWarra.

Address: Healesville-Yarra Glen Road YARRA GLEN 3775	**Owner:** Marc Besen	TarraWarra Pinot Noir	5-7 yrs
	Winemaker: Clare Holloran	Tin Cows Chardonnay	3-5 yrs
Phone: (03) 5962 3311	**Est:** 1983 **Vine Ha:** 11 **Cases:** 10,500	Tin Cows Merlot	3-5 yrs
Fax: (03) 5962 3887	**Public Hours:** 10.30am-4.30pm, weekdays	TarraWarra Chardonnay	5-7 yrs
Email: enq@tarrawarra.com.au	**Principal Varieties:** Chardonnay, Pinot Noir	Kidron "Kosher" Chardonnay	2-3 yrs
WWW: www.tarrawarra.com.au	**Principal Wines** **Potential**	Tin Cows Pinot Noir	3-5 yrs

Yarra Burn Hoddles Creek

Established in 1975 by David and Christine Fyffe, the Yarra Burn winery is situated near the small rural town of Yarra Junction, just sixty kilometres north of Melbourne. The cool climatic conditions allow Yarra Burn to produce wines of distinctive varietal character, with the delicacy, elegance and intensity expected from the Yarra Valley.

Yarra Burn was part of the renaissance of the Yarra Valley, leading the way for the region's development as one of Australia's pre-eminent wine producing districts. Since its establishment Yarra Burn has achieved many firsts including releasing the first Yarra Valley Methode Champenoise product in 1985 and the first Australian Sauvignon Blanc Semillon blend in 1987.

Today Yarra Burn's award winning range of wines includes a sparkling, five table wines and two extremely limited release 'Bastard Hill' wines. The latter, a Chardonnay and a Pinot Noir, are produced from fruit sourced from a particular block in the famous Hoddles Creek vineyard. This block is affectionately known as 'Bastard Hill' by the harvesters who have to battle with its steep incline every vintage.

Attention to detail is paramount at all stages of production at Yarra Burn, and all winemaking and viticultural techniques are constantly reviewed and improved. Drip irrigation, soil and climate analysis and sophisticated trellis systems for canopy management all ensure that the grapes being produced are of the highest quality. Subsequently the expertise of the winemaking team, and careful oak selection guarantee that the fruit will be crafted into distinctive premium wines.

Amongst the picturesque setting of rugged mountain ranges and immaculate vineyards is the rustic Yarra Burn restaurant, built from convict-hewn bluestone slabs dating back to 1860. Fabulous country fare can be enjoyed while relaxing next to a huge blazing fire in winter, while the thick stone walls provide a welcome escape from the summer sun. The restaurant is open seven days a week and also caters for private and corporate functions.

Yarra Valley Dairy

The Yarra Valley has developed into one of Australia's Premier Wine Tourism regions; until several years ago there was always something missing, that was until Mary Mooney started the boutique cheesemaking facility, with a great café deli restaurant right in the heart of the region. Before this bold move it was always difficult to get a light meal and enjoy the fresh food produce of the Region, whilst in the Yarra Valley.

Mary with her family's help has turned an unassuming 100 year old milking shed into a food and wine mecca. A large range of French and Italian style cheeses are produced from the Friesian cows which graze on the property and from hand milked goats farmed in the nearby hills.

The seasonally changing menu features loads of fresh local foods along with the Yarra Valley Dairy's own cheeses.

You're likely to find fresh local pasta, locally baked breads, homemade spiced corned beef and relishes, local tapenade, sun dried tomatoes and capsicum.

The Mooneys also specialise in pastry dishes, tartlets, terrines and their own casseroles. Their cheesecake and layered pancakes with cream centres are superb.

The rustic decor and personal service at the Dairy are great and the views on all sides of the café are truly full of country charm. Don't miss this special place on your next visit to the Yarra Valley.

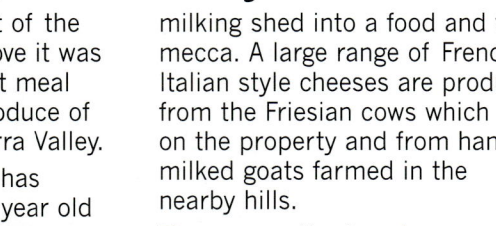

St Huberts

St Hubert's vineyard and winery was established in 1862 by Swiss wine pioneer Hubert de Castella. The wines achieved worldwide renown in 1881. They won the Emperor's Prize at the International Exhibition of that year. At one point there were 250 acres under vine and it was a premier vineyard of Australia with the cellars able to store over a million litres of wine.

The advent of cheaper table wines and the vogue for fortifieds from warmer areas saw the demise of the enterprise and the land reverted to grazing.

St Hubert's re-birth came in 1966 as one of the first Yarra Valley Renaissance Wineries. Now with a range extending from a sparkling Pinot Noir Chardonnay through to classic Yarra Valley Cabernet Sauvignon, St Hubert's reputation and the quality of their wines are once again on the very top rung of wine producers.

Yarra Ridge

Yarra Ridge now part of Beringer Blass Wine Estates, had a meteoric rise to fame since its inception in 1988 by Louis Bialkower, who for a number of years worked side by side with celebrated wine writer and fellow Yarra Valley vigneron James Halliday.

The vineyard is located in the foothills of the Christmas Hills, often referred to as the 'Yarra Ridge'. He planted five hectares to cabernet sauvignon, pinot noir and chardonnay with further plantings this grew to 50 acres by 1994. New varieties included merlot, cabernet franc and sauvignon blanc.

In 1993 Yarra Ridge purchased 100 acres of land near the Yarra Glen Racecourse which has been entirely planted.

The soils on all their Yarra Valley vineyards are the grey alluvial podsolic loams so eagerly sought after by 19th century vignerons such as Hubert de Castella, whose great grandson, Damien, is now Head Viticulturalist at Yarra Ridge.

Yarra Ridge believe strongly that quality improvements will come from the vineyard and have invested heavily in modern viticultural techniques such as the 'Scott Henry', the 'Geneva Double Curtain' and 'U' System trellises aimed at extra fruit and leaf exposure and keeping an air flow through the vines.

The Yarra Ridge wines have had unparalleled success on the Australian Wine Show circuit. The elevated tasting and hospitality area has panoramic views over the valley.

Yering Station

Yering Station is rich in history, vines were planted there by the Ryrie brothers in 1838. Donald, William and James Ryrie drove 250 head of cattle some 900 kilometres from Monaro in N.S.W and came upon the land during this journey.

They settled in the Yarra Valley two years before Melbourne was founded and planted the 600 vine cuttings they had brought with them. The brothers named the property Yering, the aboriginal name for the area. Their first wines were made in 1845 under the "Chateau Yering" label.

By 1850 an acre was under vine. At this time Yering Station covered over 30,000 acres, most of the Valley floor. Paul de Castella purchased the property in 1850, he contracted the winemaking services of Samuel de Pury and by 1860 had 51 acres under vine. In 1861 Yering won The Argus Gold Cup as Victoria's best vineyard. In 1889 Yering was awarded a "Grand Prix" at the Paris exhibition - the only one awarded outside the "Northern Hemisphere".

Unfortunately by 1896 tastes changed and premium table wines gave way to fortified wines. Paul Castella sold Yering and it reverted to a grazing property.

The Yarra Valley vineyard renaissance started in the late 1960's. The Rathbone family purchased the Yering property, the site of the

original vineyard in 1996. They have rejuvenated the vineyards which now cover 280 acres and embarked from this time on an ambitious expansion program which has seen a massive winemaking and hospitality complex built into the left bank of the Yarra River. The vaulted underground cellar is truly spectacular and has been used for large charity functions as well as for the maturation of their fast growing wine brands.

Yering Station has its own wine ranges made on site, these include Yering Station, Yarra Edge and Barak's Bridge, but there is also a strong French connection and a joint venture with the winemakers of Champagne Devaux produces a superb Methode Champenoise, Yarrabank.

The Wine Bar Restaurant and Function area sits on top of the Cellars and is constructed in truly

grand proportions, producing a long panoramic view of the valley with its high conservatory roof giving it a special spacious feel. Yering Station hosts many exhibitions and events. On the other side of the grand landscaped gardens near the entrance to the property, is the historic 140 year old wooden barn which has recently been restored, this heritage listed building is also used for exhibitions, large gatherings and a monthly farmer's market.

The original winery buildings at the northern end of the property now houses cellar door, a food and wine boutique and hosts art exhibitions with the entire commissions from the sales of art works being donated to the Leukaemia Auxiliary of the Royal Children's Hospital.

Yering Station's wines are made by Tom Carson, who has had plenty of top level Yarra Valley winemaking experience at Coldstream Hills. The wines are all excellent, I found their Cabernet Sauvignon superb. Yering Station has some interesting varieties planted including Petit Verdot, Viognier, Marsanne and Nebbiolo. Tom is assisted by Darren Rathbone and Dan Buckle, it's an energetic team getting great results.

Next door to Yering Station is the splendid Victorian home "Chateau Yering". Built in 1854, the original homestead is now one of Australia's finest country hotels, the drawing rooms are truly magnificent and Eleanore's Restaurant is top class.

Why not complete your visit to Yering Station by spoiling yourself with a night at Chateau Yering.

Address: 38 Melba Highway YERING 3770	Public Hours: 10am-5pm, daily	Chardonnay	5 yrs
Phone: (03) 9730 1107 Fax: (03) 9739 0135	Principal Varieties: Chardonnay, Pinot Noir,	Pinot Noir	5 yrs
Winemaker: Tom Carson	Merlot, Cab Sav, Cabernet Franc, Shiraz	Cabernet Merlot	8 yrs
Est: 1838 Vine Ha: 60	Principal Wines Potential	Pinot Noir Rosé E.D. Summer	

Woods Oldstyle Preserves

The proper use of condiments in creating truly great cuisine, is undoubtedly the greatest and most imaginative skill that anyone, from a great chef to the passionate amateur cook can employ. It takes their food out of the ordinary and turns it into something to marvel at.

Dianne Fitzpatrick grew up in a family passionate about food and her mother Thelma had an active hobby producing preserves mainly from her own mother's "secret" recipes. Some 20 years ago Dianne decided that her family's culinary jewels should not be hidden from the world any longer, thus was born Wood's Olde Style Preserves the name coming from her grandmothers family surname.

The business grew as did the product range extremely innovative creations from not only traditional vegetables, fruits, herbs and spices and nuts but also Australian native produce such as Lemon Myrtle, Mountain Pepperberry, Wild Lime, Quandong, Wattleseed, Illawarra Plums, Macadamia Nuts and many others, in fact the range now numbers almost 400 with 45 standard items and many exotic creations, each one fulfilling the diner's expectations. Combining quality product with innovative ideas and presentation is the key.

Chutney, pickles and relishes are usually served as accompaniments to hot and cold foods. They can also be used to add flavour to scrambled eggs, stuffing, sandwich filling, cottage cheese and savoury dips. They can also be added to stews and casseroles before cooking, sauces, marinades and glazes, cooked rice for savoury dishes and to all types of salad dressings. To provide a contrast in textures and colours amounts of dried fruits, nuts, fresh and dried herbs and spices are used. Chutneys originated in India, where their Hindu name, chatni, means "strongly spiced". They have been a familiar item in the West since the nineteenth century.

Relishes are 'mid-way' between pickles and chutneys. They can be sweet or sour, spiced or plain. The cooking time is shorter than for chutneys so ingredients tend to retain their shape.

Sauces are made in much the same way as chutneys, using similar ingredients, cooking salt and bottled vinegars. The long cooking concentrates the flavours and softens the texture, resulting in a condiment that is much darker and often more richly flavoured. Sauces have partnered all manner of foods since Roman times. The word sauce is derived from the Latin salsus meaning salty.

The sweet-sour flavour of fruit sauces, chutneys and relishes, makes them excellent partners for both game and rich meats such as duck, goose, turkey and pork. Thoughtful use of herbs and spices will often lift the condiment above the average.

Woods Preserves are seen in nearly all the great restaurants and culinary venues. The five main caterers at Stadium Australia during the Sydney 2000 Olympics used Wood's products in their cuisine. The Australian Golf Open and Presidents Cup, The Australian Tennis Open and the Australian Grand Prix caterers plus many others, all use Woods Preserves, and other products.

Wood's Products are available in their own three shops in Melbourne as well as Myer, David Jones and Daimaru and other quality food outlets.

Why not add that extra dimension to your food and wine enjoyment that Woods Preserves can help you create.

The first settlers of the new colony of Western Australia arrived in 1829 on the ship Parmelia, five years before the settlement of Victoria and South Australia.

Even before the official settlement of Perth, cuttings were planted near Fremantle and on Garden Island, but none survived. It was Charles McFaull who planted 300 cuttings at Hamilton Hill who became the state's first successful viticulturist.

In 1834, George Fletcher Moore planted the first vines in the Swan Valley, cuttings from the Cape of Good Hope in South Africa. The oldest continuously operating winery in Australia, Olive Farm, just near Perth's airport, was established in 1830 and is still going strong today. Olive Farm's founder, Thomas Walters became the first person to commercially market wine in Western Australia, but was closely followed by fellow Parmelia passenger, John Septimus Roe, the colony's first surveyor general, who founded Sandalford wines in 1840.

Many other areas of the south-west corner of the state were planted with vines in those early years, but commercially only the Swan Valley survived. The Swan Valley industry thrived and by the 1960's Western Australia was second only to South Australia in the number of wineries in the state. It was not, however, until the 1970's that the development boom in the Western Australian wine industry began.

This development was preceded by a report on the viticultural potential of a number of regions in the south west of the state by agricultural scientist, Dr John Gladstones. He highlighted a number of regions with great potential, Margaret River and Mount Barker amongst them.

A new experimental vineyard was planted by the Department of Agriculture at Forest Hill near Mount Barker in 1965. I well remember tasting two red wines made by Jack Mann at Houghton from the vineyard. That was back in 1972, the wines were several years old and Jack was most enthusiastic about the region's potential. They were certainly memorable wines.

Western Australia has seen the greatest growth in wine regions in Australia over the last three decades

with six major regions now boasting many vignerons. The Swan Valley has been joined by Margaret River, the Great Southern Region around Mount Barker, the Pemberton/Warren Valley area, the South West Coastal Plains and the Darling Ranges and Perth Hills.

The quality of Western Australian wines and the range of styles is extraordinary and although Western Australia produces less than three per cent of Australian wine production, it accounts for around twenty per cent of the nation's premium bottled wines above $16.00 per bottle. Houghton is a huge Australian premium producer, but others, including Evans & Tate, Vasse Felix, Leeuwin Estate, Goundrey, Capel Vale and the new Palandri Winery are significant Australian premium producers.

Wine tourism in Western Australia is a credit to the state, with the Margaret River region having a number of world class winery restaurants and galleries. A wine adventure around Western Australia is a rich experience, indeed. It makes the journey to the West a most worthwhile one.

 # Coastal Plains

The most fertile coastal soils, both to the north and south of Perth, have been naturally delineated by Western Australia's stately Tuart Gum trees. These massive eucalypts provide very dense timber and are a guide to would-be vignerons as to the location of the best vineyard sites.

Temperatures are moderated by proximity to the sea, and overall conditions are ideal for viticulture. The significant wineries to the south of Perth now with their own new geographic appellation · between Bunbury and the Vasse Store at the start of Margaret River are Dr Peter Pratten's Capel Vale, the Killerby Family's Killerby Vineyards and Gill Thomas' Briar Holme. Closer to Perth are Will Nairn's Peel Estate and the impressive Baldivis Estate agricultural property near Rockingham, 180 kilometres south of the city.

Several small wineries and Paul Conti's winery are on the northern outskirts of Perth at Wanneroo. The large Moondah Brook Estate of Houghton is the northern-most vineyard of this region.

Table wines produced in this region moderated by the cooling winds off the Indian Ocean share a common trait. The reds exhibit a beautiful combination of cool climate, berry-like flavours while the whites show good integration of tropical and herbaceous characters with soft acid and the full, round flavours found in wines from a warm climate area.

The strength of these coastal region wines speaks eloquently of the talent of many of the local winemakers. This fraternity has cleverly exploited the best aspects of a unique situation to produce some of Western Australia's most distinctive wines.

Coastal Plains

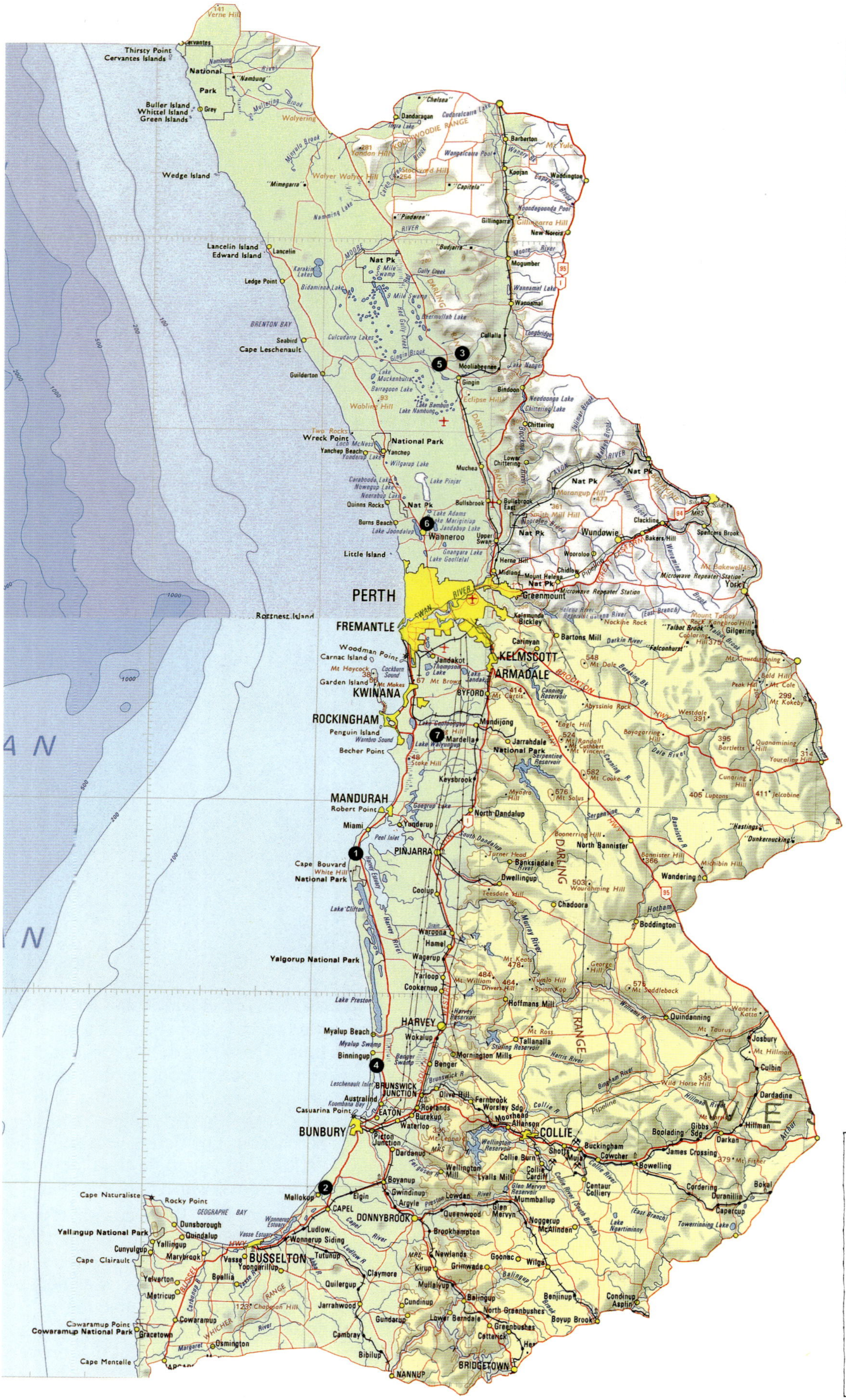

Tuart Grove

WESTERN AUSTRALIA

CHARDONNAY
1999

750ml   PRODUCE OF AUSTRALIA   14%vol

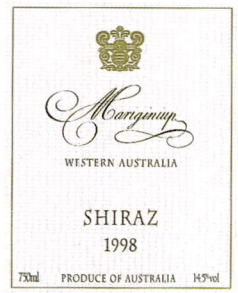

Mariginup

WESTERN AUSTRALIA

SHIRAZ
1998

750ml   PRODUCE OF AUSTRALIA   14.5%vol

Coastal Plains - WA

1. Cape Bouvard Wines
2. Capel Vale
3. Cheriton
4. Killerby Vineyards
5. Moondah Brook
6. Paul Conti
7. Peel Estate

Perth to
Great Southern
320 kms.

Western
Australia

Coastal Plains

Perth

C a p e l   V a l e

Capel Vale's splendid new winery and hospitality centre was opened in 1999 providing wine lovers travelling the long coastal highway south of Perth heading for Margaret River and beyond a great stop off point to try some great wines.

Perhaps the staggering number of medical practitioners actively involved in the wine industry says something of the beneficial effects of wine in moderation. Dr. Peter Pratten is a member of this fraternity. In addition to his medical practices he has with his wife Elizabeth, made the time to establish and manage the Capel Vale Winery and Vineyard.

Capel Vale was founded in 1974 and is located on the banks of the Capel River in the Geographe region. Vines produce excellent fruit with good yields. The Capel Vale team has long recognised the different flavours and characters produced from the various cool growing areas in the south west, and their grapes are sourced from areas where varietal flavours have proven consistently optimal. Thus the Capel Vineyards in "Geographe" produce merlot and chardonnay, the Whispering Hill Vineyard in "Mount Barker" produces riesling and shiraz and the Sheldrake Vineyard produces excellent sauvignon blanc and shiraz in the "Pemberton" region. In the Madgrigals Vineyard, Margaret River region, Cabernet based red grapes are grown

Capel Vale markets into a number of countries under the "Capel Vale" label and into the U.S.A. under the "Sheldrake" label. During the 1980's, the Pratten's established other vineyards, one on the Capel River upstream from their winery, they have called this new vineyard Capel Wellington Estate. They also established their Whispering Hill Vineyard, between Mt. Barker and the Porongurups in the Great Southern Region.

In 1995 a further 200 acres (the Sheldrake Vineyard) was planted in the Lefroy Valley, between Manjimup and Pemberton, in the high country of the south of Western Australia bringing Capel Vale's total vineyard holdings to a substantial 320 acres, covering all the major premium wine areas of the state.

In 2000, 100 acres of Cabernet Sauvignon, Merlot, Malbec, Cabernet Franc and Nebbiolo were planted at "Madrigals" vineyard, Margaret River region.

Capel Vale have won many awards in wine shows. Their 1994 Merlot was judged amongst the best 12 Merlots in the World at Vinum, with the 1993 winning gold at Zurich.

Capel Vale produces 4 ranges of wine for the Australian market: The "Layman's Hut" range, is a vintage everyday drinking range of affordable wines, the "C.V." range shows wines with varietal and vintage labelling, ready to drink, the "Capel Vale" range is premium, high quality varietal wines for cellaring or special occasions and the Black Label "Connoisseur" series are super premium varietal wines, each with a name - "Kinniard Shiraz", "Howecroft Cabernet Merlot", "Frederick Chardonnay" and "Whispering Hill Riesling".

The new winery and visitors centre is superb. Capel Vale is a premium winemaker on the move. It is a credit to its proprietors, Peter and Elizabeth Pratten.

Address: Lot 5, Stirling Estate, Mallokup Road CAPEL 6271	**Winemaker:** Nicole Esdaile	Sauvignon Blanc, Semillon, Shiraz, Verdelho
Phone: (08) 9727 1986 **Fax:** (08) 9727 1904	**Est:** 1979 **Vine Ha:** 200 **Cases:** 150,000	**Principal Wines** / **Potential**
Email: admin@capelvale.com	**Public Hours:** 10am-4.30pm, daily	"Capel Vale" — 2-8 yrs
WWW: www.capelvale.com	**Principal Varieties:** Cabernet Sauvignon, Chardonnay, Merlot, Pinot Noir, Riesling,	"CV" — Now; "Shelorake" (USA) — 2-8 yrs

Paul Conti

From humble beginnings, Paul Conti Wines has earned a reputation as one of WA's leading family owned boutique wineries.

Located 30 minutes north of Perth, the property is the original homestead of Carmelo ("Charlie") & Rosa Conti who migrated from Sicily in 1927 to raise their eight children. The original house has since been converted into a fine dining restaurant, The Conti's began growing vegetables on their property's black sandy soils.

On arriving Charlie Conti immediately planted vines and in 1948 began expanding the vineyard. The original cellar was dug by two of the Conti brothers by horse and scoop.

Son Paul learnt the traditional art of wine making and is one of Perth's pioneering premium wine producers.

In 1968 Paul began upgrading the small winery and was the first winemaker to produce premium bottled wine from Tuart soils. Early success was achieved with his award winning Mariginiup Hermitage, a wine still made from the original vines planted on the Mariginiup Vineyard in 1958.

Fruit today is exclusively sourced

from three vineyards at "Woodvale", "Mariginiup and "Carabooda". These vineyard sites have been selected for their limestone based soils and close proximity to the Indian Ocean which provides cool coastal sea breezes.

New additions to the range include Pinot Noir sourced from Pemberton's Warren Valley · constituting the Medici Ridge Range and a traditonal Méthode Champenoise Sparkling Shiraz, made from Mariginiup fruit.

For the past 7 years, Jason Conti, son of Paul, has worked closely with his father using techniques learnt from his dad, together with new technology from his studies of viticulture and winemaking.

Paul's wife Anne is the driving force behind the logistics of the business, together with daughter Berlinda, who assists with marketing and promotional activities.

Address 529 Wanneroo Road WOODVALE 6026	Est: 1948 Vine Ha: 18 Cases: 8,000	Shiraz	10+ yrs
Phone: (08) 9409 9160 Fax: (08) 9309 1634	Public Hours: 9.30am-5:30pm, Mon- Sat	Cabernet Sauvignon	8 yrs
Email: conti@eepo.com.au	Principal Varieties: Cabernet Sauvignon,	Grenache Shiraz	3 yrs
WWW: www.paulcontiwines.com.au	Muscat, Shiraz, Chenin Blanc, Chardonnay,	Chardonnay	4 yrs
Owner: Paul and Anne Conti	Grenache, Pinot Noir	Late Harvest Muscat	2 yrs
Winemaker: Paul Conti	Principal Wines Potential	Chenin Blanc	2 yrs

Killerby Vineyards

The Killerby Chardonnay is rated in Australian and New Zealand Wine Vintages (the "Little Gold Book") as "Gold Five Stars".

For many years, the Gold Book has been the ultimate guide to Australian and New Zealand wine vintages. It rates hundreds of wineries and thousands of different wines. The "Gold Five Star" rating places the Killerby Chardonnay "among the great wines of the world". The book explains the rating: "Each winestyle (label) listed is ranked out of a maximum of five stars...so that the star ranking reflects some of the earned respect for the particular label over the years of its production. A few wines of supreme quality are given "Gold Star" highlighting. In their best years, these wines are among the great wines of the world". The book goes on to rate every major vineyard in Australia and New Zealand. It pauses briefly at the Killerby Vineyards entry with the comment: "Killerby Chardonnay...one of the country's supreme wines".

The Gold Five Star rating applies not only to the current vintage, but to every vintage of the Killerby Chardonnay.

Killerby Vineyards produces four premium varietal wines, Semillon, Chardonnay, Shiraz and Cabernet Sauvignon. The Killerby winemaking philosophy is simple: to produce consistently stylish wines which provide complexity and interest.

Ben Killerby is carrying on the fine tradition of his late father Dr Barry Killerby, who established the vineyard and winery in 1973. The cellar door has a touch of Provence about it and is well worth visiting on your way to or from Margaret River.

Address: Lakes Road CAPEL 6271	Est: 1973 Vine Ha: 20	"Killerby Vineyards"	
Phone: 1800 655 722 Fax: 1800 679 578	Public Hours: 10am-5pm, daily	Semillon	10 yrs
Email: killerby@killerby.com.au	Principal Varieties: Chardonay, Cabernet	Chardonnay	7 yrs
WWW: www.killerby.com.au	Sauvignon, Shiraz, Semillon, Chardonnay	Shiraz	10 yrs
Winemaker: Paul Boulden	Principal Wines Potential	Cabernet Sauvignon	7 yrs

Peel Estate

Peel Estate is only 60 kilometres south of Perth and 3 kilometres inland from the coast at Baldivis.

Will Nairn is a personable character and has built a very personable winery in red brick with huge wooden beams, a viewing mezzanine area with wooden floors forms the characterful cellar door. The entry is via a curved brick path leading to the pergola-covered entrance. The lawns and gardens under the giant tuart gums give it a lovely settled rural feel.

The vineyards, which now cover 40 acres, were first planted in 1974 and some of the vines are now very solid citizens indeed and producing wines of great character.

I have always been a fan of chenin blanc with its refreshing apple/quince flavours and honeyed overtones. Peel Estate produce a wood matured version with just a hint of soft vanilla like oak that ages beautifully, its great. The Peel Estate Shiraz is very highly regarded being spicy and supple.

The coastal climate is ideal for Bordeaux Varieties, red and white, the minty cabernet sauvignon portrays this well. A range of other wines include a full flavoured chardonnay with elegant sweet fruit and chalky tannins from the limestone soil, a tropical style verdelho and a powerful zinfandel

with heaps of wild berry flavours which often reaches up to 15 or 16% in strength. It's a wine worth seeking out if you're a fan of this variety, its definitely one of the world's best examples.

In everything he does, Will does it his way and he does it well!!

Address: Lot 13 Fletcher Rd BALDIVIS 6171	Public Hours: 10am-5pm, daily	Wood Chenin	10 yrs
Phone: (08) 9524 1221 Fax: (08) 9524 1625	Principal Varieties: Shiraz, Cab Sav, Zinfandel,	Cabernet	10+ yrs
Owner: W.W. and M.E. Nairn	Merlot, Cab Franc, Chenin Blanc, Chard, Verdelho	Chardonnay	8 yrs
Winemaker: Will Nairn	Principal Wines Potential	Verdelho	4 yrs
Est: 1974 Vine Ha: 16 Cases: 8,000	Shiraz 10+ yrs	Zinfande	10+ yrs

Margaret River

The Margaret River region is centred around the town of Margaret River, south of Bunbury, on a large peninsula. The climate is temperate and rainfall high. Long, dry summers and high rainfall, a yearly average of more than 1,100mm, ensure crops ripen well in soils ideally suited to viticulture. These are well-drained sandy loams, over water retentive clay subsoils.

Irrigation throughout the area therefore is largely unnecessary. Even one of the State's largest vineyard of 350 acres operates successfully without any need for irrigation, this vineyard belongs to Sandalford.

As with other Australian wine-producing areas, Margaret River's wine industry is well represented by the medical profession. The initial development of the region for viticulture was recommended by a report written by Dr John Gladstones in 1965. Margaret River's first vines were planted by Dr Tom Cullity of Vasse Felix two years later. Several other medical men followed suit, including Dr Bill Pannell of Moss Wood and Dr Kevin Cullen of Cullen's.

Red wines from Margaret River have proved very successful; the best of these have been made by various wineries from cabernet sauvignon grapes, as well as cabernet franc and merlot. Shiraz is not widely grown but has achieved good results, and pinot noir has also produced excellent wines.

Of the white grape varieties, semillon and sauvignon blanc have shown consistently brilliant results,

producing fine wines of fresh, crisp styles with pronounced herbaceous flavours. The palates are rich and mouth-filling, with a frequent hint of tropical fruit, unlike some wines of this type from other regions which can tend towards a flat palate. Semillon particularly shows lifted tropical and herbaceous characters seldom seen elsewhere, with chardonnay and verdelho grapes having produced excellent wines for the region. Riesling however, proved to be less than successful when first introduced, but early problems with the variety now seem to have been overcome. The Leeuwin Estate Rhine Riesling amply demonstrates the variety's potential, while some of the late-picked rieslings are also very good. The Auslese Riesling produced by Sandalford has been awarded trophies, and continues to score close to full marks in masked tastings.

Aware of the potential and beauty of their district, the inhabitants of Margaret River have established a series of fine restaurants and accommodation houses. The cuisine of many cultures can be found in the town of Margaret River and the hotel of the same name has much to offer its guests. Similarly, the Captain Freycinet Motel offers luxurious accommodation and an excellent restaurant at reasonable prices. A number of wineries, both large and small, have constructed restaurants, art galleries and other art and craft establishments.

A trip to 'Flutes' at Brookland Valley is an absolute must - visitors can sit on the decking overlooking the lake and splendid vineyard, and enjoy

some sensational cuisine in a truly special atmosphere.

Other restaurants exist at Driftwood, Clairault, Abbey Vale, Wise Winery Amberley, Leeuwin Estate, Voyager Estate and Vasse Felix. Cullens and many of the smaller wineries also have great casual eateries, many with exceptional views in this truly beautiful region.

Fishing, surfing, bush walking and some extraordinary caves add an extra dimension to Margaret River, which now certainly vies for the title of the premier wine tourism region in Australia.

During the early 1980's, Leeuwin Estate inaugurated outdoor concerts at dusk, featuring such extraordinary performers such as the London Philharmonic Orchestra, Dame Kiri Te Kanawa and Michael Crawford. Around 7,000 delighted attendees enjoy these magnificent events, many more clamour for tickets but just can't get in. The stature and value of these events for Margaret River are inestimable. Margaret River has undergone a vineyard and wine explosion over the last few years. The giant Palandri Winery and Hospitality Complex is truly astounding, Howard Park's new winery and vineyard are breathtaking, Evans and Tate have built a large state of the art winery and Watershed Wines are in the process of a large development. Xanadu Wines has become a public company and is also in the process of enormous vineyard expansion and constructing a new winery. Margaret River is a vinous paradise, virtually without equal in the world, and its wines are indeed truly world class.

Margaret River

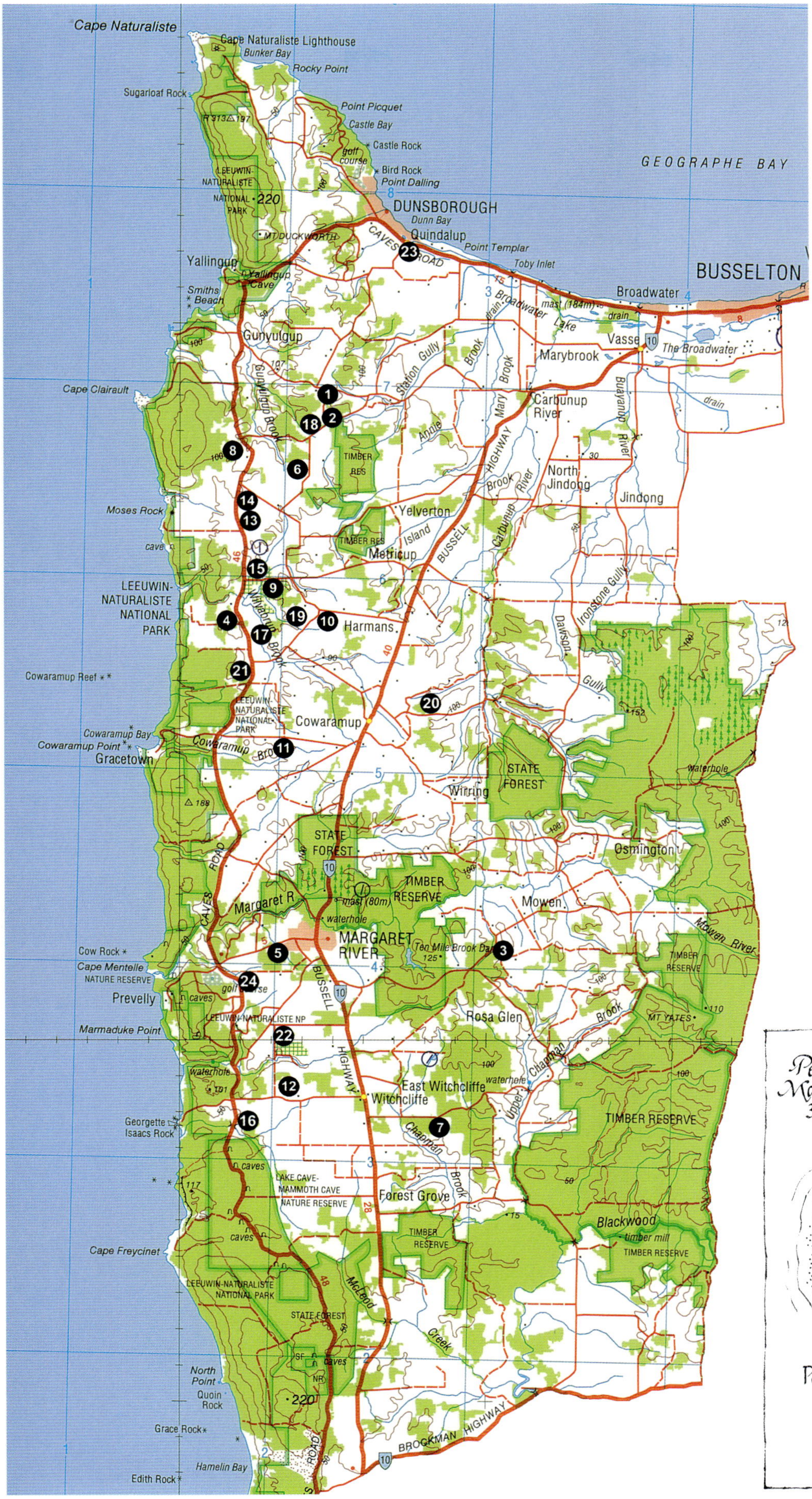

Margaret River - WA

1. Abbey Vale
2. Amberley Estate
3. Berry Farm
4. Brookland Valley
5. Cape Mentelle
6. Clairault Wines
7. Devils Lair
8. Driftwood Estate
9. Evans & Tate
10. Hayshed Hill
11. Juniper Estate
12. Leeuwin Estate
13. Lenton Brae
14. Moss Brothers
15. Moss Wood Wines
16. Redgate Wines
17. Ribbon Vale
18. Rivendell Wines
19. Sandalford
20. Treeton Estate
21. Vasse Felix
22. Voyager Estate
23. Wise Wines
24. Xanadu Wines

Perth to Margaret River: 300 kms.

Western Australia

Margaret River

Perth

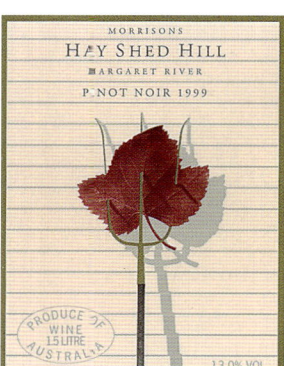

MORRISONS
HAY SHED HILL
— MARGARET RIVER —
P. NOT NOIR 1999

PRODUCE OF
WINE
1.5 LITRE
AUSTRALIA

13.0% VOL

WESTERN AUSTRALIA
1998
CABERNET SAUVIGNON
MERLOT

Art Series
LEEUWIN ESTATE
1997
MARGARET RIVER
CHARDONNAY
14.0% vol   PRODUCE OF AUSTRALIA   750mL

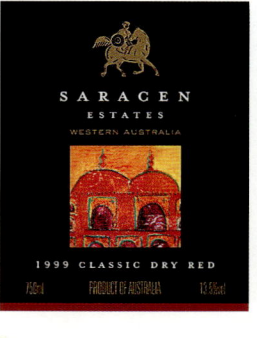

SARACEN
ESTATES
WESTERN AUSTRALIA

1999 CLASSIC DRY RED

SAMPHIRE
MARGARET RIVER
CABERNET MERLOT

WITH ITS TINY FLOWERS APPEARING
ONLY RARELY DURING SUMMER MONTHS,
THE SAMPHIRE IS UNIQUE TO THE
STONY UPLANDS, ESTUARIES AND
SEA COAST OF WESTERN AUSTRALIA.
PRODUCE OF AUSTRALIA

1998

750 ML

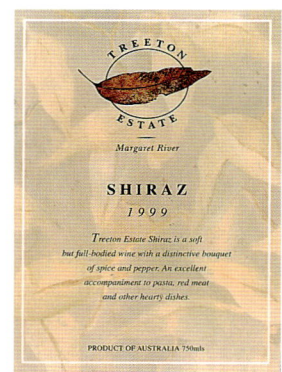

TREETON
ESTATE
Margaret River

SHIRAZ
1999

*Treeton Estate Shiraz is a soft
but full-bodied wine with a distinctive bouquet
of spice and pepper. An excellent
accompaniment to pasta, red meat
and other hearty dishes.*

PRODUCE OF AUSTRALIA 750mls

SAMPHIRE
MARGARET RIVER
VERDELHO

WITH ITS TINY FLOWERS APPEARING
ONLY RARELY DURING SUMMER MONTHS,
THE SAMPHIRE IS UNIQUE TO THE
STONY UPLANDS, ESTUARIES AND
SEA COAST OF WESTERN AUSTRALIA.
PRODUCE OF AUSTRALIA
1999

750 ML

PRODUCE OF   AUSTRALIA
MOSS WOOD
MARGARET RIVER
2000
SEMILLON
750mL

GROWN, VINTAGED & BOTTLED AT DOMAINE MOSS WOOD.
METRICUP ROAD, WILLYABRUP, WESTERN AUSTRALIA, 6280.

14.0% Vol

Clairault
MARGARET RIVER

750ml

2000
SAUVIGNON BLANC

HOTHAM
VALLEY

750 ML ~ 13.5% VOL

PRODUCE OF AUSTRALIA

MARGARET RIVER
2000
SEMILLON
SAUVIGNON BLANC

SARACEN
ESTATES
— MARGARET RIVER —

2000 SAUVIGNON BLANC

750ml   PRODUCT OF AUSTRALIA   13.5% vol

HOTHAM
VALLEY
AUSTRALIA

750mL   13.0% VOL

**SWAGMAN'S
KISS**
MARGARET RIVER
WESTERN AUSTRALIA

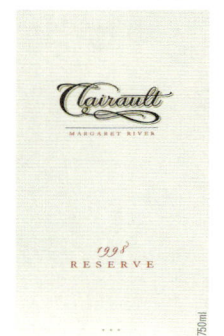

Clairault
MARGARET RIVER

1998
RESERVE

750ml

BECKETT'S
FLAT

2000   CHARDONNAY
Margaret River
WESTERN AUSTRALIA   750ml

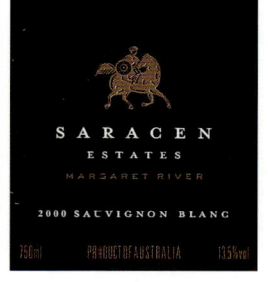

MORRISONS
HAY SHED HILL
— MARGARET RIVER —
CABERNET SAUVIGNON 1998

PRODUCE OF
WINE
750mL
AUSTRALIA

13.5% VOL

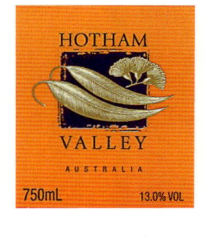

PRODUCE OF   AUSTRALIA
MOSS WOOD
MARGARET RIVER
1997
CABERNET SAUVIGNON
750mL

GROWN, VINTAGED & BOTTLED AT DOMAINE MOSS WOOD.
METRICUP ROAD, WILLYABRUP, WESTERN AUSTRALIA, 6280.

Alc. 14.0% Vol

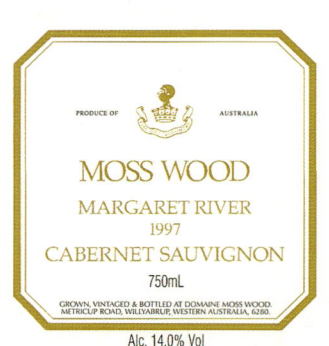

HOWARD PARK
LESTON
MARGARET RIVER
1999
SHIRAZ
14.5% VOL   750ML

TREVOR NICKOLLS

Art Series
LEEUWIN ESTATE
1996
MARGARET RIVER
CABERNET SAUVIGNON
14.5% vol   PRODUCE OF AUSTRALIA   750mL

LEEUWIN ESTATE

SIBLINGS
1999
MARGARET RIVER
SAUVIGNON BLANC SEMILLON
12% vol   PRODUCE OF AUSTRALIA   750mL

HOTHAM
VALLEY
1999
DRYANDRA WHITE
CHARDONNAY SEMILLON
WESTERN AUSTRALIA
AUSTRALIA
12.5% VOL   750 mL

BECKETT'S
FLAT

1999   CABERNET SAUVIGNON
Margaret River
WESTERN AUSTRALIA   750ml

MORRISONS
HAY SHED HILL
— MARGARET RIVER —
CHARDONNAY 1999

PRODUCE OF
WINE
750mL
AUSTRALIA

14.0% VOL

TREETON
ESTATE
Margaret River

SAUVIGNON BLANC
1999

*A Full bodied dry white wine with a
herbaceous bouquet of tropical fruit
and asparagus. The palate is well balanced
finishing smooth and crispy clean an
excellent accompaniment to white
meats and highly spiced dishes.*

12.9% ALC/VOL PRESERVATIVE (220) ADDED
CONTAINS APPROX 7.6 STANDARD DRINKS
NORTH TREETON ROAD COWARAMUP WESTERN AUSTRALIA
PRODUCT OF AUSTRALIA 750mls

Abbey Vale

Abbey Vale is one of the prettiest wineries in Margaret River. The cellar door has views over the large man-made lake and vineyards. Bill and Pam McKay have had an incredible journey leading them to their little piece of paradise.

They left Northern Ireland for Uganda just after their marriage where Bill worked as an engineer. Following this he set up his own electronics business moving on to Vancouver and finally Perth. Following the sale of his electronics business, Bill took a quite different path spending five years qualifying as a clinical psychologist.

When their son Kevin became interested in viticulture, having assisted in the planting of the nearby Amberley Vineyard, they decided to plant vines on their property nextdoor they had bought as an investment 10 years earlier in 1975.

Early in 2001 Swiss couple Jurg and Regula Hauser bought Abbey Vale, Jurg is a Professor of Economics and Regula an Architect. Their first experience with Margaret River was camping at the Meelup Beach in 1974, it began for them a love affair with the Region, which has culminated in the purchase of the superb Abbey Vale Estate.

Kevin McKay continues in his position of Chief winemaker and vineyard manager and makes the wines with some assistance from the legendary Dorham Mann who is the vineyards consultant winemaker. Kevin also works closely with Jim Brayne, chief winemaker of McWilliams, to make a Margaret River Red and White wine under the McWilliams label

On the lawns bordering the lake behind the winery, Abbey Vale occasionally hosts a prestigious concert as part of the Festival of Perth. 1994, the first, featured the Budapest Symphony Orchestra and in 1995 the Odessa Philharmonic Orchestra.

I have found the wines at Abbey Vale loaded with fruit flavours.
I particularly like the dry verdelho, with its rich tropical fruit salad of flavours and dry finish. The sauvignon blanc has won a number of awards and the cabernet sauvignon has a lovely rich round plummy character. The Abbey Vale Verdelho is a lovely fruit driven style and their semillon a more serious wine to put down for a while as it is aged for 12 months in French oak.

Address: Lot 392, Wildwood Road YALLINGUP 6282
Phone: (08) 9755 2121 **Fax:** (08) 9755 2286
Email: orders@abbeyvale.com.au

WWW: www.abbeyvale.com.au
Winemaker: K. McKay
Est: 1986   **Vine Ha:** 30
Public Hours: 10.30am-5pm, daily

Principal Varieties: Chard, Merlot, Cab Sav, Shiraz, Sauv Blanc, Sem, Verdelho, Chenin Blanc
Principal Wines
"Abbey Vale"

Amberley Estate is one of the largest and most important wineries in Margaret River. Since the first planting in 1986 on the Thornton Road property and the first vintage in 1990, Amberley has established itself as a producer of characteristic Margaret River wines.

Amberley is blessed with one of the prettiest locations in Australia, a sheltered gully resplendent with stands of imperious red gums.

The elegant white winery building is surrounded by manicured gardens and lawns which sweep down to a pond and the vineyards beyond - it looks like they were always supposed to be there and, like the wine, the staff are bright and bubbly.

A considerable area of vineyard is planted with chenin blanc. This truly underrated variety with its lifted apple and quince like flavours has performed marvels under the expert

winemaking guidance of Eddie Price, a native of Western Australia, who in 1982 became dux of the Roseworthy oenology course winning the major course prizes.

The philosophy of the Amberley label is to remain a producer of wine from the fruit grown solely in the Margaret River Appellation. The belief of the owners and management is that a steady growth pattern utilising produce from arguably one of the best growing areas in Australia will be far outweighed by the short term gains of outside blending.

The top selling chenin is accompanied by an excellent sauvignon blanc, semillon, semillon/sauvignon blanc, the Margaret River speciality, they also make a superb shiraz. Why not enjoy them as an ideal accompaniment to

a delicious lazy lunch under the verandah of the winery. Don't forget to try the rich, wild berry flavoured cabernet merlot with its lifted aromatic characters which typify this top class winemaker.

Every year in February one of Australia's great wine events takes place at Amberley it's a two day "Semillon and Seafood" Festival that features that extremely underrated grape variety "Semillon". Amberley gather semillons from makers around Australia and feature them in an indoor/outdoor bonanza complete with marquees, umbrellas and table seating for more than 700 semillon devotees each day. The setting is superb and excellent, live music completes a great day of bacchanalian enjoyment.

Amberley have certainly got their act together.

Address: Thornton Road YALLINGUP 6282	**Est:** 1986 **Vine Ha:** 32	Sav, Shiraz, Sauvignon Blanc, Semillon,
Phone: (08) 9755 2288 **Fax:** (08) 9755 2171	**Cases:** 80,000	Cabernet Franc, Chenin Blanc
Email: amberley@amberley-estate.com.au	**Public Hours:** 10am-4.30pm, daily	**Principal Wines**
Winemaker: Eddie Price and David Watson	**Principal Varieties:** Chardonnay, Merlot, Cab	Amberley Estate

Brookland Valley

Malcolm Jones is a visionary person and his vision is certainly not of the petty variety. Brookland Valley is not just pretty, it is a vinous paradise, with every detail, materially and aesthetically, perfectly in place.

In fact, it is Peter Pan who calls the tune as he plays his flute, happily gazing over the Willyabrup Brook. This beautiful symbol of eternal youth and optimism was one of the last of the wax-moulded bronze cast studies crafted back in 1893.

Malcolm graduated from Lincoln University in New Zealand in 1963 with a degree in Agricultural Science. A successful career as a Farm Management Consultant followed until some 20 years later when the desire to change his life-style led to the search for a rural retreat.

The 50-acre vineyard of close-planted manicured vines surrounding the lake is a real showpiece and produces first-rate fruit. The wines are all individually styled · the sauvignon blanc is at the tropical fruit end of the flavour spectrum, with a touch of herbaceousness, whilst the chardonnay has subtle melon and grapefruit flavours complemented by toasty hazelnut-like oak from fine French oak barriques. The cabernet/merlot/cabernet franc red is rich with cherry and plum

overtones. Recently BRL Hardy have invested in the Brookland Valley Vineyards and wine brand which is leading to much greater quantities of these exquisite wines finding their way into wine markets around the world, which gives wine drinkers a good reason to celebrate.

Malcolm and Deidre's daughter Lisa was the dux of the diploma course in hospitality and tourism at Perth's Bentley College and 'Student of the Year' in 1989.

Her first project was to create the superb 'Flutes' restaurant, gallery and function facility with her parents. Cantilevered over the lake, it overlooks the picture book valley and vineyards, it rivals any winery restaurant worldwide.

A number of beautiful villas are being built in 95 acres of wilderness bushland surrounding the Willyabrup Brook as it winds down to the Indian Ocean. Bush walking tracks through to the hilltops are now in place. I can't imagine a more idyllic stay, than at Brookland Valley, it would certainly beat keeping up with the Joneses!

Address: Caves Road WILYABRUP 6280
Phone: (08) 9755 6250 **Fax:** (08) 9755 6214
Email: brookland@brooklandvalley.com.au
Winemaker: Garry Baldwin

Est: 1984 **Vine Ha:** 20
Public Hours: Cellar Door: 10am-5pm, daily.
Flutes Café: 11am-4.30pm, Tues-Sun; from 7pm, Saturday Evenings

Principal Varieties: Chardonnay, Merlot, Cab Sav, Sauvignon Blanc, Cabernet Franc
Principal Wines
"Brookland Valley Vineyard"

Clairault Wines

Located on one of the highest points in the Cape region in the south west corner of Western Australia, Clairault is one of the original wineries in the Margaret River Region, its first vines having been planted in 1976. Cape Clairault nearby was named after French Mathematician Alexis Clairault whose calculations are still used today, 250 years later, to measure the movement of greenhouse gasses around our planet. Clairault is situated in the northern part of the region, approximately 20 kilometres north of the Margaret River township. The vineyard sits 120 metres above sea level on one of the highest points on the Cape Peninsula.

Clairault is now under the ownership of the Martin family who purchased it in June 1999. Bill Martin with wife Ena and their three sons Shane, Conor and Brian, arrived in Western Australian in 1974. Bill's skilled marketing background soon saw him appointed to a position with a wholesale liquor firm based in Perth. Then in 1980 he was licensed as part of a national operation to produce garlic bread, the first commercial venture to put such products on supermarket shelves. That business was subsequently sold, but Bill has since operated a US coast to coast specialty breadmaking operation employing 60 people.

Clairault truly is a family affair as two of Bill and Ena's sons are also involved. Conor Martin's role as Director of Operations is to coordinate the restaurant, cellar door and function facilities at Clairault, as well as being responsible for its marketing. Brian Martin is Assistant Manager of the Vineyard, and is instrumental in vineyard development.

Clairault Wines has undergone a beautiful transformation and has fast gained a reputation as a 'must' for both locals and visitors who seek true quality and a unique experience.

Clairault is the ideal place to meet friends or take your family, to enjoy the quiet charm of the vineyard and beautiful landscaped gardens with the majestic back drop of towering jarrah and marri trees.

Clairault's range of crisp, fruity white wines and beautifully structured, elegant red wines can be sampled at the strikingly attractive Cellar Door. The real temptation, however, is to stay a little longer and enjoy a glass of fine Clairault wine while dining in Clairault's Restaurant. This contemporary, stylish restaurant has a wonderful ambience, with panoramic views over the beautifully landscaped gardens and lawns, with the vineyard in the background. The Restaurant includes an alfresco dining deck with a children's playground just far enough away!

Andrea Ilott, Clairault's internationally experienced chef, will delight you with a fusion of international taste treats. In Andrea's words; "I believe a visual feast is just as important as a taste sensation.

At Clairault we create each dish individually using only the freshest and best ingredients, sourced locally and imported, to marry perfectly with Clairault's elegant wines".

Winemaker Peter Stark and his team abide by a wine making philosophy of creating balanced, perfectly structured wines that truly reflect the unique qualities of the vineyard and its fruit.

The 'flagship' Clairault Reserve, the acclaimed Clairault Cabernet Merlot, and the Swagman's Kiss Premium Red are outstanding. All are within the much loved Clairault style with lots of intensity, good weight, structure, vibrant deep, colour and soft tannins.

The Clairault Sauvignon Blanc and Semillon Sauvignon Blanc both show excellent varietal character, stunning with or without food. The Swagman's Kiss Premium White is the winery's popular Semillon Sauvignon Blanc Chardonnay blend with superb fruit flavours, and is excellent value for money.

In spring 2000, the Martins planted an extra 35 acres of vines, mainly red including Shiraz, which will add another premium wine to the Clairault stable in a year or two.

Clairault has been beautifully redeveloped by the Martin family and is a credit to them.

Address: Henry Road WILLYABRUP 6280	Cases: 30,000	Reserve	10-12 yrs
Phone: (08) 9755 6225 Fax: (08) 9755 6229	Public Hours: 10am-5pm, daily	Cabernet Merlot	5-7 yrs
Email: clairalt@clairaultwines.com.au	Principal Varieties: Cabernet Franc,	Sauvignon Blanc	3-5 yrs
Owner: Mr & Mrs Willaim & Ena Martin	Cabernet Sauvignon, Merlot, Rhine Riesling,	Semillon Sauvignon Blanc	3-5 yrs
Winemaker: Peter Stark	Riesling, Sauvignon Blanc, Semillon	Swagman's Kiss White	2-4 yrs
Est: 1976 Vine Ha: 23.5	Principal Wines Potential	Swagman's Kiss Red	3-6 yrs

Becketts Flat

Memories of the family vineyard and cellars in Europe, led Bill Ilic and his wife Noni to follow a dream of becoming Margaret River vignerons.

Their 35 acre vineyard has been planted to the grape varieties most suited to the soils and micro-climate of this central region of the Margaret River appellation. They have paid particular attention to their trellissing and pruning systems, allowing each variety to produce its best. The fruit is processed at their small, efficient well-equipped on-site winery which overlooks a meandering brook and the vineyards.

The first wines were released in 1997, with Beckett's Flat achieving immediate show success, with a Bronze for the 1997 Sauvignon Blanc/Semillon. The following year their 1998 Oak Matured Semillon/Sauvignon Blanc received a Silver, and the 1997 Cabernet (blend)

a Gold. Show success has continued with the 1998 Cabernet Sauvignon receiving a Bronze and all three of the 1999 reds receiving multiple awards, including two silvers.

Beckett's Flat is situated on the corner of the Bussell Highway and Beckett Road, just north of Metricup Road.

All wines are produced from estate-grown fruit. The vines are hand -

pruned and fruit is hand-picked. The wines are fruit driven and their styles are true to the varieties.

The tasting area is beautifully appointed and if you are looking for a great place to stay, the Ilics have a vineyard cottage, fully self contained, with verandahs looking out over the vineyard, complete with a wood fire to curl up in front in winter. Well behaved dogs are also welcome!!

Address: Beckett Road BUSSELTON 6280	Winemaker: Bill Ilic Cases: 5,000	Cabernet Sauvignon	8 yrs
Phone: (08) 9755 7402 Fax: (08) 9755 7344	Public Hours: 10am-6pm, daily	Shiraz	8 yrs
Email: bfwinery@bigpond.com	Principal Varieties: Chard, Sauvignon Blanc,	Chardonnay	5 yrs
WWW: www.beckettsflat.com.au Est: 1992	Shiraz, Cab Sav, Merlot, Semillon, Verdelho	Sauvignon Blanc Semillon	3 yrs
Owner: Bill & Noni Ilic Vine Ha: 13.9	Principal Wines Potential	Merlot	8 yrs

Cape Mentelle

David Hohnen 'the squire of Cape Mentelle', has expanded the breadth of his squiredom quite considerably in the last few years.

David began his quite remarkable career in the wine industry back in 1968 at Stonyfell Winery in South Australia. David completed his Oenology studies at the Fresno University in California and on returning to Australia in 1970 he, along with brother Mark, planted vines on the family's investment land at Margaret River. David then went to Victoria where he worked with Dominique Portet, establishing the Taltarni Vineyards.

David came back to Western Australian in 1976 and came under the spotlight when he won the Jimmy Watson Memorial Trophy with his 1982 Cabernet Sauvignon. To prove it was no fluke, David repeated the feat the following year with his 1983

wine. These awards did much to promote the Margaret River region.

In 1985, David established Cloudy

Bay in New Zealand and has produced some extraordinary sauvignon blancs. Cloudy Bay now produces a range of wines, including a fine methode champenoise, 'Pelorus'.

In 1990 Veuve Clicquot Ponsardin, the massive French champagne house, obtained a major share in Cape Mentelle, putting an indelible stamp of approval on David Hohnen's enterprises.

The Cape Mentelle range includes a shiraz and cabernet merlot, as well as the cabernet sauvignon. David also produces one of Australia's few zinfandels, a variety grown in California. This makes a huge, black, spicy red - a wine for heroes. The two Mentelle whites are the region's first semillon/sauvignon blanc blend and a full-bodied chardonnay. The new state of the art visitors centre is stunning.

Address: Wallcliffe Road MARGARET RIVER 6285	Winemaker: John Durham	Chardonnay, Merlot, Sauvignon Blanc,
Phone: (08) 9757 3266 Fax: (08) 9757 3233	Est: 1970 Vine Ha: 120	Semillon, Shiraz, Zinfandel
Email: info@capementelle.com.au	Public Hours: 10am-4.30pm, daily	Principal Wines
WWW: www.capementelle.com.au	Principal Varieties: Cabernet Sauvignon,	"Cape Mentelle"

Chapmans Creek

I first met Tony Lord in 1987 when he was the high profile founder editor and publisher of the prestigious Decanter Wine Magazine in London. He began this venture in 1974, after leaving his home town of Perth in 1970, to further his career in journalism. During his time at Decanter he became more and more impressed with the wines and progressive approach to the industry in Margaret River.

In 1992 he returned to Australia after selling Decanter, to develop Chapman's Creek, the first vines had been planted in 1990.

The winery is located on the eastern side of the renowned Willyabrup district of Margaret River and the cellar door is housed in a beautiful rustic building sensitively landscaped to blend into its creek side location.

Tony is a very individual person and wanted to make the sort of wines his long sojourn with Decanter had showed him were all too rare. He is a great fan of fruit driven styles and this is reflected in his trio of whites. His Chardonnay and Chenin Blanc are both trophy winners and his Unwooded Style Chardonnay which was one of the first in the region, is jam packed with crisp fresh fruit flavours.

Tony's Cabernet Merlot blend is a smooth silky wine with a great palate of rich cassis like berry fruit in balance with soft oak tannins.

The new Reserve range of Merlot, Cabernet and Chardonnay due for release in late 2001 will confirm Tony's aim to present at the top echelon of Australian wines.

Address: RMS 447, Yelverton Road WILLYABRUP 6280	**Public Hours:** 10:30am-4:30pm, daily	Chapman's Creek Cabernet Merlot	2-6 yrs
	Principal Varieties: Cabernet Sauvignon,	Chapman's Creek Merlot	2-10 yrs
Phone: (08) 9755 7545 **Fax:** (08) 9755 7571	Chenin Blanc, Chardonnay, Merlot	Chapman's Creek Chenin Blanc	1-5 yrs
Owner: Tony Lord **Winemaker:** Maria Melsom	**Principal Wines** **Potential**	Chapman's Creek Unoaked Chard	1-3 yrs
Est: 1990 **Vine Ha:** 10.7 **Cases:** 5,000	Chapman's Creek Chardonnay 2-6 yrs	Chapman's Creek Reserve Chard	2-10 yrs

Saracen Estate

Saracen Estates, based in the heart of the Margaret River region on the Bussell Highway at Metricup, is fortunate in that it can draw on old vines well-established over a twenty-five year period to fashion its premium wine. These vines are now at the peak of maturity and deliver the full, highly concentrated fruit flavours that characterise the winery's three premium flagship wines Sauvignon Blanc, Chardonnay and Cabernet Sauvignon. More can be expected in the future from Saracen Estates. The winery has planted an additional 200 acres, from which a second label will emerge to produce wines to complement its existing products.

The criteria in the search for land for this new vineyard was exacting. The site enjoys cool nights, warm days and a unique microclimate, with good well drained soil.

The inspiration for "Saracen Estates" as a banner for its wines stems from a philosophy of ancient origin. The Saracens of the Middle East, harassed the borders of the Roman Empire - and later those who were advancing the cause of Christianity during the Crusade, they developed into a powerful, advanced race with high social and cultural standards, in all facets of the arts and philosophy, plus some of the greatest mathematical discoveries in world history.

The Consultant winemaker is the renowned Dorham Mann, he brings his long experience gained in development and pioneering within Western Australia's premium wine regions. As a scientist he was an advisor on winemaking and grape growing with the Western Australian Department of Agriculture. As such he was involved in the planting of the first vines at the experimental vineyard at Mount Barker in 1967-68. Later as a consultant he fostered the development of large-scale vineyards in the Margaret River region.

Dorham's father was the legendary winemaker Jack Mann who created Houghton's White Burgundy, amongst many other achievements. Dorham brings all this plus his own considerable expertise to the crafting of Saracen Estates wines.

Address: Bussell Highway METRICUP 6280	**Winemaker:** D. Mann	Cabernet Sauvignon
Phone: (08) 9321 2167 **Fax:** (08) 9321 2224	**Est:** 1997 **Vine Ha:** 50	Chardonnay
Email: admin@saracenestates.com.au	**Principal Varieties:** Cabernet Sauvignon,	Sauvignon Blanc
WWW: www.saracenestates.com.au	Merlot, Chardonnay, Shiraz	Classic Red
Owner: Luke Saraceni, Elio Cazzolli	**Principal Wines**	Classic White

Devils Lair

Devil's Lair was the brainchild of Phil Sexton, a very focussed individual of great vision.

Phil, began his career as a trainee brewer at Perth's Swan Brewery he then attended the Oenology Course at the Charles Sturt University in Wagga Wagga. Phil then travelled through Europe where he hatched the idea of a boutique brewery. He later established the remarkably successful Matilda Bay Brewing Co.

His successful hospitality and brewing endeavours allowed him to become a serious vigneron, his long cherished dream. His thoroughness and vision were powerful indeed. He didn't want just any sort of vineyard. He sought a gravelly site where the vines would have to dig deep for sustenance and moisture. A particular site appealed to him. He had visited there as an anthropology student in his university days to study the ancient lair of a larger version of today's Tasmanian Devil,

now extinct on the mainland. In 1981 Phil purchased the property next door to the devil's lair, which had partly been used as a gravel pit. The location, some 20 kilometres south of Margaret River and slightly elevated, is definitely cooler than the northerly part of the region and picking occurs some several weeks later. The cabernet sauvignon is often not picked until late April.

The 100 acres of vines are planted on the steep slopes surrounding a massive lake with a surface area of

35 acres. The first red from the property was a 1990 cabernet sauvignon, which also contained a small percentage of merlot and cabernet franc. This wine was instantly successful at the annual SGIO Wine Awards in Perth, where it won the champion prize. Devil's Lair repeated this feat in 1994 with their 1993 Pinot Noir. In 1993 a "state of the art" winery was commissioned.

The unique Devil's Lair label is as individual as its rich and characterful wines. Look out for it.

Address: Rocky Road, Forrest Grove MARGARET RIVER 6285 **Phone:** (08) 9757 7573 **Fax:** (08) 9757 7533	**WWW:** www.southcorp.com.au **Owner:** Philip and Allison Sexton **Winemaker:** Janice McDonald	**Est:** 1980 **Vine Ha:** 35 **Cases:** 15,000 **Principal Varieties:** Chardonnay, Pinot Noir, Cabernet Sauvignon, Cabernet Franc, Merlot

Juniper Estate

Juniper Estate in the heart of the Margaret River winegrowing area is one of the oldest vineyards in the area. The Estate was planted by Henry and Maureen Wright in 1973, adjacent to Vasse Felix on Harmans Road South, the Wright's had migrated from Kenya to Australia in the late 1960's.

The land has a rich history. In the 19th century the road from Busselton to the south ran through what is now the vineyard and forded the Willyabrup Creek (hence the "Crossing" range of wines.) The present vineyard block was created by a subdivision by well-known West Australian family of artists, the Junipers, after whom it is now named.

Since 1999, there have been many positive changes including re-trellising, training and canopy

management, all aimed at the production of the best possible fruit. A state of the art winery and a temperature controlled barrel room has been built. The cellar door tasting area has been refurbished and now includes a kitchen.

The vineyard is on the Willyabrup gravelly loam which has produced so

many of Margaret River's best wines. The original 22 acres of cabernet sauvignon, shiraz, riesling and semillon are dry grown. Dry land viticulture is highly regarded for the depth of flavour it produces in the grapes giving concentrated flavours to the wine. Four acres of Petit Verdot, Merlot, Cabernet Franc and Malbec have been added, enabling Bordeaux blend wines to be added to the estate range. All the new plantings are also dry grown.

Vintage 2000 was the first full vintage under the Estate label. Winemaking is aimed towards depth and elegance, with extensive use of new oak giving the wine added complexity. Wine is stored in oak in the air conditioned barrel room. Juniper is a great place to enjoy wine and food outside the cellar door on the grassed areas beside the Willyabrup Creek.

Address: Harmans Rd Sth COWARAMUP 6284 **Phone:** (08) 9755 9000 **Fax:** (08) 9755 9100 **Email:** juniperestate@ozemail.com.au **WWW:** www.juniperestate.com.au **Owner:** Roger Hill, Gill Anderson & Viv Booker	**Est:** 1973 **Cases:** 8,000 **Public Hours:** 10am-5pm, daily **Principal Varieties:** Ries, Shiraz, Cab Sav, Sem **Principal Wines** **Potential** Juniper Estate Shiraz 10-15 yrs	Juniper Estate Cab Sav Juniper Estate Semillon Juniper Crossing Shiraz Juniper Crossing Cab Sav Juniper Crossing Chenin Blanc	10-15 yrs 5-10 yrs 5-10 yrs 5-10 yrs 2-5 yrs

Driftwood Estate

This impressive imposing winery seems like it has been there for much longer than is the fact. The number of awards they have won with their wines also adds weight to this appearance.

In 1987 property developer and supermarket operator Tom Galopolous and his wife Helen bought a stretch of land along Caves Road at Willyabrup, with a view to setting up a weekend retreat. Remembering his Greek grandfather's love of his own vines and wines Tom planted a few vines as a hobby. Today he has some 50 acres of beautifully tended vines, a state of the art winery, and a 200-seat brasserie to rival any winery restaurant in the world. In fact, Tom toured California, France, Italy and Greece checking out winery hospitality set-ups and he has certainly done something very special at Driftwood. The high vaulted ceiling with an atrium area overlooking the vineyards is truly spectacular. The large cellar door reception area has a grandeur and class that really impresses.

A Greek Amphitheatre complete with acropolis like columns has been constructed behind the winery amongst the gardens in front of the vineyards. Many concerts and special events are held in this magic environment.

Their Semillon Sauvignon Blanc is a very stylish polished wine with lifted aromatic jasmine and passionfruit aromas leaping out of the glass. The palate reminds me of ripe honeydew melons and tangerines, quite a wine. Their Cabernet Merlot also impressed me with its rich plum and cassis like fruit flavours, fine tannins and supple palate.

The Driftwood wines are all definitely classy, why not enjoy them at lunch or dinner in the restaurant, which also has open decking under the verandah for summer and a huge log fire for a cosy winters dining experience.

Address: Caves Road YALLINGUP 6282
Phone: (08) 9755 6323 **Fax:** (08) 9755 6343
Email: drift@iinet.net.au
WWW: www.driftwood.com.au

Winemaker: Barney Mitchell
Est: 1989 **Vine Ha:** 18 **Cases:** 20,000
Public Hours: 11am-4.30pm, daily
Principal Varieties: Chardonnay, Merlot, Cab

Sav, Shiraz, Sauvignon Blanc, Pinot Noir, Semillon, Chenin Blanc, Verdelho
Principal Wines
"Driftwood Estate"

Evans & Tate

Evans and Tate, under the guidance of Executive Chairman Franklin Tate, is one of a number of leading Australian medium sized wineries to recently successfully list on the Australian Stock Exchange. It all began with Franklin's parents. John and Toni Tate had been great fans of the early wines of Margaret River, and friends of the pioneer vigneron, Tom Cullity. In 1974, two years after establishing their Evans & Tate headquarters in the Swan Valley, they bought 70 acres of land in Margaret River, planting vines the following year.

The vineyard comprised semillon, sauvignon blanc, chardonnay, shiraz, cabernet sauvignon, cabernet franc and merlot. In 1994 the company purchased a further 250 acres of land at Jindong in the north of the region and then established 'Lionel's Vineyard' named after John Tate's late father, the first Tate to enjoy wine in Australia. This property has become the site for the company's new state of the art 8,500 tonne capacity winery. Evans and Tate have also established a further vineyard 'Alexanders' in Kaloorup. Consummate winemaker Steve Warne makes the wines.

I have been particularly impressed by the Evans & Tate Margaret River Semillon with its honey and lemon highlights and clean herbaceous flavours, it has been a most successful wine on the show circuit. The Margaret River Classic, a semillon/sauvignon blanc launched in 1987, has become one of Western Australia's best selling wines and is excellent value. But it is the cabernet sauvignon that has grabbed the limelight; the 1991 in particular had the critics swooning.

No single award has meant more to the company, however, than the trophy for the Best Red Wine of the competition received at the 2000 International wine Challenge in London for their 1999 Margaret River Shiraz - a fine accolade indeed.

The delightful cottage tasting room on Caves Road at their Wilyabrup Vineyard, Redbrook with its gorgeous gardens in the middle of the vineyard is a pretty place to drop off for a top-class tasting if you are in the region.

Address: Corner Caves & Metricup Roads MARGARET RIVER	**Est:** 1971 **Vine Ha:** Owns or controls 251	Gnangara Chenin Blanc	1-2 yrs
	Cases: 200,000	Gnangara Chardonnay	1-2 yrs
Phone: (08) 9213 1799 **Fax:** (08) 9213 1798	**Public Hours:** 10.30am-4.30pm, daily	Gnangara Shiraz	1-3 yrs
Email: et@evansandtate.com.au	**Principal Varieties:** Chard, Semillon,	Margaret River Classic	1-2 yrs
WWW: www.evansandtate.com.au	Sauvignon Blanc, Shiraz, Cabernet Sav, Merlot	Margaret River Sauv Blanc Sem up to 3 yrs	
Winemaker: Steve Warne	**Principal Wines** **Potential**	Margaret River Two Vineyards Chard up to 4 yrs	

Hotham Wines

In 1987 a group of wine enthusiasts set up a vineyard and winery, Hotham Wines at Wandering, 120 kilometres south east of Perth adding a Cellar Door in 1993, Chief amongst theses was the managing director of the newly formed Hotham Wines Ltd., Evan Cross. Hotham Wines floated on the Australian stock exchange in late 2000.

A few years earlier the Eastaught family began planting a vineyard on their picturesque property on Caves Road in the Yallingup Valley, Wildwood Estate, later a Mudbrick Winery Restaurant and four accommodation chalets were added.

In 1994 The Brown family, successful in WA Finance, development and manufacturing began setting up their Alexandra Bridge Estate Vineyards, on the Southern Outskirts of the Margaret River region, later they built a state of the art 1,000 tonne capacity winery, on a nearby property which was commissioned for the 2000 vintage.

Added to these marvelous assets a further property, of over 500 acres was purchased and planted with 245 acres of vines in 1999, Bridgeland Vineyards in the Rosa Glen area, 13 kilometers south east of the town of Margaret River, in total the current vineyard holdings of Hotham wines are over 350 acres.

Hotham market their wines under three main brands. Hotham Valley with its distinctive leaf and flower logo on an ochre colored background, inspired by the renowned Hardwood Wandoo eucalpyt trees, on the Wandering property. The second brand is Wildwood Estate and the third Alexandra Bridge.

The main winemaking activities are at the new winery (Karridale) close to Alexandra Bridge Estate. The winemaking equipment at Wandering is being relocated to the Wildwood Winery which will continue operating. The Wandering property will be sold.

The Wildwood Restaurant has enormous rustic charm with panoramic views over the vines and spectacular Yallingup Valley of the northern Margaret River Region.

The four Wildwood Chalets are set in natural bushland and built of rammed earth, they can cater for a family of four or two couples and have full facilities with open log fires for winter.

The wines are under the winemaking control of James Pennington a founder of Hotham Valley Wines who has studied microbiology at W.A.'s Murdoch University and has a degree in winemaking from Charles Sturt University in N.S.W. He also oversees the vineyards he will be assisted by Philip Tubb, who has a winemaking degree from Roseworthy in S.A. and had worked for 10 years at Leeuwin Estate before becoming winemaker at the new Karridale Winery.

Glenn Kirkwood a Charles Sturt Viticulture graduate, with plenty of experience establishing large vineyards for big companies around Australia, has just been appointed group vineyards manger, he developed the large bridgeland vineyard now part of Hotham.

Hotham Valley wines have won many medals and six trophies and will lead the stable of wines but watch out for Wildwood and Alexandra Bridge, Hotham Wines is full of expertise and great vineyards assets, exciting times are ahead for them I'm sure.

Address: Caves Road YALLINGUP 6959	Public Hours: 10:30am-4pm, daily	Hotham Valley Sem Sauv Blanc	4-6 yrs
Phone: (08) 9755 2066 Fax: (08) 9754 1389	Principal Varieties: Cab Franc, Chardonnay,	Wildwood Finale Chardonnay	6-10 yrs
WWW: www.hothamvalleywines.com	Pinot Noir, Sem, Cab Sav, Merlot, Sauv Blanc	Wildwood Finale Pinot Noir	4-6 yrs
Winemaker: James Pennington	Principal Wines Potential	Hotham Valley Cab Sav Merlot	6-8 yrs
Est: 1984 Vine Ha: 18	Hotham Valley Shiraz 4-6 yrs	Hotham Valley Semillon	4-6 yrs

Howard Park

One of Australia's most impressive new wineries is the Howard Park Margaret River winery.

I had the pleasure of seeing if a few days after its opening in early February 2000. I was struck not only by its impressive size but the symmetry of its architecture and how it had already blended beautifully into the natural bushland. The expansive tasting and entertainment area was resplendent with bowls of oranges everywhere and red packet surprises. Proprietor Jeff Burch's wife Amy, explained the winery had been opened on the first day of the Year of the Dragon, the packets were good luck symbols in her Chinese culture and the oranges represented happiness, roundness and abundance, suitable symbols for Howard Park also.

Jeff and Amy have done a mighty job in a few short years in the wine industry, after commencing with Howard Park Wines in 1994 in the Great Southern region at Denmark. They almost immediately built a beautiful new winery of 1000 tonnes capacity and a fine tasting and hospitality centre.

At the same time Jeff, who came in the Western Australian wine industry from the wine state of South Australia and a career in the packaging industry, began planting vines in the Margaret River region. The site is where their new 1000 tonne plus capacity winery and lavish entertaining area is built. There are now 140 acres of vineyards

surrounding the winery, which carry the name "Leston" named after Jeff's father.

Howard Park have three ranges of wines, their traditional Howard Park label with only three wines, from the best of their own vineyard and selected Great Southern and Margaret River fruit. There is a Riesling, a Chardonnay and a Cabernet Merlot, that has built a reputation as one of Australia's finest reds.

The second Howard Park label is "Madfish". I remember the first Madfish wine (then known as Madfish Bay), a vibrant white predominantly a Semillon and Sauvignon Blanc from the Great Southern, a 1992 vintage and most impressive.

The story goes from Aboriginal folklore that schools of small fish, herded into the shallow almost land-locked bay about 15 kms from Denmark, by larger fish, would leap from the water in a mad flurry to escape. Maybe their mad movements had something also to do with the meeting of the tides, throwing the normally calm waters into a turbulent boiling mass. Whatever the origins the name has stuck. The symbol on the Madfish labels is an Aboriginal painting of a water turtle; this represents perseverance and tolerance, again suitable symbols for Howard Park. The Madfish collection includes a Chardonnay and a Sauvignon Blanc Semillon. The reds include Shiraz, Pinot Noir and a Cabernet Sauvignon Merlot Cabernet Franc blend.

The Madfish range also includes the original Madfish wines, the "Premium White" and the "Premium Red".

As I write, Howard Park are releasing two new wines, a "Leston Shiraz" from Margaret River and a "Scotsdale Cabernet Sauvignon" from the Great Southern, the first of their regional wine series.

Howard Park export a great deal of their wine, they are doing everything with style backed up by serious capital investment. Well done Jeff and Amy.

Address: Miamup Road COWARAMUP 6284	**Public Hours:** 10am-5pm, daily	Madfish Cabernet Merlot
Phone: (08) 9755 9988 **Fax:** (08) 9755 9048	**Principal Varieties:** Cabernet Sauvignon,	Howard Park Cabernet
Email: hpw@netserv.net.au	Chardonnay, Petit Verdot, Sangiovese, Shiraz	Howard Park Leston Shiraz
Owner: Jeff & Amy Burch	**Principal Wines**	Howard Park Leston Cabernet
Winemaker: Michael Kerrigan **Est:** 1986	Madfish Shiraz	Madfish Premium Red

Leeuwin Estate

As one of Australia's leading producers of high quality varietal wines, Leeuwin has 375 acres of immaculately tended vines and a state-of-the-art winery.

The guiding philosophy of Leeuwin, since its inception in 1974 has been to produce wines of distinctive character and supreme quality. That this philosophy has been successful is apparent in the recognition and acclaim which Leeuwin has received from experts both in Australia and Overseas.

As one of the five founding wineries in the Margaret River region, the property was identified by eminent American winemaker, Robert Mondavi, as being ideal for the production of premium quality wine. With Mondavi as mentor, the Horgan family set about transforming their cattle farm into a boutique vineyard and winery. A nursery was planted in 1974 and the vineyards were planted over a five-year period from 1975. The first trial vintage was in 1978.

The mild, frost free winters, warm summers and free draining soils of the Leeuwin vineyard are ideal for the production of sauvignon blanc, chardonnay, riesling, cabernet sauvignon and pinot noir.

Leeuwin has concentrated on achieving complexity, balance and longevity in its wines through a blend of traditional and modern techniques.

Leeuwin's finest wines are known as the "Art Series" range. Paintings are commissioned from leading contemporary Australian artists to adorn the labels of these wines.

The "Art Series" wines have received much international attention and critical acclaim, with authoritative publications ranking the wines with the top 150 in the world and the top 20 in the "New World". In particular, Leeuwin's Art Series Chardonnays have twice been awarded gold medals in "Wine International Challenges", sponsored by the British publication "Wine Magazine", which awarded the Leeuwin 1986 Chardonnay the overall trophy for best Chardonnay in 1992. The wines have also received "Decanter" Magazine's highest recommendation.

Leeuwin wines are exported to numerous countries and carried in the first class of many international airlines.

Just as the pursuit of excellence manifests itself in the quality of Leeuwin wines, so too is it expressed in the aesthetic beauty of the winery, which overlooks a meadow, surrounded by a majestic forest of karri trees. Although the building is primarily a modern winery, its a uniquely Australian structure that blends harmoniously with its natural environment.

Leeuwin is famous for its annual alfresco concerts, which are performed in the natural amphitheatre in front of the winery. The tradition of the Leeuwin concerts began in 1985 when the London Philharmonic Orchestra performed alongside the kookaburras in this unique bushland setting. Since then the concerts have featured several international orchestras and leading performers, including Dame Kiri Te Kanawa, Ray Charles, Dionne Warwick, Diana Ross, Tom Jones and Michael Crawford.

Working on the principle that fine wines, food and the arts are highly complementary, Leeuwin Estate has evolved into a significant tourist attraction. The staging of the concerts has resulted in tourism awards for "Major Tourist Attraction" and recognition as best "Significant Local Event" along with a citation for its contribution to the arts.

Housed within the winery is Leeuwin's award winning restaurant. Adorning the restaurant walls is the collection of contemporary Australian art used on the labels featuring paintings from more than thirty prominent Australian artists including Sir Sidney Nolan, Lloyd Rees, John Olsen, Robert Juniper and Arthur Boyd. The restaurant has been a recipient of Gold Plate Awards and has attracted guest appearances from some of Australia's leading chefs.

The Leeuwin Estate is the venue for many art and photographic exhibitions. Leeuwin Estate is truly a vision splendid with everything carried out with personal care and attention to detail.

Leeuwin Estate is truly world class in every way.

Address: Stevens Rd MARGARET RIVER 6285
Phone: (08) 9757 6253 **Fax:** (08) 9757 6364
Email: info@leeuwinestate.com.au
WWW: www.leeuwinestate.com.au

Winemaker: Robert Cartwright
Est: 1974 **Vine Ha:** 100
Public Hours: 10am-4.30pm, daily
Principal Varieties: Chardonnay, Merlot,

Cabernet Sauvignon, Sauvignon Blanc, Pinot Noir, Riesling, Petit Verdot
Principal Wines
"Leeuwin Estate"

Hay Shed Hill

Situated in the heart of the Willyabrup Valley, home of the original Margaret River vineyards, Hay Shed Hill Estate is amongst the most picturesque and best equipped in the region.

The winery was named after the property's orginal wooden hay shed, a local landmark, which still stands high on the hill above the vineyard.

The 120-acre property was once a dairy farm and its first vines were planted in 1973. These vines supply a large portion of the Cabernet and Semillon.

In 1989 the existing vineyards were upgraded with new plantings and in 1993 the visually striking winery and cellar door were opened reflecting the character and lines of the weatherboard hay shed and residence.

Hay Shed Hill is renowned for producing outstanding single varietal wines from their estate grown vines. The wines have won numerous awards and have been selected by Qantas as in-flight wines.

In 2000 Hay Shed Hill was bought by the Sydney based Barrington Wine Company, as part of the Barrington mission to acquire and market well known premium brands from key wine growing regions around Australia.

The winemaking techniques are a blend of traditional methods and contemporary practices, with an emphasis on producing varietal fruit character.

Winemaking methods vary according to the intrinsic qualities of each grape variety, techniques include the use of cold fermentation, extended maceration, and barrel fermentation

and maturation in the finest French Oak.

Most activities around the vineyard are still done by hand. Cane pruning is carried out to promote quality.

New plantings are watered through to their first summer, but thereafter rely on rainfall only, which can result in reduced yields but ensure the quality is preserved.

The Sauvignon Blanc displays an array of intense, fresh tropical fruit character.

The Semillon shows strong regional and varietal character. The fruit is picked at two stages of ripeness, the first to capture the crisp, fresh herbaceous characters, the second to provide richness and complexity, the wine then spends 4 months in French Oak.

The Chardonnay is produced from vines of the Mendoza clone, renowned for its outstanding concentration of flavour and low yields. Oak fermentation and ten months maturation on lees in new French oak ensures a mouth filling, flavoursome wine.

The Cabernet Sauvignon is picked from two blocks with very different soil conditions. The original 1973 planting provide fruit with immense depth and structure, while the more recent planting provides intense

varietal cabernet character adding lifted aromatics to the wine, with its briary blackcurrant fruit and cedar overtones, this wine will comfortably cellar for up to ten years.

The Pinot Noir is produced from vines planted on a south facing slope, exposing the fruit to the cool southerly winds enabling the fruit to develop pronounced varietal characters. Traditional Burgundian processing techniques are used, including cold maceration and plunging the skins. To develop the complex characters that compliment the overt strawberry and plum aromas.

The Shiraz spends 14 months maturing in French oak, showing a bouquet of green peppercorns, soft mint and licorice.

While Hay Shed wines are made from estate grown fruit, they also produce a series of blended wines called Pitchfork.

Pitchfork White is an unwooded blend of Semillon, Sauvignon Blanc and Chardonnay.

Pitchfork Pink is a distinctive rose made from red grapes treated in a white grape style. Pitchfork Red is a blend of Shiraz, Cabernet and Merlot.

At Hayshed Estate it will always be quality before quantity.

Address: Harmans Mill Road Willyabrup Valley 6284
Phone: (08) 9755 6234
Fax: (08) 9755 6305
Email: info@hayshedhill.com.au
Owner: Barrington Wine Company

Winemaker: Peter Stanlake
Est: 1989 **Vine Ha:** 20 **Cases:** 30,000
Public Hours: 10:30am-5pm, daily
Principal Varieties: Cabernet Sauvignon, Sauvignon Blanc, Chardonnay, Shiraz
Principal Wines   **Potential**

Principal Wines	Potential
Hay Shed Hill Cabernet Sauvignon	10 yrs
Hay Shed Hill Pinot Noir	8 yrs
Hay Shed Hill Shiraz	8 yrs
Hay Shed Hill Chardonnay	6 yrs
Hay Shed Hill Semillon	6 yrs
Hay Shed Hill Sauvignon Blanc	1 yr

Lenton Brae

Bruce Tomlinson's many years as an architect, much of the time designing building for the harsh climate of the mining towns in the north of Western Australia, gave him a good grasp of the necessities and aesthetics for rural architecture. He has designed and constructed a modern winery and home at Lenton Brae that blends beautifully into its environment and yet is practical and very pleasing to the eye.

Bruce and his wife, Jeanette, moved down to the property to oversee its operations more closely and their son Edward, a Roseworthy graduate, is now in charge of the winemaking, aided by the expert advice of Gary Baldwin from Oenotech.

Ed had early success, in 1990 his 1988 cabernet won the SGIO trophy and a free trip to California and Bordeaux. Lenton Brae's other wines, a chardonnay and a semillon/sauvignon blanc, are also award winners.

The tasting room integrated into the winery, with the afternoon sun streaming in through the stained glass windows, is a must to visit in Margaret River. Lenton Brae sits astride a small hill (hence the world 'brae') with a stretch of water separating it from caves road, resplendent with bird life directly alongside and overlooking Mosswood.

Address: PO Box 500 MARGARET RIVER 6285 **Phone:** (08) 9755 6255 **Fax:** (08) 9755 6268 **Email:** lentonbrae@netserv.net.au	**Winemaker:** Edward Tomlinson **Est:** 1982 **Public Hours:** 10am-6pm, daily	**Principal Varieties:** Cabernet Sauvignon, Merlot, Sauvignon Blanc, Cabernet Franc, Chardonnay, Petit Verdot, Semillon

Moss Brothers

Jeff Moss spent a number of years as the vineyard manager for W.A.'s largest winery Houghton Wines planning and overseeing large vineyards in many of W.A.'s wine regions.

In 1984 with his three children Peter, David and Jane, he purchased a property in the pretty Willyabrup Valley.

Planting began in 1985, they built a home on the property and their first vintage was in 1988. The wines were made off site but the family really wanted to have their own creative input into the winemaking, so it was decided to build a winery which was completed in time for the 1989 vintage. Their vineyards are definitely some of the best in the region and their quality of the fruit is first class.

Both in the vineyards and in the winemaking the Moss family practice minimum intervention techniques, trying to harness all of natures gifts in the wines.

David and Jane are the winemaking team and Peter builds stainless steel tanks and other winery related equipment in his engineering workshop on the property, he has equipped much of the Moss Brothers Winery along with many others in the Region.

The Vineyard carries the name "Moses Rock" named after the Moses Rock on the coastline nearby.

The Moss Brothers range includes a Sauvignon Blanc, very much in the tropical fruit spectrum, Semillon a multi award winner with lots of citrus character, two Chardonnay's, a non-wooded and a premium Chardonnay partially barrel fermented. There is also a Verdelho generously flavoured with strong tropical overtones and the "Moses Rock White" a delicious blend of Verdelho, Sauvignon Blanc and Chardonnay. In the reds they have an elegant Cabernet Merlot, a benchmark wine of the Willyabrup Valley, a Shiraz, a Pinot Noir and the "Moses Rock Red" a great value blended red.

At their charming Cellar door they also sell a range of fortified wines aged in oak barrels in the winery and carrying the Bona Vista labels.

Address: Caves Road WILLYABRUP 6285 **Phone:** (08) 9755 6270 **Fax:** (08) 9755 6298 **Email:** mbv@mossbrothers.com.au	**WWW:** www.mossbrothers.com.au **Winemaker:** David & Jane Moss **Est:** 1984 **Public Hours:** 10am-5pm, daily	**Principal Varieties:** Cabernet Franc, Chardonnay, Sauvignon Blanc, Cabernet Sauvignon, Merlot, Semillon

Moss Wood Wines

Moss Wood was established by Dr. Bill Pannell and his wife, Sandra, in 1969. The first grapes planted on the 25 acre Willyabrup property were cabernet sauvignon. These were followed by pinot noir, semillon and chardonnay. Great care was taken both in choosing the site for the vineyard and the vines to be planted. As a result, fruit has been of very high quality.

The first wine, a cabernet sauvignon, was made in 1973. Later wines were made with the assistance of Roseworthy graduate, Keith Mugford who bought Moss Wood from the Pannell's some years ago. The pinot noir of Moss Wood almost defies description with its complex rich flavours, silky texture and long finish combining to make this one of the best wines of this variety in Australia. Part of the procedure employed to create this magnificent wine involves a considerable sacrifice on the part of the Mugford's in that

they thin the bunches before the grapes ripen, to lower the crop and increase the intensity of flavour in the grapes.

The other red release from Moss Wood is their cabernet sauvignon. This intense wine consistently rates as one of Australia's top ten reds, integrating deep flavours of mint and herbs, showing a floral lift in the bouquet. In recent years, the Moss Wood white wines have shown considerable development. The unwooded semillon shows complex flavours echoed by the chardonnay.

The latter wine is more complex, however, as a result of varietal differences and the careful wood ageing of half of the wine, prior to blending.

The reputation established by Bill and Sandra Pannell at Moss Wood has been carried on and enhanced by the hard work and winemaking skill of the Mugford's. Both families have made considerable contributions to the Margaret River region and the best of Moss Wood's wines are comparable to any in the world.

Address: Metricup Road WILLYABRUP 6280 **Phone:** (08) 9755 6266 **Fax:** (08) 9755 6303 **Email:** mooswood@mosswood.com.au **WWW:** www.mosswood.com.au	**Winemaker:** Keith Mugford **Est:** 1969 **Vine Ha:** 10 **Principal Varieties:** Chardonnay, Merlot,	Cabernet Sauvignon, Pinot Noir, Semillon, Cabernet Franc, Petit Verdot **Principal Wines** "Moss Wood"

Ribbon Vale

Ribbon Vale is a pretty Estate with sweeping views of the Willyabrup Valley, the name came about due to the fact the property is only 185 metres wide by 1.3 kilometers long.

The winery's symbol emblazoned on the large water tank in front of the Cellars is a distinctive Blue Wren which inhabits the vineyard.

In 2000 Ribbon Vale has had a change of ownership, now coming under the control of leading winemaker and viticulturist Keith Mugford and his wife Clare, who have also been the proprietors of icon winery Mosswood since 1985. Keith started work with Bill Pannell at Mosswood as a Roseworthy graduate in 1978. Keith has proved himself to be a very good viticulturist and a consummate winemaker. I'm sure great things are ahead for Ribbon Vale.

The vineyards were planted by John

James an industrial chemist, with the Midland brick company in 1977, ironically almost the same time Keith Mugford arrived in Margaret River.

The 1993 Ribbon Vale Sauvignon Blanc became a much celebrated wine when it won three trophies at the Perth Royal Show that year. The

Reds from Ribbon Vale have been traditionally big flavorsome wines. The Merlot standing out as the best, I am sure Keith will give them a little more elegance and complexity, with such good grapes to work with and with their care in the vineyard, I am certain the Mugfords will really revitalise Ribbon Vale.

Address: Caves Road WILLYABRUP 6284 **Phone:** (08) 9755 6272 **Fax:** (08) 9755 6337 **Email:** ribbonvale@ribbonvale.com.au **Owner:** Clare & Keith Mugford	**Winemaker:** Keith Mugford **Est:** 1977 **Vine Ha:** 7.3 **Cases:** 6,000 **Public Hours:** 10am-5pm, daily	**Principal Wines** Cab Sav/Cabernet Franc/Merlot Semillon/Sauvignon Blanc Merlot	**Potential** 7-10 yrs 7-10 yrs

Palandri Wines is one of Australia's younger wine companies, having been established in late 1999 and early 2000.

Yet, in less than two years it has established a remarkable track record, a state-of-the-art winery, one of Western Australia's largest vineyards and a national sales and marketing network.

In early 1998 Palandri Wines was only a concept. By the end of 1999 it was a fully functional wine product on company.

The driving force behind Palandri Wines has been Darrel Jarvis, former CEO of Heytesbury Pty. Ltd. and a self-styled "corporate doctor."

As Executive Chairman, Darrell Jarvis has built a strong team around him - but always with an eye firmly on good corporate structure, a motivated workforce, and a strong product and marketing focus.

A key element of that focus is the state-of-the-art winery located north of Margaret river on the busy Bussell Highway and a dedicated wine making team headed by Chief Wine Maker, Tony Carapetis.

In fact, it was Carapetis who provided much of the drive when the embryonic winery was first being established and fruit contracts with grape growers in Margaret River were being negotiated.

The result today is a showcase winery and magnificent Caller Door facility - considered by many to be one of the best anywhere in Australia.

It is a far cry from October 1999 when the current winery and Cellar Door facility was nothing more than

farm land on which cows were grazed.

Three months later that empty paddock had been transformed into a state-of-the-art, modern winery, capable of processing 1,500 tonnes of fruit a year.

By the start of the 2001 vintage, the facility had been further expanded, handling a crush of just under 3,000 tonnes.

Within the next 12-18 months, that capacity will be further increased, with the aim of expanding wine making facilities to process a minimum of 5,000 tonnes of fruit annually.

Looking back, Tony Carapetis comments: ""In October, 1999, the site was just a concrete pad in an open paddock.

"Three months later, on the morning of February 25, we started crushing Chardonnay -- I do not think anyone has built a fully functional winery in such a short time."

Importantly, the winery has been specifically designed for small batch processing, with the wine making team having the opportunity to isolate the best fruit and turn it into very special wines.

Palandri Wines

In the words of Tony Carapetis, "The aim is simple - to develop a Palandri Wines house style.

"My aim is to produce wines that are very definable from the winery and from the Margaret River or Frankland River regions."

In this regard, Tony Carapetis has few worries as the 210 hectares of vines planted at the Frankland River vineyard - 70 per cent reds and 30 per cent whites - are now bearing fruit.

By the 2002 vintage they will be a major source of fruit for Palandri Wines.

However, the Palandri Wines facility at Margaret River is much more than just a production facility - it is a major tourist attraction.

The Cellar door facility offers something for all ages -- reflecting the lifestyle wines produced by Palandri Wines.

Incorporated in the facility are mobile tasting benches which cater for small or large groups, a high-tech computer games area to entertain youngsters while their parents browse through ranges of wines, clothing and local produce and a superb restaurant.

The restaurant offers mouth-watering platter dishes and exotic individual dishes specially developed to

perfectly complement the Palandri wine ranges and prepared under the watchful eyes of a team of chefs of the highest credentials.

The idea of marrying the food and wine experience through a taste plate concept was foremost from the outset.

As a result the team of chefs have created different platters to match particular Palandri wines, providing visitors with the opportunity to learn how wines and food marry together to produce terrific taste sensations.

As Palandri Wines expands nationally and globally, it has ensured its

product range has been backed by strong marketing skills.

In late 2000, Palandri released its first commercial range - the Aurora range - a Semillon - Sauvignon Blanc, Cabernet-Shiraz and a Chardonnay.

This initial release was followed by an expansion of the Aurora range in early 2001. In turn the launch of its limited release Baldivis range occurred in April 2001.

Then, in July 2001, the company released its premium "Palandri" range -- a milestone event for Palandri Wines Limited.

The Palandri range of five wines marks the release of wines specifically sourced exclusively from grapes produced in the Margaret River region.

Importantly, this release sets a new benchmark for the company - the starting point for the premium wines of the future.

And the future looks strong, especially as Palandri wines is backed by more than 1,700 private investors who have put more than $113 million behind the company.

A further $60 million is being raised during 2001-2002. With that sort of backing, Palandri Wines is very much an organisation that aims to make a significant contribution to the development of world wine brands in Australia.

Address: Bussell HWY COWARAMUP 6285	Est: 1999 Vine Ha: 240		Palandri Shiraz	4-6 yrs
Phone: (08) 9755 5711 Fax: (08) 9755 5722	Cases: 250,000		Aurora 2000 Merlot	2-4 yrs
Email: info@palandri.com.au	Public Hours: 10am-5pm, daily		Palandri 2000 Chardonnay	4-6 yrs
WWW: www.palandri.com.au	Principal Wines	Potential	Palandri 2000 Cabernet Merlot	2-4 yrs
Winemaker: Tony Carapetis	Palandri 2000 Sauvignon Blanc	2-3 yrs	Palandri Cabernet Sauvignon	4-8 yrs

Redgate Wines

One of the most extraordinary and pleasurable experiences of my years of travel researching Pictorial Wine books occurred on Anzac Day, 1995.

My dear friend, the late Milan Roden, and I were taking some early morning photos as Redgate, making the most of the sunrise, who should appear on the doorstep of the winery but Bill Ullinger on his way to the

Anzac Day Dawn ceremony in Margaret River. In chatting with Bill, he reminisced on his last bombing raid as a 21 year old pilot in charge of a massive Lancaster bomber, 50 years earlier, in 1945, 50 years to the day, it was on Anzac Day 1945. When we asked to take his photo he said, "do you want me to put my medals on". I replied, "we won't take

your photo without them".

As we took Bill's photo, with the Australian Flat flying above the winery's outdoor tank farm, up walked our old friend Andrew Forsell with whom we spent many happy days in California.

Andrew was a winemaker for many years for the high profile Sonoma Winery, Ironhorse.

Bill's son, Paul, was next to appear on the scene. He and Andrew then took us through the wines, from the vintage just completed, Andrew's first vintage working with Paul. The wines were truly superb, they all had enormous fruit flavours and great balance. I must say the Redgate O.F.S. Semillon (Our Finest Selection) is one of the finest white wines I have ever tasted with its intense lychee like exotic aromas and full kaleidoscope of flavours.

Bill Ullinger established Redgate in 1976 at an age when many would be contemplating retirement. The property's purchase came after a long search of several hundred kilometres of Western Australia's coastline. Early teething difficulties and the first wine tax imposition in 1984 had the Ullinger's on the verge of closing the winery's doors. Then came their victory at the 1984 Adelaide Wine Show, winning the prestigious Montgomery Trophy with their 1982 Cabernet Sauvignon.

The winery doesn't have the high flying profile of its neighbours, Leeuwin Estate and Cape Mentelle, but that's changing and Bill Ullinger's 'red gate' has opened up and dropped a few top wine rockets to shake up the premium market. Make sure you track them down.

Address: Boodjidup Rd MARGARET RIVER 6285	**Est:** 1977 **Vine Ha:** 20 **Cases:** 12,000	Sauvignon Blanc Reserve — 3-5 yrs
Phone: (08) 9757 6488 **Fax:** (08) 9757 6308	**Public Hours:** 10am-5pm, daily	Classic Semillon-Sauvignon Blanc — 0-4 yrs
Email: info@redgatewines.com.au	**Principal Varieties:** Cab Franc, Cab Sav,	Semillon — 3-5 yrs
WWW: www.redgatewines.com.au	Chardonnay, Chenin Blanc, Merlot, Pinot Noir,	Late Harvest Riesling — 1-4 yrs
Owner: Ullinger Family	Sauvignon Blanc, Semillon, Shiraz	Pinot Noir — 3-6 yrs
Winemaker: Andrew Forsell	**Principal Wines** **Potential**	Cabernet Sauvignon — 5-10 yrs

Rivendell Wines

Rivendell is a beautiful refuge from the hustle and bustle of everyday life. The tranquil sheltered gardens and orchard surround the winery restaurant and gallery that are built with local timbers and blend sensitively into their environment.

The Standish family began planting vines in 1987. Their location on the North Eastern side of the main ridge is in the Yallingup area of the Margaret River Region.

The sheltered micro-climate is ideal for viticulture and their 32 acre vineyard produces really top quality, flavoursome fruit.

The first wine produced was a Semillon-Sauvignon Blanc in 1990. Rivendell also produces a Verdelho, a varietal Semillon and a varietal Sauvignon Blanc. They produce a complex red called "The Cabernets" a 60% Cabernet Sauvignon, 30% Cabernet France and 10% Merlot blend, aged in older French Alllier

and Nevers oak for 12 months. It's a fruit driven style with beautiful palate

young and developing apricot overtones as it matures.

Rivendell make a mavellous vintage port from three traditional Portuguese varieties, Touriga, Suzao and Tinta Cao. Its beautiful fruit sweetness is balanced by a clean dry finish. It's a great wine to round off your tasting before enjoying lunch in the Garden Room Bistro with its outdoor patio looking out over the inspirational terraced gardens where children can happily play. The gardens are not only there for their looks, the Standish family make their own homemade preserves from their fruit trees and berries.

Weddings and celebrations are regular events at Rivendell. The Gallery features fine examples from local artists and crafts people.

Winemaker is Mark Standish, son of the founders, Pete and Lu Standish,

richness and a soft finish: an intense mouth filling wine · pure indulgence. Their other red is a varietal Shiraz.

Another fine wine in the Rivendell stable is their "Honeysuckle". Late picked Semillon grapes are fermented leaving some residual grape sugar in the wine. It's a luscious drop that develops with age, showing fig like characters whilst

while Mark's wife Wendy also works hard in their many faceted enterprise.

If you want to stay over, Rivendell also operates the "Brandywine Lodge", providing country style accomodation for families and groups. Its bushland setting is truly charming, like the rest of their beloved Estate.

Address: Wildwood Road YALLINGUP	Winemaker: Mark Standish	Principal Wines	Potential
Phone: (08) 9755 2090 Fax: (08) 9755 2301	Est: 1987 Vine Ha: 13	The Cabernets	2-10 yrs
Email: rivendellwines@netserv.com.au	Cases: 3,000	Sauvignon Blanc	1-5 yrs
WWW: www.rivendellwines.com.au	Public Hours: 10:30am-5pm, daily	Noble Semillon	1-5 yrs

Sandalford Margaret River

One of the largest vineyards in Western Australia is the 800 acres of vines owned and operated by Sandaford Wines at Willyabrup. The vineyard is beautifully situated at the base of a circular valley. This protected site prevents damage to vines by harsh onshore winds, yet allows fruit ample exposure to the sun.

Planting commenced in 1972 under supervision of the then Managing Director, John Roe. In a recent transformation of the property, retrellising, computer controlled irrigation and the implementation of a strict vineyard regeneration program has given rise to fantastic improvements to both quality and yield.

All grapes are machine harvested at night and transported to the company's Swan Valley winery, in the cool of the night in one tonne bins, where the wines are made under the eye of experienced and skilled senior winemaker Paul Boulden.

Late in 1985, a delightful rammed earth tasting and cellar door area was constructed. The interior is furnished with polished jarrah (the local timber), and the area offers magnificent views over the vineyard. Sandalford's premium range is available, consisting of wines made from grapes grown in the Margaret River, Mount Barker and Frankland River regions. These are the Riesling, Chardonnay, Verdelho, Shiraz, Cabernet Sauvignon, Merlot, Semillon and Semillon Sauvignon Blanc. These wines represent excellent value for the consumer; their quality is consistently high and prices are very reasonable.

Address: Metricup Road WILLYABRUP 6284	**Est:** 1840 **Vine Ha:** 120 **Cases:** 90,000	Chardonnay	2-5 yrs
Phone: (08) 9374 9374 **Fax:** (08) 9274 2154	**Public Hours:** 10.30am-5pm, daily except	MR Verdelho	2-5 yrs
Email: sandalford@sandalford.com	Christmas Day and Good Friday	Cabernet Sauvignon	5-15 yrs
WWW: www.sandalford.com	**Principal Varieties:** Cab Sav, Chard, Chenin Blanc,	Riesling	5-15 yrs
Owner: Peter and Debra Prendiville	Merlot, Ries, Sav Blanc, Sem, Shiraz, Verdelho	Chardonnay	2-5 yrs
Winemaker: Paul Boulden	**Principal Wines** **Potential**	Shiraz Cabernet	

Treeton Estate

"Rralph" makes your arrival at Treeton something special. This very clever border collie leaps up onto the substantial gate post heralding your entry, it seems only right he should "keep watch" over the estate of his very maritime master, David McGowan, a former mariner and head of the School of Maritime Studies at the Fremantle Technical College.

The Margaret River region with its maritime climate seemed to be the ideal spot for David to rest his sealegs, rest probably wouldn't be the word.

David and his delightful wife Corinne bought the property in 1981 but spent only weekends and David's 12 weeks of annual leave from TAFE on the vineyard over the next 9 years. In 1992 David took a years long service leave from TAFE and returned to the fishing industry skippering, a scallop boat at Shark Bay to raise some capital to be able to build a winery to add to his vineyards. 1998 saw the first crop of sauvignon blanc, 4 acres were planted several years before.

David makes a light red, Petit rouge, in deference to his French speaking wife, it's lovely chilled. The Treeton Shiraz is a substantial wine full of wild berry flavours. Treeton also have a Chardonnay, a Semillon and make a fine Vintage Port, a favourite of David's and we enjoyed a short snort in the charming Alfresco eating area which forms part of the cellar door. You must not miss the warm hospitality and good wines from this slightly out of the way stopover. Treeton also now have a second cellar door in the small village of Cowaramup on the main Bussell Highway.

Address: Lot 1 North Treeton Road COWARAMUP 6284	**Winemaker:** David McGowan **Cases:** 4,000	Chardonnay	5 yrs
	Public Hours: 10am-6pm, daily	Shiraz	7+ yrs
Phone: (08) 9755 5481 **Fax:** (08) 9755 5051	**Principal Varieties:** Chard, Cab Sav, Shiraz,	Cabernet Sauvignon	7+ yrs
Email: treeton@netserv.net.au **Est:** 1991	Sauv Blanc, Riesling, Semillon, Chenin Blanc	Sauvignon Blanc	5 yrs
WWW: www.treetonestate.com.au **Vine Ha:** 8	**Principal Wines** **Potential**	Petit Rouge (100% Shiraz)	3 yrs

Vasse Felix

One of Australia's most beautiful winery complexes belongs to Vasse Felix, Margaret River's first vineyard and winery founded in 1967.

The winery and vineyards were purchased in 1987 by the Holmes á Court family, a most successful Western Australian Business dynasty, headed today by celebrated business woman Janet Holmes a' Court. The Holmes á Court's have done a superb job expanding the vineyards and developing the winery/hospitality centre. The Restaurant has recently been expanded and includes an outdoor timber verandah looking out over the vineyards from the top of the winery.

Vasse Felix's beginning were not so illustrious Dr Tom Cullity was the first to follow the advice from John Gladestone's Research Papers, suggesting the area was ideal for premium wine production, Cullity named the property Vasse Felix after French Seaman Thomas Vasse from the Geographe, who lost his life when a long boat overturned at the mouth of the river which now bears his name. Felix is Latin for Lucky an ironical twist, also the second name of the ships Captain Hamelin. Cullity employed a novel method of bird control, with trained Peregrine Falcons, unfortunately they never returned once let free, but the Falcon

symbol appears on the Vasse Felix label to this day.

The vineyards around the winery cover some 88 acres. The soils are gravelly loam and the moderating effect of the nearby ocean, in particular creates wonderful red wines the Vasse Felix Shiraz is not only probably the best in Margaret River but one of Australia's finest; likewise the Cabernet Sauvignon. Many of the vines are 30 years old and their character really comes through in the wines. Vasse Felix pioneered the Classic Dry White blend of Semillon and Sauvignon Blanc for which the region is famous, they also make a top class complex Chardonnay.

Apart from the vineyards at Cowaramup they have a large vineyard of 350 acres at Jindong in the north of the Margaret River Wine Region. At one stage the Holmes á Court family owned the pioneer "Forest Hill Vineyard" at Mt Barker in the Great Southern Region first

planted in 1965, these are still on a long term lease to Vasse Felix and the Forest Hill Range of wines is excellent, the Riesling and Cabernet Sauvignon are very fine wines.

Chief winemaker Clive Otto is very experienced and a great hands on operator, who leaves nothing to chance, Bob Baker is the extremely efficient General Manager and Michael Whyte the very affable sales and public relations Manager.

Vasse Felix added a very efficient new winery complex a couple of years ago which also produces Methode Champenoise.

The Underground tasting cellar with its entrance under the landscaped gardens is absolutely charming. The Café is on the ground floor of the imposing stone and timber main building, it has been recently extended, it's excellent and they also bake their own cakes, pastries and bread. The Restaurant above is spectacular and serves top class food, both enjoy wonderful views over the gardens with the Willyabrup Brook babbling by. The building also includes a large gallery which has regular exhibitions and can host functions of up to 500 people, it's truly imposing, like the rest of Vasse Felix's superb facilities. This is an impressive winery in the world wine arena.

Address: Corner Caves Road & Harmans Mill South Road COWARAMUP 6284	**Winemaker:** Cliev Otto	Classic Dry Red	5 yrs
	Est: 1967 **Vine Ha:** 175 **Cases:** 100,000	Semillon	5 yrs
Phone: (08) 9756 5000 **Fax:** (08) 9755 5425	**Public Hours:** 10am-5pm, daily	Chardonnay	
Email: info@vassefelix.com.au	**Principal Wines** **Potential**	Cabernet Merlot	
WWW: www.vassefelix.com.au	Classic Dry White 2 yrs	Cabernet Sauvignon	

Voyager Estate

Michael Wright is a patient perfectionist who leaves no stone unturned in the fulfillment of his grand vision at Voyager Estate. His extremely keen intellect and challenging mind are constantly working towards his long term goal, to make Voyager the finest Vineyard Wine and Food Estate in the world, he is well advanced on this noble Voyage.

Michael's family had humble beginnings in Australia, his forebears were tenant farmers in Scotland, which says a lot for their hardy and resilient nature. They arrived in Australia in 1854 and settled at Maldon in Central Victoria, a place of cold harsh winters, maybe reminding them of home. Late in the 1800's the

Wrights moved to Western Australia and gradually accumulated large landholdings in the wheat belt.

In the early 1960's the family's life took a remarkable turn, Michael's father Peter formed a partnership with Lang Hancock and began the exploitation of the Pilbara Iron ore deposit, the worlds largest. By the late 1980's Michael was feeling a strong need to produce a premium product of some kind, something that involved Agriculture and Tourism, he was also looking for something long term to build.

This need culminated in the purchase in 1991, of a 23 acre vineyard in Southern Margaret River near to Leewin Estate. The name of the property "Freycinet" after Captain

Freycinet a French Sea Captain who explored the coast of the region. Almost immediately Michael was faced with some problems, a legal challenge from the makers of the Spanish Sparkling Wine "Frexinet", regarding the use of the name and confusion, with the small Tasmanian winery of the same name. Michael wisely decided to rename the property "Voyager" based aptly on his family company name.

Michael then purchased some 500 acres around his regional site and put together a carefully mapped out grand plan.

In a region with some of Australia's most beautiful wineries, none quite match the stunning symmetry and fresh clean lines of Voyager Estate

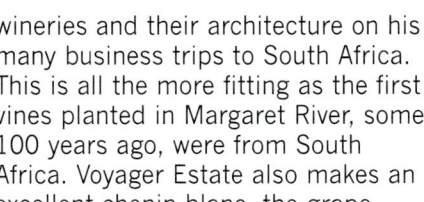

with its 'Cape Dutch' design, reminiscent of the great wineries in the Cape Province of South Africa. Michael was inspired by these

wineries and their architecture on his many business trips to South Africa. This is all the more fitting as the first vines planted in Margaret River, some 100 years ago, were from South Africa. Voyager Estate also makes an excellent chenin blanc, the grape made famous in South Africa under the name Steen.

Today the property covers a substantial contiguous 750 acres, about 260 are suitable for planting, about 170 acres are now planted and plans are for a total of 250 acres in the long term. Michael is currently exploring further land purchases in the region. His restless energy and determined, thorough approach were well evident to me on a recent visit to Voyager when I accompanied Michael, his Vineyard Manger Stephen James and world renowned Victicultural Consultant David Jordan, as they evaluated dozens of soil sample pits that had been dug on a neighboring property.

Voyager put enormous effort into their vineyard, believing very deeply that "Terrior" (the French term which encompasses everything around where the vine grows, soil structure, drainage, slope of the land, aspect and everything about the micro climate) is vital to wine quality and individuality.

Winemaker Cliff Royle joined Voyager in time for the 2000 vintage, he is extremely talented and innovative, he follows on from inaugural winemaker Stuart Pym who has gone on to Devils Lair. Cliff a Western Australian started off in the Hospitality industry and brewing, then completed his winemaking training at Charles Sturt

Voyager Estate

University at Wagga.

Cliff works very closely with Vineyards Manager Steve James and they indulge in the expensive crop limiting and quality enhancing techniques of shoot thinning, bunch thinning and exacting Vine Canopy Management, to ensure their grapes are absolutely chocked with flavour, character and beautifully balanced.

A production of 60,000 cases of premium wines is anticipated. Already the Voyager Estate wines have made a mark for themselves amongst Australia's best. The range includes a complex barrel fermented Chardonnay, a varietal Semillon with great palate length, a third of this wine is also barrel fermented, certainly it will age well. The other whites are a fresh unwooded Sauvignon Blanc Semillon (55% Sauvignon Blanc and 45% Semillon) a fresh fruit-driven Chenin Blanc and a recently released Marsanne. The first red released was a 92 vintage Cabernet Sauvignon with a touch of Merlot and Cabernet Franc blended in for softness. The wine is a firm style with loads of cassis like fruit and a hint of minty herbaceousness. The 1993, 94 and 95 have all picked up gold medals and several trophies.

Michael Wright has always wanted to produce a super premium Reserve wine, this desire came to fruition in 2000 when Voyager released their 1992 "Tom Price" Cabernet Sauvignon Merlot which had been maturing quietly for 7 years. Each year when the Vintage is suitable

(there will be no 1993) a careful selection of the best areas of the vineyards followed by a rigorous barrel selection process and 7 years maturation means this wine is in the top echelon of Australia's finest reds.

The "Tom Price" is named after the Leading American Mining Engineer Thomas Price who assisted Peter Wright and Lang Hancock in the development of the Pilbara Iron Ore Deposits and after whom Mount Tom Price is named.

At present Michael is constructing a massive underground cellar on the down slope from the main Restaurant and wine tasting building, it will provide perfect temperature and humidity for his barrel and bottle maturation needs.

The Restaurant at Voyager is truly grand and special but relaxed and friendly.

The Gardens at Voyager resplendent with roses and many exotic plants are magnificent and laid out on a grand scale. The classic Cape Dutch style architecture reminiscent of South Africa blends very effectively into the atmosphere of the complex.

Looking out over a large valley, future plans are for the gardens to extend south creating an unforgettable vista of statuesque Jarrah and Karri trees.

The Voyager of the present is spectacular but the Voyager of the future will be breathtaking.

At Voyager Estate Michael Wright has not rushed any of the necessary moves needed to make it a leading Australian wine company. I am sure the future will prove the huge investment involved has been worthwhile.

Address: Stevens Rd MARGARET RIVER 6285	Cases: 16,700-28,000	Chardonnay	2-5 yrs
Phone: (09) 385 3133 Fax: (09) 383 4029	Public Hours: 10am-5pm, daily	Cabernet Sauvignon/Merlot	5-10 yrs
Email: wine@voyagerestate.com.au	Principal Varieties: Cab Sav, Chard, Chenin	Semillon	5-10 yrs
Owner: Michael Wright Est: 1978	Blanc, Semillon, Sauv Blanc, Merlot, Shiraz	Classic White	2 yrs
Winemaker: Stuart Pym Vine Ha: 44	Principal Wines Potential	Chenin Blanc	2 yrs

Watershed

This fully integrated vineyard and winery development is one of the most exciting current events, in a region that is alive with exciting projects. Driving through the region in October 2000, I was struck by a large sign on a beautiful piece of land, five kilometres south of Margaret River on the Bussell Highway, not far from the high profile vineyards and wineries of Voyager Estate and Leeuwin Estate.

This extremely well thought out project involves highly respected winemaker John Wade, who founded the very successful Howard Park Wines in the Great Southern Region in 1986, having already held some illustrious posts in the industry, including Chief Winemaker at Wynns Coonawarra.

John has designed the winery which will be built in modular stages, culminating in a crush of around 800 tonnes · a very manageable premium wine vintage to achieve absolute top quality. By 2006 the Watershed Vineyard will be supplying all the grapes, from their own 192 acres of vines, that are being planted in 2001. The vineyard land has been very carefully chosen with the involvement of John Wade and

viticultural consultant Simon Robertson who has a viticultural degree from Charles Sturt University. Simon has held many key industry positions working for Penfolds in Coonawarra, Swanson, a high profile vineyard in California's Napa Valley and the Pertaringa Vineyards company from McLaren Vale in South Australia, one of the states largest and most successful vineyard management companies. He has also worked in the Bordeaux region and in Margaret River at Voyager Estate, Vasse Felix as Vineyard Manager and as viticulturalist at Devil's Lair since 1993.

The extremely successful wine marketer Stephen Heller, who has really put the Wise Winery from Margaret River on the map, is already working on national and international markets preparing the way for Watershed Wines.

Watershed have a magnificent site for their cellar door on the main intersection of the highway and the road leading to Voyager, Leeuwin Estate, Redgate, Xanadu Wines and Cape Mentelle.

The Watershed project will gradually expand in three stages, the winery's final capacity will be 2400 tonnes,

at which time it is planned to seek listing on the Australian stock exchange.

At present the investors in Watershed get a multifaceted holding including ownership of part of the land, part of the winery production plant and the proceeds from the sale of the wines. The other benefit is membership of the Watershed Wine Club, which includes amongst other advantages, 25% off the retail prices of the Watershed Wines. There will initially be a premium range in the $15-$20 retail price per bottle market and a super premium range somewhere over $20 per bottle.

The professionally designed packaging is certainly classy and eye catching and a huge effort has already been made in securing local and overseas markets. Agents have already been appointed within Australia and in the main overseas markets.

The Australian Tax Office has issued a product ruling which provides tax certainty for Watershed Investors.

I am most impressed with the way this whole venture has been conceived and put into action, its going to be a real Watershed of Wine.

Wise Wines

Perth Entrepreneur Ron Wise was most impressed by Dr John Gladstones research on the potential of viticulture, in the South West of WA that he sought out a sheltered property close to the ocean to plant vines. He found this on the Lee side of the prevailing winds at Eagle Bay, with magnificent views over Geographe Bay, just around the corner from Cape Naturaliste.

The sheltered northeast facing slopes overlooking the spring fed Meelup Valley have proved ideal for vines. After purchasing Geographe Estate (which was planted mainly to Cabernet in 1988) in 1992, Ron also purchased Eagle Bay Estate, next door, which already had an 8 year old vineyard including Semillon, Sauvignon Blanc, Shiraz and Merlot. The Wise Vineyards at Eagle Bay now cover 50 acres of the 150 acre property, much of which is native bushland.

Wise have been most successful with their Merlot and Shiraz but also make a very good Semillon/Sauvignon Blanc, helped by their mild maritime climate. Robert Parker selected their range of chardonnays among the top 25 in Australia.

There is also a second range of wines under the 'Coat Door' Label which includes a soft generous Cabernet/Merlot and an unwooded Chardonnay (Aquercus).

Wise has a stunning Restaurant with a balcony which is canter-levered out from the building and which can seat up to 150 people. The views over natural bushland and Geographe Bay are simply awesome. The innovate food and attentive friendly service make a meal here a very special experience. The Cellar Door with its outdoor courtyard also looking out over the bay is beautifully appointed.

Tucked amongst the woodlands surrounding the Winery complex are four unique Chalets. They are all fully equipped and each one has its own special character - The 'Tea House' sleeps 8 - 10, The 'Studio' 4 - 6, 'Potters Cottage' 4 and the cute 'Doll House' sleeps 2. There is also a delightful barbecue area amongst the Chalets. It's a very pleasant 20 minute valley walk through the bushland to Meelup Beach and a 10 minute stroll to the Wise Restaurant.

Why not extend your stay in Margaret River at this special place - you will be making a very Wise choice!!

Address: Lot 4 Eagle Bay Road EAGLE BAY 6281	Winemaker: Bruce Dukes	Eagle Bay Semillon Sauvignon Blanc 3-5 yrs
	Est: 1986 Vine Ha: 42 Cases: 35,000	Reserve Chardonnay 5+ yrs
Phone: (08) 9756 8627 Fax: (08) 9756 8770	Public Hours: 10am-5pm, daily	Cabernet Sauvignon 5+ yrs
Email: cellar@wisewine.com.au	Principal Wines Potential	Coat Door Shiraz Now-2 yrs
Owner: Ron & Sandra Wise	Eagle Bay Shiraz 5+ yrs	Coat Door Unwooded Chardonnay Now

Xanadu Wines

The Xanadu vineyard was established in 1977, by Irish doctors John and Eithne Lagan. As the winery's name suggests, this operation is more than a mere business. John and Eithne share a passion for art and literature, in addition to their love of wine. Their home houses one of the world's most extensive collections of early books and printed works and the name 'Xanadu' is taken from the epic poem by Samuel T. Coleridge.

The cellar door is constructed from local stone and boasts beautiful stained glass windows. A love of beauty has been carried over into the vineyard. In 1999 Xanadu became a public company and in 2001 it listed on the Australian Stock Exchange. There has been a huge increase in the vineyard holdings. 275 acres are now under vine, and varieties are semillon, sauvignon blanc, chardonnay, cabernet sauvignon, merlot and cabernet franc.

The first wines were made at Xanadu in 1981 and some excellent wines were produced right from the beginning. I well remember tasting the 1985 Semillon during a visit to the winery in 1986. Its huge gooseberry flavour and complexity were a knock-out. Today most of the Semillon finds it's way into the excellent 'Secession', a great Bordeaux style dry white.

Winemaker since 1990, has been the innovative Swiss, Jurg Muggli. The focus today at Xanadu is firmly on innovative quality winemaking and grapegrowing, pushing the frontiers of premium winemaking with outstanding results.

Address: Boodjidup Road MARGARET RIVER 6285 **Phone:** (08) 9757 2581 **Fax:** (08) 9757 3389 **Email:** info@xanaduwines.com.au **WWW:** www.xanaduwines.com.au	**Winemaker:** Jurg Muggli **Est:** 1977 **Vine Ha:** 130 **Cases:** 50,000 **Public Hours:** 10am-5pm, daily **Principal Varieties:** Semillon, Chardonnay, Cabernet Sauvignon, Sauvignon Blanc,	Merlot, Cabernet Franc **Principal Wines** Xanadu Xanadu Secession Xanadu Lagan Estate

The Berry Farm

In summer or winter there is no lovelier place to visit whilst you are in Margaret River than The Berry Farm. With its lush gardens of fruits and fields of berries, it's a real

Cornucopia of food and there's also a great range of fruit wines to try.

Owner Eion Lindsay is busy indeed. The Berry Farm has a delightful cottage restaurant which serves

morning and afternoon teas all day everyday, except Christmas Day, Boxing Day, New Years Day and Good Friday. Light lunches are also served from noon until 3.00 p.m.

If you visit between October and February you can pick your own strawberries or if your in Maragaret River from May to September you can gather your own Kiwi Fruit. The fruit wines range from crisp dry styles through sparkling to dessert styles and some full flavoured fortified port styles from the dark berries.

The Berry Farm also make a range of jams and conserves. Separately on the property they have a "Vinegary" where they make a distinctive range of fruit and herb vinegar's. Everything is made from fresh produce grown on the farm, which is located about 15 kms south east of the town of Margaret River, near the corner of Bessell and Rosa Glen Roads.

Make sure you put it on your agenda, for a very fruitful experience!!

Great Southern

Some 400 kms south of Perth, near the Great Southern Ocean, is a wine region of world potentia which is already producing some exciting wines.

Geographically it is the largest wine producing area in Australia, spreading between the towns of Albany, Denmark, Mt. Barker and Frankland, forming an area of some 3,600 kilometres. That's around 900,000 acres which could provide three times the current Australian wine grape harvest if it were all planted to vines. This, of course would not be possible, but it does show the area's potential.

The climate s perfect, cool with dry summers and wet winters; some supplementary irrigation is necessary, but the country lends itself to the construction of dams. In the east, the Stirling and Porongurup Ranges provide an awesome beauty unrivalled by any other Australian wine region. Its isolation adds to this feeling of grandeur.

The southern coastline is stunning and the stands of eucalypts in the west are breathtaking. Yields are low, but quality is outstanding. The five sub-regions · Albany, Stirling Ranges, Porongurup, Mt. Barker, Denmark and Frankland · support more than 20 producers, all established within the last 27 years. The first winery

in the region, Plantagenet, was commissioned in time for the 1975 vintage, with the area's first vineyards being established less than 35 years ago.

During the late 1950's the relieving horticultural adviser to the region was Bill Jamieson, later to become Western Australia's Great Southern Government Viticulturist. He was struck by the orchard region's potential for wine and followed this through over the decades. The great Maurice O'Shea from the Hunter Valley was adamant, if he had his time as a winemaker again, it would be near Albany in Western Australia.

The first vines, an experimental vineyard under Bill Jamieson's control at the Pearse family's Forest Hill property at Mt. Barker, was planted in 1965. This was followed by plantings a couple of years later by ex-Adelaide Lord Mayor, John Roche, at his Frankland River property. I tasted the first wine made from the region's grapes at the Houghton Winery with Jack Mann in 1972. A 1972 cabernet sauvignon made by him, enjoyed straight from the barrel, it was certainly impressive.

Rieslings from the Great Southern led the way with their limey intense flavours. Pinot noir has been a real star, as has chardonnay. I am sure this could be a

great region for methode champenoise. Cabernet sauvignon does well, as does shiraz and even sauvignon blanc. There are so many micro-climates and soil types, I am sure that great wines of all varieties are possible. From a wine tourist's point of view this region of natural beauty, freshness and great wines, is well worth the effort to discover.

Cellar doors have always been a little underdeveloped but during my 2000 visits I have seen this is fast changing. The new Howard Park Winery near Denmark is truly state of the art in every way. Even more impressive is the new Goundrey facility at Langton, a really world class complex. Plantagenet has had a new facade with much improved visitor facilities, Galafrey have opened a new cellar door restaurant and Matildas Meadow has a beautiful restaurant. The new West Cape Howe Winery complex is impressive as is the Somerset Hill Winery built underground with its tasting facilities in the cellar and a mushroom farm on the property, it's a great place to taste.

Nearly all the small producers have now opened cellar doors or developed their existing ones. It's a real adventure to visit the Great Southern and I always look forward to my visits there.

Great Southern - WA

1. Alkoomi Wines
2. Castle Rock
3. Fern Grove
4. Galafrey
5. Gilberts
6. Goundry Wines
7. Plantagenet
8. Somerset Hill
9. West Cape Howe
10. Wignalls

Goundrey Wines

From small beginnings, the Goundrey Wines enterprise has become not only by far the largest in the Great Southern region, but also ranks in the top three wineries in the State in terms of size, being bigger than any of the wine producers in the better known Margaret River wine region.

In the early 1970's a small five-acre vineyard of cabernet sauvignon and riesling was planted at Chapel View vineyard. The first vintage was produced in 1976 and in 1987 the company Goundrey Wines Limited, was formed, which allowed for the purchase of the Langton property. This magnificent 200 hectare hay river valley property, is now home to the main vineyard of 145 hectares including a large and modern winery which was completed in time for the 1989 vintage. The imposing winery is situated high on the valley slopes and beside it lies the historic homestead. In 1997 a magnificent new frontage to the winery was built housing one of Australia's finest cellar doors with splendid viewing

areas overlooking the barrel hall.

In 1998 the three original Goundrey vineyards were purchased by the company, these being "Windy Hill", "Chapel View" and "Williams Rest" - now "Fox River".

The combination of a cool climate and fertile soils, plus modern and effective viticultural techniques produce a high concentration of aromas and flavours. Two ranges of wine are now being produced by Goundrey, the 'Homestead Range' and a small volume under the premium 'Reserve' label.

During 2000 Goundrey Wines received over 135 awards nationally and internationally. The Schenker Trophy for the "Best Australian Wine Producer" at the International Wine and Spirit Competition in the United Kingdom - one of the worlds most prestigious awards was received in 1999. The 2000 vintage produced a record 2,701 tonnes of grapes. With the vision and the quality to succeed, Goundrey Wines is set to be a dynamic presence in the Western Australian wine industry of the future.

Address: Muir Highway MOUNT BARKER 6324	Winemaker: David Martin	Principal Wines	Potential
Phone: (08) 9851 1777 Fax: (08) 9851 1997	Est: 1971	Goundrey Unwooded Chardonnay	1-2 yrs
Email: info@goundreywines.com.au	Vine Ha: 145	Goundrey Cabernet Merlot	3-5 yrs
WWW: www.goundreywines.com.au /	Cases: 150,000	Goundrey Reserve Shiraz	5-8 yrs
www.foxriverwines.com.au	Public Hours: 10am-4.30pm, daily	Goundrey Reserve Riesling	5-10 yrs
Owner: Mr Jack Bendat	Principal Varieties: Cab Sav, Chardonnay,	Fox River Shiraz Cabernet	3-5 yrs
	Merlot, Pinot Noir, Riesling, Semillon, Shiraz	Fox River Chenin Semillon	1-2 yrs

Gilberts

The first winery one comes across after several hours driving south on the Albany Highway through the majestic Western Australian landscape is Gilberts Wines, some 18 kilometres north of Mount Barker. The statuesque Stirling and Porongurup Ranges are both visible

from the verandah of the rustic brush pole and weatherboard farm cottage tasting room.

The vineyards are set amongst a working stone fruit and apple orchard, the produce which you can taste. A Wine tasting is available daily and Fruit tasting is available January - July.

Jim and Bev Gilbert are a charming country couple, third generation horticulturists, who have a real feel for the fruit they grow naturally including the grapes that go into their wines. A crisp aromatic riesling which has won much acclaim, a full style chardonnay and a peppery shiraz with strong berry flavours that has won a number of awards.

The barbecue and picnic area is truly delightful and wine loving groups can book for a private function outside or in the cottage.

Address: RMB 438, Albany Highway KENDENUF 6323	Winemaker: Gavin Berry	Shiraz, Tawny Port	
	Est: 1985 Vine Ha: 8 Cases: 3,500	Principal Wines	Potential
Phone: (08) 9851 4028 Fax: (08) 9851 4021	Public Hours: 10am-5pm, daily (Closed	Cab/Shiraz	2+ yrs
Email: gilberts@rainbow.agn.net.au	Good Friday & Boxing Day)	Riesling	5+ yrs
Owner: Jim & Bev Gilbert	Principal Varieties: Chardonnay, Riesling,	Shiraz	5+ yrs

Galafrey

Galafrey Wines, one of the quiet achievers of the Mount Barker region, is owned and managed by Ian and Linda Tyrer, who established 12ha under vine and have a 200-tonne winery on their property. An impressive cellar door centre with sweeping views across the vineyard and beyond.

Galafrey Wines pride themselves on producing small parcels of

distinctive and consistently excellent wines. Over the years they have won many trophies and medals especially for their Rhine Riesling and Cabernet Sauvignon. The vineyard is over 20 years old, dry grown, low yielding with the wines benefiting from intensity of flavour.

The wine range includes Chardonnay, Unoaked Chardonnay, Rhine Riesling, Muller Thurgau, Pinot Noir, Shiraz,

Cabernet Sauvignon, Tawny Port and their blends Art Label Premium Dry White and Red. The Reserve Botrytis Rhine Riesling and Reserve Cabernet Sauvignon and unique hand painted magnums of older vintages of Shiraz, Cabernet Sauvignon and Rhine Riesling complete their impressive range. Kim Tyrer's paintings are featured on the Art Label labels, and some of her work is on display in the cellar sales area.

Situated only 10kms from Mount Barker, off the Muir Highway, a short drive to sample some of Mount Barker finest wines, Galafrey Wines.

Address: Quangellup Rd MT BARKER 6324	Winemaker: Ian Tyrer	Unoaked Chardonnay	4+ yrs
Phone: (08) 9851 2002	Est: 1977 Vine Ha: 11 Cases: 12,000	Muller Thrugau	2+ yrs
Fax: (08) 9851 2324	Public Hours: 10am-5pm, daily	Shiraz	10+ yrs
Email: galafrey@wn.com.au	Principal Wines Potential	Rhine Riesling	10+ yrs
Owner: Ian & Linda Tyrer	Chardonnay 6+ yrs	Pinot Noir	10+ yrs

Plantagenet

Apart from the establishment of an experimental vineyard at the Forest Hill Vineyard in 1965, Tony Smith's 'Plantagenet' was the first commercial vineyard in the Mount Barker area. Tony planted the Bouverie Vineyard at Denbarker in the late 1960's. Plantings followed at Wyjup in 1971 and three years later an old apple-packing shed in Mount Barker was purchased and Plantagenet Wines was formed.

This has since been converted into a functional, well-equipped winery which processes, bottles and provides storage space for a number of local vineyards in addition to Plantagenet.

The first Plantagenet wines were made in 1974. Gavin Berry is the highly respected current winemaker.

The introduction of the 'Omrah' Unwooded Chardonnay in 1989

proved to be a stroke of genius. It has become one of the biggest selling Western Australian whites, and appeals to those who prefer the more fruit-driven chardonnay's which generally taste better with food.

Plantagenet are concentrating more on their own wines with less contract activity now.

The winery has recently been expanded and acquired a beautiful stone frontage, complete with a

charming and larger cellar door. In 1993 a Fremantle family company, Lionel Samson & Son Ltd bought 2/3 of the partnership. Tony Smith retained his fi ownership plus the right to manage. At the same time the partnership was transformed into a private company, Plantagenet Wines Pty Ltd.

Plantagenet's production is increasing as more premium vineyards come into production in the Great Southern region.

Address: Albany HWY MOUNT BARKER 6324	Public Hours: 9am-5pm weekdays;	Riesling	7+ yrs
Phone: (08) 9851 2150 Fax: (08) 9851 1839	10am-4pm, weekends and public holidays	Mt. Barker Chardonnay	6+ yrs
Email: pknwine@rainbow.agn.net.au	Principal Varieties: Chardonnay, Sauvignon	Omrah "Unoaked" Chardonnay	3+ yrs
Winemaker: Gavin Berry	Blanc, Riesling, Cabernet Sauvignon, Shiraz,	Omrah Sauvignon Blanc	2+ yrs
Est: 1974	Pinot Noir, Merlot	Omrah Merlot/Cabernet	4+ yrs
Cases: 40,000	Principal Wines Potential	Omrah Shiraz	6+ yrs

Wignalls

I well remember riding on the back of a tray top truck through the splendid Wignalls Vineyard with my old mate, the late Milan Roden, clicking the camera as we passed row upon row of the double "Lyre Bird" trellised vines, so huge and healthy, one could only imagine great wines coming from them.

When we stopped for a look at the dark, perfect bunches of pinot noir, ripe for picking, Bill Wignall was intrigued by Milan's cameras. Many years ago he was a photo journalist before embarking on a career as a vet which led him first to Albany in 1963.

Many scoffed at his planting a vineyard "he won't get those grapes ripe". Bill proved them so wrong, his first Pinot Noir in 1985 won a gold

medal and the 1985 Chardonnay was judged the top wine at the 1987 S.G.I.O. Winemakers exhibition which won Bill and his wife Pat a trip to France where they learnt much about viticulture.

Recent times have proven that Wignalls is a major strength in winemaking fields in Australasia. Recent awards include the highest awarded Wooded Chardonnay at the Japan International Wine Challenge, and the Trophy for "Australia's Best White Wine" at the same show. Also in August 2000, Wignalls were invited and sponsored as one of eight Pinot Noir producers, selected from the new world by the USA wine industry, to showcase our wines at the famous International Pinot Noir Celebration, Oregon USA.

Address: Chester Pass Road ALBANY 6330	Est: 1982 Vine Ha: 22 Cases: 7,200	Pinot Noir	6 yrs
Phone: (08) 9841 2848 Fax: (08) 9842 9003	Public Hours: 12pm-4pm, daily	Chardonnay	8 yrs
Email: wignalls@omninet.net.au	Principal Varieties: Cab Sav, Chardonnay,	Sauvignon Blanc	2 yrs
WWW: www.wignallswines.com.au	Pinot Noir, Sauvignon Blanc, Shiraz	Cabernet Sauvignon	10 yrs
Owner: Wignall Winemaker: Bill Wignall	Principal Wines Potential	Shiraz	6 yrs

Howard Park

Howard Park now has a state of the art winery at Scotsdale Road in Denmark. After many years making wine for an extended family of vineyard owners for their own labels, up to 23 separate vignerons in some vintages, they are now concentrating solely on their prestigious Howard Park and Mad Fish labels.

Perth businessman Jeff Burch, has constructed a large state of the art winery able to crush approximately 1,000 tonnes. Set on a hillside amongst stately gums, with lawns and gardens surrounding the spacious glass conservatory style tasting area with its grand entrance is impressive indeed.

On the day of my first visit the window cleaner was at work. He told us it takes him eight hours at least to clean the lot!!

Howard Park Cabernet Sauvignon is an opulent style in the very top echelon of Australian reds and is built for the long haul with careful selection of the fruit and extended ageing in tight grained French Troncais barriques, a touch of merlot adds complexity, it's great wine.

Under the Howard Park label there is also a riesling and a chardonnay. The Mad Fish wines have unique aboriginal inspired labels. The name

comes from a local bay where the fish are often seen madly jumping to avoid the hungry feeding larger fish.

The premium white is crisp and aromatic in a white bordeaux style, the premium red is soft and generous, both are enjoying spectacular sales in the value for money arena, particularly in the U.K. The Mad Fish range has been extended and now includes a chardonnay, sauvignon blanc semillon, late harvest riesling, shiraz, pinot noir and a cabernet sauvignon/merlot/cabernet franc.

Howard Park has come a long way since its founding in a tin shed in the Great Southern in 1986.

Howard Park is a credit to the region and a sign of the exciting times that are ahead for this great area that has the potential to produce huge quantities of top class premium wines.

Address: Lot 377 Scotsdale Road DENMARK 6333	**Owner:** Jeff & Amy Burch **Est:** 1986	Howard Park Leston Shiraz (New)
Phone: (08) 9848 2345 **Fax:** (08) 9848 2964	**Winemaker:** Michael Kerrigan & James Kellie	Howard Park Scotsdale Cab Sav (New)
Email: hpw@denmarkwa.net.au	**Public Hours:** 10am-4pm, daily	Howard Park Cab Sav Merlot (Flagship)
WWW: www.howardparkwines.com.au or	**Principal Varieties:** Cab, Riesling, Chard, Shiraz	Howard Park Riesling
www.madfishwines.com.au	**Principal Wines**	Howard Park Chardonnay

∽ Somerset Hill & Mushroom Farm ∽

In 1976 Graham and Lee Upson began a small family business growing mushrooms on the outskirts of Perth, over 19 years this grew from one small growing room to 16 growing rooms employing 72 people and producing 15·20 tonnes of mushrooms a week, with a large export business particularly to South East Asia.

In the late 1980's they bought a holiday home at Denmark in the Great Southern Region of W.A. to escape from their demanding mushroom enterprise. As the 90's unfolded they found it harder and harder to go back to Perth. In 1995 they bought a beautiful property to the West of Denmark, high in the cool hills with a majestic view of the Great Southern Ocean. They then sold their mushroom business in Perth and began planting vines.

In 1997 they started a mushroom business at their vineyard and now supply restaurants and supermarkets through Southern WA with button mushrooms, field mushrooms and the nutty flavoured Swiss Brown Mushrooms.

Graham also built a delightful underground Sparkling Wine maturation cellar, incorporating one of the most characterful cellar doors in Australia.

On my visit I was most impressed with their 2000 unwooded Chardonnay, it had extremely lifted tropical flavours with hints of banana and pineapple, I rated it a gold medal, recently it has been chosen as one of the best 4 unwooded wines available in London by Richard Neill of the Daily Telegraph. I very much enjoyed their Zesty 2000 Sauvignon Blanc with its lime and kiwifruit

flavours with some jasmine floral overtones and a little cut grass and a capsicum edge to it. The 1998 Pinot Noir was gamey with some sweet conserve like berry characters.

The 2000 Semillon was probably my favourite wine, very intense tropical and citrus characters with a clean herbaceous finish.

The vineyards at Somerset Hill receive a real gift, in tonnes of compost from the mushroom farm, a most wonderful natural fertilizer and moisture retaining mulch.

The elevated location at 220 metres, near the coast means a very long growing season and late ripening up to 3 weeks later than some parts of this large region, a real bonus for the development of flavours and complexity in the grapes. With great crisp acidity the wines are all Estate grown. A real feather in the Upsons cap has been their selection to be

represented in the UK by Fields Wine Merchants, the wholesale arm of Berry Brothers and Rudd Londons oldest wine wholesaler (300 years) and suppliers to the Royal Family - Somerset Hill are their only Great Southern Supplier.

Somerset Hill have also made the regions first sparkling wine, a Methode Traditionelle that ages on tinage in the cellars, in full view, as you taste the other great Somerset Hill wines, the "Somerset Constellation" has a cosmic explosion of flavours it's a 100% Pinot Noir Cuvee, with creamy a yeasty character from 13 months on yeast lees, it's not only luscious but elegant and a great way to celebrate your visit to this beautifully conceived wine and food enterprise.

Address: 891 McLeod Road DENMARK 6333	Winemaker: Brenden Smith		Unwooded Chardonnay	3 yrs
Phone: (08) 9840 9388 Fax: (08) 9840 9394	Est: 1995	Vine Ha: 11	Sauvignon Blanc	2 yrs
Email: info@somersethillwines.com.au	Cases: 5,000		Semillon	3 yrs
WWW: www.somersethillwines.com.au	Public Hours: 11am-5pm, daily		Pinot Noir	3 yrs
Owner: Graham Upson	Principal Wines	Potential	Merlot	5 yrs

Alkoomi Wines

The Alkoomi Winery, located in the Frankland River wine region of Western Australia, lies approximately 80kms inland from the Southern Ocean. The name Alkoomi is from a local aboriginal dialect and means "The place we chose".

Merv and Judy planted their first vines in 1971 and since then have gradually increased the area so that the vineyard now consists of 180 acres of various grape varieties. The more recent plantings were essential to meet a burgeoning demand for

Alkoomi's varietal and blended wines. Great care is taken to irrigate only at those times when the vines are under severe stress. Thereby restricting the yield and facilitating the production of very high quality fruit.

Alkoomi is very much a "Family Affair" with son Wayne being responsible for viticulture, and son-in-law Rod Hallett, in charge of production. The winemaking is in the very capable hands of Michael Staniford, who has

produced some exceptional wines in the last few years. The modern winery utilizes technological developments, such as must chilling, cool fermentation and sophisticated filtration methods. Carefully selected quality oak is used for wine maturation.

Alkoomi also produces an Extra Virgin Olive Oil. The olives for this oil are hand harvested from Alkoomi's Olive Grove located on the property.

Address: Wingebellup Road, Frankland WA 6936	Est: 1971 Vine Ha: 42 Cases: 28,000	Alkoomi Blackbutt	10-12 yrs
Phone: (08) 9855 2229 Fax: (08) 9855 2284	Public Hours: 10.30am-5pm, daily	Alkoomi Cabernet Sauvignon	10-12 yrs
Email: alkcomi@wn.com.au	Principal Varieties: Cabernet, Chardonnay,	Alkoomi Jarrah Shiraz	10-12 yrs
WWW: www.alkoomiwines.com.au	Malbec, Merlot, Riesling, Sauvignon Blanc,	Frankland River Sparkling Shiraz	8 yrs
Owner: Merv and Judy Lange	Shiraz	Alkoomi Wandoo	5-7 yrs
Winemaker: Michael Staniford	Principal Wines Potential	Frankland River Chardonnay	5-7 yrs

Ferngrove

The thriving Ferngrove Vineyards Estate at Frankland River is a remarkable success story, built on the vibrant dream of a prominent South Coast pioneer farming family.

In 1996, with nearly 90 years of beef and dairy farming history behind him, Murray Burton decided to move into premium grape growing, knowing the region's productive soils, pristine environment and temperate Mediterranean climate were ideal for viticulture.

Murray mortgaged the family farm at Walpole to purchase land at Frankland River. In the following year, Frankland Valley Vineyard was established.

From the outset, Murray set his sights on achieving world's best practice in viticulture, with the ultimate goal of producing premium wines of indisputable quality for the Australian and international markets.

The vines thrived and more land was acquired just a few kilometres away,

leading to the establishment of Ferngrove Vineyard in 1998.

Development since then has been rapid, but carefully managed. A third vineyard, Vintage Park, was established at Frankland in 1999. In 2000, Murray's interests were extended to include Karri Oak Vineyard at Mt Barker.

A modern winery was established at Ferngrove in 1999 and produced its first commercial vintage in 2000.

The tourism oriented winery features rammed earth buildings, corrugated iron roofing, wide verandahs, extensive use of local timber, a floor to ceiling glass wall to allow viewing of winery operations and a lookout tower with sweeping views of the spectacular Stirling Ranges.

Murray will not believe he has succeeded until Ferngrove holds international status as one of Australia's great wine producers · a goal he, his management team and staff are determined to achieve sooner, rather than later.

The viticultural region known as the Swan Valley includes the Perth suburbs of Guildford, Bassendean and Midland and extends 15 kilometres to the north along the Swan River.

The first vines were planted by Thomas Waters at Olive Farm in 1829, the same year settlers arrived in the state.

Western Australia's first commercial vineyard was Sandalford, planted in the Swan Valley by John Septimus Roe in 1840. Houghton, however, was to become the region's most significant wine producer. The company was established when Dr John Ferguson planted vines in 1859.

Following the First World War, the small number of the area's winemaking fraternity was suddenly boosted by the arrival of many Yugoslav and other European immigrants. As a result, hundreds of small family winemaking operations came into existence. Most families sold their wine in bulk from their cellar doors, while some winemakers became more serious about commercial marketing.

In addition to these traditional winemakers and the area's larger concerns of Sandalford and Houghton, the Swan Valley now also hosts a group of winemakers and wine tourism facilities growing in importance. These include the Jane Brook Estate of Beverley and David

Atkinson, which also boasts a casual vineyard cafe. The Lamont Winery of Jack Mann's daughter Corin, also makes traditional full bodies Swan Valley styles along with having a first class restaurant run by Corin's daughter Kate. Westfield Wines, owned and operated by John Kosovich, makes consistently fine reds, whites and fortifieds, including an excellent vintage port. New wineries include Upper Reach Wines near Westfield. Swanbrook in the previous Evans & Tate Complex which also has a Restaurant, Sitella a fine Winery Restaurant Complex in the eastern side of the valley and Baskerville Wines also with an excellent Café style Restaurant.

Wine tourism in the Swan Valley has really blossomed with the World Class Novotel Vines Resort including a championship gold Course. The Mulberry Farm Complex at the Midland end of the valley is also first class and hosts many large events.

Without doubt the most significant influence on the wine industry of the Swan Valley was the indomitable and idiosyncratic Jack Mann. Jack began his winemaking career at Houghton in 1922. Fifty one vintages later, in 1972, he retired having made legendary innovations to Australia's wine industry.

In 1937, Jack produced the first vintage of Houghton's White Burgundy. The popular taste of the

day was for fortified wines, but the full-bodied flavour of the White Burgundy saw it become Australia's first widely accepted table wine.

The wine's great success owes much to Jack's winemaking philosophy and technical developments. The introduction of ideas such as cooling during fermentation and picking fruit only when completely ripe, contributed to the creation of Houghton's full-bodied wines. Jack also retained grape skins in fermenting white wines to further strengthen flavours.

Another of Jack's developments arose when attempting to crush the shrivelled grapes used in making fortified wines. An ingenious 'Mincer' was created to crush these raisined grapes, and proved very successful in the production of Jack's excellent sherries, muscats and tokays.

Jack passed on at the age of 83 years in 1989, but his wines still live on somewhere deep in my cellar.

The Swan Valley of today has much to offer the visitor. A very pleasant way to visit the larger wineries is to take a river cruise up the Swan on either the Miss Sandalford or the Lady Houghton. These vessels are delightfully furnished, and depart from Perth's Barrack Street Pier at 10.00 am. The trip is completed by 4.00 pm.

On tours to either the Sandalford or Houghton wines are available for tasting and served with lunch.

The highlight of the year for the Swan Valley is the Annual "Spring in the Valley" festival held in October. This celebration of fine wines, superb food, music, art and theatre involves many of the leading wineries, who all feature at least three different attractions at their premises. You can enjoy classical, jazz or popular music from live bands, watch magicians and street theatre, participate with potters and painters, see wood carving, tour historic buildings and participate in many other interesting activities, all of course, accompanied by the fine wines and foods of the region. Many wineries choose this time to release their new vintages and some even offer the visitor a taste of wines yet to be released.

Swan Valley

Swan Valley - WA

1. Baskerville Wines
2. Houghton Wines
3. Jane Brook Estate
4. Lamont Winery
5. Mann Wines
6. Novotel The Vines
7. Oakover
8. Sandalford Wines
9. Sitella
10. Swan Valley Cheeses
11. Swan Valley Cottages
12. Swanbrook
13. Talijanich Wines
14. Upper River
15. Westfield Wines

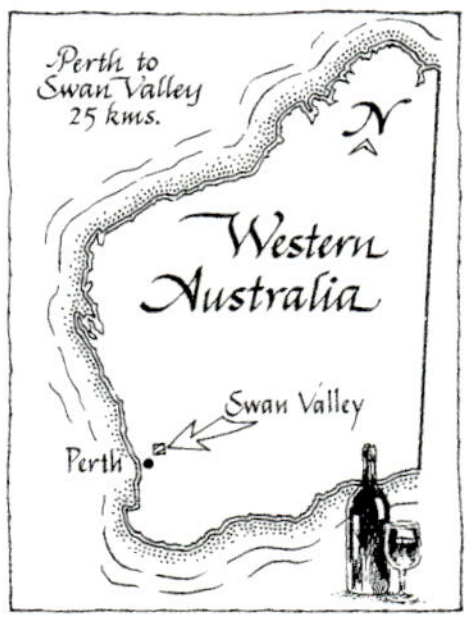

Perth to
Swan Valley
25 kms.

Western
Australia

Swan Valley

Perth

Houghton Wines

Houghton was established in 1859 by colonial surgeon Dr. John Ferguson. The vineyard was planted at Middle Swan and further developed by the founder's second son, Charles Ferguson who worked tirelessly for 50 years to improve the Vineyards and Winery.

By the time the property was purchased by the Emu Wine Company in 1950 the company had grown to a considerable size, they had already purchased the large Valencia Vineyard at Caversham. Staff remaining with the company after the takeover included winemaker Jack Mann. His white burgundy, together with the cabernet sauvignon and fortified wines, were very popular on the Australian market. Much of Houghton's other output was exported and highly successful on the overseas market.

Unfortunately, despite the company's financial success, Emu Wines did not re-channel profits into the company. The ingenuity of General Manager Ian Smith and winemakers Jack Mann and Charlie Kelly at Valencia was tested to the limit. With little but the bare necessities, excellent wine continued to be made at Houghton.

Great changes occurred four years after Jack's retirement in 1972. In 1976, the Emu Wine Company was purchased by Thomas Hardy & Sons, who immediately began work on updating winemaking equipment. Bill Hardy and, later, Jon Reynolds were appointed as the new winemakers. Having graduated as dux as the Diploma D'Oenologique course from the University of Bordeaux in France and having made

several vintages at Hardy's McLaren Vale, Bill was more than qualified to take on this new position. Jon, originally from the Hunter Valley, had also made wines at Reynella.

Without altering the award-winning style of the famous Houghton White Burgundy, Bill and Jon freshened the wine by employing up-to-date winemaking techniques. The Show Reserve Houghton White Burgundies released when fully matured, have shown just how good this Australian classic is, all have won many gold medals and trophies in wine shows.

Currently the popular Blue Stripe range of wines that includes the Houghton White Burgundy also features · Semillon Sauvignon Blanc, Frankland River Rhine Riesling, Cabernet Sauvignon and Cygnet. The Gold Reserve range includes a Cabernet Sauvignon, Chardonnay and Verdelho. There is also a "Crofters" range of wines.

The Flagship wine is the "Jack Mann" Cabernet Sauvignon an absolutely top class wine as befits Jack's contribution to The Australian Wine Industry. 1996, the first vintage, has already won 4 trophies and 11 gold medals.

The classic old cellars at Houghton and Dr. Ferguson's original home have both been beautifully restored and additions to the cellars have been tastefully handled. The Middle Swan Winery is a joy to visit and exudes an air of history. A new winery at Nannup in the south west of Western Australia had its first vintage in 2001 2,000 tonnes were crushed, soon this will rise to 5,000 tonnes.

Over the years, the company has done much to further Western Australia's wine industry, particularly in its development of regions outside the Swan Valley.

In 1994 new vineyards at Pemberton and Mount Barker were added and fruit from these properties is further enhancing the premium end of the portfolio with additional wines.

Houghton White burgundy still continues to be one of Australia's favourite whites and the 2001 vintage will be the 64th consecutive release for this famous wine.

The current winemaker is Larry Cherubino, who grew up in the Swan Valley. He is a Roseworthy graduate and has worked in Australia and overseas for BRL Hardy. Houghton continues to add lustre to the Western Australian wine industry like a star footballer in a champion team.

Baskerville Wines

with great fresh foods presented in well priced dishes, with many influences from the Mediterranean to the Middle East and Asia.

The vineyards were first established in 1972, the mature vines have had a lot of attention in the last year or two and the wines are starting to reflect this care.

The Baskerville Shiraz is a full well rounded wine, a perfect accompaniment to the Marinated Scotch Fillet Steak. The crisp and fruity Chenin Blanc is an ideal match with the Moroccan Chicken Salad, with its clean citrus finish, balancing beautifully the creamy Cajun dressing.

Baskerville produce a great blended white, Chardonnay/Verdelho its tropical and stonefruit characters combining well and just the thing with fresh grilled fish and salad.

Why not complete your visit to the Swan Valley with a lunch at Baskerville.

A little north of Lamont Wines lies the Innovative Baskerville Wines, with its Aussie Alfresco style café, providing an East meets West menu,

Address: 247 Haddrill Road BASKERVILLE 6056	**WWW:** www.baskervillewines.com.au	**Public Hours:** 10am-4pm, Thurs-Mon
Phone: (08) 9296 1348 **Fax:** (08) 9296 1035	**Winemaker:** John Griffis	**Principal Varieties**: Cab Sav, Chenin Blanc,
Email: info@baskervillewines.com.au	**Est:** 2000	Shiraz, Chardonnay, Grenache, Verdelho

Jane Brook

Beverley and David Atkinson are very focussed on their beloved Jane Brook Estate, situated at the base of the Darling Range in the beautiful Swan Valley, less than 30 minutes from Perth. They purchased the property known as "Vignacourt Wines" as newlyweds in 1972. In 1984 after a decade of replanting the vineyard to premium varieties and re-equipping the winery, the Atkinson's changed the winery name to Jane Brook, the brook which runs through the property, named by John Septimus Roe, the first Surveyor General, during his initial exploration of the upper reaches of the Swan River in September 1829. It was named in honour of Jane Currie, the wife of Capt. Mark Currie, the first Harbour Master of Fremantle.

The tasting and sales cellars are situated within this traditional rustic winery and there is an attractive vine covered courtyard and timber decking overlooking Jane Brook where lunches are served daily or inside around the open fire in winter. Lunch comprises a range of gourmet platters of cheeses, pates, fruit and salads.

Jane Brook make a classic range of varietal wines including a number of very good whites. The cabernet merlot is full bodied with soft tannins and a superb dry red shiraz, from 55-year-old vines on the property. Two excellent sparkling wines made by the traditional "methode champenoise" are produced. The Elizabeth Jane Methode Champenoise Pinot Chardonnay and the Benjamin David Methode Champenoise Shiraz. Jane Brook have their own methode champenoise equipment.

The Atkinsons two children are now heavily involved in the business. Ben Atkinson is the Viticulturalist and Elizabeth Atkinson the Business Manager. She has just introduced a Super Premium Range the "Atkinson" series the first wine being a 1997 Cabernet Sauvignon/Cabernet Franc from Pemberton.

In 1999 they purchased 75 acres of viticultural land in "Margaret River". They also source grapes from Pemberton and The Great Southern region to enhance their range of wines. The winery has recently been upgraded - Jane Brook are on the move.

Address: 229 Toodyay Rd MIDDLE SWAN 6056	**Est:** 1972 **Vine Ha:** 20 **Cases:** 20,000	Pemberton Swan Valley Sauv Blanc	5 yrs
Phone (08) 9274 1432 **Fax:** (08) 9274 1211	**Public Hours:** 10am-5pm, weekdays; 12pm-	James Vineyard Verdelho	5 yrs
Email: janebrook@janebrook.com.au	5pm, weekends & public holidays	Mount Joy Cabernet Merlot	8 yrs
WWW: www.janebrook.com.au	**Principal Varieties:** Cab Franc, Cab Sav, Chard,	Atkinson Shiraz	10 yrs
Owner: David & Beverley Atkinson	Chenin Blanc, Merlot, Sauv Blanc, Verdelho, Shiraz	Atkinson Cab Sav/Cab Franc	7 yrs
Winemaker: Julie White	**Principal Wines** **Potential**	Elizabeth Jane Pinot Chardonnay	10 yrs

Cheriton

About an hour north of Perth and less than half an hour from the Swan Valley is the Historic Cheriton Estate, its history goes back to 1843 when celebrated WA pioneer William Locke Brockman, who had emigrated from Cheriton in Kent, England, was made a land grant "Swan Location 101". He arrived with his family, seven servants, farm machinery, cows, horses, pigs, a flock of marino sheep and a complete prefabricated house. All this was a far cry from many of his fellow immigrants. The spring fed Gin-Gin Brook flows through the property all year round.

In 1904 an imposing homestead was constructed from Casuarina stone, at a cost of 2,000 pounds a true fortune in those days. Cheriton was give a new lease of life some years ago when it was purchased and restored by Jocelyn Treasure, widow of well known media executive Brian Treasure. Jocelyn has tastefully redecorated giving the rooms a colourful and comfortable air,

the fabrics she has chosen are beautiful and stylish. Some suites have ensuite bathrooms, others their own bathroom and some are shared.

Cheriton also has its own vineyard and a range of wines. There is a swimming pool for recreation or you can play croquet in the front lawn or bocce by the olive trees. For walking there is the 'Jim Gordon Trail' or a stroll watching the birds along the brook, it's only a short drive to the picturesque new Norcia with its historic monastery. The Vines Championship Golf Course and the Swan Valley wineries are also close by.

The food at Cheriton under renowned chef Albert Forster is a revelation and mine host Pauline Webb looks after your every need. Regular concerts and music recitals are held with coach transport from Perth included. Cheriton is certainly a cultural paradise.

Sittella

There are few prettier or better put together boutique winery/cafes than Sittella.

Simon and Maaike Berns have done a splendid job building the timber and earth rendered cellars and vaulted café area. Their vision and inspiration to create their wine and food mecca, came from a visit to the great winemaking regions in France.

Although innovative in design the whole complex has a feel of strong solid tradition. Their beautifully maintained vineyards slope down

from the winery which is set on a hill looking out on the valley and a brook crossed by a narrow bridge keeping the property nicely private.

Simon has equipped the winery with state of the art equipment and plenty of top quality French oak, their 10 acre vineyard is planted to Shiraz, Chardonnay and Verdelho. They also have a vineyard in Margaret River "Wildberry Springs Estate" including Cabernet Sauvignon, Semillon and Shiraz.

The first vintage was in 1998. I was most impressed with their aromatic 2000 Chenin Blanc and their Verdelho which had a lovely tropical and citrus lift. Currently the 2001 Chenin Blanc is available as well as the "Sittella Silk" their first blend of Chardonnay Verdelho and Chenin Blanc.

They have just released a 1999 Margaret River Shiraz matured in

French Oak. I'm sure it will be as successful as their Swan Valley Shiraz, already gaining much critical acclaim.

The café has a warm Mediterranean feel about it with tasteful furnishings and decorations, it opens out onto a verandah area looking out on the vines which has just been expanded, along with the kitchen to cater for increasing demand.

Vineyard and tasting tours are a regular feature at Sittella which is a worthy wine and culinary addition to the Swan Valley.

Address: 100 Barritt St HERNE HILL 6056	Cases: 1,800	Shiraz	
Phone: (08) 9296 2600 Fax: (08) 9473 0774	Public Hours: 11am-4pm, daily	Chenin Blanc	5 yrs
Owner: Simon & Maaike Berns	Principal Wines Potential	Verdelho	
Est: 1998 Vine Ha: 10	Chardonnay	Cabernet Sauvignon	

Novotel The Vines

Western Australia's premier resort is set amongst the vines at the northern end of the Swan Valley, a rural paradise, framed by the foothills of the Darling Ranges. Whilst you are well away from the hustle and bustle of city life, its only 35 minutes from Central Perth and 25 minutes from Perth's Domestic and International Airports.

The resort includes two full 18 hole golf courses, the Championship Composite Course, which has hosted a number of leading world golf events, is ranked number one of the Resort Golf Courses of Australia.

The Resort is beautifully spread out, with all the 103 suites on two levels with private balconies and breathtaking views over nature and the golf course, kangaroos even roam tamely on the lawns in the early mornings and at sunset. The rooms are spacious and superbly appointed. I can guarantee you won't want to leave.

In the area of cuisine and wine, "The Vines" excels and the prices will amaze you, they are so reasonable. The top restaurant, "The Vigneron"

opens on Friday and Saturday nights and for special events. The décor is splendid with exquisite cutlery, crockery and silver, the service is warm and friendly but not intrusive. Naturally with the French influence of Novotel, the 'sauces' are concentrated with lots of exotic flavours but I did not find them overpowering. The cuisine is basically

Mediterranean with lots of fresh produce from the valley and a stunning array of seafood from W.A.'s pristine waters.

The Vigneron hosts special dinners, particularly wine dinners, there is also a "Vigneron Club", members can accrue credits to use on their next meal. The menu at "The Vigneron" changes weekly, a big commitment

Novotel The Vines

from the executive chef and his kitchen brigade.

Their other restaurant "Muscats is open each day for lunch and dinner and every Friday and Saturday night features an International Theme Buffet, a real culinary masterpiece. For a more casual snack or a relaxing drink, there is the "Winners Bar" which has an amazing number of great local wines available by the glass or any cocktail you can imagine and a few others.

If your looking for some activities to work off all the great food and wine, there are plenty of things to do. Apart from a round of golf or brushing up your game on the driving range or putting green, you can swim in the spacious pool or relax in the heated spa, there is also a children's pool. The resort has four floodlit surface tennis courts and two top squash courts. Nearby there are horse-riding ranches or you can take a tour of the Swan Valleys historic and exciting new wineries and do a little tasting.

The vines are well set up for conferences with four separate fully equipped conference rooms.

For the more active groups there is the Merribrook Adventure training program and ropes course.

General Manger Mike Stanton fosters a strong "Excellence in Service" philosophy amongst his staff at all levels and it really shows adding to the enjoyment of your stay.

"The Vines" was justly rewarded the accolade as the "BEST RESORT IN AUSTRALIA" in 1991 at the Australian Tourism Awards, a truly prestigious achievement, and they've only got better since. Make sure you visit "The Vines" on your next trip to Perth its a very special place.

Sandalford

Sandalford's new world class tourism facility "The Sandalford Experience" was opened by the Hon. Norman Moore, W.A. Minister for Tourism in November 2000. This six million dollar development is absolutely astounding and provides all visitors with what is probably Australia's best guided winery tour, starting with a fantastic introductory video in their purpose built theatrette and continuing through information stations right through from the washing pit to the bottling line. The dynamic Prendiville family who took over the winery in 1992 are to heartily be congratulated on the magic makeover they have made.

The new tourism facilities include "The Oak Room" an impressive large banquet Hall surrounded by wine quietly maturing in oak hogsheads. Many weddings are hosted here as well as corporate gatherings. The Durack Room, named after a famous W.A. pioneering family and ancestors of the Prendivilles, also hosts gatherings. The "Cellar Emporium" ha an alfresco tasting area and sales boutique for wine and wine related products.

Sandalford was established by one of the founding fathers of Western Australia · John Septimus Roe, the state's first Surveyor General.

Septimus Roe arrived on board the Parmelia in 1829 and quickly set about establishing the site for the beautiful city of Perth. After some ten years he was rewarded for his services with the granting of a tract of land on the banks of the upper reaches of the Swan Valley. The property was named "Sandalford" after the priory in Berkshire at which his father was rector.

Vines were planted on the property but wines were made only for family consumption. The Roe Family began commercial production of wines during the 1940's and in 1971 the founders great grandson, John Roe, replanted the vineyards and re-organised the business so that Sandalford became a private company.

Sandalford

The original site is now home to Sandalford's winery and Caversham vineyard which has 15 hectares planted to chenin blanc, verdelho, semillon, merlot, shiraz and cabernet sauvignon. There are numerous tables and two fortified wines produced, including the enormously popular Sandalera and Founders Reserve Liqueur Port.

In late 1992 the complexion of the company changed dramatically. After a brief period of overseas ownership Peter Prendiville bought the winery. He transformed the vineyards, vines were re-trained to the Scott Henry trellising system, in the winery new stainless steel tanks were installed and the cooling system overhauled. Old oak was culled mercilessly and the wines improved dramatically.

On my recent visit to Sandalford I was most impressed with the further improvements they have worked hard to achieve but, above all, I was very impressed with the wines themselves - Sandalford is in good hands,

indeed. The riverboat "Miss Sandalford has had a total rebuild maintaining its classic character, it's a little like an Orient Express of the River, bringing visitors to Sandalford's Caversham vineyard and winery every day from Perth's

Barrack Street Jetty. If travelling from Perth it's only a leisurely half-hours drive.

Sandalford is again a rising star in the Western Australian premium wine scene - to the benefit of all wine lovers.

Address: 3210 West Swan Road, CAVERSHAM, WA 6055	Est: 1840	Vine Ha: 120	Principal Wines	Potential
	Cases: 90,000		Chardonnay	2-5 yrs
Phone: (08) 9374 9374 Fax: (08) 9274 2154	Public Hours: 10.30am-5pm, daily except		MR Verdelho	2-5 yrs
	Christmas Day and Good Friday		Cabernet Sauvignon	5-15 yrs
Email: sandalford@sandalford.com	Principal Varieties: Cab Sav, Chard, Chenin		Riesling	5-15 yrs
WWW: www.sandalford.com	Blanc, Merlot, Riesling, Sauv Blanc, Sem,		Chardonnay	2-5 yrs
Owner: Peter and Debra Prendiville	Shiraz, Verdelho		Shiraz Cabernet	
Winemaker: Paul Boulden				

Lamont Winery

Corin Lamont is the daughter of Western Australia's most celebrated winemaker, the late Jack Mann. Jack's forthright philosophies about wine and life are celebrated at Lamont's by Corin and her daughters Kate Lamont and Fiona Warren. Fiona's husband Mark Warren, a Charles Sturt trained winemaker makes the excellent Lamont wines.

The Lamont's are a multi talented family, their desire to excel perhaps flowing from the Mann ethos. Corin's brother Tony played cricket for Australia and older brother Dorham is a successful winemaker also in the Swan Valley.

Corin's strong interest in the Arts is highlighted in a splendid gallery at the property which showcases West Australian artists, with particular emphasis on regional artists.

Kate and Fiona cook in the highly regarded Restaurant next to the winery with views over the vineyard, and also operate a CBD retail wine and food store and a licenced restaurant in East Perth, bringing both their values and a taste of the Valley's produce to the city.

The Lamont's are a committed Swan

Valley producer, particularly known for Verdelho and Shiraz and are

sourcing fruit from other regions, notably a Frankland Riesling of much

acclaim and their blended red, The Family Reserve from Donnybrook, Harvey, Frankland and the Swan Valley.

Lamont's is a favourite venue during Spring in the Valley, the annual wine festival in October. The outdoor "Australiana" area, where great music, fine food and wine make a terrific atmosphere and you'll take away a memorable experience.

Put Lamont's on your wine tour agenda and discover this unique Swan Valley wine family.

Address: 85 Bisdee Road MILLENDON 6056
Phone: (08) 9296 4485 **Fax:** (08) 9296 1663
Email: winery@lamonts.com.au

WWW: www.lamonts.com.au
Winemaker: Mark Warren
Est: 1978

Public Hours: 10am-5pm, Wed-Sun
Principal Varieties: Cabernet Sauvignon, Muscadelle, Shiraz, Verdelho

Swanbrook

Newcomer to the Swan Valley John Andreou is certainly no newcomer to the hospitality industry having run very successful restaurants and function centres in Perth and Fremantle.

John is a truly ebullient character, he and his wife are loving their lifestyle in the Swan Valley.

Their Gnangara Cellars began their life as a bulk wine facility of the Turkich family that was bought by Evans and Tate in 1972. The winery was significantly upgraded and

gained a very good reputation producing such wines as the celebrated Gnangara Shiraz. Evans and Tate decided to centre their wines in Margaret River and in 1998 John Andreou took over the winery and surrounding vineyards of around 12 acres. Rob Marshall is the enthusiastic and talented young winemaker.

In October 2000 I had the pleasure of spending some time in Swanbrook during the spring in the valley festival. On arriving I was taken by the great festive atmosphere the Andreous had created. Behind the tasting bar, two jolly red faced gentlemen were spit roasting sides of beef, the one with a joyous proprietorial air, was non other than John Andreou. Surrounded by his many friends helping him out for the weekend it was a great event. The wines at Swanbrook like their makers are full of flavour and character.

Address: 38 Swan St HENLEY BROOK 6055	Est: 1998 Vine Ha: 4		Verdelho	4 yrs
Phone: (08) 9296 3100	Cases: 10,000		Chenin	4 yrs
Fax: (08) 9296 3099	Public Hours: 10:30am-4pm, daily		Classic White	3 yrs
Email: swanbrookwines@optusnet.com.au	Principal Wines	Potential	Classic Shiraz	8 yrs
Winemaker: Rob Marshall	Shiraz	8 yrs	Panache Grenache	8 yrs

Swan Valley Cheese Co.

The Swan Valley Cheese Company was first opened in 1999. It is situated in the heart of the valley's wine region and is a most welcome addition and tourist attraction to the Swan Valley.

Recently, the original investors in the Cheese Company were lucky enough to be able to purchase the operation in its entirety. The Portuguese born Master Cheesemaker Carlos Mendes, has been making cheeses for over twenty years and applies the traditional methods in his Mediterranean inspired creations. The Mendes family, together with the new owners, the Arbuckle and Carney families, share a "passion for wonderful cheeses".

Cow's milk is the staple ingredient in all the cheeses, with 30,000 litres being bought in each week from the lush dairy region of Augusta in the South-west of Western Australia. This milk, coupled with the expertise ensure a supreme quality product. The Award-winning cheeses produced

at the company include Mozzarella, Bocconcini, Ricotta, Fetta, various mouthwatering Romanos' and the flagship soft cheese Crescenza.

The onsite ship has been completely revamped and expansive changes in both its retail and wholesale areas have been implemented. To compliment the cheeses there is a wide range of products such as olives, olive oil, fresh baguettes, marinated artichokes, sun-dried tomatoes, freshly brewed coffee and a range of herb teas.

Another interesting side to this story is that three of the new owners are classically trained musicians, so live music throughout the year is a definite inclusion in the company's calendar.

The Swan Valley Cheese Company compliments the many restaurants and vineyards in the area. This and the regions growing popularity, makes it an essential stop on your tour of the Swan Valley.

Name: Swan Valley Cheese Co.	Address: 640 Great Northern Hwy HERNE HILL 6056	Phone: (08) 9296 0600 Fax: (08) 9296 0699

Talijancich

One of the most respected wine producing families in the Swan Valley are the Talijancich's Peter Talijancich has run their farming property at Herne Hill in the Swan Valley since he was 13 years old and his father

passed on prematurely in 1945. Peter was often up early working in the vineyards helping his mother before school. Peter's Father arrived in WA in 1926 from the Dalmatian Coast of Yugoslavia although a fisherman in his homeland like many of his countrymen who immigrated to WA he headed south to cut railway sleepers in the Jarrah Forests. After a time running a wood yard in Perth he settled in the Swan Valley in 1931 and began making bulk wines.

Peter has gradually developed the property he bought north of midland from table grapes to premium wine varieties.

In 1977 Peters son James joined the business, he planted more premium varieties and gradually took over the winemaking and changes the label from "Peters" to "Talijancich".

The Talijancich fortified's have won many accolades. Wine State voted their 1974 Tokay Australia's best, a real coup as Rutherglens respected

wines were included in the tasting.

James has re-equipped the winery with modern equipment and the premium table wines have gained a fine reputation.

The Verdelho and Semillon are very crisp clean with aromatic fruit characteristics. The Shiraz is keenly sought after being rich and plummy. Try the liqueur part style and the Tokay they are truly intense and concentrated Talijancich put on a great show for the spring in the Valley festival. The Talijancich have strength and integrity and it shows in their wines.

Address: 26 Hyem Road HERNE HILL 6056
Phone: (08) 9296 4289 **Fax:** (08) 9296 1762
Email: james@taliwine.com.au

Winemaker: James Talijancich
Est: 1932
Public Hours: 11am-5pm, Mon - Fri & Sun

Principal Varieties: Chardonnay, Chenin Blanc, Grenache, Muscadelle, Muscat, Pedro, Semillon, Shiraz, Verdelho

Westfield

John Kosovich is one of Western Australia's most respected winemakers. With his wife Mary and their son Anthony, they run an excellent small winery producing a large range of great table and fortified wines.

In the heart of the Westfield Winery, formerly the family home where John was born, a large broadaxe is displayed on a massive seven metre long wooden beam cut down by

Johns father in 1927 and fashioned by him into this integral beam of their main cellar. Having arrived in 1911, John's father had a short stint in the gold industry, followed by some years cutting railway sleepers in the Jarrah country in WA's south west. Ironically a few years back, John bought land and planted vines at Middlesex nearby the Jarrah forests, in the Manjimup - Pemberton region. The Westfield Swan Valley

property was planted by Johns father and two brothers Nick and Matt, in the 1930's the property produced dried fruits and a little wine.

John began making wine at 15 when he left school to help his ill father, by 18 he was in charge of winemaking. Today he's still a fit athletic man with an amazing 43 vintages under his belt.

The Westfield wines win many trophies, against the wines from more trendy areas in the south of WA. Their Chardonnay ages particularly well. The Verdelho is a great fruit driven style and the reds which include Merlot, Shiraz and Cabernet Sauvignon, are full bodied and worth putting down for a while. The Liqueur Muscat has an average age of around 20 years, it's a fabulous dessert wine, their Vintage Port is also worth seeking out. The Kosovich's don't say too much but their wines say plenty for them.

Address: 180 Memorial Avenue
BASKERVILLE 6056
Phone: (08) 9296 4356 **Fax:** (08) 9296 4356

Winemaker: John Kosovich
Est: 1929
Public Hours: 8:30am-5pm, Mon-Sat; 11am-4pm, Sun

Principal Varieties: Cabernet Sauvignon, Chardonnay, Chenin Blanc, Merlot, Riesling, Semillon, Shiraz, Verdelho

In virtually no time at all, an important new wine region, now supporting some 20 winemakers and a number of large vineyards of the Goliaths of the wine industry, has sprung to life. Deep in the karri, jarrah and redgum country, home of the tallest trees in Australia, lies one of the most exciting and beautiful Australian wine regions.

In the 1930's a small amount of wine was made at Middlesex in the heart of the region. Its real birth as a wine region however, came with the urging of Tony Devitt, government agricultural and viticultural expert, who proposed vineyard and winemaking trials be undertaken.

It was the recommendation by Dr Gladstones in his viticultural report in the 1960's, that the area was well suited to early ripening vines such as chardonnay and pinot noir, that prompted this move. The results came through a decade later in 1987 with flying colours. The region stretches from Donnelly River in the northwest down through Pemberton across to Middlesex and up to Manjimup. A considerable area, much of it very hilly, but with many ideal microclimates and soil structures for vineyards.

Today, BRL Hardy through Houghton have a large investment in what is one of the state's largest vineyards; no doubt Sir James Methode Champenoise is in focus for the fruit.

Domaine Chandon are sourcing fruit from a large vineyard at Manjimup. Salitage, the winery of John Horgan, is a splendid operation whose restaurant and planned winery should make it one of Australia's best large boutiques of the next century. Already its wines are world class. Gloucester Ridge have a great little winery near the extraordinary Gloucester Tree park and many other exciting developments such as Chestnut Grove and the renowned Pannell family at Picardy Wines plus Petaluma's recent buy out of Smithbrook, has seen this region with huge potential become an important part of premium Australian wine scene.

Pemberton

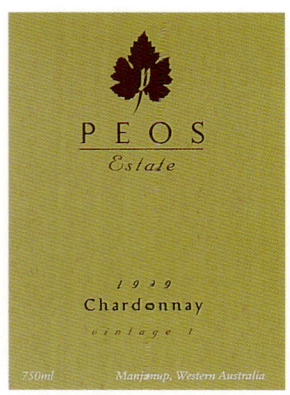

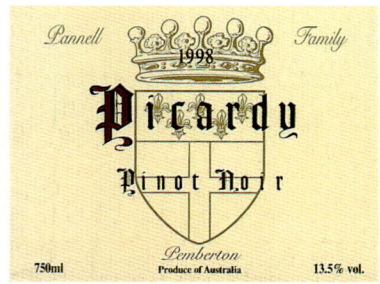

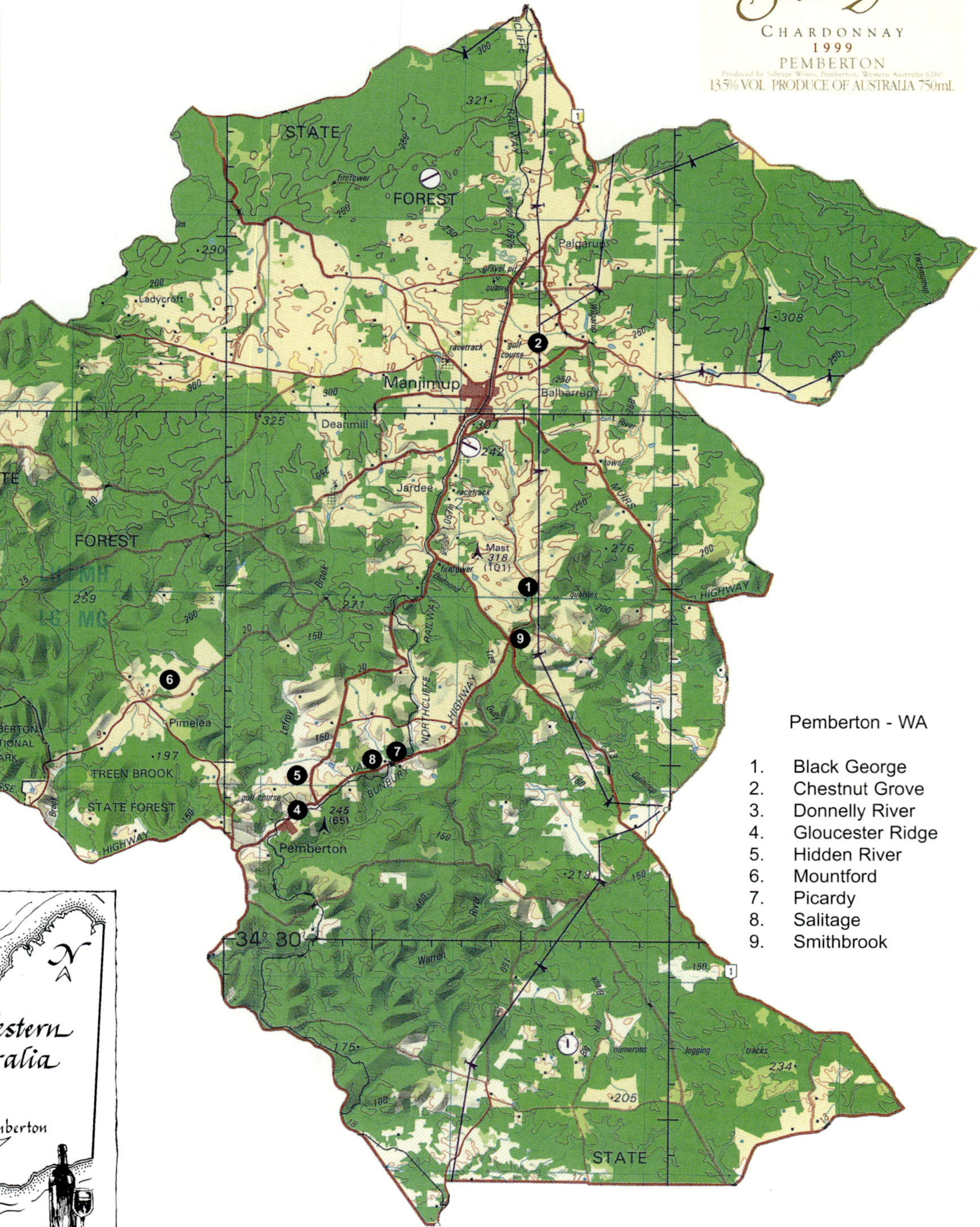

Perth to Pemberton: 340 kms.

N

Western Australia

Pemberton

Perth

Pemberton - WA

1. Black George
2. Chestnut Grove
3. Donnelly River
4. Gloucester Ridge
5. Hidden River
6. Mountford
7. Picardy
8. Salitage
9. Smithbrook

Black George - Warren River

The Pemberton region of Western Australia has always been renowned for majestic karri forests, crystal-clear streams, rich red loamy soils - providing the idyllic backdrop to the vineyard on the Black George Estate.

Located north-east of the tourist town of Pemberton, the Estate is positioned centrally in a region identified in the 1960's as having potential to produce high quality winegrapes. With a mixture of deep Karri and Jarrah / Redgum loams, adequate average rainfall, and gentle Southern Ocean breezes, the region readily attracted both Australian and International growers and winemakers after 1977.

Founders of Black George, Doug and Joy Wilson started with a vision of producing premium wines of the highest quality. Their vineyard sits atop a 240m high hill and is planted to Pinot Noir, Chardonnay, Merlot, Cabernet Franc, Sauvignon Blanc and Verdelho. In this cooler climate, the vineyard with excellent drainage and protection from occasional frosts, produces grapes of outstanding character and flavour. To control both growing and production they added a modern 300 tonne capacity winery. Here, family members - and

respected winemakers - Dr Shelley Wilson and Gregory Chinery have the latest in processing equipment at their disposal.

Black George wines have won local and overseas recognition with established markets Australia wide, in the UK and the Netherlands and the foundation has now been laid for implementing the current plan to increase production to 15000 cases per annum over the next three years.

This will enable Black George Wines to expand exports to South East Asia, other EU countries and the United States.

Expansion beyond this level is not contemplated as the Black George Team is focused with a single mind on the belief that truly premium wine must be crafted from the finest grapes, grown in the best of locations, with experienced eyes overseeing every step of the journey. In the case of Black George Pemberton Estate it is even more delightful when providence brings it all together in a beautiful and tranquil setting.

Before taking over the management of Black George Wines full time in 1994, Doug Wilson held senior management positions for 36 years with a number of Australian and overseas companies in construction, transport and distribution. He was Chairman and Chief Executive of the Western Australian Coastal Shipping Commission for 16 years, facilitating development markets for WA products throughout Australia and South East Asia. Doug was Admitted a Member to the Order of Australia for his contribution to transport and shipping in 1991.

Address: Black Georges Rd MANJIMUP 6258	**Est:** 1991 **Vine Ha:** 11 **Cases:** 7,500	Pinot Noir	2-4 yrs
Phone: (08) 9772 3569 **Fax:** (08) 9772 3102	**Public Hours:** 10am-4:45pm, daily	Captains Reserve Chardonnay	2-8 yrs
Email: blackgeorgewines@bigpond.com.au	**Principal Varieties:** Pinot Noir, Chardonnay,	Cabernet Merlot	2-10 yrs
WWW: www.warrenriverblackgeorge.com.au	Sauv Blanc, Verdelho, Merlot, Cab Franc	Verdelho	2 yrs
Winemaker: Gregory Chinery	**Principal Wines** **Potential**	Sauvignon Blanc/Chardonnay	2 yrs

Chestnut Grove

Chestnut Grove built a magnificent new winery in 1998, it is just another step in their remarkable development over recent years. Vic Kordic's tough beginnings in life prepared him well for the future and he is now one of the happiest and most contented vignerons I have met, seeing the fruits of his labour flourishing on his Manjimup farm.

During the Second World War, as a young man, he was plucked from his native Serbia to work as a forced farm labourer in Germany. Little was he to know, later in his life, farming would become his love and vocation.

In 1949 his chance to escape war-torn Europe came. He looked at the possibilities in front of him. He started at A, was it to be Argentina or Australia, happily he opted for the latter.

Arriving at Fremantle by ship through Singapore, with his wife Katharina and two children, they were without even their suitcases which never left the wharf in Italy. Vic and his family walked away with nothing into their new land.

After a stint in the Lime Kilns at Yanchep Vic moved on to the back breaking work laying railway lines in the south, often living in tents. When the opportunity came to work as a mechanic in Manjimup he jumped at the opportunity.

Through his hard work and innovative thinking he built an empire including Real Estate, a Brick-making business and Manjimup's biggest Car dealership, Kordic Holden. Early in his time at Manjimup he bought a farming property, later to the north-east of town he bought his current property which was blessed with a number of natural springs.

Whilst mainly raising cattle he was pleased to have chestnut and olive trees. On retirement in 1981 Vic took a greater interest in his farm. A study of Dr John Gladstone's recommendations led to the planting of a vineyard in 1988 and a first vintage in 1991. Today 45 acres of one of the best tended and managed vineyards I have seen is the result of Vic's labour. When Vic suffered a heart attack in 1992 his friends rallied around him and helped with picking the grapes.

In 1996 Chestnut Grove won a trophy at the Annual Sheraton Wine awards in Perth with its Pinot Noir, a complex full flavoured wine with lots of strawberry like characters. Their Verdelho won a trophy for the Best W.A. White Wine at the Perth Show in 1999 after winning the trophy as the best Verdelho in the 1996 Perth Show. The Chardonnay has loads of stonefruit with nutty overtones. The Cabernet Merlot, a 50/50 style blend, is rich, round and berry-like with hints of eucalypt and mint. The Chestnut Grove Merlot has been very successful. In one year it won Best Merlot in the Hobart and Adelaide Shows as well as the Boutique Winemakers Show and was the only Merlot awarded 5 stars by Winestate Magazine.

Chestnut Grove also produce an excellent Sauvignon Blanc plus a Madiera fortified from Verdelho and a Sparkling Methode Traditionelle from Pinot Noir and Chardonnay. I was most taken with the Verdelho which the cool climate has blessed with loads of tropical fruit flavours. Chestnut Grove have two excellent new releases with very vibrant labels a zesty white blend "Platinum" and a supple flavoursome red under the "Vermilion" label.

Chestnut Grove is an Estate that through Vic Kordic's noble endeavours is becoming world-renowned.

Address: Lot 2227 Perup Rd MANJIMUP 6258	Winemaker: Contract	Principal Varieties: Chardonnay, Merlot,
Phone: (08) 9386 3495 Fax: (08) 9386 3325	Est: 1988 Vine Ha: 18	Cabernet Sauvignon, Shiraz, Verdelho, Pinot
Email: chestnut@starwon.com.au	Public Hours: By appointment	Noir, Semillon, Sauvignon Blanc

Donnelly River

The first Winery in the Pemberton/Manjimup area was established in 1986 with plantings of 15 acres of vines. The first vintage was in 1990 with a crush of approximately 60 tons. In 1997 Matt and Ann Harsley purchased the Winery and have since increased plantings taking the output to approximately 200 tons in 2000. They retained the services of Blair Meiklejohn, one of the original developers and talented Winemaker on the property and have had considerable success with more award winning wines than any other producer in the region.

Matthew has had a career that has certainly equipped him with innovative skills. He owned and operated an International Diving company, servicing the Oil and Gas Industry, mostly in South East Asia.

Donnelly River has a very pretty location on the banks of the Donnelly River as it is crossed by the Vasse Highway. The rich river flats of silty loam have proved ideal for the vines and the pleasant rustic cellar door which has been recently expanded houses a cheerful café serving light luncheons.

Matt and Ann are delighted with their new venture to date and feel sure "The best is yet to come".

Address: Vasse Highway PEMBERTON 6260	Public Hours: 9.30am-4.50pm, daily	Cabernet	6-8 yrs
Phone: (08) 9776 2052 Fax: (08) 9776 2053	(excluding Christmas Day & Good Friday)	Pinot	4-6 yrs
Email: drw@karriweb.com.au	Principal Varieties: Chardonnay, Merlot,	Chardonnay	0-3 yrs
Owner: Matt & Ann Harsley	Cabernet Sauvignon, Sauvignon Blanc, Pinot	Sauvignon Blanc	0-3 yrs
Winemaker: Blair Meiklejohn	Noir, Semillon	Chardonnay Sem/Sauv Blend (Mist)	0-3 yrs
Est: 1986 Vine Ha: 15 Cases: 200,000	Principal Wines Potential	Cab Sav/Shiraz/Pinot (Karri)	0-5 yrs

Gloucester Ridge

It's a good thing the massive Gloucester tree does not topple over, as it would certainly add a different meaning to crushing at the pretty little winery in its shadow. At least 250,000 visitors climb this extraordinary Karri tree each year.

Don Hancock's uncle was the well-known Clare winemaker, Mick Knappstein, but Don and his wife Sue, ran a cattle farm in the Margaret River region, ironically surrounded by vineyards. They eventually searched for a vineyard site and in 1981, bought at Pemberton. Vines didn't come until four years later and only a small area was planted.

The results were excellent, so the vineyard has been expanded to 15 acres and plans are to double this. Slowly, the tourists began to drop in and the pretty little cellar door became too small, so they built a cellar door and restaurant complex mainly using local timbers. It is superb and has patio's looking over the vineyards to the grand Karri Forest. It became so busy that further expansion has been undertaken.

The Hancock's son, Michael, is vineyard manager and Brenden Smith is the contract winemaker. Quite a large range of wines are made, including a couple of semi-sweet wines that have proved most successful with the tourists pouring through each day.

Address: Burma Road PEMBERTON 6260	Public Hours: 10am-5pm, daily	Cabernets	4-5 yrs
Phone: (08) 9776 1035 Fax: (08) 9776 1390	Principal Varieties: Chardonnay, Cab Sav,	Cabernet Sauvignon	4-7 yrs
Email: gridge@karriweb.com.au	Cabernet Franc, Pinot Noir, Sauvignon Blanc	Chardonnay - Unwooded Drink	Now-2 yrs
Owner: Don and Sue Hancock Est: 1985	Principal Wines Potential	Sauvignon Blanc	Now-2 yrs
Winemaker: Brenden Smith Cases: 12,000	Wooded Chardonnay 3-5 yrs	Semillon/Sauvignon Blanc	Now-2 yrs

Hidden River

A few kilometres from Pemberton, along a series of pretty country lanes, lined with statuesque eucalyptus, lies the gorgeous Hidden River Vineyard Winery and café on a

steep slope, overlooking a natural pond of the stream passing through the property resplendent in bird life. The scene is a real gem of nature and also includes the home of proprietors the Goldring family. Philip and Sandy and daughters Holly and Jodie. Phil worked for many years with Shell and was in Darwin when Cyclone Tracy hit, he spent the best part of 20 years in Northern Western Australia.

Looking for a change of lifestyle, Phil and Sandy were back in their hometown Adelaide and made a trip up to the Barossa Valley, they were captivated by the boutique wineries and cafes and decided to look around W.A. for a location to do something similar. Hidden River is brimming over with charm and their indoor/outdoor café constructed with the glorious W.A. hardwoods and natural materials blends beautifully into its environment.

The wines are already gaining in reputation, their 1999 Chardonnay

was judged the best in its class at the Mount Barker Wine Show.

Hidden River Estate is a special discovery journey and one you should undertake.

Address: Mullineaux Rd PEMBERTON 6260	**Email:** goldring@iinet.net.au	**Public Hours:** 9am-4pm, daily (closed August)
Phone: (08) 9776 1437 **Fax:** (08) 9776 0189	**Winemaker:** Brenden Smith **Est:** 1994	**Principal Varieties:** Chardonnay, Shiraz

Mountford

I felt a real kinship with delightful, energetic couple, Andrew and Sue Mountford. They hail from the town of Honiton in Devon, the birthplace of my great-great-grandfather, the Australian Wine pioneer Thomas Hardy.

Andrew attended the Cannington Horticulture College in Somerset where he met an Australian who helped develop his growing interest in wine.

In 1983 Andrew, Sue and their two children migrated to Australia. Andrew's brother living in Denmark in the Great Southern region of Western Australia tempted them to the west. Andrew ran a landscaping business in Perth for three years, all the time looking for an opportunity to get into the wine business.

The Mountford's chose a majestic site in the Karri Country near Pemberton. The views from the hilltop location are

spectacular. They have built a substantial winery, gallery and restaurant with their own hands, even making the bricks from the gravelly soils of the property and interspersing it with huge, hard hewn karri beams.

The Mountford's also have a theatrical flair and run the "Knot in the Know" performance, featuring song, dance, music, poetry and prose.

Andrew worked at a 400 year old Cider Barn at Taunton in his homeland and also makes cider at the winery under the Tangletoe label.

John Austin, a talented photographer, is curator for the art and photographic gallery. A visit to Mountford is a must. Mountford have also won many awards including the 1992 S.G.I.O. award for the best Pemberton white wine and the 1995 Sir David Brand award for "Excellence in Tourism Development".

Address: Bamess Road PEMBERTON 6260	**Est:** 1987	Cabernet Sauvignon, Sauvignon Blanc, Pinot Noir, Cabernet Franc, Malbec
Phone: (08) 9776 1439 **Fax:** (08) 9776 1439	**Vine Ha:** 6	**Principal Wines**
Email: mountfrd@karriweb.com.au	**Public Hours:** 10am-4pm, daily	"Mountford"
Winemaker: Andrew Mountford	**Principal Varieties:** Chardonnay, Merlot,	

Peos Wines

One of the best looking vineyards I have seen travelling around Australia and New Zealand, belongs to the Peos family, in the rolling hills just west of Manjimup. The four Peos brothers are the third generation and have developed the vineyard which now consists of 92 acres as well as an olive grove next door. Their grandfather P.Y. Peos arrived in Manjimup in 1926 as a sleepercutter before moving back to farming. The Peos family have farmed in the west Manjimup district from 1951. They have seen much change in the economic climate and have adjusted their farming accordingly over the last 50 years. From originally farming tobacco, to dairy to beef to mixed horticulture, vegetables from growing potatoes, cauliflowers, beans to finally going back to grape and wine production, as the family had done on the rich soils of their native country Macedonia, for many generations. Grape growing and winemaking was their passion then on small plots of land. That passion has now transferred to developing their large vineyard in Manjimup.

Peos have released three wines under their label, an Unwooded Chardonnay, a Cabernet Sauvignon and the Peos Estate 'Four Aces' Shiraz. I am sure their beautiful vineyard and the family's understanding of horticulture and winemaking will lead to great success in the wine business.

Address: PO Box 89 MANJIMUP 6258	Winemaker: Selwyn Wines	Principal Varieties: Cabernet Sauvignon,
Phone: (08) 9772 1378 Fax: (08) 9772 1372	Est: 1996	Pinot Noir, Shiraz, Chardonnay, Sauvignon
Owner: Peos Brothers	Vine Ha: 20	Blanc, Verdelho

Smithbrook

Whilst many of the Pemberton and Manjimup producers and devotees believe Pinot Noir is the Stellar Variety of the Region, Smithbrook strongly believe that the Bordeaux varieties both red and white are most suited to the general climate and the particular "terroir" of their vineyard site. I must say in tasting their Merlot and their Sauvignon Blanc I am inclined to agree. A couple of years ago high profile Australian premium wine company Petaluma bought the Smithbrook vineyards, a large well set up vineyard comprisinng 150 acres, which includes Cabernet Sauvignon, Merlot, Cabernet Franc, Petit Verdot, Sauvignon Blanc, Semillon, Chardonnay and Pinot Noir, which is being gradually grafted over to Merlot.

Consumate winemaker Brian Croser firmly believes the varietal mix is right, his reasoning · Pemberton is warmer than Coonawarra and less continental with a smaller range of temperature change, both daily and seasonally, in other words more maritime like Bordeaux not Burgundy.

The 2000 Smithbrook Sauvignon Blanc is one of the most intriguing white wines I have tasted, with a beautiful Jasmine like bouquet, loads of pineapple and kiwifruit, reminiscent of a top French Loire Sancerre, with a dash of Semillon, half the wine spent a little time in older French oak after barrel fermentation, which has helped give the wine great complexity and interest, as well as enhancing its aging potential.

The 1999 Merlot is an exquisite wine, a deep garnet colour, with plum and cherry flavours, an intriguing almond like nuttiness and floral overtones, its silky smooth palate is simply divine.

Smithbrook is already getting good distribution to fine dining establishments around Australian and overseas. This is a wine brand to seek out, their prices are certainly very realistic for top quality.

Address: Smithbrook Rd PEMBERTON 6260	Vine Ha: 60	Principal Wines	Potential
Phone: (08) 9772 3511 Fax: (08) 9772 3579	Cases: 10,000	Smithbrook Cabernet Sauvignon	5 yrs
Email: smithbrk@karriweb.com.au	Principal Varieties: Chardonnay, Petit	Smithbrook Chardonnay	5 yrs
WWW: www.smithbrook.com.au	Verdot, Sauvignon Blanc, Shiraz, Cabernet	Smithbrook Merlot	5 yrs
Winemaker: Michael Symons	Sauvignon, Merlot, Pinot Noir, Semillon	Smithbrook Sauvignon Blanc	5 yrs

Picardy

Picardy is the extremely well thought out and executed vineyard and winery project of the well known wine family The Pannells. Dr. Bill Pannell was a true pioneer of the modern era of Western Australian wine when he planted vines on his Margaret River property Moss Wood in 1969.

He took Moss Wood to the lofty position of one of the top ten producers of premium wine in Australia, before selling it to his long term assistant winemaker Keith Mugford.

Bill has always had a love affair with France and French wines, to even having an involvement in a Burgundy wine business.

The Winery and the Villa in the middle of the Vineyard are as aesthetically pleasing as one would over hope to see, with Rhone and Provence influence. The cellars have been dug into the hillside and the floors of the barrel aging cellar have been purposely left unsealed with a gravel cover to give the area the right humidity for proper maturation.

Bill's sons have taken after their father, Stephen was for a number of years Chief Red Winemaker for BRL Hardy, his other son Dan is a trained winemaker, he along with his delightful and extremely competent wife Jodie, manage both the vineyards and the winemaking.

On our visit I was supremely impressed by the quality, richness and complexity of the wines, which all showed the vibrant colours and flavours, the low ph and the firm acidity the region produces. The Chardonnay had loads of stonefruit characters and real hazelnut overtones · delicious.

Dan makes several Pinot's from different sections of the vineyard some cropping at a lower level than others, whilst they are all full and silky in the mouth. The intensity and vinosity of the 2 tonnes/acre Cuvee was amazing, loads of cherry and raspberry characters, a deep mauve colour astonishing for a Pinot Noir

but with the genuine gamey Pinot nuances.

The "Rhone Style" Shiraz whilst bursting out with rich raspberry fruit had smooth fine tannins, partly fruit and partly from top French Oak · not American.

The Merlot/Cabernet Sauvignon/ Cabernet Franc I tried was a real blockbuster heaps of cherry and cassis with a little tomato leaf herbaceousness vibrant complex and big, definitely one for the long haul.

Picardy is set to become a true Australian icon wine brand but with the Pannell's passion and skill that doesn't amaze me at all.

Address: Corner Vasse Highway & Eastbrook Road PEMBERTON 6260
Phone: (08) 9776 0036 **Fax:** (08) 9776 0245
Email: picardy@wn.com.au
WWW: www.picardy.com.au

Winemaker: Bill and Dan Pannell
Est: 1993 **Vine Ha:** 8 **Cases:** 51,000
Public Hours: By appointment only
Principal Varieties: Cab Franc, Cab Sav, Chardonnay, Merlot, Pinot Noir, Shiraz

Principal Wines	Potential
Picardy Merlot/Cabernet	20-25 yrs
Picardy Pinot Noir	10-15 yrs
Picardy Shiraz	15-20 yrs
Picardy Chardonnay	5-10 yrs

Salitage

John Horgan is a perfectionist who never settles for second best. During the 1970's he set up Leeuwin Estate with his brother Denis, who purchased John's share in 1980. During this time, John developed a strong friendship with, and respect for, the great Robert Mondavi of California.

John also had a long-time love affair with the wines of Burgundy. In fact, along with a select group of Australians, he purchased a share in the French Burgundian Domain, La Pousse d'Or. Pousse in French is a noun meaning to shoot or grow, but also the verb means to drive somebody to do. d'Or of course is gold.

John was driven to find somewhere in his homeland where he could grow the chardonnay and pinot noir vines to make truly Burgundian style wines. He found this land and climate at Pemberton, on the most elevated ridge of the region; the gravelly soil over ironstone provides the wines with a spine, and a distinct flinty character.

John and Jenny Horgan chose the name, a combination of the first two letters of the names of their four children, Sarah, Lisa, Tamara and Gerard.

The winery at Salitage has magnificent, vaulted ceilings, as it has been designed to suit the needs of the future. Considering the already evident greatness of the wines, it was a move of considerable vision.

The wines all see some absolutely top class French oak barriques and they are at once rich and yet complex. So far, the range includes a fresh sauvignon blanc, more at the tropical fruit end of the flavour spectrum, a chardonnay rich with lemon and grapefruit flavours and toasty hazelnut overtones with some pineapple and banana tropical flavours - a real mouthful. The gamey, racy pinot noir has dark cherries bursting out. It's certainly in the best few examples of the variety in Australia. A cabernet blend is also released and an impressive wine. A second label "Treehouse" was launched several years ago and includes a shiraz which has built quite a reputation, a cabernet (a blend of Bordeaux varieties), a pinot noir and a chardonnay/verdelho blend.

Winemaker is Patrick Coutts, a Roseworthy dux, who has made wine in the south of France at Limoux, in Germany's Rhinephalz, and at Paso Robles in California, as well as the high profile Australian wineries of Brokenwood and Domain Chandon. The winery has a large open restaurant area with tasting facilities featuring many of the local timbers. Alfresco dining is available here and in the beautifully landscaped gardens surrounding the winery. Lunches are simple and classy and are served Friday through Monday.

John's son, Gerard, is involved in the marketing. Salitage have made a real impact, not only on the premium Australian Market, but in a number of prestigious International Markets.

Salitage wines have received some really top international acclaim. The Dogen of American wine writers awarded the Salitage Chardonnay 90 points and a glowing report. Wine Spectator have given the Salitage Cabernet blend 90 points. The Pinot Noir has been selected for service on Qantas in first class. Salitage Wines are on the wine lists of many of the most prestigious restaurants in New York, Chicago, Los Angeles and San Francisco, a real feather in their cap, and helping the Salitage export volume which is over 50% of their production. I take my cap off to their valiant efforts and great wines.

Address: Vasse Highway PEMBERTON 6260	**Est:** 1988 **Vine Ha:** 20 **Cases:** 12-15,000	"Salitage"
Phone: (08) 9776 1771 **Fax:** (08) 9776 1772	**Public Hours:** 10am-4pm, daily	Chardonnay 2-5 yrs
Email: salitage@salitage.com.au	**Principal Varieties:** Chardonnay, Pinot Noir,	Unwooded Chardonnay 0-2 yrs
WWW: www.salitage.com.au	Cabernet Sauvignon, Cabernet Franc, Merlot,	Pinot Noir 2-5 yrs
Owner: John and Jenny Horgan	Sauvignon Blanc, Petit Verdot	Cabernet Merlot 5-10 yrs
Winemaker: Patrick Coutts	**Principal Wines** **Potential**	Sauvignon Blanc 0-2 yrs

Tasmania

Following the development of a wine industry in New South Wales, the next State to establish viticulture was Tasmania. The state's first commercial vineyard was planted by Bartholomew Broughton in 1823, near New Town, north of Hobart. Other landowners followed suit, developing vineyards around the state, but sadly the industry was short-lived. By the 1890's Tasmania's first involvement with winemaking was over.

A re-birth of the industry occurred during the late 1950's. The first commercial vineyard was established by Claudio Alcorso in 1958, on a beautiful peninsula in the Derwent River. The property is still in existence and is now known as Moorila Estate. Encouraged by Alcorso's success, other vignerons began to plant vines and there are

now four wine producing regions. These are the Pipers River area north-east of Launceston, the Tamar Valley north of Launceston, the East Coast and finally Southern Tasmania - the area around Hobart - comprising the Derwent Valley, Coal Valley and the Huon · d'Entrecasteau Valleys. A large percentage of the production comes from the Pipers River region.

Although the State's production is relatively small, there are more than 70 wine producers and many more vineyards, and the industry is growing fast with the guidance and assistance of a very supportive State Government. The quality of Tasmanian wine has been of such a standard that mainland winemakers have had to take notice. Some wines have been exceptional.

It has been widely assumed that Tasmania's cool wet climate would prevent viticulture. This is far from the truth, as many areas of the State experience a mild climate, comparable with some parts of the mainland. All Tasmanian regions can be quite warm in some years, and surprisingly, in some seasons can experience drought conditions. Tasmanian wine styles are many, but the methode champenoise wines are absolutely outstanding, and many mainland wineries are either sourcing grapes or wines in Tasmania to use in their sparkling wine blends. Although Tasmania's winemakers cannot hope to compete with the volume of wine produced on the mainland, their wines are certainly capable of taking on the best in quality terms.

Northern Tasmania

There are now two main regions in the north of Tasmania that have vineyards and make wine. The chief of these is the Pipers River region, some 35 kilometres north-east of Launceston. The climate is ideal for viticulture. The soils are generally rich and red, but also drain very well. The country is generally quite hilly and the north easterly-facing slopes can be planted to give a better aspect to the sun and protect the vines from at times, severe south westerly winds.

Many of the vineyards have windbreaks of poplars which provide good growing season protection and add to the magnificent autumn kaleidoscope of colour this region enjoys. The red soils, the green, yellow and amber tones of the vine leaves, the deep blue skies and the fluffy white clouds are truly spectacular.

The region is by far the biggest producer in Tasmania, accounting for about 70 per cent of wine production. One of the first vineyard/wineries established was Heemskerk, back in 1975, a venture between Graham Wiltshire and the Fesq family wine business in Sydney. For a time the French Champagne House of Louis Roederer were involved, but today, Tasmanian winemaker Andrew Pirie, holds the reins.

Dr Andrew Pirie, who has a PhD in viticulture, established Pipers Brook Wines in 1974. Other large players are the Clover Hill vineyards of Dominique Portet's Taltarni Vineyard in Victoria and Ninth Island Winery. Other smaller boutique producers such as Dalrymple make up the balance. In all, around ten wine producers cover the region.

Probably the prettiest viticultural area in Australia, and perhaps the world, is that surrounding the Tamar Estuary. The vineyards generally are planted on the relatively steep slopes of the eastern shores of this estuary which varies from several kilometres to several hundred metres in width. Many of these wineries have hospitality operations with restaurants and even accommodation. The active bird-life requires netting of the vines (or very active deterrents) to guard the valuable crop. The grapes in this region have a very long ripening period and often achieve high degrees of sugar combined with good acid levels, the winemaker's dream.

Wineries such as the Tamar Ridge Vineyards and Winery of dynamic Tasmanian businessman Joe Chromy, Marion's and Strathlynn make the most of their locations. Being less than half an hour from Launceston make a visit essential. The Lake Barrington Vineyard is the first in north-western Tasmania (really more north central). This beautiful vineyard and cute winery and tasting room overlooks the large Lake Barrington. With mountains all around, it's like being in the Swiss Alps. Of the northern Tasmanian wines, chardonnay, pinot noir and methode champenoise stand out but good riesling, sauvignon blanc, shiraz, merlot and cabernet sauvignon can be produced in the various microclimates that the region possesses.

Northern Tasmania

PIPERS BROOK VINEYARD
1999 RIESLING
Tasmania

Northern Tasmania - TAS

1. Clover Hill
2. Dalrymple
3. Delamere
4. Holm Oak
5. Marions
6. Pipers Brook
7. Rosevears Estate
8. St Matthias
9. Tamar Ridge

1997

St.M

Cabernet Merlot
1999
ST MATTHIAS CHURCH 1842 TAMAR VALLEY TASMANIA

TASMANIA

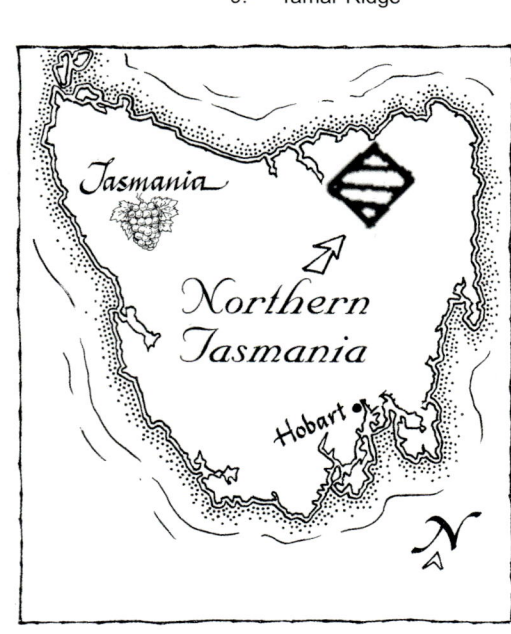

CLOVER HILL
TASMANIA

1998 CHARDONNAY
TASMANIA

464

Clover Hill

The quest for superior quality fruit to produce a super premium Australian sparkling wine led Taltarni proprietor John Goelet to the Pipers River region in North Eastern Tasmania, after a 25 year search. The 190-acre property he purchased in 1986 is a prime hillside site on rich red volcanic soils, known as Clover Hill.

Located at Lebrina, Clover Hill has 52 acres so far planted to the three premium grape varieties chardonnay, pinot noir and pinot meunier. An on-site winery facility processes the grapes into still base wines, the conversion to sparkling wine being completed at Taltarni in Victoria. The results so far have been exciting. The three classic varieties comprise the finished blend. The first vintage in

1991 won the Grand Championship Trophy at the Inaugural Cairns Wine Show and the 1992 (Gold Medal - Hobart, Trophy - Perth and Trophy - Adelaide) provided quick evidence that Clover Hill was on its way to becoming one of the very finest Australian sparkling wines.

In 1998 John Goelet made a further move in Tasmania when he purchased a further vineyard at Lalla Gully. This vineyard tucked away in a picturesque valley near to Clover Hill is producing a chardonnay with lots of stonefruit and fig flavours, quite nutty and complex, the 1999 I have tried is superb. In 1999 the first vintage of sauvignon blanc was produced, it's a vivid racy fruit driven wine again with some fig characters,

really zesty and benefitting from Taltarni's long experience dealing successfully with this highly strung variety.

Recently John Goelet has joined with Michael MacKenzie, a managing partner of Champagne Jacqueson & Fils, to purchase a 150-acre property at Middle Tea Tree, in the emerging coal river region near Hobart. Their careful research has made them very confident vines to be planted on this property will provide them with top quality grapes for the Clover Hill Methode Champenoise wines and the Lalla Gully range of premium table wines. I am sure I will add a further dimension to what are already really top class Australian wines.

Address: 60 Clover Hill Road LEBRINA 7254	**Winemaker:** Shane Clohesy	**Public Hours:** Appointment Only
Phone: (03) 6395 6114 **Fax:** (03) 6395 6257	**Est:** 1986 **Vine Ha:** 20	**Principal Varieties:** Chardonnay, Pinot Noir,
Owner: Mr John Goelet	**Cases:** 3,000	Pinot Meunier

Dalrymple

At first sight this impressive vineyard reminded me of a Roman amphitheatre. The rows of vines are in perfect symmetry and the vines are like soldiers standing guard over the developing winery and home of cancer specialist, Dr. Bertel Sundstrup and his wife, Anne. The

very knowledgeable Jill Mitchell, who for many years produced the outstanding Melbourne radio program of Ross Campbell, has joined the Sundstrup's to help sell the wines.

Stretched across several hundred

metres at the peak of this beautifully balanced hill of vines is a long sign of shadecloth that clearly reads, from the road many hundred metres below, 'Dalrymple Vineyard'. It is impressive indeed.

The establishment of the vineyard, close to the biggest Tasmania producer, Pipers Brook Vineyard, began in 1987. The plantings include pinot noir, chardonnay and sauvignon blanc. The first vintage releases were in 1991 and all wines have won medals in Tasmanian or mainland wine shows. At first, contract winemakers were used, but following the completion of a new winery at Dalrymple in 1997, Bertel Sundstrup has made all wines on-site.

We have certainly seen some great wines from this well-organised venture in recent vintages.

Address: 1337 Pipers Brook Rd PIPERS BROOK 7254	Winemaker: Bertel Sundstrup		Principal Wines	Potential
	Est: 1987	Vine Ha: 12	Pinot Noir	2005
Phone: (03) 6382 7222 Fax: (03) 6382 7222	Cases: 4,000		Pinot Noir Special Bin	2007
Email: dalrymple.wine@microtech.com.au	Public Hours: 10am-5pm, daily		Chardonnay	2007
WWW: www.dalrymplevineyards.com.au	Principal Varieties: Chardonnay, Pinot Noir,		Unwooded Chardonnay	2004
Owner: Dr Bertel and Mrs Anne Sundstrup	Sauvignon Blanc		Sauvignon Blanc	2004

Delamere

Richard Richardons's first contact with the Tasmanian wine industry was way back in 1973 at Sydney University when he was having morning coffee with Andrew Pirie, founder of Pipers Brook, the successful wine company that pioneered Northern Tasmanian viticulture and winemaking.

Andrew was studying an Agricultural Science degree in Horticulture, whereas Richard was studying Agricultural Chemistry, both went on to gain a Ph.D. After working in Miami in the U.S.A. researching into the protein structure of milk, he returned to Australia in the late 1970's and took a position at Royal Sydney Hospital as a Post Doctoral Fellow.

But research grants were hard to come by, and his thoughts kept coming back to his discussion with Andrew Pirie about vines and wines being climate specific and his visit to Pipers Brook in 1974, when he had

seen the young vines, battling with the bracken fern to get established. He and his wife made a decision and in 1983 bought a property and began planting vines Pipers Brook.

Dallas is an artist who specialises printmaking etching from zinc plate; she has designed the striking abstract Delamere label, which captures a sensuous beauty, which is exactly how the Richardsons see their wine. They feel Tasmanian wine has come a long way, with some of the

frost varieties planted in their district including Cabernet Sauvignon now all uprooted or grafted over.

Delamere specialize in the two wines they believe Pipers Brook produces better than any other Australian wine region, Chardonnay and Methode Champanoise sparkling wines from Pinot Noir and Chardonnay. Their thoughts are echoed by Ed Carr the sparkling winemaker from BRL Hardy who purchased recently the Rochcombe Vineyards and Winery from Andrew Pirie. BRL have bought wines from Delamere for a number of years and have valued their fruit sufficiently to use it in their super premium sparkling Arras.

Richard concentrates a lot on the palate of his wines, not just the aromas, he feels texture and length of flavour are very important for the enjoyment of wine with food.

Richard's wines are a true reflection of Tasmania, his vineyards and most importantly himself.

Address: 4238 Bridport Rd PIPERS BROOK 7254	Email: delamere@telstra.easymail.com.au	Public Hours: 10am-5pm, daily
Phone: (03) 6382 7190 Fax: (03) 6382 7250	Winemaker: Richard Richardson Est: 1983	Principal Varieties: Chardonnay, Pinot Noir

Holm Oak

Nicholas Butler has a splendid little winery and a gorgeous vineyard on the northern reaches of the Tamar Estuary, near Rowella. The name is taken from an evergreen oak tree just near the winery. Many other oaks line the driveway of the winery and the vineyard entrance off the main road is one of the prettiest in Australia.

Nick had a brush with fame, so to speak, when the then Prime Minister, Paul Keating, who is not a big wine drinker, took a shine to his 1992 Cabernet during an ALP conference in Hobart, where Keating was attending a birthday party for journalists, Peter Harvey and Paul Bongiorno, when the Holm Oak Cabernet captured his palate. Not long afterwards an official order arrived from Canberra and Holm Oak became a regular visitor at the Lodge for official functions.

Nick is a keen, enthusiastic and creative winemaker and makes wines for a number of other small vineyards. If you want to see a charming small winery at work, in a beautiful location, visit Holm Oak. You could also take a leaf out of the Politician's book and have Holm Oak at home.

Address: 11 West Bay Road ROWELLA 7270	**Winemaker:** Nicholas Butler	**Public Hours:** 12 pm-5 pm, daily
Phone: (03) 6394 7577 **Fax:** (03) 6394 7350	**Est:** 1983 **Vine Ha:** 6 **Cases:** 3,000	**Principal Varieties:** Pinot Noir, Cab Sav, Ries

Marions

Captured by the magic of the Tamar River Valley and it's fine wine growing potential as travellers in 1979, Mark and Marion Semmens sold their home in Los Angeles and established a vineyard on the banks of the Tamar at Spring Bay. Thus began the task of transforming their "jungle bush rock heap" into the "loveliest vineyard location in the nation". They produce wines entirely estate grown and bottled that are handmade, stylish and delicious. Their location, protected by the valley's formation and the broad expanse of the Tamar estuary, offers the slow ripening process necessary to develop maximum flavour characteristics in the fruit. Most of their work is done in the vineyard manipulating the vine canopy to assure a natural balance of the grape's composition.

The vineyards are planted to Pinot Noir, Chardonnay, Cabernet Sauvignon, Muller Thurgau, Merlot, Cabernet Franc, Cascade, Zinfandel and Pinot Gris. The wines are made in combination with traditional and modern techniques, minimal handling assuring the greatest retention of natural flavours of the grape. New French Oak is purchased yearly to complement those flavours and assist the slow maturation process. Marion's Vineyard has been developed as a full wine retreat which includes an amphitheatre/stage, jetty, BBQ and wine tasting facilities in a bush setting, accommodation chalets and a combination restaurant/reception centre catering for up to 300, built atop the winery. Their terraced rockery gardens and magnificent river/mountain/bush views complement the facilities and assure your visit to Marion's Vineyard will be a very pleasant one indeed!!

Address: 51 Foreshore Drive DEVIOT 7275	**Cases:** 2,500	**Principal Wines**	**Potential**
Phone: (03) 6394 7434 **Fax:** (03) 6394 7434	**Public Hours:** 10am-5pm, daily	Cabernet Sauvignon/Merlot	15 yrs
Owner: Mark & Marion	**Principal Varieties:** Cabernet Sauvignon,	Chardonnay	5 yrs
Winemaker: Mark & Marion Semmens	Chardonnay, Müller Thurgau, Pinot Gris, Pinot	Pinot Noir	8 yrs
Est: 1980 **Vine Ha:** 8	Noir, Zinfandel	Gewürztraminer	5 yrs

Pipers Brook

Dr Andrew Pirie is generally acknowledged as Australia's most learned viticulturist, and is the country's first holder of a PhD in that subject. Before establishing his own vineyard, Andrew conducted an exhaustive Australia-wide search for the site most suited to producing European-style wines. He decided on Pipers Brook, to the northeast of Launceston, in 1974.

The wisdom of this decision is quickly evident when sampling any Pipers Brook wines. The demand for these wines is strong, so they are often hard to find. Andrew's prime objective has been to produce high quality, long-ageing wines, using viticultural techniques and site locations similar to those in the great French areas of Bordeaux, Burgundy and Alsace. Pipers Brook expanded in the 1980's opening the Strathlynn Wine Centre set amongst vineyards on the banks of the Tamar River a truly magnificent setting. The two vineyards Strathlynn and the Peir Vineyard supply Pipers Brook with grapes. Certainly their "terroir" is entirely different from Pipers Brook. The Pipers Brook Vineyards include those around the winery as well as the Pipers Hill, Ninth Island Vineyard, The Bird Vineyard and the Timperon and Lueva Vineyards nearby and also the Buchanan

Pipers Brook

Vineyard in the Tamar Valley.

Several years ago Pipers Brook became a publicly listed wine company one of its first actions was the acquisition of two of the other large wineries in Tasmania namely Pipers Brook's neighbour "Heemskerk" and its sister winery not far away "Rochecombe". The Rochecombe winery and vineyards have since been sold to BRL Hardy.

The Ninth Island wines are from Northern Tasmanian vineyards largely owned by Pipers Brook. The Ninth Island Tamar Cabernet, from the warmer Tamar estuary microclimate is a great cool climate cabernet. Ninth Island also produce a Pinot Grigio, Sauvignon Blanc, Chardonnay, Riesling and a Pinot Noir. These wines are all top flight and a great statement of the varietal and regional characteristics of both Pipers Brook and the Tamar.

The winemaking techniques are modern with state of the art equipment, using fine French oak for some of the wines.

The Pipers Brook Vineyard labels include a chardonnay called the 'Summit', from 27 year old vines growing on the stony summit of Pipers Brook vineyard and only appearing in the best yeas, a flinty French Alsace-style riesling for which the vineyard became famous.

Pipers Brook labels in fact now fall into 3 categories. The "Single Site" wines, "The Summit" Chardonnay, already mentioned and "The Blackwood" Pinot Noir. These wines represent the pinnacle of wine quality when one site with the right vine and the right "terroir" is managed perfectly giving wines of great power and complexity. These wines show a distinct individual vineyard character and have enormous ageing potential.

The next Pipers Brook label is the "Reserve". Small blends of privileged "terroir" sites these include The Pinot Noir Reserve, Chardonnay Reserve and a Reserve Merlot, the 2000 vintage being the first release. These wines have great strength of regional and varietal character.

The third range are the "Estate" wines a Pinot Noir (formerly Pellion) Chardonnay, Riesling, Gewürztraminer, Pinot Gris, Sauvignon Blanc and a Cabernet.

The region has been recognised as providing some of the best fruit in the world for Methode Traditionelle sparkling wines. Andrew Pirie has dabbled in sparkling a little and presented a part of his PhD thesis on the similarities of the region viticulturally, climatically and soil wise to champagne. He has now taken a big leap forward with

Heemskerk, he inherited the wonderful "Jansz" Sparkling wine a joint project with Louis Rederer from France.

Andrew has been working for many years on the ultimate Methode Traditionelle sparkling and has just released the "Pirie" in both a vintage and a non-vintage Cuvee.

The long growing season slow ripening and retention of crisp fruit acids is essential for great sparkling wines also so are the classic champagne varieties. Pinot Noir, for body and flavour, Chardonnay for "spice", delicacy and lifted fruit flavours and Pinot Meuniere to round off the wines. Andrew has certain South East sloping vineyards devoted to "Pirie" their climatic summation and growing period is almost identical to champagne (within 1 - 2%). The soils although not chalky like champagne have very similar drainage and moisture retention properties. Very importantly the humidity that helps the wines produce delicate flavours in the grapes is much higher than in other Australia cool climate regions a real bonus for "Pirie". If you want to celebrate with the best go for the "Pirie".

Andrew Pirie is a perfectionist, his Pipers Brook and Ninth Island wines reflect this and you the wine drinker are the beneficiary.

Address: Pipers Brook LEBRINA 7254	Public Hours: 10am-5pm, daily (Except Christmas Day)	Pirie Vintage Sparkling	3-5 yrs
Phone: (03) 6332 4444 Fax: (03) 6334 9112		Pipers Brook Riesling	5-10 yrs
Email: info@pbv.com.au	Principal Varieties: Chardonnay,	Pipers Brook Pinot Noir	8-10 yrs
WWW: www.pbv.com.au	Gewürztraminer, Pinot Gris, Pinot Noir,	Pipers Brook Chardonnay	3-8 yrs
Winemaker: Dr Andrew Pirie	Riesling, Sauvignon Blanc	Ninth Island Pinot Noir	2-3 yrs
Est: 1974 Vine Ha: 220 Cases: 100,000	Principal Wines Potential	Ninth Island Chardonnay	2 yrs

Tamar Ridge

Tamar Ridge wines is a new Tasmanian wine company with its roots firmly planted in the mainstream of Tasmanian viticulture. While the name may be new the organization behind the company has accumulated years of experience in the wine industry and has the knowledge and resources to achieve its goal. The goal is quite simple - to produce premium and super-premium wines exemplifying the structure and elegance that are the hallmarks of true cool climate winemaking.

The company owns over 220 acres of land on the west bank of the Tamar River approximately 45 kilometres north of Launceston at a location known as 'Kayena'. Of this area 153 acres are planted including an extra 16 acres of Riesling planted in 2001 to help overcome the severe shortfall in supply currently being experienced with this variety. Two large storage dams with a total capacity of 1 million hectoliters have been constructed to ensure adequate supply of water to the vineyard.

To maximize the quality of fruit from the vineyard they have retained the services of Dr Richard Smart (one of the world's foremost viticultural consultants) to advise on vineyard set up and ongoing maintenance programmes. On his advice, the entire vineyard has been trellised using the Scott Henry system specifically designed to maximize fruit exposure and enhance ripeness levels in cooler regions. Crops from this vineyard have been excellent showing good ripeness levels and pronounced varietal fruit flavours.

Wines are made using the best available expertise and resources. The winemaker for the first four vintages from 1998 to 2001 was Julian Alcorso who had previously built a considerable reputation as the owner and winemaker of Moorilla Estate near Hobart. He has extensive experience in cool climate winemaking and has in recent years gained additional experience in a number of consultancy and contract winemaking roles in Europe. In February 2001 the winemaking team was strengthened by the addition of Michael Fogarty as winemaker to provide support to Julian. Julian has now moved back to Hobart to set up

his own contract winemaking operation in the Coal River Valley with Michael Fogarty continuing in the winemaking role.

A little over 100 tonnes of grapes were crushed in the 1998 vintage. These wines were made using leased facilities at Dalrymple Winery in the Pipers Brook region.

A new winery was completed at the West Tamar site in time to receive fruit from the 1999 vintage with just over 200 tonnes being processed. The winery has already been expanded to increase capacity. A little over 600 tonnes of fruit was processed during the 2001 vintage with about 380 tonnes being for Tamar Ridge branded wines with the rest being processed on behalf of other growers. Contract winemaking for other growers will continue to form an important part of the operation.

Tamar Ridge is owned by Josef Chromy. Joe is a successful Tasmanian businessman who founded Blue Ribbon Meats and built it into one of the largest and most successful companies in the state. In 1994 he floated Blue Ribbon but kept a considerable interest in the company and retained the position of Chairman. His passion is the Tasmanian wine industry and some

Tamar Ridge

years ago he saw its enormous potential. Purchasing the Heemskerk (& Jansz), Rochecombe and Buchanan's vineyards and wineries and formed Tamar Valley Wines (later renamed as the Heemskerk Wine Group). Under his ownership the Heemskerk Group underwent a transformation with new planting's, improved vineyard practices and considerable investment in the construction of a vastly improved winemaking facility, which would cater for the anticipated growth of the company into the next century.

The Heemskerk Group enjoyed considerable critical acclaim for its wines with the highlight being the naming of the 1995 Heemskerk Chardonnay as the Australasian Chardonnay of the Year by Winestate magazine in 1997. Another of the companies products was Jansz, a methode champenoise sparkling wine recognised as one of the best of this style produced in Australia. In

1998 Joe sold the considerable assets of the Heemskerk Group to their expanding neighbour Pipers Brook Vineyards.

The combination of Heemskerk's considerable vineyard and production assets and Pipers Brook's market demand was a logical one and Joe Chromy decided the time was right to sell. However, he was certainly not ready to quit the wine industry. The decision was made to retain a vineyard and some brands. Joe is continuing with his dream to establish a super premium brand that will enhance the already considerable reputation of the Tasmanian wine industry and allow it to fulfill its even more considerable potential.

Joe established the Tamar Ridge vineyard in 1994, in the West Tamar region to take advantage of the milder, frost-free climate and favorable growing conditions of the

area. These conditions provide optimum grape ripening for table and sparkling wine production.

Tamar Ridge have had much success in wine shows including most successful exhibitor in the 2001 Tasmanian wine show. In 3 years they have already won 5 trophies and 78 gold, silver and bronze medals.

Tamar have 3 ranges of wines as well as the Tamar Ridge label they produce a Devil's Corner Range and a prestigious Josef Chromy Selection wines. As well as Riesling, Chardonnay, Pinot Noir and Cabernet Sauvignon they produce an excellent Sauvignon Blanc a variety not commonly seen in Tasmania. They also make a late harvest Riesling and several award winning Methode Traditionelle Sparkling wines.

Tamar Ridge are well focused and have the resources and ability to become a genuine top level Australian wine producer.

Address: Auburn Road KAYENA 7270	Public Hours: 10am-5pm, daily (Closed	Tamar Ridge Riesling	10 yrs
Phone: (03) 6334 6208	Christmas Day & Good Friday)	Tamar Ridge Sauvignon Blanc	2 yrs
Fax: (03) 6334 6050	Principal Varieties: Cabernet Sauvignon,	Tamar Ridge Cabernet Sauvignon	5 yrs
Email: taste@tamarridgewines.com.au	Chardonnay, Pinot Noir, Riesling, Sauvignon	Tamar Ridge Pinot Noir	5 yrs
Winemaker: Michael Fogarty	Blanc	Tamar Ridge Chardonnay	4 yrs
Est: 1994 Vine Ha: 62 Cases: 15,000	Principal Wines Potential	Tamar Ridge Unwooded Chardonnay	2 yrs

Rosevears Estate

Dr Michael Beamish settled in Tasmania from the United Kingdom in 1976. His strong interest in wine led him to purchase the Glengarry Vineyard in 1990 and following on from this the Notley Gorge Vineyard in 1994. His passion for fine wine and food and a belief in Tasmania as a food and wine destination, led to the development of Rosevears Estate.

Rosevears Estate was constructed to give visitors a unique Tasmanian food and wine experience by combing the vineyard, winemaking, wine tasting and fine food in a setting that must be seen to be truly appreciated. It was officially opened by Premier Jim Bacon in October 1999. Rosevears Estate features a 200 seat Restaurant and Function centre, a working Winery and extensive vine plantings.

With sweeping views of the river, valley and the surrounding mountains, Rosevears Estate offers a stunning a la carte menu, lunches, winery tours, wedding and function facilities and cellar door sales.

Rosevears Estate has new label and logo; 'The Jester' which depicts the Estate and the skills required to juggle the weather and viticulture with winemaking.

Rosevears Estate is located 15 minutes from Launceston and offers an exceptional tourism experience, helping Tasmania to be one of the world's premier tourist destinations.

Address: PO Box 1231 LAUNCESTON 7250	**Public Hours:** 10am-4pm daily (including Christmas)	Rosevears Estate Pinot Noir	5 yrs
Phone: (03) 6330 1800 **Fax:** (03) 6330 1810	**Principal Varieties:** Cabernet Sauvignon,	Rosevears Estate Riesling	2-4 yrs
Owner: Michael Beamish, Roderick Cuthbert, Roger Martin	Pinot Noir, Sauvignon Blanc, Chardonnay, Riesling	Rosevears Estate Cab Sav	4-8 yrs
Winemaker: Jim Chatto, Shane McKorrow		Rosevears Estate Sparkling	2-3 yrs
Vine Ha: 24 **Cases:** 10,000	**Principal Wines** **Potential**	Rosevears Estate Sauvignon Blanc	1-2 yrs
		Rosevears Estate Chardonnay	2-4 yrs

St Matthias

One of the first vineyards established on the glorious Tamar Estuary, north of Launceston was St Matthias. Vines were first planted in 1983. Today the vineyards cover 21 acres of the sun bathed north east facing slopes of the Estuary. This unique microclimate and "Terrior" can create extremely powerful wines with the long hours of sunshine, which not only shines directly on the vines, but also reflects off the wide expanse of water which also moderates the climate and helps avert spring frosts.

The St Matthias range is quite extensive so there is plenty to try, if you make the short 15 minute drive from downtown Launceston. The St Matthias Brut Methode Traditionnelle is a creamy yet crisp and elegant sparkling wine. The whites include Riesling, Chardonnay and a blended dry white "Cuvee Printemps" crisp and fresh. In the reds they produce a Cabernet Merlot and a Pinot Noir.

St Matthias is part of the Morilla Estate group and some of the Morilla wines use fruit from their Tamar vineyards. The Moorilla Estate Syrah from Tamar grapes is superb.

The recently expanded cellar door at St Matthias also offers Tasmanian platters to accompany your tasting, giving you all the more reason to visit this pretty estate.

Eastern Tasmania

The Eastern Coast of Tasmania has a surprisingly mild climate with much more sun, less wind and rainfall than either the Southern or Northern Regions of Tasmania. The soils are generally lighter with well drained Sandy loams predominating. These conditions with the moderating effect of the warm southerly flowing coastal current in the Tasman Sea have proved ideal for a wide range of varieties from Riesling through to Cabernet Sauvignon.

The region was pioneered by Abalone

Diver Geoff Bull in 1980 and his Freycinet Vineyards and Winery have been most successful with varieties from Muller Thurgau, Riesling, Chardonnay, Pinot Noir, Merlot to

Cabernet Sauvignon all producing excellent wines.

Coombend Estate just down the road from Freycinet was established in 1985 and Apsley Gorge Vineyard with its winery in a former Fisheries building on the Harbour at Bicheno have been later additions.

Eastern Tasmania's superb climate and viticultural conditions will surely see many more vineyards in the years to come. The region is truly a beautiful place to visit and I urge you to do so.

Eastern Tasmania - TAS

1. Apsley Gorge / Bicheno Winery
2. Coombend
3. Freycinet

Aquatas Salmon

Since Aquatas first started operating in 1987, it has experienced considerable growth to become the second largest Atlantic Salmon farming operations in Tasmania.

Over the 2001-2002 financial year, the company will farm in excess of 1,000,000 smolt (juvenile fish) and will harvest over 2800 tonnes of Atlantic Salmon. Its main farming operations are situated in the northern end of the D'Entrecasteaux Channel, just south of Hobart.

The clean waters in which Aquatas' fish are farmed provide a natural advantage over Northern Hemisphere producers. Aquatas salmon are free from disease and pollution while the conditions provide the ideal environment for fast, high quality growth.

The process of preparing products for smoking is meticulous. Each fish is individually filleted, pin boned and cured. Each slice of the Premium pre-sliced cold smoked products is individually inspected ensuring that any imperfect pieces are removed. This process guarantees a consistent quality product.

The highest levels of hygiene are maintained in the processing operations, with strict rules and procedures adhered to at all times.

Aquatas' innovative culture has lead it to develop a native Australian product. Lemon Myrtle Cold Smoked Atlantic Salmon combines the fine dining experience of traditionally oak smoked Atlantic salmon with the mellow lemon lime flavours of Australia's own Lemon Myrtle leaf sprinkled on top. The result is a subtle citrus after taste complimented by a succulent, smooth texture that is second to none.

Oak Smoked Pastrami Atlantic Salmon is another recent addition to Aquatas' product range. This product introduces traditionally smoked salmon to a spicy topping which includes pepper, coriander and mustard seeds. Once again the salmon is gently smoked over oak chips, allowing the spices to blend with the oak smoked flavour of the salmon. The final product has a spicy taste without the heat and a succulent smooth texture.

Being a pioneering company, Aquatas is continually developing new products.

Aquatas is a growing and professional company setting the standard in Australia and overseas with high quality Tasmanian products.

Innovation, quality and a wide range of products are the key to Aquatas'

success.

Apart from fresh, chilled Atlantic Salmon, Aquatas offers a wide variety of traditionally smoked Atlantic Salmon and smoked Ocean Trout products packaged in sizes ranging from 100g to whole sides to cater for the retail and catering sectors of the market.

In addition Aquatas also offers a unique range of Hot Smoked Atlantic Salmon products. The hot Smoked Atlantic Salmon sides are available in four unique flavours; Creole, Mediterranean, Apricot and Teriyaki. Hot smoking is not a process commonly associated with Atlantic salmon but has proved very successful for Aquatas. The process involves cooking the product during smoking. It is different from the method used to produce the better known traditionally cold smoked salmon where lower temperatures do not cook the salmon fillet. These products have developed an excellent reputation in many of the leading hotels and restaurants in Australia and overseas.

The many and varied Aquatas Salmon products match superbly with Tasmania's spectacular Sparkling wines and the crisp dry Chardonnay's, Riesling and Sauvignon Blanc's.

Bicheno / Apsley Gorge

One of the worlds most spectacularly situated wineries is the Aplsey Gorge Winery at "The Gulch" the pretty, serene, seaport of Bicheno, you can gaze out at the fishing trawlers as you taste their crisp Chardonnay and their classy aromatic Pinot Noir.

Brian Franklin made his first wines in 1993. His Apsley Gorge Vineyard is located inland from Bicheno on Tasmania's east coast. It's at the end of a north east facing valley at the entrance to the Apsley Gorge National Park. The wines, mostly Chardonnay and Pinot Noir benefit from the unique microclimate of this pristine site surrounded by the Park.

Modern trellising techniques combined with the natural features of the valley produce wines with an extraordinary concentration of fruit flavours. Quality is of paramount importance and the berries are hand picked to minimize damage. The first vintage was rewarded with Bronze medals at the Tasmanian Wine Show. All of the later vintages have received Silver and Gold medals at the Royal Hobart Wine Show and the Tasmanian Wine Show. The 1995 Chardonnay won the trophy for the best white wine at the Hobart Show.

When travelling along the beautiful East Coast of Tasmania don't forget to make Bicheno winery a compulsory "port of call".

Address: The Gulch BICHENO 7215 **Phone:** (03) 6375 1221 **Fax:** (03) 6375 1589 **Email:** agv@tassie.net.au **Owner:** Brian Franklin	**Winemaker:** Brian Franklin **Est:** 1980 **Vine Ha:** 5 **Cases:** 2,000	**Public Hours:** 10am-6pm, daily (Summer) **Principal Wines** **Potential** Apsley Gorge Pinot Noir 5-7 yrs Apsley Gorge Chardonnay 5-7 yrs

Coombend

Coombend is a family property dating back to 1841, run by John & Jo Fenn-Smith. The property comprises 5000 acres of improved pasture. The vineyard was planted in 1985.

Coombend enjoys a mild maritime climate with an average annual rainfall of 30 inches. Located on the 42nd parallel south the central East Coast has more sunshine hours than other Tasmanian regions. Theses climatic condition make Coombend the perfect location for producing high quality fruit.

The first commercial picking of Cabernet Sauvignon grapes was in 1990, and its subsequent release was awarded a gold medal at the 1992 Royal Hobart wine Show. 1998 saw the first vintage of Sauvignon Blanc and Riesling. To coincide with this release the Coombend Sales Centre, before Christmas in 1998, it is open from 10.00 am to 5.00 pm daily.

To compliment Coombends premium wines, olives trees have been planted approximately 3000 trees were planted in 1996. The seven varieties are mainly for oil production, two are for eating and pickling purposes.

Coombend also has two very comfortable, self-contained cottage available for accommodation. They are ideal for family holidays with reasonable rates available including breakfast. You can relax in a peaceful environment and enjoy dinner delivered to your cottage. The Coombend cottage has two bedrooms, and commands a glorious view of the farm from it's location amongst the olive grove. Make Coombend your stop over on your Tasmanian Wine Adventure.

Address: Coombend SWANSEA 7190 **Phone:** (03) 6257 8881 **Fax:** (03) 6257 8484	**Winemaker:** Andrew Hood **Est:** 1985 **Public Hours:** 9am-5pm, daily	**Principal Varieties:** Cab Franc, Cab Sav, Riesling, Sauvignon Blanc, Shiraz

Freycinet

Geoff Bull is an individualist who has had a most interesting life. His first career was as an award-winning photo-journalist. Then a desire for the great outdoors led him to become an abalone diver off the east cost of Tasmania.

In 1980 he began planting vines on the steep slopes of his property near Bicheno on Tasmania's East Coast. In a step by step process he established a small winery which grew gradually under the large cypress trees at the foot of the steep slopes.

The two winery buildings include a splendid café style tasting area. Geoff and Susan's daughter Lindy, studied winemaking. She has a degree from the famous Roseworthy College, as does Lindy's husband, Claudio Radenti.

Freycinet make an excellent Riesling from 20 year old vines and have planted Schonburger, a new variety and also make a lovely spicy Riesling

Schonburger. The Chardonnay, Pinot Noir and Cabernet Sauvignon are also excellent. The Freycinet Vineyard overlooks the spectacular Freycinet National Park area and coastline. Freycinet Vineyard/Winery is situated in a unique microclimate. "It is an inverted 'U' shape, opening at the lower end and rising to close at the opposite end, with a mini valley between the sides of the 'U'. On the 42 south latitude line, the heat degree summation is a low 1250 degree days, but the sunshine hours are high and the growing season extends into May. The rain falls in the winter and the site is frost free, largely wind protected and a sun trap during summer.

New winemaking equipment and top class French oak barriques in the skillful hands of the two young winemakers are making the most of superb grapes from Geoff's extremely well managed vineyards. Recent

Merlot plantings add complexity to the Cabernet Sauvignon wine produced from the original twenty year old vines.

James Halliday, a leading Australian wine writer has rated the vineyard 5 stars. All their wines are produced from fruit off their own vineyards. The vineyard is hand pruned and harvested by hand. The Radenti sparkling wine is produced to the traditional Methode Champenoise process. Freycinet purchased small scale champagne equipment new from France which is employed in the production of the Radenti. The Radenti spends 4 years on yeast lees in the bottle.

The vineyard is renowned for its production of Burgundy style wines, mainly the Pinot Noir. They also produce an excellent Chardonnay produced in the traditional white Burgundian method. The Chardonnay fruit is fermented in French Oak and allowed to stay in contact with the lees, which are stirred every week for 12 months. The wine also undergoes a malolactic fermentation. The process produces a complex rich full bodied cool climate Chardonnay.

Freycinet Vineyard recently decided to produce a straight varietal Riesling. The 2000 Riesling is an excellent example of a fully ripened rich cool climate Riesling. Qantas has selected this wine for use on its 1st Class International flights. These wines are drinking very well however they have the ability to age beautifully given a good cellaring environment.

Address: Tasman Highway BICHENO 7215
Phone: (03) 6257 8574 **Fax:** (03) 6257 8454
Email: freycinetwines@tassie.net.au

Owner: Geoff and Sue Bull
Winemaker: Claudio Radenti/Lindy Bull
Est: 1980 **Vine Ha:** 7

Public Hours: 9am-5pm, daily
Principal Varieties: Cabernet Sauvignon, Chardonnay, Merlot, Pinot Noir, Riesling

Southern Tasmania

Southern Tasmanian wine regions surround Hobart. The first vineyard in Tasmania was planted by fabric baron, Claudio Alcorso, at Berriedale on the banks of the Derwent River, in a northern suburb of Hobart in 1958. Further up the Derwent Valley are several vineyards and wineries, including Meadowbank and Stefano Lubiana.

The next area planted was the Coal Valley, east of the Derwent, near Richmond and Campania. The fine Domaine A Stoney Vineyard is here and the Victorian Domaine Chandon's expanding Tolpuddle Vineyards, along with several other small wine ventures. Further

towards Port Arthur is the spectacular Bream Creek Vineyard of Fred Peacock.

The other Southern Region is the Huon Valley and d'Entrecasteau Valleys, some 30 kilometres south of Hobart on the peninsula between the Huon River and Bruny Island. A fine

winery and vineyard in this region is the Panorama Vineyard of Michael and Sharon Vishacki.

Microclimates in these very cold viticultural regions · by world standards · is critical. Long sunshine hours in the summer help the equally long growing season, but the aspect of the slope and protection from the howling westerly winds is essential. The moderating effect of the many estuaries also plays an important role, helping produce some great wines · not without the viticulturist losing a little sleep. A number of wineries now have hospitality adjuncts helping make a visit a complete experience.

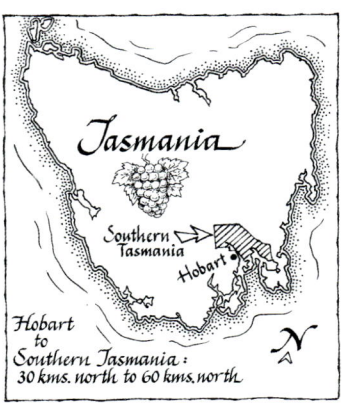

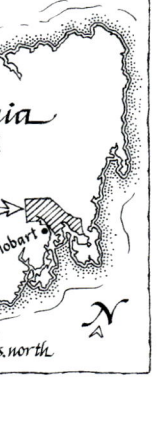

Southern Tasmania - TAS

1.   Bream Creek Vineyard
2.   Domaine A Stoney Vineyard
3.   Morilla
4.   Panorama Vineyard
5.   Potters Cottage
6.   Stefano Lubiano

Bream Creek

Fred Peacock definitely has Australia's premier vineyard vista. Planted in the early 1970's Bream Creek Vineyard is one of the longest established commercial vineyards in Tasmania and is definitely one of the most picturesque in Australia. Situated on the East Coast with the same latitude as Hobart, the vineyard enjoys a north easterly aspect overlooking Marion Bay and Maria Island.

The original 5 hectares were planted mainly to Riesling and Cabernet Sauvignon, with smaller areas of Pinot Noir and Chardonnay. As the planted area has grown, so has the range of varieties. Traminer is now produced along with the rarely encountered but elegantly flavoursome Schonburger. The recent plantings of Sauvignon Blanc have now seen the first wine of this variety released.

Bream Creek Vineyard enjoys a very long, mild growing season with no risk of damaging spring or autumn frost. This coupled with the age of the vines, results in grapes with intense varietal fruit flavours, an attribute reflected in the quality of the wines. While the main pickings occur in late April and May, it is not unusual to finish picking Riesling in early June.

You can taste the Bream Creek wines at the gorgeous "Potters Croft", down the road a little towards Port Arthur and located in the quiet fishing village of Dunalley set amongst the gum trees. Share the panoramic view with the sea eagles, take a walk along the rocky foreshore of this waterfront retreat, enjoy a tasting of the Bream Creek wines and pick up some wine for your cellar.

Potters Croft has a cafe and stylish self-contained accommodation. Make this a stop on your journey. Bream Creek Vineyard is a sight you should experience, then travel on to Potters Croft for a taste of wines.

Address: 321 Marion Bay Road BREAM CREEK 7175	**Email:** peacockf@mpx.com.au **Est:** 1973	**Public Hours:** By appointment
Phone: (03) 6231 4646 **Fax:** (03) 6231 4646	**Owner:** Fred Peacock **Vine Ha:** 7 **Winemaker:** Steve Lubiana **Cases:** 3,000	**Principal Varieties**: Chardonnay, Pinot Noir, Riesling, Sauvignon Blanc, Schonburger

Domaine A Stoney Vineyard

Stoney Vineyard began its life as the property of George and Priscilla Park in 1973. In 1988 Ruth and Peter Althaus tasted the wines at a comparative tasting on a trip from their native Switzerland. The fell in love with them and Tasmania. When they heard the property was on the market a year later they did not hesitate. Peter was a senior executive with IBM in charge of the Customer Engineering Department in Zurich. Peter is a great fan of Bordeaux Wines and 70 per cent of the property is planted to red Bordeaux varieties, cabernet sauvignon, merlot, cabernet franc and petit verdot. A further 20 per cent is pinot noir with only 10 per cent in sauvignon blanc.

The soils are stony, well drained with a thin layer of rich black clay and low rainfall. The dry conditions with loads of sunshine and the north and east-facing slopes produce outstanding fruit. Peter is a fastidious winemaker and his wines are fantastic. The winery includes an area for Functions and Entertainment

from 15 to 60 guests can be received for set luncheons, dinners and wine appreciation classes. A Swiss trained professional chef takes care that the standard of the food matches the top quality of the wines. This is a winery with its act very much together.

Moorilla Estate

Moorilla Estate has been synonymous with quality and style since being established by art and textile entrepreneur Claudio Alcorso, in 1958.

Moorilla is located twelve kilometres north of the capital city, Hobart, with true waterfront on a private peninsula of the picturesque and tranquil Derwent River. Moorilla specialises in hand crafted cool climate wines, fine food and generous and warm hospitality. Moorilla is an Aboriginal name meaning 'a stone by water'. Traces of Aboriginal camp sites can be found along Moorilla's banks, overlooking the River Derwent.

After much experimentation, Claudio found that wine produced at Moorilla was so good, that he turned his efforts to full time production of fine quality table wines, under the 'Moorilla Estate' label.

Today, Moorilla is the most famous and one of the largest Tasmanian wineries, with an annual crush of in excess of 150 tonnes of grapes. It is no coincidence that wines of distinction are produced in Tasmania. Moorilla, which is situated along the 42nd parallel, is on a similar latitude to the famous wine producing regions of Europe.

Moorilla's temperate climate allows for the slow and perfect ripening of the grape varieties, that make the world's finest table wines ·especially the Pinot Noir.

At Moorilla, thanks to Tasmania's lingering Autumns, it is possible to leave the grapes on the vines as late as May before picking.

While Claudio Alcorso is recognised as the founder of the Tasmanian wine industry, it should be amended to read: founder of the modern day commercial Tasmanian wine industry, because vines were planted in Hobart, Tasmania, with the arrival of the first white settlers. In 1798, George Bass, on board the brig The Norfolk sailed up the estuary of the Derwent, he observed the environment carefully and entered in his diary the comment: "Being a stiff close soil, it is perhaps adapted to the growth of grape vines rather than grain".

The first 200 vines were planted at Moorilla in 1958 on a block situated near the back of the Wine Centre. Today there are 63 acres (some 250,000 vines). The vineyard is exceptionally labour intensive and grapes are hand harvested, birds are a major problem and nets are placed over the vines prior to harvest.

Moorilla has four individual self-contained chalets, purpose designed and built with privacy, indulgence, relaxation and comfort in mind.

Generous in space, light and elegant, all with luxury features like spa baths for two in stunning granite, glass bathrooms and king size beds to help you recuperate.

The two, one bedroom chalets are ideal for that special occasion, while the two chalets, with two bedrooms, comfortably accommodate a family of four or two couples travelling together.

You can bathe in the sunrise from your private balcony, stroll after breakfast in the vineyard, chat with the winemaker and build up an appetite for lunch in Moorilla's award winning restaurant.

Moorilla also has a museum where the curator guides you on a journey through ancient civilisations, a celebration of life and art that will stimulate your mind and senses.

Moorilla is an indulgent retreat, a cocoon catering to every whim and a base from which to explore nearby Richmond, Mount Wellington and Salamanca Place, or further afield to Port Arthur, World Heritage areas and the beautiful Derwent Valley. Why not plan your escape to Moorilla soon.

Address: 655 Main Road, Berriedale HOBART 7000 **Phone:** (03) 6249 2949 **Fax:** (03) 6249 4093	**Owner:** Alain Rousseau **Winemaker:** Alain Rousseau **Est:** 1958 **Vine Ha:** 12 **Cases:** 12,000	**Public Hours:** 9am-5pm, daily **Principal Varieties:** Ries, Gewürztraminer, Chardonnay, Pinot Noir, Cab Sav

Tasmanian Abalone Fishery

One of the joys of living in Australia is the ease of access to the wonderful array of food prepared and offered by the Asian cuisine. In neighbouring Asian countries, abalone is a luxury product that is very highly valued, particularly if it's grown wild, harvested and supplied live.

Abalone, when cooked, is milky-moist, tender and mild - somewhat like lobster, though sweeter to the palate. Taste-wise, abalone is also a distant cousin to calamari. A little care is required in its preparation, but then light sautéing or steaming is all that is needed to create a culinary delicacy and a special eating experience - one that will leave you longing for more.

The quality and freshness of wild abalone meat, together with its scarcity, makes it a high-premium food item. Whilst traditionally appearing on the menus of exclusive restaurants in Asia, interest is growing in Australia, where some of our most innovative chefs are using fresh abalone to create a variety of new and exciting dishes, showcasing the product and their talents.

So market demand for abalone continues to grow, but where to get it?

Did you know that over 40% of the world's wild harvested abalone comes from Australia and currently provides our producers with an export income of about $A180 million per annum?1 The Australian Abalone Industry is run by a relatively small number of licensed fishermen, about half of whom operate in Tasmania. They abide by the tight controls and regulations that protect the existing ecology and enforce responsible fishing practices.

The natural elements of the cold, pristine waters of Tasmania provide a perfect environment and these fishermen are acknowledged as producers of the world's finest abalone. They also enjoy a reputation, both nationally and internationally, for managing one of the best wild fisheries in the world and their steadily improving catch statistics indicate they are going from strength to strength. Licensed fishermen have quotas, currently set at 800kg in Tasmania and they usually sell their catch directly to a distributor. However, despite their unique ability to supply an exclusive premium quality product, live and in the shell, return prices to the producer are many times less than the end consumer, or more importantly distributor, pays in Asia.

Showing true Australian entrepreneurial spirit, some of Tasmania's abalone producers have recently teamed with another Australian-owned company, Abalone Australia Direct (www.abalonedirect.com), a company that provides direct marketing of their products to the restaurant marketplace and utilises Internet technology systems to facilitate direct trading between the producers and their end users.

Abalone Australia Direct is revolutionising the distribution supply chain in a way that enables producers of wild abalone to translate their natural advantages into sound economic gains.

This new venture moves them into the 21st Century and beyond. It will help lift the prices of Tasmanian abalone, give the abalone fishermen a much greater return on their unique produce and position them rightfully on the world market.

If you've never tasted fresh grilled abalone with a crisp award winning Tasmanian Riesling or a rich Tasmanian Chardonnay or for that matter, with abalone cooked in any fashion, you haven't lived. Make sure you enjoy this marvelous gourmet treat as soon as possible.

Panorama Vineyard

The Panorama Vineyard is located on the eastern bank of the Huon River about 45 minutes south of Hobart, in a sheltered region that was once the centre of high quality stonefruit orchards and apples supplying the export market.

Located just below the 43 degrees latitude the vineyard enjoys an exceptional microclimate. In a low altitude area it has a cool temperate climate with moderate summers, very high sunshine hours and mild winters. The long slow ripening period allows for optimal development of fruit flavours. Young couple Michael and Sharon Vishacki have done a great job with the vineyard, winery and cellar door.

In keeping with Michael's philosophy the vineyard is not too large and does not prevent him from adopting a totally hands-on approach, each shoot is placed by hand.

To maximise ripeness and to ensure top quality fruit at vintage, Michael removes leaves in the canopy, to expose the fruit to sunlight and nets are placed over each row, when the grapes are almost ripe, to protect them from the birds. Although time-consuming Michael considers these measures are worth the effort and it is certainly reflected in the quality of the wine.

Naturally the grapes are harvested by hand and only fruit in pristine condition is used. Pruning also still done by hand, which is yet another opportunity for Michael to inspect the vines and monitor their condition. During maturation in premium French and American Oak, the wines are constantly monitored and the barrels topped up to deal with the inevitable evaporation. The end result is a wine which has a very little preservative and of superior quality.

Panorama Vineyard produce a selection of elegant wines including a gold medal winning Pinot Noir, bronze medal winning Chardonnay, a Sauvignon Blanc and Soft Apple wines, fruit Ports and Liqueurs.

Cellar door sales are available daily, (closed Tuesday) and the beautiful appointed wine tasting room is set in the magnificent surroundings of the vineyard.

Why not take a pleasant 45 minute drive south of Hobart and enjoy some of the most spectacular views Tasmania has to offer, and visit the Vishacki's picturesque Panorama Vineyard.

Stefano Lubiana

Formed in 1990, Stefano Lubiana Wines is owned and operated by husband and wife team, Steve and Monique Lubiana.

Located 25 minutes north of Hobart on the Western banks of the Derwent River, their 170 hectare property is home to both a thriving young family and a healthy enterprise, focusing on the production of hand crafted true cool-climate, still and sparkling wine.

After making wine in South Australia for 3 years, the young couple moved to Tasmania in search of Australia's most ideal cool climate site. Steve's first impression of the Derwent region was the fabulous quality of strawberries and stone fruit; this helped make the decision to move to Granton a little more obvious.

In spring 1990 a small vineyard of Pinot Noir and Chardonnay were planted and since, Sauvignon Blanc, Riesling, Merlot, Cabernet Franc, Pinot Grigio and Nebbiolo have been

added totalling 12 hectares. Granton's latitude of 43 degrees South enables the vineyard to enjoy extended sun exposure due to the extra day length. The vertical shoot positioned vines are laid out on gently undulating slopes in narrow rows running north south. The close proximity to the river offers excellent cold air drainage and frost protection and provides a moderating influence on the vineyards mesoclimate, cooling the site in summer and warming it during winter. Harvest usually occurs from mid-March to mid-May and crop levels are kept less than 2 kilos per vine.

Steve believes the wine is made in the vineyard and winemakers are merely caretakers, helping the wine to reflect the 'terroir'. The vineyard will soon be completely organic and Steve prefers to use traditional winemaking techniques in order to capture the true personality of the wines.

The Stefano Lubiana range consists of two sparkling wines made in the traditional way, a Germanic style Riesling, Pinot Grigio, Sauvignon Blanc, and at the Burgundy end is two Chardonnay's and two pinot Noir's at two different price points but with equal esteem. When tasting Steve's wines one cannot help but think food is a major influence.

Stefano Lubiana Wines is considered by many as Tasmania's top producer. Their wines are getting better each year and therefore becoming harder to find. A winemaking legacy of over 200 years, attention to detail and pursuit for excellence is quickly gaining Steve Lubiana a firm place amongst Australia's cult favourites.

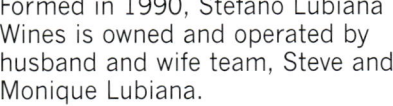

Address: 60 Rowbottoms Rd GRANTON 7030	**Public Hours:** 10am-5pm, daily	NV Brut	
Phone: (03) 6263 7457 **Fax:** (03) 6263 7430	**Principal Varieties:** Merlot, Pinot Noir, Sauv	Pinot Grigo	2-4 yrs
Email: wine@stefanolubiana.com **Est:** 1990	Blanc, Chardonnay, Pinot Grigio, Riesling	Riesling	2-4 yrs
WWW: www.stefanolubiana.com **Vine Ha:** 12	**Principal Wines** **Potential**	Chardonnay	3-6 yrs
Winemaker: Steve Lubiana **Cases:** 8,000	Vintage Brut	Pinot Noir	4-8 yrs

Tassal Tasmanian Salmon

In 1983, a report to the Tasmanian Fisheries Development Authority recommended a salmon farming industry could be successfully developed in Tasmania. As a result, the government assisted with the establishment of a sea farm at Dover in the south of Tasmania and a hatchery at Wayatinah in the central highlands.

The first successful introduction of Atlantic Salmon (salmo salar) occurred when fertilised salmon eggs were purchased from the Gaden Hatchery in New South Wales in 1984. These eggs were from stock originally imported in the early 1960's from Nova Scotia, Canada. After hatching, the salmon were quarantined for several months and checked thoroughly for disease. They proved to be free of all major viral and bacterial diseases and were put into sea pens for growing to harvest size. Theses early stocks are the basis of Tassal's current disease-free species.

Tassal Limited was established in 1987 as a public company listed on the Australian Stock Exchange. The company is vertically integrated from financial involvement in hatchery operations, through to farming, processing, value-adding, distribution and marketing of a range of salmon products.

The first commercial harvest of 53 tonnes was taken in the summer of 1986/87. The Tasmanian industry now produces almost 10,000 tonnes per annum, of which Tassal accounts for over 65%.

Tassa produces over some 6,500 tonnes of salmon from its Tasmanian operations each year. Of this

approximately 2,000 tonnes is exported to markets throughout the western Pacific Region. Locally there is an increasing demand for smoked salmon and value added food products.

The Company has a highly respected team of marine biologists and experienced personnel who have an impressive number of years' experience in perfecting the growing of salmon.

Research and development projects have led to many pioneering innovations in both fish husbandry and farm technology, Tassal remains the leader in its field and continues to register improved growth and survival rates for its salmon.

With a delicate flavour, rich colour and fine even texture, Royal Tasmanian salmon is high in Omega-3 polyunsaturated oils that reduce blood fats in the human body, providing many health benefits. Royal Tasmanian salmon are raised naturally and free from any chemical, hormonal or artificial additives under the Royal Tasmanian brand. In addition to the primary processing centre at Dover, Tassal has opened a new value-added processing centre at

Hounville, south of Hobart. New world-class technology allows Tassal to deliver increased production capacity and a broader range of "Royal Tasmanian" salmon products.

"Royal Tasmanian" Salmon is recognised in the major Asian fish markets as synonymous with perfection, matching the finest in the world for its consistent quality, colour, taste and texture. "Royal Tasmanian" salmon is considered superior in quality, appearance and flavour.

For the smoked salmon products, a specially developed mixture of Australian hardwoods imparts a mellow, smoked flavour and rich natural colour. In addition to quality fresh, head on, gilled and gutted salmon, Tassal offers a range of fillets and skinless, boneless portions. Tassal have also just released an exciting new Hot Smoked Salmon range. Their products are also available in Australian supermarkets, as well as leading Restaurants and Hotels.

In 1994, a wholly owned subsidiary office was opened in Japan. Tassal's commitment to quality is evidenced by the successful completion of the World's Best Practice program in May 1996, followed by ISO9002 certification in June 1996. This program is part of ongoing cultural and continuous improvement projects.

Tassal's "Royal Tasmanian" salmon, both fresh and smoked, is the perfect companion for the splendid sparkling wines for which Tasmania is fast gaining a world wide reputation, as well as their exciting Riesling, Chardonnay and other fine white table wines.

Queensland

Wine production first began on a commercial level in Queensland in the unlikely location of Roma, almost 450 kilometres to the north-west of Brisbane. The venture was founded by Samuel Bassett in 1863. Vine cuttings were provided by Bassett's uncle who had an established vineyard in the Hunter Valley. By the time Samuel's son, William, took control of the company in 1912, 'Romavilla' was a thriving business, with more than 450 acres under vine. William Bassett had received winemaking tuition from the great Leo Buring and his wines were highly sought-after. Romavilla has remained constantly in production. This seemed in doubt only after William's death in 1973, but a group of Sydney businessmen purchased the property two years later, and production continued.

While Romavilla is Queensland's longest operating winery, the vast majority of the state's industry is situated around the towns of Stanthorpe and Ballandean, near the border of New South Wales. The region is known as the 'Granite Belt', owing to its granitic soils and its location on a small elevated plateau in the Great Dividing Range. Altitudes vary from 800 to 940 metres above sea level, making the area one of the highest wine-producing districts in Australia. Generally therefore, the climate is cool and not dissimilar to that experienced by the Central Highlands of New South Wales. Distance from the sea can result in harsh winters, and even occasional snow. The average maximum temperature during summer months is only 26 degrees centigrade and soils are decomposed granite varieties.

From a small bulk wine industry, began by the early European settlers, wine has now become a fully-fledged industry, with larger vineyards and wineries being established. The industry has expanded considerably and the Granite Belt now boasts more than 25 commercial wineries. Winemakers of the region are united in their desire to exploit the unique Queensland climate. Many innovative techniques are being employed and wines released so far show successful evidence of these efforts.

Every year on the first and second weekend of October the industry has its "Spring Wine Festival" attracting many wine and food enthusiasts to the region. This is followed on the third weekend by the "Australian Small Winemakers Show" attracting over 900 entries involving every State in Australia.

The first Sunday in May boasts the extremely successful "Opera At Sunset", attracting over 2,000 opera and wine lovers to the wineries.

The Granite Belt region is a unique contributor to Australia's wine industry. Vignerons are highly motivated and justifiably proud of their region. Some of the wines produced are of exceptional quality and are sure to become more widely respected in the near future.

In recent years there have been some considerable vineyard and winery developments around Kingaroy and in the hinterlands of both the Gold Coast and the Sunshine Coast.

Queensland

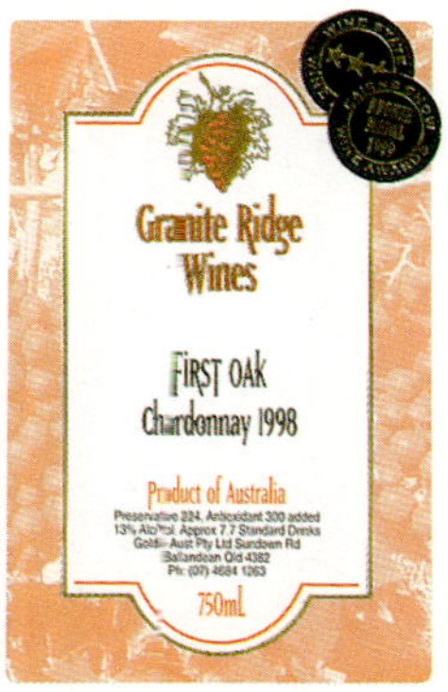

Granite Ridge Wines

FIRST OAK
Chardonnay 1998

Product of Australia

Preservative 204, Antioxidant 300 added
13% Alc/Vol Approx 7.7 Standard Drinks
Goldn-Aust Pty Ltd Sundown Rd
Ballandean Qld 4382
Ph: (07) 4684 1263
750mL

Robinsons Family

1999
SHIRAZ CABERNET

Queensland

1.   Bald Mountain Vineyards
2.   Ballandean Estate Winery
3.   Felsberg
4.   Golden Grove Winery
5.   Granite Ridge
6.   Heritage Wines
7.   Hidden Creek
8.   Kominos Wines
9.   Mount View
10. Preston Peak
11. Robinsons Family Vineyards
12. Stanthorpe Wine Co.

Ballandean Estate

Angelo Puglisi was the major influence in the renaissance of the Queensland Wine Industry in the 1970's and 80's.

Angelo's grandfather Salvadore Cardillo established the vineyard in 1930. In 1969-70 Angelo planted premium classic wine varieties and made the first wines from these in 1972, his 1975 vintage was notable as two of his wines won gold medals at the Brisbane Show. In 1977 Angelo was awarded a Churchill fellowship and travelled throughout Europe studying winemaking. For some years the winery went under the name Sundown Valley Vineyards.

Today Ballandean Estate is greatly expanded and the fourth generation of the family are involved. Angelo's hardworking wife Mary, their daughters Leanne and her husband Mario who looks after the cellar operations plus Robyn and her husband Ian Henderson who is assistant winemaker, are all heavily involved.

Ballandean also make some excellent late picked styles and great fortifieds including Port and Muscat.

The winery now sports a characterful café, Ballandean Estate is a vibrant and interesting place to visit.

Address: Sundown road BALLANDEAN 4382 **Phone:** (07) 4684 1226 **Fax:** (07) 4684 1288 **Email:** enquiries@ballandean-estate.com.au **WWW:** www.ballandean-estate.com.au	**Owner:** Angelo and Mary Puglisi **Winemaker:** Angelo Puglisi & Adam Chapman **Est:** 1970 **Vine Ha:** 18 **Cases:** 6,000	**Public Hours:** 9am-5pm, daily **Principal Varieties:** Shiraz, Cabernet Sauvignon, Sylvaner, Sauvignon Blanc, Muscat, Semillon

Felsberg

Otto and Anne Haag are a couple brimming over with positive energy. Their winery is spectacularly located on top of a precipitous Ridge, looking out over the Glen Aplin Valley. The tasting and Hospitality areas have truly breathtaking views.

Otto of Bavarian origin was the long time chief brewer for Castlemaine Brewery so there's not much he doesn't understand about fermentation and he has certainly put it to good use in creating a range of exciting wines and a Mead made from highland honey.

During our visit he was busy constructing a Bell Tower as part of a hospitality area where light lunches and refreshments are now served.

The Haags bought the property as a holiday retreat in 1983. They planted vines and today have 18 acres under vine. The winery was completed in 1991.

Otto's Germanic style Riesling and Gewurztraminer are truly spicy and aromatic, their Chardonnay is likewise very lifted. They also make a Merlot and a Cabernet Sauvignon as well as other varieties. Felsberg is a place to visit to imbibe in the view as well as the wines and bathe in the Haags positive energy.

Address: Townsend's Rd GLEN APLIN 4381 **Phone:** (07) 4683 4332 **Fax:** (07) 4683 4377 **Email:** felsberg@ozemail.com.au **Est:** 1983 **Owner:** Otto & Anne Haag **Vine Ha:** 7 **Winemaker:** Otto Haag **Cases:** 1,600	**Public Hours:** 9:30am-4:30pm, daily **Principal Varieties:** Cab Sav, Chard, Gewürztraminer, Merlot, Rhine Riesling, Shiraz **Principal Wines** **Potential** Felsberg Chardonnay 2-5 yrs	Felsberg Traminer Felsberg Shiraz Felsberg Riesling Felsberg Cab/Shiraz Felsberg Merlot	2-5 yrs 5-7 yrs 2-5 yrs 5-7 yrs 5-7 yrs

Golden Grove

Sam and Grace Constanzo have created a vibrant multifaceted vineyard, winery and hospitality complex in the heart of Ballandean, the traditional capital of the Granite Belt wine region. Sam's father Mario arrived in Queensland from Italy in the 1940's as a 17 year old, after cutting cane at Ingham he came to

Stanthorpe, where he met his wife to be Mila. In 1949 they bought a 120 acre block where they grew table grapes and stonefruit. In the early 1970's Mario planted the first Shiraz in the region, his three sons grew up to love winemaking.

In 1986 Sam and Grace bought the family property. On a trip to

California they became fired up with the idea of a premium wine, food and hospitality business. In 1991 the focus really changed, more table grape vines were removed to make way for Chardonnay, Merlot, Cabernet Sauvignon, Semillon and Sauvignon Blanc. They have also planted the Burnett Valley's first vineyard at Mundabrah.

In their hospitality area they hold many pre-booked and special functions, such as a

'Sicilian Vintage Lunch' and a 'Walk In The Cloud's' re-enactment (from the film featuring a Napa Valley Vineyard). They also have a cook your own barbecue facility.

Their wine club launched in 1998 also hosts dinners.

The wines are great and son Raymond whom is studying oenology at Charles Sturt University is now involved in the winemaking, the future looks bright at Golden Grove.

Address: Sundown Rd BALLANDEAN 4382	WWW: www.goldengrovee.com.au	Principal Varieties: Cabernet Franc,
Phone: (07) 4684 1291 Fax: (07) 4684 1247	Winemaker: Sam Costanzo Est: 1976	Cabernet Sauvignon, Chardonnay, Merlot,
Email: goldengrove@halenet.com.au	Public Hours: 9am-5pm, daily	Muscat, Sauvignon Blanc, Semillon, Shiraz

Granite Ridge

Dennis Ferguson established Granite Ridge Wines, originally Delana - Fergusor Estate Wines, in 1996.

The winery is one of the best to visit in Australia, from the pleasantly rustic wooden tasting bar you can

see all the winemaking processes, from crushing to fermentation, maturation, bottling and labelling going on around you as you taste.

Granite Ridge is a friendly family winery. Dennis is Chief Executive and Winemaker, he is assisted in the winemaking and production area by Julianne Ferguson, whilst the viticulturalist is "Fergie" Ferguson.

The Granite Ridge Wines have been very successful in wine shows, both the 1996 and 1997 Cabernet Sauvignons were voted Queensland's best and the winery was appointed official supplier of the Queensland Parliamentary Wine for 1998.

The Winery is housed in a pretty 'Australiana Style' Building surrounded by landscaped native gardens resplendent with large wine barrels at the entrance.

Address: Sundown Rd BALLANDEAN 4382	Winemaker: Dennis & Juliane Ferguson	1st Oak Chardonnay
Phone: (07) 4684 1263 Fax: (07) 4684 1250	Est: 1995 Vine Ha: 4 Cases: 1,000	Granite Range - Cabernet Sauvignon
Email: graniteridge@flexi.net.au	Public Hours: 9am-5pm, daily	The Ridge - Shiraz/Cabernet Sauvignon
WWW: www.graniteridgewines.com.au	Principal Wines	Granite Amber - Liquer Muscat
Owner: Dennis & Juliane Ferguson	Goldies Unwooded Chardonnay	Granite Rock - Shiraz

Heritage Wines

The Winery at Heritage exudes character and charm. The decor and furnishings in the cellar door and hospitality area bring back a strong feeling of yesteryear, it is warm and cosy in winter and a respite from the searing sun in summer.

The buildings began their life as cold storage rooms for apples so they are well insulated and ideal for winemaking and the maturation of the wine.

Bryce and Paddy Kassulke began planting their vineyards at Cottonvale in 1993, on well drained granite soils, they began with Chardonnay, Merlot, Shiraz and Cabernet Sauvignon, Semillon Sauvignon Blanc. Malbec and Cabernet Franc have since been added.

Heritage serve lunch plus morning and afternoon teas to groups who book, they also have country style barbecue and picnic facilities for

visitors.

Jim Barnes is the personable winemaker who ferments many of his wines in expensive new oak.

Heritage have also just opened a second cellar door at Mount Tambourine. Make sure you visit one of their locations when you are in Queensland and enjoy their good taste in wine and hospitality.

Address: Granite Belt Dr COTTONVALE 4375	Winemaker: Jim Barnes		Heritage Estate Shiraz	3-4 yrs
	Est: 1992 Vine Ha: 4 Cases: 5,000		Heritage Estate Cabernet Franc	3-4 yrs
Phone: (07) 4685 2197 Fax: (07) 4685 2112	Public Hours: 9am-5pm, daily		Heritage Estate Merlot	3-4 yrs
Email: heritage@halenet.com.au	Principal Wines	Potential	Heritage Estate Chardonnay	2-3 yrs
Owner: Bryce & Paddy Kassulke	Heritage Estate Semillon	2-3 yrs	Heritage Estate Classic Dry White	1-2 yrs

Hidden Creek

David and Wendy Cull are busy professional people who sought a pretty hideaway in the country to escape their high pressure lives.

They found an idyllic spot overlooking the Severn River Valley and Girraween National Park where they bought a 40 acre property.

They have built a lovely holiday home and a charming winery and café, overlooking their lake, which serves innovative Mediterranean cuisine for lunch and excellent coffee on a daily basis.

Whilst they specialize in Chardonnay and Shiraz they also produce Semillon, Verdelho, Merlot and

Nebbiolo as well as fortified wines including a Muscat.

David looks after the vineyard himself and assists in the winemaking. Wendy is involved in the food and hospitality.

Hidden Creek is a magic place so make sure you seek it out.

Address: Eukey Road BALLANDEAN 4382	WWW: www.hiddencreek.com.au	Public Holidays
Phone: (07) 4684 1383 Fax: (07) 4684 1355	Winemaker: Mark Ravenscroft Est: 1995	Principal Varieties: Cab Sav, Chard, Merlot,
Email: info@hiddencreek.com.au	Public Hours: 10am-4pm, Weekends &	Muscat, Nebbiolo, Semillon, Shiraz, Verdelho

Kominos Wines

One of the modern day pioneering wineries in the unique Stanthorpe wine region of southern Queensland is Kominos. The vineyards are located at 850 metres above sea level and even receive the occasional sprinkling of snow in this comparatively cool viticultural area, long known for its top quality stonefruit.

Tony Comino and family established their first plantings in 1976, with Tony putting his Bachelor of Agricultural Science degree to good use. He and his personable wife Mary now run the vineyards and the superb new winery they have built in a classic colonial Australian style.

In October 1999 their 98 Merlot was awarded a Gold Medal and champion dry Red at the Australian

Smallwinemakers Show . This was the best Red from 864 exhibits and 160 Australian boutique wineries. Three days later a savage hailstorm devastated the winery vineyard.

Their Vintage 2000 was almost totally lost with that freak hailstorm, not long before vintage. Tony and Mary are philosophical people who have taken this major set back with admirable good grace, they deserve success.

Their excellent wines · both red and white have made quite an impact worldwide. They make quite a range from classic varieties and have a beautifully appointed "Natural" tasting room. Their hospitality is second to none.

Address: New England Hwy SEVERNLEA 4380	**Winemaker:** Tony Comino **Cases:** 5,000	**Principal Wines**	**Potential**
Phone: (07) 4683 4311 **Fax:** (07) 4683 4291	**Public Hours:** 8am-4:30pm, Weekdays;	Cabernet Sauvignon	10 yrs
Email: kominoswines@bigpond.com	8:30am-5pm, Weekends	Vin Doux	10 yrs
WWW: www.kominoswines.com.au **Est:** 1976	**Principal Varieties:** Riesling, Chardonnay,	Shiraz	10 yrs
Owner: Comino Family **Vine Ha:** 12	Pinot Noir, Cabernet Sauvignon, Merlot	Chardonnay	8 yrs

Mountview Wines

While Mountview offers a full range of red and white table wines, it's our sparkling wines, made in the methode champenoise, that draws many visitors to experience our special brand of hospitality.

Set among Pine trees, the red cedar barn style winery enjoys great views and stands on the site of the original Mountview vineyards established in

1921.

Visitors entering the wine tasting room are cosseted admist the range of winemaking equipment and oak barrels, providing that authentic winery experience.

Wines include Shiraz, Merlot and Cabernet also Chardonnay, Semillon and Sauvignon Blanc with 4 champagne styles · Chardonnay

Royal, Shiraz Royal Bianco and a Sparkling Pear Cider.

Sometimes one finds the greatest wineries and wines in the most unlikely places because the people who create them care a lot about what they do and put all of themselves into the enterprise. Pauline Stewart's Mountview Wines is such a place.

Address: Mt. Stirling Rd GLEN APLIN 4381	**WWW:** www.mountviewwines.com.au	days School & Public Holidays)
Phone (07) 4683 4316 **Fax:** (07) 4683 4111	**Vine Ha:** 2	**Principal Varieties:** Shiraz, Cab Sav, Merlot,
Email: pauline@mountviewwines.com.au	**Public Hours:** 9:30am-4:30pm, Fri-Mon (7	Chardonnay, Semillon, Sauvignon Blanc

Preston Peak

Preston Peak stunned the wine world when their first Chardonnay, their 1997 Barrel fermented Chardonnay won a gold medal at the 1998 Royal

Melbourne Wine Show - Australia's biggest ever Wine Show and in the largest class with 248 entries, their gold was one of only six awarded,

the other five going to prestigious classics such as Rosemount Roxburgh and Tyrrells Vat 47. Winemaker at their Wyberba ('Devils Elbow') Winery in the Granite belt, a young woman, Phillipa Hambleton should be justly proud.

Enthusiastic owners of Preston Peak Ashley Smith and Kym Thumpkin are from Toowoomba and have also planted vineyards and opened a cellar door with hospitality and function facilities at their Preston Peak location outside Toowoomba. They serve vineyard platters and homemade cakes, coffee and tea with tastings. The center is surrounded by ornamental trees, an olive grove, rose gardens as well as an extensive vineyard.

Extensions to the cellar are already underway, a small crop of Shiraz was picked from their Toowoomba Vineyard in 2000. I'm sure future vintages of Preston Peak will dazzle just like their 1997 Chardonnay.

Address: 31 Preston Peak Lane PRESTON 4352	**WWW:** www.prestonpeak.com	**Est:** 1999 **Vine Ha:** 5
Phone: (07) 4630 9499 **Fax:** (07) 4630 9499	**Owner:** Ashley Smith & Kym Thumpkin	**Public Hours:** 11am-3pm, Weekdays; 10am-5pm, Weekends
Email: info@prestonpeak.com	**Winemaker:** Rod McPherson & Phillipa Hamilton	

Stanthorpe Wine Co.

The Granite Belt has more than 24 wineries in a climate that sees four distinct seasons, with crisp winters, cool summers, fresh springs and colourful autumns, it is one of Australia's most dynamic wine making regions.

The Stanthorpe Wine Centre is located on the northern edge of the region almost the first wine establishment you find when driving from Brisbane it's a great place to stop and orient your visit to the region. The center is nestled amongst nature, stonefruit and apple orchards. The friendly staff of wine enthusiasts, headed by manager Bill Higgins give you a great introduction to the boutique wineries and wines of the Granite Belt. You can also purchase a number of limited release wines exclusive to the region. Preston Peak wines feature strongly, the Centre has its own educational

vineyard, where you can see how 9 different grape varieties are grown.

The center has a large antique cast iron fire to warm you in winter and a

Regional Art and Craft Gallery. You can also buy coffee and snacks to keep you going on your Granite Belt discovery journey.

		Principal Wines	Potential
Address: Granite Belt Drive THULIMBAH 4376	**Est:** 1997 **Vine Ha:** 4 **Cases:** 2,500	Summit Estate Shiraz	10 yrs
Phone: (07) 4683 2011 **Fax:** (07) 4683 2600	**Public Hours:** 9:30am-5pm, daily	Stanthorpe Wine Co. Emily Rose	4 yrs
Email: stanwine@halenet.com.au	**Principal Varieties:** Cabernet Sauvignon,	Summit Estate Pinot	10 yrs
Winemaker: Andrew Hickenbotham & Phillipa Hambleton	Merlot, Pinot Noir, Shiraz, Chardonnay, Petit Verdot, Semillon, Tempranello	Summit Estate Cabernet/Merlot	8 yrs

Robinsons Family

John and Heather Robinson were true modern day Australian wine pioneers when they established their vineyards at Ballandean in 1969.

John lived in France from 1963-66 and worked in Beaujolais, Burgundy and Bordeaux returning to Australia with a real passion to make his own wine. In 1971 he worked with Wine Legend Max Lake at his Hunter Valley Winery.

Heather comes from the wine pioneering Salter family who established Saltram's Wines in 1859 and ran it until 1950.

The Robinsons made their first wine in 1974. In 1975 they won a gold medal at the Brisbane Show with a Cabernet/Shiraz/Pinot blend. John and Heather introduced Chardonnay, Pinot Noir and Cabernet Sauvignon to Queensland in the early 1970's to compliment the existing Shiraz plantings. Today the Robinson's vineyards cover 35 acres, quite large by Queensland standards.

Robinson's Methode Traditionnelle Chardonnay/Pinot Noir Sparkling is a consistent wine show winner, they also produce an unwooded Chardonnay, a Shiraz and a Cabernet Sauvignon.

Daughter Anne Robinson who has a degree in landscape architecture and is studying viticulture, runs the vineyards. Son Craig is winemaker he has worked for Hardys in McLaren Vale, Houghtons in W.A. and made wine in California.

Robinson's have a great track record and are well set for the bright future of Queensland wines.

Address: PO Box 57, Curtin Road BALLANDEAN 4382 **Phone:** (07) 4684 1216 **Fax:** (07) 4684 1216 **Owner:** JW PR & PM Robinson **Winemaker:** Craig Robinson **Est:** 1969 **Vine Ha:** 10 **Cases:** 3,000	**Public Hours:** 10am-5pm daily (except Good Friday & Christmas Day) **Principal Varieties:** Cabernet Sauvignon, Gamay, Pinot Noir, Semillon, Traminer, Chardonnay, Merlot, Sauvignon Blanc, Shiraz **Principal Wines** Potential	Vintage Brut Cabernet Sauvignon Shiraz Unwooded Chardonnay Wooded Chardonnay Shiraz Cabernet	0-5 yrs 5-15 yrs 5-10 yrs 0-2 yrs 2-6 yrs 0-5 yrs

Mt Tamborine

There cannot be much in common between the frosty climate of Macedon in Victoria and Mount Tamborine in the hinterland hills of the Gold Coast. For some years Roger Hart had a winery at Lancefield in Victoria, before buying the Mt Tamborine property in 1990. Whilst Mt Tambornie has a small vineyard at their picturesque property with its awesome views of the coast, they also have 120 acres of vines at Ballandean and 60 acres of vines at Severn Hills, both in the Granite Belt. Roger's father was a part owner of Woodleys Wines in Adelaide and Roger studied Agricultural Science at Adelaide University, before working at the C.S.I.R.O. in Horticultural research.

Mt Tamborine is owned by 14 families and fast expanding, 15 wines at least are produced and wine tourism at the cellar door and exports are booming.

The Winery is expanding and technically very well equipped. Vintage is expected to grow to 700 tonnes in 2002.

A Café Restaurant was opened in 1999 and it makes it even more enjoyable to visit Mt Tamborine, particularly if you're staying on the Gold Coast.

Address: 32 Hartley Rd NTH TAMBORINE 4272 **Phone:** (07) 5545 3981 **Fax:** (07) 5545 3311 **Email:** sales@mttamborinewinery.com.au	**WWW:** www.mttamborinewinery.com.au **Winemaker:** Bruce Humphrey-Smith **Est:** 1991	**Public Hours:** 10am-4pm, Mon-Sat Principal Varieties: Cabernet Franc, Cabernet Sauvignon, Chardonnay, Merlot, Shiraz

Classic Wines & Blends

One of the most complex skills acquired by Australia's most talented winemakers has been the art of blending wine. Among the great blenders in the history of Australia's wine industry I would include Leo Buring, the late Maurice O'Shea from Mount Pleasant in the Hunter Valley (now owned by McWilliam's); Colin Preece from Seppelt at Great Western; Colin Haselgrove and Roger Warren from Thomas Hardy & Sons; Penfolds' great Max Schubert; Yalumba's Rudi Kronberger; and of course, the irrepressible Wolf Blass. In the modern ear of Australian wine undoubtedly Andrew Garrett stands out.

These men and others from today's top winemaking fraternity such as Brian Croser, John Duval, Brian Walsh and Peter Dawson all have in common the ability to recognise compatibility between two or more wines and blend them in the appropriate proportions, so that the end result is superior to any of the single components. Similarly, these winemakers share the responsibility of deciding the regional origin of fruit used. Blending possibilities are therefore virtually infinite and great winemaking skill is required to be successful in this regard. During the varietal table wine boom of the 1970's, the blending of wines was often frowned upon. The phenomenal success of Wolf Blass must be attributed then both to his winemaking brilliance and marketing genius. Fortunately, attitudes have now broadened and Australia's great blends are once again receiving the attention they deserve. The great classic Hunter Valley/McLaren Vale and Hunter/Barossa Valley blends have almost vanished. They re being replaced by exciting blends such as Nagambie Victoria/Coonawarra, Coonawarra/Barossa Valley, Coonawarra/Clare and Coonawarra/McLaren Vale. Fruit from South Australia's Langhorne Creek remains popular with blenders of red wines. Australia's blended wines are among the best in the world and add a fascinating dimension to the country's output.

Peter Rumball Wines

Peter Rumball is an Australian specialist Methode Champenoise Sparkling winemaker, who led the renaissance of sparkling red wines in the 1980's, when sparkling reds had almost disappeared from the market through the "Cold Duck" debacle. His style has made him famous. Peter loves sparkling reds so much it is now the majority of sparkling wine that he produces.

His sparkling reds are strong in varietal character. Shiraz is used exclusively. Big, full basewines are selected for depth of colour and fruit character. As a result, the wines have a very full palate complex, with fruit tannin, sweetness and fine bubbles, Peter places great emphasis on these four characters of the wine. The interaction between the disgorged wine and the liqueuring is also of great importance to Peter, he adds a special formula "liqueur" . The wine has medium oak character without being overpowering, spending approximately 12 months in American and French oak. The Final "sparkling red" wine will age and improve in the bottle for another three years, although he palate is set up for maximum balance at the time of purchase.

The base wines are sourced from Coonawarra, the Barossa Valley and

McLaren Vale. Expert contracted growers grow all the grapes. Peter considers a more consistent product can be achieved by cross blending basewines from different areas and vineyards.

Sparkling Wines undergo two fermentations. During the primary fermentation the basewines are made as a normal dry reds then transported to Adelaide for blending.

During the secondary fermentation, pure yeast is used, a small amount of sugar is added to the shiraz wine, which is then filled into heavyweight bottles. Fermentation is completed after about three weeks. The wine spends a minimum 6-8 months on yeast lees prior to disgorging. The non-vintage Peter Rumball Sparkling Shiraz, spends less time on lees than the 100% Coonawarra Vintage Sparkling Shiraz. After Liqueuring the wine is bottle aged for 6 months.

Peter Rumball is the master of sparkling reds, I hope you celebrate this at an appropriate moment - That's anytime!!

Cockatoo Ridge

Cockatoo Ridge wines reflect the real taste of Australia - fruit-driven with complexity and depth of flavour.

Established in 1991, Cockatoo Ridge's original aim still remains, to make classic Australian wines of consistent quality, varietal character and fresh, up-front fruit flavour. Cockatoo Ridge wines are made using the traditional grape varieties of Chardonnay, Cabernet Sauvignon, Merlot, Shiraz and Pinot Noir, they complement a variety of cuisines and occasions.

Cockatoo Ridge's distinctive packaging provides a strong link with its Australian origins. the eye-catching painting featured on the label was painted by a local Australian artist, Russell Morrison, and is a fitting tribute to the untouched beauty and vivid colours of the Australian outback.

In 10 years, Cockatoo Ridge has become recognised as one of Australia's biggest selling sparkling wine brands. The Sparkling Brut NV continues to set new standards for the sparkling wine category with bold, contemporary packaging and popular style. Cockatoo Ridge also produce fine table wines.

The ripe and complex Shiraz combines classic spicy and peppery characters, with earthy fruit sweetness. A generous wine, it features sweet plums and cloves on the nose. On the palate, soft grainy tannins and subtle mocha vanillin oak complement the rich fruit flavours.

The Chardonnay is a lively fruit driven wine, displaying fresh melons and figs on the nose, with a generous palate of peaches and nectarines. Subtle toasty vanillin oak brings complexity to this Chardonnay and partial Malolactic fermentation adds a soft and creamy texture to the finish, complementing the sweet, spicy fruit.

The Cabernet Sauvignon Merlot has an enticing aroma of cedar and spice with hints of berry and aniseed. The palate is soft and rich with generous berry flavours of raspberry and mulberry. Supple tannins add texture and complexity to this classic blend.

Cockatoo Ridge also make a sparkling red from Cabernet Sauvignon it bursts with lifted fruit characters of red berries and spice. Enriched by bottle age on lees, the palate shows excellent depth of fruit flavour with soft velvety tannins and a chocolaty richness that compliments the long clean finish. It was awarded the Best Sparkling Red wine of the year at the International Wine Challenge in London in 1999. A unique Australian experience and ideal with Roast Turkey and Leg Ham with cranberry sauce.

The traditional Sparkling NV Brut, with its subtle pink hue, has an enticing bouquet of melons and toast. With a dry, full flavoured palate, this wine shows a refreshing crispness with a lingering finish. Bottle fermentation and subsequent resting on lees has provided the natural effervescence and soft creaminess so desirable in a quality, sparkling wine its great with canapes, fresh oysters.

Cockatoo Ridge has just released a Premium sparkling wine under the 'Eyrie' banner (means a nest perched up high). 'Eyrie' is the pinnacle of the sparkling winemaking endeavours at Cockatoo Ridge. Great depth, finesse and elegance are obtained by skilfully blending the finest premium cool climate Pinot noir and Chardonnay grapes from South Australia, Victoria and Tasmania.

'Eyrie' is an assemblage of the finest Pinot Noir and Chardonnay, shows a delicate bead and creamy mousse with strawberry fruit characters, crisp citrus-like acidity and nutty nuances on the nose. The palate is rich in stone fruit flavours with biscuits and honey balanced by a citric acidity. Extended ageing on lees gives the wine a rich and creamy mouthfeel, complementing the long dry finish, and adding depth and elegance.

Cockatoo Ridge also produce some Reserve wines made from small parcels of premium Limestone Coast fruit, skilfully selected for and handcrafted into distinctive, regional wines.

The Reserve Shiraz has a distinctive pepper and clove bouquet with sweet violet and plum aromas backed with vanillan oak. Intense Shiraz fruit characters are influenced by subtle smoky oak, with a mid-palate of violets and plums, and a lingering peppery finish.

The Reserve Chardonnay is rich and luscious showing subtle influences of oak maturation and Malolactic Fermentation balanced with crisp citrus fruits. Aroma's of lemon peel, figs and spice lead to a "peaches and cream" mid palate with a soft textured finish.

"Cockatoo Ridge" is an exciting 'World Brand' of Australian Wines, representing extremely high quality at very affordable prices wherever they are sold globally.

Andrew Garrett Group

Mercurial would be an understatement when referring to Andrew Garrett. His vision and energy have taken him through some troubled waters, in the last two decades of the Australian Wine Industry, his resilience and never say die attitude have stood him well.

Always innovative, Andrew seems to have the knack of being able to bring a brand of wine to life. Whilst some see this as luck, there is obviously a lot more to it. A big part of this, is the fact Andrew sources his grapes from his own and contract growers, in top premium cool climate regions, he does not stint on the raw material, great grapes!! Andrew is also a trained and talented winemaker, he started his career in the early 1980's making wine for Tolleys Pedare. He then began his own enterprise buying the old Romalo Sparkling Wine Cellars next to Penfolds at Magill and the McLarens on the Lake Winery complex at McLaren Vale. After a time with Suntory as a partner, he sold to Mildara Blass, retaining the McLarens on the Lake complex.

His biggest moves since this 1995 buyout were setting up large vineyards in the Yarra Valley and a home at Springwood Park in the Adelaide Hills, where he is planting vineyards. Andrew has also launched a number of very successful quality wine brands.

A recent launch has been a McLaren Vale based range, "Kelly's Promise" named in honour of Dr Alexander Kelly, a pioneer of McLaren Vale, who arrived in SA in 1840 as a medical graduate from Edinburgh in Scotland. He planted vines firstly at

Morphett Vale and then in McLaren Vale, a large venture, named "The Tintara Vineyard Company" which was bought by Thomas Hardy in 1876.

One of Andrews prized possessions is a copy of Dr Kelly's book "Winegrowing in Australia" written in 1867 which was fortunately saved from a disastrous fire that destroyed Andrew's Romalo Cellars in 1988.

The Yarra Valley vineyards produce Andrew "Yarra Glen" Range the top wines are in "The Grand Cabernet Sauvignon" and "The Yarra Glen Chardonnay". He also produces a N.V. Brut Chardonnay, a Sauvignon Blanc, Pinot Noir, Shiraz and an unoaked Chardonnay. The cellar door is

currently at the beautiful Yarra Glen Grand Hotel, plans are afoot for a cellar door at the vineyard.

The "Kelly's Promise" Range has two levels a Reserve Range comprising a Grenache from old dry grown bush vines and a Cabernet Sauvignon. The premium range at value for money prices, includes a Chardonnay, a Shiraz and a Cabernet Merlot.

Andrew produces a premium Range under his Adelaide Hills "Springwood Park" Label including a crisp Sauvignon Blanc, a Chardonnay, a Pinot Noir and a Botrytised White.

Another range from Clare is marketed under the "Martindale Hall" label Riesling, Sauvignon Blanc and Chardonnay.

Andrew also has an interest in the Macedon Ranges area in Victoria producing a Sauvignon Blanc-Chardonnay blend, a barrel fermented Chardonnay and a Pinot Noir under his "Macedon Ridge" label.

In the fighting varietal market he is represented by his "Ironwood Label" of South Eastern Australian wines, Chardonnay, White Shiraz - a Rose style, Shiraz and Cabernet Sauvignon.

To top off the lot the two finest Andrew Garrett Wines bear the names of his two sons super premiums both, "Nicholas" a McLaren Vale Shiraz - the best of the vintage and "Tom" a King Valley Merlot a really silky drop.

Andrew Garrett has added an extra dimension to Australian wine, he is a seriously good winemaker, so search out his wines, there is sure to be one in your price bracket to suit your taste.

Yangarra Park

At Vin Expo 2001, the world's largest wine exhibition held biannually, I ran into my good friend John Grant the former General Manager Marketing for Southcorp Wines. He had just been appointed President of Kendall Jackson, one of the most prestigious and largest global premium wine companies, started by the amazing Jess Jackson, a real human dynamo. I well remember visiting their winery, then in Lake County in Northern California, when I was researching my North American Wine Pictorial Atlas in 1987. I was most impressed with their wines already winning awards, their "California Chardonnay" was a wonderfully balanced generous wine and I bought and drank plenty of it during my two years in California.

I was delighted to learn of their new Australian Venture "Yangarra Park" based out of Clarendon just South of Adelaide, Kendall Jackson recently appointed a young wine maker to run their Australian operations, Peter Fraser formerly the Chief Winemaker at Norman's Wines and for whom I have great respect.

Fraser was in the thick of the fray during the late1990s when Australia was steam-rolling the wine world with increasingly successful production and marketing campaigns. His role in

making his native land a wine giant, made him a natural choice to help usher in Kendall-Jackson Wine Estates venture down under. "Peter brings a deft and cosmopolitan style to the wines of Yangarra Park, a style that comes from rich experience as cellar hand, winemaker, winejudge and consultant," said Kendall-Jackson Winemaster Randy Ullom. "His insights about Australian terroir clearly show in his excellent first vintages". Fraser has spent most of his career as a winemaker for Normans Wines Ltd. His leadership at Normans saw a steep increase in listings at major supermarkets in the United Kingdom, and a soaring rate of competition awards, including the trophy for Red Wine of the Year at the 1998 London International Wine Challenge. Earlier, he also worked in Australia for Woodstock and St. Hallett. Fraser graduated from the prestigious University of Adelaide with a Bachelor's Degree in Oenology. He has direct responsibility for the portfolio of Yangarra Park wines, which arrived on the world market in September 2001. His approach to winemaking meshes well with Kendall-Jackson's and ensures consistency and quality, "We offer exceptional value for money," Fraser said. "We give people

the opportunity to taste the flavours of different regions, the generosity of the fruit. It's much the same thing Kendall-Jackson is already famous for" Yangarra Park has four varietals, all priced retail under $10. Included are a Cabernet Sauvignon, Merlot, Shiraz and Chardonnay, all from the 2000 vintage. The wines were first shown at this year's Vinexpo and the London International Wine Fair, where they received strong attention from world wine media and retailers. Yangarra Park translates from a local Australian dialect roughly as "earth" although when applied to wines the concept of richness "from the earth" comes into play." Perhaps the strongest pillar of winemaking is selecting the right fruit from choice vineyards", Fraser said.

Peter has worked hard to establish ties with growers in South Eastern Australia during all his winemaking posts, and brings the same approach and contacts to Yangarra Park. Fraser seeks out the prized fruit from each leading wine region and blends it into bottlings that show off premier varietal flavors. The guiding philosophy is "The best Australian varietal wines under $10." In the years to come, perhaps as early as 2002, a "Reserve Tier" will be launched featuring Kendall-Jackson's Flavor Domaine philosophy translated down under as "The Best Australian Varietal Wines from the Best Appellations." At the end of the day, it's a source of pride and satisfaction for the new Kendall-Jackson winemaker.

Kendall-Jackson are set to make a real impact on the world scene with "Yangarra Park" Look out for these exceptionally good value premium wines wherever you are.

Foreword to NZ Wines

What the New Zealand wine industry lacks in size it makes up in dynamism. Producing only 0.2% of the worlds wine, the country attracts a much larger share of attention in the wine world.

The reason is that New Zealand wines have striking attributes that distinguish them from all others. The unique combination of the cool climate, relatively infertile soil types and astute winemaking produces intense, crisp flavours quite unlike the wines that made the neighboring Australian wine industry famous.

The distinctiveness of New Zealand wines allows the country to develop a niche alongside the worlds more established producers, rather than competing head to head. This approach has worked wonders for our industry, which saw the area under vine more than double in the decade up to 2000. In the same time, the number of wineries nearly trebled to 358 and wine exports increased almost fivefold. In the next five years, exports are expected to double again.

Complementing this growth is recognition of the value and possibilities of wine tourism. A national initiative to develop this aspect of the New Zealand wine experience, should see wine tourism becoming one of the country's major attractions, for local and overseas visitors.

Despite its forward-looking nature, the New Zealand wine industry has always sought to take the best of the world wine traditions on board, through winemaking partnerships and ongoing contact with wineries in both the Old and New World.

The one belief we all share, is that making wine is fundamentally about creating experiences that enrich and enhance the enjoyment of life. I trust that this book will give you some indication of the rich variety of such experiences the New Zealand wine industry has to offer.

Peter Hubscher

Chairman · Wine Institute of New Zealand

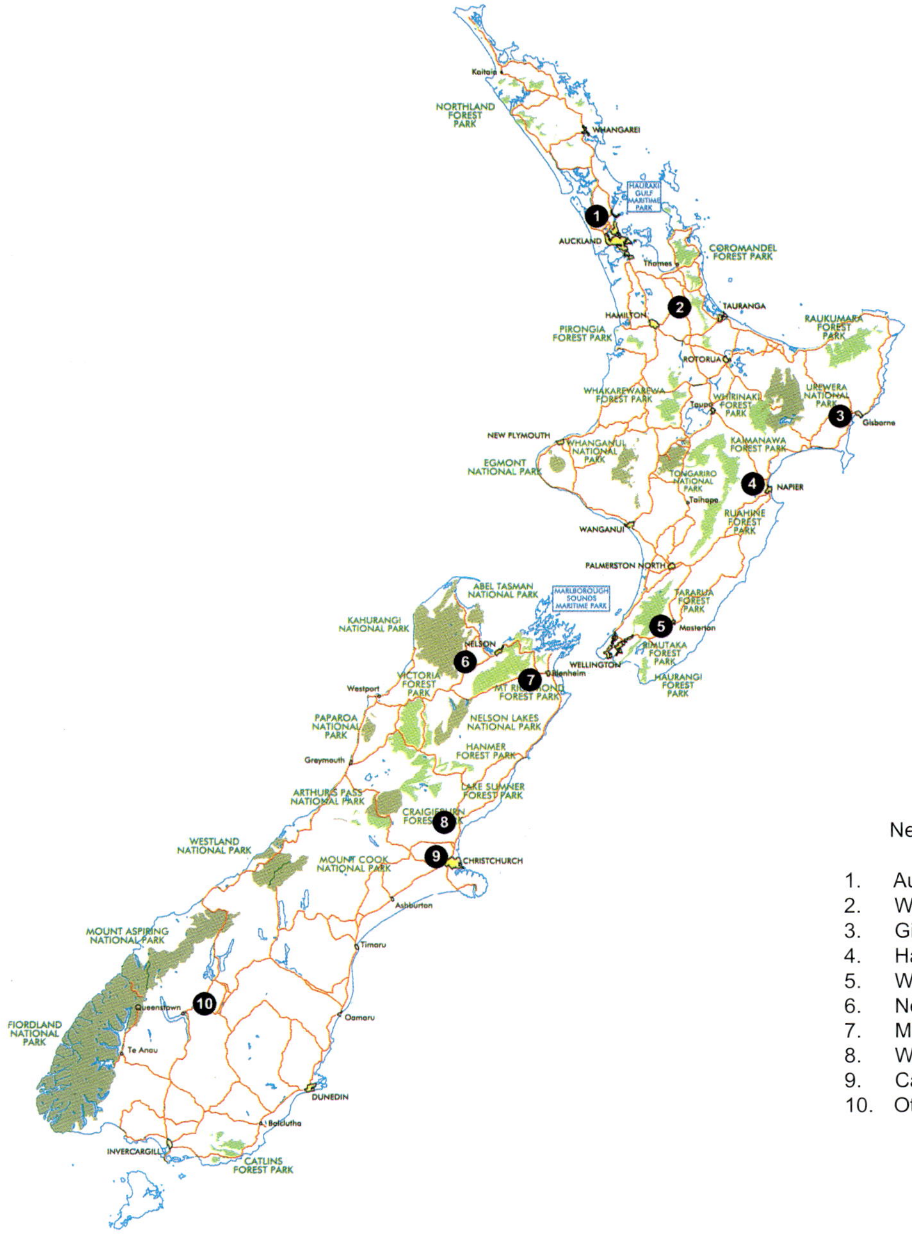

New Zealand

1. Auckland
2. Waikato
3. Gisborne
4. Hawkes Bay
5. Wairarapa
6. Nelson
7. Marlborough
8. Waipara
9. Canterbury
10. Otago

New Zealand

New Zealand has undergone a vinous explosion in the last 10 years of the Millennium. Today there are around 360 active commercial wineries and maybe close to 400 wine producers in total. In 1994 the total area and vines was 16,700 acres by 2000 this had expanded to over 25,000. The export success of New Zealand wines has been dramatic, in 1986 the export sales were NZ$4 million this had expanded to over NZ$125 million by 2000.

New Zealand has an extremely strong agricultural economy based on sheep and dairy products. Wine is however fast gaining momentum. There are 10 main wine regions almost equally spread between the North and south Islands, a spread of over 1800 kms from Kaitaia in the north almost a sub tropical climate to southern Otago certainly with an Antarctic chill about it. The scenery in the wine regions is truly breathtaking and I trust this pictorial expose will bring this to life for you, along with introducing you many of the characters of this vibrant growing industry.

The first vines were planted in 1819

by an English Missionary Samuel Marsden on the north east coast of the North Island at Kerikeri. The first wines however were made by James Busby, a British wine pioneer, who had already had a hand in the establishment of the Australian Wine Industry. He made his first New Zealand wines in 1836 at Waitangi selling wine to the British troops stationed nearby.

The industry like Australia has had its boom times but also its tribulations. Phylloxera took its toll in the early 1900's which ironically was also a time local wines gained one of their largest market shares ever, at around 25% of wine consumed.

The first plantings in Marlborough began in 1973 it is now the largest wine region by far, with 40% of the national vineyard. The electrifying Sauvignon Blancs made there have excited the wine world and secured a very good niche in wine markets, internationally. Hawkes Bay has also enjoyed exceptional growth over recent years its Cabernet Sauvignons and Merlots are certainly world class.

Gisborne is renowned for its Chardonnays but certainly Chardonnay and Pinot Noir seems to excel in all New Zealand regions. Problems in viticulture due to the high rainfall and humidity have been handled very well, in recent years with organic vineyard techniques and good canopy management, to the fore.

New Zealand's plans to double its production by 2010 and quadruple its wine exports are a far cry from 1986, when a surplus of wine led to a government sponsored vine pull scheme, with the country losing 25% of its vines, fortunately many of these were not premium varieties in the right locations. Today the picture is entirely different, viticulturally and gives New Zealand an ideal springboard for its assault on world wine markets. Fortunately New Zealanders are also appreciating the quality of their own wines and now drinking less imported wine. I look forward to my visits to New Zealand in the years to come I am certain I will see even more dramatic developments.

La Bonne Cuisine

The story of La Bonne Cuisine is one of European technology and New Zealand passion, of family commitment and international friendships, staff loyalty and a business philosophy based around quality and good taste.

Back in the 70s when pate was literally a foreign word to most New Zealanders Earl and Jo Meek were looking to invest and work in a business with a future. They found it in a small production kitchen in an Auckland waterside suburb, where pate was being made and supplied to restaurants and delicatessens.

To Earl and Jo gourmet food seemed like a product with a distinct future and they entered into a partnership with the owners.

The product was cooked on the stove top, frozen, and sold under the Breton brand. Fresh pate with its short shelf life was not an option but the partners recognized a huge opportunity in the 'fresh' market segment. They advertised in the UK for the expertise and this materialised in the form of French Master Chef Jean Conil whose image is now the logo for the Master Chef range.

This was the Meek's · and the country's introduction to European-style pates, oven-baked, rapidly cooled and packed immediately. In a lucky coincidence of timing, vacuum packing technology became available at the same time. The result was a

fresh pate product with a vastly improved texture, a good shelf life and nationwide distribution.

In the mid-80s when their partners retired Earl and Jo headed to a Paris Food Fair with a mission to extend their gourmet food knowledge. In true New Zealand style they simply asked for advice and were invited by two brothers who owned a major Belgian company to visit their facility. This was the beginning of a true sharing of ideas and information, and of lifetime friendships between the two families.

When they came up with the idea of gourmet salami snacks as a product range, instead of undertaking all the development themselves the Meeks looked round for the technology and the expertise. A Product Development Consultant for a major US snack company was lured to the antipodes for an extended holiday to help develop what became Master Chef Salami Nibbles and Little Ripper Salami Sticks.

The next tasty initiative was Dips and Hummus products. Another investigative trip to the UK and another international friendship later and there's a whole new range of products rushing out of supermarket chillers. There are 14 creative combinations like roasted garlic and onion gourmet dip, roasted capsicum and tomato hummus dip, wholegrain mustard and honey dip (does amazing things to a boiled potato), black olive hummus.

La Bonne Cuisine now operates out of purpose-built premises in East Auckland with separate kitchens for each product range and computerized systems controlling many of the critical functions. Over half the 25 staff have been with the company for over 10 years · some for 20!

The machinery's European, the recipes, techniques and inspiration come from everywhere but the passion is pure New Zealand.

Earl and Jo Meek enjoy identifying trends and making them happen, they accept the challenge of legislative requirements around food preparation and packaging, human resource management, health and safety legislation, and they know that good gourmet food depends on good people and technology.

The lifelong friendships, the fun, the people and the fact that their business is their passion, is all icing on the product. And a truly delicious range it is too.

Mainland Cheese

New Zealand is renowned as a clean, green country. The clean air, pastures and water make it an ideal environment for the production of quality dairy products. Over 3 million cows on approximately 15,000 dairy farms span the country, from the mighty Waikato and Taranaki regions of the North Island to the Canterbury Plains and Otago on the West Coast of the South Island.

Year-round pasture grazing is possible in New Zealand due to the country's considerable natural advantages. The warm, moist climate promotes pasture growth, and the relatively mild temperatures enable cows to be grazed outdoors all year round. The end result is that the purest and freshest milk is produced, from which delicious Mainland cheese is made.

Mainland has been supplying Australia and New Zealand with premium quality Mainland cheese since 1963 and more recently with pure spreadable butter since 1997.

The Mainland cheese makers are proud of the fact that they take special care and time when maturing Mainland cheeses. The time taken ensures that the cheeses develop their rich full flavours, which are distinctive to Mainland products.

Products include the delicious crumbly texture of Mainland Vintage Cheddar Cheese, which is a full bodied mature cheddar with an extra sharp taste profile that has been aged for up to 24 months, plus the sharp, clean taste of Mainland Special Reserve Extra Tasty Cheddar Cheese which has a slightly crumbly texture that has been aged for up to 20 months. Both these cheeses are a perfect accompaniment to a Cabernet Sauvignon or a Shiraz. For something different, why not try Mainland Smoked Cheddar Cheese, which has a mature cheddar flavour and been specially smoked which provides the perfect aroma when consuming crusty bread, crackers and Chardonnay.

Mainland cheese requires some care when storing, therefore the product should be stored at or below 4 degrees Celsius at all times. However prior to consumption (usually about 30 minutes) I recommend that cheese be bought up to room temperature. This enables the full flavours and aromas of the cheese to fully develop and be appreciated.

Once the cheese is opened, it will not last to the expiry date printed on the product. This is because the cheese will then be exposed to oxygen (Mainland prevent this by vacuum packing the product). Once it is open and oxygen is present, cheese provides a wonderful medium for the growth of surface yeast and moulds

Mainland Cheese

it is moist and contains nutrients which suit their growth.

Therefore, once opened, it is recommended that the pack be covered with plastic wrap and stored in an airtight container. It should also be stored in the cooler parts of the refrigerator - not in the doors where it is continually exposed to the ambient temperatures when opened.

For more information regarding their premium quality cheeses, Mainland welcome calls on their consumer information line on 1800 633 275 (in Australia).

Mainland is your friend in the fridge, just waiting to be enjoyed with a premium New Zealand or Australian Wine!!

PREMIUM **mainland** QUALITY CHEESE

Special Reserve **EXTRA TASTY**

Aged for up to 20 months

PREMIUM **mainland** QUALITY CHEESE

CHEDDAR MASTER'S **SMOKED** CHEDDAR

The team at Mainland have selected this fine cheese for the complexity of matured cheddar flavour and enhanced it with the flavours of the smoke house. A truly complimentary combination of flavours to be enjoyed by the most demanding palate.

250g NET

BIN 049

PREMIUM **mainland** QUALITY CHEESE

VINTAGE TASTY

A rich, full bodied, mature Cheddar. Complements good food and

Vineyards surround New Zealand's capital city on all sides. There are now vineyards spanning some 450 kilometers from Kaitiaia in the northlands to Hamilton in the south, Waikeke Island in the East to Waimauku in the West.

Whilst the Auckland Regions combined, only account for less than 5% of the National Vineyard, the region is far more important on a winemaking sense. All the large New Zealand wine companies notably Montana/Corbans, The Villa Maria Group and Nobilo/Selaks have their head offices and blending facilities, as well, many large New Zealand wineries have a base in the region, bringing in a large percentage of their grape supplies and wine, from the larger growing regions of Gisborne and Hawkes Bay as well as Marlborough and other regions in the South Island.

Auckland Regions have proved that with improved viticulture practices, particularly canopy management and organic disease control, great wines of all style can be produced. Waikeke Island one of the prettiest places I have ever been to in my life, produces very good wines. The West Auckland regions produce excellent Chardonnay and other varieties. The Northern regions have expanded greatly in recent years and the area around Matakana is now a fully fledged wine region.

Wine tourism and facilities including cafes and restaurants is very strong in all the Auckland regions, so when you are in New Zealand's leading city, don't forget to visit at least one of these wonderful wine regions.

Auckland

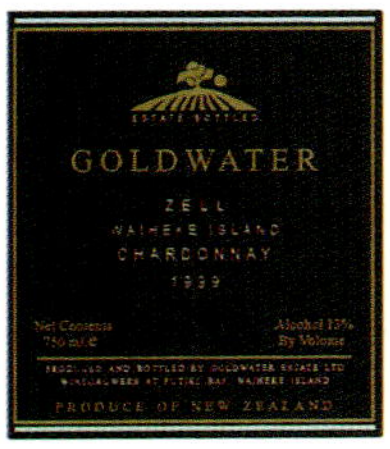

GOLDWATER
WAIHEKE ISLAND
CABERNET SAUVIGNON
AND
MERLOT
1998

PRODUCE OF NEW ZEALAND

MATAKANA ESTATE
NEW ZEALAND

Pinot Gris

1999

2000

Marlborough
SAUVIGNON BLANC

WEST BROOK

WINE OF NEW ZEALAND

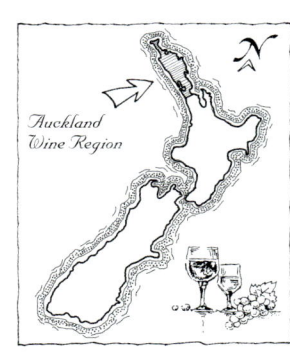

Auckland
Wine Region

GOLDWATER
ZELL
WAIHEKE ISLAND
CHARDONNAY
1999

PRODUCE OF NEW ZEALAND

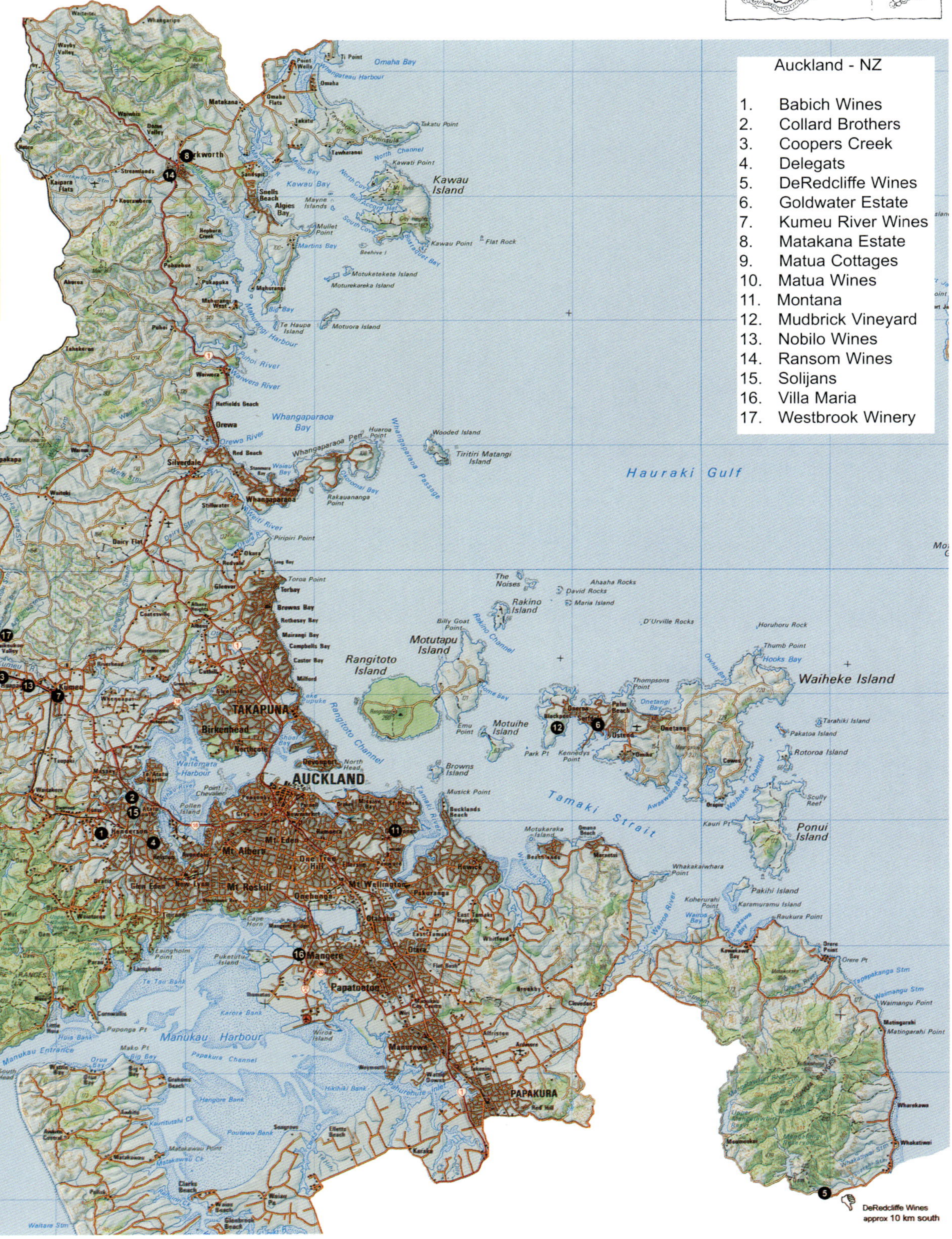

Auckland - NZ

1. Babich Wines
2. Collard Brothers
3. Coopers Creek
4. Delegats
5. DeRedcliffe Wines
6. Goldwater Estate
7. Kumeu River Wines
8. Matakana Estate
9. Matua Cottages
10. Matua Wines
11. Montana
12. Mudbrick Vineyard
13. Nobilo Wines
14. Ransom Wines
15. Solijans
16. Villa Maria
17. Westbrook Winery

DeRedcliffe Wines
approx 10 km south

Montana Wines

Montana is New Zealand's leading winemaker, not only in terms of the variety, volume and value of the wines the company produces, but also as an innovator and standard bearer.

The company produces a range of over 350 wines at its five wineries, sourcing grapes from Montana's own vineyards as well as from growers. These vineyards are spread across New Zealand's three major wine regions, Hawke's Bay, Gisborne and Marlborough.

In fact, it was Montana who planted Marlborough's very first commercial vineyards in 1973. The country's signature wine, Marlborough Sauvignon Blanc, was also first produced by Montana. Their original is still the most exported version of this distinctive wine style.

Apart from varietal Pinot Noir, Cabernet Sauvignon, Chardonnay and Riesling wines, Montana also creates Deutz methode traditionnelle in Marlborough, made in association with the House of Deutz in France. In Hawke's Bay the company produces Bordeaux-style red wines with input from French masters

Cordier, as well as Chardonnay and Semillon for its exclusive Sauternes-style wine, Virtu. Gisborne is Chardonnay country, with Montana Gisborne Chardonnay, first made by current managing director Peter Hubscher in the early 1970's still the most popular. Gisborne is also home to Montana's Gewürztraminer and Semillon varietal wines. The company's single most successful wine, Lindauer methode traditionelle, draws on fruit from all these regions and is finished at the company's winery in Auckland.

The quality of Montana's wines saw the company being named White Winemaker of the year, at the International Wine Challenge in London, twice in the space of three years in the late 1990's.

Montana' vineyard holdings, winery capacity and brand portfolio received a significant boost when the company acquired Corbans Wines in November 2000. This winery, dating back to 1902, has developed along similar lines to Montana, with wineries and vineyards in the same regions. Its internationally known brands include Corbans and Stoneleigh.

To serve its export customers, Montana has offices in the UK and USA, as well as a sizable sales force linked to their subsidiary Montana Wines Australia.

For the visitor, both Montana's Brancott Winery in Marlborough and Church Road Winery in Hawke's Bay offer unique attractions. The Church Road Winery, home of the boutique wine range of the same name, boasts the only wine museum in New Zealand as well as the imposing Tom McDonald Cellar.

Down in Marlborough, the Brancott Winery provides a natural focal point for wine tourism in the region. Here visitors can see the only Coquard Champagne press in the Southern Hemisphere, as well as the world's first grape tipper tanks. These revolutionary drainer tanks, first used for the 2000 vintage, decant directly into presses, to cut down handling of grapes, speed up production and give winemakers greater control over maceration periods.

Montana is a world recognised premium maker, who have earned well their highly respected reputation.

Villa Maria

Villa Maria Estate is now New Zealand's second largest winery, following Montana's takeover of Corbans.

George Fistonich is a human dynamo. He founded Villa Maria in 1961 and is still the owner and extremely active Managing Director today. It was our great pleasure to call in on him at the winery, on his 60th birthday, he was hard at work as usual. Since the early 1980's, Villa Maria has been the most successful exhibitor in wine shows in New Zealand and overseas, and is today New Zealand's leading award winner.

George who is reknowned for achieving industry firsts, was amongst those who first realised the potential to make premium wines in New Zealand, for both local and overseas markets.

Another initiative for George and Villa Maria was being the first New Zealand Winery to pay its contract growers on the quality of their grapes, not just on the tonnage supplied. This led to another venture

in 1993 which saw Villa Maria become a joint promoter, of a public share offering, to develop the 105 acre Seddon Vineyard development in New Zealand's Marlborough grape growing region. In a second, larger float in 1998 "Terra Vitae", Villa Maria are assisting the development of a 190 acre vineyard in Marlborough's Awatere Valley, plus two vineyards in another prime grape growing region, Hawke's Bay. Plantings in Hawke's Bay include a Merlot vineyard in the well publicised Gimblett Gravels area (recently recognised as a new appellation). Villa Maria also own their own vineyards in the Gimblett Gravels, one of which is "Twyford Gravels". A second of the Terra Vitae

vineyards in Hawke's Bay is "Keltern" which is planted in approx. 120 acres of Chardonnay.

Villa Maria has an unrelenting passion to produce quality wines. Realising that it takes more than just good winemaking to produce quality, a passion to succeed begins in the vineyard. Astute site selection is followed by superior vineyard management, and then complemented by expert winemaking.

Villa Maria, have also built a large state-of-the-art winery in the Marlborough region. I will be covering all these wineries and wines in the Regional Chapters.

Nobilo Wines

What started off as a small family winery making a large array of wines, is now New Zealand's second largest wine group. A few years ago Nobilo took over Selaks Wines including the ultra modern, large, state of the art "Drylands Estate" Winery in Marlborough. In 2000 the large Australian based international wine company BRL Hardy, who already owned a share of Nobilo bought the entire company. The expertise of BRL and the capital injection, will only further enhance the quality of the very good Nobilo and Selaks

Wines.

Nobilo was founded in 1943. During the 1970's brothers Nick, Steve and Mark made a very successful assault on the growing premium wine market, often with innovative wines and labels which have included the successful "White Cloud" brand. Most of the Nobilo fruit comes from Marlborough, Gisborne and Hawkes Bay. The wines are made both at the Huapai Winery near Auckland, which has an excellent cellar door and the Drylands Estate Winery in

Marlborough.

The top ranges are the Selaks Founders Reserve range comprising Trophy-winning Chardonnay, an oak-aged Sauvignon Blanc, a Trophy-winning Noble Riesling and a sophisticated Merlot and the Nobilo Icon Series range, showing a world-class Trophy winning Sauvignon Blanc and Chardonnay. The Drylands and Selaks Premium Selection ranges are proving to be one of New Zealand's most popular brands. There are two other ranges which represent fantastic value, Fall Harvest and Fernleaf both featuring very good Sauvignon Blancs.

The Nobilo Wine Group is gaining ground quickly on world markets, always a strong and pioneer New Zealand wine exporter, the increased BRL Hardy involvement will certainly strengthen this push even further.

Address: Station Road HUAPAI	**Winemaker:** Darryl Woolley	Nobilo Fall Harvest Range
Phone: +64 9 412 6666 **Fax:** +64 9 412 7124	**Est:** 1943	Icon Series Range
Email: nobilo@nobilo.co.nz	**Public Hours:** 9am-5pm, daily	Selaks Premium Selection Range
WWW: www.nobilo.co.nz	**Principal Wines**	Noiblo Fernleaf Range
Owner: B.R.L. Hardy	White Cloud Range	House of Nobilo Range

Collard Brothers

Lionel Collard is one of the gentlemen of the New Zealand wine industry. His family winery is on Lincoln Road, the main Highway of the Henderson Wine region.

The Collards are people of the earth, their business was founded in 1910 as a Horticultural enterprise by J.W. Collard and it was not until 1946 that they began as winemakers. The Collards have great respect for nature and the importance of growing good grapes. Collards winemaking philosophy is

traditionalist, yet their winery is very well equipped. In the vineyard they have developed many new varieties. They have won many gold medals and trophies in Australia and New Zealand.

The winery is surrounded by the home vineyard but they also have a large vineyard at Waimauka northwest of Auckland, called Rothesay. Some grapes are purchased from Hawkes Bay, Te Kauwhata and Marlborough, they have an extensive range, for a

moderately small boutique winery. Winemaker for the last 25 years is Lionel's son Bruce, also a respected wine judge, his other son Geoffrey is the Assistant Winemaker and Viticulturalist.

The Rothesay Chardonnay is their flagship, they also produce an excellent fruit driven Sauvignon Blanc from Rothesay, in the tropical spectrum and quite un-Marlborough like. The Rothesay Cabernet Sauvignon is also a very good full style. The company pioneered Chenin Blanc and Rhine Riesling and won New Zealand's first gold medals for both varieties.

In 1999 a Botrytised late Harvest Riesling was produced that has won many accolades. Their other wines are all very well made and extraordinary value for money, and exported to many countries.

Address: 303 Lincoln Road HENDERSON	**Vine Ha:** 20	Rothesay Viognier
Phone: +64 9 838 8341	**Public Hours:** 9am-5pm, Mon-Sat; 11am-	Hawkes Bay Chenin Blanc
Fax: +64 9 837 5840	5pm, Sun & Public Holidays	Rothesay Chardonnay
Winemaker: Bruce Collard & Geoffrey Collard	**Principal Wines**	Rothesay Cabernet Sauvignon
Est: 1910	Rothesay Sauvignon Blanc	Hawkes Bay Chardonnay

Soljans

My most vibrant visit to a New Zealand Winery was my last at Soljans wines, after 17 action packed days in 10 wines regions, visiting 150 wineries. Tony Soljan is a passionate, exuberant individual, we found him wearing his barbecue hat behind the grill cooking for a large group, who had just arrived on a visit to his winery. Tony leaps into any task in his business that needs doing and his infectious enthusiasm certainly rubs off on his staff.

Right in the heart of the West Auckland/Henderson traditional wine region, the vineyards were established by Tony's late father Frank in 1937.

Soljans source grapes from selected vineyards in New Zealand's leading wine regions, to supplement those from their own Estate. Apart from a range of excellent table wines, they

produce some very fine Methode Champenoise sparkling wines.

Winemaker is Matt Ussher who studied the art of winemaking in Australia and spent four vintages producing award-winning wines in France, then spent a vintage in both Argentina and Chile as a wine consultant.

I was most impressed with the Marlborough Sauvignon Blanc, very zesty and spicy and the Barrique Reserve Chardonnay with complex tropical flavours with a hint of apricot, with cashew and a fresh French bread like character on the palate, easily in the gold medal league.

The Hawkes Bay Barrique Reserve Cabernet Merlot was a knock out wine - superb Bordeaux like with loads of mulberry and cassis aromas and flavours.

Soljans are very serious about their wines, but you can have lots of fun at their winery as well as catering for functions, there is a lovely wine garden picnic area. Make sure you find Tony and tap into his joyous energy.

Address: 263 Lincoln Rd HENDERSON	**Winemaker:** Matt Ussher	**Cases:** 20,000	Barrique Reserve Merlot	5-8 yrs
Phone: +64 9 838 8365 **Fax:** +64 9 838 8366	**Public Hours:** 9am–5:30pm, Mon-Sat; 11am-		Estate Pinotage	2-5 yrs
Email: cellar@soljans.co.nz	5pm, Sun		Barrique Reserve Chardonnay	4-6 yrs
WWW: www.soljans.com	**Principal Wines**	**Potential**	Barrique Reserve Cabernet Merlot	
Owner: Tony Soljan **Est:** 1937	Legacy Methode Traditionnelle	4-8 yrs	Estate Cabernet Merlot	

Babich Wines

One of the larger traditional New Zealand wineries is Babich Wines Ltd., on the outskirts of the fast expanding city of Auckland.

The Babich family are strong and forthright and go about their business in a quiet no nonsense way. That is not to say they are conservative, as their wines are on the cutting edge of quality and technique. The wines I tasted from barrel at their winery in late 1999 particularly their 1998 Red wines, were exceptional and you could easily sense they were made for the long haul and would do marvellous things if you put them down to mature in your Cellar.

As I sat on top of the Babich's Tank Farm with my photographer, I had a strong sense of the family's commitment as I chatted with brothers Peter and Joe. Peter is now taking a back seat a little, he started work at the winery in August 1949 when the New Zealand wine industry was entirely different, horses were still being used occasionally in the vineyards and there was not one stainless steel tank. 90% of the wines they made then were fortified, in 1997 they ceased making fortified's altogether.

Apart from their Auckland Vineyards, Babich have vineyards in the sought after Gimblett Road area of Hawkes

Bay for Reds and the Awatere Valley in Marlborough for their Whites.

Joe started work in 1958 and in Peter's words "Joe was a bloody good winemaker, so I looked after the vineyards, administration and marketing, we were fortunate that way".

Joe reminisced that some years ago he used to jump from tank to tank on the tank farm with a two inch hose in hand, today he would "go off his brain" if he saw his staff do it, so the industry has changed.

David Babich, Peter's middle son, has recently joined Babich Wines and is the first third-generation family member to take up a permanent position with the company. David has a strong sales and marketing background, a degree in winemaking from Roseworthy College, and a Bcom. in marketing and management from Auckland University.

After our stint on the stainless steel tanks, we went into the cool barrel aging cellars to taste some wines. The first we tried was a 1998 Babich Winemakers Reserve Syrah, the wine displayed purple and mauve colour, it was intriguing, its vibrant peppery, raspberry and currant like intensity superb, I rated it 94 out of 100. The 1998 Irongate a blend of 78% Cab Sav. 15% Merlot and 7% Cabernet Franc was also a splendid wine with loads of cassis and cherry flavours, quite aromatic with floral overtones of violets and roses. The 1999 Pinot Noir Marlborough was no means overshadowed by the two blockbuster Reds I had just tried, its colour quite deep and mauve, it showed lots of spicy cherry fruit characters with a cedar wood like fragrance and subtle "Herbes de Provence" overtones.

A wine that really surprised me was a 1999 Pinotage from the Gimblett Road · Hawkes Bay region, a very concentrated vinous wine, in a rich Rhone Valley style, released under their Winemakers Reserve Label.

Neill Culley is the respected Babich winemaker, he has a BSc., Dip.Wine from Roseworthy College, plus a postgraduate MBA from Auckland University.

Two of the top Babich wines each year are their Patriarch Chardonnay and Patriarch Cabernet Sauvignon.

The Babich family can be relied upon to give you top quality at very affordable prices.

Address: Babich Road HENDERSON	**Winemaker:** Neill Culley	**Principal Wines**
Phone: +64 9 833 7859 **Fax:** +64 9 833 9929	**Est:** 1916 **Vine Ha:** 125 **Cases:** 85,000	The Patriarch
Email: info@babichwines.co.nz	**Public Hours:** 9am-5pm, Mon-Sat; 11am-5pm, Sun	Irongate
WWW: www.babichwines.co.nz	**Principal Varieties:** Cab, Merlot, Pinot Noir,	Winemakers Reserve
Owner: Peter & Joe Babich	Riesling, Chard, Pinot Gris, Pinotage, Syrah	Babich Varietals

Coopers Creek

One of the most complete and interesting visit and tastings I made whilst in New Zealand was to the Coopers Creek Winery, with proprietor Andrew Hendry and winemaker Simon Nunns. They were both celebrating winning the Busby Trophy for the best 1997 or older wine, at the Liquorland Natural Wine Show in Canberra Australia. Their 1997 Chardonnay had triumphed. Ironically James Busby came to New Zealand, and planted the first vines, after being a pioneer in the Australian Wine Industry's very early days of the 19th Century.

Simon's first vintage at Coopers Creek was in 1997, he actually studied Veterinary Science and Zoology before studying Winemaking Science, winning the Jason Winter Memorial award in his graduation year in 1995.

The winery on the main road at Huapai on the outskirts of Auckland has expanded greatly in recent years. On our visit we saw their brand new state of the art bottling line in operation, which can bottle up to 1,400 dozen bottles a day. Work was soon to commence on a new barrel and bottle maturation cellar, partly built into the hillside at their pretty location. The sales and tasting area overlook beautiful gardens with outside entertaining facilities, a lake and the vineyards. During the summer months the gardens are resplendent with sculptures of all sorts, taking part in an annual art exhibition.

The production at Coopers Creek has grown to over 700 tonnes each vintage and comes not only from their vineyards at Huapai, which are currently expanding, due to the purchase of the block next door. They also have their own vineyards at Middle Road and on Highway 50 in Hawkes Bay. Coopers Creek contract growers in Gisborne, Hawkes Bay and Marlborough to supplement their own vineyards and to satisfy the needs of their large range of wines that now number over twenty.

Our tasting started with the cutely named "Fat Cat Chardonnay", suitably enough as we tasted, "Merlot" the vineyard cat was lounging on top of her cage of Chardonnay. Certainly the wine, at a very friendly price, was no slouch, showing lots of Jasmine like aromas and tropical fruit flavours, a delightful mouthfilling style. It's a big and bold wine that has won Gold in its class yet retails for under NZ$15. We went on to taste the Sauvignon Blanc Reserve with subtle wood treatment, an easy gold medal quality wine, with melons and stonefruit shining out. You will find their standard Sauvignon on the Elite class on Virgin Atlantic Airlines.

The 1999 Hawkes Bay Riesling really took one by surprise with a slight botrytis inspired concentration, to its citrus blossom bouquet and honey and lime flavours. I voted it 95.5 out of 100, the best New Zealand Riesling I'd tasted.

The 1998 Swamp Reserve Chardonnay, an icon wine for Coopers Creek, from their own vineyard at Hawkes Bay, really shone with its peach stonefruit characters, balanced with subtle vanilla bean highlights and a long citrus finish (96.5 out of 100). The "Wild Ferment" Chardonnay, only using the wild yeast on the grape skins was interesting and complex.

The reds tasted, included a Pinot Noir and a Merlot from Hawkes Bay, both very fruit driven. The 1998 Hawkes Bay Cabernet Sauvignon (85%) Cabernet Franc (15%), had lots of cassis with some mint characters and firm tannin. The Hawkes Bay Reserve Merlot was bursting out with plum and raspberry, complemented by toasty oak - delicious. The 1998 Reserve Cabernet (75%) Merlot (20%) Cabernet Franc (5%) got my top vote 95.5 out of 100, with its cassis flavours complemented by cedar and cigar box - tobacco overtones with a hint of dark chocolate and licorice, a very rich and complex wine.

We finished with a couple of excellent late picked wines, a late Harvest Riesling with minimal botrytis and refreshing lime citrus flavours with hints of honey and apricot. The 1998 Late Harvest Semillon from Gisborne, had some genuine intensity with luscious peach and apricot flavours. Coopers Creek will soon release a Pinot Gris and a Syrah.

Coopers Creek are planning a café to compliment their tasting area, which will make it an even more rewarding visit when your in Auckland.

Address: 601 State Highway 16 HUAPAI	Winemaker: Simon Nunns	CC Riesling	3-6 yrs
Phone: +64 9 412 8560	Est: 1980 Vine Ha: 24.5	CC Hawkes Bay Chardonnay	2-4 yrs
Fax: +64 9 412 8375	Cases: 60,000	CC Gisborne Chardonnay	1-3 yrs
Email: info@cooperscreek.co.nz	Public Hours: 10am-5.30pm, Mon-Fri;	CC Semillon Chardonnay	1-3 yrs
WWW: www.cooperscreek.co.nz	10.30am-5.30pm Weekends	CC Reserve Riesling	3-6 yrs
Owner: Andrew & Cynthia Hendry	Principal Wines Potential	CC Swamp Reserve Chardonnay	3-5 yrs

Kumeu River Wines

Mick and Kate Brajkovick arrived in New Zealand from the Hugo Salvery Dalmation coast in 1938. After a time, whilst Mick did some backbreaking work, digging Kauri Gum in the northern Regions of New Zealand, they arrived in the Kumeu Valley 20 km northwest of Auckland, in the early 1940's. They both worked in vineyards and orchards in the region to raise the capital needed to buy their own property which they did in 1944. They gradually expanded the vineyards when Mick died prematurely in 1949 their young son Mate helped his mother lending the vines. Mate unfortunately died in 1992 but his mother well into her nineties still lives on the property where she can see her grandchildren running an internationally successful winery and vineyards, assisted by their mother Melba, Mates widow. The fourth generation of the Brajkoviscs Kate's great grandchildren are now growing up amongst the vines.

Michael Brajovich the winemakers has already had a most distinguished career in wine in 1982 he graduated from South Australia Roseworthy College Oenology degree course, he travelled to France working in both the Bordeaux and Burgundy regions and in 1989 became New Zealands first Master of Wines, conquering this extremely vigorous course.

Michael pays much tribute to his late father a wine industry legend who

received an OBE for services to wine in 1985, Mate was an extremely good viticulturist, the solid foundations he laid in the vineyards are now being built on by son Milan who has a degree in chemical engineering as well as vineyard experience in Bordeaux and Burgundy, he also worked for a time with the New Zealand Dairy Board. The other brother Paul has a degree in Marketing and has worked in the Wine Trade in England and Europe, he has come home to manage the sales and marketing for the family business. Melba's daughter Marijana has a commerce degree, she became Director of sales at Auckland's prestigious Regent Hotel in 1989 after 5 years worked there. With all this expertise and commitment in the family, it's easy to see why Kumeu River wines are so good and successful with remarkable results, particularly in the U.S.A. where their Kumeu River Chardonnay is

renowned, having being marked by the prestigious wine spectator, in its top 100 wines of the year four times.

The wines Michael explains are made with a judicious blend of science and the arts. All the vineyards are hard pruned and hand picked. The whites are bunch pressed, a time consuming process but giving great quality advantages, both the whites and reds are fermented with their own indigenous yeasts, present in the vineyards. The Chardonnay and Sauvignon Blanc both undergo fermentation in French Oak Barriques. The reds are given long extended maceration on the skins, before being drained and pressed. Both the reds and whites are put through Malolactic fermentation, softening their acids and adding to their complexity. I am sure it is in carefully guiding theses natural winemaking processes, that Michael gets such complex and interesting wines.

The Kumeu River Merlot I found exceptional, it comes out under their less expensive Brajkovich label. The Kumeu River Range includes a Pinot Noir as well as the Chardonnay. The ultimate Kumeu River Wines, as you can imagine, pays homage to Mate and his contribution not only to Kumeu River but New Zealand's whole wine industry. Mates vineyard Chardonnay is simply one of New Zealands finest wines, from a very fine family.

Address: 55 Highway 16 KUMEU
Phone: +64 9 412 8415 **Fax:** +64 9 412 7627
Email: paul@kumeuriver.co.nz

WWW: www.kumeuriver.co.nz
Winemaker: Michael Brajkovich
Est: 1944 **Vine Ha:** 25

Public Hours: 9am-5:30pm, Mon-Sat
Principal Varieties: Cab Franc, Chardonnay, Malbec, Merlot, Pinot Grigio, Pinot Noir

Matua Valley Wines

The two really "stand out" characters of the New Zealand Wine Industry are Bill and Ross Spence. Their warmth, generosity and hospitality are legendary. The Spences were early starters in the modern New Zealand Wine Industry, when they founded their wine enterprise at Waimauka in the early 1970's, crushing their first grapes in 1973.

Bill and Ross are innovative types who see no reason for not trying something new. They were the first New Zealand Winery to produce a Sauvignon Blanc, now the world wide signature wine of their nation.

In 1990 they made a bold move into the Marlborough Region launching Shingle Peak Wines which have become a stunning success.

The Matua Valley Winery is a vinous mecca, not to be missed if you find yourself anywhere near Auckland. It's set in a very pretty valley just far enough away from the city to have true rural charm.

The tasting cellars are warm and friendly, the attitude of everyone at Matua Valley is welcoming indeed. The picnic area is most pleasant and relaxing and has facilities for a game of petarque or croquet as part of your picnic or when you barbecue on the facilities provided, there is even a childrens playground to keep them amused.

If you are after a very special experience, in the grounds of the winery there is a very special restaurant "The Hunting Lodge" set in

a gracious 130 year old Victorian Villa and surrounded by gorgeous gardens. In summer you can dine on the verandahs or in winter beside the log fire. The food is in the innovate style of the Matua Valley wines, featuring fresh local produce and a very distinct New Zealand flavour.

If you feel like totally relaxing after lunch and to stay a day or so in the region, Bill and his vivacious wife Eileen, have a number of marvelous fully equipped vineyard cottages with heaps of rustic charm, just across from the main Matua Vineyard. I can speak from personal experience, they are the best vineyard accommodation I have seen anywhere in the world.

The Matua Valley Wines have loads of character like their makers and all the critics in New Zealand rank them in the top echelon of premium offerings.

The Flagship wines are their Ararimu Chardonnay and their Ararimu Merlot Cabernet from the best vineyard selections of their vineyards, just north west of the winery in the Ararimu Valley. These are intense and complex with top French oak maturation evident and will definitely improve even further with a few years in the bottle.

Appropriately the next range under Ararimu is called Innovator, the Pinot Noir from the Wairarapa region is particularly impressive, but there are several other wines in the range. Matua Valley have another range from their "Matheson" Vineyard in Hawkes Bay which features a spicy Grenache, a full bodied Chardonnay and a wooded Sauvignon Blanc. The

other labels are Judd Estate well known for the Chardonnay and a fighting varietal label "Eastern Bays".

Matua Valley have had great success on the International market, a compliment not only to their quality and value for money, but the hard work and persistence of the Spence Brothers - more power to them.

Address: Waikoukou Valley Rd WAIMAUKU	Est: 1974 Vine Ha: 140 Cases: 150,000	Ararimu Merlot/Cabernet Sauvignon	6 yrs
Phone: +64 9 411 8301 Fax: +64 9 411 7982	Public Hours: 9am-5pm Mon-Sat; 11am-4:30pm Sun	Ararimu Chardonnay	6 yrs
Email: sales@matua.co.nz	Principal Varieties: Cabernet Sauvignon,	Matua Matheson Cabernet/Merlot	4 yrs
WWW: www.matua.co.nz	Chardonnay, Grenache, Malbec, Merlot, Pinot	Matua Matheson Sauvignon Blanc	3 yrs
Owner: Spence & Robertson families	Gris, Pinot Noir, Riesling, Sauvignon Blanc	Matua Matheson Chardonnay	5 yrs
Winemaker: Mark Robertson	Principal Wines Potential	Matua Judd Estate Chardonnay	6 yrs

Vineyard Cottages

The most beautiful vineyard hideaway I have had the pleasure of staying in are the Vineyard Cottages, set amongst the vines each side of a stream near the Matua Valley Winery.

Bill Spence, the joint Chief Executive of Matua Valley and his delightful hard working wife Eileen, have built seven wonderful self contained cottages. Their construction is classy but rustic, with oiled timbers and other natural materials. During our stay Eileen was busy, with a large brush in hand, giving the natural New Zealand wooden exteriors a preserving drink.

The Victorian character with the use of wood and country print furnishings with earthy themes and wine colours, sets off their situation superbly. The landscaping with trees, shrubs and flowers means your outlook is beautiful but also very private, as each cottage is well separated from the others. They are located in the Waikoukou Valley which is truly peaceful with a serene bucolic air about it yet only 30 minutes from downtown Auckland.

Each cottage has an outdoor private patio at the rear with a gas barbecue and table setting. There is a fire place inside to give a cosy atmosphere in winter.

The separate bedroom has a king size bed and there is a fold out double bed in the main lounge and living area which includes a dining room table setting. The ambiance of these cottages makes them a true haven of peace and a great escape if you are by yourself or with a group where you can book a number of the cottages. You are in the heart of wine country with a number of high quality premium wineries to visit and taste at, such as Matua Valley, Kumeu River, Coopers Creek, Nobilo's or the new Westbrook Winery not far away, plus a number of others.

If you are a golf fan, four of New Zealand's best and most beautiful golf courses are just a long iron away. The Muriwai club perched on the cliffs above the surf is truly spectacular.

Other things to do include fishing, hot air ballooning, clay pigeon shooting, even a game of petanque or croquet, just the other side of the vineyard in Matua Valley.s gardens, or a quiet walk in the nearby forests.

The nearby beaches stretch for miles secluded by warm sand dunes. The dining in the region is also very fine indeed. One of Auckland's best restaurants, the Historic Hunting Lodge, is only a stroll away, whilst a number of wineries in the area have cafes and eateries, plus there are other restaurants serving fresh, typically New Zealand, dishes.

The pantries of the excellent kitchens in the cottages are well stocked or you can forage locally and whip up your own gourmet feast.

The Vineyard cottages are the place to escape to, you are certain to take away a marvelous memory of your stay.

Goldwater Estate

Goldwater Estate was established by Kim and Jeanette Goldwater in 1978, when they planted the first vines on the gorgeous Waiheke Island, in the middle of Auckland harbour. After producing some excellent wines, including some of the best Cabernets and Merlots produced in New Zealand and a great Chardonnay, the Goldwaters expanded their wine interests setting up a production base in Marlborough in 1992. They now produce some fine Marlborough Sauvignon Blanc and Chardonnay to compliment their Waihike range, they now have 100 acres, planted under contract at Marlborough.

The Goldwater Waiheke vineyards of 35 acres are truly spectacular overlooking the pretty Putiki Bay. Goldwater have also recently contracted a further 20 acres of vineyards in the Gimblett Gravels

region of Hawkes Bay, predominatley Merlot with some Cabernet & Syrah

The Waiheke Island Cabernet/Merlot/Cabernet France blend and Esslin Merlot are certainly in the top few New Zealand Reds, they also produce their Zell Chardonnay from Waiheke grapes. The Marlborough Wines include the intense Dog Point Sauvignon Blanc and the stylish Roseland Chardonnay.

A visit to Goldwater on Waiheke, a short half hours ferry ride from Auckland, is now enhanced at the Goldwater Cellar door as you can now purchase platters of fine cheeses and smoked meats, to enjoy with the wines.

Having met Kim and Jeanette at many wine promotions around the world, I have noticed their extremely pleasant and informative approach is backed by a persistent energy to make even greater wines, one cannot help but admire them.

Address: 18 Causeway Road PUTIKI BAY	Est: 1978	Vine Ha: 11	Principal Wines	Potential
Phone: +64 9 372 7493 Fax: +64 9 372 6827	Cases: 26,000		Waiheke Island Esslin Merlot	5-15+ yrs
Email: info@goldwaterwine.com	Public Hours: 11am-4pm, during summer		Waiheke Island Cab Sav	5-15+ yrs
WWW: www.goldwaterwine.com	Principal Varieties: Cabernet Sauvignon,		Waiheke Island Zell Chardonnay	5 yrs
Owner: Kim & Jeanette Goldwater	Merlot, Cabernet Franc, Chardonnay,		Marlborough Roseland Chardonnay	3-5 yrs
Winemaker: Kim Goldwater	Sauvignon Blanc		Marlborough Dog Point Sauv Blanc	Now

Mudbrick Vineyard

I will always have lasting memories of viewing sunset over the city of Auckland and Auckland Harbour through the vines from Mudbrick Vineyards cellar door and then enjoying a splendid meal in their very classy restaurant.

They have one of the world's truly exciting locations. Their mudbrick buildings blend beautifully into the landscape.

Mudbrick's wines are making quite an impact in the premium market, led by their opulent plummy reserve Merlot and a soft, rich complex Chardonnay. They also produce a firm varietal Malbec- a rarity, a Cabernet Sauvignon Merlot with some herbaceousness and a blended Red under the Shepherds Point Label, acknowledging their location. This Cabernet Sauvignon/Merlot/Syrah blend is an earthy style ideal for cellar aging.

New vintage releases include a single variety syrah, a blended Reserve Merlot / Cabernet Sauvignon / Malbec / Cabernet Franc and a very appealing Cabernets blend.

The restaurant menu changes

seasonally and features lots of seafood and game. The chef also uses lots of fresh herbs from the wineries garden. Mudbrick is a fine place to travel to for a very special treat, if you're in Auckland at any time.

Address: Church Bay Road ONEROA	Owner: Nick & Robyn Jones	Principal Wines
Phone: +64 9 372 9050 Fax: +64 9 372 9051	Winemaker: James Rowan	Mudbrick Reserve Merlot Cab/Malbick Syrah
Email: mudbrick@ihug.co.nz	Vine Ha: 3 Cases: 700	Mudbrick Cabernet Sauvignon Franc
WWW www.mudbrick.co.nz Est: 1992	Public Hours: 10am-4pm, Weekends	Shepherd Point Cabernet Sauvignon Merlot

Matakana Estate

Travelling north of Auckland to explore this fast expanding premium wine region, I was struck by a most impressive new vineyard with a winery under construction, Matakana Estate.

This venture has been extremely well thought out with considerable vision by Kevin Fitzgerald, his wife Pat Vegar Fitzgerald and her sons Peter and Paul Vegar. They have put a lot of research into the terroir of their vineyard land before planting and have planted Semillon, Pinot Gris and Syrah, less common varieties in New Zealand, as well as the more traditional varieties of Chardonnay, Cabernet Sauvignon, Merlot, Cabernet Franc and Malbec.

The vineyards are hand pruned to limit production and bunch thinned for the same reason to give intensity of flavour to the grapes. Leaf plucking by hand ensures the grapes get sufficient exposure to the sun, to gain ripe fruit flavours. The vineyards are hand picked several times at vintage, to ensure even ripeness. The wines are carefully hand crafted and top class new French oak barriques are used. The Matakana free draining clay underlies the vineyards providing ideal soil conditions.

Luka Lunjevich, Pat Vegar's grandfather, sailed from Croatia to New Zealand in 1902, he almost didn't make it being ship wrecked near the North Cape. A strong swimmer, he also saved the life of a young girl on board. He spent the rest of his life in north of Kaitaia planting a vineyard and making his own wine. His son Fred, Pat's father, carried on making the wine, I am sure they would be proud of the Matakana Estate Pat and her family have created.

The first wines released from the 1999 vintage have received rave reviews. The new winery with a Mediterranean feel about it and classy cellars door, with superb views over the slopes of vines makes a visit to Matakana a must.

Ransom Wines

Ransom is the first Matakana vineyard and winery you find driving north from Auckland, on the Main Highway One. It takes only about 40 minutes to get there. The sheltered north facing slopes have proved ideal for the vineyard, which now covers 20acres. The first wines were made in 1996.

Robin and Marion Ransom have built an attractive stone winery with great views over their valley of vines. The initial processing facility was constructed in 1997, a couple of years later they added a hospitality area, including catering facilities as well as an office and an apartment. A striking tower above the winery is on the drawing board.

On my visit I was most impressed by their Clos de Valerie Pinot Gris (a little play on words as the winery is located on Valerie close), it had lots of intense honeysuckle aromas and flavours. The Dark Summit Cabernet Sauvignon/Merlot had a deep mauve colour with rich mulberry, cassis and dark cherry fruit aromas and flavours, with a hint of cedar and tobacco leaf, a complex interesting and mouth filling wine.

Ransom also make two Chardonnays, a fruit driven style "Gumfield" and a Barrique Chardonnay, a real Red wine drinkers White, rich and creamy with some toasty wood influences. Ransom is one of the best and most established wineries in this exciting new area.

I had trouble finding many Matakana wineries but not Ransom.

Address: 46 Valerie Close WARKWORTH
Phone: +64 9 425 8862 **Fax:** +64 9 425 8862
Email: ransom.wines@xtra.co.nz

Winemaker: Robin Ransom
Est: 1993 **Vine Ha:** 8
Public Hours: 9am-6pm, daily

Principal Varieties: Cabernet Franc, Cabernet Sauvignon, Chardonnay, Malbec, Merlot, Pinot Gris

West Brook Winery

The 2000 vintage was a milestone for West Brook wines, they made wine in their brand new winery in the Ararimu Valley near Waimauku for the first time

West Brook is a traditional family winery founded in 1937 in the Henderson region, now part of the outer suburbs of Auckland.

The new winery is surrounded by a new vineyard, which will shortly come into production, supplementing West Brook's grape intake. The vineyard of 15 acres has been planted to Merlot, Malbec and Chardonnay, which should enhance even further the ultra premium West Brook wines that have been wining gold medals in recent years.

Winemaker and Manager is Anthony Ivicevich, who has initiated many innovative moves bringing West Brook forward into the modern premium wine era. Anthony's son is

following the winemaking tradition and is currently chief winemaker for the large important premium producer Delegat.

The new West Brook Winery has a tasting room and gallery looking out

over the vineyards and winemaking facility. Plans are afoot for a restaurant in the complex.

West Brook have gained quite a reputation for their Chardonnay, with their barrique fermented version, a blend of Henderson and Marlborough fruit, being a rich complex style.

West Brook also have a super premium label "Blue Ridge" which includes a Tangy Marlborough Sauvignon Blanc and a zesty Marlborough Riesling. They also make one of my favorite varieties, Chenin Blanc from Hawke's Bay grapes. Their 1998 Merlot and Cabernet Merlot have shown they are no slouch in the red wine arena either.

Why not duck out to their new winery vineyards, its pretty rural location is only 25 minutes drive out of Auckland.

		Potential
Address: 215 Ararimu Valley Rd WAIMAUKU	**Winemaker:** Anthony Ivicevich	Blue Ridge Merlot — 4-8 yrs
Phone: +64 9 411 9924 **Fax:** +64 9 411 9925	**Est:** 1937 **Vine Ha:** 6 **Cases:** 14,000	Blue Ridge Chardonnay — 3-7 yrs
Email: info@westbrook.co.nz	**Public Hours:** 10am-5pm, Mon-Sat; 11am-5pm, Sun	Blue Ridge Sauvignon Blanc — 2-3 yrs
WWW: www.westbrook.co.nz		Blue Ridge Riesling — 3-6 yrs
Owner: Anthony & Susan Ivicevich	**Principal Wines**	Blue Ridge Cabernet/Merlot — 4-7 yrs

De Redcliffe Wines

One of the most spectacular winery Resorts in the world is the De Redcliffe Winery and Hotel du Vin. The whole complex is stylish with the accent on luxury.

De Redcliffe was established some 24 years ago by Chris Canning, who produced New Zealand's first Cabernet Merlot Blend. They have vineyards in leading New Zealand Regions. The Home Vineyard at the winery site in the Mangatawhiri Valley about 45 minutes drive South of Auckland. The De Redcliffe vineyards in the prestigious Gimblett road area of Hawkes Bay specialise in red grapes, whilst their Marlborough vineyards specialise in Riesling and Sauvignon Blanc. Their Chardonnay and Pinot Noir come from the "Home Vineyard".

The Hotel was established in 1987 inspired by the great wine estates of Europe it's distinctive and elegant with a focus on wine and food. The rooms are truly sumptuous. Activities include swimming, patanque, tennis, day pigeon shooting, cycling or you

can attack a Confidence Course.

The Marlborough sourced Riesling is very aromatic and the Hawkes Bay

Cabernet Merlot a full rich style. Why not take a pleasant drive form Auckland and discover this Vinous paradise for yourself.

Waikato & Bay of Plenty

The other side of the Bombay Hills south of Auckland lies the rolling rural countryside of the Waikato, the regions centre is Hamilton, New Zealand's fifth largest city. It's only about 45 minutes drive to the nearest wineries from Auckland. The splendid winery resort DeRedcliffe and their Hotel du Vin is a great classy gourmet escape near Hamilton, Viligrad wines have a characterful indoor-outdoor restaurant, hidden away in the Hills is the Ohinemuri Estate at Paeroa which has a quaint teahouse style café. The Rogapai historic winery makes some great wines including a selection of sweet botrytised wines which do very well in the region. All wine styles are made in the region but whites in the aromatic spectrum do very well.

The Bay of Plenty continues around the coast to the east from Waikato towards the delightful seaside resort town of Tauranga. The sweeping bays and beaches are awesome particularly at sunset. The showpiece wineries of Mills Reef, which also caters for functions and has a superb restaurant and Morton Estate are both classy by any standards in the wine world. They also offer a large range of wines from the Bay of Plenty and vineyards in other leading New Zealand Regions.

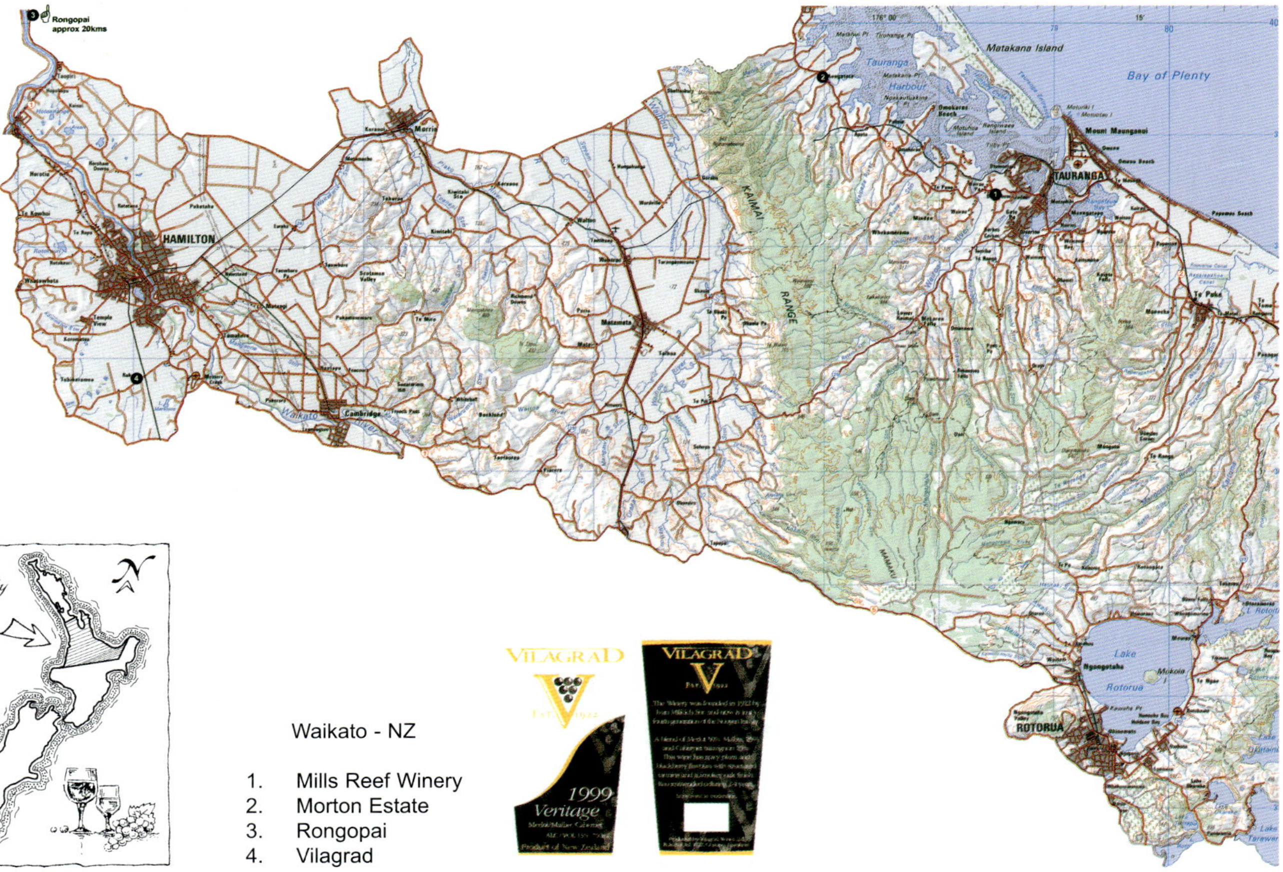

Waikato and Bay of Plenty Wine Region

Waikato - NZ

1. Mills Reef Winery
2. Morton Estate
3. Rongopai
4. Vilagrad

Rongopai

In 1903 almost 100 years ago Rongopai began its life as the

Government funded Viticultural Research Station · Te Kauwhata.

Tom Van Dam was the government viticulturist from 1978-1986. In 1985 the research station closed and Tom took it over turning it into a commercial winery. The winery has 10 acres of their own vines and contract three local growers and one in Gisborne.

Rongopai have made quite a reputation for their Botrytised wines. I had the pleasure of trying some of these on my visit, the 1997 Botrytised Riesling was a real revelation with a medium deep gold colour. Its concentrated nectar and honey like character was nicely balanced by grapefruit like citrus characters, with a piquant quince like edge, complex and most importantly luscious. I rated it 93 out of 100. Another interesting wine was the

1997 Botrytised Chardonnay, full of luscious peach and apricot nectar flavours, a unique style. The 1999 Botrytised selection, a blend of Chardonnay and Muller Thurgau, was also a great wine, needing a little time to fill out.

I was also impressed with the 1998 Sauvignon Blanc "Te Kauwhata" with honey, melon and passionfruit, one of the most fruit driven New Zealand Sauvignons I have seen. The 1999 Gold medal winning Chardonnay with 25% Gisborne fruit again was fruit driven, it had been chosen to be served on Air New Zealand, quite an honour.

Rongopai have a tasting and sales area on the main road a couple of kilometers from the winery, but make sure you visit both and check out a little of the early history of New Zealand's Wine Industry.

Address: 55 Te Kauwhata Road TE KAUWHATA	**Est:** 1982	**Vine Ha:** 4	Chardonnay	5 yrs
Phone: +64 7 826 3981 **Fax:** +64 7 825 3462	**Public Hours:** 9am-5pm weekdays; 10am-		Sauvignon Blanc	2 yrs
Email: rongopaiwine@xtra.co.nz	5pm Saturdays; 11am-4pm Sundays		Riesling	8 yrs
WWW: www.rongopaiwines.co.nz	**Principal Varieties:** Chardonnay, Merlot,		Botrytised Chardonnay	10-15 yrs
Owner: Tom Van Dam	Riesling, Malbec, Pinot Noir, Sauvignon Blanc		Pinot Noir	5 yrs
Winemaker: Tom Van Dam	**Principal Wines**	**Potential**	Merlot Malbec	5-8 yrs

Vilagrad

Over 70 years ago Dalmatian settlers, Ivan and Pera Millicich established a vineyard at Ohaupo close to Hamilton, New Zealand's 5th largest city. Today the third generation Pieter Nooyen, his wife Nelda and their three sons Jacob, Kristian and Adam, operate a wine enterprise which includes a hospitality centre with a distinct rustic Mediterranean flavour, it opens for lunch on Sundays, when the spit roast turns, adding a special atmosphere. The Nooyens also cater for many weddings, conferences and private functions of all sorts.

The vineyards cover some 12 acres and are supplemented by grapes from local growers. Vilagrad have an excellent Reserve Range of wines, which includes Chardonnay, Gewarztraminer, Pinot Noir and a Cabernet Sauvignon/Merlot/Malbec blend.

The reception area is vine covered and particularly picturesque in Autumn, it really comes to life in April, during a yearly wine and food

festival, maybe this is not a bad time

to visit the Nooyens special place.

Mills Reef Winery

Mills Reef is a truly spectacular winery and restaurant complex, it is a major tourist attraction being right on the outskirts of the Bay of Plenty tourist mecca of Tauranga.

The Preston family began their enterprise as fruit wine producers, tasting their kiwifruit dry white. I can see why they have been successful. Paddy Preston and his son Tim began making wine together in 1981 but Paddy's winemaking hobby goes back over 30 years. The first vintage under the Mills Reef label was in 1989, they found success early and have won more than 100 medals for their wines and a number of trophies.

About half of Mills Reef grape supply comes from their own vineyards at Hawkes Bay the rest from selected Hawkes Bay growers.

The wines include several ranges the "Moffat Road Selection are lighter in style, drink now wines. They also have a "Reserve" range for the more serious wine enthusiast and a top of

the tree label "Elspeth" only released when the vintage for a particular variety is considered outstanding.

The new varieties are Chardonnay, Sauvignon Blanc, Riesling, Cabernet Sauvignon, Merlot, Pinot Noir and a Syrah that appears under the Eslspeth label that has won considerable acclaim. Mills Reef produce a trophy winning Methode Champenoise and have both a vintage and non vintage release.

Their state of the art winery includes a 500 barrel maturation cellar. It was built in 1995 the same year as the truly magnificent 150 seat Restaurant which has additional patios, for outdoor eating, amongst the splendid 20 acres of landscaped gardens. Paddy, helped by his daughter Melissa, plus sons Warren and Tim, have made Mills Reef a revelation in wine, food and culture hosting many art and music events.

Morton Estate

Morton Estate is housed in captivating Cape Dutch inspired building close to the beautiful Bay of Plenty, about 25 kilometres north of the pretty resort town of Tauranga. Morton is almost unique amongst New Zealand's larger wineries (they rank in the top ten size wise, with a 2000 vintage of 1,550 tonnes), as they use only grapes from their own vineyards, which total an impressive 750 acres. The largest vineyard is their spectacular River View Vineyard

on the free draining shingle soils of the Ngaruroro River, in the Hinterland area of Hawkes Bay.

They also have a 100-acre vineyard in the heart of the Wairau plains in the Marlborough Region. This Stonecreek vineyard provides fruit for their Sauvignon Blanc.

Morton Estate have become justly famous for their Flagship brand "Black Label" I remember tasting their first vintage, a 1983 Black Label Chardonnay in Melbourne in

the early 1980's, at a combined New Zealand promotion and being most impressed by its richness balance and complexity.

Current owners John and Alison Coney have invested heavily in every area of Morton Estate. Their classic 1930's, original art deco head office in Auckland was formerly owned by a brewery, it has a unique barrel room for tastings and entertainment, like everything at Morton Estate it is first class.

Gisborne

Gisborne is often referred to as the Chardonnay capital of New Zealand. In fact over half the vines planted are Chardonnay, a far cry from the 1980's when Muller-Thurgau dominated the region and it was virtually only regarded as a bulk wine region, with the exception of the flag flown by quality individual producers, like Milton Vineyard and Matawhero Wines. Most of the vineyards in the long valleys of Gisborne are owned by or supply the larger New Zealand

wineries, making wine which is to a certain degree produced to a formula and price.

Whilst Gisborne was devastated by phylloxera before it played havoc in Hawkes Bay and Marlborough, today over 90% of the vines are grafted on to phylloxera resistant American rootstocks. Another advantage gained by Gisborne through adversity happened in the mid 1980's, when a "vine pull" scheme sponsored by the New Zealand government, due to

wine surpless, led to many bulk wine varieties being pulled up in the Gisborne Region, to be replaced by Chardonnay and other premium classic varieties.

Wine tourism is not a major part of the Gisborne scene, there are a few boutique wineries, which are very individual and worth visiting. The top shelf Acton Estate, which incorporates the Parker M.C. wine operations has superb accommodation.

Gisborne - NZ

1. The Colosseum
2. Matawhero Wines
3. Milton Vineyard

Matawhero Wines

Dennis Irwin is an absolute character, a very creative man not short of courage, never bowing to convention in anything he tackles.

The tasting area at Matawhero is in part of Dennis home, it's a magic mixture of obscure antiques and memorabilia, it's real trip down memory lane, a visit you will always remember.

Dennis is not interested in lightweight wines, he builds character into all his wines and often ages them in barrel on bottle for some years a rarity in New Zealand.

I first met Dennis in the early 1980's when he was on a promotional visit to Australia, he left a lasting impression. A few years ago he had a serious car accident and now gets around with a distinct limp but it certainly hasn't slowed him up.

Dennis was a pioneer in the mid 1970's when he made his first Gisbourne wines, his Gewurtztraminer took the wine world by storm. His Reserve wines have always been successful and the Chardonnay particularly so. I like his Syrah a lot and very good Bordeaux blend "Bridge Estate".

Address: Riverpoint Road RD 1 MATAWHERO **Phone:** +64 6 868 8366 **Fax:** +64 6 867 9856	**Winemaker:** Denis Irwin **Est:** 1975 **Vine Ha:** 32 **Public Hours:** 11am-4:30pm, Weekdays; 11am-5pm, Sat	**Principal Varieties:** Cabernet Franc, Cabernet Sauvignon, Chardonnay, Malbec, Merlot, Pinot Noir, Sauvignon Blanc, Semillon, Shiraz

The Colosseum

Dennis Irwin the genuine wine legend of the Gisborne region has always felt the region lacked facilities for Wine Tourism, Restaurants and Cafes there are rare indeed.

Although almost as big in area of vines planted at Hawkes Bay there are only 10 or so wineries as versus Hawkes Bays 34. Wine tourism facilities in the area are also dismally lacking.

On my visit on the eve of the new Millennium, my photographer and I found Dennis hard at work on a Sunday, wearing his builder's hat, busy on the construction site. We shared a drop of Red straight from the bottle as no glasses were to be found, it was a wet and windy day but Dennis and his companion were not perturbed, the dome like shell of the Colosseum was taking shape. Now it is a delightful Way Stop, a classy but casual eatery to enjoy the local produce on your visit. Well done Dennis once again a poineer of good taste.

Millton Vineyard

James and Annie Millton planted their first vineyard in the Gisborne Region in 1984, on the site of the first vineyards in the area more than 100 years before.

The Millton vineyard was the first New Zealand Vineyard to obtain Bio-Gro status, they use bio dynamic viticultural techniques that avoid the use of systemic sprays, insecticides and chemical fertilizers. They also process their grapes using very little preservatives such as sulphur dioxide.

The Millton wines are individual in style with concentrated flavours and with the integrity their organic methods produce.

We were led through a most enlightening and lively tasting by their resident mine host "Richard Chardonnay" complete with this French beret and a host with wonderful wine, food and fun anecdotes from his many years as a purser on Air New Zealand.

The Opau vineyard Riesling with just a slight hint of sweetness was just delicious. Millton have four separate vineyards in the region and use all their own grapes. The top of the range Clos de St. Anne Chardonnay impressed me greatly with ripe tropical flavours and a crisp quince like finish.

Richard enthused over their dry Rose made with Pinot Noir and Chardonnay, it certainly deserved his praise and one wonders why we don't drink more of this style in our Southern summers. The Clos de St Anne Pinot Noir and a full bodied Malbec also impressed. I hope your visit to Millton will be as rewarding as ours.

Address: Papatu Road MANUTUKE	**Email:** info@milton.bpc.co.nz	**Principal Varieties:** Cabernet Sauvignon,
Phone: +64 6 862 8680	**Winemaker:** James Millton	Chardonnay, Chenin Blanc, Malbec, Merlot,
Fax: +64 6 862 8869	**Est:** 1984	Pinot Noir, Riesling

Hawkes Bay

most recognised wine regions. Awards gained on the world scene by Hawke's Bay wines reflect this.

The Southern Hawke's Bay wineries around Havelock North, on the slopes of Te Mata Peak, enjoy north facing slopes and well drained, volcanic soils. They produce exceptional Reds, the Te Mata Coleraine in particular is world class.

There are also a number of vineyards along the coast from south to north, producing more herbaceous Reds and Whites. In recent times a central Hawke's Bay sub-region has emerged further inland, in the foothills of the coastal ranges which have a cooler general climate and colder nights, producing wines of more elegance.

Hawke's Bay can produce top wines of all styles, from all varieties in its many microclimates and the unique "Terrior" of its many vineyard sites. The region has New Zealand's longest continuous wine history going back to the mid-1800's.

Certainly vineyard expansion and the construction of wineries, with wine tourism facilities such as the splendid Sileni Estates, is mind blowing, well over a billion dollars of investment has gone into the region in recent years. Many wineries large and small have cafes and restaurants. The Historic Mission Estate Winery and Restaurant is worth visiting as is the nearby Church Road Winery, which has New Zealand's only wine museum.

There is a sense of happening in Hawke's Bay, which gets the adrenaline pumping, I had the privelege of tasting the incredible 1998 Red wines in barrel during my visit, anyone who doubts the potential of New Zealand to make great Reds, should have been with me.

Hawke's Bay in many ways has a similarity to the great French wine region of Bordeaux, certainly supporting the massive plantings of recent years of Bordeaux Red varieties, particularly Merlot and Cabernet Sauvignon. The Hawke's Bay wine region is situated around the towns of Napier and Hastings and has a number of distinct sub-regions. The area which has experienced the most dramatic growth in vineyard planting, is around Gimblett Road, were the flat alluvial plains have a layer of grey shale and shingle soils, with a deep gravel base. These soils are free draining, hold heat overnight and reflect heat and light onto the vines above during the day, this leads to super ripe grapes from the late ripening Bordeaux Red varieties, in a climate which is generally cool. In warm years such as 1998 these Reds are rich opulent styles, which equal anything produced in the world's

  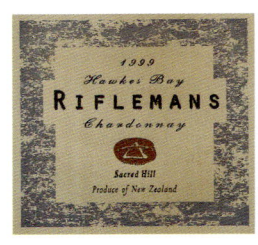  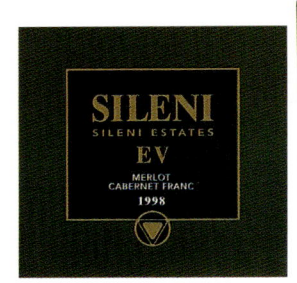 

Hawkes Bay

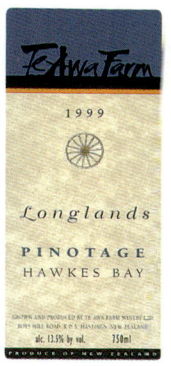

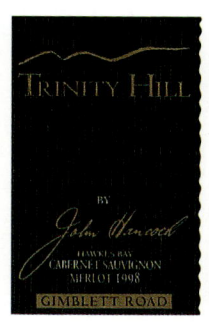

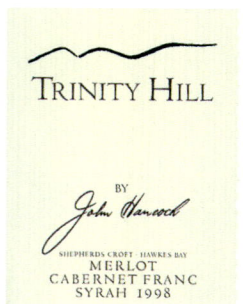

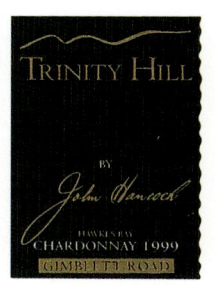

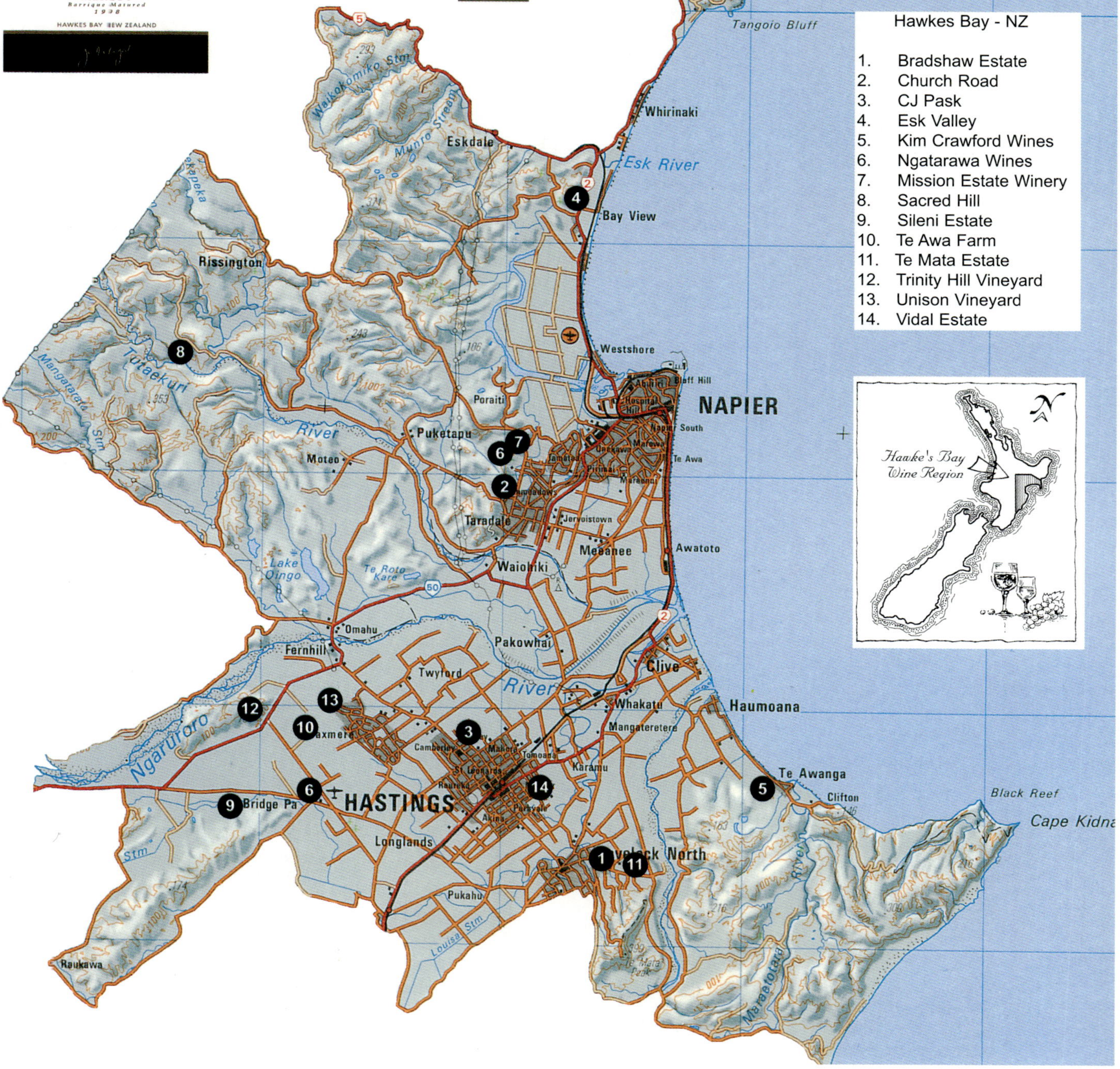

Hawkes Bay - NZ

1. Bradshaw Estate
2. Church Road
3. CJ Pask
4. Esk Valley
5. Kim Crawford Wines
6. Ngatarawa Wines
7. Mission Estate Winery
8. Sacred Hill
9. Sileni Estate
10. Te Awa Farm
11. Te Mata Estate
12. Trinity Hill Vineyard
13. Unison Vineyard
14. Vidal Estate

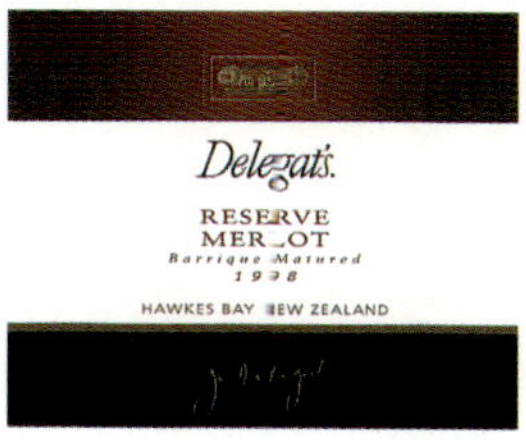

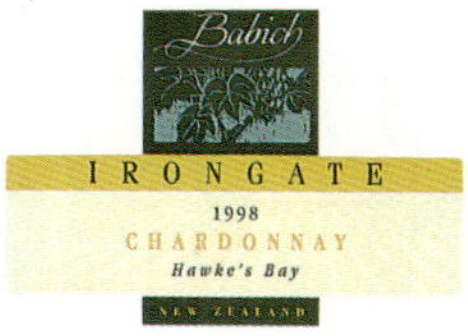

Hawke's Bay Wine Region

Bradshaw Estate

During our visit to Hawkes Bay, we were struck by a very pretty winery just up the road from the high profile Te Mata Estate, in fact their historic homestead and vineyards were part of the Te Mata Station, the 1912 homestead was the Station managers residence.

The Vidal Family planted the vineyards in 1936 and again totally replanted it in the 1980's. Wayne and Judy Bradshaw bought the property from The Vidals in 1991.

The Bradshaw's have constructed a modern state of the art winery and a hospitality/restaurant complex, which opens every Friday and Saturday for dinner all year and lunch every day in summer and Tuesday to Sunday in winter. We did not have the pleasure of dining there but heard very good reports about the food.

The Bradshaw's wines have received a good deal of critical acclaim. Their 1998 Reserve Chardonnay received a

top five star rating from Cuisine Annual, a big rich concentrated wine.

Their 1996 Reserve Merlot/Cabernet Sauvignon received 4 stars. All the wines are made on site mainly from their own 10 acre vineyard, supplemented by selected local growers.

Watch out for Bradshaw who are quietly making strong progress, make sure you drop in for a tasting and a meal when you're in the Hawkes Bay Region.

Address: RD 12, 291 Te Mata Road HAVELOCK NORTH Phone: +64 6 877 5795 Fax: +64 6 877 3317	Email: hawkesbaywine@xtra.co.nz Est: 1994 Public Hours: 10am-3:30pm, daily	Principal Varieties: Cabernet Franc, Cabernet Sauvignon, Chardonnay, Gewürztraminer, Merlot, Sauvignon Blanc

Esk Valley

Esk Valley is part of George Fistonich's Villa Maria Group, it however runs completely autonomously under creative winemaker Gordon Russell, who's first taste of the beverage industry was running the cellar of a traditional English Pub in London's Fleet Street

The Esk Valley Winery was built in the 1940's by an Englishman Robert Bird, who had planted vines as part of his market gardens in the 1930's. The concrete open fermenting vats are prized by Gordon, who uses them for all his small batches of red wines, which also then gives him many options for blending the final wines.

Gordon pays a lot of attention to the wines "texture" · the balance and harmony of the wine, together with its complexity and palate interest.

Esk Valley are renowned for their reds, the top wine "The Terraces" a

Merlot dominated wine, comes from the sun drenched north facing slopes of the Natural amphitheatre first planted by Robert Bird in the 1930's. "The Terraces" 1995 was rated New

Zealand's best wine in 1997 by the respected Cuisine Annual. It is not produced every year. I tasted the 1998 Terraces on my visit an enormous wine with deep blue mauve colour, quite floral with rich cassis and plum like fruit, with distinct but subtle spices · a gem. Esk Valley also produce a super premium Reserve Range. The Reserve Merlot-Malbec-Cabernet Sauvignon Blend is also one of NZ's best Red wines and has won the annual Cuisine Magazine NZ Red tasting in 1994,1996,1997 and 2001. The Black Label premium range includes a number of varietal and blended Reds and Whites and a very good Rose. The Botrytis Chenin Blanc I tasted, a 1998 was not picked until the 19th June and fermented in New French Oak Barriques, truly concentrated luscious wine with vanilla character coming from the wood, a world beater, well done Esk Valley.

Address: Main State Highway 1 BAYVIEW Phone: +64 6 836 6411 Fax: +64 6 836 6413 Winemaker: Gordon Russell	Est: 1933 Public Hours: 9am-5:30pm, daily (Summer); 9:45am-5pm, daily (Winter)	Principal Varieties: Cabernet Franc, Cabernet Sauvignon, Chenin Blanc, Malbec, Merlot, Riesling, Sauvignon Blanc

Kim Crawford Wines

Kim Crawford is a highly credentialed and respected New Zealand winemaker. In 1999 he finally found a home for his wines, a beautiful modern contemporary designed wine center, with an airy spacious tasting area looking out over the Te Awanga Beach and Hawkes Bay. Kim has a range of wines that have been hugely successful, particularly on the export market.

For many years until 1998 Kim was Chief winemaker for Coopers Creek bringing them much success. He started his Kim Crawford label in 1996. He also sources grapes from the renowned Tietjen vineyard in the

Gisborne region, his 1997 Tietjen Gisborne Chardonnay took all before it a at the prestigious Australian National wine show winning the trophy for the "Best Dry White Tablewine" his 1998 Marlborough Sauvignon Blanc won a gold medal at London's International wine challenge the first ever current vintage New Zealand wine to do so. I tried his 1999 Te Awanga Chardonnay awarding it 93.5/100 it had loads of nectarine and melon with a toasty finish, superb. The Tietjen 1998 was even more intense 95.5/100.

The 1998 Wicken Estate Cabernet Franc had huge cherry and plum

flavours with floral overtones and some spice another 90+ wine.

The top Kim Crawford "Tane" (maori for Lord of the Forest) a Merlot Cabernet Franc blend was exquisite, a beautifully crafted silky red with plenty of power · 94/100. The Reka (maori for honey) Botrytised Riesling in half bottles was crisp as well as luscious, with lime and lemon and hints of apricot in the background.

Kim Crawford hand crafts his wines with character and style. The range also includes Sauvignon Blanc, Chardonnay, Methode Traditionnelle, Pinot Noir and Pinot Gris from Marlborough.

Address: Clifton Road, RD2 HASTINGS
Phone: +64 6 875 0553 **Fax:** +64 9 875 1188
Email: jason@kimcrawfordwines.co.nz

WWW: www.kimcrawfordwines.co.nz
Winemaker: Kim Crawford
Est: 1996 **Vine Ha:** 30

Principal Varieties: Cabernet Franc, Chardonnay, Merlot, Pinot Noir, Riesling, Sauvignon Blanc, Semillon

Delegat's Hawkes Bay

Delegat's is a modern, dynamic family wine business that has grown over 50 years to be one of New Zealand's five largest wine companies. Brother and sister team, Jim and Rosemari Delegat, own and manage the company which is growing very quickly through exports of its super premium Oyster Bay Marlborough and Delegat's labels to international markets in the U.K., North America and Asia Pacific.

To keep pace with the growth, and plan for the future, the company is making major vineyard and winery investments in the country's two leading wine regions · Hawkes Bay and Marlborough. Delegat's philosophy is to have a limited range of premium and super premium varietal wines and to focus on the grape varieties for which each region is renowned.

Currently, the flagship label for the Delegat's family brand is the Reserve range of wines. The Reserve

Chardonnay, Merlot and Cabernet Sauvignon wines are handcrafted from specially selected Hawkes Bay grapes while a new Reserve Sauvignon Blanc from Marlborough grapes is due for release in late 2001.

Delegat's Reserve Chardonnay is barrique fermented and the two reds are barrique matured in top French oak, which is used very subtly. Winemaker, Michael Ivicevich, and his

winemaking team, know how to let the top class, ripe fruit do the 'talking'. At under NZ$20 per bottle the Reserve range is outstanding value.

Delegat's also have a range of premium varietals based on Hawkes Bay grapes · fresh, fruity wines with generous varietal flavours. A chardonnay and a cabernet merlot blend are included · both matured in French oak.

The Delegat's Hawkes Bay vineyards feature a diverse range of soils, from heavier clays to free draining river shingles · ideal for allowing the winemaking team to express regional harmony and terroir. The company's Highway 50 and Gimblett Road vineyards are in the newly named 'Gimblett Gravels Winegrowing District', west of the city of Hastings · a small select area of vineyards which is quickly gaining a reputation for the quality of its Bordeaux reds · merlot and cabernet sauvignon.

Mission Estate Winery

Mission Estate is New Zealand's oldest operating winery, founded by the Marist Fathers in 1851. Mission firstly operated to produce sacramental wines and wines for use within the church, which seems only suitable for a religious order that was founded in France.

In the latter part of the 19th century the brothers bowed to public pressure and began selling some wine to the public. Today Mission Estate is a reasonably large winery producing several ranges of premium wines which sell extremely well and rank in the top level of New Zealand's wines for both quality and value for money.

The winery's location on the property and is now in the Classic 19th Century Victorian weatherboard building. The fully restored former seminary building also houses museum, restaurant, café, conference facilities and craft gallery.

The history and operation of the mission can be discovered on a guided tour of the museum and underground cellar. The restaurant and café are open daily from 10.00 a.m. until late.

The Mission Estate wines cover three separate ranges. The Mission Estate label in the entry-level price wise of premium wines, is great value, top quality at extremely affordable prices. The range includes Sauvignon Blanc, Riesling, Chardonnay, Pinot Gris, Gewurztramminer, Cabernet Sauvignon a Cabernet Sauvignon-Merlot and a varietal Merlot.

The Reserve Range wines often rank in the top few New Zealand wines, although Mission also have a super premium range above their Reserve called Jewelstone. The Reserve Range is quite extensive including Chardonnay, Semillon, Reisling, Pinot Gris, Sauvignon Blanc, Merlot, Cabernet Sauvignon and a Cabernet Sauvignon-Merlot. The 1998 Reserve Cabernet Sauvignon was awarded prestigious 5 stars by the respected Cuisine Wine Annual.

The crowning range Jewelstone, is Mission's ultimate Statement, at present the range includes Chardonnay, Syrah and a Cabernt Sauvignon -Merlot.

The team at the Estate truly understand their mission, make it yours to seek out their wonderful wines.

Address: 198 Church Road GREENMEADOWS
Phone: +64 6 844 2259 **Fax:** +64 6 844 6023
Email: missionwinery@clear.net.nz
Winemaker: Paul Mooney

Est: 1851
Vine Ha: 35
Cases: 63,000
Public Hours: 9am-5:30pm, daily

Principal Varieties: Cabernet Merlot, Cabernet Sauvignon, Chardonnay, Gewürztraminer, Merlot, Pinot Gris, Riesling, Sauvignon Blanc, Syrah

Ngatarawa Wines

2001, makes it 20 years since Ngatarawa crushed its first grapes as the pioneer of the Ngatarawa region of Hawkes Bay. Winemaker is Alwyn Corban a fourth generation member of the famous Corban wine family. Alwyn and his cousin Brian Corban recently bought out their partners, the Glazebrook family and now own the winery and vineyards, outright. The winery "The Stables" is over 100 years old and was built as stables for racehorses. The landscaped gardens in front feature a long lily pond and fountain it is a magnificent country estate.

Ngatarawa recently introduced a super premium range under the "Alwyn Reserve" Label, only released in exceptional years and from exceptional varieties in that vintage. The first release includes a Chardonnay, Merlot and a Cabernet Sauvignon all from the opulent 1998 vintage and a Noble Harvest

(botrytised) Riesling in half bottles from the 1994 Vintage, the wines are all rated at the very top of Hawkes Bay's produce.

The next range is under the "Glazebrook" banner this range was extended in 2000 to include a Sauvignon Blanc and a Syrah. The

other range of wines is under "The Stables" name and often top quality at affordable prices. The wines I found all had excellent balance and the older wines I tried, had certainly held up well. The Stables Winery has a special feel about it, a timeless elegance, its important to visit here when in the region.

Address: R05 Ngatarawa Rd, RD5 HASTINGS	**Owner:** Alwyn & Bryan Corban	**Public Hours:** 11am-5pm Monday & Sunday
Phone: +64 6 879 7603 **Fax:** +64 6 879 6675	**Winemaker:** Alwyn Corban	(closed Christmas Day)
Email: ngatarawawines@clear.net.nz	**Est:** 1981	**Principal Varieties:** Chardonnay, Riesling,
WWW: www.ngatarawawines.co.nz	**Cases:** 30,000	Cabernet Sauvignon, Merlot, Sauvignon Blanc

CJ Pask

Chris Pask is a quiet achiever a powerhouse of positive energy in partnership with Kate Radburnd a South Australian winemaker, who has been in Hawkes Bay with C J Pask for many years and has recently also taken on the role of Managing Director.

I was most impressed with the quality of the Pask Wines, from their highest priced Reserve Wines to the great value for money. "Roys Hill" red, a Cabernet-Merlot-Malbec blend and one of the real gems of New

Zealand's "Value" wines.

The 1998 Reds I tried in barrel were just sensational very round but with immense power, long, strong wines. Their 1998 Reserve Merlot was recently rewarded at the huge, prestigious International Wine Challenge in London, it outpointed all the world wines of "Bordeaux and Cabernet Merlot" Styles to win the trophy, a real winner for New Zealand, Hawkes bay and the Gimblett Road Vineyard area that Chris Pask pioneered in 1982. The deep river shingle soils, left by the river when it changed direction after the 1851 earthquake, reflect and retain heat, giving the grapes extra strength and ripe characters compared with other areas of Hawks Bay.

Between the 'Reserve' wines, which also includes a great Cabernet

Sauvignon and a Chardonnay and the 'Roys Hill' label, Pask produce their Gimblett Road range which includes Chardonnay, Merlot, Cabernet Merlot and Pinot Noir. The Pinot Noir I found a lovely mouth filling meaty style, which I like in this variety.

When you visit C J Pask make sure to venture out the back to see Chris's Locomotive, he's a mechanical and railway wizard and restores old steam engines, powerful like his wines.

Address: 1133 Omahu Road HASTINGS	**Winemaker:** Kate Radburnd	Chardonnay, Malbec, Merlot, Pinot Noir	
Phone: +64 6 879 7906 **Fax:** +64 6 879 6428	**Est:** 1985 **Vine Ha:** 50 **Cases:** 35,000	**Principal Wines**	**Potential**
Email: info@cjpaskwinery.co.nz	**Public Hours:** 9am-5pm weekdays, 10am-	CJPASK Reserve Range	5+ yrs
WWW: www.cjpaskwinery.co.nz	5pm Sat & Public Holidays, 11am-4pm Sun	Roys Hill Range	
Owner: Chris Pask, Kate Radburnd, John Benton	**Principal Varieties:** Cab Franc, Cab Sav,	Gimslett Rd Range	3-5 yrs

Sileni Estates

One of the worlds most striking modern winery buildings constructed in recent times must be the splendid Sileni Estates Winery and Epicurean centre nestled below the foothills of the central north island ranges in Hawkes Bay.

Everything at Sileni has been done with great style in a grand manner, the boldness of its creator, top flight businessman and pharmaceutical scientist Graeme Avery, is breathtaking.

Sileni already have 250 acres of its own vineyard and their production in 2000 grew to 170 tonnes. The wineries capacity is 1000 tonnes, but Graeme is in no hurry to get to this level, even when he does 80% of the production will come from his own grapes and will be at Super premium quality levels.

The wines so far released are headed by their ultimate statement the "E.V. (Exceptional Vintage) Merlot/Cabernet Franc" a supple wine with intense plum/berry flavours, the 1998 is a powerhouse. The Sileni 2000 Semillon has some barrel fermentation and is a leader in this style in New Zealand. It will age extremely well. The 1999 Sileni Chardonnay is a complex wine also

with admirable intensity.

The Epicurean centre is truly multi faceted and everything has been conceived and put into action in a thoughtful and professional manner, no detail has been too small to miss the careful attention of Graeme and his manager/winemaker Grant Edmonds.

The centre includes two restaurants, culinary gardens, a gourmet food store "Vinotica", a wine education centre, a wine tasting area and a

culinary school. In 2000 a visit and demonstration by celebrity Chef Jamie Oliver · "The Naked Chef" was a huge success.

Sileni Estates would do any state of the art winery complex in the Napa Valley or any other leading world wine region proud. It is one of the most important developments in the wine industry of New Zealand and providing an example for others to follow to truly help their great Industry "Come of Age". Sileni is Sublime !!

Address: 2016 Maraekakaho Road RD1 HASTINGS	Winemaker: Grant Edmonds/Nigel Davies/Elanor Dodd	Principal Wines	Potential
Phone: +64 6 879 8768 Fax: +64 6 879 7187	Est: 1997 Vine Ha: 100 Cases: 65,000	EV Merlot/Cabernet Franc	10-15 yrs
Email: sileni.estates@xtra.co.nz	Public Hours: 10am-5pm, daily	Sileni Merlot/Franc/Cabernet	7-10 yrs
WWW: www.sileni.co.nz	Principal Varieties: Cab Sav, Merlot,	Sileni Chardonnay	4-6 yrs
Owner: Graeme Avery	Semillon, Cab Franc, Chardonnay, Pinot Noir	Pourriture Noble	2-4 yrs
		Sileni Semillon	3-6 yrs

Sacred Hill

Sacred Hill has one of New Zealand's finest Winery Restaurants, set in native bushland, with a delightful outside dining area where one can relax in the dappled light, filtering through the trees, its quite an experience particularly in late summer.

Sacred Hill wines have grown in range and stature in recent years. The enterprise is a family affair founded by David Mason in 1986 on the Whitecliffs overlooking the river. The families property "Dartmoor" is near the small village of Puketapu, Maori for Sacred Hill hence the name.

Sacred Hill have three ranges of wine, much like many New Zealand premium producers. The entry level goes under the Whitecliffs label, with a Sauvignon Blanc, Chardonnay and Merlot. Then comes the Sacred Hill label, which include several barrel fermented wines, a Sauvignon Blanc, Chardonnay and a Basket Press

Merlot. The super premium Reserve Range includes a Sauvignon Blanc under the "Sauvage" label, Rifleman's Chardonnay and Brokenstone Merlot. There area several wines only available at cellar door including a

Syrah and a Pinot Noir. In suitable years they also produce fabulous Botrytised wines from Semillon and Riesling. Sacred Heart certainly have some heavenly wines.

Address: Dartmoor Road, RD 6 NAPIER	Email: enquiries@sacredhill.com	Public Hours: 11am-5pm, Dec-Feb
Phone: +64 6 844 0138	Winemaker: Tony Bish	Principal Varieties: Cabernet Sauvignon,
Fax: +64 6 844 3271	Est: 1986	Chardonnay, Malbec, Merlot, Sauvignon Blanc

Te Mata Estate

One of New Zealand's oldest, most historic and highest profile premium wineries is Te Mata Estate.

In 1892 Bernard Chambers planted the first vines. His father John Chambers from Derbyshire, initially settled in South Australia and went on to make a fortune at Bendigo in the early 1850's making and sharpening mining tools during the gold rush. After an exploratory trip to New Zealand, looking for land to invest his profits in and make a home for his family, he returned in 1854 and bought 18,250 acres including slopes of Te Mata Peak in Hawkes Bay. By the early 1900's Te Mata were winning gold medals in international wine shows.

John Buck as a young man worked for the English wine firm Stowells of Chelsea. In 1974 after establishing himself as the leading New Zealand wine judge and wine columnist, he and fellow wine judge Michael Morris bought the then for sale Te Mata Estate. Buck and Morris rejuvenated the vineyards and planted new areas

where once Chambers had vines. The winery has been beautifully restored and expanded to it reminds me of a top Bordeaux Chais. Long time winemkaer is Australian Peter Cowley I tasted the 1998 Coleraine Cabernet

Merlot from barrel and have to say it is one of the finest red wines I've ever tried.

The stunning cellar door recently constructed is a great place to try the sublime Te Mata Wines.

Te Awa Farm

Te Awa Farm has quickly become one of New Zea and's most highly regarded premium wine producers, if this was not enough, it is also home to one of New Zealand's finest Chefs and having eaten in their classy rustic bistro area, I can only say its was a truly memorable wine and food experience.

The foundations of Te Awa Farm started many years ago. Ian Lawson began growing premium wine grapes in 1980 when he planted both Chardonnay and Sauvignon Blanc, by the mid 1980's he had added Chenin Blanc and Cabernet Franc. He was joined by his son Gus and as the years went by their passion to produce their own premium wines from their own vineyards grew. They also developed a desire to produce Bordeaux style wines and in 1992 purchased Te Awa Farm, carefully chosen because of its location on "Roys Hill" right in the heart of the Gimblett Gravels wine growing district with its deep river shale, renowned today for producing world class Bordeaux style Reds. They planted immediately and the first wines were made from the property in 1995. The vineyards now cover 120 acres and Te Awa only make their wine from their own vineyard.

The soil structure varies considerably on the property and Lawson's spent

a great deal of time chosing the perfect "Terroir" for each variety. Te Awa are also blessed with a very talented winemaker, perfectly suited to the task of making complex Bordeaux style Reds. Jenny Dobson a New Zealander has spent 16 years in France, making wine in Bordeaux and Burgundy and was winemaker at the highly respected Bordeaux property Chateau Senejac.

Te Awa Farm have several ranges. The main label is "Longlands" although in the mainstream price wise for premium wines, they are often very much in the Top Echelon of all New Zealand wines. The "Longlands" labels include Sauvignon Blanc, Chardonnay, Merlot, Cabernet Merlot Pinotage and Syrah, their super premium wines include "Frontier Chardonnay", which comes from 5 different sites in their vineyards planted to 3 different clones, all picked separately and handled individually, before a rigorous selection of the best parcels to produce a great wine. The top Te Awa Farm Red is their "Boundary" a Merlot dominant Bordeaux style wine, made from Cabernet Sauvignon and Cabernet Franc, again carefully chosen sites are used, with daily monitoring to ensure picking at the ultimate moment for each parcel, the Merlot from a gravelly ridge achieves incredible ripeness and

richness every year.

Jenny Dobson concentrates on complexity as well as bold fruit flavours, her Reds certainly have a silky balanced structure.

The winery includes a cellar shop that is worth a wander. The winery restaurant is one of New Zealand's finest eateries. The winery includes a cellar shop that is worth a wander. The winery restaurant has established a reputation as one of New Zealand's finest eateries. Lunch at Te Awa Farm provides the experience of stunning Hawkes Bay wine matched with fabulous cuisine based principally around local Hawkes Bay produce. If you've tasted "Pacific Oyster Potato Soufflé with Chardonnay cream" with a Frontier Chardonnay, you've certainly pushed your own wine and food experiences past another Frontier. The boundaries of your culinary enjoyment will explode, when you taste his "Grilled Marinated Lamb on soft Polenta with a Merlot essence", a glass of the sublime "Boundary" Red in hand to slide it down.

Te Awa Farm has been aptly named, taken from the Maori "Te Awa O Te Atua" literally means "River of God" describing the mysterious subterranean streams that feed the Te Awa farm's vines, helping to create their Sublime wines.

Address: Roys Hill Rd, SH50, RD5, HASTINGS	**Est:** 1992 **Vine Ha:** 46 **Cases:** 25,000	Longlands Sauvignon Blanc
Phone: +64 6 879 7602 **Fax:** +64 6 879 7756	**Public Hours:** 9am-5pm, daily	Frontier Sauvignon Blanc
Email: winery@teawafarm.co.nz	**Principal Varieties:** Cabernet Sauvignon,	Longlands Chardonnay
WWW: www.teawafarm.co.nz	Malbec, Pinotage, Syrah, Cabernet Franc,	Frontier Chardonnay
Owner: Lawson Family	Chardonnay, Merlot, Sauvignon Blanc	Longlands Merlot
Winemaker: Jenny Dobson	**Principal Wines Potential**	Longlands Syrah

Trinity Hill Vineyard

John Hancock graduated from Roseworthy's Oenology diploma in 1973 the same year as winemaking legends John Duval of Penfolds and Geoff Weaver. After a time making wine for Leo Buring he came to New Zealand in 1979, working as winemaker for Delegats and then Morton Estate for around 15 years.

In 1993 John and several associates bought 45 acres of bare land in the Gimblett Road area of Hawkes Bay, later in 1997 they bought 25 further acres, already under vine.

The first grapes were crushed in 1996. Trinity Hill has developed a world class reputation in a few short years. Their Syrah is absolutely outstanding as are their Gimblett Road Merlot, Cabernet Sauvignon and Chardonnay. Under the Trinity Hill label they also make a Wairarapa Riesling. An excellent second label "Shepherds Croft" includes a Merlot/Cabernet/Syrah Blend a Sauvignon Blanc and a Chardonnay.

Trinity Hill have been most successful on the International Wine scene and are listed on the wine lists of such esteemed restaurants as "Lucas Carton" in Paris, "Gordon Ramseys" in London, "Jean-George" in New York and even at the "French Laundry" in the Napa Valley perhaps America's best Restaurant.

I found the wines not only absolutely top quality but also extremely good value for money. It's certainly worth visiting their interesting and innovative tasting and sales area to seek them out. The winery also has an excellent landscaped picnic area, nestled under the imposing Ridge of Hills behind the Cellars.

Address: 2396 State HWY 50, RD5 HASTINGS	Winemaker: Warren Gibson & John Hancock	Shepherds Croft Sauvignon Blanc	3 yrs
Phone: +64 6 879 7778 Fax: +64 6 879 7770	Est: 1993 Vine Ha: 30 Cases: 35,000	Shepherds Croft Chardonnay	3 yrs
Email: trinityhill@xtra.co.nz	Public Hours: 10am-5pm daily	Shepherds Croft Merlot/Franc/Syrah	3-5 yrs
WWW: www.trinityhill.co.nz	Principal Varieties: Chardonnay, Sauvignon	Gimblett Road Chardonnay	3-5 yrs
Owner: John & Jennifer Hancock,Trevor &	Blanc, Cabernet Sauvignon, Merlot, Syrah	Gimblett Road Cab Sav/Merlot	5+ yrs
Hanne Janes, Robert & Robyn Wilson	Principal Wines Potential	Gimblett Road Merlot	5+ yrs

Unison Vineyard

When we visited vibrant young couple   Bruce and Anna-Barbara Helliwell,

they were excavating gravelly shale soils, next to their winery and typical of the Gimblett Road red wine area, to build an underground cellar to age their wines, which has now been completed.

The Helliwells are red wine specialists producing two outstanding red blends from Merlot, Cabernet and Syrah, they grow in their 15 acre vineyard.

Bruce & Anna-Barbara met whilst making wine in Tuscany.

They have planted their vines in the very close European way and limit their yields to produce concentrated wines.

Their standard label simply called "Unison" is complex and full. Their other and top wine "Unison Selection" has also received rave reviews, the 1998 particularly, is absolutely outstanding.

Unison is a true family boutique and a special place to visit.

Address: 2⁻63 Hwy 50, RD 5 HASTINGS **Phone:** +64 6 879 7913 **Fax:** +64 6 879 7913 **Email:** unison.vineyard@xtra.co.nz	**Winemaker:** Bruce & Anne-Barbara Helliwell **Est:** 1993 **Vine Ha:** 6	**Public Hours:** 9am-5pm, daily **Principal Varieties:** Cabernet Sauvignon, Merlot, Shiraz

Vidal Estate

Situated right in the middle of the Hawkes Bay town of Hastings, it also boasts New Zealand's first Winery Bar Restaurant, opened in 1979. Having enjoyed a meal or two there, I can vouch for its quality and very enjoyable ambience.

Vidal is a vital part of George Fistonich's Villa Maria Group, whilst the winery owns some 50 acres of vines, they have a number of growers under contract, they are also starting to take advantage of grapes from the 'Villa Maria' inspired large vineyard ventures, in the Hawkes Bay region.

The Vidal "Reserve Label" wines have long been recognised as amongst New Zealand's finest wines. The "Reserve" Cabernet Sauvignon/Merlot and the 'Lyons Vineyard Reserve" Merlot/Cabernet Franc, are two extremely fine Bordeaux style wines. The "Reserve" Chardonnay has a long pedigree of success.

Vidal also produce a fine Botrytised

Noble Semillon in years when conditions are right, seek out this wine particularly, it is exceptional.

Vidal have made wine since 1905 their track record is impeccable and their future bright.

Address: 913 St Aubyns St East HASTINGS **Phone:** +64 6 876 8105 **Fax:** +64 6 876 5312 **Winemaker:** Rod McDonald **Est:** 1905	**Public Hours:** 11am-6pm, Mon-Sat; 10:30am-5pm, Sun **Principal Varieties:** Cabernet Franc,	Cabernet Sauvignon, Chardonnay, Chenin Blanc, Malbec, Merlot, Pinot Gris, Pinot Noir, Riesling, Sauvignon Blanc, Semillon

Wairarapa

Wairarapa is the general area of the South Eastern Portion of New Zealand's North Island. It incorporates the Martinborough wine region, one of New Zealand's highest profile wine regions for outweighing in importance. The area of vines planted which accounted for only about 2% of the Nations Vineyard area in 2000.

Wairarapa does very well with Pinot Noir and the aromatic whites such as Riesling, Gewuztraminer and Pinot Gris, maybe this has something to do with its more continental climate than most New Zealand wine regions.

Martinborough has some 23 wineries, who all produce very individual wines. The soil structure varies considerably from rather heavy clay based soil, to River Shale with large stones and many other types.

The Martinborough makers are an eclectic bunch fiercely individual and proud of their wines. The variation from vintage to vintage is more marked than most regions.

Martinborough is probably the worlds most accessible wine region, most of the wineries are literally in the heart of the historic and pretty town, vinerayds and all on the streets interspersed with housing. You can visit a large majority on foot, which is a real advantage during the famous festival "Toast Martinborough" each November. On my visit in mid November there was a sense of excitement in the air as the wineries were busy erecting marquees and preparing for the wine, food, music and cultural extravaganza. New Vineyards plantings are roaring ahead, soon Martinborough will boast size as well as quality.

Wairarapa - NZ

1. Margrain Wines
2. Pallisern Estate
3. Solestone Estate
4. Te Kairanga

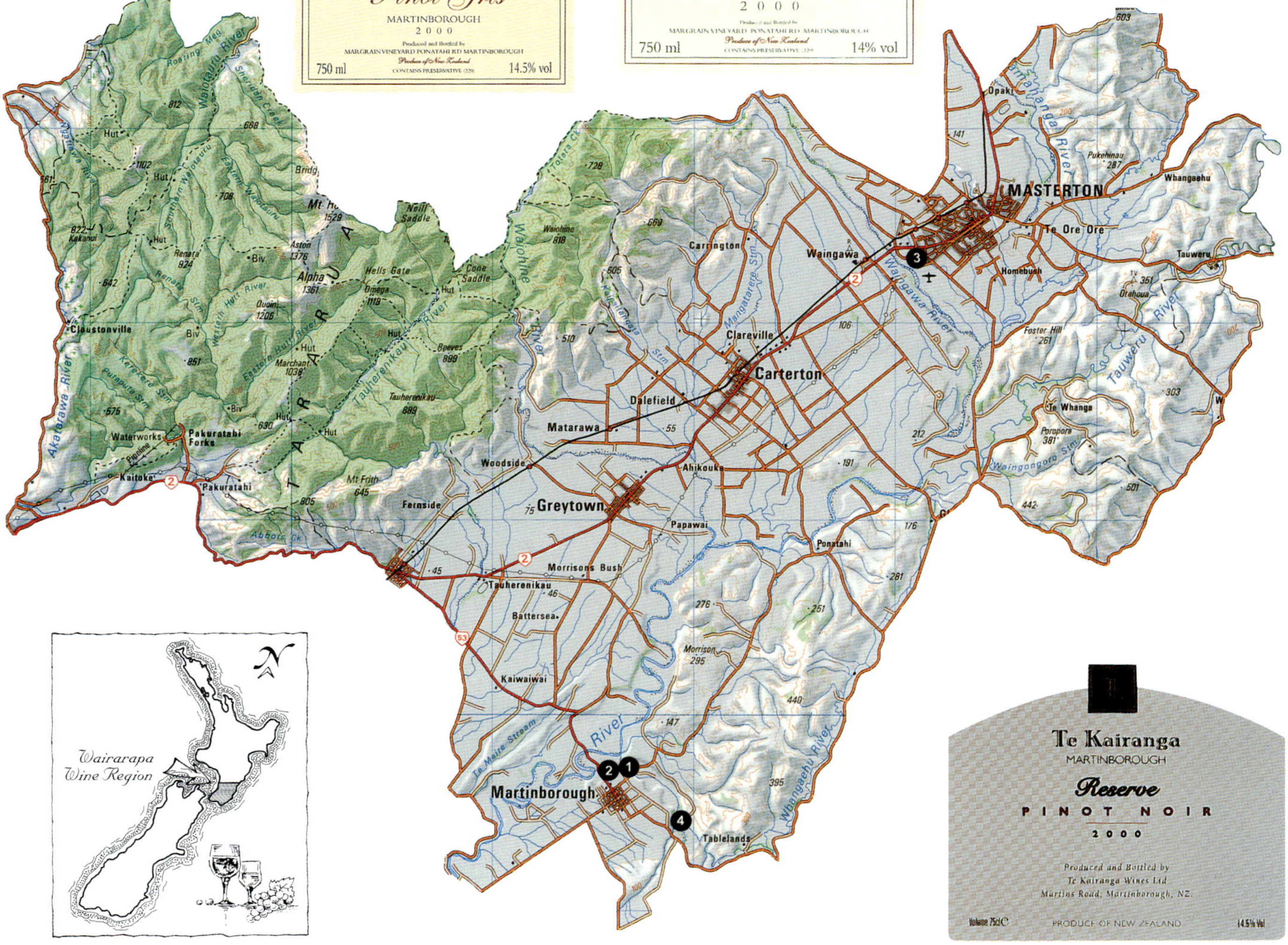

MARGRAIN

Pinot Gris

MARTINBOROUGH

2000

Produced and Bottled by
MARGRAIN VINEYARD PONATAHI RD MARTINBOROUGH
Produce of New Zealand

750 ml   14.5% vol
CONTAINS PRESERVATIVE (220)

MARGRAIN

Pinot Noir

MARTINBOROUGH

2000

Produced and Bottled by
MARGRAIN VINEYARD PONATAHI RD, MARTINBOROUGH
Produce of New Zealand

750 ml   14% vol
CONTAINS PRESERVATIVE (220)

Wairarapa Wine Region

Te Kairanga

MARTINBOROUGH

Reserve

PINOT NOIR

2000

Produced and Bottled by
Te Kairanga Wines Ltd
Martins Road, Martinborough, NZ.

Volume 750 ml   PRODUCT OF NEW ZEALAND   14.5% Vol

Margrain Wines

Margrain has expanded significantly over the last couple of years, with the purchase of Chifney Vineyard and a lease of the Hawthornthwaite Vineyard. Their vintage has more than tripled in size in 2000 although still not large.

Graham Margrain decided to change his lifestyle after 25 years in the building industry, with wife Daryl they bought a property in the edge of the Martinborough Terraces, with beautiful views over the Huangaroa River and the distant mountains.

Graham put his building expertise to good use and apart from constructing a winery built eight self-contained accommodation units located on the Ridge, with exceptional views. Seven more have since been added to giving the Margrains 15 in total.

An old woolshed has been converted to a function and conference centre and many corporate groups are using it during the week.

Winemaker is the talented and affable Strat Canning who is reveling in the expanded operation. The Margrain Merlot is particularly full round and complex as is their Pinot Noir. Strat also produces a "Proprietors Selection" Range. The Riesling has captured many fans, they also make a Pinot Gris and a Chardonnay. Make Margrain a stop over on your New Zealand Wine pilgrimage, you won't be disappointed.

Address: Ponatahi Road MARTINBOROUGH
Phone: +64 6 306 9292 **Fax:** +64 6 309 9297
Email: margrain@xtra.co.nz

WWW: www.margrainvineyard.co.nz
Winemaker: Strat Canning **Est:** 1992
Public Hours: 10am-5pm, Weekends

Principal Varieties: Chardonnay, Chenin Blanc, Gewürztraminer, Merlot, Pinot Gris, Pinot Noir, Riesling

Palliser Estate

Palliser is Martinborough's largest and certainly one of its finest wine producers. At present they have 215 acres under vine, now supplying all their own requirements, this control from the viticulture to the finished wine shows through in the consistently high quality of Palliser's whole range of wines.

Palliser make one of New Zealand's finest Methode Traditionnelle Sparkling wines. They also produce a consistently excellent Sauvignon Blanc, which shows loads of fruit in the tropical spectrum. The Palliser Riesling is an elegant wine with crisp citrus characters. Apart from a Chardonnay they make a complex Pinot Noir which is always amongst the best examples of the variety produced in New Zealand.

Palliser also have a second label "Pencarrow" the wines are a little more straight forward but with excellent balance and good varietal character.

Winemaker Alan Johnson is thoughtful and thorough in his work and his wines reflect this care.

The Palliser tasting area is beautifully appointed and their courtyard garden a top spot to relax and enjoy the wines.

Address: Kitchener St MARTINBOROUGH
Phone: +64 6 306 9019 Fax: +64 6 306 9946
Email: palliser@palliser.co.nz

WWW: www.palliser.co.nz
Winemaker: Allan Johnson **Est:** 1989
Public Hours: 10am-4:30pm, saily; 10:30am-

6pm, Oct-Apr
Principal Varieties: Chardonnay, Pinot Gris, Pinot Noir, Riesling, Sauvignon Blanc

Solestone Estate

The Solestone "Sol" for sun and "stone" for the river stones that are in abundance in their vineyard, which is managed very tightly by Winemaker Luc Desbonnets, whose family were wool traders in the Northern French City of Lille. Luc has the vines on very low trellises and close planted. The suns reflection from the stones and their heat absorption and radiation at night plus shoot and bunch thinning, gives low yielding crops of intensely flavoured grapes, which is evident in the wine.

Luc has also spent some years working in well known French regions, including Pomerol and the Middle European wine regions of Hungary, Moldova and Rumania.

The winery boasts an innovative "slow food" café featuring organic food from the region, cooked in the wood fired pizza oven.

I was particularly impressed with the Sauvignon Blanc with its exotic Lychee and Loquat oriental flavours

and crisp finish. Their reds really impressed me with their intense color and fruit characters, the 1998 Reserve Cabernet Franc "blew me out of the water" with its rose like floral aromas and dense black cherry flavours I scored it 95.5/100.

Solstone is a bright light on the Wairarapa Region which will shine into the future.

Address: 119 Solway Crescent MASTERTON **Phone:** +64 6 377 5505 **Fax:** +64 6 377 7504 **Email:** solstone@xtra.co.nz	**Winemaker:** Luc Desbonnets **Est:** 1982 **Public Hours:** 9am-5pm, Weekdays; 11am-4pm, Weekends	**Principal Varieties:** Cabernet Franc, Cabernet Sauvignon, Chardonnay, Merlot, Pinot Noir, Sauvignon Blanc

Te Kairanga

One of the more established Martinborough wineries is Te Kairanga nestled in a sheltered Valley on the Western outskirts of the region. The name in fact means good soil and plentiful food. The winery and wines have gone through a renaissance over recent years, with more vineyards being purchased. In 1999/2000 20 acres of new vineyards were planted adding to their existing 80 acres. This will expand further to a total of 120 acres.

Whilst Cabernet Sauvignon is not generally a Martinborough specialty, the Te Kairanga 1998 won the trophy for the best wine in the 2000 New Zealand Wine Society Royal Easter Show, although the grapes in future will be sourced from Hawkes Bay as the Martinborough Vines were grafted over in 1999.

Te Kairanga are well respected for their rich complex Chardonnay and

make a Reserve wine as well as their normal label, much of the new plantings have been Pinot Noir and this variety, for which the region is most renowned, will be a focal point of their winemaking development.

The winery and cellar door have loads of old world charm and you will receive a warm welcome at Te Kairanga.

Address: Martins Road MARTINBOROUGH **Phone:** +64 6 306 9122 **Fax:** +64 6 306 9322 **Email:** info@tekairanga.co.nz	**WWW:** www.tkwine.co.nz **Winemaker:** Peter Caldwell **Est:** 1984 **Vine Ha:** 40	**Public Hours:** 10am-5pm, daily **Principal Varieties:** Chardonnay, Pinot Noir, Riesling, Sauvignon Blanc

Nelson

landscape.

Nelson wineries are an eclectic bunch from the extremely small individual boutiques operations to the main stream Seifried Estate with its 250 acres of vineyards and a 900 tonne crush.

Wine tourism is alive and well in the region with many cafes, function and accommodation facilities at the wineries. The new Waimea Estates with its 110 acre vineyards plus a classy café under food wizard, Derek Sheperd, is an exciting development.

Nelson Wineries really come alive at the weekends with lots of music and other events, it's a region not to leave off your wine touring agenda. A wide range of wine styles reflect the myriad of microclimates in this region.

Vying with Waikeke Island as New Zealand's prettiest wine region is

Nelson with its undulating coastal Hills reminiscent of a Tuscan

NELSON
PINOT NOIR
1999
WINE OF NEW ZEALAND

WAIMEA ESTATES 2000
SAUVIGNON BLANC
WINE OF NEW ZEALAND

Nelson Wine Region

Nelson - NZ

1. Kahurangi
2. Seifried
3. Waimea Estate

Kahurangi

Kahurangi is Maori for treasured possession, which is exactly what Amanda and Greg Day consider their Estate which they purchased in November 1998.

Kahurangi is the original family home vineyard and winery of the Regional leaders the Seifried family who first planted vines on the property in the early 1970's.

The Winery café is full of character and serves Tuscan style meats reflecting the uncanny resemblance of its setting to Tuscany. The Days have planted olive trees with a view to making their own olive oil, to use in their restaurant and to produce olive products for sale in their cellar door.

The Riesling and Gewürztraminer from mature vines are both intense and aromatic. Kahurangi also produce Chardonnay and Pinot Noir. They are planting a new vineyard of around 25 acres in the Upper Moutere Valley. The main varieties being Pinot Noir, Pinot Gris, Sauvignon Blanc and Chardonnay.

Amanda Day has used her obvious talents in interior design and décor to turn the characterful cottage in the vineyard into a beautiful retreat which can sleep six, its certainly a great spot to stay over before you move on to Marlborough.

Address: Sunrise Rd UPPER MOUTERE	Est: 1998 Vine Ha: 12.5 Cases: 7,800	Chardonnay	5-8 yrs
Phone: +64 3 543 2980 Fax: +64 3 543 2981	Public Hours: 11am-5pm, daily (Summer);	Riesling	3-7 yrs
Email: kahurangi.estate@xtra.co.nz	Winter weekends only - closed June-August	Dry Riesling	2-5 yrs
WWW: www.kahurangiwine.com	Principal Varieties: Chardonnay, Pinot Noir,	Sauvignon Blanc	2-4 yrs
Owner: Amanda & Greg Day	Sauvignon Blanc, Gewürztraminer, Riesling	Unwooded Chardonnay	2-3 yrs
Winemaker: Saralinda MacMillan	Principal Wines Potential	Pinot Noir	3-5 yrs

Waimea Estate

Waimea Estates was established by a family heavily involved in orchards in the Nelson region, they figured their skills in horticulture combined with the ideal grape growing country of the Waimea plains, would lead them to produce outstanding wine. They have certainly not been disappointed with a Riesling from their first vintage in 1997 winning a trophy for New Zealand's top Riesling in the 1998 Liquorland Easter Wine Show.

In 2000 they sold part of their large 200 acre vineyard they had developed to McCashins the Nelson Brewer, who have started their own winemaking business.

Waimea's Winery and hospitality complex was opened by Prime Minister, the Honourable Jenny Shipley on 18th November 1998. They also took the trophy for the best wine in the Christchurch show,

held to identify New Zealand's best Sauvignon Blanc, with their 1998 Sauvignon Blanc, tasting it at the winery, I was most impressed with its intense gooseberry and passionfruit aromas and flavours. Waimea are working hard to establish themselves as New Zealand's top producers of Pinot Noir, in a mainstream style and price.

The winery café under chef Derek Sheperd is doing exciting things with the bountiful fresh produce of the Nelson Region.

Address: 22 Appleby Highway HOPE	Winemaker: Michael Brown	Principal Varieties: Cabernet Franc,
Phone: +64 3 544 1791 Fax: +64 3 544 6385	Est: 1993	Cabernet Sauvignon, Chardonnay,
Email: waimeaestates@ts.co.nz	Vine Ha: 48	Gewürztraminer, Malbec, Merlot, Pinot Noir,
WWW: www.waimeaestates.co.nz	Public Hours: 10am-5pm, daily	Riesling, Sauvignon Blanc

Seifried

Hermann Seifried is one of the hardest working most down to earth winemakers you'd ever be likely to find. On the day of our visit he was busy in the winery fixing some machinery as well as dealing with other winemaking and bottling chores. Seifried grow nearly all their own grapes in their 250 acres of vineyards, along with making all their wines, they also construct all their stainless steel tanks and some other equipment on site.

In the viticulture area they also produce their own grafted cuttings, in their own vine nursery. They have five different vineyard locations with varieties to match the "Terrior" of each, planting is continuing as they expand their wine production.

Hermann gained his degree in winemaking at Weinsburg in Germany in 1968, before travelling to South Africa where he worked for the Giant KWV, in their "small table wine" cellar.

In 1993 Seifried built a grand hospitality and function center at their new location on Redwood Road Appleby. The restaurant is first class and opens 7 days as week for lunch all year round, plus nightly for dinner in summer and weekends only for dinner in winter.

In 2000 Seifried continued their success in International wine shows, winning two gold medals at the London International wine competition, probably the world's largest wine show, where only five other New Zealand wines won gold medals.

Seifried run a comprehensive tour of the vineyards and winery for visitors, it's a great way to get a more detailed knowledge of vineyards and winemaking.

Seifried have a three tiered range of premium wines, the "Old Coach Road" range is at the entry price level. The unwooded Chardonnay has been particularly successful. The "Seifried Estate" range is in the mainstream, price wise but includes innovative wines, like their "Icewine", a German influenced dessert wine made from frozen grapes. The "Winemakers Selection" label is their flagship, with the Sauvignon Blanc standing out .

Seifried wines I've found of consistently outstanding quality and great value for money.

Why not visit Seifried, take the tour, taste the wines and stay for lunch or dinner.

Address: Redwood Road APPLEBY
Phone: +64 3 544 5599 **Fax:** +64 3 544 5522
Email: wines@seifried.co.nz
Owner: Hermann & Agnes Seifried

Winemaker: Chris Seifried
Est: 1976 **Vine Ha:** 100
Public Hours: 10am-5pm daily
Principal Varieties: Cabernet Sauvignon,

Gewürztraminer, Pinot Noir, Chardonnay,
Merlot, Sauvignon Blanc
Principal Wines **Potential**
Seifried Chardonnay 4 yrs

Marlborough

The Marlborough wine region only came to life in 1973 when Montana planted the first vines. The real boom in planting started after Cloudy Bay released their first Sauvignon Blanc in 1985 and began making a real statement on world wine markets.

The region reminds me much of California's Napa Valley, with its elongated valley surrounded by Mountains on three sides and a wide shallow bay on the other, it also has its share of mists in autumn that contribute to botrytised wines of exceptional quality.

Soils vary but are basically river loam and silt interspersed with round river stones reminiscent of "Chateau Neuf du Pape" these aid drainage plus retain and emit heat particularly at night. Mild wet winters lead to cool dry summers with lots of sunlight, it's a paradise for the vine.

With over 9000 acres under vine Marlborough is by far New Zealand's largest wine region, accounting for around 40% of the nations vineyard area.

The main Wairau Valley is fast filling with vines and the price of land has skyrocketed, a number of satilite valleys and being developed specifically the Awatere Valley to the south, bordering on the coast, but other valleys and some of the foothills are now being developed.

Marlborough is developing into a true, international wine tourism destination, many wineries have café restaurants and a growing number have classy vineyard accommodation facilities. There are also many up-market bed and breakfast establishments and plenty of innovative restaurants. Olive groves are springing up everywhere and the ideal horticultural conditions are fostering the growing of fresh vegetables, fruits and herbs, it's nature's paradise.

Apart from Sauvignon Blanc which accounts for over a third of the production. Chardonnay and Pinot Noir are the next two stars, which are also being used to produce an expanding quantity of Methode Traditionnelle sparkling wines. Riesling is often overlooked, it produces vibrant exciting wines, particularly the botrytised variety.

Marlborough also has a special quality of light, which leads to breathtakingly beautiful landscape scenes, magnificently captured by one of the world's best wine photographers, Kevin Judd. Kevin, a top class winemaker, was also responsible for the first Sauvignon Blanc, at Cloudy Bay, that put Marlborough on the map as a world class wine region.

Marlborough

Marlborough

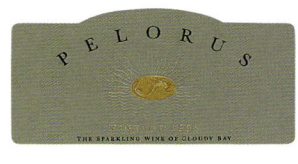
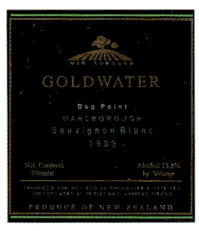

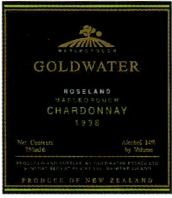

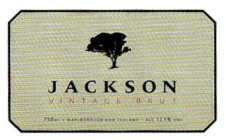

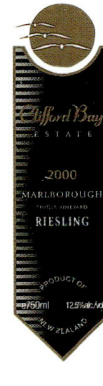

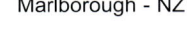

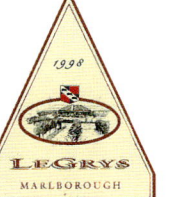

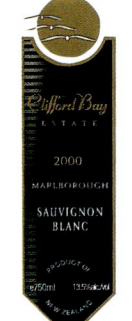
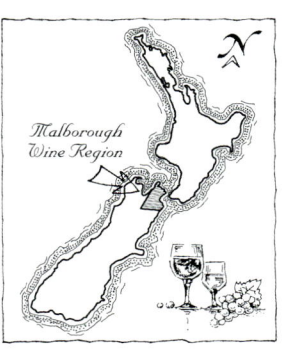

Marlborough - NZ

1. Allan Scott Wines
2. Brancott Montana
3. Cellier Le Brun
4. Clifford Bay
5. Cloudy Bay
6. Domaine Georges Michel
7. Drylands Estate
8. Forrest Estate
9. Framingham
10. Grove Mill
11. Huia Wines
12. Hunters Wines
13. Isabel
14. Jackson Estate
15. Lawsons
16. Le Brun Family
17. Mudhouse - Le Grys
18. Nautilas Estate
19. Ponder Estate
20. Shingle Peak
21. Stoneleigh Vineyard
22. Vavasour Wines
23. Villa Maria Winery
24. Wairau River
25. Whitehaven Wine Co.
26. Wither Hills

Allan Scott Wines

administration.

Their daughter Victoria ably assists Catherine in the sales and hospitality side. Victoria, together with husband Daniel control the cellar door and restaurant complex.

The Scotts son Joshua has a diploma in viticulture and winemaking achieved at the Marlborough polytech and is involved in the winemaking. Youngest daughter Sara is currently studying but is a helping hand in all aspects of the establishment.

In 1997 Allan Scott Wines saw the release of an excellent sparkling Methode Traditionnelle and 'prestige' range of wines including Cabernet Sauvignon, Chardonnay and Merlot along with the original Allan Scott Chardonnay, Sauvignon, Riesling, Pinot Noir and Autumn Riesling.

I found their Sauvignon Blanc to be very much in the tropical spectrum, with some exotic Jasmine and Lychee characters, plus pineapple, passionfruit and citrus flavours, very much my style, the Chardonnay I found also very fruit driven with melon and apricot flavours and a spicy toasty finish · delicious.

They also make a top late picked Autumn Riesling, some vintages are very concentrated, when the "noble rot", botrytis, is more prevalent. Their other Riesling is dry crisp and aromatic, a great food wine.

The family owned company Allan Scott Wines and Estates Ltd in Jacksons Road, Marlborough, has fast cemented its place among the province's top wine producers.

A family venture established in 1990 and managed by Catherine and Allan Scott. Allan Scott is a pioneer of the Marlborough wine region who has been a leader in every aspect of its development.

Catherine is born and raised in the Marlborough region. She is involved

in the winemaking process, sales and

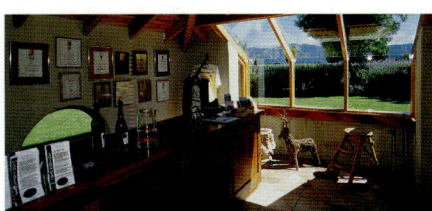

Address: Jacksons Road RD3 BLENHEIM	Winemaker: Graeme Bradshaw		Allan Scott Chardonnay	5 yrs
Phone: +64 3 572 9054 Fax: +64 3 572 9053	Est: 1990	Cases: 60,000	Allan Scott Sauvignon	2 yrs
Email: scott.wines@xtra.co.nz	Public Hours: 9am-4:30pm, daily		Allan Scott Riesling	10 yrs
WWW: www.allanscott.co.nz	Principal Wines	Potential	Methode Traditional	10 yrs
Owner: Allan & Catherine Scott	Prestige Chardonnay	6 yrs	Autumn Riesling Late Harvest	6 yrs

Clifford Bay

Eric Bowers left a long career in the oil industry to become a viticulturalist and vigneron in the Marlborough region, he and wife Beverley, along with some partners, bought 50 acres of land in a river flood plain near the coast in the Awatere Valley.

They began planting in 1994. The first wine, a Sauvignon Blanc, was made by Glenn Thomas at the nearby Vavasour Winery, took all before it, 3 gold medals in three wine shows, they ferment a small percentage of their Sauvignon Blanc in French oak barriques giving a lift and complexity. The '98,'99 and 2000 have all received rave reviews from the critics.

1998 Vintage saw the first Chardonnay, with their single vineyard Chardonnay, a wine with real weight and richness, assisted by fermentation and maturation, in new plus 2 year old French oak casks,

complimenting the strong peach and melon flavours of the fruit. The 1999 and 2000 vintages have shown even more complexity and interest.

In 1999 Clifford Bay Estate made their first Riesling, a fresh intense

wine with crisp lime/citrus characters and floral overtones, a wine which is sure to age well, if you can keep your hands off it that long!!

Clifford Bay are white wine champions.

Address: 26 Rapaura Road BLENHEIM	**Owner:** Eric & Beverley Bowers	Sauvignon Blanc
Phone: +64 3 572 7148 **Fax:** +64 3 572 7138	**Winemaker:** Glenn Thomas	**Principal Wines Potential**
Restaurant Phone: +64 3 572 7132	**Est:** 1994 **Vine Ha:** 20 **Cases:** 10,000	Clifford Bay Estate Sauvignon Blanc 2-3 yrs
Email: clifford.bay.estate@xtra.co.nz	**Public Hours:** 10am-5pm daily	Clifford Bay Estate Chardonnay 5 yrs
WWW: www.cliffordbay.co.nz	**Principal Varieties:** Riesling, Chardonnay,	Clifford Bay Estate Riesling 5 yrs

Huia Wines

Huia is owned and operated by Claire and Mike Allan, who studied at Roseworthy in South Australia. Their enterprise has gone through some amazing growth phases since they first started making wine in 1996.

They began with a vineyard of 21 acres of Raupara Road and made their wine off site, in the Awatere Valley at Vavasour Winery.

In 1998, they redesigned two off the rack farm sheds into an impressive looking winery and cellar door sales area.

The first wine to really capture the wine drinkers imagination was their Gewurztraminer, a full flavoured spicy and yet dry wine. Claire and Mark concentrate on getting their grapes fully ripe, then hand pick and whole bunch press most of them. This is an expensive and time consuming

process but it is also suitable for their Methode Traditionnelle Brut, Chardonnay, Riesling and Pinot Gris. Huia also produces a complex Pinot Noir and flavoursome Marlborough Sauvignon Blanc.

The rustic cellar door has much character and charm. It is open over summer months and is a great place to try Claire and Mike's very personal hand crafted wines.

Address: Boyces Road, RD3 BLENHEIM	**Est:** 1996 **Vine Ha:** 33 **Cases:** 14,500	Huia Sauvignon Blanc	5 yrs
Phone: +64 3 572 8326 **Fax:** +64 3 5728 331	**Public Hours:** 11am-5pm, daily (Summer);	Huia Gewürztraminer	10 yrs
Email: wine@huia.net.nz	Winter reduced hours	Huia Reisling	8 yrs
WWW: www.huia.net.nz	**Principal Varieties:** Gewürztraminer, Pinot	Huia Pinot Gris	8 yrs
Owner: Claires & Mike Allan	Noir, Sauv Blanc, Chard, Pinot Gris, Riesling	Huia Chardonnay	5 yrs
Winemaker: Claire & Mike Allan	**Principal Wines** **Potential**	Huia Pinot Noir	5 yrs

Cloudy Bay

If any one winery has put New Zealand wines firmly on the world wine map it is Cloudy Bay.

David Hohnen became a stellar red wine producer in Margaret River with Cape Mentelle vineyards, which he established in 1972. His 1982 Cabernet Merlot won the Jimmy Watson Memorial Trophy, Australia's most prestigious red wine award, to show it was no fluke he went on to win it again the next year with his 1983 vintage.

David was looking for a location to make a world beating white wine, he settled on Marlborough, after tasting some sauvignon blancs given to him by a group of Marlborough winemakers visiting Margaret River. He set up Cloudy Bay and crushed his first grapes in 1985.

Today Cloudy Bay Vineyards is owned by French Champagne house Veuve Cliquot Ponsardin. Cloudy Bay is a specialist premium wine producer and together with its sister winery Cape Mentelle, shares a commitment to 'wines of region'. The winery and vineyards are situated in the Wairau Valley in Marlborough, with it's unique and cool maritime climate and the longest hours of sunshine of any place in New Zealand.

Cloudy Bay has 325 acres of estate vineyards and long term supply agreements with five Wairau Valley growers. The main varieties grown are Sauvignon Blanc, Chardonnay and Pinot Noir with lesser quantities of Semillon, Riesling and Gewurztraminer, the annual crush is around 1200 tonnes.

The winery takes its name from the bay at the eastern extremity of the Wairau Valley, named Cloudy Bay by Captain Cook on his voyage to New Zealand in 1770.

Cloudy Bay is export oriented with 20 markets worldwide, the principal ones being Australia, United Kingdom, USA, Europe and Japan.

Winemaker at Cloudy Bay since its inception is Kevin Judd one of New Zealand's most respected winemakers, who created the now legendary Cloudy Bay Sauvignon Blanc. Kevin is a passionate perfectionist, whose contribution to New Zealand's wine industry is well acknowledged by his industry peers.

In 1986 the highly successful Sauvignon Blanc was joined by Cloudy Bay Chardonnay and subsequently Cloudy Bay Pinot Noir was introduced. Kevin is responsible for the day-to-day management of the company and also oversees the production of Pelorus, Cloudy Bay's stunning sparkling wine, first made in 1987, and heralded as one of the pre-eminent sparkling styles of the Antipodes.

Trained at Roseworthy Agricultural College, Kevin first made wine at Chateau Reynella in South Australia, he moved to New Zealand to join Selaks Wines in Auckland in 1983, before becoming the inaugural winemaker at Cloudy Bay in 1985. His 1996 Sauvignon Blanc was rated by the respected Wine Spectator Magazine as one of the 10 finest wines in the world, released in 1997, sharing this honour with such wines as Chateau d'Yquem and Robert Mondavi Reserve Chardonnay.

He is an active participant in national industry activities and is one of the world's finest wine photographers.

Cloudy Bay will continue to expand. The company believes that the future success of specialist wineries lies in the production of premium wines from varieties best suited to specific regions. Emphasis is placed on individual fruit character and the development of a recognisable estate wine style. To say they have been successful in this mission is a gross understatement!!

Address: PO Box 376 BLENHEIM	**Winemaker:** Kevin Judd & James Healy	Cloudy Bay Sauvignon Blanc
Phone: +64 3 520 9149	**Est:** 1985 **Vine Ha:** 135	Cloudy Bay Pinot Noir
Fax: +64 3 520 9040	**Cases:** 100,000	Pelorus N.V
Email: info@cloudybay.co.nz	**Public Hours:** 10am-4:30pm, daily	Cloudy Bay Chardonnay
WWW: www.cloudybay.co.nz	**Principal Wines**	Cloudy Bay Te Koko

Domaine Georges Michel

In 1998 Georges Michel purchased the winery and vineyards of Merlen Wines. Georges has a winery in Beaujolais, in his French homeland and a chain of hotels. After doing considerable work on his Marlborough winery and putting in a full restaurant, he now makes Marlborough his home, whilst travelling frequently to oversee his worldwide wine and hospitality businesses.

The Domaine Sauvignon Blanc is definitely in the tropical spectrum whilst "La Reserve" Chardonnay shows the influence of fermentation in French (naturally) oak barriques. A Pinot Noir has been added with the 2000 vintage.

The Cellar Sales area and restaurant have loads of French character and charm and you can also buy two of George's French wines, "Chateau du Grand Mont" Beaujolais and "Chateau des Pethieres" Brouilly. The restaurant is an ideal place to try the

French wines along with the   Domaines local wines.

Address: Vintage Lane, RD 3 BLENHEIM	Email: georgesmichel@xtra.co.nz	Public Hours: 9am-5pm, daily
Phone: +64 3 572 7230	Winemaker: Guy Brac de la Perriere	Principal Varieties: Chardonnay, Pinot Noir,
Fax: +64 3 572 7231	Est: 1988	Sauvignon Blanc

Le Brun Family

Daniel Le Brun was a pioneer of Methode Traditionnelle sparkling wines, in New Zealand, when he brought his finely honed Champagne making making skills from his French homeland and founded Cellier Le Brun in the Marlborough Region. Whilst he has sold this business some years ago he and his wife Adele have built a beautiful Sparkling wine facility on Rapaura Road. The Le Brun's first vintage was 1996. They only use grapes grown in their own 10 acre vineyard, solely for their Methode Traditionnelle production.

The first wine released in 2000 was their "Daniel No. 1" Methode Traditionnelle Blanc de Blancs, they have since followed this up with a "1996 Vintage Methode Traditionnelle"made from a Pinot Noir/Chardonnay Cuvee.

Daniels skills and experience in Champenoise production and his hand crafting of his wines, leads to finely balanced elegant methode traditionelles, with fine bead, elegant flavours and creamy overtones from subtle yeast autolysis.

These are sparkling wines to truly celebrate.

| Address: 169 Rapaura Rd, RD 3 MARLBOROUGH | Email: lbfe@voyager.co.nz | Public Hours: 10am-4pm, daily (Summer) |
| Phone: +64 3 572 9876 Fax: +64 3 572 9875 | Winemaker: Daniel Le Brun | Principal Varieties: Chardonnay |

Cellier Le Brun

Cellier Le Brun is one of New Zealand's original sparkling wine producers, who have done fine things in a climate ideally suited to sparkling wine production. These days they also produce a range of premium table wines under the "Terrace Road" label.

The crush at Cellier Le Brun has increased dramatically in recent years. They now have a substantial 50 acres under vine.

The cellars also sport a successful restaurant that has undergone substantial renovations recently. Both the restaurant and cellars are built into the hillside, giving ideal cool conditions in summer and creating a special atmosphere for the maturation on tirage, of their methode traditionelle, sparkling wines.

The "Daniel Le Brun 1995 Millennium Cuvee" has been a great success as has their Blanc de Blancs Methode Traditionnelle. They also produce a "Brut Tache" with a touch of "salmon pink" colour.

Cellier Le Brun is a great place to have a pre lunch or dinner "Champers" and stay for a meal.

Address: PO BOX 33 RENWICK	**WWW:** www.lebrun.co.nz	**Public Hours:** 9am-5pm, daily
Phone: +64 3 572 8859 **Fax:** +64 3 572 8814	**Winemaker:** Allan McWilliams	**Principal Varieties:** Chardonnay, Chenin
Email: lebrun@xtra.co.nz	**Est:** 1985	Blanc, Pinot Meunier, Pinot Noir, Sauv Blanc

Jackson Estate

John Stichbury's grandfather Adam Jackson brought a property on Jackson Road over 120 years ago, he was already farming in the area. Today the 105 acre vineyard which is one of the few non-irrigated in the region, produces concentrated flavours, on the rich river silts.

The Jackson Estate Sauvignon Blanc which was first produced in 1991 has gained many awards and is always one of the finest in the region. The wines are made by fastidious and talented Australian winemaker Martin Shaw, who with his cousin,

Micheal Hill-Smith, has a high profile winery in Australia, specialisng in Sauvignon Blanc. Martin was for many years Chief winemaker for the high profile Petaluma winery of Brian Croser.

Jackson Estate also produce a very good Chardonnay plus a Chardonnay Reserve in exceptional years, a Riesling plus a botrytis Riesling in suitable years, a Pinot Noir and a fine vintage Brut Sparkling, methode traditionnelle.

Jackson Estate wines do not have their own cellar door but their wines are available at Cellier Le Brun.

Address: Jacksons Road MARLBOROUGH	**Winemaker:** Martin Shaw	Sauvignon Blanc	3-5 yrs
Phone: +64 3 572 8287 **Fax:** +64 3 572 9500	**Est:** 1989 **Vine Ha:** 60 **Cases:** 25,000	Chardonnay	5-7 yrs
Email: jacksone@voyager.co.nz	**Principal Varieties:** Pinot Noir, Sauvignon	Reisling (Marlborough Dry)	5-7 yrs
WWW: www.jacksonestate.co.nz	Blanc, Chardonnay, Riesling	Pinot Noir	5-7 yrs
Owner: John Stichbury	**Principal Wines** **Potential**	Jackson Vintage	5-7 yrs

Oyster Bay Estate

Oyster Bay wines from the Marlborough region are gaining a growing following in many sophisticated and wine savvy international markets. The label is owned by the Delegat's family wine company and was launched with the 1990 vintage (The Sauvignon Blanc immediately winning the accolade of 'Best Sauvignon Blanc worldwide' at The International Wine & Spirit Competition in London). The Oyster Bay range features a sauvignon blanc and a chardonnay with the exciting prospect of a pinot noir being added within the next couple of years.

The Oyster Bay philosophy is to produce fine distinctly regional wines that are both elegant and assertive, with powerful fruit flavours, wines you can drink on release and which have the structure and balance to reward cellaring · in short, the styles that have made Marlborough famous.

The vineyards are planted in the prime central Wairau Valley on shallow stony soils over deep layers of free draining river shingle, ideal for reducing vine vigour and encouraging the sauvignon blanc, chardonnay and pinot noir grapes to achieve maximum concentrated fruit flavours. The aspect of the land, the direction of the vine rows, spacing, and trellis configuration together with the techniques of pruning, canopy and soil moisture management being followed, mean the grapes harvested are absolutely top class.

Oyster Bay Sauvignon Blanc has received plenty of critical acclaim and is recognised as one of the finest examples of this icon New Zealand wine style. It has lots of lively zesty penetrating fruit aromas and flavours with fresh ripe melon with a nice capsicum edge and a lingering finish. The wine is bottled immediately after winemaking to retain all the fruit flavours and aromas.

Oyster Bay Chardonnay has the typically Marlborough characters of incisive ripe fruit, which is nicely balanced by top quality oak used in a sensitive manner. During their 6 months in oak the wines are lees stirred to help them achieve maximum softness and integration but there is no malo-lactic fermentation to make sure the crisp fruit flavours are retained. The fruit is beautifully balanced by a svelte vanilla toastiness from the oak.

Delegat's are responding to the international success of Oyster Bay with significant new Marlborough investments. In 1999 Delegat's promoted the public float of Oyster Bay Marlborough Vineyards Limited. This vineyard owning company, in which Delegat's has a 30% shareholding, is progressively developing a 250 hectare plus vineyard in the heart of the Wairau Valley. The vineyard is projected to eventually yield approximately 59% sauvignon blanc, 33% chardonnay and 8% pinot noir.

In addition, Delegat's has also recently unveiled plans to build a new state-of-the-art winery in the Wairau Valley · the NZ$12 million first stage is expected to be ready for the 2003 harvest.

Drylands Estate

The Drylands Winery was built as a state of the art facility in 1995. It is one of the largest winemaking facilities in New Zealand and makes much of the premium wines of the Nobilo/Selaks group owned by Australian giant premium wines producer BRL Hardy Ltd.

The site of the original winery was "Rosetree Cottage" and one of the original roses still grows outside the winery. The Rosetree property was once farmed by ancestors of Nobilo executive Peter McDonald.

The 40 acre Dyrlands Vineyard was planted in 1980/81 largely to Sauvignon Blanc and it is one of the oldest vineyards in the region mostly planted on its own roots, not grafted, certainly the Sauvignon Blanc it produces is concentrated and truly outstanding every year. The alluvial soils provide the finer characters which are the heart of the Sauvignon Blanc.

Long time winemaker is Darryl Woolley a talented Australian, who is right at home in Marlborough. He oversees a large range of wines under the Selaks and Nobilo brands, many of which are of gold medal quality at very affordable prices.

The Selaks "Premium Selection" range, at less than NZ$15, is exceptional value. It includes an award winning Sauvignon Blanc, Chardonnay, Riesling, Cabernet Sauvignon, a Methode Traditionnelle and an amazing Ice Wine, made by freezing the grapes in a tank and separating the water, in the form of ice crystals, from the grape sugars, flavours and acid, making a concentrated sweet dessert wine that is beautifully crisp and most affordable, at not much over NZ$15 per half bottle.

The next range up the premium ladder is the "Drylands" label, which includes a Pinot Noir, Merlot, Chardonnay, Pinot Gris and Pinot Noir.

The Flagship label is the Selaks "Founders Reserve" which includes an oak aged Sauvignon Blanc, always an intense wine, there is also a Merlot, a Chardonnay and a Noble Riesling.

Drylands is a very well set up winery, with an excellent cellar sales and tasting area, it's well worth checking out, I'm sure you'll find the wine for you at a price to suit.

Address: Hammerichs Road RAPAURA	**Winemaker:** Brian Vieceli **Vine Ha:** 130	**Principal Varieties:** Cabernet Sauvignon,
Phone: −64 3 570 5252 **Fax:** +64 3 570 5272	**Public Hours:** 9am-5pm, Mon-Sat; 11am-	Chardonnay, Gewürztraminer, Merlot, Pinot
WWW: www.nobilo.co.nz **Est:** 1996	4pm, Sun	Noir, Riesling, Sauvignon Blanc, Semillon

Grove Mill

Grove Mill is one of the larger and more established wine producers in the Marlborough region making their first vintage in 1988. Their vineyard holdings have expanded considerably in recent years and they now cover 165 acres, much of which is still coming into production. Grove Mill have an increasing number of excellent growers who work closely with their viticulturalist and winemaker.

The Grove Mill complex is very well put together and houses New Zealand's only 'Vine Library', outside the tasting room. It features ten individual rows of different grape varieties. Visitors can see, taste and smell the grapes whilst tasting the wines they are made from.

Grove Mill also has a showpiece "Wetland" covering 2.5 acres of beautiful ponds. 3,000 native trees and shrubs have been planted and it has become the home to many native birds, including Grey and Shoveler ducks, Shags, Pukekos, New Zealand Tree Frogs and the Southern Bell Frog, which is also featured on the winery's labels. The wetland has just won the 2001 Habitat Enhancement Award, at the Marlborough Rural

Environment Awards. A boardwalk will be constructed in the future through this wonderful wetland, which is connected by a pathway through a native plant museum to the Vine Library. It's an enjoyable and educational stroll.

Grove Mill are doing a great job with the exciting Pinot Gris grape (they were the first in the region to plant this grape variety) which produces a lively fruit driven style that slides down smoothly indeed. The Grove Mill Chardonnay is also a very successful wine. Naturally Grove Mill

produce the icon Marlborough variety Sauvignon Blanc, being the first to win the New Zealand Champion Wine of Show, also winning Blue Gold at the Sydney 'Top 100' four years out of the past five. This wine has also been named in the Top 10 Wines of The World with Oysters, 3 years running, at Washington's "Old Ebbitt Grill" awards in the USA. In their main range they also have a silky Merlot with loads of plummy fruit showing some subtle classy oak handling.

Grove Mill have a second range of wines under the Sanctuary label. These wines often win awards and are selling at extraordinarily reasonable prices. As well as a Sauvignon Blanc and a Chardonnay they also produce an off-dry fragrant Riesling. The Sanctuary range also includes a very good Pinotage/Pinot Noir blend, these wines are mainstream in style and well worth the trip to Grove Mill to try them.

Grove Mill is a very professionally run operation with great wines, which promotes itself well on world wine markets and is a credit to New Zealand's wine industry.

Address: PO Box 67 Waihopai Valley Road, RENWICK	**Winemaker:** David Pearce	Grove Mill Marlborough Sauv Blanc	4 yrs
	Est: 1988 **Vine Ha:** 100 **Cases:** 75,000	Grove Mill Marlborough Chardonnay	2-4 yrs
Phone: +64 3 572 8200	**Public Hours:** 11am-5pm, daily	Grove Mill Marlborough Riesling	6 yrs
Fax: +64 3 572 8211	**Principal Varieties:** Pinot Gris, Riesling,	Grove Mill Marlborough Pinot Gris	4-6 yrs
Email: info@grovemill.co.nz	Chardonnay, Pinot Noir, Sauvignon Blanc	Grove Mill Marlborough Pinot Noir	4 yrs
WWW: www.grovemill.co.nz	**Principal Wines** **Potential**	Sanctuary Marlborough Sauv Blanc	2-3 yrs

Forrest Estate

Doctor's John and Brigid Forrest's winemaking team are amongst the most highly technically trained winemakers in New Zealand, they are also delightful people, passionate about their wines and keen to share their enthusiasm and knowledge with all who visit their special Estate, where every visitor gets a unique, structured wine tasting.

They recently opened a beautiful new hospitality and wine education complex in front of their efficient and friendly winery.

The Forrest Estate was established in 1988, although the Forrest family has deep roots in Marlborough, arriving with the first wave of European settlers to farm the land. Born in Marlborough, John has enjoyed an international career in biochemistry, before returning home where he has successfully combined

his family farming heritage, with the technical skills of the scientist to winegrowing.

The family's 175 acres of vines and winery lie in the centre of the Wairau River valley near Renwick, 10 kilometers from Blenheim.

The Forrest's winegrowing philosophy is to produce fully ripened grapes and then, with creative winemaking, give a personal expression to their fresh varietal fruit characters.

Forrest Estate have a wide range of wines for a moderately small producer. Some are mainstream others not, such as their Malbec, I tasted the 1999 out of Barrel, with John and was most impressed by its huge Cassis fruit and its restrained fine tannins. Forrest also produce a very good Rose. The Forrests also have a joint venture with Australian Viticulturist Bob Newton, "Newton Forrest" in the renowned Gimblett Road area of Hawkes Bay. Their cornerstone Cabernet Merlot is a regular gold medal winner and available at the winery for tasting and purchase, along with all the other wines.

Address: Blicks Road, RENWICK	**Est:** 1988	Sauvignon Blanc	
Phone: +64 3 572 9084 **Fax:** +64 3 572 9086	**Vine Ha:** 60	Estate Dry Riesling	5-7 yrs
Email: forrestj@voyager.co.nz	**Public Hours:** 10am-4:30pm daily	Chardonnay	3-5 yrs
WWW: www.forrest.co.nz	**Principal Varieties:** Pinot Noir, Sauvignon	Gewürztraminer	2-4 yrs
Owner: John & Brigid Forrest	Blanc, Riesling	Pinot Noir	2-5 yrs
Winemaker: John Forrest	**Principal Wines** **Potential**	Botrytised Semillon/Sauvignon Blanc	2-4 yrs

Framingham

Framingham is a show piece winery, an absolute joy to the eye, where no detail has been left to chance. You enter the enclosed courtyard through a portal in the walled garden. Immediately you are struck by the neat profusion of colourful flowers, looked after by in house gardener Jane White, who designed the garden with Director Rex Brooke-Taylor. The entire garden is replanted twice a year with 1,500 annuals which Jane raises from seed in her own propagation shed. On the southern side of the winery is a native garden showcasing over 100 New Zealand native species occurring in the Marlborough Region.

When one enters the winery reception and tasting area the warm rich décor and furnishings provide an ideal environment to taste the exciting wines. There is also a

warmly lit underground cellar.

Framingham's aromatic whites, not surprisingly, exhibit lots of floral character and are clean and fresh. The dry, medium dry and Reserve late harvest Riesling (with botrytis influence) are all rated in the absolute top echelon of New Zealand's aromatic wines, they have been joined by a Gewürztraminer and

a Pinot Gris.

The Framingham reds include Pinot Noir, Merlot and the interesting Italian Red. Montepulciano. Recently an extra 300 acres of land has been purchased and planting of more aromatic white varieties is underway.

Framingham is an essential stop on your Marlborough meanderings.

Address: Conders Bend Road RENWICK	**Public Hours:** 10am-5pm daily (Summer);	Framingham Sauvignon Blanc	5 yrs
Phone: +64 3 572 8884 Fax: +64 3 572 9884	11am-4pm daily (Winter)	Framingham Classic Riesling	5 yrs
Email: framwine@voyager.co.nz	**Principal Varieties:** Riesling, Sauvignon	Framingham Pinot Noir	5 yrs
WWW: www.framingham.co.nz	Blanc, Pinot Gris, Gewürztraminer, Pinot Noir,	Framingham Pinot Gris	5 yrs
Winemaker: Antony Mackenzie	Chardonnay, Merlot	Framingham Gewürztraminer	5 yrs
Est: 1994 **Vine Ha:** 40 **Cases:** 25,000	**Principal Wines** **Potential**	Framingham Dry Riesling	10 yrs

Hunters Wines

If the New Zealand wine industry had a royal family, the Queen would certainly be Jane Hunter O.B.E. who was recognised by the British Royal family in 1993 for her contribution to New Zealand viticulture. Jane has the style of a true diplomat and spends much of her time travelling the world promoting New Zealand wine and her beloved Hunter's Wines.

Jane has her feet very firmly based in the soil. She grew up on her family's vineyards in Barmera in South Australia's Riverland, which her father still runs, as well as having a 10 acre vineyard near Blenheim, supplying Hunters.

Jane never planned to be involved with vineyards. She has a degree in Agricultural Science from Adelaide University and started her career in farming on the isolated West Coast South Australian town of "Streaky Bay". She then opted for viticulture and at the tender age of 27 travelled to New Zealand to work for Montana as their national viticulturalist.

She met and married Ernie Hunter who had hotels in Christchurch and had started New Zealand's first discount liquor chain. In 1983 they launched their winery and made their first wines, with borrowed equipment from an old cider factory in Christchurch.

Four years later, after Ernie's sudden death, Jane took over the management of Hunter's Wines. The winery has continued to grow in size,

annual output and reputation. Hunters are well set with 37 hectares of its own vineyards and 46 hectares under contract in the Wairau Valley.

To date, Hunters Wines have won more than 60 gold medals at national and international wine competitions, as well as a host of other awards.

Jane takes the most pride in having received the trophy for the best Sauvignon Blanc, at the New Zealand National Wine Show in 1989. Only bottled ten days before the show, it also went on to top the Decanter magazine tasting in England, out of 130 Sauvignon Blancs tasted from around the world.

Hunter's Wines 1991 Sauvignon Blanc achieved unprecedented honours by winning both a gold medal and the Marquis de Goulaine Trophy as the best Sauvignon Blanc in the world at the 1992 International Wine & Spirit Competition.

In 1995 Hunter's Wines claimed another international success, by gaining the inaugural Black Diamond Award at the 1995 InterVine International Wine Competition in North America. Hunter's were one of only nine wineries world wide to win the three gold medals required to qualify for the top award.

In 1997 in London, Jane launced a new blend of Methode Champenoise, an innovative product specifically designed by the team at Hunter's

Wines for the British market, called Miru Miru (Maori for "bubble"). The wine has been a great success, with Miru Miru 1995 winning a Gold Medal and the James Rogers Memorial Trophy at the International Wine Challenge in the UK in 1998 and in 2001 Miru Miru 1997 won a Gold Medal at the Sunday Times Wine Club.

Visitors are welcome to spend time at the winery. As well as tasting current wines, visitors can enjoy a meal at Hunter's restaurant, cool off in the pool during Marlborough's summer and just relax in the beautiful native garden setting. There is also Artist in Residence, Clarry Neame, to visit.

Jane's hard work, drive and commitment to the Hunter's Wines quality standards has led to the success of the winery over the past ten years. It is her expertise and that of the team at Hunter's Wines, which ensures the consistently high quality of the wines produced and the hospitality facilities, which ensures recognition of the winery as one of world standing.

Jane's hard work drive and commitment to the Hunters Wines quality standards has led to the success of the winery over the past ten years. It is her expertise and that of the team at Hunter's Wines, which ensures the consistently high quality of the wines produced and the hospitality facilities, which ensures recognition of the winery as one of world standing.

Address: Rapaura Road BLENHEIM	Est: 1979 Vine Ha: 37 Cases: 44,000	Hunters Sauvignon Blanc	2 yrs
Phone: +64 3 572 8489 Fax: +64 3 572 8457	Public Hours: 9:30am-4:30pm Mon-Sat,	Winemakers Selection Sauv Blanc	4 yrs
Email: hunters@voyager.co.nz	10am-4pm Sun	Hunters Chardonnay	5 yrs
WWW: www.hunters.co.nz	Principal Varieties: Chardonnay, Merlot,	Hunters Pinot Noir	4-5 yrs
Owner: Jane Hunter O.B.E; Hon. D.Sc	Pinot Noir, Riesling, Sauvignon Blanc	Hunters Brut	6 yrs
Winemaker: Gary Duke	Principal Wines Potential	Hunters Riesling	3-4 yrs

Isabel

Isabel Estate Vineyard was established in 1982 for the production of premium classical grape varieties.

Prior to the 1994 vintage, Proprietor Michael Tiller, then an airline pilot with Air New Zealand, together with his wife Robyn, operated Isabel Estate successfully as a contract grape growing vineyard, supplying some of Marlborough's leading wine producers with premium fruit. The character and individuality of their grapes, derived from vineyard location, encouraged them to produce and market their own wine under the Isabel Estate label. They regard this as the most natural of evolutionary steps.

Isabel Estate wines are produced from the vineyards plantings of Sauvignon Blanc, Chardonnay, Pinot Gris, Riesling and Pinot Noir when vintage conditions are just right - a late harvest Sauvignon Blanc is produced called "Noble Sauvage".

Isabel Estate Vineyard is located on the Omaka Terrace, just south of the township of Renwick. This site is unusual in Marlborough as it combines deep free-draining gravels with a narrow layer of calcium rich clay in the subsoil. The clay layer acts as a barrier preventing excessive water loss, reducing the need for irrigation in the hot, windy weather.

The vineyard is also planted to a higher vine density and has approximately twice the number of vines per acre than is usual in Marlborough. This allows for lower yields per vine, giving much sought after concentration and depth to the wines.

Isabel Estate Vineyard is one of the largest privately owned vineyards in Marlborough. It's an Estate with all its aspects very much together and great wines.

Address: 72 Hawkesbury Road RENWICK	**Winemaker:** Michael Tiller		Isabel Chardonnay	8 yrs
Phone: +64 3 572 8300 **Fax:** +64 3 572 8383	**Est:** 1982 **Vine Ha:** 60 **Cases:** 20,000		Isabel Pinot Gris	3-4 yrs
Email: admin@isabelestate.com	**Public Hours:** 10am-4pm, daily (phone first)		Isabel Pinot Noir	8 yrs
WWW: www.isabelestate.com	**Principal Wines**	**Potential**	Isabel Dry Riesling	3-4 yrs
Owner: Tiller Family	Isabel Sauvignon Blanc	3-4 yrs	Isabel Sauvage	5+ yrs

Lawsons

Ross and Barbara Lawson began as grapegrowers early in the development of Marlborough as a wine region, planting vines in 1980.They became winemakers in 1992 with a small vintage of 15 tonnes, which has now grown to around 400 tonnes.

The wines have been received well, with many show successes. Recent vintages of Sauvignon Blanc, Chardonnay, Riesling and Gewürztraminer show excellent depth of fruit and complexity evidence of the variety of winemaking techniques utilised. The 1999 Sauvignon Blanc won almost every Sauvignon Blanc trophy, worldwide.

Their state of the art winery has automatically controlled refrigeration, insulated barrel hall, processing equipment including Delta Crusher Destemmer, Diemme Tank Press and a hydraulic lifting receival bin to minimise fruit maceration. A fully serviced laboratory is also on site, 80 tonnes per day can be handled during vintage. The wine is all bottled on site at the Winery.

The Winery also has a modern cellar door facility where all the wines are available for tasting and purchase.

Lawson's also operates a mail order sales facility with regular newsletters and new release information, why not join up.

Address Alabama Road BLENHEIM	**Est:** 1992 **Cases:** 25,000		Marlborough Sauvignon Blanc	2 yrs
Phone: +64 3 578 7674 Fax: +64 3 578 7603	**Public Hours:** 10am-5pm daily		Marlborough Chardonnay	3 yrs
Email: wine@lawsonsdryhills.co.nz	**Principal Varieties:** Chardonnay, Pinot Gris,		Marlborough Riesling	5 yrs
WWW: www.lawsonsdryhills.co.nz	Riesling, Gewürztraminer, Pinot Noir,		Marlborough Gewürztraminer	5 yrs
Owner: Ross & Barbara Lawson & shareholders	Sauvignon Blanc		Marlborough Pinot Noir	3-6 yrs
Winemaker: Mike Just & Adrian Baker	**Principal Wines**	**Potential**	Marlborough Pinot Gris	4 yrs

Mudhouse - Le Grys

John and Jennifer Joslin arrived in New Zealand after cruising the world for six years in their yacht "Dancing Wave", in a search for the ideal place to live. They decided after a brief visit that Marlborough was 'it' and bought land, whereupon they developed Le Grys Vineyard. It was here they also built their unusual and beautiful mud-block house.

After successfully chartering their yacht in the Caribbean, John & Jennifer decided to commence a homestay accommodation in their mud-block home. Such was the success of their vineyard homestays, the Joslins built a self-contained lodge similar in style and construction to the main house for guests who prefer complete seclusion and peace within the vineyard setting.

The Le Grys vineyard was established in 1993 and is planted with

Marlborough's three main varieties, Sauvignon Blanc, Chardonnay and the emerging star, Pinot Noir.

The first Le Grys Sauvignon Blanc was released in August 1996 and the Chardonnay in February 1997. Both wines won awards and were successfully exported to the UK.

The Mudhouse label was launched in 1997 as demand for the wine in the UK grew. Both labels have proven successful in their own right, winning awards including two golds and the '97 Le Grys winning Best Sauvignon Blanc 'Wines of the Year' trophy in Australia in 1998. The Mudhouse

2000 vintage Sauvignon Blanc, was awarded the trophy at the International Wine and Spirits competition in the UK. The wines have all received very favourable reviews in the national and international press.

With more vines maturing, the range now includes a Pinot Noir and Merlot both very exciting wines, rapidly selling out each year.

The Le Grys & Mudhouse Wines are also available by mail order and selected wine outlets with wine tasting available at the vineyard by appointment or at the winery.

Address: Conders Bend Road RENWICK	Winemaker: Matt Thomson	Principal Wines	Potential
Phone: +64 3 572 9490 Fax: +64 3 572 9491	Est: 1996 Vine Ha: 8 Cases: 14,500	Marlborough Sauvignon Blanc	18 mths
Email: wine@mudhouse.co.nz	Public Hours: All year	Legrys Marlborough Sauv Blanc	2-3 yrs
WWW: www.mudhouse.co.nz	Principal Varieties: Merlot, Sauvignon Blanc,	Black Swan Reserve Pinot Noir	6-8 yrs
Owner: John & Jennifer Joslin	Chardonnay, Pinot Noir	Black Swan Reserve Merlot	6-7 yrs

Ponder Estate

Ponder Estate was established by Mike and Diane Ponder in 1987 and covers more than 90 acres of vineyards and olive groves. In 1994 after five years of producing quality award winning grapes for a major NZ winery, the Ponders completed their dream by producing their own wine and creating history with their first commercial pressing of Extra Virgin Olive Oil.

The Estate was already attracting media and visitor attention for its attractive plantings and eye-catching architecture. The Shed Gallery opened in 1994 for art, wine, olive oil, gifts and nursery sales of olives and lavenders and to offer a unique attraction for visitors to Marlborough.

Ponder Estate's award winning Sauvignon Blanc and Chardonnay enjoy an enviable reputation in both Great Britain and Australia where

over 60% of the production is sold. Their Artists Reserve range of wines are only produced in the very best vintages from hand selected grapes. Currently the range consists of Artist's Reserve Chardonnay, Pinot Noir and Merlot.

Mike and Diane now have olive groves

comprising over six thousand trees, planted alongside their vineyards. The olives are hand harvested in May, June and July when they are at their ripest and cold pressed by their own mill on the Estate. This is open seasonally to view oil pressing.

For over 20 years Mike Ponder has achieved international success as one of New Zealand's most acclaimed artiest. Visitors to the Ponder Estate have the opportunity to view and purchase Michael's latest oils or watercolours which are on display at the Shed Gallery. A number of fine limited edition prints of his paintings are available. Mike has also written a book on olive oil which is available at the shed.

What better way to view the exhibition than to combine it with a tasting of Ponder Estate wines and olive oil?

Address: New Renwick Road BLENHEIM	Est: 1987 Vine Ha: 25 Cases: 15,000	Ponder Estate Artists Reserve Merlot	6 yrs
Phone: +64 3572 8642 Fax: +64 3572 9034	Public Hours: daily, 9:30am-5pm, summer;	Ponder Estate Marlborough Sauv Blanc	2 yrs
Email: ponder.estate@xtra.co.nz	10am-4:30pm, winter	Ponder Estate Marlborough Chard	4 yrs
WWW: www.ponder.co.nz	Principal Varieties: Chardonnay, Merlot,	Ponder Estate Classic Riesling	6 yrs
Owner: Mike & Di Ponder	Pinot Noir, Riesling, Sauvignon Blanc	Ponder Estate Marlborough Pinot Noir	6 yrs
Winemaker: Alan McCorkindale	Principal Wines Potential	Ponder Estate Artists Reserve Chard	5 yrs

Nautilus Estate

Noir, Nautilus now have some almost 70 acres of their own and contract growers vineyards planted with the latest clones of pinot noir. I am sure exciting pinot noirs are on the horizon.

The value packed "Twin Islands" label includes Sauvignon Blanc, Chardonnay, Pinot Noir a N.V. Methode Traditionnelle and a Merlot Cabernet Franc, a blend of Hawkes Bay and Marlborough Fruit.

Nautilus is a very professional operation as befits its high pedigree ownership. The wines have been very successful in wine shows and in many overseas markets particularly Australia, United Kingdom and the U.S.A.

Nautilus is a venture begun in 1985 by "Negociants" an arm of the Hill-Smith family, founders of Yalumba wines in the Barossa Valley South Australia in 1849.

From less than 2000 litres of wine produced in 1985, the production is now risen to around 350,000 litres.

Whilst Sauvignon Blanc was the total initial focus, the Nautilus Range now includes Chardonnay, Pinot Gris, Pinot Noir and a Cabernet Sauvignon/Merlot as well as a NV Cuvee Marlborough Brut Sparkling. Recent vintages have seen a second brand "Twin Islands" created blending wines from various regions in New Zealand's north and south islands.

Nautilas have some 75 acres of their own Marlborough vineyards and contract a number of dedicated, quality growers.

The wines have been made under winemaker Clive Jones at the contract winery - Rapaura Vintners in which Nautilus is a large shareholder. In 2000 Nautilus constructed a new specialist Pinot Noir winery, next door to the Rapaura Vintners facility. This new facility is the only one like it in New Zealand and also includes Administration offices and a cellar door facility with an underground storage area.

With the increased focus on Pinot

Address: 12 Rapaura Road RENWICK	**Est:** 1985	**Vine Ha:** 30		Nautilus Chardonnay	2-5 yrs
Phone: +64 3 572 9364 **Fax:** +64 3 572 9374	**Cases:** 50,000			Nautilus Pinot Noir	3-5 yrs
Email: sales@nautilusestate.com	**Public Hours:** 10am-5pm, daily			Nautilus Cabernet/Merlot	5-7 yrs
WWW: www.nautilusestate.com	**Principal Wines**		**Potential**	Nautilus Cuvee Marlborough Brut NV	
Winemaker: Clive Jones	Nautilus Sauvignon Blanc		up to 3 yrs	Nautilus Pinot Gris	2-5 yrs

Stoneleigh Vineyard

New Zealand's best known winemaking area, Marlborough, is home to Stoneleigh Vineyards award winning range of wine. Stoneleigh Vineyards is situated on the banks of the Wairau River beneath the imposing Richmond Ranges in Marlborough.

On the site of a former riverbed, Stoneleigh Vineyards takes its name from the abundance of stones which line the land. These stones lend the wines its unique character. While the Marlborough climate is the underlying factor for the exceptional quality of wines, the stones beneath the vines temper the coolness of the region by reflecting sunlight onto the fruit speeding up the ripening process.

Marlborough's world-renowned terroir of cool temperatures, high annual sunshine hours and crisp coastal climate, combined with Stoneleigh Vineyards unique stony soil, produces elegant wines that capture the essence of the region.

Internationally, Marlborough is renown for its icon wine varietal Sauvignon Blanc, with its distinctive combination of fresh, lively acidity and full fruit flavours. Stoneleigh Vineyards Marlborough Sauvignon Blanc is something of a quality benchmark for all New Zealand

Sauvignon Blanc and is available in more countries around the world than any other New Zealand wine. Other classic cool climate varietals such as Chardonnay, Riesling and Pinot Noir also flourish in this region.

The majority of Stoneleigh Vineyards' land is planted in Sauvignon Blanc, followed by Chardonnay, Riesling and Pinot Noir alongside small parcels of Gewürztraminer, Cabernet Sauvignon, Merlot, Cabernet Franc, Malbec, Pinot Gris and Pinot Meunier.

Exported to over 30 countries, the multi-award-winning Stoneleigh Vineyards range - Sauvignon Blanc, Chardonnay, Riesling and Pinot Noir - has received a lot of attention on the international wine stage including Best Buy recommendations from one of the world's leading wine magazines, Wine Spectator, for the 1998 and 1999 vintages of Stoneleigh Vineyards Sauvignon Blanc.

Nationally, wines from every vintage have received critical acclaim and won awards too. Most recently, Stoneleigh Vineyards Marlborough Sauvignon Blanc 2000 won gold, the Champion Sauvignon Trophy and Champion Commercial White Wine Trophy at the 2000 Air New Zealand

Wine Awards. The same wine also won gold at the Liquorland Top 100 competition. Stoneleigh Vineyards Marlborough Riesling 1999 won Gold at the Air New Zealand Wine Awards and Silver at the 2000 Royal Easter Wine Show.

The success of the Stoneleigh Vineyards can be credited to the exceptional quality of the wines produced and the consistency in delivering pure Marlborough flavours.

Visit the Brancott Visitors Centre, on State Highway One, Blenheim, to sample the award-winning range of Stoneleigh Vineyards wines. Brancott also offers winery tours where you'll see the only French Coquard grape press in the Southern Hemisphere and the first bulk grape tipper tanks in the world. Savour a meal with distinct Marlborough flavours, matched with some of New Zealand's best wine, in the cafe or restaurant or buy a unique item to remember your visit by, or wine that you can enjoy later.

To stay abreast of Stoneleigh Vineyards news and Marlborough events bookmark www.stoneleigh.co.nz. The site has up-to-date information on Stoneleigh Vineyards' latest releases, tasting notes and competition results and awards.

Vavasour Wines

Vavasour Wines pioneered grape growing in the Awatere Valley, which is situated approximately 30 kilometres south east of Blenheim on the flood plain and ancient terraces of the Awatere river. To the north is the coastline of Clifford Bay and to the south the mountainous Kaikoura Ranges.

On the morning of our visit, after a late snowfall in the surrounding mountains, we came across the Vavasour Vineyard team busily planting a new vineyard. Over recent years the company has increased its own vineyards by over 100 acres taking their total vineyard area to 133 acres.

Peter Vavasour, the founder of Vavasour Wines traces his ancestry back to 1066 and the days of

William the Conqueror, where one of his forebears was thought to be a taster for Williams's court.

Peter became involved in the industry in 1986 when he planted the first grapes in the Awatere Valley and harvested the first crop in 1989.

Winemaker is the highly regarded Glenn Thomas who has been with the company since its inception and over the years had produced many award winning wines.

Vavasour's success has encouraged many others to plant in the Awatere Valley, which has built an enviable reputation for its wines in a very short time.

The Vavasour wines have a unique character coming from the vineyards location, soil type and microclimate. The free draining soils, a mild

maritime climate, long sunshine hours, relatively low rainfull and shelter from the cold westerly winds help create the distinctively Vavasour characters.

The wines exhibit strong floral characters and are less herbaceous than their Wairau Valley neighbours and are complimented by showing some interesting flinty and mineral flavours.

The company produces two ranges, one under the Vavasour label with its distinctive cockerel brand and the other under the Dashwood label.

The company had built up a strong following over a short number of years and its wines can be found, in addition to the New Zealand market, those of Australia, USA and the UK.

Address: Redwood Pass Seddon BLENHEIM	**Est:** 1986 **Vine Ha:** 26 **Cases:** 35,000	Vavasour Sauvignon Blanc	0-5 yrs
Phone: +64 3 575 7481 **Fax:** +64 3 575 7240	**Public Hours:** 10am-4pm, daily (Summer);	Vavasour Chardonnay	0-3 yrs
Email: vavasour@vavasour.com	10am-4pm, Mon-Sat (Winter)	Vavasour Pinot Noir	0-4 yrs
WWW: www.vavasour.com	**Principal Varieties:** Cabernet, Pinot Noir,	Vavasour Reisling	0-5+ yrs
Owner: Public Unlisted Company	Sauvignon Blanc, Chardonnay, Riesling	Dashwood Sauvignon Blanc	0-2 yrs
Winemaker: Glen Thomas	**Principal Wines** **Potential**	Dashwood Chardonnay	0-2 yrs

Villa Maria Winery

With the takeover of Corbans by Montana, the Villa Maria Group is now New Zealand's second largest winemaker.

In 1999 Villa Maria crushed the first grapes at its new Marlborough Winery, literally as the walls were going up around the tanks and fermentation cellar. 2,300 tonnes were crushed by a very talented winemaking team, under chief winemaker Michelle Richardson, a graduate science degree holder from Massey University, who travelled the world, before gaining her postgraduate Diploma in Wine Science from Roseworthy College in South Australia. She then worked three vintages for Cassegrain in New South Wales, Australia plus a vintage in France, in the Bergerac region, as a "Flying Winemaker".

She began at Villa Maria in 1992 becoming Senior Assistant winemaker in 1993 and winemaker in 1994. In 1998 she became group winemaker of all Villa Maria winemaking operations including Esk Valley and Vidal Estate wineries. Michelle follows the winemaking philosophy of minimum intrusion in the process of turning premium grapes into great wines, sensitively using oak and techniques such as malolactic fermentation to enhance the wines, not overpower them.

For many years Villa Maria has been the most successful New Zealand exhibitor in wine shows both in New Zealand and overseas. In 1993, owner and managing director George Fistonich, who founded Villa Maria in 1961, was awarded "Winemaker of the Show" at the Liquorland Royal Easter show. In 1997 and 1998, as Group Winemaker, Michelle Richardson achieved the same feat. In their annual awards, the Australian Winestate Magazine also awarded Michelle the accolade of top New Zealand Winemaker in 1998,1999 and 2000.

Villa Maria have an increasingly strong viticultural base through large vineyard ventures in prime locations in both the Marlborough and Hawkes Bay regions.

Two of the finest wines Michelle and

her team make are the Reserve Marlborough Sauvignon Blanc and their Reserve Noble Riesling. The "Reserve" wines are only made when vintage conditions allow varieties to really shine. The Marlborough Reserve Chardonnay is also exceptional and the Reserve Hawkes Bay Cabernet Sauvignon/Merlot is always a great wine. More recently the winemaking team have been producing Pinot Noir wines and their perseverance was rewarded with the trophy for top Pinot Noir at the Royal Easter Show Awards in 2000.

Villa Maria also have a "Cellar Selection" range of wines, somewhat less expensive than the Reserve Range but also excellent and made to complement food. The Cellar Selection range covers most varieties and styles including a Pinot Noir from Marlborough.

The least expensive Villa Maria wines

appear under the "Private Bin" label, which includes all the mainstream varieties along with Pinot Gris andGewürztraminer. It is very hard to find a lame duck amongst the Villa Maria wines · there isn't one.

Villa Maria's new Marlborough Winery is a true state of the art facility, with its striking simplicity of design and operation it has been beautifully conceived and the cellar door is bright, airy and has a distinct quality feel about it. One must make it an obligatory call on their Marlborough tour.

Address: Corner Paynters Road & New Renwich Road BLENHEIM
Phone: +64 3 577 9530 **Fax:** +64 3 577 9585

Email: enquiries@villamaria.co.nz
Winemaker: George Geris
Public Hours: 10am-5pm, daily

Principal Varieties: Cabernet Sauvignon, Chardonnay, Gewürztraminer, Pinot Noir, Riesling, Sauvignon Blanc

Wairau River

Phil and Chris Rose have the easy relaxed air successful rural people develop, they were pioneer grape growers in the Marlborough region in 1977 and now have 250 acres of fine established vineyard, they limit their yields to produce grapes with intense varietal flavours.

The wines are all made at the Rapaura Vintners facility, of which they are a large shareholder, giving them full control of the winemaking as well as the grapegrowing. It is not a wonder with this control and their desire to be seen as a top premium New Zealand producer on world markets (they visit often on promotional trips), that they have succeeded in being a leading Marlborough producer.

Phil and Chris have also created a fine cellar door and restaurant complex, which also promotes Shingle Peak and a select number of other wines, it's ideally situated on the corner of the main entry to the region from Nelson and Rapaura Road, with its large array of wineries. They are also the closest winery to the Wairau River.

Apart from a fine Sauvignon Blanc that has won many awards they a have a very consistent Range and some excellent Botrytised wines in favorable years.

Address: Cnr of Rapaura Rd & SH 6 BLENHEIM	**Winemaker:** John Belsham	Reserve
Phone: +64 3 572 9800 **Fax:** +64 3 572 9885	**Est:** 1991 **Vine Ha:** 100 **Cases:** 30,000	Sauvignon Blanc
Email: office@wairauriverwines.com	**Public Hours:** 10am-5pm, daily	Chardonnay
WWW: www.wairauriverwines.com	**Principal Wines**	Riesling
Owner: Phil & Chris Rose	Sauvignon Blanc Reserve & Chardonnay	Borytised Riesling Reserve

Shingle Peak

The extremely successful and affable Spence Brothers Ross and Bill, created the Shingle Peak label in 1990 in recognition of the growing international demand for Marlborough wines from New Zealand.

Shingle Peak was named after one of the mountains in the Kaikoura Range, which can be sighted from the Wairau plains where most Marlborough fruit is grown. As with most premium wine producing regions, Shingle Peak is founded on a strong viticultural base, where the grapes develop the unique characteristics which identify the wines so clearly with Marlborough.

Production has grown significantly with shipments to the United Kingdom, Australia, Canada and the USA making up the largest markets. It is expected that the production will double by 2003 and further growth after this will make the brand one of the largest in the region.

The wines are made at Rapaura Vintners, the superbly equipped winery, in which Shingle Peak has a substantial shareholding. The wines are matured and bottled under their control at the Matua Valley winery in the Auckland region.

The wines are top premium quality at very realistic prices and have quickly gained excellent distribution in the domestic and international markets.

Along with the mainstream Sauvignon Blanc and Pinot Noir, a Chardonnay, Riesling and Pinot Gris are also produced.

Address: Rapaura Road BLENHEIM	& Beringer Wine Estates	**Cases:** 50,000
Phone: +64 9 411 8301 **Fax:** +64 9 411 7982	**Winemaker:** Mark Robertson	**Principal Varieties:** Chardonnay, Pinot Gris,
Owner: Ross & Bill Spence, Mark Robertson	**Est:** 1990 **Vine Ha:** 131	Pinot Noir, Riesling, Sauvignon Blanc

Wither Hills

As I write, Brent Morris is building a state of the art winery on the Wither Hills vineyards his father established in 1975, the first contract vineyards in the Marlborough region on the Southern side of the Wairau Valley.

Brent is by any reasoning a rising star if not a superstar of New Zealand wine, with an urbane flair for promotion as well as finely honed technical winemaking skills, a capacity for hard work and a big vision.

Brent launched Wither Hills in 1994 he was then chief winemaker for the demanding Delegat Wine family.

Brents wines have been spectacularly successful in wine shows particularly his 1998 Marlborough Pinot Noir was successful in the Sydney Top 100 wines competition in 1999. The same wine took all before it winning the trophy for the best wine from 1200 wines (with 74 gold medals

and 12 trophy wines amongst them) at the Air New Zealand wine show.

Brent and his father have 200 acres of mature vines to select the best fruit from and another 100 acres of land to plant if they wish.

The Wither Hills range so far includes just a Sauvignon Blanc a Chardonnay

and the Pinot Noir. Brent is already selling a lot of premium wines in the USA, into top restaurants under the "White Linen" brand.

Brent is assisted by the talented and highly qualified Ben Glover a Marlborough native. They make a great team and with Wither Hills wines, the world is their oyster.

Address: 16 Salisbury Street HERNE BAY	**Winemaker:** Brent Marris		Blanc, Pinot Noir	
Phone: +64 9 378 0857 **Fax:** +64 9 378 0857	**Est:** 1994	**Vine Ha:** 65	**Principal Wines**	**Potential**
Email: winery@witherhills.co.nz	**Cases:** 20,000		Wither Hills Sauvignon Blanc	1-2 yrs
WWW: www.witherhills.co.nz	**Public Hours:** By apopintment only		Wither Hills Chardonnay	3-5 yrs
Owner: Brent & John Marris	**Principal Varieties:** Chardonnay, Sauvignon		Wither Hills Pinot Noir	4-6 yrs

Whitehaven Wine Co.

Established in 1994, by Greg and Sue White, Whitehaven has grown into an export driven company with a very strong reputation for quality. Simon Waghorn, a leading winemaker who left a senior position with Corbans Wines to assist them, joined the Whites in their new venture. In the early years Whitehaven sourced grapes from a group of contract growers and this

continues to be its main source of supply. However in the last two years Whitehaven has purchased some 100 acres of their own vineyards.

Their single Vineyard Reserve Sauvignon Blanc and Marlborough Sauvignon Blanc feature regularly in the top half dozen of the many Marlborough Sauvignon Blancs produced. They also produce a consistently good Chardonnay, a

Pinot Gris, Riesling, Gewürztraminer and a Pinot Noir.

The Whitehaven complex in the heart of Blenheim also includes an excellent Alfresco café with a cozy indoor section for winter. The Whites have recently taken control of the cellar door and restaurant side of the business and a new manager and chefs are already proving a big success, with innovative food and friendly service.

Whitehaven's latest plans include a new 2,500 tonne winery which will be operational for the 2002 vintage.

Address: Blicks Road RENWICK	**Est:** 1994	**Vine Ha:** 40	Whitehaven Sur Sauvignon Blanc
Phone: +64 3 572 9592 **Fax:** +64 3 572 9572	**Cases:** 25,000		Whitehaven Sur Pinot Gris
Email: greg@whitehaven.co.nz	**Public Hours:** 11am-5pm, daily		Whitehaven Sur Gewürztraminer
Owner: Greg & Sue White	**Principal Wines**		Whitehaven Riesling
Winemaker: Simon Waghorn	Whitehaven Sauvignon Blanc		Whitehaven Chardonnay

Waipara

Waipara is located on the Canterbury plains, some 65 kilometres north of Christchurch, The Teviotdale hills form an attractive backdrop to the region, as well as protecting it from harsh south westerly weather. The attractive undulating terrain provides many northerly aspects creating ideal terroir, when combined with the warm north westerly winds.

The region has a remarkable range of soils from river silts laden with shingle and river stones to clay and loam over limestone. Many different grape varieties and wine styles do well in various parts of the region, Pinot Noir, Chardonnay and Riesling certainly shine out.

The region has expanded greatly in the number of producers and area under vine in recent years. The substantial Canterbury House vineyards, with 150 acres of vines, a large winery and restaurant hospitality complex has helped bring the region to life. Pegasus Bay is a very good producer, with a splendid restaurant. The many interesting small wineries, often with hospitality and accommodation, plus the natural beauty of the region makes Waipara a great place to visit.

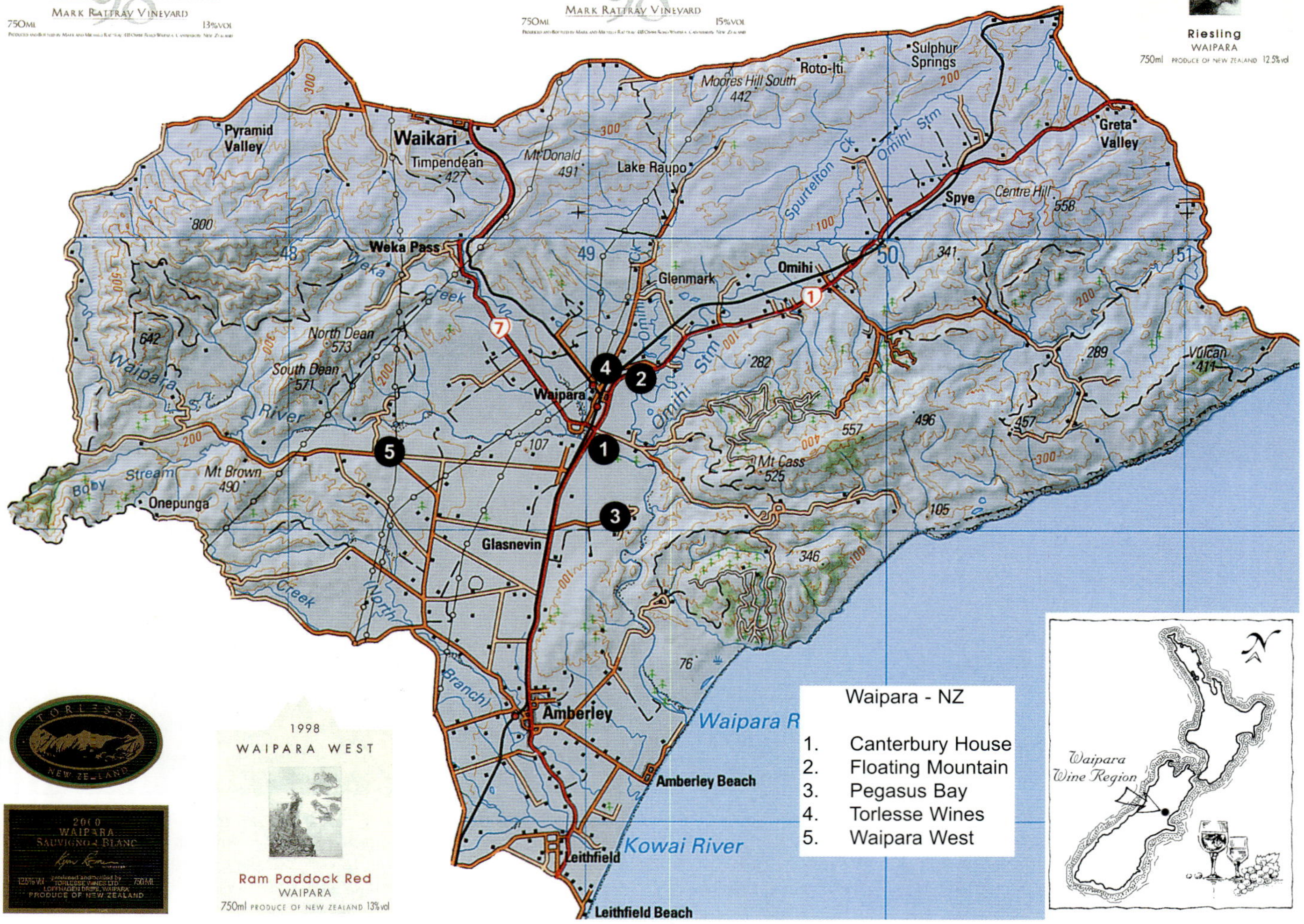

Waipara - NZ

1. Canterbury House
2. Floating Mountain
3. Pegasus Bay
4. Torlesse Wines
5. Waipara West

Canterbury House

Michael and Nancy Reids holiday in New Zealand in the early 1990's, turned into a major project for them and a third career for Michael, in his own words "his last". Wine to Michael had been long term love affair and hobby, it is now his business.

At Amberley in the heart of the Waipara Wine district, Michael has built a most impressive winery and hospitality centre including a magnificent restaurant and function area.

Already 170 acres are under vine and plans are for this to expand 270 acres. The first vines went in the ground in 1994. Pinot Noir is the main focus but Chardonnay Sauvignon Blanc and Riesling were also planted, with Pinot Gris and Merlot being added the following year.

The complex will be expanded over the next few years to incorporate an enlarged restaurant and function area, a barrel hall and a vineyard enclosed in a cloistered courtyard.

Canterbury House have a talented team under General Manager Kathleen Corsbie, the viticulturist is Jean-Luc Dufour trained in

Switzerland, he has worked in vineyards in his homeland, France and the United States. Winemaker Mark Rattray whose youthful good looks belie his wealth of experience, starting at the Hamilton Winery, then situated in a suburb of Adelaide South Australia, where he began his career waxing oak vats, back in 1969. He has studied in Geisenheim

Germany and worked at a number of large and small New Zealand wineries, over four decades. Michael Reid has reserved the best job for himself as "taster", giving the final nod to wines before bottling.

The soils of the vineyard are chiefly sandy loams over well drained gravel,only grapes from the estate are used giving full control to the winemaker.

I found the Pinot Gris had a deep gold colour with lots of tropical guava and melon flavors with a crisp finish. The Sauvignon Blanc from the 1998 vintage was a real stunner as was the 1999, again both very tropical. The Chardonnay showed exotic banana and pineapple, creamy with a vanilla like palate and a long finish definitely in the gold medal league. The Pinot Noir had heaps of cherry fruit, it was warm and mouthfilling, with plenty of spicy and gamey flavours. The Merlot was equally impressive with some interesting smokey earthy and truffle like characters adding complexity to the plummy fruit.

Canterbury House export a good deal of wine and are growing in a sensible ordered manner, it is an impressive estate by any world standards and a must visit when in Waipara.

Address: State Highway 1 WAIPARA	Owner: Michael Reid	Riesling
Phone: +64 3 314 6900	Winemaker: Mark Rattray	Sauvignon Blanc
Fax: +64 3 314 6905	Est: 1994 Vine Ha: 68 Cases: 50,000	Chardonnay
Email: canterburyhouse@attglobal.net	Principal Wines	Pinot Noir
WWW: www.canterburyhouse.com	Pinot Gris	Merlot

Floating Mountain

Floating Mountain began its life as Waipara Springs in 1989, founded by Mark and Michelle Rattray. Mark is one of New Zealand's truly consummate winemakers. His winemaking experience goes back to South Australia in the late 1960's.After study at Geisenhemin Germany he worked for Montana for a number of years, followed by 7 years as Penfold New Zealand's winemaker manager until 1985. He then made wine for St. Helena in the Canterbury area and Waipara Springs before building his own winery in 1993. He is also winemaker at the high profile Canterbury House, by far Waipara's biggest vineyard and winery.

Floating Mountain takes its name from the Maori name "Maukatere" for Mt Grey that floats above the winter clouds and Mark's vineyard and winery.

Mark grows his vines with strictly limited crops of intensely flavoured grapes, I found his wines complex, strong and long in flavour, absolute gems. The tasty Chardonnay, a Mendoza clone, had many layers of melon and grapefruit flavours with cashew and hazelnut overtones, a rich luscious drop (96/100). The Pinot Noir was concentrated, full of dark cherry and plum flavours with some cedar and cigar box characters, very gamey, definitely my style of Pinot, which would be just superb with quail, pheasant or pigeon. I scored this wine a 1998, 97/100.

Mark Rattray is quietly producing some of New Zealand's finest wines · seek him out!!

Address: 418 Omihi Road WAIPARA	Owner: Mark & Michelle Rattray **Vine Ha:** 4	Principal Wines	Potential
Phone: +64 3 314 6710 **Fax:** +64 3 314 6710	**Winemaker:** Mark Rattray **Cases:** 2,000	Floating Mountain Pinot Noir	7 yrs
Email: floatingmountain@mail.com	**Public Hours:** By appointment	Floating Mountain Chardonnay	5 yrs
WWW: www.floatingmountain.com **Est:** 1993	**Principal Varieties:** Pinot Noir, Chard, Sauv Blanc	Floating Mountain Sauvignon	3 yrs

Pegasus Bay

Pegasus Bay is by any definition a top New Zealand Wine producer, which also houses one of the finest New Zealand winery restaurants, run by Chef Edward Donaldson son of the founders Ivan and Chris Donaldson.

Professor Ivan Donaldson is a prominent wine judge and writer, he and his wife Chris who is very active in the family enterprise and their four sons, planted vines in the mid 1980's, making their first wines in 1991. The soils are sandy loam, which is heavily interspersed with sizable round stones, giving it good heat reflecting and retention properties. This combined with proximity to the coast and shelter from the cool sea breezes, gives Pegasus Bay a unique "Terroir" where ripening many grape varieties, even in cool years, is little problem.

The winemaking team consists of son Matthew, trained at Adelaide University and his fiance Lynnette also a trained oenologist. Their wines are spectacular and often distinctly individual in style. I found the Sauvignon Blanc (70%) / Semillon (30%) to be absolutely outstanding with honey, citrus and passionfruit flavours leaping out of the glass, a little wood age gives it a really nice palate richness 94.5/100. Their

Chardonnay which spends about 14 months in a combination of new and older French oak barriques, just bursts out with melon and apricot fruit, with a nutty creamy cashew like palate, highlighted by smoky oak and butterscotch overtones, it's a real mouthful of flavour 92/100.

Their top Pinot Noir "Prima Donna" is a rich meaty style, with loads of dark cherries. They also produce a great Cabernet Merlot and a special selection of this wine under the "Maestro" label, both fabulous Bordeaux style reds. The 1998 "Maestro" had deep mauve colour, cassis, cherry fruit flavours with cedar and minty confectionery overtones and a hint of herbaceousness · sublime 94/100.

The "Magic Castle" buildings and beautiful gardens and lake only add to this special family wine domain.

Address: Stockgrove Road, RD2, Waipara AMBERLEY	Winemaker: Matthew Donaldson & Lynnette Hudson	Cabernet/Merlot
	Est: 1986 **Vine Ha:** 35 **Cases:** 12,000	Chardonnay
Phone: +64 3 314 6869 **Fax:** +64 3 314 6869	**Public Hours:** 10am-5pm, daily	Sauvignon/Semillon
Email: info@pegasusbay.co.nz	**Principal Wines**	Riesling
WWW: www.pegasusbay.com	Pinot Noir	Botrytised Chardonnay Finale

Torlesse Wines

Kym Rayner's family are long time McLaren Vale vineyard folk from South Australia and for many years ran the Tintara Vineyards of my own family's former wine enterprise.

Kym showed us through the new Torlesse winery and cellar door complex, under construction, on a rainy November Sunday in 1999, you could sense this was a wine producer on the move.

Torlesse is owned by a group of shareholders with skills in viticulture, horticulture, engineering, environmental management and accounting, a great blend of talents for a vineyard and wine business. Between them they have 45 acres of vines some more than 15 years old.

The wines are divided into several ranges, most of the top "Reserve" wines are vineyard and grower

designated. They also make wines from Marlborough vineyards and other selected South Island Vineyards. The "Reserve" Cabernet Sauvignon Merlot has developed a good reputation, deep coloured full flavoured red, maybe benefiting from Kym's McLaren Vale experience. The gamey Pinot Noir, Sauvignon Blanc and two styles of Riesling (one slightly sweet) have also gained recognition. They also make Pinot Gris and Chardonnay. So whether you choose Wine Tasting at Waipara, the Whale Watch experience at Kaikoura or the alpine thermal delights of Hanmer Springs, Torlesse is the ideal way to break your journey.

The new cellars and tasting room in the centre of the region just off the main road is worth visiting.

Address: Loffhagen Drive WAIPARA	**Public Hours:** 11am-4pm, Fri-Sun	Sauvignon Blanc
Phone: +64 3 314 6929 **Fax:** +64 3 377 1595	**Principal Wines**	Pinot Gris
Email: krayner@xtra.co.nz **Vine Ha:** 18	Chardonnay Waipara Reserve	Cabernet/Merlot
Winemaker: Kym Rayner **Cases:** 8,000	Pinot Noir	Reserve Port

Waipara West

After Paul Tutton and his sister Victoria bought their property in 1989, at the western extremity of the Waipara Valley, they discovered their great great uncle, a sheep baron, had owned it some 70 years before.

The vines are planted on the river flood plain and slopes sheltered by a precipitous ridge to the south plus mountains to the west and north.

Paul runs a successful wine merchants business in London, where he lives with his artist wife Olge Sienke. I met him at Vin Expo in 1999 and was most impressed by his wide wine knowledge. The property is run by sister Vic and her husband viticulturalist Lindsay Hill. Their 52 acre vineyard on four distinct soil types, with many microclimates, produces some excellent and interesting wines. The Pinot Noir is a

full style with lots of dark cherry character, complex and spicy. The Chardonnay and Sauvignon Blanc are also vibrant and fruit driven. They also make a blended red, mainly from Cabernet Sauvignon Called "Ran Paddock Red", its got plenty of flavour with a slightly herbaceous

finish. Peter Evans is the talented young winemaker a 1984 Roseworthy Oenology graduate.

Waipara West export 90% of their wines so its worth looking for them in major United Kingdom, European and North American wine markets.

Address: 376 RMB Paddock Road WAIPARA	**Est:** 1989	**Vine Ha:** 22	Pinot Noir	5 yrs
Phone: +64 3 314 8699 **Fax:** +64 3 314 8692	**Cases:** 6,000		Chardonnay	5-8 yrs
Email: waiparawest@xtra.co.nz	**Public Hours:** 10am-4pm, Weekdays		Riesling	5 yrs
WWW: www.waiparawest.com	**Principal Varieties:** Cab Sav, Merlot,		Ram Paddock Red	5 yrs
Owner: Tutton Sienko & Hill	Riesling, Cab Franc, Chardonnay, Pinot Noir		Sauvignon Blanc	2 yrs
Winemaker: Petter Evans	**Principal Wines**	**Potential**	Cabernet Franc	5 yrs

Canterbury

The Canterbury region proper, surrounds the beautiful city of Christchurch, which was my first port of call in New Zealand, reminding me somewhat of my home town Adelaide.

Whilst the region covers a large physical area, stretching east, down the beautiful banks Peninsula to the stunning French Farm Winery and Restaurant at Akaroa Harbour, west to Oxford, north to Woodend and south to the Rakaia River. Mostly the wineries are small but the hospitality is generous and many have cafes restaurants and other wine tourism facilities.

The soils and microclimates vary enormously and a great number of wine styles are successfully produced. The largest winery by far is Giesen in 1999 they crushed 750 tonnes which is being greatly expanded mainly through a new winery and vineyards they have established in Marlborough, they crushed over 2000 tonnes in 2001.

Canterbury is a great place to spend a few lazy days of wine and roses.

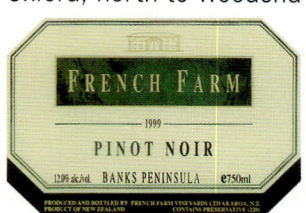

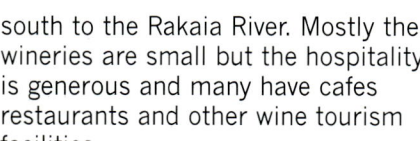

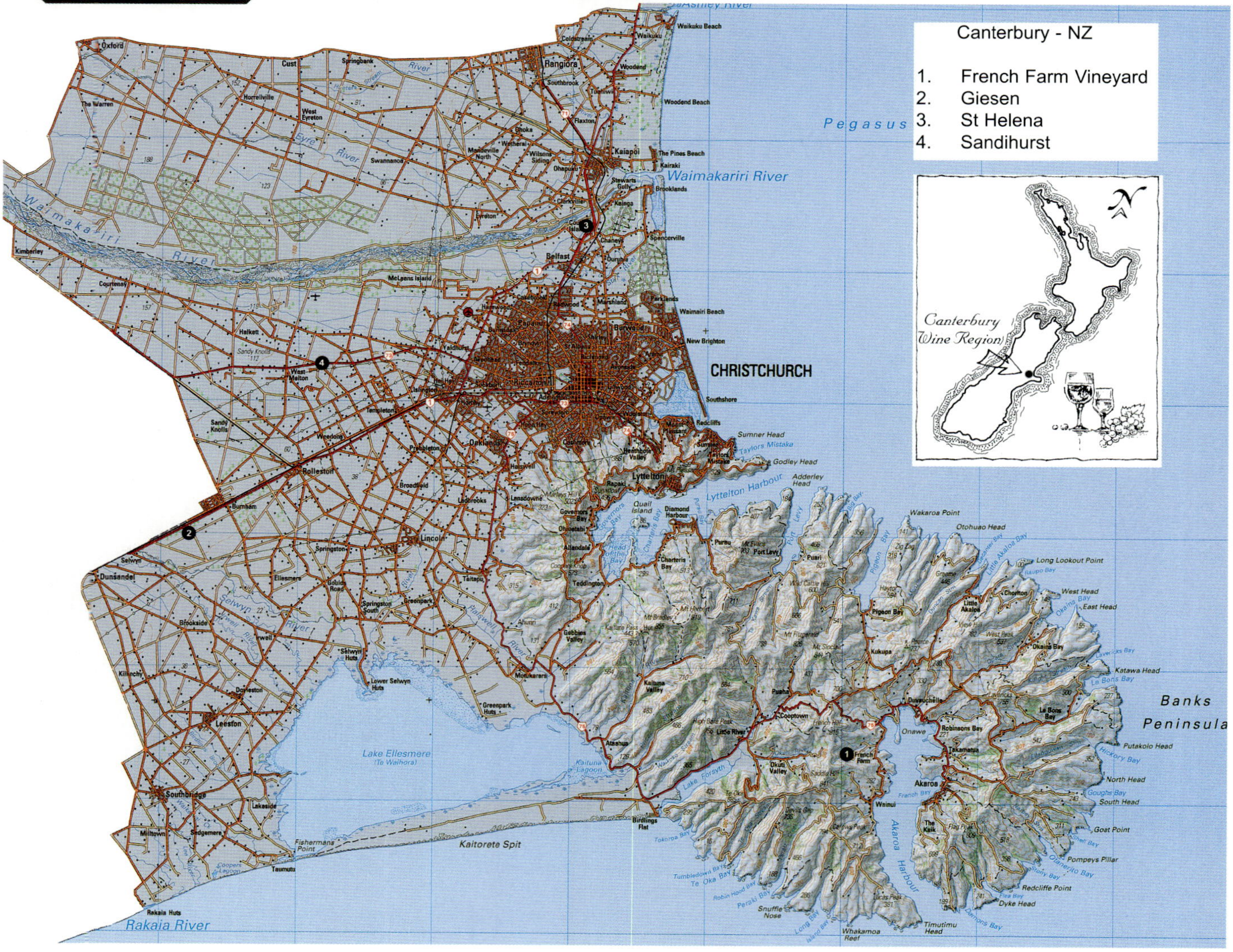

Canterbury - NZ

1. French Farm Vineyard
2. Giesen
3. St Helena
4. Sandihurst

French Farm Vineyard

French Farm is one of the most beautiful winery and restaurant complexes I have seen anywhere in the world. The gardens and outdoor patio look out over the awesome Akaroa Harbour an ancient volcanic crater, both Akaroa and Duvauchelle were established by French settlers. French Farm was created to reflect the French style so fiercely protected by the local residents.

The French Farm buildings have a grand French Provincial style about them. The mature trees and French Farm stream running alongside just adds to the charm. The main restaurant is warm and friendly but with a grandeur created by its high vaulted ceilings. It seats over 100 and seating can be expanded considerably by incorporating the outdoor area in summer. French Farm is just the place to host a gathering or hold a wedding or other special function.

The food is truly sensational under renowned chef Matthew Fairey, who is also General Manager. Not only does Matthew produce classic dishes and sauces in the French tradition, he also creates some innovative dishes in the traditional wood fired Pizza oven,you can even get his creations · take away · if you want to visit the harbour and have a casual "picnic style"meal.

The French Farm vineyards enjoy a warm sheltered micro-climate on the sun drenched slopes, on volcanic soils. Both the Pinot Noir and Chardonnay produced have intense fruit driven flavours. The winery also produces a very good Riesling, Sauvignon Blanc and an excellent Rose, which is just the thing chilled with an alfresco lunch on the terrace.

French Farm also make wines for a number of small vineyards on the Bank's Peninsula including the wines of Sunnybrae Vineyard which are sold at the French Farm cellar door under the "Akaroa Harbour" label.

French Farm is less than an hours spectacular drive from Christchurch. When you come to the peak of the hills and se the Akaroa Harbour open out before you, it's a truly breathtaking sight, preparing you well for the magic of the French Farm Winery and Restaurant, which will be add a memorable experience of your life.

Address: French Farm Valley Rd WAINUI Phone: +64 3 304 5784 Fax: +64 3 304 5785 Email: enquiries@frenchfarm.co.nz WWW: www.frenchfarm.co.nz	Owner: James & Emily Jane Ullrich Winemaker: Mark Leonard Est: 1991 Vine Ha: 8 Cases: 2,000 Public Hours: 10am-5pm daily	Principal Varieties: Pinot Noir, Chardonnay	
		Principal Wines	Potential
		Chardonny	2-4 yrs
		Pinot Noir	3-5 yrs

St Helena

Robin and Bernice Moody are enthusiastic and passionate about their vineyards and wine and blessed with an entrepreneurial flair in its promotion.Theirs was the first vineyard and winery established in the Canterbury region, crushing its first harvest in 1978. The winery cellar door exhudes a friendly family atmosphere, where the true enjoyment of wines is celebrated.

The focus at St Helena over recent years has been very much on Pinot Noir, which now covers more than half the area of their expanded 75 acre vineyard. The vineyard has been re-trellised, giving riper fruit with more tropical character. The winery has also undergone an upgrading process, under the eye of their very experienced and respected winemaker Alan McCorkindale, the dux of the 1983 Roseworthy Oenology course and former winemaker and manager for Corbans, in the Marlborough Region.

The Moody's Pinot push was rewarded in 1999 when British Airways chose their 1998 Pinot Noir for their "long haul" flights, one of only six wines selected from 600 submitted.

St Helena also produce Riesling, Pinot Blanc, Pinto Gris and Chardonnay as well as an excellent blended dry white under the "Southern Alps" banner and a Marlborough grown Sauvignon Blanc.

St Helena is a winery where you will be looked after and learn a lot on your visit.

Address: Coutts Island RD CHRISTCHURCH
Phone: +64 3 323 8202 **Fax:** +64 3 323 8252
Email: sthelena@xtra.co.nz

Winemaker: Alan McCorkindale
Est: 1978
Public Hours: 10am-5pm, daily

Principal Varieties: Chardonnay, Müller Thurgau, Pinot Gris, Pinot Noir, Riesling, Sauvignon Blanc

Sandihurst

John Brough is a hands on viticulturalist and winemaker, on the day of our visit, he stood out like a beacon, in his full length yellow vineyard attire, busy treating his vines. John only uses grapes grown on his own 40 acre vineyard, the wines are also fermented, matured and bottled, on site in his winery.

Sandihurst have become renowned for their Pinot Noir, particularly their "Premium Selection" the 1997 vintage being awarded 5 stars · the top rating in the "Cuisine Annual' they also have a "Sandihurst" Pinot Label.

John's other wines are mainly the more aromatic Alsace varieties, Riesling, Gewürztraminer and Pinot Gris. The Riesling shows plenty of lime citrus flavours and some nice honey like character, being not quite dry. The Gewürztraminer is spicy and dry and the Pinot Gris shows lots of concentrated marmalade like characters, with tropical overtones a really mouthfilling style.

Sandihurst are finding many receptive export markets for their fine wines.

Address: Main West Coast Road WEST MELTON
Phone: +64 3 347 8289 **Fax:** +64 3 347 8289
Email: sales@sandihurstwines.co.nz

WWW: www.sandihurstwines.co.nz
Owner: John & Joan Brough
Winemaker: Andrew Meggitt
Est: 1988 **Vine Ha:** 16

Public Hours: Tasting & Sales 11am-4:30pm Sat-Sun; Weekdays by appointment
Principal Varieties: Gewürztraminer, Pinot Gris, Pinot Noir, Riesling

Otago

Otago is the world's most southerly wine region located in the rugged Southern Alps of New Zealand's South Island. Some of the vineyard sites are quite scary, wedged between towering stony peaks and huge abysses. The sun catching aspects of these sites and patches of stony soil amongst the rocks are keenly sought after.

Although a late starter as a region, with the first wines only being made in the mid to late 1980's, planting is roaring ahead and the region now has 27 wineries and many more vineyards. In area of vines Otago is the fourth largest region in New Zealand, behind Marlborough, Hawkes Bay and Gisborne.

The winters can be harsh but the summers, although short, are hot with long sunshine hours and cool nights. This continental climate when combined with good vineyard sites creates exceptional wines, particularly pinots noir which often shows distinct Burgurdian characters but the full gamut of classic European varieties do well, in one microclimate or another. Wine tourism is thriving in the region particularly near to New Zealand's snow capital and summer mountain resort Queenstown.

Gibbson Valley wines, is spectacular, with its cellars dug into the mountain side and top cellar restaurant (its in fact the most visited winery in New Zealand or Australia). Many other wineries also have great wine tourism facilities, with its exceptional scenery interesting wineries and great wine. Otago is a wine tourist's Mecca. A good time to visit is during January or February when the "Otago Wine Festival" takes place.

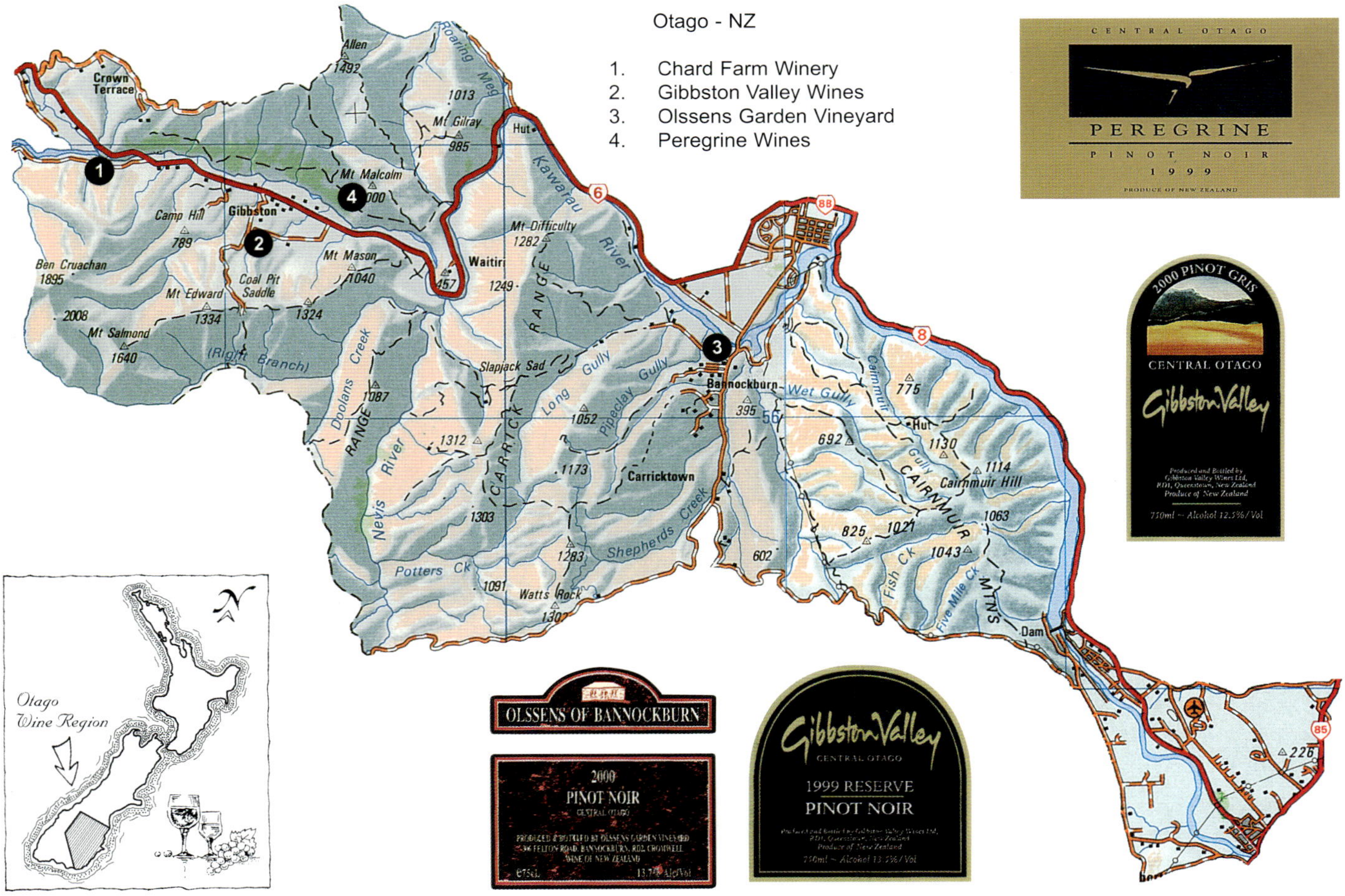

Otago - NZ

1. Chard Farm Winery
2. Gibbston Valley Wines
3. Olssens Garden Vineyard
4. Peregrine Wines

Chard Farm Winery

Chard Farm was established in 1987 by Rob & Greg Hay. Initially most locals thought it was pie in the sky stuff and it was even overheard in the local pub that Chard Farm as a vineyard was a "waste of bloody good merino country". That "wasted merino country" is now producing around 120,000 bottles of wine every year. Rob studied winemaking in Germany in the early 80's, before returning to look for a piece of land that would emulate, as best as possible the unique continental climate of the Burgundy and Alsace regions of France. At the time, a quick visit to Otago confirmed his gut feeling that the area had the necessary "terroir" (the very complex local interaction of soil and climate at each individual site) that produces the greatness or otherwise in the wines of the world.

Select areas of Otago are probably most similar to the classic premium wine regions of Burgundy, Alsace, Southern German and Champagne - home of some of the greatest wines in the world. However, most of Otago is not suitable for growing grapes and only the warm north facing, frost free slopes of the inland basins and river terraces have proved to be suitable.

The major danger for the growers in Otago is unseasonal frosts. Chard Farm is one of the regions most frost free sites, this was a major factor convincing Rob & Greg that the site was right in 1987. The north facing,

sloping land allows the cold air, generated at night, to slide off into the Kawarau River which acts as a large "conveyor belt" to carry the cold air away.

Chard Farm have enjoyed many successes in wine shows, a gold medal in the 1997 Air New Zealand Wine awards for the 1996 "Bragato" Reserve Pinot Noir. The same wine acheived a first place, 5 star rating and top Pinot Noir from the South Island, at the annual New Zealand/Australian Winestate tasting, held in Auckland in Feb 98, also being runner up in the 1999 Bragato awards, and receiving 3rd place in the final of the Australasian Pinot Noir "Wine of the Year" awards, in September 99. The "Finla Mor" 98 won the inaugural Mike Wolter Pinot Noir Trophy for champion Pinot Noir at the Bragato Wine Awards and the "Judge & Jury" Chardonnay 98 was selected in the same month to accompany the main course at the APEC conference dinner September 15 1999.

Chard Farm also lays claim to producing the first genuine Ice wine in the Southern Hemisphere. In 1992 some Riesling grapes were harvested on the shortest day of the year - June 22 at - 10C in the frozen state and pressed while still frozen.

Chard Farm are currently embarking on a major vineyard push into the Cromwell and Alexandra areas to

help meet projected demand into the next century. 28 acres have been planted in the Lowburn area with new clones of Pinot Noir, Pinot Gris and Riesling and several more are being planted in the Cromwell area. The future Chard Farm emphasis will be on single vineyard Pinot Noir from these areas in "vintage" years. The future for Pinot Gris also looks very exciting as it requires a coolish climate like it's Pinot Noir parentage in order to obtain greatness.

Chard Farm are also partners in Otago's largest vineyard development. The Amisfield Vineyard development in Lowburn near Cromwell. Around 375 acres are being developed.

Chard Farm has also formed a joint venture company with local businessman John Darby to develop a premium, large scale methode champenoise operation using Otago fruit, the first wine was released in September 1999. The Otago area has long been touted by wine experts,as the "Epernay" or Champagne capital of the Southern Hemisphere.

Chard Farm's exceptional location, don't be frightened by the River Chasm and "bungy jumpers", the drive to the winery, the vineyard vista the warm hospitality and great wines make the trip more than worth the trouble.

Address: Chard Road GIBBSTON	Winemaker: Rob Hay & John Wallace	Chard Farm Pinot Noir
Phone: +64 3 442 6100 Fax: +64 3 441 8400	Est: 1987 Vine Ha: 25 Cases: 15,000	Chard Farm Pinot Gris
Email: sales@chardfarm.co.nz	Public Hours: 10am-5pm, daily	Chard Farm Chardonnay
WWW: www.chardfarm.co.nz	Principal Wines	Chard Farm Riesling

Gibbston Valley Wines

As one of New Zealand's leading boutique wine producers, Gibbston Valley Winery, Restaurant and Wine Caves offers visitors a total quality winery experience.

The Gibbston Valley Winery is situated in the Kawarau Gorge on the main Queenstown-Cromwell Highway just 20 minutes drive from the popular resort town of Queenstown. It is perhaps the most visited winery in New Zealand or Australia.

The first experimental vines were planted in 1981 and the first commercial quantities of wine released in 1987. The company Gibbston Valley Wines Ltd was formed in 1990 and the winery and restaurant opened in December 1990.

As part of its ongoing commitment to the production of quality wines Gibbston Valley opened New Zealand's largest underground wine caves in December 1995. Over 1500 kilograms of explosives were used to blast 1400 cubic metres of schist rock from the hillside, to create the underground cellars which can now house up to 500 barrels.

With a stable year-round temperature

of 14 degrees the caves provide a near perfect environment for barrel ageing Pinot Noir and Chardonnay, as well as providing an exciting new visitor attraction for the Queenstown area. Visitors are personally hosted on a relaxed informative tour of the winery, vineyard and wine cave, culminating with wine tasting underground.

The restaurant at Gibbston Valley has become an integral part of the Southern Lakes dining experience. The restaurant is open for lunch daily featuring both courtyard and inside dining, with all areas providing a perfect setting for sole use by conference groups, wedding parties and private dinners. The kitchen brigade led by executive chef Mark Sage, offer menus with a strong emphasis placed on fresh local produce and ingredients,with great importance being placed on matching dishes with wines produced in the winery.

The wine caves and restaurant are currently being expanded and a cheese making facility is being opened where visitors can see cheeses being made.

Grapes are sourced from a range of vineyard sites throughout Otago, Gibbston Valley's own vineyards at Bendigo, Alexandra and the Home Block at Gibbston now stretch over 125 acres. 70% is planted in Pinot Noir with the rest in Riesling, Pinot Gris, Chardonnay and Sauvignon Blanc.

Kiwi winemaker Grant Taylor returned to New Zealand in 1993 after 15 years in the Napa Valley in the U.S.A. Now a "veteran" of the fledgling Otago winemaking fraternity his aims are simply put "to produce wine which express the region and the terroir through the fruit character". The dry, continental climate is exciting and the emergence of Pinot Noir as a key variety for the region, means the winemaking team are continually focused on producing wines of the highest possible quality.

Their early commitment to quality winemaking practices has paid dividends. Gibbston Valley Wines have been awarded over 70 medals at national and international wine shows. Over 30 medals have been for the Pinot Noir variety, including 9 gold medals and 8 trophies. The Reserve Pinot Noir has won a number of trophies at the Royal Easter Show, including champion wine of the show twice plus champion wine of the show (Japan International Wine Challenge). In 2001 at the world's largest wine competition, the London International Wine Challenge, the 2000 Reserve Pinot Noir won the Pinot Trophy · acknowledging it as the world's best, the 1999 Reserve Pinot also won a gold!! Approximately 200 tonne of fruit is processed through the winery each year resulting in 15,000 cases of finished wine. Extensions to the winery are currently underway that will double that capacity.

The wines are now shipped to overseas destinations including the UK, USA, Australia, Japan Singapore, Canada and Fiji. Gibbston Valley is an exemplory wine producer and wine tourism destination.

Address: RD 1 GIBBSTON
Phone: +64 3 442 6910 **Fax:** +64 3 442 6909
Email: gvwltd@gibbston-valley-wines.co.nz

WWW: www.gvwines.co.nz
Winemaker: Grant Taylor **Est:** 1987
Public Hours: 10am-5:30pm, daily

Principal Varieties: Chardonnay, Gewürztraminer, Pinot Gris, Pinot Noir, Riesling, Sauvignon Blanc

Olssens Garden Vineyard

John Olssen and Heather McPherson have created a rural haven in the rugged Bannockburn region, their 12 acres of gardens providing a real oasis amongst the stark dry craggy hills. The tasting room at the vineyard is serene and decorated with intriguing art of all sorts. During the summer months light food is served at tables outside the tasting room. People are also encouraged to bring their own picnic and take advantage of the shelter and shade provided by the gardens.

The first crop from their 25 acre vineyard came in 1994, for the first three vintage the grapes were supplied to Chard Farm. In 1997 the first wines appeared under the Bannockburn" label made totally from their own grapes, by winemaker Duncan Forsyth at Chard Farm. This year has seen an exciting new phase in Olssens development with the

commissioning of their own winery and the appointment of Peter Bartle as winemaker.

For a small boutique producer Olssens make a wide range of wines all of which have received critical acclaim. However it is the consistently high quality of their Pinot Noir which is establishing Olssens reputation in this fast growing wine producing area. The full bodied Slapjack Creek Reserve Pinot Noir is an excellent example of the high standards being set. Their

1998 Pinot Noir was voted best Pinot and overall champion wine at the Bragato awards last year. Karen Olssen their viticulturalist has twice won the Mike Wolter trophy at these same awards for growing the Pinot grapes used in the top placed wine. In addition to producing world class Pinot Noir Olssens also produce a full flavoured Chardonnay, a 'sancerre style' herbaceous Sauvignon Blanc, a favourite accompaniment to summer time food, a mouth-filling aromatic Gewürztraminer and a dry crisp Riesling. Two recent additions to the label are Desert Gold, a Late Harvest Riesling, which has received high praise and Robert the Bruce a robust blended red which lives up to its name.

Olssen's Vineyard is a paradise and a refreshing stop over in the dry desert like Bannockburn region.

Address: 306 Felton Rd BANNOCKBURN	Est: 1990 Vine Ha: 10		
Phone: −64 3 445 1716 Fax: +64 3 445 0050	Cases: 4,500	Chardonnay	4-6 yrs
Email: wine@olssens.co.nz	Public Hours: 10am-5pm, daily (Summer);	Sauvignon Blanc	2 yrs
WWW: www.olsens.co.nz	11am-4pm, daily (Winter)	Riesling	4-6 yrs
Owner: John Olssen & Heather McPherson	Principal Wines Potential	Gewürztraminer	2-4 yrs
Winemaker: Peter Bartle	Pinot Noir 4-5 yrs	Desert Gold - Late Harvest Riesling	4-6 yrs

Peregrine Wines

On our visit to Peregrine the vineyards and characterful old stone buildings were very much in a state of development. Two years later 75 acres are under vine and the historic stone cottage and woolshed have been lovingly restored. Peregrine is expanding fast with another 190 acres of vineyards under contract being planted, mainly in the Cromwell area of Central Otago.

The first vintage from Peregrine got off to a flying start in 1998. Their Sauvignon Blanc outshone most of the Marlborough stars, when it won a gold medal at the Air New Zealand wine awards, also gaining a rare 5 star rating from Cuisine Magazine. Peregrine also produce a fruit driven, tropical style Pinot Gris, a crisp elegant Riesling and a gamey Pinot Noir.

Peregrine's slogan, "Wines with

Altitude" is very appropriate they have reached for the high ground in

every way and certainly found it.

Address: Kawarau Gorge Rd, RD1 QUEENSTOWN	Winemaker: Rudi Bauer	Peregrine Pinot Gris	0-4 yrs
Phone: +64 3 442 4000 Fax: +64 3 442 4038	Est: 1998 Cases: 8,500	Peregrine Chardonnay	0-5 yrs
Email: peregrine@xtra.co.nz	Public Hours: 10am-5pm, daily	Peregrine Sauvignon Blanc	0-2 yrs
WWW: www.peregrinewines.co.nz	Principal Wines Potential	Peregrine Riesling	0-4 yrs
Owner: Greg Hay, Adam Peren & Phillip Anderson	Peregrine Pinot Noir 0-5 yrs	Peregrine Gewürztraminer	0-4 yrs

The Who's Who Of Wine

Vine cuttings arrived in Australia with the first fleet in 1788 and were planted somewhat unsuccessfully, at Farm Cove, not far from where Sydney's Opera House now stands. One of the early pioneers of Australia's wine industry was James Busby who went on to found the New Zealand Wine Industry. Over two hundred years of development of the Wine Industries of Australia and New Zealand there have been noteable contributions by many men and women.

The fields of Research, Viticulture, Winemaking, supply of essential products and services and the promotion of Wine have all been vital to the astounding development of the wine industry in both countries. Growth has been spectacular in the last decade but only because a solid and strong foundation has been laid in all areas by outstanding people.

The Who's Who of Wine begins with a section devoted to the most outstanding contributors to the Australian Wine Industry, both past and present, it is by no means exhaustive and as such as author and publisher, I apologise to anyone who feels a particular persons contribution has been overlooked. I

have worked on this project for almost 5 years, it has proved a difficult task and one which retrospectively I may not have undertaken, had I known what was in front of me. Apart from "The Legends of Wine" there is a section listing prominent people in the Wine Industry of today in both countries. The people featured are those who have accepted the opportunity to support this unique publication without whose help it would not have been possible to publish. As publisher I have gone to inordinate and expensive lengths to make sure every person in all areas of the wine industry has had the opportunity for a small investment to be included, alas I have not been able to present entries on all the people who should be present, none-the-less an impressive number of worthy entries are included.

My earnest wish is this 1st edition will provide the impetus necessary for a truly representative and even more valuable 2nd edition "Who's Who of Wine" to be published in several years time.

I also thank most sincerely a number of prominent wine industry organisations and suppliers for their

support and part sponsorship of this "Who's Who Section", Amorim Cork Australia, The Wolf Blass Foundation, Booth Transport, Collotype Labels and Mono Pumps Australia. Each has a feature outlining the valuable role they play in Australia's Wine Industry.

My personal philosophy, very much supported by my travels through the wine industries of the world, over many years, is that the most important ingredient in the creation of premium wines is not climate, soil, state of the art equipment or any other physical ingredient it is people with their ingenuity, hard work and perseverance.

So often, particularly when travelling with my wonderful friend, photographer and philosopher, the late Milan Roden, we found truly great wines in regions and from grape varieties the experts say good wines can never be made from, in Milan's words (I first used to treat with some cynicism) "Thomas you know the wines are only a reflection of the people who make them". How true it is, and so to those who have made the wines of Australia and New Zealand so great, I'm sure you would like to make their acquaintance.

The Legends Of Wine

Thomas William Carlyon Angove

Position: Chairman
Organisation: Angove's Pty Ltd
DOB: Renmark 8th Aug, 1917
Education/Honours: Holdfast Bay Prep. School, Wykeham Prep School and St Peters College, R.D Oen, Roseworthy Agricultural College, gaining all prizes awarded in the course: The Leo Buring Gold Medal for the highest aggregate work in all diploma subjects, the R.H. Martin Tasting Prize and the Karl Weidenhofer Prize for Individual Study for his project on brandy distillation. The project was highly creditable and was later published and subsequently reprinted in booklet form.
Career History: February 1941 became a Director of Angove's Pty Ltd, September 1941 he enlisted in the Royal Australian Air Force as a trainee pilot and served until discharged in September 1944 with rank Flight Lieutenant F/LT, 1946 became Managing Director of Angove's Limited, 1969 commenced the development on the River Murray of the largest single vineyard in Australia. After some years of quiet experimenting, the company released a world first, Tom Angove had the idea of a plastic or flexible bag inside a rigid cardboard box as a way of selling wine. The dream became reality in 1965 and the ingeniousness of the idea is clearly demonstrated by the hold which the soft pack now has in the table wine market place, 1977 he was awarded the Queen Elizabeth II Silver Jubilee Medal for services to the wine industry (1952-1977), he retired as Managing Director of Angove's Pty Ltd in January 1983 and was succeeded by his son John. He continues as Chairman of the Board of Directors. He is recognised by the industry as having had tremendous influence in the development of the River Murray area.
Hobbies/Clubs: Boating and all river activities. Adelaide Club. Naval and Military Club.

Brian Joseph Barry

Position: Director/Winemaker
Organisation: Jud's Hill Nominees Pty Ltd
Date of Birth: Murray Bridge, SA 15th February, 1927
Education/Honours: Leaving Honours, Diploma Oenology, Foseworthy 1948, Hons.
Directorates: Jud's Hill Nominees Pty Ltd
Career History: March 1948 graduated Roseworthy, R.D. Oen (Hons), 1948-1952, Chemist and Assistant Winemaker, Hamiltons Ewell Vineyards, 1952-1976, Technical Manager, Berri Co-operative Winery and Distillery Ltd, 1976-1980, Operations director, Leasingham Stanley Winery, 1980 - current Jud's Hill Nominees Pty Ltd, 1961-2001 Wine Judge
Hobbies/Clubs: Tennis, Cricket, Football, Horse Races, Petanque

Wolfgang Franz Otto Blass

Organisation: Wolf Blass & Associates
DOB: East Germany 2nd Sep, 1934
Education/Honours: High School
Career History: 1949 - East Germany, apprenticeship wine-making and viticulture, 1953-54 Wine University - Master of Wine - Kellermeister Diploma, Wurzburg, 1954, Sparkling Winemaker & Kellermeister, Germany, 1957 Wine Chemist and Cellar Superintendent, London - Bristol, 1960 job offers as sparkling wine expert - Australia or Venezuela (South America), 1961 first Diploma Holder - Wine & Spirit (London) migrated to Australia, 1961-1963 Kaiser Stuhl Co-op, Pearl Wines and Sparkling Wine development, 1964-1969, first freelance technical adviser, operated a selling arm under the name "Selected Wine Distributor", 1969-1973 Manager & Winemaker, United Distillers Tollano, Table Wine production, heralded the "Golden Boy" in the new era, 1973 resigned and started his own business with a $2,000 overdraft, 1974 won 3 consecutive Jimmy Watson Trophies, 1974 (Melbourne) 1974, 1975, 1976, 1976 John Glaetzer joined Blass, Bilyara Vineyards adopts Eaglehawk Label, National distribution Network in all States, Export - first exported in mid 1970's to New Zealand, Fiji, Hong Kong, Singapore, Malaysia and Papua New Guinea, 1977 change of style and development of a new Rhine Riesling, 1984-1985 1.6 million bottles were sold, 1984 Wolf Blass Wines became a Public Company, 1985 establishment of the Wolf Blass headquarters, National Marketing Award for Excellence, International partnership with Remy Martin, France and formation of Remy/Blass sales distribution - a National Company, 1986 50% acquisition of the independent Australian Bottling Company, 1987 South Australian Great Achievements Award in Commerce, 1989 Finalist in National Business Entrepreneur of the Year Award, Sydney, 1990 New Zealand joint venture Wine Company in the Marlborough Region between Corbans Wines and Wolf Blass Wines International, joint venture with one of the World's largest Wine and Spirit Manufacturers and Distributors - Joseph E. Seagrams & Sons Inc, 1991 personally initiated Australia's very first Public Museum of the Wine Industry, formation of Mildara Blass Limited - merged with Mildara, formation of Wolf Blass & Associates Pty Ltd, release of the biography "Wolf Blass - A Journey in Wine", 1992 acclaimed International Winemaker of the Year, awarded the Robert Mondavi Trophy, 1994 Founder Chairman of the $1,000,000 Wolf Blass Foundation, 1996 takeover - Mildara Blass was acquired by the CUB Fosters Corporation, Wolf Blass Foundation staged the inaugural International Wine & Health Conference "Medically, is wine just another alcoholic beverage", awarded an Honorary Doctorate of Applied Science, 1997 awarded the Inaugural 'Legend of Langhorne Creek Honour', currently Ambassador for Wolf Blass Wines International, participating in promotion, overseas development and maintaining the quality style of the winemaking production.

Lindsay Stanley Booth

Position: Founder
Organisation: L S Booth Wine Transport
Date of Birth: 30th Aug, 1918 - 27th Mar, 1999 (dec.)
Education/Honours: Reynella Primary School (7 yrs)

Eric Brand

Position: Chief Executive Officer (retired)
Career History: Eric arrived in the Coonawarra in 1950 when he married Bill Redman's daughter Nancy. He bought a small block of orchards and vineyards from the Redman family. He began making his own wine in 1966 with equipment and support from Hardy's Wines. In the late 1960's he launched one of Coonawarra's first boutique wines under the "Laira" label. Always a supporter of the region, he is still actively involved, even though well into his eighties.

Harry Gena Brown

Position: Deceased - Managing Director - Founder
Organisation H.G. Brown & Sons Pty Ltd - est. 1964 - sold 1979
Date of Birth: Sydney, Australia 28th Nov, 1918
Career History: Harry started in the liquor business below the legal drinking age. In fact he worked for Johnnie Walker Senior at Walker's Wine Bar (and later Rhinecastle Wines) washing bottles out the back. He graduated to selling bulk wine in the cellar - customers would bring in their empty flagons and Harry would fill them from barrels. While working for Johnnie Walker he made lifelong friendships with people, indeed if anyone can claim to have put Wolf Blass on the map, it is Harry Brown - Wolf's first wholesaler in NSW. Early on Harry had important influence on the Tulloch family's success, he helped build their brand identity and boosted their sales. In 1939 he was at the first meeting of the Wine & Food Society of NSW and in 1947 was involved in the beginnings of The Wine Society, which originally operated out of Rhinecastle's offices and warehouse. Later, Harry set up his own wholesale distribution business, H.G. Brown & Sons, based at Gibbes Street, Chatswood, where there was a resident chef and guests were regularly wined and dined by Harry, his wife Simone and sons Robin & Roger. The Browns were not only the leading distributors of Australian wines, they had importing rights for some of the great wines of the world, such as Deinhard, Mouton-Rothschild, Joseph Drouhin, Trimbach, Laurent-Perrier, KWV, Prosper Maufoux, Fonseca port and Mateus Rosé. He made frequent buying trips to Europe. He began his own table wine brand in 1966 originally made by Jim Ingolcby. In 1974 Harry's son Robin died suddenly, throwing the business into disarray. Harry was forced to sell the company in 1979, and H.J. Heinz, the baked-bean maker which then owned Stanley Leasingham, took over. Harry and Roger continued to work for H.G. Brown-Stanley Leasingham until 1981, when Harry went to work for the Tyrrells and Roger started his own wholesaling business, Roger Brown Wine Agencies.
Hobbies/Clubs: Royal Sydney Yacht Squadron

The Legends Of Wine

John Francis Brown

Position: Founder of Brown Brothers

Organisation: Brown Brothers

Date of Birth: Hurdle Creek, 18th June 1867

Education/Honours: Attended the primary school near the family's Hurdle Creek property, which has long since gone out of existence. He involved himself in a good deal of self-taught education, particularly in regard to accounting and bookkeeping

Directorates: Director of Wangaratta Flour Milling for a period in the 1930's.

Hobbies/Clubs: His Oxley Shire activities were his main interest apart from growing grapes and making and selling his wine, Milawa Football Club

Hermann Paul Leopold Buring

Position: Deceased 1961

Organisation: Leo Buring

Date Of Birth: South Australia 7th October, 1876

Education/Honours: Prince Alfred College (1884-1894), Roseworthy Agricultural College (1894-1896), Dux of Oenology 1896, Roseworthy Diploma of Agriculture 1896, Roseworthy Diploma of Oenology 1937

Career History: He was a highly skilled winemaker and is often described as "Australia's Ambassador for Wine" because he was one of the first to export Australian wine to many countries as far back as the early 1900's. Gained practical experience in Europe before settling back in Australia at Minchinbury in 1902. Four years later his wines earned 6 gold medals at The Brewers and Wine Exhibition in London. He finally achieved his dream at the age of 68 when he bought the Orange Grove Winery at Tanunda, in the Barossa Valley which he re-named "Chateau Leonay". Over the years he established a reputation as Australia's foremost maker of Riesling - the flagship being Leo Buring Leonay. They combine intense fruit flavours with great elegance. His influence in introducing Australia to table wine has been far reaching. His influence on the industry, ranging from technical advice to government reports, resulted in many improvements.

James Busby

Career History: An English immigrant to Australia he was one of the founders of the Australian Wine Industry in New South Wales in the early 1800's. He travelled to New Zealand where he made New Zealand's first wines in 1836 at Waitangi on New Zealand's North Island, selling the wines to British troops stationed nearby.

William Bruce Chambers

Position: Director

Organisation: Chambers Rosewood Winery

Date of Birth: Rutherglen 5th June, 1933

Education/Honours: Roseworthy, Diploma of Oenology

Hobbies/Clubs: Naval & Military Club

Garry Crittenden

Position: Chief Executive

Organisation: Dromana Estate

Career History: An early pioneer of the modern era of wine on Victoria's Mornington Peninsula, founding Dromana Estate Vineyards in 1982. A former nurseryman and proprietor of one of Victoria' largest commercial nurseries he has established many unusual and seldom seen grape varieties, particularly those eminating from Italy. He has been a leader in the making and marketing of Italian varietals and received recognition and a number of awards for this work, also publishing a book on the subject. Garry has also been a Director of Domaine Chandon in the Yarra Valley. He and wife Margaret have pioneered the winery café-food concept and Wine and Food tourism, in an innovative and classy manner.

Brian Croser

Position: Chief Executive

Organisation: Petaluma Wines

Date of Birth: Born 1948

Education/Honours: Adelaide University - Agricultural Science (Hons), 1971 - Davis University, California

Career History: One of the most influential individuals of the modern era of Australian wine. An honours graduate in Agricultural Science from the Adelaide University he joined Thomas Hardy & Sons in 1970 travelling to Davis University in 1971 where he studied, going on to Europe on a study tour. He returned to Australia becoming Chief Winemaker briefly for Hardy's before leaving to inaugurate the wine degree course at Wagga (now Charles Sturt University) in 1976. Whilst still at Charles Sturt he began Petaluma Wines now an extremely successful premium, publicly listed, wine company. His work in the technology of white wine making revolutionized Australian White Wines in the 1970's. He has led many Industry lobbies to the National Government and is a former President of the Winemakers Federation of Australia. A Champion of the Industry.

Len Evans, A.O., O.B.E.

Position: Chief Executive Officer, Winemaker

Organisation: Evans Family Wines

Date of Birth: Born 1930's

Career History: The most influential person in the Australian Wine Industry in the last half of the 20th century. Len almost became a professional golfer in New Zealand before wine became his life. His Bulletin Place Wine & Food mecca focussed Australian's on wine in its true content in the 1960's, he went on to found the Rothbury Wine Society and

Winery in the Lower Hunter pioneering wine and food functions on a grand scale. His erudite and entertaining manner and extraordinary public speaking ability combined with his extraordinary palate and wine knowledge has helped immeasurably the development and expansion of the Australian Wine Industry and helped gain its preeminent position in the world of wine. Awarded the O.B.E. and the O.A. for his services to the wine industry.

Gustav Gramp

Position: Deceased

Organisation: G. Gramp & Sons Ltd (now Orlando)

Date of Birth: Barossa Valley, SA 1850

History: Gustav was the eldest of seven children between Johann Gramp and his wife. In 1874 Gustav married and his father gave him 40 acres as a wedding present. Gustav steadily extended his vineyards so that production reached 3,200 gallons in 1892 and had more than doubled within a decade. As his operations expanded Johann Gramp integrated his wine making with his son until in 1877 Gustav took over from his famous father, and paved that way for the next, crucial era of expansion of Australian wines. He maintained the traditions from the new base at Rowland Flat, planting new areas of vineyard and increasing fermenting and storage capacity. As public tastes changed throughout the years, Gustav enlarged the range of his wines. He built substantial cellars in the 1880's and enlarged them as the business flourished. These original buildings have been incorporated into the heart of the modern Orlando complex. Then in 1912 the business was sufficiently prosperous to warrant conversion into a limited company, and so G. Gramp & Sons Ltd was born. Gustav's most famous wine was his Carte Blanche, a hock-style white which became synonymous with consistency and reliability to such an extent that it was one of the first Australian wines to be bought on label alone. Gustav took his fathers' legacy, what would become the Orlando story to the next stage.

James Halliday

Position: Lawyer, Wine Writer, Wine Judge

Career History: Australia's most prominent and respected wine writer and wine judge. A lawyer by profession, his keen interest in wine led him to be one of the three founding partners of the legendary Brokenwood Wines in the Lower Hunter Valley, NSW in 1970. He began writing books and articles on wine in the 1970's. His compendium of Australia's Wineries and his yearly wine annual have been extremely successful as has his Australian and New Zealand Wine Atlas. He wrote for The Australian Newspaper on wine for a number of years. In 1985 he established Coldstream Hills Vineyards and Winery in Victoria's Yarra Valley, an icon wine producer, now owned by Southcorp Wines. James is still actively involved along with his wine, judging and prolific wine writing.

The Legends Of Wine

Richard Hamilton

Position: Founder
Organisation: Hamilton's Ewell Vineyards
Date of Birth: England
Career History: Richard established his Ewell Vineyards and Winery at Marion, a suburb of Adelaide, in 1837, the same year John Reynell established Reynella Wines, the first two wineries in the South Australian colony, founded only one year earlier. Whilst his company was sold to Mildara in the 1970's many of his descendants are involved in the wine industry including Dr Richard Hamilton who's Hamilton Wine Group manage one of Richard's (the founder) original vineyards at Marion where the vines are well over 100 years old. Mark Hamilton and Hugh Hamilton also own and operate wine companies.

Sir James Gilbert Hardy

Position: Company Director - formerly Director/Manager NSW/Eastern States ("Wine Company Executive")
Organisation: Thomas Hardy & Sons Pty Ltd, subsequently BRL Hardy Ltd
Date of Birth: Seacliff, SA, 20th November, 1932
Education/Honours: St Peters College, Adelaide, Australian Society of Accountants, Order of the British Empire (OBE), Knight Bachelor (KT)
Directorates: Former Chairman Royal Society for the Blind, NSW, Former Grand Master Freemasons Lodge, NSW
Hobbies/Clubs Royal Sydney Yacht Squadron, "505" World Yachting Champion 1966, America's Cup Helmsman "Gretel II" 1970, "Southern Cross" 1974, "Southern Cross II" 1977, Member Australia II Team, Winner America's Cup 1983, Holder of many Industry, Community & Sporting positions

Thomas Hardy

Position: Deceased 10th January, 1912
Organisation: Thomas Hardy & Sons Pty Ltd
Date of Birth: Gittisham, Devon, England 12th Jan, 1830
History: 1850-1851 workman, Reynell Farm, 1852-1852 Goldfields (Forest Creek, Vic), 1853 Founded winemaking and horticultural enterprise at Bankside, SA, 1876 took over Tintara Vineyard Company, 1878 bought Motlock's Flour Mill, McLaren Vale, by 1893 Thomas Hardy & Sons processed Australia's largest vintage - 315,000 gallons
Hobbies/Clubs: Olive Growing, Olive Oil Production, other Horticultural Crops, Gardening, Travel, wrote a number of books including "The Vineyards and Wine Cellars of California"

Colin Haselgrove

Position: Winemaker, Director, M.D./C.E.O.
Organisation: Thomas Hardy & Sons Pty. Ltd., Emu Wines, Walter Reynell & Sons Pty. Ltd.
Date of Birth: Born 1904 - Deceased December 1982
Education/Honours: Roseworthy College (Diploma of Agriculture Dux) 1924, Université de Montpellier - Post Graduate Diploma, Order of the British Empire (OBE)
Directorates: Thomas Hardy & Sons, Mildara Wines, Australian Wine Research Institute, Reynella Wines, Australian Wine Board
Career History: Worked and studied in Cognac - France and Algeria before holding many Company and Industry positions.
Hobbies/Clubs: Royal South Australian Yacht Squadron, Winner of the 1950 Sydney-Hobart Yacht Race in "Nerida".

Ian Laurie Hickinbotham

Position: Oenologist, Wine Educator
Organisation: Hickinbotham Winemakers Pty Ltd - retired
Date of Birth: Horsham, Vic, 23rd March, 1929
Education/Honours: Roseworthy Diploma of Oenology, Order of Australia OAM, Honorary Life Membership American Society for Enology & Viticulture
Career History: Ian has contributed much to the progress of Australian winemaking in four States, he even exported the first Tasmanian wine from grapes transported across and vinified near Geelong in 1982, he is also the first Australian oenologist to be awarded the prestigious Honorary Life Membership of the American Society of Enology and Viticulture. Some experts believe Ian was the first oenologist in no less than four of Australia's now classical wine regions, Coonawarra, Hunter Valley, Geelong and Mornington Peninsula, his pioneering also included developing a new way of packaging 200ml bottles then selling them to airlines whereby tourists tasted up to 200 different Australian wines while in flight. His family company, purchased wines from winegrowers in six States and applied winegrowers front labels and a Hickinbotham Winemakers' back label story, a scheme unique in the world. Due to Ian's adoption of Australian invented technology (a machine for removing air from empty bottles and a new type of screw cap) passengers enjoyed superior quality wines on Ansett, Qantas, British Airways and Lufthansa. While with Penfolds he initiated development of the Bag-in-the-Box package concept and though the company subsequently abandoned the project, later to become known as the Tablecask, 70% of Australia's table wines were sold in this form. When managing Kaiser Stuhl he invented the transfer machine for Champagne making, subsequently adapted by a German machinery company, and was first to apply an hermetic centrifuge to sparkling wine

when he made the inaugural Sparkling Ringolde and Gala Spumante (Australia's first such wine style). He also introduced acknowledgement of grapegrowers of superior quality grapes on labels, as the 'Individual Vineyard Wines'. His greatest contribution to winemaking was his inaugural encouragement of the natural bacterial fermentation. In later years, Ian founded the Wine Press Club of Victoria, while he continues to stage wine appreciation seminars at Hickinbotham's Dromana winery and is Features Writer of the Australian Society of Wine Education's quarterly.

Robert Wyndham Hill Smith

Position: Chief Executive Officer/Proprietor
Organisation: Yalumba Wine Company
Date of Birth: Adelaide 29th October, 1951
Education/Honours: Angaston Primary School, St Peters College, BB (Marketing) - University of SA 1985, Stanford University 1994
Directorates: Lord Nelson Brewery Hotel, Erlistoun Gold, Vintage Bloodstock
Career History: School, University, Travelled Europe, AWBC 1993-1995, AME 1995-1998, AWEC 1996-2001+, SATRA 1997-2000, SACA 2000
Hobbies/Clubs: Cricket, Football, Thoroughbreds, Art, Food, Travel, Wine, SACA, Groucho Club, RAGC, Tanunda Golf Club, VRC, SAJC

Warren John

Career History: Warren is one of Australia's most respected Coopers making fine oak barrels for the Wine Industry. He has fought hard in a family business, that like all coopers, went through many years, when survival was difficult. Leading winemakers like Wolf Blass have sworn by the quality of his barrels and the many gold medals their wines have won speaks loudly for the quality of his work. His son Peter is carrying on the family's fine tradition.

Dr Alexander Charles Kelly

Position: Director/Manager, Managing Director, Chief Executive Officer, Founder
Organisation: Tintara Vineyard Company
Date of Birth: Born Dunbar, Scotland, 1811 - Deceased 9th October, 1877
Education/Honours: M.D. Edinburgh University, 1832
Career History: A pioneer of South Australian wine and a crusader for the health benefits of wine particularly the ironstone rich red wines produced in the southern vales south of Adelaide. His great vision led to the entrepreneurial establishment of the Tintara Vineyard Company. Unfortunately, although the vineyards and winery were very well established commercially, it was not a success, being bought at auction by Thomas Hardy in 1876.

The Legends Of Wine

John Kilgour

Position: Winemaker, Senior Winemaker
Organisation: Thomas Hardy & Sons
DOB: Darwin 9th November, 1910, Deceased 5th August, 1995
Education/Honours: Roseworthy Diploma of Agriculture 1932

Career History For many years was winemaker at Stonyfell under Henry Martin, he became famed for his fortified wines later to become winemaker for the Emu Wine Company running their Tatachilla Winery. His innovative style, ability and desire to share his discoveries and experience with others assisted and inspired many up and coming young winemakers. He pioneered the Ion exchange and Colour Spectro Photometry technology techniques. The Tasting Room at the Adelaide TAFE College was named after him.
Hobbies/Clubs: President Bacchus Club Adelaide 1955-1956

Max Lake

Organisation: Lake's Folly
Date of Birth: Born1924
Career History: From 1960, became Chairman Judges International Wine, Expovin 1977, Great Britain 1986, Wines of the Americas 1985-199, initial member of the National Wine Show advisory committee. Honorary Life Member Royal Agricultural Society Tasmania, Chairman subcommittee National Health & Medical Research Council for the revision of Wine & Spirit standards 1981-1982, NSW Government Award for distinguished service to the Wine Industry 1997. First wine publication "Claret Style in Australia", 1959, Author 12 books "classic Wines of Australia" 1966, Australia's all-time best 101 books (Bulleting 1991, Flavour 1991), has also appeared in Japanese, German and Portuguese editions. Cited Encyc. Brit. Year book, Definitive work on Food and Wine Flavour due 2002, "Australia's own philosopher in the kitchen" John Newton, founder Asian-Pacific Zone International Wine & Food Society. Max Lake founded Lake's Folly in 1963. This and his writing clearly were in the vanguard of the resurgence of the Cabernet Sauvignon and Chardonnay varieties in Australia. It was the first of the family small vineyards to sell its own production to the public, and its success, and shared experience influenced the hundreds of boutique wineries that are now such an adornment of Australian wine here and overseas.

Peter Leon Lehmann

Position: Founder and Deputy Chairman
Organisation: Peter Lehmann Wines Ltd
Date of Birth: Angaston 18th August, 1930
Education/Honours:
Member Order of Australia (AM), First List of the Order
Directorates: Peter Lehmann Wines Ltd
Career History: 1947-1959 commenced winemaking at Yalumba - training under Rudi Kronberger, 1959-1979 Winemaker/Manager Saltram & Production Manager Dalgety Wine Estates 1972-1979, founded Masterson 1977 to crush grower's fruit for 1978 vintage and 1979 vintage at Saltram, President - Barossa Vintage Festival 1974-1978, founded Masterson Barossa Vignerons 1979 and built winery, first vintage 1980 on present Tanunda site, 1982 name changed to Peter Lehmann Wines, various partners through 1980's, 1992 majority partner M S McLeod decides to sell, 1993 float of Peter Lehmann Wines Ltd, now a very successful public company
Hobbies/Clubs: Gardening, Reading, Classical Music

Dr Henry Lindeman

Career History: One of Australia's pioneering wine Doctors, a Royal Naval Surgeon, he settled in the Hunter Valley in 1842 establishing vineyards at Cawarra, Coolatta, Catawba, Warrawee and Kirkton. He went on to purchase the Ben Ean Winery in 1912, from where Lindemans expanded into one of Australia's largest and most successful wine companies. Today its many wine enterprises are part of the Southcorp Wine Group. "You make us smile Dr Lindeman".

Brian McGuigan AM

Position: Managing Director

Organisation: Brian McGuigan Wines Ltd
Date of Birth: Newcastle 2nd July, 1942
Career History: Brian McGuigan established the Wyndham Estate wine company at Dalwood in the Hunter Valley in the 1970's. As Managing Director he built one of the most successful wine companies in Australia producing in excess of 1,250,000 cases annually. Under Brian and his wife Fay, Wyndham became one of the leading exporters of Australian wine. Following the sale of Wyndham in 1991 Brian established a new company, Brian McGuigan Wines Ltd, in 1992. Total sales are now approaching 800,000 cases. He was awarded the Order of Australia Medal in the 1988 Queens Birthday Honours, voted the NSW winemaker of the Year, named NSW Outstanding Liquor Industry Executive, Foundation member of the Hunter Economic Development Corporation, Executive of the Hunter Valley Vineyard Association for 25 years, (four periods as Chairman), Businessman of the Year for Northern NSW for the Year 1997, his company was awarded the Enterprise Award by Newcastle Council of Commerce - 1984, past Director of the Australian Rural Group Ltd, Member of the NSW Wine Industry Association, his Company being awarded Exporter of the Year for 1986, awarded Rotary Annual Award for Vocational Excellence - 1994, current Chairman of the

Mater Miscricordia Hospital in Newcastle and heavily involved in the development of the Pokolbin community's new pipeline to carry water from the Hunter River to the Pokolbin region. He also chairs a committee to develop a similar pipeline to the Broke/Fordwich area.

Hobbies/Clubs: Newcastle Club

Samuel McWilliam

Position: Founder
Organisation: McWilliams Wines
Career History: Planted vineyards at Corowa on the River Murray in New South Wales in 1877 establishing a family wine dynasty that still remains in family hands today. In 1913, son J.J. McWilliam drove a bullock dray with 40,000 cuttings to Hanwood near Griffith and established the Riverina Wine Industry.

Jack Mann

Position: Winemaker
Organisation: Houghton Wines
Date of Birth: Perth, Australia 19th March, 1906 - Deceased 1989
Education/Honours: Middle Swan Primary School, Midland Junction High School, Member of the British Empire (MBE) 1964
Career History: Created Houghton White Burgundy in 1937 which became the market leader and yardstick for Australian white wines. Was a pioneer in many innovative winemaking spheres such as the temperature control of white wine fermentation. Famous also for his warm generous red table wines, many of which attest to his skill long after his death. He inspired many winemakers and promoted constantly the health and social benefits of sensible wine consumption.
Hobbies/Clubs: Cricket, Shooting, Verdi, Swan Valley Vintners, W.A. Cricket Association

Charles Henry (Mick) Morris

Position: Chief Executive Officer (retired)
Organisation: Morris Wines
Date of Birth: 1st July, 1928
Career History: Descendant of wine pioneer, George Morris, who established the grand Fairfield Winery in the 1870's. Mick's grandfather, Charles, established Morris Wines at Mia Mia. Mick is one of the true stalwarts of the Victorian and Rutherglen wine industries who stoically produced vintage after vintage of great and often unappreciated full bodied reds, whites and fortified wines for 5 decades from the 1940's to the end of the 1980's. His son David carries on the tradition today.

The Legends Of Wine

Dan Murphy

Career History: A determined, resolute and resilient figure, Dan revolutionised the selling promotion and marketing of Australian wine when he established "The Vintage Club", in a huge historic arcade in Melbourne's Prahran, in the late 1950's. It grew to almost 100,000 members. Dan bottled his own wines for the club and also championed and promoted proprietary brands of premium table wine. For many years his wine column in Tuesday's Age Newspaper was compulsory reading for the wine enthusiast. His concept launched in the 1980's of the Wine Warehouse at Alplington followed by other Melbourne suburbs took wine marketing in the retail sense to another level. These stores have now been purchased by Woolworths and Dan has finally retired. The 'doyen' of the retail wine industry

Robert Oatley

Position: Founder
Organisation: Rosemount Estate Wines
Career History: Robert founded Rosemount Estate Wines in the Upper Hunter Valley, NSW in 1969. He built his company into one of Australia's largest premium wine companies with vineyards and wineries in many different regions. He made Rosemount one of the worlds best known premium wine producers with enormous export sales. In 2001 he oversaw the merging of Rosemount with Southcorp Wines, Australia's largest producer, which has now been substantially strengthened by this merger.

Maurice O'Shea

Position: Winemaker, Manager
Organisation: Mount Pleasant Wines
Date of Birth: Deceased · 1956
Education/Honours: University of Montpellier, France
Career History: Of French origin, he returned to France to study winemaking at Montpellier in 1921, following the purchase by his family of the Mount Pleasant Vineyards and Winery in the Lower Hunter Valley, established by Charles Frig in 1880. He became the most celebrated winemaker of his time showing an uncanny skill for blending wines to create classics. In 1932 he sold half the business to McWilliams, later they purchased the business outright. Maurice remained as Winemaker and Manager until his death in 1956. The longevity of his wines ensures even today they can amaze the most vigorous critics.

Ira John Pendrigh, AM, FAICD

Position: Chairman
Organisation: BRL Hardy Ltd
DOB: Monaco 1st April, 1931
Education/Honours: Bedford School (UK) · O & C Matriculation, HMS · Conway · Leaving Certificate, University of London · Foreign Going Navigation Officers Certificate A.S.A., Member of the Order of Australia (AM)
Directorates: National Wine Centre Inc.
Career History: 1949-1953 · British Merchant Navy · Navigation Officer (RNR), 1953-1969 · General Manager & Director, C.H. Smith & Co Pty Ltd Ships Agents, Lloyds Agent, N.Tasmania, 1969-1981 · Regional Manager, Terminal Properties of Aust. Container Terminal & Depot Operators, Port Adel. S.A. (Trans Ocean Terminals & Freightbases) 1981-1992 · Managing Director & Chief Executive, Berri Renmano, consolidated cooperative wineries Ltd & associated companies, 1985-1992 · Managing Director, Valley Growers Cooperative Ltd, 1986-1992 Councillor, Winemakers Federation of Australia, 1988-1994 · Director, Wine Trust of Australia, 1988-1996 · Director, Australian Wine & Brandy Corporation, Chairman 1993-1996, Dep. Chair 1992-1993, Chairman 1993-1996 · Australian Wine Exporters council, Chairman 1992-1996 · International Trade & Technical Advisory Committee, 1991-1995 Chairman, Australian Horticultural Policy Council, 1992-1995 · Member, Federal Government, 'E.C./Australia' Wine agreement, negotiating team, 1992 · date · Director & current Chairman, BRL Hardy Ltd, 1994-1995 · Chairman, S.A. Ports Corporatisation task force, 1996 · date · Director, National Wine Centre Inc., 1992 · date, self employed, Consultant & Company Director
Hobbies/Clubs: Duplicate Bridges, S.A. Bridge Association

Dr Christopher Rawson Penfold

Position: Deceased · March 1870 · age 59
Organisation: Penfolds
Date of Birth: 1811
Education/Honours: Studied medicine at St Bartholomew's Hospital, London
History: Emigrated to South Australia at the age of 33 with his wife Mary and daughter Georgina. They arrived in the colony, founded only eight years before, aboard the Taglioni on August 8, 1844. They had purchased 500 acres at Magill in the foothills of the Mount Lofty ranges about five miles from the infant settlement of Adelaide for £1200. Some 200 acres were already under crops and even then Magill was considered choice real estate. Before leaving Britain he had obtained vine cuttings from the south of France and these were planted around the site of the modest stone cottage he built in 1845.
The couple called this house The Grange, after Mary's home in England. Dr Penfold built up his medical practice and made fortified wines · port and sherry for his patients. As the demand for his wine grew he expanded the vineyards and increased production. At some stage in the 1850's, wine probably took over from medicine as the family's chief source of income. Dr Penfold died at Magill in March 1870, at the age of 59, after many years of poor health. Mary Penfold assumed control of the still-growing wine business, with help from Georgina's husband Thomas Hyland.

Ron Potter

Career History: Designer of much of today's innovative Australian winemaking equipment which has put Australia at the top of the world's premium wine producing nations. The "Potter Tank" for draining and fermentation is an Australian Legend. He became the first winemaker at the Miranda winery in Griffith, NSW in the early 1950's.

Guenter Prass, AM

Position: Oenologist, General Manager (former)
Organisation: Barossa Valley Estates
Date of Birth: Breitscheid, Germany Nov 20th, 1926
Education/Honours: Oppenheim/Rhein. Dip. Viticulture and Oenology
Career History: 1946-1955 work experience · winemaker/cellarmaster Estate Winery, Mosel, Germany, consultant winemaker to winery supplier Seitz Werke, winemaking experience in various mediterranean countries, 1955 table winemaker Orlando Wines, Rowland Flat, Barossa Valley, 1959-1979 Production Manager, Technical Director, Orlando Wines. Part of management team which created wine styles Barossa Pearl, Starwine, Coolabah, Jacob's Creek, Carrington, St Helga, St Hugo, 1979-1987 Managing Director, Orlando Wines responsible for company performance, actively involved in developing export markets for Australian wines, 1988 Chairman, Orlando Wines, 1989-1992 Director of Trading, Thomas Hardy & Sons, 1992-1995 General Manager, Barossa Valley Estates. Invested Member of the Order of Australia for services to the Australian wine industry, AM, 1991, Member of the Barossa Valley Wine fraternity, Barons of the Barossa

Colin Preece

Position: Winemaker 1923-1963
Organisation: B. Seppelt & Sons
Date of Birth: Deceased 7th September, 1979
Career History: Colin Preece devoted his entire working life to Seppelt. He became a legend in his own lifetime because of the great wines he produced at Great Western. After a distinguished career of 30 years, he was forced to retire due to ill health. Wine industry commentators label him "Master" and rank him with three other greats · Maurice O'Shea (Mt Pleasant), Roger Warren (Hardy's) and Max Schubert (Penfolds).

Bill Redman

Date of Birth: Born 1887 · Deceased 1979
Career History: Arrived in Coonawarra in 1901, the year of John Riddoch's death. In 1907 he became head cellarman at Riddochs Yallum Park and purchased his own 40 acre block from Riddoch's Estate. Around 1910 he produced his first wine using an old cheese press and fermented it in hogsheads from Douglas A Tolley who purchased the wine for one shilling per gallon. From 1919 when Yallum was purchased by Chateau Tanunda and stopped producing, Redman remained

The Legends Of Wine

Coonawarra's only winemaker until 1945 when Woodley's purchased Yallum Estate and recommenced winemaking. In all he presided over 65 vintages.

John Reynell

Position: Founder, Master, Owner
Organisation: Reynell Farm (became Walter Reynell & Sons Pty Ltd after his death)
Date of Birth: Bristol, England 9th February, 1809, died 15th June 1873

John Riddoch

Position: Deceased - 1901
Organisation: Wynns Coonawarra
Date of Birth: Banffshire, Scotland October 1826
History: What is now Wynns Coonawarra Estate was founded by Scottish pioneer John Riddoch, who noticed the fertility of a small strip of red soil - terra rossa - in the far south-east of South Australia. He planted vineyards in 1891 and completed the estate's three-gabled winery in 1896. Riddoch died in 1901 and Coonawarra languished for the first half of this century. Coonawarra's revival began in 1951 when Melbourne wine merchants Samuel and David Wynn purchased Riddoch's original vineyards and winery and renamed the property Wynns Coonawarra Estate.

Edmund Roth

Career History: Granted 92 acres of land near Mudgee in 1858. This "Vine Dresser" from Germany founded the Mudgee wine industry. The discovery of gold in the region in 1872 did not sway him from his vinous path. By 1880 six of the thirteen wineries in the region were run by Roth and his sons. The family's connection with wine in the region continued for close on 100 years.

Max Schubert

Position: Chief Winemaker Retired
Organisation: Penfolds
DOB: Barossa Valley, 1915
Education/Honours: 1950 - studied sherry making in Spain, 1984 was made a Member of the Order of Australia, 1988 named London's Decanter Magazine "Man of the Year", 1990 Maurice O'Shea Award, South Australian Achiever of the Year
History: As the creator of Penfolds Grange Hermitage, Max Schubert is arguably the most important and influential figure in the modern Australian wine industry. Almost single-handedly Schubert lifted Australia's table wine industry out of mediocrity in the 1950s. Appointed Penfolds Chief Winemaker in 1948, Schubert 'retired' in 1975 but was retained as a consultant and kept an office at Penfolds' original winery at Magill near his home until shortly before his death. An early interest in the smells and tastes of wine and winemaking was kindled by life among a sea of vines and he joined Penfolds at Nuriootpa as a messenger boy in 1931, when the Depression was at

its height. Before long he was promoted to the position of chemist's assistant and within two years had moved to the Magill winery. He studied chemistry at night in the city. He was appointed an assistant winemaker at 25 and Production Manager (equivalent to Chief Winemaker) in 1948 at the age of 33. In 1950 Schubert was sent to study sherry making in Spain. On his way back he visited Bordeaux where he was taken under the wing of Christian Cruse, one of the most respected and highly qualified wine mend in France. Schubert returned from France and developed Grange Hermitage beginning with the 1951 vintage. He introduced a number of winemaking techniques for the first time in Australia. The costs of making Grange were high and Schubert was ordered to cease production before the 1957 vintage. However, he continued to make the wine in secret until production resumed officially with the 1960 vintage. In 1962 Penfolds entered the 1955 wine in the Sydney Show - it won a gold medal. With 35 trophies and championships, 117 gold and 97 other medals, Grange remains the most successful Australian show red of all time. As Chief Winemaker through the 1950s and 1960s Schubert also led development of the red wine 'family'. As recently as 1982 he designed the Magill Estate (first vintage 1983). In 1984 Schubert was made a Member of the Order of Australia for his services to the wine industry and in 1988 he received international recognition when London's Decanter magazine named him Man of the Year. In 1990 Schubert received the inaugural McWilliams-sponsored Maurice O'Shea Award for his contribution to the Australian wine industry, the same year he was named South Australian Achiever of the Year as part of the National Australia Day Council's Australia Day Awards. Max Schubert passed away at the age of 79 in March 1994.

William Douglas (Doug) Seabrook

Position: Managing Director (Owner)
Organisation: W.J. Seabrook & Son
Date of Birth: Melbourne 30th January, 1923
Career History: Doug commenced work in the family business, W.J. Seabrook & Son at an early age and worked in the company all his life except during Military Service. After his father Tom died in 1967, Doug changed the direction of the company to be more open in sales to the public. Doug dedicated his life to wine, advising wine makers in an expanding industry and also advising students and anyone else who was interested. He was Chairman of Judges at the Royal Melbourne Wine Show for about 30 years, a record not yet reached by any other.
Hobbies/Clubs: Wine/Garden, Athenaem

Oscar Benno Seppelt

Position: Founder - Seppelt
Organisation: Seppelt
Date of Birth: Deceased
History: 1849 Joseph Seppelt and his family migrated to Australia from Silesia in Eastern Europe, 1851 Joseph purchased land and planted his first vines at what is now Seppeltsfield in the Barossa Valley, 1852

the first cellar was built round and over the dairy at Seppeltsfield, 1865 Joseph Best purchased and named the "Great Western Vineyard" in Victoria and started building cellars, by this time Seppelt was the biggest winery in South Australia, 1868 Joseph Seppelt died. His son, Benno, at 21 years of age took over the family business, 1877 Seppeltsfield's high-tech distillery opened, doubling efficiency, 1878 Para Liqueur Port was laid down for the first time, not to be disturbed for 100 years, 1878 Port Store Cellar completed at Seppeltsfield, 1880 Seppelt wines were first entered into a wine show, winning 22 firsts and 53 other awards out of 95 exhibits, 1887 Joseph Best died and the Great Western property was purchased by Ballarat businessman Hans Irvine, 1892 the foundation stone of the new building was laid, which would provide cellaring, bottling, labelling and packing facilities as well as laboratory at Great Western, Sparkling Burgundy first made at Great Western, 1900 Seppelt became the largest winery in Australia, producing 2 million litres per annum, 1902 Hans Irvine, of Great Western and Benno Seppelt became friends and colleagues, 1908 Seppeltsfield winery had doubled in size again, employing 1700 people, Great Western Sparkling Burgundy sold for 60 shillings per case, 1912 Great Western Sparkling Burgundy exported to New Zealand, 1914 Seppelt expanded in Victoria purchasing vineyards at Rutherglen, 1916 Seppelt purchased Chateau Tanunda distillery for brandy production, 1918 Hans Irvine retired, Seppelt took over the Great Western Cellars, stock and vineyards, 1922 Seppelt pioneered vineyards in southern NSW, at Barooga and Qualco in South Australia, 1964 Seppelt planted the Keppoch vineyard, Padthaway, Seppelt pioneered the Drumborg vineyard in southern Victoria, 1978 the first 100 year old Para Liqueur Port was released, 1980 Seppelt purchased land and planted the Partalunga vineyard in the Adelaide Hills, 1983 Ian McKenzie became Chief Winemaker at Seppelt, 1986 first release of Salinger Vintage Brut, Seppelt's premium methode champenoise wine, 1994 Seppelt released Viva 1 and Viva 2 - a whole new concept in fortifieds, 1997 the inaugural Seppelt Contemporary Art Awards at the Museum of Contemporary Art, Sydney, 1998 launch of new varieties from Drumborg Vineyard - Pinot Grigio and Sauvignon Blanc

Samuel Smith

Position: Founder, Brewer, Winemaker
Organisation: Yalumba
Date of Birth: Wareham, Dorset, UK, 17th July, 1812 - deceased
Career History: Born and educated in the village of Wareham, Master brewer at the local brewery house. Migrated to South Australia in 1847 aboard "China", worked for Angas at Lindsay Park & Tarrawatta, travelled to goldfields (Bendigo), found gold and left Angas to tend vines and wines, started in 1849 at Yalumba, the rest is history.
Hobbies/Clubs: Gardening

The Legends Of Wine

Karl Stockhausen

Position: Winemaker
Organisation: Briar Ridge Vineyard
Date of Birth: Hamburg, Germany 26th January, 1930
Education/Honours: 1946-1948 Commercial High School · Hamburg, 1958-1962 Accountancy Certificate, 1986 one year Marketing · University of NSW
Hobbies/Clubs: Skiing, Golf

Murray Davey Tyrrell, AM

Position: Chairman
Organisation: Tyrrell's Vineyards Pty Ltd
Date of Birth: Cessnock 10th February, 1921
Education/Honours: Maitland Boys High School, Order of Australia Medal 1986, Graham Gregory Trophy for Service to the NSW Wine Industry, 1994, NSW Wine Industry Award for Industry Excellence & Distinguished Service, 1995, Hunter Regional Tourism Organisation Award for Outstanding Contribution to Regional Tourism by an Individual, 1996
Career History: Lifetime in the wine industry.
Hobbies/Clubs: Cricket, Rugby League, Tennis, Beef Cattle Grazing, Tattersall's Club, North Sydney Club

John Vickery

Position: Richmond Grove Chief Winemaker
Organisation: Orlando Wyndham Group Pty Ltd
DOB: Adelaide 31st October, 1932
Education/Honours: Roseworthy, Diploma in Agriculture · Oenology
Career History: John started his winemaking career in 1955 and has a long and proud record as one of Australia's greatest makers of white wines, notably Rieslings, backed up by an equally impressive reputation with reds. His famous "DW" series whites of the 1960's and 1970's were among the greatest Rieslings ever made in Australia. He has also spent 8 years making wines in Coonawarra, and his scores of medals and trophies include a Jimmy Watson Trophy from the Melbourne Wine Show in 1981.
Hobbies/Clubs: Farming, Grapegrowing, Collecting Vintage English Motorcycles, Enjoying Wine

James Calexte Watson

Position: Musician, Wine Merchant
Organisation: Founder in 1935 of Jimmy Watson's Wine Bar
Date of Birth: Melbourne 18th October, 1903 · deceased 22nd February, 1962
Education/Honours: Merit Certificate, Napier Street School, Fitzroy
Career History: Jim was brought up in a family environment of hospitality. He became a highly regarded professional flautist having been tutored by John Amadio a celebrated artist. Because of economic circumstances he bought a business with an Australian Wine License in Lygon Street, Carlton. He had a passion for promoting Australian Wine and this was the beginning of his love of teaching Melburnians the pleasure of enjoying Australian table wine. He was an innovative and industrious man who entertained many famous people at the Carlton Wine Bar and was a legend in his own time. He purchased a reception venue (Ascot House) in the late 1940's and thoroughly enjoyed the mix of food, wine and music. After his death, his many friends contributed to a fund for a memorial trophy at the Royal Melbourne Wine Show acknowledging his contribution to the Australian Wine Industry and in particular the selection of young red wine of the previous years vintage to bottle and cellar.
Hobbies/Clubs: Photography, Engineering, Sailing, Royal St Kilda Yacht Club

George Wyndham

Position: Founder
Organisation: Dalwood Wines
Date of Birth: Dinton, Wiltshire, United Kingdom, 1801
Career History: George Wyndham immigrated to Australia with wife Margaret in 1827 and reached Sydney on Boxing Day that year. In 1828 his first vines were planted along the Hunter River, using 600 vine cuttings given to him by James Busby. George purchased "Annandale" in 1830. A farm of 2,000 acres and renamed it "Dalwood" after a portion of his father's Dinton Estate in England. It was here that he built his home "Dalwood House". The first vintage was produced in 1831, which due to the extremely hot conditions, was "promised to make good vinegar". However, seven years after the first wines were planted, Dalwood Wines released its first vintage to rave reviews and by the mid 1800's was exporting to England and India. Also in 1831, Wyndham settled a 100,000 acre property "Bukkulla" near Inverell and established a vineyard from vines brought from Dalwood. By 1860 Wyndham's total vineyards holdings were producing 11,000 gallons of wines. Dalwood's vine plantings again expanded and became the second largest vineyard in the colony. Following George Wyndham's death on 24th December 1860 (aged 69) the properties gradually passed out of Wyndham hands and by 1892 only Bukkulla remained. In 1892 Dalwood was awarded the coveted Gold Medal for best Australian wine at Bordeaux in France. George Wyndham led the way in promoting the fledging Australian wine industry. To honour George Wyndham's memorable achievements, Dalwood Wines was renamed Wyndham Estate in 1970 · one hundred years after George Wyndham's death.

David Wynn

Position: Deceased
Organisation: Wynns Coonawarra
Date of Birth: 21st January, 1915
Education/Honours: Wesley & Adelaide University
History: In 1951 Samuel and David Wynn purchased John Riddoch's original vineyards and winery and renamed the property Wynns Coonawarra Estate. The Wynns recognised the intrinsic qualities of Coonawarra wines · their richness and intensity of fruit character and set out to build an independent identity in the region. If it were not for their bold and courageous purchase the winery would have become a wool shed and the vineyards a sheep run. David Wynn, then in his mid-30s, had gradually taken control of the business as his father moved closer to retirement. He set about his daunting task in Coonawarra with clear-sightedness and determination. He was Australia's first wine producer to use the word 'Estate' to indicate that what was in the bottle came from the place named on the label. He also commissioned the Melbourne artist Richard Beck to produce a woodcut of the winery facade. This illustration has appeared on every Wynns Coonawarra Estate label since, making it one of Australia's most recognisable · wine symbols. By the early 1960s, Coonawarra's dark age was well and truly over. Wynns also gradually increased its holdings and by 1981 was the largest grower in the district with 440 hectares under vine. Riddoch's vineyards are the core of today's Wynns Coonawarra Estate, with his winery · essentially unchanged · forming the centerpiece of the operation. They created the famous label that has made John Riddoch's winery one of Australia's best-known buildings.

Samuel Wynn

Position: Deceased
Organisation: Wynns Coonawarra
Date of Birth: Poland 4th April, 1892
Education/Honours: No formal education, Hebrew School in Poland
History: In 1951 Samuel and David Wynn purchased John Riddoch's original vineyards and winery and renamed the property Wynns Coonawarra Estate. The Wynns recognised the intrinsic qualities of Coonawarra wines · their richness and intensity of fruit character and set out to build an independent identity in the region. If it were not for their bold and courageous purchase the winery would have become a wool shed and the vineyards a sheep run. David Wynn, then in his mid-30s, had gradually taken control of the business as his father moved closer to retirement. He set about his daunting task in Coonawarra with clear-sightedness and determination. He was Australia's first wine producer to use the word 'Estate' to indicate that what was in the bottle came from the place named on the label. He also commissioned the Melbourne artist Richard Beck to produce a woodcut of the winery facade. This illustration has appeared on every Wynns Coonawarra Estate label since, making it one of Australia's most recognisable · wine symbols. By the early 1960s, Coonawarra's dark age was well and truly over. Wynns also gradually increased its holdings and by 1981 was the largest grower in the district with 440 hectares under vine. Riddoch's vineyards are the core of today's Wynns Coonawarra Estate, with his winery · essentially unchanged · forming the centerpiece of the operation. They created the famous label that has made John Riddoch's winery one of Australia's best-known buildings.

Perc McGuigan -
Still going strong

Jack Mann (1906 -1989)
Presided over 65 Vintages.
"A winemaker is a humble servant of nature; his role
is to give nature the opportunity to produce the best
possible wine. Nature creates, man only guides."

Mono Pumps Australia

Mono Pumps (Australia) Pty Ltd is a division of Mono Pumps Limited which in turn is owned by Halliburton, Dallas, Texas, U.S.A. Mono Pumps Limited, originally known as J & E Arnfield Limited has been based at Guide Bridge, Audenshaw, Manchester, England since 1938. The Arnfield brothers began a business in 1865 in Derbyshire manufacturing water wheels, and then textile machinery as the industrial revolution reached its peak. From this base the Company expanded to provide general engineering services and in 1935 accepted the first orders for manufacture of the newly invented progressive cavity positive displacement pump. This invention, by the French mathematician Rene Moineau, had been seized upon by the British entrepreneur, John North, who secured the rights to the patent for Great Britain and much of the Commonwealth, for Mono Pumps Limited. Today Mono Pumps Ltd is one of the world's largest manufacturers of progressive cavity positive displacement pumps. Mono Pumps Limited Companies are located at Audenshaw, Australia and New Zealand. The Company also has a branch office in Dublin, Eire. Mono Pumps (Australia) Pty Ltd was founded in 1959 with the company partially manufacturing and totally assembling progressive cavity positive displacement pumps in Melbourne for the Australian market. When the company opened its sales, manufacture and service centre on a new site in 1964, it was already operating sales branch offices in all states except Tasmania and Northern Territory. By 1967 Mono Pumps (Australia) Pty Ltd had completed its sales representation in all states. In 1980 Mono Pumps (Australia) Pty Ltd completed its totally local production facilities programme with the opening of its Stator Manufacturing Centre on the eight-acre site shared with its manufacturing centre and Head Office in Melbourne. Mono Pumps (Australia) Pty Ltd manufacture the key rotors and stators entirely in-house in both Melbourne and England. By maintaining sole responsibility for these, and other critical components, the Company is able to maintain their legendary pump reliability reputation which is crucial to so many of their customers' businesses. It has been this combination of manufacturing excellence and professional sales representation that has enabled Mono Pumps (Australia) Pty Ltd to open up the Australian and Export markets for its range of progressive cavity positive displacement pump.

I remember seeing my first mono-pump in 1969 at Hardy's McLaren Vale, whilst working my first vintage, it's powerful quiet efficiency in stark contrast to the cumbersome piston pumps huffing and puffing away at the wine.

Mono Pumps are used in many different industries, in fact wine only accounts for about 15% of the Australian turnover of the company.

One of the outstanding qualities of a mono pump is the ability to handle thick liquids and liquids with solids, such as crushed grapes with the skins and grape juice combined, called the "must".

Mono Pumps are used extensively in the Mining Industry, the Waste Water Industry and in Agriculture, an amazing new pump is the "sun-sub" a solar powered submersible stainless steel pump which runs directly from solar panels without batteries. The system is much more efficient than the traditional windmill, plus cheaper to install and maintain, another great

advantage is the pump works most efficiently in hot weather when water is most in demand. For remote locations the new sun-sub range of solar pumps has been a godsend.

Mono Pump Australia has undergone dramatic growth in supply to the wine industry in recent years, mainly due to their Mono "Winery Pump" concept, totally packaging the pump with a purpose designed trolley with dual wheels for stability that can even be pulled over 4 inch wine hoses without losing its balance. The Pump is also bi-directional, the variable speed shaft is electronically

controlled to allow very slow speed pumping ideal for premium wine work and can be adjusted with finger tip control, to pump incredibly large volumes for such a compact pump, ideal at vintage time.

Mono Pumps asked dozens of winemakers what their ideal pump set up would be and this research led to the release of the "Winery Pump" concept in 1997 its been a huge success. The concept has been well named because one mono pump can in fact take care of all the pumping needs in a winery, from handling the juice and skins "must" to the thick lees after fermentation and pressings, to the delicate task of filling individual wooden casks such as barriques and hogsheads.

Mono Pumps are extremely smooth and gentle in their operation and also don't allow air into the wine. Many winemakers swear by them and wouldn't use anything else.

Mono Pumps also produce a "Wide Throat" range ideal for use under the crusher to take the crushed grapes and juice to the drainer or fermentation vessel. These pumps have an open section on top with a long "hopper" to feed in the semi solid material such as pressings, a stainless steel "auger" takes the material into the pumps inlet chamber. These "wide throat" pumps, range from small boutiques styles to massive pumps for the giants of the industry. They are universally acclaimed and are also used in the food processing, paper, waste water and mining industries. The easily adjustable variable speed facility of the "wide throat" is a huge advantage and can be automatically adjusted electronically in the crushing pit, a vital need in any winery.

For wineries that need to move large quantities of wine the "Mono-Packo" centrifugal wine transfer pump (which can also be mounted in a purpose built trolley) is ideal, it's compact and extremely powerful.

Another innovative Mono concept is the "Wine Turnover Pump" range, they are the perfect pumps for pumping wines from the base of the fermentation tank to an irrigation system which sprays over the cap of skins, in the top of the tank to extract colour and flavour from the skins, in a circulating system.

Mono Pumps are the wine industry pump specialists and their innovative approach and focus on customer needs has enabled them to produce outstanding pumps. Mono's manufacturing precision and their reliability are legendary. The Melbourne Manufacturing and service centre gives Mono another great advantage, in giving great customer service. Mono Pumps have met the challenge presented by the dramatic growth of the wine industry and their future looks bright indeed.

Amorim Cork Australia

Amorim Cork Australia is a wholly owned subsidiary of the world's leading cork producer, the Portugal-based Amorim.

Amorim Cork Australia, which began its life in 1911 as Cork & Seals, leads the way in innovative technology, production and quality control in the Australian cork industry.

Its modern facilities in the Melbourne suburb of Dandenong house a state-of-the-art cork manufacturing factory - the only one in Australia - which produces the new generation Amorim Twin Top® cork, a high quality 'technical' cork that combines the best raw material with Amorim's cutting-edge technology.

That's a very long way from the company that J Vogt and Co established in 1911. The focus then was on the manufacturing of stoppers and the cork waste (75% of the base raw material) was recycled to produce insulation corkboard, composition cork and expansion cork.

Cork & Seals' operations included cool room construction, a floor-laying division and an injection moulding plant to produce Bar Top corks for use in wines, spirits and liqueurs - fortified wine in Australia represented 80% of all wines produced in this era.

During the rapid growth of the table wine industry in the 1960s, Cork & Seals introduced Filtra corks and continued research into wine cork

treatments resulting in a world first - gamma radiation, and a microwave process to sterilise wine corks. Patent No. 572470, dated 30th August, 1983.

Further developments include the introduction of the first preformed heat shrink capsules to the Australian market.

Part of Amorim since 1998, Amorim Cork Australia is at the forefront of technological advances in cork production, investing in research, development and quality control and understands the need to continually adapt to meet the changing demands of the Australian wine industry.

An example of this commitment is the Amorim Cork Australian produced Twin Top. Its genesis lies in the nine years of research that resulted in the highly successful Amorim SPARK® cork for sparkling wines.

Made from the best quality raw material, Twin Top® corks feature discs of fine natural cork cut across

Amorim Cork Australia

the grain, at either end of a high-grade granulated cork body.

Twin Top® discs are subject to the world's most advanced cork production technology - including the highly efficient INOS II washing process that is exclusive to Amorim.

Utilising a revolutionary form of 'hydrodynamic extraction' to remove contaminants from the cork, INOS II is the result of six years of intensive scientific and technological research.

INOS II completely washes the inner section of the cork, pumping a purified solution into and out of the cork's lenticels or pores. The pumping action extracts any resident particles. The purified hot water extracts any substances that could otherwise be dissolved by the wine and affect its flavour.

A competitively priced product that retains all the beneficial properties of natural cork, Twin Top® also enhances the on going supply of cork through better utilisation of the raw material.

Whilst cork is an ideal wine stopper, a very small percentage of corks can still adversely effect wine quality.

Amorim is applying considerable resources to eliminating contamination in cork. . The strategy is to attack this at every point in the cork production process.

A great deal of research has been done around the world in recent years to isolate the causes of contamination. Amorim is getting close to a solution.

At Amorim's two newly opened primary processing facilities in

Alentejo (in the south of Portugal), cork from each property is stacked separately, away from direct contact with the soil, and is allocated a unique code that it retains throughout production and distribution. In future Amorim will be able to track an individual cork from the forest to the bottle.

These initiatives will allow Amorim to build a complete profile of cork quality and yield from each forest, identify differences and choose the best raw material.

Amorim's initiatives have significantly reduced the incidence of taint in Amorim corks, to an average of less than half a percent over the past seven years. Current efforts focus on minimising the opportunities for contamination.

Amorim has also established `rigorous and comprehensive quality control procedures, recognised by the ISO 9002 accreditation of all of its factories in Portugal. Its distribution companies undertake additional quality control and laboratory testing. Packaging materials are also tested to ensure maximum protection for the corks

during transit.

Finally, Amorim maintains a research and development program, in which it currently invests $US 6 million a year. This R&D program pursues continuous improvement in Amorim's products and processes.

Amorim's totally professional approach is paying dividends ensuring the traditional natural stopper for wine - Cork will do its job even better in years to come.

Lindsay Booth, his sons and grandsons have revolutionised the handling transportation and storage of wines. Lindsay passed on in 1999 but has left a huge legacy in the area of logistics necessary, for the massive expansion the wine industry is undergoing at present.

Lindsay launched into wine transport in 1936, it was a natural extension of his entrepreneurial nature. In the 1930's he operated vineyards in the Reynella area for Mostyn Owen, also carting wood for the winemakers of the region mainly for use in their distilleries. During vintage time he also carted grapes to the wineries for many vineyard owners.

In 1941 Lindsay also secured a job, working for Penfolds Wines, buying grapes and also carting grapes for them, plus managing their grape receiving depot at Burbank, now a Southern suburb of Adelaide.

In 1948 he established his own vineyards at Morphett Vale planting them with Grenache on the advice of Penfolds chief Leslie Penfold Hyland. By this time he had a fleet of trucks, basically only used during vintage time for carting grapes and wine in wooden hogsheads.

In chatting recently with Managing Director Brian Booth he reminisced over the extraordinary development of the company he has seen in his lifetime. He harked back to his own childhood and seeing d'Arry Osborn on his first working day in 1944, loading hogsheads of wine on to his father Lindsay's truck at the d'Arenberg winery.

Brian Booth

Lindsay Booth

Booth's Transport

By 1957 eldest son Devron had begun working with his father and by 1959 younger son Brian had joined the business. Wanting to get more use out of the family's trucks the boys began driving them to Sydney themselves.

Brian reminisced on his first trip to Sydney, taking a bulk tanker load of dry red wine from Penfolds Auldana Cellars in Adelaide to the Penfolds Minchinbury Cellars west of Sydney for the production of "Sparkling Burgundy". This was back in 1964, both cellars have since been closed and the land sold for housing.

In 1968 Lindsay formed a company with all 7 members of his family, by this time Devron and Brian had moved into general freight as an addition to its bulk transport business. Lindsay began taking a back seat in 1970 to concentrate on his vineyards at McLaren Vale.

In 1989 Booth took over the wine division of United Transport, to become the largest wine carrier in Australia

Until 1979 Booths transported wine in "cross tanks" on their own bases, placed on tray top trucks, in this year they purchased their first "Road Tanker". Over the last 21 years their fleet has grown astronomically from this simple road tanker to 125 tankers, 18 carting milk produce, with at the remainder carrying a staggering half a billion litres of wine a year. The busiest time is during vintage and the post vintage period, from late January until July.

Booth have also moved into the specialised storage of packaged wine in huge temperature and humidity controlled buildings, providing the wine industry with vital logistical support for its massive expansion.

In 2000 Devron decided it was time to take a step back and he purchased most of the wine storage facilities of the company, that he had created with Brian. Devron now runs these, as well as working on an innovative concept for a unique folding protective railings system for bulk transport vehicles, worldwide.

Brian is busy running Booth Transport's vibrant 60 million dollar transport business with his four sons, the eldest Mitchell runs the Melbourne depot, Peter is in Adelaide, Cameron in Brisbane and the youngest Damien in Sydney.

In August 2001 Booth brought a half share in the ABC Bottling and wine storage business near their head office at Lonsdale, south of Adelaide, this has also added to their other considerable logistical storage assets.

Booth Transport have a great team, who have a very friendly down to earth way of dealing with their clients. The Booth family are a tremendous asset to Australia's wine industry and deserve all the spectacular success they have quietly achieved.

Devron Booth

Collotype Labels

EST. 1903

Collotype Labels is dedicated to providing the World's Best Premium Label Solutions for Global Markets through leadership in Quality, Service and Innovation.

Heritage

In 1903, a small print shop took its name from the best reproduction process of the day, Collotype.

Today, that print shop has grown to become the world's most awarded label printer.

Collotype Labels is the leading printer of premium wet glue and self adhesive labels. Their dedication and innovative approach to the art and craft of printing means they are recognised internationally as providing the benchmark for world's best practice in premium label quality and service solutions.

Since printing their first wine and spirit labels in the 1930s, Collotype has driven many of the innovations that have seen labels evolve from a simple description of content to 'little works of art' playing a vital role in the marketing mix.

Located in several premium wine producing regions around the world and linked via the latest in information technology, Collotype is proudly supporting an expanding global market.

Collotype is privately owned and actively run by a Board of Directors dedicated to the printing industry. While justifiably proud of their heritage, they know that their future depends on satisfying the demands of their customers and the market place not only today, but also tomorrow and into the future.

Quality

You can be assured that your labels will be more than 'little works of art',

they will also meet all technical and functional demands placed upon them.

There may be many printers who can produce a beautifully printed label, however quality of print really comes down to consistency. Every label must be as good as the next, within a single print run, and from one print run to the next.

Even after passing the careful eye of a master printer and continuous on-line computer monitoring, their quality assurance programme · certified to ISO 9001 · ensures excellence in every label which adorns your product. Their quality is achieved with a strong commitment to the environment. This is supported by their ISO 14001 accreditation.

A beautiful label is wasted if it doesn't retain its quality finish, through the process of bottling and transportation, until it reaches the consumer. Collotype's knowledge of the rigours and demands placed upon labels enables them to advise their clients on what solutions best satisfy their needs as both manufacturers and marketers. While the ultimate recognition comes from their clients returning to Collotype again and again for premium label solutions, their peers in the label and printing industry have made them the World's most awarded premium label printer. Their quality shines.

Service

The greatest label solutions rely on more than craft and knowledge. At the heart of Collotype's philosophy is a concept that has been one of their cornerstones and the foundation of our continued success · service.

From the moment you first contact Collotype until your product is in the hands of the consumer, you have the undivided attention of the Collotype team in achieving your objectives.

With superior quality offset printing on both wet glue and self adhesive label stocks · plus a comprehensive range of processes and embellishment techniques · Collotype can advise you on how best to achieve the perfect look and feel for your product.

Naturally, their fast turn-around

SCREEN INKS

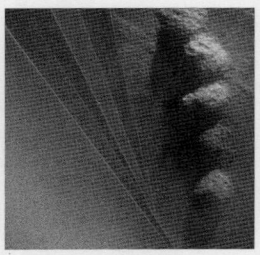

BRONZING

VARNISHES

GRAINING

EMBOSSING

Collotype Labels

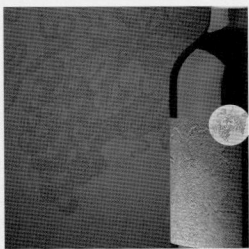

FOIL ART

WINE FIND

DNA SMARTMARK

WEBRUNNER

COLLOTEMPS

times and guaranteed delivery will satisfy the most demanding production schedule.

At every stage, Collotype will liaise with your production, bottling and packaging representatives

to make sure that your labels are guaranteed to meet the physical demands of application, shipping and storage.

Warehousing facilities allow you to achieve true economy of scale through large runs, and their despatch service will have your labels anywhere in the world on time and in mint condition.

With current production capabilities in excess of one billion labels per year, and established long term relationships with many of the world's leading wine and spirit companies, Collotype have the experience, know how and processes to provide any label requirements to satisfy your needs.

You deserve the best service and their aim is to give it to you.

Innovation

With their commitment to innovation and continuous improvement, the future holds even greater promise.

Through their use of innovative techniques and materials, Collotype is the driving force behind many of the breakthroughs in wine label design and production.

Collotype pioneered the printing of high quality, embellished self adhesive labels for wine and the use of specialty papers for wine and spirit labels.

It is Collotype's standards for label performance in application and transportation that the entire industry measures itself by.

You can use the services of Collotype's research and development team to take your labels to the very edge of printing technology.

Imagine the possibilities and advantages Collotype's range of processes and services can provide - not only for wine and spirit labels, but also labels in product areas such as luxury goods, gourmet foods, premium beverages and personal care.

Peter Teakle
Chairman

Nigel Vinecombe
Managing Director

David Maher
Sales Director

John Frankhuisen
Technical Director

www.collotype.com

Wolf Blass Foundation

The Wolf Blass Foundation was formed in 1995. Wolf Blass marked his 60th birthday by initiating the Foundation, as a vehicle for the betterment of the Australian wine industry and donated the sum of one million dollars towards the Foundation Fund.

The Foundation is a unique and autonomous initiative, which is highly relevant to the key objectives within the industry 'Strategy 2025' Plan and provides a range of tangible benefits to the industry. It is quite distinct from all other industry bodies because it is private, politically and commercially independent and takes a 'whole of industry' approach. The Foundation however, complements

and affiliates with existing bodies for maximum effectiveness.

Most importantly, the Chief Executive of the Winemakers Federation of Australia is a Trustee (Director) of the Wolf Blass Foundation. The Foundation is fortunate to have members on the Board who play leading roles within the Australian wine industry:

Wolf Blass AM

Guenter Prass AM

Ian Sutton

It is anticipated that an Executive Officer will be appointed to manage the Foundation's projects and coordinate its expansion and resource attraction program. As the

Foundations activities gather momentum and new projects are initiated, the Foundation will attract interest and build its networks, to further strengthen its capacity and capability. It is intended that the Wolf Blass Foundation will operate from the National Wine Centre when completed.

The Foundation has a short but impressive record of achievement and a solid profile. It plans and operates strategically to attract resources and partnerships to deliver maximum 'value added' benefits to the industry. The Foundation's success, its record to date and its objective demonstrate its serious intent to achieve the advancement of

Wolf Blass Foundation

the Australian wine industry. Financial resources have been derived in the first instance from sound management of the Foundation investment fund. Although the Foundation is only in its sixth year of operation the Board has allocated over $300,000 from profits generated via sound investment of the original million dollars. The Board is proud to report that the initial investment has grown to nearly two million dollars, however a strict criteria has been set that funding will be allocated from the interest received on funds employed.

A number of important projects have been funded to date these include the "International Wine and Health Conference - Wine Australia, Sydney 1996". This inaugural event titled 'Medically, Is Wine Just Another Alcohol Beverage' attracted prominent national and international epidemiologists and research scientists from the USA, UK, France, Denmark and Australia. The foundation contributed $85,000 to this landmark initiative.

"Taste Theatres" - Wine Australia, Melbourne 1998 and 2000 - the Wolf Blass Foundation has financially supported the highly successful "Taste Theatres" run by the Australian Society of Wine Education (ASWE) by providing major sponsorship for this important program at Wine Australia in 1998 and 2000. The well coordinated, integrated education program demonstrates the Wolf Blass Foundations, is dedicated to advancing excellence and prosperity for the Australian wine industry. It provides an opportunity to educate consumers about wine styles and their composition, with a 'moderation' message being emphasised. The foundation has invested $170,000 in this project.

"Ongoing International Student/Lecturer/Winemaker Exchange" - Pursuing the same theme of education, this international exchange project demonstrates the Foundation's commitment to excellence in the industry, by encouraging the interchange of ideas and methodologies between winemaking students, lectures and winemakers from different countries.

The Foundation commits $10,000 per annum to this exchange program.

"Treading out the Vintage" Historical Project. An initiative of the National Wine Center and the Wolf Blass Foundation, is a national project that seeks to record the memories of Australia's wine industry pioneers and characters. those who have played significant roles in its development, it is imperative that theses stories are recorded now, before many are lost forever. Over the next six years 100 key figures, in the Australia Wine Industry will be interviewed on broadcast quality tape and videoptaped by professional historians. Industry leaders have compiled a list of key wine personalities from all Australian States and Territories.

These people represent every facet of the industry - corporate leaders, winemakers, merchants, suppliers, educators, personalities, restaurateurs, growers, transport operators, contractors, fruit pickers and labourers, coopers, viticulturists, managers and accountants, marketing and sales personnel - including design and packaging personnel and media. Their input will provide a true and living picture of the industry's heritage and its colourful past.

The resulting historical information will be used in exhibitions in the National Wine Center, on the official wine industry's web site, at key libraries and in educational and tourism packages. A major publication will also be compiled by multi-award winning historian, Rob Linn, which will be of widespread interest to the public, consumers and wine enthusiasts alike. This project will be a living memorial to the heritage of Australia's wine industry. The Foundation has committed seed

capital with the anticipation that the industry will support this uniquely valuable project up to $250,000.

"National Riesling Challenge" - The inaugural Hyatt Hotel Canberra - 'National Riesling Challenge', was conducted in October 2000, with 81 companies entering 137 Rieslings. Based on the success of this event, a powerful Committee has been formed to organise the next Challenge in February 2002, with the aim of eventually extending the event to international status. Riesling has suffered a decline in popularity over the past two decades and yet the Australian, flavorsome, high quality Rieslings are one of the greatest assets of the Australian wine industry. The Foundation supports this initiative to re-ignite, revitalise and promote the status of this style so that, in future, Australia will be recognised as a top producer of a consistent, quality Riesling style. The Foundation has committed $5,000 p.a. over the next five years and will act as a catalyst to secure major sponsors for this event.

The Australian Society for Viticulture and Oenology is Australia's professional society for winemakers, viticulturists and those in wine industry research. ASVO runs three seminars each year on various issues and is an equal partner, with the Australian Wine Research Institute, in the triennial Australian Wine Industry Technical Conference.

In August 2001 the ASVO held a seminar in Melbourne to discuss future directions for Australian wine shows, which has attracted an impressive group of representatives from the industry. The Foundation has agreed to contribute $2000 towards the cost of this important seminar.

The Foundation has donated funds to support this publication, the "Who's Who of Wine - Australia & New Zealand" including the "Legends of Wine" section, helping it come to fruition.

Funds have also been provided to grant scholarships affiliated within the wine industry.

The Foundation has already helped the Australian Wine Industry advance in so many areas and will continue to do so - Ein Prosit Wolf!!

WOLF BLASS
FOUNDATION INC.

The Who's Who of Wine

Gaetano (Caj) Amadio

Position: Proprietor
Organisation: Chain of Ponds Wines Pty Ltd
DOB: Adelaide 28th March, 1939
Education/Honours: Secondary College Education, Wine Making
Directorates: Caj Amadio & Genny Amadio
Career History: Caj Amadio's father, Giovanni Amadio, migrated from Italy (Marche region) in 1927. He produced commercial dry table wine in South Australia from the mid-1930s to the late fifties. Caj Amadio made wine as an amateur in the seventies, winning many awards including two Masters Awards. Caj pioneered viticulture in the area of Gumeracha in the Adelaide Hills in 1985, by planting a 3 acre pilot vineyard of 9 varieties called "Gumeracha Vineyards", and initiated a further 150 acre planting adjacent to his pilot vineyard in 1988. He produced his first vintage in 1993 and went on to launch his Chain of Ponds label in 1995. Chain of Ponds Wines is now the Most Awarded Boutique Winery in Australia. He has succeeded in attracting world markets, including the attention of the Americans by being chosen by the Wine Spectator Magazine for their high quality wines. Their 1997 Chardonnay was chosen in the "Top 100 Wines of the World" achieving the rating of 16th. Decanter Magazine (UK) invited Caj Amadio, as one of the 50 Rising Stars of the world, to attend their "Rising Stars" event in London, May 2001. Chain of Ponds Wines produces around 15,000 cases per year. His latest venture is a further 150 acres planted at Kersbrook in 1998/99 with a further 180 acres planned. Kersbrook is within the Adelaide Hills Wine Region.
Hobbies/Clubs: Fishing, Cooking, Travelling France & Italy, Glenelg Golf Club, Ferrari Car Club

John C Angove

Position: Managing Director
Orrganisation: Angove's Pty Ltd
DOB: Adelaide, 21st February 1947
Education/Honours: St Peter's College 1957-1965, Adelaide University (BSc) 1966-1968, Post Graduate Commerce Course 1969, Degree B.Sc. Majoring in Organic Chemistry ·

Microbiology
Directorates: St Agnes Wines Pty Ltd, Lyrup Wine Co. Pty. Ltd., Cole & Woodham Pty Ltd
Career History: Worked in numerous company departments during school and university vacations, after studies spent 18 months in Europe and USA, following vintage activity and wine industry supplies, commenced with company in 1971 in sales and marketing, developed company wholesale distribution system across Australia, appointed a Director in 1971, appointed Managing Director in 1983.
Hobbies/Clubs: Family, The Murray River, Boating, Skiing (Water & Snow), Golf, Adelaide Club, Royal Adelaide Golf Club, Renmark Golf Club, Renmark Club

Brenton Baker

Position: Group Manager - Viticulture
Organisation: BRL Hardy Ltd
DOB: Adelaide 2nd Sept, 1945
Education/Honours: Roseworthy - Diploma of Agriculture (Horticulture 1966), Roseworthy Agricultural College, SA, Graduate Diploma of Extension, 1974, Hawkesbury Agricultural College, NSW, Graduate Management Development Programme 1983, SA Public Service
Directorates: Director Willunga Basin Water Company
History/Career: July 1966 - December 1971 - Field Officer Vegetables with SA Department of Agriculture - vegetable research and extension throughout SA, January 1971 - May 1984 - Senior Horticultural Advisor with SA Department of Agriculture, June 1984 - June 1999 - Thomas Hardy & Sons Group - Viticulturist, July 1992 - present - BRL Hardy Ltd Group Manager - Viticulture, responsible for management of all Company viticultural activities Australia wide.

Jack M Bendat

Position: Chairman/Proprietor
Organisation: Goundrey Wines Pty Ltd
DOB: Illinois, California 6th May, 1925
Education/Honours: Obtained a Bachelor of Business Administration from Woodbury College, Los Angeles, California
Directorates: Goundrey Wines
Career History: Former Chairman of GWN, Former Chairman of 94.5FM
Hobbies/Clubs: Royal Perth Yacht Club

Gregory Christopher Bishop

Position: Managing Director - Winery/Resort
Organisation: Coolangatta Estate
DOB: Nowra 15th April, 1957
Education/Honours: Up to Year 10 - Bomaderry High School, Years 11 & 12 - The Scots School Bathurst
Directorates: Coolangatta Estate
Career History: After leaving school in 1974 Greg returned to Coolangatta Estate to manage the families Resort, re-established the 1st new age vineyard. In 1988 after extensive consultations with leading Industry figures including Dr Richard Smart and the Tyrrells Family he developed a passion for viticulture which has led to consistent quality wine production. The Estate's wines are made at Tyrrells, the current focus is on wine
Hobbies/Clubs: Rugby, Food & Wine

Grant Walker Burge

Position: Proprietor & Chief Winemaker
Organisation: Grant Burge Wines Pty Ltd
DOB: Adelaide 20th January, 1951
Education/Honours: St Peters College, Roseworthy
Directorates: Barossa Infrastructure Ltd
Career History: In 1951, Grant was born into the Burge winemaking family. After leaving school, he served his winemaking apprenticeship under his father, Colin, at the family's Wilsford winery before moving on to Glenloth. Grant then went on to Southern Vales (now Tatachilla), teaming up with another passionate young winemaker, Ian Wilson. Together Grant and Ian purchased the Krondorf winery and transformed it into one of the major innovative forces in the Australian wine industry. When the Krondorf operation was taken over by the Mildara group in 1986, Grant and his wife, Helen, retained the surrounding vineyards and Grant stayed on as a director of Mildara until 1988 when he re-established himself as Grant Burge Wines, which is based at the historic Moorooroo Cellars, on the banks of Jacobs Creek and right in the heart of the Barossa Valley.
Hobbies/Club: South Australian Cricket Association, Norwood Football Club

Brad Camer

Position: Director - Asia
Organisation: Southcorp Wines
Education/Honours: Bachelor of Commerce, with a major in Marketing, University of NSW.
Career History: Product Manager, Masterfood, 1989 joined Southcorp Wines and has held a number of roles including Executive General Manager of Marketing, General Manager of E-Business, Penfolds Brand Manager, Marketing Manager of the Table Wines Category, currently Director, Southcorp Wines' Asian Region
Hobbies/Clubs: Golf, Rugby Union & Cricket

William Calabria

Position: Company Director/Winemaker

Organisation: Westend Estate Wines

DOB: Griffith 5th March, 1948

Directorates: Billabong Bottle Shop

Career History: 37 years in winemaking at Westend Estate, driving force in producing high quality dry reds, cabernet sauvignon and shiraz as well as sauvignon blanc and chardonnay from Riverina fruit plus golden mist botrytis collecting over 8 trophies, 32 gold medals, 46 silver and 76 bronze at National Wine Shows over the last 5 years. One of the leaders for the Riverina Region.

Hobbies/Clubs: Music, Sport, Basketball, Boxing, Playing Guitar, Non-drinker, Ex-boxer · Riverina Champion

Chris Cameron

Position: Managing Director & Chief Winemaker

Organisation: Pepper Tree Wines

DOB: Hunter Valley, NSW 12th June, 1956

Directorates: Pepper Tree Wines Pty Ltd, Audrey Wilkinson Vineyard Pty Ltd, Peppertree Coonawarra Vineyards Pty Ltd, Barform Pty Ltd, Hunter Wine Country Private Irrigation District

Career History: Has been in the industry since 1978 and has a wealth of experience, not only in winemaking

but in marketing and sales. This marketing flair has developed the labels and overall package, pioneering in Australia the use of latest innovations such as blue and ruby red bottles, coloured supremecorq and instant custom labelling.

Hobbies/Clubs: Golf, Rugby, Reading, Cooking & Photography

John Casella

Position: Chief Executive Officer

Organisation: Casella Wines Pty Ltd

DOB: Brisbane Qld, 19th February, 1959

Education/Honours: Tertiary

Directorates: Casella Wines Pty Ltd; Casella Management Pty Ltd

Career History: After University education, started working for a large winery in the Riverina in NSW where the size of the business expanded rapidly. Returned to the family business in 1993 with the aim of turning a small Mum & Dad winery into a "State of the Art" modern winery, built with the latest technology. The Family run business has grown from processing 200 tonnes to 25,000 tonnes in just 7 short years.

Hobbies/Clubs: Family, Golf, Clay Target Shooting

John Baptiste Cassegrain

Position: Managing Director

Organisation: Cassegrain Wines

DOB: Wauchope NSW, 14th January, 1956

Letitia Cecchini

Position: Proprietor & Winemaker

Organisation: Serenella Wines, Pokolbin, Lower Hunter NSW.

Douglas Harold Collett

Position: Retired Winemaker

Organisation: Retired

DOB: South Perth, WA 25th June 1920

Education/Honours: Roseworthy Agricultural College, Ecole National d'Agriculture · Montpellier

Career History: For many years one of Australia's leading consultant winemakers. Founder of the Woodstock Winery with his son Scott. Author of a fascinating autobiography "Astonishing luck · in the face of incredible odds". In 1943 he was commissioned in the RAAF and saw service as a Hurricane and Spitfire pilot.

Hobbies/Clubs: Fishing and Jazz

Steve Clarkson

Position: Richmond Grove Winery Manager/Winemaker

Organisation: Orlando Wyndham Group Ltd

Education/Honours: Yr 12 Penola High School, Bachelor of Applied Science Oenology, Roseworthy 1986-1988

Career History: Born and raised in Coonawarra, South Australia, lived on a sheep and cattle property, developed an interest in chemistry and winemaking at school. Gained a vintage position in a Coonawarra winery as a Lab. Technician and Cellar Hand. Over the next seven years worked in four grape growing regions and graduated from Roseworthy. Commenced winemaking in McLaren Vale prior to moving to Wyndham Estate, Hunter Valley. In seven years managed wineries and made wine for Wyndham Estate and Richmond Grove labels. Relocated to the Barossa Valley in 1997 as both Winemaker and Manager of Richmond Grove Barossa Winery.

Hobbies/Clubs: Any ball sports

The Who's Who of Wine

Tony Cominc

Position: Proprietor & Winemaker
Organisation: Kominos Wines, Severnlea, Stanthorpe, Queensland

Peter Cowan

Position: Managing Director Australasia/Asia Region
Organisation: Southcorp Wine Group, ASIA Pacific
DOB: South Africa, 1st April, 1954
Career History: 17 years with Johnson & Johnson in various marketing general management and global/regional executive roles, including the last 5 years as Sales/Marketing Director for Australasia and Vice President, Asia Pacific for key categories, Group Managing Director, New Zealand Milk, which is the Consumer Business Unit of the New Zealand Dairy Board, 2001 Regional Director Asia Pacific, Southcorp Wine Group

Harry Guy Darling

Position: Manager/Owner
Organisation: Koombahla Vineyard Pty Ltd

DOB: Melbourne Victoria 1st September, 1925
Education/Honours: B.Mech E (Hons), Melbourne University 1950
Directorates: Koombahla Vineyard, Darling Estate Wines, King Valley Wines
Career History: 1943-1947 Royal Australian Navy, 1950-1962 Senior Scientist, Australian Defence Scientific Service, 1962-1980 Engineering Manager, N.C.L. Ltd, 1980 Grape Grower, 1984-1994 President, K.V.G.A. Inc., 1990 Boutique Winemaker, 1994 Member Geographical Indications Committee AWBC,1998-2000 Chairman W.G.C.A. Inc,
Hobbies/Clubs: M.C.C., R.A.C.V.

Peter James Dawson

Position: Group Chief Winemaker
Organisation: BRL Hardy Ltd
DOB: Geelong, Victoria 10th December, 1955
Education/Honours: 1978 Bachelor of Science LaTrobe University, 1983 Bachelor of Applied Science (Wine Science) Riverina College of Advanced Education (now Charles Sturt University), 1995 International Red Winemaker of the Year, International Wine Challenge, London, 1997 International Red Winemaker of the Year, International Wine Challenge, London
Career History: 1976 Cellar Foreman, Thomas Hardy & Sons, 1978-1982 Quality Manager and Packaging Manager, 1982-1985 Winemaker, Houghton Wines, WA, 1984 Vintage Winemaker, J-P Moueix, Chateau Petrus, Pomeral, France, 1990-1994 Winemaker, Domaine de la Baume, France, 1985-1992 Senior Winemaker, Houghton Wines, WA, 1992-1993 Regional Manager, WA, BRL Hardy Ltd, 1993-current Group Chief Winemaker, BRL Hardy Ltd
Hobbies/Clubs: Beef cattle breeding, LandCare Australia, Australian painting, Wine & food, Member Lord Baden-Powell Society

Robin Day

Position: International Wine Development Director -

Pernod Ricard
Organisation: Orlando Wyndham Group Pty Ltd
DOB: Gawler 14th July, 1948
Education/Honours: Bachelor of Agricultural Science, University of Adelaide, Bachelor of Wine Science, Charles Sturt University
Directorates: Orlando Wyndham, Australian Wine & Brandy Corporation, Australian Wine Research Institute
Career History: International Wine Development Director for Pernod Ricard and a Director of Orlando Wyndham with whom he spent 20 years as Winemaker and Technical Director. Since 1994 has been responsible for development of wine operations in South Africa, Chile, California, Hungary and France. In 1994 he was the first Australian to open the Nederburg Auction in South Africa. He is proprietor of Domain Day at Mt Crawford in the Adelaide Hills, SA and operates an international consultancy to the wine industry, Domain Day Consulting
Hobbies/Clubs: Writing, France and it's Culture, Wines of the World, Public Speaking, Classic Motor Cars, Tennis & Swimming

Tony Devitt

Position: Co-proprietor
Organisation: Ashbrook Estate, Willyabrup, Margaret River, WA
Career History: W.A. Government Viticulturist and Wine Judge

Leon Deans

Position: Company Winemaker
Organisation: Orlando Wyndham Group Pty Ltd
DOB: Adelaide, SA 22nd July, 1956
Education/Honours: 1979 - Graduate in Bachelor of Applied Science in Oenology, Roseworthy Agricultural College, SA, 1987 - Graduate Diploma of Business Administration, SA Institute of Technology, SA, RH Martin Memorial Prize for Sensory Evaluation; Australian Wine Consumers' Cooperative Society Prize
Directorates: Shea-Oak Rise Vineyards Pty Ltd
Career History: Commenced work for Orlando Wyndham in 1979 and held various positions until 1996 including Orlando Winemaker in charge of the group wine production carried out in South Australia. This included the management of the vintage make and two South Australian wineries, plus strong

involvement in wine styles and practices, as well as juice and wine purchases. Other roles have included White Winemaker (responsible for bottled white and sparkling wines); Operations Winemaker, Rowland Flat and Winemaker/Grower Liaison Officer at Orlando Wines, Griffith

Hobbies/Clubs: Fishing, Bird Watching & Competitive Target Shooting, Metropolitan Rifle Club

Brian William de Mamiel

Position: Australian Trading Manager

Organisation: BRL Hardy Wine Co

DOB: Southern Cross, WA 2nd July, 1943

Directorates: Australian Liquor Merchants Association

Career History: Prior to entering into the wine industry was employed in an accounting role within the wholesale pharmaceutical and airline industries. Held various sales/marketing roles with Valencia Vineyards/Houghton Wines, the most recent of which was National Sales Manager (1969-1983). Transferred to Sydney as State Manager, Thomas Hardy & Son from 1983 and was appointed State Manager, BRL Hardy in 1992. Was appointed to National Sales Manager - BRL Hardy (1994-1999). In April 1999 was appointed to the present position of Australian Trading Manager - BRL Hardy.

Tod Dexter

Position: Chief Executive, Chief Winemaker

Organisation: Stonier Wines

DOB: Melbourne, Australia 22nd August, 1956

Career History: 1979-1986 Assistant Winemaker, Cakebread Cellars, Napa, California, 1986-1986, Cellar Foreman, Brown Bros, Milawa, Vic, 1987, Winemaker, Elgee Park Wines, Vic, 1988 - current, Winemaker, Stoniers Winery, Vic

Hobbies/Clubs: Surfing, Windsurfing, Skiing, Golf, Tennis, Reading, Good Food, Family, Holidays

Peter Strickland Dennis

Position: Owner/Manager

Organisation: Dennis Wines

DOB: Adelaide 18th January, 1951

Education/Honours: Scotch College - Leaving certificate

Career History: Left school

1969 and worked for Ryecroft for 2 years in winery and vineyard, Jockaroo 18 mths Victoria, Deck boy on Explosive Ship, Brown Brothers - Milawa, Tullochs - Hunter Valley, Vindana - Monash, SA, travelled overseas 3 years working in Hotels and Oil Rigs including New Zealand, took up present position in 1979

Hobbies/Clubs: Flying, Gliding, Walking & Swimming

John Duval

Position: Winemaker

Organisation: Penfolds/Southcorp

DOB: November 1950

Education/Honours: 1991 WINE magazine named him Red Winemaker of the Year at the International WINE Challenge, also in the UK, 1989 named International Winemaker of the Year at Britain's International Wine & Spirit Competition

Career History: 1974 - Assistant Winemaker, Nuriootpa, Barossa Valley, 1986 - Chief Winemaker, Penfolds. Acknowledged as one of the best winemakers working in Australia today. He is known internationally for his accomplished palate and has judged at the Adelaide, Sydney, Canberra and Perth wine shows.

Robert Victor Edwards

Position: Marketing Director

Organisation: Peter Lehmann Wines Ltd

DOB: Adelaide 21st August, 1946

Education/Honours: B.Commerce, Melbourne University

Directorates: Director, Peter Lehmann Wines Ltd

Career History: Worked in the wine industry for 20 years in marketing and selling, Marketing Manager - Peter Lehmann Wines 1995, Director Peter Lehmann Wines 1999 - current

Christopher Thomas Eerden

Position: Managing Director

Organisation: Lace Fine Wine Merchants Ltd

DOB: Adelaide, SA 24th December, 1960

Education/Honours;

Completed Matriculation in 1977 at Murray Bridge High School, South Australia, Bachelor of Science degree at Adelaide University, South Australia, completing first year only

Directorates: Lace Fine Wine Merchants Ltd

Career History: 1979-1983 Clerk and member of "The Promising Young Officers Scheme", Commonwealth Banking Corporation, SA, 1981-1983 casual employment undertaking duties as food and drink service and bar work, G.V.C.D. Nominees Pty Ltd, SA,

1983 -1988 full time employment, G.V.C.D. undertaking the following positions, Manager, The Drumminor Restaurant, Waiter/Manager 1983-1985, Manager, Vittorio's Restaurant & Cocktail Bar 1985-1987, Wine Expo Centre, Manager, Stonyfell Winery Complex 1987-1988, Acting General Manager, Stonyfell Winery Complex June 1988 - August 1988, 1987 & 1988 Judge, South Australian Student Waiter of the Year competition, 1987 Judge, The Australian Student Waiter of the Year Competition, 1988-1989 European Holiday, 1989-1992 Manager, Drumminor Restaurant, 1992 commenced the company Lace Fine Wine Merchants Ltd

Hobbies/Clubs: Classical Music, Art, Architecture & Literature

John Scott Ellis

Position: Chief Executive Officer

Organisation: The Hanging Rock Winery Pty Ltd

DOB: Newcastle, NSW 15th February, 1947

Education/Honours: Ivanhoe Grammar School - Matriculation, Roseworthy College - Diploma of Agriculture, Diploma of Oenology (HI)

Directorates: The Hanging Rock Winery Pty Ltd

Career History: Graduated Dux Roseworthy Agricultural College 1971, Winemaker at Augustine Barossa Valley Estates (now Krondorf), Yalumba, Saxonvale, first winemaker for Rosemount Estate 1975-1978, then Tisdall Wines 1979-1984, Executive Officer Victorian Wine Industry Association 1984-1985, Chief Executive Officer and Winemaker - The Hanging Rock Winery 1987 - present.

Hobbies/Clubs: Motor Vehicles

Peter Wier Fergusson

Position: Marketing Director

Organisation: Fergusson Winery

DOB: Melbourne 8th September, 1948

Education/Honours: Diploma Applied Chemistry, Adjunct Professor Swinbourne University of Technology Lilydale

Career History: Founded Fergusson Winery 1968

Hobbies/Clubs: Sports Cars, Hot Air Ballooning, R.A.C.V., MG Car Club

David George Farnhill

Position: Chief Executive Officer, Winemaker
Organisation: Cathcart Ridge Estate

DOB: Sydney, NSW 30th November, 1949
Education/Honours: Scotch College, Melbourne, Prahran College of Technology, Charles Sturt Pookie College
Directorates: Belfast Brewery Ltd
Career History: Owner Winemaker Cathcart Ridge established 1978, over 20 vintages in Victoria and South Australia. Won in excess of 100 medals including, Gold World Wine Championship Chicago, Gold Top Shiraz Victoria, Concours Des Vin, Best in Class, Top in Category Winestate 95, 96, 97, 98, advisor to the Dean at Deakin University in Wine Science
Hobbies/Clubs: Wine Education, Classic Cars, Timber boats, Australian Yachting Association, Port Fairy Yacht Club

Andrew Garrett

Position: Chief Executive
Organisation: Andrew Garrett Vineyard Estates
Education/Honours: Graduate of Roseworthy College
Career History: Winemaker and successful entrepreneur in the Australian Wine Industry

Howard Aubrey Haese

Position: Proprietor
Organisation: Barossa Settlers
DOB: Gawler, SA 5th September, 1927
Education/Honours: Intermediate Standard, Gawler High School, Higher Rank Examination to Petty Officer · R.A.N.
Career History: Active involvement in the Agricultural Bureau of SA being Past Secretary and President · Past Secretary of Local Church · Past Committee Member of Tanunda AH & F Society · Past Breeder of British Sheep. Past supporter of Primary & Secondary Schools locally, dedicated grape grower eventually establishing own winery, 1983. President of local branch Liberal Club.
Hobbies/Clubs: Food & Wines · establishing a rose garden, property beautification, member of S.A.B.A. Bridge Club, Ex Navi mens Association · R.S.L. · SABA

Peter Hall

Position: Chief Winemaker
Organisation: Brian McGuigan Wines Ltd

Mark Eric Hamilton

Position: Proprietor / Solicitor / Vigneron / Vintner
Organisation: Hamilton's Ewell Vineyards
DOB: Melbourne 4th April, 1952

Education/Honours: Secondary School and Matriculation with Commonwealth Scholarship · Geelong Grammar School, Victoria, Bachelor of Law, University of Adelaide, Master of Laws (Commercial) University of Adelaide
Directorates: State Heritage Authority (SA)
Career History: Commercial Solicitor, Grope Hamilton Lawyers Adelaide, Proprietor Hamilton's Ewell Vineyards
Hobbies/Clubs: Running, Wine, Art & Music, Adelaide Club Inc., Royal Adelaide Golf Club Inc.

Richard Burton Hamilton

Position: Managing Director/Plastic Surgeon
Organisation: Hamilton Wine Group, Leconfield Coonawarra
DOB: 9th March, 1947

Education/Honours: St Peters College, University of Adelaide 1965-1969, Christchurch Medical School, New Zealand, Goltenburg University, Sweden, Flinders University, Adelaide
Directorates: Hamilton Wine Group, Hamilton Estate Vineyards, Leconfield Coonawarra
Hobbies/Clubs: Adelaide Club

Geoffrey Michael Hardy

Position: Viticulturalist / Vigneron / Owner
Organisation: Geoff Hardy Pty Ltd/Pertaringa Vineyards
DOB: Adelaide 5th April, 1956
Education/Honours: St Peters College · Secondary, Roseworthy Agricultural College · Tertiary, Assoc. Dip. In Wine Marketing
Directorates: Wirrega Vineyards, Vintech Pty Ltd, Barossa Vintners, McLaren Vale & Fleurieu Wine Ind. Ltd, Kuitpo Vineyards, Geoff Hardy Pty Ltd
Career History: After leaving St Peters College, commenced work experience in the wine industry then studied Wine Production and Marketing at Roseworthy College, travelled to Europe for 6 months on a study tour in 1978, worked as a grapegrower, liaison officer for 9 years, purchased and managed Pertaringa Vineyard then planted a number of other vineyards around South Australia for a number of owners and himself, established a vine nursery business since 1981 and a viticultural consulting business since 1982, makes wine at Wirra Wirra and Barossa Vintners where he has a part ownership, currently has the brands Geoff Hardy, Pertaringa & Wirrega.
Hobbies/Clubs: Golf, Tennis, Surfing, Fishing, Diving, McLaren Vale Bacchus Club, Blackwood Golf Club, McCracken Golf Club, Maxwell Tennis Club

Thomas Keith Hardy

Position: Chief Executive Officer
Organisation: Vintage Image Productions
DOB: Adelaide 5th April, 1949
Education/Honours: St Peters College · Adelaide, South Australian Institute of Technology
Career History: 1968-1972 Laboratory Technician, Asst. Accountant, Thomas Hardy & Sons, 1973-1979 Sales Promotions, Melbourne, 1979-1982, Sales Manager, Perth, 1982-1986 Wine Negociant Melbourne, Marketing Manager "Nick's Wine Merchants", 1987-1989 USA, Canada compiling The Pictorial Atlas of North American Wines, 1989-1992 Proprietor the "Chateau de Fleurac" Hotel, Restaurant, Cognac France, 1993-2001 Wine Negociant · Author/Publisher based in Adelaide
Hobbies/Clubs: Sailing · represented Australia, Golf, Travel, Lacrosse · represented Australia, Royal South Australian Yacht Squadron, Wirrina Golf Club

William David Hardy

Position: Corporate Oenologist

Organisation: BRL Hardy Ltd

DOB: Adelaide 23rd November, 1950

Education/Honours: St Peter's College, Adelaide 1960-1967, University of Adelaide · Bachelor of Agricultural Science · 1972, Université de Bordeaux · Diplome National d'Oenologue · 1973

Career History: 1972 Trainee Winemaker Tintara Cellars, McLaren Vale, travelled to Bordeaux, France to undertake the Diplome National d'Oenologue at the Université de Bordeaux, extensive tour of European viticultural areas, 1973 vintage at Chateaux Bouscaut and Haut Brion, Winemaker Tintara Cellars, Senior Winemaker Houghton Wines, WA, returned to South Australia with winemaking responsibilities broadening to include supervision of vintage operations at the company's country sites at Waikerie and Padthaway, co-ordination of the rebuilding of the winemaking and distallation facilities at the company's headquarters at Reynella and responsibility for all fortified wines and brandy produced by the company, seven years later, the company established a base in France by acquisition of Domaine de la Baume in the Languedoc-Roussillon area and Bill was chosen to manage this project during the early years of establishment and growth, resided in France for the initial vintage under Hardy's ownership in 1990 and five vintages later returned once again to the Hardy Head Office in SA where he is currently Corporate oenologist dealing with technical communications and activities involving the wine trade, press, clients, staff and the public both in Australia and around the world.

Hobbies/Clubs: Golf, Bushwalking, Hunting, Adelaide Club, Bacchus Club, SA Wine & Food Society, S.A. Field and Game

Andrew Walter Harris

Position: Principal

Organisation: Andrew Harris Vineyards

DOB: Coonabarabran, 18th August, 1962

Education/Honours: Rowena Public School, The Kings School, Parramatta

Hobbies/Clubs: Golf, Skiing & Travel

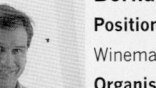

Bernard Hickin

Position: Group White & Sparkling Winemaker

Organisation: Orlando Wyndham Group Pty Ltd

DOB: Melbourne 13th July, 1953

Education/Honours: 1975 · Graduate in Oenology, Roseworthy Agricultural College, SA

Career History: Commenced work at Orlando's Griffith winery as an Assistant Winemaker. Later developed some of the highly successful Botrytis Semillon wines for the company with major show successes between 1985 & 1987. In 1987 moved to Orlando's Rowland Flat winery in the Barossa Valley as an Operations Winemaker, assisting in white wines and in the preparation of sparkling wines such as Orlando Carrington and Orlando Trilogy. 1994 appointed Senior White & Sparkling Winemaker and took on responsibility for the whole Group in 1997.

Hobbies/Clubs: Sailing and Sailboarding, Running, Fly Fishing and Keeping Fit

Robert Ian Churchill Hirst

Position: Chairman, Managing Director

Organisation: Tucker Seabrook (Aust) Pty Ltd

DOB: Sydney, NSW 19th August, 1946

Education/Honours: Kings School · Leaving Certificate, Sydney University · Matriculation, Institute of Chartered Accountants · Member · Chartered Accountant (ACA), Macquarie University · Master of Business Administration (MBA)

Directorates: Board Member · Liquor Merchants Association of Australia, Stedmans Hospitality Personnel and Training Pty Ltd, 4 Liquor.com.au

Career History: 1964-1972 Coopers & Lybrand, Cartered Accountants, Sydney, 1972-1974 Royal Australian Army, 1974-1976 Rothmans Group of Companies, Melbourne, 1976 · present Tucker Seabrook Aust., Sydney

Hobbies/Clubs: Naval & Military, Sydney Cricket & Football Ground/Stadium, Mosman Rowing Club, Carbine Club

Ian Clifford Hongell

Position: Winemaker

Organisation: Peter Lehmann Wines Ltd

Education/Honours: Nuriootpa High School 1984-1988, Roseworthy College 1990-1992

Career History: 1990-1992 Roseworthy College, 1993 Contract Winemaker Southcorp Wines, 1993-1998 Winemaker Cranswick Estate Winery, 1998 · current Winemaker Peter Lehmann Wines

Hobbies/Clubs: Wine, Food, Outdoors, Water Skiing, Motorcycles, Cars, Hunting, Shooting & Fishing

Anthony James Hooper

Position: Senior Orlando White Winemaker

Organisation: Orlando Wyndham Group Pty Ltd

DOB: Adelaide, SA 28th October, 1964

Education/Honours: 1986 · Bachelor of Applied Science (Oenology), Roseworthy Agricultural College, SA; Post Graduate Diploma in Viticulture, Charles Sturt University

Career History: Before commencing work for Orlando Wyndham in 1999, held positions with Lindemans, Seppelts Great Western, Berri Co-Op, McWilliams Wines, Villa Maria Estate, Esk Valley Estate, Yarra Burn Vineyards and Highfield Estate. Has held the position of White Winemaker for Orlando Wyndham since his commencement with the company and has recently been promoted to Senior Orlando White Winemaker

Hobbies/Clubs: Scuba Diving

Michael Hope

Position: Managing Director

Organisation: Hope Estate

DOB: Cowra, NSW 12th June, 1962

Education/Honours: Bachelor of Pharmacy · Sydney University

Career History: Studied Pharmacy at Sydney University in 1981/1983 and in 1985 he established a Pharmacy chain in Sydney and the Central Coast, 1994 purchased a small vineyard in Broke/Fordwich. From this small enterprise has grown Hope Estate Pty Ltd Vineyard & Winery with 87.9 hectares under vine, some 30 yrs old, Michael & team are producing gold medal winning premium wines. In 2000 purchased Virgin Hills, Macedon Ranges Vic, he is now a major player in the Australian Wine Industry to vineyards in NSW, Vic & WA

Hobbies/Clubs: Golf & 5 Day Test Matches

(Meredith) Jane Hunter (nee Arnold)

Position: Managing Director

Organisation: Hunter's Wines (NZ) Ltd

DOB: Barmera, South Australia 27th May, 1954

Education/Honours: Cobdogla Primary School, St Peter's Collegiate Girls' School (Adelaide), Adelaide University (B.AG.SC) Torrens C.A.E. (Dip.T), O.B.E. 1993 Honorary Doctorate Science (Massey) 1997

Career History: 1976-1979 T.A.F.E. (Adelaide), 1980-1981 Teaching · New Zealand, 1981-1983 Owner Restaurant · New Zealand, 1983-1987 National Viticulturist Montana Wines (NZ), 1987 Owner/Viticulturist, Hunter's Wines (NZ) Ltd

Hobbies/Clubs: Cooking, Gardening & Reading

Angus Murray Kennedy

Position: Operations & Technical Director
Organisation: BRL Hardy Ltd
DOB: Tamworth, NSW 8th September, 1946
Education/Honours: The Scots College, Sydney (1957-1963), University of Sydney · B.Engineering (Chem), University of Auckland · B.Commerce, University of Hawaii · Advanced Management Programme
Directorates: ERL Hardy, Barossa Valley Estate, Brookland Valley, Domaine De La Baume, Pacific Wine Partners
Career History: 1968-1981 · CSR Ltd, Shift Superintendent · Chelsea Sugar Refinery, Shift Superintendent · Yarraville, Sugar Refinery, Development Officer · Refinery Section, Head Chemist · New Farm Sugar Refinery, Senior Development Officer · Technical Services, Production Manager · Glanville Sugar Refinery, 1981-1988 B Seppelt & Sons Ltd · Operations Manager and Production manager, 1988 - 1992 · Operations Manager, Berri Renmano Limited, 1992 · current BRL Hardy Ltd, 1992 · Group Operations & Technical Manager, 1994 · Operations and Technical Director
Hobbies/Clubs: Tennis, Literature, Theatre & Philately

Peter John

Position: Chief Executive
Organisation: A P John & Sons Pty Ltd, Coopers Tanunda, Barossa Valley, South Australia

Malcolm Jones

Position: Managing Director
Organisation: Brookland Valley Estate

Phillip Jones

Position: Chief Executive/Winemaker
Organisation: Bass Phillip Wines

Sam Kurtz

Position: Group Red and Fortified Winemaker
Organisation: Orlando Wyndham Group Pty Ltd
DOB: Tanunda, South Australia 1969
Education/Honours: Bachelor of Applied Science (Wine Science), Roseworthy Agricultural College, South Australia; 1995 & 2001 · completed the WRI Advanced Wine Assessment Course
Career History: Commenced work for Orlando Wyndham in 1988 as a Cellarhand in the Barossa Valley. Following study at college he held positions as a Cellarhand at Saxonvale in the Hunter Valley (1991), Assistant Winemaker at Wickham Hill Winery at Griffith (1992) and Winemaking Intern at Simi Winery in the Sonoma Valley in the USA (1992). Between 1993 and 1997 was a White Winemaker at Orlando Wines in the Barossa Valley, plus travelled to Kavar, Hungary for red and white winemaking in 1996. From 1998 to 1999 was in charge of red winemaking at Orlando's Rowland Flat Winery and in 2000 was appointed to overseeing all the red and fortified wine production for the Orlando Wyndham Group across Australia.
Hobbies/Clubs: Hiking, Camping, Gardening & Motor Sport

Philip Leslie Laffer

Position: Chief Winemaker/Director of Viticulture and Winemaking
Organisation: Orlando Wyndham Group Pty Ltd
DOB: 1st October, 1940
Education/Honours: Scotch College, South Australia; 1961 · Graduate of Agriculture, Roseworthy Agricultural College, South Australia; 1963 · Graduate in Oenology, Roseworthy Agricultural College, South Australia
Directorates: Orlando Wyndham Group Pty Ltd
Career History: Employed in the wine industry since 1963, initially with Lindemans Wines Pty Ltd as a winemaker. Resigned from Lindemans in 1990 and commenced employment with Orlando Wyndham Group Pty Ltd with the position of Operations Director until 1992 when he held the position of Company Winemaker. In 1995 he was appointed to Chief Winemaker and Director of Viticulture and Winemaking.

Keith M. Lambert

Position: Managing Director & Chief Executive Officer
Organisation: Southcorp Limited
DOB: Edinburgh, Scotland 1955
Education/Honours: Upper Canada College, Toronto, the Richard Ivey School of Business Administration at the University of Western Ontario and attended the Advanced Management Program at Harvard. He is also a member of the Ontario Institute of Chartered Accountants and qualified while at Coopers & Lybrand
Career History: 1983-1989 · Senior Executive · Carling O'Keefe, 1989-1993 · Senior Vice President · Molson Breweries, 1993-1997 · Senior Vice-President, Strategy and Development · Foster's Brewing Group Ltd, 1997-2001 · Chief Executive Officer · Rosemount Estates Pty Ltd, 2001 · Managing Director & Chief Executive Officer ·Southcorp Limited
Hobbies/Clubs: Travel, Wine, Skiing & Boating

Leonie Anne Lange

Position: Winemaker
Organisation: Peter Lehmann Wines Ltd
DOB: Gawler, South Australia 7th July, 1952
Education/Honours 4th Year High School
Career History: Commenced work 1969 as a laboratory Assistant in a Food Processing Manufacturer in Adelaide, SA. In 1972 started as a Laboratory Technician at Saltram Wines, Angaston, SA under the leadership of Peter Lehmann. In 1979 Peter Lehmann started up his own Winery in Tanunda, SA where I held the position of Laboratory Supervisor for 6fi years and then transferred over to the Winemaking division under the watchful eyes of Peter Lehmann and Chief Winemaker Andrew Wigan. All training has been 'in house' from my superiors.
Hobbies/Clubs: Gardening & Cooking

Dr Chris Laurie

Position: Founder & Former Chief Executive
Organisation: Hillstowe Wines, Adelaide Hills & McLaren Vale
Career History: Descendant of wine pioneer Buxton Forbes Laurie

Ian Eric Leask

Position: Director
Organisation: Pertaringa Wines
DOB: Gosford 1940
Directorates: Breakneck Creek Vineyard, McLaren Vale Picker
Career History: Grape growing experience initially Hunter Valley and last 25 years in McLaren Vale. Established the first mechanical grape harvesting business in McLaren Vale, 28 vintages completed
Hobbies/Clubs: Classic Cars and Beef Cattle

Douglas McCaig Lehmann

Position: Managing Director
Organisation: Peter Lehmann Wines Ltd
DOB: Angaston 6th March, 1952
Education/Honours: Matriculation
Directorates: Peter Lehmann Wines Ltd
Career History: 1971 - commenced employment in Wine Industry, 1975-1977 - Assistant Winemaker, Angle Vale Vineyards, 1977-1990 - Winemaker, Basedow Wines and Manager Basedow 1983-1993, 1990 - Chief Executive Officer, McLeod Wine Group (Peter Lehmann, Basedow & Hoffman) 1993 - Managing Director, Peter Lehmann Wines Ltd
Hobbies/Clubs: Motorsport, River Boats, Variety Club of South Australia, Sporting Car Club of SA, Bacchus, Club, Barossa Branch

Margaret Elizabeth Lehmann

Position: Public Relations
Organisation: Peter Lehmann Wines Pty Ltd
DOB: Adelaide 1st Nov 1942
Education/Honours: BA (Adelaide), Dip Ed (Queensland), Jaguar/Gourmet Traveller Award
Directorates: Alt. Director, Peter Lehmann Wines
Career History: Public Relations Manager for Peter Lehmann Wines and alternate Director for Peter Lehmann. Received the Jaguar/Gourmet Traveller Award for Excellence in the category "Innovation in Travel", 2000. At present is in her second term as Councillor for the Barossa Council, is on a variety of committees associated with Council, a member of the Regional Development Board, Chair of 'Food Barossa' Inc. Has convened many committees for specific Barossa events and media launches for Barossa Vintage Festival Tasting Australia, Barossa Under the Stars, Barossa London visit, was a member of the State Libraries' Board 1985-1992, Deputy Chair 1997-1992 serving with Chairmen Jim Crawford and Des Ross, previously been the South Australian member of the Kelty Federal Taskforce on Regional Development, Councillor of the National Museum, Canberra, and the South Australian member of the National Advisory Council to the ABC
Hobbies/Clubs: Reading, Classical Music & Australian Flora

Fay McGuigan JP

Position: Export Marketing Manager
Organisation: Brian McGuigan Wines Ltd
DOB: Cessnock (Hunter Valley) 2nd April, 1943
Education/Honours: H.S.C., 2 yrs Winemaking, Dale Carnegie Marketing Course
Career History: Under Fay's guidance the export of McGuigan Wines is increasing by some 30% per year. Fay was Export Manager at Wyndham Estate for some 10 years. She took the Companies export sales from a nil base to an annual turnover of $16 million over a period of eight years and established links with 28 countries. In the eight years since she has joined her husband, Brian, in the publicly listed Company, she has secured trade arrangements with twelve countries including USA, UK, Sweden, Norway, New Zealand, Philippines, Thailand, Fiji, the Pacific Islands and more recently Taiwan and China. The United States and the United Kingdom being the McGuigan Company's largest markets. Fay was one of the early pioneers of wine exports and has been hailed as an ambassador of Australian wine in overseas markets. She has been recognised on a number of occasions and more recently was awarded the New South Wales Telstra Businesswoman of the Year Award for the AusIndustry Section. During 1999 Fay was honoured with an "Australia Export Heroes" Award by the Australian Institute of Export. For 3 years, Fay was on the committee of the Prime Minister's "Supermarkets to Asia Council". She regularly travels Internationally to gauge the requirements of her customers so as to ensure that McGuigan Wines vineyard plantings and winemaking processes are in step with her customers wants and needs.
Hobbies/Clubs: Tennis

Lisa Anne McGuigan

Position: Brand Manager
Organisation: Tempus Two Wines
DOB: Scone, Australia 11th January, 1967
Education/Honours: Associate Diploma Hospitality and Catering Management
Directorates: Director of Brian McGuigan Wines
Career History: Worked in middle management in 5 star Hotels for 8 years, spent 2 years working for McGuigan Wines first setting up and managing the Hunter Cellars and then became Marketing Director for the company in 1997. Set up boutique wine brand called Tempus Two Wines and is currently the Brand Manager
Hobbies/Clubs: Cello

Percival Alfred McGuigan

Position: Manager
Organisation: Penfolds Wines Pty Ltd
DOB: Rosebrook, via Maitland, NSW 16th November, 1913
Education/Honours: Primary - Mistletoe Farm Public School, Pokolbin - 1919-1924, Marist Brothers - Maitland 1925-1931 (L.C. Standard), Mid 1930's completed a correspondence course in Dairy Chemistry and Bacteriology through O.A. Mendelssohn & Associates of Sydney
Career History: 1931-1933 Clerk at Branxton Butter Factory, transferred to "Oak" Butter Factory at Hekham as Cream Clerk 1933-1941, September 1941 appointed Manager of Penfolds Wines Hunter River Vineyards by Frank Penfold-Hyland, a position occupied for 27 years, in the mid 1960's, together with Ivan Combet they inspected many prospective vineyard properties and the Company decided to purchase a 723 acre property at Wybong, some 17 miles from Muswellbrook. In September 1970 he personally planted the first vines in the Upper Hunter since the 1920's. During the next 6 years they planted 280 acres with some 10 varieties. On the 12th of February 1968 he and his wife purchased the Penfolds Dalwood vineyard and he retired from Penfolds. In 1970 he sold the property to his son Brian McGuigan, Mr Digby Matheson and Mr Tim Allen. He continued to do P.R. for Brian until 1975 and then retired to Nelson Bay.
Hobbies/Clubs: Nine years as Real Estate Salesman 1975-1984 - Nelson Bay, Branxion Lions Club (1957-1970) Charter Member, Rutherford Probus Club - 1986-1990, Patron McGuigan Wines 'Club 2000'.

The Who's Who of Wine

Ian McKenzie

Position: Winemaker · Consultant to Southcorp Wines
Organisation: Seppelt / Southcorp Wines
Education/Honours: Diploma of Oenology, Roseworthy College
Career History: Trainee Winemaker, Berri-Renmano (now BRL Hardy). He remained at Berri-Renmano Co-operative for 24 years, completing a 3 year Roseworthy College Diploma of Oenology and working short stints at Orlando, Lubiana & Emu wines. Mid 70's Show Judge and Chairman of Judges for the Perth, Adelaide, Barossa, McLaren Vale, Riverland, Ballarat, Lilydale, Hunter Valley & Victorian Wine Shows, 1976 Chief Winemaker Berri-Renmano, 1983 Chief Winemaker, Seppelt Great Western Winery, 1991-1995 Chairman, National Australian Wine Show, Canberra

Hylton McLean

Position: White Winemaker
Organisation: Orlando Wyndham Group Pty Ltd
DOB: Wollongong, NSW 27th October, 1951
Education/Honours: Bachelor of Arts (Economics and Financial Studies), Macquarie University, Sydney, NSW, Bachelor of Arts Hons (Earth Sciences), Macquarie University, Sydney, NSW, Diploma of Applied Science (Wine Science), Charles Sturt University, Wagga Wagga, NSW
Career History: 1986-1990 · Eduvin Wine Consultants and Educators before becoming a Lecturer for Roseworthy Agricultural College/University of Adelaide for the term from 1990 to 1999. Before this time has previously worked for Allandale Winery (1980), Mildara Wines (1985) and Heemskerk Wines (1986). Currently undertaking part time studies in a PhD at Adelaide University, SA
Hobbies/Clubs: Co-author of circa. 10 secondary school text books on Environmental Geography and Economics, Macmillan & co; Author/Co-author of circa. 6 scientific papers in oenology, topics ranging from the nature of cork taint to the metabolism of agrochemicals by grapevines.

Kevin Peter McLintock

Position: Chief Executive Officer
Organisation: McWilliam's Wines Pty Ltd
DOB: Aliwal North 26th Dec, 1949
Education/Honours: Marist Brothers Observatory · South Africa, Harvard University · Business School PMD (USA)
Directorates: Liquor Merchants Association · McWilliam's Wines Pty Ltd · 4 Liquor.Com. · Mount Pleasant Pty Ltd · Barwang International Pty Ltd · Bodega Wines Pty Ltd
Career History: Group General Manager · Kersaf Liquor Holdings, Managing Director · Remy Blass Associates, Director · Tucker & Co, Chief Executive Officer · McWilliam's Wines
Hobbies/Clubs: Golf, Skiing, Rugby & Wine, Harvard Club of Australia, Pymble Golf Club, City Tattersalls Club

Stephen Brian Millar

Position: Managing Director
Organisation: BRL Hardy Ltd
DOB: Adelaide 18th November, 1943
Education/Honours: Qualified Certified Practising Accountant, Diploma of Management (Kettering University of Michigan USA)
Career History: 1992 following the merger of Berri Renmano Limited and Thomas Hardy & Sons Pty Ltd Stephen was appointed Managing Director of the new company following his success as CEO of the Berri Renmano Group, Chairman of overseas subsidiary companies in the UK, France, Canada & USA, Deputy Chairman of the Australian Wine Export Council, Chairman of the Packaging Committee of the Winemakers' Federation of Australia, a member of the Minister's Advisory Council on Customs, President of the Australian Wine & Brandy Producers Association and on the Board of Nobilo Wines Limited (New Zealand) and SA Employers Chamber of Commerce and Industry.
Hobbies/Clubs: Football & Tennis

Brian Miller

Position: Marketing Manager
Organisation: Andrew Garrett Vineyard Estates
Career History: Former Executive with Seppelts Wines, Mitchelton Wines and Dorado Wines, an active promoter of Australian wine since the early 1970's.

Graeme John Morris

Position: Managing Director
Organisation: Winery Supplies
DOB: Melbourne 26th February, 1949
Education/Honours: Primary · Fawkner State School, Secondary · Fawkner Technical School, Matriculation · Preston Institute of Technology, Diploma of Applied Chemistry, Bachelor of Science (Applied Chemistry), Diploma of Education
Directorates: Winery Supplies
Career History: 1968 · Trainee Chemist, C.U.B., commenced part-time studies at the Royal Melbourne Institute of Technology, 1976 achieved both a Diploma and a Degree in Applied Chemistry, promoted to Head of Department · Raw Materials Analysis at the Group Technical Centre in Bouverie Street, Carlton, promoted to Brewer at the Victoria Plant, Melbourne, 1977 joined the teaching profession after obtaining a Diploma of Education, 1980 enrolled at William Anglis College Melbourne in both the Basic & Advanced Wine courses, 1980-1988 vintages at Bianchet Winery assisting with grapegrowing and winemaking etc, 1982 initiated the first scientific, technical winemaking classes in Victoria held at Dandenong College of TAFE, 1986 Sales Representative · Robert Bryce & Co, 1989 opened Winery Supplies Pty Ltd
Hobbies/Clubs: Winemaking, Wine tasting, Tennis, Golf, Snow Skiing, Reading & Wine Education

James Francis Murphy

Position: Sole Proprietor
Organisation: Jim Murphy Market Cellars
DOB: Boorowa 13th December, 1947
Education/Honours: Boorowa Convent (St Josephs)
Career History: Involved in the wine industry since 1967, 17 yrs at the ANU Staff Centre · Manager, 1980-1984 Chairman of the Management Committee · Restaurant and Catering Association, Chairman of CanTrade, member of the Centenary of Federation Committee, member of the Canberra Business Council, ACT & Region Chamber of Commerce and Industry, Board member of the ACT Science and Technology Council, 1988 appointed Honorary Ambassador for Canberra, member of the Chief Minister's business delegations to Canberra's Sister City in Japan, Nara and China, 1988 represented Canberra at the 1998 Global Business Opportunities Convention in Osaka, Japan
Hobbies/Clubs: Football · all codes, Wines & Fine dining

The Who's Who of Wine

Paul Nightingale

Position: Partner
Organisation: Nightingale Wines
DOB: Sydney 25h November, 1948
Education/Honours: Leaving Certificate · Punchbowl Boys High 1965, Wagga Wagga Teachers College 1968, dip School Administration UNE 1984, Grape Growing TAFE 1997, Winemaking and Appreciation 1998, Administration (Distinction & Special Commendation)
Directorates: Nightingale Press Pty Ltd, Nightingale Software Pty Ltd, Blackline Masters Pty Ltd, Foundation of Australian Manufacturing Education
Career History: Former School Teacher who now writes and publishes school text books. Also produces and distributes educational CD-ROMS for primary schools worldwide. As an indulgence, became interested in wine as a result of a lost wager with his wife, Gail, over a well-known wine label. Instead of paying his wager in cash, he bought shares in the company. Over the past nine years, the passion for the wine industry built up to the point where he learned how to grow grapes, planted a vineyard and built a winery. On weekends, Paul can be found at Nightingale Wines with his wife, Gail. The weekend at the Vineyard and Cellar Door are an escape from the busy weekday world of publishing.
Hobbies/Clubs: Wines, Grape Growing, Rugby League, Rugby Union, Cricket, Water Polo and relaxing with people

Dr Philip Anthony Norrie

Position: Doctor / Vigneron / Historian "The Wine Doctor"
Organisation: Self employed GP, Pendarves Estate
DOB: Sydney 5th February, 1953
Education/Honours: Knox Grammar School, MB, BS, (University of NSW), MSc (University of Sydney), M Soc Sc (Hons) Charles Sturt University (Wagga Wagga), PhD Candidate (University of Western Sydney, Richmond)
Directorates: Philip Norrie Pty Ltd, P. Norrie Services

Pty Ltd, Pendarves Estate Pty Ltd
Career History: 1971 · commenced medical studies at the University of NSW, where he trained and did his internship at St Vincent's Hospital, gained his Bachelor of Medicine and Bachelor of Surgery degrees, 1980 gained an Australian Family Planning Association Certificate and established his own solo family/general practice surgery, 1986, together with his wife, Belinda, founded Pendarves Estate and pursued his great interest in wine and health by researching the biographies of all the over 180 doctors in Australia, who have founded vineyards, resulting in a book called "Australia's Wine Doctors", he then went on to write 7 books, 1990 "Vineyards of Sydney", 1993 "Lindeman", 1994 "Penfold", 1996 "Leo Buring", 1998 "Wine and Health Diary Annually", 2000 "Wine and Health · A new look at an Old Medicine", 2000 "Doctor Norrie's advice on Wine and Health · Thinking and Drinking Health", 1992 became the first graduate from the newly formed History & Philosophy of Science Department, University of Sydney,1997 completed his second Master's Degree, a Master of Social Science with Honours from Charles Sturt University, continues to write articles on wine and health and is the unofficial medical spokesman giving talks about wine and health and is also a lecturer and a Ph.D. research fellow in the wine course at the School of Food Sciences, Faculty of Food & Environmental Sciences, University of Western Sydney, 2001 produced World's first Wine and Health wall poster and started marketing · "The Wine Doctor" brand.
Hobbies/Clubs: Travel, Movies & Trains

James David O'Dea

Position: Managing Director
Organisation: Windowrie Viticultural Services
DOB: Sydney 17th December, 1939
Education/Honours: Leaving Certificate · St Ignatius College, Sydney, H.D.A. Hawkesbury Agricultural College, Post Graduate · Kanzas City University USA
Directorates: Chairman · Board Lyndon Community, President · Cowra Region Vineyard Association, President · Canowindra P A & H Association, Executive · N.S.W. Wine Industry Association, Chairman · NSW WIA Water Committee
Career History: 1960 · Graduated Hawkesbury, 2 yrs studying Agriculture in the USA, 1962 moved to Windowrie, 1988 planted 12ha vineyard, 1997 own/manage 250ha vineyard, established vineyards for many investors including Brian McGuigan · Managing Company "Windowrie Viticultural Services", supply grapes to Arrowfield Wines, Charles Sturt University Winery & Brokenwood Wines 1998 Built the First Winery in the Cowra Region for Vintage 1999. Now processing over 4,000 tonnes for Companies including

Hardy's, Simeon, Brokenwood, McGuigans and many smaller wine company's. We make all our labels which include:- Windowrie Family Reserve, Windowrie Estate, Windowrie The Mill, Windowrie Platinum Series, Windowrie Lachlan.
Hobbies/Clubs: Rugby, Golf, Swimming & Classical Music

Chester d'Arenberg Osborn

Position: Chief Winemaker & Viticulturist
Organisation: d'Arenberg Wines Pty Ltd
DOB: Adelaide 1st July, 1962
Education/Honours: Prince Alfred College, Roseworthy Agricultural College (Bachelor of Applied Science in Oenology 1983)
Career History: 1982 Vintage Assistant at Tulloch's, 1983 Vintage Assistant at Hardy's Chateau Reynella, 1984 Viticultural and Oenological tour of European wine regions in France, Italy, Germany and Spain, 1984 Chief Winemaker, d'Arenberg Wines. Outside of his other wine pursuits including wine tasting and judging at the Adelaide Wine Show and as a Panel Chair & Super Juror at the London International Wine Challenge Chester also serves in various capabilities at the McLaren Vale Winemaker's Association, 1990 crowned McLaren Vale Bushing King, winner of the 1996 Hyatt/Advertiser South Australian Wine of the Year Award and 1999 Hyatt/Advertiser South Australian Wine of the Year Award, 1998 announced Winestate magazine's Inaugural Australian Winemaker of the Year and runner up in 1999, short-listed for the International Wine & Spirits Competition 1998 and 1999 International Winemaker of the year. d'Arenberg won in two consecutive years (1999 and 2000) The Wine Society Perpetual Trophy for the Most Successful Winery of the Competition at the Sydney International Top 100 Competition. June 2000 saw Chester Osborn voted Person of the Year at the 8th Annual Hospice du Rhone celebration (Pasa Robles, USA), in recognition of outstanding contribution to Rhone Wines. d'Arenberg was awarded the inaugural wine.com Hall of Fame Award in August 2000.
Hobbies/Clubs: Photography, Wine tasting & judging. Artistic endeavours and appreciation. Appreciation of eclectic music. Finds time to keep up with all of the latest gadgets and technological innovations, as well as voraciously reading as many scientific publications as time will permit.

The Who's Who of Wine

Francis d'Arenberg Osborn

Position: Managing Director
Organisation d'Arenberg Wines Pty Ltd
DOB: Adelaide 27th December, 1926
Education/Honours: McLaren Vale Primary, Morphett Vale Higher Primary, Prince Alfred College - Matriculation, 1995 invested as a Patron of the Australian Wine Industry in, "Honour of an outstanding contribution to the affairs of the Australian Wine Industry", two years after completing his 50th consecutive vintage in 1993, 1978 awarded the Queen's Jubilee Medal for services to the South Australian Wine Industry.
Career History: 1943 started making wine in the family business, 1957 - full management and control of d'Arenberg Wines, 1958 joined the Wine & Brandy Producers Association of South Australia and has been treasurer, vice president & president and is now an honorary life member. d'Arry was a delegate to the Federal Wine and Brandy Producers Council in the 1960's and also a founding member of the Australian Wine & Brandy Producer's Association when it was formed in the 1970's, as well as a member of the executive, and honorary treasurer. For 28 years d'Arry was a councillor on the South Australian Chamber of Commerce representing the wine industry, and was a foundation member and chair of the McLaren Vale Wine Bushing Festival as well as serving as chairperson of the McLaren Vale Winemakers Association, a member of the McLaren Vale Water Resources committee, a member of the Economic Development Authority Wine Industry inquiry and continues to serve in numerous official capacities.
Hobbies/Clubs: Fishing

Neil Warren Pike

Position: Director / Winemaker
Organisation: Pikes Wines
DOB: Mt Gambier 4th September, 1959

Education/Honours: St Peters College, Naracoorte High School (Secondary Education), Roseworthy College RAWM (Tertiary Education)

Directorates: Pikes Vintners Pty Ltd, Pikes Beer Co. Pty Ltd, Pikes Consultancy Services Pty Ltd
Career History: 24 Vintages - Wynns 1978, Quelltaler 1980-1981, Mitchells 1982-1993 inc., Pikes 1985-2001 inc., Chateau Haut Brion 1988, established Pikes Wines in 1984
Hobbies/Clubs: Golf, Aussie Rules Football & Cooking

Christian Porta

Position: Chairman/Chief Executive Officer
Organisation: Orlando Wyndham Group Pty Ltd
DOB: Sarralbe, France 3rd July, 1962
Education/Honours: MBA Ecole Superieure of Commerce, Paris
Directorates: Simeon Wines, French Australian Chamber of Commerce, Orlando Wyndham Group Pty Ltd
Career History: 1984-1988 Paris Consultant, Arthur Andersen, 1988-1993 Financial Controller, Pernod Ricard, 1993-1998 Finance & Administration Director, Pernod Ricard, 1998-1999 Managing Director, Campbell Distillers, London, 1999 - current Chief Executive Officer, Orlando Wyndham Group

Warren Dean Randall

Position: Winemaker
Organisation: Tinlins Wines Pty Ltd
DOB: Adelaide 19th September, 1956
Education/Honours: Secondary - Norwood High School, Tertiary - Bachelor of Agricultural Science (Adelaide University - 1977), Bachelor of Wine Science (Charles Sturt University - 1981)
Directorates: Director - Tinlins Wines Pty Ltd, McLaren Vale, SA, Garden Gully Great Western Vineyards Pty Ltd, Currency Rise Vineyards, Currency Creek, SA
Career History: 1978-1979 Assistant Winemaker/Cellarhand, Wynns Reynella, 1980-1981 Winemaker, Seaview Champagne Cellars Magill, 1981-1982 Champagne maker, Lindemans Wines Sydney, 1982-1989 Champagne maker, Seppelt Wines Great Western, 1989-1994 Chief Winemaker, Andrew Garrett Wines McLaren Vale, 1995 - current Winemaker/Director, Tinlins Wines McLaren Vale

Hobbies/Clubs: Physical fitness, Porsche enthusiast & Crows fan

Gary Roberts

Position: Sales Director - Australasia
Organisation: Southcorp Wines
Career History: Project Co-ordinator, Tooth & Co, General Manager Trading NSW & NSW State Manager, Penfolds Wine Group, 1991 - Sales Director-Australasia, Southcorp Wines,

Edgar Frederick Riek

Position: Retired ex Viticulturist/Owner Lake George Winery
DOB: Napier, New Zealand 1st May, 1920
Education/Honours: Brisbane Grammar School, D.SC - University of Queensland, OAM (1996) for service to the wine industry and to science
Career History: 1944-1954 Part-time Lecturer at University of Queensland and Canberra University College, 1945-1978 Research Scientist CSIRO (Entomologist & Biologist), 1964 visiting Professor University of California, Berkeley, 1973 Visiting Professor University of Florida, Tallahassee, 1954 Foundation member Canberra Wine & Food Club, 1957 Author of the Canberra Gardener, Honorary Life Member Canberra Horticultural Society,1971 Established Lake George Vineyard (and subsequent winery) with main emphasis on Burgundy varieties. Also grew wild grape species from America and Asia for the distinctive flavours of their grapes. An early advocate of sword culture and the importance of soil structure. 1974 Foundation (and 1977 Honorary Life) member of Canberra District Winegrowers' Association (1978) erroneously changed to Vignerons' Association), 1976-1981 Judge at Rutherglen Wine Show, Chairman of Judges 1981, special interest in fortified wines, 1974 established the Canberra Wine Show - a regional show, 1977-1987 Initiated and organised the Australian National Wine Show, 1981-1983 Research and development grant to study extraction of wood flavours and their utilisation in wine, continue as a consultant to that show.
Hobbies/Clubs: Fly Fishing, Gardening & Bridge

The Who's Who of Wine

William (Bill) Ryan

Position: Chief Executive

Organisation: Ryan Family Wines

Career History: An extremely successful Hotelier in New South Wales who established Broke Estate Vineyards and Wines at Broke in the Lower Hunter Valley, now known as Ryan Family Wines. Bill still manages the enterprise with his wife Bliss and with the assistance of his sons William and Matthew and daughter Fiona. He lives in a classic colonial home 'Minimbah' in the Hunter Valley.

Philip Leslie Shaw

Position: Winemaker/Director

Organisation: Rosemount Estate

DOB: Adelaide, Australia 17th July, 1947

Education/Honours: Roseworthy Agriculture, Roseworthy Oenology, 1986 & 2000 awarded the Robert Mondavi Award as "Winemaker of the Year" at the International Wine and Spirit Competition in London, 1999 Qantas/Wine Magazine's Australian Winemaker of the Year award, 2000 recipient of the Graham Gregory Trophy for "outstanding contribution to the Australian Wine Industry"

Directorates: Rosemount

Career History: At an early age worked in wineries after school, washing bottles to earn pocket money and experimenting with his own wine brews. After graduating from Roseworthy he worked for Lindemans 1970-1982, 1982 - current Winemaker, Rosemount Estate. After being instrumental in the development of the prestigious chardonnay wines from Rosemount's premium vineyard, Roxburgh the latter part of the 1980's and 1990's saw Philip's attention turn to perfecting the red wines coming from Rosemount's stable. In 1990 he took a leading role in the move towards cool climate grape growing and winemaking in Australia by planting the largest vineyard on the slopes

of Mt Canobolas in the mountain district of Orange.

Hobbies/Clubs: Most sports, Bush Walking, Fly Fishing, Cooking & Gardening Design

Stephen Ross Shelmerdine

Position: Managing Director

Organisation: Shelmerdine Vineyards Pty Ltd

DOB: Melbourne, Victoria 11th November, 1950

Education/Honours: Secondary - Melbourne Grammar School, Tertiary - Melbourne University BA (Hons) 1972

Directorates: (1995-1997) President, Winemakers' Federation of Australia, (1991-1995) Chairman, Victorian Wine Industry Association, (1993 -) Chairman, Victorian Wineries Tourism Council, (1992 - 1998) Board Member, Australian Wine & Brandy Corporation, (1989 -) Board Member, Victorian Wine Industry Association, (1993 -) Member, Premier of Victoria's Food Industry Advisory Council, (1976-1988) Director, Laradoc Pty Ltd (1991-1994) Director, Mitchelton Partnership, (1991-1994) Director, Barclay Investment, (1989 -) Director, Shelmerdine Vineyards Pty Ltd, (1994 -) Director, Mitchelton Wines Pty Ltd, (1994 -) Director, Petaluma Limited

Hobbies/Clubs: Melbourne Club, MCC

K. Brian Stonier A.O.

Position: Executive Chairman

Organisation: Stonier Wines Pty Ltd

DOB: Prospect, South Australia 24th July, 1932

Education/Honours: Melbourne Grammar School, Melbourne University (LL.B.1954), FCA, AO 1980

Career History: Chartered Accountant 1961-65, Publisher 1965-98 (Macmillan Australia, Sun Books)

Hobbies/Clubs: Reading, Writing & Accounting

Malcolm Chancellor Stopp

Position: National Sales Manager

Organisation: Peter Lehmann Wines Limited

DOB: Tasmania 7th January, 1960

Education/Honours: The Hutchins School, Hobart, Tasmania - Matriculation, Roseworthy Agricultural College, RAWM Winemarketing Diploma

Directorates: Sugarloaf Holdings Pty Ltd

Career History: Employed in wine industry, full time, since 1978, heritage is from 6 generations of family

Wine & Spirits Merchants in Tasmania - E Chancellor Pty Ltd (Est 1873), Roseworthy graduate in Wine Marketing, associated with Peter Lehmann Wines since 1991 and National Sales Manager since 1996, worked in 4 vintages making wine (3 in Australia, 1 in France), worked in UK wine trade for 18 months based in London (1988/1989) - H Sichel & Son Pty Ltd, prior to joining Peter Lehmann Wines Limited in 1996 worked for Samuel Smith & Sons (7 years), Baker Liquor Merchants/Inchcape Liquor Marketing (7 years)

Hobbies/Clubs: Golf, Tennis, Cricket, Wine & Bridge

Dr Bertel Sundstrup

Position: Owner/Winemaker

Organisation: Dalrymple Vineyards

DOB: Wondai, Queensland 24th January, 1931

Education/Honours: MBBS, FRCR, FRACR, Diploma of Viticulture & Oenology, Charles Sturt University

Directorates: Director W.P. Holman Clinic Research Funds

Career History: Graduated MBBS University of Sydney in 1955. After hospital experience moved into General Practice until 1965 when began specialising in cancer treatment. Director of Launceston Peter MacCallum Clinic from 1972 - 1985, then Director of Launceston Holman Clinic for Cancer. Retired 1998.

Set up Dalrymple Vineyards in 1987, and became winemaker in 1996.

Hobbies/Clubs: Rowing Coach, Windsurfing, Bush Walking, Skiing.

Franklin J Tate

Position: Chairman and Chief Executive Officer

Organisation: Evans & Tate Ltd

DOB: Perth, Western Australia 2nd October, 1961

Education/Honours: Curtin University, Perth, WA, Bachelor of Business, Majoring in Marketing

Directorates: Evans & Tate Ltd

Career History: 1987 - current, Wine Industry

Hobbies/Clubs: Sailing, Reading, Travel & Wine

Eric Vivian Hamill (Viv) Thomson

Position: Managing Director
Organisation: Best's Wines · Great Western
DOB: Swan Hill, Victoria 1st July, 1938
Education/Honours: Great Western Primary School, Stawell High School, Wesley College, Melbourne, Roseworthy Agricultural College, S.A
Career History: In 1944 the Family moved from Lake Boga to "Concongella" Great Western where Viv and his family still reside, 1959-1960 travelled overseas · 1 year in East Africa, mainly Kenya, 9 months in England & Europe, 1972 commenced judging in National & District Shows, since then he has judged at nearly all major wine shows. He is ably assisted at Best's Wines by his wife Christine, their two sons and daughter. Viv has also been Chairman of the Ararat Apex Club, Great Western Primary School, Stawell Secondary College and the Victorian Wine Industry Association.
Hobbies/Clubs: Great Western Football Club (Best & Fairest 1960)

Jonathan William Tolley

Position: Director
Organisation: Jonathan Tolley Wine Merchant
DOB: Adelaide, 4th February, 1950
Education/Honours: 1956-1967 St Peters College, 1968 SA Institute of Technology · Diploma of Accounting, 1968 Wine & Brandy Producers Association Wine Course Diploma, 1982 Australian Institute of Management · Marketing, Sharebroking Operators Course, 1992 University of Adelaide, Office

of Continuing Education · Marketing Development
Directorates: Jonathan & Jude Tolley
Career History: 1968-1971 Sharebrokers Operator & Clerk, 1971-1972 Sharebrokers Operator & Clerk, London UK & travelled extensively overseas, 1972-1974 Liquor Control Service Organisation, Adelaide, 1974-1983 SA Manager, Tolley Wines Pty Ltd, 1983-1995 National Sales & Marketing Director, Tolley Wines Pty Ltd, 1996 · Present Director, Jonathan Tolley Wine Merchant
Hobbies/Clubs: All sport · Football (Aussie), Golf, Cricket, Horse Racing Thoroughbred/Standard Bred (Harness), Popular Music, Contempary Art and Wine

Walter Reginald Tonkin

Position: Managing Director
Organisation: Tonkins Currency Creek Wines
DOB: Strathalbyn, South Australia 28th February, 1934
Education/Honours: Macclesfield Primary School, Mt Barker High School
Directorates: Chairman · Currency Creek Grapegrowers & Winemakers Assoc.
Hobbies/Clubs: SAJC (Strathalbyn Racing Club Committee Member)

Tom Van Der Hoek

Position: Coolabah, Fortified & Beverage Winemaker
Organisation: Orlando Wyndham Group Pty Ltd

Kees Van De Scheur

Position: General Manager/Chief Winemaker
Organisation: Bimbadgen Estate Wine
DOB: Holland, 14th April, 1952
Career History: 1971-1975 Sales, The Rothbury Estate, 1976-1977 Wine Sales, H G Brown & Sons, 1978-1986 Winemaker, The Robson Vineyard, 1987-1993 developed Briar Ridge Vineyard as General

Manager/Winemaker, 1995 · current, developed Van de Scheur Wines as Managing Director/Winemaker, 1997 · current, developed Bimbadgen Estate Wines, Lower Hunter Valley · Chief Winemaker/General Manager
Hobbies/Clubs: Food, Wine & Music

Pieter van Gent

Position: Winemaker/Manager
Organisation: Storeton Pty Ltd T/as Pieter van Gent Winery & Vineyard
DOB: Holland, 1st March, 1937
Education/Honours: 4yr Management Course
Career History: 1960-1970 Apprenticeship in wine, learning his skills in the laboratory and cellars, Penfolds Wines, 1970-1978 Winemaker, Craigmoor Wines, 1979 · current Winemaker/Managing Director, Pieter van Gent Winery & Vineyard

Richard John Ward

Position: Managing Director
Organisation: Kitchener Wines Ltd
DOB: Wellington, New Zealand 27th July, 1938
Education/Honours: Scots College, Wellington
Directorates: Director · Vavasour Wines Ltd, Director · Riverstone Vineyards Ltd
Career History: 1964-1968 Managing Director, Mercer Enterprises, 1968-1981 Managing Director, Avalon Wines & Spirits, 1969-1973 Directorship · John Buck Ltd, Wine Reseller & Wine Consultant, 1970-1973 Directorship · Western Park Tavern Ltd, 1979-1981 P.S.I.S. Representative on Nobilo Vintners Ltd Marketing Committee, 1981-1984 Wellington Regional Manager, Wilson Neill Wines & Spirits & Wilson Neill Ltd, 1984-1987 Managing Director, Tavern Management Independent Taverns Ltd, 1984-1987 Director Willis Street Lodge, United Food & Chemical Workers Enterprises Ltd, 1987 Wine & Spirit Industry Consultant, 1987-1989 General Manager, Negociants NZ Ltd, 1990 Director, Vavasour Wines Ltd, 1990 Managing Director, Kitchener Wines Ltd
Hobbies/Clubs: Tennis, Skiing

Ronald George Westwood

Position: Managing Director

Organisation: Westwood Wine Agencies Pty Ltd

DOB: Wedderburn, Victoria 3rd March, 1932

Education/Honours: Carey Grammar School, Melbourne Boys High School, Associate Fellow · Australian Institute of Management, Associate Fellow · Catering Institute of Australia

Directorates: Westwood Wine Agencies

Career History: 1948-1951 Junior Clerk, HM Department of Trade & Customs, Melbourne, 1951-1957 Apprentice Assistant, Retail Store Manager, Crooks National Stores, 1957-1958 Trainee Executive G.J. Coles, Melbourne, 1958-1960 Departmental Manager, G.J. Coles, Queensland, 1960-1963 Sales & Merchandising Representative, Key Accounts Representative, Arnotts Biscuits, Melbourne, 1963-1965 Field Sales Supervisor, Gerber Baby Foods (Petersville), Victoria, 1965-1972 Assistant Branch Manager · Victoria & Tasmania, Member National Marketing Committee, Orlando Wines, 1972-1974 General Manager, Emerald Wholesale Wine & Spirits, Victoria, 1974 Partner/Manager, Robwood Abbey Licensed Restaurant, Diamond Creek, Victoria, 1974-1976 Manager, Victoria, Tasmania, Northern Territory, Member National Marketing Committee, Penfold Wines, 1976 Overseas study, European Wine Regions, 1977 established Westwood Wine Agencies · acting as broker for several Australian & European winemakers, 1979-1980 Consultant General Manager, Campbells of Rutherglen, 1993 Managing Director Westwood Wine Agencies Pty Ltd, Licensed Wholesale Wine & Spirit Distributors.

Hobbies/Clubs: Classical Music, Opera, Australian Rules Football, History of Wine, Reading, Royal Automobile Club of Victoria, Carlton Football & Cricket Social Club, Les Amis du Vin (Australia) · Founder.

Mark B. Whisson

Position: Managing Director

Organisation: Whisson Lake Pty Ltd

Education/Honours: B.Sc in Biochemistry & Botany · Adelaide University 1973-1975, Honours in Botany · Adelaide University 1976, MSc in Plant Biochemistry · University of Alberta (Canada) 1977-1981, Soil Science, Wine Production, Horticulture · TAFE Waite Institute 1984.

Directorates: Mark Whisson

Career History: 1983-1989 Petaluma · 1983 started as a Vineyard Hand, 1984 appointed Acting Vineyard Manager, 1984 appointed Vineyard Manager in Northern Piccadilly Valley planting seven new vineyards, 1986 appointed vineyard Manager of Ten Hills Vineyards, 1988 appointed Viticulturlist in Clare, Piccadilly & Coonawarra Regions, 1989-1991 · Woods Hills vineyards · Vineyard Manager/Viticultralist, 1991 · present Trig Point Viticultural Management · owned and operating business which contracts to develop, manage and sell fruit of clients vineyards which currently number 26, all in the Adelaide Hills, 1986 · present Whisson Lake · November 1985 planted own vineyard at Carey Gully, it profitably sells grapes to Southcorp and Orlando and has produced wine under Whisson Lake label since 1989, 1989/1999 Whisson · planted another vineyard at the bottom of Whisson Lake Vineyard and successfully produced wine under the Whisson Label · sold fruit to d'Arenberg for 2001 vintage.

Hobbies/Clubs: Car Racing (Driving) · classic and historic, Fine Wine and Fine Dining, S.A. Sporting Car Club, Porsche Club SA, ANWR

Andrew Douglas Wigan

Position: Chief Winemaker

Organisation: Peter Lehmann wines

DOB: Ararat, Victoria 12th August, 1949

Education/Honours: B.Applied Science (Applied Chemistry) Ballarat, Diploma of Oenology (Roseworthy)

Directorates: Alternate Director, Peter Lehmann Wines Ltd

Career History: 1973-1975 Cellar & Lab. Assistant Krondorf Wines, 1976-1979 Winemaker, Saltram, 1980? Senior Winemaker, thence Chief Winemaker Peter Lehmann Wines and part of the team responsible for the full range of Peter Lehmann Wines from day 1 of the company. Highlights · winning Jimmy Watson Trophy 1990 with 1989 Stonewell Shiraz, 7 International Wine & Spirit Competition trophies, Red Wine of the Year, International Wine Challenge, 2000, Top Wine, Red or White, Adelaide National Wine Show 2000, nomination Qantas/Wine Magazine Winemaker of the Year, at least 6 wines in Wine Spectator Top 100. Major influences in career: Peter Lehmann, Colin Preece & Jim Irvine

Hobbies/Clubs: Barossa Valley Golf Club

David Woods

Position: International Trading Director

Organisation: BRL Hardy Ltd

DOB: Scotland, 21st Aug, 1953

Directorates: Nobilo Wine Group, Pacific Wine Partners, Barossa Valley Estates, Domaine de la Baume

Career History: Joined the Hardy Group in April 1987 as Sales and Marketing Manager at Houghton Wines, based in Perth. Following the merger of Thomas Hardy's three sales divisions he returned to Adelaide as National Sales Manager for the Group. He maintained this role for the newly formed BRL Hardy Group in July 1992 and subsequently was given responsibility for Australian marketing. Appointed to the Board in September 1994, he was responsible for all sales and marketing matters in Australia, including public relations, cellar door sales and bulk wines sales to other wineries until his appointment to the role of International Trading Director in April 1999. In October 1998 David was appointed a Director of Nobilo Wine Group, a New Zealand wine company which BRL Hardy subsequently purchased. He is also a Director of Barossa Valley Estates, Domaine de la Baume and Pacific Wine Partners, three of BRL Hardy's joint ventures. Previous experience in the Australian wine industry included 2fi years as National Sales Manager with Wolf Blass Wines and 3 years with Sydney-based Australian Liquor Marketers, a distributor-importer for a broad range of domestic and international wines, spirits and beers. Prior to his arrival in Australia, David was involved in sales and marketing in the music and construction industries in the UK.

Timothy Edmund Hardy Yule

Position: General Manager

Organisation: Trinity Wine Agency

DOB: Adelaide, South Australia 15th July, 1961

Education/Honours: Secondary Education · Dover College, Dover Kent UK

Hobbies/Clubs: Queensland Wine Press Club, Reading, Golf, Cooking

**Milan Roden with
the Jimmy Watson
Throphy**

Robert Mondavi on his
82nd Birthday with
author Tom Hardy

605

Peter Lehmann
"A living legend"

Index

Index

WHO'S WHO